THE GLOBE AND MAIL

REPORT ON BUSINESS

CANADA COMPANY

HANDBOOK

1   9   9   3

Production Editor
Alan Husdal

Publisher
Michael J. Ryan

Copyright © 1993

GLOBE AND MAIL PUBLISHING
444 Front Street West
Toronto, Ontario
M5V 2S9
(416) 585-5250
Fax: (416) 585-5249

ISSN 0847-2831
ISBN 0-921925-45-X

Cover design and cover illustration by Doris Diehl-Palozzi.

Printed and bound in Canada by General Printers.

Our Research Services Let You See Investment Opportunities For Yourself.

There was a time when all anyone expected of a discount broker was savings. Green Line® Investor Services Inc. delivered savings, then and now, with commissions up to 83%* less than full-commission brokers.

Today, to be successful, investors need and want more timely information, and Green Line delivers again, with a range of research services that build real value into the savings we're famous for.

An eye on the markets. At Green Line, we are committed to supplying our clients with everything they need to make their own informed decisions. We offer;

- investment seminars in major cities
- Financial Post Investor Reports covering 500 TSE listed companies
- Standard & Poor's Research Reports

covering 4,000 U.S. companies
- complimentary quarterly economic research reports
- a series of handy reference guides to track the performance of Canadian and U.S. equities, foreign equities, and mutual funds.

You can also choose from a wide selection of investment research products featured in our Green Line Investment Research Catalogue at significant savings.

Call Green Line and let us look out for you. For more information on Green Line and a free copy of our Investment Research Catalogue, call us today at **1-800-465-LINE**.

GREEN LINE
CANADA'S LARGEST DISCOUNT BROKER

Table of Contents

Preface vii

Introduction viii

Major Industry Sections

Mines 1

Precious Metals 25

Oil & Gas 65

Forestry.. 131

Food, Beverages & Tobacco 153

Household & Leisure Goods 171

Automotive.. 181

Biotechnology & Pharmaceuticals... 189

Steel, Metal & Machinery 197

Electrical & Electronic.. 211

Chemicals.. 235

Packaging & Containers.. 243

Real Estate Developers & Managers 251

Transportation 269

Pipelines.. 279

Utilities.. 287

Communications & Media... 313

Wholesale Distributors.. 341

Retailing.. 351

Banks & Trusts.. 375

Investing, Financing & Leasing.. 393

Insurance 419

Management Companies 433

Computer Software & Processing 461

Consulting 473

Industrial, nec (Not Elsewhere Classified)... 481

Company Index 507

Report on Business 1000 .... ROB-1

Definitions of Financial Terms.. ROB-107

Globe and Mail Publishing © 1993

This is the fifth edition of the **Report on Business Canada Company Handbook.** The financial analysts who worked on the Handbook this year were David Curry, John F. Grennan, Kevin Grennan, Vivian Hood, G. Trevor Leong, Sean T. McLoughlin, Douglas Tripp, and Tsang Kwong-Ping. Mary-Jane Wilson was our corporate information coordinator. Software development and support was provided by Helena Huiqun Jin, Sham Arora, and Gerry ter Hofstede. We would like to thank Angela Bianchi, Joanne Hamill, Carlie Oreskovich, and Donna Hymers. Special thanks go to Josée Gauthier.

Globe and Mail Publishing markets a number of targeted directories and reference standards including **Business Connexions, Canadian Federal Government Handbook, Canadian Parliamentary Guide,** and **The Guide to the Canadian Financial Services Industry.**

Globe Information Services is constantly collecting and analyzing financial information and news on thousands of Canadian companies. For up-to-date information on companies in the **Handbook** and other Canadian companies contact our Client Services Department: (416) 585-5345 Toronto; (800) 268-9128 Canada; (800) 456-9190 U.S.; and (416) 585-5249 Fax.

Selection and arrangement of companies

The white pages of the **Report on Business Canada Company Handbook** provide current news, ratios and price performance charts, and annual and quarterly financial information for 414 major Canadian public companies. These companies include the current TSE 300 and all former TSE 300 companies since 1984 that remain publicly traded.

One full page is devoted to each company. Companies are grouped by industry and arranged alphabetically, within each industry. The **Handbook** uses the same industry groupings as the **Report on Business Corporate Database**. A company index follows this section of the **Handbook**.

The earnings table preceeding each section lists each company in that industry group. The table lists earnings per share for the current year and the mean earnings estimates for the subsequent two fiscal years. Earnings estimates are provided by I/B/E/S, the Institutional Brokers Estimate System. Following each earnings table are industry summaries compiled by both Globe Information Services and INVESTEXT.

The colour pages are an alphabetical directory of all the companies that appeared in the July 1993 **Report on Business 1000**, including public and private companies, crown corporations, and cooperatives. Each entry lists the address, company type, industry segment, description of business, senior executive, and total revenue from the most recent annual report.

Sources of information

The bulk of information in the **Handbook** is provided from a range of Info Globe Online databases including: the **Report on Business Corporate Database, The Globe and Mail Online**, and **Marketscan Plus**.

Globe Information Services is constantly gathering and organizing financial information and news on thousands of Canadian companies. For up-to-date information on companies included in the **Canada Company Handbook** and other Canadian companies contact our Client Services department:

- (416) 585-5345 Toronto
- (800) 268-8043 Ontario
- (800) 268-9128 Canada
- (800) 456-9190 U.S.
- (416) 585-5249 FAX

The **Institutional Brokers Estimate System (I/B/E/S)**, created in 1971, is the authoritative source monitoring earnings estimates on more than 13,000 companies of interest to institutional investors world-wide. The estimates are produced by 5,500 professional analysts from the research departments of more than 600 leading brokerage and investment firms in 39 countries around the globe. The database, which contains more than 200,000 estimates, is updated daily in order to maintain the most current data related to earnings forecasts. The I/B/E/S universe is continually expanding as analysts broaden their coverage into new areas and as new brokerage firms are added to the system.

The **INVESTEXT** database was employed in the compilation of the **Handbook**. INVESTEXT is a database which offers the complete text of company and industry reports written by analysts at more than 150 of the world's leading investment banks and consulting and research firms. INVESTEXT currently includes over 210,000 reports which cover 12,000 companies and 53 industries. Copies of all reports are available online or from Thomson Financial Networks.

INVESTEXT
Thomson Financial Networks
11 Farnsworth Street
Boston, MA 02210
(800) 544-5651 Canada
(800) 662-7878 U.S.
011 44 071 815-3860 U.K.
(617) 330-1986 FAX

The following section includes a sample company page with sections labelled for your convenience. Major sections are:

- Summary stock market information
- Fundamental information
- Stock graphs
- Business description
- Current news synopsis
- General information.

Sample Company Page

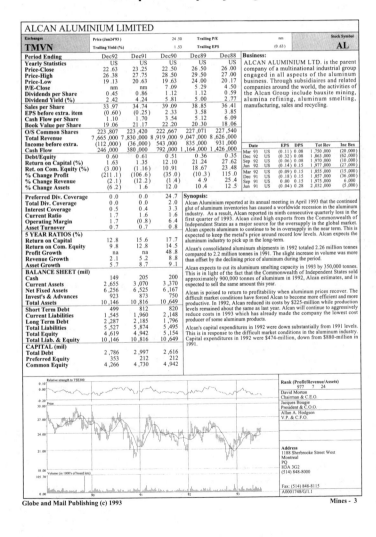

ALCAN ALUMINIUM LIMITED

Exchanges	Price (Jun24'93)		24 .50	Trailing P/E		nm	Stock Symbol
TMVN	Trailing Yield (%)		1 .53	Trailing EPS		(0 .63)	AL

Period Ending	Dec92	Dec91	Dec90	Dec89	Dec88
Yearly Statistics	US	US	US	US	US
Price-Close	22 .63	23 .25	22 .50	26 .50	26 .00
Price-High	26 .38	27 .75	28 .50	29 .50	27 .00
Price-Low	19 .13	20 .63	19 .63	24 .00	20 .17
P/E-Close	nm	nm	7 .09	5 .29	4 .50
Dividends per Share	0 .45	0 .86	1 .12	1 .12	0 .59
Dividend Yield (%)	2 .42	4 .24	5 .81	5 .00	2 .77
Sales per Share	33 .97	34 .74	39 .09	38 .85	36 .41
EPS before extra. item	(0 .60)	(0 .25)	2 .33	3 .58	3 .85
Cash Flow per Share	1 .10	1 .70	3 .54	5 .12	6 .09
Book Value per Share	19 .06	21 .17	22 .20	20 .30	18 .06
O/S Common Shares	223 ,807	223 ,420	222 ,667	227 ,071	227 ,540
Total Revenue	7 ,665 ,000	7 ,830 ,000	8 ,919 ,000	9 ,047 ,000	8 ,626 ,000
Income before extra.	(112 ,000)	(36 ,000)	543 ,000	835 ,000	931 ,000
Cash Flow	246 ,000	380 ,000	792 ,000	1 ,164 ,000	1 ,426 ,000
Debt/Equity	0 .60	0 .61	0 .51	0 .36	0 .35
Return on Capital (%)	1 .63	1 .35	12 .10	21 .24	27 .62
Ret. on Com. Equity (%)	(3 .00)	(1 .16)	10 .91	18 .67	23 .48
% Change Profit	(211 .1)	(106 .6)	(35 .0)	(10 .3)	115 .0
% Change Revenue	(2 .1)	(12 .2)	(1 .4)	4 .9	25 .4
% Change Assets	(6 .2)	1 .6	12 .0	10 .4	12 .5
Preferred Div. Coverage	0 .0	0 .0	24 .7		
Total Div. Coverage	0 .0	0 .0	2 .0		
Interest Coverage	0 .5	0 .4	3 .3		
Current Ratio	1 .7	1 .6	1 .6		
Operating Margin	1 .7	(0 .8)	6 .4		
Asset Turnover	0 .7	0 .7	0 .8		
5 YEAR RATIOS (%)					
Return on Capital	12 .8	15 .6	17 .7		
Return on Com. Equity	9 .8	12 .8	14 .5		
Profit Growth	na	na	48 .8		
Revenue Growth	2 .1	5 .2	8 .8		
Asset Growth	5 .7	8 .7	9 .1		
BALANCE SHEET (mil)					
Cash	149	205	200		
Current Assets	2 ,655	3 ,070	3 ,370		
Net Fixed Assets	6 ,256	6 ,525	6 ,167		
Invest's & Advances	923	873	750		
Total Assets	10 ,146	10 ,816	10 ,649		
Short Term Debt	499	812	820		
Current Liabilities	1 ,545	1 ,960	2 ,148		
Long Term Debt	2 ,287	2 ,185	1 ,796		
Total Liabilities	5 ,527	5 ,874	5 ,495		
Total Equity	4 ,619	4 ,942	5 ,154		
Total Liab. & Equity	10 ,146	10 ,816	10 ,649		
CAPITAL (mil)					
Total Debt	2 ,786	2 ,997	2 ,616		
Preferred Equity	353	212	212		
Common Equity	4 ,266	4 ,730	4 ,942		

Business:

ALCAN ALUMINIUM LTD. is the parent company of a multinational industrial group engaged in all aspects of the aluminum business. Through subsidiaires and related companies around the world, the activities of the Alcan Group include bauxite mining, alumina refining, aluminum smelting, manufacturing, sales and recycling.

Date		EPS	DPS	Tot Rev	Inc Bex
Mar 93	US	(0 .11)	0 .08	1 ,750 ,000	(20 ,000)
Dec 92	US	(0 .32)	0 .08	1 ,863 ,000	(62 ,000)
Sep 92	US	(0 .06)	0 .08	1 ,970 ,000	(10 ,000)
Jun 92	US	(0 .14)	0 .15	1 ,977 ,000	(27 ,000)
Mar 92	US	(0 .09)	0 .15	1 ,855 ,000	(15 ,000)
Dec 91	US	(0 .18)	0 .15	1 ,857 ,000	(36 ,000)
Sep 91	US	0 .00	0 .15	1 ,975 ,000	6 ,000
Jun 91	US	(0 .04)	0 .28	2 ,032 ,000	(5 ,000)

Synopsis:

Alcan Aluminium reported at its annual meeting in April 1993 that the continued glut of aluminum inventories has caused a worldwide recession in the aluminum industry. As a result, Alcan reported its ninth consecutive quarterly loss in the first quarter of 1993. Alcan cited high exports from the Commonwealth of Independent States as a major source for the oversupply in the global market. Alcan expects aluminum to continue to be in oversupply in the near term. This is expected to keep the metal's price around record low levels. Alcan expects the aluminum industry to pick up in the long-term.

Alcan's consolidated aluminum shipments in 1992 totaled 2.26 million tonnes compared to 2.2 million tonnes in 1991. The slight increase in volume was more than offset by the declining price of aluminum during the period.

Alcan expects to cut its aluminum smelting capacity in 1993 by 350,000 tonnes. This is in light of the fact that the Commonwealth of Independent States sold approximately 900,000 tonnes of aluminum in 1992, Alcan estimates, and is expected to sell the same amount this year.

Alcan is poised to return to profitability when aluminum prices recover. The difficult market conditions have forced Alcan to become more efficient and more productive. In 1992, Alcan reduced its costs by $225-million while production levels remained about the same as last year. Alcan will continue to aggressively reduce costs in 1993 which has already made the company the lowest cost producer of some aluminum products.

Alcan's capital expenditures in 1992 were down substantially from 1991 levels. This is in response to the difficult market conditions in the aluminum industry. Capital expenditures in 1992 were $474-million, down from $880-million in 1991.

Rank (Profit/Revenue/Assets)
977   7   24

David Morton
Chairman & C.E.O.

Jacques Bougie
President & C.O.O.

Allan A. Hodgson
V.P. & C.F.O.

Address
1188 Sherbrooke Street West
Montreal
PQ
H3A 3G2
(514) 848-8000

Fax: (514) 848-8115
A0001748/G/1.1

Globe and Mail Publishing (c) 1993

Mines - 3

Stock Market Information

This section gives the ticker symbol and the Canadian and American stock exchanges where the company stock is listed. The primary exchange is listed first. The latest closing market price date for the majority of companies in the **Handbook** is June 24, 1993.

Stock exchange codes are: **T**-Toronto; **M**- Montreal; **V**-Vancouver; **W**-Winnipeg; **Z**-Alberta; **A**-American; **N**-New York; and **Q**-Nasdaq.

Fundamental Information

The fundamental information is derived from a company's annual and quarterly financial statements. Financial items are indicated as dollar amounts, percentages, or ratios. Dollar amounts are reported in Canadian currency and in thousands of dollars, unless otherwise indicated. For ratio calculations, figures are converted to Canadian dollars and annualized. Annual and quarterly information is restated or reclassified where applicable. Share information is split adjusted. Financial items having negative values are enclosed in parentheses.

Certain financial information is not available for all companies. The following codes may be used when a number does not appear: **na** - not available; **nc** - no common shares trading; **nd** - no debt; **nm** - not meaningful; **np** - no preferred shares; and **nt** - no shares trading.

The **Handbook** uses four different presentations to reflect the differences in financial reporting requirements for different types of companies. They are: Banks; Finance (eg. trust, insurance and investment companies); Real Estate Management and Development; and General (eg. industrial, resource and communications companies).

For a detailed explanation of each financial item, please refer to the **Definitions of Financial Terms** beginning on page ROB-107.

The **Yearly Statistics** section contains five years of financial information. All financial items in this section apply to all companies in the **Handbook**.

The section beginning with **Preferred Dividend Coverage** contains three years of financial ratios. Preferred Dividend Coverage and Total Dividend Coverage apply to all companies. All other financial items in this section are presentation specific.

The **5 Year Ratios** section contains three years of key ratios. All financial items in this section apply to all companies.

The **Balance Sheet** and **Capital** sections contain three years of financial information. Two items — Total Equity and Total Liabilities — apply to all companies. All other financial items in this section are presentation specific.

The **Quarterly** section contains information from the eight most recent quarterly financial statements. All financial items apply to all companies. Quarterly data represent the incremental period between the dates given.

Stock Graphs

The graphs in the **Handbook** are designed so that price and volume movements for each stock can be seen at a glance for each week during the past five years, or since the stock has been publicly traded. Market information is taken from the primary exchange on which the stock trades. The information is current as of June 25, 1993.

Three graphs are displayed for each of the companies in the **Handbook**. The graphs display three types of information:

- strength compared to the TSE 300
- stock price
- stock volume, in thousands of board lots.

Relative strength is calculated by dividing the stock price by the TSE 300 index. The result of this division is the ratio between the stock price and the TSE 300 index. The relative strength indicator is then adjusted to normalize the value by subtracting the beginning ratio from each day's value. The result of this adjustment is to set the day-one value at zero for easier analysis. When the relative strength indicator is moving up, the stock is performing better than the TSE 300 index. When the indicator is level, the stock is performing the same as the TSE 300 index. When the indicator is moving down, the stock is performing worse than the TSE 300 index.

The stock price graph displays the high, low, and close prices, as well as the five-week (solid line) and 40-week (dotted line) moving averages. All prices have been stock split adjusted. A logarithmic scale is used to better facilitate the analysis of price movements. Wherever a company name change, merger, or amalgamation has occurred, every effort has been made to display the complete price history of the company stock.

The volume graph displays the volume of shares traded, in thousands of board lots, during each week. The highest recorded volume for the stock during the five-year period, rounded up to the nearest hundred, is displayed on the vertical axis.

Business Description

This section provides an overview of a company's line of business. It lists primary and secondary activities, and gives the location of company operations, mines, properties, and markets. The business description may also list company products and include subsidiary and major shareholder information.

Current News Synopsis

The synopsis, or summary, provides context for all other company information and covers any or all of the following:

- industry trends
- company events (eg. sales contracts, take-overs, share offerings, layoffs)
- key executive appointments
- fundamental information on a company's geographic and product divisions.

This section provides a 12-month capsule of company events. The majority of summaries cover events from July 1992 to June 1993. Where possible, changes were made to summaries up to the date of printing.

General Information

This section provides an investor with the means to obtain additional information on a given company. Included are company rankings of profit, revenue, and assets from the latest **Report on Business 1000**, the names and titles of up to five top company officers, and the head office address, phone, and fax number.

Intstitutional Brokers Estimate System (I/B/E/S)

The Institutional Brokers Estimate System (I/B/E/S), created in 1971, is the authoritative source of comparative earnings expectations data in the business community. From a single product with a promising future it has become a range of portfolio management tools relied upon by thousands of analysts and investors throughout the world.

Global I/B/E/S is a compendiuum of earnings and growth rate forecasts on all publicly-traded corporations followed by securities analysts. It remains the only source of reliable, consistent, and timely world-wide earnings expectations. Global I/B/E/S contains individual and consensus earnings expectations data on more than 13,000 publicly-traded corporations in 39 countries.

Global I/B/E/S earnings-per-share data is primarily obtained from over 5,500 analysts working for approximately 600 leading investment firms worldwide. I/B/E/S calculates the consensus information which summarizes analysts' estimates on a firm, industry, economic sector, and market level. In addition to mean estimates for the current fiscal-year, Global I/B/E/S provides up-to-date earnings forecasts for the next five fiscal year periods, the rate of growth in earnings over the next five years, and quarterly estimate data.

Because earnings expectations drive stock prices, Global I/B/E/S earnings forecasts are a key element in the investment decision-making process. Consensus forecast revisions can provide the early warning of change in earnings expectations essential to identifying new investment opportunities and to avoiding unpleasant earnings surprises.

Intstitutional Brokers Estimate System (I/B/E/S) — Canadian Edition

The I/B/E/S database has provided earnings forecasts and the consensus derived from these forecasts in Canada since 1984. Currently, data for 400 Ca-nadian corporations is included in the active files. Annual earnings, quarterly earnings, and long term growth forecasts are now made by securities analysts who are employed by 53 participating Canadian and U.S. institutional brokerage and research firms whose data are compiled for this comprehensive database. All these 5,000 individual estimates for these companies are included in this database. I/B/E/S is continually updated each day for daily, weekly, and monthly publication. The Canadian Edition is available in hard copy and in a wide variety of computer readable formats, both detail (analyst-by-analyst) and summary (consensus).

Page	Company	$	Latest year end	Earnings per Share		
				Actual	Estimate this year	Estimate next year
3	Alcan Aluminium	$US	9212	(0.31)	(0.16)	0.82
4	Arimetco International		9212	0.08	0.19	0.65
5	Brenda Mines		9212	0.58	1.00	0.50
6	Brunswick Mining and Smelting		9212	0.55	0.06	0.53
7	Cameco		9212	1.03	1.38	1.38
8	Canada Tungsten Mining		9301	(1.88)	n.a.	n.a.
9	Cominco		9212	(0.21)	(0.45)	0.60
10	Denison Mines		9212	0.28	n.a.	n.a.
11	Dia Met Minerals		9301	0.00	n.a.	n.a.
12	Gibraltar Mines		9212	0.25	0.03	0.42
13	Granges		9212	0.00	0.08	0.23
14	Hudson Bay Mining and Smelting		9206	0.39	n.a.	n.a.
15	Inco	$US	9212	(0.04)	(0.25)	1.24
16	Kerr Addison Mines		9212	(0.20)	0.84	0.68
17	Metall Mining		9212	0.26	0.19	0.56
18	Potash Corporation of Saskatchewan		9212	1.50	1.37	1.82
19	Princeton Mining		9212	(0.05)	(0.31)	(0.15)
20	Rio Algom		9212	0.85	0.76	1.30
21	Teck		9212	0.30	0.43	0.79
22	Westmin Resources		9212	(0.71)	(0.20)	0.42

Estimates from I/B/E/S Inc., 345 Hudson St., New York, NY 10014 (212) 243-3335. In Canada: 6 Lansing Square, Ste. 235, Willowdale, ON M2J 1T5 (416) 496-0977.

Mines

Nonferrous Metals & Mining - Industry Report [May-18-1993].
MERRILL LYNCH CAPITAL MARKETS - reported by Roling, D. A.
The copper industry continues to operate at capacity and the
aluminum industry at about 90%. Volumes have been strong
reflecting continued strong demand. It is true that prices have
weakened, more so in some metals than others, but for the most
part (in aluminum and nickel) that has been due to significant
increases in supply out of the Commonwealth of Independent
States. A reason for taking issue with the weak commodity
price argument as it relates to the earnings potential of the
metals companies is that it ignores the tremendous improvement made in productivity during the past five-plus years and
the resulting reduction in costs. Most nonferrous metals companies are well positioned to report significantly higher earnings during the next few years. [RN 1331817]

Nonferrous Metals & Mining - Industry Report [Apr-27-1993].
MERRILL LYNCH CAPITAL MARKETS reported by Roling, D. A.
The intermediate and long term fundamentals remain intact
and other factors are coming into play, such as the recovery in
the U.S. economy and the belief that inventory reduction by
European and Japanese consumers has run its course. For the
most part, the companies in the nonferrous industry have
lowered their costs of production and strengthened their balance sheets, putting them in a strong position to capitalize on
the recovery when it arrives. In 1Q:93, earnings were again
turning out to be less than originally anticipated. The poor first
quarter results for some of the copper companies was a result
of record levels of rainfall that caused a shortfall of about
40,000 metric tons (mt) of production and higher costs. Also
impacting results were lower metal prices. Nonferrous metals
prices for 1Q:93 averaged somewhat lower than for 1Q:92 and
4Q:92. [RN 1326561]

Metal Stock Strategies - Industry Report [Apr-14-1993].
PAINEWEBBER INC. reported by Marcus, P.F.
Copper prices on the London Metal Exchange are down about
$0.04 (U.S.) per pound, and traders report that there has been
massive selling by the Chinese buyers, merchants and producers. However, copper is still the only industrial metal price that
is not depressed in price. Most other prices are at levels far
below long-term market clearing levels. Copper production is
up sharply from 1989 peak levels and is expected to continue
to rise, especially given sizable future additions to mining
capacity. Copper production in 1993 is expected to be up 11%
from 1989 levels versus a 3.7% rise for aluminum, a 3%
decline for nickel and a 2.2% decline for steel. There is no
shortage of copper smelting capacity, as evidenced by the drop
in spot treatment and refining charges. [RN 1323894]

Metal Stock Strategies - Industry Report [Mar-30-1993].
PAINEWEBBER INC. reported by Marcus, P.F.
Evidence is accumulating that aluminum demand in the West
in 1993 will be up moderately at best, with a decline no
surprise. Demand is probably still sliding in Japan, and it is off
in Western Europe. Hence, with inventories at huge levels on
the London Metal Exchange at 1.7 million tonnes, aluminum
inventories on a weeks' supply basis are up to 11. Spot
aluminum ingot on the LME remains depressed at $0.52 (U.S.)
per pound for the week of March 30, 1993 despite some good
news about production problems in the C.I.S. The spot ingot
price is low enough to continue to drag down the prices of
flat-rolled products such as can sheet and common alloy sheet.
[RN 1321490]

Canada: Metals & Minerals - Industry Report [Mar-17-1993].
BBN JAMES CAPEL INC. reported by Ortslan, T.S.
Demand for metals is expected to remain weak during the
remainder of 1993, except in the U.S. Metal inventories are at
record highs, but, relative to the annualized consumption
levels, the respective ratios for each metal have not yet dete-
riorated to the levels seen in the mid-1970s or between 1982
and 1986. A generalized sustained recovery is not expected
before 1994, with inventories returning to normal levels by
late 1994 or 1995. [RN 1317400]

Global Nonferrous Metals & Mining Monthly - Industry Report
[Feb-23-1993]. MERRILL LYNCH CAPITAL MARKETS reported by Roling, D.A., et al
On average, the nonferrous metals and mining industry has
remained profitable throughout the recession and the anemic
recovery period to date. The combination of those two items
(demand and costs) has resulted in the industry weathering
both the recession and slow recovery in good shape. With
limited exception, balance sheets are healthy, cash flow is
adequate, capital expenditure needs are limited, and earnings
are being recorded. Based upon fundamentals, the copper
group is the strongest subset in the industry while aluminum
is the weakest subset. As a result of the differing fundamentals
and recent performance, aluminum may have significantly
higher upside potential ahead. [RN 1305997]

ALCAN ALUMINIUM LIMITED

Exchanges	Price (Jun24'93)	24.50	Trailing P/E	nm	Stock Symbol
TMVN	Trailing Yield (%)	1.53	Trailing EPS	(0.63)	**AL**

Period Ending	Dec92	Dec91	Dec90	Dec89	Dec88
Yearly Statistics	US	US	US	US	US
Price-Close	22.63	23.25	22.50	26.50	26.00
Price-High	26.38	27.75	28.50	29.50	27.00
Price-Low	19.13	20.63	19.63	24.00	20.17
P/E-Close	nm	nm	7.09	5.29	4.50
Dividends per Share	0.45	0.86	1.12	1.12	0.59
Dividend Yield (%)	2.42	4.24	5.81	5.00	2.77
Sales per Share	33.97	34.74	39.09	38.85	36.41
EPS before extra. item	(0.60)	(0.25)	2.33	3.58	3.85
Cash Flow per Share	1.10	1.70	3.54	5.12	6.09
Book Value per Share	19.06	21.17	22.20	20.30	18.06
O/S Common Shares	223,807	223,420	222,667	227,071	227,540
Total Revenue	7,665,000	7,830,000	8,919,000	9,047,000	8,626,000
Income before extra.	(112,000)	(36,000)	543,000	835,000	931,000
Cash Flow	246,000	380,000	792,000	1,164,000	1,426,000
Debt/Equity	0.60	0.61	0.51	0.36	0.35
Return on Capital (%)	1.63	1.35	12.10	21.24	27.62
Ret. on Com. Equity (%)	(3.00)	(1.16)	10.91	18.67	23.48
% Change Profit	(211.1)	(106.6)	(35.0)	(10.3)	115.0
% Change Revenue	(2.1)	(12.2)	(1.4)	4.9	25.4
% Change Assets	(6.2)	1.6	12.0	10.4	12.5

Business:

ALCAN ALUMINIUM LTD. is the parent company of a multinational industrial group engaged in all aspects of the aluminum business. Through subsidiaires and related companies around the world, the activities of the Alcan Group include bauxite mining, alumina refining, aluminum smelting, manufacturing, sales and recycling.

Date		EPS	DPS	Tot Rev	Inc Bex
Mar 93	US	(0.11)	0.08	1,750,000	(20,000)
Dec 92	US	(0.32)	0.08	1,863,000	(62,000)
Sep 92	US	(0.06)	0.08	1,970,000	(10,000)
Jun 92	US	(0.14)	0.15	1,977,000	(27,000)
Mar 92	US	(0.09)	0.15	1,855,000	(15,000)
Dec 91	US	(0.18)	0.15	1,857,000	(36,000)
Sep 91	US	0.00	0.15	1,975,000	6,000
Jun 91	US	(0.04)	0.28	2,032,000	(5,000)

Preferred Div. Coverage	0.0	0.0	24.7
Total Div. Coverage	0.0	0.0	2.0
Interest Coverage	0.5	0.4	3.3
Current Ratio	1.7	1.6	1.6
Operating Margin	1.7	(0.8)	6.4
Asset Turnover	0.7	0.7	0.8
5 YEAR RATIOS (%)			
Return on Capital	12.8	15.6	17.7
Return on Com. Equity	9.8	12.8	14.5
Profit Growth	na	na	48.8
Revenue Growth	2.1	5.2	8.8
Asset Growth	5.7	8.7	9.1
BALANCE SHEET (mil)			
Cash	149	205	200
Current Assets	2,655	3,070	3,370
Net Fixed Assets	6,256	6,525	6,167
Invest's & Advances	923	873	750
Total Assets	10,146	10,816	10,649
Short Term Debt	499	812	820
Current Liabilities	1,545	1,960	2,148
Long Term Debt	2,287	2,185	1,796
Total Liabilities	5,527	5,874	5,495
Total Equity	4,619	4,942	5,154
Total Liab. & Equity	10,146	10,816	10,649
CAPITAL (mil)			
Total Debt	2,786	2,997	2,616
Preferred Equity	353	212	212
Common Equity	4,266	4,730	4,942

Synopsis:

Alcan Aluminium reported at its annual meeting in April 1993 that the continued glut of aluminum inventories has caused a worldwide recession in the aluminum industry. As a result, Alcan reported its ninth consecutive quarterly loss in the first quarter of 1993. Alcan cited high exports from the Commonwealth of Independent States as a major source for the oversupply in the global market. Alcan expects aluminum to continue to be in oversupply in the near term. This is expected to keep the metal's price around record low levels. Alcan expects the aluminum industry to pick up in the long-term.

Alcan's consolidated aluminum shipments in 1992 totaled 2.26 million tonnes compared to 2.2 million tonnes in 1991. The slight increase in volume was more than offset by the declining price of aluminum during the period.

Alcan expects to cut its aluminum smelting capacity in 1993 by 350,000 tonnes. This is in light of the fact that the Commonwealth of Independent States sold approximately 900,000 tonnes of aluminum in 1992, Alcan estimates, and is expected to sell the same amount this year.

Alcan is poised to return to profitability when aluminum prices recover. The difficult market conditions have forced Alcan to become more efficient and more productive. In 1992, Alcan reduced its costs by $225-million while production levels remained about the same as last year. Alcan will continue to aggressively reduce costs in 1993 which has already made the company the lowest cost producer of some aluminum products.

Alcan's capital expenditures in 1992 were down substantially from 1991 levels. This is in response to the difficult market conditions in the aluminum industry. Capital expenditures in 1992 were $474-million, down from $880-million in 1991.

Relative strength to TSE300 / Price / Volume (in 1000's of board lots)

Rank (Profit/Revenue/Assets)
977   7   24

David Morton
Chairman & C.E.O.

Jacques Bougie
President & C.O.O.

Allan A. Hodgson
V.P. & C.F.O.

Address
1188 Sherbrooke Street West
Montreal
PQ
H3A 3G2
(514) 848-8000

Fax: (514) 848-8115
A0001748/G/1.1

ARIMETCO INTERNATIONAL INC.

Exchanges	Price (Jun24'93)	2 .56	Trailing P/E	80 .00	Stock Symbol
T	Trailing Yield (%)	0 .00	Trailing EPS	0 .03	**ARX**

Period Ending	Dec92	Dec91	Dec90	Dec89
Yearly Statistics	US	US	US	US /8M
Price-Close	3 .35	3 .70	1 .30	n t
Price-High	5 .75	4 .50	1 .80	n t
Price-Low	2 .85	1 .25	1 .00	n t
P/E-Close	32 .43	nm	nm	n t
Dividends per Share	0 .00	0 .00	0 .00	0 .00
Dividend Yield (%)	0 .00	0 .00	0 .00	0 .00
Sales per Share	0 .92	0 .56	0 .34	0 .54
EPS before extra. item	0 .07	(0 .02)	(0 .08)	(0 .63)
Cash Flow per Share	0 .17	0 .03	(0 .05)	(0 .88)
Book Value per Share	1 .51	0 .85	0 .76	1 .98
O/S Common Shares	26 ,397	20 ,399	17 ,295	1 ,250
Total Revenue	22 ,597	10 ,498	4 ,904	539
Income before extra.	1 ,661	(432)	(1 ,181)	(789)
Cash Flow	3 ,911	616	(646)	(735)
Debt/Equity	0 .32	0 .80	0 .31	4 .39
Return on Capital (%)	4 .94	0 .01	(3 .08)	na
Ret. on Com. Equity (%)	5 .82	(2 .85)	(15 .18)	na
% Change Profit	484 .1	63 .4	0 .3	na
% Change Revenue	115 .2	114 .1	506 .3	na
% Change Assets	64 .2	78 .5	33 .7	na

Date		EPS	DPS	Tot Rev	Inc Bex
Mar 93	US	(0 .01)	0 .00	5 ,479	(191)
Dec 92	US	0 .01	0 .00	4 ,054	275
Sep 92	US	0 .06	0 .00	10 ,266	1 ,338
Jun 92	US	(0 .02)	0 .00	4 ,550	432
Mar 92	US	(0 .02)	0 .00	3 ,751	(384)
Dec 91	US	0 .03	0 .00	3 ,252	388
Sep 91	US	(0 .03)	0 .00	2 ,761	(489)
Jun 91	US	(0 .01)	0 .00	2 ,510	(121)

Preferred Div. Coverage	np	np	np
Total Div. Coverage	na	na	na
Interest Coverage	1 .9	0 .0	0 .0
Current Ratio	3 .0	1 .0	0 .3
Operating Margin	6 .1	(2 .1)	(11 .4)
Asset Turnover	0 .4	0 .3	0 .2
5 YEAR RATIOS (%)			
Return on Capital	na	na	na
Return on Com. Equity	na	na	na
Profit Growth	na	na	na
Revenue Growth	na	na	na
Asset Growth	na	na	na
BALANCE SHEET (000)			
Cash	7 ,944	3 ,385	499
Current Assets	20 ,267	7 ,328	1 ,316
Net Fixed Assets	34 ,286	26 ,552	18 ,089
Invest's & Advances	1 ,499	0	0
Total Assets	56 ,872	34 ,630	19 ,404
Short Term Debt	2 ,420	3 ,663	1 ,764
Current Liabilities	6 ,689	7 ,193	4 ,093
Long Term Debt	10 ,368	10 ,148	2 ,223
Total Liabilities	17 ,058	17 ,341	6 ,316
Total Equity	39 ,814	17 ,289	13 ,089
Total Liab. & Equity	56 ,872	34 ,630	19 ,404
CAPITAL (000)			
Total Debt	12 ,788	13 ,811	3 ,987
Preferred Equity	0	0	0
Common Equity	39 ,814	17 ,289	13 ,089

Business:

ARIMETCO INTERNATIONAL INC. is a natural resource company engaged in the production of cathode copper through acid leaching of predominantly copper oxide ores, followed by solvent extraction and electrowinning. The company has interests in five mineral properties, three of which contain former producing copper mines.

Synopsis:

In March 1993, Arimetco International and Breakwater Resources announced they will not renew their one-year contract under which Arimetco manages Breakwater's operations. The company said it could now concentrate on its core U.S. copper, industrial minerals and engineering and construction operations.

During 1992, Arimetco produced and sold a total of 17.9 million pounds of cathode copper. Production figures were significantly less than ones forecast. Arimetco attributed lower production to delays in the granting of permits for its leach pads in Nevada. Arimetco expects copper production at the company's properties to increase in 1993.

In November 1992, Arimetco, Breakwater and Nova Gold Resources entered into a joint venture to process ore from Nova Gold's Murray Brook property. Breakwater and Arimetco will hold a 25% interest in the joint venture, with NovaGold controlling the other 50%. The ore will be processed by East West Caribou Mining, a subsidiary of Breakwater Resources. As part of the agreement, Arimetco and Breakwater subscribed for $500,000 worth of Nova Gold shares. Arimetco purchased Breakwater's portion of the subscription in exchange for a promissory note from Breakwater. The Murray Brook deposit is estimated to contain about 25 million pounds of copper.

Arimetco has mining interests in both Nevada and Arizona. Over 51% of production in 1992 was generated from the Yerington property located in Nevada. Production at Arimetco's Johnson Camp property was responsible for almost 46% of copper production in 1992.

Relative strength to TSE300

Price

Volume (in 1000's of board lots)

Rank (Profit/Revenue/Assets)
361   573   472

H. Roy Shipes
Chairman, C.E.O. & President
John D. Bracale
V.P., C.F.O. And Secretary

Address
6245 East Broadway Blvd.
Suite 350
Tucson
AZ
85711
(602) 745-8882

Fax: (602) 745-0315
01000829/G/1.2

BRENDA MINES LTD.

Exchanges	Price (Jun24'93)		14 .75	Trailing P/E		28 .92	Stock Symbol
TV	Trailing Yield (%)		0 .00	Trailing EPS		0 .51	**BND**

Period Ending	Dec92	Dec91	Dec90	Dec89	Dec88
Yearly Statistics					
Price-Close	13 .00	14 .25	12 .25	20 .50	24 .25
Price-High	14 .00	15 .68	20 .25	24 .50	24 .88
Price-Low	12 .50	11 .00	11 .50	19 .25	17 .75
P/E-Close	22 .41	nm	nm	nm	8 .08
Dividends per Share	0 .00	0 .00	0 .00	0 .10	0 .50
Dividend Yield (%)	0 .00	0 .00	0 .00	0 .49	2 .06
Sales per Share	0 .93	1 .26	6 .63	13 .04	17 .49
EPS before extra. item	0 .58	(0 .38)	(0 .30)	(1 .93)	3 .00
Cash Flow per Share	1 .47	1 .49	2 .19	0 .60	4 .05
Book Value per Share	20 .51	19 .92	20 .31	20 .61	22 .64
O/S Common Shares	4,887	4,887	4,887	4,887	4,887
Total Revenue	10,573	14,227	50,621	72,332	99,241
Income before extra.	2,852	(1,871)	(1,476)	(9,424)	14,628
Cash Flow	7,186	7,292	10,697	2,944	19,737
Debt/Equity	nd	nd	nd	nd	nd
Return on Capital (%)	4 .35	(2 .70)	(0 .88)	(11 .23)	22 .90
Ret. on Com. Equity (%)	2 .89	(1 .90)	(1 .48)	(8 .92)	14 .02
% Change Profit	252 .4	(26 .8)	84 .3	(164 .4)	150 .0
% Change Revenue	(25 .7)	(71 .9)	(30 .0)	(27 .1)	11 .3
% Change Assets	3 .0	4 .7	(6 .2)	(12 .6)	9 .2
Preferred Div. Coverage	np	np	np		
Total Div. Coverage	na	na	na		
Interest Coverage	nd	nd	nd		
Current Ratio	39 .4	95 .6	100 .9		
Operating Margin	(38 .2)	(171 .2)	(12 .6)		
Asset Turnover	0 .0	0 .1	0 .3		
5 YEAR RATIOS (%)					
Return on Capital	2 .5	4 .1	5 .6		
Return on Com. Equity	0 .9	1 .6	2 .5		
Profit Growth	(13 .4)	na	na		
Revenue Growth	(34 .9)	(28 .3)	12 .9		
Asset Growth	(0 .8)	(2 .3)	(2 .7)		
BALANCE SHEET (000)					
Cash	102,098	100,655	94,987		
Current Assets	110,266	106,486	106,340		
Net Fixed Assets	1,903	3,188	4,861		
Invest's & Advances	0	0	200		
Total Assets	120,673	117,181	111,936		
Short Term Debt	0	0	0		
Current Liabilities	2,798	1,114	1,054		
Long Term Debt	0	0	0		
Total Liabilities	20,454	19,814	12,698		
Total Equity	100,219	97,367	99,238		
Total Liab. & Equity	120,673	117,181	111,936		
CAPITAL (000)					
Total Debt	0	0	0		
Preferred Equity	0	0	0		
Common Equity	100,219	97,367	99,238		

Business:

BRENDA MINES LTD. is a natural resources company. Its mining and milling operation in British Columbia is currently in the reclamation stage. The company is engaged in oil and gas production in Australia. Its consulting group provides mechanical maintenance, equipment sales, and environment and process control services to mining companies worldwide. Noranda Inc. owns 76% of the company.

Date	EPS	DPS	Tot Rev	Inc Bex
Mar 93	0 .27	0 .00	4,676	1,314
Dec 92	(0 .16)	0 .00	1,149	(775)
Sep 92	0 .15	0 .00	3,040	741
Jun 92	0 .25	0 .00	3,030	1,247
Mar 92	0 .34	0 .00	3,354	1,639
Dec 91	(1 .12)	0 .00	1,534	(5,470)
Sep 91	0 .11	0 .00	3,782	499
Jun 91	0 .30	0 .00	3,758	1,478

Synopsis:

For the year ended December 31, 1993, Brenda Mines reported earnings, but none of its revenues came from mining activities. Revenues for 1992 were derived from Brenda's oil interest in Australia and short-term investment income.

Brenda's oil interest consists of a 1.09% joint venture interest in the Jabiru, Challis and Cassini projects in the Timor Sea off the northwestern coast of Australia. Brenda's share of crude oil sales dipped to 484 barrels per day in 1992, compared to 650 barrels per day in 1991. The lower share is a result of declining field production rates.

Brenda's exploration expenditures in 1992 fell to $900,000 from $2.5-million in 1991. The declining figures reflect lower spending in both the Noranda Exploration and Minnova Inc. joint ventures.

Brenda's oil production is forecasted to be lower in 1993. The company's share of production for 1993 is estimated at 150,400 barrels, down from 177,036 barrels in 1992. At the end of 1992, Brenda had cash and short-term investments equaling $102.1-million. The company expects to maintain its existing investments, subject to ongoing determination of profitability.

Relative strength to TSE300 / Price / Volume (in 1000's of board lots) charts

Rank (Profit/Revenue/Assets)
319   689   387

Bernard O. Brynelsen
Chairman
David L. Bumstead
President

Address
P.O. Box 755
BCE Place
Toronto
ON
M5J 2T3
(416) 982-7111

Fax: (416) 982-7490
B0003445/G/1.2

BRUNSWICK MINING AND SMELTING CORPORATION LIMITED

Exchanges	Price (Jun24'93)	8.37	Trailing P/E	46.53	Stock Symbol
TM	Trailing Yield (%)	5.67	Trailing EPS	0.18	**BMS**

Period Ending	Dec92	Dec91	Dec90	Dec89	Dec88
Yearly Statistics					
Price-Close	8.75	7.00	8.00	10.63	11.50
Price-High	10.50	9.38	11.00	14.50	13.50
Price-Low	7.00	6.50	6.75	10.25	9.50
P/E-Close	21.34	nm	12.50	13.28	13.22
Dividends per Share	0.50	0.25	0.70	0.70	0.40
Dividend Yield (%)	5.71	3.57	8.75	6.59	3.48
Sales per Share	7.95	4.54	7.20	8.72	9.35
EPS before extra. item	0.41	(0.53)	0.64	0.80	0.87
Cash Flow per Share	1.15	(0.41)	1.22	1.41	1.47
Book Value per Share	5.91	5.96	6.74	6.70	6.37
O/S Common Shares	39,924	39,096	38,979	37,792	35,872
Total Revenue	338,656	188,711	285,773	345,006	339,011
Income before extra.	16,176	(20,836)	25,021	29,671	31,041
Cash Flow	45,611	(15,845)	47,371	52,256	52,380
Debt/Equity	0.26	0.39	0.04	0.13	0.29
Return on Capital (%)	9.46	(13.15)	11.91	14.07	17.81
Ret. on Com. Equity (%)	6.90	(8.40)	9.70	12.32	14.41
% Change Profit	177.6	(183.3)	(15.7)	(4.4)	58.0
% Change Revenue	79.5	(34.0)	(17.2)	1.8	20.9
% Change Assets	(0.6)	14.0	(9.8)	3.0	1.7

Preferred Div. Coverage	np	np	np
Total Div. Coverage	0.8	0.0	0.9
Interest Coverage	7.2	0.0	15.3
Current Ratio	1.8	1.7	6.4
Operating Margin	7.6	(24.6)	10.5
Asset Turnover	0.7	0.4	0.7
5 YEAR RATIOS (%)			
Return on Capital	8.0	8.0	9.6
Return on Com. Equity	7.0	7.6	8.6
Profit Growth	(3.8)	na	36.4
Revenue Growth	3.8	(3.8)	6.3
Asset Growth	1.3	3.7	1.8
BALANCE SHEET (000)			
Cash	70,815	71,206	71,362
Current Assets	185,104	190,290	133,693
Net Fixed Assets	244,396	241,567	244,936
Invest's & Advances	0	0	0
Total Assets	429,591	431,977	378,773
Short Term Debt	53,541	81,105	1,359
Current Liabilities	101,060	115,353	20,904
Long Term Debt	8,050	9,649	10,184
Total Liabilities	193,595	198,854	115,946
Total Equity	235,996	233,123	262,827
Total Liab. & Equity	429,591	431,977	378,773
CAPITAL (000)			
Total Debt	61,591	90,754	11,543
Preferred Equity	0	0	0
Common Equity	235,996	233,123	262,827

Date	EPS	DPS	Tot Rev	Inc Bex
Mar 93	(0.17)	0.00	63,847	(6,770)
Dec 92	(0.15)	0.33	65,920	(6,080)
Sep 92	0.21	0.00	89,426	8,414
Jun 92	0.29	0.15	102,500	11,460
Mar 92	0.06	0.00	80,810	2,382
Dec 91	0.01	0.10	77,704	172
Sep 91	(0.17)	0.00	55,603	(6,571)
Jun 91	(0.26)	0.15	32,142	(10,123)

Business:

BRUNSWICK MINING AND SMELTING CORP. LTD. is engaged in mining and metallurgical operations at its facilities in New Brunswick. The company mines lead, zinc, silver, and copper and smelts lead. The company also makes diammonium phosphate, a fertilizer. Brunswick is 65% owned by Noranda Inc.

Synopsis:

In late May 1993, Brunswick Mining and Smelting Corp. Ltd. told shareholders at its annual meeting that unless new sources of ore are found, production will have to be cut. Brunswick Mining employs some 2,000 people in northern New Brunswick. In response to this possible cut, Brunswick's president said at least $37.5-million in exploration costs will be spent over the next five years. The exploration program will take place near the Brunswick Mine and another mine operated by Health Steele, a subsidiary.

In April 1993, Brunswick announced its intention to enter into a 50/50 joint venture with Noranda Exploration. The two companies will explore the wellknown Buchans base metal area in Newfoundland. Preliminary field work is underway, which reflects Brunswick's commitment to base metal exploration in Eastern Canada.

Brunswick Mining spent $6.6-million on exploration for the year ended December 1992. This is up slightly from the previous year. Brunswick aims to replace the depleted ore reserves either by expanding existing ore bodies or through the discovery of new ones.

For the year ended December 1992, Brunswick had export sales of almost $201-million. This is up sharply from the 1991 figure of $114.5-million.

The outlook for Brunswick Mining depends upon demand for the metals it produces and the price it receives for them. Since metals are an industrial product, demand and price are directly related to the general level of economic activity.

Rank (Profit/Revenue/Assets)
138   212   228

John C. White
Chairman

John K. Carrington
President & C.E.O.

A.R. Thomas
V.P., Finance

Address
P.O. Box 3000
Bathurst
NB
E2A 3Z8
(506) 546-6671

Fax: (506) 548-8379
B0004526/G/1.1

CAMECO CORPORATION

Exchanges	Price (Jun24'93)	21.37	Trailing P/E	133.59	Stock Symbol
TM	Trailing Yield (%)	2.34	Trailing EPS	0.16	**CCO**

Period Ending	Dec92	Dec91	Dec90	Dec89	Dec88
Yearly Statistics					
Price-Close	17.54	13.50	na	na	na
Price-High	18.38	15.50	na	na	na
Price-Low	13.50	13.13	na	na	na
P/E-Close	116.93	13.11	n t	n t	n t
Dividends per Share	0.50	0.25	0.00	1.15	0.00
Dividend Yield (%)	2.85	1.85	0.00	na	0.00
Sales per Share	5.87	6.12	7.60	7.84	5.91
EPS before extra. item	0.15	1.03	2.21	0.58	na
Cash Flow per Share	2.45	2.68	2.37	4.28	1.48
Book Value per Share	21.48	21.83	23.55	21.34	21.57
O/S Common Shares	51,981	51,934	41,534	41,534	40,004
Total Revenue	247,098	301,173	373,090	319,488	252,584
Income before extra.	7,970	47,893	91,621	23,519	56,321
Cash Flow	127,242	124,406	98,553	174,441	59,061
Debt/Equity	0.15	0.14	0.36	0.59	0.74
Return on Capital (%)	1.50	5.05	9.07	5.33	8.81
Ret. on Com. Equity (%)	0.71	4.54	9.83	2.69	11.11
% Change Profit	(83.4)	(47.7)	289.6	(58.2)	(5.5)
% Change Revenue	(18.0)	(19.3)	16.8	26.5	26.2
% Change Assets	0.2	(3.2)	(6.4)	(3.4)	109.0

Preferred Div. Coverage	np	np	np
Total Div. Coverage	0.3	3.7	na
Interest Coverage	1.6	3.6	3.6
Current Ratio	6.8	4.7	5.1
Operating Margin	26.1	21.9	24.1
Asset Turnover	0.2	0.2	0.2
5 YEAR RATIOS (%)			
Return on Capital	6.0	na	na
Return on Com. Equity	5.8	na	na
Profit Growth	(33.2)	na	na
Revenue Growth	4.3	na	na
Asset Growth	12.8	na	na
BALANCE SHEET (000)			
Cash	45,008	0	0
Current Assets	264,731	229,571	264,323
Net Fixed Assets	991,613	1,039,838	1,076,047
Invest's & Advances	0	0	0
Total Assets	1,376,483	1,373,996	1,419,192
Short Term Debt	0	13,287	13,263
Current Liabilities	38,779	48,623	51,625
Long Term Debt	169,591	148,938	340,957
Total Liabilities	259,977	240,224	441,220
Total Equity	1,116,506	1,133,772	977,972
Total Liab. & Equity	1,376,483	1,373,996	1,419,192
CAPITAL (000)			
Total Debt	169,591	162,225	354,220
Preferred Equity	0	0	0
Common Equity	1,116,506	1,133,772	977,972

Business:

CAMECO CORP. is one of the world's largest uranium producers, supplying about 10% of the western world's uranium consumption requirements. It has mining operations in Saskatchewan and processing facilities in Ontario where uranium concentrates are converted to fuel products for nuclear power plants. Cameco is 42% owned by public shareholders.

Date	EPS	DPS	Tot Rev	Inc Bex
Mar 93	0.35	0.13	52,809	18,345
Dec 92	(0.44)	0.13	120,643	(22,796)
Sep 92	0.14	0.13	48,221	7,377
Jun 92	0.11	0.13	49,374	5,720
Mar 92	0.34	0.13	88,092	17,669
Dec 91	0.38	0.13	102,012	18,919
Sep 91	0.33	0.13	69,827	16,891
Jun 91	0.12	0.00	60,376	4,895

Synopsis:

In May 1993, shareholders of Cameco Corporation were pleased to hear that the federal government was selling half of its stake in the company. The $102.5-million deal will leave Ottawa with five million shares of Cameco, or 9.6% of the total outstanding shares. Investors were pleased with the sale and the reduced government ownership of Cameco. Public ownership of Cameco will rise to 51.1% from 41.9% after the deal closes on June 7, 1993.

In April 1993, the Toronto Stock Exchange requested and received additional information regarding Cameco's 1992 exploration program at the Fort a la Corne diamond project in central Saskatchewan. The joint venture property, held by Cameco, Monopros Limited and Uranerz Exploration and Mining Limited, has been the subject of speculation concerning the possibility of profitable diamond mining. Results of the 1992 exploration program, released on April 15, 1993, showed yields of 138 macro diamonds with a total weight of 7.610 carats. The largest stone recovered had a weight of 0.985 carats.

In March 1993, The Northern Miner reported that reserves at Cameco's mineral properties had fallen. As of January 1,1993, Cameco's share of uranium reserves from five deposits was 460 million pounds. This represents a drop of 7%, or 35 million pounds, compared with one year ago. The drop is attributed to the sale of Cameco's 20% interest in the Cluff Lake project, which accounted for eight million pounds and the reduced reserves at the Eagle Point project.

A new treaty signed by the United States and Canada,in early March 1993, will enable Canadian companies to sell uranium to Taiwan. The agreement allows Canada to bypass its official policy of not selling nuclear materials to any country that has not signed the Nuclear Non-Proliferation Treaty by channeling sales through the U.S. This is welcome news for Cameco, which is one of the lowest-cost producers of uranium in the world.

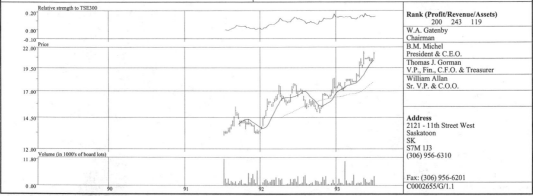

Rank (Profit/Revenue/Assets)		
200	243	119

W.A. Gatenby
Chairman
B.M. Michel
President & C.E.O.
Thomas J. Gorman
V.P., Fin., C.F.O. & Treasurer
William Allan
Sr. V.P. & C.O.O.

Address
2121 - 11th Street West
Saskatoon
SK
S7M 1J3
(306) 956-6310

Fax: (306) 956-6201
C0002655/G/1.1

CANADA TUNGSTEN INC.

Exchanges	Price (Jun24'93)	1.47	Trailing P/E	nm	Stock Symbol
TM	Trailing Yield (%)	0.00	Trailing EPS	(1.90)	**CTG**

Period Ending	Jan93	Dec91	Dec90	Dec89	Dec88
Yearly Statistics					
Price-Close	1.50	3.00	2.00	5.50	6.50
Price-High	3.10	3.50	5.25	8.50	7.50
Price-Low	1.35	2.00	1.50	4.80	4.50
P/E-Close	nm	nm	nm	nm	nm
Dividends per Share	0.19	0.20	0.20	0.20	0.20
Dividend Yield (%)	12.67	6.67	10.00	3.64	3.08
Sales per Share	0.88	0.86	0.41	0.60	0.59
EPS before extra. item	(1.88)	(0.12)	(0.33)	(0.28)	(0.10)
Cash Flow per Share	(0.21)	0.04	(0.26)	(0.17)	(0.01)
Book Value per Share	1.49	3.58	4.04	4.54	5.00
O/S Common Shares	29,806	20,756	18,942	18,239	17,678
Total Revenue	19,715	18,044	8,085	11,985	11,910
Income before extra.	(41,211)	(2,451)	(6,316)	(5,089)	(1,806)
Cash Flow	(4,630)	825	(4,691)	(2,979)	(144)
Debt/Equity	0.02	0.01	0.02	0.02	0.02
Return on Capital (%)	(68.33)	(3.09)	(7.55)	(5.60)	(1.81)
Ret. on Com. Equity (%)	(69.45)	(3.25)	(7.93)	(5.95)	(2.04)
% Change Profit	(1,581.4)	61.2	(24.1)	(181.8)	38.3
% Change Revenue	9.3	123.2	(32.5)	0.6	4.8
% Change Assets	(39.1)	4.0	0.0	(4.9)	(0.1)

Preferred Div. Coverage	np	np	np
Total Div. Coverage	0.0	0.0	0.0
Interest Coverage	0.0	0.0	0.0
Current Ratio	5.2	7.0	17.2
Operating Margin	(18.7)	(7.0)	(54.0)
Asset Turnover	0.4	0.2	0.1
5 YEAR RATIOS (%)			
Return on Capital	(17.3)	(4.2)	(8.8)
Return on Com. Equity	(17.7)	(4.5)	(9.7)
Profit Growth	na	na	na
Revenue Growth	11.6	(3.8)	(23.0)
Asset Growth	(11.5)	(3.2)	11.9
BALANCE SHEET (000)			
Cash	9,113	8,281	4,438
Current Assets	14,260	16,471	13,812
Net Fixed Assets	36,222	64,682	60,686
Invest's & Advances	575	694	6,172
Total Assets	51,057	83,862	80,670
Short Term Debt	0	0	0
Current Liabilities	2,747	2,353	802
Long Term Debt	946	867	1,741
Total Liabilities	6,620	9,618	4,131
Total Equity	44,437	74,244	76,539
Total Liab. & Equity	51,057	83,862	80,670
CAPITAL (000)			
Total Debt	946	867	1,741
Preferred Equity	0	0	0
Common Equity	44,437	74,244	76,539

Business:

CANADA TUNGSTEN is a tungsten mining company. The primary assets owned by Canada Tungsten include a tungsten mine, two other undeveloped tungsten ore bodies, a 50% interest in the Aurora Partnership Mine and the Kremzar gold mine, as well as a diversified inventory of royalty interests and exploration properties. The tungsten mine at Tungsten and the Kremzar gold mine are on a care and maintenance basis.

Date	EPS	DPS	Tot Rev	Inc Bex
Mar 93	(0.03)	0.00	2,815	(1,027)
Jan 93	(0.06)	0.00	5,210	(1,362)
Sep 92	(1.77)	0.00	4,843	(38,645)
Jun 92	(0.04)	0.00	3,989	(1,041)
Mar 92	(0.01)	0.19	5,673	(163)
Dec 91	(0.03)	0.00	6,288	(522)
Sep 91	(0.03)	0.00	5,543	(689)
Jun 91	(0.03)	0.00	3,786	(619)

Synopsis:

At the end of 1992, Canada Tungsten Mining Corporation announced that it will proceed with a planned amalgamation with Canamax Resources Inc. and Minerex Resources Ltd. The deal will see Canada Tungsten and Minerex Resources Ltd. combine their assets to form a new company named Minerex Resources Inc. The new company will be a wholly owned subsidiary of Canada Tungsten. The reorganization will be fully completed effective January 1, 1993. The terms of the reorganization are as follows: shareholders of Canada Tungsten Mining will receive one common shares of Canada Tungsten Inc. for each Canada Tungsten Mining share held; shareholders of Canamax will receive 0.2 common shares of Canada Tungsten Inc. for each Canamax common share held.; and shareholders of Minerex will receive 0.5 common shares of Canada Tungsten Inc. for each Minerex common share held.

Canada Tungsten's primary assets include a world class tungsten mine and two other undeveloped tungsten ore bodies, a 50% interest in the Aurora Partnership mine and the Kremzar gold mine, as well as a diversified inventory of exploration properties and royalty interests. Canada Tungsten's mine in Tungsten, Northwest Territories, and the Kremzar gold mine have both been placed on a care and maintenance basis. Resumption of operations at these mines will require a significant rise in metal prices.

Canada Tungsten operates in both Canada and the United States. Sales of the company's current principal products, which are tungsten and gold, are primarily in the United States. In contrast, almost 90% of Canada Tungsten's assets are located in Canada.

Relative strength to TSE300 / Price / Volume (in 1000's of board lots) charts

Rank (Profit/Revenue/Assets)
948 616 537

Douglas A. Berlis
Chairman Of The Board

Wayne D. Lenton
President & C.E.O.

Udo E. Von Doehren
Vice President, Finance

John C. Devitt
Vice President, Operations

Address
Suite 1600
Oceanic Plaza
1066 West Hastings St.
Vancouver
BC
V6E 3X1
(604) 689-0046
Fax: (604) 688-8370
C0002354/G/1.2

COMINCO LTD.

Exchanges		Price (Jun24'93)		15.37		Trailing P/E		nm		Stock Symbol
TMVA		Trailing Yield (%)		2.93		Trailing EPS		(0.82)		**CLT**

Period Ending	Dec92	Dec91	Dec90	Dec89	Dec88
Yearly Statistics					
Price-Close	17.75	21.38	21.25	27.25	25.00
Price-High	23.50	25.75	28.00	32.13	25.13
Price-Low	17.13	19.50	19.13	22.50	12.75
P/E-Close	nm	nm	32.69	10.32	9.77
Dividends per Share	0.40	0.50	0.50	0.50	0.30
Dividend Yield (%)	2.25	2.34	2.35	1.84	1.20
Sales per Share	18.47	17.76	17.69	20.09	21.22
EPS before extra. item	(0.42)	(0.56)	0.65	2.64	2.56
Cash Flow per Share	1.18	0.62	2.52	5.41	5.50
Book Value per Share	12.37	12.85	13.97	13.83	11.85
O/S Common Shares	79,456	79,440	79,333	79,331	79,085
Total Revenue	1,554,646	1,335,017	1,417,545	1,609,704	1,667,938
Income before extra.	(30,167)	(41,309)	54,756	214,615	213,472
Cash Flow	93,526	45,773	199,949	428,336	430,653
Debt/Equity	0.61	0.60	0.44	0.36	0.28
Return on Capital (%)	2.30	(0.29)	6.83	22.83	26.10
Ret. on Com. Equity (%)	(3.33)	(4.20)	4.65	20.59	24.03
% Change Profit	27.0	(175.4)	(74.5)	0.5	164.7
% Change Revenue	16.5	(5.8)	(11.9)	(3.5)	26.9
% Change Assets	(2.5)	0.2	0.4	17.3	10.0
Preferred Div. Coverage	0.0	0.0	15.8		
Total Div. Coverage	0.0	0.0	1.3		
Interest Coverage	0.9	0.0	2.3		
Current Ratio	1.8	1.7	1.8		
Operating Margin	0.3	(2.4)	7.6		
Asset Turnover	0.6	0.5	0.6		
5 YEAR RATIOS (%)					
Return on Capital	11.6	13.6	13.7		
Return on Com. Equity	8.3	11.1	9.6		
Profit Growth	na	na	27.0		
Revenue Growth	3.4	0.1	(0.6)		
Asset Growth	4.7	6.6	4.2		
BALANCE SHEET (000)					
Cash	18,969	28,183	48,201		
Current Assets	682,375	689,312	671,676		
Net Fixed Assets	1,658,794	1,659,929	1,657,431		
Invest's & Advances	48,743	116,354	129,556		
Total Assets	2,432,567	2,495,311	2,490,351		
Short Term Debt	156,727	193,982	154,043		
Current Liabilities	382,758	395,871	374,993		
Long Term Debt	542,423	544,352	428,369		
Total Liabilities	1,281,752	1,271,540	1,177,488		
Total Equity	1,150,815	1,223,771	1,312,863		
Total Liab. & Equity	2,432,567	2,495,311	2,490,351		
CAPITAL (000)					
Total Debt	699,150	738,334	582,412		
Preferred Equity	167,692	203,188	204,851		
Common Equity	983,123	1,020,583	1,108,012		

Business:

COMINCO LTD. is an integrated natural resource company with activities in mining, smelting and refining, mineral exploration, and fertilizer production. The company produces zinc and lead. It also mines copper and other metals at mines in Canada, the United States, Mexico and Spain. The company sells fertilizers under the Elephant Brand in Canada and under generic names in the United States.

Date	EPS	DPS	Tot Rev	Inc Bex
Mar 93	(0.47)	0.00	291,500	(36,800)
Dec 92	(1.21)	0.20	365,644	(95,167)
Sep 92	0.64	0.20	425,800	51,800
Jun 92	0.22	0.20	419,000	18,100
Mar 92	(0.07)	0.00	336,300	(4,900)
Dec 91	(0.21)	0.25	351,920	(16,309)
Sep 91	(0.29)	0.00	307,100	(22,100)
Jun 91	0.08	0.25	391,300	7,300

Synopsis:

In late May 1993, Cominco announced it would cut an additional 100 jobs from its money-losing Trail, B.C., lead-zinc operation. This follows a dramatic restructuring of the Trail operation in 1992 which saw 632 jobs eliminated in an effort to ensure business viability at the mine. Cominco plans to cut additional jobs over the next three to four years at Trail in the face of severely depressed market conditions.

In late April 1993, Cominco announced it finally decided to scrap its inoperative, $135-million QSL lead smelter in Trail, B.C. The smelter has been out of service since March 1990. As a result of the problems with its smelter in Trail and the need to finance its share of the $360-million (U.S.) Quebrada Blanca copper project in Chile, The Dominion Bond Rating Service reduced the rating on Cominco's senior debt to triple-B (high) from A (low), and the rating on the preferred shares from Pfd-3 to Pfd-2.

Cominco's Quebrada Blanca copper project has now moved into the major phase of its construction, according to the company's first quarter report for 1993. Engineering at the property is 90% completed with on site power generation equipment delivered and ready for installation. The project is on schedule with initial production set for the first half of 1994. When the Quebrada Blanca mine is completed it is expected to produce 165 million pounds of high-grade cathode copper annually. Cominco has a 38.25% participating interest in the property.

Cominco's main industry segments are mining and integrated metals, and fertilizers. In 1992, Cominco reported that almost 76% of total sales were generated from the mining and integrated sector with the remainder coming from the fertilizer business. These percentages are roughly at the same level as last year.

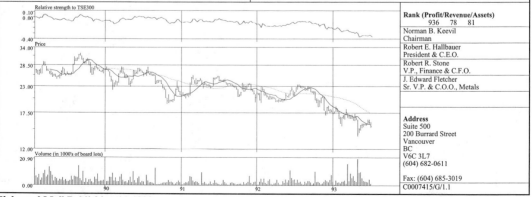

Rank (Profit/Revenue/Assets)
936   78   81

Norman B. Keevil
Chairman

Robert E. Hallbauer
President & C.E.O.

Robert R. Stone
V.P., Finance & C.F.O.

J. Edward Fletcher
Sr. V.P. & C.O.O., Metals

Address
Suite 500
200 Burrard Street
Vancouver
BC
V6C 3L7
(604) 682-0611

Fax: (604) 685-3019
C0007415/G/1.1

DENISON MINES LIMITED

Exchanges	Price (Jun24'93)	0.35	Trailing P/E	nm	Stock Symbol
TM	Trailing Yield (%)	0.00	Trailing EPS	(0.28)	**DEN.B**

Period Ending	Dec92	Dec91	Dec90	Dec89	Dec88
Yearly Statistics					
Price-Close	0.16	0.22	0.70	4.00	4.90
Price-High	0.35	1.00	3.45	6.88	6.75
Price-Low	0.07	0.20	0.45	3.70	4.35
P/E-Close	0.57	nm	nm	nm	nm
Dividends per Share	0.00	0.00	0.00	0.24	0.24
Dividend Yield (%)	0.00	0.00	0.00	6.00	4.86
Sales per Share	2.50	5.03	4.93	4.91	8.14
EPS before extra. item	0.28	(1.71)	(4.83)	(0.47)	(2.71)
Cash Flow per Share	(0.12)	0.69	0.31	0.74	1.41
Book Value per Share	(3.16)	(3.80)	(2.38)	2.38	3.01
O/S Common Shares	64,143	64,143	64,143	64,143	53,344
Total Revenue	206,613	317,038	318,282	336,904	441,017
Income before extra.	36,751	(91,144)	(291,268)	(4,278)	(120,256)
Cash Flow	(7,601)	44,513	19,730	47,409	73,613
Debt/Equity	na	na	6.35	0.52	0.67
Return on Capital (%)	97.51	(14.05)	(64.41)	5.89	(8.13)
Ret. on Com. Equity (%)	na	na	nm	(19.23)	(67.50)
% Change Profit	140.3	68.7	(6,708.5)	96.4	(541.2)
% Change Revenue	(34.8)	(0.4)	(5.5)	(23.6)	(4.0)
% Change Assets	(7.4)	(19.4)	(36.4)	(21.8)	(16.1)
Preferred Div. Coverage	na	na	0.0		
Total Div. Coverage	na	na	0.0		
Interest Coverage	10.3	0.0	0.0		
Current Ratio	1.2	1.1	1.9		
Operating Margin	12.8	(5.3)	(36.7)		
Asset Turnover	0.4	0.7	0.5		
5 YEAR RATIOS (%)					
Return on Capital	3.4	(14.0)	(10.6)		
Return on Com. Equity	na	na	nm		
Profit Growth	6.2	na	na		
Revenue Growth	(14.8)	(5.4)	(10.8)		
Asset Growth	(20.8)	(21.5)	(18.4)		
BALANCE SHEET (000)					
Cash	19,718	23,341	22,930		
Current Assets	48,229	84,393	121,202		
Net Fixed Assets	31,261	142,906	457,631		
Invest's & Advances	1,787	4,121	8,145		
Total Assets	437,838	473,027	586,978		
Short Term Debt	0	5,468	7,865		
Current Liabilities	40,141	76,089	64,829		
Long Term Debt	80,449	122,950	211,260		
Total Liabilities	457,720	529,660	552,467		
Total Equity	(19,882)	(56,633)	34,511		
Total Liab. & Equity	437,838	473,027	586,978		
CAPITAL (000)					
Total Debt	80,449	128,418	219,125		
Preferred Equity	182,511	186,861	186,861		
Common Equity	(202,393)	(243,494)	(152,350)		

Business:

DENISON MINES LTD. is a Canadian energy resources company. It has uranium deposits in Saskatchewan and Australia, uranium recovery operations in Louisiana and oil and gas operations in Greece. Roman Corp. Ltd. of Toronto is the company's largest shareholder.

Date	EPS	DPS	Tot Rev	Inc Bex
Mar 93	(0.07)	0.00	22,348	28
Dec 92	(0.06)	0.00	28,462	955
Sep 92	(0.04)	0.00	27,324	1,792
Jun 92	(0.11)	0.00	36,311	(2,118)
Mar 92	0.49	0.00	115,959	36,122
Dec 91	(1.22)	0.00	81,601	(73,406)
Sep 91	(0.38)	0.00	68,333	(19,655)
Jun 91	(0.08)	0.00	98,818	(1,073)

Synopsis:

Denison's earning potential is dependent upon an arbitration case being heard between Denison and Ontario Hydro. The arbitration case began in April 1993 and is expected to last several months. Denison alleges that the utility owes the company up to $350-million in undepreciated capital costs because of its decision to end a long-term uranium supply contract. The possibility of receiving an award from the arbitration panel has become Denison's major asset. The company's only other assets are producing oil and gas wells and interests in non-producing uranium properties. Creditors who hold Denison's large debt are also hoping for a positive result from the panel. Denison owes some $186-million in liabilities consisting of bank loans, mortgages and reclamation costs.

In the first quarter of 1993, Denison Mines completed negotiation with Total Cie Miniera regarding two uranium mines located in Saskatchewan. Denison says it now owns a 19.5% interest in the Midwest uranium project and a 22.5% interest in the McClean uranium project. The two properties have combined reserves of more than 80 million pounds of uranium oxide.

Uranium sales for the year ended 1992 were sharply lower because of the drop in sales to Ontario Hydro. Denison sold 838,855 pounds of uranium to Ontario Hydro in 1992, down from 1,998,096 pounds in 1991. Denison did record profits in 1992, but the results were inflated by gains arising on the sale of various assets in the period.

Relative strength to TSE300

Price

Volume (in 1000's of board lots)

Rank (Profit/Revenue/Assets)
970   217   216

Helen E. Roman-Barber
Chairman

William James
President & C.E.O.

R.B. Keeler
V.P., Controller

Address
National Bank Building
150 York Street
Suite 1508
Toronto
ON
M5H 3S5
(416) 865-1991
Fax: (416) 865-0632
D0000940/G/1.4

DIA MET MINERALS LTD

Exchanges	Price (Jun24'93)	53.50	Trailing P/E	53500.00	Stock Symbol
TV	Trailing Yield (%)	0.00	Trailing EPS	0.00	DMM

Period Ending	Jan93	Jan92	Jan91
Yearly Statistics			
Price-Close	38.50	9.00	0.26
Price-High	60.00	9.13	0.72
Price-Low	4.60	0.32	0.20
P/E-Close	38,500.00	1,800.00	260.00
Dividends per Share	0.00	0.00	0.00
Dividend Yield (%)	0.00	0.00	0.00
Sales per Share	na	na	na
EPS before extra. item	0.00	0.01	0.00
Cash Flow per Share	0.00	(0.00)	0.00
Book Value per Share	0.49	0.36	0.35
O/S Common Shares	10,183	9,359	8,572
Total Revenue	24	60	7
Income before extra.	6	47	5
Cash Flow	6	(13)	7
Debt/Equity	nd	nd	0.03
Return on Capital (%)	0.16	1.46	na
Ret. on Com. Equity (%)	0.16	1.48	na
% Change Profit	(86.2)	892.5	na
% Change Revenue	(59.5)	755.8	na
% Change Assets	46.6	10.7	na

Preferred Div. Coverage	np	np	np
Total Div. Coverage	na	na	na
Interest Coverage	nd	nd	na
Current Ratio	14.8	5.0	0.7
Operating Margin	26.9	na	68.1
Asset Turnover	na	na	na
5 YEAR RATIOS (%)			
Return on Capital	na	na	na
Return on Com. Equity	na	na	na
Profit Growth	na	na	na
Revenue Growth	na	na	na
Asset Growth	na	na	na
BALANCE SHEET			
Cash	1,335,645	144,522	0
Current Assets	1,424,972	215,701	150,830
Net Fixed Assets	3,802,958	3,350,422	3,070,146
Invest's & Advances	0	0	0
Total Assets	5,227,930	3,566,123	3,220,976
Short Term Debt	0	0	90,848
Current Liabilities	96,469	43,171	210,175
Long Term Debt	0	0	0
Total Liabilities	270,229	198,971	210,175
Total Equity	4,957,701	3,367,152	3,010,801
Total Liab. & Equity	5,227,930	3,566,123	3,220,976
CAPITAL			
Total Debt	0	0	90,848
Preferred Equity	0	0	0
Common Equity	4,957,701	3,367,152	3,010,801

Business:

DIA MET MINERALS LTD. is in the mineral exploration business with a special interest in diamonds. Its principal properties are located in the Northwest Territories.

Date	EPS	DPS	Tot Rev	Inc Bex
Jan 93	0.00	0.00	1	(3)
Oct 92	0.00	0.00	5	1
Jul 92	0.00	0.00	18	17
Apr 92	(0.00)	0.00	0	(9)
Jan 92	0.01	0.00	60	54
Oct 91	0.00	0.00	0	(1)
Jul 91	0.00	0.00	0	(1)
Apr 91	(0.00)	0.00	0	(6)

Synopsis:

Dia Met Minerals Ltd. plans to construct a pilot plant in the Lac de Gras area of the Northwest Territories and perform tests on two 5,000-tonne bulk samples in early 1994. The tests will help the company decide whether a profitable diamond mine could be built. Mining industry experts have said that a sample of 5,000 carats of diamonds is required to provide proof that a mine is economically viable while others estimate that up to 10,000 carats have to be sampled. Dia Met reported that it obtained more than one carat of diamonds for each tonne mined from one of its kimberlite pipes. Dia Met reported that it acquired 62.11 carats from a 49.8-tonne sample taken from Pipe Four and 31% of the diamonds were of gem quality. A sample weighing 179.7 tonnes was taken from Pipe Three, with the diamonds weighing 61.28 carats and 33% of the carats were of gem quality. Dia Met will have the commercial worth of samples evaluated as part of its feasibility study. Bulk samples from two other pipes were reported but they were not as rich.

The project in the Northwest Territories is a diamond joint venture and is being developed by its joint venture partner BHP Minerals Canada Ltd. In 1990 an agreement was reached between Dia Met and The Broken Hill Proprietary Company Limited (BHP). The agreement has BHP funding all exploration, at a $2-million (U.S.) per year minimum through to mine feasibility, and earning a 51% interest. BHP will also finance mine construction costs up to $500-million (U.S.) on behalf of the joint venture. Under the agreement, Dia Met will receive 29% of the diamonds, after direct mining costs and the repayment of mine financing, from the first mine. Dia Met must provide mine financing over $500-million (U.S.) and for subsequent mines for its proportionate interest. BHP is an international producer of minerals, steel and petroleum products and is active in more than 50 countries.

Dia Met agreed to a private placement of 350,000 common shares at $39 a share to European investors through First Marathon Securities Ltd.

Relative strength to TSE300

Price

Volume (in 1000's of board lots)

Rank (Profit/Revenue/Assets)		

Charles E. Fipke
Chairman

James E. Eccott
President

Address
1605 Powick Road
Kelowna
BC
V1X 4L1
(604) 861-8660

Fax: (604) 861-3649
D0015566/G/1.4

GIBRALTAR MINES LIMITED

Exchanges	Price (Jun24'93)	4.75	Trailing P/E	22.62	Stock Symbol
TV	Trailing Yield (%)	0.00	Trailing EPS	0.21	**GBM**

Period Ending	Dec92	Dec91	Dec90	Dec89	Dec88
Yearly Statistics					
Price-Close	5.00	6.25	6.88	9.63	12.00
Price-High	8.20	8.75	11.38	13.00	12.75
Price-Low	4.75	5.50	6.25	9.13	8.50
P/E-Close	19.23	23.15	8.38	4.77	17.39
Dividends per Share	0.05	0.20	0.50	2.90	0.40
Dividend Yield (%)	1.00	3.20	7.27	30.13	3.33
Sales per Share	5.47	5.60	6.72	8.28	3.93
EPS before extra. item	0.26	0.27	0.82	2.02	0.69
Cash Flow per Share	1.37	1.08	1.31	2.47	1.31
Book Value per Share	5.60	5.39	5.32	5.00	5.88
O/S Common Shares	12,041	12,041	12,041	12,041	12,041
Total Revenue	67,338	69,136	84,558	104,712	50,013
Income before extra.	3,107	3,244	9,888	24,310	8,339
Cash Flow	16,501	12,947	15,825	29,798	15,750
Debt/Equity	nd	nd	nd	nd	nd
Return on Capital (%)	10.31	8.16	31.88	61.60	15.82
Ret. on Com. Equity (%)	4.70	5.03	15.92	37.13	12.08
% Change Profit	(4.2)	(67.2)	(59.3)	191.5	96.2
% Change Revenue	(2.6)	(18.2)	(19.2)	109.4	(32.4)
% Change Assets	7.9	(2.8)	(5.9)	4.3	(3.1)

Date	EPS	DPS	Tot Rev	Inc Bex
Mar 93	0.03	0.00	11,246	424
Dec 92	0.07	0.00	19,170	863
Sep 92	0.09	0.00	15,812	1,119
Jun 92	0.02	0.00	17,120	261
Mar 92	0.07	0.05	15,236	865
Dec 91	0.03	0.05	20,147	339
Sep 91	0.08	0.05	17,655	904
Jun 91	0.02	0.05	17,113	258

	Dec92	Dec91	Dec90
Preferred Div. Coverage	np	np	np
Total Div. Coverage	5.2	1.3	1.6
Interest Coverage	nd	nd	nd
Current Ratio	4.7	4.6	3.9
Operating Margin	8.1	5.3	19.8
Asset Turnover	0.7	0.8	0.9
5 YEAR RATIOS (%)			
Return on Capital	25.6	25.5	21.0
Return on Com. Equity	15.0	15.3	12.9
Profit Growth	(6.1)	17.3	na
Revenue Growth	(1.9)	3.7	5.4
Asset Growth	(0.1)	0.5	(0.5)
BALANCE SHEET (000)			
Cash	9,958	11,526	31,279
Current Assets	28,476	26,835	44,618
Net Fixed Assets	58,343	54,039	39,808
Invest's & Advances	8,000	0	0
Total Assets	94,853	87,916	90,409
Short Term Debt	0	0	0
Current Liabilities	6,032	5,803	11,570
Long Term Debt	0	0	0
Total Liabilities	27,480	23,048	26,377
Total Equity	67,373	64,868	64,032
Total Liab. & Equity	94,853	87,916	90,409
CAPITAL (000)			
Total Debt	0	0	0
Preferred Equity	0	0	0
Common Equity	67,373	64,868	64,032

Business:

GIBRALTAR MINES LTD. is a copper and molybdenum mining company. It has operations and exploration activities in British Columbia. Placer Dome Inc. of Vancouver owns 68.1% of the company's shares.

Synopsis:

In May 1993, Gibraltar Mines announced that it will suspend mining activities at its McLeese Lake property in British Columbia. The shut-down will last 24 days and begin on July 23, 1993. Gibraltar stated the closure was necessary in order to conserve cash during a period of weak copper prices and low ore grades at the mine.

For the year ended December 31, 1993, Gibraltar produced 70.9 million pounds of copper in concentrate, compared with 63.4 million pounds for the same period last year. Gibraltar attributes the increase to higher mill throughput and an increase in head grades. Cathode copper production fell in the year to 6.9 million pounds compared with the 1991 level of 7.3 million pounds. Molybdenum production declined to 376,000 pounds from 808,000 pounds in 1991. Declining grades and poor market conditions led to the closing of the molycircuit in late 1992 with the mine not expected to operate in 1993.

At present mining levels, Gibraltar can sustain mining operations for another 12 years. Proven and probable reserves in three zones are about 162.6 million tons grading 0.301% copper and 0.0084% molybdenum at a strip ratio of 1.2-to-1. Gibraltar reserves do not include the North zone. At present market conditions, the North zone is uneconomical to mine. The zone also has a 30% net profit interest belonging to Newcoast Silver Mines.

As of December 31, 1992, Gibraltar had in place forward sales contracts for 2.2 million pounds of copper averaging $1.02 (U.S.) per pound covering the period through January 1993, and put options exercisable by the company covering 6.6 million pounds of copper at an average strike price of $1.10 (U.S.) per pound and expiring through February 1993.

Rank (Profit/Revenue/Assets)
309 430 426

Ian G. Austin
President

Address
P.O. Box 49330
Bentall Postal Station
Vancouver
BC
V7X 1P1
(604) 682-7082

Fax: (604) 682-7092
G0001435/G/1.2

GRANGES INC.

Exchanges	Price (Jun24'93)	3.40	Trailing P/E	nm	Stock Symbol
TA	Trailing Yield (%)	0.00	Trailing EPS	(0.07)	**GXL**

Period Ending	Dec92	Dec91	Dec90	Dec89	Dec88
Yearly Statistics					
Price-Close	1.80	1.20	1.44	2.60	3.60
Price-High	2.20	1.95	2.65	3.85	9.25
Price-Low	1.00	1.13	1.20	2.20	3.00
P/E-Close	nm	nm	nm	nm	nm
Dividends per Share	0.00	0.00	0.00	0.00	0.00
Dividend Yield (%)	0.00	0.00	0.00	0.00	0.00
Sales per Share	1.88	1.68	1.86	2.28	2.34
EPS before extra. item	0.00	(0.79)	(0.05)	(0.28)	(0.61)
Cash Flow per Share	0.27	0.13	0.34	0.62	0.45
Book Value per Share	1.86	1.83	2.57	3.70	3.80
O/S Common Shares	33,807	33,888	33,888	33,888	23,007
Total Revenue	65,465	60,581	70,389	69,820	52,196
Income before extra.	50	(26,689)	(1,603)	(8,146)	(13,494)
Cash Flow	9,203	4,350	11,584	18,011	9,893
Debt/Equity	0.25	0.17	0.23	0.33	0.39
Return on Capital (%)	1.42	(28.45)	0.36	(3.60)	(12.34)
Ret. on Com. Equity (%)	0.08	(35.79)	(1.51)	(7.66)	(16.13)
% Change Profit	100.2	(1,564.9)	80.3	39.6	(1,022.4)
% Change Revenue	8.1	(13.9)	0.8	33.8	141.8
% Change Assets	6.2	(31.1)	(32.6)	35.2	(4.2)

	Dec92	Dec91	Dec90
Preferred Div. Coverage	np	np	np
Total Div. Coverage	na	na	na
Interest Coverage	1.2	0.0	0.2
Current Ratio	2.5	2.4	4.3
Operating Margin	(0.4)	(51.6)	(9.0)
Asset Turnover	0.7	0.7	0.5
5 YEAR RATIOS (%)			
Return on Capital	(8.5)	(8.2)	(1.9)
Return on Com. Equity	(12.2)	(11.7)	(3.9)
Profit Growth	(49.1)	na	na
Revenue Growth	24.8	44.0	52.8
Asset Growth	(8.6)	(0.9)	36.1
BALANCE SHEET (000)			
Cash	35,885	29,877	36,207
Current Assets	51,324	43,949	51,648
Net Fixed Assets	34,977	37,304	65,983
Invest's & Advances	0	0	0
Total Assets	86,301	81,253	117,918
Short Term Debt	14,773	10,352	4,713
Current Liabilities	20,408	18,393	12,057
Long Term Debt	629	244	15,107
Total Liabilities	23,556	19,285	30,736
Total Equity	62,745	61,968	87,182
Total Liab. & Equity	86,301	81,253	117,918
CAPITAL (000)			
Total Debt	15,402	10,596	19,820
Preferred Equity	0	0	0
Common Equity	62,745	61,968	87,182

Business:

GRANGES INC. is a base and precious metals mining company. Its principal mining operations and sources of earnings are its 29% joint venture interest in the Trout Lake mine in Canada (copper, zinc, gold and silver) and the Crofoot/Lewis mine in the U.S. which produces gold. Crofoot/Lewis is held through its 67% owned Hycroft Resources & Development Corp.

Date	EPS	DPS	Tot Rev	Inc Bex
Mar 93	(0.10)	0.00	11,963	(3,330)
Dec 92	(0.04)	0.00	15,558	(1,236)
Sep 92	0.01	0.00	16,793	381
Jun 92	0.06	0.00	18,017	1,936
Mar 92	(0.03)	0.00	14,784	(1,031)
Dec 91	(0.02)	0.00	15,893	(525)
Sep 91	(0.66)	0.00	14,178	(22,293)
Jun 91	(0.07)	0.00	14,663	(2,244)

Synopsis:

Granges reported that its first quarter production results for 1993 were down compared to the same period last year. Granges produced 19,423 ounces of gold in the first three months of the year down 25% from last year. Silver production was also down, at 21% below 1992 levels to 68,271 ounces recovered. Copper production totaled 1.9 million pounds in the quarter, down 9% over last year. Zinc production, however, was up 27% in the period to reach 8.5 million pounds.

Granges attributes these lower figures to poor weather conditions which delayed production at the Crofoot/Lewis mine located in Nevada and weak gold, copper and zinc prices. Granges expects lost production at the Crofoot/Lewis mine to be caught up later in the year.

The Crofoot mine is expected to produce approximately 100,000 ounces of gold in 1993, which is about the same level as last year. Granges' 1992 gold production reached a record level of 110,896 ounces. Operating costs per ounce of gold recovered are expected to be the same as 1992 levels. Capital expenditures at the mine are expected to be $1.5-million in 1993.

In February 1993, Granges settled a lawsuit that started in 1989 with Oxford Acquisitions Inc. Granges settled the suit by issuing 150,000 Granges shares to the plaintiff. The original lawsuit alleged the plaintiff had a prior right to purchase a 9.167% interest in the Trout Lake mine that Granges acquired from Outokumpu Mines Ltd.

For the year ended December 31, 1992, Canadian sales accounted for 29% of total sales for Granges with the remainder being generated in the United States. As of December 31, 1992, assets held in Canada accounted for almost 77% of Granges total assets. The other assets were in the United States.

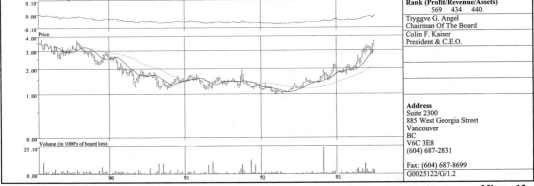

Rank (Profit/Revenue/Assets)
569   434   440

Tryggve G. Angel
Chairman Of The Board

Colin F. Kaiser
President & C.E.O.

Address
Suite 2300
885 West Georgia Street
Vancouver
BC
V6C 3E8
(604) 687-2831

Fax: (604) 687-8699
G0025122/G/1.2

HUDSON BAY MINING AND SMELTING CO., LIMITED

Exchanges	Price (Jun24'93)		4.45	Trailing P/E		4.31	Stock Symbol
T	Trailing Yield (%)		0.00	Trailing EPS		1.03	**HBM.S**

Period Ending	Jun92	Jun91	Dec90	Dec89	Dec88
Yearly Statistics		6M			
Price-Close	6.50	3.90	5.00	8.13	10.13
Price-High	6.88	6.63	8.38	11.25	10.13
Price-Low	3.50	3.75	5.00	8.13	7.13
P/E-Close	16.67	nm	3.29	2.09	4.38
Dividends per Share	0.00	0.00	0.14	0.11	1.84
Dividend Yield (%)	0.00	0.00	2.84	1.29	18.17
Sales per Share	37.16	36.64	38.53	41.35	37.70
EPS before extra. item	0.39	(16.09)	1.52	3.89	2.31
Cash Flow per Share	2.98	2.08	5.43	7.72	4.79
Book Value per Share	9.56	9.17	25.26	23.81	19.95
O/S Common Shares	10,903	10,903	10,903	10,903	10,861
Total Revenue	407,371	202,278	423,157	455,442	412,054
Income before extra.	4,204	(175,426)	16,582	42,351	25,073
Cash Flow	32,485	11,314	59,197	84,030	52,071
Debt/Equity	0.33	0.33	0.10	0.03	nd
Return on Capital (%)	3.18	(187.70)	9.04	27.23	16.74
Ret. on Com. Equity (%)	4.12	(186.91)	6.19	17.78	11.83
% Change Profit	101.2	(2,215.9)	(60.8)	68.9	(29.9)
% Change Revenue	0.7	(4.4)	(7.1)	10.5	20.1
% Change Assets	23.8	(50.0)	1.5	17.8	16.1

Date	EPS	DPS	Tot Rev	Inc Bex
Mar 93	(0.14)	0.00	88,855	(1,424)
Dec 92	0.33	0.00	97,532	3,330
Sep 92	1.14	0.00	107,039	11,427
Jun 92	(0.29)	0.00	110,987	(3,263)
Mar 92	0.70	0.00	96,228	4,561
Dec 91	(0.35)	0.00	97,008	(3,514)
Sep 91	(0.09)	0.00	103,224	(906)
Jun 91	(15.56)	0.00	103,595	(170,130)

Preferred Div. Coverage	np	np	np
Total Div. Coverage	na	na	22.4
Interest Coverage	na	na	na
Current Ratio	1.6	2.0	2.2
Operating Margin	2.3	(13.6)	5.4
Asset Turnover	1.6	2.0	1.0
5 YEAR RATIOS (%)			
Return on Capital	(26.3)	(22.9)	12.5
Return on Com. Equity	(29.4)	(26.3)	8.9
Profit Growth	(34.9)	na	23.8
Revenue Growth	3.5	7.2	7.8
Asset Growth	(3.0)	(5.1)	2.9
BALANCE SHEET (000)			
Cash	0	7,287	15,323
Current Assets	132,640	141,480	150,064
Net Fixed Assets	112,373	56,106	246,494
Invest's & Advances	0	0	0
Total Assets	249,554	201,552	403,065
Short Term Debt	3,609	1,200	0
Current Liabilities	80,593	70,080	68,840
Long Term Debt	30,253	31,472	26,400
Total Liabilities	145,350	101,552	127,639
Total Equity	104,204	100,000	275,426
Total Liab. & Equity	249,554	201,552	403,065
CAPITAL (000)			
Total Debt	33,862	32,672	26,400
Preferred Equity	0	0	0
Common Equity	104,204	100,000	275,426

Business:

HUDSON BAY MINING AND SMELTING CO. LTD. is a natural resources company. The company mines and processes copper, zinc, gold, silver and nickel at sites in northern Manitoba. It also operates a zinc oxide plant in Ontario. The company has a partial interest in a tantalum and spodumene mine in southeastern Manitoba. Minorco beneficially owns all of the company's common shares.

Synopsis:

In late January 1993, Hudson Bay Mining and Smelting Co. Limited announced it will need additional ore concentrates for its new zinc plant now under construction, and its existing copper smelter in Flin Flon, Manitoba. This follows the closure of two mines in Manitoba in the last 18 months, and two others in the Snow Lake division which are approaching the end of their productive lives. Hudson Bay Mining replaces existing ore bodies with its policy of saturation geophysics. The policy has never failed to produce replacement ore bodies in the past.

Hudson Bay Mining's new zinc plant in Flin Flon is expected to cost $171-million, up from the original estimate of $120-million. The company stated that certain aspects of the environmental improvement project have turned out to be more expensive than it expected. The company also announced in late 1992, that 600 employees could be laid off over the next 16 months because of mine closures and reduced staff requirements related to the smelter upgrades.

Proven and probable reserves for Hudson Bay's Flin Flon/Snow Lake mines, as of June 30, 1992, are 9.5 million tonnes grading 1.4% copper, 5.6% zinc and minor precious metals. The figures for the Ruttan mine are 8.3 million tonnes at 1.4% copper and 1.8% zinc, with no precious metals reported. The Namew Lake nickel mine, 60% owned by Hudson Bay, is scheduled to deplete its reserves in late 1993.

All of Hudson Bay's operations are carried out in Canada. For the 12 months ended June 30, 1992, sales to Canadian customers represented 35% of total net sales. Exports to the U.S. totaled 53% of total sales with the remainder being exported to Europe.

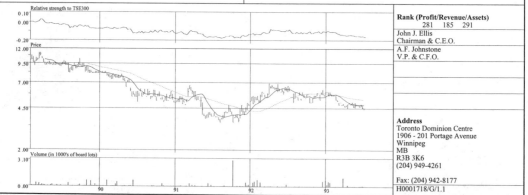

Rank (Profit/Revenue/Assets)
281 185 291

John J. Ellis
Chairman & C.E.O.

A.F. Johnstone
V.P. & C.F.O.

Address
Toronto Dominion Centre
1906 - 201 Portage Avenue
Winnipeg
MB
R3B 3K6
(204) 949-4261

Fax: (204) 942-8177
H0001718/G/1.1

INCO LIMITED

Exchanges	Price (Jun24'93)	29 .12	Trailing P/E	nm	Stock Symbol
TMN	Trailing Yield (%)	2.40	Trailing EPS	(0 .44)	**N**

Period Ending	Dec92	Dec91	Dec90	Dec89	Dec88
Yearly Statistics	US	US	US	US	US
Price-Close	28 .50	35 .25	29 .38	31 .38	31 .00
Price-High	39 .50	43 .88	36 .88	44 .25	42 .50
Price-Low	24 .50	27 .50	26 .00	30 .00	22 .13
P/E-Close	nm	36 .32	5 .16	3 .15	2 .98
Dividends per Share	0.85	1 .00	1 .00	0.85	10 .70
Dividend Yield (%)	3 .62	3 .25	3 .97	3 .20	42 .32
Sales per Share	23 .63	28 .48	29 .80	37 .53	30 .96
EPS before extra. item	(0.21)	0.74	4 .18	7 .11	6 .92
Cash Flow per Share	2.96	3 .63	5 .16	8 .87	8 .14
Book Value per Share	14 .71	15 .70	15 .78	12 .33	6 .51
O/S Common Shares	109 ,292	106 ,247	104 ,438	104 ,574	105 ,851
Total Revenue	2 ,622 ,238	3 ,053 ,420	3 ,335 ,086	4 ,064 ,459	3 ,348 ,168
Income before extra.	(17 ,612)	82 ,648	441 ,217	753 ,404	735 ,427
Cash Flow	320 ,489	382 ,219	538 ,443	932 ,633	858 ,288
Debt/Equity	0.68	0.73	0 .59	0 .74	0 .96
Return on Capital (%)	3 .99	7 .57	30 .59	72 .70	75 .95
Ret. on Com. Equity (%)	(1 .36)	4 .68	0 .00	75 .60	82 .32
% Change Profit	(121 .3)	(81 .3)	(41 .4)	2 .4	487 .2
% Change Revenue	(14 .1)	(8 .4)	(17 .9)	21 .4	83 .4
% Change Assets	(7 .4)	10 .8	10 .7	(10 .1)	36 .2
Preferred Div. Coverage	0 .0	16 .3	84 .7		
Total Div. Coverage	0 .0	0.8	4 .0		
Interest Coverage	1 .0	1 .8	7 .0		
Current Ratio	2 .1	1 .5	1 .9		
Operating Margin	2 .8	6 .5	18 .9		
Asset Turnover	0 .6	0 .7	0 .8		
5 YEAR RATIOS (%)					
Return on Capital	38 .2	40 .2	39 .8		
Return on Com. Equity	38 .2	40 .6	39 .4		
Profit Growth	na	241 .9	53 .2		
Revenue Growth	7 .5	15 .4	16 .7		
Asset Growth	6 .8	8 .5	5 .6		
BALANCE SHEET (000)					
Cash	34 ,889	31 ,148	70 ,472		
Current Assets	1 ,139 ,629	1 ,449 ,356	1 ,354 ,265		
Net Fixed Assets	2 ,576 ,078	2 ,598 ,146	2 ,450 ,100		
Invest's & Advances	240 ,889	225 ,831	148 ,660		
Total Assets	4 ,161 ,278	4 ,494 ,840	4 ,058 ,493		
Short Term Debt	60 ,076	279 ,644	115 ,507		
Current Liabilities	541 ,973	941 ,476	719 ,501		
Long Term Debt	1 ,081 ,038	990 ,758	892 ,516		
Total Liabilities	2 ,490 ,638	2 ,760 ,921	2 ,341 ,588		
Total Equity	1 ,670 ,640	1 ,733 ,919	1 ,716 ,905		
Total Liab. & Equity	4 ,161 ,278	4 ,494 ,840	4 ,058 ,493		
CAPITAL (000)					
Total Debt	1 ,141 ,114	1 ,270 ,402	1 ,008 ,023		
Preferred Equity	62 ,592	65 ,763	69 ,183		
Common Equity	1 ,608 ,048	1 ,668 ,156	1 ,647 ,722		

Business:

INCO LIMITED is a producer of nickel, copper, precious metals and cobalt. It also makes wrought and mechanically alloyed nickel alloys and manufactures blades, rings, discs and other forged and precision machined components. The company also produces sulphuric acid and liquid sulphur dioxide. The company has properties, operations and markets around the world.

Date		EPS	DPS	Tot Rev	Inc Bex
Mar 93	US	(0.22)	0.10	557 ,218	(22 ,589)
Dec 92	US	(0.28)	0.10	630 ,028	(28 ,960)
Sep 92	US	0.09	0.25	612 ,231	10 ,621
Jun 92	US	(0.03)	0.25	680 ,865	(1 ,432)
Mar 92	US	0.01	0.25	699 ,748	2 ,159
Dec 91	US	(0.07)	0.25	713 ,170	(5 ,732)
Sep 91	US	0.03	0.25	663 ,630	4 ,503
Jun 91	US	0.28	0.25	820 ,048	30 ,313

Synopsis:

In late March 1993, Inco Limited announced a number of steps to reduce costs, enhance customer service and improve profitability in its alloy business unit, Inco Alloys International (IAI). These initiatives, which include employment reductions and a reorganization of IAI, are being implemented to improve efficiency and reduce costs while providing more reliable and timely delivery to customers. The goal is to reduce costs to a level at which IAI can break even in today's difficult market conditions. Through this plan, Inco expects employment levels in 1993 to drop by 340 people or 12% of the existing workforce at IAI.

In February 1993, Inco announced it will spent $40.1-million over the next two years to reopen the Garson Mine, one of its high-grade ore bodies in the Sudbury region. The first phase of the reopening involves mining 4.8 million tons of ore grading 1.58% nickel and 1.09% copper. When the Garson Mine is in full production in late 1995, it is scheduled to produce 2,000 tons of ore per day for the next nine years.

Sales by geographic region for 1992 were: Canada, $274-million; the United States, $852-million; Europe, $778-million; and other, $655-million. Sales figures are after elimination of sales between geographic areas. Total net sales in Canada were $1,667-million including exports to the U.S. of $557-million and to Europe of $574-million.

Inco's 1992 (1991) deliveries were: nickel, 473 (507) million pounds; copper, 244 (254) million pounds; cobalt, 3.09 (3.07) million pounds; platinum-group metals, 314,000 (332,000) troy ounces; and gold, 40,000 (76,000) troy ounces.

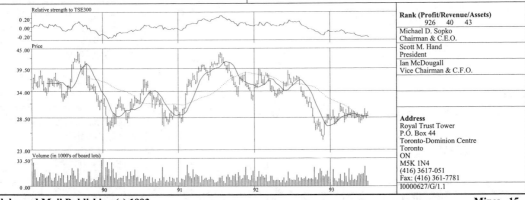

Rank (Profit/Revenue/Assets)
926   40   43
Michael D. Sopko
Chairman & C.E.O.
Scott M. Hand
President
Ian McDougall
Vice Chairman & C.F.O.

Address
Royal Trust Tower
P.O. Box 44
Toronto-Dominion Centre
Toronto
ON
M5K 1N4
(416) 3617-051
Fax: (416) 361-7781
I0000627/G/1.1

KERR ADDISON MINES LIMITED

Exchanges	Price (Jun24'93)	20 .25	Trailing P/E	8 .13	Stock Symbol
T	Trailing Yield (%)	2 .96	Trailing EPS	2 .49	**KER**

Period Ending	Dec92	Dec91	Dec90	Dec89	Dec88
Yearly Statistics					
Price-Close	16 .00	15 .50	15 .75	20 .25	22 .00
Price-High	19 .25	17 .38	21 .00	23 .75	22 .88
Price-Low	14 .50	13 .50	14 .38	18 .13	17 .38
P/E-Close	9 .14	86 .11	15 .75	28 .13	36 .67
Dividends per Share	0 .60	0 .60	0 .60	0 .60	0 .60
Dividend Yield (%)	3 .75	3 .87	3 .81	2 .96	2 .73
Sales per Share	0 .92	0 .67	12 .05	7 .50	6 .27
EPS before extra. item	1 .75	0 .18	1 .00	0 .72	0 .60
Cash Flow per Share	(0 .17)	(0 .14)	4 .99	1 .71	1 .53
Book Value per Share	21 .09	19 .94	20 .37	19 .97	19 .85
O/S Common Shares	17 ,593	17 ,590	17 ,559	17 ,548	17 ,545
Total Revenue	20 ,226	29 ,980	252 ,017	163 ,537	134 ,382
Income before extra.	30 ,699	3 ,207	17 ,611	12 ,639	10 ,509
Cash Flow	(3 ,018)	(2 ,496)	87 ,543	30 ,043	26 ,712
Debt/Equity	nd	0 .17	0 .21	0 .36	0 .36
Return on Capital (%)	8 .94	2 .04	5 .50	4 .29	5 .01
Ret. on Com. Equity (%)	8 .51	0 .91	4 .97	3 .62	3 .02
% Change Profit	857 .3	(81 .8)	39 .3	20 .3	(53 .8)
% Change Revenue	(32 .5)	(88 .1)	54 .1	21 .7	5 .0
% Change Assets	(8 .6)	(32 .5)	(5 .1)	(3 .0)	(1 .8)

Date	EPS	DPS	Tot Rev	Inc Bex
Mar 93	0.66	0.15	16 ,657	11 ,549
Dec 92	1.87	0.15	3 ,704	32 ,758
Sep 92	0.10	0.15	0	1 ,838
Jun 92	(0.14)	0.15	35 ,864	(2 ,500)
Mar 92	(0.08)	0.15	4 ,938	(1 ,397)
Dec 91	(0.15)	0.15	7 ,760	(2 ,629)
Sep 91	(0.07)	0.15	0	(1 ,269)
Jun 91	0.09	0.15	47 ,301	1 ,629

Preferred Div. Coverage	np	np	np
Total Div. Coverage	2 .9	0 .3	1 .7
Interest Coverage	9 .3	0 .9	1 .4
Current Ratio	79 .3	0 .9	7 .8
Operating Margin	(10 .1)	(59 .3)	1 .0
Asset Turnover	0 .0	0 .0	0 .3
5 YEAR RATIOS (%)			
Return on Capital	5 .2	5 .1	5 .2
Return on Com. Equity	4 .2	3 .8	4 .0
Profit Growth	6 .2	(9 .0)	48 .2
Revenue Growth	(31 .0)	(16 .3)	38 .2
Asset Growth	(11 .0)	(3 .9)	10 .1
BALANCE SHEET (000)			
Cash	73 ,850	0	89 ,718
Current Assets	173 ,103	12 ,801	164 ,048
Net Fixed Assets	25 ,889	25 ,499	157 ,019
Invest's & Advances	169 ,791	266 ,299	285 ,688
Total Assets	388 ,139	424 ,658	629 ,146
Short Term Debt	0	13 ,226	0
Current Liabilities	2 ,182	14 ,155	21 ,004
Long Term Debt	0	45 ,000	75 ,000
Total Liabilities	17 ,143	73 ,851	271 ,465
Total Equity	370 ,996	350 ,807	357 ,681
Total Liab. & Equity	388 ,139	424 ,658	629 ,146
CAPITAL (000)			
Total Debt	0	58 ,226	75 ,000
Preferred Equity	0	0	0
Common Equity	370 ,996	350 ,807	357 ,681

Business:

KERR ADDISON MINES LIMITED has interests in Canadian companies in the natural resources sector and joint-venture interests in undeveloped mineral properties in Canada, the United States, and Central America.

Synopsis:

In May 1993, Kerr Addison Mines Limited announced it had sold its exploration assets to Metal Mining Corporation for $23.5-million and other considerations. The assets included in the purchase are Kerr Addison's interest in the Troilus gold property in Quebec; its interest in the Petaquilla copper property in Panama; its grassroots exploration properties in Canada, the United States and Latin America; and its investments in Adrian Resources Ltd., MSV Resources Inc. and RFC Resources Finance Corp. Prior to the sale, all of Kerr Addison's exploration assets were held jointly with Metall Mining, formerly Minnova.

Following the sale of Kerr Addison Mining's interest in Minnova and its interest in Anderson Exploration, the company is no longer directly involved in the mining business. Kerr Addison's president says the company is talking with its major shareholders regarding a corporate reorganization.

In February 1993, Kerr Addison sold its 30% interest in Anderson Exploration through a secondary offering to a group led by Nesbitt Thomson. Kerr Addison will sell its 6,202,281 common shares of Anderson Exploration for $14.75 per share. The proceeds of $91.5-million will be held in cash until Kerr Addison decides on the direction the company will take in the future.

Rank (Profit/Revenue/Assets)
91   612   243

D.L. Bumstead
Chairman Of The Board

Andre Y. Fortier
President & C.E.O.

Address
Suite 2700
1 Adelaide Street East
Toronto
ON
M5C 2Z6
(416) 982-7270

Fax: (416) 982-7498
K0000647/G/1.2

For further company information, call Globe Information Services 1-800-268-9128 or (416)585-5345

METALL MINING CORPORATION

Exchanges	Price (Jun24'93)		11.00	Trailing P/E		25.00	Stock Symbol
TM	Trailing Yield (%)		0.00	Trailing EPS		0.44	**MLM**

Period Ending	Dec92	Dec91	Dec90	Dec89	Dec88
Yearly Statistics					
Price-Close	12.75	10.38	12.13	12.25	11.00
Price-High	14.25	13.13	15.25	14.38	11.63
Price-Low	10.38	10.00	10.88	11.25	8.75
P/E-Close	31.10	29.64	173.21	13.46	13.25
Dividends per Share	0.00	0.00	0.00	0.00	0.00
Dividend Yield (%)	0.00	0.00	0.00	0.00	0.00
Sales per Share	5.11	4.08	4.24	2.96	na
EPS before extra. item	0.41	0.35	0.07	0.91	0.83
Cash Flow per Share	0.72	0.11	0.09	0.58	0.41
Book Value per Share	12.96	12.36	11.94	12.13	11.30
O/S Common Shares	57,554	44,415	39,415	37,714	37,714
Total Revenue	312,786	215,515	190,744	131,900	16,626
Income before extra.	22,237	15,162	2,864	34,304	31,480
Cash Flow	38,937	4,665	3,711	21,768	15,285
Debt/Equity	0.36	0.35	0.48	0.57	0.07
Return on Capital (%)	5.99	4.65	3.73	8.83	9.22
Ret. on Com. Equity (%)	3.43	2.97	0.62	7.76	7.78
% Change Profit	46.7	429.4	(91.7)	9.0	118.6
% Change Revenue	45.1	13.0	44.6	693.3	(46.7)
% Change Assets	50.8	6.3	4.0	49.9	9.5

Business:			

Business:
METALL MINING is engaged in the exploration, development and production of minerals internationally. It operates mines mainly in North America, Europe and Australasia, producing copper, zinc, gold, lead, silver and industrial minerals. The company also has major holdings in Teck Corp. and M.I.M. Holdings. Metallgesellschaft AG of Germany owns 68.63% of the company.

Date	EPS	DPS	Tot Rev	Inc Bex
Mar 93	0.05	0.00	72,488	2,818
Dec 92	0.18	0.00	104,350	9,778
Sep 92	0.15	0.00	95,932	8,586
Jun 92	0.06	0.00	54,293	3,179
Mar 92	0.02	0.00	58,211	694
Dec 91	0.02	0.00	45,540	1,026
Sep 91	0.39	0.00	75,986	16,626
Jun 91	0.04	0.00	51,239	1,478

	Dec92	Dec91	Dec90
Preferred Div. Coverage	np	np	np
Total Div. Coverage	na	na	na
Interest Coverage	2.8	1.9	1.3
Current Ratio	2.0	1.6	1.6
Operating Margin	1.9	(9.3)	(5.8)
Asset Turnover	0.2	0.2	0.2
5 YEAR RATIOS (%)			
Return on Capital	6.5	na	na
Return on Com. Equity	4.5	na	na
Profit Growth	9.1	na	na
Revenue Growth	58.6	na	na
Asset Growth	22.2	na	na
BALANCE SHEET (000)			
Cash	174,536	98,649	100,216
Current Assets	288,927	184,295	160,731
Net Fixed Assets	413,815	210,940	203,627
Invest's & Advances	525,947	431,467	406,795
Total Assets	1,263,532	837,950	788,147
Short Term Debt	57,144	29,338	22,903
Current Liabilities	144,175	112,581	99,776
Long Term Debt	209,364	163,579	204,135
Total Liabilities	517,525	288,994	317,576
Total Equity	746,007	548,956	470,571
Total Liab. & Equity	1,263,532	837,950	788,147
CAPITAL (000)			
Total Debt	266,508	192,917	227,038
Preferred Equity	0	0	0
Common Equity	746,007	548,956	470,571

Synopsis:

In May 1993, Metall Mining purchased Kerr Addison's exploration assets for $23.5-million and other considerations. The exploration assets sold by Kerr Addison include: its interest in the Troilus gold property in Quebec; its interest in the Petaquilla copper property in Panama; its exploration properties in Canada, the United States and Latin America; and its investments in Adrian Resources Ltd., MSV Inc., and RFC Resources Finance Corporation.

In early May 1993, minority shareholders of Minnova Inc. overwhelmingly accepted the offer to amalgamate with Metall Mining. The deal, worth about $110-million, was approved by 99.9% of shares over all. The agreement will allow Metall Mining to combine Minnova's exploration expertise and ore reserves with the company's international marketing and financial strength, says Metall Mining's president.

In May 1993, Metall Mining announced it is considering the construction of a new smelter at its 87.3% owned Copper Range Mine in Michigan. The new smelter, which would cost about $200-million (U.S.), would allow Metall to refine more copper at a lower price. An alternative to a new smelter would be the modification of existing facilities in order to meet environmental standards. These pollution control modifications would cost Metall Mining about $15-million. Copper reserves and production at the Copper Range Mine are estimated to last approximately 30 years.

For the year ended December 31, 1992, Metall had the following production results. Metall Mining's share of copper production was 109,000 tonnes, up from 83,000 tonnes in 1991. Gold production rose from 138,000 ounces in 1991 to 199,000 ounces in 1992. Zinc production remained at about the same level as last year with 74,000 tonnes produced. Lead and silver production in 1992 was 38,000 tonnes and 3,808 ounces respectively. Metall also produced 1.3 million tonnes of coal in 1992, up sharply from the 491,000 tonnes produced in 1991.

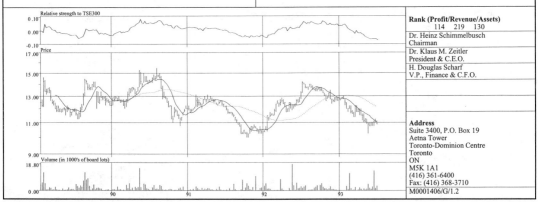

Rank (Profit/Revenue/Assets)
114   219   130

Dr. Heinz Schimmelbusch
Chairman

Dr. Klaus M. Zeitler
President & C.E.O.

H. Douglas Scharf
V.P., Finance & C.F.O.

Address
Suite 3400, P.O. Box 19
Aetna Tower
Toronto-Dominion Centre
Toronto
ON
M5K 1A1
(416) 361-6400
Fax: (416) 368-3710
M0001406/G/1.2

POTASH CORPORATION OF SASKATCHEWAN INC.

Exchanges	Price (Jun24'93)		25.75	Trailing P/E		18.13	Stock Symbol
TMN	Trailing Yield (%)		2.80	Trailing EPS		1.42	**POT**

Period Ending	Dec92	Dec91	Dec90	Dec89	Dec88
Yearly Statistics					
Price-Close	25.75	21.13	15.88	15.38	n t
Price-High	27.38	21.25	16.63	18.00	n t
Price-Low	21.00	15.38	13.00	14.50	n t
P/E-Close	17.17	18.06	23.01	6.46	n t
Dividends per Share	0.72	0.72	0.72	3.21	0.00
Dividend Yield (%)	2.80	3.41	4.54	20.89	0.00
Sales per Share	9.56	7.92	7.66	9.21	0.00
EPS before extra. item	1.50	1.17	0.69	2.38	na
Cash Flow per Share	2.58	2.18	1.72	3.53	0.00
Book Value per Share	29.58	28.82	28.37	30.02	na
O/S Common Shares	38,737	38,674	38,669	35,000	0
Total Revenue	382,836	311,840	288,750	334,807	370,919
Income before extra.	58,176	45,183	25,443	83,416	106,120
Cash Flow	99,921	84,313	63,362	123,646	157,211
Debt/Equity	0.08	0.10	0.13	0.18	0.09
Return on Capital (%)	5.83	4.55	4.01	7.65	9.21
Ret. on Com. Equity (%)	5.15	4.09	2.37	7.39	na
% Change Profit	28.8	77.6	(69.5)	(21.4)	612.4
% Change Revenue	22.8	8.0	(13.8)	(9.7)	41.2
% Change Assets	1.8	(1.8)	(0.1)	(4.4)	2.2

Date	EPS	DPS	Tot Rev	Inc Bex
Mar 93	0.21	0.18	94,635	8,003
Dec 92	0.30	0.18	78,115	11,806
Sep 92	0.42	0.18	96,055	16,366
Jun 92	0.49	0.18	120,682	18,638
Mar 92	0.29	0.18	87,984	11,366
Dec 91	0.19	0.18	72,054	7,551
Sep 91	0.25	0.18	72,246	9,568
Jun 91	0.41	0.18	91,892	15,739

Preferred Div. Coverage	np	np	np
Total Div. Coverage	2.1	1.6	1.0
Interest Coverage	6.1	3.7	2.3
Current Ratio	2.6	2.1	1.4
Operating Margin	18.8	18.0	17.2
Asset Turnover	0.3	0.2	0.2
5 YEAR RATIOS (%)			
Return on Capital	6.2	5.3	3.4
Return on Com. Equity	na	na	na
Profit Growth	31.4	40.5	na
Revenue Growth	7.8	10.0	7.5
Asset Growth	(0.5)	(0.9)	(0.3)
BALANCE SHEET (000)			
Cash	9,460	5,021	3,706
Current Assets	178,998	144,408	141,217
Net Fixed Assets	1,091,309	1,106,879	1,131,192
Invest's & Advances	4,178	1,810	1,742
Total Assets	1,283,631	1,260,778	1,283,334
Short Term Debt	25,756	35,737	56,159
Current Liabilities	69,404	70,036	98,537
Long Term Debt	68,597	76,346	87,818
Total Liabilities	138,001	146,382	186,355
Total Equity	1,145,630	1,114,396	1,096,979
Total Liab. & Equity	1,283,631	1,260,778	1,283,334
CAPITAL (000)			
Total Debt	94,353	112,083	143,977
Preferred Equity	0	0	0
Common Equity	1,145,630	1,114,396	1,096,979

Business:

POTASH CORPORATION OF SASKATCHEWAN INC. along with its subsidiary PCS Sales, is a leading publicly owned North American company engaged in the mining, production and sale of potash to agricultural and industrial markets in North America and around the world. The company represents 8% to 10% of world potash production, 15% of world capacity and 40% of the world's excess capacity.

Synopsis:

In April 1993, Potash Corporation was one of a number of potash companies named as defendants relating to a complaint filed with the United States District Court in Minnesota. The complaint alleges a conspiracy among the 14 defendants to fix the price of potash purchased by the plaintiffs as well as potash purchased by the members of a class proposed by the plaintiffs. The complaint also states the price fixing began in 1987 and continued thereafter. The complaint seeks undisclosed damages and other relief. As of early April 1993, Potash Corporation had not yet been served notice.

Potash Corporation announced that 1992 results were positively affected by increases in both domestic sales and export prices. In 1992, Potash Corporation sold 3.8 million tonnes of potash, down 2% compared to last year. Domestic volumes were up 10% in 1992 which more than offset declines in export volumes. Export volumes were down 9.5% in 1992, reflecting a drop in world demand and increased competition from the Commonwealth of Independent States.

Potash Corporation operates five mines in Saskatchewan, four of which it owns. The company has the ability to produce 9.2 million tonnes of muriate of potash annually, approximately 15% of the world's capacity. International export sales are made through Canpotex Limited, a sales agency for all Saskatchewan potash producers.

During 1992, sales to the United States accounted for over 50% of total sales. International sales accounted for 47% of sales in 1992. The remainder was sold in Canada. Almost all of the company's assets are held in Canada.

Relative strength to TSE300 / Price / Volume (in 1000's of board lots) chart, 1990–1993.

Rank (Profit/Revenue/Assets)
58   194   128

Charles E. Childers
Chairman, President & C.E.O.

Barry E. Humphreys
Sr. V.P., Finance & Treasurer

Address
PCS Tower
Suite 500
122 - 1st Avenue South
Saskatoon
SK
S7K 7G3
(306) 933-8500
Fax: (306) 933-8877
P0014021/G/1.6

For further company information, call Globe Information Services 1-800-268-9128 or (416)585-5345

PRINCETON MINING CORPORATION

Exchanges	Price (Jun24'93)	0.48	Trailing P/E	nm	Stock Symbol
T	Trailing Yield (%)	0.00	Trailing EPS	(0.18)	**PMC**

Period Ending	Dec92	Dec91	Dec90	Dec89	Dec88
Yearly Statistics					
Price-Close	1.45	0.85	3.25	4.95	5.88
Price-High	1.90	3.35	5.13	5.38	5.88
Price-Low	0.50	0.28	3.00	4.95	1.65
P/E-Close	nm	nm	6.92	3.26	4.49
Dividends per Share	0.00	0.00	0.16	0.40	0.00
Dividend Yield (%)	0.00	0.00	4.92	8.08	0.00
Sales per Share	2.12	1.24	2.70	6.99	6.79
EPS before extra. item	(0.04)	(3.58)	0.47	1.52	1.31
Cash Flow per Share	0.04	(0.41)	0.11	1.97	1.97
Book Value per Share	0.81	0.83	4.47	4.15	3.49
O/S Common Shares	31,079	31,079	23,404	22,697	17,805
Total Revenue	66,921	32,870	64,108	148,869	112,313
Income before extra.	(1,273)	(91,381)	10,808	30,602	22,210
Cash Flow	1,281	(10,400)	2,644	39,366	32,372
Debt/Equity	0.62	0.61	0.39	0.33	0.12
Return on Capital (%)	0.80	(96.28)	8.07	42.57	48.07
Ret. on Com. Equity (%)	(4.98)	(140.17)	10.87	38.69	44.61
% Change Profit	98.6	(945.5)	(64.7)	37.8	497.2
% Change Revenue	103.6	(48.7)	(56.9)	32.5	93.2
% Change Assets	(3.6)	(73.3)	14.3	30.0	60.1

Preferred Div. Coverage	np	np	np
Total Div. Coverage	na	na	3.0
Interest Coverage	0.2	0.0	na
Current Ratio	2.4	2.4	1.7
Operating Margin	(1.0)	(38.0)	(1.2)
Asset Turnover	1.4	0.6	0.3
5 YEAR RATIOS (%)			
Return on Capital	0.6	4.8	24.0
Return on Com. Equity	(10.2)	(7.3)	19.2
Profit Growth	na	na	69.3
Revenue Growth	2.8	(7.6)	0.9
Asset Growth	(9.4)	(9.7)	17.2
BALANCE SHEET (000)			
Cash	3,591	6,588	0
Current Assets	16,119	18,489	38,628
Net Fixed Assets	28,067	27,739	135,210
Invest's & Advances	1,122	1,067	14,893
Total Assets	48,693	50,533	189,024
Short Term Debt	748	405	3,348
Current Liabilities	6,629	7,740	22,998
Long Term Debt	14,829	15,369	37,197
Total Liabilities	23,444	24,662	84,508
Total Equity	25,249	25,871	104,516
Total Liab. & Equity	48,693	50,533	189,024
CAPITAL (000)			
Total Debt	15,577	15,774	40,545
Preferred Equity	0	0	0
Common Equity	25,249	25,871	104,516

Business:

PRINCETON MINING CORP. is a mining company with two operating mines in British Columbia. The Similco mine produces copper and some gold and silver as a by-product. The Cassiar mine produces chrysotile asbestos fibre. The company has a 19.6% equity interest in Rea Gold Corporation.

Date	EPS	DPS	Tot Rev	Inc Bex
Mar 93	(0.13)	0.00	13,513	(3,933)
Dec 92	(0.09)	0.00	15,359	(2,759)
Sep 92	0.01	0.00	17,916	411
Jun 92	0.03	0.00	17,444	1,091
Mar 92	0.00	0.00	16,354	(16)
Dec 91	(2.96)	0.00	162	(76,670)
Sep 91	(0.31)	0.00	1,271	(7,412)
Jun 91	(0.21)	0.00	9,527	(4,988)

Synopsis:

In May 1993, Princeton Mining was served with a demand for payment of $6.3-million relating to a debt swap agreement in the bankruptcy of Cassiar Mining. The demand for payment was served by the trustee in the bankruptcy of Cassiar. The dispute centers around an undischarged inter-company loan between Princeton Mining and San Antonio Gold. Princeton has stated that it intends to defend any legal action with respect to the trustee's demands.

In April 1993, Minera Princeton Chile Limitada, a wholly owned subsidiary of Princeton Mining, announced it had received assay results from the recent drilling program conducted at its Rio Lluta project in Chile. Drilling results support previous findings that the property has a high potential to host a large porphyry copper system. The most significant results indicate copper grades as high as 0.12% copper.

Following a proposed merger in late 1992, Princeton Mining has decided not to proceed with a plan to acquire the Luz del Cobre copper deposit in Mexico. Princeton stated that drilling results on the property did reveal ore grades, but they failed to indicate total reserves at the site.

According to a long term agreement signed with Mitsubishi Materials Corporation, all of Princeton Mining's copper production is sold to the Japanese company. Prices are set in relation to world copper and precious metal markets.

As of December 31, 1993, Princeton Mining operated in two business sectors: the mining of copper and precious metals; and the mining of asbestos. Over 93% of revenues in 1992 were generated from the copper and precious metals sector. Asbestos mining accounted for the remaining revenues in 1992.

Relative strength to TSE300 / Price / Volume (in 1000's of board lots)

Rank (Profit/Revenue/Assets)
716   431   544

George C. Stevens
Chairman

James C. O'Rourke
President & C.E.O.

Robert A. Watts
Vice President & C.F.O.

Address
Suite 2000
1055 West Hastings Street
Vancouver
BC
V6E 3V3
(604) 688-2511

Fax: (604) 688-4769
P0000482/G/1.2

RIO ALGOM LIMITED

| Exchanges | Price (Jun24'93) | 18.25 | Trailing P/E | 20.28 | Stock Symbol |
| **TMA** | Trailing Yield (%) | 4.11 | Trailing EPS | 0.90 | **ROM** |

Period Ending	Dec92	Dec91	Dec90	Dec89	Dec88
Yearly Statistics					
Price-Close	17.38	16.38	18.50	22.75	24.00
Price-High	18.50	22.88	22.88	27.00	25.00
Price-Low	15.13	14.25	16.00	22.25	18.25
P/E-Close	20.44	32.12	9.59	9.89	9.34
Dividends per Share	0.70	7.05	1.05	0.95	0.70
Dividend Yield (%)	4.03	43.04	5.68	4.18	2.92
Sales per Share	23.51	23.64	30.19	39.14	45.30
EPS before extra. item	0.85	0.51	1.93	2.30	2.57
Cash Flow per Share	2.15	2.09	4.75	4.31	5.40
Book Value per Share	14.46	13.84	20.24	19.73	19.33
O/S Common Shares	43,736	43,736	43,736	43,736	43,736
Total Revenue	1,048,998	1,059,592	1,377,970	1,753,482	2,011,175
Income before extra.	39,380	24,495	87,286	104,602	114,773
Cash Flow	94,085	91,346	207,893	188,415	235,778
Debt/Equity	0.78	0.73	0.56	0.63	0.67
Return on Capital (%)	7.13	5.30	12.37	13.54	17.67
Ret. on Com. Equity (%)	6.02	3.00	9.67	11.75	14.21
% Change Profit	60.8	(71.9)	(16.6)	(8.9)	23.3
% Change Revenue	(1.0)	(23.1)	(21.4)	(12.8)	28.2
% Change Assets	7.6	(19.7)	(5.0)	(0.4)	0.6

Preferred Div. Coverage	18.6	11.5	31.2		
Total Div. Coverage	1.2	0.1	1.8		
Interest Coverage	5.3	2.9	5.1		
Current Ratio	2.4	2.9	3.8		
Operating Margin	6.6	6.6	11.6		
Asset Turnover	0.6	0.7	0.7		
5 YEAR RATIOS (%)					
Return on Capital	11.2	12.3	13.5		
Return on Com. Equity	8.9	10.3	12.3		
Profit Growth	(15.9)	(23.0)	(0.3)		
Revenue Growth	(7.8)	(5.4)	1.8		
Asset Growth	(3.9)	(4.9)	1.5		
BALANCE SHEET (000)					
Cash	235,909	182,792	355,253		
Current Assets	619,607	615,832	975,726		
Net Fixed Assets	1,020,966	907,385	935,262		
Invest's & Advances	8,735	8,582	13,917		
Total Assets	1,711,163	1,590,567	1,980,641		
Short Term Debt	44,554	42,487	43,308		
Current Liabilities	257,836	215,657	258,785		
Long Term Debt	470,182	417,597	470,469		
Total Liabilities	1,052,593	958,792	1,068,724		
Total Equity	658,570	631,775	911,917		
Total Liab. & Equity	1,711,163	1,590,567	1,980,641		
CAPITAL (000)					
Total Debt	514,736	460,084	513,777		
Preferred Equity	26,384	26,562	26,722		
Common Equity	632,186	605,213	885,195		

Business:

RIO ALGOM LTD. is a North American mining corporation with interests in the mining of uranium, copper, molybdenum, potash, and coal. Rio Algom also operates metals distribution businesses in Canada, the United States, Australia, and New Zealand.

Date	EPS	DPS	Tot Rev	Inc Bex
Mar 93	0.15	0.00	258,480	7,018
Dec 92	0.22	0.35	266,230	10,144
Sep 92	0.36	0.00	268,544	16,175
Jun 92	0.17	0.35	264,193	8,203
Mar 92	0.10	0.00	243,194	4,858
Dec 91	0.29	0.40	264,465	13,174
Sep 91	(0.22)	0.00	252,066	(9,102)
Jun 91	0.13	6.65	267,750	6,387

Synopsis:

In March 1993, Rio Algom said it expects copper production at its $290-million (U.S.) Cerro Colorado project in Chile to begin by the end of 1993. The mine is expected to be fully developed by June 1994, when it will yield approximately 40,000 tonnes of copper annually and is expected to have a life of about 23 years. Reserves at the Cerro Colorado property contain 79 million tonnes grading 1.39% copper. Finished cathode copper has already been pre-sold for a 14-year period based on London Metal Exchange prices at delivery date.

Rio Algom is also considering an expansion at the Cerro Colorado project. The company believes that a 50% expansion could be achieved at a cost of between $35-million (U.S.) and $50-million (U.S.).

In 1992, Rio Algom's share of copper production was 126.5 million pounds. Operating profits from copper sales accounted for 42% of total operating profits for the company in 1992. Operating profits from uranium sales contributed 31% of total operating profits in 1992. Two years ago, copper profits accounted for only 31% of total operating profits with uranium accounting for 54%. In 1992, Rio Algom's copper production came from the company's one-third interest in the Highland Valley Mine in British Columbia. Future increases in copper production from the Cerro Colorado project are expected to add significantly to the company's operating profits.

In the first quarter of 1993, Potash Company of America (PCA), Rio Algom's potash producer, was one of a number of defendants included in a class action suit filed in the United States. The suit alleges that the defendants conspired to fix potash prices beginning in 1987. PCA denies the allegations and will defend itself in court.

At Rio Algom's annual meeting held in April 1993, shareholders approved and adopted a Shareholder Protection Rights Plan. The plan is intended to protect the company from takeovers.

Relative strength to TSE300

Price

Volume (in 1000's of board lots)

Rank (Profit/Revenue/Assets)
74   99   104

Gordon C. Gray
Chairman

Colin A. Macaulay
President & C.E.O.

Michael S. Parrett
V.P., C.F.O.

Address
120 Adelaide Street West
Suite 2600
Toronto
ON
M5H 1W5
(416) 367-4000

Fax: (416) 365-6870
R0001889/G/1.4

TECK CORPORATION

Exchanges	Price (Jun24'93)		21.37	Trailing P/E		71.25	Stock Symbol
TMV	Trailing Yield (%)		0.94	Trailing EPS		0.30	**TEK.B**

Period Ending	Dec92	Dec91	Dec90	Dec89	Dec88
Yearly Statistics					
Price-Close	17.00	18.13	20.88	26.50	17.75
Price-High	22.13	23.00	28.50	28.00	17.75
Price-Low	16.38	17.00	19.38	17.13	13.00
P/E-Close	56.67	40.29	18.98	20.23	13.25
Dividends per Share	0.20	0.20	0.20	0.18	0.14
Dividend Yield (%)	1.18	1.10	0.96	0.68	0.79
Sales per Share	4.14	4.64	5.62	5.11	4.48
EPS before extra. item	0.30	0.45	1.10	1.31	1.34
Cash Flow per Share	1.40	1.50	2.06	1.89	1.94
Book Value per Share	9.97	9.81	8.86	7.91	6.69
O/S Common Shares	84,307	81,503	77,123	76,679	76,266
Total Revenue	377,576	396,365	474,060	414,263	347,360
Income before extra.	25,517	36,826	90,568	106,394	105,428
Cash Flow	114,817	118,517	158,723	144,222	143,448
Debt/Equity	0.31	0.09	0.09	0.04	0.26
Return on Capital (%)	5.88	8.42	19.41	23.74	26.20
Ret. on Com. Equity (%)	3.02	4.77	13.14	17.92	24.70
% Change Profit	(30.7)	(59.3)	(14.9)	0.9	213.4
% Change Revenue	(4.7)	(16.4)	14.4	19.3	70.7
% Change Assets	16.6	2.1	13.1	0.1	61.3
Preferred Div. Coverage	np	25.0	15.6		
Total Div. Coverage	1.5	2.1	4.3		
Interest Coverage	4.5	10.4	22.1		
Current Ratio	4.9	3.3	1.6		
Operating Margin	18.2	20.4	27.3		
Asset Turnover	0.2	0.3	0.4		
5 YEAR RATIOS (%)					
Return on Capital	16.7	18.0	18.3		
Return on Com. Equity	12.7	14.0	14.3		
Profit Growth	(5.4)	9.6	41.3		
Revenue Growth	13.1	16.4	16.7		
Asset Growth	16.7	18.1	18.7		
BALANCE SHEET (000)					
Cash	214,762	132,595	95,083		
Current Assets	288,532	206,369	170,869		
Net Fixed Assets	724,841	558,404	583,600		
Invest's & Advances	362,589	415,600	401,662		
Total Assets	1,375,962	1,180,373	1,156,131		
Short Term Debt	9,425	11,857	18,914		
Current Liabilities	58,449	63,272	108,507		
Long Term Debt	253,546	61,684	43,776		
Total Liabilities	535,227	356,231	448,339		
Total Equity	840,735	824,142	707,792		
Total Liab. & Equity	1,375,962	1,180,373	1,156,131		
CAPITAL (000)					
Total Debt	262,971	73,541	62,690		
Preferred Equity	0	24,606	24,606		
Common Equity	840,735	799,536	683,186		

Business:

TECK CORP. is a mining company which has interests in 10 mines in Canada producing gold, silver, copper, zinc, lead, niobium and coal. Investments include a 22% interest in Cominco Ltd. and a 44% interest in Golden Knight Resources Inc., both of Vancouver. Teck also produces oil and gas in Western Canada through its 67% interest in Trilogy Resources Corp. of Calgary.

Date	EPS	DPS	Tot Rev	Inc Bex
Dec 92	(0.11)	0.10	99,012	(9,091)
Sep 92	0.16	0.00	100,626	13,820
Jun 92	0.14	0.10	87,513	11,969
Mar 92	0.11	0.00	90,425	8,819
Dec 91	0.07	0.10	92,413	6,423
Sep 91	0.07	0.10	99,763	6,126
Jun 91	0.17	0.10	100,634	13,335
Mar 91	0.14	0.00	103,555	10,942

Synopsis:

In late 1992, Elkview Coal Corporation, a wholly owned subsidiary of Teck Corporation, acquired a 100% interest in the Elkview coal mine. Total considerations for the mine include: a payment of $37-million of which $26-million is held as a loan to the mine; the assumption by Elkview of a project debt of $27.5-million (U.S.) of which $10-million (U.S.) is guaranteed by the company; and the granting to the project leaders of a net profit royalty interest in the mine of 43% reducing to 33% after $50-million in royalties have been paid.

For the year ended December 31, 1992, Teck's share of gold production was 379,800 ounces, down from 441,060 ounces in 1991. Copper production in 1992 fell over 19% compared to last year. In 1992 Teck's share of copper production was over 52 million pounds. Other production figures for the year include: over 33 million pounds of zinc; over 10 million pounds of lead; 292,206 ounces of silver; and 556,000 pounds of molybdenum. Teck expects gold production in 1993 to fall to 345,250 ounces recovered. Estimated copper production in 1993 will be around the same level as last year.

During 1992, Teck invested $17-million in exploration expenses. A total of 66% of these expenditures were devoted to North American exploration. The remainder was spent on foreign exploration, particularly in Latin America. In 1991, 94% of budgeted exploration was devoted to North America. This trend of reducing exploration in North America and increasing it in Latin America is expected to continue in 1993.

Teck's export sales for the year ended 1992 amounted to $177-million, compared to $186-million in 1991.

Relative strength to TSE300

Price

Volume (in 1000's of board lots)

Rank (Profit/Revenue/Assets)

111   197   120

Norman B. Keevil
Chairman, President & C.E.O.

David A. Thompson
Sr. V.P. & C.F.O.

Address
6th Floor
200 Burrard Street
Vancouver
BC
V6C 3L9
(604) 687-1117

Fax: (604) 687-6100
T0000566/G/1.2

WESTMIN RESOURCES LIMITED

Exchanges	Price (Jun24'93)	5.00	Trailing P/E	nm	Stock Symbol
TV	Trailing Yield (%)	4.00	Trailing EPS	(0.83)	WMI

Period Ending	Dec92	Dec91	Dec90	Dec89	Dec88
Yearly Statistics					
Price-Close	5.50	3.35	2.10	8.75	9.25
Price-High	6.13	6.25	8.88	12.00	11.50
Price-Low	3.40	1.55	1.55	8.75	8.50
P/E-Close	nm	nm	nm	7.48	462.50
Dividends per Share	0.20	0.20	0.20	0.20	0.20
Dividend Yield (%)	3.64	5.97	9.52	2.29	2.16
Sales per Share	2.08	2.42	2.83	2.64	2.93
EPS before extra. item	(0.71)	(1.02)	(2.50)	1.17	0.02
Cash Flow per Share	0.16	(0.16)	0.45	0.23	1.56
Book Value per Share	0.69	1.44	2.52	5.19	4.19
O/S Common Shares	42,969	41,258	39,221	39,205	39,101
Total Revenue	105,724	122,768	139,631	113,663	125,423
Income before extra.	(18,108)	(26,286)	(80,841)	63,555	17,843
Cash Flow	6,691	(6,302)	17,838	9,029	60,833
Debt/Equity	1.11	0.75	0.42	0.38	0.78
Return on Capital (%)	(1.01)	(2.12)	(13.41)	11.36	4.21
Ret. on Com. Equity (%)	(67.39)	(51.93)	(64.96)	25.02	0.42
% Change Profit	31.1	67.5	(227.2)	256.2	(18.2)
% Change Revenue	(13.9)	(12.1)	22.8	(9.4)	(34.2)
% Change Assets	(33.3)	(4.3)	(30.6)	(19.8)	3.5
Preferred Div. Coverage	0.0	0.0	0.0		
Total Div. Coverage	0.0	0.0	0.0		
Interest Coverage	0.0	0.0	0.0		
Current Ratio	0.5	0.3	0.4		
Operating Margin	(25.3)	(35.0)	(14.7)		
Asset Turnover	0.3	0.2	0.2		
5 YEAR RATIOS (%)					
Return on Capital	(0.2)	1.4	2.9		
Return on Com. Equity	(31.8)	(17.7)	(8.3)		
Profit Growth	na	na	na		
Revenue Growth	(11.1)	(8.3)	(3.9)		
Asset Growth	(18.2)	(12.6)	(11.9)		
BALANCE SHEET (000)					
Cash	102	113	952		
Current Assets	26,290	17,997	16,276		
Net Fixed Assets	159,858	173,432	195,547		
Invest's & Advances	109,582	261,715	263,334		
Total Assets	303,357	454,515	475,157		
Short Term Debt	37,661	52,150	17,500		
Current Liabilities	49,142	65,181	45,043		
Long Term Debt	114,992	136,850	107,200		
Total Liabilities	165,918	202,031	174,945		
Total Equity	137,439	252,484	300,212		
Total Liab. & Equity	303,357	454,515	475,157		
CAPITAL (000)					
Total Debt	152,653	189,000	124,700		
Preferred Equity	107,804	193,268	201,525		
Common Equity	29,635	59,216	98,687		

Business:

WESTMIN RESOURCES LTD. is a mining company with two producing properties. Myra falls produces copper and zinc concentrates, and the Premier Gold project produces gold and silver. Brascade Resources Inc. of Toronto is the company's major shareholder.

Date	EPS	DPS	Tot Rev	Inc Bex
Mar 93	(0.28)	0.05	18,950	(9,902)
Dec 92	(0.16)	0.05	24,944	(4,666)
Sep 92	(0.25)	0.05	21,880	(7,667)
Jun 92	(0.14)	0.05	28,736	(2,543)
Mar 92	(0.16)	0.05	30,163	(3,233)
Dec 91	(0.18)	0.05	29,869	(4,520)
Sep 91	(0.37)	0.05	27,509	(10,734)
Jun 91	(0.24)	0.05	32,587	(5,850)

Synopsis:

Effective April 24, 1993, Westmin Resources locked out its unionized employees at the Myra Falls Mine. The lockout affects 364 unionized employees at the mine near Campbell River, B.C. The two parties could not negotiate a new collective agreement despite the help of a government mediator. The previous collective agreement ended March 31, 1993. Before the lockout, Westmin served layoff notices in an effort to streamline production in the face of difficult international metal markets. The Myra Falls Mine produces zinc and copper, as well as gold and silver byproducts.

After first milling 1.17 million tonnes of ore last year, Westmin has upgraded reserve totals at Myra Falls. As of December 31, 1992, the property had proven and probable reserves of 12.5 million tonnes grading 2.1 grams of gold per tonne, 45.6 grams of silver per tonne, 1.9% copper per tonne, 0.5% lead per tonne and 6.3% zinc per tonne. The significant increase was the result of an additional 2.5 million tonnes of high-grade reserves that was found on the property.

Westmin's Premier Gold project was operating at 25% capacity in the first quarter of 1993. As a result, production figures at the mine were down compared to last year. The project milled 40,704 tonnes in the first quarter compared to 140,244 tonnes in the first quarter of 1992. Operating costs at the project fell compared to last year due to the closure of the open pit.

Production results for 1993 depend upon resolving the labor dispute at Myra Falls.

Relative strength to TSE300

Price

Volume (in 1000's of board lots)

Rank (Profit/Revenue/Assets)
915 371 271

Paul M. Marshall
Chairman Of The Board

Walter Segsworth
President

Ross A. Mitchell
V.P., Finance & Treasurer

Address
P.O. Box 49066
1055 Dunsmuir Street
Suite 904
Vancouver
BC
V7X 1C4
(604) 681-2253
Fax: (604) 681-0357
W0002192/G/1.2

Page	Company	$	Latest year end	Earnings per Share Actual	Estimate this year	Estimate next year
27	Agnico-Eagle Mines		9212	0.22	0.26	0.40
28	American Barrick Resources	$US	9212	0.62	0.79	0.92
29	Aur Resources		9209	(0.30)	(0.08)	0.08
30	Bachelor Lake Gold Mines		9212	(1.15)	n.a.	n.a.
31	Belmoral Mines		9212	(0.07)	n.a.	n.a.
32	Bema Gold		9112	(0.10)	(0.08)	(0.10)
33	Breakwater Resources		9112	(0.55)	n.a.	n.a.
34	Cambior		9212	0.37	0.46	0.70
35	Campbell Resources		9212	(0.01)	n.a.	n.a.
36	Cominco Resources		9212	(0.16)	(0.18)	(0.01)
37	Cornucopia Resources		9212	0.31	n.a.	n.a.
38	Dickenson Mines		9212	0.15	0.20	0.29
39	Echo Bay Mines		9212	(0.11)	(0.09)	0.04
40	Equity Silver Mines		9212	(0.05)	0.03	n.a.
41	Euro-Nevada Mining		9303	0.30	0.45	0.56
42	Franco-Nevada Mining		9303	1.25	1.62	2.04
43	Glamis Gold		9206	0.20	0.20	0.34
44	Goldcorp		9212	0.12	n.a.	n.a.
45	Golden Knight Resources		9212	0.10	0.29	0.39
46	Golden Star Resources	$US 18M	9212	(1.30)	n.a.	n.a.
47	Hemlo Gold Mines		9212	0.43	0.41	0.39
48	Lac Minerals		9212	0.09	0.09	0.17
49	MinVen Gold		9212	(0.21)	(0.20)	(0.08)
50	Muscocho Explorations		9212	(0.06)	n.a.	n.a.
51	Northgate Exploration		9212	(0.30)	n.a.	n.a.
52	Pegasus Gold	$US	9212	0.38	0.37	0.60
53	Pioneer Metals		9112	2.44	n.a.	n.a.
54	Placer Dome		9212	0.47	0.39	0.47
55	Quebec Sturgeon River Mines		9212	(0.17)	n.a.	n.a.
56	Rayrock Yellowknife Resources		9212	0.26	0.29	0.45
57	Royal Oak Mines		9212	0.19	0.18	0.34
58	Sonora Gold		9212	(0.01)	(0.25)	(0.23)
59	TVX Gold		9212	0.06	0.11	0.15
60	United Keno Hill Mines		9212	(0.20)	n.a.	n.a.
61	Viceroy Resource		9303	0.30	0.41	0.59
62	Wharf Resources		9212	0.23	0.29	0.36

Estimates from I/B/E/S Inc., 345 Hudson St., New York, NY 10014 (212) 243-3335. In Canada: 6 Lansing Square, Ste. 235, Willowdale, ON M2J 1T5 (416) 496-0977.

Gold & Gold Shares - Industry Report [Apr-28-1993]. MER-RILL LYNCH CAPITAL MARKETS reported by Myers, W.G.
The recent strong rise in the price of gold has been driven by technical factors. The traditional fundamental drivers of the gold price, inflation and the value of the US dollar, are not nearly as favorably disposed to higher gold prices at the present time. Another factor that could be driving gold prices at the present time is the developing stalemate on President Clinton's economic policies. The gold speculators appear to view the President's lack of success at getting his economic agenda backed by Congress as anegative for the US dollar. [RN 1326642]

Gold Monthly - Industry Report [Apr-1-1993]. MERRILL LYNCH CAPITAL MARKETS reported by Myers, W.G.
Higher inflation has most often led to higher gold prices, and conversely, a falling trend in inflation has weakened the price of gold. The average rate of inflation in the USA for 1993 is likely to be under 3%. The recent strength in the gold price seems to have been started by the commodity funds, both in the USA and in Europe. Newcrest's gold output and sales are likely to improve in 1993, because of the treatment of at least 20,000 tonnes of the copper/gold concentrate that the company has been stockpiling at its Telfer mine in Western Australia. This could add to the expected increase in production from the company's ordinary mine production. [RN 1318327]

Gold Market (The) - Industry Report [Mar-24-1993]. SHEAR-SON LEHMAN BROTHERS, INC. reported by Phizackerley, J., et al
The gold share market is seeing a good period which got going late in 1992. It was started by the perception that gold stocks were oversold. Gold was trading at or below $330 (U.S.) per oz, and analysts started doing things like adding up the value of the trucks and grinding mills, and sold the inherent value issue. 1Q:93 earnings for the gold industry will be poor. The 1993 U.S. gold mining industry cash production cost forecast is $230 (U.S.) per oz. The gold sector has shrugged off the political wranglings currently proceeding in the U.S., which aim to tax the gold mining industry as a means to reach the required U.S. deficit savings. President Clinton would establish a 12.5% royalty on the gross value of the hardrock minerals taken from public lands. [RN 1317833]

Canada: Gold & Silver - Industry Report [Mar-17-1993]. BBN JAMES CAPEL INC. reported by Ortslan, T.S.
Over the past twelve months, the price of gold languished in response to the high real returns in hard currency and a lack of both inflation and strong economic growth. Central banks still carry some 35,000 tonnes of gold in a market that does about 2,000 tonnes in annual volume. The Marxist capitalism in China is doing well, with demand of almost 400 tonnes annually. It is on the way to doubling over the next five years. China could be the biggest consumer of gold, with only 100 tonnes of domestic production; on a per-capita basis, it is globally still in the lower ranks. LAC continues to suffer from a lack of reserve growth, while Placer has the ounce problem of production and political issues concerning Placer Pacific in Papua New Guinea. Each has a strong asset base, and their weaknesses are well defined. LAC has reserve expansion potential in Quebec, Nevada and Chile. Placer Dome will both rationalize and expand, and it should be able to settle the ownership issue of the Porgera mine with the Papua New Guinea government at a monetary value reflecting market conditions. [RN 1317401]

International Gold - Industry Report [Mar-1-1993]. THE FIRST BOSTON CORPORATION reported by Reeve, T.
Gold markets were active in February 1993, with continued strong physical offtake, particularly in China and elsewhere in the Far East. Demand was also good in the Middle East. High levels of physical demand are expected to continue throughout 1993. In February, American Barrick increased its forecast of future production for 1996 to 2 million ounces of gold. Placer Dome increased its ore reserves at Pipeline, Zaldivar, and Dome. A partial estimate of resources in anticipated by midyear 1993 at the company's Las Cristinas project in Venezuela. [RN 1312693]

Gold Monthly - Industry Report [Feb-25-1993]. MERRILL LYNCH CAPITAL MARKETS reported by Myers, W.G.
There is a slow change underway in the supply/demand fundamentals for gold which could favor higher gold prices over the longer term. These changes include continued strong jewelry demand at prices below $400 an ounce, a peaking of newly mined supply, smaller gold sales from the CIS countries, and the possibility of a new shortage of oil developing in the second half of the 1990's. Stock price data are provided by company. [RN 1304950]

AGNICO-EAGLE MINES LIMITED

Exchanges	Price (Jun24'93)		12 .50	Trailing P/E		50 .00	Stock Symbol
TMQ	Trailing Yield (%)		0 .60	Trailing EPS		0 .25	**AGE**

Period Ending	Dec92	Dec91	Dec90	Dec89	Dec88
Yearly Statistics					
Price-Close	5 .50	4 .40	7 .13	9 .88	12 .00
Price-High	6 .75	7 .50	12 .88	13 .13	22 .00
Price-Low	3 .95	4 .00	5 .13	8 .38	11 .38
P/E-Close	25 .00	nm	nm	nm	nm
Dividends per Share	0 .12	0 .09	0 .09	0 .12	0 .37
Dividend Yield (%)	2 .09	1 .96	1 .24	1 .19	3 .08
Sales per Share	2 .49	2 .73	2 .71	2 .38	3 .27
EPS before extra. item	0 .22	(2 .86)	(1 .82)	(0 .66)	(0 .39)
Cash Flow per Share	0 .50	0 .28	0 .40	0 .10	0 .30
Book Value per Share	1 .40	1 .16	4 .45	5 .66	4 .94
O/S Common Shares	31 ,029	30 ,721	30 ,711	25 ,890	16 ,032
Total Revenue	71 ,675	58 ,779	62 ,699	37 ,102	46 ,104
Income before extra.	6 ,210	(81 ,904)	(47 ,687)	(10 ,072)	(5 ,559)
Cash Flow	13 ,955	7 ,988	10 ,383	1 ,572	4 ,253
Debt/Equity	0 .44	0 .56	0 .13	0 .16	0 .24
Return on Capital (%)	15 .00	(76 .84)	(27 .92)	(12 .17)	(6 .99)
Ret. on Com. Equity (%)	15 .74	(95 .04)	(33 .66)	(8 .92)	(7 .47)
% Change Profit	107 .6	(71 .8)	(373 .5)	(81 .2)	(157 .2)
% Change Revenue	21 .9	(6 .3)	69 .0	(19 .5)	(18 .9)
% Change Assets	9 .7	(47 .6)	(5 .4)	62 .0	27 .2

Date	EPS	DPS	Tot Rev	Inc Bex
Mar 93	0 .01	0 .00	15 ,876	344
Dec 92	0 .01	0 .00	16 ,296	268
Sep 92	0 .13	0 .00	19 ,626	3 ,748
Jun 92	0 .10	0 .12	18 ,613	2 ,670
Mar 92	(0 .02)	0 .00	16 ,564	(476)
Dec 91	(2 .74)	0 .00	3 ,977	(78 ,647)
Sep 91	0 .01	0 .00	20 ,071	442
Jun 91	0 .01	0 .09	19 ,230	441

	Dec92	Dec91	Dec90
Preferred Div. Coverage	np	np	np
Total Div. Coverage	1 .7	0 .0	0 .0
Interest Coverage	5 .5	0 .0	0 .0
Current Ratio	0 .6	0 .4	1 .4
Operating Margin	11 .7	(78 .3)	(43 .8)
Asset Turnover	0 .7	0 .8	0 .4
5 YEAR RATIOS (%)			
Return on Capital	(21 .8)	(20 .3)	(2 .4)
Return on Com. Equity	(25 .9)	(26 .0)	(5 .3)
Profit Growth	(8 .6)	na	na
Revenue Growth	4 .7	3 .9	5 .7
Asset Growth	2 .3	2 .3	18 .6
BALANCE SHEET (000)			
Cash	4 ,610	0	14 ,929
Current Assets	15 ,291	10 ,244	26 ,040
Net Fixed Assets	82 ,463	80 ,168	127 ,892
Invest's & Advances	4 ,032	3 ,354	25 ,029
Total Assets	102 ,826	93 ,766	178 ,961
Short Term Debt	6 ,100	7 ,496	5 ,209
Current Liabilities	25 ,551	25 ,738	18 ,477
Long Term Debt	12 ,929	12 ,466	11 ,970
Total Liabilities	59 ,496	58 ,186	42 ,187
Total Equity	43 ,330	35 ,580	136 ,774
Total Liab. & Equity	102 ,826	93 ,766	178 ,961
CAPITAL (000)			
Total Debt	19 ,029	19 ,962	17 ,179
Preferred Equity	0	0	0
Common Equity	43 ,330	35 ,580	136 ,774

Business:

AGNICO-EAGLE MINES LTD. is a precious metals mining company. It has gold operations in Joutel and Cadillac, Quebec. Exploration activities are focused in Quebec and Ontario. The company has a 59% interest in Goldex Mines Ltd.

Synopsis:

It was reported in early April 1993 that Agnico-Eagle Mines plans to expand its LaRonde gold mine located in Val d'Or, Quebec. The expansion is expected to cost $50-million and take three years to complete. The project is being considered because of a major new ore body that was discovered on the property. The new deposit is the most significant finding since the dicovery of the original ore body. The new deposit also contains silver, zinc and copper.

In early June 1993, Agnico-Eagle announced it had filed a preliminary prospectus for an offering of 4,250,000 common shares. The offering will be made in the United States and Canada. Agnico-Eagle said the proceeds from the sale will be used to repay bank debt, finance exploration and development projects and other purposes. The offering is expected to be completed by late June 1993.

During 1992, Agnico-Eagle produced 171,251 ounces of gold. The average cost per ounce of gold produced was $229 (U.S.). Over 78% of this production came from the company's LaRonde Division with the remainder being mined at Agnico-Eagle's Joutel Division. Agnico-Eagle estimates 1993 gold production to be 155,000 ounces. The slight drop is attributed to scaled down operations at the Joutel Division. Proven and probable reserves at LaRonde total more than six million tons averaging 0.187 ounces of gold per ton. Agnico-Eagle estimates reserves at the company's Joutel Division total 241,924 tons of proven and probable ore. The average grade of these reserves is 0.20 ounces of gold per ton.

In January 1993, Agnico-Eagle sold its 40% interest in certain mineral claims in Quebec to Goldex Mines Ltd. In exchange for the claims, Goldex will issue Agnico-Eagle 1,652,174 common shares of Goldex, through a flow-through share agreement, and Agnico-Eagle will advance Goldex $150,000.

Rank (Profit/Revenue/Assets)
233   424   414

Paul Penna
President & Managing Director
Sean Boyd
C.F.O. & Treasurer

Address
Suite 2302
401 Bay Street
P.O. Box 102
Toronto
ON
M5H 2Y4
(416) 947-1212
Fax: (416) 367-4681
A0000738/G/2.0

AMERICAN BARRICK RESOURCES CORPORATION

Exchanges	Price (Jun24'93)	30 .75	Trailing P/E	43 .93	Stock Symbol
TMN	Trailing Yield (%)	0 .34	Trailing EPS	0 .70	**ABX**

Period Ending	Dec92	Dec91	Dec90	Dec89	Dec88
Yearly Statistics	US	US	US	US	US
Price-Close	19 .63	16 .00	12 .69	9 .19	4 .91
Price-High	19 .94	16 .06	14 .13	10 .00	7 .19
Price-Low	13 .19	10 .56	8 .94	4 .88	4 .56
P/E-Close	26 .06	41 .08	48 .33	55 .51	30 .90
Dividends per Share	0 .07	0 .06	0 .04	0 .03	0 .02
Dividend Yield (%)	0 .33	0 .34	0 .32	0 .33	0 .41
Sales per Share	1 .91	1 .26	0 .97	0 .85	0 .63
EPS before extra. item	0 .62	0 .34	0 .23	0 .14	0 .13
Cash Flow per Share	0 .89	0 .58	0 .45	0 .35	0 .28
Book Value per Share	3 .50	2 .98	2 .41	1 .92	1 .66
O/S Common Shares	283 ,779	281 ,837	267 ,987	256 ,630	235 ,424
Total Revenue	553 ,767	368 ,686	283 ,111	218 ,527	162 ,878
Income before extra.	174 ,940	92 ,440	58 ,205	33 ,735	30 ,495
Cash Flow	252 ,025	157 ,784	117 ,323	84 ,707	65 ,714
Debt/Equity	0 .34	0 .37	0 .63	0 .18	0 .24
Return on Capital (%)	18 .72	11 .30	11 .07	10 .39	10 .46
Ret. on Com. Equity (%)	19 .08	12 .45	10 .24	7 .65	8 .38
% Change Profit	89 .2	58 .8	72 .5	10 .6	48 .3
% Change Revenue	50 .2	30 .2	29 .6	34 .2	46 .6
% Change Assets	15 .2	13 .9	13 .0	44 .9	3 .7

Preferred Div. Coverage	np	np	np
Total Div. Coverage	9 .5	6 .2	5 .2
Interest Coverage	25 .0	13 .2	7 .1
Current Ratio	2 .5	2 .9	3 .5
Operating Margin	40 .5	30 .4	23 .4
Asset Turnover	0 .4	0 .3	0 .2
5 YEAR RATIOS (%)			
Return on Capital	12 .4	10 .7	10 .7
Return on Com. Equity	11 .6	9 .6	9 .8
Profit Growth	53 .4	51 .9	80 .3
Revenue Growth	37 .8	38 .3	46 .4
Asset Growth	17 .3	32 .7	47 .4
BALANCE SHEET (000)			
Cash	288 ,023	252 ,140	311 ,778
Current Assets	353 ,371	328 ,447	391 ,231
Net Fixed Assets	1 ,094 ,402	921 ,701	716 ,046
Invest's & Advances	0	0	0
Total Assets	1 ,504 ,293	1 ,306 ,337	1 ,146 ,883
Short Term Debt	77 ,185	45 ,256	77 ,038
Current Liabilities	138 ,772	112 ,261	111 ,501
Long Term Debt	260 ,098	262 ,996	331 ,401
Total Liabilities	511 ,564	465 ,684	502 ,007
Total Equity	992 ,729	840 ,653	644 ,876
Total Liab. & Equity	1 ,504 ,293	1 ,306 ,337	1 ,146 ,883
CAPITAL (000)			
Total Debt	337 ,283	308 ,252	408 ,439
Preferred Equity	0	0	0
Common Equity	992 ,729	840 ,653	644 ,876

Business:

AMERICAN BARRICK RESOURCES CORP. is a gold mining company. Its principal producing mines are the Goldstrike mine in Nevada, the Mercur mine in Utah and the Holt-McDermott mine in Ontario. The company has other mining interests in Ontario, Quebec and Nevada. Its exploration activities are focused in the areas surrounding the mines.

Date		EPS	DPS	Tot Rev	Inc Bex
Mar 93	US	0 .16	0 .04	147 ,962	46 ,065
Dec 92	US	0 .24	0 .00	202 ,198	65 ,533
Sep 92	US	0 .18	0 .03	146 ,504	49 ,494
Jun 92	US	0 .13	0 .03	118 ,601	36 ,754
Mar 92	US	0 .08	0 .00	86 ,464	23 ,159
Dec 91	US	0 .09	0 .01	94 ,290	24 ,082
Sep 91	US	0 .10	0 .03	99 ,465	28 ,194
Jun 91	US	0 .10	0 .03	94 ,404	24 ,571

Synopsis:

During the first quarter of 1993, American Barrick announced that gold production at the Goldstrike mine doubled compared to the same period last year. Gold production at Goldstrike in the first quarter of 1993 was 307,773 ounces, up from 151,838 ounces in the first quarter of 1992. American Barrick's total gold production during the first quarter was 354,839 ounces, compared to 202,505 ounces in 1992. Operating costs were $174 (U.S.) per ounce compared with $199 (U.S.) in 1992.

During 1992, American Barrick produced 1.3 million ounces of gold, a new record for the company and almost 68% higher than in 1991. Operating costs were $164 (U.S.) per ounce during 1992, compared to $205 (U.S.) in 1991. American Barrick expects to produce 1.5 million ounces of gold in 1993. Long-term forecasts put American Barrick's production at 2 million ounces annually by 1995.

As of December 31, 1992, American Barrick had more than 27 million ounces of gold in its ore reserves. Almost 78% of American Barrick's gold reserves are held at the Goldstrike mine in Nevada. The remaining share of gold production stems from interests in other gold mines located in Ontario, Utah and Nevada.

American Barrick continues to use hedging strategies to stabilize the price it receives for its gold. This strategy has generated substantial profits over the last few years. In the first quarter of 1993, American Barrick sold its gold at a realized price of $410 (U.S.) per ounce, compared with the average price of gold during the period of $330 (U.S.) an ounce. American Barrick says its production is fully hedged until the end of 1994 at a realized price of over $400 (U.S.) per ounce.

In the first quarter of 1993, American Barrick raised the cash dividend by 23% to 4 cents, paid semi-annually. The board of directors also authorized a two-for-one split of the common shares that was effected through a stock dividend on March 1, 1993.

Relative strength to TSE300

Price

Volume (in 1000's of board lots)

Rank (Profit/Revenue/Assets)
12   133   96

Peter Munk
Chairman & C.E.O.

Robert M. Smith
President & C.O.O.

Gregory C. Wilkins
Exec. V.P. & C.F.O.

Address
24 Hazelton Avenue
Toronto
ON
M5R 2E2
(416) 923-9400

Fax: (416) 923-8511
B0015879/G/2.0

AUR RESOURCES INC.

Exchanges	Price (Jun24'93)		4.30	Trailing P/E		nm	Stock Symbol
TM	Trailing Yield (%)		0.00	Trailing EPS		(0.22)	**AUR**

Period Ending	Sep92	Sep91	Sep90	Sep89	Sep88
Yearly Statistics					
Price-Close	3.05	3.15	3.50	5.19	1.90
Price-High	3.45	4.30	7.32	6.50	5.44
Price-Low	1.95	2.90	3.05	1.38	1.88
P/E-Close	nm	nm	nm	518.70	54.29
Dividends per Share	0.00	0.00	0.00	0.00	0.00
Dividend Yield (%)	0.00	0.00	0.00	0.00	0.00
Sales per Share	0.45	0.36	0.21	0.04	na
EPS before extra. item	(0.30)	(0.20)	(0.97)	0.01	0.04
Cash Flow per Share	(0.11)	(0.03)	(0.02)	0.02	0.07
Book Value per Share	0.83	1.12	1.30	2.09	1.69
O/S Common Shares	46,171	45,904	45,533	40,158	32,734
Total Revenue	22,043	21,911	16,506	5,782	3,972
Income before extra.	(13,383)	(8,921)	(40,890)	362	1,102
Cash Flow	(5,042)	(1,127)	(866)	630	2,061
Debt/Equity	nd	nd	nd	0.00	0.00
Return on Capital (%)	(29.69)	(20.62)	(57.55)	1.27	3.89
Ret. on Com. Equity (%)	(29.83)	(16.17)	(57.19)	0.52	2.16
% Change Profit	(50.0)	78.2	nm	(67.1)	(21.1)
% Change Revenue	0.6	32.7	185.5	45.6	(18.0)
% Change Assets	(23.2)	(14.7)	(28.9)	35.4	37.2

	Sep92	Sep91	Sep90
Preferred Div. Coverage	np	np	np
Total Div. Coverage	na	na	na
Interest Coverage	nd	nd	0.0
Current Ratio	5.5	3.8	8.1
Operating Margin	(56.4)	(63.2)	(401.2)
Asset Turnover	0.5	0.3	0.1
5 YEAR RATIOS (%)			
Return on Capital	(20.5)	(12.7)	(5.4)
Return on Com. Equity	(20.1)	(13.2)	(8.4)
Profit Growth	na	na	na
Revenue Growth	35.4	58.7	96.3
Asset Growth	(2.9)	30.6	50.9
BALANCE SHEET (000)			
Cash	23,477	15,298	29,446
Current Assets	27,329	20,081	37,774
Net Fixed Assets	12,881	29,893	23,562
Invest's & Advances	3,228	6,556	4,933
Total Assets	43,439	56,530	66,269
Short Term Debt	0	0	0
Current Liabilities	4,935	5,295	4,663
Long Term Debt	0	0	0
Total Liabilities	4,935	5,295	7,163
Total Equity	38,504	51,236	59,106
Total Liab. & Equity	43,439	56,530	66,269
CAPITAL (000)			
Total Debt	0	0	0
Preferred Equity	0	0	0
Common Equity	38,504	51,236	59,106

Business:

AUR RESOURCES INC. is a mineral resources exploration, development and mining company with two producing gold mines and many other gold, base metal and diamond properties in Val d'Or, Quebec. Aur, as the operator in a joint venture, is developing a large copper-zinc mine on the Louvicourt property near Val d'Or.

Date	EPS	DPS	Tot Rev	Inc Bex
Mar 93	0.00	0.00	3,895	29
Dec 92	0.01	0.00	6,154	256
Sep 92	(0.19)	0.00	5,218	(8,478)
Jun 92	(0.04)	0.00	4,824	(1,828)
Mar 92	(0.05)	0.00	5,667	(2,102)
Dec 91	(0.02)	0.00	6,333	(976)
Sep 91	(0.19)	0.00	5,991	(8,154)
Jun 91	(0.01)	0.00	5,239	(125)

Synopsis:

Aur's share of gold production for the six months ended March 31, 1993, was 19,336 ounces. The gold was recovered from the Norlartic, Ferderber and Dumont gold mines. The Norlartic mine closed in January 1993 because of depleted reserves. The Ferderber and Dumont gold mines were originally expected to close in June 1993 but will operate beyond the June 1993 closing date until ore reserves have been depleted.

Aur's exploration efforts in the first six months of fiscal 1993 were focused on the company's gold and base metals project in northern Quebec and on the base metals land holdings in Maine. Development of the world class Louvicourt copper-zinc-gold deposit in Quebec is on schedule for a July 1994 opening. Expenditures are projected to average approximately $13-million per month for the rest of 1993. Aur is required to provide 30% of these costs after August 1993, when Teck is expected to have fulfilled its $55-million expenditure commitment to earn a 25% interest in Louvicourt. The $350-million project is expected to be the biggest copper producer in the province of Quebec.

In February 1993, Aur entered into a joint venture agreement with Consolidated Abitibi Resources and Thunderwood Resources. The agreement states Abitibi and Thunderwood can earn a 25% interest in Aur's McConnell diamond project in the Northwest Territories. The two companies must each provide up to $250,000 for land acquisition this year and incur $500,000 in exploration expenditures on the project in each of 1993, 1994 and 1995. Aur expects to spent $1.5-million on exploration work relating to the property in 1993.

Relative strength to TSE300 / Price / Volume (in 1000's of board lots)

Rank (Profit/Revenue/Assets)
904   604   571

James W. Gill
President

Address
Suite 2501
1 Adelaide Street East
Toronto
ON
M5C 2V9
(416) 362-2614

Fax: (416) 367-0427
A0015314/G/2.0

BACHELOR LAKE GOLD MINES INC.

Exchanges	Price (Jun24'93)	0.21	Trailing P/E	nm	Stock Symbol
M	Trailing Yield (%)	0.00	Trailing EPS	(1.14)	**BLG**

Period Ending	Dec92	Dec91	Dec90	Dec89	Dec88
Yearly Statistics					
Price-Close	0.06	0.07	0.18	0.50	1.15
Price-High	0.20	0.25	0.65	1.25	2.75
Price-Low	0.01	0.05	0.15	0.31	1.10
P/E-Close	nm	nm	nm	nm	nm
Dividends per Share	0.00	0.00	0.00	0.00	0.00
Dividend Yield (%)	0.00	0.00	0.00	0.00	0.00
Sales per Share	0.16	na	na	0.68	1.32
EPS before extra. item	(1.15)	(0.11)	(0.38)	(0.42)	(0.13)
Cash Flow per Share	(0.07)	(0.10)	(0.18)	(0.32)	0.02
Book Value per Share	(1.09)	0.06	0.17	0.56	0.97
O/S Common Shares	8,648	8,523	8,398	8,273	8,148
Total Revenue	1,214	484	6	5,625	10,479
Income before extra.	(9,912)	(958)	(3,213)	(3,414)	(1,113)
Cash Flow	(600)	(829)	(1,506)	(2,593)	183
Debt/Equity	na	12.39	4.19	0.70	0.32
Return on Capital (%)	(436.13)	(6.22)	(33.00)	(30.43)	(6.03)
Ret. on Com. Equity (%)	na	(97.26)	(105.90)	(54.50)	(14.05)
% Change Profit	(935.0)	70.2	5.9	(206.8)	91.4
% Change Revenue	151.1	7,644.8	(99.9)	(46.3)	257.3
% Change Assets	(99.8)	(3.8)	(21.7)	(13.5)	8.7

Business:
BACHELOR LAKE GOLD MINES INC. is a gold mining company. Its principal producing mine is the Bachelor Lake mine, located in Lesueur Township, Que., about 500 kilometres northwest of Montreal. The company has other properties in the same area. The company owns a 74.1% interest in Western Premium Resources Corp. of Toronto.

Date	EPS	DPS	Tot Rev	Inc Bex
Mar 93	(0.01)	0.00	0	(123)
Dec 92	(0.02)	0.00	1	(218)
Sep 92	(0.02)	0.00	1	(165)
Jun 92	(1.09)	0.00	588	(9,329)
Mar 92	(0.02)	0.00	618	(201)
Dec 91	(0.05)	0.00	153	(468)
Sep 91	(0.02)	0.00	66	(171)
Jun 91	0.00	0.00	263	15

	Dec92	Dec91	Dec90
Preferred Div. Coverage	np	np	np
Total Div. Coverage	na	na	na
Interest Coverage	0.0	0.0	0.0
Current Ratio	0.0	0.0	0.1
Operating Margin	(676.2)	na	na
Asset Turnover	62.5	na	na
5 YEAR RATIOS (%)			
Return on Capital	(102.4)	(32.0)	(31.0)
Return on Com. Equity	na	(73.5)	(54.9)
Profit Growth	na	na	na
Revenue Growth	(5.8)	(39.7)	(100.0)
Asset Growth	(100.0)	(14.0)	(15.1)
BALANCE SHEET			
Cash	12,418	33,461	43,364
Current Assets	21,948	189,294	574,681
Net Fixed Assets	2	9,307,118	9,298,656
Invest's & Advances	0	0	0
Total Assets	21,950	9,496,412	9,873,337
Short Term Debt	4,303,283	3,889,812	3,593,689
Current Liabilities	6,903,828	6,480,840	5,919,403
Long Term Debt	2,500,000	2,500,000	2,500,000
Total Liabilities	9,403,828	8,980,840	8,419,403
Total Equity	(9,381,878)	515,572	1,453,934
Total Liab. & Equity	21,950	9,496,412	9,873,337
CAPITAL			
Total Debt	6,803,283	6,389,812	6,093,689
Preferred Equity	0	0	0
Common Equity	(9,381,878)	515,572	1,453,934

Synopsis:

For the year ended December 31, 1992, Bachelor Lake Gold Mines produced and sold a total of 3,412 ounces of gold. The average production cost per ounce of gold was $382 per ounce. Bachelor Lake mined and processed the gold ore at the nearby Minnova Inc. mill.

In August 1993, Bachelor Lake suspended gold mine operations at its Bachelor Lake Mine. When the mine closed, Bachelor Lake had proven mineral reserves of 232,370 tons averaging 0.204 ounces of gold per ton. The company also had a further one million tons of drill indicating ore grading 0.267 ounces per ton.

In 1992, Bachelor Lake's shares were delisted on the Toronto Stock Exchange. The company terminated the share listing in an effort to reduce administration costs. The shares continue to trade on the Montreal Exchange.

In order for Bachelor Lake Mine to reopen, gold prices will have to rise significantly higher than early 1993 levels. The company will continue to explore the possibility of resuming operations at the mine.

Relative strength to TSE300 / Price / Volume (in 1000's of board lots)

Rank (Profit/Revenue/Assets)
619 907 868

Herbert S Gasser
President

C.E. Peter Earl
V.P., Finance & Secretary

Address
166 Pearl Street
Toronto
ON
M5H 1L3
(416) 597-0969

Fax: (416) 597-1776
B0000102/G/2.0

For further company information, call Globe Information Services 1-800-268-9128 or (416)585-5345

BELMORAL MINES LTD.

Exchanges	Price (Jun24'93)	0.17	Trailing P/E	nm	Stock Symbol
TM	Trailing Yield (%)	0.00	Trailing EPS	(0.07)	**BME**

Period Ending	Dec92	Dec91	Dec90	Dec89	Dec88
Yearly Statistics					
Price-Close	0.08	0.11	0.16	0.73	1.33
Price-High	0.18	0.25	0.85	1.98	3.25
Price-Low	0.06	0.09	0.13	0.56	1.22
P/E-Close	nm	nm	nm	nm	nm
Dividends per Share	0.00	0.00	0.00	0.00	0.00
Dividend Yield (%)	0.00	0.00	0.00	0.00	0.00
Sales per Share	0.21	0.14	0.43	0.44	0.67
EPS before extra. item	(0.07)	(0.12)	(0.63)	(0.91)	(0.21)
Cash Flow per Share	(0.04)	(0.04)	(0.08)	(0.17)	0.05
Book Value per Share	(0.11)	(0.04)	0.08	0.70	1.56
O/S Common Shares	47,206	47,206	46,943	44,898	38,718
Total Revenue	11,954	8,179	21,689	19,147	27,089
Income before extra.	(3,402)	(5,664)	(29,096)	(34,581)	(7,849)
Cash Flow	(2,107)	(1,986)	(3,630)	(6,727)	2,055
Debt/Equity	na	na	0.54	0.27	nd
Return on Capital (%)	(1,042.42)	(143.77)	(124.12)	(68.80)	(11.41)
Ret. on Com. Equity (%)	na	(520.59)	(165.76)	(75.55)	(12.78)
% Change Profit	39.9	80.5	15.9	(340.6)	(445.6)
% Change Revenue	46.2	(62.3)	13.3	(29.3)	(16.3)
% Change Assets	(48.4)	(44.6)	(81.4)	(30.2)	(0.8)

Preferred Div. Coverage	np	np	np
Total Div. Coverage	na	na	na
Interest Coverage	0.0	0.0	0.0
Current Ratio	0.2	0.5	1.1
Operating Margin	(22.2)	(33.6)	(11.7)
Asset Turnover	3.8	1.3	2.2
5 YEAR RATIOS (%)			
Return on Capital	(278.1)	(68.0)	(37.9)
Return on Com. Equity	na	(153.6)	(45.5)
Profit Growth	na	na	na
Revenue Growth	(18.1)	(21.9)	(0.4)
Asset Growth	(48.9)	(30.9)	(18.0)
BALANCE SHEET			
Cash	371,000	775,000	0
Current Assets	1,353,000	2,377,000	3,379,000
Net Fixed Assets	964,000	2,100,000	4,706,000
Invest's & Advances	275,000	550,000	994,000
Total Assets	2,592,000	5,027,000	9,079,000
Short Term Debt	3,450,000	1,650,000	95,000
Current Liabilities	7,420,000	4,653,000	3,177,000
Long Term Debt	300,000	2,100,000	2,000,000
Total Liabilities	7,720,000	6,753,000	5,177,000
Total Equity	(5,128,000)	(1,726,000)	3,902,000
Total Liab. & Equity	2,592,000	5,027,000	9,079,000
CAPITAL			
Total Debt	3,750,000	3,750,000	2,095,000
Preferred Equity	0	0	0
Common Equity	(5,128,000)	(1,726,000)	3,902,000

Business:

BELMORAL MINES LTD. is engaged in the acquisition and development of mineral properties and the exploration for and production of gold. Its principal mineral holdings and business activities are in Quebec and Arizona.

Date	EPS	DPS	Tot Rev	Inc Bex
Mar 93	0.00	0.00	3,211	49
Dec 92	(0.03)	0.00	2,238	(1,503)
Sep 92	(0.02)	0.00	2,728	(744)
Jun 92	(0.02)	0.00	3,206	(1,010)
Mar 92	(0.00)	0.00	3,784	(145)
Dec 91	(0.07)	0.00	141	(3,187)
Sep 91	0.02	0.00	2,899	922
Jun 91	(0.03)	0.00	2,590	(1,558)

Synopsis:

Belmoral Mines stated in its 1992 annual report that the company cannot meet its financial obligations given its current structure. Belmoral will be asking shareholders at the its annual meeting to approve a change in the company's focus from mining to oil and gas. The change in focus follows from an agreement with Geopetrol Resources Inc. and Aur Resources, signed in March 1993.

The agreement takes a major step in reducing Belmoral's debt as well as enabling it to pursue an interest in the oil and gas industry. The deal states that Geopetrol would purchase Belmoral's debt to Aur Resources, and Aur would acquire Belmoral's 50% share of Aur's mining assets. Geopetrol would then convert the debt into common shares of Belmoral and become a shareholder with approximately 49% of the company's outstanding common shares.

Belmoral's share of gold production in calendar 1992 totaled 23,849 ounces. Joint venture operating costs declined to $398 per ounce from $475 per ounce in the previous year. The drop in operating cost reflects a drop in exploration costs for the year.

Belmoral's ore reserves as of September 30, 1993, the end of the Aur-Belmoral fiscal year, totaled 132,000 tons of proven and probable reserves averaging 0.27 ounces of gold per ton. Mining during fiscal 1992 reduced reserves by 198,000 tons. At current production levels, the reserves will be exhausted during the second half of 1993.

The transaction involving Belmoral, Geopetrol and Aur, and the future direction of the company are subject to shareholder approval, and will be decided at Belmoral's annual and special meeting set for June 25, 1993.

Relative strength to TSE300
Price
Volume (in 1000's of board lots)

Rank (Profit/Revenue/Assets)
918   615   873

J. Gordon Strasser
President & C.E.O.
R. Paul Middleton
V.P./C.F.O. & Secretary

Address
Suite 1215
111 Richmond Street West
Toronto
ON
M5H 2G4
(416) 364-0444

Fax: (416) 364-2753
B0009647/G/2.0

BEMA GOLD CORPORATION

Exchanges	Price (Jun24'93)	1.90	Trailing P/E	nm	Stock Symbol
TV	Trailing Yield (%)	0.00	Trailing EPS	(0.29)	**BGO**

Period Ending	Dec92	Dec91	Dec90	Dec89	Dec88
Yearly Statistics					
Price-Close	0.85	1.56	2.95	2.40	1.50
Price-High	2.10	3.20	4.60	2.95	1.80
Price-Low	0.71	1.32	1.85	0.96	1.49
P/E-Close	nm	nm	nm	nm	nm
Dividends per Share	0.00	0.00	0.00	0.00	0.00
Dividend Yield (%)	0.00	0.00	0.00	0.00	0.00
Sales per Share	0.15	0.26	0.45	0.20	na
EPS before extra. item	(0.28)	(0.10)	(0.03)	(0.11)	(0.11)
Cash Flow per Share	(0.05)	(0.02)	0.01	0.01	0.06
Book Value per Share	0.71	0.98	1.00	0.89	0.91
O/S Common Shares	31,398	30,738	28,091	24,108	18,983
Total Revenue	5,609	7,792	11,539	3,254	(325)
Income before extra.	(8,605)	(3,030)	(726)	(2,286)	(1,912)
Cash Flow	(1,710)	(639)	234	144	(1,059)
Debt/Equity	1.09	0.88	0.44	0.23	0.01
Return on Capital (%)	(14.65)	(4.63)	(0.62)	(9.67)	(13.39)
Ret. on Com. Equity (%)	(32.84)	(10.42)	(2.93)	(11.84)	(13.45)
% Change Profit	(184.0)	(317.3)	68.2	(19.6)	(69.7)
% Change Revenue	(28.0)	(32.5)	254.6	1,102.4	(222.4)
% Change Assets	(15.9)	31.7	56.9	53.5	63.4

Date	EPS	DPS	Tot Rev	Inc Bex
Mar 93	(0.02)	0.00	520	(743)
Dec 92	(0.21)	0.00	815	(6,334)
Sep 92	(0.03)	0.00	1,386	(1,166)
Jun 92	(0.03)	0.00	1,226	(877)
Mar 92	(0.01)	0.00	1,770	(227)
Dec 91	(0.05)	0.00	2,249	(1,466)
Sep 91	(0.02)	0.00	1,895	(747)
Jun 91	(0.02)	0.00	1,839	(488)

	Dec92	Dec91	Dec90
Preferred Div. Coverage	np	np	np
Total Div. Coverage	na	na	na
Interest Coverage	0.0	0.0	0.0
Current Ratio	0.9	2.2	1.5
Operating Margin	(106.1)	(32.1)	(1.2)
Asset Turnover	0.1	0.1	0.3
5 YEAR RATIOS (%)			
Return on Capital	(8.6)	na	na
Return on Com. Equity	(14.3)	na	na
Profit Growth	na	na	na
Revenue Growth	84.1	na	na
Asset Growth	34.2	na	na
BALANCE SHEET (000)			
Cash	240	5,643	5,529
Current Assets	2,914	9,625	7,066
Net Fixed Assets	41,636	41,583	31,164
Invest's & Advances	1,878	4,477	4,549
Total Assets	49,790	59,174	44,943
Short Term Debt	1,272	2,210	2,605
Current Liabilities	3,279	4,399	4,675
Long Term Debt	23,209	24,055	9,710
Total Liabilities	27,371	29,185	16,762
Total Equity	22,418	29,989	28,181
Total Liab. & Equity	49,790	59,174	44,943
CAPITAL (000)			
Total Debt	24,481	26,265	12,314
Preferred Equity	0	0	0
Common Equity	22,418	29,989	28,181

Business:

BEMA GOLD CORPORATION is the result of the amalgamation of Amir Mines Ltd., Bema International Resources Inc. and Normine Resources Ltd. It is engaged in the exploration and development of gold and silver properties in the United States and Canada. The main focus of activity concerns three heap leach gold mines in Idaho.

Synopsis:

In January 1993, Bema Gold along with Amax Gold and Cia Minera Refugio (C.M.R.) completed agreements whereby Amax Gold purchased C.M.R.'s 50% interest in the Refugio property. Amax then became partners with Bema to jointly finance and develop the property in Chile. The Amax Gold / C.M.R. deal relates to the Verde, Pancho and Guanaco gold deposits. Bema and Amax Gold will own and operate the Refugio property through a jointly held Chilean subsidiary company, Cia Minera Maricunga.

The majority of Bema's gold reserves come from its 50% owned Refugio Property in Chile. Reserves there total 8.6 million contained ounces of gold in the geological reserve category. The development of the Refugio project will increase Bema's gold production from 11,000 ounces of gold equivaent in 1992 to about 120,000 ounces annually for the next two to three years. The estimated average operating cost per ounce of gold recovered will be $175 (U.S.).

All of Bema's revenues in 1992 were derived from the Champagne Mine in Idaho. Production at the mine ceased in February 1992. As of December 31, 1992, 40% of Bema's assets were located in the United States. Over 38% of the company's assets were located in Chile with the remainder in Canada.

In March 1993, Bema proposed to renogotiate the $5.6-million of convertible debentures maturing May 31, 1993, so as to extend the maturity date by two years to May 31, 1995. The convertible debentures will carry the original 9% coupon while lowering the conversion rate to $1.00 per share. Bema says discussions to date indicate most holders of the debenture agree to the terms.

Rank (Profit/Revenue/Assets)
871   772   541

Clive T. Johnson
Chairman & C.E.O.

Barry D. Rayment
President & C.O.O.

Address
Box 48
1400 - 510 Burrard Street
Vancouver
BC
V6C 3A8
(604) 681-8371

Fax: (604) 681-6209
01002528/G/2.0

Relative strength to TSE300

Price

Volume (in 1000's of board lots)

BREAKWATER RESOURCES LTD.

Exchanges	Price (Jun24'93)	0 .21	Trailing P/E	nm	Stock Symbol
TVQ	Trailing Yield (%)	0 .00	Trailing EPS	(0 .42)	**BWR**

Period Ending	Dec91	Dec90	Dec89	Dec88	Dec87
Yearly Statistics					
Price-Close	0 .21	0 .70	2 .50	3 .85	4 .55
Price-High	0 .72	2 .85	4 .85	6 .38	13 .50
Price-Low	0 .17	0 .58	2 .01	3 .70	4 .00
P/E-Close	nm	nm	9 .62	48 .13	23 .95
Dividends per Share	0 .00	0 .00	0 .05	0 .10	0 .05
Dividend Yield (%)	0 .00	0 .00	2 .00	2 .60	1 .10
Sales per Share	0 .93	1 .20	1 .22	1 .23	1 .34
EPS before extra. item	(0 .55)	(1 .17)	0 .26	0 .08	0 .19
Cash Flow per Share	(0 .06)	0 .23	0 .49	0 .61	0 .58
Book Value per Share	0 .20	0 .77	1 .96	2 .94	3 .40
O/S Common Shares	68 ,520	68 ,520	61 ,096	30 ,912	26 ,759
Total Revenue	64 ,581	81 ,747	86 ,412	35 ,962	32 ,103
Income before extra.	(37 ,383)	(75 ,391)	15 ,277	2 ,282	4 ,203
Cash Flow	(4 ,150)	14 ,621	29 ,950	17 ,050	13 ,196
Debt/Equity	5 .10	1 .15	0 .35	0 .34	0 .36
Return on Capital (%)	(39 .23)	(51 .32)	16 .03	7 .46	10 .26
Ret. on Com. Equity (%)	(112 .54)	(87 .16)	14 .50	2 .51	5 .95
% Change Profit	50 .4	(593 .5)	569 .5	(45 .7)	411 .3
% Change Revenue	(21 .0)	(5 .4)	140 .3	12 .0	39 .3
% Change Assets	(28 .3)	(17 .5)	31 .8	0 .8	72 .8

Preferred Div. Coverage	np	np	np
Total Div. Coverage	na	na	4 .9
Interest Coverage	0 .0	0 .0	7 .3
Current Ratio	0 .5	1 .1	3 .6
Operating Margin	(55 .0)	(12 .8)	17 .0
Asset Turnover	0 .6	0 .5	0 .4
5 YEAR RATIOS (%)			
Return on Capital	(11 .4)	(2 .4)	na
Return on Com. Equity	(35 .3)	(12 .5)	na
Profit Growth	na	na	na
Revenue Growth	22 .9	205 .3	na
Asset Growth	6 .3	17 .3	na
BALANCE SHEET (000)			
Cash	3 ,634	6 ,448	33 ,989
Current Assets	25 ,847	33 ,889	56 ,587
Net Fixed Assets	68 ,932	101 ,215	103 ,534
Invest's & Advances	9 ,478	11 ,480	18 ,856
Total Assets	107 ,225	149 ,525	181 ,297
Short Term Debt	37 ,928	8 ,242	7 ,245
Current Liabilities	57 ,065	29 ,686	15 ,546
Long Term Debt	30 ,198	52 ,673	34 ,085
Total Liabilities	93 ,858	96 ,459	61 ,363
Total Equity	13 ,367	53 ,066	119 ,934
Total Liab. & Equity	107 ,225	149 ,525	181 ,297
CAPITAL (000)			
Total Debt	68 ,126	60 ,935	41 ,330
Preferred Equity	0	0	0
Common Equity	13 ,367	53 ,066	119 ,934

Business:

BREAKWATER RESOURCES LTD. is a mining company which has a 49% interest in the gold producing Cannon Mine in Washington State. The company also has mineral properties in Canada including the Estrades Mine in Quebec.

Date	EPS	DPS	Tot Rev	Inc Bex
Sep 92	(0 .02)	0 .00	17 ,169	(2 ,185)
Jun 92	(0 .06)	0 .00	13 ,795	(2 ,416)
Mar 92	(0 .02)	0 .00	14 ,395	(1 ,518)
Dec 91	(0 .32)	0 .00	10 ,620	(21 ,344)
Sep 91	(0 .05)	0 .00	16 ,274	(3 ,642)
Jun 91	(0 .11)	0 .00	21 ,897	(7 ,387)
Mar 91	(0 .07)	0 .00	16 ,023	(5 ,010)
Dec 90	(1 .27)	0 .00	26 ,936	(81 ,934)

Synopsis:

In March 1993, Breakwater Resources Ltd. and Arimetco International Inc. announced they will not renew their one-year management contract, under which Arimetco manages Breakwater operations. The decision was mutual and enables both companies to focus on their own operations. Breakwater will now concentrate on its zinc, lead, and precious metals businesses.

In December 1992, Breakwater announced plans to restart mining at its Estrades precious metals, zinc and copper mine in Quebec. The decision follows an engineering review of the ore reserves as well as a feasibility study on the project. The ore reserves have been confirmed in the proved and probable category at 276,000 tonnes grading 7.47 grams a tonne gold, 215.33 grams of silver, 0.88% copper, 1.34% lead and 13.16% zinc. Production is scheduled for March 1993.

In November 1992, Breakwater, Arimetco and Nova Gold Resources entered into a joint venture to process ore from Nova Gold's Murray Brook Property. Breakwater and Arimetco will hold a 25% interest in the joint venture with NovaGold controlling the other 50%. The ore will be processed by East West Caribou Mining, a subsidiary of Breakwater Resources. As part of the agreement, Arimetco and Breakwater subscribed for $500,000 worth of Nova Gold shares. Arimetco purchased Breakwater's portion of the subscription in exchange for a promissory note from Breakwater. The Murray Brook deposit is estimated to contain about 25 million pounds of copper.

Relative strength to TSE300 / Price / Volume (in 1000's of board lots)

Rank (Profit/Revenue/Assets)
941 438 409

H.R. Shipes
Chairman

Russell D. Alley
President & C.O.O.

Address
6179 East Broadway Blvd.
2nd Floor
Tucson
AZ
85711
(602) 745-0774

Fax: (602) 745-0863
B0012021/G/2.0

CAMBIOR INC.

Exchanges	Price (Jun24'93)	18.50	Trailing P/E	nm	Stock Symbol
TM	Trailing Yield (%)	0.76	Trailing EPS	(0.23)	**CBJ**

Period Ending	Dec92	Dec91	Dec90	Dec89	Dec88
Yearly Statistics					
Price-Close	12.13	9.25	12.00	14.75	12.13
Price-High	12.75	11.88	20.50	16.25	18.88
Price-Low	7.00	8.25	9.75	11.38	11.38
P/E-Close	nm	20.56	15.39	20.21	15.96
Dividends per Share	0.14	0.14	0.13	0.12	0.11
Dividend Yield (%)	1.16	1.51	1.08	0.81	0.91
Sales per Share	5.45	5.32	4.53	4.69	4.60
EPS before extra. item	(0.13)	0.45	0.78	0.73	0.76
Cash Flow per Share	1.64	1.52	1.65	1.45	1.52
Book Value per Share	9.76	10.29	9.98	9.25	7.77
O/S Common Shares	36,877	30,711	30,711	29,960	23,655
Total Revenue	189,288	169,093	152,639	116,883	109,839
Income before extra.	(4,391)	13,920	23,991	17,661	17,969
Cash Flow	55,270	46,765	50,548	34,970	35,709
Debt/Equity	0.44	0.12	0.05	0.07	0.04
Return on Capital (%)	(0.34)	4.48	8.31	7.80	10.36
Ret. on Com. Equity (%)	(1.30)	4.47	8.22	7.66	10.36
% Change Profit	(131.5)	(42.0)	35.8	(1.7)	(17.8)
% Change Revenue	11.9	10.8	30.6	6.4	18.7
% Change Assets	49.2	12.0	6.5	41.6	(0.8)

Preferred Div. Coverage	np	np	np
Total Div. Coverage	0.0	3.2	6.0
Interest Coverage	0.0	20.4	21.3
Current Ratio	2.1	2.9	3.3
Operating Margin	(5.0)	5.7	12.3
Asset Turnover	0.3	0.4	0.4
5 YEAR RATIOS (%)			
Return on Capital	6.1	8.9	na
Return on Com. Equity	5.9	9.1	na
Profit Growth	na	(8.0)	na
Revenue Growth	15.3	16.8	na
Asset Growth	20.1	22.5	na
BALANCE SHEET (000)			
Cash	66,262	48,409	72,412
Current Assets	123,163	79,967	110,185
Net Fixed Assets	468,659	310,268	235,194
Invest's & Advances	1,096	3,801	5,274
Total Assets	603,052	404,170	360,787
Short Term Debt	23,791	3,430	6,411
Current Liabilities	58,979	27,588	33,187
Long Term Debt	135,452	35,407	8,099
Total Liabilities	243,326	88,042	54,360
Total Equity	359,726	316,128	306,427
Total Liab. & Equity	603,052	404,170	360,787
CAPITAL (000)			
Total Debt	159,243	38,837	14,510
Preferred Equity	0	0	0
Common Equity	359,726	316,128	306,427

Business:

CAMBIOR INC. is a major Canadian gold producer with interests in eight mines in production or under development. The mines are in the Val d'Or and Rouyn-Noranda regions of Quebec, as well as Alaska. The company has other properties in Quebec and the United States. The company has a joint interest in the Niobec mine, near Chicoutimi, Que., the only niobium mine in North America.

Date	EPS	DPS	Tot Rev	Inc Bex
Mar 93	0.02	0.00	54,465	876
Dec 92	(0.47)	0.07	44,501	(15,493)
Sep 92	0.06	0.07	47,359	2,027
Jun 92	0.16	0.07	52,153	5,176
Mar 92	0.13	0.00	43,854	3,899
Dec 91	0.00	0.07	42,685	31
Sep 91	0.10	0.07	46,565	3,165
Jun 91	0.21	0.07	43,518	6,401

Synopsis:

In May 1993, it was reported that Cambior's Omai gold project located in Guyana began commercial production. The property, operated and 65% held by Cambior, is expected to become the largest gold mine in South America. Production began January 16, 1993, with the first gold bar being produced on February 1, 1993. The Omai project is expected to produce, by open-pit, 260,000 ounces of gold annually. Cambior expects output from Omai to almost double the company's total gold production in 1993 to a level of 620,000 ounces. In 1992, Cambior produced 354,298 ounces of gold.

Reserves at the Omai gold project are estimated at two million contained ounces of gold, enough to last approximately 10 years. Budgeted production costs are $200 (U.S.) per ounce of gold. Over the last 18 months, Cambior has spent about $180-million to get the property into production.

On May 6, 1993, shareholders of Cambior approved a shareholder protection rights plan adopted by the company's board of directors in March 1993. The plan is designed to protect shareholders from unfair takeover tactics.

Cambior also stated at its 1993 annual meeting that it expects to spend about $17-million on exploration in 1993. Approximately $7-million of the 1993 exploration budget will be spent in Canada. Exploration expenditures in both Mexico and Chile are to be about $4-million each. The remaining $2-million will be spent in the United States.

In March 1993, Cambior announced it was going ahead with construction on its Carlota copper mine located in Arizona. Capital expenses for construction and deposit development are estimated at $82-million (U.S.). Commercial production is scheduled for the first quarter of 1995 with annual production to be 30,000 tons of copper for the first 10 years of mining.

Rank (Profit/Revenue/Assets)
825   283   196

Gilles Mercure
Chairman Of The Board
Louis P. Gignac
President & C.E.O.

Address
Suite 850
800 Rene-Levesque Blvd. West
Montreal
PQ
H3B 1X9
(514) 878-3166

Fax: (514) 878-3324
C0000622/G/2.0

CAMPBELL RESOURCES INC.

Exchanges	Price (Jun24'93)		1.11	Trailing P/E		nm	Stock Symbol
TMN	Trailing Yield (%)		0.00	Trailing EPS		(0.02)	**CCH**

Period Ending	Dec92	Dec91	Dec90	Dec89	Dec88
Yearly Statistics					
Price-Close	0.38	0.46	0.42	0.88	0.85
Price-High	0.63	0.60	1.25	1.30	2.31
Price-Low	0.38	0.33	0.35	0.68	0.75
P/E-Close	nm	15.33	nm	22.00	nm
Dividends per Share	0.00	0.00	0.00	0.00	0.00
Dividend Yield (%)	0.00	0.00	0.00	0.00	0.00
Sales per Share	0.35	0.41	0.48	0.53	0.68
EPS before extra. item	(0.01)	0.03	(0.34)	0.04	(1.13)
Cash Flow per Share	0.02	0.24	0.04	0.09	(0.14)
Book Value per Share	0.69	0.70	0.66	1.07	1.09
O/S Common Shares	99,298	99,226	98,642	77,670	54,841
Total Revenue	35,625	44,562	45,557	45,783	41,730
Income before extra.	(910)	3,324	(26,965)	3,001	(60,868)
Cash Flow	2,011	23,891	3,509	6,468	(7,531)
Debt/Equity	0.02	0.10	0.46	0.33	0.40
Return on Capital (%)	(0.79)	5.63	(23.08)	6.73	(55.56)
Ret. on Com. Equity (%)	(1.33)	4.95	(36.43)	4.21	(70.72)
% Change Profit	(127.4)	112.3	(998.5)	104.9	nm
% Change Revenue	(20.1)	(2.2)	(0.5)	9.7	(11.1)
% Change Assets	(9.6)	(11.4)	(12.0)	24.1	(35.7)

Preferred Div. Coverage	np	np	np
Total Div. Coverage	na	na	na
Interest Coverage	0.0	3.7	0.0
Current Ratio	1.4	2.3	1.6
Operating Margin	(3.5)	3.3	(83.5)
Asset Turnover	0.4	0.4	0.3
5 YEAR RATIOS (%)			
Return on Capital	(13.4)	(12.8)	(13.8)
Return on Com. Equity	(19.9)	(19.6)	(20.7)
Profit Growth	na	na	na
Revenue Growth	(5.4)	9.8	(2.5)
Asset Growth	(10.9)	(6.4)	(3.0)
BALANCE SHEET (000)			
Cash	4,593	12,330	7,299
Current Assets	10,508	24,705	14,747
Net Fixed Assets	70,648	65,687	68,320
Invest's & Advances	5,795	5,786	25,542
Total Assets	86,951	96,178	108,609
Short Term Debt	1,506	5,407	2,400
Current Liabilities	7,486	10,800	9,199
Long Term Debt	0	1,369	27,721
Total Liabilities	18,786	27,136	43,331
Total Equity	68,165	69,042	65,278
Total Liab. & Equity	86,951	96,178	108,609
CAPITAL (000)			
Total Debt	1,506	6,776	30,121
Preferred Equity	0	0	0
Common Equity	68,165	69,042	65,278

Business:

CAMPBELL RESOURCES INC. is a gold mining and natural resources company. Campbell operates the Joe Mann gold mine near Chibougamau, Quebec. Campbell has other properties in Canada and Mexico. Northgate Exploration Ltd. of Toronto has a 34% interest in the company.

Date	EPS	DPS	Tot Rev	Inc Bex
Mar 93	(0.00)	0.00	8,097	(255)
Dec 92	(0.01)	0.00	7,339	(1,189)
Sep 92	(0.01)	0.00	7,392	(567)
Jun 92	0.00	0.00	9,487	176
Mar 92	0.01	0.00	11,249	670
Dec 91	0.01	0.00	11,962	1,075
Sep 91	0.01	0.00	9,950	943
Jun 91	0.00	0.00	10,840	266

Synopsis:

Campbell Resources announced at the company's annual meeting in May 1993 that it expects to spend between $10-million to $12-million over the next two years to develop the Joe Mann Mine in Northern Quebec. The development plan should raise the mine's gold production to around 70,000 to 75,000 ounces of gold a year. During 1992, Campbell's gold production from the Joe Mann Mine was 70,000 ounces, down from 87,000 ounces in 1991. The company estimates its total gold production in 1993 will be 68,000 ounces, which includes 6,000 ounces from Mexico.

Gold and copper production at the Joe Mann Mine declined by over 20% in 1992, compared to last year. During 1992, the mine produced 70,200 ounces of gold and 1.2 million pounds of copper. In 1991, the mine produced 87,500 ounces of gold and 1.5 million pounds of copper. Campbell attributes the decline in production to the lack of development work at the mine.

In an attempt to raise money to further develop the Joe Mann Mine in Quebec, Campbell sold a graduated net smelter return royalty on production at the Joe Mann mine to Repadre Capital in April 1993. Repadre Capital will pay Campbell Resources $3-million for a royalty which will be 1.8% at gold prices up to $500 per ounce, increasing to 3.6% at $625 per ounce.

Besides the development work at the Joe Mann Mine, Campbell continues to hold an extensive portfolio of mineral properties in Mexico. At the La Colorada property in northwestern Mexico, Campbell's joint venture partner is earning a 70% interest in the project by putting the mine into production. The mine is expected to start production in mid-1993. Campbell's 30% interest in the property is expected to be worth about 7,000 ounces of gold, with an operating cost to be about $200 (U.S.) per ounce.

Relative strength to TSE300
Price
Volume (in 1000's of board lots)

Rank (Profit/Revenue/Assets)
693   527   436

John F. Kearney
Chairman Of The Board
John O. Kachmar
President
Patrick D. Downey
V.P. & C.F.O.

Address
Suite 2701
P.O Box 498
1 First Canadian Place
Toronto
ON
M5X 1E5
(416) 366-5201
Fax: (416) 367-3294
C0001051/G/2.0

COMINCO RESOURCES INTERNATIONAL LIMITED

Exchanges	Price (Jun24'93)	2.05	Trailing P/E	nm	Stock Symbol
TV	Trailing Yield (%)	0.00	Trailing EPS	(0.16)	**COR**

Period Ending	Dec92	Dec91	Dec90	Dec89	Dec88	Business:
Yearly Statistics						COMINCO RESOURCES INTERNATIONAL
Price-Close	2.20	1.75	1.65	3.70	2.25	LIMITED operates in the mining industry
Price-High	2.80	2.45	3.60	4.10	3.25	producing ferro-nickel, copper, gold and silver
Price-Low	1.80	1.15	1.50	2.31	1.71	and conducting exploration for base metals,
P/E-Close	nm	nm	nm	nm	nm	precious metals and industrial metals. The
Dividends per Share	0.00	0.00	0.00	0.00	0.00	company is actively exploring mineral
Dividend Yield (%)	0.00	0.00	0.00	0.00	0.00	properties in the U.S., Chile, Mexico, Bolivia,
Sales per Share	1.05	1.01	0.56	0.32	0.38	Ireland and Turkey. Cominco Ltd. holds a
EPS before extra. item	(0.17)	(0.10)	(0.65)	(0.35)	(0.30)	59.2% interest in the company.
Cash Flow per Share	(0.10)	0.06	(0.35)	(0.18)	(0.14)	
Book Value per Share	1.55	1.53	1.63	2.09	2.37	
O/S Common Shares	59,869	51,535	51,535	40,518	32,401	
Total Revenue	63,608	52,221	28,101	14,762	15,036	
Income before extra.	(9,355)	(4,966)	(30,698)	(13,145)	(9,605)	

Date	EPS	DPS	Tot Rev	Inc Bex
Mar 93	(0.06)	0.00	7,629	(3,856)
Dec 92	(0.10)	0.00	15,664	(5,399)
Sep 92	0.04	0.00	18,538	1,723
Jun 92	(0.04)	0.00	15,287	(1,911)
Mar 92	(0.07)	0.00	14,424	(3,768)
Dec 91	(0.06)	0.00	15,751	(2,542)
Sep 91	0.00	0.00	12,514	(76)
Jun 91	0.00	0.00	14,105	(269)

	Dec92	Dec91	Dec90	Dec89	Dec88
Cash Flow	(5,368)	2,959	(16,590)	(6,889)	(4,554)
Debt/Equity	0.12	0.12	0.06	0.08	0.09
Return on Capital (%)	(6.64)	(2.89)	(34.79)	(14.75)	(11.00)
Ret. on Com. Equity (%)	(10.91)	(6.11)	(36.44)	(16.28)	(11.65)
% Change Profit	(88.4)	83.8	(133.5)	(36.9)	(52.1)
% Change Revenue	21.8	85.8	90.4	(1.8)	(31.9)
% Change Assets	10.4	6.2	0.3	10.9	(4.5)

	Dec92	Dec91	Dec90
Preferred Div. Coverage	np	np	np
Total Div. Coverage	na	na	na
Interest Coverage	0.0	na	na
Current Ratio	2.1	1.5	4.0
Operating Margin	(18.8)	(5.4)	(87.4)
Asset Turnover	0.5	0.5	0.3
5 YEAR RATIOS (%)			
Return on Capital	(14.0)	na	na
Return on Com. Equity	(16.3)	na	na
Profit Growth	na	na	na
Revenue Growth	23.6	na	na
Asset Growth	4.4	na	na
BALANCE SHEET (000)			
Cash	6,609	8,774	14,444
Current Assets	31,944	29,892	28,872
Net Fixed Assets	79,372	46,030	43,126
Invest's & Advances	2,395	10,425	6,517
Total Assets	113,711	103,025	97,007
Short Term Debt	5,382	6,985	1,556
Current Liabilities	14,998	20,095	7,133
Long Term Debt	5,727	2,350	3,501
Total Liabilities	21,020	24,255	13,180
Total Equity	92,691	78,770	83,827
Total Liab. & Equity	113,711	103,025	97,007
CAPITAL (000)			
Total Debt	11,109	9,335	5,057
Preferred Equity	0	0	0
Common Equity	92,691	78,770	83,827

Synopsis:

In April 1993, Cominco Resources International Ltd. announced it had reopened the Glenbrook nickel smelter in Riddle, Oregon. The refinery was closed for two months and will reopen and operate at only two-thirds capacity. The refinery had been a primary source of revenues for Cominco Resources International. As a result of it being closed for two of the first three months of the year, first quarter revenues in 1993 dropped to about half the level recorded in the first quarter of 1991. The smelter was closed because of difficult conditions in the nickel industry.

In 1993, Cominco Ltd. expects to spend more than $15-million on exploration expenditures under its control. Of that total, Cominco Resources' share is about $5.7-million. Although exploration is planned for the United States and Mexico, the company's efforts will be concentrated in Turkey and Chile. In 1992, Cominco Resources formed a three-year joint venture to explore copper deposits in Chile.

After first receiving favorable drilling results for its 100% owned Cerattepe copper property in Turkey, Cominco Resources announced in April 1993, that it will conduct metallurgical and engineering studies at the property. The studies will be carried out in an attempt to make a production decision relating to the property. The focus is on the main high-grade zone of 1.2 million tonnes averaging 10% copper. The property also has gold and silver reserves overlying the copper deposit.

In 1992, Cominco Resources produced almost 10 million pounds of nickel contained in ferronickel. This is up from 7 million pounds in 1991. The company attributes the increase to higher grades of ore from the Glenbrook open pit.

Rank (Profit/Revenue/Assets)
882 439 395

George D. Tikkanen
President
Bryan Morris
Vice President, Finance

Address
Suite 400
200 Burrard Street
Vancouver
BC
V6C 3L7
(604) 682-0611

Fax: (604) 844-2516
01001142/G/2.0

CORNUCOPIA RESOURCES LTD.

Exchanges	Price (Jun24'93)	2.85	Trailing P/E	9.13	Stock Symbol
T	Trailing Yield (%)	0.00	Trailing EPS	0.31	**CNP**

Period Ending	Dec92	Dec91	Dec90	Dec89	Dec88
Yearly Statistics	US	US	US	US	US
Price-Close	1.60	0.33	0.70	1.90	1.85
Price-High	1.60	0.82	2.40	2.75	4.95
Price-Low	0.30	0.20	0.54	1.08	1.70
P/E-Close	3.50	nm	nm	nm	nm
Dividends per Share	0.00	0.00	0.00	0.00	0.00
Dividend Yield (%)	0.00	0.00	0.00	0.00	0.00
Sales per Share	0.06	na	na	na	na
EPS before extra. item	0.31	(0.09)	(0.22)	(0.22)	(0.04)
Cash Flow per Share	(0.04)	(0.04)	(0.05)	(0.01)	(0.04)
Book Value per Share	0.44	0.14	0.23	0.45	0.59
O/S Common Shares	20,230	19,371	19,371	19,371	17,128
Total Revenue	8,359	212	94	306	232
Income before extra.	6,004	(1,777)	(4,297)	(4,041)	(730)
Cash Flow	(760)	(796)	(904)	(232)	(668)
Debt/Equity	nd	nd	nd	nd	nd
Return on Capital (%)	112.72	(49.99)	(65.18)	(42.73)	(7.11)
Ret. on Com. Equity (%)	103.60	(49.99)	(65.18)	(42.97)	(7.11)
% Change Profit	437.8	58.6	(6.3)	(453.8)	nm
% Change Revenue	3,849.6	124.7	(69.2)	31.9	na
% Change Assets	247.4	(42.3)	(45.7)	(13.6)	(11.6)

Date		EPS	DPS	Tot Rev	Inc Bex
Mar 93	US	0.00	0.00	558	35
Dec 92	US	(0.01)	0.00	685	(115)
Sep 92	US	0.00	0.00	719	76
Jun 92	US	0.32	0.00	6,935	6,276
Mar 92	US	(0.01)	0.00	20	(234)
Dec 91	US	(0.05)	0.00	52	(1,081)
Sep 91	US	(0.01)	0.00	38	(170)
Jun 91	US	(0.02)	0.00	64	(298)

	Dec92	Dec91	Dec90
Preferred Div. Coverage	np	np	np
Total Div. Coverage	na	na	na
Interest Coverage	nd	nd	nd
Current Ratio	12.4	19.1	8.4
Operating Margin	(35.4)	na	na
Asset Turnover	0.1	na	na
5 YEAR RATIOS (%)			
Return on Capital	(10.5)	(33.0)	(25.7)
Return on Com. Equity	(12.3)	(33.1)	(25.8)
Profit Growth	na	na	na
Revenue Growth	na	na	na
Asset Growth	(3.7)	(18.0)	10.3
BALANCE SHEET			
Cash	7,366,121	975,078	2,401,004
Current Assets	8,271,585	1,792,708	2,849,663
Net Fixed Assets	1,278,313	780,325	994,772
Invest's & Advances	39,186	187,500	937,500
Total Assets	9,589,084	2,760,533	4,781,935
Short Term Debt	0	0	0
Current Liabilities	665,853	93,692	337,615
Long Term Debt	0	0	0
Total Liabilities	665,853	93,692	337,615
Total Equity	8,923,231	2,666,841	4,444,320
Total Liab. & Equity	9,589,084	2,760,533	4,781,935
CAPITAL			
Total Debt	0	0	0
Preferred Equity	0	0	0
Common Equity	8,923,231	2,666,841	4,444,320

Business:

CORNUCOPIA RESOURCES LTD. is a precious metals exploration company. Current operations centre on the Ivanhoe property located on the Carlin Gold Trend in north-central Nevada. The company has other properties in Alaska and Nevada.

Synopsis:

In late May 1993, Cornucopia Resources signed an agreement with U.S. Gold for an option to acquire a 55% interest in the Tonkin Springs Mine and mill in Eureka County, Nevada. Cornucopia can earn the interest by paying $5-million to U.S. Gold with $500,000 due when the option is exercised, by June 30, 1993, and the balance due, plus interest, in the next four years payable in quarterly installments. Tonkin Springs first opened in 1989 but was closed in mid-1990 because the operation was uneconomical. Cornucopia believes it can mine the reserves at an estimated $222 (U.S.) per ounce. Preliminary indications reveal a sulphide resource of approximately 3 million tons grading 0.095 ounces of gold per ton.

In April 1993, Cornucopia announced it had negotiated an option to purchase a 100% interest in the Mary Drinkwater gold deposit near Silver Peaks, Nevada. Cornucopia has until May 30, 1993, to exercise its option. If exercised, Cornucopia will be required to pay the property vendor an aggregate of $230,000 and assume responsibility for annual advance royalties and operating costs. To maintain its interest, Cornucopia will be required to make a production decision within five years of the option's exercise date.

After the closure of the Hollister Mine in May 1992, Cornucopia's operating profits have come from the leach pads located on the property. Since the start of the Newmont/Cornucopia Ivanhoe mining venture on June 23, 1992, Cornucopia's share of production totaled 3,666 ounces of gold. The leach pads are expected to continue production throughout 1993.

Relative strength to TSE300 / Price / Volume (in 1000's of board lots)

Rank (Profit/Revenue/Assets)
208   697   812

Andrew F.B. Milligan
President & C.E.O.

Shannon M. Ross
C.F.O.

Address
Suite 520, Marine Building
355 Burrard Street
Vancouver
BC
V6C 2G8
(604) 687-0619

Fax: (604) 681-4170
C0057738/G/2.0

DICKENSON MINES LIMITED

Exchanges	Price (Jun24'93)	6.87	Trailing P/E	31.25	Stock Symbol
TA	Trailing Yield (%)	0.00	Trailing EPS	0.22	**DML.A**

Period Ending	Dec92	Dec91	Dec90	Dec89	Dec88
Yearly Statistics					
Price-Close	4.00	3.50	3.90	6.25	5.38
Price-High	5.38	4.13	7.00	7.75	8.13
Price-Low	3.40	2.50	3.63	4.55	4.20
P/E-Close	26.67	8.14	nm	16.03	15.81
Dividends per Share	0.00	0.00	0.00	0.00	0.05
Dividend Yield (%)	0.00	0.00	0.00	0.00	0.93
Sales per Share	3.45	3.51	3.42	3.46	3.16
EPS before extra. item	0.15	0.43	(2.23)	0.39	0.34
Cash Flow per Share	0.28	0.58	0.26	0.51	0.68
Book Value per Share	3.50	3.35	2.92	5.15	4.36
O/S Common Shares	17,513	17,513	17,513	17,513	15,119
Total Revenue	61,336	62,874	60,909	60,264	46,454
Income before extra.	2,682	7,510	(39,134)	6,064	4,806
Cash Flow	4,878	10,133	4,532	7,910	9,648
Debt/Equity	0.64	0.83	0.99	0.25	0.35
Return on Capital (%)	5.71	10.72	(44.01)	11.15	9.07
Ret. on Com. Equity (%)	4.47	13.69	(55.37)	7.77	7.55
% Change Profit	(64.3)	0.0	(745.4)	26.2	(25.3)
% Change Revenue	(2.4)	3.2	1.1	29.7	5.4
% Change Assets	(7.9)	6.7	(34.6)	9.1	60.2

Preferred Div. Coverage	np	np	np
Total Div. Coverage	na	na	na
Interest Coverage	2.0	3.9	0.0
Current Ratio	0.9	0.9	2.7
Operating Margin	7.4	14.5	(77.3)
Asset Turnover	0.5	0.5	0.5
5 YEAR RATIOS (%)			
Return on Capital	(1.5)	0.4	0.8
Return on Com. Equity	(4.4)	(3.0)	(3.6)
Profit Growth	(16.1)	12.6	na
Revenue Growth	6.8	12.3	14.5
Asset Growth	2.3	6.5	11.7
BALANCE SHEET (000)			
Cash	6,422	15,374	7,628
Current Assets	19,536	28,764	20,690
Net Fixed Assets	47,999	48,064	46,615
Invest's & Advances	45,123	45,490	46,965
Total Assets	112,658	122,318	114,688
Short Term Debt	14,388	23,124	0
Current Liabilities	21,973	31,178	7,791
Long Term Debt	24,995	25,299	50,343
Total Liabilities	51,357	63,699	63,579
Total Equity	61,301	58,619	51,109
Total Liab. & Equity	112,658	122,318	114,688
CAPITAL (000)			
Total Debt	39,383	48,423	50,343
Preferred Equity	0	0	0
Common Equity	61,301	58,619	51,109

Business:

DICKENSON MINES LIMITED is a natural resource mining and exploration company. It owns the Red Lake gold mine in Ontario, the Havelock lime operation in New Brunswick, and Saskatchewan Minerals, a sodium sulphate producer in Saskatchewan. The company manages and owns 36.2% of Wharf Resources Ltd. of Toronto, which has a heap leach gold mine in South Dakota.

Date	EPS	DPS	Tot Rev	Inc Bex
Mar 93	0.09	0.00	15,352	1,635
Dec 92	0.08	0.00	14,934	1,540
Sep 92	0.03	0.00	16,661	528
Jun 92	0.02	0.00	15,942	349
Mar 92	0.02	0.00	13,799	265
Dec 91	0.08	0.00	15,104	1,293
Sep 91	0.12	0.00	16,429	2,184
Jun 91	0.14	0.00	16,954	2,472

Synopsis:

Dickenson Mines reported that its 1992 share of gold production increased slightly to 111,872 ounces from 108,477 ounces in 1991. Dickenson's gold production is generated through its 100% owned Arthur White Mine, located near Red Lake, Ontario, and its 36.2% interest in Wharf Resources. The Red Lake property produced 75,052 ounces of gold in 1992, compared with 74,605 ounces in 1991. Wharf's share of gold production at its mine in 1992 totaled 95,186 ounces, a new record for the mine. Cash costs there fell by 12% over last year to $183 (U.S.) in 1992. Dickenson's share of total gold production in 1993 is expected to top 123,000 ounces.

Dickenson's Red Lake Mine is its major asset. Proven and probable reserves at the mine total 3.1 million tons grading 0.32 ounces of gold per ton. The mine also has one million tons of reserves in the possible category. At present production levels, the Red Lake Mine has enough reserves to last almost 14 years.

All of Dickenson's operations are based in Canada with product sales primarily being generated within Canada, except for approximately 53% of industrial mineral product sales which were to customers in the United States.

Rank (Profit/Revenue/Assets)
328   446   396

Robert R. McEwen
Chairman, President & C.E.O.
Rolando C. Francisco
Sr. V.P. & C.F.O.
John F. Cook
V.P., Operations

Address
Suite 2700
145 King Street West
Toronto
ON
M5H 1J8
(416) 361-0402

Fax: (416) 361-5741
D0001061/G/2.0

ECHO BAY MINES LTD.

Exchanges	Price (Jun24'93)	14.75	Trailing P/E	nm	Stock Symbol
TMZA	Trailing Yield (%)	0.51	Trailing EPS	(0.30)	**ECO**

Period Ending	Dec92	Dec91	Dec90	Dec89	Dec88
Yearly Statistics	US	US	US	US	US
Price-Close	6.25	8.63	10.38	21.25	16.75
Price-High	9.75	11.63	24.88	23.50	30.88
Price-Low	5.38	7.63	8.25	15.25	15.63
P/E-Close	nm	107.81	nm	112.43	24.42
Dividends per Share	0.08	0.08	0.08	0.07	0.07
Dividend Yield (%)	1.20	0.87	0.72	0.34	0.42
Sales per Share	2.97	3.12	3.42	3.00	2.76
EPS before extra. item	(0.30)	0.07	(0.60)	0.16	0.56
Cash Flow per Share	0.73	0.87	0.91	0.97	0.93
Book Value per Share	4.19	4.68	4.47	5.15	5.02
O/S Common Shares	105,169	105,146	99,117	99,048	98,874
Total Revenue	313,179	328,391	339,783	299,369	287,230
Income before extra.	(31,721)	6,793	(59,670)	16,020	54,426
Cash Flow	76,500	87,799	90,512	96,097	90,334
Debt/Equity	0.50	0.48	0.02	0.02	0.00
Return on Capital (%)	(3.76)	3.03	(11.49)	5.95	15.96
Ret. on Com. Equity (%)	(6.81)	1.45	(12.53)	3.18	12.68
% Change Profit	(567.0)	111.4	(472.5)	(70.6)	12.3
% Change Revenue	(4.6)	(3.4)	13.5	4.2	33.5
% Change Assets	7.0	(3.7)	(8.4)	14.8	49.2

Date		EPS	DPS	Tot Rev	Inc Bex
Mar 93	US	(0.02)	0.00	83,992	(2,207)
Dec 92	US	(0.24)	0.04	79,891	(25,249)
Sep 92	US	(0.04)	0.04	75,254	(4,311)
Jun 92	US	0.00	0.04	86,277	(415)
Mar 92	US	(0.02)	0.00	71,000	(1,700)
Dec 91	US	(0.04)	0.04	74,317	(4,617)
Sep 91	US	0.02	0.04	80,379	2,327
Jun 91	US	0.05	0.03	82,039	4,726

Preferred Div. Coverage	np	np	np
Total Div. Coverage	0.0	0.9	0.0
Interest Coverage	0.0	2.2	0.0
Current Ratio	1.4	0.8	0.7
Operating Margin	(0.3)	5.5	8.5
Asset Turnover	0.3	0.4	0.4
5 YEAR RATIOS (%)			
Return on Capital	1.9	6.2	8.6
Return on Com. Equity	(0.4)	4.2	6.6
Profit Growth	na	(23.5)	na
Revenue Growth	7.7	21.1	32.2
Asset Growth	10.0	16.0	30.3
BALANCE SHEET (000)			
Cash	60,293	0	11,094
Current Assets	105,095	56,246	68,376
Net Fixed Assets	764,132	791,437	813,881
Invest's & Advances	63,798	21,949	19,138
Total Assets	936,585	875,031	908,688
Short Term Debt	9,388	9,994	0
Current Liabilities	73,986	70,376	103,856
Long Term Debt	210,696	223,686	9,181
Total Liabilities	496,292	383,486	465,548
Total Equity	440,293	491,545	443,140
Total Liab. & Equity	936,585	875,031	908,688
CAPITAL (000)			
Total Debt	220,084	233,680	9,181
Preferred Equity	0	0	0
Common Equity	440,293	491,545	443,140

Business:

ECHO BAY MINES LTD. is a gold mining company. It has 10 producing mines in the United States and Canada. The company has mines in Ontario, the Northwest Territories, Colorado, Washington and Nevada. It has other properties in North America under development. The company currently owns 33% of the Muscocho Group of companies including Muscocho Explorations Ltd. of Toronto.

Synopsis:

In the first quarter ended March 31, 1993, Echo Bay Mines reported that gold production rose to 193,051 ounces, compared with 168,370 ounces in the same period last year. Also, silver production more than doubled in the quarter to 4.7 million ounces from 2.1 million. Echo Bay said higher levels of production were the result of improved productivity at all four of its operating mines. The improved production figures, though, were affected sharply by lower gold prices in the period.

Exploration expenses in the first quarter of 1993, more than doubled the level of last year. Echo Bay spent $1.6-million (U.S.) on exporation in the first quarter compared to $600,000 (U.S.) in the first quarter of 1992. The company is exploring opportunities in Mexico, Latin America, Russia and North America.

At the beginning of 1993, Echo Bay operated or had an interest in the Lupin mine in the Northwest Territories, the Kettle Rive mine, and the McCoy/Cove and Round Mountain deposits in Nevada. As of the end of 1992, total reserves at these mines equal 7.2 million ounces of gold. Echo Bay is also involved in two advanced projects in Alaska. They are the 100% owned Alaska-Juneau project and the 50% owned Kensington deposit in southeast Alaska.

In January 1993, Echo Bay announced the write-down of its investment in the Kettle River gold mine. This follows an announcement by Crown Resources that it was withdrawing from the Kettle River joint venture. Echo Bay now controls 100% of the property. The $14.9-million write-down relates to the scaled down production rates at which the mine will be operated. The mill operating rate will be reduced by 25% now that Echo Bay must develop and finance the property by itself. Gold production will drop to a level of about 65,000 ounces in 1993, compared with 85,000 ounces in 1992.

Relative strength to TSE300

Price

Volume (in 1000's of board lots)

Rank (Profit/Revenue/Assets)
944   195   137

Robert Frederick Calman
Chairman

John Zigarlick
President & C.E.O.

Richard C. Kraus
Exec. V.P. & C.F.O.

Peter Clarke
Senior V.P., Operations

Address
370 Seventeenth Street
Denver
CO
80202
(303) 592-8058

Fax: (303) 592-8090
E0000405/G/2.0

EQUITY SILVER MINES LIMITED

Exchanges	Price (Jun24'93)		1.20	Trailing P/E		nm	Stock Symbol
TV	Trailing Yield (%)		16.67	Trailing EPS		(0.10)	**EST.A**

Period Ending	Dec92	Dec91	Dec90	Dec89	Dec88
Yearly Statistics					
Price-Close	0.75	1.06	0.84	4.20	4.10
Price-High	1.13	1.60	4.40	4.80	6.88
Price-Low	0.65	0.63	0.65	3.60	4.00
P/E-Close	nm	9.64	2.80	6.67	13.23
Dividends per Share	0.20	0.20	0.20	0.20	0.20
Dividend Yield (%)	26.67	18.87	23.81	4.76	4.88
Sales per Share	1.05	1.47	2.63	2.74	2.57
EPS before extra. item	(0.12)	0.11	0.30	0.63	0.31
Cash Flow per Share	0.19	0.39	0.94	1.23	1.11
Book Value per Share	1.41	1.73	1.81	1.74	1.30
O/S Common Shares	32,523	32,523	32,523	32,523	32,522
Total Revenue	39,509	54,069	91,573	93,324	85,229
Income before extra.	(3,881)	3,625	10,058	22,105	12,171
Cash Flow	6,089	12,543	30,596	40,121	36,110
Debt/Equity	nd	0.00	0.03	0.02	0.03
Return on Capital (%)	(11.50)	6.95	32.00	46.71	30.05
Ret. on Com. Equity (%)	(7.62)	6.30	17.10	41.76	24.45
% Change Profit	(207.1)	(64.0)	(54.5)	81.6	100.9
% Change Revenue	(26.9)	(41.0)	(1.9)	9.5	14.2
% Change Assets	(9.0)	(8.0)	(4.7)	31.1	(2.8)

Business:

EQUITY SILVER MINES LTD. is a natural resources company. It operates a silver-gold-copper mine in British Columbia. The company has exploration activities in British Columbia and Newfoundland. Placer Dome Inc. of Vancouver owns 58.8% cent of the company's common shares.

Date	EPS	DPS	Tot Rev	Inc Bex
Mar 93	0.01	0.05	5,421	177
Dec 92	(0.10)	0.05	11,508	(3,325)
Sep 92	0.00	0.05	9,071	14
Jun 92	(0.01)	0.05	7,150	(200)
Mar 92	(0.04)	0.05	11,780	(1,113)
Dec 91	(0.03)	0.05	10,582	(880)
Sep 91	0.01	0.05	11,474	318
Jun 91	0.04	0.05	16,388	1,370

	Dec92	Dec91	Dec90
Preferred Div. Coverage	np	np	np
Total Div. Coverage	0.0	0.6	1.5
Interest Coverage	nd	145.5	119.9
Current Ratio	8.1	4.4	4.0
Operating Margin	(33.1)	(4.7)	18.5
Asset Turnover	0.4	0.5	0.9
5 YEAR RATIOS (%)			
Return on Capital	20.8	26.1	26.0
Return on Com. Equity	16.4	20.4	19.2
Profit Growth	na	7.6	30.1
Revenue Growth	(12.0)	(3.3)	11.2
Asset Growth	0.3	(7.7)	(7.3)
BALANCE SHEET (000)			
Cash	19,543	31,442	47,336
Current Assets	39,869	41,467	53,883
Net Fixed Assets	1,012	7,849	17,420
Invest's & Advances	2,220	2,217	71
Total Assets	80,911	88,913	96,637
Short Term Debt	0	174	1,784
Current Liabilities	4,939	9,457	13,628
Long Term Debt	0	0	182
Total Liabilities	35,171	32,787	37,631
Total Equity	45,740	56,126	59,006
Total Liab. & Equity	80,911	88,913	96,637
CAPITAL (000)			
Total Debt	0	174	1,966
Preferred Equity	0	0	0
Common Equity	45,740	56,126	59,006

Synopsis:

At Equity Silver's annual meeting held in May 1993, the company stated that it does not expect mining operations to continue after 1993. Current reserves are almost depleted at the Huston, British Columbia, operation and there is no information to indicate additional sources of underground ore. As of December 31, 1992, the property had proven and probable reserves totaling 316,000 tons grading 4.31 ounces of silver per ton, 0.123 ounces of gold per ton and 0.46% copper per ton, based on an 8.75 ounces of silver-equivalent grade.

Equity Silver will continue to explore the Huston area for additional ore reserves in 1993. A regional program is planned and is expected to cost $900,000 in 1993. Equity Silver spent $533,000 on exploration expenditures in 1992.

Equity Silver's metal production fell in 1992 compared with 1991. This decline was attributed to lower mill throughput and a lower silver grade associated with the closing of the mine. In 1992, the company produced 3.1 million ounces of silver, down almost 45% from last year. Gold production dropped 11.5% in the year to a level of 49,200 ounces recovered. Copper production remained at about the same level as last year with over 10 million pounds produced. Sales volumes of silver and copper in 1993 are expected to be at about 60% of 1992 levels. Gold is expected to be at approximately 70% of 1992 production levels.

In 1992 and 1991, 74% of Equity Silver's sales were exported to a Japanese smelter.

Rank (Profit/Revenue/Assets)
817 508 453

Winslow W. Bennett
Chairman Of The Board

C. Henry Brehaut
President & C.E.O.

Arthur W. Brown
V.P., Operations

Address
P.O. Box 49330
Bentall Postal Station
Vancouver
BC
V7X 1P1
(604) 682-7082

Fax: (604) 682-7092
E0004172/G/2.0

EURO-NEVADA MINING CORPORATION LIMITED

Exchanges	Price (Jun24'93)	28.00	Trailing P/E	93.33	Stock Symbol
T	Trailing Yield (%)	0.18	Trailing EPS	0.30	**EN**

Period Ending	Mar93	Mar92	Mar91	Mar90	Mar89
Yearly Statistics					
Price-Close	22.63	15.50	12.00	13.00	3.80
Price-High	23.00	19.00	17.38	14.88	7.50
Price-Low	14.00	11.13	8.00	3.00	3.25
P/E-Close	87.02	59.62	70.59	144.44	nm
Dividends per Share	0.05	0.06	0.02	0.00	0.00
Dividend Yield (%)	0.22	0.39	0.17	0.00	0.00
Sales per Share	na	na	na	na	na
EPS before extra. item	0.30	0.26	0.17	0.09	(0.08)
Cash Flow per Share	0.58	0.34	0.27	0.26	(0.02)
Book Value per Share	5.21	5.39	3.20	2.36	1.26
O/S Common Shares	15,569	14,056	13,854	12,799	10,594
Total Revenue	11,325	8,363	4,795	3,429	932
Income before extra.	4,609	3,613	2,205	966	(718)
Cash Flow	9,141	4,685	3,634	2,813	(198)
Debt/Equity	nd	0.13	0.22	nd	0.74
Return on Capital (%)	8.83	7.90	7.43	7.21	(0.97)
Ret. on Com. Equity (%)	5.87	6.02	5.92	4.44	(6.57)
% Change Profit	27.6	63.9	128.3	234.5	(124.2)
% Change Revenue	35.4	74.4	39.8	267.9	361.1
% Change Assets	(2.6)	58.7	79.6	32.1	167.7

Preferred Div. Coverage	np	np	np		
Total Div. Coverage	5.9	8.6	8.0		
Interest Coverage	na	na	na		
Current Ratio	37.4	4.7	26.7		
Operating Margin	47.1	47.9	44.9		
Asset Turnover	na	na	na		
5 YEAR RATIOS (%)					
Return on Capital	6.1	na	na		
Return on Com. Equity	3.1	na	na		
Profit Growth	na	na	na		
Revenue Growth	123.7	na	na		
Asset Growth	57.9	na	na		
BALANCE SHEET (000)					
Cash	46,770	39,678	21,272		
Current Assets	48,453	50,453	21,729		
Net Fixed Assets	36,790	37,035	24,570		
Invest's & Advances	0	0	8,814		
Total Assets	85,243	87,488	55,113		
Short Term Debt	0	9,500	0		
Current Liabilities	1,294	10,856	814		
Long Term Debt	0	0	9,500		
Total Liabilities	4,141	11,673	10,849		
Total Equity	81,102	75,815	44,264		
Total Liab. & Equity	85,243	87,488	55,113		
CAPITAL (000)					
Total Debt	0	9,500	9,500		
Preferred Equity	0	0	0		
Common Equity	81,102	75,815	44,264		

Business:

EURO-NEVADA MINING CORPORATION LIMITED's main objective is to seek out royalties on precious metal deposits in Nevada, the southwestern U.S., and Canada. It holds royalties on 25 properties including a 4% NSR (Net Smelter Royalty) and a 5% NPI (Net Profit Interest) on the Meikle Mine in the Carlin Gold Belt of Nevada.

Date	EPS	DPS	Tot Rev	Inc Bex
Mar 93	0.05	0.05	1,965	782
Dec 92	0.07	0.00	3,003	1,137
Sep 92	0.11	0.00	3,590	1,608
Jun 92	0.07	0.00	2,767	1,082
Mar 92	0.06	0.03	2,367	902
Dec 91	0.05	0.00	2,343	685
Sep 91	0.06	0.00	1,526	835
Jun 91	0.09	0.00	2,956	1,191

Synopsis:

In May 1993, Euro-Nevada Mining announced that it had issued two million special warrants pursuant to a previous agreement made with Gordon Capital, First Marathon Securities, Midland Walwyn and Toronto Dominion Securities. The special warrants, worth gross proceeds of $50-million, were issued at $25 per warrant. Each special warrant is convertible into a common share and an ordinary warrant. Two ordinary warrants entitles the holder to purchase an additional common share of Euro-Nevada at $32 per share. The ordinary warrants are good for five years.

Euro-Nevada is a gold royalty company. Its holdings include 30 royalty properties in some of the best gold producing regions in North America. These regions include the Carlin trend in Nevada, the Hemlo belt in Northern Ontario and the Eskay Creek property in British Columbia. Euro-Nevada has 10 royalty properties currently in production with the remainder to be developed in the future. Euro-Nevada's share of gold reserves relating to its portfolio of royalty properties totals almost 2.2 million contained ounces.

In March 1993, Euro-Nevada purchased a package of three royalties from a U.S.-based oil company. The royalty properties are: the Corbin-Wickes property, in which Euro-Nevada holds a 2.4% Net Smelter Return (NSR) royalty; the Tuxedo property, in which the company holds a 2% NSR royalty; and the Sellers Mountain property, in which Euro-Nevada holds a 3% NSR royalty. All three properties are in the United States.

Relative strength to TSE300

Price

Volume (in 1000's of board lots)

Rank (Profit/Revenue/Assets)
268   681   443

Seymour Schulich
Chairman Of The Board

Pierre Lassonde
President & C.E.O.

Ron W. Binns
V.P., Finance & C.F.O.

Address
20 Eglinton Avenue West
Suite 1900
P.O. Box 2005
Toronto
ON
M4R 1K8
(416) 480-6480
Fax: (416) 488-6598
01001620/G/2.0

FRANCO-NEVADA MINING CORPORATION LIMITED

Exchanges	Price (Jun24'93)	61.87	Trailing P/E	49.50	Stock Symbol
T	Trailing Yield (%)	0.97	Trailing EPS	1.25	**FN**

Period Ending	Mar93	Mar92	Mar91	Mar90	Mar89
Yearly Statistics					
Price-Close	39.88	24.63	17.25	21.50	9.50
Price-High	40.00	28.50	22.75	23.00	11.13
Price-Low	23.00	15.38	12.00	8.50	6.50
P/E-Close	31.90	41.04	43.13	74.14	73.08
Dividends per Share	0.60	0.30	0.20	0.10	0.05
Dividend Yield (%)	1.51	1.22	1.16	0.47	0.53
Sales per Share	na	na	na	na	na
EPS before extra. item	1.25	0.60	0.40	0.29	0.13
Cash Flow per Share	1.24	0.59	0.39	0.27	0.13
Book Value per Share	7.71	4.30	1.79	1.67	0.68
O/S Common Shares	14,022	12,737	12,677	12,177	12,177
Total Revenue	25,491	11,685	7,881	5,935	3,203
Income before extra.	17,233	7,562	5,065	3,519	1,516
Cash Flow	17,056	7,489	4,864	3,262	1,568
Debt/Equity	nd	0.05	0.26	0.43	nd
Return on Capital (%)	28.82	24.22	24.44	27.35	30.57
Ret. on Com. Equity (%)	21.15	19.50	23.55	24.69	18.75
% Change Profit	127.9	49.3	43.9	132.1	1,070.1
% Change Revenue	118.2	48.3	32.8	85.3	213.5
% Change Assets	89.8	101.0	(2.6)	56.3	136.3
Preferred Div. Coverage	np	np	np		
Total Div. Coverage	2.0	2.0	2.0		
Interest Coverage	745.7	140.9	53.8		
Current Ratio	43.2	12.5	5.9		
Operating Margin	92.3	87.7	86.2		
Asset Turnover	na	na	na		
5 YEAR RATIOS (%)					
Return on Capital	27.1	21.6	15.9		
Return on Com. Equity	21.5	17.6	12.9		
Profit Growth	165.8	169.7	na		
Revenue Growth	90.2	87.3	na		
Asset Growth	68.8	49.7	39.2		
BALANCE SHEET (000)					
Cash	81,922	40,081	18,572		
Current Assets	84,273	44,151	19,589		
Net Fixed Assets	16,517	7,218	4,763		
Invest's & Advances	10,268	7,157	4,583		
Total Assets	111,058	58,526	29,113		
Short Term Debt	0	2,660	3,018		
Current Liabilities	1,953	3,543	3,347		
Long Term Debt	0	0	2,867		
Total Liabilities	2,931	3,708	6,379		
Total Equity	108,127	54,818	22,734		
Total Liab. & Equity	111,058	58,526	29,113		
CAPITAL (000)					
Total Debt	0	2,660	5,885		
Preferred Equity	0	0	0		
Common Equity	108,127	54,818	22,734		

Date	EPS	DPS	Tot Rev	Inc Bex
Mar 93	0.25	0.60	5,686	3,494
Dec 92	0.45	0.00	8,499	6,215
Sep 92	0.30	0.00	6,092	4,150
Jun 92	0.25	0.00	5,214	3,374
Mar 92	0.15	0.30	2,879	1,803
Dec 91	0.15	0.00	2,905	1,873
Sep 91	0.16	0.00	3,007	2,046
Jun 91	0.15	0.00	2,894	1,840

Business:

FRANCO-NEVADA MINING CORP. LTD. is a gold exploration and mining company. The company has interests in the Carlin Gold Belt in Nevada, including the Goldstrike Mine operated by American Barrick Resources Corp. It owns 620 acres of land adjacent to the Williams and Golden Giant Mines near Hemlo, Ontario. It owns 36% of Redstone Resources Inc. of Toronto.

Synopsis:

In March 1993, Franco-Nevada Mining announced plans to raise approximately $38-million through an offering of special warrants. The agreement was entered into with First Marathon Securities, Gordon Capital and Nesbitt Thomson. Franco-Nevada will issue one million special warrants at $38 each. Each special warrant will be converted into one common share and one-half of an ordinary warrant to purchase an additional common share at $50 per share, excercisable for five years. Franco-Nevada expects to use most of the proceeds to maintain cash balances while the company acquires new gold royalties over the next few months.

Franco-Nevada's main assets are the royalty and net profit interests in the Goldstrike Mine located in Nevada. The mine is operated by American Barrick Resources. Franco-Nevada holds a 4% Net Smelter Return royalty and a 5% Net Profit Interest on the largest gold mine outside of Africa with estimated reserves of over 21 million contained ounces of gold. The mine produced 1.1 million ounces of gold in 1992, up from 546,000 ounces in 1991. Production is expected to rise to 1.3 million ounces in 1993 and increase to a level of 1.8 million ounces of gold production annually by 1995.

In January 1993, Franco-Nevada completed the acquisition of a new 6% Net Profit Interest at the Goldstrike Mine. The deal relates to the western extension of the mine. Reserves at the site total three million contained ounces in the proven category with an additional 1.5 million ounces in the geological reserve category. Franco-Nevada issued 225,000 shares in exchange for the royalty.

Relative strength to TSE300 / Price / Volume (in 1000's of board lots)

Rank (Profit/Revenue/Assets)
134   583   400

Seymour Schulich
Chairman & C.E.O.

Pierre Lassonde
President & C.O.O.

Ronald W. Binns
V.P., Finance & C.F.O.

Address
20 Eglinton Ave. West
Suite 1900
P.O. Box 2005
Toronto
ON
M4R 1K8
(416) 480-6480
Fax: (416) 488-6598
F0007001/G/2.0

GLAMIS GOLD LTD.

Exchanges	Price (Jun24'93)		9 .62	Trailing P/E		53 .47	Stock Symbol
TN	Trailing Yield (%)		0 .62	Trailing EPS		0 .18	**GLG**

Period Ending	Jun92	Jun91	Jun90	Jun89	Jun88
Yearly Statistics					
Price-Close	3 .55	3 .45	2 .62	1 .23	3 .95
Price-High	4 .75	3 .70	3 .40	3 .95	9 .50
Price-Low	3 .05	2 .20	1 .00	1 .15	3 .80
P/E-Close	35 .50	11 .13	8 .45	nm	65 .83
Dividends per Share	0 .06	0 .04	0 .00	0 .00	0 .00
Dividend Yield (%)	1 .69	1 .16	0 .00	0 .00	0 .00
Sales per Share	1 .91	1 .73	1 .19	0 .86	0 .84
EPS before extra. item	0 .10	0 .31	0 .31	(0 .32)	0 .06
Cash Flow per Share	0 .70	0 .73	0 .46	0 .12	0 .21
Book Value per Share	1 .86	1 .81	1 .54	1 .24	1 .56
O/S Common Shares	17 ,350	16 ,816	16 ,380	16 ,282	16 ,282
Total Revenue	33 ,231	30 ,077	20 ,942	15 ,414	14 ,237
Income before extra.	1 ,647	5 ,176	4 ,991	(5 ,214)	1 ,036
Cash Flow	12 ,009	12 ,295	7 ,551	1 ,886	3 ,354
Debt/Equity	0 .59	0 .30	0 .22	0 .00	0 .01
Return on Capital (%)	6 .82	19 .36	28 .68	(29 .33)	5 .95
Ret. on Com. Equity (%)	5 .25	18 .57	21 .98	(22 .92)	4 .24
% Change Profit	(68 .2)	3 .7	195 .7	(603 .3)	(43 .5)
% Change Revenue	10 .5	43 .6	35 .9	8 .3	(7 .4)
% Change Assets	30 .2	23 .4	3 .0	11 .6	4 .2

Preferred Div. Coverage	np	np	np
Total Div. Coverage	1 .6	7 .8	na
Interest Coverage	2 .9	16 .9	9 .8
Current Ratio	6 .2	1 .7	1 .3
Operating Margin	8 .9	20 .5	30 .9
Asset Turnover	0 .6	0 .7	0 .6
5 YEAR RATIOS (%)			
Return on Capital	6 .3	7 .8	8 .3
Return on Com. Equity	5 .4	6 .0	4 .7
Profit Growth	(2 .1)	19 .0	18 .1
Revenue Growth	16 .6	18 .7	13 .5
Asset Growth	13 .9	11 .4	17 .8
BALANCE SHEET (000)			
Cash	6 ,142	70	5 ,614
Current Assets	15 ,781	5 ,125	10 ,079
Net Fixed Assets	37 ,179	35 ,171	21 ,074
Invest's & Advances	1 ,242	1 ,242	2 ,433
Total Assets	55 ,474	42 ,610	34 ,517
Short Term Debt	80	772	5 ,274
Current Liabilities	2 ,538	3 ,012	8 ,000
Long Term Debt	19 ,044	8 ,362	390
Total Liabilities	23 ,247	12 ,126	9 ,257
Total Equity	32 ,227	30 ,484	25 ,260
Total Liab. & Equity	55 ,474	42 ,610	34 ,517
CAPITAL (000)			
Total Debt	19 ,124	9 ,134	5 ,664
Preferred Equity	0	0	0
Common Equity	32 ,227	30 ,484	25 ,260

Business:

GLAMIS GOLD LTD. is a gold mining company. It has two producing open pit, heap leach gold mines in California, the Picacho, in Imperial County in S.E. California and Yellow Aster in Kern County, about 100 miles north of Los Angeles. A third property, the Alto, located in Calaveras County, California, is mined out.

Date	EPS	DPS	Tot Rev	Inc Bex
Mar 93	0 .01	0 .00	7 ,629	223
Dec 92	0 .05	0 .00	8 ,746	757
Sep 92	0 .07	0 .06	9 ,351	1 ,294
Jun 92	0 .05	0 .00	10 ,681	782
Mar 92	0 .00	0 .00	8 ,489	(18)
Dec 91	0 .04	0 .00	7 ,484	574
Sep 91	0 .04	0 .06	7 ,853	739
Jun 91	0 .10	0 .00	9 ,443	1 ,745

Synopsis:

Glamis Gold's production figures for the quarter ended March 31, 1993, reveal that 16,820 ounces of gold were recovered compared to 18,100 ounces over the same period last year. Average cash costs per ounce of production for the nine months ended March 31, 1993, were $190 (U.S.) compared to $176 (U.S.) from the previous third quarter.

In the first quarter of 1993, construction of the $4.3-million Baltic Mine heap leach pads and processing facilities was delayed by bad weather. The initial start-up was scheduled for June 1993. The Baltic Mine, when fully operational, will add approximately 40,000 ounces of gold per year to Glamis's total production. Glamis's gold production for fiscal 1994 is expected to top 100,000 ounces of gold recovered.

Glamis's other properties include the Picacho Mine in California, the Yellow Aster Mine in California and the Cieneguita gold property in Mexico.

In January 1993, Glamis's shares were listed on the New York Stock Exchange.

Relative strength to TSE300 / Price / Volume (in 1000's of board lots)

Rank (Profit/Revenue/Assets)		
	379 540 515	

Chester F. Millar
Chairman

A. Dan Rovig
President & C.E.O.

Lorne B. Anderson
C.F.O. & Treasurer

Address
3324 - Four Bentall Centre
1055 Dunsmuir Street
P.O. Box 49287
Vancouver
BC
V7X 1L3
(604) 681-3541
Fax: (604) 681-9306
G0009788/G/2.0

GOLDCORP INC.

Exchanges	Price (Jun24'93)	7.87	Trailing P/E	11.75	Stock Symbol
TM	Trailing Yield (%)	0.00	Trailing EPS	0.67	**G**

Period Ending	Dec92	Dec91	Dec90	Dec89	Dec88
Yearly Statistics					
Price-Close	2.62	3.10	4.15	5.00	6.00
Price-High	3.70	4.45	6.50	6.50	8.88
Price-Low	2.55	2.97	3.85	3.20	5.50
P/E-Close	21.83	nm	nm	nm	150.00
Dividends per Share	0.00	0.00	0.00	0.00	0.00
Dividend Yield (%)	0.00	0.00	0.00	0.00	0.00
Sales per Share	6.01	5.40	3.42	2.48	na
EPS before extra. item	0.12	(0.46)	(3.45)	(0.90)	0.04
Cash Flow per Share	1.01	1.06	0.32	0.14	0.04
Book Value per Share	6.29	6.02	6.46	9.20	8.80
O/S Common Shares	17,428	17,428	17,541	17,541	17,540
Total Revenue	109,187	96,989	66,265	35,757	2,746
Income before extra.	2,079	(8,039)	(60,485)	(15,706)	767
Cash Flow	17,660	18,587	5,681	2,508	767
Debt/Equity	0.60	0.49	0.44	0.14	nd
Return on Capital (%)	4.00	(1.86)	(41.08)	(4.28)	0.50
Ret. on Com. Equity (%)	1.94	(7.37)	(44.03)	(9.95)	0.42
% Change Profit	125.9	86.7	(285.1)	(2,147.9)	(28.3)
% Change Revenue	12.6	46.4	85.3	1,202.0	(29.8)
% Change Assets	10.7	16.0	(29.4)	77.3	(30.2)

	Dec92	Dec91	Dec90
Preferred Div. Coverage	np	np	np
Total Div. Coverage	na	na	na
Interest Coverage	2.2	0.0	0.0
Current Ratio	2.0	2.4	9.5
Operating Margin	5.6	10.1	(135.2)
Asset Turnover	0.4	0.4	0.3
5 YEAR RATIOS (%)			
Return on Capital	(8.5)	(9.2)	(8.6)
Return on Com. Equity	(11.8)	(12.1)	(10.5)
Profit Growth	14.2	na	na
Revenue Growth	94.6	99.4	96.1
Asset Growth	2.3	3.8	5.5
BALANCE SHEET (000)			
Cash	48,943	59,378	47,881
Current Assets	78,880	87,096	82,560
Net Fixed Assets	164,418	137,357	50,416
Invest's & Advances	3,733	0	62,026
Total Assets	250,802	226,596	195,420
Short Term Debt	21,897	22,857	0
Current Liabilities	39,164	35,608	8,713
Long Term Debt	43,405	29,446	49,673
Total Liabilities	141,130	119,812	82,063
Total Equity	109,672	104,880	113,357
Total Liab. & Equity	250,802	226,596	195,420
CAPITAL (000)			
Total Debt	65,302	52,303	49,673
Preferred Equity	0	0	0
Common Equity	109,672	104,880	113,357

Business:

GOLDCORP INC. is an investment company that provides opportunities to invest in a managed portfolio of gold-related investments.

Date	EPS	DPS	Tot Rev	Inc Bex
Mar 93	0.41	0.00	32,420	7,155
Dec 92	0.02	0.00	31,030	333
Sep 92	0.13	0.00	33,116	2,280
Jun 92	0.11	0.00	27,288	1,866
Mar 92	(0.14)	0.00	21,932	(2,400)
Dec 91	0.02	0.00	24,971	415
Sep 91	(0.46)	0.00	28,499	(8,018)
Jun 91	0.26	0.00	32,150	4,562

Synopsis:

On October 8, 1992, Goldcorp Inc's gold reserves increased through Wharf Mine's 60% acquisition of the Golden Reward Mine. Management changes at the Red Lake Mine and high production costs effected profit margins in 1992. The industrial minerals division, a source valuable cash flow for Goldcorp, hopes an increase in market demand for sodium sulphate and limestone products will push its profit margins. The company's 1993 first quarter results showed positive growth due to an increase in gold production, reduced operating costs, higher revenues and increasing gold prices.

Goldcorp plans to increase its total 1993 gold production by 26%, cut its debt by year-end to $49-million from $65-million, lower its cash operating costs at the Red Lake and Wharf mines, and expand its exploration properties portfolio. Goldcorp now has exploration properties in Colorado, New Mexico and Nevada. It spent $1.3-million on these properties in 1992.

Goldcorp's share of gold production totaled 92,798 ounces in 1992 compared to 87,815 ounces in 1991. About 72% of Goldcorp's revenues come from gold sales, with the remainder from interest income. Total gold reserves increased by 17% in 1992 to 1.9 million ounces.

Goldcorp controls three producing gold mines, two exploration companies and two industrial mineral operations.

Relative strength to TSE300

Price

Volume (in 1000's of board lots)

Rank (Profit/Revenue/Assets)
354   361   290

Robert R. McEwen
President, Chairman & C.E.O.

Address
Suite 2700
145 King Street West
Toronto
ON
M5H 1J8
(416) 865-0326

Fax: (416) 865-9636
G0017192/G/2.0

GOLDEN KNIGHT RESOURCES INC.

Exchanges	Price (Jun24'93)	11 .75	Trailing P/E	78 .33	Stock Symbol
TMVQ	Trailing Yield (%)	0 .00	Trailing EPS	0 .15	**GKR**

Period Ending	Dec92	Dec91	Dec90	Dec89	Dec88
Yearly Statistics					6M
Price-Close	6 .75	9 .38	11 .75	11 .38	8 .75
Price-High	9 .50	13 .63	15 .63	12 .00	12 .13
Price-Low	6 .13	8 .50	10 .50	7 .50	8 .13
P/E-Close	67 .50	28 .41	39 .17	54 .17	145 .83
Dividends per Share	0 .00	0 .00	0 .00	0 .00	0 .00
Dividend Yield (%)	0 .00	0 .00	0 .00	0 .00	0 .00
Sales per Share	1 .12	1 .62	1 .27	0 .87	na
EPS before extra. item	0 .10	0 .33	0 .30	0 .21	0 .03
Cash Flow per Share	0 .42	0 .83	0 .60	0 .39	0 .11
Book Value per Share	5 .66	5 .56	5 .23	4 .87	4 .58
O/S Common Shares	12 ,167	12 ,167	12 ,167	11 ,972	11 ,743
Total Revenue	14 ,550	20 ,761	16 ,316	11 ,662	827
Income before extra.	1 ,181	4 ,015	3 ,577	2 ,486	364
Cash Flow	5 ,099	10 ,155	7 ,255	4 ,667	662
Debt/Equity	nd	nd	nd	nd	nd
Return on Capital (%)	2 .90	8 .84	8 .52	6 .70	2 .54
Ret. on Com. Equity (%)	1 .73	6 .12	5 .87	4 .44	1 .40
% Change Profit	(70 .6)	12 .2	43 .9	241 .5	(40 .1)
% Change Revenue	(29 .9)	27 .2	39 .9	605 .1	(34 .0)
% Change Assets	3 .9	8 .3	7 .1	15 .1	3 .5
Preferred Div. Coverage	np	np	np		
Total Div. Coverage	na	na	na		
Interest Coverage	nd	nd	nd		
Current Ratio	15 .2	10 .5	7 .4		
Operating Margin	7 .8	24 .0	27 .4		
Asset Turnover	0 .2	0 .3	0 .2		
5 YEAR RATIOS (%)					
Return on Capital	5 .9	6 .7	na		
Return on Com. Equity	3 .9	4 .3	na		
Profit Growth	(0 .6)	na	na		
Revenue Growth	42 .2	na	na		
Asset Growth	7 .4	35 .4	147 .8		
BALANCE SHEET (000)					
Cash	17 ,514	16 ,741	9 ,985		
Current Assets	23 ,095	19 ,671	13 ,374		
Net Fixed Assets	55 ,012	55 ,522	56 ,062		
Invest's & Advances	0	0	0		
Total Assets	78 ,107	75 ,193	69 ,436		
Short Term Debt	0	0	0		
Current Liabilities	1 ,520	1 ,865	1 ,799		
Long Term Debt	0	0	0		
Total Liabilities	9 ,292	7 ,559	5 ,817		
Total Equity	68 ,815	67 ,634	63 ,619		
Total Liab. & Equity	78 ,107	75 ,193	69 ,436		
CAPITAL (000)					
Total Debt	0	0	0		
Preferred Equity	0	0	0		
Common Equity	68 ,815	67 ,634	63 ,619		

Business:

GOLDEN KNIGHT RESOURCES INC. is a gold mining company. It has a 40% interest in Les Mines Casa Berardi in northwestern Quebec. TVX Gold Inc. holds the remaining interest in the mines. The Golden Knight/Inco joint venture also has other interests in the area.

Date	EPS	DPS	Tot Rev	Inc Bex
Mar 93	0 .09	0 .00	5 ,542	1 ,055
Dec 92	0 .01	0 .00	3 ,319	99
Jun 92	0 .03	0 .00	3 ,603	337
Mar 92	0 .02	0 .00	4 ,047	265
Dec 91	0 .08	0 .00	6 ,586	974
Sep 91	0 .08	0 .00	4 ,493	964
Jun 91	0 .10	0 .00	5 ,257	1 ,279
Mar 91	0 .07	0 .00	4 ,425	798

Synopsis:

After a record loss in 1992, Golden Knight Resources Inc. is planning to re-start operations at its East mine project in Quebec this summer. Production was suspended in April 1992 when surface material penetrated through a fault zone into the mine. An extensive $6.9-million rehabilitation project should ensure the mine will function as normal. Golden Knight's share of the costs amount to $2.8-million.The shutdown severely affected 1992 production figures for Golden Knight. The company has a 40% interest in the Casa Berardi joint venture project in Quebec. The mines are operated by TVX Gold Inc, a subsidiary of Inco Limited.

Golden Knight's first quarter earnings in 1993 showed the company's recovery well underway, with earnings of $1.1-million, a sharp increase from $265,000 earned in the same period in 1992. The boost in production is partially due to the higher ore grade, 0.42 ounces per tonne compared to 0.22 ounces per tonne in the same period in 1992.

Exploration work proved successful for Golden Knight in 1992, with the discovery of two new gold bearing zones north of the Casa Berardi fault. The deposits will be further explored and delineated in 1993. The surface program is budgeted at $900,000. An underground exploration and development program, if approved, would cost $14-million.

Golden Knight's share of gold production dropped to 32,802 ounces in 1992, compared to 47,278 ounces in 1991. The East Mine closure caused mining revenues to fall by $6-million last year to $13.6-million, and net earnings to drop to $1.2-million in 1992 from $4-million in 1991. The mine closure brought operating costs down in 1992 to $8.9-million from $10.2-million in 1991. Costs per ounce increased from $215 to $273 per ounce.

Relative strength to TSE300 / Price / Volume (in 1000's of board lots) charts

Rank (Profit/Revenue/Assets)
408   659   460

Norman B. Keevil Jr.
Chairman

John G. Taylor
V.P., Finance

Address
Suite 600
200 Burrard Street
Vancouver
BC
V6C 3L9
(604) 687-1117

Fax: (604) 687-6100
G0017738/G/2.0

GOLDEN STAR RESOURCES LTD.

Exchanges	Price (Jun24'93)		14.37	Trailing P/E		nm	Stock Symbol
TM	Trailing Yield (%)		0.00	Trailing EPS		(0.07)	**GSC**

Period Ending	Dec92	Jun91	Jun90	Jun89	Jun88	Business:
Yearly Statistics	US/18M					GOLDEN STAR RESOURCES LTD. is
Price-Close	7.00	2.40	2.00	4.20	8.00	involved in the acquisition, exploration and
Price-High	7.00	2.40	3.90	4.20	11.50	development of precious and base metals
Price-Low	2.15	0.71	0.80	1.85	2.15	properties in Guyana.
P/E-Close	nm	nm	nm	nm	200.00	
Dividends per Share	0.00	0.00	0.00	0.00	0.00	
Dividend Yield (%)	0.00	0.00	0.00	0.00	0.00	
Sales per Share	na	na	na	0.39	na	
EPS before extra. item	(1.30)	(0.24)	(0.90)	(0.88)	0.04	
Cash Flow per Share	(0.16)	(0.14)	(0.19)	(0.12)	0.08	
Book Value per Share	1.13	2.22	2.49	3.74	4.54	
O/S Common Shares	14,763	6,663	6,273	5,508	5,132	
Total Revenue	383	259	1,197	3,009	1,110	
Income before extra.	(15,376)	(1,592)	(5,680)	(4,692)	135	
Cash Flow	(2,886)	(915)	(1,096)	(647)	327	

Date	EPS	DPS	Tot Rev	Inc Bex
Mar 92	(0.02)	0.00	164	(341)
Dec 91	(0.03)	0.00	(68)	(354)
Sep 91	(0.01)	0.00	94	(187)
Jun 91	(0.01)	0.00	102	(151)
Mar 91	(0.05)	0.00	23	(638)
Dec 90	(0.03)	0.00	52	(480)
Sep 90	(0.03)	0.00	83	(322)
Jun 90	(0.28)	0.00	266	(3,780)

	Dec92	Jun91	Jun90	Jun89	Jun88
Debt/Equity	0.10	0.14	0.10	0.10	nd
Return on Capital (%)	(59.94)	(9.28)	(28.40)	(18.72)	1.72
Ret. on Com. Equity (%)	(67.76)	(10.47)	(31.37)	(21.39)	0.86
% Change Profit	(666.1)	72.0	(21.0)	(3,566.8)	126.2
% Change Revenue	17.3	(78.3)	(60.2)	170.9	2,217.2
% Change Assets	34.9	(1.0)	(21.7)	(1.4)	183.3

				Synopsis:
Preferred Div. Coverage	np	np	np	
Total Div. Coverage	na	na	na	
Interest Coverage	0.0	na	na	
Current Ratio	1.6	1.6	3.3	
Operating Margin	na	(2,915.9)	(16.9)	
Asset Turnover	na	na	na	

Golden Star Resources Ltd. reported a $1.6-million (U.S.) first quarter loss in 1993, citing a $1.1-million (U.S.) loss of equity in the Omai Gold Mine in Guyana. Golden Star has a 30% stake in Omai, Cambior Inc. of Montreal has a 65% interest and the Guyana government holds the remaining 5%.

5 YEAR RATIOS (%)

Return on Capital	(22.9)	(12.9)	na
Return on Com. Equity	(26.0)	(14.4)	na
Profit Growth	na	na	na
Revenue Growth	44.6	61.7	na
Asset Growth	23.9	39.9	na

In 1993 Golden Star signed a $1.1-million (U.S.) deal to buy two properties in French Guyana. Golden Star has the option for a 100% interest in the second property upon completion of a feasibility study.

As of March 6, 1993, Golden Star had cash and short-term investments of $15.3-million (U.S.) and $1-million (U.S.), respectively. The $10.5-million (U.S.) it hoped to raise by placing 1.2 million special warrants was to be used toward new acquisitions and exploration, possibly in French Guyana, Surinam and Venezuela. In February 1993 Golden Star began drilling at its Surinam property.

BALANCE SHEET (000)

	Dec92	Jun91	Jun90
Cash	3,793	1,169	2,472
Current Assets	4,148	2,039	5,100
Net Fixed Assets	9,681	15,872	13,140
Invest's & Advances	5,391	195	42
Total Assets	19,221	18,107	18,282
Short Term Debt	1,663	0	704
Current Liabilities	2,535	1,308	1,528
Long Term Debt	0	2,000	900
Total Liabilities	2,535	3,308	2,671
Total Equity	16,686	14,799	15,611
Total Liab. & Equity	19,221	18,107	18,282

Its 1993 gold production target is 260,000 ounces at an operating cost of $200 (U.S.) per ounce. Proven and probable mineable reserves at Omai are 2.2 million ounces of gold with 10 years of probable reserves.

CAPITAL (000)

	Dec92	Jun91	Jun90
Total Debt	1,663	2,000	1,603
Preferred Equity	0	0	0
Common Equity	16,686	14,799	15,611

Relative strength to TSE300

Price

Volume (in 1000's of board lots)

Rank (Profit/Revenue/Assets)
901   925   678

David K. Fagin
Chairman & C.E.O.

David A. Fennell
President & Secretary

Christopher W. Taylor
Treasurer & Controller

Address
One Norwest Center
1700 Lincoln Street
Suite 1950
Denver
CO
80203
(303) 830-9000
Fax: (303) 830-9022
S0039081/G/2.0

HEMLO GOLD MINES INC.

Exchanges	Price (Jun24'93)	12.62	Trailing P/E	27.45	Stock Symbol
TM	Trailing Yield (%)	1.58	Trailing EPS	0.46	HEM

Period Ending	Dec92	Dec91	Dec90	Dec89	Dec88
Yearly Statistics					
Price-Close	7.88	11.50	11.25	17.63	10.75
Price-High	11.75	12.00	20.38	19.88	18.00
Price-Low	7.38	7.38	9.00	11.00	10.50
P/E-Close	18.31	76.67	41.67	47.64	21.50
Dividends per Share	0.20	0.20	0.20	0.20	0.20
Dividend Yield (%)	2.54	1.74	1.78	1.14	1.86
Sales per Share	2.19	2.17	2.32	2.20	2.22
EPS before extra. item	0.43	0.15	0.27	0.37	0.50
Cash Flow per Share	0.72	0.76	0.87	0.67	0.88
Book Value per Share	2.75	2.50	2.16	2.08	1.91
O/S Common Shares	96,761	96,568	87,630	87,516	87,516
Total Revenue	220,825	202,866	215,832	199,084	201,134
Income before extra.	41,941	13,725	23,636	32,780	43,972
Cash Flow	69,370	71,013	75,797	58,491	76,918
Debt/Equity	0.26	0.34	0.53	nd	nd
Return on Capital (%)	21.78	10.37	23.10	32.93	53.34
Ret. on Com. Equity (%)	16.54	6.37	12.71	18.76	28.82
% Change Profit	205.6	(41.9)	(27.9)	(25.5)	(23.5)
% Change Revenue	8.9	(6.0)	8.4	(1.0)	(10.2)
% Change Assets	4.1	8.4	0.1	2.6	6.7

Preferred Div. Coverage	np	np	np
Total Div. Coverage	2.2	0.7	1.4
Interest Coverage	63.0	20.5	23.8
Current Ratio	1.8	2.7	2.1
Operating Margin	29.6	27.7	31.0
Asset Turnover	0.4	0.4	0.4
5 YEAR RATIOS (%)			
Return on Capital	28.3	43.6	na
Return on Com. Equity	16.6	23.6	na
Profit Growth	(6.1)	na	na
Revenue Growth	(0.3)	na	na
Asset Growth	4.3	10.1	na
BALANCE SHEET (000)			
Cash	92,658	117,312	101,841
Current Assets	142,106	157,572	114,791
Net Fixed Assets	312,017	325,448	292,717
Invest's & Advances	66,964	17,470	53,962
Total Assets	521,087	500,490	461,901
Short Term Debt	39,796	35,941	25,425
Current Liabilities	79,319	57,369	55,550
Long Term Debt	29,755	46,526	75,863
Total Liabilities	255,350	258,980	272,307
Total Equity	265,737	241,510	189,594
Total Liab. & Equity	521,087	500,490	461,901
CAPITAL (000)			
Total Debt	69,551	82,467	101,288
Preferred Equity	0	0	0
Common Equity	265,737	241,510	189,594

Business:

HEMLO GOLD MINES INC. is a gold mining company. It owns and operates the Golden Giant Mine in the Hemlo area of northwestern Ontario. It also owns 55% of the operations of the Silica mine near Rouyn-Noranda, Quebec. Other projects include the Holloway joint venture in Ontario and the New World project in Montana. Noranda Inc. is the company's major shareholder.

Date	EPS	DPS	Tot Rev	Inc Bex
Mar 93	0.13	0.00	59,206	12,662
Dec 92	0.10	0.10	55,514	10,443
Sep 92	0.13	0.00	60,956	11,890
Jun 92	0.10	0.10	50,482	9,688
Mar 92	0.10	0.00	52,734	9,920
Dec 91	(0.17)	0.10	50,056	(16,030)
Sep 91	0.13	0.00	58,111	12,915
Jun 91	0.10	0.10	53,675	8,612

Synopsis:

Hemlo Gold Mines Inc. plans to pour millions of dollars during 1993 into developing the Holloway project, in which it has a 58% direct and indirect interest. It should provide 80,000 ounces of gold annually. Hemlo's share of expenditures on the Holloway project is expected to be $4.5-million in 1993, with an additional $24-million slated for 1994 and 1995. A $12-million underground exploration and ore reserve validation program at Holloway was slated for completion in December 1993. Holloway is expected to be producing by 1995.

Plans are underway to develop the New World property in Montana. Hemlo has a 60% interest in this project owned by Crown Butte Resources. It's expected to produce 80,000 ounces of gold annually by 1996. Hemlo invested $16-million in exploration studies in 1992, and expects to spend $15-million in 1993.

Hemlo's 1992 gold reserves totaled 5 million ounces, production shot up by 2% from 1991 to 451,400 ounces, and its operating costs fell to $113 (U.S.) per ounce from $124 (U.S.) per ounce in 1991. Gold reserves at the Golden Giant Mine should last for 13 more years. Reserves at the Sildor Mine in Quebec are sufficient for six more years of production.

Relative strength to TSE300 / Price / Volume (in 1000's of board lots) charts

Rank (Profit/Revenue/Assets)
70   259   205

Alex G. Balogh
Chairman Of The Board

Ian D. Bayer
President & C.E.O.

Michael C. Proctor
V.P., Finance

John Keyer
Mine Manager - Golden Giant

Address
Suite 2902
1 Adelaide Street East
Toronto
ON
M5C 2Z9
(416) 982-7116

Fax: (416) 982-7388
H0000930/G/2.0

LAC MINERALS LTD.

Exchanges		Price (Jun24'93)		12.75	Trailing P/E		212.50	Stock Symbol
TMN		Trailing Yield (%)		0.94	Trailing EPS		0.06	**LAC**

Period Ending	Dec92	Dec91	Dec90	Dec89	Dec88
Yearly Statistics	US	US	US	US	US
Price-Close	6.75	9.13	10.25	13.88	12.25
Price-High	9.75	10.50	16.00	14.63	16.13
Price-Low	6.50	7.38	7.38	10.63	10.25
P/E-Close	61.93	66.61	nm	37.91	23.79
Dividends per Share	0.11	0.19	0.19	0.11	0.10
Dividend Yield (%)	1.63	2.08	1.85	0.79	0.82
Sales per Share	3.26	3.78	3.71	1.82	1.77
EPS before extra. item	0.09	0.12	(0.53)	0.31	0.42
Cash Flow per Share	0.89	1.04	1.16	0.66	0.74
Book Value per Share	5.14	5.30	4.85	5.54	3.57
O/S Common Shares	147,218	146,922	121,256	121,094	92,255
Total Revenue	507,211	511,119	483,620	239,983	216,138
Income before extra.	12,744	15,429	(64,315)	30,525	38,428
Cash Flow	131,128	131,544	140,759	64,874	68,278
Debt/Equity	0.48	0.42	0.72	0.27	0.16
Return on Capital (%)	3.19	5.74	(3.87)	9.81	19.14
Ret. on Com. Equity (%)	1.66	2.26	(10.22)	6.11	12.27
% Change Profit	(17.4)	124.0	(310.7)	(20.6)	21.9
% Change Revenue	(0.8)	5.7	101.5	11.0	14.9
% Change Assets	(0.4)	(0.6)	(11.7)	127.9	7.1

Date		EPS	DPS	Tot Rev	Inc Bex
Mar 93	US	0.00	0.00	125,324	642
Dec 92	US	0.04	0.07	133,231	5,768
Sep 92	US	(0.01)	0.00	118,613	(1,123)
Jun 92	US	0.03	0.05	128,281	4,407
Mar 92	US	0.03	0.00	129,864	3,692
Dec 91	US	0.01	0.10	126,347	2,024
Sep 91	US	0.05	0.00	130,565	6,166
Jun 91	US	0.04	0.11	129,206	5,057

Preferred Div. Coverage	np	np	np		
Total Div. Coverage	0.8	0.6	0.0		
Interest Coverage	2.3	3.4	0.0		
Current Ratio	3.7	2.0	1.8		
Operating Margin	3.3	6.5	(18.8)		
Asset Turnover	0.4	0.4	0.3		
5 YEAR RATIOS (%)					
Return on Capital	6.8	9.9	10.9		
Return on Com. Equity	2.4	4.5	5.1		
Profit Growth	(16.7)	4.9	na		
Revenue Growth	21.9	28.1	30.3		
Asset Growth	16.3	25.1	28.3		
BALANCE SHEET (000)					
Cash	401,249	310,925	245,912		
Current Assets	542,312	445,855	397,629		
Net Fixed Assets	775,058	883,268	933,328		
Invest's & Advances	0	0	0		
Total Assets	1,341,037	1,346,438	1,354,695		
Short Term Debt	93,931	161,767	162,654		
Current Liabilities	144,667	226,067	221,491		
Long Term Debt	270,100	166,897	260,931		
Total Liabilities	584,844	568,375	766,313		
Total Equity	756,193	778,063	588,382		
Total Liab. & Equity	1,341,037	1,346,438	1,354,695		
CAPITAL (000)					
Total Debt	364,031	328,664	423,585		
Preferred Equity	0	0	0		
Common Equity	756,193	778,063	588,382		

Business:

LAC MINERALS's financial results include those of its gold mining operations in Canada, the U.S. and Chile, as well as its zinc mine in Chile and limestone quarry in Canada. Lac's principal source of revenue is the sale of gold it produces.

Synopsis:

In March 1993, Lac Minerals Ltd. reported a major gold discovery at its Nevada project in Chile, but production isn't expected for several years. The grade of the deposit ranged from 0.01 ounces per tonne to 1.1 ounces per tonne. Lac is looking to expand its mining operations by investing between $100-million (U.S.) to $400-million (U.S.) in joint venture projects, in possibly 25 countries. Lac already has operations in Canada, Chile and the United States.

The Lac owned El Indio mine in Chile is the richest gold reserve in South America producing 223,688 ounces in 1992, but 1993 first quarter results showed gold production at El Indio down, due primarily to lower headgrades.

Lac's main objective for 1993 is to reduce cash production costs to $190 (U.S.) per ounce, increase its reserves, increase the operating cash flow by $15-million (U.S.) and decrease its debt by $40-million (U.S.). Lac's 1993 earnings are expected to fall below its 1992 figures largely due to higher U.S. taxes and increasing exploration costs.

Lac's 1992 cash production costs fell to $213 (U.S.) per ounce. It's gold production shot up to 1.135 million ounces. Lac's gold reserves totaled 10.2 million ounces in 1992.

Relative strength to TSE300 / Price / Volume (in 1000's of board lots) charts

Rank (Profit/Revenue/Assets)
143   139   105

Peter A. Allen
President & C.E.O.
J. Gordon Maw
Sr. V.P & C.F.O.
Gerald J. Gauthier
Sr. V.P., North American Ops.

Address
Royal Bank Plaza
21st Floor, North Tower
P.O. Box 156
Toronto
ON
M5J 2J4
(416) 777-2400
Fax: (416) 777-2405
L0000657/G/2.0

MINVEN GOLD CORPORATION

Exchanges	Price (Jun24'93)		0.47	Trailing P/E		nm	Stock Symbol
TVA	Trailing Yield (%)		0.00	Trailing EPS		(0.22)	**MVG**

Period Ending	Dec92	Dec91	Dec90	Dec89	Dec88
Yearly Statistics	US	US	US		
Price-Close	0.32	0.32	0.75	3.85	3.70
Price-High	0.75	1.06	4.00	4.35	4.80
Price-Low	0.25	0.30	0.53	2.85	3.35
P/E-Close	nm	nm	nm	nm	370.00
Dividends per Share	0.00	0.00	0.00	0.00	0.00
Dividend Yield (%)	0.00	0.00	0.00	0.00	0.00
Sales per Share	0.80	0.93	1.32	1.58	1.86
EPS before extra. item	(0.22)	(0.98)	(0.11)	(0.54)	0.01
Cash Flow per Share	0.00	(0.02)	0.07	0.18	0.28
Book Value per Share	0.36	0.60	1.76	1.87	2.73
O/S Common Shares	47,490	37,285	28,901	28,901	24,720
Total Revenue	33,229	31,810	38,403	42,955	36,508
Income before extra.	(8,991)	(33,507)	(3,265)	(14,200)	91
Cash Flow	26	(819)	1,893	4,848	4,920
Debt/Equity	1.27	1.10	0.41	0.32	0.23
Return on Capital (%)	(14.99)	(55.31)	(3.86)	(21.86)	0.60
Ret. on Com. Equity (%)	(45.41)	(91.58)	(6.75)	(23.38)	0.18
% Change Profit	73.2	(926.2)	73.2	nm	(98.2)
% Change Revenue	4.5	(17.2)	4.4	17.7	(6.5)
% Change Assets	(14.8)	(27.9)	17.4	(24.9)	71.6

	Date		EPS	DPS	Tot Rev	Inc Bex
	Mar 93	US	(0.04)	0.00	2,469	(1,914)
	Dec 92	US	(0.13)	0.00	7,389	(5,548)
	Sep 92	US	0.03	0.00	13,363	1,060
	Jun 92	US	(0.08)	0.00	6,828	(2,988)
	Mar 92	US	(0.04)	0.00	5,648	(1,515)
	Dec 91	US	(0.02)	0.00	11,085	(1,640)
	Sep 91	US	(0.77)	0.00	10,628	(28,382)
	Jun 91	US	(0.08)	0.00	5,291	(2,823)

Preferred Div. Coverage	np	np	np
Total Div. Coverage	na	na	na
Interest Coverage	0.0	0.0	0.0
Current Ratio	0.2	0.4	0.7
Operating Margin	(24.7)	(104.6)	(7.6)
Asset Turnover	0.7	0.6	0.5
5 YEAR RATIOS (%)			
Return on Capital	(19.1)	(8.5)	12.7
Return on Com. Equity	(33.4)	(20.1)	3.2
Profit Growth	na	na	na
Revenue Growth	(0.2)	8.4	275.2
Asset Growth	(1.5)	14.3	32.2
BALANCE SHEET (000)			
Cash	1,203	1,552	940
Current Assets	4,792	6,824	7,124
Net Fixed Assets	39,990	46,251	67,809
Invest's & Advances	0	0	1,290
Total Assets	48,804	57,276	79,428
Short Term Debt	20,494	9,456	3,034
Current Liabilities	27,938	19,262	10,278
Long Term Debt	1,333	15,266	17,751
Total Liabilities	31,661	34,823	28,706
Total Equity	17,143	22,453	50,722
Total Liab. & Equity	48,804	57,276	79,428
CAPITAL (000)			
Total Debt	21,827	24,722	20,785
Preferred Equity	0	0	0
Common Equity	17,143	22,453	50,722

Business:

MINVEN GOLD CORP. was formed in 1988 through the amalgamation of Brohm Resources Inc. and MFC Mining Finance Corp. The company has interests in gold mines located in Idaho, South Dakota, California and British Columbia.

Synopsis:

In February 1993, MinVen Gold Corporation announced a corporate reorganization plan to seek new financing. As of May 25, 1993, MinVen's restructuring plan included raising $11-million (U.S.) through the issue of senior exchangeable promissory notes. This plan was approved by the Toronto Stock Exchange. A principal revision included reducing the share-exchange ratio for its existing shareholders.

On October 8, 1992, MinVen acquired the remaining interest in the Golden Reward Mine for circa $17.4-million (U.S.). The company later sold 60% of the mine to Wharf Resources Ltd. for $21.25-million (U.S.), much of which was used to pay off debts. As of December 31, 1992, MinVen had a working capital deficit of $23.1-million (U.S.).

In 1992 MinVen sold 89,772 ounces of gold and 122,673 ounces of silver. Cash operating costs were reduced from $362 (U.S.) to $321(U.S.) per ounce. Its Stibnite Mine in Idaho produced 27,651 ounces of gold in 1992, the Gilt Edge Mine produced 26,836 ounces of gold, but it ceased operation as of January 1993 since all permitted oxide ore reserves had been mined. MinVen's 40% share of Golden Reward Mine production totaled 24,909 ounces of gold. A total of 9,084 gold ounces was produced at the Cactus Mine in California. The mine closed in February 1992 due to the exhaustion of its ore reserves.

Relative strength to TSE300 / Price / Volume (in 1000's of board lots) chart

Rank (Profit/Revenue/Assets)		
895	505	496

Paul A. Bailly
Chairman

Alan R. Bell
President & C.E.O.

Robert R. Gilmore
V.P., Finance & C.F.O.

Address
Suite 2450
410 - 17th Street
Denver
CO
80202
(303) 573-0221

Fax: (303) 573-1012
C0059152/G/2.0

MUSCOCHO EXPLORATIONS LTD.

Exchanges	Price (Jun24'93)	0.35	Trailing P/E	nm	Stock Symbol
TQ	Trailing Yield (%)	0.00	Trailing EPS	(0.12)	**MUS**

Period Ending	Dec92	Dec91	Dec90	Dec89	Dec88
Yearly Statistics					
Price-Close	0.05	0.07	0.07	2.00	4.05
Price-High	0.09	0.11	1.90	4.05	4.25
Price-Low	0.03	0.03	0.02	1.35	2.80
P/E-Close	nm	nm	nm	nm	nm
Dividends per Share	0.00	0.00	0.00	0.00	0.00
Dividend Yield (%)	0.00	0.00	0.00	0.00	0.00
Sales per Share	0.08	0.17	0.20	0.34	0.28
EPS before extra. item	(0.06)	(0.32)	(1.09)	(1.23)	(0.07)
Cash Flow per Share	(0.03)	(0.07)	(1.06)	(0.99)	0.11
Book Value per Share	0.07	0.07	0.15	1.23	2.45
O/S Common Shares	43,634	41,045	31,406	31,134	30,965
Total Revenue	3,260	6,277	6,809	15,386	13,636
Income before extra.	(2,586)	(10,897)	(33,930)	(38,021)	(1,950)
Cash Flow	(1,410)	(2,343)	(33,210)	(30,608)	2,863
Debt/Equity	1.65	1.65	0.90	0.09	nd
Return on Capital (%)	(26.69)	(124.37)	(131.28)	(64.21)	(2.99)
Ret. on Com. Equity (%)	(83.70)	(286.48)	(157.69)	(66.60)	(3.16)
% Change Profit	76.3	67.9	10.8	(1,849.8)	(515.1)
% Change Revenue	(48.1)	(7.8)	(55.7)	12.8	31.0
% Change Assets	(19.1)	(42.1)	(63.9)	(37.6)	58.9

Preferred Div. Coverage	np	np	np
Total Div. Coverage	na	na	na
Interest Coverage	0.0	0.0	0.0
Current Ratio	0.0	0.1	0.2
Operating Margin	(39.7)	(147.2)	(354.0)
Asset Turnover	0.4	0.5	0.3
5 YEAR RATIOS (%)			
Return on Capital	(69.9)	(64.8)	(40.2)
Return on Com. Equity	(119.5)	(103.0)	(46.2)
Profit Growth	na	na	na
Revenue Growth	(20.8)	(5.1)	(2.2)
Asset Growth	(30.2)	(13.4)	1.2
BALANCE SHEET (000)			
Cash	0	0	0
Current Assets	45	527	2,430
Net Fixed Assets	6,111	7,346	14,052
Invest's & Advances	2,704	2,575	1,392
Total Assets	8,860	10,953	18,910
Short Term Debt	5,228	4,965	4,159
Current Liabilities	5,686	7,947	14,309
Long Term Debt	0	0	0
Total Liabilities	5,686	7,947	14,309
Total Equity	3,173	3,007	4,601
Total Liab. & Equity	8,860	10,953	18,910
CAPITAL (000)			
Total Debt	5,228	4,965	4,159
Preferred Equity	0	0	0
Common Equity	3,173	3,007	4,601

Business:

MUSCOCHO EXPLORATIONS LTD. is principally engaged in the exploration, development and mining of gold properties. It operates the Magino Gold Mine and the Magnacon Gold Mine (which has recently closed) in Ontario. The company has other properties in Ontario, Quebec and Newfoundland. Muscocho has a 25% interest in MacMillan Gold Corp. of Vancouver.

Date	EPS	DPS	Tot Rev	Inc Bex
Mar 93	(0.01)	0.00	(203)	(439)
Mar 92	(0.01)	0.00	1,433	(600)
Dec 91	(0.26)	0.00	1,205	(8,512)
Sep 91	0.16	0.00	10,456	7,684
Jun 91	(0.01)	0.00	1,849	(448)
Mar 91	(0.03)	0.00	1,546	(841)
Dec 90	(0.39)	0.00	390	(12,032)
Sep 90	(0.64)	0.00	2,434	(19,878)

Synopsis:

Declining gold prices and reduced ore grades forced Muscocho Explorations Ltd. to suspend operations at its 50% owned Magino gold mine on September 8, 1992. Additional exploration and development work will be required before production can resume. Property wide reserves stand at 673,927 tons averaging 0.163 ounces of gold per ton.

The 38% owned Magnacon Mine will re-open when economic conditions improve. It was closed down in May 1992. There was no further revenue from gold sales.

Additional gains on the settlement of debts and other corporate activities enabled the company to post a modest profit of $37,142 in 1992. Muscocho will be financing its activities primarily from asset sales and recoveries.

Relative strength to TSE300 / Price / Volume (in 1000's of board lots)

Rank (Profit/Revenue/Assets)
894   756   842

J.T. Flanagan
President

Address
Suite 1210
111 Richmond St. West
Toronto
ON
M5H 2G4
(416) 363-1124

M0014546/G/2.0

For further company information, call Globe Information Services 1-800-268-9128 or (416)585-5345

NORTHGATE EXPLORATION LIMITED

Exchanges	Price (Jun24'93)	1.85	Trailing P/E	nm	Stock Symbol
TMN	Trailing Yield (%)	0.00	Trailing EPS	(0.33)	**NGX**

Period Ending	Dec92	Dec91	Dec90	Dec89	Dec88
Yearly Statistics					
Price-Close	0.64	0.95	1.42	7.25	6.38
Price-High	0.95	2.20	8.63	8.50	8.50
Price-Low	0.63	0.85	1.25	5.63	6.25
P/E-Close	nm	nm	nm	17.26	63.75
Dividends per Share	0.00	0.00	0.00	0.00	0.58
Dividend Yield (%)	0.00	0.00	0.00	0.00	9.10
Sales per Share	na	0.74	0.78	0.25	0.05
EPS before extra. item	(0.30)	(3.17)	(5.33)	0.42	0.10
Cash Flow per Share	(0.12)	0.06	0.37	0.39	(0.04)
Book Value per Share	0.78	1.15	4.26	9.24	9.19
O/S Common Shares	27,982	22,367	22,294	22,071	22,012
Total Revenue	8,253	22,364	26,615	20,967	20,641
Income before extra.	(8,261)	(70,724)	(118,233)	9,442	2,262
Cash Flow	(3,146)	1,434	8,095	8,620	(913)
Debt/Equity	1.94	2.10	0.65	0.69	0.27
Return on Capital (%)	(5.91)	(59.01)	(45.37)	4.23	4.47
Ret. on Com. Equity (%)	(34.93)	(117.27)	(79.12)	4.65	1.11
% Change Profit	88.3	40.2	(1,352.2)	317.4	(96.0)
% Change Revenue	(63.1)	(16.0)	26.9	1.6	(84.1)
% Change Assets	(20.9)	(48.6)	(60.4)	37.1	35.8

Date	EPS	DPS	Tot Rev	Inc Bex
Mar 93	(0.06)	0.00	622	(1,783)
Dec 92	(0.20)	0.00	4,565	(5,500)
Sep 92	(0.03)	0.00	197	(704)
Jun 92	(0.04)	0.00	937	(1,242)
Mar 92	(0.03)	0.00	1,225	(747)
Dec 91	(3.09)	0.00	4,395	(68,942)
Sep 91	(0.03)	0.00	5,465	(649)
Jun 91	0.01	0.00	6,209	164

Preferred Div. Coverage	np	np	np
Total Div. Coverage	na	na	na
Interest Coverage	0.0	0.0	0.0
Current Ratio	11.2	6.3	2.9
Operating Margin	na	(45.2)	(31.9)
Asset Turnover	na	0.2	0.1
5 YEAR RATIOS (%)			
Return on Capital	(20.3)	(9.7)	2.1
Return on Com. Equity	(45.1)	(30.1)	(8.6)
Profit Growth	na	na	na
Revenue Growth	(42.5)	(19.5)	(15.0)
Asset Growth	(21.5)	(5.7)	4.2
BALANCE SHEET (000)			
Cash	32,208	33,012	33,326
Current Assets	33,561	34,198	44,255
Net Fixed Assets	58	449	26,196
Invest's & Advances	37,445	55,152	104,278
Total Assets	71,064	89,799	174,729
Short Term Debt	0	0	8,393
Current Liabilities	3,004	5,469	15,465
Long Term Debt	42,157	53,710	53,710
Total Liabilities	49,381	64,179	79,728
Total Equity	21,683	25,620	95,001
Total Liab. & Equity	71,064	89,799	174,729
CAPITAL (000)			
Total Debt	42,157	53,710	62,103
Preferred Equity	0	0	0
Common Equity	21,683	25,620	95,001

Business:

NORTHGATE EXPLORATION LTD. is a gold mining company with mines in Califronia, Quebec, and Chile. It also has exploration activites in those areas and the Northwest Territories. The company has investments in several other gold companies including ABM Gold Corp. of Vancouver, Campbell Resources Inc. of Chibougamau, Que., Sonora Gold Corp. of Jamestown, Calif., and Geddes Resources Ltd.

Synopsis:

In mid-1993 Northgate Exploration Limited announced it was selling its 34% equity stake in Campbell Resources Inc., which operates the Joe Mann gold-copper mine in Quebec and several exploration projects in Mexico. The deal is subject to regulatory approval. Campbell produced 13,000 ounces of gold in the first quarter of 1993 compared with 26,900 ounces same period in 1992.

At the company's May 1993 annual meeting, Northgate announced it had received $10-million in cash proceeds from the sale of its 40% holding in Geddes Resources Ltd. Northgate agreed in 1993 to sell Colomac mine to Royal Oak Mines Inc. It's expected that 80% of the proceeds will go to the banks to pay off debts. Further asset sales may be necessary to meet its debt repayment.

As of March 31, 1993, Northgate had a working capital of $29.1-million, including $31.5 million in cash and $37-million in investments. Long-term subordinated debentures totaled $42.2-million. The Geddes and Colomac sales increased its cash to approximately $43-million.

Northgate raised more than $12-million in sales of its non-core assets in 1992. Its long term debt was reduced by $11.5-million through the re-purchase of 85% of its outstanding convertible debentures at a discount. Nonetheless it reported a $1.7-million loss in the first quarter of 1993, $1-million higher than same period in 1992. Northgate reported a net loss in 1992 as a result of market declines in metal prices, declining reserves and the recession. Hardest hit were Campbell Resources Inc. and Sonora Gold Corp. Investment income rose to $8-million in 1992 because of the repurchase of its convertible debentures..

Production forecast at the Joe Mann and Jamestown mines for 1993 is 178,000 ounces.

Relative strength to TSE300

Price

Volume (in 1000's of board lots)

Rank (Profit/Revenue/Assets)		
868	719	477

John F. Kearney
Chairman Of The Board

John Kachmar
President & C.E.O.

Sylvester P. Boland
Exec. V.P. & C.F.O.

J.O. Kachmar
Exec. V.P. & C.O.O.

Address
Suite 2701, P.O. Box 143
1 First Canadian Place
Toronto
ON
M5X 1C7
(416) 362-6683

Fax: (416) 367-3250
N0003283/G/2.0

PEGASUS GOLD INC.

Exchanges	Price (Jun24'93)		28.50	Trailing P/E		nm	Stock Symbol
TMA	Trailing Yield (%)		0.35	Trailing EPS		(0.25)	**PGU**

Period Ending	Dec92	Dec91	Dec90	Dec89	Dec88
Yearly Statistics	US	US	US	US	US
Price-Close	18.75	14.25	14.88	15.38	13.75
Price-High	22.75	16.13	18.50	17.88	23.13
Price-Low	13.50	11.00	10.88	10.50	13.38
P/E-Close	nm	33.69	nm	31.77	17.00
Dividends per Share	0.10	0.10	0.10	0.10	0.10
Dividend Yield (%)	0.53	0.70	0.67	0.65	0.73
Sales per Share	6.29	5.95	6.95	7.44	6.84
EPS before extra. item	(0.22)	0.37	(1.55)	0.41	0.66
Cash Flow per Share	1.56	1.42	1.61	1.60	1.46
Book Value per Share	9.31	8.82	8.04	9.66	9.29
O/S Common Shares	31,473	27,857	24,701	24,151	23,886
Total Revenue	184,574	158,034	155,871	178,401	173,310
Income before extra.	(6,341)	9,599	(38,172)	9,763	15,606
Cash Flow	45,139	37,235	39,800	38,378	34,791
Debt/Equity	0.22	0.29	0.24	0.14	0.17
Return on Capital (%)	(1.88)	5.21	(13.89)	6.77	9.85
Ret. on Com. Equity (%)	(2.35)	4.32	(17.69)	4.29	7.34
% Change Profit	(166.1)	125.1	(491.0)	(37.4)	7.7
% Change Revenue	16.8	1.4	(12.6)	2.9	49.5
% Change Assets	12.2	26.9	(4.5)	2.2	5.8

Preferred Div. Coverage	np	np	np
Total Div. Coverage	0.0	3.4	0.0
Interest Coverage	0.0	2.4	0.0
Current Ratio	3.8	4.7	3.0
Operating Margin	(5.9)	8.2	(11.8)
Asset Turnover	0.5	0.4	0.6
5 YEAR RATIOS (%)			
Return on Capital	1.2	3.6	3.6
Return on Com. Equity	(0.8)	1.8	2.4
Profit Growth	na	15.6	na
Revenue Growth	9.7	33.6	52.5
Asset Growth	8.0	12.9	28.0
BALANCE SHEET (000)			
Cash	109,753	64,814	10,443
Current Assets	168,569	121,973	63,031
Net Fixed Assets	175,242	197,310	180,701
Invest's & Advances	47,960	24,507	26,090
Total Assets	394,022	351,072	276,554
Short Term Debt	21,196	5,614	0
Current Liabilities	44,042	25,842	20,937
Long Term Debt	41,799	65,412	48,231
Total Liabilities	100,883	105,421	78,061
Total Equity	293,139	245,651	198,493
Total Liab. & Equity	394,022	351,072	276,554
CAPITAL (000)			
Total Debt	62,995	71,026	48,231
Preferred Equity	0	0	0
Common Equity	293,139	245,651	198,493

Business:

PEGASUS GOLD INC. is a precious metals mining company. It has gold, silver, zinc and lead mines in Montana, Idaho, Nevada and Australia. The company has exploration activities in the western United States, Australia and Chile.

Date		EPS	DPS	Tot Rev	Inc Bex
Mar 93	US	(0.01)	0.10	33,153	(449)
Dec 92	US	0.12	0.00	45,304	3,235
Sep 92	US	(0.54)	0.00	52,605	(15,377)
Jun 92	US	0.18	0.00	51,968	4,827
Mar 92	US	0.11	0.00	34,396	2,953
Dec 91	US	0.13	0.00	42,448	3,309
Sep 91	US	0.11	0.00	47,646	3,078
Jun 91	US	0.11	0.00	43,715	2,834

Synopsis:

On April 1, 1993, Pegasus Gold Inc. purchased VenturesTrident II L.P.'s investment in Zapopan NL of Australia in exchange for 1.75 million common shares of Pegasus and $4.65-million (U.S.) in notes from MinVen Gold Corp. for a total cost of $31-million (U.S.). In 1992, Pegasus purchased 38% equity in Zapopan for $20.9-million (U.S.). Pegasus now holds 60.7% of the outstanding shares of Zapopan. The mine is expected to produce 90,000 gold ounces in 1993.

Pegasus reported a net loss of $6.3-million (U.S.) in 1992, after a $19.2-million (U.S.) after-tax write-off for the Ortiz joint venture project in New Mexico. Pegasus terminated its joint venture agreement with Lac Minerals on the Ortiz project in Mexico in 1992. On October 15, 1992 Pegasus raised $53-million (U.S.) by selling 3.25 million common shares in Canada and Europe, to repay a long-term $21.2-million (U.S.) debt. The balance goes to fund major capital projects.

Pegasus reported a first quarter loss of $449,000 (U.S.) in 1993, compared to a $3-million (U.S.) profit for the same period in 1992. Gold production for the period totaled 67,600 ounces. Cash operating costs for the first quarter increased to $229 (U.S.) per ounce from $221 (U.S.) in 992 because of lower byproduct credits.

Pegasus spent a total of $9.1-million (U.S.) on exploration in 1992. Its 1993 exploration budget is $13-million (U.S). Pegasus plans to spend $7.5-million (U.S.) on capital additions on operating properties and $6.3-million (U.S.) on the Zortman Extension and for developing existing sites. Two U.S. projects, Emigrant and Garnet, were disappointing in 1992 and may be dropped in 1993. A total of 19 new projects were generated in 1992.

Little change is expected for existing operations in 1993. Gold production is expected to hit 400,000 ounces in 1993, reaching 500,000 ounces by 1995. Gold reserves stand at 3.8 million ounces, good for another six years of production. Cash operating costs came down to $214 (U.S.) per ounce in 1992.

Relative strength to TSE300

Price

Volume (in 1000's of board lots)

Rank (Profit/Revenue/Assets)
860   258   213

Werner G. Nennecker
President & C.E.O.

John L. Azlant
V.P., Finance & C.F.O.

Steven W. Benning
Exec. V.P., Operations

Allan Park
V.P., Exploration

Address
Suite 400
North 9 Post Street
Spokane
WA
99201
(509) 624-4653

Fax: (509) 838-8317
P0001798/G/2.0

PIONEER METALS CORPORATION

Exchanges	Price (Jun24'93)	0.55	Trailing P/E	1.03	Stock Symbol
T	Trailing Yield (%)	0.00	Trailing EPS	0.53	**PSM**

Period Ending	Dec91	Dec90	Dec89	Dec88	Dec87
Yearly Statistics					
Price-Close	0.18	0.13	0.44	2.95	11.13
Price-High	0.24	0.44	2.90	10.50	16.75
Price-Low	0.03	0.03	0.40	2.70	4.65
P/E-Close	0.07	nm	nm	nm	35.89
Dividends per Share	0.00	0.00	0.00	0.00	0.00
Dividend Yield (%)	0.00	0.00	0.00	0.00	0.00
Sales per Share	na	na	na	0.10	0.91
EPS before extra. item	2.44	(0.98)	(3.58)	(1.41)	0.31
Cash Flow per Share	(0.03)	(0.29)	(0.05)	0.07	0.41
Book Value per Share	0.02	(2.20)	(1.27)	2.15	4.07
O/S Common Shares	43,079	23,392	23,130	18,854	13,981
Total Revenue	56,281	5,955	7,462	4,233	13,083
Income before extra.	55,644	(22,898)	(79,939)	(25,091)	4,053
Cash Flow	(627)	(6,816)	(1,064)	1,162	5,309
Debt/Equity	nd	na	na	0.33	0.00
Return on Capital (%)	na	na	(430.41)	(46.10)	17.38
Ret. on Com. Equity (%)	na	na	(1,419.89)	(51.52)	12.55
% Change Profit	343.0	71.4	(218.6)	(719.0)	55.5
% Change Revenue	845.0	(20.2)	76.3	(67.6)	15.7
% Change Assets	(86.5)	(68.9)	(70.0)	33.6	471.3

Date	EPS	DPS	Tot Rev	Inc Bex
Mar 92	0.00	0.00	162	96
Sep 91	0.03	0.00	2	567
Jun 91	0.01	0.00	1,678	436
Mar 91	0.49	0.00	12	11,397
Dec 90	(0.73)	0.00	4,452	(17,027)
Sep 90	(0.19)	0.00	4,578	(4,583)
Jun 90	(0.25)	0.00	3,084	(5,591)
Mar 90	0.19	0.00	8,083	4,303

	Dec91	Dec90	Dec89
Preferred Div. Coverage	np	np	np
Total Div. Coverage	na	na	na
Interest Coverage	nd	0.0	0.0
Current Ratio	0.5	0.0	0.1
Operating Margin	na	na	na
Asset Turnover	na	na	na
5 YEAR RATIOS (%)			
Return on Capital	na	na	(81.2)
Return on Com. Equity	na	na	(288.5)
Profit Growth	84.4	na	na
Revenue Growth	37.9	189.3	na
Asset Growth	(38.1)	17.2	105.6
BALANCE SHEET (000)			
Cash	5	176	1,452
Current Assets	44	1,829	2,867
Net Fixed Assets	1,029	5,664	17,959
Invest's & Advances	0	0	4,557
Total Assets	1,118	8,287	26,643
Short Term Debt	0	30,646	12,379
Current Liabilities	91	58,820	54,707
Long Term Debt	0	0	0
Total Liabilities	91	59,730	55,963
Total Equity	1,028	(51,443)	(29,320)
Total Liab. & Equity	1,118	8,287	26,643
CAPITAL (000)			
Total Debt	0	30,646	12,379
Preferred Equity	0	0	0
Common Equity	1,028	(51,443)	(29,320)

Business:

PIONEER METALS CORP. is a gold mining company. It has producing mines in British Columbia, Idaho and Manitoba and exploration activities in New Mexico and British Columbia.

Synopsis:

Pioneer Metals Corporation is continuing with its restructuring plan, with hopes to reactivate operations at its 100% owned Puffy Lake gold mine. This mine has been dormant since 1989, when a forest fire hit the site. Repair costs could total $1.6-million. Pioneer is studying several alternatives for financing the reactivation, including joint venture proposals. It will also be paying close attention to further exploring its Galore Creek project and the Fish Lake project.

Puffy Lake's mineral reserves at a cut off of 3.5 grams per tonne is estimated to be 1.484 million tonnes of proven and probable reserves averaging 7.5 grams per tonne with an additional 673,000 tonnes of possible reserves averaging 7.01 grams per tonne, for a total contained gold reserve of 497,588 troy ounces.

Pioneer Metals Corporation reported a loss of $102,000 in 1992 compared to earnings of $56-million in 1991, due in part from a gain on debt settlement. During the third quarter of 1992, Pioneer recorded a loss of $113,000 compared to earnings of $12.4-million for same period in 1991. In early 1992, approximately $21-million of Pioneer's debt was forgiven by the Chase Manhattan Bank of Canada. Since restructuring began, Pioneer has eliminated more than $60-million of debt.

Rank (Profit/Revenue/Assets)
902   620   893

Stephen H. Sorensen
Chairman, President & C.E.O.

Address
Suite 1770
401 West Georgia St.
Vancouver
BC
V6B 5A1
(604) 669-3383

Fax: (604) 669-1240
P0025667/G/2.0

PLACER DOME INC.

Exchanges	Price (Jun24'93)		25.75	Trailing P/E		54.79	Stock Symbol
TMVN	Trailing Yield (%)		1.01	Trailing EPS		0.47	**PDG**

Period Ending	Dec92	Dec91	Dec90	Dec89	Dec88
Yearly Statistics	US	US	US		
Price-Close	14.75	12.63	19.75	21.13	15.75
Price-High	15.50	19.38	25.00	23.00	20.25
Price-Low	10.75	11.13	15.50	14.25	13.88
P/E-Close	25.83	nm	24.17	39.86	13.58
Dividends per Share	0.26	0.26	0.30	0.30	0.23
Dividend Yield (%)	1.76	2.06	1.52	1.42	1.43
Sales per Share	4.31	4.10	3.96	3.85	3.08
EPS before extra. item	0.47	(1.00)	0.70	0.53	1.16
Cash Flow per Share	1.46	1.25	1.31	1.22	0.99
Book Value per Share	6.15	6.26	7.45	8.16	8.09
O/S Common Shares	237,116	236,736	236,395	234,800	234,512
Total Revenue	1,090,000	1,030,000	1,031,300	1,011,300	921,600
Income before extra.	111,000	(236,000)	164,600	125,100	262,400
Cash Flow	345,000	295,000	308,200	286,300	224,400
Debt/Equity	0.08	0.21	0.19	0.16	0.09
Return on Capital (%)	9.21	(12.22)	12.29	10.15	18.26
Ret. on Com. Equity (%)	7.55	(14.56)	9.71	6.56	15.59
% Change Profit	147.0	(243.4)	53.6	(52.3)	65.9
% Change Revenue	5.8	(0.1)	19.1	9.7	(7.8)
% Change Assets	(9.8)	(14.0)	9.0	6.3	23.3

Date		EPS	DPS	Tot Rev	Inc Bex
Mar 93	US	0.05	0.07	228,000	11,000
Dec 92	US	0.18	0.07	253,000	43,000
Sep 92	US	0.14	0.07	284,000	33,000
Jun 92	US	0.10	0.07	283,000	24,000
Mar 92	US	0.05	0.07	267,000	11,000
Dec 91	US	(1.20)	0.07	286,000	(283,000)
Sep 91		0.07	0.08	300,400	15,900
Jun 91		0.09	0.08	287,200	20,400

Preferred Div. Coverage	np	np	np
Total Div. Coverage	1.8	0.0	2.7
Interest Coverage	7.8	0.0	10.4
Current Ratio	3.8	3.8	4.1
Operating Margin	11.8	(28.1)	9.5
Asset Turnover	0.5	0.4	0.3
5 YEAR RATIOS (%)			
Return on Capital	7.5	8.3	na
Return on Com. Equity	5.0	5.7	na
Profit Growth	(3.2)	na	na
Revenue Growth	4.9	7.7	na
Asset Growth	2.1	5.4	na
BALANCE SHEET (000)			
Cash	477,000	623,000	784,900
Current Assets	757,000	885,000	1,000,600
Net Fixed Assets	1,138,000	1,179,000	1,439,600
Invest's & Advances	83,000	109,000	157,700
Total Assets	2,067,000	2,291,000	2,662,800
Short Term Debt	46,000	60,000	32,800
Current Liabilities	201,000	235,000	241,200
Long Term Debt	69,000	250,000	309,800
Total Liabilities	608,000	810,000	901,200
Total Equity	1,459,000	1,481,000	1,761,600
Total Liab. & Equity	2,067,000	2,291,000	2,662,800
CAPITAL (000)			
Total Debt	115,000	310,000	342,600
Preferred Equity	0	0	0
Common Equity	1,459,000	1,481,000	1,761,600

Business:

PLACER DOME INC. is a gold mining company, which also produces significant quantities of silver, copper and molybdenum. The company has producing gold mines in Canada, the United States, Australia, Chile, and Papua New Guinea. Exploration activites are underway in North and South America, Australia, South-East Asia and Africa.

Synopsis:

The biggest challenge facing Placer Dome Inc. in 1993 is the political climate in Papua New Guinea. In 1992 the government of the island increased its share in the Porgera gold mine to 25% in an attempt to keep tighter control on its natural resources.

Placer had a disastrous year with the Mount Milligan gold and copper property, and planned to shut down the Dona Lake gold mine in Ontario this year. Placer sold its 49% interest in Minera Real de Angeles AS de CV to Empresas Frisco of Mexico for $4.5-million (U.S.) in May 1993. Placer bought all of the Mulatos gold properties previously controlled by Minera estimated to contain 800,000 gold ounces for $5-million (U.S.). The Big Bell and Marigold properties were sold in 1992. Placer Dome has agreed to buy gold properties in Nevada from USMX Inc. for $15-million (U.S.). They contain 244,000 ounces of gold in proven and probable reserves.

Placer completed a feasibility study on the 60% owned Pipeline gold deposit and has budgeted $250-million for development. Mineable ore reserves are 35.3 million tons grading 0.120 ounces of gold per ton with a 12-year production span. The Dome Mine and Zaliwar feasibility studies were slated for completion. The 50% owned Zaliwar copper project in Chile will cost $500-million to develop.

1993 first quarter results show Placer's net earnings at $11-million sales revenues were down because of lower sales volumes. Cash flow stood at $78-million (U.S.).

1992 gold production was 1.9 million ounces, expected to fall to 1.8 million ounces in 1993 because of output decline from Porgera, and lower ore grades at some properties. Output will continue falling in 1994 and 1995. Average cash production costs in 1992 were $186 (U.S.). Gold reserves stand at 18.4 million ounces.

Rank (Profit/Revenue/Assets)
25   85   74

Robert M. Franklin
Chairman
John M. Willson
President & C.E.O.
Ian G. Austin
Sr. V.P., Finance & C.F.O.
Arthur W. Brown
V.P., Canadian Operations

Address
1600 - 1055 Dunsmuir Street
P.O. Box 49330
Bentall Postal Station
Vancouver
BC
V7X 1P1
(604) 682-7082
Fax: (604) 682-7092
P0001699/G/2.0

QUEBEC STURGEON RIVER MINES LIMITED

Exchanges	Price (Jun24'93)	0.60	Trailing P/E	nm	Stock Symbol
TQ	Trailing Yield (%)	0.00	Trailing EPS	(0.18)	**QSR**

Period Ending	Dec92	Dec91	Dec90	Dec89	Dec88
Yearly Statistics					
Price-Close	0.23	0.23	0.47	1.20	2.05
Price-High	0.70	0.50	1.55	2.35	4.00
Price-Low	0.12	0.11	0.35	0.95	2.00
P/E-Close	nm	nm	nm	nm	nm
Dividends per Share	0.00	0.00	0.00	0.00	0.00
Dividend Yield (%)	0.00	0.00	0.00	0.00	0.00
Sales per Share	1.32	0.95	1.30	0.90	1.13
EPS before extra. item	(0.17)	(0.20)	(0.95)	(0.22)	(0.11)
Cash Flow per Share	0.19	(0.10)	0.08	(0.28)	0.06
Book Value per Share	0.43	0.61	0.41	1.36	1.58
O/S Common Shares	9,958	9,651	9,352	9,304	9,304
Total Revenue	13,043	10,163	13,650	9,888	12,204
Income before extra.	(1,668)	(1,896)	(8,863)	(2,063)	(1,058)
Cash Flow	1,824	(948)	758	(2,631)	596
Debt/Equity	0.61	2.50	6.51	2.18	1.63
Return on Capital (%)	(10.02)	(5.87)	(22.34)	(7.01)	0.30
Ret. on Com. Equity (%)	(32.72)	(39.02)	(107.66)	(15.09)	(7.03)
% Change Profit	12.0	78.6	(329.7)	(95.1)	26.5
% Change Revenue	28.3	(25.5)	38.0	(19.0)	82.3
% Change Assets	(77.9)	(8.6)	(51.1)	(8.8)	49.0

Business:

QUEBEC STURGEON RIVER MINES LTD. is a gold mining and exploration company. It has a controlling interest in the Bachelor Lake mine in Lesueur Township, PQ. The company has a 51.7% interest in Bachelor Lake Gold Mines Inc. of Montreal and a 54% interest in St. Andrew Goldfields Ltd. of Toronto.

Date	EPS	DPS	Tot Rev	Inc Bex
Mar 93	(0.03)	0.00	115	(348)
Dec 92	0.74	0.00	(84)	7,247
Sep 92	0.04	0.00	4,259	255
Jun 92	(0.93)	0.00	4,797	(8,958)
Mar 92	(0.02)	0.00	4,072	(212)
Dec 91	(0.05)	0.00	3,317	(476)
Sep 91	0.04	0.00	2,516	349
Jun 91	(0.08)	0.00	2,521	(731)

Preferred Div. Coverage	np	np	np
Total Div. Coverage	na	na	na
Interest Coverage	0.0	0.0	0.0
Current Ratio	0.0	0.3	0.6
Operating Margin	(6.5)	(42.1)	(142.4)
Asset Turnover	1.8	0.3	0.3
5 YEAR RATIOS (%)			
Return on Capital	(9.0)	(6.0)	(3.3)
Return on Com. Equity	(40.3)	(35.6)	(27.5)
Profit Growth	na	na	na
Revenue Growth	14.2	(2.6)	5.0
Asset Growth	(33.3)	(8.5)	(6.0)
BALANCE SHEET (000)			
Cash	5	1,011	609
Current Assets	12	2,445	3,436
Net Fixed Assets	123	28,400	28,871
Invest's & Advances	6,898	0	1,480
Total Assets	7,033	31,827	34,815
Short Term Debt	861	983	323
Current Liabilities	949	7,006	5,868
Long Term Debt	1,782	13,750	24,556
Total Liabilities	2,731	25,932	30,992
Total Equity	4,303	5,895	3,822
Total Liab. & Equity	7,033	31,827	34,815
CAPITAL (000)			
Total Debt	2,643	14,733	24,879
Preferred Equity	0	0	0
Common Equity	4,303	5,895	3,822

Synopsis:

Quebec Sturgeon River Mines Limited reported a loss of $9.17-million for the six months ended June 30, 1992, compared to a loss of $1.76-million for the same period in 1991. The company's subsidiaries produced $8.8-million of bullion revenue and recorded a consolidated mine operating profit of $1.4-million during this period.

In 1992 activities at the Bachelor Lake Mine in Quebec were suspended. A partner is needed before mining can resume.

Relative strength to TSE300

Price

Volume (in 1000's of board lots)

Rank (Profit/Revenue/Assets)
747   699   627

G. Warren Armstrong
President

C.E. Peter Earl
V.P., Finance

Address
166 Pearl Street
Toronto
ON
M5H 1L3
(416) 597-0969

Fax: (416) 597-1776
Q0000425/G/2.0

RAYROCK YELLOWKNIFE RESOURCES INC.

Exchanges	Price (Jun24'93)	15.00	Trailing P/E	83.33	Stock Symbol
T	Trailing Yield (%)	0.00	Trailing EPS	0.18	RAY

Period Ending	Dec92	Dec91	Dec90	Dec89	Dec88
Yearly Statistics					
Price-Close	10.13	4.90	8.88	10.50	6.25
Price-High	10.25	8.75	11.00	12.00	10.88
Price-Low	4.95	4.70	7.13	5.88	6.00
P/E-Close	38.94	32.67	26.10	32.81	9.19
Dividends per Share	0.00	0.00	0.00	0.00	0.00
Dividend Yield (%)	0.00	0.00	0.00	0.00	0.00
Sales per Share	10.60	8.30	8.73	5.12	3.19
EPS before extra. item	0.26	0.15	0.34	0.32	0.68
Cash Flow per Share	2.44	1.54	1.72	0.95	0.92
Book Value per Share	7.86	7.16	7.03	5.52	5.40
O/S Common Shares	10,760	9,033	9,079	11,747	11,413
Total Revenue	102,869	76,348	84,845	58,079	38,093
Income before extra.	2,476	1,400	3,166	3,171	6,612
Cash Flow	22,447	13,982	15,572	9,268	8,850
Debt/Equity	0.46	0.62	0.62	0.59	0.45
Return on Capital (%)	6.45	4.97	9.12	8.60	12.52
Ret. on Com. Equity (%)	3.30	2.14	4.86	4.92	11.15
% Change Profit	76.9	(55.8)	(0.2)	(52.0)	(4.5)
% Change Revenue	34.7	(10.0)	46.1	52.5	(3.6)
% Change Assets	28.0	1.0	31.6	19.7	10.5
Preferred Div. Coverage	145.6	53.8	77.2		
Total Div. Coverage	145.6	53.8	77.2		
Interest Coverage	2.6	1.8	2.8		
Current Ratio	2.1	3.4	3.2		
Operating Margin	4.2	5.5	8.1		
Asset Turnover	0.5	0.5	0.5		
5 YEAR RATIOS (%)					
Return on Capital	8.3	10.3	11.1		
Return on Com. Equity	5.3	7.2	7.9		
Profit Growth	(18.6)	(12.3)	(23.0)		
Revenue Growth	21.1	18.7	31.8		
Asset Growth	17.6	21.6	21.9		
BALANCE SHEET (000)					
Cash	22,164	11,884	19,736		
Current Assets	51,625	34,095	37,518		
Net Fixed Assets	155,892	104,939	101,592		
Invest's & Advances	2,366	2,240	2,180		
Total Assets	210,270	164,254	162,656		
Short Term Debt	5,052	0	0		
Current Liabilities	24,397	10,070	11,595		
Long Term Debt	34,284	40,297	39,677		
Total Liabilities	125,302	99,252	98,418		
Total Equity	84,968	65,002	64,238		
Total Liab. & Equity	210,270	164,254	162,656		
CAPITAL (000)					
Total Debt	39,336	40,297	39,677		
Preferred Equity	375	375	375		
Common Equity	84,593	64,627	63,863		

Business:

RAYROCK YELLOWKNIFE RESOURCES INC. is a gold mining company. It operates open-pit gold mines in Nevada and owns Western Ag-Minerals Co. of Houston, an agricultural mineral producer. It also has a 50.3% interest in Mineral Rayrock Inc., a Central and South American gold and copper exploration company, and a 49.5% voting interest in Discovery West Corp., an oil and gas company.

Date	EPS	DPS	Tot Rev	Inc Bex
Mar 93	(0.09)	0.00	23,824	(1,320)
Dec 92	0.21	0.00	33,508	2,021
Sep 92	(0.07)	0.00	21,259	(641)
Jun 92	0.13	0.00	26,971	1,214
Mar 92	(0.01)	0.00	21,293	(118)
Dec 91	0.07	0.00	20,699	676
Sep 91	(0.08)	0.00	14,882	(726)
Jun 91	0.11	0.00	20,773	1,030

Synopsis:

In 1992 Rayrock Yellowknife Resources Inc. acquired a 66.66% majority interest in the Marigold gold mine in Nevada through a property swap and a $17.5-million (U.S.) acquisition.

On January 1, 1993, Discovery West Corp. agreed to purchase all of Rayrock's oil and gas assets for an amount in excess of $1-million. Rayrock owns 40% of Discovery, an investment worth $63-million. The 69% owned Minera Rayrock Inc. made an equity issue of $25-million in early 1993 and planned to borrow $18-million (U.S.) to finance the Ivan copper mine in Chile. Production is set to begin in 1994, with the potential of mining 22 million pounds per year. A feasibility study on the newly acquired Sierra Valenzuela project shows a significant new copper discovery, with grades of 1% to 3%. Further drilling is planned in 1993.

Rayrock's working capital was $27.2-million and its cash flow increased as a result of increased activity at Marigold, Discovery and Minera in 1992. Rayrock's equity rose by $20-million in 1992, through a combination of a $15-million equity issue and the weak Canadian dollar.

Rayrock's 1992 gold production share increased to 82,300 ounces resulting from the Marigold purchase. Operating costs were $222 (U.S.) per ounce in 1992, down from $289 (U.S.) per ounce in 1991.

Relative strength to TSE300

Price

Volume (in 1000's of board lots)

Rank (Profit/Revenue/Assets)
337   376   313

H. Earl Joudrie
Chairman Of The Board

David R. Crombie
President & C.E.O.

C. Bruce Burton
V.P. & C.F.O.

David A. Hutton
V.P., Explorat'n & Development

Address
30 Soudan Avenue
Suite 500
Toronto
ON
M4S 1V6
(416) 489-0022

Fax: (416) 489-0096
R0000435/G/2.0

ROYAL OAK MINES INC.

Exchanges	Price (Jun24'93)		7.37	Trailing P/E		70.91	Stock Symbol
TA	Trailing Yield (%)		0.00	Trailing EPS		0.10	**RYO**

Period Ending	Dec92	Dec91	Dec90	Dec89	Dec88
Yearly Statistics					
Price-Close	1.95	1.58	0.70	0.50	0.42
Price-High	2.62	1.70	1.32	0.79	0.72
Price-Low	1.41	0.66	0.40	0.29	0.34
P/E-Close	10.83	6.32	nm	nm	nm
Dividends per Share	0.00	0.00	0.00	0.00	0.00
Dividend Yield (%)	0.00	0.00	0.00	0.00	0.00
Sales per Share	1.81	2.79	2.08	na	na
EPS before extra. item	0.18	0.25	(0.17)	(0.04)	(0.04)
Cash Flow per Share	0.22	0.48	(0.09)	(0.02)	0.00
Book Value per Share	1.17	0.88	0.77	0.31	0.33
O/S Common Shares	69,947	56,118	20,599	6,295	4,776
Total Revenue	114,423	97,649	18,160	154	77
Income before extra.	11,437	8,641	(1,443)	(165)	(165)
Cash Flow	13,593	16,598	(788)	(96)	28
Debt/Equity	nd	nd	1.24	nd	nd
Return on Capital (%)	17.60	26.65	(5.04)	(9.37)	(10.17)
Ret. on Com. Equity (%)	17.43	26.52	(16.19)	(9.37)	(10.17)
% Change Profit	32.4	698.8	(774.5)	0.0	(195.6)
% Change Revenue	17.2	437.7	nm	100.4	94.6
% Change Assets	49.9	(22.0)	4,740.5	24.3	(10.4)

Date	EPS	DPS	Tot Rev	Inc Bex
Mar 93	0.02	0.00	29,132	1,236
Dec 92	0.03	0.00	35,622	2,154
Sep 92	0.05	0.00	30,188	2,937
Jun 92	0.01	0.00	20,657	740
Mar 92	0.10	0.00	27,471	5,606
Dec 91	0.08	0.00	25,113	4,005
Sep 91	0.04	0.00	22,923	2,372
Jun 91	0.03	0.00	24,472	694

	Dec92	Dec91	Dec90
Preferred Div. Coverage	np	np	np
Total Div. Coverage	na	na	na
Interest Coverage	nd	4.4	0.0
Current Ratio	1.7	1.4	1.0
Operating Margin	12.5	14.6	(10.7)
Asset Turnover	1.0	1.3	0.2
5 YEAR RATIOS (%)			
Return on Capital	3.9	(0.3)	(22.3)
Return on Com. Equity	1.6	(2.6)	(33.4)
Profit Growth	na	na	na
Revenue Growth	392.5	255.9	182.0
Asset Growth	129.0	116.4	126.5
BALANCE SHEET (000)			
Cash	12,719	4,935	6,373
Current Assets	33,348	15,669	24,565
Net Fixed Assets	77,547	58,200	70,188
Invest's & Advances	775	311	239
Total Assets	111,670	74,484	95,551
Short Term Debt	0	0	9,825
Current Liabilities	19,433	11,523	25,821
Long Term Debt	0	0	9,825
Total Liabilities	29,735	25,211	79,665
Total Equity	81,935	49,273	15,886
Total Liab. & Equity	111,670	74,484	95,551
CAPITAL (000)			
Total Debt	0	0	19,650
Preferred Equity	0	0	0
Common Equity	81,935	49,273	15,886

Business:

ROYAL OAK MINES INC. is a gold mining and production company.

Synopsis:

First quarter results for 1993 show unusual losses for Royal Oak Mines Inc., which continues to operate using strike breakers. On May 23, 1992, a legal work stoppage began at the Giant Gold Mine near Yellowknife, Northwest Territories, which had not been resolved as of mid-1993. The company has continued to operate the mine using replacement workers and some staff. On September 18, 1992, an explosion at the mine killed nine miners. The deaths are being investigated as homicides.

In 1992, Royal Oak acquired and re-opened the Hope Brook Mine in Newfoundland. The mine is capable of producing over 120,000 ounces of gold annually. In May 1993 it purchased controlling interest in Geddes Resources Ltd. for $10-million. Royal Oak bought its 39.3% stake in Geddes from Northgate Exploration Ltd. Geddes is the developer of the controversial Windy Craggy copper-gold mining project in British Columbia, where it wants to build a $550-million open-pit and underground copper and gold mine. However, Geddes has encountered opposition from environmentalist groups who want to preserve the area as a wilderness site.

On April 1993, Royal completed the purchase of the Colomac gold mine in Yellowknife. The mine will be re-opened in 1994 at an estimated capital cost of $15-million. Production is expected to begin in March 1994, with a potential of 180,000 ounces of gold per year.

Royal's 1992 gold production totaled 245,469 ounces, an increase of 26% from 1991. It forecasts 320,000 gold ounces for 1993. Royal Oak reduced its cash operating costs by 7% from $327 (U.S.) per ounce in 1991 to $304 (U.S.) per ounce in 1992. The Hope purchase increased mineable reserves by over 1 million ounces.

Relative strength to TSE300 / Price / Volume (in 1000's of board lots)

Rank (Profit/Revenue/Assets)		
164	352	399

Margaret K. Witte
Chairman, President & C.E.O.

Christopher A. Serin
C.F.O.

John R. Smrke
V.P., Operations

Address
1425 West Pender Street
2nd Floor
Vancouver
BC
V6G 2S3
(604) 682-8320

Fax: (604) 682-4286
H0002415/G/2.0

SONORA GOLD CORP.

Exchanges	Price (Jun24'93)	0.27	Trailing P/E	nm	Stock Symbol
TVQ	Trailing Yield (%)	0.00	Trailing EPS	(0.06)	**SON**

Period Ending	Dec92	Dec91	Dec90	Dec89	Dec88
Yearly Statistics					
Price-Close	0.12	0.20	0.25	1.80	1.80
Price-High	0.25	0.45	1.85	2.35	8.25
Price-Low	0.08	0.15	0.15	1.30	1.60
P/E-Close	nm	nm	nm	nm	nm
Dividends per Share	0.00	0.00	0.00	0.00	0.00
Dividend Yield (%)	0.00	0.00	0.00	0.00	0.00
Sales per Share	1.88	1.85	1.64	1.87	2.04
EPS before extra. item	(0.01)	(0.96)	(1.32)	(0.11)	(3.03)
Cash Flow per Share	0.21	0.18	(0.13)	0.15	0.14
Book Value per Share	(1.66)	(1.65)	(0.69)	0.63	0.73
O/S Common Shares	20,262	20,262	20,262	20,262	20,262
Total Revenue	38,093	37,970	33,900	39,150	37,858
Income before extra.	(276)	(19,366)	(26,662)	(2,192)	(53,820)
Cash Flow	4,161	3,656	(2,700)	3,138	2,484
Debt/Equity	na	na	na	3.20	2.68
Return on Capital (%)	30.53	(88.27)	(55.55)	3.05	(65.41)
Ret. on Com. Equity (%)	na	na	na	(15.94)	(152.23)
% Change Profit	98.6	27.4	(1,116.3)	95.9	(894.8)
% Change Revenue	0.3	12.0	(13.4)	3.4	522.2
% Change Assets	(14.9)	(46.5)	(38.0)	(4.6)	(37.8)
Preferred Div. Coverage	np	np	np		
Total Div. Coverage	na	na	na		
Interest Coverage	0.9	0.0	0.0		
Current Ratio	0.2	0.5	0.2		
Operating Margin	8.0	(42.8)	(69.3)		
Asset Turnover	2.1	1.7	0.8		
5 YEAR RATIOS (%)					
Return on Capital	(35.1)	(42.1)	na		
Return on Com. Equity	na	na	na		
Profit Growth	na	na	na		
Revenue Growth	44.3	na	na		
Asset Growth	(30.1)	(24.7)	88.5		
BALANCE SHEET (000)					
Cash	2,022	2,659	688		
Current Assets	8,960	9,561	6,660		
Net Fixed Assets	9,421	12,035	32,915		
Invest's & Advances	0	0	0		
Total Assets	18,381	21,596	40,348		
Short Term Debt	38,709	9,707	32,000		
Current Liabilities	45,781	17,438	38,740		
Long Term Debt	6,108	30,858	9,779		
Total Liabilities	52,029	54,968	54,354		
Total Equity	(33,648)	(33,372)	(14,006)		
Total Liab. & Equity	18,381	21,596	40,348		
CAPITAL (000)					
Total Debt	44,817	40,565	41,779		
Preferred Equity	0	0	0		
Common Equity	(33,648)	(33,372)	(14,006)		

Business:

SONORA GOLD CORP. is a gold mining company which holds a 70% interest in and is the operator of the Jamestown mine 120 miles east of San Francisco, California. NorthWest Gold Corp., a subsidiary of Northgate Exploration Limited, owns 42% of the outstanding shares of the company.

Date	EPS	DPS	Tot Rev	Inc Bex
Mar 93	(0.05)	0.00	8,370	(1,055)
Dec 92	0.01	0.00	9,679	167
Sep 92	(0.03)	0.00	8,958	(699)
Jun 92	0.01	0.00	9,740	177
Mar 92	0.00	0.00	9,779	79
Dec 91	(0.91)	0.00	10,889	(18,316)
Sep 91	(0.00)	0.00	9,773	(299)
Jun 91	0.01	0.00	9,436	108

Synopsis:

Sonora Gold Corp.'s ability to continue operations depends on its support from NorthWest, its major shareholder, on restructuring its $25.6-million debt. As of December 31, 1992, Sonora had a shareholder's deficiency of $33.6-million and a working capital deficiency of $36.8-million.

The main source of cash in 1992 came from NorthWest's advances of $2.2-million, and funds from operations, used to reduce $4.9-million in long term debt and other liabilities.

Sonora did not proceed with the development of the Dutch-App/Nyman and Jumper ore bodies because of low 1991 gold prices.

Sonora's 1992 gold production at the Jamestown Mine fell from 132,000 ounces to 129,000 ounces. Production 1993 is expected to total 114,000 ounces. Proven and mineable reserves at Jamestown at the end of 1992 were 2.89 million tonnes at a grade of 0.065 ounces per tonne. Operating cost per ounce of gold increased to $244 (U.S.) in 1992 compared with $237 (U.S.) in 1991. Cash flow in 1992 was $4.9-million, up from 1991. Sonora's increased 1992 revenues are attributed to a low Canadian dollar. Future cash flow from the Jamestown mine will depend on the strength of gold prices, and U.S. dollar exchange rate.

Relative strength to TSE300

Price

Volume (in 1000's of board lots)

Rank (Profit/Revenue/Assets)
616   515   729

John F. Kearney
Chairman, C.E.O. & President

Patrick D. Downey
Exec. V.P. & C.F.O.

John O. Kachmar
Exec. V.P. & C.O.O.

Address
Suite 2701
P.O. Box 143
1 First Canadian Place
Toronto
ON
M5X 1C7
(416) 362-7203
Fax: (416) 362-7938
S0017384/G/2.0

TVX GOLD INC.

Exchanges	Price (Jun24'93)		5 .00	Trailing P/E		62 .50	Stock Symbol
TM	Trailing Yield (%)		0 .00	Trailing EPS		0 .08	**TVX**

Period Ending	Dec92	Dec91	Jan91	Dec89	Dec88
Yearly Statistics	US	US /51W	US	US	US
Price-Close	2 .65	3 .60	5 .00	7 .63	5 .50
Price-High	4 .00	5 .00	8 .25	8 .38	11 .75
Price-Low	2 .30	3 .05	3 .80	4 .70	5 .00
P/E-Close	27 .32	63 .16	28 .74	nm	12 .14
Dividends per Share	0 .00	0 .00	0 .00	0 .00	0 .00
Dividend Yield (%)	0 .00	0 .00	0 .00	0 .00	0 .00
Sales per Share	1 .12	0 .81	0 .59	na	na
EPS before extra. item	0 .08	0 .05	0 .15	(0 .10)	0 .37
Cash Flow per Share	0 .36	0 .36	0 .27	0 .12	0 .02
Book Value per Share	1 .49	1 .41	1 .37	1 .39	3 .93
O/S Common Shares	134 ,032	134 ,032	134 ,038	47 ,334	31 ,015
Total Revenue	156 ,443	110 ,678	60 ,999	(4 ,456)	23 ,772
Income before extra.	10 ,402	6 ,405	12 ,786	(4 ,210)	11 ,186
Cash Flow	49 ,438	46 ,842	24 ,819	5 ,165	540
Debt/Equity	0 .81	1 .02	0 .98	nd	0 .17
Return on Capital (%)	0 .00	5 .60	8 .40	(5 .55)	8 .80
Ret. on Com. Equity (%)	5 .34	3 .51	10 .28	(4 .49)	11 .25
% Change Profit	59 .3	(48 .9)	403 .7	(137 .6)	152 .8
% Change Revenue	38 .6	85 .0	1 ,468 .9	(118 .7)	540 .6
% Change Assets	(6 .1)	7 .5	432 .7	(66 .6)	137 .5

Business:

TVX GOLD INC. is a precious metals producer. It has six producing gold mines: two in North America; three in Brazil; and one in Chile.

Date		EPS	DPS	Tot Rev	Inc Bex
Mar 93	US	0 .02	0 .00	36 ,087	2 ,015
Dec 92	US	0 .02	0 .00	40 ,705	3 ,011
Sep 92	US	0 .02	0 .00	38 ,481	2 ,417
Jun 92	US	0 .02	0 .00	37 ,333	1 ,848
Mar 92	US	0 .02	0 .00	40 ,487	3 ,126
Dec 91	US	0 .00	0 .00	44 ,207	31
Sep 91	US	0 .02	0 .00	26 ,463	2 ,024
Jun 91	US	0 .02	0 .00	21 ,819	2 ,935

Preferred Div. Coverage	np	np	np
Total Div. Coverage	na	na	na
Interest Coverage	1 .9	2 .0	9 .1
Current Ratio	0 .6	0 .6	0 .7
Operating Margin	20 .5	22 .8	20 .1
Asset Turnover	0 .4	0 .2	0 .1
5 YEAR RATIOS (%)			
Return on Capital	5 .3	(2 .7)	(5 .8)
Return on Com. Equity	5 .2	(4 .0)	(7 .8)
Profit Growth	na	na	na
Revenue Growth	111 .0	na	200 .2
Asset Growth	33 .6	65 .9	67 .1
BALANCE SHEET (000)			
Cash	16 ,395	10 ,332	14 ,371
Current Assets	49 ,938	49 ,404	38 ,346
Net Fixed Assets	347 ,464	377 ,382	350 ,484
Invest's & Advances	0	0	0
Total Assets	413 ,862	440 ,884	410 ,312
Short Term Debt	65 ,352	50 ,262	26 ,653
Current Liabilities	86 ,522	77 ,118	54 ,411
Long Term Debt	97 ,166	143 ,605	152 ,922
Total Liabilities	213 ,932	251 ,356	227 ,170
Total Equity	199 ,930	189 ,528	183 ,142
Total Liab. & Equity	413 ,862	440 ,884	410 ,312
CAPITAL (000)			
Total Debt	162 ,518	193 ,867	179 ,575
Preferred Equity	0	0	0
Common Equity	199 ,930	189 ,528	183 ,142

Synopsis:

During 1992 TVX Gold Inc. spent $2.4-million (U.S.) of its own money, out of a total $4-million (U.S.) on exploring six producing mines in North and South America. It found new mineral deposits at Casa Berardi and Mineral Hill. A new satellite ore zone was discovered at La Coipa, in Chile.

TVX suspended operations at Casa Berardi in Quebec on April 25, 1992, after overburden material flowed into the mine, which had produced 48,000 ounces of gold up to that date.

Gold production in 1992 totaled 314,0000 ounces of gold and 8.1 million ounces of silver. This increase from 1991 resulted from higher production at its new plant at La Coipa, Chile, which it jointly owns with Placer Dome. Production costs in 1992 fell to $179 (U.S.) per ounce of gold from $198 (U.S.) in 1991.

In 1993, TVX Gold expects to produce 410,000 ounces of gold equivalent at an average cost between $180 (U.S.) and $190 (U.S.) per ounce.

TVX uses a hedging program which reduces price risk and ensures that operations remain viable during periods of low metal prices. In 1992 this method enhanced revenues by $8.1-million (U.S.), compared to $5.7-million (U.S.) in 1991.

Relative strength to TSE300

Price

Volume (in 1000's of board lots)

Rank (Profit/Revenue/Assets)
157   281   204

Eike F. Batista
Chairman

Martin H. Robinson
President & C.E.O.

Glenn A. Ives
V.P., Finance

Address
Suite 4300
161 Bay Street
Toronto
ON
M5j 2S1
(416) 366-8160

Fax: (416) 366-8163
T0009889/G/2.0

UNITED KENO HILL MINES LIMITED

Exchanges	Price (Jun24'93)	3.60	Trailing P/E	nm	Stock Symbol
T	Trailing Yield (%)	0.00	Trailing EPS	(0.24)	**UKH**

Period Ending	Dec92	Dec91	Dec90	Dec89	Dec88
Yearly Statistics					
Price-Close	0.45	0.55	1.00	3.65	6.50
Price-High	0.96	1.50	3.65	6.38	10.25
Price-Low	0.40	0.40	0.90	3.20	5.88
P/E-Close	nm	nm	nm	nm	nm
Dividends per Share	0.00	0.00	0.00	0.00	0.00
Dividend Yield (%)	0.00	0.00	0.00	0.00	0.00
Sales per Share	na	na	na	0.29	4.82
EPS before extra. item	(0.20)	(0.05)	(0.43)	(0.97)	(3.54)
Cash Flow per Share	(0.23)	(0.29)	(0.36)	(0.91)	(3.14)
Book Value per Share	0.37	0.56	0.61	1.04	0.32
O/S Common Shares	7,129	7,129	7,129	7,129	3,753
Total Revenue	400	2,014	703	2,409	18,254
Income before extra.	(1,414)	(350)	(3,041)	(5,639)	(12,912)
Cash Flow	(1,637)	(2,069)	(2,564)	(5,276)	(11,442)
Debt/Equity	0.83	0.22	0.31	nd	3.75
Return on Capital (%)	(27.67)	(6.59)	(46.31)	(86.53)	(139.20)
Ret. on Com. Equity (%)	(42.76)	(8.36)	(51.68)	(131.31)	(183.06)
% Change Profit	(304.0)	88.5	46.1	56.3	(169.5)
% Change Revenue	(80.1)	186.5	(70.8)	(86.8)	(14.0)
% Change Assets	(4.9)	(27.6)	4.0	(37.6)	(15.5)

Preferred Div. Coverage	np	np	np
Total Div. Coverage	na	na	na
Interest Coverage	0.0	na	na
Current Ratio	0.2	0.3	0.6
Operating Margin	na	na	na
Asset Turnover	na	na	na
5 YEAR RATIOS (%)			
Return on Capital	(61.3)	(62.8)	(64.1)
Return on Com. Equity	(83.4)	(82.0)	(82.9)
Profit Growth	na	na	na
Revenue Growth	(55.2)	(33.3)	(44.0)
Asset Growth	(17.7)	(17.4)	(11.6)

BALANCE SHEET			
Cash	0	34,000	0
Current Assets	445,000	545,000	1,618,000
Net Fixed Assets	5,015,000	5,217,000	5,484,000
Invest's & Advances	0	0	0
Total Assets	5,567,000	5,854,000	8,087,000
Short Term Debt	2,169,000	874,000	1,364,000
Current Liabilities	2,967,000	1,840,000	2,823,000
Long Term Debt	0	0	0
Total Liabilities	2,967,000	1,840,000	3,723,000
Total Equity	2,600,000	4,014,000	4,364,000
Total Liab. & Equity	5,567,000	5,854,000	8,087,000
CAPITAL			
Total Debt	2,169,000	874,000	1,364,000
Preferred Equity	0	0	0
Common Equity	2,600,000	4,014,000	4,364,000

Business:

UNITED KENO HILL MINES LTD. is a silver and lead mining company. It has operations in the Mayo district of the Yukon and exploration activities in the Yukon and Nevada. Falconbridge Ltd. of Toronto owns 44.9% of the company's common shares.

Date	EPS	DPS	Tot Rev	Inc Bex
Mar 93	(0.06)	0.00	(46)	(412)
Dec 92	(0.08)	0.00	168	(494)
Sep 92	(0.05)	0.00	69	(375)
Jun 92	(0.05)	0.00	62	(375)
Mar 92	(0.02)	0.00	101	(170)
Dec 91	0.01	0.00	(4)	106
Sep 91	(0.07)	0.00	168	(474)
Jun 91	0.08	0.00	1,215	544

Synopsis:

United Keno Hill Mines Limited reported a consolidated net loss in 1992 of more than $1-million, resulting from the suspension of mining activity and commercial production. No revenues were reported as a result. There was no mineral production, but activity will resume once economic conditions improve.

Proven and probable reserves at its Elsa property total 322,000 tons grading 28 ounces of silver per ton and 4.6% lead. Silver remains its primary product. A further deficit is predicted in 1993.

Relative strength to TSE300 / Price / Volume (in 1000's of board lots)

Rank (Profit/Revenue/Assets)		
720	918	980

Stephen F. Powell
President & C.F.O.

Address
196 Adelaide Street West
Toronto
ON
M5H 1W7
(416) 351-1762

Fax: (416) 351-1766
U0001293/G/2.0

VICEROY RESOURCE CORPORATION

Exchanges	Price (Jun24'93)	10.75	Trailing P/E	68.91	Stock Symbol
TV	Trailing Yield (%)	0.00	Trailing EPS	0.16	**VOY**

Period Ending	Mar92	Mar91	Mar90	Mar89	Mar88
Yearly Statistics					
Price-Close	4.30	4.25	4.10	6.13	9.13
Price-High	5.50	6.00	6.13	11.25	25.00
Price-Low	2.90	3.55	3.25	4.00	7.00
P/E-Close	nm	nm	nm	111.36	268.38
Dividends per Share	0.00	0.00	0.00	0.00	0.00
Dividend Yield (%)	0.00	0.00	0.00	0.00	0.00
Sales per Share	na	na	na	na	na
EPS before extra. item	(0.10)	(0.06)	(0.01)	0.06	0.03
Cash Flow per Share	(0.09)	(0.05)	0.00	0.06	0.04
Book Value per Share	2.14	2.01	2.71	2.72	2.66
O/S Common Shares	17,732	15,712	14,502	14,502	14,497
Total Revenue	520	585	1,061	1,564	1,171
Income before extra.	(1,688)	(909)	(151)	801	460
Cash Flow	(1,571)	(823)	42	891	511
Debt/Equity	0.83	nd	0.28	0.26	0.00
Return on Capital (%)	(3.36)	(2.22)	(0.30)	1.81	2.41
Ret. on Com. Equity (%)	(4.86)	(2.57)	(0.39)	2.05	1.79
% Change Profit	(85.7)	(500.6)	(118.9)	74.0	184.6
% Change Revenue	(11.1)	(44.9)	(32.2)	33.6	564.4
% Change Assets	121.7	(35.5)	1.6	25.6	192.3
Preferred Div. Coverage	np	np	np		
Total Div. Coverage	na	na	na		
Interest Coverage	na	nd	na		
Current Ratio	4.0	12.8	1.5		
Operating Margin	na	na	na		
Asset Turnover	na	na	na		
5 YEAR RATIOS (%)					
Return on Capital	(0.3)	(1.0)	(1.6)		
Return on Com. Equity	(0.8)	(1.2)	(1.7)		
Profit Growth	na	na	na		
Revenue Growth	24.1	24.0	28.7		
Asset Growth	39.7	58.9	78.7		
BALANCE SHEET (000)					
Cash	10,696	7,598	17,249		
Current Assets	15,953	17,761	17,344		
Net Fixed Assets	55,484	14,123	33,757		
Invest's & Advances	0	0	0		
Total Assets	73,041	32,946	51,101		
Short Term Debt	31	0	11,052		
Current Liabilities	3,961	1,387	11,873		
Long Term Debt	31,188	0	0		
Total Liabilities	35,180	1,387	11,873		
Total Equity	37,861	31,559	39,228		
Total Liab. & Equity	73,041	32,946	51,101		
CAPITAL (000)					
Total Debt	31,219	0	11,052		
Preferred Equity	0	0	0		
Common Equity	37,861	31,559	39,228		

Business:

VICEROY RESOURCE CORP. is a natural resources company. Its wholly owned subsidiary, Viceroy Gold Corp. of Las Vegas, is developing a gold mine at the Castle Mountain Project in San Bernardino County, California, with a predicted output of 100,000 ounces per year.

Date	EPS	DPS	Tot Rev	Inc Bex
Dec 92	0.04	0.00	8,547	775
Sep 92	0.09	0.00	9,262	1,549
Jun 92	0.07	0.00	7,867	1,207
Mar 92	(0.04)	0.00	105	(783)
Dec 91	(0.02)	0.00	129	(311)
Sep 91	(0.02)	0.00	158	(344)
Jun 91	(0.04)	0.00	115	(686)
Mar 91	(0.03)	0.00	112	(490)

Synopsis:

Viceroy Resource Corporation produced 104,105 gold ounces during its first year of operations at its Castle Mountain Gold Mine in California. Viceroy is operator and 75% owner of the mine. It started gold production in April 1992.

Viceroy will possibly implement a communication circuit this year to further enhance recovery rates from the higher-grade ore and to increase overall gold production.

In October 1992, Viceroy raised $4.5-million on the exercise of warrants, increasing its working capital to more than $14-million.

As of May 1992, Viceroy's possible reserves remained at 13.4 million tons grading 0.046 ounces of gold per ton.

Relative strength to TSE300 / Price / Volume (in 1000's of board lots)

Rank (Profit/Revenue/Assets)
738 907 470

D. Ross Fitzpatrick
President & C.E.O.

J. Christopher Mitchell
Senior Vice President

Paul F. Saxton
Senior Vice President

Address
Suite 880
999 West Hastings Street
Vancouver
BC
V6C 2W2
(604) 688-9780

Fax: (604) 682-3941
V0003263/G/2.0

WHARF RESOURCES LTD.

Exchanges	Price (Jun24'93)		11.75	Trailing P/E		65.28	Stock Symbol
TQ	Trailing Yield (%)		0.85	Trailing EPS		0.18	**WFR**

Period Ending	Dec92	Dec91	Dec90	Dec89	Dec88
Yearly Statistics	US	US	US	US	US
Price-Close	6.25	5.75	5.63	6.25	5.25
Price-High	6.75	6.38	7.25	7.75	6.87
Price-Low	5.00	4.75	5.00	4.60	4.15
P/E-Close	22.40	15.21	nm	17.08	10.19
Dividends per Share	0.10	0.30	0.00	0.00	0.00
Dividend Yield (%)	1.60	5.22	0.00	0.00	0.00
Sales per Share	1.93	1.90	1.56	1.67	1.43
EPS before extra. item	0.23	0.33	(0.33)	0.31	0.42
Cash Flow per Share	0.54	0.65	0.55	0.63	0.66
Book Value per Share	2.51	2.39	2.36	2.67	2.33
O/S Common Shares	18,951	18,941	18,941	18,816	17,403
Total Revenue	37,714	37,948	31,207	31,667	26,755
Income before extra.	4,643	6,641	(5,822)	5,971	7,850
Cash Flow	10,309	12,323	10,386	11,071	11,773
Debt/Equity	0.28	0.02	0.02	0.03	0.06
Return on Capital (%)	10.74	16.52	(7.96)	15.65	21.61
Ret. on Com. Equity (%)	9.20	13.89	(13.09)	12.30	20.45
% Change Profit	(30.1)	214.1	(197.5)	(23.9)	84.0
% Change Revenue	(0.6)	21.6	(1.5)	18.4	24.0
% Change Assets	41.0	2.5	(11.4)	19.0	20.7

Period Ending					
Preferred Div. Coverage	np	np	np		
Total Div. Coverage	2.0	1.1	0.0		
Interest Coverage	30.3	92.2	0.0		
Current Ratio	1.2	4.6	6.3		
Operating Margin	14.2	17.4	19.0		
Asset Turnover	0.5	0.6	0.5		
5 YEAR RATIOS (%)					
Return on Capital	11.3	12.0	11.3		
Return on Com. Equity	8.5	10.2	11.9		
Profit Growth	1.7	29.7	na		
Revenue Growth	11.8	31.2	39.3		
Asset Growth	12.9	15.0	25.8		
BALANCE SHEET (000)					
Cash	7,615	10,840	11,877		
Current Assets	15,716	17,539	18,149		
Net Fixed Assets	56,166	36,326	34,585		
Invest's & Advances	3,731	0	0		
Total Assets	78,226	55,492	54,141		
Short Term Debt	3,855	349	455		
Current Liabilities	13,132	3,840	2,873		
Long Term Debt	10,619	381	629		
Total Liabilities	26,186	5,873	5,082		
Total Equity	47,646	45,225	44,665		
Total Liab. & Equity	78,226	55,492	54,141		
CAPITAL (000)					
Total Debt	14,474	730	1,084		
Preferred Equity	0	0	0		
Common Equity	47,646	45,225	44,665		

Business:

WHARF RESOURCES LTD. is a precious metals mining company. It owns and operates two adjoining gold mines in Lawrence County, South Dakota, namely, the Wharf Mine (100% owned) and the Golden Reward Mine(60% owned). Wharf is 36% owned by Dickenson Mines Limited, and 15% owned by Goldcorp Inc.

Date		EPS	DPS	Tot Rev	Inc Bex
Mar 93	US	0.01	0.00	8,262	186
Dec 92	US	0.07	0.00	11,503	1,422
Sep 92	US	0.12	0.00	11,654	2,298
Jun 92	US	(0.02)	0.10	7,293	(251)
Mar 92	US	0.06	0.00	7,264	1,174
Dec 91	US	0.06	0.00	9,098	1,305
Sep 91	US	0.10	0.30	10,461	1,999
Jun 91	US	0.08	0.00	10,202	1,628

Synopsis:

Wharf Resources Ltd.'s 1993 first quarter results showed a decline in earnings affected in part by the operating loss incurred at the Golden Reward Mine and lower gold prices. Gold production at the Wharf Mine during the period climbed by 13% and cash production costs fell by 7%. Its gold production totaled 16,504 ounces. Production at the Golden Reward Mine totaled 3,498 ounces of gold, and its cash production costs came to $511 (U.S.) per ounce.

On October 8, 1992, Wharf acquired a 60% interest in the Golden Reward Mine from MinVen Gold Corporation. Wharf was appointed manager of the operation. In 1992, Wharf initiated the permitting of the $5-million (U.S.) Clinton gold development project in South Dakota, which is expected to be producing by 1995. Its deposits are currently estimated to contain 858,000 ounces of proven, probable and possible gold reserves.

Wharf's estimated gold production for 1993 is 124,000 ounces at an average cash production cost of $210 (U.S.) per ounce. Total estimated gold reserves at end of 1992 stood at 2.5 million ounces.

Golden Reward is expected to adversely affect the company's earnings in 1993. Positive growth is expected in 1994.

Rank (Profit/Revenue/Assets)
242   488   419

Robert R. McEwen
Chairman, President & C.E.O.
Rolando C. Francisco
Sr. V.P. & C.F.O.

Address
Suite 2700
145 King Street West
Toronto
ON
M5H 1J8
(416) 361-0402

Fax: (416) 361-5741
W0002465/G/2.0

For further company information, call Globe Information Services 1-800-268-9128 or (416)585-5345

Page	Company	$	Latest year end	Earnings per Share Actual	Estimate this year	Estimate next year
67	Alberta Energy		9212	0.53	0.83	1.12
68	Anderson Exploration		9209	0.17	0.48	0.64
69	Bow Valley Industries		9212	0.22	0.10	0.61
70	Cabre Exploration		9207	0.30	0.63	0.77
71	Canada Southern Petroleum		9206	(0.12)	n.a.	n.a.
72	Canadian Natural Resources		9212	1.04	0.55	1.51
73	Canadian Occidental Peteroleum		9212	0.26	0.54	1.47
74	Canadian Roxy Petroleum		9212	(0.11)	n.a.	n.a.
75	Chauvco Resources		9212	0.53	0.68	0.81
76	Chieftain International	$US	9212	0.04	0.08	0.18
77	Cimarron Petroleum		9204	0.03	0.06	0.15
78	Co-Enerco Resources		9212	0.35	0.55	0.68
79	Coho Resources		9212	0.05	0.29	0.36
80	Computalog		9212	(0.32)	n.a.	n.a.
81	Conwest Exploration		9212	0.72	0.73	1.08
82	Czar Resources		9212	0.10	n.a.	n.a.
83	Discovery West		9212	0.17	0.28	0.31
84	Dorset Exploration		9212	0.27	0.49	0.70
85	Dreco Energy Services	$US	9208	1.05	1.21	1.53
86	Elan Energy		9212	0.44	0.81	0.99
87	Excel Energy		9212	0.04	0.30	0.53
88	Gulf Canada Resources		9212	(0.55)	(0.08)	0.07
89	Hillcrest Resources		9211	0.23	0.39	0.40
90	Home Oil		9212	0.38	0.40	0.60
91	Horsham		9212	0.48	0.73	0.94
92	Imperial Oil		9212	1.01	2.06	2.56
93	International Colin Energy		9206	0.51	n.a.	n.a.
94	International Petroluem		9209	(0.12)	0.09	0.12
95	Inverness Petroleum		9212	0.13	0.26	0.38
96	Mark Resources		9212	(0.29)	0.16	0.36
97	Morgan Hydrocarbons		9212	0.11	n.a.	n.a.
98	Morrison Petroleums		9212	0.90	0.99	1.21
99	Norcen Engery Resources		9212	0.42	0.79	0.99
100	North Canadian Oils		9212	0.12	0.18	0.49
101	Northstar Energy		9212	0.31	n.a.	n.a.
102	Nowsco Well Services		9212	1.23	0.72	1.00
103	Numac Oil & Gas		9212	0.08	0.18	0.21
104	Ocelot Energy		9212	0.20	0.43	0.52
105	Omega Hydrocarbons		9212	0.07	n.a.	n.a.
106	PanCanadian Petroleum		9212	1.37	1.83	2.22
107	Paramount Resources		9212	0.23	0.30	0.45
108	Pe Ben Oilfield Services		9212	(0.03)	n.a.	n.a.
109	Petro-Canada		9212	0.28	0.42	0.56
110	Pinnacle Resources		9212	0.52	0.77	1.07
111	Poco Petroleums		9212	(1.55)	0.07	0.20
112	Precambrian Shield Resources		9212	(0.66)	n.a.	n.a.
113	Ranchmen's Resources		9212	(0.07)	0.15	0.25
114	Ranger Oil	$US	9212	0.25	0.18	0.20
115	Renaissance Energy		9212	0.35	0.67	0.96
116	Rigel Energy		9212	0.28	0.52	0.78
117	Rio Alto Exploration		9112	(0.09)	0.32	0.45
118	Saskatchewan Oil and Gas		9212	(0.57)	(0.18)	0.17
119	Sceptre Resources		9212	(0.64)	0.29	0.46
120	Scurry-Rainbow Oil		9212	0.66	n.a.	n.a.
121	Shell Canada		9212	0.72	1.08	1.84
122	Suncor		9212	(0.01)	0.86	1.79
123	Talisman Energy		9212	0.32	0.51	0.75
124	Tarragon Oil and Gas		9212	0.27	0.42	0.60
125	Total Petroleum (North America)	$US	9212	0.03	0.31	0.55
126	Tri Link Resources		9303	0.29	0.73	0.92
127	Triton Canada Resources		9205	(0.39)	n.a.	n.a.
128	Ulster Petroleums		9212	0.07	0.13	0.23

Estimates from I/B/E/S Inc., 345 Hudson St., New York, NY 10014 (212) 243-3335. In Canada: 6 Lansing Square, Ste. 235, Willowdale, ON M2J 1T5 (416) 496-0977.

Oil & Gas

Weekly Natural Gas Monitor - Industry Report [May-4-1993]. MERRILL LYNCH CAPITAL MARKETS reported by Olson, J.E., et al

In 1Q:93, earnings were strong, with few shortfalls. Natural gas stocks have done about five time better than the U.S. market over the past year, with not much distinction among producers, pipelines and LDC's. [RN 1331067]

Exploration & Production Company Outlook - Industry Report [Apr-2-1993]. PAINEWEBBER INC. reported by Bradshaw, D.C., et al

1Q:93 numbers from exploration and production companies will be sharply ahead of the 1992 level, signifying that operational sensitivity to better energy pricing will be an underappreciated element of the prospects for the energy group in the future. The natural gas market bears little resemblance to a yearago with average composite spot prices for 1Q:93 standing at $1.87 (U.S.) per Mcf — up nearly 50% from the $1.26 (U.S.) per Mcf in 1992. Although the uptick in natural gas realizations will have a dramatic effect on first quarter operational results, significant acquisitions, successes with the drill bit and continued cost vigilance should propel the numbers for some ahead of the pack. [RN 1321486]

Canada: Oil And Gas Market Outlook - Industry Report [Mar-24-1993]. WOOD GUNDY INC. reported by Mathieson, D., et al

Driven by solid industry fundamentals, the oil sector has recorded good share price performance so far in 1993. The junior oils, which have consistently outperformed since late in 1988, continue to improve in terms of relative performance, while the senior oil producers have begun to make up some lost ground, and have increased an average of 21% over the last seven months. As a result of this appreciation, many companies have discounted not only 1993 results, but a large portion of 1994 expectations as well. [RN 1316837]

Canadian World Oil Markets Perspective - Industry Report [Mar-18-1993]. WOOD GUNDY INC. reported by Mathieson, D., et al

Today's oil markets are facing the most complex challenges of the past decade. The markets must address the effective re-entry of Iraq into world oil markets, the level of productiion emanating from the formerSoviet Union, threats of increasing tax burdens in the U.S. and Europe, and the prospects of pipeline apportionments in Canada. All of these factors contribute to an oil market that is extremely volatile and difficult to forecast. The most encouraging feature of the current environment in the Canadian oil patch is that companies have stopped focussing on the direction of commodity prices over which they have no control. Instead, the emphasis is on areas they control directly, such as operating and overhead costs. All sectors of the industry have been successful at cutting the underlying cost of operating so as to provide sustainable improvements in cash flow. [RN 1316095]

Canadian Oil And Gas Review: March - Industry Report [Mar-17-1993]. BBN JAMES CAPEL INC. reported by Gowland, D., et al

Refining and marketing profits have improved for the group due to across-the-board cost-cutting measures, and to the elimination of operations that produced only minimal marginal revenues. Downstream operations are much better suited for the size and growth level of the marketplace they serve, but further cost cutting and efficiency measures will be required. Relatively stable prices for both the inputs and outputs of this area of operations have helped return the group to marginal refining and marketing profitability. But downstream operations continue to be a difficult business, and there will notbe a profit or return on equity level to be achieved before an economic recovery and further refining and marketing downsizing. [RN 1316119]

Gas Assessments & Strategies - Industry Report [Mar-15-1993]. KIDDER, PEABODY & COMPANY, INCORPORATED reported by Barone, R.J., et al

With the U.S. government no longer regulating wellhead prices and with the existence of supplies no longer an issue, the 1990s will be a period of growth for the natural gas industry. Natural gas consumption in the U.S. will increase 14% to 21.8 trillion cubic feet (TCF) in 1995, up from 19.1 TCF in 1991. The largest growth is expected to occur in the power generation sector. The cost of generating a kilowatt-hour with a natural gas-fired combined cycle unit is substantially less than with a coal-powered unit. According to the Utility Data Institute, approximately 44,800 megawatts of gas-fired generating capacity is planned for the 1990s. [RN 1313168]

Integrated Oils: Int'l and Domestic - Industry Report [Mar-1-1993]. THE FIRST BOSTON CORPORATION reported by Clark, J.F.

Calendar 1993 should prove to be a transition year for the integrated oils. The integrated companies should benefit from improved financial flexibility resulting from the restructuring of 1992 — expense cuts, capital spending cuts, dividend reductions, and asset sales. However, close examination of company cash flow tables reveals that while conditions have improved, most companies remain on the edge of self-funding, even at reduced expense and expenditure levels. [RN 1312705]

ALBERTA ENERGY COMPANY LTD.

Exchanges	Price (Jun24'93)		21.37	Trailing P/E		36.85	Stock Symbol
TMVZ	Trailing Yield (%)		1.64	Trailing EPS		0.58	**AEC**

Period Ending	Dec92	Dec91	Dec90	Dec89	Dec88
Yearly Statistics					
Price-Close	16.25	12.50	16.88	19.88	15.75
Price-High	17.00	16.88	20.25	22.75	19.50
Price-Low	9.75	11.50	15.50	15.63	13.63
P/E-Close	30.66	104.17	23.44	38.23	30.29
Dividends per Share	0.35	0.33	0.33	0.33	0.30
Dividend Yield (%)	2.15	2.64	1.96	1.66	1.91
Sales per Share	8.26	7.68	8.48	8.05	4.78
EPS before extra. item	0.53	0.12	0.72	0.52	0.52
Cash Flow per Share	3.28	2.46	3.08	2.98	3.38
Book Value per Share	11.99	11.74	11.94	11.50	10.68
O/S Common Shares	69,389	68,026	66,785	65,850	59,774
Total Revenue	570,300	519,600	565,400	511,200	481,900
Income before extra.	42,200	13,800	53,600	37,300	36,100
Cash Flow	225,300	165,800	204,000	187,100	196,200
Debt/Equity	0.50	0.72	0.73	0.69	0.84
Return on Capital (%)	6.13	4.65	9.73	8.63	7.65
Ret. on Com. Equity (%)	4.47	1.00	6.15	4.30	5.28
% Change Profit	205.8	(74.3)	43.7	3.3	(40.3)
% Change Revenue	9.8	(8.1)	10.6	6.1	2.1
% Change Assets	(6.3)	(0.9)	3.9	3.7	3.9

Date	EPS	DPS	Tot Rev	Inc Bex
Mar 93	0.13	0.00	129,900	10,600
Dec 92	0.05	0.00	153,200	4,900
Sep 92	0.18	0.00	135,500	14,000
Jun 92	0.22	0.35	147,800	16,500
Mar 92	0.08	0.00	131,000	6,800
Dec 91	0.03	0.00	134,400	3,300
Sep 91	0.03	0.00	117,700	3,800
Jun 91	0.00	0.33	131,400	1,300

Preferred Div. Coverage	7.3	2.4	9.2
Total Div. Coverage	1.4	0.5	1.9
Interest Coverage	2.5	1.3	2.4
Current Ratio	1.2	1.1	1.1
Operating Margin	20.8	14.7	21.8
Asset Turnover	0.3	0.3	0.3
5 YEAR RATIOS (%)			
Return on Capital	7.4	8.6	10.0
Return on Com. Equity	4.2	5.6	6.9
Profit Growth	(7.0)	(22.0)	(7.9)
Revenue Growth	3.8	1.8	0.1
Asset Growth	0.7	1.2	0.7
BALANCE SHEET (000)			
Cash	16,600	18,600	29,800
Current Assets	123,100	123,800	151,500
Net Fixed Assets	1,576,900	1,687,300	1,704,200
Invest's & Advances	194,200	231,600	209,800
Total Assets	1,932,900	2,063,100	2,082,200
Short Term Debt	2,900	16,300	40,800
Current Liabilities	104,900	110,200	142,500
Long Term Debt	449,600	609,600	595,900
Total Liabilities	1,025,800	1,189,600	1,210,000
Total Equity	907,100	873,500	872,200
Total Liab. & Equity	1,932,900	2,063,100	2,082,200
CAPITAL (000)			
Total Debt	452,500	625,900	636,700
Preferred Equity	75,000	75,000	75,000
Common Equity	832,100	798,500	797,200

Business:

ALBERTA ENERGY CO. LTD. participates in Canada's natural gas, oil, pipelines, forest products and petrochemicals industries. AEC is among the top ten oil and gas companies in Canada in terms of reserves, production levels and exploratory landholdings, as well as Alberta's largest intraprovincial transporter of oil.

Synopsis:

Alberta Energy Company has begun development of the Caribou Lake project in northeastern Alberta due to increased gas demand in North America, impending California and Pacific Northwest markets, and its continued focus on the natural gas business. The project, which will have a capacity of 55 million cubic feet per day, should be onstream in late 1993. In addition, Alberta Energy (AEC), will spend $40-million to increase its underground storage at Suffield, Alberta, to 500 million cubic feet, by early 1994. AEC began narrowing its focus by disposing of some of its non-core assets in 1992. Interests in a contract drilling company and a coal venture were sold, and its interest in Chieftain International was reduced to 22%. The company recently announced its plans to spin off a fertilizer venture in which it has a 25% stake. It will realize about $30-million from the sale and hold a 10% stake in the new company.

Net earnings and cash flow for the first quarter of 1993 jumped 60% and 20% over 1992, respectively, despite reduced output from Syncrude, a synthetic oil producer. Factors influencing these results were higher oil and gas prices, record gas production and record prices for lumber and a $3.1-million reduction in interest expense.

The 206% jump in net earnings for 1992 was primarily due to increased activity levels in the oil, gas and forest products operations. During 1992, AEC's produced natural gas sales averaged 300 million cubic feet per day while average oil and natural gas liquids sales were 25,759 barrels per day. Pipeline revenues of $84.2-million maintained the same level as in 1991 and are not expected increase in 1993.

Revenues net of royalties by operation in 1992 were: oil and gas 33%; Syncrude 28%; pipelines 15%; forest products 14%; and other 10%. AEC's 1992 asset base by product was: natural gas 53%; Syncrude, 16%; pipelines, 13%; conventional oil, 3%; and other, 15%.

Rank (Profit/Revenue/Assets)
69   145   95

David E. Mitchell
President & C.E.O.
John D. Watson
V.P., Finance & C.F.O.

Address
Suite 2400
639 - 5th Avenue S.W.
Calgary
AB
T2P 0M9
(403) 266-8111

Fax: (403) 266-8154
A0001293/G/3.2

ANDERSON EXPLORATION LTD.

Exchanges	Price (Jun24'93)		27.25	Trailing P/E		77.86	Stock Symbol
T	Trailing Yield (%)		0.00	Trailing EPS		0.35	**AXL**

Period Ending	Sep92	Sep91	Sep90	Sep89	Sep88
Yearly Statistics					
Price-Close	12.88	11.25	18.38	17.25	11.38
Price-High	13.25	17.88	20.00	18.00	12.00
Price-Low	7.00	10.50	16.50	10.38	10.50
P/E-Close	80.47	38.79	25.52	28.28	27.74
Dividends per Share	0.00	0.00	0.00	0.00	0.00
Dividend Yield (%)	0.00	0.00	0.00	0.00	0.00
Sales per Share	4.75	4.59	4.54	3.66	3.60
EPS before extra. item	0.16	0.29	0.72	0.61	0.41
Cash Flow per Share	1.93	1.77	2.09	1.71	1.57
Book Value per Share	9.48	9.33	9.96	7.22	6.61
O/S Common Shares	20,705	20,564	18,333	18,137	18,117
Total Revenue	95,599	94,377	88,837	70,064	64,872
Income before extra.	3,208	5,971	13,209	10,988	7,309
Cash Flow	38,661	36,264	38,188	31,023	27,977
Debt/Equity	0.78	0.38	0.41	0.61	0.73
Return on Capital (%)	6.13	10.08	15.35	14.24	12.86
Ret. on Com. Equity (%)	1.65	3.19	8.42	8.77	6.42
% Change Profit	(46.3)	(54.8)	20.2	50.3	16.8
% Change Revenue	1.3	6.2	26.8	8.0	6.1
% Change Assets	20.6	0.7	17.6	4.4	4.6

Business:

ANDERSON EXPLORATION LTD. is an oil and gas exploration and production company with emphasis placed on natural gas. It has producing wells and exploration activities in Alberta. Company chairman, J.C. Anderson, owns 17.2% of the company's shares.

Date	EPS	DPS	Tot Rev	Inc Bex
Mar 93	0.12	0.00	35,993	2,495
Dec 92	0.13	0.00	30,961	2,630
Sep 92	0.14	0.00	27,425	2,721
Jun 92	(0.04)	0.00	25,152	(865)
Mar 92	0.03	0.00	22,655	597
Dec 91	0.04	0.00	20,367	755
Sep 91	(0.03)	0.00	15,472	(656)
Jun 91	0.02	0.00	18,360	612

Preferred Div. Coverage	np	np	np	
Total Div. Coverage	na	na	na	
Interest Coverage	1.7	3.0	3.2	
Current Ratio	1.2	1.1	1.2	
Operating Margin	19.4	27.5	36.1	
Asset Turnover	0.2	0.2	0.2	
5 YEAR RATIOS (%)				
Return on Capital	11.7	12.9	na	
Return on Com. Equity	5.7	6.6	na	
Profit Growth	(12.6)	15.4	na	
Revenue Growth	9.3	9.0	na	
Asset Growth	9.2	5.2	na	
BALANCE SHEET (000)				
Cash	0	8,762	10,828	
Current Assets	13,558	18,384	24,944	
Net Fixed Assets	439,777	357,500	348,177	
Invest's & Advances	0	0	0	
Total Assets	453,335	375,884	373,121	
Short Term Debt	205	0	0	
Current Liabilities	11,237	16,495	21,523	
Long Term Debt	153,000	73,000	75,000	
Total Liabilities	257,069	184,102	190,449	
Total Equity	196,266	191,782	182,672	
Total Liab. & Equity	453,335	375,884	373,121	
CAPITAL (000)				
Total Debt	153,205	73,000	75,000	
Preferred Equity	0	0	0	
Common Equity	196,266	191,782	182,672	

Synopsis:

While Anderson is pursuing several oil projects, it is currently focusing on natural gas development projects which will increase gas deliverability. These projects are associated with existing and acquired properties in the company's traditional areas of operation, on the Peace River Arch of Alberta and in east-central Alberta. Anderson expects relatively higher volumes of gas production for the remainder of the year, due in part to these projects which have the potential to increase production by approximately 40 million cubic feet per day.

According to Anderson Exploration, market conditions are in place for a turnaround in the gas business. The company expects the U.S. to face a serious deliverability shortfall caused by declining reserves and productive capacity in the U.S.and increased consumption. Mexico, which is capable of gas self-sufficiency, is now importing gas from the U.S. This creates additional pressure on U.S. supply, which can be made up by Canadian gas. Anderson has positioned itself to meet the increased energy needs and to profit from these exploits.

1992 was highlighted by the purchase and integration of Columbia Gas Development of Canada Ltd. into Anderson's operations. Gas properties from the Columbia acquisition contributed 40 million cubic feet per day for the fiscal quarter ending March 1993, versus 27 million cubic feet per day in the comparable quarter in 1992, the first quarter after the acquisition.

During fiscal 1992 (1991), Anderson's average daily production consisted of 5,748 (5,428) barrels of oil and natural gas liquids, and 111 (77) million cubic feet of natural gas. At its September 1992 (1991) year-end, Anderson had 25.4 (22.3) million barrels of proven and probable oil and natural gas liquid reserves, and 1,033 (907) billion cubic feet of proven and probable natural gas reserves.

Anderson's revenues by resource in 1992 (1991) were: gas, 60% (50%); and oil and natural gas liquids, 40% (50%).

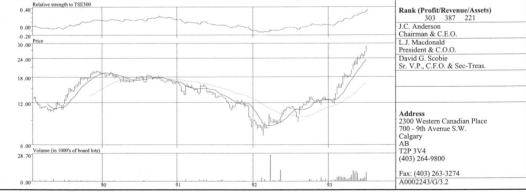

Rank (Profit/Revenue/Assets)
303   387   221

J.C. Anderson
Chairman & C.E.O.

L.J. Macdonald
President & C.O.O.

David G. Scobie
Sr. V.P., C.F.O. & Sec-Treas.

Address
2300 Western Canadian Place
700 - 9th Avenue S.W.
Calgary
AB
T2P 3V4
(403) 264-9800

Fax: (403) 263-3274
A0002243/G/3.2

BOW VALLEY ENERGY INC.

Exchanges	Price (Jun24'93)	14.62	Trailing P/E	60.94	Stock Symbol
TMA	Trailing Yield (%)	0.00	Trailing EPS	0.24	**BVI**

Period Ending	Dec92	Dec91	Dec90	Dec89	Dec88
Yearly Statistics					
Price-Close	9.50	13.75	14.50	14.13	12.75
Price-High	11.63	15.38	16.25	16.25	16.00
Price-Low	8.63	12.63	12.50	12.00	11.63
P/E-Close	45.24	nm	30.85	83.09	nm
Dividends per Share	0.00	0.00	0.00	0.12	0.23
Dividend Yield (%)	0.00	0.00	0.00	0.81	1.80
Sales per Share	5.14	5.95	8.20	6.63	6.91
EPS before extra. item	0.21	(3.31)	0.47	0.17	(0.22)
Cash Flow per Share	2.34	2.80	4.28	3.58	3.22
Book Value per Share	3.05	3.50	8.32	6.34	7.14
O/S Common Shares	54,017	53,940	51,090	50,826	50,316
Total Revenue	305,800	341,600	442,700	364,200	346,800
Income before extra.	29,700	(258,700)	49,700	25,700	10,300
Cash Flow	126,400	147,400	218,100	182,300	148,800
Debt/Equity	0.24	0.21	0.12	0.09	0.11
Return on Capital (%)	5.27	(18.85)	10.77	7.44	5.57
Ret. on Com. Equity (%)	9.96	(87.95)	10.12	2.94	(3.02)
% Change Profit	111.5	(620.5)	93.4	149.5	(73.5)
% Change Revenue	(10.5)	(22.8)	21.6	5.0	1.0
% Change Assets	3.6	(13.7)	15.8	(2.5)	35.6

Date	EPS	DPS	Tot Rev	Inc Bex
Mar 93	0.04	0.00	73,400	6,400
Dec 92	0.22	0.00	91,900	21,800
Sep 92	(0.02)	0.00	68,900	1,300
Jun 92	0.00	0.00	70,900	2,800
Mar 92	0.01	0.00	74,300	3,800
Dec 91	(3.31)	0.00	73,700	(267,000)
Sep 91	(0.02)	0.00	75,100	1,100
Jun 91	0.01	0.00	86,100	3,800

Preferred Div. Coverage	2.5	0.0	4.2
Total Div. Coverage	2.5	0.0	4.2
Interest Coverage	3.8	0.0	8.1
Current Ratio	1.6	2.3	2.7
Operating Margin	13.8	(70.7)	24.8
Asset Turnover	0.2	0.2	0.3
5 YEAR RATIOS (%)			
Return on Capital	2.0	3.1	4.7
Return on Com. Equity	(13.6)	(14.2)	(5.8)
Profit Growth	(5.3)	na	11.1
Revenue Growth	(2.3)	(5.3)	(4.0)
Asset Growth	6.5	7.7	2.5
BALANCE SHEET (000)			
Cash	100,600	176,000	181,600
Current Assets	192,300	244,100	255,700
Net Fixed Assets	1,150,300	1,051,800	1,245,700
Invest's & Advances	0	0	0
Total Assets	1,342,600	1,295,900	1,501,400
Short Term Debt	19,900	18,300	18,300
Current Liabilities	120,600	107,200	94,200
Long Term Debt	184,600	149,100	107,900
Total Liabilities	502,800	478,200	407,900
Total Equity	839,800	817,700	1,093,500
Total Liab. & Equity	1,342,600	1,295,900	1,501,400
CAPITAL (000)			
Total Debt	204,500	167,400	126,200
Preferred Equity	675,100	628,800	668,400
Common Equity	164,700	188,900	425,100

Business:

BOW VALLEY ENERGY INC. is an international natural resource company. It is engaged in the exploration, production and marketing of oil and natural gas. It operates primarily in Canada, the United Kingdom, and Indonesia. British Gas (Canada) Ltd. owns 33% of the company's outstanding voting shares.

Synopsis:

Bow Valley's focus for 1993 will be in international exploration and production. The company is relying on increased production, mainly from existing properties, to power growth. New projects in Indonesia and East Brae, in the North Sea, are expected to increase oil production to more than 40,000 barrels per day in 1994. The new East Brae field is scheduled to start producing in December 1993, with an initial rate of 11,700 barrels daily while the project in Indonesia will contribute 5,700 barrels daily. Gas production is expected to reach 200 million cubic feet per day in 1994 as a result of North Sea production at Brae and in the Netherlands. The company expects that these production increases should result in a near doubling of oil production, funds and net income generated in 1994 over 1993.

Capital expenditures for planned projects in 1993 will total over $255-million. $200-million will be allocated to development activities and the balance to exploration. Spending obligations will drop to $150-million in 1994 as projects are completed.

To provide for long-term growth, Bow Valley is planning to add a fifth international project to its properties. Areas under consideration include South America, Asia and North Africa. The company's acquisition of Great West Energy Ltd., in November 1992, represents a downstream extension for its sales into core markets in both Canada and the U.S.

During 1992 (1991) Bow Valley's average daily production by resource was: oil, 24,838 (29,411) barrels; and natural gas, 160.2 (166.1) million cubic feet. At the end of 1992 (1991), Bow Valley had gross proven and probable oil reserves totaling 149.3 (161.6) million barrels and 1,453 (1,518) billion cubic feet of natural gas reserves. During 1992, (1991), Bow Valley's contributions to operating revenue by geographic market were: the U.K., 39% (43%); Canada, 38% (37%); Indonesia, 22% (19%); and other international markets, 2% (1%).

Relative strength to TSE300 / Price / Volume (in 1000's of board lots) chart, 1990–1993

Rank (Profit/Revenue/Assets)
96   222   123

Frederick Huycke
Chairman
Robert G. Welty
President & C.E.O.
Gordon A. Milne
Senior V.P. & C.F.O.
J. Lindsay Milne
Sr. V.P., Oil & Gas Ops.

Address
1800, 321 - 6th Avenue S.W.
P.O. Box 6610
Station D
Calgary
AB
T2P 3R2
(403) 261-6100
Fax: (403) 261-6105
B0002899/G/3.2

CABRE EXPLORATION LTD.

Exchanges	Price (Jun24'93)	18.00	Trailing P/E	32.14	Stock Symbol
T	Trailing Yield (%)	0.00	Trailing EPS	0.56	CBE

Period Ending	Ju l92	Ju l91	Ju l90	Ju l89	Ju l88
Yearly Statistics					
Price-Close	11.25	8.25	8.13	4.40	3.75
Price-High	11.25	9.13	8.63	4.60	7.38
Price-Low	8.25	7.13	4.05	2.50	3.45
P/E-Close	37.50	27.50	23.90	31.43	37.50
Dividends per Share	0.00	0.00	0.00	0.00	0.00
Dividend Yield (%)	0.00	0.00	0.00	0.00	0.00
Sales per Share	1.88	1.60	1.27	1.32	1.02
EPS before extra. item	0.30	0.30	0.34	0.14	0.10
Cash Flow per Share	1.24	1.22	1.02	0.89	0.72
Book Value per Share	5.39	4.79	3.88	3.01	2.86
O/S Common Shares	14,159	12,843	9,856	5,897	5,889
Total Revenue	26,811	21,485	11,748	7,784	5,674
Income before extra.	3,912	3,723	3,004	1,067	770
Cash Flow	16,777	15,189	8,642	5,273	3,871
Debt/Equity	0.20	nd	nd	0.04	0.12
Return on Capital (%)	7.93	12.66	14.87	8.07	5.85
Ret. on Com. Equity (%)	5.67	7.46	10.34	4.89	3.51
% Change Profit	5.1	23.9	181.5	38.6	(32.3)
% Change Revenue	24.8	82.9	50.9	37.2	27.8
% Change Assets	48.8	60.3	68.9	2.1	17.2

Preferred Div. Coverage	na	np	np	
Total Div. Coverage	na	na	27.3	
Interest Coverage	5.1	97.2	27.9	
Current Ratio	0.8	2.8	4.3	
Operating Margin	22.7	29.4	38.0	
Asset Turnover	0.2	0.3	0.2	
5 YEAR RATIOS (%)				
Return on Capital	9.9	11.0	10.1	
Return on Com. Equity	6.4	7.1	6.4	
Profit Growth	28.0	54.6	30.2	
Revenue Growth	43.2	48.6	27.5	
Asset Growth	36.9	33.7	22.8	
BALANCE SHEET (000)				
Cash	721	9,783	9,964	
Current Assets	8,725	14,487	13,551	
Net Fixed Assets	97,763	60,760	33,302	
Invest's & Advances	5,400	0	0	
Total Assets	112,057	75,326	46,998	
Short Term Debt	0	0	0	
Current Liabilities	10,775	5,196	3,157	
Long Term Debt	15,297	0	0	
Total Liabilities	35,690	13,781	8,721	
Total Equity	76,367	61,545	38,277	
Total Liab. & Equity	112,057	75,326	46,998	
CAPITAL (000)				
Total Debt	15,297	0	0	
Preferred Equity	6	0	0	
Common Equity	76,361	61,545	38,277	

Business:

CABRE EXPLORATION LTD. is engaged in acquiring petroleum and natural gas rights and in conducting exploration and development on those rights in Alberta, Saskatchewan and British Columbia.

Date	EPS	DPS	Tot Rev	Inc Bex
Jan 93	0.17	0.00	9,398	2,357
Oct 92	0.23	0.00	10,689	3,245
Jul 92	0.10	0.00	10,190	1,376
Apr 92	0.06	0.00	6,306	676
Jan 92	0.09	0.00	5,747	1,206
Oct 91	0.08	0.00	5,231	982
Jul 91	0.01	0.00	4,935	57
Apr 91	0.00	0.00	3,862	102

Synopsis:

Recent changes to Alberta's oil and gas royalty scheme, announced in October 1992, reduce royalties by one-third on oil discovered after September 30, 1992. In addition, a one-year royalty holiday applies to exploratory wells in this group.

Cabre, which operates primarily in Alberta, derives most of its revenues from oil and has an active drilling program. It expects to benefit from this new royalty category. Cabre continues to focus on the exploration and development of light and medium crude oil in Alberta. According to Cabre, North American markets for light and medium crude exceed production capacity and are therefore virtually assured.

At current oil and gas prices, the company anticipates record results in 1993. Management expects oil and gas production rates to increase in the second half of fiscal 1993 as a result of its recent drilling successes, proposed drilling activity and latest asset acquisition. Polaris Petroleums Ltd., which was acquired in February 1993 through a share swap, could add another 7% to daily oil output and 60% to natural gas production.

Cabre attributes the continued improvement in its financial performance to increased oil production and gas sales, which reflect in part the acquisition of the Canadian assets of Coho Resources Ltd. in 1992. Coho accounted for approximately 41% of the oil and 64% of the gas production increase in Cabre's latest six-month period ending January 1993.

During fiscal 1992, (1991), Cabre's average daily production of oil and natural gas liquids was 4,049 (2,573) barrels, and average daily production of natural gas was 13 (8.3) million cubic feet. At its 1992 (1991) fiscal year end, Cabre had proven and probable oil reserves totaling 13.1 (8) million barrels, and 94.2 (64) billion cubic feet of natural gas reserves.

Relative strength to TSE300 / Price / Volume (in 1000's of board lots) charts

Rank (Profit/Revenue/Assets)
285   576   398

Harry B. Wheeler
President & C.E.O.

J. Douglas Kay
Executive Vice President

Address
Suite 1400
700 - 9th Avenue S.W.
Calgary
AB
T2P 3V4
(403) 231-8800

Fax: (403) 263-4865
C0024445/G/3.2

For further company information, call Globe Information Services 1-800-268-9128 or (416)585-5345

CANADA SOUTHERN PETROLEUM LTD.

Exchanges	Price (Jun24'93)	5.50	Trailing P/E	nm	Stock Symbol
T	Trailing Yield (%)	0.00	Trailing EPS	(0.08)	**CSW**

Period Ending	Jun92	Jun91	Jun90	Jun89	Jun88
Yearly Statistics					
Price-Close	3.50	2.65	2.20	3.15	7.00
Price-High	5.38	4.00	3.65	7.50	9.50
Price-Low	2.31	2.05	2.15	3.05	1.80
P/E-Close	nm	88.33	nm	nm	nm
Dividends per Share	0.00	0.00	0.00	0.00	0.00
Dividend Yield (%)	0.00	0.00	0.00	0.00	0.00
Sales per Share	0.10	0.13	0.13	0.12	0.14
EPS before extra. item	(0.12)	0.03	(0.07)	(0.10)	(0.01)
Cash Flow per Share	(0.04)	0.06	(0.01)	(0.04)	0.02
Book Value per Share	1.15	1.27	1.22	1.25	1.35
O/S Common Shares	12,346	12,346	12,272	11,990	11,990
Total Revenue	1,894	3,146	2,214	2,036	2,283
Income before extra.	(1,431)	426	(821)	(1,181)	(129)
Cash Flow	(542)	791	(128)	(526)	182
Debt/Equity	nd	nd	nd	nd	nd
Return on Capital (%)	(9.59)	2.78	(5.47)	(7.57)	(0.18)
Ret. on Com. Equity (%)	(9.59)	2.78	(5.47)	(7.57)	(0.91)
% Change Profit	(436.0)	151.9	30.5	(813.3)	(3,018.7)
% Change Revenue	(39.8)	42.1	8.7	(10.8)	10.2
% Change Assets	(9.3)	3.2	1.3	(6.2)	28.9

Date	EPS	DPS	Tot Rev	Inc Bex
Mar 93	(0.01)	0.00	644	(105)
Dec 92	(0.01)	0.00	705	(160)
Sep 92	(0.00)	0.00	492	(29)
Jun 92	(0.06)	0.00	444	(665)
Mar 92	(0.02)	0.00	496	(206)
Dec 91	(0.02)	0.00	516	(259)
Sep 91	(0.02)	0.00	407	(301)
Jun 91	0.01	0.00	753	64

	Jun92	Jun91	Jun90
Preferred Div. Coverage	np	np	np
Total Div. Coverage	na	na	na
Interest Coverage	nd	nd	nd
Current Ratio	13.2	11.9	9.2
Operating Margin	(115.1)	(0.2)	(70.9)
Asset Turnover	0.1	0.1	0.1
5 YEAR RATIOS (%)			
Return on Capital	(4.0)	(1.9)	(1.4)
Return on Com. Equity	(4.2)	(2.2)	(2.4)
Profit Growth	na	13.2	na
Revenue Growth	(1.8)	2.9	(4.9)
Asset Growth	2.8	4.8	5.3
BALANCE SHEET (000)			
Cash	3,569	4,626	4,632
Current Assets	4,247	5,306	5,215
Net Fixed Assets	9,020	9,368	9,234
Invest's & Advances	1,326	1,412	1,132
Total Assets	14,593	16,086	15,581
Short Term Debt	0	0	0
Current Liabilities	322	446	566
Long Term Debt	0	0	0
Total Liabilities	385	446	566
Total Equity	14,208	15,639	15,015
Total Liab. & Equity	14,593	16,086	15,581
CAPITAL (000)			
Total Debt	0	0	0
Preferred Equity	0	0	0
Common Equity	14,208	15,639	15,015

Business:

CANADA SOUTHERN PETROLEUM LTD. is a petroleum exploration and production company. The company has producing oil and gas wells in northeastern British Columbia. It has other properties in the Yukon, the Arctic Islands, Alberta and the Northern Territory, Australia.

Synopsis:

Canada Southern Petroleum reported that the 47% increase in operating revenue for the third quarter ending March 1993 was due to the increase in proceeds from carried-interest properties in British Columbia. This increase in revenue was not sufficient to offset the 59% increase in depletion and depreciation, lower interest income, a foreign exchange loss, and a mandatory provision for site restoration costs.

The company's June 1992 year-end loss is attributable principally to a 42% reduction in operating revenues, which in turn was caused by a drop in proceeds from carried-interest properties and lower oil prices. The reduced carried-interest income was the consequence of capital improvements to these properties, which were funded directly out of operating revenue.

Canada Southern continued to evaluate and acquire new oil and gas prospects on Crown Lands in B.C. and Alberta. Additional seismic work was completed on these prospects and more is planned for 1993.

During 1992, the company recorded write-downs totaling $365,000 relating to oil and gas properties in Australia and mineral properties in Canada, based on the current potential of those interests. The company also reported a $233,000 increase in other costs and expenditures, due in part to the expense of the ongoing litigation involving the Kotaneelee gas field.

After a one-year delay, Canada Southern's lawsuit against its working-interest partners of the Kotaneelee gas field in the Yukon is proceeding. The suit, filed in 1990, is seeking the surrender of the partners' interests in the field as well as compensation for the loss of income by Canada Southern as a result of the delay in marketing the gas. The Kotaneelee gas field, which had been shut-in since 1980, began production in February 1991. As at June 1992, (1991) Canada Southern had proven oil reserves of 532,000 (550,695) barrels and natural gas reserves of 33.75 (45.16) billion cubic feet.

Rank (Profit/Revenue/Assets)
721   863   774

Charles J. Horne
President

Address
Suite 1410
One Palliser Square
125 - 9th Avenue S.E.
Calgary
AB
T2G 0P6
(403) 269-7741
Fax: (403) 261-5667
C0002192/G/3.2

CANADIAN NATURAL RESOURCES LIMITED

Exchanges	Price (Jun24'93)	19.50	Trailing P/E	52.70	Stock Symbol
T	Trailing Yield (%)	0.00	Trailing EPS	0.37	**CNQ**

Period Ending	Dec92	Dec91	Dec90	Dec89	Dec88
Yearly Statistics					
Price-Close	7.38	3.84	1.80	0.95	0.09
Price-High	7.50	4.38	2.20	0.98	0.13
Price-Low	3.63	1.63	0.95	0.09	0.05
P/E-Close	27.32	20.20	13.33	19.00	17.50
Dividends per Share	0.00	0.00	0.00	0.00	0.00
Dividend Yield (%)	0.00	0.00	0.00	0.00	0.00
Sales per Share	1.50	0.94	0.56	0.18	0.13
EPS before extra. item	0.27	0.19	0.14	0.05	0.01
Cash Flow per Share	0.81	0.50	0.30	0.10	0.05
Book Value per Share	1.50	0.92	0.48	0.18	(0.02)
O/S Common Shares	54,442	49,044	41,886	34,958	25,006
Total Revenue	77,197	40,321	21,064	6,279	3,033
Income before extra.	13,923	8,030	5,019	1,708	195
Cash Flow	41,776	21,324	11,023	3,257	1,148
Debt/Equity	0.74	0.79	0.74	0.45	1.96
Return on Capital (%)	25.46	24.90	38.68	36.43	18.41
Ret. on Com. Equity (%)	21.98	24.58	37.98	54.18	na
% Change Profit	73.4	60.0	193.9	775.9	149.0
% Change Revenue	91.5	91.4	235.5	107.0	(12.8)
% Change Assets	73.6	111.6	202.2	122.1	(13.4)

Date	EPS	DPS	Tot Rev	Inc Bex
Mar 93	0.14	0.00	31,108	7,254
Dec 92	0.10	0.00	26,907	5,713
Sep 92	0.07	0.00	20,988	3,595
Jun 92	0.06	0.00	15,848	2,655
Mar 92	0.04	0.00	13,453	1,960
Dec 91	0.06	0.00	14,652	2,482
Sep 91	0.04	0.00	9,545	1,523
Jun 91	0.05	0.00	7,811	1,966

Preferred Div. Coverage	np	np	np
Total Div. Coverage	na	na	na
Interest Coverage	7.4	5.7	6.0
Current Ratio	0.8	1.0	0.8
Operating Margin	36.6	35.4	39.9
Asset Turnover	0.4	0.4	0.4
5 YEAR RATIOS (%)			
Return on Capital	28.8	27.0	23.5
Return on Com. Equity	na	na	na
Profit Growth	181.8	192.2	121.5
Revenue Growth	85.9	61.5	35.5
Asset Growth	84.4	52.0	28.8
BALANCE SHEET (000)			
Cash	9	40	51
Current Assets	9,338	7,883	4,458
Net Fixed Assets	163,848	91,881	42,695
Invest's & Advances	0	0	0
Total Assets	173,186	99,763	47,153
Short Term Debt	0	0	0
Current Liabilities	11,317	8,242	5,633
Long Term Debt	60,478	35,561	14,938
Total Liabilities	91,735	54,540	27,023
Total Equity	81,451	45,224	20,130
Total Liab. & Equity	173,186	99,763	47,153
CAPITAL (000)			
Total Debt	60,478	35,561	14,938
Preferred Equity	0	0	0
Common Equity	81,451	45,224	20,130

Business:

CANADIAN NATURAL RESOURCES LIMITED is engaged in the exploration for, and development and production of oil and gas. The company has land holdings in Alberta and British Columbia.

Synopsis:

Canadian Natural Resources continues to focus its efforts on expanding its productive asset base where the majority of the company's activities are carried out - northeastern B.C. and northwestern Alberta. A capital expenditure program of $74- $85-million is slated for the company's ongoing property acquisition and exploration and development programs, which includes the drilling of up to 120 wells. These expenditures are to be funded through a combination of cash flow, available bank financing and the issuing of common share equity, such as the issue completed recently.

Canadian Natural completed the sale of two million common shares at $27.50 per share for gross proceeds of $55-million in May 1993. The proceeds will initially be applied to reduce outstanding bank indebtedness.

Drilling activity together with its property acquisition program to date have added proven and probable reserves in excess of 152 billion cubic feet of natural gas and 8.5 million barrels of oil and natural gas liquids (NGL) to the company's reserve base. Current production volumes from these reserves are approximately 155 million cubic feet of natural gas per day and 7,500 barrels of oil and NGL per day.

During fiscal 1992 (1991), Canadian Natural's average gross daily production of natural gas was 93.5 (57.3) million cubic feet per day, and average gross daily production of oil and NGL was 4,184 (1,681) barrels per day. At its 1992 (1991) fiscal year-end, the company had 358 (210) billion cubic feet of natural gas reserves and 18.7 (9.3) million barrels of proven and probable oil reserves.

Contributions to revenue by commodity in 1992 (1991) were: natural gas, 59% (67%); and oil and natural gas liquids, 41% (33%).

Relative strength to TSE300 / Price / Volume (in 1000's of board lots)

Rank (Profit/Revenue/Assets)
151   412   337

Allan P. Markin
Chairman

John G. Langille
President

Keith A. J. Macphail
Vice President, Operations

Address
Suite 1710
300 - 5th Avenue S.W.
Calgary
AB
T2P 3C4
(403) 221-2100

Fax: (403) 233-8941
C0003899/G/3.2

For further company information, call Globe Information Services 1-800-268-9128 or (416)585-5345

CANADIAN OCCIDENTAL PETROLEUM LTD.

Exchanges	Price (Jun24'93)		29 .00	Trailing P/E		107.41	Stock Symbol
TMA	Trailing Yield (%)		1.38	Trailing EPS		0.27	**CXY**

Period Ending	Dec92	Dec91	Dec90	Dec89	Dec88
Yearly Statistics					
Price-Close	25 .13	27 .13	14 .50	20 .38	16 .25
Price-High	30 .25	27 .75	20 .25	22 .25	20 .75
Price-Low	23 .88	13 .50	13 .38	16 .00	15 .25
P/E-Close	96 .64	77 .50	30 .85	35 .13	28 .02
Dividends per Share	0 .40	0 .40	0 .40	0 .40	0 .40
Dividend Yield (%)	1 .59	1 .48	2 .76	1 .96	2 .46
Sales per Share	7 .78	8 .42	8 .80	8 .23	8 .32
EPS before extra. item	0 .26	0 .35	0 .47	0 .58	0 .58
Cash Flow per Share	2 .02	2 .42	3 .24	2 .99	2 .78
Book Value per Share	10 .46	10 .43	10 .54	10 .25	10 .35
O/S Common Shares	66 ,933	66 ,696	66 ,628	66 ,849	66 ,818
Total Revenue	563 ,800	593 ,176	651 ,669	591 ,191	739 ,681
Income before extra.	17 ,267	23 ,101	31 ,573	38 ,732	38 ,949
Cash Flow	135 ,049	161 ,330	216 ,258	200 ,125	185 ,536
Debt/Equity	1 .29	0 .61	0 .42	0 .43	0 .31
Return on Capital (%)	3 .42	4 .37	7 .93	9 .64	11 .29
Ret. on Com. Equity (%)	2 .47	3 .30	4 .55	5 .63	5 .65
% Change Profit	(25 .3)	(26 .8)	(18 .5)	(0 .6)	(32 .8)
% Change Revenue	(5 .0)	(9 .0)	10 .2	(20 .1)	23 .5
% Change Assets	34 .3	5 .1	3 .3	3 .4	(8 .3)

Preferred Div. Coverage	np	np	np
Total Div. Coverage	0 .6	0 .9	1 .2
Interest Coverage	1 .1	1 .9	2 .1
Current Ratio	1 .8	1 .4	1 .2
Operating Margin	0 .5	2 .5	2 .4
Asset Turnover	0 .3	0 .4	0 .4
5 YEAR RATIOS (%)			
Return on Capital	7 .3	8 .9	10 .1
Return on Com. Equity	4 .3	5 .5	6 .1
Profit Growth	(21 .6)	(10 .8)	(22 .9)
Revenue Growth	(1 .2)	2 .0	(0 .5)
Asset Growth	6 .7	2 .3	2 .4
BALANCE SHEET (000)			
Cash	285 ,045	47 ,809	21 ,921
Current Assets	453 ,313	222 ,492	193 ,715
Net Fixed Assets	1 ,530 ,812	1 ,272 ,498	1 ,226 ,164
Invest's & Advances	0	0	0
Total Assets	2 ,045 ,065	1 ,522 ,766	1 ,448 ,998
Short Term Debt	79 ,476	37 ,486	24 ,412
Current Liabilities	248 ,740	157 ,713	157 ,142
Long Term Debt	819 ,612	383 ,508	270 ,683
Total Liabilities	1 ,345 ,115	826 ,999	746 ,456
Total Equity	699 ,950	695 ,767	702 ,542
Total Liab. & Equity	2 ,045 ,065	1 ,522 ,766	1 ,448 ,998
CAPITAL (000)			
Total Debt	899 ,088	420 ,994	295 ,095
Preferred Equity	0	0	0
Common Equity	699 ,950	695 ,767	702 ,542

Business:

CANADIAN OCCIDENTAL PETROLUEM LTD. is an energy and chemicals company. It has oil and gas and sulphur operations in North America, South America, the North Sea and the Middle East, and oil sands interests in Alberta. The company also supplies bleaching agents to the pulp and paper industry and thermoset plastics and polyvinyl chloride film to markets in North America.

Date	EPS	DPS	Tot Rev	Inc Bex
Mar 93	0 .03	0 .10	135 ,208	1 ,983
Dec 92	0 .11	0 .10	164 ,900	7 ,347
Sep 92	0 .12	0 .10	128 ,444	7 ,660
Jun 92	0 .01	0 .10	125 ,504	1 ,136
Mar 92	0 .02	0 .10	144 ,952	1 ,124
Dec 91	0 .11	0 .10	158 ,835	6 ,830
Sep 91	0 .11	0 .10	137 ,221	7 ,415
Jun 91	0 .01	0 .10	134 ,856	881

Synopsis:

Continued growth in reserves and production is a priority for Canadian Occidental Petroleum Ltd. (CanOxy). Substantial portions of the Yemen and Ecuador contract areas remain to be explored while high potential areas in Pakistan and Romania await drilling. International oil and gas projects, which are slated for start-up in 1993, are expected to triple the company's daily oil production to approximately 100,000 barrels per day. These same projects are to stabilize natural gas production at approximately 200 million cubic feet per day by the end of 1993.

The 1993 capital program, anticipated to be worth about $500-million, is expected to be financed from cash flow from operations and arranged long-term lines of credit. The main focus on capital spending during 1993 will be on the completion of projects in the Republic of Yemen, the North Sea and Ecuador. Additional costs will be incurred in the development of the Eugene Island area of the U.S. Gulf Coast and in exploration activities currently planned in the Republic of Yemen, Pakistan, Romania and Indonesia.

CanOxy expects crude oil prices to remain near current levels until renewed oil demand growth is achieved. Natural gas prices in Canada, low throughout much of 1992, have begun to rebound due to greater access to U.S. markets and below normal temperatures in much of North America.

During fiscal 1992 (1991), CanOxy's average gross daily production by resource was: natural gas, 195.1 (200.3) million cubic feet; oil and gas liquids, 22,100 (21,200) barrels; and 12,900 (11,900) barrels of synthetic oil. At its 1992 (1991) fiscal year-end, the company's total proven and probable reserves by resource were: 930.8 (980.1) billion cubic feet of natural gas; 319.4 (214.3) million barrels of oil and gas liquids; and 133.7 (134.8) million barrels of synthetic oil.

1992 sales contributions by operation were: oil and gas, 52%; alternative fuels, 21%; and chemicals, 27%.

Relative strength to TSE300 / Price / Volume (in 1000's of board lots) chart 1990–1993

Rank (Profit/Revenue/Assets)
133   146   93

Dr. Ray R. Irani
Chairman Of The Board

Victor J. Zaleschuk
Sr. V.P., Finance & C.F.O.

Jim Taylor
Executive V.P. & C.O.O.

Address
Suite 1500
635 - 8th Avenue S.W.
Calgary
AB
T2P 3Z1
(403) 234-6700

Fax: (403) 263-8673
C0003900/G/3.2

CANADIAN ROXY PETROLEUM LTD.

Exchanges	Price (Jun24'93)	4.50	Trailing P/E	nm	Stock Symbol
TZ	Trailing Yield (%)	0.00	Trailing EPS	(0.08)	**CNR**

Period Ending	Dec92	Dec91	Dec90	Dec89	Dec88
Yearly Statistics					
Price-Close	5.00	6.50	7.13	7.00	7.00
Price-High	7.50	7.13	7.75	7.63	9.25
Price-Low	4.75	4.90	5.75	6.38	6.38
P/E-Close	nm	nm	101.79	350.00	nm
Dividends per Share	0.00	0.00	0.00	0.00	0.00
Dividend Yield (%)	0.00	0.00	0.00	0.00	0.00
Sales per Share	1.55	1.65	1.93	1.69	1.46
EPS before extra. item	(0.11)	(2.65)	0.07	0.02	(0.07)
Cash Flow per Share	0.76	0.85	1.15	0.98	0.73
Book Value per Share	6.70	6.81	9.46	9.49	9.47
O/S Common Shares	14,136	14,136	14,136	14,136	14,136
Total Revenue	22,302	23,767	27,706	24,599	21,279
Income before extra.	(1,485)	(37,431)	1,031	247	(1,010)
Cash Flow	10,784	12,040	16,222	13,786	10,254
Debt/Equity	0.16	0.24	0.17	0.19	0.20
Return on Capital (%)	1.19	(35.88)	3.97	3.06	1.32
Ret. on Com. Equity (%)	(1.56)	(32.56)	0.77	0.18	(0.75)
% Change Profit	96.0	(3,730.6)	317.4	124.5	(161.9)
% Change Revenue	(6.2)	(14.2)	12.6	15.6	(10.3)
% Change Assets	(5.1)	(28.7)	0.7	0.5	1.8

Date	EPS	DPS	Tot Rev	Inc Bex
Mar 93	(0.02)	0.00	5,257	(314)
Dec 92	0.00	0.00	6,261	40
Sep 92	(0.03)	0.00	5,561	(436)
Jun 92	(0.03)	0.00	5,385	(436)
Mar 92	(0.05)	0.00	5,095	(653)
Dec 91	(2.56)	0.00	5,525	(36,193)
Sep 91	(0.05)	0.00	5,105	(670)
Jun 91	(0.01)	0.00	5,883	(468)

	Dec92	Dec91	Dec90
Preferred Div. Coverage	np	np	np
Total Div. Coverage	na	na	na
Interest Coverage	1.1	0.0	2.2
Current Ratio	0.3	0.2	0.3
Operating Margin	4.3	(207.6)	22.6
Asset Turnover	0.2	0.2	0.1
5 YEAR RATIOS (%)			
Return on Capital	(5.3)	(4.5)	3.4
Return on Com. Equity	(6.8)	(6.2)	0.4
Profit Growth	na	na	na
Revenue Growth	(1.3)	3.5	(0.5)
Asset Growth	(7.1)	(5.9)	(0.2)
BALANCE SHEET (000)			
Cash	0	37	3,282
Current Assets	6,063	4,394	9,139
Net Fixed Assets	124,271	131,998	182,841
Invest's & Advances	0	982	752
Total Assets	130,334	137,374	192,732
Short Term Debt	12,754	20,340	20,322
Current Liabilities	17,623	23,996	27,993
Long Term Debt	2,177	2,277	2,118
Total Liabilities	35,563	41,118	59,045
Total Equity	94,771	96,256	133,687
Total Liab. & Equity	130,334	137,374	192,732
CAPITAL (000)			
Total Debt	14,931	22,617	22,440
Preferred Equity	0	0	0
Common Equity	94,771	96,256	133,687

Business:

CANADIAN ROXY PETROLEUM LTD. is an oil and gas exploration company. The company's operations are focused in Western Canada. Westcoast Petroleum Ltd. owns 82.6% of the company's shares.

Synopsis:

Canadian Roxy will focus its activities on exploitation of existing core assets and lower-risk oil and natural gas exploration projects in 1993. As part of its ongoing asset rationalization program, Canadian Roxy recently sold 75% of its oil and gas producing equipment and facilities to Westcoast Petroleum Ltd., (Westcoast owns 82.6% of Canadian Roxy) for $10-million. Canadian Roxy will lease back the same assets for 10 years. In early 1993, a 10% interest in the Wabasca oil pipeline and the company's Trout and Kidney properties in Alberta were sold for approximately $5-million. The net proceeds from the divestment of non-core properties will be reinvested to acquire new properties or increase ownership in existing core areas.

The company is hopeful that the increase in natural gas prices in late 1992 reflect a narrowing of the supply and demand imbalance which has persisted since deregulation of the gas markets in 1985. Canadian Roxy expects a modest growth of natural gas prices in 1993 and an average price of $21 (U.S.) per barrel for West Texas Intermediate crude. The new Alberta royalty structure which became effective in October 1992 is expected to benefit a junior such as Canadian Roxy. There is a permanent 12-month royalty holiday for crude oil exploration wells and a reduction of about one-third in royalties for new crude oil discoveries.

The 1992 annual results reflect a decline in production levels, depressed commodity prices and a $34.9-million after tax write-down of proven reserves.

Average daily production by resource during 1992 (1991) was: oil, 2,372 (2,424) barrels; and natural gas, 16.9 (17.3) million cubic feet. At the end of 1992 (1991), gross proven and probable reserves were: oil, 12.2 (12.8) million barrels; and 82.8 (97.9) billion cubic feet of natural gas reserves. Contributions to revenue, net of royalties, in 1993 were: crude oil and natural gas liquids, 65%; natural gas, 33%; and other, 2%.

Relative strength to TSE300 / Price / Volume (in 1000's of board lots) chart

Rank (Profit/Revenue/Assets)
723   601   378

I.J. Koop
Chairman, President & C.E.O.

Stephen J. Letwin
V.P., Fin., Secty. & C.F.O.

Address
Suite 2700
Canada Trust Tower
421 - 7th Ave. S.W.
Calgary
AB
T2P 4K9
(403) 260-9400
Fax: (403) 260-9418
R0002788/G/3.2

CHAUVCO RESOURCES LTD.

Exchanges	Price (Jun24'93)	17.37	Trailing P/E	28.96	Stock Symbol
TMZ	Trailing Yield (%)	0.00	Trailing EPS	0.60	CHA

Period Ending	Dec92	Dec91	Dec90	Dec89	Dec88
Yearly Statistics					
Price-Close	12.88	11.00	8.25	5.88	2.50
Price-High	14.13	12.25	9.13	6.25	2.88
Price-Low	9.88	8.13	5.25	2.50	2.00
P/E-Close	24.29	29.33	17.74	35.61	33.33
Dividends per Share	0.00	0.00	0.00	0.00	0.00
Dividend Yield (%)	0.00	0.00	0.00	0.00	0.00
Sales per Share	3.36	2.95	2.35	0.98	0.64
EPS before extra. item	0.53	0.38	0.47	0.17	0.08
Cash Flow per Share	1.84	1.69	1.29	0.60	0.36
Book Value per Share	5.03	3.84	3.06	1.80	1.63
O/S Common Shares	43,745	39,034	36,141	26,837	26,688
Total Revenue	144,380	114,561	81,115	26,967	17,555
Income before extra.	22,614	14,402	15,715	4,450	1,910
Cash Flow	78,253	64,622	43,697	16,121	9,550
Debt/Equity	0.24	0.36	0.35	0.38	0.29
Return on Capital (%)	15.60	18.18	27.12	13.42	6.29
Ret. on Com. Equity (%)	12.23	11.05	19.78	9.72	4.56
% Change Profit	57.0	(8.4)	253.1	133.0	(50.2)
% Change Revenue	26.0	41.2	200.8	53.6	16.3
% Change Assets	29.9	36.0	100.6	19.2	21.4

Preferred Div. Coverage	np	np	np
Total Div. Coverage	na	na	na
Interest Coverage	6.8	4.7	3.4
Current Ratio	1.0	0.7	0.6
Operating Margin	24.9	27.5	36.0
Asset Turnover	0.4	0.4	0.4
5 YEAR RATIOS (%)			
Return on Capital	16.1	15.8	14.7
Return on Com. Equity	11.5	11.1	10.8
Profit Growth	42.6	49.8	76.1
Revenue Growth	57.1	60.1	83.7
Asset Growth	38.6	35.6	72.1
BALANCE SHEET (000)			
Cash	471	449	0
Current Assets	17,309	11,065	11,979
Net Fixed Assets	314,628	244,402	175,868
Invest's & Advances	115	115	115
Total Assets	332,052	255,582	187,962
Short Term Debt	1,452	0	2,248
Current Liabilities	16,678	15,747	21,014
Long Term Debt	50,303	53,427	36,506
Total Liabilities	112,094	105,655	77,268
Total Equity	219,958	149,927	110,694
Total Liab. & Equity	332,052	255,582	187,962
CAPITAL (000)			
Total Debt	51,755	53,427	38,754
Preferred Equity	0	0	0
Common Equity	219,958	149,927	110,694

Business:

CHAUVCO RESOURCES LTD. is an oil and gas exploration and production company. It has producing oil and gas wells in Alberta, Saskatchewan and British Columbia. The company has additional undeveloped properties in those three provinces and Manitoba. Chauvco recently acquired a 23.34% interest in a production concession in Argentina.

Date	EPS	DPS	Tot Rev	Inc Bex
Mar 93	0.13	0.00	36,847	5,688
Dec 92	0.15	0.00	40,657	6,843
Sep 92	0.19	0.00	38,408	7,935
Jun 92	0.13	0.00	36,229	5,489
Mar 92	0.06	0.00	29,086	2,347
Dec 91	0.03	0.00	27,142	1,042
Sep 91	0.14	0.00	30,712	5,491
Jun 91	0.12	0.00	29,585	4,578

Synopsis:

Chauvco achieved its strongest annual performance in 1992 with record levels of cash flow and earnings. A highlight was the acquisition of production and exploration properties in Argentina, which has established an international presence for Chauvco. This interest produces more than 1,900 barrels of oil a day, as well as 23.8 million cubic feet of gas. With the deregulation of the natural gas industry in Argentina, Chauvco feels that this addition will provide significant prospects for long term growth. Currently, the company is evaluating natural gas marketing options for its gas reserves.

The improvement in financial results for the first quarter 1993 was primarily due to higher natural gas prices and increased gas production volumes in Canada. The increase in volume resulted from the Woods Petroleum of Canada acquisitions in the third quarter 1992, higher takes by system aggregators and new wells tied-in in late 1992.

Further exploitation of the company's asset base in Canada and Argentina is expected to increase daily production to 20,800 barrels of oil and to 46 million cubic feet of natural gas. Production estimates are anticipated to generate cash flow of $85-million and earnings of $27-million in 1993.

The 1993 capital program of $85-million is expected to be funded from cash flow. Of this amount, committed capital expenditures account for less than $30-million.

Average gross daily production in 1992 (1991) was: crude oil and natural gas liquids 18,144 (13,832) barrels; and natural gas, 37.6 (13.6) million cubic feet. Gross proven and probable reserves in 1992 (1991) were: crude oil and natural gas liquids, 52.5 (42.8) million barrels; and natural gas, 466.6 (113.8) billion cubic feet.

Rank (Profit/Revenue/Assets)
113   319   261

Guy J. Turcotte
Chairman & C.E.O.

D. Nolan Blades
President & C.O.O.

James K. Wilson
V.P., Finance & C.F.O.

Address
Suite 2900
255 - 5th Avenue S.W.
Calgary
AB
T2P 3G6
(403) 231-3100

Fax: (403) 269-9497
C0016637/G/3.2

Globe and Mail Publishing (c) 1993

Oil & Gas - 75

CHIEFTAIN INTERNATIONAL, INC.

Exchanges	Price (Jun24'93)		25 .87	Trailing P/E		323 .44	Stock Symbol
TZA	Trailing Yield (%)		0 .00	Trailing EPS		0 .08	**CID**

Period Ending	Dec92	Dec91	Dec90	Dec89
Yearly Statistics	US	US	US	US
Price-Close	22 .00	16 .25	22 .00	23 .13
Price-High	23 .75	22 .13	28 .25	23 .13
Price-Low	14 .25	13 .25	20 .75	14 .25
P/E-Close	377 .17	nm	20 .98	184 .47
Dividends per Share	0 .00	0 .00	0 .00	0 .00
Dividend Yield (%)	0 .00	0 .00	0 .00	0 .00
Sales per Share	4 .01	3 .47	4 .62	1 .51
EPS before extra. item	0 .04	(0 .58)	0 .77	0 .09
Cash Flow per Share	2 .32	2 .21	3 .38	0 .99
Book Value per Share	13 .90	13 .40	13 .98	13 .21
O/S Common Shares	10 ,988	9 ,488	9 ,488	9 ,488
Total Revenue	40 ,592	35 ,429	46 ,972	18 ,619
Income before extra.	437	(5 ,492)	7 ,324	828
Cash Flow	22 ,601	20 ,948	32 ,073	9 ,403
Debt/Equity	nd	nd	nd	nd
Return on Capital (%)	1 .10	(6 .22)	9 .02	na
Ret. on Com. Equity (%)	0 .31	(4 .23)	5 .68	na
% Change Profit	108 .0	(175 .0)	784 .5	na
% Change Revenue	14 .6	(24 .6)	152 .3	na
% Change Assets	71 .0	(8 .8)	11 .0	na

Date		EPS	DPS	Tot Rev	Inc Bex
Mar 93	US	(0 .04)	0 .00	10 ,204	(476)
Dec 92	US	0 .07	0 .00	11 ,921	694
Sep 92	US	0 .03	0 .00	7 ,868	334
Jun 92	US	0 .02	0 .00	8 ,241	161
Mar 92	US	(0 .08)	0 .00	6 ,228	(752)
Dec 91	US	(0 .59)	0 .00	9 ,952	(5 ,615)
Sep 91	US	(0 .01)	0 .00	5 ,942	(34)
Jun 91	US	(0 .03)	0 .00	5 ,588	(357)

Preferred Div. Coverage	np	np	np	
Total Div. Coverage	na	na	na	
Interest Coverage	nd	nd	nd	
Current Ratio	22 .1	15 .8	7 .3	
Operating Margin	2 .1	(31 .3)	21 .1	
Asset Turnover	0 .2	0 .2	0 .3	
5 YEAR RATIOS (%)				
Return on Capital	na	na	na	
Return on Com. Equity	na	na	na	
Profit Growth	na	na	na	
Revenue Growth	na	na	na	
Asset Growth	na	na	na	
BALANCE SHEET (000)				
Cash	114 ,750	27 ,185	38 ,828	
Current Assets	122 ,672	33 ,770	47 ,499	
Net Fixed Assets	98 ,341	94 ,377	93 ,364	
Invest's & Advances	0	0	0	
Total Assets	225 ,050	131 ,604	144 ,380	
Short Term Debt	0	0	0	
Current Liabilities	5 ,555	2 ,134	6 ,525	
Long Term Debt	0	0	0	
Total Liabilities	72 ,308	4 ,459	11 ,743	
Total Equity	152 ,742	127 ,145	132 ,637	
Total Liab. & Equity	225 ,050	131 ,604	144 ,380	
CAPITAL (000)				
Total Debt	0	0	0	
Preferred Equity	0	0	0	
Common Equity	152 ,742	127 ,145	132 ,637	

Business:

CHIEFTAIN INTERNATIONAL, INC. is a Canadian company based in Alberta and is engaged in oil and gas exploration and development in the United States, the North Sea, Libya and Peru.

Synopsis:

Chieftain's 1993 approved capital expenditures budget of $90-million includes $65-million designated for acquisitions of U.S. producing properties. The balance of $25-million is authorized for exploration and development expenditures of which $17.5-million is directed to the U.S. and $7.5-million to international ventures. Funding for these investments has been provided by equity financing. During the fourth quarter of 1992, the company and its subsidiary, Chieftain International Funding Corp. collectively raised $88-million (U.S.) through public offerings.

The company believes U.S. natural gas prices will improve as a result of reduced deliverability that was caused by a sustained period of low capital expenditures and drilling activity in the U.S. In addition, the American Gas Association has estimated that U.S. gas demand has grown by 23% from 1986 through 1992, despite a relatively weak economy through much of this period. Since the Persian Gulf crisis and the resulting price volatility, prices for oil and natural gas liquids have stabilized around the $20 per barrel level for the last two and one-half years. The company anticipates no dramatic change in oil prices for the foreseeable future and oil and natural gas liquids production is expected to be relatively flat.

The 50% increase in gas production in the first quarter 1993 over the comparable period in 1992, was largely in response to a 30% increase in the average wellhead price realized by Chieftain - $1.80 (U.S.) per thousand cubic feet. The financial results also reflect a $1.6-million payment in preferred share dividends.

During 1992 (1991) average daily production by resource was: oil, 1,800 (1,720) barrels; and natural gas, 41 (34) million cubic feet. At the end of 1992 (1991), gross proven and probable oil reserves totaled 7 (7.3) million barrels, natural gas reserves totaled 96 (92) billion cubic feet. Chieftain's 1992 revenues by source were: natural gas 65%; oil and natural gas liquids, 31%; and interest and other, 4%.

Rank (Profit/Revenue/Assets)
489   476   280

David E. Mitchell
Chairman

Stanley A. Milner
President & C.E.O.

Edward L. Hahn
V.P., Finance & Treasurer

Gerald W. Youell
Sr. V.P., Explorat'n & Prod'n

Address
1201 Toronto-Dominion Tower
Edmonton Centre
Edmonton
AB
T5J 2Z1
(403) 425-1950

Fax: (403) 429-4681
C0002656/G/3.2

For further company information, call Globe Information Services 1-800-268-9128 or (416)585-5345

CIMARRON PETROLEUM LTD.

Exchanges	Price (Jun24'93)	9.62	Trailing P/E	192.50	Stock Symbol
T	Trailing Yield (%)	0.00	Trailing EPS	0.05	**CIR**

Period Ending	Apr92	Apr91	Apr90	Apr89	Apr88
Yearly Statistics					
Price-Close	9.50	12.00	8.50	5.25	6.00
Price-High	14.25	13.50	11.00	6.63	8.37
Price-Low	9.50	8.63	5.13	4.50	4.05
P/E-Close	950.00	150.00	36.96	40.39	33.33
Dividends per Share	0.00	0.10	0.10	0.10	0.10
Dividend Yield (%)	0.00	0.83	1.18	1.91	1.67
Sales per Share	1.98	2.52	2.52	1.86	1.68
EPS before extra. item	0.01	0.08	0.23	0.13	0.18
Cash Flow per Share	0.96	1.39	1.38	0.95	1.07
Book Value per Share	5.18	5.17	4.54	3.51	3.48
O/S Common Shares	7,674	7,661	6,822	4,964	4,957
Total Revenue	15,169	19,967	14,208	9,399	8,909
Income before extra.	45	564	1,307	663	900
Cash Flow	7,374	10,339	7,731	4,717	5,323
Debt/Equity	0.14	0.00	0.01	0.51	0.29
Return on Capital (%)	(0.26)	1.04	7.78	4.74	7.10
Ret. on Com. Equity (%)	0.11	1.60	5.40	3.82	5.29
% Change Profit	(92.0)	(56.8)	97.1	(26.3)	(59.8)
% Change Revenue	(24.0)	40.5	51.2	5.5	0.8
% Change Assets	3.4	23.7	16.2	21.2	5.1

Date	EPS	DPS	Tot Rev	Inc Bex
Jan 93	0.02	0.00	4,261	179
Oct 92	(0.02)	0.00	3,937	(201)
Jul 92	0.04	0.00	3,600	322
Apr 92	0.01	0.00	3,129	60
Jan 92	(0.02)	0.00	3,554	(192)
Oct 91	0.02	0.00	4,459	165
Jul 91	0.00	0.00	4,027	12
Apr 91	(0.17)	0.10	3,924	(1,279)

Preferred Div. Coverage	np	np	np
Total Div. Coverage	0.0	0.7	1.9
Interest Coverage	0.0	6.3	4.5
Current Ratio	0.4	0.8	1.0
Operating Margin	(0.8)	(4.6)	14.8
Asset Turnover	0.3	0.4	0.3
5 YEAR RATIOS (%)			
Return on Capital	4.1	8.3	11.1
Return on Com. Equity	3.2	6.6	9.0
Profit Growth	(54.7)	(17.8)	(16.9)
Revenue Growth	11.3	12.6	4.6
Asset Growth	13.5	20.2	17.2
BALANCE SHEET (000)			
Cash	386	925	904
Current Assets	4,062	5,740	5,325
Net Fixed Assets	49,380	45,944	36,450
Invest's & Advances	0	0	0
Total Assets	53,442	51,684	41,775
Short Term Debt	5,612	0	31
Current Liabilities	9,057	6,787	5,548
Long Term Debt	61	91	122
Total Liabilities	13,688	12,063	10,774
Total Equity	39,754	39,621	31,001
Total Liab. & Equity	53,442	51,684	41,775
CAPITAL (000)			
Total Debt	5,673	91	153
Preferred Equity	0	0	0
Common Equity	39,754	39,621	31,001

Business:

CIMARRON PETROLEUM LTD. is engaged in the exploration for and development of oil and gas properties in Canada.

Synopsis:

Cimarron Petroleum Ltd.'s financial results for the third quarter reflect an improvement in oil and gas production levels, increases in commodity prices, and a reduction in dry hole and operating costs. Interest expense increased as the company financed expenditures for acquisitions through use of its line of credit. Developments in the fourth quarter include two new gas discoveries, one in Northern Alberta and the other on its Enchant property.

Cimarron's capital budget for the fourth quarter is set at approximately $3-million, which will include $500,000 to increase its interest in the Lynburn area acquired in the second quarter. Cimarron expects to drill five wells in the fourth quarter, three of which are development and two exploratory.

Fiscal 1992 financial results reflect the depressed industry conditions prevalent in North America, during the latter part of 1991 and early months of 1992. For Cimarron, the low product prices offset oil production increases and inhibited growth in natural gas production levels. In response to these conditions, capital spending was reduced by 32%, operating costs were reduced by 20%, and the dividend normally paid out in April was terminated. The company refocused its efforts on developing its core areas.

During the nine-month period ending January 1993 (1992), the average price per barrel of oil and natural gas liquids was $19.74 ($18.78). The average price per thousand cubic feet of natural gas was $1.38 ($1.34). Average production for this same period was 1,531 barrels per day of oil and natural gas liquids, and 9 million cubic feet per day of natural gas.

During the year ending April 30, 1992 (1991), average daily production by resource was: oil and natural gas liquids, 1,555 (1,465) barrels; and natural gas, 10.1 (12.2) million cubic feet. At its 1992 (1991) fiscal year end, its gross proven and probable reserves by resource were: 5.3 (5.4) million barrels of crude oil and liquids; and 73 (62) billion cubic feet of natural gas.

Relative strength to TSE300

Price

Volume (in 1000's of board lots)

Rank (Profit/Revenue/Assets)		
572	652	525

R.W. Pawliw
President & C.E.O.

C.D. Ripplinger
C.F.O., Controller & Secty.

K.J. Edinga
Exec. V.P. & C.O.O.

Address
Suite 800
400 - 3rd Avenue S.W.
Calgary
AB
T2P 4H2
(403) 265-8900

Fax: (403) 266-2780
C0014546/G/3.2

CO-ENERCO RESOURCES LTD.

Exchanges	Price (Jun24'93)		13.12	Trailing P/E		32.89	Stock Symbol
TZ	Trailing Yield (%)		0.00	Trailing EPS		0.40	COE

Period Ending	Dec92	Dec91	Dec90	Dec89	Dec88
Yearly Statistics					
Price-Close	11.00	8.00	4.95	5.00	3.70
Price-High	12.88	8.88	6.00	5.38	5.00
Price-Low	7.38	4.50	4.40	3.50	3.60
P/E-Close	31.43	nm	nm	nm	nm
Dividends per Share	0.00	0.00	0.00	0.00	0.00
Dividend Yield (%)	0.00	0.00	0.00	0.00	0.00
Sales per Share	4.44	4.17	3.59	2.48	1.96
EPS before extra. item	0.35	(2.93)	(0.08)	(0.16)	(0.20)
Cash Flow per Share	2.14	1.63	1.55	1.08	0.93
Book Value per Share	6.51	4.81	7.69	7.87	8.28
O/S Common Shares	22,811	18,158	14,805	14,255	13,501
Total Revenue	90,653	69,276	51,955	34,927	26,572
Income before extra.	8,230	(46,729)	1,385	244	(692)
Cash Flow	43,745	27,152	22,440	15,029	12,362
Debt/Equity	0.34	0.32	0.32	0.29	0.25
Return on Capital (%)	12.24	(38.78)	5.26	3.53	1.33
Ret. on Com. Equity (%)	6.06	(48.40)	(0.99)	(1.97)	(2.38)
% Change Profit	117.6	(3,473.9)	467.6	135.3	(157.8)
% Change Revenue	30.9	33.3	48.8	31.4	(2.0)
% Change Assets	35.9	(22.7)	4.4	1.9	3.1

Date	EPS	DPS	Tot Rev	Inc Bex
Mar 93	0.09	0.00	24,137	2,136
Dec 92	0.08	0.00	25,180	1,764
Sep 92	0.12	0.00	24,094	2,690
Jun 92	0.11	0.00	22,620	2,451
Mar 92	0.05	0.00	18,853	1,325
Dec 91	(2.73)	0.00	18,011	(44,882)
Sep 91	(0.05)	0.00	17,484	(352)
Jun 91	(0.11)	0.00	18,208	(1,195)

Preferred Div. Coverage	np	0.0	0.6
Total Div. Coverage	7.6	0.0	0.6
Interest Coverage	5.3	0.0	2.0
Current Ratio	0.8	0.8	1.0
Operating Margin	23.5	(92.0)	0.0
Asset Turnover	0.4	0.4	0.2
5 YEAR RATIOS (%)			
Return on Capital	(3.3)	(5.2)	1.1
Return on Com. Equity	(9.5)	(10.9)	(3.2)
Profit Growth	47.0	na	(10.1)
Revenue Growth	27.3	24.7	7.6
Asset Growth	2.8	(0.9)	1.7
BALANCE SHEET (000)			
Cash	492	1,200	2,242
Current Assets	19,491	17,840	18,056
Net Fixed Assets	213,646	154,084	204,318
Invest's & Advances	0	0	0
Total Assets	233,666	171,924	222,374
Short Term Debt	0	0	1,870
Current Liabilities	23,379	21,105	17,659
Long Term Debt	50,990	36,409	42,266
Total Liabilities	85,277	59,566	83,518
Total Equity	148,389	112,358	138,856
Total Liab. & Equity	233,666	171,924	222,374
CAPITAL (000)			
Total Debt	50,990	36,409	44,136
Preferred Equity	0	25,000	25,000
Common Equity	148,389	87,358	113,856

Business:

CO-ENERCO RESOURCES LTD. is an intermediate-sized oil and gas company. Exploration and production activities are focused in Alberta, southeastern Saskatchewan and northeastern British Columbia.

Synopsis:

In February 1993, Cooperative Energy Corporation sold its remaining 5.3 million common shares of Co-enerco to a syndicate of underwriters on a bought deal basis. This effectively distributes Cooperative Energy's stake to the public.

To further capitalize on its dominant position in the Zama area of Alberta, Co-enerco acquired a major producing property for a cash consideration of $29.1-million in 1992. The acquisition included 4.5 million barrels of oil and natural gas liquids, 11.5 billion cubic feet of gas, 17,000 net acres of non-producing lands and 1,000 kilometres of seismic. The Zama area continues to be the focus of the company's operation and drilling activity.

Of the 1992 increase in the company's production of oil and liquids, two-thirds was the result of its drilling and recompletion program and the balance came from acquisitions. The reduced volumes of gas sales resulted from lower productivity in two areas: Clarke Lake and the Iosegun fields. Existing producing properties provided 99% of the total volume. To offset this decline, the company is seeking a property acquisition close to one of its existing fields that would help restore gas reserves. Such an acquisition is expected to be made in first half of 1993 at a cost of about $30-million.

During 1992 (1991) average daily production by resource was: oil, 9,375 (6,497) barrels; and natural gas, 35.8 (39.3) million cubic feet. At the end of 1992 (1991), gross proven and probable reserves were: oil, 23.8 (15) million barrels; and natural gas, 136.1 (135.9) billion cubic feet.

1992 (1991) revenues by operation were: crude oil and natural gas liquids, 80% (72%); and natural gas, 20% (28%).

Relative strength to TSE300 / Price / Volume (in 1000's of board lots) chart

Rank (Profit/Revenue/Assets)
198 394 301

Vernon J. Leland
Chairman

David Q. Martin
President & C.E.O.

Allan E. Dobson
V.P., Finance

Address
Suite 1600
530 - 8th Avenue S.W.
Calgary
AB
T2P 3S8
(403) 266-7800

Fax: (403) 266-7900
C0037061/G/3.2

COHO RESOURCES LIMITED

Exchanges	Price (Jun24'93)	2.60	Trailing P/E	32.50	Stock Symbol
TMZ	Trailing Yield (%)	0.00	Trailing EPS	0.08	**COH**

Period Ending	Dec92	Dec91	Dec90	Dec89	Dec88
Yearly Statistics					
Price-Close	1.70	1.15	3.55	6.50	4.50
Price-High	2.50	3.60	7.50	7.50	5.25
Price-Low	0.95	1.10	3.30	5.00	1.35
P/E-Close	28.33	nm	10.44	108.33	nm
Dividends per Share	0.00	0.00	0.00	0.00	0.00
Dividend Yield (%)	0.00	0.00	0.00	0.00	0.00
Sales per Share	1.40	1.59	1.76	1.47	1.14
EPS before extra. item	0.06	(1.91)	0.34	0.06	(0.01)
Cash Flow per Share	0.53	0.50	0.71	0.58	0.42
Book Value per Share	1.10	0.78	2.81	2.38	2.18
O/S Common Shares	31,429	28,324	28,324	27,857	21,968
Total Revenue	41,136	47,631	63,257	38,204	24,316
Income before extra.	1,759	(53,712)	10,053	2,569	1,686
Cash Flow	15,306	14,100	19,787	14,993	8,377
Debt/Equity	2.06	3.36	0.66	0.91	0.74
Return on Capital (%)	8.56	(42.21)	17.45	9.20	6.38
Ret. on Com. Equity (%)	5.84	(106.36)	13.14	1.94	(2.92)
% Change Profit	103.3	(634.3)	291.3	52.4	377.3
% Change Revenue	(13.6)	(24.7)	65.6	57.1	66.4
% Change Assets	6.2	(27.8)	20.5	19.0	21.1
Preferred Div. Coverage	17.1	0.0	21.4		
Total Div. Coverage	17.1	0.0	21.4		
Interest Coverage	2.1	0.0	4.1		
Current Ratio	2.0	0.4	0.9		
Operating Margin	26.1	(107.0)	25.2		
Asset Turnover	0.3	0.3	0.3		
5 YEAR RATIOS (%)					
Return on Capital	(0.1)	(1.0)	7.7		
Return on Com. Equity	(17.7)	(19.8)	0.4		
Profit Growth	na	na	75.1		
Revenue Growth	22.9	38.8	38.7		
Asset Growth	5.8	5.0	11.6		
BALANCE SHEET (000)					
Cash	9,668	4,423	4,307		
Current Assets	14,912	12,976	21,445		
Net Fixed Assets	121,361	114,674	155,093		
Invest's & Advances	0	1,449	2,018		
Total Assets	137,894	129,865	179,937		
Short Term Debt	0	20,424	435		
Current Liabilities	7,643	28,882	23,278		
Long Term Debt	71,497	57,946	53,809		
Total Liabilities	103,200	106,517	97,799		
Total Equity	34,694	23,348	82,138		
Total Liab. & Equity	137,894	129,865	179,937		
CAPITAL (000)					
Total Debt	71,497	78,368	54,244		
Preferred Equity	27	1,325	2,623		
Common Equity	34,667	22,023	79,515		

Business:

COHO RESOURCES LTD. is an oil and gas company whose major asset is a 68% ownership in Coho Resources, Inc., an active United States oil and gas company.

Date	EPS	DPS	Tot Rev	Inc Bex
Mar 93	0.03	0.00	11,325	880
Dec 92	0.02	0.00	11,231	640
Sep 92	0.02	0.00	10,831	682
Jun 92	0.01	0.00	10,766	372
Mar 92	0.00	0.00	8,042	65
Dec 91	(0.94)	0.00	12,585	(26,374)
Sep 91	(0.93)	0.00	11,920	(26,182)
Jun 91	(0.04)	0.00	10,764	(1,045)

Synopsis:

Coho Resources Ltd. sold its Canadian oil and gas assets to Cabre Exploration Ltd. for $26.5-million in February 1992. The sale completes a phase of the corporation's restructuring program. Coho's main objective is to regain acceptance in financial markets as a sound, viable company with potential from its two assets: a 67.5% ownership in Coho Resources Inc., (a U.S. oil and gas company), and a sizable working interest in Tunisia, North Africa. As part of the restructuring, Coho is reviewing a possible merger with its subsidiary, Coho Resources Inc.

A capital budget of $28.5-million was approved for 1993. Of this amount, $23.2-million will be allocated to Coho Resources Inc. and will be funded by the company's $23.3-million projected cash flow. A $5.3-million capital program has been allocated to exploration activities in Tunisia. These funds are provided by a $5.6-million public offering completed in October 1992.

Disposition of Coho's Canadian assets had an impact on the overall financial results for 1992. However, the company's U.S. operations recorded increases in production, reserves and cash flows.

The following figures reflect the company's U.S. operations. Average gross daily production in 1992 was: crude oil and natural gas liquids 5,460 barrels; and natural gas, 3.2 million cubic feet. Gross proven and probable reserves in 1992 were: crude oil and natural gas liquids, 45.5 million barrels; and natural gas, 39.8 billion cubic feet.

Relative strength to TSE300 / Price / Volume (in 1000's of board lots)

Rank (Profit/Revenue/Assets)
373   502   369

K. H. Lambert
Chairman Of The Board

Douglas R. Martin
Sr. V.P. & C.F.O.

Address
Suite 3700
700 - 2nd Street S.W.
Calgary
AB
T2P 2W2
(403) 261-9800

Fax: (403) 261-0980
C0009031/G/3.2

COMPUTALOG LTD.

Exchanges	Price (Jun24'93)	3.75	Trailing P/E	nm	Stock Symbol
T	Trailing Yield (%)	0.00	Trailing EPS	(0.11)	**CGH**

Period Ending	Dec92	Dec91	Dec90	Dec89	Dec88
Yearly Statistics					
Price-Close	0.44	0.93	3.50	3.90	5.00
Price-High	1.10	3.70	5.00	5.50	6.50
Price-Low	0.35	0.75	2.80	3.50	3.80
P/E-Close	nm	nm	nm	nm	50.00
Dividends per Share	0.00	0.00	0.00	0.00	0.00
Dividend Yield (%)	0.00	0.00	0.00	0.00	0.00
Sales per Share	2.14	2.86	3.53	3.01	3.28
EPS before extra. item	(0.32)	(1.07)	(0.93)	(0.63)	0.10
Cash Flow per Share	(0.06)	(0.25)	0.06	(0.32)	0.49
Book Value per Share	1.50	1.81	2.91	3.75	4.41
O/S Common Shares	26,933	26,933	26,913	23,113	22,678
Total Revenue	58,434	84,840	86,125	69,266	78,434
Income before extra.	(8,617)	(28,780)	(23,739)	(14,666)	2,203
Cash Flow	(1,746)	(6,628)	1,401	(7,275)	11,217
Debt/Equity	0.37	0.23	0.30	0.25	nd
Return on Capital (%)	(12.68)	(28.13)	(22.92)	(17.59)	4.42
Ret. on Com. Equity (%)	(19.33)	(45.31)	(28.80)	(15.72)	2.23
% Change Profit	70.1	(21.2)	(61.9)	(765.7)	(26.6)
% Change Revenue	(31.1)	(1.5)	24.3	(11.7)	8.1
% Change Assets	(6.7)	(39.0)	(2.2)	0.3	(0.8)

Preferred Div. Coverage	np	np	np
Total Div. Coverage	na	na	na
Interest Coverage	0.0	0.0	0.0
Current Ratio	2.0	1.9	2.8
Operating Margin	(12.0)	(12.8)	(9.9)
Asset Turnover	0.9	1.1	0.8
5 YEAR RATIOS (%)			
Return on Capital	(15.4)	(11.3)	(7.1)
Return on Com. Equity	(21.4)	(16.8)	(8.8)
Profit Growth	na	na	na
Revenue Growth	(4.3)	8.0	(2.5)
Asset Growth	(11.2)	(0.6)	4.5
BALANCE SHEET (000)			
Cash	1,592	284	2,786
Current Assets	32,938	33,627	62,625
Net Fixed Assets	31,074	35,781	41,723
Invest's & Advances	616	327	5,960
Total Assets	65,578	70,250	115,183
Short Term Debt	6,999	8,000	8,887
Current Liabilities	16,865	18,115	22,296
Long Term Debt	8,000	2,983	14,657
Total Liabilities	25,218	21,435	36,953
Total Equity	40,360	48,815	78,230
Total Liab. & Equity	65,578	70,250	115,183
CAPITAL (000)			
Total Debt	14,999	10,983	23,544
Preferred Equity	0	0	0
Common Equity	40,360	48,815	78,230

Business:

COMPUTALOG LTD. provides oil and gas field services to the Canadian, United States and international markets. Services include logging of oil and gas wells to determine quality and quantity of hydrocarbons present and the provision of directional drilling services. The company also manufactures specialized downhole tools and surface computer systems for its own operations and other clients.

Date	EPS	DPS	Tot Rev	Inc Bex
Mar 93	0.17	0.00	24,348	4,713
Dec 92	0.00	0.00	17,520	98
Sep 92	(0.10)	0.00	12,790	(2,756)
Jun 92	(0.18)	0.00	11,661	(4,734)
Mar 92	(0.05)	0.00	16,463	(1,225)
Dec 91	0.05	0.00	22,453	1,331
Sep 91	(0.12)	0.00	17,883	(3,314)
Jun 91	(0.92)	0.00	18,360	(26,653)

Synopsis:

Computalog benefited in 1992 from earlier decisions to reorganize its operations and was successful in attracting new business partners. The company worked to reduce costs during 1992, while expenditures by the North American oilfield industry were well below levels of the preceding decade for drilling of new wells and for the workover of producing wells.

During November 1992, Computalog entered into an agreement with Trimac Limited and CLOG Partners, L.P. under which they will jointly loan up to $12-million to the company. The first $6-million of borrowings will bear interest at 10% with drawings above that will be at 12.5%. The first $6-million of drawings are repayable at the end of three years, with the balance repayable at the end of year four. Computalog anticipates that it will benefit from its association with these two companies through expanded business conducts, access to additional strategic opportunities and the ability to exploit new technology. In December 1992, Computalog issued to CLOG Partners and Trimac 8,000,000 warrants each to purchase up to 8,000,000 common shares at an exercise price of 50 cents.

Computalog Wireline Products, the company's manufacturing division, introduced a number of new products for sale to independent wireline companies during 1992. Computalog Wireline also used its expertise and capability to win non-oilfield related work.

Drilling rig counts in both Canada and United States were higher in the beginning of 1993 compared to 1992 and general expectations are that there will be an overall improvement in the industry in 1993. Computalog expects to maintain its historical market share. Computalog will re-emphasize its research program to complete the transition to self reliance in the tool and technology field.

In 1992 total operating revenues (net loss) by geographic location were: Canada, 47% (50%); the U.S., 45% (30%); and international, 8% (20%).

Rank (Profit/Revenue/Assets)		
873	450	487

C. Victor Kloepfer
Chairman Of The Board

Glynn G. Davies
Vice President & C.O.O.

Address
Suite 800
600 - 6th Avenue S.W.
Calgary
AB
T2P 0S5
(403) 265-6060

Fax: (403) 237-8493
C0007960/G/3.3

CONWEST EXPLORATION COMPANY LIMITED

Exchanges	Price (Jun24'93)		25.00	Trailing P/E		36.23	Stock Symbol
T	Trailing Yield (%)		0.96	Trailing EPS		0.69	**CEX.B**

Period Ending	Dec92	Dec91	Dec90	Dec89	Dec88
Yearly Statistics					
Price-Close	10.00	9.13	13.75	13.75	10.00
Price-High	11.50	14.63	15.38	15.00	13.25
Price-Low	8.00	8.88	11.50	10.00	9.38
P/E-Close	13.89	nm	38.19	17.63	10.10
Dividends per Share	0.24	0.48	0.46	0.44	0.44
Dividend Yield (%)	2.40	5.26	3.35	3.20	4.40
Sales per Share	4.51	4.46	6.25	6.51	6.76
EPS before extra. item	0.72	(0.86)	0.36	0.78	0.99
Cash Flow per Share	2.13	1.41	2.35	2.83	3.36
Book Value per Share	10.43	9.96	11.15	11.85	11.57
O/S Common Shares	19,906	19,706	19,702	13,914	13,654
Total Revenue	108,850	75,145	103,110	103,225	97,700
Income before extra.	13,971	(15,852)	6,129	10,301	12,713
Cash Flow	40,174	26,427	37,860	39,050	42,633
Debt/Equity	0.70	0.75	0.56	0.63	0.52
Return on Capital (%)	8.20	(2.85)	6.61	10.56	12.99
Ret. on Com. Equity (%)	6.73	(7.80)	3.03	6.19	8.50
% Change Profit	188.1	(358.6)	(40.5)	(19.0)	(62.5)
% Change Revenue	44.9	(27.1)	(0.1)	5.7	(7.5)
% Change Assets	3.4	(0.8)	7.8	9.2	15.0

Preferred Div. Coverage	36.7	0.0	20.4
Total Div. Coverage	2.7	0.0	0.7
Interest Coverage	2.4	0.0	1.8
Current Ratio	3.4	2.6	2.8
Operating Margin	10.6	(1.0)	23.6
Asset Turnover	0.2	0.2	0.2
5 YEAR RATIOS (%)			
Return on Capital	7.1	11.4	14.2
Return on Com. Equity	3.3	7.2	10.2
Profit Growth	(16.3)	na	(16.2)
Revenue Growth	0.5	22.5	25.5
Asset Growth	6.7	23.1	25.4
BALANCE SHEET (000)			
Cash	24,309	16,647	23,141
Current Assets	55,556	52,576	64,693
Net Fixed Assets	300,457	278,416	260,875
Invest's & Advances	63,586	75,221	83,651
Total Assets	421,618	407,874	411,040
Short Term Debt	353	0	0
Current Liabilities	16,242	19,935	23,090
Long Term Debt	149,129	152,190	127,000
Total Liabilities	207,661	205,134	186,411
Total Equity	213,957	202,740	224,629
Total Liab. & Equity	421,618	407,874	411,040
CAPITAL (000)			
Total Debt	149,482	152,190	127,000
Preferred Equity	6,299	6,400	5,000
Common Equity	207,658	196,340	219,629

Business:

CONWEST EXPLORATION CO. LTD. is a natural resources company. Conwest produces oil and gas, mines zinc and is involved in the development of small hydroelectric projects. Conwest owns 24.3% of Faraday Resources Inc. Faraday owns a 49.8% voting interest and an 18% equity interest in Conwest.

Date	EPS	DPS	Tot Rev	Inc Bex
Mar 93	0.22	0.06	29,202	4,210
Dec 92	0.02	0.06	21,281	547
Sep 92	0.11	0.06	24,881	2,224
Jun 92	0.34	0.06	32,502	6,459
Mar 92	0.25	0.06	30,186	4,741
Dec 91	(0.79)	0.12	11,975	(14,805)
Sep 91	(0.11)	0.12	19,927	(2,008)
Jun 91	(0.01)	0.12	17,409	(22)

Synopsis:

Conwest Exploration Company Limited and its controlling shareholder Faraday Resources Inc. jointly announced in June 1993 that they will amalgamate. The amalgamated company would continue to be known as Conwest. The amalgamation would result in the elimination of the multiple voting/subordinate voting capital structure of Conwest and the intercorporate holdings between Conwest and Faraday.

The most significant development during 1992 was in the oil and gas division where natural gas condensate discoveries in northwestern Alberta resulted in a 45% increase in natural gas reserves and a 21% increase in oil and natural gas liquids reserves. These discoveries did not affect oil and gas revenues and net production income in 1992. Conwest expects the increased reserves will result in higher production rates, revenues and net production income in 1993 and future years.

During 1992 (1991) average daily production was: oil and natural gas liquids, 5,600 (5,900) barrels; natural gas, 37.8 (33.4) million cubic feet; and zinc 92,100 (98,200) tonnes. At the end of 1992 (1991), the company's proven and probable reserves were: oil and natural gas liquids, 34.5 (28) million barrels; natural gas, 415 (284) billion cubic feet; and zinc ore, 2,319 (2,420) tonnes.

1992 (1991) contributions to operating revenue by segment were: oil and gas, 47% (65%); mining, 31% (46%); hydro, 4% (1%); and other, 18% (-12%).

Relative strength to TSE300 / Price / Volume (in 1000's of board lots)

Rank (Profit/Revenue/Assets)
150   364   230

M.P. Connell
Chairman Of The Board

John C. Lamacraft
President & C.E.O.

Address
Suite 2000
95 Wellington Street West
Toronto
ON
M5J 2N7
(416) 362-6721

Fax: (416) 362-0069
C0010506/G/3.2

CZAR RESOURCES LTD.

Exchanges	Price (Jun24'93)		2.23	Trailing P/E		18.58	Stock Symbol
T	Trailing Yield (%)		0.00	Trailing EPS		0.12	CZR

Period Ending	Dec92	Dec91	Dec90	Dec89	Dec88
Yearly Statistics					
Price-Close	0.94	0.53	1.13	1.44	1.23
Price-High	1.29	1.20	1.50	1.54	2.00
Price-Low	0.40	0.41	0.93	1.02	1.10
P/E-Close	9.40	nm	22.60	28.80	24.60
Dividends per Share	0.00	0.00	0.00	0.00	0.00
Dividend Yield (%)	0.00	0.00	0.00	0.00	0.00
Sales per Share	1.10	0.73	0.72	0.81	0.63
EPS before extra. item	0.10	(0.01)	0.05	0.05	0.05
Cash Flow per Share	0.43	0.18	0.21	0.24	0.18
Book Value per Share	0.45	0.25	0.26	0.19	(0.19)
O/S Common Shares	42,817	36,445	36,280	35,556	27,637
Total Revenue	29,923	27,243	26,916	24,323	18,813
Income before extra.	3,701	(387)	1,637	1,301	1,472
Cash Flow	11,466	6,693	7,669	6,799	5,061
Debt/Equity	1.92	4.92	4.88	6.80	na
Return on Capital (%)	14.25	10.53	13.68	21.77	185.37
Ret. on Com. Equity (%)	26.18	(4.25)	20.46	163.34	na
% Change Profit	1,056.3	(123.6)	25.8	(11.6)	nm
% Change Revenue	9.8	1.2	10.7	29.3	23.0
% Change Assets	8.6	(1.1)	7.8	13.6	29.1

Preferred Div. Coverage	np	np	np
Total Div. Coverage	na	na	na
Interest Coverage	1.9	0.9	1.3
Current Ratio	0.9	0.5	0.7
Operating Margin	26.0	20.4	26.1
Asset Turnover	0.4	0.4	0.4
5 YEAR RATIOS (%)			
Return on Capital	49.1	na	na
Return on Com. Equity	na	na	na
Profit Growth	610.1	na	39.6
Revenue Growth	14.3	13.3	9.6
Asset Growth	11.1	9.2	9.8
BALANCE SHEET (000)			
Cash	4,974	0	0
Current Assets	12,691	5,697	9,142
Net Fixed Assets	58,047	59,303	56,486
Invest's & Advances	0	0	0
Total Assets	71,006	65,375	66,110
Short Term Debt	948	989	894
Current Liabilities	14,655	12,441	12,306
Long Term Debt	36,044	43,242	44,248
Total Liabilities	51,717	56,387	56,866
Total Equity	19,289	8,988	9,244
Total Liab. & Equity	71,006	65,375	66,110
CAPITAL (000)			
Total Debt	36,992	44,231	45,142
Preferred Equity	0	0	0
Common Equity	19,289	8,988	9,244

Business:

CZAR RESOURCES LTD. is a natural gas exploration and production company. The company has producing wells in Alberta and British Columbia. It also has exploration activities in the two provinces. The company markets gas to industrial customers in Alberta, British Columbia and the United States.

Date	EPS	DPS	Tot Rev	Inc Bex
Mar 93	0.04	0.00	8,711	1,809
Dec 92	0.05	0.00	9,065	1,878
Sep 92	0.01	0.00	6,625	426
Jun 92	0.02	0.00	6,816	675
Mar 92	0.02	0.00	7,417	722
Dec 91	0.02	0.00	7,966	698
Sep 91	(0.04)	0.00	5,473	(1,399)
Jun 91	(0.01)	0.00	6,269	(555)

Synopsis:

Czar's strategy is to build a natural gas reserves base and revenue stream that will enable it to participate in the recovery and growth of the natural gas industry in Canada. In 1992, Czar reduced expenditures on exploration, development and acquisitions in favor of debt reduction. With increased gas prices, Czar has returned to a more balanced approach with an increased exploration and development program planned for 1993.

The highlight of the 1992 acquisition program was the purchase of assets in the July Lake portion of the Helmet field. This purchase, together with a subsequent acquisition of other interests in the Helmet area, added approximately 9.7 billion cubic feet of net gas reserves.

The results of first quarter 1993 reflect higher natural gas prices and production, as well as substantially lower interest charges on the company's debt. Lower interest expense resulted from the $12-million debt reduction during 1992 and fixed interest rates on Czar's remaining debt.

Czar's average daily gross production in 1992 (1991) was: crude oil and natural gas liquids, 366 (291) barrels; and natural gas, 45 (44.2) million cubic feet. Gross proven and probable reserves at the end of 1992 (1991) were : oil and natural gas liquids, 1.2 (1.3261) million stock tank barrels; and natural gas, 201 (205) billion cubic feet.

The distribution of gas sales by geographic region was: B.C., 25.7%; U.S. Northeast, 21.6%; California, 18.2%; Alberta, 15.6%; U.S. Midwest, 10.8%; U.S. Pacific Northwest, 6.6%; and Eastern Canada, 1.5%.

Relative strength to TSE300

Price

Volume (in 1000's of board lots)

Rank (Profit/Revenue/Assets)
288 561 479

Robert W. Lamond
Chairman, President & C.E.O.

Charles A. Teare
Exec. V.P. & C.F.O.

P. Richard Ewacha
V.P., Production

Address
Suite 2100
144 - 4th Avenue S.W.
Calgary
AB
T2P 3N4
(403) 265-0270

C0012102/G/3.2

DISCOVERY WEST CORP.

Exchanges	Price (Jun24'93)		7.25	Trailing P/E		36.25	Stock Symbol
T	Trailing Yield (%)		0.00	Trailing EPS		0.20	DSW

Period Ending	Dec92	Dec91	Dec90	Dec89	Dec88
Yearly Statistics					
Price-Close	5.00	1.55	1.55	1.50	1.11
Price-High	5.88	2.00	2.40	1.80	1.91
Price-Low	1.50	1.35	1.35	1.05	1.02
P/E-Close	29.41	17.22	4.43	21.43	15.86
Dividends per Share	0.00	0.00	0.00	0.00	0.00
Dividend Yield (%)	0.00	0.00	0.00	0.00	0.00
Sales per Share	0.87	0.66	0.65	0.44	0.40
EPS before extra. item	0.17	0.09	0.35	0.07	0.07
Cash Flow per Share	0.54	0.37	0.37	0.24	0.19
Book Value per Share	2.13	1.90	1.83	1.42	1.37
O/S Common Shares	31,054	23,021	23,100	19,421	19,421
Total Revenue	20,774	13,671	12,499	8,253	7,274
Income before extra.	4,258	1,775	6,306	1,287	1,238
Cash Flow	12,597	7,430	6,596	3,986	3,083
Debt/Equity	nd	0.18	0.18	0.28	0.29
Return on Capital (%)	10.60	5.66	18.15	4.51	3.61
Ret. on Com. Equity (%)	7.68	4.01	17.86	4.50	4.05
% Change Profit	139.9	(71.9)	390.0	4.0	36.6
% Change Revenue	52.0	9.4	51.4	13.5	(8.9)
% Change Assets	28.0	2.1	24.4	(0.2)	3.6

Date	EPS	DPS	Tot Rev	Inc Bex
Mar 93	0.05	0.00	8,029	1,394
Dec 92	0.08	0.00	7,312	2,135
Sep 92	0.03	0.00	5,583	854
Jun 92	0.04	0.00	4,241	1,104
Mar 92	0.02	0.00	3,658	165
Dec 91	0.04	0.00	3,660	690
Sep 91	0.00	0.00	3,154	38
Jun 91	0.02	0.00	3,391	477

	Dec92	Dec91	Dec90
Preferred Div. Coverage	118.3	36.2	110.6
Total Div. Coverage	118.3	36.2	110.6
Interest Coverage	16.5	4.4	7.7
Current Ratio	1.8	0.8	1.5
Operating Margin	27.6	17.1	24.4
Asset Turnover	0.2	0.2	0.2
5 YEAR RATIOS (%)			
Return on Capital	8.5	7.2	4.2
Return on Com. Equity	7.6	6.6	3.6
Profit Growth	36.3	36.7	81.2
Revenue Growth	21.0	12.1	32.1
Asset Growth	10.9	9.5	32.9
BALANCE SHEET (000)			
Cash	9,126	378	1,213
Current Assets	12,558	1,928	4,064
Net Fixed Assets	56,793	48,531	44,749
Invest's & Advances	15,740	15,854	16,098
Total Assets	85,256	66,632	65,271
Short Term Debt	0	0	0
Current Liabilities	7,079	2,444	2,803
Long Term Debt	0	7,950	7,950
Total Liabilities	18,558	21,908	21,968
Total Equity	66,698	44,724	43,303
Total Liab. & Equity	85,256	66,632	65,271
CAPITAL (000)			
Total Debt	0	7,950	7,950
Preferred Equity	500	990	990
Common Equity	66,198	43,734	42,313

Business:

DISCOVERY WEST CORP. is engaged in the development of and participation in the operation of oil and gas properties primarily in Alberta. It also has a 34.8% voting interest in Rayrock Yellowknife Resources Inc., a mining and exploration and development company.

Synopsis:

Discovery West Corp. will maintain an active exploration and development program through the remainder of 1993. It is anticipated that 50 to 60 company-operated wells will be drilled this year with the company maintaining average interests in the 60% to 70% range. Approximately 25% of these are expected to be wildcat wells.

Although oil will be the primary focus of company activity this year, Discovery will be increasingly more active in gas exploration. Also, a strong effort will be made to tie-in existing gas reserves. Discovery is seeking approval to construct a 10 million cubic foot per day sweet gas facility with associated gathering lines and a 14 mile pipeline to tie into the Nova pipeline system. The total cost of this project is an estimated $3.6-million. As a result of recent successes in the general Halkirck/Stettler area of east central Alberta, Discovery has increased its undeveloped land holding in this area to 26,000 acres.

Along with its ongoing gas project at Halkirck/Stettler, the company will begin marketing gas from the Sugden, Red Willow and Whitecourt areas around June 1993. These projects are expected to yield approximately three million cubic feet of gas per day.

Effective January 1993, the company purchased from its parent, Rayrock Yellowknife Resources Inc., all of its oil and certain of its gas interests for cash consideration of approximately $1-million. This purchase has increased Discovery's working interest oil and natural gas liquids production by approximately 60 barrels of oil per day and gas production by 1.1 million cubic feet per day.

During fiscal 1992, average daily production by resource was: oil and natural gas liquids, 2,407 barrels; and natural gas, 7.473 million cubic feet. At its 1992 (1991) fiscal year end, the company's gross proven and probable reserves by resource were: 6.6 (4.7) million barrels of crude oil and natural gas liquids; and 37.5 (31.6) billion cubic feet of natural gas.

Rank (Profit/Revenue/Assets)
277   608   442

David R. Crombie
President & C.E.O.

C. Bruce Burton
V.P. & C.F.O.

O. Michael Isaac
Exec. V.P.

Address
30 Soudan Avenue
Suite 500
Toronto
ON
M4S 1V6
(416) 489-0022

Fax: (416) 489-0096
D0001223/G/3.2

DORSET EXPLORATION LTD.

Exchanges	Price (Jun24'93)	18.37	Trailing P/E	54.04	Stock Symbol
T	Trailing Yield (%)	0.00	Trailing EPS	0.34	**DXL**

Period Ending	Dec92	Dec91	Dec90	Dec89	Dec88
Yearly Statistics					
Price-Close	10.50	3.80	0.95	0.74	0.80
Price-High	11.13	4.20	1.15	1.00	0.85
Price-Low	3.55	0.70	0.55	0.30	0.70
P/E-Close	38.89	63.33	nm	nm	nm
Dividends per Share	0.00	0.00	0.00	0.00	0.00
Dividend Yield (%)	0.00	0.00	0.00	0.00	0.00
Sales per Share	1.05	0.58	0.54	0.44	1.13
EPS before extra. item	0.27	0.06	(1.07)	(0.07)	(0.04)
Cash Flow per Share	0.74	0.32	0.25	0.14	0.47
Book Value per Share	1.88	1.55	1.98	2.79	7.04
O/S Common Shares	24,859	24,422	13,790	12,907	5,090
Total Revenue	26,090	13,373	7,438	5,545	5,841
Income before extra.	6,764	1,363	(14,528)	(852)	(362)
Cash Flow	18,344	7,263	3,452	1,699	2,405
Debt/Equity	0.38	0.24	0.31	0.22	0.32
Return on Capital (%)	22.05	9.24	(34.61)	0.03	na
Ret. on Com. Equity (%)	15.97	4.18	(45.94)	(2.37)	na
% Change Profit	396.3	109.4	(1,605.2)	(135.4)	na
% Change Revenue	95.1	79.8	34.1	(5.1)	na
% Change Assets	42.0	31.2	(13.1)	(7.5)	na

Date	EPS	DPS	Tot Rev	Inc Bex
Mar 93	0.10	0.00	8,920	2,429
Dec 92	0.11	0.00	5,238	2,898
Sep 92	0.08	0.00	7,065	1,944
Jun 92	0.05	0.00	9,977	1,234
Mar 92	0.03	0.00	4,527	688
Dec 91	0.03	0.00	4,451	783
Sep 91	0.02	0.00	3,032	323
Jun 91	(0.01)	0.00	2,979	(123)

	Dec92	Dec91	Dec90
Preferred Div. Coverage	np	np	np
Total Div. Coverage	na	na	na
Interest Coverage	13.5	3.5	0.0
Current Ratio	0.7	0.8	1.6
Operating Margin	47.1	26.7	(191.5)
Asset Turnover	0.3	0.2	0.2
5 YEAR RATIOS (%)			
Return on Capital	na	na	na
Return on Com. Equity	na	na	na
Profit Growth	na	na	na
Revenue Growth	na	na	na
Asset Growth	na	na	na
BALANCE SHEET (000)			
Cash	0	155	3,033
Current Assets	3,672	2,997	4,424
Net Fixed Assets	71,941	50,894	35,787
Invest's & Advances	2,040	800	1,466
Total Assets	77,653	54,691	41,677
Short Term Debt	0	0	0
Current Liabilities	5,042	3,905	2,726
Long Term Debt	17,779	9,077	8,431
Total Liabilities	30,834	16,797	14,408
Total Equity	46,819	37,894	27,269
Total Liab. & Equity	77,653	54,691	41,677
CAPITAL (000)			
Total Debt	17,779	9,077	8,431
Preferred Equity	0	0	0
Common Equity	46,819	37,894	27,269

Business:

DORSET EXPLORATION LTD. is involved with the exploration for and development of oil and gas reserves.

Synopsis:

Dorset Exploration continues to balance acquisition, exploitation and exploration opportunities with more emphasis on exploration activities initiated in previous years. In 1993, the company expects proved oil and gas reserves additions to more than double annual production. Both oil and gas production are expected to increase by 80%, due to new wells coming on stream at Bon Accord, Manor and Soda Lake.

Net proceeds of approximately $30-million from the sale of 1.7 million common shares at $18.25 per share in May 1993, has resulted in the company increasing its 1993 capital budget program to $65-million. Expenditures will include the drilling of 60 wells to exploit previously acquired properties, complete assessments of earlier discoveries, and undertake new exploration on recent acquisitions.

Dorset reported record oil and gas revenues, earnings and cash flow for fiscal 1992. Production gains more than offset the 5% decline in oil and 1% decline in gas prices received by the company in 1992. Significant reductions in operating and overhead costs, production expenses declined to $3.54 a barrel of oil equivalent from $4.81 in 1991, were due to substantial increases in two of the company's major areas where existing facilities had excess capacity.

During fiscal 1992 (1991), average daily production by resource was: oil and natural gas liquids, 2,948 (1,315) barrels; and natural gas, 16.7 (10.8) million cubic feet. At its 1992 (1991) fiscal year end, the company's gross proven and probable reserves by resource were: 8 (5.4) billion barrels of crude oil and natural gas liquids; and 88.7 (63.9) billion cubic feet of natural gas.

Relative strength to TSE300 / Price / Volume (in 1000's of board lots)

Rank (Profit/Revenue/Assets)
221 579 463

Edward L. Molnar
Chairman, President & C.E.O.

George D. Ziroff
Controller & C.F.O.

Wayne B. Jessee
Executive Vice President

Address
205 - 5th Avenue S.W.
Suite 3600
Calgary
AB
T2P 2V7
(403) 267-0700

Fax: (403) 267-0777
01002510/G/3.2

DRECO ENERGY SERVICES LTD.

Exchanges	Price (Jun24'93)	29.00	Trailing P/E	24.58	Stock Symbol
TQ	Trailing Yield (%)	0.00	Trailing EPS	1.18	**DRE.A**

Period Ending	Aug92	Aug91	Aug90	Aug89	Aug88
Yearly Statistics	US	US	US	US	US
Price-Close	14.38	12.00	10.25	3.00	n t
Price-High	17.50	19.25	11.25	3.00	n t
Price-Low	8.75	8.25	2.05	1.30	n t
P/E-Close	9.94	6.88	11.19	6.18	n t
Dividends per Share	0.00	0.00	0.00	0.00	0.00
Dividend Yield (%)	0.00	0.00	0.00	0.00	0.00
Sales per Share	10.91	13.76	10.16	8.60	5.76
EPS before extra. item	1.05	1.31	0.67	0.34	0.01
Cash Flow per Share	1.43	1.88	1.17	0.82	0.24
Book Value per Share	6.76	5.94	4.23	3.50	3.02
O/S Common Shares	6,089	6,085	4,695	4,672	4,666
Total Revenue	69,465	78,854	49,064	42,353	28,808
Income before extra.	6,452	7,402	3,218	1,621	67
Cash Flow	8,674	10,635	5,615	3,979	1,144
Debt/Equity	0.07	0.08	0.47	0.52	0.77
Return on Capital (%)	16.49	23.58	16.45	11.61	5.08
Ret. on Com. Equity (%)	16.69	26.43	17.78	10.65	0.49
% Change Profit	(12.8)	130.0	98.5	2,319.4	101.3
% Change Revenue	(11.9)	60.7	15.8	47.0	9.4
% Change Assets	15.6	28.2	24.9	(3.6)	(10.0)

Date		EPS	DPS	Tot Rev	Inc Bex
May 93	US	0.40	0.00	22,718	2,532
Feb 93	US	0.27	0.00	23,138	1,695
Nov 92	US	0.27	0.00	19,701	1,666
Aug 92	US	0.24	0.00	17,548	1,442
May 92	US	0.25	0.00	17,968	1,546
Feb 92	US	0.30	0.00	18,590	1,824
Nov 91	US	0.27	0.00	15,198	1,640
Aug 91	US	0.32	0.00	19,935	1,962

Preferred Div. Coverage	np	np	np
Total Div. Coverage	na	na	na
Interest Coverage	21.6	13.6	3.9
Current Ratio	3.4	3.7	1.8
Operating Margin	6.9	10.2	9.0
Asset Turnover	1.2	1.6	1.3
5 YEAR RATIOS (%)			
Return on Capital	14.6	9.1	na
Return on Com. Equity	14.4	4.5	na
Profit Growth	186.7	204.5	na
Revenue Growth	21.3	11.0	na
Asset Growth	9.9	(0.1)	na
BALANCE SHEET (000)			
Cash	6,980	1,836	0
Current Assets	36,437	30,111	19,690
Net Fixed Assets	17,370	16,989	15,226
Invest's & Advances	0	0	0
Total Assets	54,592	47,211	36,821
Short Term Debt	130	93	3,352
Current Liabilities	10,843	8,206	10,918
Long Term Debt	2,579	2,848	6,057
Total Liabilities	13,422	11,054	16,975
Total Equity	41,170	36,157	19,846
Total Liab. & Equity	54,592	47,211	36,821
CAPITAL (000)			
Total Debt	2,709	2,941	9,409
Preferred Equity	0	0	0
Common Equity	41,170	36,157	19,846

Business:

DRECO ENERGY SERVICES LTD. participates in two principal business segments: drilling and well servicing equipment; and downhole drilling products.

Synopsis:

Dreco Energy Services experienced lower activity levels in the drilling and well servicing equipment segment during 1992. These levels were due to reduced capital spending in the industry, which resulted in many projects the company expected to bid on being deferred or canceled. The company had lower downhole rental revenues in 1992. The company believes that even with gas prices strengthening recently in North America, it is uncertain whether prices are at a level to stimulate increased drilling and demand for downhole products.

The company's Norwegian joint venture completed the manufacture of an automated offshore platform drilling facility in 1992 for $25-million and received a $95-million contract expected to be completed in 1994, for a platform in the Troll Field in the Norwegian sector of the North Sea. During 1992, the joint venture also established a subsidiary in the United Kingdom to pursue opportunities for platform drilling facilities in the U.K. sector of the North Sea.

During fiscal 1993, Dreco received a $8.7-million (U.S.) contract for a mobile semi-automated drilling rig for use in Oman, a $6.9-million (U.S.) contract for two mobile drilling rigs for use in the Tyumen region of Western Siberia, contracts with two Russian firms for the construction of twenty workover rigs for Western Siberia for $13.7-million (U.S.) and a $13-million (U.S.) purchase order for two derricks and accessories for the Hibernia field. The contracts are for engineering and construction and will be completed in the fall of 1993.

1992 total revenues (operating profit) by segment were: drilling and well servicing equipment, 79% (49%); and downhole products, 21% (51%). Total revenues (operating profit) by geographic area of operation were: the United States, 35% (27%); and Canada, 65% (73%). Export sales to international clients in 1992 were 89% of total Canadian sales, and 27% of total U.S. sales. The majority of export sales from North America are to Africa, Asia and the Middle East.

Relative strength to TSE300

Price

Volume (in 1000's of board lots)

Rank (Profit/Revenue/Assets)		
204	407	488

Frederick W. Pheasey
Chairman Of The Board

Franklin L. Kobie
President & C.E.O.

Daryl W. Ferko
V.P., Fin., C.F.O. & Treasurer

Address
3716 - 93 Street
Edmonton
AB
T6E 5N3
(403) 463-2065

Fax: (403) 463-3276
01002039/G/3.3

ELAN ENERGY INC.

Exchanges	Price (Jun24'93)	17.87	Trailing P/E	26.68	Stock Symbol
TM	Trailing Yield (%)	0.00	Trailing EPS	0.67	**ELN**

Period Ending	Dec92	Dec91	Dec90	Dec89	Dec88
Yearly Statistics					
Price-Close	10.88	8.50	4.30	3.45	2.40
Price-High	11.63	9.50	5.25	3.45	4.30
Price-Low	7.75	3.75	3.35	2.25	2.05
P/E-Close	24.72	50.00	9.56	19.17	nm
Dividends per Share	0.00	0.00	0.00	0.00	0.00
Dividend Yield (%)	0.00	0.00	0.00	0.00	0.00
Sales per Share	2.19	2.02	1.78	1.26	0.75
EPS before extra. item	0.44	0.17	0.45	0.18	(1.32)
Cash Flow per Share	1.39	0.98	0.99	0.66	0.27
Book Value per Share	4.50	4.18	3.61	3.05	2.85
O/S Common Shares	36,849	29,964	24,935	21,253	21,253
Total Revenue	78,760	52,465	40,795	26,836	15,909
Income before extra.	16,053	4,483	10,340	4,204	(28,036)
Cash Flow	50,236	25,493	22,681	14,040	5,833
Debt/Equity	0.38	0.61	1.00	0.72	0.22
Return on Capital (%)	9.84	7.15	12.08	10.01	(32.08)
Ret. on Com. Equity (%)	11.03	4.16	13.35	6.70	(37.56)
% Change Profit	258.1	(56.6)	146.0	115.0	(3,843.1)
% Change Revenue	50.1	28.6	52.0	68.7	8.9
% Change Assets	12.9	16.8	57.1	51.5	(26.9)

Preferred Div. Coverage	na	na	na		
Total Div. Coverage	na	na	na		
Interest Coverage	5.2	1.6	2.6		
Current Ratio	0.6	0.6	1.2		
Operating Margin	27.1	26.3	43.3		
Asset Turnover	0.3	0.2	0.2		
5 YEAR RATIOS (%)					
Return on Capital	1.4	(0.3)	(16.1)		
Return on Com. Equity	(0.5)	(2.1)	na		
Profit Growth	84.6	na	51.7		
Revenue Growth	40.0	37.9	41.8		
Asset Growth	18.0	28.7	35.8		

BALANCE SHEET (000)

	Dec92	Dec91	Dec90
Cash	122	271	63
Current Assets	10,359	8,933	7,565
Net Fixed Assets	233,299	205,758	179,392
Invest's & Advances	3,846	4,225	423
Total Assets	247,504	219,252	187,760
Short Term Debt	0	0	0
Current Liabilities	17,356	15,731	6,410
Long Term Debt	62,700	76,900	90,300
Total Liabilities	81,471	93,654	97,519
Total Equity	166,033	125,598	90,241
Total Liab. & Equity	247,504	219,252	187,760

CAPITAL (000)

	Dec92	Dec91	Dec90
Total Debt	62,700	76,900	90,300
Preferred Equity	217	217	223
Common Equity	165,816	125,381	90,018

Business:

ELAN ENERGY INC. is an oil and gas exploration and production company. It has operations and exploration activities in Alberta and Saskatchewan. Lasmo plc of the United Kingdom controls 22% of the outstanding common shares.

Date	EPS	DPS	Tot Rev	Inc Bex
Mar 93	0.26	0.00	30,307	8,445
Dec 92	0.11	0.00	23,163	5,083
Sep 92	0.14	0.00	21,091	5,145
Jun 92	0.16	0.00	19,404	5,323
Mar 92	0.02	0.00	15,102	502
Dec 91	0.01	0.00	15,169	423
Sep 91	0.11	0.00	14,846	2,843
Jun 91	0.03	0.00	11,307	669

Synopsis:

Elan Energy's record revenue and earnings for the first quarter of fiscal 1993 reflect higher oil and gas production. The increase in production resulted from a combination of increased drilling activities and from the acquisition of OMV (Canada) Ltd.. The acquisition of OMV, which was finalized in March 1993 for net consideration of $151-million, added an average of 6,000 barrels per day of crude oil and natural gas liquids and 10 million cubic feet per day of natural gas to production for the first quarter. The acquisition increases Elan's oil and natural gas liquid reserves by 68%, almost triples natural gas reserves, and adds over 126,000 net acres to the company's undeveloped land base. The acquisition was primarily funded by a nine million common share issue in February 1993, which yielded $108-million in proceeds. Other borrowings were used to fund the rest of the acquisition.

Additional increases in production were obtained through other acquisitions. Elan increased its working interest in the light-oil producing Nipisi region of northern Alberta (acquired from Chevron Canada Resources Ltd.), late in 1992. This interest added 500 barrels of oil per day to the first quarter production average. At the same time, working interests were also acquired at the House Mountain region of northern Alberta, which added almost 500 barrels per day of light oil production.

For 1993, Elan will continue to focus its drilling program on oil prospects where horizontal technology can be applied. Horizontal or directional wells can tap a larger area of an oil pool, allowing it to drain more efficiently. It can also be more cost-efficient, producing as much as several vertical wells.

During fiscal 1992 (1991), average daily production by resource was: oil and natural gas liquids, 14,000 (9,250) barrels; and natural gas, 6.8 (6.9) million cubic feet. At its 1992 (1991) fiscal year end, the company's gross proven and probable reserves by resource were: 42.8 (36.5) million barrels of crude oil and natural gas liquids; and 40.2 (47.2) billion cubic feet of natural gas.

Relative strength to TSE300 / Price / Volume (in 1000's of board lots) chart

Rank (Profit/Revenue/Assets)		
139	411	293

Dennis G. Flanagan
Chairman & C.E.O.

Verne G. Johnson
President & C.O.O.

Curtis W. Hicks
V.P., Finance

Address
Suite 4100
150 - 6th Avenue S.W.
Calgary
AB
T2P 3Y7
(403) 266-8500

Fax: (403) 262-7337
O0000950/G/3.2

EXCEL ENERGY INC.

Exchanges	Price (Jun24'93)	9.62	Trailing P/E	87.46	Stock Symbol
T	Trailing Yield (%)	0.00	Trailing EPS	0.11	**EEI**

Period Ending	Dec92	Dec91	Dec90	Dec89	Dec88
Yearly Statistics					
Price-Close	2.43	0.80	1.00	1.25	0.82
Price-High	2.58	1.30	1.55	1.45	1.35
Price-Low	0.55	0.80	0.80	0.77	0.56
P/E-Close	60.75	nm	6.67	15.63	82.00
Dividends per Share	0.00	0.00	0.00	0.00	0.00
Dividend Yield (%)	0.00	0.00	0.00	0.00	0.00
Sales per Share	0.62	0.54	0.49	0.35	0.26
EPS before extra. item	0.04	(0.60)	0.15	0.08	0.01
Cash Flow per Share	0.28	0.17	0.30	0.18	0.12
Book Value per Share	1.25	1.26	1.88	1.72	1.64
O/S Common Shares	14,751	10,210	9,821	9,821	9,821
Total Revenue	6,976	5,329	5,225	4,178	3,781
Income before extra.	456	(5,920)	1,521	753	107
Cash Flow	3,095	1,631	2,978	1,765	980
Debt/Equity	0.19	0.40	0.26	nd	nd
Return on Capital (%)	5.38	(25.56)	7.68	4.59	1.25
Ret. on Com. Equity (%)	2.91	(37.88)	8.61	4.56	1.02
% Change Profit	107.7	(489.2)	102.0	603.7	(98.3)
% Change Revenue	30.9	2.0	25.1	10.5	52.6
% Change Assets	26.6	(18.2)	32.7	6.5	4.9

Preferred Div. Coverage	np	np	np
Total Div. Coverage	na	na	na
Interest Coverage	2.9	0.0	771.5
Current Ratio	1.1	0.4	0.7
Operating Margin	15.4	(98.9)	29.5
Asset Turnover	0.3	0.3	0.2
5 YEAR RATIOS (%)			
Return on Capital	(1.3)	4.0	8.5
Return on Com. Equity	(4.2)	na	na
Profit Growth	(40.6)	na	(14.3)
Revenue Growth	22.9	(19.7)	(25.9)
Asset Growth	8.9	(7.7)	(34.9)
BALANCE SHEET (000)			
Cash	2,994	174	119
Current Assets	5,259	1,338	1,101
Net Fixed Assets	19,625	18,312	22,910
Invest's & Advances	0	0	0
Total Assets	24,884	19,650	24,011
Short Term Debt	1,800	1,620	950
Current Liabilities	4,780	3,310	1,693
Long Term Debt	1,620	3,497	3,900
Total Liabilities	6,400	6,807	5,593
Total Equity	18,484	12,843	18,418
Total Liab. & Equity	24,884	19,650	24,011
CAPITAL (000)			
Total Debt	3,420	5,117	4,850
Preferred Equity	0	0	0
Common Equity	18,484	12,843	18,418

Business:

EXCEL ENERGY INC. is an oil and gas exploration and production company. It has producing oil and gas assets in Canada and the United States and land holdings in Alberta, British Columbia and Saskatchewan. The company has oil sands leases in the Ardmore-Muriel Lake region of Alberta.

Date	EPS	DPS	Tot Rev	Inc Bex
Mar 93	0.07	0.00	2,982	1,076
Dec 92	0.03	0.00	2,129	353
Sep 92	0.01	0.00	1,727	73
Jun 92	0.00	0.00	1,522	(61)
Mar 92	0.00	0.00	1,598	91
Dec 91	(0.06)	0.00	1,420	(5,857)
Sep 91	0.00	0.00	1,198	(117)
Jun 91	0.00	0.00	1,303	(53)

Synopsis:

In 1993 Excel Energy's focus continues to be the development of existing interests combined with the acquisition of strategic oil and gas properties. The company has budgeted for participation in 27 (15 net) wells in Alberta and British Columbia in 1993. Proceeds of $12.3-million, which resulted from the issue of three million special warrants in early 1993, will enable the company to proceed with its principal development drilling program and facilities construction in the Birch area of B.C., and Cadottte, Garrington, Ronalane and Sylvan Lake, all in Alberta. In May 1993, Excel added to its asset base by agreeing to acquire the petroleum and natural gas assets of Carmangay Oil Ltd. in the Birch area, and the Sutton and Larne/Zama areas of Alberta for $9.5-million.

Excel's capital expenditure program is expected to increase oil and gas production to approximately 2,000 barrels of oil and 12 million cubic feet of natural gas per day by December 1993. The $12-million capital budget will be financed from cash flow from operations, common share issues and established lines of credit.

As of February 1993, the company's aggressive drilling program which included the participation in 14 wells, resulted in 4 oil wells and 7 gas wells, for a success rate of 80%. This success has more than doubled Excel's reserves.

During fiscal 1992 (1991), average daily production by resource was: oil and natural gas liquids 480 (431) barrels; and natural gas, 7 (4.3) million cubic feet. At its 1992 (1991) fiscal year end, the company's gross proven and probable reserves by resource were: 1,864,000 (850,000) barrels of crude oil and natural gas liquids; and 23,453 (24,360) million cubic feet of natural gas.

Relative strength to TSE300

Price

Volume (in 1000's of board lots)

Rank (Profit/Revenue/Assets)
497   742   674

John J. Fleming
Chairman & C.E.O.

John Andriuk
President & C.O.O.

Richard K. Jaggard
Secretary & V.P., Finance

Address
Suite 1500
340 - 12th Avenue S.W.
Calgary
AB
T2R 1L5
(403) 269-8850

Fax: (403) 264-1088
D0003192/G/3.2

GULF CANADA RESOURCES LIMITED

Exchanges	Price (Jun24'93)	5.25	Trailing P/E	nm	Stock Symbol
TMZ	Trailing Yield (%)	0.00	Trailing EPS	(2.40)	**GOU**

Period Ending	Dec92	Dec91	Dec90	Dec89	Dec88
Yearly Statistics					
Price-Close	4.15	10.25	10.63	15.88	14.50
Price-High	10.88	10.63	17.38	16.88	18.63
Price-Low	3.60	6.00	10.00	14.00	12.63
P/E-Close	nm	nm	nm	nm	nm
Dividends per Share	0.10	0.40	0.40	0.40	0.40
Dividend Yield (%)	2.41	3.90	3.77	2.52	2.76
Sales per Share	4.38	5.01	5.59	5.04	4.40
EPS before extra. item	(2.16)	(0.84)	(0.82)	(0.35)	0.00
Cash Flow per Share	2.09	2.09	3.25	2.69	2.64
Book Value per Share	3.89	5.97	7.19	8.40	9.21
O/S Common Shares	162,748	158,623	155,876	155,876	155,876
Total Revenue	940,000	1,057,000	956,000	959,000	917,000
Income before extra.	(302,000)	(63,000)	(23,000)	46,000	67,000
Cash Flow	339,000	328,000	507,000	419,000	409,000
Debt/Equity	1.42	1.17	0.44	0.19	0.36
Return on Capital (%)	(8.22)	1.92	2.03	4.87	4.14
Ret. on Com. Equity (%)	(44.30)	(12.68)	(10.54)	(3.93)	(0.27)
% Change Profit	(379.4)	(173.9)	(150.0)	(31.3)	(60.8)
% Change Revenue	(11.1)	10.6	(0.3)	4.6	8.1
% Change Assets	(13.8)	4.2	13.4	(10.3)	12.6
Preferred Div. Coverage	0.0	0.0	0.0		
Total Div. Coverage	0.0	0.0	0.0		
Interest Coverage	0.0	0.6	0.6		
Current Ratio	1.7	1.7	0.8		
Operating Margin	(38.3)	(9.9)	3.8		
Asset Turnover	0.2	0.2	0.2		
5 YEAR RATIOS (%)					
Return on Capital	0.9	3.9	3.5		
Return on Com. Equity	(14.3)	(4.0)	(0.8)		
Profit Growth	na	na	na		
Revenue Growth	2.0	4.7	(20.5)		
Asset Growth	0.5	2.6	(10.4)		
BALANCE SHEET (000)					
Cash	396,000	858,000	0		
Current Assets	656,000	1,070,000	320,000		
Net Fixed Assets	2,360,000	2,484,000	2,738,000		
Invest's & Advances	185,000	336,000	661,000		
Total Assets	3,384,000	3,926,000	3,767,000		
Short Term Debt	147,000	298,000	41,000		
Current Liabilities	382,000	646,000	407,000		
Long Term Debt	1,570,000	1,478,000	902,000		
Total Liabilities	2,174,000	2,402,000	1,643,000		
Total Equity	1,210,000	1,524,000	2,124,000		
Total Liab. & Equity	3,384,000	3,926,000	3,767,000		
CAPITAL (000)					
Total Debt	1,717,000	1,776,000	943,000		
Preferred Equity	577,000	577,000	1,004,000		
Common Equity	633,000	947,000	1,120,000		

Date	EPS	DPS	Tot Rev	Inc Bex
Mar 93	(0.34)	0.00	182,000	(47,000)
Dec 92	(1.78)	0.00	245,000	(277,000)
Sep 92	0.03	0.00	243,000	18,000
Jun 92	(0.31)	0.00	192,000	(39,000)
Mar 92	(0.10)	0.10	179,000	(4,000)
Dec 91	(0.87)	0.10	237,000	(115,000)
Sep 91	(0.05)	0.10	223,000	5,000
Jun 91	0.17	0.10	308,000	47,000

Business:

GULF CANADA RESOURCES LTD. is an oil and gas production and exploration company. The company is a producer of crude oil, natural gas liquids and natural gas in Western Canada. It also has producing oil wells in Indonesia. The company has exploration activities in Western Canada, the Arctic, the East Coast, Southeast Asia and Africa.

Synopsis:

While Olympia & York Developments Ltd.'s placed its 75% stake in Gulf in the custody of Toronto-Dominion Bank as collateral against a $2.5-billion (U.S.) loan, Gulf has been dealing with problems of its own. Long-term debt grew to $1.5-billion and short-term debt to $94-million at year-end. Gulf is taking steps to strengthen its balance sheet by restructuring capital through equity sourcing, selling assets to reduce debt and tightening its focus internationally and in Western Canada.

Gulf restated its loss for the first quarter 1993 to $47-million which reflects the sale of its stake in Home Oil Co. for $145-million in April 1993. The restated loss includes a $33-million write-down in the carrying value of Home.

Gulf hopes to increase liquids production beyond 100,000 barrels per day in 1993. However, pipeline limitations which threatened market access in late 1992 are expected to continue. The company expects oil prices to remain volatile due to global uncertainties, with liquids prices averaging about the same or slightly higher than 1992 levels. Gulf expects a modest increase in gas production and although natural gas prices have begun to recover, Gulf believes competitive forces will restrain price increases in the short term.

The 1992 loss includes non-recurring after-tax losses of $280-million, reflecting the final Hibernia write-down, a reduction in the carrying value of Gulf's northern drilling system and a provision relating to its previous investment in Home Oil. Results were positively affected by higher liquid sales volumes, reduced costs, improved drilling system performance and a favorable tax settlement. 1992 gross daily production was: oil and natural gas liquids, 96,800 barrels; and natural gas, 319.1 million cubic feet. At 1992 year-end, gross proven and probable reserves by resource were: crude oil and natural gas liquids, 840 million barrels; and natural gas, 4.8 trillion cubic feet.

Relative strength to TSE300 / Price / Volume (in 1000's of board lots)

Rank (Profit/Revenue/Assets)
992   109   60

Robert J. Butler
Chairman
C.E. Shultz
President & C.E.O.
A.R. Sello
V.P., Finance & C.F.O.

Address
401 - 9th Avenue S.W.
P.O. Box 130
Calgary
AB
T2P 2H7
(403) 233-4000

Fax: (403) 233-5143
G0003506/G/3.2

HILLCREST RESOURCES LTD.

Exchanges	Price (Jun24'93)	8.12	Trailing P/E	30.09	Stock Symbol
TZ	Trailing Yield (%)	0.00	Trailing EPS	0.27	**HRT**

Period Ending	Nov92	Nov91	Nov90	Nov89	Nov88
Yearly Statistics					
Price-Close	3.85	3.75	1.95	1.80	1.20
Price-High	4.25	3.90	2.00	2.25	2.00
Price-Low	2.75	1.75	1.30	1.15	0.79
P/E-Close	16.04	20.83	12.19	nm	15.00
Dividends per Share	0.00	0.00	0.00	0.00	0.00
Dividend Yield (%)	0.00	0.00	0.00	0.00	0.00
Sales per Share	0.93	1.01	0.87	0.60	0.42
EPS before extra. item	0.24	0.18	0.16	(0.06)	0.08
Cash Flow per Share	0.58	0.56	0.43	0.22	0.16
Book Value per Share	1.97	1.46	1.07	0.75	0.62
O/S Common Shares	18,516	15,951	9,913	7,526	6,112
Total Revenue	15,992	12,883	8,397	3,954	2,952
Income before extra.	4,245	2,529	1,812	(95)	595
Cash Flow	9,960	7,004	4,202	1,433	942
Debt/Equity	0.13	0.23	0.30	0.51	0.20
Return on Capital (%)	12.86	12.21	13.77	2.94	14.59
Ret. on Com. Equity (%)	13.56	13.13	18.49	(7.93)	15.04
% Change Profit	67.8	39.6	1,998.9	(116.0)	260.0
% Change Revenue	24.1	53.4	112.4	33.9	41.6
% Change Assets	60.5	44.2	64.2	50.3	65.9

Date	EPS	DPS	Tot Rev	Inc Bex
Feb 93	0.08	0.00	5,937	1,470
Nov 92	0.07	0.00	4,479	1,197
Aug 92	0.07	0.00	4,046	1,296
May 92	0.05	0.00	3,551	905
Feb 92	0.05	0.00	3,917	846
Nov 91	0.04	0.00	3,653	669
Aug 91	0.07	0.00	3,274	914
May 91	0.02	0.00	2,931	328

Preferred Div. Coverage	21.2	8.1	5.9
Total Div. Coverage	21.2	8.1	5.9
Interest Coverage	8.8	5.0	4.3
Current Ratio	0.2	0.5	0.5
Operating Margin	29.4	23.7	28.4
Asset Turnover	0.3	0.3	0.3
5 YEAR RATIOS (%)			
Return on Capital	11.3	12.5	(9.0)
Return on Com. Equity	10.5	na	na
Profit Growth	91.4	na	na
Revenue Growth	50.2	37.9	20.6
Asset Growth	56.7	54.3	5.5
BALANCE SHEET (000)			
Cash	0	0	2,495
Current Assets	3,189	3,646	2,495
Net Fixed Assets	55,967	33,220	22,756
Invest's & Advances	0	0	0
Total Assets	59,156	36,866	25,564
Short Term Debt	401	936	228
Current Liabilities	15,973	6,696	5,149
Long Term Debt	4,550	4,900	4,550
Total Liabilities	20,708	11,666	9,699
Total Equity	38,448	25,200	15,865
Total Liab. & Equity	59,156	36,866	25,564
CAPITAL (000)			
Total Debt	4,951	5,836	4,778
Preferred Equity	1,993	1,993	5,275
Common Equity	36,455	23,207	10,589

Business:

HILLCREST RESOURCES is engaged in oil and gas exploration and production. The company has oil and gas properties in Alberta and British Columbia and mining properties in the Northwest Territories.

Synopsis:

Oil projects have been the primary target of Hillcrest's exploration program during the past few years as they offered the greatest potential to generate immediate cash flow. However, since natural gas markets in Canada and the United States have been steadily improving, Hillcrest is formulating a more balanced exploration program between oil and natural gas.

During fiscal 1993, Hillcrest will focus exploration efforts in the Gift, Bellis and Provost/Halkirk areas of Alberta and will pursue new areas in central Alberta with the potential for liquid rich natural gas and light gravity crude oil. A $12.5-million budget has been approved for exploration and development activities.

Management anticipates revenues in fiscal 1993 to exceed $26 million and cash flow from operations to exceed $14-million. Hillcrest's forecast is based on a $19.50 price for West Texas Intermediate crude oil and a $1.25 per thousand cubic foot average price of natural gas. Total production for 1993 is forecast to increase by about 70%, primarily as a result of a recent acquistion of oil producing properties in southeast Saskatchewan, and a successful exploration well drilled in the Carstairs area of Alberta. Oil and liquids production is expected to reach more than 2,800 barrels per day and natural gas production to exceed 12.5 million feet per day.

Despite lower product prices and natural gas volumes in fiscal 1992, oil and gas production revenue jumped 25% from 1991. This improvement was attributed to a 43% increase in crude oil sales and a 49% increase in crude oil production volume.

During 1992 (1991) Hillcrest's average daily production by resource was: crude oil and natural gas liquids, 1,648 (1,105) barrels; and natural gas, 1,130 (1,160) cubic feet. At its 1992 (1991) year end, total gross proven and probable reserves by commodity were: 8.2 (3.041) million barrels of crude oil and liquids and 35,030 (35,025) million cubic feet of natural gas.

Relative strength to TSE300 / Price / Volume (in 1000's of board lots)

Rank (Profit/Revenue/Assets)		
278	644	502

James Palmer
Chairman

Colin F. Ogilvy
President & C.E.O.

S. Blair Patrick
V.P., Finance & Secretary

Address
Suite 1800
407 - 2nd Street S.W.
Calgary
AB
T2P 2Y3
(403) 299-2222

Fax: (403) 265-9595
S0000556/G/3.2

HOME OIL COMPANY LIMITED

Exchanges	Price (Jun24'93)	21 .50	Trailing P/E	71 .67	Stock Symbol
TA	Trailing Yield (%)	0 .00	Trailing EPS	0 .30	**HOC**

Period Ending	Dec92	Dec91	Dec90	Dec89
Yearly Statistics				
Price-Close	15 .00	15 .00	n t	n t
Price-High	16 .63	18 .38	n t	n t
Price-Low	13 .75	14 .13	n t	n t
P/E-Close	88 .24	nm	n t	n t
Dividends per Share	0 .00	0 .06	0 .25	0 .01
Dividend Yield (%)	0 .00	0 .40	n t	n t
Sales per Share	6 .89	6 .71	8 .22	0 .32
EPS before extra. item	0 .17	(0 .01)	1 .68	1 .10
Cash Flow per Share	3 .48	2 .93	4 .61	0 .20
Book Value per Share	10 .09	9 .91	15 .64	0 .34
O/S Common Shares	39 ,644	39 ,644	39 ,637	839 ,259
Total Revenue	281 ,200	273 ,100	333 ,600	277 ,700
Income before extra.	6 ,900	(400)	66 ,400	43 ,700
Cash Flow	138 ,000	116 ,000	182 ,500	164 ,600
Debt/Equity	1 .07	1 .35	0 .48	0 .45
Return on Capital (%)	7 .28	5 .90	15 .42	na
Ret. on Com. Equity (%)	1 .74	(0 .16)	14 .28	na
% Change Profit	1 ,825 .0	(100 .6)	51 .9	na
% Change Revenue	3 .0	(18 .1)	20 .1	na
% Change Assets	(6 .8)	(0 .8)	5 .1	na

Preferred Div. Coverage	np	np	np
Total Div. Coverage	na	0 .0	5 .7
Interest Coverage	1 .4	1 .0	3 .1
Current Ratio	0 .8	1 .2	0 .6
Operating Margin	21 .9	22 .4	40 .3
Asset Turnover	0 .2	0 .2	0 .2
5 YEAR RATIOS (%)			
Return on Capital	na	na	na
Return on Com. Equity	na	na	na
Profit Growth	na	na	na
Revenue Growth	na	na	na
Asset Growth	na	na	na
BALANCE SHEET (000)			
Cash	0	0	0
Current Assets	63 ,300	92 ,400	95 ,400
Net Fixed Assets	1 ,304 ,700	1 ,375 ,700	1 ,386 ,400
Invest's & Advances	13 ,300	13 ,800	22 ,500
Total Assets	1 ,390 ,500	1 ,492 ,400	1 ,504 ,300
Short Term Debt	1 ,700	3 ,300	61 ,500
Current Liabilities	74 ,600	78 ,000	152 ,700
Long Term Debt	426 ,500	527 ,700	236 ,000
Total Liabilities	990 ,600	1 ,099 ,400	884 ,400
Total Equity	399 ,900	393 ,000	619 ,900
Total Liab. & Equity	1 ,390 ,500	1 ,492 ,400	1 ,504 ,300
CAPITAL (000)			
Total Debt	428 ,200	531 ,000	297 ,500
Preferred Equity	0	0	0
Common Equity	399 ,900	393 ,000	619 ,900

Business:

HOME OIL COMPANY LIMITED explores for, produces, transports and markets crude oil, natural gas and related products. With operations in British Columbia, Alberta, Saskatchewan and Manitoba, Home Oil operates six of its largest properties, nine natural gas processing plants and two regional pipeline systems. It operates and owns 88% of Scurry-Rainbow Oil Ltd. It also owns 50% of Federated Pipe Lines Ltd.

Date	EPS	DPS	Tot Rev	Inc Bex
Mar 93	0 .13	0 .00	75 ,300	5 ,000
Dec 92	0 .04	0 .00	79 ,700	1 ,700
Sep 92	0 .07	0 .00	69 ,000	2 ,800
Jun 92	0 .06	0 .00	66 ,500	2 ,200
Mar 92	0 .00	0 .00	66 ,000	200
Dec 91	0 .03	0 .00	70 ,200	1 ,200
Sep 91	(0 .08)	0 .00	65 ,100	(3 ,000)
Jun 91	(0 .07)	0 .00	62 ,500	(2 ,800)

Synopsis:

Home Oil Ltd. expects to benefit from a tighter capital structure, renewed exploration and rising natural gas prices in 1993. The disposal of the Reichmann family's 59.7% interest in Home Oil (through Gulf Canada Resources Limited and Olympia & York Developments Limited) in May 1993 ended a period of uncertainty regarding the ownership of Home. The Reichmann family had put the company up for sale in 1992, but their holding fell to creditors with the demise of their real estate empire.

During 1992, Home addressed the substantial debt it inherited when it was spun off from Interhome Energy Inc. in May 1991. Debt was reduced to $426.5-million at the end of 1992 from a high of $540-million. This figure is expected to fall to less than $370-million by the end of this year. Home also plans to continue its property rationalization, selling assets worth about $40-million in 1993. About $20-million of the proceeds will be used for acquisitions that complement the company's 36 core holdings.

Total capital spending will be $120-million in 1993, up from $86-million in 1992. Home expects to drill 120 wells, up from 70 last year and is shifting back toward natural gas. According to the company, each 10 cent improvement in the price of natural gas means an extra $4-million in profit and $5-million in cash flow. Home hit record daily gas production of 250 million cubic feet in the first three months of 1993, and had an average price of $1.72 for each thousand cubic feet. Many of the company's gas sales contracts were for terms of one year and will be renegotiated this fall, when Home hopes to reap the gains of higher prices.

In 1992 (1991), Home Oil's average daily production was: crude oil, 22,839 (23,763) barrels; natural gas liquids, 8,034 (6,588) barrels; and natural gas 214.2 (172.8) million cubic feet. At year-end total proven and probable reserves: crude oil, 63.6 (73.4) million barrels; natural gas liquids, 25.3 (25.5) million barrels; and natural gas, 1,094.7 (1,207.4) billion cubic feet.

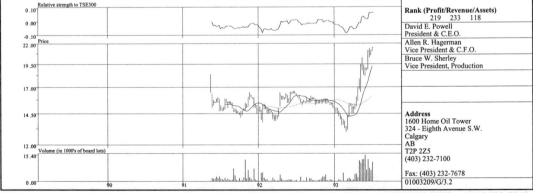

Rank (Profit/Revenue/Assets)
219   233   118

David E. Powell
President & C.E.O.
Allen R. Hagerman
Vice President & C.F.O.
Bruce W. Sherley
Vice President, Production

Address
1600 Home Oil Tower
324 - Eighth Avenue S.W.
Calgary
AB
T2P 2Z5
(403) 232-7100

Fax: (403) 232-7678
01003209/G/3.2

HORSHAM CORPORATION (THE)

Exchanges	Price (Jun24'93)		15.62	Trailing P/E		40.06	Stock Symbol
TMN	Trailing Yield (%)		0.00	Trailing EPS		0.39	**HSM**

Period Ending	Dec92	Dec91	Dec90	Dec89	Dec88
Yearly Statistics	US	US	US	US	US
Price-Close	11.13	10.50	9.13	11.63	7.00
Price-High	11.63	11.88	12.38	12.13	8.00
Price-Low	8.00	8.00	6.75	6.75	4.80
P/E-Close	22.34	13.11	11.34	13.11	30.17
Dividends per Share	0.00	0.00	0.00	0.00	0.00
Dividend Yield (%)	0.00	0.00	0.00	0.00	0.00
Sales per Share	25.49	27.83	32.93	25.78	2.95
EPS before extra. item	0.41	0.70	0.69	0.75	0.19
Cash Flow per Share	0.36	1.05	0.81	1.25	0.24
Book Value per Share	5.09	4.92	4.24	3.56	2.19
O/S Common Shares	89,407	87,861	84,703	84,665	76,195
Total Revenue	2,328,953	2,482,789	2,832,007	2,097,710	191,516
Income before extra.	36,245	61,442	58,157	60,058	11,719
Cash Flow	31,803	91,636	68,787	100,124	15,115
Debt/Equity	1.07	0.99	0.84	1.00	2.00
Return on Capital (%)	7.23	15.25	19.49	24.39	7.62
Ret. on Com. Equity (%)	8.17	15.54	17.62	25.64	8.82
% Change Profit	(41.0)	5.6	(3.2)	412.5	166.3
% Change Revenue	(6.2)	(12.3)	35.0	995.3	3,442.0
% Change Assets	2.9	23.8	15.2	20.8	506.5

Preferred Div. Coverage	np	np	np
Total Div. Coverage	na	na	na
Interest Coverage	1.4	3.4	3.2
Current Ratio	1.9	3.5	2.5
Operating Margin	1.3	4.3	4.5
Asset Turnover	1.9	2.2	3.0
5 YEAR RATIOS (%)			
Return on Capital	14.8	14.6	14.4
Return on Com. Equity	15.2	14.9	15.3
Profit Growth	52.4	89.3	52.5
Revenue Growth	236.4	271.7	219.5
Asset Growth	60.7	105.7	164.1
BALANCE SHEET (000)			
Cash	285,187	365,202	280,963
Current Assets	516,175	574,003	447,542
Net Fixed Assets	401,550	303,517	251,487
Invest's & Advances	226,002	206,470	191,568
Total Assets	1,165,252	1,132,238	914,607
Short Term Debt	85,239	289	0
Current Liabilities	271,751	164,478	180,206
Long Term Debt	401,514	426,619	301,907
Total Liabilities	710,254	700,051	555,795
Total Equity	454,998	432,187	358,812
Total Liab. & Equity	1,165,252	1,132,238	914,607
CAPITAL (000)			
Total Debt	486,753	426,908	301,907
Preferred Equity	0	0	0
Common Equity	454,998	432,187	358,812

Business:

HORSHAM CORP. is an investment company which invests in large established businesses. The company has a 20% equity interest in American Barrick Resources Corp. of Toronto, a 100% interest in Clark Oil & Refining Corp. of St. Louis, Missouri, a petroleum products company and a 100% interest in Horsham Properties GmbH, a German property development company.

Date		EPS	DPS	Tot Rev	Inc Bex
Mar 93	US	0.08	0.00	608,379	6,824
Dec 92	US	0.14	0.00	569,441	12,595
Sep 92	US	0.04	0.00	629,515	3,712
Jun 92	US	0.13	0.00	586,032	11,784
Mar 92	US	0.09	0.00	509,712	8,154
Dec 91	US	0.20	0.00	639,405	17,855
Sep 91	US	0.17	0.00	609,731	15,115
Jun 91	US	0.18	0.00	653,323	15,164

Synopsis:

Late in December 1992, Horsham purchased the remaining 40% of Clark Oil and Refining Corp., bringing Horsham's ownership of Clark to 100%. The Clark purchase was refinanced by a $125-million debt issue at the subsidiary level. The debt is secured by shares of Clark and is without recourse to Horsham.

The U.S. Clean Air Act amendments of 1990 state that diesel fuel sold for on-road vehicles must contain less than an average of 0.05% sulphur by October 1993. Because of the uncertainty of margins for the reformulated fuel, Clark has focused its efforts on the off-road market which is allowed under law to use conventional diesel products. As a result, Clark has postponed more than $70-million of capital spending on refinery modifications required to make the low sulphur product.

Infrastructure work began in March 1993 at Horsham's 600-acre business park project, Bradenburg Park, in Germany. Horsham expects to make this project self-financing through land sales which include a prepaid sale to Coca-Cola for a distribution centre.

Refined product prices continued to be weak through 1992 due to declining crude prices and an unseasonably warm winter in the U.S. Refining and retail margins were also negatively impacted by a sluggish U.S. economy and higher industry throughput relative to 1991. Clark's profit fell by $26-million despite strong refinery production in 1992. During 1992, Clark's refining division processed 142,400 barrels of oil per day. This 10% increase was partly due to maintenance turnarounds at Clark's two refineries in 1991.

Horsham's share of American Barrick's net earnings in 1992 (1991) was $34.1-million (U.S.) ($18.4-million (U.S.)). Horsham also recorded a $0.9-million (U.S.) dilution gain resulting from the sale of shares by American Barrick at prices in excess of their carrying value on Horsham's books. A combination of increased production, gold price hedging and lower operating and depreciation costs contributed to American Barrick's increase in earnings.

Relative strength to TSE300 / Price / Volume (in 1000's of board lots) chart

Rank (Profit/Revenue/Assets)		
66	47	112

Peter Munk
Chairman & C.E.O.
Paul D. Melnuk
President & C.O.O.
Eric D. Sigurdson
V.P. & C.F.O.

Address
24 Hazelton Avenue
Toronto
ON
M5R 2E2
(416) 924-6665

Fax: (416) 924-2842
U0001475/G/3.1

IMPERIAL OIL LIMITED

Exchanges	Price (Jun24'93)		47.75	Trailing P/E		40.47	Stock Symbol
TMVA	Trailing Yield (%)		3.77	Trailing EPS		1.18	**IMO**

Period Ending	Dec92	Dec91	Dec90	Dec89	Dec88
Yearly Statistics					
Price-Close	40.68	40.00	58.63	64.00	50.00
Price-High	48.13	61.13	67.63	64.13	63.50
Price-Low	37.75	38.75	53.25	48.63	45.00
P/E-Close	40.27	47.62	43.75	25.20	16.34
Dividends per Share	1.80	1.80	1.80	1.80	1.80
Dividend Yield (%)	4.43	4.50	3.07	2.81	3.60
Sales per Share	46.18	48.84	58.81	55.83	41.53
EPS before extra. item	1.01	0.84	1.34	2.54	3.06
Cash Flow per Share	5.92	5.14	3.53	7.55	7.32
Book Value per Share	34.23	35.03	35.80	37.86	34.99
O/S Common Shares (mil)	194	194	192	190	164
Total Revenue ($mil)	9,026	9,592	11,674	10,126	7,173
Income before extra. ($mil)	195	162	256	456	501
Cash Flow ($mil)	1,148	993	673	1,353	1,199
Debt/Equity	0.34	0.36	0.57	0.56	0.14
Return on Capital (%)	6.76	5.04	7.11	13.05	13.76
Ret. on Com. Equity (%)	2.91	2.37	3.65	7.06	8.87
% Change Profit	20.4	(36.7)	(43.9)	(9.0)	(32.8)
% Change Revenue	(5.9)	(17.8)	15.3	41.2	(6.5)
% Change Assets	(2.5)	(6.7)	(6.9)	61.6	1.7

Preferred Div. Coverage	np	np	np
Total Div. Coverage	0.6	0.5	0.7
Interest Coverage	3.9	2.2	2.3
Current Ratio	1.7	1.3	1.0
Operating Margin	6.4	5.4	6.1
Asset Turnover	0.7	0.7	0.8
5 YEAR RATIOS (%)			
Return on Capital	9.1	11.8	12.9
Return on Com. Equity	5.0	7.2	7.8
Profit Growth	(23.6)	(10.7)	(16.9)
Revenue Growth	3.2	6.2	5.8
Asset Growth	6.8	9.3	9.5
BALANCE SHEET (mil)			
Cash	1,022	293	2
Current Assets	2,638	2,127	2,403
Net Fixed Assets	9,965	10,760	11,378
Invest's & Advances	216	245	296
Total Assets	13,192	13,532	14,509
Short Term Debt	0	58	365
Current Liabilities	1,563	1,639	2,441
Long Term Debt	2,243	2,356	3,518
Total Liabilities	6,556	6,742	7,644
Total Equity	6,636	6,790	6,865
Total Liab. & Equity	13,192	13,532	14,509
CAPITAL (mil)			
Total Debt	2,243	2,414	3,883
Preferred Equity	0	0	0
Common Equity	6,636	6,790	6,865

Business:

IMPERIAL OIL LTD. is an integrated oil company. Its diversified activities fall under three groups. The resource division engages in the exploration and production of crude oil and natural gas. The petroleum division manages refines, markets and distributes crude oil refined products. The chemicals division makes and markets various chemicals. Exxon Corp. owns 69% of the company.

Date	EPS	DPS	Tot Rev	Inc Bex
Mar 93	0.38	0.45	2,174,000	73,000
Dec 92	0.27	0.45	2,361,000	51,000
Sep 92	0.23	0.45	2,281,000	46,000
Jun 92	0.30	0.45	2,320,000	58,000
Mar 92	0.21	0.45	2,067,000	40,000
Dec 91	(0.64)	0.45	2,301,000	(124,000)
Sep 91	0.44	0.45	2,352,000	85,000
Jun 91	0.03	0.45	2,347,000	5,000

Synopsis:

Imperial Oil anticipates further cutbacks will fuel profit gains in 1993. The company announced plans to cut 1,000 of its 4,600 gasoline stations in addition to the 360 closed last year. Overcapacity among Canadian refiners and low demand caused by the economic downturn has resulted in the company's decision to permanently close its 44,000 barrel-a-day Ioco refinery in Vancouver during the second half of 1994. The site will be used as a storage and distribution centre for products such as asphalt and bulk lubricants. Spare capacity at the company's Strathcona refinery in Alberta will be used to serve Ioco's customers in southern B.C. The costs involved in suspending operations at Ioco will result in a $54-million after-tax charge against the company's second quarter profit.

Capital outlays are expected to rise to $585-million in 1993, a 25% increase from 1992. A portion of this amount will go toward resuming the Cold Lake heavy oil plant expansion. Cold Lake production is expected to rise to 91,000 barrels a day by mid-year and to 104,000 barrels per day by the end of 1994.

The $289-million cash flow provided from operating activities during the first quarter 1993 was used to reduce debt by $114-million and to increase its cash and marketable securities balance which stood at $1-billion at the end of 1992. Imperial expects to announce later this year specific measures to translate this large balance into improved shareholder return.

1992 (1991) gross daily production by resource was: oil and natural gas liquids, 302,000 (318,000) barrels; and natural gas, 561 (641) million cubic feet. At 1992 (1991) year-end, gross proven reserves by resource were: crude oil and natural gas liquids, 1,866 (1,985) million barrels; and natural gas, 3,236 (4,184) billion cubic feet.

Imperial's revenues before inter-segment sales (net earnings/loss) by business segment were: natural resources, 7% (77%); petroleum products, 81% (48%); chemicals, 10% (7%); and corporate and other, 2% (-32%).

Relative strength to TSE300

Price

Volume (in 1000's of board lots)

Rank (Profit/Revenue/Assets)		
14	10	23

R.B. Peterson
Chairman & C.E.O.

R.A. Brenneman
President

Address
111 St. Clair Avenue West
Toronto
ON
M5W 1K3
(416) 968-4111

Fax: (416) 968-5228
I0000445/G/3.1

INTERNATIONAL COLIN ENERGY CORPORATION

Exchanges	Price (Jun24'93)		23.62	Trailing P/E		29.53	Stock Symbol
TA	Trailing Yield (%)		0.00	Trailing EPS		0.80	**KCN**

Period Ending	Jun92	Jun91	Jun90	Jun89	Jun88
Yearly Statistics					
Price-Close	9.75	3.35	3.60	3.87	1.50
Price-High	10.00	3.65	7.65	3.90	2.85
Price-Low	3.55	1.50	2.85	1.44	0.45
P/E-Close	19.12	14.57	20.00	32.25	nm
Dividends per Share	0.00	0.00	0.00	0.00	0.00
Dividend Yield (%)	0.00	0.00	0.00	0.00	0.00
Sales per Share	2.24	1.77	0.94	4.16	1.24
EPS before extra. item	0.51	0.23	0.18	0.12	(0.06)
Cash Flow per Share	1.53	1.00	0.62	0.65	0.03
Book Value per Share	3.26	1.93	1.72	0.94	0.76
O/S Common Shares	7,335	3,118	3,097	1,755	1,687
Total Revenue	11,893	5,613	3,513	7,094	1,864
Income before extra.	2,772	904	694	373	(74)
Cash Flow	8,054	3,100	2,244	1,110	42
Debt/Equity	0.67	1.26	0.70	0.25	0.21
Return on Capital (%)	17.24	13.73	9.05	14.63	(6.97)
Ret. on Com. Equity (%)	17.88	12.40	13.95	25.45	(10.35)
% Change Profit	206.8	30.3	86.0	603.5	64.9
% Change Revenue	111.9	59.8	(50.5)	280.6	8,570.3
% Change Assets	115.3	36.8	82.6	124.0	285.1

	Jun92	Jun91	Jun90
Preferred Div. Coverage	np	4.5	3.3
Total Div. Coverage	29.3	4.5	3.3
Interest Coverage	7.7	2.8	10.5
Current Ratio	0.7	0.6	0.8
Operating Margin	42.1	37.3	24.7
Asset Turnover	0.3	0.3	0.2
5 YEAR RATIOS (%)			
Return on Capital	9.5	5.4	(0.8)
Return on Com. Equity	11.9	5.5	(11.5)
Profit Growth	143.8	122.3	na
Revenue Growth	253.7	(12.2)	(28.0)
Asset Growth	115.4	6.3	(9.0)
BALANCE SHEET (000)			
Cash	111	71	742
Current Assets	3,225	1,442	3,100
Net Fixed Assets	40,784	18,648	11,463
Invest's & Advances	45	345	384
Total Assets	44,074	20,470	14,959
Short Term Debt	1,516	543	1,406
Current Liabilities	4,360	2,603	4,125
Long Term Debt	14,516	9,604	3,659
Total Liabilities	20,154	12,435	7,715
Total Equity	23,920	8,035	7,244
Total Liab. & Equity	44,074	20,470	14,959
CAPITAL (000)			
Total Debt	16,032	10,147	5,065
Preferred Equity	0	2,007	1,927
Common Equity	23,920	6,028	5,317

Business:

INTERNATIONAL COLIN ENERGY CORPORATION is involved in oil and gas exploration and development.

Date	EPS	DPS	Tot Rev	Inc Bex
Mar 93	0.26	0.00	10,247	2,527
Dec 92	0.21	0.00	8,475	2,083
Sep 92	0.15	0.00	5,896	1,069
Jun 92	0.18	0.00	3,649	1,151
Mar 92	0.11	0.00	2,976	608
Dec 91	0.13	0.00	3,101	672
Sep 91	0.09	0.00	2,173	342
Jun 91	0.15	0.00	2,230	501

Synopsis:

International Colin Energy's strategy is based on growth through acquisitions and development. The company recently purchased Olympia Energy Ventures Ltd., a private oil and gas company and in May of this year acquired a major oil and gas company's interest in the Adsett and Bougie Creek areas of northeastern B.C. for $19-million. The company said this acquisition includes 40,000 net acres of land and about nine million cubic feet a day of gas production. A further four shut-in gas wells will be brought on stream early in 1994, adding an additional six million cubic feet of gas per day to production.

Over the last three months, the company's development expenditures have focused on the Kidney and Panny areas in Northern Alberta. Both properties were acquired subsequent to the 1992 year end, and thus are not included in the financial results for this period. During the first quarter 1993, 29 wells were drilled resulting in 25 oil producers and four dry holes. 22 wells have been drilled by the end of June 1993. At present, International Colin is evaluating eight additional drilling locations at Kidney, which will be drilled by the end of June 1993.

Record growth in International Colin's production, earnings and cash flow for the third quarter 1993 reflect the impact of the company's acquisitions and development activities and operating efficiencies. Production averaged 5,919 barrels of oil per day, (BOPD), up 159% from the 2,288 BOPD averaged in the March 1992 quarter.

1992 (1991) average daily production before royalties: 1,686 (733) barrels of oil equivalents per day. At the 1992 (1991) year end, the company reported gross proven and probable oil reserves totaling 11 (3.8) million barrels and 2.7 (2.9) million cubic feet of natural gas reserves.

Relative strength to TSE300

Price

Volume (in 1000's of board lots)

Rank (Profit/Revenue/Assets)
322   677   567

John P. McGrain
Chairman

Thomas J. Jacobson
President

Paul D. Wright
V.P., Finance

Address
Suite 1210
333 - 11th Avenue S.W.
Calgary
AB
T2R 1L9
(403) 269-6822

Fax: (403) 263-1410
D0001132/G/3.2

INTERNATIONAL PETROLEUM CORPORATION

Exchanges	Price (Jun24'93)	2.08	Trailing P/E	nm	Stock Symbol
TQ	Trailing Yield (%)	0.00	Trailing EPS	(0.68)	**IRP**

Period Ending	Sep92	Sep91	Sep90	Sep89	Sep88
Yearly Statistics	US	US	US	US	US/11M
Price-Close	3.70	5.63	2.40	2.65	3.80
Price-High	7.25	6.25	3.00	4.15	5.60
Price-Low	3.50	1.60	1.80	2.10	3.90
P/E-Close	nm	nm	nm	nm	nm
Dividends per Share	0.00	0.00	0.00	0.00	0.00
Dividend Yield (%)	0.00	0.00	0.00	0.00	0.00
Sales per Share	0.05	0.09	0.07	0.08	0.26
EPS before extra. item	(0.10)	(0.32)	(0.31)	(0.20)	(0.75)
Cash Flow per Share	(0.07)	(0.07)	(0.02)	(0.06)	0.06
Book Value per Share	1.50	1.65	1.29	1.32	1.42
O/S Common Shares	31,704	23,933	23,483	17,158	15,873
Total Revenue	4,165	2,753	(100)	4,092	9,531
Income before extra.	(2,856)	(7,439)	(5,628)	(3,154)	(10,777)
Cash Flow	(1,967)	(1,676)	(278)	(1,066)	776
Debt/Equity	0.01	0.02	0.02	0.03	0.01
Return on Capital (%)	(6.41)	(20.92)	(20.60)	(13.35)	(47.71)
Ret. on Com. Equity (%)	(6.58)	(21.36)	(21.27)	(13.95)	(51.00)
% Change Profit	61.6	(32.2)	(78.4)	73.2	(128.9)
% Change Revenue	51.3	2,856.9	(102.4)	(60.6)	(16.7)
% Change Assets	16.9	29.3	39.3	(5.8)	6.1

Preferred Div. Coverage	np	np	np		
Total Div. Coverage	na	na	na		
Interest Coverage	0.0	0.0	0.0		
Current Ratio	6.0	3.5	2.6		
Operating Margin	(161.7)	(100.6)	(224.3)		
Asset Turnover	0.0	0.0	0.0		
5 YEAR RATIOS (%)					
Return on Capital	(21.8)	(23.9)	(25.7)		
Return on Com. Equity	(22.8)	(25.8)	(29.2)		
Profit Growth	na	na	na		
Revenue Growth	(19.7)	(27.5)	na		
Asset Growth	16.0	8.7	(2.6)		
BALANCE SHEET (000)					
Cash	16,017	3,430	12,335		
Current Assets	20,896	25,496	13,951		
Net Fixed Assets	36,174	21,648	21,687		
Invest's & Advances	0	0	0		
Total Assets	57,070	48,816	37,764		
Short Term Debt	405	733	449		
Current Liabilities	3,486	7,277	5,292		
Long Term Debt	0	0	0		
Total Liabilities	9,678	9,445	7,462		
Total Equity	47,393	39,371	30,302		
Total Liab. & Equity	57,070	48,816	37,764		
CAPITAL (000)					
Total Debt	405	733	449		
Preferred Equity	0	0	0		
Common Equity	47,393	39,371	30,302		

Business:

INTERNATIONAL PETROLEUM CORP. is involved in the acquisition, exploration and development of oil and gas properties. Properties are located in the Middle and Far East, North and West Africa, North and South America and Europe.

Date		EPS	DPS	Tot Rev	Inc Bex
Mar 93	US	(0.54)	0.00	1,352	(742)
Dec 92	US	(0.04)	0.00	1,366	(1,337)
Sep 92	US	(0.08)	0.00	327	(2,193)
Jun 92	US	(0.02)	0.00	570	(551)
Mar 92	US	0.03	0.00	1,840	828
Dec 91	US	(0.03)	0.00	678	(940)
Sep 91	US	(0.21)	0.00	(994)	(4,792)
Jun 91	US	(0.03)	0.00	807	(729)

Synopsis:

International Petroleum Corporation's, (IPC) strategy of concentrating on international exploration has proven to be a wise one. There is a growing shift of exploration expenditures by larger oil companies from North America to the international arena.

IPC announced in June 1993 that it intends to issue by way of private placement four million units at a price of $2 per unit, each unit consisting of one common share and one-half a share purchase warrant. The proceeds of the placement will be utilized in connection with the recent acquisition of the Welton Field, a producing oil field onshore the United Kingdom, and for general corporate purposes.

The main source of revenue in 1992 was service income generated by the company's technical centre; technical and management services are provided to joint ventures in concessions operated by IPC. The decrease in service revenues in 1992 resulted primarily from reduced exploration activity in company operated joint ventures as opposed to wholly owned concessions. IPC anticipates that service income will continue to be a primary source of funds during 1993, together with proceeds from farm outs of concession interests, until the start up of production from the Bukha Field offshore Oman.

Relative strength to TSE300 / Price / Volume (in 1000's of board lots)

Rank (Profit/Revenue/Assets)
807   786   476

Adolf H. Lundin
Chairman
Ian H. Lundin
President
Nigel R. McCue
Chief Financial Officer

Address
Suite 1320
885 West Georgia Street
Vancouver
BC
V6C 3E8
(604) 689-7842

Fax: (604) 689-4250
01000209/G/3.2

INVERNESS PETROLEUM LTD.

Exchanges	Price (Jun24'93)	12.12	Trailing P/E	57.74	Stock Symbol
TM	Trailing Yield (%)	0.00	Trailing EPS	0.21	**IES**

Period Ending	Dec92	Dec91	Dec90	Jun90	Jun89
Yearly Statistics			6M		
Price-Close	7.75	5.88	6.25	5.75	4.00
Price-High	8.25	7.25	7.50	6.25	5.50
Price-Low	4.75	5.00	5.75	3.85	3.30
P/E-Close	59.62	nm	10.42	57.50	nm
Dividends per Share	0.00	0.00	0.00	0.00	0.00
Dividend Yield (%)	0.00	0.00	0.00	0.00	0.00
Sales per Share	2.45	2.48	3.55	2.35	1.90
EPS before extra. item	0.13	(1.79)	0.30	0.10	(0.06)
Cash Flow per Share	1.22	1.19	2.10	1.26	0.99
Book Value per Share	3.77	3.39	3.77	3.47	3.33
O/S Common Shares	27,786	24,842	10,681	10,634	10,109
Total Revenue	63,490	43,867	19,023	24,905	19,749
Income before extra.	4,282	(30,062)	3,658	2,152	648
Cash Flow	31,394	20,814	11,193	12,985	10,012
Debt/Equity	0.37	0.59	0.77	0.50	0.53
Return on Capital (%)	6.82	(19.27)	19.07	8.73	4.90
Ret. on Com. Equity (%)	3.48	(50.26)	16.55	2.82	(1.66)
% Change Profit	114.2	(510.9)	240.0	232.1	(68.3)
% Change Revenue	44.7	15.3	52.8	26.1	(7.5)
% Change Assets	0.6	79.2	26.1	0.5	0.6

Business:

INVERNESS PETROLEUM LTD. is involved in the acquisition, exploration and development of oil and gas properties.

Date	EPS	DPS	Tot Rev	Inc Bex
Mar 93	0.05	0.00	18,015	1,591
Dec 92	0.08	0.00	18,122	2,199
Sep 92	0.04	0.00	16,650	1,309
Jun 92	0.04	0.00	14,827	1,211
Mar 92	(0.03)	0.00	13,826	(437)
Dec 91	(1.76)	0.00	15,631	(29,815)
Sep 91	0.01	0.00	13,735	549
Jun 91	(0.09)	0.00	6,611	(754)

Preferred Div. Coverage	4.3	0.0	7.9
Total Div. Coverage	4.3	0.0	7.9
Interest Coverage	3.1	0.0	6.5
Current Ratio	0.8	0.8	1.0
Operating Margin	16.7	(55.2)	39.9
Asset Turnover	0.3	0.2	0.3
5 YEAR RATIOS (%)			
Return on Capital	4.0	4.5	8.3
Return on Com. Equity	(5.8)	(6.0)	2.7
Profit Growth	15.9	na	110.0
Revenue Growth	24.3	40.1	23.5
Asset Growth	18.1	22.3	16.6
BALANCE SHEET (000)			
Cash	0	0	0
Current Assets	14,200	17,365	8,330
Net Fixed Assets	185,466	180,548	101,819
Invest's & Advances	0	0	0
Total Assets	199,666	198,405	110,724
Short Term Debt	0	0	0
Current Liabilities	17,654	20,707	8,066
Long Term Debt	42,923	58,132	39,044
Total Liabilities	84,656	99,816	60,124
Total Equity	115,010	98,589	50,600
Total Liab. & Equity	199,666	198,405	110,724
CAPITAL (000)			
Total Debt	42,923	58,132	39,044
Preferred Equity	10,393	14,341	10,287
Common Equity	104,617	84,248	40,313

Synopsis:

Inverness Petroleum is refocusing on natural gas exploration while continuing to maintain a balance of oil and gas production. The company views natural gas as its long-term business due to improved markets and available exploration prospects. Also, the popularity of natural gas continues to grow with consumers because of its price and with governments for environmental reasons.

Plans for 1993 include an aggressive exploration and development program. Inverness is also actively pursuing reserve acquisitions that have the potential to generate immediate cash flow required to fund development of existing properties situated in Alberta, Saskatchewan and British Columbia. The $42-million capital budget slated for these activities is to be primarily funded from operating cash flow estimated at $42.4-million for 1993.

Increases of up to 18% and 35% in oil and gas production levels, respectively, have been targeted for this year. Inverness expects oil prices to remain relatively stable and natural gas prices to improve steadily.

Fiscal 1992 was highlighted by record levels of production volumes, revenue, cash flow and earnings reflecting the company's expanding asset base and operating activities.

During 1992 (1991), Inverness' average daily production by resource was: natural gas, 52 (37.2) million cubic feet; and crude oil and natural gas liquids, 5,928 (4,404) barrels. At its 1992 (1991) year-end, total gross proven and probable reserves by commodity were: 200.1 (195.1) billion cubic feet of natural gas; and 13.8 (11.5) million barrels of crude oil and liquids.

Relative strength to TSE300

Price

Volume (in 1000's of board lots)

Rank (Profit/Revenue/Assets)
276   440   318

William J. Anderson
Chairman, President & C.E.O.

R. Ross Liland
V.P., Finance

Murray M. Frame
Exec. V.P. & C.O.O.

Address
Suite 2200
400 - 3rd Avenue S.W.
Calgary
AB
T2P 4H2
(403) 294-3800

Fax: (403) 264-1810
I0001899/G/3.2

MARK RESOURCES INC.

Exchanges	Price (Jun24'93)	11.25	Trailing P/E	nm	Stock Symbol
T	Trailing Yield (%)	0.00	Trailing EPS	(0.19)	**MKC**

Period Ending	Dec92	Dec91	Dec90	Dec89	Dec88
Yearly Statistics					
Price-Close	5.25	6.25	9.50	10.13	9.00
Price-High	6.25	9.75	12.75	10.50	11.00
Price-Low	4.50	5.75	9.00	7.25	7.00
P/E-Close	nm	nm	67.86	506.25	450.00
Dividends per Share	0.00	0.00	0.00	0.00	0.00
Dividend Yield (%)	0.00	0.00	0.00	0.00	0.00
Sales per Share	4.13	4.04	4.16	2.94	2.41
EPS before extra. item	(0.29)	(2.65)	0.14	0.02	0.02
Cash Flow per Share	1.31	1.48	1.73	1.42	1.19
Book Value per Share	5.59	5.88	8.53	8.39	8.25
O/S Common Shares	26,634	26,539	26,465	26,185	22,902
Total Revenue	109,863	107,193	109,639	69,237	52,816
Income before extra.	(7,611)	(70,260)	3,570	459	338
Cash Flow	34,832	39,131	45,711	32,910	25,572
Debt/Equity	1.14	1.11	0.69	0.68	0.69
Return on Capital (%)	3.07	(26.93)	5.89	4.58	3.85
Ret. on Com. Equity (%)	(4.99)	(36.81)	1.60	0.23	0.19
% Change Profit	89.2	(2,068.1)	677.8	35.8	(96.4)
% Change Revenue	2.5	(2.2)	58.4	31.1	3.9
% Change Assets	(1.8)	(20.0)	4.6	12.6	15.2

	Date	EPS	DPS	Tot Rev	Inc Bex
	Mar 93	0.05	0.00	27,644	1,269
	Dec 92	(0.27)	0.00	32,249	(7,070)
	Sep 92	0.02	0.00	26,607	412
	Jun 92	0.01	0.00	24,914	349
	Mar 92	(0.05)	0.00	26,093	(1,302)
	Dec 91	(2.59)	0.00	27,615	(68,579)
	Sep 91	(0.03)	0.00	23,645	(982)
	Jun 91	(0.02)	0.00	25,664	(511)

	Dec92	Dec91	Dec90
Preferred Div. Coverage	np	np	np
Total Div. Coverage	na	na	na
Interest Coverage	0.7	0.0	1.5
Current Ratio	0.9	0.8	0.4
Operating Margin	12.3	(90.3)	20.5
Asset Turnover	0.3	0.3	0.2
5 YEAR RATIOS (%)			
Return on Capital	(1.9)	(0.9)	0.5
Return on Com. Equity	(8.0)	(5.9)	(5.2)
Profit Growth	na	na	(15.2)
Revenue Growth	16.6	31.6	28.0
Asset Growth	1.3	2.7	15.8
BALANCE SHEET (000)			
Cash	0	0	824
Current Assets	61,706	12,258	13,871
Net Fixed Assets	347,837	404,658	507,579
Invest's & Advances	0	0	0
Total Assets	411,396	418,921	523,651
Short Term Debt	51,321	1,278	11,555
Current Liabilities	69,797	15,332	37,198
Long Term Debt	118,490	172,006	143,629
Total Liabilities	262,472	262,888	297,929
Total Equity	148,924	156,033	225,722
Total Liab. & Equity	411,396	418,921	523,651
CAPITAL (000)			
Total Debt	169,811	173,284	155,184
Preferred Equity	0	0	0
Common Equity	148,924	156,033	225,722

Business:

MARK RESOURCES INC. is an oil and gas exploration, development and production company. It has producing wells and exploration activities primarily in Western Canada. The company holds an 88% interest in Precambrian Shield Resources Limited of Calgary. Union Energy Inc. of Toronto is the company's major shareholder.

Synopsis:

Mark Resources announced in May 1993 the terms of a proposed amalgamation of its wholly owned subsidiary, 468714 Alberta Inc. with its 88% held subsidiary, Precambrian Shield Resources Limited. Mark proposes to pay $14.3-million to buy out the minority shareholders of Precambrian. In order to finance this purchase, reduce debt and fund operating activities, Mark recently closed an issue of six million special warrants for net proceeds of approximately $47-million.

Mark has shifted its focus from exploration to development of existing core properties and light oil acquisitions. Each objective was allocated 35% of Mark's $40-million capital budget for 1993. Major development and projects in Saskatchewan and Alberta are expected to result in increased production to an average 10,500 barrels per day and cash flow growth to $40-million in 1993.

Increased cost efficiencies are resulting from the asset rationalization program and cost control measures initiated in 1992. Per-unit gas production costs will be significantly reduced as a result of the disposition of its Sandhills property in December 1992. Proceeds of $50-million from this disposition are being applied to reduce bank debt. Dispositions, totaling $3-million year-to-date, of non-core properties, including low interest shallow gas and mature heavy oil, were completed and funds redeployed to acquisitions.

In October 1992, Mark's former parent company, Union Energy Inc., closed the sale of $88-million of debentures. The debentures, exchangeable for Mark common shares held by Union, effectively distribute Union's 58% stake to the public.

During 1992 (1991) average daily production by resource was: oil, 9,576 (9,468) barrels; and natural gas, 85 (82) million cubic feet. At the end of 1992 (1991), gross proven and probable reserves totaled 43 (42) million barrels of oil, and 475 (468) billion cubic feet of natural gas.

Relative strength to TSE300

Price

Volume (in 1000's of board lots)

Rank (Profit/Revenue/Assets)
859   359   234

James W. Leech
Chairman

Daryl E. Birnie
President & C.E.O.

Daniel T. Tsubouchi
Sr. V.P., Corp. Aff. & Finance

I. Lorne Levorson
Sr. V.P., Explor. & Prod.

Address
Suite 1300
800 - 5th Avenue S.W.
Calgary
AB
T2P 4A4
(403) 267-1500

Fax: (403) 269-2297
B0002273/G/3.2

MORGAN HYDROCARBONS INC.

Exchanges	Price (Jun24'93)		6.75	Trailing P/E		48.21	Stock Symbol
TMZ	Trailing Yield (%)		0.00	Trailing EPS		0.14	**MHI**

Period Ending	Dec92	Dec91	Dec90	Dec89	Dec88
Yearly Statistics					
Price-Close	5.25	5.25	6.50	3.95	3.50
Price-High	5.75	6.63	7.88	4.10	4.50
Price-Low	3.90	4.40	3.70	3.05	2.70
P/E-Close	47.73	nm	27.08	20.79	35.00
Dividends per Share	0.00	0.00	0.00	0.00	0.00
Dividend Yield (%)	0.00	0.00	0.00	0.00	0.00
Sales per Share	1.91	1.92	1.94	1.60	1.52
EPS before extra. item	0.11	(0.06)	0.24	0.19	0.10
Cash Flow per Share	0.78	0.49	0.85	0.62	0.50
Book Value per Share	3.17	3.26	2.94	2.71	2.50
O/S Common Shares	32,611	24,555	20,593	20,520	20,250
Total Revenue	57,075	43,663	39,801	32,451	25,435
Income before extra.	3,406	(1,318)	4,901	3,903	2,363
Cash Flow	23,386	11,119	17,467	12,532	8,219
Debt/Equity	0.57	0.64	0.75	0.60	0.38
Return on Capital (%)	6.39	1.10	10.25	8.62	6.05
Ret. on Com. Equity (%)	3.71	(1.88)	8.44	7.34	4.03
% Change Profit	358.4	(126.9)	25.6	65.2	(34.6)
% Change Revenue	30.7	9.7	22.6	27.6	15.0
% Change Assets	34.1	14.2	22.2	25.1	24.8

Business:

MORGAN HYDROCARBONS INC. is an oil and gas exploration and production company. It has producing wells and exploration activities in Alberta and Saskatchewan. The company markets natural gas in Canada and the United States.

Date	EPS	DPS	Tot Rev	Inc Bex
Mar 93	0.02	0.00	14,605	544
Dec 92	0.05	0.00	15,027	1,783
Sep 92	0.04	0.00	14,435	982
Jun 92	0.03	0.00	13,514	818
Mar 92	(0.01)	0.00	9,398	(177)
Dec 91	(0.06)	0.00	10,246	(1,340)
Sep 91	0.03	0.00	11,287	717
Jun 91	(0.02)	0.00	10,054	(529)

	Dec92	Dec91	Dec90
Preferred Div. Coverage	np	np	np
Total Div. Coverage	na	na	na
Interest Coverage	1.8	0.3	2.2
Current Ratio	1.1	1.2	1.0
Operating Margin	16.4	3.0	25.1
Asset Turnover	0.3	0.3	0.3
5 YEAR RATIOS (%)			
Return on Capital	6.5	7.4	7.2
Return on Com. Equity	4.3	5.5	1.8
Profit Growth	(1.2)	na	37.8
Revenue Growth	20.8	16.8	14.8
Asset Growth	23.8	16.8	6.8
BALANCE SHEET (000)			
Cash	5,714	1,230	1,663
Current Assets	13,058	7,500	11,706
Net Fixed Assets	178,500	134,957	112,706
Invest's & Advances	250	250	250
Total Assets	192,241	143,367	125,547
Short Term Debt	0	0	0
Current Liabilities	11,942	6,102	11,539
Long Term Debt	59,411	50,911	45,111
Total Liabilities	88,768	63,387	64,976
Total Equity	103,472	79,979	60,571
Total Liab. & Equity	192,241	143,367	125,547
CAPITAL (000)			
Total Debt	59,411	50,911	45,111
Preferred Equity	0	0	0
Common Equity	103,472	79,979	60,571

Synopsis:

With current production levels, and active exploration programs, Morgan Hydrocarbons anticipates cash flow from operations to exceed $30-million in 1993. The demand for Morgan's heavy oil continues to increase and the company expects this to result in improved pricing throughout 1993. The colder than normal temperatures in late 1992 and early 1993, and the low levels of natural gas storage caused an uncharacteristic surge in natural gas demand and price. Morgan expects to see a tightening of supply and possibly shortages of natural gas this year, if drilling levels in the U.S. continue at present low levels. Morgan anticipates higher average natural gas prices in 1993 with a potential for price surges.

Capital expenditures in 1992 were higher than 1991 primarily due to the Eagle Lake and Norex acquisitions. With renewed emphasis on exploration in 1993, Morgan intends to spend approximately $12-milion to $15-million towards exploration activities. Exploration drilling will focus primarily on the Senlac/Long Lake area of west central Saskatchewan, with the objective of doubling current productions levels within the next 24 months. Current daily output levels are at 7,600 barrels of oil and 27 million cubic feet of natural gas. Approximately $18-million to $22-million has been budgeted for development which will include light oil infill drilling and restimulation at Eagle Lake, heavy oil horizontal drilling at Senlac and Long Lake and natural gas development at its Bilawchuk and Manning areas of Alberta. These activities will be financed through internally generated cash flow, supplemented with joint venture funding.

Morgan's average daily net production in 1992 (1991) was: crude oil and natural gas liquids, 6,600 (4,940) barrels; and natural gas 24.1 (23.4) million cubic feet. Net proven and probable reserves at the end of 1992 (1991) were: oil and natural gas liquids, 15.8 (14.3) million barrels; and natural gas 130.4 (128.2) billion cubic feet. 1992 (1991) revenues by operating segment were: oil and gas liquids, 66% (53%); natural gas, 18% (23%); and natural gas processing, 15% (23%).

Relative strength to TSE300

Price

Volume (in 1000's of board lots)

Rank (Profit/Revenue/Assets)
299   453   325

Vernon L. Horte
Chairman

William A. Trickett
President & C.E.O.

Allen Emes
V.P., Finance

Address
2200 Bow Valley Square II
205 - 5th Avenue S.W.
Calgary
AB
T2P 2V7
(403) 298-8300

Fax: (403) 298-8390
M0015445/G/3.2

MORRISON PETROLEUMS LTD.

Exchanges	Price (Jun24'93)	12.87	Trailing P/E	33.86	Stock Symbol
T	Trailing Yield (%)	0.23	Trailing EPS	0.38	**MRP**

Period Ending	Dec92	Dec91	Dec90	Dec89	Dec88
Yearly Statistics					
Price-Close	8.50	4.13	3.58	3.00	2.42
Price-High	8.80	4.33	4.33	3.00	2.67
Price-Low	4.00	3.17	2.71	1.18	1.75
P/E-Close	27.42	17.19	12.80	16.98	30.21
Dividends per Share	0.03	0.03	0.00	0.00	0.00
Dividend Yield (%)	0.39	0.81	0.00	0.00	0.00
Sales per Share	1.46	0.96	0.87	0.67	0.35
EPS before extra. item	0.31	0.24	0.28	0.18	0.08
Cash Flow per Share	0.89	0.64	0.60	0.41	0.31
Book Value per Share	2.47	2.00	1.79	1.51	1.18
O/S Common Shares	47,148	40,929	40,749	40,164	33,405
Total Revenue	68,807	41,518	36,559	23,420	12,386
Income before extra.	14,024	9,839	11,344	6,043	2,656
Cash Flow	40,484	25,968	24,367	14,064	6,755
Debt/Equity	0.27	0.01	0.01	0.03	0.06
Return on Capital (%)	21.53	19.76	22.32	16.54	8.57
Ret. on Com. Equity (%)	14.15	12.71	16.96	12.08	7.00
% Change Profit	42.5	(13.3)	87.7	127.6	(22.8)
% Change Revenue	65.7	13.6	56.1	89.1	7.5
% Change Assets	73.1	12.8	23.8	46.4	11.1

Business:
MORRISON PETROLEUM LTD. is an independent petroleum explorer and producer whose main area of activity is in Alberta and northeastern British Columbia. Most of the company's revenues result from the sale of light and medium crude oil.

Date	EPS	DPS	Tot Rev	Inc Bex
Mar 93	0.11	0.03	23,386	5,082
Dec 92	0.13	0.00	26,603	5,848
Sep 92	0.10	0.00	23,497	4,621
Jun 92	0.05	0.00	10,094	2,100
Mar 92	0.04	0.03	8,613	1,456
Dec 91	0.10	0.00	12,044	3,981
Sep 91	0.05	0.00	11,171	2,175
Jun 91	0.03	0.03	9,259	1,323

Preferred Div. Coverage	np	np	np	
Total Div. Coverage	10.3	7.2	na	
Interest Coverage	11.6	na	na	
Current Ratio	1.2	1.6	1.4	
Operating Margin	33.3	33.6	39.7	
Asset Turnover	0.3	0.3	0.4	
5 YEAR RATIOS (%)				
Return on Capital	17.7	16.4	13.3	
Return on Com. Equity	12.6	11.7	9.8	
Profit Growth	32.5	60.2	22.5	
Revenue Growth	42.9	40.2	23.6	
Asset Growth	31.4	22.2	18.9	
BALANCE SHEET (000)				
Cash	3,119	5,221	9,144	
Current Assets	22,667	17,544	18,711	
Net Fixed Assets	165,712	90,400	78,474	
Invest's & Advances	6,129	4,453	2,456	
Total Assets	194,508	112,396	99,641	
Short Term Debt	1,090	852	933	
Current Liabilities	19,228	11,121	12,915	
Long Term Debt	30,004	0	0	
Total Liabilities	78,006	30,616	26,650	
Total Equity	116,502	81,780	72,991	
Total Liab. & Equity	194,508	112,396	99,641	
CAPITAL (000)				
Total Debt	31,094	852	933	
Preferred Equity	0	0	0	
Common Equity	116,502	81,780	72,991	

Synopsis:

The increase in revenue for Morrison Petroleums in 1992 was attributed to higher oil and gas production. Acquisitions of $66.5-million and successful exploration and development of areas such as Thompson Lake and Long Coulee, both in Alberta, have had a significant impact on the company's financial performance. The Thompson field is also responsible for much of the growth in first quarter 1993 cash flow. With the drilling of 60 new wells currently underway, the Thompson field is expected to produce, temporarily, 20,000 barrels of oil a day and generate $40-million in cash flow in 1993.

Morrison expects the consolidation within the oil and gas industry to continue during the next few years. This activity will create opportunities for companies to strategically acquire valuable oil and gas producing properties and undeveloped acreage. However, the company believes it will become increasingly difficult to acquire such assets due to increased interest in natural gas properties and a larger number of potential buyers. Morrison will continue to pursue key oil and gas acquisitions in 1993.

Morrison's capital expenditure program for exploration and development, excluding acquisitions of producing properties, is expected to be $35-million in 1993, with 25% targeted to exploration and 75% for development. This program is to be financed by an estimated pre-tax cash flow of $60-million.

A three-for-one share split was approved by shareholders in May 1993. After the split, Morrison will have about 47.1 million shares outstanding.

1992 (1991) daily production by resource was: oil and natural gas liquids, 7,968 (5,237) barrels; and natural gas, 19.5 (5) million cubic feet. At 1992 (1991) year end, total gross proven and probable reserves by resource were: crude oil and natural gas liquids, 19.9 (10.4) million barrels and natural gas, 132.3 (61.2) billion cubic feet.

Relative strength to TSE300

Price

Volume (in 1000's of board lots)

Rank (Profit/Revenue/Assets)
149   427   322

A. Gordon Stollery
Chairman & C.E.O.

Walter Deboni
President & C.O.O.

David R. Schick
V.P., Finance & C.F.O.

Address
Suite 2900
400 - 3rd Avenue S.W.
Calgary
AB
T2P 4H2
(403) 262-5242

Fax: (403) 237-0466
M0005162/G/3.2

NORCEN ENERGY RESOURCES LIMITED

Exchanges	Price (Jun24'93)		21 .25	Trailing P/E		36 .64	Stock Symbol
TMA	Trailing Yield (%)		2 .82	Trailing EPS		0 .58	**NCN**

Period Ending	Dec92	Dec91	Dec90	Dec89	Dec88
Yearly Statistics					
Price-Close	17 .50	23 .50	22 .88	25 .38	18 .88
Price-High	23 .75	26 .63	25 .38	27 .75	21 .50
Price-Low	16 .50	19 .88	16 .88	18 .38	16 .63
P/E-Close	35 .71	47 .96	12 .04	14 .59	13 .20
Dividends per Share	0 .60	0 .60	0 .55	0 .50	0 .50
Dividend Yield (%)	3 .43	2 .55	2 .40	1 .97	2 .65
Sales per Share	14 .70	15 .33	16 .60	13 .22	11 .51
EPS before extra. item	0 .49	0 .49	1 .90	1 .74	1 .43
Cash Flow per Share	4 .84	4 .66	6 .01	5 .12	4 .17
Book Value per Share	17 .23	17 .66	17 .77	16 .41	15 .14
O/S Common Shares	69 ,653	60 ,100	59 ,412	59 ,100	58 ,638
Total Revenue	1 ,009 ,090	978 ,497	1 ,050 ,297	845 ,066	736 ,902
Income before extra.	38 ,857	44 ,064	129 ,188	110 ,213	91 ,744
Cash Flow	316 ,775	279 ,212	356 ,143	300 ,702	244 ,174
Debt/Equity	0 .92	0 .90	1 .00	0 .88	0 .78
Return on Capital (%)	7 .14	7 .30	13 .49	13 .50	12 .29
Ret. on Com. Equity (%)	2 .82	2 .76	11 .09	10 .99	9 .74
% Change Profit	(11 .8)	(65 .9)	17 .2	20 .1	(7 .5)
% Change Revenue	3 .1	(6 .8)	24 .3	14 .7	0 .3
% Change Assets	4 .9	1 .6	15 .0	12 .8	3 .7

Date	EPS	DPS	Tot Rev	Inc Bex
Mar 93	0.33	0.15	314 ,619	24 ,101
Dec 92	0.18	0.15	301 ,285	13 ,483
Sep 92	0.04	0.15	227 ,653	3 ,954
Jun 92	0.03	0.15	221 ,909	3 ,318
Mar 92	0.25	0.15	256 ,595	18 ,102
Dec 91	0.03	0.15	259 ,834	5 ,237
Sep 91	0.00	0.15	208 ,598	3 ,683
Jun 91	(0.09)	0.15	206 ,348	(1 ,834)

Preferred Div. Coverage	5 .6	3 .0	7 .7
Total Div. Coverage	0 .8	0 .9	2 .6
Interest Coverage	1 .9	2 .2	4 .0
Current Ratio	1 .5	1 .1	1 .2
Operating Margin	17 .6	16 .8	27 .5
Asset Turnover	0 .3	0 .3	0 .3
5 YEAR RATIOS (%)			
Return on Capital	10 .7	12 .1	12 .8
Return on Com. Equity	7 .5	9 .2	9 .7
Profit Growth	(17 .2)	(2 .5)	1 .5
Revenue Growth	6 .5	9 .6	9 .5
Asset Growth	7 .4	7 .1	6 .4
BALANCE SHEET (000)			
Cash	90 ,850	12 ,065	7 ,253
Current Assets	335 ,261	215 ,620	246 ,271
Net Fixed Assets	2 ,457 ,521	2 ,488 ,651	2 ,407 ,256
Invest's & Advances	269 ,093	247 ,436	246 ,430
Total Assets	3 ,200 ,853	3 ,050 ,329	3 ,002 ,946
Short Term Debt	63 ,874	54 ,020	193 ,981
Current Liabilities	225 ,497	203 ,598	208 ,822
Long Term Debt	1 ,143 ,381	1 ,085 ,267	1 ,056 ,164
Total Liabilities	1 ,890 ,500	1 ,789 ,057	1 ,747 ,246
Total Equity	1 ,310 ,353	1 ,261 ,272	1 ,255 ,700
Total Liab. & Equity	3 ,200 ,853	3 ,050 ,329	3 ,002 ,946
CAPITAL (000)			
Total Debt	1 ,207 ,255	1 ,139 ,287	1 ,250 ,145
Preferred Equity	110 ,099	200 ,000	200 ,000
Common Equity	1 ,200 ,254	1 ,061 ,272	1 ,055 ,700

Business:

NORCEN ENERGY RESOURCES LTD. is a major resource enterprise with three business segments: oil and gas; propane marketing; and mineral resources. In its core oil and gas business, Norcen exlores, develops, and produces in Canada, the U.S., Australia, and Argentina. Superior Propane distributes propane across Canada and the U.S. Norcen holds an 11% equity interest in Iron Ore Company of Canada.

Synopsis:

In April 1993, in a joint statement issued by Norcen Energy Resources Limited and North Canadian Oils Limited, it was announced that the operations and staff of the two companies would be integrated by July 1, 1993. North Canadian's financial results will appear on Norcen's books from the beginning of April. Norcen, which is controlled by the Edper Bronfman empire, became a controlling shareholder in North Canadian in April when the Bronfmans consolidated their energy investments. Norcen's strength in oil and its international presence will complement North Canadian's presence in the natural gas and cogeneration markets.

The improvement in Norcen's first quarter 1993 financial performance resulted primarily from production gains, higher prices for natural gas and oil and gas liquids and a sharp rise in propane volumes sold.

Norcen plans to spend $83-million on exploration this year, apportioning 39% for Canada and splitting the remainder between U.S. and other international projects. Its development budget totals $129.4-million, of which 77% will be spent in Canada.

Average daily production in 1992 (1991) was: oil and gas liquids, 56,400 (54,500) barrels; and natural gas, 291.3 (251.2) million cubic feet. Gross established reserves in 1992 (1991) were: oil and gas liquids, 199.3 (193.8) million barrels; and natural gas, 1,752 (1,785) billion cubic feet.

Contributions to sales and other revenues (contributions to operating income/loss) in 1992 by geographic segment were: Canada, 80% (90%); United States, 15% (2%); Australia, 5% (8%); and other international, 1% (-1%). Contributions to sales and other revenues (contribution to operating income) by business segment were: oil and gas, 50% (76%); propane marketing, 45% (10%); mineral resources, 4% (14%) and investment and other revenues, 1% (-).

Relative strength to TSE300 / Price / Volume (in 1000's of board lots) chart, 1990–1993.

Rank (Profit/Revenue/Assets)		
76	103	64

Edward G. Battle
Chairman Of The Board

Barry D. Cochrane
President & C.E.O.

Paul H. Palmer
Sr. V.P. & C.F.O.

J. Gerhard Schopp
V.P., Operations

Address
715 - 5th Avenue S.W.
Calgary
AB
T2P 2X7
(403) 231-0111

Fax: (403) 231-0187
N0002475/G/3.2

NORTH CANADIAN OILS LIMITED

Exchanges	Price (Jun24'93)	16.50	Trailing P/E	nm	Stock Symbol
TMA	Trailing Yield (%)	1.21	Trailing EPS	(0.37)	**NCO**

Period Ending	Dec92	Dec91	Dec90	Dec89	Dec88
Yearly Statistics					
Price-Close	11.38	10.63	15.00	23.00	18.88
Price-High	17.25	16.70	23.50	25.00	21.50
Price-Low	8.38	10.50	13.75	18.25	16.75
P/E-Close	94.79	42.52	23.44	42.59	28.17
Dividends per Share	0.20	0.20	0.20	0.20	0.20
Dividend Yield (%)	1.76	1.88	1.33	0.87	1.06
Sales per Share	9.63	8.39	7.00	3.82	4.01
EPS before extra. item	0.12	0.25	0.64	0.54	0.67
Cash Flow per Share	2.64	2.45	2.57	2.61	2.88
Book Value per Share	16.67	16.68	16.64	15.90	14.10
O/S Common Shares	36,574	36,534	36,596	35,371	27,487
Total Revenue	375,700	328,800	290,200	148,895	142,731
Income before extra.	11,000	16,900	32,800	27,967	30,280
Cash Flow	96,600	89,300	93,700	78,833	78,687
Debt/Equity	0.28	0.25	0.34	0.25	0.23
Return on Capital (%)	3.31	4.75	7.10	6.68	7.55
Ret. on Com. Equity (%)	0.71	1.49	4.00	3.46	4.84
% Change Profit	(34.9)	(48.5)	17.3	(7.6)	15.1
% Change Revenue	14.3	13.3	94.9	4.3	16.0
% Change Assets	4.2	(2.1)	11.5	16.9	6.2
Preferred Div. Coverage	1.6	2.2	3.5		
Total Div. Coverage	0.8	1.1	2.0		
Interest Coverage	2.3	2.5	3.1		
Current Ratio	1.0	2.6	1.6		
Operating Margin	4.6	7.9	12.4		
Asset Turnover	0.3	0.3	0.2		
5 YEAR RATIOS (%)					
Return on Capital	5.9	6.6	7.2		
Return on Com. Equity	2.9	3.6	3.8		
Profit Growth	(16.1)	0.0	7.3		
Revenue Growth	24.9	24.0	15.1		
Asset Growth	7.1	7.6	7.1		
BALANCE SHEET (000)					
Cash	0	120,500	120,100		
Current Assets	99,800	196,200	240,100		
Net Fixed Assets	880,300	831,800	808,400		
Invest's & Advances	159,900	65,000	65,000		
Total Assets	1,148,500	1,101,900	1,125,800		
Short Term Debt	0	0	67,500		
Current Liabilities	98,500	74,300	146,200		
Long Term Debt	202,200	177,800	172,400		
Total Liabilities	437,400	390,300	413,700		
Total Equity	711,100	711,600	712,100		
Total Liab. & Equity	1,148,500	1,101,900	1,125,800		
CAPITAL (000)					
Total Debt	202,200	177,800	239,900		
Preferred Equity	101,300	102,300	103,300		
Common Equity	609,800	609,300	608,800		

Business:

NORTH CANADIAN OILS LIMITED is a senior exploration, production, marketing and power cogeneration company. Exploration activity is concentrated in the Western Sedimentary Basin of Canada, while marketing and cogeneration activities have an North American focus.

Date	EPS	DPS	Tot Rev	Inc Bex
Mar 93	(0.48)	0.00	94,400	(15,800)
Dec 92	(0.03)	0.10	120,200	400
Sep 92	0.08	0.10	89,200	4,600
Jun 92	0.06	0.10	88,300	4,100
Mar 92	(0.07)	0.00	78,000	1,000
Dec 91	0.07	0.00	84,100	4,400
Sep 91	0.03	0.10	75,000	3,000
Jun 91	0.02	0.10	80,300	2,800

Synopsis:

In April 1993, in a joint statement issued by North Canadian and Norcen Energy Resources Limited, it was announced that the operations and staff of the two companies would be integrated by July 1, 1993. North Canadian's operations would be rolled into Norcen. Norcen, which is controlled by the Edper Bronfman empire, became a controlling shareholder in North Canadian in April 1993 when the Bronfmans consolidated their energy investments. North Canadian's strength in natural gas and presence in the cogeneration market will complement Norcen's strengths in the oil and international markets.

First quarter financial results reflect a $9.5-million provision for potential marketing losses resulting from gas contracts negotiated during the summer of 1992. North Canadians's production had fallen short of sales. When prices were low, the company easily made up the difference on the spot market. With rising prices, however, not only was North Canadian paying more on the spot market, but it also found it difficult to find adequate supplies to make up the 50 million cubic feet of gas it was short each day. This situation will continue until the current contracts expire in October 1993. Other provisions applied in the first quarter include an accounting change, legal and financial costs related to the Norcen deal and a write-down on a Los Angeles cogeneration facility. North Canadian also wrote down the value of its $70-million investment portfolio by $3 million. About 75% of the holdings are in Edper-related companies,

Cost-savings from the management agreement with Norcen are expected to improve the company's financial results. Natural gas production is expected to improve by November 1994, when the capacity of a gas plant in northwest Alberta is expanded. Daily production for 1993 is expected be 235 million cubic feet of gas and 7,200 barrels a day of crude oil and natural gas liquids.

Relative strength to TSE300 / Price / Volume (in 1000's of board lots) chart, 1990–1993

Rank (Profit/Revenue/Assets)
171 198 143

Paul M. Marshall
Chairman

Norman R. Gish
President & C.E.O.

G. Barry Padley
Sr. V.P., C.F.O. & Corp. Sec.

Address
Suite 700
112 - 4th Avenue S.W.
Calgary
AB
T2P 4B2
(403) 261-3100

Fax: (403) 261-3351
N0002819/G/3.2

NORTHSTAR ENERGY CORPORATION

Exchanges	Price (Jun24'93)		28.50	Trailing P/E		67.86	Stock Symbol
TZ	Trailing Yield (%)		0.00	Trailing EPS		0.42	**NEN**

Period Ending	Dec92	Dec91	Dec90	Dec89	Dec88
Yearly Statistics					
Price-Close	11.13	4.75	4.60	5.75	2.75
Price-High	11.13	5.00	6.75	5.75	3.60
Price-Low	4.50	4.10	4.60	2.90	2.50
P/E-Close	35.89	33.93	25.56	63.89	34.38
Dividends per Share	0.00	0.00	0.00	0.00	0.00
Dividend Yield (%)	0.00	0.00	0.00	0.00	0.00
Sales per Share	1.79	1.19	1.21	1.83	0.81
EPS before extra. item	0.31	0.14	0.18	0.09	0.08
Cash Flow per Share	1.30	0.86	0.95	0.83	0.60
Book Value per Share	4.73	4.26	4.13	4.50	3.62
O/S Common Shares	15,894	14,170	14,177	11,774	11,744
Total Revenue	35,369	25,062	24,843	21,575	17,298
Income before extra.	4,699	2,061	3,158	1,670	1,487
Cash Flow	19,494	12,128	13,188	9,781	6,921
Debt/Equity	0.12	0.09	0.11	0.02	0.30
Return on Capital (%)	11.05	6.06	9.18	8.55	6.41
Ret. on Com. Equity (%)	6.93	3.22	4.56	2.20	2.08
% Change Profit	128.0	(34.7)	89.1	12.3	16.5
% Change Revenue	41.1	0.9	15.1	24.7	26.1
% Change Assets	24.4	(12.5)	21.0	13.8	19.7

Business:

NORTHSTAR ENERGY CORP. is engaged in petroleum and natural gas exploration, production, processing and marketing. The company's principal reserves and land holdings are in Alberta.

Date	EPS	DPS	Tot Rev	Inc Bex
Mar 93	0.16	0.00	14,270	2,496
Dec 92	0.16	0.00	13,407	2,403
Sep 92	0.06	0.00	8,559	966
Jun 92	0.04	0.00	6,714	621
Mar 92	0.05	0.00	6,689	709
Dec 91	0.04	0.00	6,855	483
Sep 91	0.03	0.00	5,606	474
Jun 91	0.02	0.00	5,530	298

	Dec92	Dec91	Dec90
Preferred Div. Coverage	np	np	5.1
Total Div. Coverage	na	14.1	5.1
Interest Coverage	13.4	5.7	8.6
Current Ratio	0.8	1.2	0.6
Operating Margin	23.4	16.7	24.7
Asset Turnover	0.2	0.2	0.2
5 YEAR RATIOS (%)			
Return on Capital	8.2	7.5	7.6
Return on Com. Equity	3.8	2.8	1.7
Profit Growth	29.8	124.6	27.2
Revenue Growth	20.8	16.1	23.8
Asset Growth	12.3	12.4	10.9
BALANCE SHEET (000)			
Cash	267	0	0
Current Assets	9,249	10,702	8,476
Net Fixed Assets	107,458	85,937	98,599
Invest's & Advances	3,466	0	3,420
Total Assets	120,173	96,639	110,495
Short Term Debt	1,233	1,891	1,620
Current Liabilities	11,731	8,798	14,791
Long Term Debt	7,608	3,393	5,348
Total Liabilities	44,975	36,245	44,676
Total Equity	75,198	60,394	65,819
Total Liab. & Equity	120,173	96,639	110,495
CAPITAL (000)			
Total Debt	8,841	5,284	6,968
Preferred Equity	0	0	7,211
Common Equity	75,198	60,394	58,608

Synopsis:

Record growth in production, earnings and cash flow for the first quarter of 1993 for Northstar Energy were attributed to production gains and higher gas and oil prices. Production increases resulted primarily from new properties at Hamburg, Robin/Long Coulee, Gilby and David, all situated in Alberta, which were added over the course of 1992 and 1993 to date.

Northstar's capital budget for 1993 is $25-million, balanced between exploration and development expenditures. This budget also includes $3-million to be used towards the construction of a 102 megawatt cogeneration facility in Windsor, Ontario. The company's interest in this facility resulted from the acquisition of PowerLink Corporation and its Canadian affiliates in July 1992. Construction of the facility will begin in the second half of 1993. The investment in cogeneration provides a natural hedge against volatility in gas prices, (cogeneration profitability increases in low price gas markets). The company has targeted new property acquisitions of a further $20-million to $50-million for 1993.

1992 (1991) average daily production before royalties was: oil and natural gas liquids, 1,019 (535) barrels; and natural gas, 39,700 (25,800) cubic feet. At the 1992 (1991) year end, the company reported gross proven and probable oil reserves totaling 4.8 (2.1) million barrels; and 221.1 (171.1) billion cubic feet of natural gas reserves.

Relative strength to TSE300

Price

Volume (in 1000's of board lots)

Rank (Profit/Revenue/Assets)
263   530   390

John A. Hagg
Chairman & C.E.O.

S. Barry Jackson
President & C.O.O.

Brian K. Lemke
V.P., Finance & Secretary

Address
Suite 300
535 - 7th Avenue S.W.
Calgary
AB
T2P 0Y4
(403) 298-0500

Fax: (403) 298-0599
G0012859/G/3.2

NOWSCO WELL SERVICE LTD.

Exchanges	Price (Jun24'93)		21.37	Trailing P/E		17.24	Stock Symbol
TQ	Trailing Yield (%)		0.70	Trailing EPS		1.24	**NWS**

Period Ending	Dec92	Dec91	Dec90	Dec89	Dec88
Yearly Statistics					
Price-Close	11.00	10.25	14.63	15.75	13.50
Price-High	11.75	16.00	18.50	17.13	19.00
Price-Low	7.00	9.50	13.25	12.50	12.25
P/E-Close	16.92	nm	38.49	175.00	14.36
Dividends per Share	0.15	0.14	0.14	0.24	0.24
Dividend Yield (%)	1.36	1.37	0.96	1.52	1.78
Sales per Share	12.88	12.77	12.35	9.29	10.23
EPS before extra. item	0.65	(0.35)	0.38	0.09	0.94
Cash Flow per Share	1.94	0.42	1.14	0.96	1.59
Book Value per Share	9.51	9.22	9.80	9.17	9.83
O/S Common Shares	16,418	16,272	16,124	16,076	16,051
Total Revenue	225,433	223,558	220,059	171,106	174,921
Income before extra.	10,707	(5,636)	6,165	1,485	15,053
Cash Flow	31,774	6,783	18,401	15,441	25,580
Debt/Equity	0.32	1.02	1.00	1.11	0.95
Return on Capital (%)	7.94	3.94	10.16	4.87	8.33
Ret. on Com. Equity (%)	7.00	(3.66)	4.04	0.97	9.43
% Change Profit	290.0	(191.4)	315.2	(90.1)	8.1
% Change Revenue	0.8	1.6	28.6	(2.2)	14.7
% Change Assets	(29.3)	(2.4)	4.8	0.5	38.8

Date	EPS	DPS	Tot Rev	Inc Bex
Mar 93	0.30	0.00	61,121	5,013
Dec 92	0.29	0.15	63,642	4,833
Sep 92	0.24	0.00	57,867	3,981
Jun 92	0.41	0.00	57,626	6,578
Mar 92	(0.29)	0.00	46,298	(4,685)
Dec 91	(0.57)	0.00	53,322	(9,179)
Sep 91	0.37	0.00	56,265	5,916
Jun 91	(0.39)	0.07	48,458	(6,297)

Preferred Div. Coverage	np	np	np	
Total Div. Coverage	4.3	0.0	2.7	
Interest Coverage	2.2	0.7	1.5	
Current Ratio	2.0	2.8	3.5	
Operating Margin	4.6	(2.5)	6.3	
Asset Turnover	0.9	0.6	0.6	
5 YEAR RATIOS (%)				
Return on Capital	7.0	7.8	8.3	
Return on Com. Equity	3.6	4.3	6.2	
Profit Growth	(5.1)	na	(20.5)	
Revenue Growth	8.1	7.5	1.6	
Asset Growth	0.1	15.4	7.8	
BALANCE SHEET (000)				
Cash	23,622	116,466	127,072	
Current Assets	101,696	198,835	222,745	
Net Fixed Assets	111,556	124,845	111,992	
Invest's & Advances	11,136	0	0	
Total Assets	243,838	344,715	353,119	
Short Term Debt	15,142	32,154	28,500	
Current Liabilities	50,467	69,930	62,927	
Long Term Debt	35,081	120,638	128,648	
Total Liabilities	87,718	194,772	195,154	
Total Equity	156,120	149,943	157,965	
Total Liab. & Equity	243,838	344,715	353,119	
CAPITAL (000)				
Total Debt	50,223	152,792	157,148	
Preferred Equity	0	0	0	
Common Equity	156,120	149,943	157,965	

Business:

NOWSCO WELL SERVICE LTD. is an oil and gas service company. It provides specialized products, equipment and technology to the oil and gas industry and to the pipeline, mining and industrial sectors. The company has operations in North America, United Kingdom Europe, Middle East, North Africa and Southeast Asia.

Synopsis:

Nowsco Well Service maintained its market share in traditional service lines in 1992, however, it began to concentrate more on the pipeline, industrial and coiled tubing services that it believes has the greater growth potential. Nowsco also feels that integrated product line management and the efficient application of research and development will enable the company to capitalize on these and other markets.

In 1992, the largest portion of total operating profit came from revenue generated outside of North America, primarily in Britain and Europe and from operations in Southeast Asia. Nowsco added two joint ventures during the year in Argentina and Russia. Political and economic uncertainties in some of these regions remain a question mark, but Nowsco believes the downside risks are limited. During 1992 Nowsco expanded Southeast Asia's cementing operations and introduced industrial and pipeline services. In Europe, Nowsco closed and consolidated certain unprofitable operations, thereby increasing overall profitability from the segment.

North American activity has remained fairly constant over the past few years, representing an average of 50% of total revenue. Nowsco believes the signs are positive for natural gas pricing levels in North America to be sufficient to stimulate the natural gas industry in the future. With the strengthening of natural gas prices, drilling activity is expected to improve in both Canada and the United States. Nowsco meanwhile transferred some of its under-used North American equipment to Argentina, Australia, the U.K. and Vietnam.

Operations segment revenues in 1992 by geographic segment were: Canada, 33%; the U.S., 11%; and international, 56%. Operating income in 1992 by geographic segment was: Canada, -75%; the U.S., 27%; and international, 148%. Total operating income in 1992 included financial segment income of $3.6-million. Service activity as a percentage of operating revenue in 1992 was: pipeline service, 21%; cementing, stimulation and coiled tubing, 55%; and other, 24%.

Rank (Profit/Revenue/Assets)
173 255 295
S. Patrick Shouldice
Chairman & C.E.O.
R.F. Simard
President & C.O.O.
A.J. Robertson
V.P. Treasurer & C.F.O.

Address
Suite 2750
801 - 6th Avenue S.W.
Calgary
AB
T2P 4L8
(403) 261-2990

Fax: (403) 262-8066
N0003809/G/3.3

For further company information, call Globe Information Services 1-800-268-9128 or (416)585-5345

NUMAC OIL & GAS LTD.

Exchanges	Price (Jun24'93)	8 .00	Trailing P/E	72 .73	Stock Symbol
TMA	Trailing Yield (%)	0 .00	Trailing EPS	0 .11	**NMC**

Period Ending	Dec92	Dec91	Dec90	Dec89	Dec88
Yearly Statistics					
Price-Close	6 .00	5 .88	6 .25	9 .75	8 .25
Price-High	6 .38	7 .00	9 .63	11 .37	11 .00
Price-Low	4 .75	4 .75	5 .75	8 .50	8 .25
P/E-Close	75 .00	nm	34 .72	139 .29	48 .53
Dividends per Share	0 .00	0 .00	0 .00	0 .00	0 .00
Dividend Yield (%)	0 .00	0 .00	0 .00	0 .00	0 .00
Sales per Share	1 .67	1 .74	1 .96	1 .62	1 .55
EPS before extra. item	0 .08	(2 .34)	0 .18	0 .07	0 .17
Cash Flow per Share	0 .87	0 .83	1 .16	0 .83	0 .94
Book Value per Share	4 .53	4 .32	6 .68	6 .54	6 .94
O/S Common Shares	33 ,048	26 ,448	26 ,177	25 ,585	25 ,543
Total Revenue	46 ,511	46 ,047	50 ,943	43 ,528	43 ,159
Income before extra.	2 ,326	(61 ,766)	4 ,703	1 ,878	4 ,399
Cash Flow	24 ,398	21 ,965	29 ,815	21 ,168	23 ,950
Debt/Equity	0 .46	0 .88	0 .49	0 .44	0 .29
Return on Capital (%)	3 .94	(39 .77)	4 .75	2 .27	3 .48
Ret. on Com. Equity (%)	1 .76	(42 .74)	2 .75	1 .09	2 .51
% Change Profit	103 .8	(1 ,413 .3)	150 .4	(57 .3)	(40 .3)
% Change Revenue	1 .0	(9 .6)	17 .0	0 .9	0 .8
% Change Assets	1 .3	(25 .5)	6 .7	5 .5	2 .0

Preferred Div. Coverage	np	np	np
Total Div. Coverage	na	na	na
Interest Coverage	1 .1	0 .0	1 .3
Current Ratio	0 .9	0 .5	0 .9
Operating Margin	18 .8	(202 .5)	23 .3
Asset Turnover	0 .2	0 .2	0 .1
5 YEAR RATIOS (%)			
Return on Capital	(5 .1)	(4 .4)	4 .4
Return on Com. Equity	(6 .9)	(6 .3)	2 .5
Profit Growth	(20 .6)	na	(21 .8)
Revenue Growth	1 .6	4 .0	(7 .2)
Asset Growth	(2 .9)	0 .6	6 .3
BALANCE SHEET (000)			
Cash	0	0	0
Current Assets	6 ,755	8 ,701	15 ,905
Net Fixed Assets	254 ,620	244 ,662	321 ,635
Invest's & Advances	56	4 ,605	8 ,849
Total Assets	262 ,111	258 ,721	347 ,215
Short Term Debt	1 ,060	6 ,787	4 ,173
Current Liabilities	7 ,617	16 ,336	18 ,037
Long Term Debt	68 ,000	93 ,455	82 ,126
Total Liabilities	112 ,416	144 ,466	172 ,451
Total Equity	149 ,695	114 ,255	174 ,764
Total Liab. & Equity	262 ,111	258 ,721	347 ,215
CAPITAL (000)			
Total Debt	69 ,060	100 ,242	86 ,299
Preferred Equity	0	0	0
Common Equity	149 ,695	114 ,255	174 ,764

Business:

NUMAC OIL AND GAS LTD. is a diversified natural resources company. It has oil and gas exploration and production operations in Alberta, British Columbia and Saskatchewan. uranium exploration in northern Saskatchewan and heavy oil recovery technology.

Date	EPS	DPS	Tot Rev	Inc Bex
Mar 93	0 .06	0 .00	14 ,476	2 ,110
Dec 92	(0 .02)	0 .00	11 ,697	(343)
Sep 92	0 .05	0 .00	11 ,430	1 ,303
Jun 92	0 .02	0 .00	11 ,727	624
Mar 92	0 .03	0 .00	11 ,450	742
Dec 91	(2 .33)	0 .00	11 ,762	(61 ,548)
Sep 91	(0 .01)	0 .00	10 ,954	(240)
Jun 91	(0 .01)	0 .00	11 ,079	(337)

Synopsis:

Numac Oil & Gas Ltd. and Westcoast Petroleum Ltd. have agreed to merge, an arrangement that will allow their major Hong Kong shareholders to consolidate their holdings in one company. Under the plan of arrangement announced in May 1993, each Numac share would be exchanged for one Westcoast share. The merged company would operate under the Numac name. Although Numac's head office is currently in Edmonton, the new company headquarters would be in Calgary, where Westcoast Petroleum is based.

The major Hong Kong shareholders are Cheng Yu-tung, who owns 24.95% of Numac and 23.75% of Westcoast Petroleum, and the Doo family which owns 15% of Numac's common shares, 50% of its principal convertible debentures and 23.75% of Westcoast Petroleum. Mr. Cheng and the Doo family have owned the Numac shares since 1991, when they bought the control block from the Edper Bronfman empire's Consolidated Enfield Corp. Westcoast Petroleum became a private company in February 1993, when it was sold by its Vancouver-based parent, Westcoast Energy Inc., for $247.5-million. The merger will bring those assets back into public trading. About 14% of the newly created company's shares will be widely held.

The company will seek opportunities in China and expects to build on Westcoast Petroleum's ventures in Indonesia and Libya. The combined companies would have had cash flow of $25.2-million in the first three months of 1993. Numac's contribution to this figure will rise substantially as its investment in the Caroline gas field in Alberta begins production this spring. The merged company's reserves would total about 72.9 million barrels of crude oil and liquids, and 738.3 billion cubic feet of natural gas.

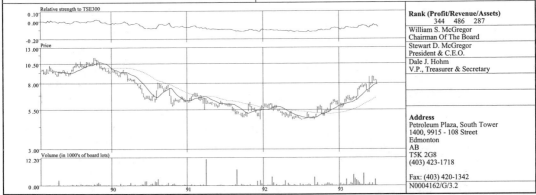

Rank (Profit/Revenue/Assets)
344   486   287
William S. McGregor
Chairman Of The Board
Stewart D. McGregor
President & C.E.O.
Dale J. Hohm
V.P., Treasurer & Secretary

Address
Petroleum Plaza, South Tower
1400, 9915 - 108 Street
Edmonton
AB
T5K 2G8
(403) 423-1718

Fax: (403) 420-1342
N0004162/G/3.2

OCELOT ENERGY INC.

Exchanges	Price (Jun24'93)	15.50	Trailing P/E	55.36	Stock Symbol
TM	Trailing Yield (%)	0.00	Trailing EPS	0.28	**OCE.B**

Period Ending	Dec92	Dec91
Yearly Statistics		14W
Price-Close	7.00	3.95
Price-High	7.25	4.50
Price-Low	3.80	3.70
P/E-Close	35.00	1.69
Dividends per Share	0.00	0.00
Dividend Yield (%)	0.00	0.00
Sales per Share	5.80	12.78
EPS before extra. item	0.20	0.63
Cash Flow per Share	0.95	3.63
Book Value per Share	3.96	3.65
O/S Common Shares	26,426	15,702
Total Revenue	139,341	57,753
Income before extra.	4,745	10,491
Cash Flow	22,607	16,355
Debt/Equity	0.61	2.00
Return on Capital (%)	10.67	na
Ret. on Com. Equity (%)	5.86	na
% Change Profit	(87.8)	na
% Change Revenue	(35.0)	na
% Change Assets	0.5	na

	Dec92	Dec91
Preferred Div. Coverage	np	np
Total Div. Coverage	na	na
Interest Coverage	1.9	4.7
Current Ratio	1.4	1.7
Operating Margin	12.2	29.5
Asset Turnover	0.7	1.1
5 YEAR RATIOS (%)		
Return on Capital	na	na
Return on Com. Equity	na	na
Profit Growth	na	na
Revenue Growth	na	na
Asset Growth	na	na
BALANCE SHEET (000)		
Cash	6,274	16,176
Current Assets	42,184	46,565
Net Fixed Assets	155,433	150,634
Invest's & Advances	0	0
Total Assets	199,826	198,737
Short Term Debt	4,050	3,378
Current Liabilities	30,709	27,445
Long Term Debt	60,137	111,339
Total Liabilities	95,090	141,474
Total Equity	104,736	57,263
Total Liab. & Equity	199,826	198,737
CAPITAL (000)		
Total Debt	64,187	114,717
Preferred Equity	0	0
Common Equity	104,736	57,263

Business:

OCELOT ENERGY INC. is engaged in the acquisition, exploration, development and production of natural gas. It has properties in Alberta and British Columbia and in Africa. It also operates Lynx Energy drilling and oil field services and O.J. Pipelines.

Date	EPS	DPS	Tot Rev	Inc Bex
Mar 93	0.26	0.00	103,471	6,908
Dec 92	0.07	0.00	31,906	1,739
Sep 92	0.01	0.00	33,354	561
Jun 92	(0.06)	0.00	18,601	(1,295)
Mar 92	0.18	0.00	55,318	3,740

Synopsis:

Ocelot's strong financial performance during the first quarter of 1993 was attributed primarily to improved revenues from the company's core business of natural gas and crude oil production. Increased production volumes resulted primarily from the Sylvan Lake acquisition, acquired from Encor Inc. in January 1993. The acquisition includes proven and probable reserves of seven million barrels of oil and natural gas liquids, 52.5 billion cubic feet of natural gas, a large gas plant, three oil batteries and three satellites. The daily production of 2,000 barrels of oil and natural gas liquids and 10 million cubic feet of natural gas from 61 oil wells and 32 gas wells currently producing, increases Ocelot's net production by 60%. Ocelot views the acquisition as a major step in its plan to become a senior independent Canadian energy producer.

In March 1993, the company announced its intention to spin off four of its oilfield service divisions, (excluding O.J. Pipelines) into a separately traded public company to be called Lynx Energy Services Corp. If approved by shareholders, Lynx will begin operations July 1, 1993.

The bulk of Ocelot's $60-million capital budget for 1993 will be spent on further exploration and development activities in B.C. and Alberta.

In the longer term Ocelot is focusing on a number of African development projects that will produce natural gas for electricity generation. In July 1993, it will submit an application for a $300-million project with TransCanada PipeLines Ltd. to develop an offshore gas field and pipeline in Tanzania. Ocelot's share of this project would be about $25-million, of which half would be spent in 1994, pending Tanzanian government approval. Under the proposal, the World Bank would back the project. Ocelot is also considering a proposal to operate a gas field offshore from Cameroon, as well as a project to develop a gas field in Poland.

Rank (Profit/Revenue/Assets)
262   323   317

W. David Lyons
President & C.E.O.

Douglas A. Cutts
V.P. Finance & C.F.O.

Glenn D. Gradeen
Exec. V.P. & C.O.O.

Address
Suite 3300
Bow Valley Square II
205 - 5th Avenue S.W.
Calgary
AB
T2P 4V7
(403) 299-5700
Fax: (403) 299-5750
01003210/G/3.2

For further company information, call Globe Information Services 1-800-268-9128 or (416)585-5345

OMEGA HYDROCARBONS LTD.

Exchanges	Price (Jun24'93)	3.80	Trailing P/E	27.14	Stock Symbol
T	Trailing Yield (%)	0.00	Trailing EPS	0.14	**OMH**

Period Ending	Dec92	Dec91	Dec90	Dec89	Dec88
Yearly Statistics					
Price-Close	2.90	2.75	2.95	3.55	3.00
Price-High	3.70	3.70	4.35	3.80	6.25
Price-Low	2.10	2.45	2.75	2.10	2.70
P/E-Close	41.43	nm	11.80	118.33	nm
Dividends per Share	0.00	0.00	0.00	0.00	0.00
Dividend Yield (%)	0.00	0.00	0.00	0.00	0.00
Sales per Share	1.62	1.60	2.03	1.54	1.33
EPS before extra. item	0.07	(0.98)	0.25	0.03	(1.13)
Cash Flow per Share	0.65	0.61	0.97	0.54	0.38
Book Value per Share	3.38	3.31	4.28	4.03	4.00
O/S Common Shares	13,485	13,492	13,195	13,053	13,053
Total Revenue	22,213	22,242	27,418	20,776	18,098
Income before extra.	953	(13,211)	3,218	393	(14,775)
Cash Flow	8,759	8,170	12,711	7,079	5,011
Debt/Equity	0.42	0.47	0.34	0.40	0.44
Return on Capital (%)	5.66	(32.09)	10.43	4.34	(31.64)
Ret. on Com. Equity (%)	2.11	(26.11)	5.90	0.75	(24.78)
% Change Profit	107.2	(510.5)	718.8	102.7	(734.9)
% Change Revenue	(0.1)	(18.9)	32.0	14.8	(28.6)
% Change Assets	(0.6)	(20.8)	2.4	0.4	(22.0)

Preferred Div. Coverage	np	np	np
Total Div. Coverage	na	na	na
Interest Coverage	2.2	0.0	2.4
Current Ratio	0.8	0.8	0.5
Operating Margin	15.0	2.6	26.2
Asset Turnover	0.3	0.3	0.3
5 YEAR RATIOS (%)			
Return on Capital	(8.7)	(8.3)	(0.1)
Return on Com. Equity	(8.4)	(8.1)	(1.9)
Profit Growth	(16.4)	na	(24.6)
Revenue Growth	(2.6)	(2.7)	(12.0)
Asset Growth	(8.8)	(7.9)	(5.2)
BALANCE SHEET (000)			
Cash	0	0	0
Current Assets	2,835	3,278	4,009
Net Fixed Assets	76,831	75,246	95,652
Invest's & Advances	0	0	0
Total Assets	79,666	80,116	101,163
Short Term Debt	0	0	3,250
Current Liabilities	3,733	4,208	7,531
Long Term Debt	19,227	21,016	16,200
Total Liabilities	34,033	35,418	44,661
Total Equity	45,633	44,698	56,502
Total Liab. & Equity	79,666	80,116	101,163
CAPITAL (000)			
Total Debt	19,227	21,016	19,450
Preferred Equity	0	0	0
Common Equity	45,633	44,698	56,502

Business:

OMEGA HYDROCARBONS LTD. is an oil and gas exploration and production company. It has wells and exploration activities in Alberta, Saskatchewan, and Manitoba.

Date	EPS	DPS	Tot Rev	Inc Bex
Mar 93	0.02	0.00	5,278	248
Dec 92	0.04	0.00	6,060	482
Sep 92	0.06	0.00	6,011	792
Jun 92	0.02	0.00	5,511	352
Mar 92	(0.02)	0.00	4,633	(286)
Dec 91	(0.09)	0.00	5,749	(13,350)
Sep 91	0.02	0.00	5,943	226
Jun 91	(0.02)	0.00	4,996	(244)

Synopsis:

Omega Hydrocarbons intends to expand exploration in 1993 into the more gas prone regions of southwestern and west-central Alberta, and to evaluate some of the better oil prospects in its traditional core areas of southwestern Manitoba and the eastern plains of Alberta. Omega hopes these efforts will result in a better balance between oil and gas prospects in inventory by year end.

Funds generated from operations doubled to $2.2-million during the first quarter of 1993, over the same period last year. The increase was attributed to higher prices and lower costs. Daily average production levels of 3,000 barrels of oil and 5.4 million cubic feet of gas were relatively stable compared to the daily averages for 1992.

Omega's gross capital expenditures fell during 1992 to $7.6-million from $11.5-million. Omega spent $641,000 on land acquisitions in 1992, compared with $3.3-million in 1991. During 1992, Omega earned $181,000 from the disposition of interests in small producing properties and other assets no longer required in its operations, compared with $139,000 in 1991.

Omega ceased operations that were not material to it in North Dakota in 1992, but intends to retain its Certificate of Authority to transact business in that state. Omega does not conduct operations in any other foreign jurisdictions. During 1992, Omega purchased 7,300 Common Shares for aggregate cash consideration of $18,000, reducing the number of outstanding Common Shares to 13.48 million by year end.

Average daily production before royalties in 1992 (1991) was: oil and natural gas liquids, 3,000 (3,200) barrels; natural gas, 6.2 (5.6) million cubic feet. Gross proven and probable reserves in 1992 (1991) were: oil and natural gas liquids, 11.3 (12.1) million barrels; natural gas, 70.7 (72.9) billion cubic feet. Contributions to gross production revenues in 1992 (1991) by product were: crude oil and natural gas liquids, 87% (89%); and natural gas, 13% (11%).

Relative strength to TSE300 / Price / Volume (in 1000's of board lots)

Rank (Profit/Revenue/Assets)
429   603   455

Thomas J. (Jack) Hall
Chairman & C.E.O.

Dennis E. Hall
President

John L. Maclagan
V.P., Finance

Address
Suite 1300
Sun Life Plaza III
112 - 4th Avenue S.W.
Calgary
AB
T2P 0H3
(403) 261-0743
Fax: (403) 264-5691
O0000778/G/3.2

PANCANADIAN PETROLEUM LIMITED

Exchanges	Price (Jun24'93)	42.75	Trailing P/E	25.15	Stock Symbol
TMZV	Trailing Yield (%)	1.40	Trailing EPS	1.70	**PCP**

Period Ending	Dec92	Dec91	Dec90	Dec89	Dec88
Yearly Statistics					
Price-Close	33.50	24.50	30.38	28.75	26.25
Price-High	33.50	34.00	32.00	32.00	28.13
Price-Low	23.00	22.38	25.25	24.25	23.13
P/E-Close	24.45	64.47	17.97	27.12	26.25
Dividends per Share	0.60	0.60	0.60	0.60	0.60
Dividend Yield (%)	1.79	2.45	1.98	2.09	2.29
Sales per Share	7.57	6.77	7.58	6.25	5.42
EPS before extra. item	1.37	0.38	1.69	1.06	1.00
Cash Flow per Share	3.92	3.38	3.95	3.11	2.86
Book Value per Share	13.41	12.64	12.86	11.76	11.30
O/S Common Shares	124,920	124,910	124,910	124,900	124,900
Total Revenue	951,100	852,700	951,800	787,500	690,400
Income before extra.	170,600	47,500	211,600	133,000	124,500
Cash Flow	490,300	422,400	493,600	389,000	357,200
Debt/Equity	0.21	0.20	0.17	0.24	0.29
Return on Capital (%)	14.97	7.14	19.94	13.59	12.81
Ret. on Com. Equity (%)	10.49	2.98	13.76	9.23	8.98
% Change Profit	259.2	(77.6)	59.1	6.8	(31.3)
% Change Revenue	11.5	(10.4)	20.9	14.1	(1.2)
% Change Assets	5.5	0.9	6.0	2.3	13.6

Date	EPS	DPS	Tot Rev	Inc Bex
Mar 93	0.49	0.15	266,200	61,300
Dec 92	0.56	0.15	296,900	69,100
Sep 92	0.34	0.15	236,000	43,200
Jun 92	0.31	0.15	217,800	37,800
Mar 92	0.16	0.15	200,800	20,500
Dec 91	(0.54)	0.15	215,700	(67,900)
Sep 91	0.26	0.15	203,000	33,200
Jun 91	0.27	0.15	191,400	33,100

Preferred Div. Coverage	np	np	np
Total Div. Coverage	2.3	0.6	2.8
Interest Coverage	10.4	5.3	9.8
Current Ratio	1.5	0.7	0.8
Operating Margin	30.8	27.5	38.5
Asset Turnover	0.3	0.3	0.3
5 YEAR RATIOS (%)			
Return on Capital	13.7	15.2	16.5
Return on Com. Equity	9.1	9.8	10.1
Profit Growth	(1.2)	(4.7)	(7.2)
Revenue Growth	6.3	3.5	(3.5)
Asset Growth	5.5	6.4	4.4
BALANCE SHEET (000)			
Cash	64,000	0	20,900
Current Assets	290,400	165,300	185,400
Net Fixed Assets	2,739,100	2,719,200	2,685,300
Invest's & Advances	0	0	0
Total Assets	3,086,500	2,925,400	2,899,100
Short Term Debt	0	39,600	17,700
Current Liabilities	190,800	233,400	227,700
Long Term Debt	352,800	274,100	257,100
Total Liabilities	1,411,800	1,346,700	1,293,000
Total Equity	1,674,700	1,578,700	1,606,100
Total Liab. & Equity	3,086,500	2,925,400	2,899,100
CAPITAL (000)			
Total Debt	352,800	313,700	274,800
Preferred Equity	0	0	0
Common Equity	1,674,700	1,578,700	1,606,100

Business:

PANCANADIAN PETROLEUM LIMITED is engaged, directly and through subsidiaries, in the exploration for development, production and marketing of crude oil, natural gas, natural gas liquids and sulphur. It is a major producer of crude oil and natural gas in Canada and augments its conventional and synthetic crude oil operations with international projects.

Synopsis:

PanCanadian Petroleum predicts a 30% increase in oil production and a 7 to 8% growth in natural gas in 1993. The company plans to drill 900 wells in 1993, about double the number it drilled in 1992. PanCanadian expects its 1993 capital spending budget to increase 25% from 1992 to $425-million, of which $45-million will be spent overseas and more than $120-million on gas projects.

An exploration agreement was signed with Petrofina in late 1992, giving the company a 15% working interest in 3.8 million acres in exploratory blocks in the Sirte Basin, Libya (where U.S.-based firms cannot invest). The work commitment includes 8,500 kilometers of seismic, and a 12-well drilling program. The company's 25% stake in the Russian joint venture exceeds 4,000 barrels daily, which is expected to rise to 6,000 barrels daily by the end of 1993. PanCanadian is examining other projects in the former Soviet Union.

PanCanadian announced in May 1993 that it is offering for sale Langevin Resources, a wholly owned subsidiary. Total proven and probable reserves are in the order of 4 million barrels of oil and natural gas liquids and 200 billion cubic feet of natural gas. During 1992, the Langevin properties produced 2,000 barrels of oil and natural gas liquids and 28 million cubic feet of natural gas daily.

Net daily production in 1992 (1991) was: conventional crude oil, 70,588 (57,377) barrels; natural gas liquids, 20,197 (18,099) barrels; synthetic crude oil, 17,872 (16,514) barrels; natural gas, 449 (348) million cubic feet. Gross established reserves in 1992 (1991) were: conventional crude oil and natural gas liquids, 200.1 (172.9) million barrels; natural gas, 2,291 (2,392) billion cubic feet; synthetic crude oil, 163.6 (169.9) million barrels permitted. Contributions to total revenues in 1992 (1991) by product segment were: conventional crude oil, 49% (49%); synthetic crude oil, 16% (16%); natural gas liquids, 12% (12%); natural gas, 22% (19%); and other, 1% (4%).

Relative strength to TSE300 / Price / Volume (in 1000's of board lots) chart

Rank (Profit/Revenue/Assets)		
20	107	69

David P. O'Brien
Chairman, President & C.E.O.

Michael A. Grandin
Sr. V.P. & C.F.O.

Guido A. Montemurro
Sr. V.P., Operations

Address
P.O. Box 2850
Calgary
AB
T2P 2S5
(403) 290-2000

Fax: (403) 290-2950
P0000960/G/3.2

PARAMOUNT RESOURCES LTD.

Exchanges	Price (Jun24'93)		24.75	Trailing P/E		70.71	Stock Symbol
T	Trailing Yield (%)		0.40	Trailing EPS		0.35	**POU**

Period Ending	Dec92	Dec91	Dec90	Dec89	Apr89
Yearly Statistics					8M
Price-Close	10.75	7.25	9.75	9.50	5.00
Price-High	11.00	11.00	10.25	9.50	5.00
Price-Low	5.00	6.38	7.50	5.00	2.58
P/E-Close	53.75	45.31	23.21	26.39	17.86
Dividends per Share	0.10	0.10	0.20	0.20	0.13
Dividend Yield (%)	0.93	1.38	2.05	2.11	2.60
Sales per Share	2.78	2.40	2.69	2.31	1.60
EPS before extra. item	0.20	0.16	0.42	0.24	0.28
Cash Flow per Share	1.36	1.24	1.42	1.27	0.86
Book Value per Share	2.35	2.05	1.97	1.74	1.71
O/S Common Shares	14,363	11,900	11,754	11,670	11,630
Total Revenue	38,978	30,049	33,151	18,730	20,765
Income before extra.	2,821	1,880	4,972	2,738	3,274
Cash Flow	19,275	14,708	16,613	9,865	9,989
Debt/Equity	1.30	1.57	1.31	1.66	1.43
Return on Capital (%)	13.08	9.51	23.38	19.29	18.19
Ret. on Com. Equity (%)	0.00	7.90	22.86	20.45	17.30
% Change Profit	50.1	(62.2)	21.0	25.5	1.2
% Change Revenue	29.7	(9.4)	18.0	35.3	17.9
% Change Assets	19.8	2.8	8.4	9.9	32.5

Preferred Div. Coverage	np	np	np
Total Div. Coverage	2.0	1.6	2.1
Interest Coverage	2.4	1.4	2.6
Current Ratio	0.8	1.0	0.7
Operating Margin	24.4	14.0	34.8
Asset Turnover	0.4	0.3	0.4
5 YEAR RATIOS (%)			
Return on Capital	16.7	18.1	20.1
Return on Com. Equity	15.6	17.5	20.5
Profit Growth	(2.7)	(10.5)	11.8
Revenue Growth	17.2	13.0	15.8
Asset Growth	14.1	10.9	11.0
BALANCE SHEET (000)			
Cash	2	9	48
Current Assets	11,147	10,901	13,001
Net Fixed Assets	95,583	73,330	71,014
Invest's & Advances	2,856	7,011	5,455
Total Assets	110,202	92,011	89,470
Short Term Debt	0	0	131
Current Liabilities	13,923	10,590	17,572
Long Term Debt	43,818	38,431	30,245
Total Liabilities	76,420	67,574	66,307
Total Equity	33,782	24,437	23,163
Total Liab. & Equity	110,202	92,011	89,470
CAPITAL (000)			
Total Debt	43,818	38,431	30,376
Preferred Equity	0	0	0
Common Equity	33,782	24,437	23,163

Business:

PARAMOUNT RESOURCES LTD. is a public Canadian resource company engaged in the exploration for and the development and production of petroleum and natural gas, principally in Western Canada.

Date	EPS	DPS	Tot Rev	Inc Bex
Mar 93	0.13	0.00	15,422	1,845
Dec 92	0.11	0.10	14,417	1,585
Sep 92	0.05	0.00	8,421	711
Jun 92	0.06	0.00	7,812	747
Mar 92	(0.02)	0.00	8,347	(222)
Dec 91	0.04	0.10	7,873	420
Sep 91	0.02	0.00	6,443	250
Jun 91	0.09	0.00	7,806	1,099

Synopsis:

Paramount Resources purchased an additional working interest in 130 gas wells (70 producing and 60 shut-in), equity interest in eight gas plants and 29,000 net acres from Trilogy Resources for $7-million plus adjustments effective February 1, 1993. The properties acquired are concentrated in northeastern Alberta where Paramount and Trilogy had been joint venture partners. Gas production from wells included in this transaction produced a net 7.2 million cubic feet per day during 1992. This acquisition supports Paramount's ongoing effort to increase net production with its core shallow gas producing region.

Total capital expenditures in 1992 fell 17% from 1991 to $13-million. Funds were split: 59% to exploration and development projects that were internally derived; and 41% to property acquisition.

Paramount sold a record amount of natural gas during the first quarter of 1993. Sales averaged 101 million cubic feet per day, an improvement of 14 million cubic feet per day over the same period last year. Higher 1993 gas sales are attributed to new productive capacity and the sale of storage gas. Gas left in storage as of December 1992 generated sales equivalent to 8 million cubic feet per day during this quarter. Sales are expected to average 95 to 105 million cubic feet per day throughout 1993. Gas prices averaged $1.61 per thousand cubic feet for the quarter ending March 31, 1993, a 57% increase over average prices during the first quarter of 1992. Gas prices are expected to remain at this level for 1993, but the market is extremely volatile.

Average gross daily production in 1992 (1991) was: crude oil and natural gas liquids, 61.1 (60.5) barrels; natural gas, 87.2 (72.3) million cubic feet. Gross proven and probable additional reserves as at December 31, 1992 (January 1, 1992) were: oil and natural gas liquids, 939,000 (671,000) barrels; and natural gas, 390 (339) billion cubic feet. Paramount generates 99% of its revenue from the sale of natural gas and 1% from the sale of oil and natural gas liquids.

Relative strength to TSE300 / Price / Volume (in 1000's of board lots)

Rank (Profit/Revenue/Assets)
320 510 402

C.H. Riddell
Chairman & President

Address
4000 First Canadian Centre
350 - 7th Avenue S.W.
Calgary
AB
T2P 3W5
(403) 266-2047

Fax: (403) 262-7994
P0004728/G/3.2

PE BEN OILFIELD SERVICES LTD.

Exchanges	Price (Jun24'93)	4.15	Trailing P/E	37.73	Stock Symbol
T	Trailing Yield (%)	0.00	Trailing EPS	0.11	**PBN**

Period Ending	Dec92	Dec91	Dec90	Dec89	Dec88
Yearly Statistics					
Price-Close	0.55	1.25	0.55	0.85	1.05
Price-High	1.25	1.40	1.20	1.45	1.40
Price-Low	0.48	0.25	0.45	0.55	0.85
P/E-Close	nm	7.81	nm	9.44	nm
Dividends per Share	0.00	0.00	0.00	0.00	0.00
Dividend Yield (%)	0.00	0.00	0.00	0.00	0.00
Sales per Share	4.35	5.92	3.79	10.67	9.16
EPS before extra. item	(0.03)	0.16	(0.82)	0.09	(0.13)
Cash Flow per Share	0.04	0.52	0.11	0.10	0.04
Book Value per Share	0.73	0.76	0.60	1.42	1.33
O/S Common Shares	3,020	3,020	3,020	3,020	3,020
Total Revenue	13,142	17,909	11,450	32,244	27,703
Income before extra.	(100)	488	(2,472)	258	(386)
Cash Flow	116	1,576	318	290	113
Debt/Equity	0.41	0.60	2.32	1.04	0.75
Return on Capital (%)	(1.62)	23.78	(32.18)	4.08	(2.22)
Ret. on Com. Equity (%)	(4.46)	23.81	(81.27)	6.22	(9.35)
% Change Profit	(120.5)	119.7	(1,057.3)	166.9	(853.2)
% Change Revenue	(26.6)	56.4	(64.5)	16.4	57.9
% Change Assets	(10.1)	(34.4)	(44.9)	29.8	33.0

Preferred Div. Coverage	np	np	np
Total Div. Coverage	na	na	na
Interest Coverage	0.0	7.5	0.0
Current Ratio	1.7	1.4	1.2
Operating Margin	(0.5)	10.1	1.5
Asset Turnover	2.8	3.4	1.4
5 YEAR RATIOS (%)			
Return on Capital	(1.6)	(0.3)	(7.1)
Return on Com. Equity	(13.0)	(11.9)	(20.4)
Profit Growth	na	na	na
Revenue Growth	(5.6)	22.2	6.4
Asset Growth	(11.0)	(6.3)	7.1
BALANCE SHEET			
Cash	502,794	1,747,673	1,553,119
Current Assets	3,222,846	3,878,990	5,740,005
Net Fixed Assets	1,381,496	1,181,148	1,963,175
Invest's & Advances	57,018	107,033	150,906
Total Assets	4,690,324	5,220,090	7,955,973
Short Term Debt	306,500	1,170,000	2,785,000
Current Liabilities	1,904,023	2,715,750	4,739,860
Long Term Debt	592,107	210,026	1,410,000
Total Liabilities	2,496,130	2,925,776	6,149,860
Total Equity	2,194,194	2,294,314	1,806,113
Total Liab. & Equity	4,690,324	5,220,090	7,955,973
CAPITAL			
Total Debt	898,607	1,380,026	4,195,000
Preferred Equity	0	0	0
Common Equity	2,194,194	2,294,314	1,806,113

Business:

PE BEN OILFIELD SERVICES LTD. is engaged in the transportation and field warehousing of drill pipe and casing for the petroleum industry. It also is engaged in the transportation and stockpiling of pipeline material for the oil and gas transmission industry. The company operates in Western and Central Canada.

Date	EPS	DPS	Tot Rev	Inc Bex
Mar 93	0.23	0.00	5,615	697
Dec 92	0.00	0.00	2,974	(3)
Sep 92	0.00	0.00	2,689	(2)
Jun 92	(0.12)	0.00	1,782	(370)
Mar 92	0.09	0.00	5,697	276
Dec 91	(0.10)	0.00	3,427	(287)
Sep 91	0.21	0.00	6,848	627
Jun 91	(0.08)	0.00	(189)	(248)

Synopsis:

During 1993, Pe Ben Oilfield Services expects an improvement in oilfield activity. This was partly the result of the Alberta royalty rebate plan introduced in 1992, which enhanced natural gas pricing levels, and lower interest rates. Management's primary focus in 1993 will be to complete their restructuring of oilfield operations.

The company has secured stringing subcontracts in conjunction with the construction of 109 kilometeres of 1067 millimetre O.D. (42") pipeline in Ontario for the first quarter of 1993, and the stockpiling of approximately 140 kilometres of 1219 millimetre O.D. (48") pipe in Manitoba and Saskatchewan to be undertaken between February and July. Several other pipeline projects are scheduled for the balance of the year, with tenders for the summer to be called at the end of the first quarter.

The 1992 the merger of oilfield operations expanded Pe Ben's scope of services, but no immediate net income contribution was realized, due to costs of reorganization. Pipeline subcontracting declined by $4.9-million in 1992, contract transportation levels remained unchanged, and a 37% increase in demand for specialized and light oilfield services was registered.

In 1992, a total of 657 kilometres of large diameter pipeline transmission pipe was hauled, stockpiled or strung in Western Canada and Ontario. On a comparative basis, 1,507 kilometres of transmission pipe was hauled, stockpiled or strung in 1991. The available work volume was relatively the same between the two periods and Pe Ben's bidding practices remained unaltered, however competitive pricing both undermined available margins on the work secured and precluded participation on many other projects.

Relative strength to TSE300 / Price / Volume (in 1000's of board lots)

Rank (Profit/Revenue/Assets)
449   634   996

Graham R. Dawson
Chairman

Address
4510 - 17 Street
P.O. Box 5805 Stn "L"
Edmonton
AB
T6P 1X5
(403) 440-4425

Fax: (403) 440-1134
P0001536/G/3.3

PETRO-CANADA

Exchanges	Price (Jun24'93)	12.00	Trailing P/E	279.07	Stock Symbol
TMVZW	Trailing Yield (%)	1.09	Trailing EPS	0.04	**PCA**

Period Ending	Dec92	Dec91	Dec90	Dec89	Dec88
Yearly Statistics					
Price-Close	8.13	9.50	n t	n t	n t
Price-High	10.88	13.25	n t	n t	n t
Price-Low	7.88	9.00	n t	n t	n t
P/E-Close	203.13	nm	n t	n t	n t
Dividends per Share	0.13	0.20	0.26	0.27	0.00
Dividend Yield (%)	1.60	2.11	n t	n t	0.00
Sales per Share	20.96	24.76	33.78	29.51	3,754.91
EPS before extra. item	0.04	(3.08)	1.02	0.12	na
Cash Flow per Share	2.31	1.41	3.57	2.75	501.83
Book Value per Share	10.72	11.58	15.03	14.46	1,410.60
O/S Common Shares	246,463	215,295	171,831	164,425	1,243
Total Revenue	4,710,000	4,984,000	5,873,000	5,026,000	4,801,000
Income before extra.	9,000	(598,000)	176,000	20,000	(11,000)
Cash Flow	502,000	274,000	601,000	452,000	624,000
Debt/Equity	0.40	0.68	0.89	0.88	0.74
Return on Capital (%)	4.50	(16.91)	13.20	6.36	3.32
Ret. on Com. Equity (%)	0.35	(23.57)	7.10	0.97	(0.90)
% Change Profit	101.5	(439.8)	780.0	281.8	(105.2)
% Change Revenue	(5.5)	(15.1)	16.9	4.7	(5.5)
% Change Assets	(11.3)	(17.1)	7.9	(0.1)	(20.1)

Preferred Div. Coverage	np	np	np
Total Div. Coverage	0.3	0.0	3.9
Interest Coverage	1.5	0.0	2.2
Current Ratio	1.0	1.3	1.0
Operating Margin	2.9	(3.1)	7.5
Asset Turnover	0.9	0.8	0.8
5 YEAR RATIOS (%)			
Return on Capital	2.1	3.3	8.9
Return on Com. Equity	(3.2)	(2.1)	3.6
Profit Growth	(47.0)	na	na
Revenue Growth	(1.5)	(0.8)	1.8
Asset Growth	(8.7)	(5.8)	(3.9)
BALANCE SHEET (000)			
Cash	82,000	0	36,000
Current Assets	1,156,000	1,330,000	1,821,000
Net Fixed Assets	3,865,000	4,084,000	4,778,000
Invest's & Advances	80,000	453,000	504,000
Total Assets	5,350,000	6,034,000	7,278,000
Short Term Debt	175,000	130,000	705,000
Current Liabilities	1,108,000	987,000	1,851,000
Long Term Debt	868,000	1,562,000	1,586,000
Total Liabilities	2,707,000	3,541,000	4,696,000
Total Equity	2,643,000	2,493,000	2,582,000
Total Liab. & Equity	5,350,000	6,034,000	7,278,000
CAPITAL (000)			
Total Debt	1,043,000	1,692,000	2,291,000
Preferred Equity	0	0	0
Common Equity	2,643,000	2,493,000	2,582,000

Business:

PETRO-CANADA is the largest Canadian controlled integrated oil and gas company. It is involved in the exploration, development, production and marketing of crude oil, natural gas, natural gas liquids, synthetic oil, bitumen and sulphur. The company owns and operates four major refineries and has the second largest refining capacity in Canada, and produces a range of fuels, lubricants, and other products.

Date	EPS	DPS	Tot Rev	Inc Bex
Mar 93	0.16	0.03	1,171,000	40,000
Dec 92	0.12	0.03	1,250,000	27,000
Sep 92	(0.27)	0.03	1,201,000	(56,000)
Jun 92	0.03	0.03	1,138,000	6,000
Mar 92	0.15	0.03	1,132,000	32,000
Dec 91	(1.83)	0.03	1,249,000	(364,000)
Sep 91	(0.41)	0.03	1,224,000	(85,000)
Jun 91	(0.46)	0.00	1,169,000	(97,000)

Synopsis:

Petro-Canada is focusing on oil and gas development prospects in Western Canada and future consolidation in the gasoline refining and marketing businesses for 1993. The company expects little change in oil prices and a gradual but sustained recovery in natural gas prices. Petrocan also expects natural gas exports to increase to meet rising U.S. demand as pipeline expansions come on line. Refinery closings are reducing Canada's products supply surplus.

Petro-Canada plans to invest 33% of its $540-million capital expenditure budget to maintain or improve refining and marketing reliability and profitability. The company expects to have its refinery operations at 90% capacity by the end of this year. About 32% of the capital budget is slated for the Hibernia offshore development project (net of grants), and another 30% goes to maintain or enhance oil and gas production in its core properties. Capital expenditures are to be financed by cash flow.

Petrocan reduced its debt by 60% from 1990 levels as a result of refinancing of debt, asset sales such as its investment in Westcoast Energy and some ownership in the Syncrude oil sands. The return to profitability and 77% increase in cash flow were due in part to a $306-million drop in operating and overhead costs and the closure or divestment of 534 retail and 61 wholesale outlets. Petrocan continues to focus on cost control and debt management.

Average daily production in 1992 (1991) was: crude oil and field natural gas liquids, net before royalties, 79,800 (92,500) barrels; natural gas, 517 (524) million cubic feet; and sulphur, 800 (1,100) tons. Proved reserves, net before royalties, in 1992 (1991) were: crude oil and field natural gas liquids, 417.3 (423) million barrels; natural gas, 2.4 (2.7) trillion cubic feet; and sulphur 5.2 (6.1) million tons. Revenues (operating earnings before depreciation, exploration and interest expense) in 1992, by segment were: natural resources, 8% (67%); refined products, 85% (31%); and corporate and other, 7% (2%).

Relative strength to TSE300 / Price / Volume (in 1000's of board lots)

Rank (Profit/Revenue/Assets)
190   27   41

A.E. Barroll
Chairman

James M. Stanford
President & C.E.O.

Wesley R. Twiss
Sr. V.P. & C.F.O.

Address
P.O. Box 2844
Calgary
AB
T2P 3E3
(403) 296-4040

Fax: (403) 296-3061
P0015657/G/3.1

PINNACLE RESOURCES LTD.

Exchanges	Price (Jun24'93)		22.25	Trailing P/E		34.77	Stock Symbol
TZ	Trailing Yield (%)		0.00	Trailing EPS		0.64	**PNN**

Period Ending	Dec92	Dec91	Dec90	Dec89	Dec88
Yearly Statistics					
Price-Close	15.25	7.00	4.00	3.25	0.85
Price-High	16.38	8.00	5.25	3.50	1.30
Price-Low	6.63	2.65	3.40	0.87	0.60
P/E-Close	28.77	35.00	14.29	19.12	nm
Dividends per Share	0.00	0.00	0.00	0.00	0.00
Dividend Yield (%)	0.00	0.00	0.00	0.00	0.00
Sales per Share	2.43	1.47	1.39	1.02	0.50
EPS before extra. item	0.53	0.20	0.28	0.17	(0.02)
Cash Flow per Share	1.54	0.82	0.92	0.66	0.18
Book Value per Share	4.26	2.44	1.46	0.78	0.35
O/S Common Shares	14,620	12,823	9,209	7,577	5,089
Total Revenue	33,642	17,605	12,528	7,348	2,445
Income before extra.	6,933	2,327	2,297	1,125	(63)
Cash Flow	20,113	8,870	7,415	4,343	751
Debt/Equity	nd	nd	nd	nd	0.31
Return on Capital (%)	21.31	15.86	25.23	16.94	(1.29)
Ret. on Com. Equity (%)	14.63	9.73	23.71	29.15	(4.24)
% Change Profit	198.0	1.3	104.3	1,889.1	na
% Change Revenue	91.1	40.5	70.5	200.5	na
% Change Assets	92.6	38.9	66.1	31.9	162.8

	Dec92	Dec91	Dec90
Preferred Div. Coverage	np	15.7	na
Total Div. Coverage	82.5	15.7	na
Interest Coverage	108.4	5.0	11.8
Current Ratio	2.1	1.2	0.4
Operating Margin	26.0	15.3	20.4
Asset Turnover	0.4	0.4	0.4
5 YEAR RATIOS (%)			
Return on Capital	15.6	na	na
Return on Com. Equity	14.6	na	na
Profit Growth	na	na	na
Revenue Growth	na	na	na
Asset Growth	72.7	na	na
BALANCE SHEET (000)			
Cash	21,821	2,314	418
Current Assets	27,043	5,175	3,423
Net Fixed Assets	57,440	38,688	28,145
Invest's & Advances	0	0	0
Total Assets	84,483	43,863	31,568
Short Term Debt	0	0	0
Current Liabilities	12,768	4,401	7,707
Long Term Debt	0	0	0
Total Liabilities	22,158	10,505	13,172
Total Equity	62,325	33,358	18,396
Total Liab. & Equity	84,483	43,863	31,568
CAPITAL (000)			
Total Debt	0	0	0
Preferred Equity	0	2,020	4,944
Common Equity	62,325	31,338	13,452

Business:

PINNACLE RESOURCES LTD. is involved in oil and gas exploration and development prospects in Alberta.

Date	EPS	DPS	Tot Rev	Inc Bex
Mar 93	0.17	0.00	12,392	2,508
Dec 92	0.19	0.00	10,998	2,425
Sep 92	0.18	0.00	9,875	2,344
Jun 92	0.10	0.00	7,034	1,351
Mar 92	0.06	0.00	5,735	813
Dec 91	0.07	0.00	6,011	855
Sep 91	0.07	0.00	4,573	771
Jun 91	0.03	0.00	3,736	388

Synopsis:

Pinnacle Resources expects to increase oil production by 62% in 1993 to an average 6,500 barrels per day. It also expects to almost triple natural gas production from its proven reserve base to an average 23 million cubic feet per day in 1993. For the first quarter of 1993, Pinnacle drilled a total of 61 gross wells, which include 23 oil wells, 20 gas wells and 18 dry holes. The company plans to spend $62-million in 1993 on capital expenditures, a 120% increase over 1992.

Pinnacle received gross proceeds of $24-million in December 1992, for the issuance of 1.6 million Common Shares. As at March 31, 1993, Pinnacle had 14.9 million Common Shares outstanding.

The Government of Alberta announced changes to the oil and gas royalty system in October 1992. Effective January 1, 1993, Crown royalty rates became price sensitive for oil and natural gas production from pools discovered before October 1, 1992. Royalty rates would drop to 14% for oil and 16% for natural gas at reference prices below $14 per barrel of oil and $1 per thousand cubic feet of gas. Also, exploratory wells which discover new oil pools after October 1, 1992, will qualify for a one-year royalty holiday. Production after this time will be subject to a newly defined third-tier royalty rate, which could enhance Pinnacle's future cash flows depending on how successful the company is. Royalties as an average percentage of 1992 sales were 24% for oil and 18% for gas.

Average daily production in 1992 (1991) was: crude oil, 4,018 (1,827) barrels; natural gas, 8.4 (8.3) million cubic feet. Proven and probable reserves in 1992 (1991) were: crude oil, 6.64 (4.07) million barrels; natural gas, 69.1 (45.7) billion cubic feet. The company's oil and gas exploration, development and production activities are all conducted in Canada. Sales in 1992 (1991) by product were: oil, 88% (79%); natural gas, 12% (21%). On the basis of increased production forecasts and stable prices, Pinnacle predicts record petroleum and natural gas sales in 1993 of $58-million, an 83% increase over 1992 results.

Rank (Profit/Revenue/Assets)
216   539   445

Richard J.S. Wigington
Chairman, President & C.E.O.
Stuart G. Clark
Exec. V.P., C.F.O. & Treasurer

Address
Suite 1100
801 - 6th Avenue S.W.
Monenco Place
Calgary
AB
T2P 3W2
(403) 265-5300
Fax: (403) 262-2563
01000587/G/3.2

For further company information, call Globe Information Services 1-800-268-9128 or (416)585-5345

POCO PETROLEUMS LTD.

Exchanges					Stock Symbol
TMZ	Price (Jun24'93)	9.37	Trailing P/E	nm	**POC**
	Trailing Yield (%)	0.53	Trailing EPS	(1.46)	

Period Ending	Dec92	Dec91	Dec90	Dec89	Dec88
Yearly Statistics					
Price-Close	4.60	5.63	8.13	8.75	8.25
Price-High	5.88	8.63	8.88	9.50	13.25
Price-Low	3.50	5.00	5.75	6.50	7.25
P/E-Close	nm	140.63	38.69	54.69	nm
Dividends per Share	0.10	0.13	0.00	0.00	0.00
Dividend Yield (%)	2.17	2.31	0.00	0.00	0.00
Sales per Share	3.21	3.62	3.72	3.01	4.08
EPS before extra. item	(1.55)	0.04	0.21	0.16	(0.38)
Cash Flow per Share	1.26	1.54	1.92	1.56	1.47
Book Value per Share	5.35	7.39	7.37	7.16	6.42
O/S Common Shares	77,924	60,352	41,587	41,128	27,608
Total Revenue	204,783	190,787	154,218	103,734	97,164
Income before extra.	(97,512)	127	11,205	8,173	(6,385)
Cash Flow	80,386	80,559	79,490	53,556	34,949
Debt/Equity	0.51	0.65	0.34	0.23	0.86
Return on Capital (%)	(19.03)	5.29	9.32	5.85	2.23
Ret. on Com. Equity (%)	(22.91)	(0.50)	2.83	2.32	(6.20)
% Change Profit	nm	(98.9)	37.1	228.0	(213.4)
% Change Revenue	7.3	23.7	48.7	6.8	30.5
% Change Assets	(19.7)	67.0	16.3	3.8	18.4

	Date	EPS	DPS	Tot Rev	Inc Bex
	Mar 93	0.02	0.00	56,363	1,544
	Dec 92	(1.45)	0.00	50,410	(92,327)
	Sep 92	(0.02)	0.00	51,837	(991)
	Jun 92	(0.01)	0.05	51,102	(574)
	Mar 92	(0.07)	0.05	51,434	(3,620)
	Dec 91	(0.03)	0.13	51,162	(4,917)
	Sep 91	0.01	0.00	49,545	976
	Jun 91	0.01	0.00	43,852	1,428

	Dec92	Dec91	Dec90
Preferred Div. Coverage	0.0	0.1	4.1
Total Div. Coverage	0.0	0.0	4.1
Interest Coverage	0.0	1.6	4.9
Current Ratio	0.9	1.0	1.9
Operating Margin	(65.0)	16.3	25.6
Asset Turnover	0.3	0.2	0.3
5 YEAR RATIOS (%)			
Return on Capital	0.7	6.3	9.4
Return on Com. Equity	(4.9)	0.4	5.5
Profit Growth	na	(58.7)	16.4
Revenue Growth	22.4	29.6	35.4
Asset Growth	13.8	39.8	33.5
BALANCE SHEET (000)			
Cash	0	0	0
Current Assets	32,128	33,133	22,040
Net Fixed Assets	649,659	825,991	495,507
Invest's & Advances	0	0	0
Total Assets	696,121	866,716	519,117
Short Term Debt	8,391	11,247	1,128
Current Liabilities	34,688	33,092	11,505
Long Term Debt	209,887	285,683	113,528
Total Liabilities	266,347	407,307	183,733
Total Equity	429,774	459,409	335,384
Total Liab. & Equity	696,121	866,716	519,117
CAPITAL (000)			
Total Debt	218,278	296,930	114,656
Preferred Equity	13,084	13,188	29,025
Common Equity	416,690	446,221	306,359

Business:

POCO PETROLEUMS LTD. is an oil and gas exploration development and production company. It has producing wells and land holdings in Alberta, Saskatchewan and northeastern British Columbia. The company markets natural gas to customers in Canada and the United States.

Synopsis:

Poco Petroleums signed a letter of intent to purchase properties in the Brazeau river area of Alberta. Once the transaction closes May 31, 1993, the company will begin to exploit the 3 million barrels of liquids and 81 billion cubic feet of natural gas included in the deal. The properties daily produce 850 barrels of liquids and 23 million cubic feet of gas. Poco plans to increase production through the drilling of new wells and the re-completion of others. The first quarter results for 1993 include, the impact of the acquired assets, effective January 1, 1993.

Poco replaced through acquisitions and exploration over 128% of its 1992 production of 11.5 million barrels of oil equivalent. However, the year-end independent engineering evaluation eliminated 100,000 barrels of liquids and 34.2 billion cubic feet of natural gas reserves, and shifted significant reserves from the proven category to the probable. The proven rate for 1992 (1991) was: crude oil and natural gas liquids, 72% (81%); and natural gas, 75% (86%).

Average liquid sales for the first quarter of 1993 increased 5% over the fourth quarter 1992 average, and natural gas sales were up 16%. Natural gas prices rose steadily during this period, but liquid prices were down 8% compared to the final quarter last year. Poco believes it will improve earnings in 1993 owing to higher production levels. Oil and liquids production is expected to reach 19,500 barrels a day in 1993, up from an average 18,500 barrels a day in 1992. Natural gas production is estimated to reach 185 million cubic feet a day by the end of 1993, and to average 160 million for the year.

Average daily sales in 1992 (1991) were: crude oil and natural gas liquids, 17,756 (14,890) barrels; and natural gas, 137.7 (128.5) million cubic feet. Gross proven and probable reserves in 1992 (1991) were: oil and gas liquids, 42.4 (42.4) million barrels; and natural gas, 664.4 (758.3) billion cubic feet. Contributions to net revenue in 1992 (1991) by product were: crude oil and natural gas liquids, 59% (57%); natural gas, 36% (34%); and other, 5% (9%).

Relative strength to TSE300 / Price / Volume (in 1000's of board lots)

Rank (Profit/Revenue/Assets)
972   270   183

Arne R. Nielsen
Chairman

Craig W. Stewart
President & C.O.O.

John W. Ferguson
V.P. & C.F.O.

Address
Suite 3500
250 - 6th Avenue S.W.
Calgary
AB
T2P 3H7
(403) 260-8000

Fax: (403) 263-2708
P0003112/G/3.2

PRECAMBRIAN SHIELD RESOURCES LIMITED

Exchanges	Price (Jun24'93)		3.10	Trailing P/E		nm	Stock Symbol
T	Trailing Yield (%)		0.00	Trailing EPS		(0.63)	**PCB**

Period Ending	Dec92	Dec91	Dec90	Dec89	Dec88
Yearly Statistics					
Price-Close	1.80	2.35	2.55	2.90	2.00
Price-High	2.30	2.60	3.55	3.25	3.15
Price-Low	1.30	1.90	2.35	2.00	2.00
P/E-Close	nm	nm	31.88	32.22	40.00
Dividends per Share	0.00	0.00	0.00	0.00	0.00
Dividend Yield (%)	0.00	0.00	0.00	0.00	0.00
Sales per Share	1.27	1.17	1.19	0.82	0.76
EPS before extra. item	(0.66)	(0.26)	0.08	0.09	0.05
Cash Flow per Share	0.48	0.44	0.52	0.46	0.36
Book Value per Share	1.86	2.52	2.78	2.70	2.61
O/S Common Shares	36,657	36,657	36,657	36,657	36,657
Total Revenue	7,061	42,767	43,445	30,318	24,931
Income before extra.	(24,038)	(9,710)	2,912	3,446	1,636
Cash Flow	17,419	16,034	19,113	16,856	11,767
Debt/Equity	0.83	0.68	0.61	0.58	0.45
Return on Capital (%)	(22.95)	(5.26)	7.78	8.01	6.23
Ret. on Com. Equity (%)	(29.94)	(9.99)	2.90	3.54	1.98
% Change Profit	(147.6)	(433.4)	(15.5)	110.6	(53.4)
% Change Revenue	(83.5)	(1.6)	43.3	21.6	0.6
% Change Assets	(22.0)	(8.5)	6.0	11.3	(1.1)

Business:

PRECAMBRIAN SHIELD RESOURCES LIMITED is an oil and natural gas exploration and development company active primarily in Western Canada. Mark Resources Inc. of Calgary holds an 88% interest in the company.

Date	EPS	DPS	Tot Rev	Inc Bex
Mar 93	0.03	0.00	8,580	951
Dec 92	(0.66)	0.00	12,863	(23,948)
Sep 92	0.00	0.00	11,443	30
Jun 92	0.00	0.00	10,590	8
Mar 92	0.00	0.00	11,829	(128)
Dec 91	(0.27)	0.00	11,017	(9,908)
Sep 91	0.00	0.00	10,158	(32)
Jun 91	0.01	0.00	10,219	259

	Dec92	Dec91	Dec90
Preferred Div. Coverage	np	np	np
Total Div. Coverage	na	na	na
Interest Coverage	0.0	0.0	1.8
Current Ratio	1.0	0.8	0.3
Operating Margin	16.1	(19.6)	28.7
Asset Turnover	0.3	0.2	0.2
5 YEAR RATIOS (%)			
Return on Capital	(1.2)	4.8	1.0
Return on Com. Equity	(6.3)	0.3	(5.4)
Profit Growth	na	na	(16.9)
Revenue Growth	(22.3)	11.5	5.8
Asset Growth	(3.6)	(2.2)	(4.2)
BALANCE SHEET (000)			
Cash	0	0	302
Current Assets	53,585	2,524	4,548
Net Fixed Assets	96,100	189,338	205,029
Invest's & Advances	0	0	0
Total Assets	149,685	191,862	209,587
Short Term Debt	50,988	715	11,086
Current Liabilities	54,943	3,075	17,429
Long Term Debt	5,631	62,285	51,046
Total Liabilities	81,418	99,557	107,572
Total Equity	68,267	92,305	102,015
Total Liab. & Equity	149,685	191,862	209,587
CAPITAL (000)			
Total Debt	56,619	63,000	62,132
Preferred Equity	0	0	0
Common Equity	68,267	92,305	102,015

Synopsis:

Mark Resources, of Calgary announced in May 1993 the terms of a proposed amalgamation of its wholly owned subsidiary, 468714 Alberta Inc. with its 88% held subsidiary, Precambrian Shield Resources Limited. Mark proposes to pay $14.3-million to buy out Precambrian's minority shareholders. Shareholders will be entitled to receive $3.25 a share in cash. Precambrian's board has accepted a recommendation by an independent directors' committee that the board accept Mark's offer and submit it to shareholders for approval.

Precambrian's 27% decline in oil and gas revenues for the first quarter of 1993 was attributed to reduced production levels in both commodities. This decline was offset by increases in commodity prices, and reductions in production, depreciation, depletion and interest expenses.

Precambrian's 1992 net loss resulted from the loss on sale of the Sandhills gas property at the end of December 1992. The $50-million proceeds of disposition, previously held in escrow, were released in April 1993 and used to pay down debt.

Daily production levels in 1992 (1991) were: oil and natural gas liquids, 3,766 (3,472) barrels; and natural gas, 44.5 (39.9) million cubic feet. Total proven and probable reserves at year-end were: oil and natural gas liquids, 12.7 (11.9) million barrels and natural gas; 165.3 (162.4) billion cubic feet. Natural gas reserves exclude 233.5 billion cubic feet of reserves at Sandhills which was sold effective December 1992.

Relative strength to TSE300 / Price / Volume (in 1000's of board lots) charts 1990–1993.

Rank (Profit/Revenue/Assets)
885   498   328

Barry W. Harrison
Chairman

Daryl E. Birnie
President & C.E.O.

Daniel T. Tsubouchi
Sr. V.P., Corp. Affairs & Fin.

Address
Suite 1300
800 - 5th Avenue S.W.
Calgary
AB
T2P 4A4
(403) 267-1500

Fax: (403) 269-2297
P0004011/G/3.2

RANCHMEN'S RESOURCES LTD.

Exchanges	Price (Jun24'93)	6.00	Trailing P/E	300.00	Stock Symbol
TZ	Trailing Yield (%)	0.00	Trailing EPS	0.02	**RRL**

Period Ending	Dec92	Dec91	Dec90	Dec89	Dec88
Yearly Statistics					
Price-Close	4.00	4.70	8.38	8.38	4.35
Price-High	5.63	8.37	9.25	8.38	7.62
Price-Low	3.70	4.40	7.12	4.30	4.25
P/E-Close	nm	nm	167.50	nm	nm
Dividends per Share	0.00	0.00	0.23	0.17	0.00
Dividend Yield (%)	0.00	0.00	2.75	2.03	0.00
Sales per Share	3.01	3.15	3.35	2.58	2.82
EPS before extra. item	(0.07)	(0.95)	0.05	(0.05)	(0.06)
Cash Flow per Share	1.28	0.86	1.53	1.22	1.17
Book Value per Share	3.46	3.42	4.24	4.74	6.16
O/S Common Shares	20,235	15,985	15,487	15,175	12,971
Total Revenue	51,746	49,043	51,692	40,240	31,969
Income before extra.	265	(13,228)	2,773	1,239	1,338
Cash Flow	22,412	13,492	23,482	18,320	12,795
Debt/Equity	0.29	0.71	0.48	nd	0.04
Return on Capital (%)	2.33	(7.18)	3.87	1.48	2.04
Ret. on Com. Equity (%)	(1.93)	(24.79)	1.14	(1.03)	(1.39)
% Change Profit	102.0	(577.0)	123.8	(7.4)	(67.8)
% Change Revenue	5.5	(5.1)	28.5	25.9	32.5
% Change Assets	(6.8)	(6.2)	40.4	(10.0)	37.9

Date	EPS	DPS	Tot Rev	Inc Bex
Mar 93	0.02	0.00	12,500	800
Dec 92	(0.05)	0.00	12,546	(535)
Sep 92	0.00	0.00	13,700	400
Jun 92	0.05	0.00	13,700	1,200
Mar 92	(0.07)	0.00	11,800	(800)
Dec 91	(0.54)	0.00	12,143	(8,128)
Sep 91	(0.19)	0.00	11,300	(2,600)
Jun 91	(0.15)	0.00	12,400	(1,900)

Preferred Div. Coverage	0.2	0.0	1.4
Total Div. Coverage	0.2	0.0	0.5
Interest Coverage	1.3	0.0	3.3
Current Ratio	0.9	0.9	1.2
Operating Margin	6.8	(14.1)	8.5
Asset Turnover	0.4	0.4	0.3
5 YEAR RATIOS (%)			
Return on Capital	0.5	2.1	4.6
Return on Com. Equity	(5.6)	(2.5)	2.8
Profit Growth	(42.5)	na	28.2
Revenue Growth	16.4	20.9	14.6
Asset Growth	8.8	11.5	11.8
BALANCE SHEET (000)			
Cash	35	0	3,067
Current Assets	10,878	8,364	14,598
Net Fixed Assets	117,823	129,843	132,745
Invest's & Advances	11	53	61
Total Assets	128,961	138,303	147,454
Short Term Debt	0	305	100
Current Liabilities	11,943	9,412	12,110
Long Term Debt	24,790	49,398	40,846
Total Liabilities	44,305	68,215	62,581
Total Equity	84,656	70,088	84,873
Total Liab. & Equity	128,961	138,303	147,454
CAPITAL (000)			
Total Debt	24,790	49,703	40,946
Preferred Equity	14,730	15,350	19,203
Common Equity	69,926	54,738	65,670

Business:

RANCHMEN'S RESOURCES LTD. is an oil and gas exploration and production company. It has producing wells in Alberta and Saskatchewan, and other land holdings in Alberta, Saskatchewan, Manitoba and Labrador. Total S.A. of Paris, France, holds approximately 52% of the company's common shares.

Synopsis:

Ranchmen's Resources gained independence from its major shareholder, Total S.A. of France, when Total sold its 52.3% control block of 10.6 million Common Shares to a group of brokers in April 1993, for $50-million. The sale will result in a secondary distribution of Ranchmen's Common Shares through special warrants.

The company raised $16.4-million in 1992 from the issuance of 4.2 million Common Shares. The funds were used to repay bank debt. The company's long-term debt declined to 29% of equity at the end of 1992 from 70% of equity at the end of 1991.

In an effort to concentrate on the development of core assets in areas where the company has a significant interest, Ranchmen's undertook a property rationalization program in early 1992. As a result of trades, acquisitions and dispositions, the company increased its interest in 22 properties, eliminated its interest in 71 others, and reduced its gross wells by 960 and net wells by 108.

The reduced property holdings together with revised production estimates caused proven oil reserves to fall 14% in 1992, and proven gas reserves to drop 20%. First quarter 1993 production of oil and natural gas liquids dipped 6% to 5,440 barrels per day, and natural gas slipped 6% to an average of 33.9 million cubic feet per day over the same period last year. Results for the first quarter of 1993 included a 38% increase in cash flow and a $1.6-million improvement in earnings over the 1992 first quarter, largely owing to improved oil and gas prices, and lower operating costs and interest charges.

Average daily production in 1992 (1991) was: crude oil and natural gas liquids, 5,600 (5,570) barrels; and natural gas, 34.4 (33) million cubic feet. Gross proven and probable reserves in 1992 (1991) were: crude oil and natural gas liquids, 14.4 (16.2) million barrels; and natural gas, 139.9 (174.1) billion cubic feet. Contributions to gross revenue in 1992 (1991) by product were: crude oil and natural gas liquids, 68% (67%); and natural gas, 32% (33%).

Relative strength to TSE300 / Price / Volume (in 1000's of board lots)

Rank (Profit/Revenue/Assets)		
530	466	380

Jean-Bernard Keller
Chairman Of The Board

Kerry E. Sully
President & C.E.O.

Peter H. Ryder
V.P., Finance & C.F.O.

Terry D. Brooker
V.P. & C.O.O.

Address
Suite 1000
333 - 11th Avenue S.W.
Calgary
AB
T2R 1L9
(403) 267-9400

Fax: (403) 267-9444
R0000253/G/3.2

RANGER OIL LIMITED

Exchanges	Price (Jun24'93)	6.62	Trailing P/E	27.60	Stock Symbol
TMN	Trailing Yield (%)	1.21	Trailing EPS	0.24	**RGO**

Period Ending	Dec92	Dec91	Dec90	Dec89	Dec88
Yearly Statistics	US	US	US	US	US
Price-Close	7.00	8.75	8.00	6.88	6.00
Price-High	9.38	10.00	9.63	7.75	7.88
Price-Low	6.38	7.00	6.63	6.00	5.38
P/E-Close	19.80	112.31	12.76	18.22	33.29
Dividends per Share	0.08	0.08	0.06	0.00	0.00
Dividend Yield (%)	1.39	1.05	0.88	0.00	0.00
Sales per Share	1.53	1.22	1.81	1.64	1.20
EPS before extra. item	0.24	0.06	0.46	0.27	0.12
Cash Flow per Share	1.22	0.82	1.07	0.84	0.67
Book Value per Share	4.55	4.39	4.36	3.69	2.71
O/S Common Shares	98,486	98,461	97,118	84,636	74,635
Total Revenue	170,505	135,812	185,538	149,602	107,141
Income before extra.	23,486	5,794	42,445	23,233	10,204
Cash Flow	120,018	80,047	94,452	66,925	50,356
Debt/Equity	0.08	0.01	0.03	0.25	0.44
Return on Capital (%)	3.85	1.43	10.80	10.76	7.18
Ret. on Com. Equity (%)	5.34	1.27	11.16	8.49	4.52
% Change Profit	305.4	(86.3)	82.7	127.7	(38.0)
% Change Revenue	25.5	(26.8)	24.0	39.6	(3.5)
% Change Assets	8.7	0.2	4.2	23.2	(2.6)

Preferred Div. Coverage	np	np	30.8
Total Div. Coverage	3.0	0.7	6.6
Interest Coverage	14.0	3.4	8.9
Current Ratio	2.0	2.1	4.2
Operating Margin	6.0	1.2	22.0
Asset Turnover	0.2	0.2	0.3
5 YEAR RATIOS (%)			
Return on Capital	6.8	8.4	9.1
Return on Com. Equity	6.2	6.8	7.0
Profit Growth	7.4	1.2	76.8
Revenue Growth	8.9	5.9	1.2
Asset Growth	6.3	7.0	3.1
BALANCE SHEET (000)			
Cash	12,729	58,174	168,075
Current Assets	56,550	92,844	197,184
Net Fixed Assets	577,578	490,105	383,547
Invest's & Advances	7,199	6,954	8,066
Total Assets	641,327	589,903	588,797
Short Term Debt	1,695	2,710	5,700
Current Liabilities	28,712	44,198	46,672
Long Term Debt	33,000	3,108	6,324
Total Liabilities	193,497	157,840	150,656
Total Equity	447,830	432,063	438,141
Total Liab. & Equity	641,327	589,903	588,797
CAPITAL (000)			
Total Debt	34,695	5,818	12,024
Preferred Equity	0	0	14,923
Common Equity	447,830	432,063	423,218

Business:

RANGER OIL LTD. is an oil and gas exploration and production company. The company has producing wells in North America and the United Kingdom. Exploration areas include North America, the United Kingdom, France, and the Netherlands.

Date		EPS	DPS	Tot Rev	Inc Bex
Mar 93	US	0.07	0.08	48,028	7,109
Dec 92	US	0.07	0.00	45,660	6,716
Sep 92	US	0.02	0.00	44,139	1,876
Jun 92	US	0.08	0.00	41,240	7,395
Mar 92	US	0.08	0.08	37,770	7,499
Dec 91	US	(0.08)	0.00	36,900	(8,188)
Sep 91	US	0.06	0.00	30,703	5,895
Jun 91	US	0.03	0.00	29,087	3,412

Synopsis:

Ranger Oil is reducing exploration spending in the North Sea in light of proposed tax changes announced by the British government in March 1993. Companies engaged in exploration will no longer receive a tax credit on profits from existing fields. Ranger received $33-million (U.S.) in tax repayments in 1992, but will receive no refund under the new rules. However, the Petroleum Revenue Tax charged on current oil and gas production will be reduced to 50% from 75% on July 1, 1993, and the tax will be abolished on fields given development consent after March 16, 1993.

Oil and gas revenues before royalties climbed by 32% in the first quarter of 1993, without any tax recovery. The tax recovery for the same period in 1992 totaled $13.5-million. The higher revenues are attributed to improved levels of oil and natural gas production, partly owing to the utilization of oil and gas assets acquired for $57-million (U.S.) from Calgary-based MLC Oil and Gas, in July 1992. The acquisition includes proved and probable reserves of 7.9 million barrels of oil and natural gas liquids and 89 billion cubic feet of natural gas.

Average daily production in 1992 (1991) in the United Kingdom was: oil and natural gas liquids, 10,210 (10,108) barrels; natural gas, 22.4 (1.7) million cubic feet. Average daily production in 1992 (1991) in North America was: oil and natural gas liquids, 3,650 (2,655) barrels; natural gas, 71.7 (56.6) million cubic feet. Gross proved and probable reserves in 1992 (1991) were: crude oil and natural gas liquids, 47.1 (35.8) million barrels; natural gas, 445.0 (401.9) billion cubic feet. Of the 1992 proved and probable reserves, the United Kingdom properties account for 67% of the crude oil and natural gas liquids reserves, while the North American properties account for 74% of the natural gas reserves.

Contributions to total revenues in 1992 (1991) by geographic segment were: the U.K., 66% (63%); North America, 29% (30%); and corporate, 5% (7%).

Relative strength to TSE300 / Price / Volume (in 1000's of board lots) chart, 1990–1993.

Rank (Profit/Revenue/Assets)
101 268 171

Simon Reisman
Chairman
Fred J. Dyment
President & C.O.O.

Address
2700 Esso Plaza East
425 First Street S.W.
Calgary
AB
T2P 3L8
(403) 232-5200

Fax: (403) 263-0090
R0000324/G/3.2

RENAISSANCE ENERGY LTD.

Exchanges	Price (Jun24'93)	34 .00	Trailing P/E	73 .91	Stock Symbol
TM	Trailing Yield (%)	0 .00	Trailing EPS	0 .46	**RES**

Period Ending	Dec92	Dec91	Dec90	Dec89	Dec88
Yearly Statistics					
Price-Close	18 .63	13 .13	15 .75	12 .88	6 .44
Price-High	19 .75	17 .13	16 .50	12 .88	8 .94
Price-Low	12 .25	11 .88	12 .00	6 .31	5 .25
P/E-Close	53 .21	41 .03	41 .45	41 .53	47 .69
Dividends per Share	0 .00	0 .00	0 .00	0 .00	0 .00
Dividend Yield (%)	0 .00	0 .00	0 .00	0 .00	0 .00
Sales per Share	3 .76	3 .21	3 .00	2 .25	1 .68
EPS before extra. item	0 .35	0 .32	0 .38	0 .31	0 .14
Cash Flow per Share	1 .91	1 .67	1 .43	1 .16	0 .80
Book Value per Share	6 .04	4 .78	3 .84	3 .45	3 .13
O/S Common Shares	74 ,668	65 ,046	60 ,330	58 ,705	57 ,732
Total Revenue	266 ,071	206 ,679	179 ,961	130 ,632	86 ,247
Income before extra.	24 ,552	20 ,805	22 ,812	17 ,915	7 ,935
Cash Flow	135 ,152	107 ,005	86 ,012	67 ,415	41 ,035
Debt/Equity	0 .41	0 .55	0 .54	0 .42	0 .42
Return on Capital (%)	9 .51	11 .58	14 .56	13 .05	8 .05
Ret. on Com. Equity (%)	6 .44	7 .67	10 .51	9 .36	4 .56
% Change Profit	18 .0	(8 .8)	27 .3	125 .8	(26 .7)
% Change Revenue	28 .7	14 .8	37 .8	51 .5	52 .8
% Change Assets	33 .0	34 .0	25 .6	13 .7	49 .9

Business:

RENAISSANCE ENERGY LTD. is an oil and gas exploration, development and production company. It has producing wells in Alberta, and sells natural gas to markets in Alberta, Eastern Canada, and the United States. Exploration activities focus on the plains area of Alberta.

Date	EPS	DPS	Tot Rev	Inc Bex
Mar 93	0 .13	0 .00	84 ,041	10 ,050
Dec 92	0 .15	0 .00	83 ,095	10 ,434
Sep 92	0 .11	0 .00	69 ,374	8 ,333
Jun 92	0 .07	0 .00	60 ,740	4 ,748
Mar 92	0 .02	0 .00	52 ,862	1 ,037
Dec 91	0 .02	0 .00	50 ,139	1 ,916
Sep 91	0 .07	0 .00	47 ,872	4 ,232
Jun 91	0 .12	0 .00	51 ,247	7 ,770

	Dec92	Dec91	Dec90
Preferred Div. Coverage	np	np	np
Total Div. Coverage	na	na	na
Interest Coverage	4 .6	5 .0	3 .1
Current Ratio	0 .6	0 .5	1 .0
Operating Margin	20 .5	23 .0	26 .0
Asset Turnover	0 .4	0 .4	0 .4
5 YEAR RATIOS (%)			
Return on Capital	11 .3	12 .5	12 .6
Return on Com. Equity	7 .7	8 .4	8 .2
Profit Growth	17 .8	34 .3	56 .0
Revenue Growth	36 .3	45 .2	40 .2
Asset Growth	30 .7	37 .6	36 .5
BALANCE SHEET (000)			
Cash	120	60	365
Current Assets	25 ,619	12 ,744	28 ,472
Net Fixed Assets	709 ,939	540 ,340	384 ,400
Invest's & Advances	0	0	0
Total Assets	735 ,558	553 ,084	412 ,872
Short Term Debt	0	0	0
Current Liabilities	41 ,599	27 ,364	27 ,601
Long Term Debt	182 ,743	169 ,715	124 ,229
Total Liabilities	284 ,408	242 ,175	180 ,956
Total Equity	451 ,150	310 ,909	231 ,916
Total Liab. & Equity	735 ,558	553 ,084	412 ,872
CAPITAL (000)			
Total Debt	182 ,743	169 ,715	124 ,229
Preferred Equity	0	0	0
Common Equity	451 ,150	310 ,909	231 ,916

Synopsis:

Renaissance Energy plans to spend $325-million on capital projects in 1993, a 24% increase over 1992. Financing will come indirectly from a $198-million equity issue of 7.5 million Common Shares scheduled to close May 19, 1993. The bulk of the proceeds will be used to pay down debt which stood at $242-million at the end of the first quarter of 1993, up 22% from the 1992 first quarter.

The company's 1992 drilling program resulted in 154 successful natural gas wells, and it hopes to drill in excess of 850 wells in 1993 of which 500 will be natural gas prospects. Renaissance has a total of 2.16 million net acres of undeveloped land, of which 70% is natural gas prone. The company believes these properties will yield at least 1.5 trillion cubic feet of additional gas reserves. Much of the company's future exploration effort will continue to be directed to natural gas prospects.

Gross revenues increased 59% to $84-million for the first quarter of 1993 over the same period last year, cash flow increased 92% to $45-million, and net income increased 869% to $10-million. The gains are largely a result of tightly focused operations, split between oil and gas production in the Plains area of Alberta.

Average daily production in 1992 (1991) was: oil, 25,900 (18,683) barrels; and natural gas, 212.2 (176.4) million cubic feet. Gross proven and probable reserves in 1992 (1991) were: oil and liquids, 119.2 (76.9) million barrels; and natural gas, 961.3 (732.3) billion cubic feet.

Contributions to gross revenue in 1992 (1991) were: oil, 60% (52%); natural gas, 40% (40%); oil hedging, - (9%); and other, - (-1%). Natural gas sales volume in 1992 (1991) by market segment was: U.S. export, 38% (29%); Eastern Canada industrial, 29% (28%); Alberta/Saskatchewan industrial, 12% (13%); system utilities, 13% (13%); and spot, 8% (17%). Pipeline capacity for natural gas exports to the U.S. are being expanded so that by 1994 all Canadian natural gas will have access to the North American market.

Rank (Profit/Revenue/Assets)
112   237   179

Ronald G. Greene
Chairman

Clayton H. Woitas
President & C.E.O.

John A. Thomson
Sr. V.P., Finance & C.F.O.

Address
Suite 3300
400 - 3rd Avenue S.W.
Calgary
AB
T2P 4H2
(403) 267-1400

Fax: (403) 267-1468
R0012081/G/3.2

RIGEL ENERGY CORPORATION

Exchanges	Price (Jun24'93)		23 .25	Trailing P/E		61 .18	Stock Symbol
TMA	Trailing Yield (%)		0 .00	Trailing EPS		0 .38	**RJL**

Period Ending	Dec92	Dec91	Dec90
Yearly Statistics			
Price-Close	10 .25	6 .13	n t
Price-High	10 .50	7 .25	n t
Price-Low	4 .80	5 .25	n t
P/E-Close	36 .61	32 .26	n t
Dividends per Share	0 .00	0 .00	0 .00
Dividend Yield (%)	0 .00	0 .00	0 .00
Sales per Share	2 .71	2 .61	2 .66
EPS before extra. item	0 .28	0 .19	0 .43
Cash Flow per Share	1 .40	1 .21	1 .45
Book Value per Share	3 .29	3 .01	4 .58
O/S Common Shares	35 ,352	35 ,251	35 ,251
Total Revenue	97 ,498	94 ,391	98 ,077
Income before extra.	9 ,843	6 ,831	15 ,333
Cash Flow	49 ,230	42 ,759	51 ,182
Debt/Equity	0 .19	0 .27	nd
Return on Capital (%)	13 .92	10 .12	na
Ret. on Com. Equity (%)	8 .86	5 .11	na
% Change Profit	44 .1	(55 .4)	na
% Change Revenue	3 .3	(3 .8)	na
% Change Assets	(3 .8)	(11 .3)	na
Preferred Div. Coverage	np	np	np
Total Div. Coverage	na	na	na
Interest Coverage	11 .1	8 .0	41 .9
Current Ratio	1 .3	1 .3	1 .2
Operating Margin	18 .1	17 .5	29 .7
Asset Turnover	0 .5	0 .4	0 .4
5 YEAR RATIOS (%)			
Return on Capital	na	na	na
Return on Com. Equity	na	na	na
Profit Growth	na	na	na
Revenue Growth	na	na	na
Asset Growth	na	na	na
BALANCE SHEET (000)			
Cash	2 ,691	3 ,851	1 ,011
Current Assets	14 ,590	16 ,057	14 ,783
Net Fixed Assets	196 ,602	203 ,686	205 ,383
Invest's & Advances	0	0	26 ,066
Total Assets	211 ,386	219 ,755	247 ,856
Short Term Debt	0	0	0
Current Liabilities	11 ,602	12 ,298	12 ,150
Long Term Debt	22 ,140	29 ,000	0
Total Liabilities	95 ,087	113 ,839	86 ,447
Total Equity	116 ,299	105 ,916	161 ,409
Total Liab. & Equity	211 ,386	219 ,755	247 ,856
CAPITAL (000)			
Total Debt	22 ,140	29 ,000	0
Preferred Equity	0	0	0
Common Equity	116 ,299	105 ,916	161 ,409

Business:

RIGEL ENERGY CORPORATION is in the business of exploration, development, production and marketing of oil and gas in Canada.

Date	EPS	DPS	Tot Rev	Inc Bex
Mar 93	0.15	0.00	27 ,674	5 ,334
Dec 92	0.11	0.00	28 ,411	3 ,702
Sep 92	0.06	0.00	22 ,952	2 ,004
Jun 92	0.06	0.00	23 ,063	2 ,245
Mar 92	0.05	0.00	23 ,072	1 ,892
Dec 91	0.03	0.00	23 ,848	1 ,134
Sep 91	0.06	0.00	21 ,609	2 ,016
Jun 91	0.03	0.00	20 ,956	1 ,024

Synopsis:

Total Canada Oil & Gas agreed to change its name to Rigel Energy Corporation prior to July 31, 1993, as a result of the sale by Total S.A. of France of its 53% control block of 18.8 million Common Shares to an underwriting syndicate in February 1993 for $183-million.

The company acquired Total Energold in 1992, increasing its unused tax pools by $78-million. The company expects to defer all income taxes for the next four years and to reduce its effective tax rate for a similar period through the use of these pools. The 1993 effective tax rate is expected to be less than 20%, while the 1992 rate was 43%.

Capital expenditures in 1992 were $32.9-million, compared with $34.9-million in 1991. Asset dispositions totaled $2.4-million in 1992, and $3-million in 1991. The 1993 capital program is budgeted at $48.6-million. During the first quarter of 1993, the company acquired 19,300 net acres of undeveloped land with an average working interest of 59%. The company participated in 46 wells, compared to 15 wells in the same period last year.

Net revenue after royalties increased 21% from the 1992 first quarter to $23.2-million. Higher production levels of crude oil, condensate and natural gas, combined with higher prices for all products, contributed to the gain. Long term debt remained unchanged from 1992 year-end at $22-million, with working capital of $4.9-million. Average daily production in 1992 (1991) was: crude oil and natural gas liquids, 9,156 (8,395) barrels; and natural gas, 65.1 (65) million cubic feet. Gross proven and probable reserves in 1992 (1991) were: crude oil, condensates and natural gas liquids, 35.6 (34.6) million barrels; natural gas, 341 (381.1) billion cubic feet. Contributions to gross production revenues in 1992 (1991) by product were: crude oil and condensates, 57% (55%); natural gas, 37% (37%); and natural gas liquids, 6% (8%). Major gas markets in 1992 by geographical area were: the U.S., 77%; and Canada, 33%.

Relative strength to TSE300 / Price / Volume (in 1000's of board lots)

Rank (Profit/Revenue/Assets)
187 382 312

Donald T. West
President & C.E.O.

Donald R. Gardner
V.P., Finance, C.F.O., Sec.

Address
Suite 700
639 Fifth Avenue S.W.
Calgary
AB
T2P 0M9
(403) 267-3000

Fax: (403) 267-3006
01003159/G/3.2

RIO ALTO EXPLORATION LTD.

Exchanges	Price (Jun24'93)	11.37	Trailing P/E	63.19	Stock Symbol
T	Trailing Yield (%)	0.00	Trailing EPS	0.18	**RAX**

Period Ending	Dec92	Dec91	Dec90	Dec89	Dec88
Yearly Statistics					
Price-Close	3.45	0.92	0.42	0.15	0.41
Price-High	3.55	1.30	0.60	0.48	1.55
Price-Low	0.80	0.31	0.12	0.13	0.25
P/E-Close	31.36	306.67	nm	nm	nm
Dividends per Share	0.00	0.00	0.00	0.00	0.00
Dividend Yield (%)	0.00	0.00	0.00	0.00	0.00
Sales per Share	0.32	0.05	0.09	0.11	0.11
EPS before extra. item	0.11	0.00	(0.11)	(0.03)	(0.10)
Cash Flow per Share	0.23	0.02	0.03	0.01	0.02
Book Value per Share	0.54	0.40	0.29	0.49	0.51
O/S Common Shares	35,997	34,303	15,770	10,770	10,770
Total Revenue	11,117	1,167	(128)	1,228	1,323
Income before extra.	3,876	59	(1,411)	(290)	(1,096)
Cash Flow	7,962	303	356	97	186
Debt/Equity	1.20	0.05	0.19	0.21	0.20
Return on Capital (%)	16.65	1.70	(21.31)	(1.92)	(14.01)
Ret. on Com. Equity (%)	23.48	0.65	(28.80)	(5.38)	(18.14)
% Change Profit	6,438.7	104.2	(387.1)	73.6	(913.6)
% Change Revenue	852.6	1,014.3	(110.4)	(7.1)	(29.3)
% Change Assets	137.9	255.8	(25.8)	(0.7)	(9.6)

Date	EPS	DPS	Tot Rev	Inc Bex
Mar 93	0.09	0.00	8,363	3,138
Dec 92	0.05	0.00	4,825	1,816
Sep 92	0.02	0.00	2,359	613
Jun 92	0.02	0.00	2,427	785
Mar 92	0.02	0.00	1,940	663
Dec 91	0.00	0.00	433	1
Sep 91	0.00	0.00	281	24
Jun 91	0.00	0.00	260	4

	Dec92	Dec91	Dec90
Preferred Div. Coverage	np	np	np
Total Div. Coverage	na	na	na
Interest Coverage	5.5	1.5	0.0
Current Ratio	1.0	1.1	3.3
Operating Margin	42.5	14.4	10.3
Asset Turnover	0.2	0.0	0.2
5 YEAR RATIOS (%)			
Return on Capital	(3.8)	(6.3)	(29.5)
Return on Com. Equity	(5.6)	(9.8)	(34.5)
Profit Growth	95.8	na	na
Revenue Growth	42.8	(14.9)	na
Asset Growth	41.4	30.5	(20.6)
BALANCE SHEET (000)			
Cash	2,307	373	1,094
Current Assets	7,069	6,489	1,326
Net Fixed Assets	41,253	13,714	4,273
Invest's & Advances	0	0	0
Total Assets	48,322	20,312	5,708
Short Term Debt	984	244	244
Current Liabilities	6,879	6,078	407
Long Term Debt	22,169	400	624
Total Liabilities	29,048	6,570	1,149
Total Equity	19,274	13,742	4,559
Total Liab. & Equity	48,322	20,312	5,708
CAPITAL (000)			
Total Debt	23,153	644	869
Preferred Equity	0	0	0
Common Equity	19,274	13,742	4,559

Business:

RIO ALTO EXPLORATION LTD. is an oil and gas exploration and production company. It has wells and properties in Alberta and Saskatchewan.

Synopsis:

Rio Alto Exploration has established a new core area in the Ante Creek region of Alberta, where it purchased an average working interest of 75% in 91,000 acres of land effective January 1, 1993. With its acquisition, the company assumed the operations on May 1, 1993, of four gas plants, four compressor stations and three oil batteries. The property produces 11 million cubic feet of natural gas per day and 1,000 barrels of oil and natural gas liquids per day net to Rio Alto.

Rio Alto also purchased effective January, 1, 1993, an average 45% working interest in 133,000 acres of land near its existing operations at West Kirby and Duncan. The property contains 15 shut-in gas wells, most of which were successfully tested. A new gas plant is expected to be constructed in this area during the winter of 1993/94. As a result of recent acquisition and development activities, Rio Alto expects to increase average production in 1993 to over 70 million cubic feet of natural gas per day and 1,050 barrels per day of oil and natural gas liquids.

During the first quarter of 1993, Rio Alto issued two million Common Shares at $6.25 per share. Proceeds of the issue, which closed April 16, 1993, were used to reduce bank indebtedness. Pro forma to the recent acquisitions and the proceeds of the share issue, the company's long-term debt will be $25-million, giving it a present debt to cash flow ratio of 1:1.

Capital expenditures in 1992 of $32-million included $20-million of property acquisitions and $12-million of development activities. The program was financed through cash flow (25%), bank debt (69%), and proceeds of share issuance (6%).

Average daily production in 1992 (1991) was: oil and natural gas liquids, 99 (150) barrels; and natural gas, 27.5 (3.5) million cubic feet. Gross proven and probable reserves in 1992 (1991) were: oil and gas liquids, 259,200 (640,000) barrels; and natural gas, 122.7 (22) billion cubic feet.

Relative strength to TSE300 / Price / Volume (in 1000's of board lots)

Rank (Profit/Revenue/Assets)
286 683 546

Richard T. Cones
President & C.E.O.

Address
Suite 350
717 - 7th Avenue S.W.
Calgary
AB
T2P 0Z3
(403) 264-8780

Fax: (403) 261-7626
R0001990/G/3.2

SASKATCHEWAN OIL AND GAS CORPORATION

Exchanges	Price (Jun24'93)	10.37	Trailing P/E	nm	Stock Symbol
TM	Trailing Yield (%)	0.00	Trailing EPS	(0.47)	**SKO**

Period Ending	Dec92	Dec91	Dec90	Dec89	Dec88
Yearly Statistics					
Price-Close	4.85	6.63	13.00	13.88	8.50
Price-High	6.25	13.00	16.13	15.00	10.25
Price-Low	4.25	6.00	12.38	8.25	6.88
P/E-Close	nm	nm	61.91	277.60	nm
Dividends per Share	0.00	0.00	0.00	0.00	0.00
Dividend Yield (%)	0.00	0.00	0.00	0.00	0.00
Sales per Share	5.68	4.68	5.52	4.90	3.30
EPS before extra. item	(0.57)	(1.10)	0.21	0.05	(0.41)
Cash Flow per Share	1.58	1.21	2.09	1.85	1.00
Book Value per Share	6.69	7.27	10.85	10.48	9.57
O/S Common Shares	68,700	68,364	68,146	56,759	39,254
Total Revenue	389,200	319,900	346,691	229,054	115,786
Income before extra.	(39,000)	(74,900)	14,723	7,740	(8,721)
Cash Flow	107,900	82,600	130,363	83,643	34,752
Debt/Equity	0.89	0.91	0.48	0.54	0.43
Return on Capital (%)	0.78	(2.80)	7.29	4.85	0.26
Ret. on Com. Equity (%)	(8.16)	(12.12)	1.96	0.47	(4.52)
% Change Profit	47.9	(608.7)	90.2	188.8	(165.6)
% Change Revenue	21.7	(7.7)	51.4	97.8	(4.2)
% Change Assets	(4.3)	(10.8)	10.3	68.2	83.0

Date	EPS	DPS	Tot Rev	Inc Bex
Mar 93	(0.11)	0.00	87,500	(7,700)
Dec 92	(0.23)	0.00	103,900	(16,000)
Sep 92	(0.04)	0.00	106,700	(2,600)
Jun 92	(0.09)	0.00	98,400	(6,400)
Mar 92	(0.29)	0.00	80,100	(20,100)
Dec 92	(0.94)	0.00	95,100	(64,200)
Sep 91	(0.08)	0.00	75,300	(5,500)
Jun 91	(0.05)	0.00	71,200	(3,700)

Preferred Div. Coverage	np	np	np
Total Div. Coverage	na	na	8.9
Interest Coverage	0.2	0.0	1.8
Current Ratio	0.9	0.9	0.8
Operating Margin	2.1	(8.6)	22.6
Asset Turnover	0.4	0.3	0.3
5 YEAR RATIOS (%)			
Return on Capital	2.1	3.7	4.5
Return on Com. Equity	(4.5)	(2.1)	(0.7)
Profit Growth	na	na	(17.8)
Revenue Growth	26.3	30.8	15.7
Asset Growth	23.7	30.9	34.6
BALANCE SHEET (000)			
Cash	0	0	0
Current Assets	132,700	100,200	94,631
Net Fixed Assets	943,800	1,024,800	1,166,174
Invest's & Advances	0	0	0
Total Assets	1,076,500	1,125,000	1,260,805
Short Term Debt	11,100	11,100	11,100
Current Liabilities	155,000	112,200	123,792
Long Term Debt	396,600	441,700	341,925
Total Liabilities	617,000	628,200	521,522
Total Equity	459,500	496,800	739,283
Total Liab. & Equity	1,076,500	1,125,000	1,260,805
CAPITAL (000)			
Total Debt	407,700	452,800	353,025
Preferred Equity	0	0	0
Common Equity	459,500	496,800	739,283

Business:

SASKATCHEWAN OIL AND GAS CORP. is an oil and gas exploration and production company. It has producing wells and exploration activities in Western Canada. The company markets its production across North America. The Saskatchewan Oil and Gas Corporation Amendment Act, 1992, allows ownership of the voting shares of the company to a maximum of 35% for non-citizens of Canada.

Synopsis:

Saskoil reduced retained earnings by $223.6-million in 1992 as a result of changing from the full cost method of accounting for the cost of its crude and natural gas properties to the successful efforts method. The company retroactively changed methods on December 31, 1992. Under full cost accounting, all the costs of energy exploration and development are capitalized and depleted. Using the successful efforts method, only those costs directly related to adding crude oil and natural gas reserves are capitalized and depleted or depreciated over the life of the reserves. All other expenditures are expensed to earnings during the period in which they are earned. Using full cost assumptions, Saskoil's 1992 loss would have been $37.3-million, compared with $23-8-million in 1991. The losses under the method now used were $39-million in 1992 and $74.9-million in 1991.

Saskoil hopes to cut its long-term debt to the $350-million range in 1993, from nearly $400-million in 1992, by cutting costs and selling non-strategic assets. During 1992, Saskoil sold $27.3-million of non-strategic properties. Capital programs for 1993 are budgeted at $78-million, a 32% rise over 1992.

Total revenue rose 9% in the first quarter of 1993 compared to the first quarter of 1992, mainly because increased oil production and better oil prices resulted in oil revenues of $54.6-million, up from $47.4-million the year before. This increase was offset by lower natural gas revenues of $27.2-million, down from $29.6-million, owing to slightly lower natural gas production and prices.

Average daily sales in 1992 (1991) were: crude oil and natural gas liquids, 39,800 (32,700) barrels; and natural gas, 239.9 (241.4) million cubic feet. Proven and probable reserves in 1992 (1991) were: crude oil and natural gas liquids, 208.9 (205.1) million barrels; and natural gas, 1,273.7 (1,377.8) billion cubic feet. Contributions to revenues before royalties in 1992 (1991) by product were: crude oil, 61% (55%); natural gas, 30% (41%); and other, 9% (4%).

Relative strength to TSE300 / Price / Volume (in 1000's of board lots)

Rank (Profit/Revenue/Assets)
945   191   150
Theodore M. Hanlon — Chairman
Theodore H. Renner — President & C.E.O.
C.J. Byrne McNamara — V.P., Finance & C.F.O.

Address
1777 Victoria Avenue
P.O. Box 1550
Regina
SK
S4P 3C4
(306) 781-8200

Fax: (306) 781-8364
S0038455/G/3.2

SCEPTRE RESOURCES LIMITED

Exchanges	Price (Jun24'93)		11.75	Trailing P/E		7.99	Stock Symbol
TMA	Trailing Yield (%)		0.00	Trailing EPS		1.47	**SRL**

Period Ending	Dec92	Dec91	Dec90	Dec89	Dec88
Yearly Statistics					
Price-Close	5.63	17.00	37.00	51.25	32.00
Price-High	17.50	41.50	51.25	56.25	49.00
Price-Low	4.40	15.50	32.00	31.50	30.00
P/E-Close	nm	nm	46.25	nm	80.00
Dividends per Share	0.00	0.00	0.00	0.00	0.00
Dividend Yield (%)	0.00	0.00	0.00	0.00	0.00
Sales per Share	11.30	20.92	27.15	28.57	18.97
EPS before extra. item	(0.04)	(22.89)	0.80	(4.00)	0.40
Cash Flow per Share	3.75	5.61	10.05	8.50	8.10
Book Value per Share	5.05	7.49	30.31	25.83	28.78
O/S Common Shares	52,321	9,358	9,358	6,961	5,798
Total Revenue	181,755	198,516	246,445	199,730	110,714
Income before extra.	307	(210,502)	11,309	(24,169)	6,289
Cash Flow	60,262	52,458	91,098	59,039	46,950
Debt/Equity	0.60	2.88	1.05	2.01	0.92
Return on Capital (%)	6.33	(30.98)	7.58	3.27	4.23
Ret. on Com. Equity (%)	(0.36)	(121.13)	3.25	(16.13)	1.55
% Change Profit	100.1	(1,961.4)	146.8	(484.3)	(24.0)
% Change Revenue	(8.4)	(19.4)	23.4	80.4	36.4
% Change Assets	(9.5)	(30.2)	(3.7)	61.9	3.6
Preferred Div. Coverage	np	0.0	3.0
Total Div. Coverage	0.3	0.0	3.0
Interest Coverage	1.0	0.0	1.3
Current Ratio	0.8	0.8	1.1
Operating Margin	15.1	(86.7)	21.0
Asset Turnover	0.4	0.4	0.3
5 YEAR RATIOS (%)			
Return on Capital	(1.9)	(1.4)	7.1
Return on Com. Equity	(26.6)	(25.4)	3.0
Profit Growth	(48.3)	na	21.5
Revenue Growth	17.4	23.2	17.3
Asset Growth	0.4	16.4	23.6
BALANCE SHEET (000)			
Cash	519	5,921	1,993
Current Assets	28,470	36,115	62,970
Net Fixed Assets	440,938	478,830	676,389
Invest's & Advances	0	0	0
Total Assets	469,408	518,780	743,677
Short Term Debt	0	0	14,480
Current Liabilities	33,925	43,401	57,481
Long Term Debt	157,628	339,677	335,787
Total Liabilities	205,095	400,811	410,680
Total Equity	264,313	117,969	332,997
Total Liab. & Equity	469,408	518,780	743,677
CAPITAL (000)			
Total Debt	157,628	339,677	350,267
Preferred Equity	0	47,894	49,394
Common Equity	264,313	70,075	283,603

Business:

SCEPTRE RESOURCES LTD. is an oil and gas exploration and production company. The company has producing wells in Western Canada. It has exploration activities in Western Canada, Indonesia, Pakistan, Egypt and Bolivia. The company sells its production in the North American market.

Date	EPS	DPS	Tot Rev	Inc Bex
Mar 93	1.10	0.00	49,200	5,724
Dec 92	0.56	0.00	48,101	2,971
Sep 92	0.01	0.00	45,288	1,107
Jun 92	(0.20)	0.00	44,840	(1,026)
Mar 92	(0.40)	0.00	43,526	(2,745)
Dec 91	(11.18)	0.00	51,165	(104,639)
Sep 91	(0.30)	0.00	46,006	(2,227)
Jun 91	(11.20)	0.00	48,590	(103,653)

Synopsis:

Sceptre Resources had a target of early July 1993 for closing an agreement to purchase Gulf Canada's oil and gas producing properties and facilities in southeast Saskatchewan for $65-million. These properties currently produce 5,000 barrels per day of light and medium crude oil. The company plans an active exploration and development program after closing.

Sceptre's planned 1993 capital program of $70-million was doubled to $145-million. The 1993 exploration and development program will increase 75% to $70-million, and the remaining allocation relates to the southeast Saskatchewan and other core area property acquisitions. As part of a strategy developed in 1992 to focus on core areas with enhanced economic returns, the 1992 capital program of $41-million was lower than the $70-million allocated for 1991.

Sceptre's international operations were eliminated during 1992. The disposition program, which began in mid-1992, had total sales of $21.9-million. The program included the sale of oil and gas interests in the U.S., as well as Canadian properties with 25.5 billion cubic feet of natural gas and 1.7 million barrels of oil and liquid reserves.

First quarter crude oil production levels fell to 15,655 barrels per day in 1993 from 17,849 in 1992. First quarter natural gas production dropped to 133.7 million cubic feet per day in 1993 compared to 137.1 in 1992, owing to the disposition of non-core properties.

Average daily production in 1992 (1991) was: crude oil and natural gas liquids, 18,970 (20,923) barrels; natural gas, 126 (122) million cubic feet. Proven and probable reserves in 1992 (1991) were: crude oil and gas liquids, 69 (65) million barrels; natural gas, 646 (723) billion cubic feet.

Gross product revenue before royalties in 1992 (1991) by product was: crude oil and liquids, 65% (68%); and natural gas, 35% (32%).

Relative strength to TSE300 / Price / Volume (in 1000's of board lots)

Rank (Profit/Revenue/Assets)
521 287 217

Maurice J. Leclair
Chairman

Grant D. Billing
President & C.E.O.

Stanley G. Weber
V.P. Fin., C.F.O. & Corp. Sec.

Address
Suite 2000
400 - 3rd Avenue S.W.
Calgary
AB
T2P 4H2
(403) 298-9800

Fax: (403) 290-1106
S0000627/G/3.2

SCURRY-RAINBOW OIL LIMITED

Exchanges	Price (Jun24'93)	23.50	Trailing P/E	33.57	Stock Symbol
TA	Trailing Yield (%)	2.13	Trailing EPS	0.70	**SCR**

Period Ending	Dec92	Dec91	Dec90	Dec89	Dec88
Yearly Statistics					
Price-Close	16.25	17.50	24.25	25.25	18.25
Price-High	17.75	25.00	31.00	25.25	20.88
Price-Low	16.00	17.50	24.00	17.88	14.63
P/E-Close	24.62	24.65	14.44	17.91	16.30
Dividends per Share	0.50	0.50	0.50	0.50	1.00
Dividend Yield (%)	3.08	2.86	2.06	1.98	5.48
Sales per Share	5.50	5.24	6.28	5.22	4.98
EPS before extra. item	0.66	0.71	1.68	1.41	1.12
Cash Flow per Share	3.17	3.21	4.27	3.72	3.57
Book Value per Share	17.72	17.57	17.36	16.18	15.27
O/S Common Shares	13,462	13,462	13,462	13,462	13,462
Total Revenue	74,568	71,703	86,454	72,817	70,277
Income before extra.	8,824	9,535	22,632	18,979	15,112
Cash Flow	42,736	43,265	57,424	50,117	48,122
Debt/Equity	nd	0.06	0.01	0.00	0.00
Return on Capital (%)	7.06	7.80	17.39	14.22	12.37
Ret. on Com. Equity (%)	3.72	4.06	10.03	8.97	7.38
% Change Profit	(7.5)	(57.9)	19.2	25.6	(34.7)
% Change Revenue	4.0	(17.1)	18.7	3.6	(13.5)
% Change Assets	(1.2)	2.3	8.7	8.5	(3.8)

Date	EPS	DPS	Tot Rev	Inc Bex
Mar 93	0.18	0.00	19,167	2,361
Dec 92	0.23	0.25	22,826	3,050
Sep 92	0.17	0.00	17,516	2,276
Jun 92	0.12	0.25	17,043	1,635
Mar 92	0.14	0.00	17,183	1,863
Dec 91	0.18	0.25	17,200	2,370
Sep 91	0.07	0.00	16,485	966
Jun 91	0.09	0.25	16,221	1,156

	Dec92	Dec91	Dec90
Preferred Div. Coverage	np	np	np
Total Div. Coverage	1.3	1.4	3.4
Interest Coverage	20.3	13.0	34.7
Current Ratio	0.8	0.6	0.6
Operating Margin	23.4	25.3	44.6
Asset Turnover	0.2	0.2	0.2
5 YEAR RATIOS (%)			
Return on Capital	11.8	14.6	16.2
Return on Com. Equity	6.8	8.4	9.4
Profit Growth	(17.6)	(10.8)	4.9
Revenue Growth	(1.7)	2.2	1.6
Asset Growth	2.7	4.3	3.9
BALANCE SHEET (000)			
Cash	18	0	0
Current Assets	16,358	15,520	15,738
Net Fixed Assets	367,761	371,973	362,983
Invest's & Advances	0	1,366	1,212
Total Assets	384,171	388,859	379,933
Short Term Debt	0	13,906	3,235
Current Liabilities	19,794	26,625	25,789
Long Term Debt	0	0	0
Total Liabilities	145,579	152,360	146,238
Total Equity	238,592	236,499	233,695
Total Liab. & Equity	384,171	388,859	379,933
CAPITAL (000)			
Total Debt	0	13,906	3,235
Preferred Equity	0	0	0
Common Equity	238,592	236,499	233,695

Business:

SCURRY-RAINBOW OIL LTD. is an oil and gas exploration and production company. The company has producing wells in British Columbia and the Prairie provinces. The company is 88.1% owned by Home Oil Limited of Calgary.

Synopsis:

Scurry-Rainbow Oil expects that environmental regulations passed by the Alberta government in 1992 will be in place by mid to late 1993. These regulations will likely increase the length and cost of project approvals because of greater public input and requirements for environmental impact assessments on individual projects.

Through its asset rationalization program, the company acquired $16-million of additional interests in 1992, and generated proceeds of $10-million from the sale of minor interest properties. The net effect was the addition of incremental productive capacity of almost 400 barrels of oil per day and 2.5 million cubic feet of natural gas per day, together with a 12% drop in unit operating costs. However, proved reserves declined 13% for crude oil and natural gas liquids, and 6% for natural gas from 1991 levels.

Proved crude oil reserves fell a further 3.2 million barrels during the first quarter of 1993, as a result of the $15-million sale of 50 non-strategic properties in southeastern Saskatchewan, containing 800 wells. Proved and probable natural gas reserves increased 7 billion cubic feet to a total of 538 billion cubic feet as a result of a $2-million acquisition of a 100% interest in developed acreage in Alberta.

The company's exploration and development program will jump by 70% to $37-million in 1993. Exploration expenditures totaled $10-million in 1992, and development expenditures totaled $12-million.

Average daily production in 1992 (1991) was: crude oil, 7,051 (7,208) barrels; natural gas, 56.8 (43) million cubic feet; and natural gas liquids, 1,150 (1,095) barrels. Proved reserves in 1992 (1991) were: crude oil, 15.3 (18.2) million barrels; natural gas liquids, 7 (7.3) million barrels; natural gas, 338 (358) billion cubic feet; and sulphur, 1.04 (1.07) million long tons. Contributions to operating revenue in 1992 (1991) by segment were: crude oil, 57% (65%); natural gas, 36% (26%); and natural gas liquids, 7% (6%).

Relative strength to TSE300

Price

Volume (in 1000's of board lots)

Rank (Profit/Revenue/Assets)
191   417   245

David E. Powell
President & C.E.O.

Allen R. Hagerman
Vice President & C.F.O.

Address
1600 Home Oil Tower
324 - 8th Avenue S.W.
Calgary
AB
T2P 2Z5
(403) 232-7101

Fax: (403) 232-7678
S0001273/G/3.2

SHELL CANADA LIMITED

Exchanges	Price (Jun24'93)	39.50	Trailing P/E	49.38	Stock Symbol
TMVZ	Trailing Yield (%)	2.28	Trailing EPS	0.80	**SHC**

Period Ending	Dec92	Dec91	Dec90	Dec89	Dec88
Yearly Statistics					
Price-Close	34.63	38.50	37.00	42.00	42.50
Price-High	46.00	45.50	42.75	49.38	43.38
Price-Low	34.00	34.50	34.38	38.50	35.50
P/E-Close	48.09	nm	13.41	22.22	11.27
Dividends per Share	0.90	0.90	0.90	0.90	0.80
Dividend Yield (%)	2.60	2.34	2.43	2.14	1.88
Sales per Share	40.08	42.23	48.00	43.23	44.38
EPS before extra. item	0.72	(1.12)	2.76	1.89	3.77
Cash Flow per Share	3.54	3.22	6.87	5.73	7.08
Book Value per Share	26.73	26.91	28.94	27.44	34.98
O/S Common Shares	112,092	112,078	112,048	112,048	84,686
Total Revenue	4,657,000	4,844,000	5,441,000	4,917,000	5,060,000
Income before extra.	80,000	(126,000)	309,000	212,000	427,000
Cash Flow	397,000	361,000	770,000	642,000	793,000
Debt/Equity	0.48	0.43	0.32	0.30	0.27
Return on Capital (%)	4.22	(0.72)	14.17	11.26	21.18
Ret. on Com. Equity (%)	2.66	(4.03)	9.78	7.02	15.10
% Change Profit	163.5	(140.8)	45.8	(50.4)	22.0
% Change Revenue	(3.9)	(11.0)	10.7	(2.8)	4.2
% Change Assets	1.9	(3.9)	8.5	0.9	1.9

Date	EPS	DPS	Tot Rev	Inc Bex
Mar 93	0.13	0.00	1,151,000	15,000
Dec 92	0.83	0.45	1,355,000	92,000
Sep 92	(0.05)	0.00	1,222,000	(5,000)
Jun 92	(0.11)	0.45	1,051,000	(12,000)
Mar 92	0.05	0.00	993,000	5,000
Dec 91	0.64	0.45	1,195,000	71,000
Sep 91	0.19	0.00	1,195,000	22,000
Jun 91	(1.64)	0.45	1,150,000	(184,000)

Preferred Div. Coverage	na	na	na
Total Div. Coverage	0.8	0.0	3.1
Interest Coverage	1.5	0.0	6.4
Current Ratio	1.8	1.8	2.5
Operating Margin	2.6	(0.1)	10.7
Asset Turnover	0.7	0.8	0.9
5 YEAR RATIOS (%)			
Return on Capital	10.0	13.0	15.7
Return on Com. Equity	6.1	8.3	10.3
Profit Growth	(25.6)	na	16.2
Revenue Growth	(0.9)	0.1	(2.3)
Asset Growth	1.8	2.4	1.1
BALANCE SHEET (000)			
Cash	128,000	36,000	44,000
Current Assets	1,516,000	1,492,000	1,980,000
Net Fixed Assets	4,349,000	4,292,000	4,040,000
Invest's & Advances	159,000	126,000	129,000
Total Assets	6,024,000	5,910,000	6,149,000
Short Term Debt	147,000	188,000	12,000
Current Liabilities	849,000	828,000	792,000
Long Term Debt	1,277,000	1,102,000	1,040,000
Total Liabilities	3,027,000	2,893,000	2,905,000
Total Equity	2,997,000	3,017,000	3,244,000
Total Liab. & Equity	6,024,000	5,910,000	6,149,000
CAPITAL (000)			
Total Debt	1,424,000	1,290,000	1,052,000
Preferred Equity	1,000	1,000	1,000
Common Equity	2,996,000	3,016,000	3,243,000

Business:

SHELL CANADA LTD. is an integrated oil company. It has oil and gas exploration and production operations in Western Canada. The oil products division operates refineries and a network of service stations. The chemicals division produces petrochemicals for markets worldwide. Shell Investments Ltd., a wholly owned subsidiary of Shell Petroleum NV of the Netherlands, is the major shareholder.

Synopsis:

Under the terms of a deal which is still being negotiated, Shell Canada Limited will buy 350 Pay Less and Canadian Turbo gasoline stations throughout western Canada, along with the Turbo refinery outside Calgary, a lubricants re-refinery in Edmonton, and a gasoline distribution centre. Shell also gains 300 employees. In return, Shell is transferring its home-heating business on Vancouver Island to Pay Less. The acquisition will take Shell from a 13% market share in Western Canada to just over 20%.

Shell announced in June 1993 that it intends to sell the remaining 60,000 hectares of land in the Elk Valley area of southeastern British Columbia over the next two to three years. The land disposition is consistent with the company's plan to focus on its core oil and natural gas properties and its earlier decision to withdraw from the coal industry.

Shell expects improved earnings and profitability in 1993 and beyond because of increasing cost reductions due to restructuring, new revenue from the 73% owned Caroline gas project, and lower interest costs as a result of debt repayments.

Average gross daily production in 1992 (1991) was: crude oil and natural gas liquids, 9,569 (10,100) cubic metres; natural gas, 20.3 (19.6) million cubic metres; and sulphur, 3,657 (3,510) tonnes. Gross proved reserves in 1992 (1991) were: crude oil and condensates, 25.8 (28.6) million cubic metres; natural gas liquids, 25.7 (27.3) million cubic metres; natural gas, 94.1 (101.6) billion cubic metres; and sulphur 33.5 (31.7) million tonnes.

Shell's revenues by division in 1992 before inter-segment sales (operating profit) were: resources, 12% (63%); oil products, 74% (26%); chemicals, 13% (5%); and corporate, 1% (6%). Corporate revenue is mainly dividend and interest income. 1991 revenues by division before inter-segment sales (operating profit) were: resources, 13% (89%); oil products, 73% (-1%); chemicals, 13% (3%); and corporate 1% (9%).

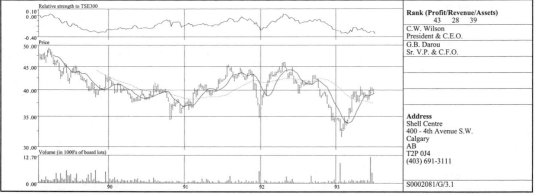

Rank (Profit/Revenue/Assets)		
43	28	39

C.W. Wilson
President & C.E.O.
G.B. Darou
Sr. V.P. & C.F.O.

Address
Shell Centre
400 - 4th Avenue S.W.
Calgary
AB
T2P 0J4
(403) 691-3111

S0002081/G/3.1

SUNCOR INC.

Exchanges	Price (Jun24'93)	31.12	Trailing P/E	nm	Stock Symbol
TMVZ	Trailing Yield (%)	3.34	Trailing EPS	(4.06)	**SU**

Period Ending	Dec92	Dec91	Dec90	Dec89	Dec88
Yearly Statistics					
Price-Close	n t	n t	n t	n t	n t
Price-High	n t	n t	n t	n t	n t
Price-Low	n t	n t	n t	n t	n t
P/E-Close	nm	n t	n t	n t	nm
Dividends per Share	1.04	1.05	0.40	0.39	0.40
Dividend Yield (%)	n t	n t	n t	n t	n t
Sales per Share	28.23	28.76	32.29	27.60	25.20
EPS before extra. item	(4.19)	1.42	2.27	1.05	(0.94)
Cash Flow per Share	3.55	6.11	6.31	4.85	1.52
Book Value per Share	17.20	22.44	22.07	20.19	19.08
O/S Common Shares	54,428	54,374	54,374	54,374	53,248
Total Revenue	1,539,000	1,566,000	1,759,000	1,488,000	1,345,000
Income before extra.	(228,000)	77,000	124,000	57,000	(49,000)
Cash Flow	193,000	332,000	343,000	261,000	81,000
Debt/Equity	0.21	0.12	0.20	0.21	0.31
Return on Capital (%)	(25.01)	9.97	14.27	8.53	(2.41)
Ret. on Com. Equity (%)	(21.15)	6.28	10.71	5.30	(4.76)
% Change Profit	(396.1)	(37.9)	117.5	216.3	(202.1)
% Change Revenue	(1.7)	(11.0)	18.2	10.6	(1.8)
% Change Assets	(13.0)	(0.9)	9.4	2.1	(2.7)

Preferred Div. Coverage	np	77.0	124.0
Total Div. Coverage	0.0	1.4	5.6
Interest Coverage	0.0	8.3	6.4
Current Ratio	1.1	1.3	1.5
Operating Margin	2.8	8.9	11.2
Asset Turnover	0.8	0.7	0.8
5 YEAR RATIOS (%)			
Return on Capital	1.1	7.5	6.0
Return on Com. Equity	(0.7)	4.4	3.0
Profit Growth	na	na	41.3
Revenue Growth	2.3	6.2	3.6
Asset Growth	(1.4)	1.2	0.0
BALANCE SHEET (000)			
Cash	0	2,000	28,000
Current Assets	373,000	378,000	470,000
Net Fixed Assets	1,342,000	1,598,000	1,519,000
Invest's & Advances	30,000	29,000	0
Total Assets	1,947,000	2,238,000	2,259,000
Short Term Debt	26,000	18,000	23,000
Current Liabilities	342,000	298,000	324,000
Long Term Debt	171,000	134,000	222,000
Total Liabilities	1,011,000	1,012,000	1,053,000
Total Equity	936,000	1,226,000	1,206,000
Total Liab. & Equity	1,947,000	2,238,000	2,259,000
CAPITAL (000)			
Total Debt	197,000	152,000	245,000
Preferred Equity	0	6,000	6,000
Common Equity	936,000	1,220,000	1,200,000

Business:

SUNCOR INC. is a Canadian integrated oil and gas company. It explores for and produces conventional crude oil and natural gas in Western Canada where it also operates the world's first commercial oil sands plant. Suncor markets natural gas in Canada and the U.S. It has a refinery in Sarnia, Ontario, it manufactures and distributes fuels, petrochemicals, and heating oil under the Sunoco and Sunchem brands.

Date	EPS	DPS	Tot Rev	Inc Bex
Mar 93	0.24	0.26	379,000	13,000
Dec 92	0.18	0.26	426,000	9,000
Sep 92	(4.20)	0.26	388,000	(228,000)
Jun 92	(0.28)	0.26	361,000	(15,000)
Mar 92	0.11	0.26	361,000	6,000
Dec 91	0.10	1.05	402,000	5,000
Sep 91	0.49	0.00	378,000	27,000
Jun 91	0.25	0.00	398,000	13,000

Synopsis:

Refined products demand was flat in Suncor's primary markets of Ontario and Quebec in 1992. Weak demand and a surplus of both service stations and refining capacity have forced the industry to announce significant rationalizations of station networks and refineries. To address this concern, Suncor will be conducting a strategic review of its downstream operations in 1993. Both Sun Company, Inc. of Philadelphia and the Ontario Energy Corporation sold their stakes in Suncor Inc. during the year.

Suncor's net loss for 1992 was attributed to lower revenues from Sunoco Group, a higher Crown royalty rate on synthetic crude oil, the impact of interruptions at its oil sands plant, and the inclusion in 1991 of a gain from the disposition of its chemical shipping business. The loss also included a $238-million after tax restructuring charge.

Allocation of the 1993 $214-million capital budget by operation is as follows: oil sands operations, 48%; resources group, 34%; and Sunoco group, 18%.

Average gross daily production in 1992 (1991) was: synthetic crude oil, 58,500 (60,600) barrels; crude oil and natural gas liquids, 12,700 (11,400) barrels; and natural gas, 147 (105) million cubic feet. Gross proven reserves in 1992 (1991) were: synthetic crude oil, 276 (256) million barrels; crude oil and natural gas liquids, 42 (39) million barrels; and natural gas, 617 (490) billion cubic feet.

Contributions to sales and other operating revenues excluding federal sales tax (earnings before income taxes) in 1992 by segment were: oil sands group, 9% (-31%); resources group, 5% (-64%); and Sunoco Group, 86% (5%). Contributions to sales and other operating revenues excluding federal sales tax (earnings before income taxes) in 1991 by segment were: oil sands group, 10% (58%); resources group, 3% (7 %); and Sunoco group 87%, (35%).

Rank (Profit/Revenue/Assets)
987   79   94

Richard L. George
Chairman, President & C.E.O.

Timothy R. Hughes
Senior Vice President & C.F.O.

Address
36 York Mills Road
North York
ON
M2P 2C5
(416) 733-7300

Fax: (416) 733-0958
S0005839/G/3.1

TALISMAN ENERGY INC.

Exchanges	Price (Jun24'93)	30.00	Trailing P/E	88.24	Stock Symbol
TMV	Trailing Yield (%)	0.00	Trailing EPS	0.34	**TLM**

Period Ending	Dec92	Dec91	Dec90	Dec89	Dec88
Yearly Statistics					
Price-Close	15.38	12.00	16.63	20.75	18.00
Price-High	15.50	18.00	22.00	22.50	22.50
Price-Low	10.50	11.50	15.38	15.25	14.50
P/E-Close	69.89	nm	30.79	57.64	163.64
Dividends per Share	0.00	0.19	0.19	0.15	0.23
Dividend Yield (%)	0.00	1.58	1.14	0.72	1.25
Sales per Share	4.50	3.97	5.33	7.50	6.60
EPS before extra. item	0.22	(3.40)	0.54	0.36	0.11
Cash Flow per Share	1.77	1.10	1.94	2.39	2.33
Book Value per Share	6.25	6.02	9.61	9.55	9.33
O/S Common Shares	50,466	50,466	50,462	50,434	50,361
Total Revenue	245,061	106,887	285,308	401,226	347,559
Income before extra.	11,178	(171,539)	27,434	17,929	5,529
Cash Flow	89,284	55,622	98,056	120,481	117,341
Debt/Equity	0.00	0.60	0.22	0.40	0.36
Return on Capital (%)	6.74	(40.45)	7.55	4.05	1.74
Ret. on Com. Equity (%)	3.61	(43.48)	5.68	3.77	1.18
% Change Profit	106.5	(725.3)	53.0	224.3	(87.6)
% Change Revenue	129.3	(62.5)	(28.9)	15.4	(2.5)
% Change Assets	(25.3)	(26.6)	(9.2)	2.2	4.3

Date	EPS	DPS	Tot Rev	Inc Bex
Mar 93	0.16	0.00	63,150	7,869
Dec 92	0.06	0.00	65,037	2,912
Sep 92	0.05	0.00	59,251	2,292
Jun 92	0.07	0.00	57,968	3,719
Mar 92	0.04	0.00	56,983	1,970
Dec 91	(2.81)	0.00	(53,919)	(141,577)
Sep 91	(0.28)	0.10	51,539	(14,180)
Jun 91	(0.19)	0.00	51,967	(9,533)

Preferred Div. Coverage	np	np	np	
Total Div. Coverage	na	0.0	2.9	
Interest Coverage	2.0	0.0	4.8	
Current Ratio	1.0	2.5	3.5	
Operating Margin	11.4	(24.7)	5.3	
Asset Turnover	0.5	0.3	0.3	
5 YEAR RATIOS (%)				
Return on Capital	(4.1)	(2.8)	6.5	
Return on Com. Equity	(5.8)	(4.3)	5.4	
Profit Growth	(24.2)	na	(6.8)	
Revenue Growth	(7.2)	(17.9)	(7.5)	
Asset Growth	(12.0)	(1.7)	8.0	
BALANCE SHEET (000)				
Cash	7,528	2,351	49,403	
Current Assets	55,477	126,964	227,875	
Net Fixed Assets	325,392	351,818	455,583	
Invest's & Advances	11,098	81,634	113,713	
Total Assets	446,390	597,705	814,671	
Short Term Debt	228	71	494	
Current Liabilities	57,367	50,952	65,448	
Long Term Debt	0	181,431	105,197	
Total Liabilities	131,237	293,730	329,620	
Total Equity	315,153	303,975	485,051	
Total Liab. & Equity	446,390	597,705	814,671	
CAPITAL (000)				
Total Debt	228	181,502	105,691	
Preferred Equity	0	0	0	
Common Equity	315,153	303,975	485,051	

Business:

TALISMAN ENERGY INC. produces crude oil, natural gas and sulphur in western Canada. It has exploration interests in western Canada, the Northwest Territories and Ontario. British Petroleum Company plc, through a subsidiary, is the majority shareholder.

Synopsis:

Talisman Energy, the former BP Canada, severed all formal links with British Petroleum (BP) in 1992 and proceeded into 1993 as a fully Canadian company. BP sold its holding in BP Canada on the understanding that the company would change its name because it would no longer be part of the BP group of companies.

Talisman received court approval on May 20, 1993, to merge with Encor Inc. As part of the deal, Talisman agreed to issue a total of 15.2 million shares to all Encor shareholders. After the deal is complete, Talisman will have 65.7 million Common Shares outstanding. The merger will more than double Talisman's crude oil and natural gas liquids output, increase its natural gas production by 65%, and double its oil and gas reserves. Encor has proven reserves of 77 million barrels of oil and convertible liquids, 530 billion cubic feet of natural gas and 20 million barrels of synthetic oil. All of Encor's debt will be assumed by Talisman which, according to pro forma financial statements, will have a debt of $300-million, and a cash flow of $148-million. Talisman eliminated its long-term debt in 1992 with proceeds from the sale of mining assets and of the preferred share portfolio.

Independence from BP allows Talisman to operate outside Canada. During the first quarter of 1993, Talisman used $13.7-million from its 1993 capital budget to enter into two partner-operated, joint ventures in Cuba where it hopes to exploit potentially prolific oil bearing structures. Capital expenditures totaled $45.9-million for this quarter, up from $12.5-million a year ago.

Average daily production in 1992 (1991) was: crude oil and natural gas liquids, 16,402 (16,059) barrels; natural gas, 210 (170) million cubic feet. Proven and probable reserves in 1992 (1991) were: oil and gas liquids, 48.5 (46.9) million barrels; natural gas, 1,033 (959.4) billion cubic feet; sulphur, 2.4 (2) million tons. Contributions to net revenue in 1992 (1991) by product were: oil and natural gas liquids, 47% (52%); gas, 46% (35%); other, 7% (13%).

Relative strength to TSE300

Price

Volume (in 1000's of board lots)

Rank (Profit/Revenue/Assets)		
168	245	224

David A. Claydon
Chairman & C.E.O.

Dr. James Buckee
President & C.O.O.

W.I. Bobye
V.P., Finance & C.F.O.

Address
Suite 2400
855 - 2nd Street S.W.
Calgary
AB
T2P 4J9
(403) 237-1234

Fax: (403) 237-1902
B0016718/G/3.2

TARRAGON OIL AND GAS LIMITED

Exchanges: T

	Price (Jun24'93)	19.00	Trailing P/E	57.58	Stock Symbol
	Trailing Yield (%)	0.00	Trailing EPS	0.33	TN

Business:
TARRAGON OIL AND GAS holds petroleum and natural gas properties.

Period Ending	Dec92	Dec91	Dec90	Dec89	Dec88
Yearly Statistics					
Price-Close	8.25	4.07	2.40	3.60	4.20
Price-High	8.38	4.25	3.80	5.20	5.60
Price-Low	3.63	2.00	2.00	2.80	4.20
P/E-Close	30.00	45.14	nm	nm	nm
Dividends per Share	0.00	0.00	0.00	0.00	0.00
Dividend Yield (%)	0.00	0.00	0.00	0.00	0.00
Sales per Share	1.21	0.90	0.42	0.55	1.04
EPS before extra. item	0.28	0.09	0.00	0.00	(0.48)
Cash Flow per Share	0.75	0.45	0.21	0.17	0.12
Book Value per Share	3.03	2.25	2.08	1.75	1.28
O/S Common Shares	24,294	20,704	17,432	14,550	3,318
Total Revenue	29,130	17,454	7,768	5,849	3,922
Income before extra.	6,503	2,078	428	132	(1,005)
Cash Flow	17,635	8,595	3,527	1,376	349
Debt/Equity	0.36	0.41	0.19	nd	1.48
Return on Capital (%)	13.55	8.69	3.99	3.76	(0.61)
Ret. on Com. Equity (%)	10.83	4.15	(1.47)	(4,107.43)	(44.10)
% Change Profit	212.9	385.5	224.2	113.1	(1,290.8)
% Change Revenue	66.9	124.7	32.8	49.1	228.7
% Change Assets	51.5	52.7	28.6	33.5	(5.8)

Date	EPS	DPS	Tot Rev	Inc Bex
Mar 93	0.08	0.00	11,154	2,316
Dec 92	0.11	0.00	10,670	2,904
Sep 92	0.09	0.00	8,127	2,102
Jun 92	0.05	0.00	5,182	1,150
Mar 92	0.03	0.00	5,151	574
Dec 91	0.05	0.00	5,135	952
Sep 91	0.03	0.00	4,943	511
Jun 91	0.00	0.00	4,395	378

	Dec92	Dec91	Dec90
Preferred Div. Coverage	np	np	0.5
Total Div. Coverage	na	5.8	0.5
Interest Coverage	8.6	3.3	5.6
Current Ratio	4.0	4.9	1.3
Operating Margin	37.1	27.1	11.3
Asset Turnover	0.2	0.2	0.1
5 YEAR RATIOS (%)			
Return on Capital	5.9	4.2	2.4
Return on Com. Equity	(827.6)	(827.8)	(898.2)
Profit Growth	138.4	na	na
Revenue Growth	89.4	83.3	29.7
Asset Growth	30.2	na	39.7
BALANCE SHEET (000)			
Cash	650	0	6
Current Assets	26,593	16,390	4,540
Net Fixed Assets	92,395	61,588	45,933
Invest's & Advances	1,680	1,680	1,680
Total Assets	120,668	79,658	52,153
Short Term Debt	0	0	0
Current Liabilities	6,648	3,339	3,582
Long Term Debt	26,392	18,921	7,529
Total Liabilities	47,213	33,043	12,019
Total Equity	73,455	46,615	40,134
Total Liab. & Equity	120,668	79,658	52,153
CAPITAL (000)			
Total Debt	26,392	18,921	7,529
Preferred Equity	0	0	3,899
Common Equity	73,455	46,615	36,235

Synopsis:
Tarragon Oil and Gas will almost double in size once its purchase of Opinac Exploration for $122-million is completed on July 1, 1993. The purchase will almost quadruple Tarragon's gas production, resulting in an almost equal split between oil and gas for the acquisition. The company issued $85-million worth of stock to help pay for the acquisition.

Significant production gains were realized in the first quarter of 1993. Daily oil production increased 137% over the same period last year to 5,373 barrels, and daily gas production was up 69% to 21.1 million cubic feet. The most significant production gain was from the properties acquired for $17-million in southeast Saskatchewan, which contributed 1,475 barrels per day. Closing is scheduled for mid-June, 1993, however operating results for these properties have been accrued in the first quarter since the effective acquisition date is January 1, 1993.

Capital expenditures totaled $36-million in the first quarter of 1993, including $17-million for the southeast Saskatchewan acquisition. Based on internal estimates, six million barrels of proved oil reserves and 22.8 billion cubic feet of proved gas reserves have been added during this period at a cost of $4.18 per barrel equivalent. The minimum capital program for 1993 increased to $65-million and could rise to $80-million, depending on the success of future exploration and production purchase efforts. The 1992 capital program totaled $38-million, and resulted in an increase in production of 75 barrels of oil per day for each $1-million expended.

Average daily production in 1992 (1991) was: oil, 3,108 (1,825) barrels; and gas, 13.5 (8.6) million cubic feet. Proven and probable reserves in 1992 (1991) were: oil, 13.5 (10.5) million barrels; and gas, 140.5 (87.1) billion cubic feet.

Contributions to revenue before royalties in 1992 (1991) by product were: oil, 77% (79%); and gas, 23% (21%).

Rank (Profit/Revenue/Assets)
222   565   388

Joseph L. Rotman
Chairman
Ed Chwyl
President & C.E.O.
Raymond T. Chan
V.P., Finance & Secretary

Address
500 - 4th Avenue S.W.
Suite 2500
Calgary
AB
T2P 2V6
(403) 237-5570

Fax: (403) 262-5324
N0000940/G/3.2

TOTAL PETROLEUM (NORTH AMERICA) LTD.

Exchanges	Price (Jun24'93)	9 .37	Trailing P/E	26 .04	Stock Symbol
TMA	Trailing Yield (%)	2 .13	Trailing EPS	0 .36	**TPN**

Period Ending	Dec92	Dec91	Dec90	Dec89	Dec88
Yearly Statistics	US	US	US	US	US
Price-Close	7 .50	12 .63	23 .25	32 .63	24 .50
Price-High	13 .38	29 .50	33 .75	36 .25	24 .63
Price-Low	5 .13	12 .50	22 .75	24 .25	17 .50
P/E-Close	171 .44	nm	14 .71	15 .44	6 .39
Dividends per Share	0 .30	0 .80	0 .80	0 .65	0 .40
Dividend Yield (%)	4 .86	7 .26	4 .02	2 .36	2 .00
Sales per Share	65 .04	73 .92	87 .09	78 .85	73 .51
EPS before extra. item	0 .03	(0 .45)	1 .16	1 .51	2 .55
Cash Flow per Share	1 .60	1 .64	3 .49	4 .97	6 .66
Book Value per Share	11 .28	11 .68	14 .30	13 .81	10 .61
O/S Common Shares	37 ,422	36 ,288	30 ,983	30 ,140	24 ,823
Total Revenue	2 ,397 ,000	2 ,486 ,200	2 ,657 ,700	2 ,170 ,600	1 ,833 ,540
Income before extra.	2 ,100	(11 ,500)	42 ,000	48 ,200	72 ,749
Cash Flow	58 ,800	55 ,000	106 ,600	136 ,400	163 ,633
Debt/Equity	0 .61	0 .41	0 .22	0 .35	0 .55
Return on Capital (%)	2 .33	(0 .63)	11 .36	13 .81	21 .66
Ret. on Com. Equity (%)	0 .33	(3 .01)	8 .24	12 .18	28 .43
% Change Profit	118 .3	(127 .4)	(12 .9)	(33 .7)	371 .2
% Change Revenue	(3 .6)	(6 .5)	22 .4	18 .4	4 .9
% Change Assets	3 .9	(9 .6)	(0 .4)	20 .1	(5 .0)

Preferred Div. Coverage	3 .0	0 .0	6 .4
Total Div. Coverage	0 .2	0 .0	1 .4
Interest Coverage	1 .3	0 .0	6 .4
Current Ratio	1 .2	1 .1	1 .1
Operating Margin	0 .6	(0 .1)	2 .6
Asset Turnover	2 .2	2 .4	2 .3
5 YEAR RATIOS (%)			
Return on Capital	9 .7	9 .2	11 .7
Return on Com. Equity	9 .2	5 .8	na
Profit Growth	na	na	(5 .2)
Revenue Growth	6 .5	9 .2	2 .2
Asset Growth	1 .2	2 .5	5 .4
BALANCE SHEET (000)			
Cash	17 ,700	9 ,200	26 ,500
Current Assets	368 ,000	390 ,200	427 ,800
Net Fixed Assets	702 ,800	640 ,700	623 ,100
Invest's & Advances	0	0	0
Total Assets	1 ,080 ,900	1 ,040 ,400	1 ,151 ,200
Short Term Debt	0	0	0
Current Liabilities	316 ,700	361 ,100	405 ,400
Long Term Debt	264 ,200	177 ,800	124 ,100
Total Liabilities	645 ,800	603 ,300	596 ,200
Total Equity	435 ,100	437 ,100	555 ,000
Total Liab. & Equity	1 ,080 ,900	1 ,040 ,400	1 ,151 ,200
CAPITAL (000)			
Total Debt	264 ,200	177 ,800	124 ,100
Preferred Equity	13 ,100	13 ,100	111 ,900
Common Equity	422 ,000	424 ,000	443 ,100

Business:

TOTAL PETROLEUM (NORTH AMERICA) LTD. is an integrated petroleum company with exploration and production operations in Western Canada and refinery and marketing operations in the central United States. The company sells its petroleum products under the brand names Total, Vickers and Apco. Total Cie Francaise des Petroles of France owns 51% of the company's voting shares.

Date		EPS	DPS	Tot Rev	Inc Bex
Mar 93	US	(0 .15)	0 .00	514 ,800	(5 ,300)
Dec 92	US	0 .08	0 .00	584 ,400	3 ,200
Sep 92	US	0 .15	0 .10	649 ,200	5 ,800
Jun 92	US	0 .28	0 .10	635 ,800	10 ,500
Mar 92	US	(0 .48)	0 .10	527 ,600	(17 ,400)
Dec 91	US	(0 .32)	0 .20	609 ,300	(10 ,700)
Sep 91	US	0 .10	0 .20	656 ,800	3 ,300
Jun 91	US	0 .17	0 .20	631 ,700	6 ,600

Synopsis:

Total Petroleum (North America) Ltd.'s performance continued to improve largely as a result of ongoing programs initiated in 1992. These programs focused on corporate cost controls, enhanced supply and trading activities, and the restructuring of its marketing network.

A corporate reorganization that took place during the summer of 1992, led to the creation of four profit centres: crude oil supply; refining; product supply; and marketing. At the same time, the company started the construction of new crude oil pipelines and new hydrotreating units in two of its refineries, for start-up during the summer of 1993. These projects will enable the company to meet U.S. regulations that require the reduction of sulphur content in diesel fuel used in on-road vehicles by October 1, 1993. In addition, this will provide the company with the ability to process high sulphur, less expensive crude oils, resulting in reduced feedstock costs.

Total Petroleum finalized contract negotiations in April 1993, under which Total will acquire the Town and Country network of gasoline/convenience stores located in the central U.S. The transaction is expected to be completed by June 1993, and fits with the company's strategy of consolidating its retail operations in marketing areas with direct supplies from its refineries. The restructuring also calls for the rebranding of all stores under the Total name.

Approximately half of the increase in net income for the company's first quarter of 1993 is related to the acquisition of Total Energold Corporation, which is expected to reduce Total Canada's effective tax rate for a period of up to four years. Increased crude oil production, and higher prices over 1992 levels contributed to the improvement in both cash flow and net income for the period.

As of the fourth quarter of 1992, the dividend on the Common Shares has been suspended.

Relative strength to TSE300

Price

Volume (in 1000's of board lots)

Rank (Profit/Revenue/Assets)
334   44   121

Philippe Dunoyer
Chairman, President & C.E.O.

Richard E. Dana
Sr. V.P., Finance

Address
999 - 18th Street
Denver
CO
80202
(303) 291-2000

T0002162/G/3.1

TRI LINK RESOURCES LTD.

Exchanges	Price (Jun24'93)	14.50	Trailing P/E	65.91	Stock Symbol
T	Trailing Yield (%)	0.00	Trailing EPS	0.22	**TLR.A**

Period Ending	Mar92	Mar91	Mar90	Mar89	Mar88
Yearly Statistics					
Price-Close	5.88	4.95	nt	nt	nt
Price-High	6.75	6.50	nt	nt	nt
Price-Low	4.90	4.20	nt	nt	nt
P/E-Close	53.41	12.07	nt	nt	nt
Dividends per Share	0.00	0.00	0.02	0.00	0.05
Dividend Yield (%)	0.00	0.00	nt	0.00	nt
Sales per Share	1.43	2.28	1.91	1.41	1.40
EPS before extra. item	0.11	0.41	0.17	0.01	0.16
Cash Flow per Share	0.66	1.33	0.93	0.63	0.69
Book Value per Share	4.48	3.18	2.11	1.96	1.65
O/S Common Shares	11,094	8,089	4,345	4,345	3,837
Total Revenue	13,682	14,172	8,309	5,776	5,363
Income before extra.	1,165	2,859	1,167	482	957
Cash Flow	6,378	8,255	4,028	2,558	2,640
Debt/Equity	0.25	0.44	0.67	0.46	0.43
Return on Capital (%)	4.73	17.17	10.42	5.26	na
Ret. on Com. Equity (%)	3.09	15.16	8.38	0.77	na
% Change Profit	(59.2)	145.0	142.2	(49.6)	na
% Change Revenue	(3.5)	70.6	43.8	7.7	na
% Change Assets	49.6	37.8	27.9	14.0	na

Business:

TRI LINK RESOURCES LTD. is an independent oil and natural gas exploration, development and production company operating primarily in Saskatchewan and Alberta.

Date	EPS	DPS	Tot Rev	Inc Bex
Dec 92	0.08	0.00	7,227	1,112
Sep 92	0.06	0.00	6,171	660
Jun 92	0.05	0.00	5,123	684
Mar 92	0.03	0.00	3,720	313
Dec 91	0.04	0.00	3,599	321
Sep 91	0.03	0.00	3,433	254
Jun 91	0.03	0.00	2,931	278
Mar 91	0.01	0.00	3,201	38

Preferred Div. Coverage	np	np	2.7
Total Div. Coverage	na	13.4	2.3
Interest Coverage	3.5	7.0	2.9
Current Ratio	1.1	0.6	0.3
Operating Margin	17.2	37.7	29.2
Asset Turnover	0.2	0.3	0.2
5 YEAR RATIOS (%)			
Return on Capital	na	na	na
Return on Com. Equity	na	na	na
Profit Growth	na	na	na
Revenue Growth	na	na	na
Asset Growth	na	na	na
BALANCE SHEET (000)			
Cash	266	0	0
Current Assets	3,114	3,356	1,881
Net Fixed Assets	59,486	43,721	32,259
Invest's & Advances	436	414	330
Total Assets	71,036	47,492	34,471
Short Term Debt	0	843	1,392
Current Liabilities	2,797	5,445	5,928
Long Term Debt	12,550	10,376	8,766
Total Liabilities	21,308	21,746	19,293
Total Equity	49,728	25,746	15,177
Total Liab. & Equity	71,036	47,492	34,471
CAPITAL (000)			
Total Debt	12,550	11,219	10,158
Preferred Equity	0	0	5,995
Common Equity	49,728	25,746	9,182

Synopsis:

Tri Link Resources enjoyed a production growth rate of 80% to an average of 4,680 barrels of oil per day for the year ended March 31, 1993. The company focused its drilling program during fiscal 1992 on the Hazelwood/Moose Valley area of southeast Saskatchewan, and will continue to do so in fiscal 1993. For the third quarter ending December 31, 1992, Tri Link drilled 35 wells, resulting in 13 vertical oil wells, 6 horizontal oil wells, 4 holes cased for horizontal re-entry, and 12 dry holes.

Tri Link plans to double its capital budget to $40-million for the fiscal year beginning April 1, 1993. Of this amount, $22-million is allocated to vertical development drilling and horizontal drilling, which is designed to grow production and cash flow through the year. A further $11-million is allocated to new exploration, with at least 15 new pool prospects to be drilled, and $7-million is allocated to facilities construction.

Tri Link reported a 122% increase on cash flow to $14.1-million for fiscal 1993, largely owing to increased production during the latter half of the fiscal year. Tri Link added 13 million barrels of new reserves during this period, of which six million equivalent barrels were added through acquisitions made after fiscal 1992. The company financed the $13-million cost of the acquisitions through its bank line of credit and an $8-million equity issue.

During fiscal 1993, Tri Link completed two Common Share issues totaling $23.3-million, and a $20-million Special Warrant issue. The Special Warrants were converted to 1.4 million Common Shares in April 1993, after the fiscal year-end. Net proceeds of $19-million on the Special Warrant issue will be applied to repay bank debt in full for general corporate purposes.

Approximately 96% of Tri Link's production base is light and medium gravity oil. Oil equivalent reserves in 1993 (1992) were 28.7 (17.8) million barrels. For the year ending March 31, 1993, gas production averaged two million cubic feet per day.

Relative strength to TSE300 / Price / Volume (in 1000's of board lots)

Rank (Profit/Revenue/Assets)
410   660   478

Gary W. Burns
President & C.E.O.

H. Garth Wiggins
V.P., Finance, Sec.-Treas.

Address
10th Floor
550 - 6th Avenue S.W.
Calgary
AB
T2P 0S2
(403) 262-4601

01003045/G/3.2

TRITON CANADA RESOURCES LTD.

Exchanges	Price (Jun24'93)		2.80	Trailing P/E		nm	Stock Symbol
TMZ	Trailing Yield (%)		0.00	Trailing EPS		(0.23)	**TTN**

Period Ending	May92	May91	May90	May89	May88
Yearly Statistics					
Price-Close	0.65	0.75	1.80	1.57	1.95
Price-High	0.90	2.00	2.45	2.25	2.90
Price-Low	0.30	0.60	1.50	1.35	1.35
P/E-Close	nm	nm	30.00	nm	nm
Dividends per Share	0.00	0.00	0.00	0.00	0.00
Dividend Yield (%)	0.00	0.00	0.00	0.00	0.00
Sales per Share	1.05	1.40	1.29	1.22	1.31
EPS before extra. item	(0.39)	(0.14)	0.06	(0.22)	(0.12)
Cash Flow per Share	0.16	0.32	0.41	0.45	0.61
Book Value per Share	0.67	1.11	1.25	1.18	1.40
O/S Common Shares	39,790	23,905	23,849	23,758	23,660
Total Revenue	31,675	38,080	52,187	48,440	47,367
Income before extra.	(7,705)	(645)	4,417	(2,265)	200
Cash Flow	3,925	7,755	9,665	10,660	13,808
Debt/Equity	0.41	0.58	0.32	1.06	0.91
Return on Capital (%)	(10.74)	4.45	14.15	1.89	4.12
Ret. on Com. Equity (%)	(36.75)	(11.92)	5.10	(17.04)	(8.00)
% Change Profit	(1,094.6)	(114.6)	295.0	(1,232.5)	(93.6)
% Change Revenue	(16.8)	(27.0)	7.7	2.3	4.2
% Change Assets	(14.3)	(4.8)	(19.7)	(9.4)	7.5

Date	EPS	DPS	Tot Rev	Inc Bex
Feb 93	0.00	0.00	8,124	612
Nov 92	(0.01)	0.00	6,406	(2)
Aug 92	(0.01)	0.00	5,944	57
May 92	(0.21)	0.00	11,945	(5,030)
Feb 92	(0.07)	0.00	7,170	(1,170)
Nov 91	(0.07)	0.00	6,873	(1,177)
Aug 91	(0.04)	0.00	7,187	(328)
May 91	(0.05)	0.00	15,700	(743)

	May92	May91	May90
Preferred Div. Coverage	0.0	0.0	1.5
Total Div. Coverage	0.0	0.0	1.5
Interest Coverage	0.0	0.9	2.4
Current Ratio	0.9	0.7	1.0
Operating Margin	(31.3)	3.8	6.7
Asset Turnover	0.3	0.4	0.3
5 YEAR RATIOS (%)			
Return on Capital	2.8	6.7	1.9
Return on Com. Equity	(13.7)	(6.2)	(39.3)
Profit Growth	na	na	4.6
Revenue Growth	(7.0)	1.0	2.9
Asset Growth	(8.6)	(3.5)	(4.5)
BALANCE SHEET (000)			
Cash	0	0	350
Current Assets	3,805	5,960	8,010
Net Fixed Assets	59,820	71,810	75,610
Invest's & Advances	15,465	14,625	13,425
Total Assets	79,310	92,560	97,275
Short Term Debt	335	1,475	890
Current Liabilities	4,102	8,277	7,859
Long Term Debt	18,440	24,920	17,295
Total Liabilities	33,964	47,376	39,903
Total Equity	45,346	45,184	57,372
Total Liab. & Equity	79,310	92,560	97,275
CAPITAL (000)			
Total Debt	18,775	26,395	18,185
Preferred Equity	18,622	18,770	27,678
Common Equity	26,724	26,414	29,694

Business:

TRITON CANADA RESOURCES LTD. is an oil and gas exploration and production company. It also markets natural gas. The company has producing wells and exploration activities in Western Canada.

Synopsis:

Triton Canada Resources expects its financial performance to continue to improve through the fiscal year beginning June 1, 1993, led by increased oil production, higher gas prices and lower costs. The company participated in 18 wells in the third quarter ending February 1993, resulting in 9 gross (2 net) oil wells and 5 gross (5 net) gas wells.

Net earnings for the nine months ending February 1993 increased to $667,000 from a $2.7-million loss, and funds flow from operations increased to $6.8-million from $3.5-million for the prior year period. Both earnings and funds flow were reduced by $240,000 in the third quarter due to a one-time provision relating to prior periods. Triton attributes the changes to higher oil and lower gas production, and reduced general, administrative and interest expenses.

Average wellhead gas prices increased 3% for the first nine months of fiscal 1993 over 1992. However, the average for February 1993 was 17% higher than the average for fiscal 1992. Gas production fell 10% to 46.4 million cubic feet per day during this period. Oil prices increased 9% over the same period last year. Average oil production increased 6% to 989 barrels per day, but average production for February 1993 was up 45% to 1,261 barrels per day over February 1992 due to new discoveries.

Contributions to revenue after royalties for the nine months ending February 1993 (February 1992) were: oil, 20% (14%); gas, 58% (62%); Alberta royalty tax credit, 6% (6%); gas marketing, 9% (11%); and other, 7% (7%).

Total reserves before royalties for the year ending May 1992 were: conventional oil, 3.1 million barrels; and gas, 115.6 billion cubic feet. All gas reserves are in Alberta.

Rank (Profit/Revenue/Assets)
860 546 458

David E. Gore
Chairman
J. Joseph Ciavarra, Jr.
President & C.E.O.
Robert D. Matheson
V.P., Admin., Secty. & C.F.O.

Address
4th Floor
Bow Valley Square III
255 - 5th Avenue S.W.
Calgary
AB
T2P 3G6
(403) 261-5500
Fax: (403) 264-3013
C0029839/G/3.2

ULSTER PETROLEUMS LTD.

Exchanges	Price (Jun24'93)	5.87	Trailing P/E	73.44	Stock Symbol
T	Trailing Yield (%)	0.00	Trailing EPS	0.08	ULP

Period Ending	Dec92	Dec91	Dec90	Dec89	Dec88	Business:
Yearly Statistics						ULSTER PETROLEUMS LTD. is an oil and
Price-Close	3.30	2.70	3.30	3.10	1.86	gas exploration and production company. Its
Price-High	3.40	3.45	3.95	3.20	2.69	producing wells and exploration activities are
Price-Low	1.85	2.45	2.40	1.75	1.55	located in Alberta. The company sells natural
P/E-Close	47.14	67.50	22.00	28.18	31.00	gas to customers in Alberta and the United
Dividends per Share	0.00	0.00	0.00	0.00	0.00	States.
Dividend Yield (%)	0.00	0.00	0.00	0.00	0.00	
Sales per Share	0.69	0.55	0.61	0.55	0.37	
EPS before extra. item	0.07	0.04	0.15	0.11	0.06	
Cash Flow per Share	0.42	0.32	0.42	0.34	0.21	
Book Value per Share	2.60	2.54	2.54	2.29	2.18	
O/S Common Shares	33,954	33,942	33,389	30,363	29,459	

Income before extra.	2,350	1,310	4,757	3,357	1,728	
Total Revenue	23,267	18,784	19,905	16,414	11,466	

Cash Flow	14,425	10,781	13,561	9,989	6,254	Date	EPS	DPS	Tot Rev	Inc Bex
Debt/Equity	0.44	0.31	0.13	0.19	0.12	Mar 93	0.03	0.00	6,956	1,232
Return on Capital (%)	4.88	3.98	9.13	7.73	4.50	Dec 92	0.02	0.00	6,635	806
Ret. on Com. Equity (%)	2.69	1.53	6.17	5.03	2.73	Sep 92	0.01	0.00	5,747	424
% Change Profit	79.4	(72.5)	41.7	94.3	(32.0)	Jun 92	0.02	0.00	5,786	734
% Change Revenue	23.9	(5.6)	21.3	43.2	11.0	Mar 92	0.01	0.00	5,099	386
% Change Assets	12.4	16.8	17.1	17.4	2.6	Dec 91	0.00	0.00	4,565	(26)
						Sep 91	0.00	0.00	4,568	168
						Jun 91	0.01	0.00	4,558	281

				Synopsis:
Preferred Div. Coverage	np	np	np	
Total Div. Coverage	na	na	na	
Interest Coverage	2.2	2.2	6.6	
Current Ratio	0.6	0.5	1.1	
Operating Margin	25.2	22.1	40.8	
Asset Turnover	0.2	0.2	0.2	
5 YEAR RATIOS (%)				
Return on Capital	6.0	6.7	6.9	
Return on Com. Equity	3.6	4.1	4.4	
Profit Growth	(1.6)	7.5	19.2	
Revenue Growth	17.6	24.2	20.8	
Asset Growth	13.0	23.6	21.2	
BALANCE SHEET (000)				
Cash	8	35	62	
Current Assets	2,977	2,716	6,503	
Net Fixed Assets	136,869	121,721	100,078	
Invest's & Advances	0	0	0	
Total Assets	139,846	124,437	106,581	
Short Term Debt	0	0	0	
Current Liabilities	4,969	5,027	5,661	
Long Term Debt	39,107	26,966	10,571	
Total Liabilities	51,438	38,403	21,843	
Total Equity	88,408	86,034	84,738	
Total Liab. & Equity	139,846	124,437	106,581	
CAPITAL (000)				
Total Debt	39,107	26,966	10,571	
Preferred Equity	0	0	0	
Common Equity	88,408	86,034	84,738	

Synopsis:

Ulster Petroleums completed a rights offering of 6.8 million Common Shares in January 1993, netting it $18-million. Of that amount, $8-million was used to finance purchases at Retlaw and Delia in Alberta, which increased gas reserves by 15 billion cubic feet and crude oil reserves by 200,000 barrels.

During the first quarter ending March 1993, Ulster also issued a Notice of Redemption to its debenture holders, which resulted in the conversion of its $5-million of outstanding convertible debentures into 1.6 million Common Shares. These two transactions increased Ulster's shareholders' equity to $113.2-million (represented by 42.4 million Common Shares outstanding), and reduced long-term debt to $16-million. On a pro forma basis, after giving effect to these two transactions, Ulster's net asset value is $3.85 per Common Share, compared with $4.10 without them.

Ulster invested $26-million, net of disposals, acquiring oil and natural gas properties in 1992. These additions were financed from cash provided by operations of $14-million, and the remainder from bank advances. Acquisitions are expected to total $25-million in 1993, and will be financed mainly from cash flow from operations.

Natural gas production jumped 37% to an average 30.3 million cubic feet per day in the first quarter of 1993, and natural gas prices rose 16%. Crude oil production increased 10% to an average 2,200 barrels per day, and crude oil prices increased 13%. These factors contributed to a 219% jump in net earnings to $1.2-million over the same period in 1992.

Average daily production in 1992 (1991) was: crude oil, 2,000 (1,500) barrels; and natural gas, 23.9 (20.8) million cubic feet. Gross proven and probable reserves in 1992 (1991) were: crude oil, 6.3 (5.7) million barrels; and natural gas, 145.2 (132) billion cubic feet. Ulster is not predisposed to either crude oil or natural gas projects, but pursues opportunities offering the greatest long-term returns.

Relative strength to TSE300 / Price / Volume (in 1000's of board lots)

Rank (Profit/Revenue/Assets)
343   595   364
Donne C. Traxel
President
Bob Woima
V.P., Finance & Administration

Address
Suite 1400
144 - 4th Avenue S.W.
Sun Life Plaza I
Calgary
AB
T2P 3N4
(403) 269-0400
Fax: (403) 264-5835
U0000283/G/3.2

Page	Company	$	Latest year end	Earnings per Share Actual	Estimate this year	Estimate next year
133	Abitibi-Price		9212	(3.02)	(0.90)	0.60
134	Canadian Pacific Forest		9212	(4.83)	(2.61)	0.64
135	Canfor		9212	(1.89)	2.44	4.35
136	Cascades		9212	0.50	0.00	0.52
137	Crestbrook Forest		9212	(0.59)	0.86	1.01
138	Doman Industries		9212	0.88	1.24	2.29
139	Domtar		9212	(1.36)	(0.42)	0.38
140	Donohue		9212	(0.47)	0.86	1.88
141	Fletcher Challenge Canada		9206	(1.26)	(0.20)	1.03
142	International Forest		9212	0.18	1.98	2.48
143	MacMillan Bloedel		9212	(0.52)	0.54	1.56
144	Noranda Forest		9212	(0.77)	0.45	1.10
145	Repap Enterprises		9212	(2.84)	(1.08)	(0.02)
146	Rolland		9212	(2.58)	0.50	n.a.
147	Slocan Forest		9212	0.47	3.36	4.72
148	Tembec		9209	(1.36)	(0.98)	0.80
149	Weldwood of Canada		9212	0.47	1.62	2.36
150	West Fraser Timber		9212	0.54	3.54	4.87

Estimates from I/B/E/S Inc., 345 Hudson St., New York, NY 10014 (212) 243-3335. In Canada: 6 Lansing Square, Ste. 235, Willowdale, ON M2J 1T5 (416) 496-0977.

Forestry

Calling British Columbia the "Brazil of the North" European Green Party politicians have called for a boycott of B.C. lumber, pulp and paper products. The European Greens said they will pressure paper consumers, such as magazine publishers, to demand that their suppliers end destructive forestry practices in the province. The comments have angered the B.C. government and forest industry, who have called the boycott totally irresponsible and have vowed to do whatever has to be done to protect one of the industry's principal international markets. The most recent statistics available show that in 1991 B.C. producers shipped about $500-million worth of wood products, including lumber and plywood, to the European Community, and more than $1-billion worth of pulp and paper.

Canada won a major victory recently in a critical trade battle with the United States, as a binational panel ruled that the Canadian softwood lumber industry was not benefiting from unfair subsidies. The softwood battle, the longest-running trade dispute between the two countries, started in 1986 when Ottawa imposed a 15% export tax on Canadian shipments to avoid the imposition of similar duties by the United States. The government lifted the export tax late in 1991, with the hope that U.S. concerns about Canadian practices had softened. Washington immediately launched a trade case against numerous provinces, particularly British Columbia, where the softwood industry is most important. In 1992, Canadian companies shipped $4.4-billion worth of softwood to the U.S., and in the past 12 months they have paid more than $200-million in border duties. Despite the 6.51% duty imposed last May, shipments to the United States actually increased last year by 14.6%, giving the Canadian companies 29.3% of the U.S. market.

The federal government announced that it is giving Canada's forest industry $46.5-million to help develop new technologies and to promote environmentaly sound practices and products. The industry will get $45-million over five years to support research and development, and another $1.5-million to help the Canadian Pulp and Paper Association fund its European office in Brussels. The Canadian forest industry, which sold about $35-billion worth of products last year, spends about $100-million a year on research and development, not including government funds.

The Canadian forest industry is highly cyclical and is only recently recovering from a deep downturn. The pulp and paper sector - the largest segment of Canada's forest industry - has had a particularly difficult two years, losing about $3.7-billion.

Forestry giant Domtar Inc. is set to invest about $200-million in "a major world breakthrough" technology that will allow it to make recycled fine paper with little or no de-inking. The Montreal-based company is believed to have secured world licencing rights for the process and plans to install it almost immediately at its two major fine-paper mills in Windsor, Quebec, and Cornwall, Ontario.

Paper & Forest Products: 1Q Earnings Preview - Industry Report [Apr-8-1993]. MERRILL LYNCH CAPITAL MARKETS reported by Chao, S.

Record wood products profits are expected for 1Q:93, due to record prices. Wood products prices have been declining in recent weeks due to weakening demand as building activity has been hurt by severe winter storms across the country. Prices should stabilize and firm somewhat in the fall of 1993, but not to exceed 1Q:93 highs. There are a number of new linerboard and corrugating medium capacity expansion plans being contemplated at various companies that may be approved by the end of 1993. [RN 1319703]

Paper & Forest Products - Industry Report [Mar-25-1993]. WOOD GUNDY INC. reported by Duncan, R.

U.S. lumber prices in early 1993 are averaging $475 (U.S.) per M. Bad weather in British Columbia could drive prices even higher in 2Q:93. North American demand has risen moderately during 1Q:93, and prices have increased more than 100% from the 1992 average. Offshore demand has deteriorated. Prices for these grades are up 14%-26% from 1992 averages. Later in 1993, Japanese demand is expected to increase, and in 1994, higher European demand should lead to stronger prices. [RN 1316997]

Paper & Forest Products - Industry Report [Mar-24-1993]. PRUDENTIAL SECURITIES INC. reported by Rogers, M.S., et al

The increase in industrial production, the key determinant of demand, is the primary favorable factor in the outlook. Should industrial production continue to move higher, linerboard prices could be raised in 3Q:92 but a 4Q:92 increase is more likely given the rise in mill inventories in the past two months. [RN 1317461]

Paper & Forest Products - Industry Report [Mar-24-1993]. BROWN BROTHERS HARRIMAN & CO. reported by McAuley, K.F.

Lumber prices have risen 50% since the start of 1993. Prices for panels are up 15%. Market pulp prices declined beneath historic lows during the period. Uncoated free sheet and newsprint prices increased in March. Although box prices and demand remained firm, linerboard prices decreased about $10 (U.S.) to $20 (U.S.) per ton. The $30 (U.S.) per ton increase is not expected to go into effect on April 1, 1993, as earlier planned, although prices should rise $10 (U.S.) to $15 (U.S.) per ton late in the spring. [RN 1317027]

ABITIBI-PRICE INC.

Exchanges	Price (Jun24'93)	14.25	Trailing P/E	nm	Stock Symbol
TMVN	Trailing Yield (%)	3.51	Trailing EPS	(3.01)	**A**

Period Ending	Dec92	Dec91	Dec90	Dec89	Dec88
Yearly Statistics					
Price-Close	14.50	14.63	12.00	13.25	19.25
Price-High	15.50	16.75	16.25	21.50	28.00
Price-Low	11.25	11.25	12.00	13.13	18.50
P/E-Close	nm	nm	nm	18.93	7.40
Dividends per Share	0.50	0.50	0.50	1.00	1.00
Dividend Yield (%)	3.45	3.42	4.17	7.55	5.20
Sales per Share	24.18	23.89	44.58	47.03	47.68
EPS before extra. item	(3.19)	(1.12)	(0.76)	0.70	2.60
Cash Flow per Share	(1.21)	0.33	0.95	3.03	5.68
Book Value per Share	10.76	14.45	16.07	17.33	17.50
O/S Common Shares	69,267	69,267	69,267	69,267	69,266
Total Revenue	1,632,100	1,667,000	3,092,400	3,277,000	3,323,600
Income before extra.	(219,300)	(75,900)	(50,400)	54,200	188,200
Cash Flow	(84,100)	22,600	65,700	210,000	393,700
Debt/Equity	0.51	0.43	0.49	0.48	0.40
Return on Capital (%)	(22.64)	(4.91)	(1.33)	7.83	20.37
Ret. on Com. Equity (%)	(25.30)	(7.34)	(4.55)	4.02	15.62
% Change Profit	(188.9)	(50.6)	(193.0)	(71.2)	49.7
% Change Revenue	(2.1)	(46.1)	(5.6)	(1.4)	10.7
% Change Assets	(19.5)	(12.7)	(3.2)	(2.9)	3.9

Business:

ABITIBI-PRICE INC. is an integrated forest products company. It manufactures and markets newsprint and uncoated groundwood papers. The company operates in North America and has markets in 32 countries.

Date	EPS	DPS	Tot Rev	Inc Bex
Mar 93	(0.42)	0.13	462,400	(28,800)
Dec 92	(0.99)	0.13	428,800	(67,700)
Sep 92	(1.00)	0.13	425,500	(68,700)
Jun 92	(0.60)	0.13	680,500	(41,300)
Mar 92	(0.61)	0.13	368,300	(41,600)
Dec 91	(0.70)	0.13	371,800	(48,100)
Sep 91	(0.25)	0.13	406,900	(16,600)
Jun 91	(0.08)	0.13	738,600	(5,700)

	Dec92	Dec91	Dec90
Preferred Div. Coverage	0.0	0.0	0.0
Total Div. Coverage	0.0	0.0	0.0
Interest Coverage	0.0	0.0	0.0
Current Ratio	1.2	1.8	1.3
Operating Margin	(8.8)	(1.5)	0.8
Asset Turnover	1.0	0.8	1.2
5 YEAR RATIOS (%)			
Return on Capital	(0.1)	7.6	11.7
Return on Com. Equity	(3.5)	3.8	7.4
Profit Growth	na	na	na
Revenue Growth	(11.5)	(9.8)	3.7
Asset Growth	(7.3)	(0.4)	3.5
BALANCE SHEET (000)			
Cash	120,000	0	0
Current Assets	453,000	761,200	716,100
Net Fixed Assets	946,300	1,073,800	1,373,700
Invest's & Advances	226,700	219,900	252,100
Total Assets	1,738,100	2,159,800	2,472,900
Short Term Debt	12,200	68,600	172,200
Current Liabilities	385,200	419,800	537,600
Long Term Debt	375,600	368,600	388,600
Total Liabilities	973,300	1,137,900	1,332,700
Total Equity	764,800	1,021,900	1,140,200
Total Liab. & Equity	1,738,100	2,159,800	2,472,900
CAPITAL (000)			
Total Debt	387,800	437,200	560,800
Preferred Equity	19,500	21,100	27,200
Common Equity	745,300	1,000,800	1,113,000

Synopsis:

Abitibi-Price hopes that a return to its core business as a maker of groundwood papers, such as newsprint and telephone directory paper, will restore it to profitability. In 1992, the company sold two of its three merchant business groups (paper distribution and industrial products distribution) for $340-million, and its Building Products division for over $120-million. Net cash proceeds totaling $351-million were used to reduce debt.

Prices for all its paper products declined by more than $90 Canadian a tonne on average in 1992. The company sold 1.8 million tonnes of newsprint (1.6 tonnes in 1991), and 412,000 tonnes of uncoated groundwood papers (402,000 tonnes in 1991).

While Abitibi's losses nearly tripled to $219-million for 1992, the company believes that its first quarter results for the period ending Mar. 31, 1993, show the impact of its restructuring efforts. First quarter sales of $471-million by product were: newsprint, 51%; groundwood papers, 15%; office products and converted products, 23%; and lumber and other, 11%.

During the first quarter of 1993, both prices and volumes in newsprint markets showed signs of improvement as U.S. consumption grew by 2.7% in the first two months. Over 70% of the company's production is sold in the United States. But improvements in demand and pricing for the company's uncoated groundwood papers lagged those for newsprint largely because retailers, publishers and printers continue to use lower cost newsprint in place of uncoated groundwood grades. This was reflected by a 35% increase in newsprint sales to commercial printers and markets.

The company faces uncertainty in terms of who will end up with controlling interest. The Reichmann family's Olympia and York Developments Ltd. lost control of Abitibi in a court-approved debt restructuring of the real estate company. A banking group led by Hongkong and Shanghai Banking Corp. is considering options for disposing of the controlling block of shares.

Relative strength to TSE300

Price

Volume (in 1000's of board lots)

Rank (Profit/Revenue/Assets)
986   75   101

Bernd K. Koken
Chairman Of The Board

Ronald Y. Oberlander
President & C.E.O.

Eileen A. Mercier
Sr. V.P. & C.F.O.

Address
207 Queens Quay West
Suite 680
P.O. Box 102
Toronto
ON
M5J 2P5
(416) 369-6700
Fax: (416) 369-6794
A0000192/G/4.1

CANADIAN PACIFIC FOREST PRODUCTS LIMITED

Exchanges	Price (Jun24'93)	20.37	Trailing P/E	nm	Stock Symbol
TM	Trailing Yield (%)	1.47	Trailing EPS	(4.59)	**PFP**

Period Ending	Dec92	Dec91	Dec90	Dec89	Dec88
Yearly Statistics					
Price-Close	22.50	24.25	28.00	39.50	42.00
Price-High	28.50	35.00	40.00	49.50	54.50
Price-Low	20.00	22.00	27.50	35.75	39.50
P/E-Close	nm	nm	nm	7.88	5.71
Dividends per Share	0.40	0.40	1.15	2.60	2.50
Dividend Yield (%)	1.78	1.65	4.11	6.58	5.95
Sales per Share	35.47	45.03	47.74	65.43	68.38
EPS before extra. item	(4.82)	(13.00)	(0.21)	5.01	7.36
Cash Flow per Share	(2.86)	(5.16)	5.14	9.67	11.38
Book Value per Share	19.05	23.83	37.23	38.55	36.05
O/S Common Shares	52,459	43,959	43,959	43,959	43,959
Total Revenue	1,749,700	1,926,900	2,051,200	2,883,700	3,013,500
Income before extra.	(248,000)	(571,500)	(9,400)	220,100	323,400
Cash Flow	(147,400)	(226,800)	226,000	425,100	500,200
Debt/Equity	1.48	1.20	0.51	0.34	0.21
Return on Capital (%)	(11.09)	(32.08)	1.50	18.38	30.58
Ret. on Com. Equity (%)	(24.23)	(42.58)	(0.56)	13.42	21.95
% Change Profit	56.6	(5,979.8)	(104.3)	(31.9)	51.1
% Change Revenue	(9.2)	(6.1)	(28.9)	(4.3)	8.6
% Change Assets	1.2	(9.1)	6.3	10.7	3.9

Date	EPS	DPS	Tot Rev	Inc Bex
Mar 93	(1.23)	0.00	429,600	(64,800)
Dec 92	(1.13)	0.10	444,900	(59,500)
Sep 92	(1.10)	0.10	447,200	(57,900)
Jun 92	(1.13)	0.10	450,000	(59,500)
Mar 92	(1.47)	0.10	413,400	(71,100)
Dec 91	(10.56)	0.10	466,700	(464,000)
Sep 91	(0.02)	0.10	506,000	(1,000)
Jun 91	(1.28)	0.10	490,700	(56,400)

Preferred Div. Coverage	np	np	np
Total Div. Coverage	0.0	0.0	0.0
Interest Coverage	0.0	0.0	0.5
Current Ratio	1.5	1.9	1.8
Operating Margin	(10.4)	(40.4)	3.5
Asset Turnover	0.6	0.7	0.6
5 YEAR RATIOS (%)			
Return on Capital	1.5	11.4	20.7
Return on Com. Equity	(6.4)	3.5	13.8
Profit Growth	na	na	na
Revenue Growth	(8.8)	24.8	28.2
Asset Growth	2.3	30.9	33.5
BALANCE SHEET (000)			
Cash	0	0	0
Current Assets	601,200	727,200	710,600
Net Fixed Assets	2,117,800	2,072,300	2,437,500
Invest's & Advances	160,500	143,700	96,300
Total Assets	3,000,800	2,965,000	3,263,300
Short Term Debt	88,000	34,900	172,600
Current Liabilities	388,600	383,600	398,700
Long Term Debt	1,392,200	1,216,700	667,100
Total Liabilities	2,001,600	1,917,400	1,626,600
Total Equity	999,200	1,047,600	1,636,700
Total Liab. & Equity	3,000,800	2,965,000	3,263,300
CAPITAL (000)			
Total Debt	1,480,200	1,251,600	839,700
Preferred Equity	0	0	0
Common Equity	999,200	1,047,600	1,636,700

Business:

CANADIAN PACIFIC FOREST PRODUCTS LTD. is an integrated forest products company. Products include newsprint, pulp, paperboard and packaging, white paper and lumber. The company has mills in New Brunswick, Quebec, Ontario, British Columbia and Washington. It exports to 40 countries, but chiefly to the United States. Canadian Pacific Ltd. has an 60% interest.

Synopsis:

Canadian Pacific Forest Products is continuing its efforts to improve productivity and cut costs, but sees no chance of turning a profit in 1993. The company needs better prices for its pulp and paper products, but pulp markets remain very difficult with inventories at their highest level in more than 20 years. Prices for pulp are also being driven down because the world's producers can now supply about five million tonnes more than buyers need. Since the third quarter of 1992, list prices for pulp have fallen by 25%.

For the first quarter ending March 31, 1993, the company shipped 171 tonnes of pulp, down from the 208 tonnes shipped the year before. Newsprint shipments rose to 249 tonnes from 231 tonnes for the same period. CP Forest expects newsprint consumption in North America to continue to rise through the balance of 1993 due to increased newspaper advertising driven by an improving economy. Lumber shipments climbed from 77 million board feet for the first quarter of 1992, to 90 million board feet for the same period this year. Wood products consumption is expected to continue to improve with the economic recovery in North America, but stable demand is forecast for the Japanese market.

All of the company's manufacturing facilities are located in Canada, with the exception of the Ponderay Newsprint Company joint venture in the United States. In 1992, CP Forest had export sales of $841-million to the United States ($930-million in 1991), and $555-million to other countries ($573-million in 1991). The breakdown of 1992 sales of $1,826-million by product was: newsprint, 31%; pulp, 25%; white paper, 10%; paperboard and packaging, 19%; wood products, 12%; and other, 3%.

CP Forest is North America's largest supplier of recycled-content newsprint, capable of producing 900,000 tonnes each year. As part of its recycling initiatives, CP Forest utilizes its de-inking plants to remove some 330,000 tonnes of old magazines and newspapers from the waste stream annually.

Rank (Profit/Revenue/Assets)
989 70 70

Michel Belanger
Chairman

Paul E. Gagne
President & C.E.O.

David G. Toole
Sr. V.P. & C.F.O.

Address
1155 Metcalfe Street
Montreal
PQ
H3B 2X1
(514) 878-4811

Fax: (514) 878-4850
G0002394/G/4.1

For further company information, call Globe Information Services 1-800-268-9128 or (416)585-5345

CANFOR CORPORATION

Exchanges	Price (Jun24'93)	39.75	Trailing P/E	nm	Stock Symbol
TV	Trailing Yield (%)	1.31	Trailing EPS	(0.88)	**CFP**

Period Ending	Dec92	Dec91	Dec90	Dec89	Dec88
Yearly Statistics					
Price-Close	27.00	25.38	21.75	25.75	25.63
Price-High	29.75	29.75	29.88	31.38	30.50
Price-Low	24.00	19.38	20.00	23.38	22.50
P/E-Close	nm	nm	310.71	6.47	6.09
Dividends per Share	0.52	0.45	0.55	0.70	0.55
Dividend Yield (%)	1.91	1.77	2.53	2.72	2.15
Sales per Share	35.44	34.70	38.73	40.45	47.77
EPS before extra. item	(1.89)	(4.18)	0.07	3.98	4.21
Cash Flow per Share	1.29	(1.34)	4.32	2.19	6.83
Book Value per Share	19.78	21.70	25.90	26.38	23.16
O/S Common Shares	28,436	25,869	22,844	22,818	22,729
Total Revenue	948,656	767,548	922,379	979,904	1,133,146
Income before extra.	(49,894)	(99,053)	3,798	96,351	101,564
Cash Flow	35,446	(31,705)	98,563	49,906	154,945
Debt/Equity	0.68	0.63	0.41	0.46	0.27
Return on Capital (%)	(2.18)	(14.73)	4.66	22.30	24.74
Ret. on Com. Equity (%)	(9.26)	(17.57)	0.26	16.06	21.43
% Change Profit	49.6	(2,708.0)	(96.1)	(5.1)	(1.1)
% Change Revenue	23.6	(16.8)	(5.9)	(13.5)	(9.5)
% Change Assets	4.2	0.9	(4.8)	0.0	25.9

Date	EPS	DPS	Tot Rev	Inc Bex
Mar 93	0.57	0.00	265,500	16,800
Dec 92	(0.29)	0.25	254,013	(7,694)
Sep 92	(0.82)	0.00	220,600	(22,200)
Jun 92	(0.34)	0.27	267,300	(9,100)
Mar 92	(0.44)	0.00	205,700	(10,900)
Dec 91	(1.30)	0.25	173,006	(22,353)
Sep 91	(1.42)	0.00	190,406	(34,500)
Jun 91	(0.71)	0.20	199,500	(15,700)

	Dec92	Dec91	Dec90
Preferred Div. Coverage	0.0	0.0	1.7
Total Div. Coverage	0.0	0.0	0.3
Interest Coverage	0.0	0.0	1.5
Current Ratio	1.4	1.4	1.8
Operating Margin	2.0	(8.8)	0.5
Asset Turnover	0.8	0.7	0.7
5 YEAR RATIOS (%)			
Return on Capital	7.0	14.2	20.1
Return on Com. Equity	2.2	10.1	14.5
Profit Growth	na	na	(13.9)
Revenue Growth	(5.4)	(6.3)	(3.7)
Asset Growth	6.5	8.3	5.7
BALANCE SHEET (000)			
Cash	8,470	5,208	4,155
Current Assets	337,694	286,118	295,412
Net Fixed Assets	572,123	593,590	593,926
Invest's & Advances	324,570	327,387	308,638
Total Assets	1,270,358	1,219,338	1,208,449
Short Term Debt	100,912	103,252	32,513
Current Liabilities	236,729	198,412	159,910
Long Term Debt	298,611	267,513	221,032
Total Liabilities	684,288	633,526	591,832
Total Equity	586,070	585,812	616,617
Total Liab. & Equity	1,270,358	1,219,338	1,208,449
CAPITAL (000)			
Total Debt	399,523	370,765	253,545
Preferred Equity	23,500	24,500	25,000
Common Equity	562,570	561,312	591,617

Business:

CANFOR CORP. is an integrated forest products company. It produces kraft pulp and sack kraft paper, lumber and other wood and wood fibre products. Canfor has facilities in British Columbia, northern Alberta and northwestern United States. It has pulp sales offices in Canada, Europe and Japan. Canfor owns half of a pulp and newsprint company and half a Canadian building materials distribution company.

Synopsis:

Canfor sees 1992 as a transition year for the company. A new senior management team was put in place mid-year, and a reorganization of the company along product lines was implemented.

In the pulp and sack kraft paper segment, the operating loss for 1992 was reduced by $3-million to $8-million. This loss includes a $6-million devaluation of year-end pulp and chip inventories to net realizable values, which were lower than cost. Prices for sack kraft paper were generally stable during 1992. Production in 1992 was 85,000 tonnes, compared to 91,000 tonnes in 1991.

In the wood and wood products segment, income from 1992 operations improved by $92-million over 1991. An increase in lumber prices contributed $81-million to the improved operating income. However the 7% countervailing duty on softwood lumber exports to the U.S. cost the company $19-million in 1992, compared to $2-million in export charges for the previous year. For the first quarter of 1993, this duty cost Canfor $8-million before income taxes.

Some of the environmentally friendly products that the Canfor produces include lawn turf made from wood mulch, and car door panels made with recycled wood scraps, sawdust and shavings. The company hopes to hit $30-million to $50-million in annual sales for car parts within three to five years.

1992 (1991) sales by product line were: pulp and sack kraft paper, 23% (29%); lumber, 51% (44%); plywood and hardboard, 1% (2%); building materials purchased for resale, 21% (22%); and miscellaneous, 4% (3%). 1992 (1991) sales by market were: the United States, 52% (41%); Europe, 19% (25%); Canada, 14% (17%); the Far East, 14% (16%); and other, 1% (1%).

Relative strength to TSE300 / Price / Volume (in 1000's of board lots)

Rank (Profit/Revenue/Assets)
955   108   129

Peter J.G. Bentley
Chairman & C.E.O.

Arild S. Nielssen
President & C.O.O.

A. Gordon Armstrong
Sr. V.P., Finance

Address
2900 - 1055 Dunsmuir Street
P.O. Box 49420
Bentall Postal Station
Vancouver
BC
V7X 1B5
(604) 661-5241
Fax: (604) 661-5273
C0035314/G/4.2

CASCADES INC.

Exchanges	Price (Jun24'93)	5.87	Trailing P/E	15.46	Stock Symbol
TM	Trailing Yield (%)	0.00	Trailing EPS	0.38	CAS

Period Ending	Dec92	Dec91	Dec90	Dec89	Dec88
Yearly Statistics					
Price-Close	6.75	6.00	4.10	5.13	5.50
Price-High	8.50	6.50	5.38	7.50	7.25
Price-Low	5.25	3.80	3.13	5.00	4.85
P/E-Close	13.78	nm	9.76	8.27	7.75
Dividends per Share	0.00	0.00	0.00	0.00	0.00
Dividend Yield (%)	0.00	0.00	0.00	0.00	0.00
Sales per Share	16.50	15.67	16.94	14.12	12.19
EPS before extra. item	0.49	(0.03)	0.42	0.62	0.71
Cash Flow per Share	0.68	1.02	1.27	1.16	1.42
Book Value per Share	5.70	5.14	5.22	4.56	3.91
O/S Common Shares	54,749	54,637	48,288	48,288	48,288
Total Revenue	939,292	818,392	833,227	691,851	592,887
Income before extra.	28,235	(1,559)	20,126	29,887	34,463
Cash Flow	37,351	52,449	61,541	55,914	68,744
Debt/Equity	1.85	1.47	1.69	1.39	1.20
Return on Capital (%)	7.89	7.59	12.92	14.43	18.10
Ret. on Com. Equity (%)	9.01	(0.59)	8.52	14.61	19.88
% Change Profit	1,911.1	(107.7)	(32.7)	(13.3)	60.1
% Change Revenue	14.8	(1.8)	20.4	16.7	11.3
% Change Assets	84.0	3.0	29.1	28.4	15.8

Preferred Div. Coverage	18.3	np	np
Total Div. Coverage	18.3	na	na
Interest Coverage	1.7	1.2	1.7
Current Ratio	1.3	1.4	1.6
Operating Margin	3.8	8.4	9.4
Asset Turnover	0.5	0.9	0.9
5 YEAR RATIOS (%)			
Return on Capital	12.2	13.7	16.5
Return on Com. Equity	10.3	11.6	16.3
Profit Growth	5.6	na	0.7
Revenue Growth	12.0	13.0	25.4
Asset Growth	29.4	19.8	35.7
BALANCE SHEET (000)			
Cash	54,405	60,595	67,667
Current Assets	566,530	348,025	339,724
Net Fixed Assets	1,057,048	499,324	449,001
Invest's & Advances	50,259	59,136	41,979
Total Assets	1,713,312	931,360	904,174
Short Term Debt	178,846	91,588	66,304
Current Liabilities	429,531	245,384	208,543
Long Term Debt	616,985	320,780	360,865
Total Liabilities	1,283,089	650,401	651,990
Total Equity	430,223	280,959	252,184
Total Liab. & Equity	1,713,312	931,360	904,174
CAPITAL (000)			
Total Debt	795,831	412,368	427,169
Preferred Equity	118,397	0	0
Common Equity	311,826	280,959	252,184

Business:

CASCADES INC. is a pulp and paper company. It also operates in the packaging and building materials industry. The company has operations in Canada, the United States, France, Belgium and Sweden. Its products include bleached pulp, coated folding boxboard, corrugated cardboard and kraft paper. The company has markets in Canada, the United States, continental Europe and Sweden.

Date	EPS	DPS	Tot Rev	Inc Bex
Mar 93	(0.01)	0.00	421,469	847
Dec 92	0.24	0.00	285,520	14,583
Sep 92	0.02	0.00	219,789	1,313
Jun 92	0.13	0.00	217,008	6,920
Mar 92	0.10	0.00	216,975	5,419
Dec 91	0.06	0.00	192,870	3,419
Sep 91	(0.16)	0.00	198,773	(8,390)
Jun 91	0.13	0.00	206,491	2,591

Synopsis:

Cascades plans to restructure its various groups over the next three to four years. In the meantime, the company plans to continue to focus on recovery, and manufacturing products using recycled materials. Cascades believes that the demand for recycled products has just begun, and that demand will remain strong.

Cascades acquired Paperboard Industries Corporation in December 1992. The company created Cascades Paperboard International (CPI) to regroup 24 Cascades boxboard mills around the world. CPI is among the 10 largest integrated producers of boxboard in the world and is the largest producer in Canada. The company is looking to sell off as many as eight of those plants, which employ 1,250 people and represent roughly $300-million of CPI's total annual sales of about $1-billion.

In 1992, Cascades also took control of Rolland Inc., one of Canada's largest manufacturers of fine paper. Combined with the acquisition of mills and the purchase of equity in packaging and conversion companies, Cascades doubled its assets from $931-million in 1991 to $2-billion in 1992. This figure includes assets of $577.5-million for Paperboard Industries and $133.1-million for Rolland.

The boxboard group, combined with the subsidiary CPI, generated sales of $430-million or 48% of total sales in 1992, compared with $442-million or 55% in 1991. Combined sales for sectors other than the boxboard group jumped by $108-million or 29%.

By geographical segment, 51% of 1992 revenue was generated by the group's Canadian operations, 38% by European subsidiaries, and 11% by the U.S. units. The widespread slump in prices for the company's main products in North America and the sharp drop in boxboard prices in Europe eroded the company's consolidated gross margin before amortization, which dropped from 30% in 1991 to 26% in 1992. The company experienced its worst economic conditions in Europe, where total demand for boxboard fell 5%, and prices dropped an average of 7%.

Relative strength to TSE300 / Price / Volume (in 1000's of board lots)

Rank (Profit/Revenue/Assets)
102 111 102

Bernard Lemaire
Chairman Of The Board

Laurent Lemaire
President & C.E.O.

Andre Belzile
Corp. Dir., Finance

Martin Pelletier
V.P., Operations

Address
404, Rue Marie-Victorin
C.P. 30
Kingsey-Falls
PQ
J0A 1B0
(819) 363-2245

Fax: (819) 363-5155
C0027546/G/4.1

CRESTBROOK FOREST INDUSTRIES LTD.

Exchanges	Price (Jun24'93)	14 .75	Trailing P/E	nm	Stock Symbol
TV	Trailing Yield (%)	1 .02	Trailing EPS	(0 .04)	**CFI**

Period Ending	Dec92	Dec91	Dec90	Dec89	Dec88
Yearly Statistics					
Price-Close	12 .00	13 .75	17 .50	21 .50	16 .38
Price-High	15 .75	21 .00	22 .00	25 .00	19 .50
Price-Low	10 .25	12 .00	14 .75	17 .00	13 .00
P/E-Close	nm	nm	12 .41	5 .11	4 .06
Dividends per Share	0 .15	0 .60	0 .60	0 .60	0 .60
Dividend Yield (%)	1 .25	4 .36	3 .43	2 .79	3 .66
Sales per Share	15 .46	17 .23	28 .83	34 .36	32 .87
EPS before extra. item	(0 .59)	(1 .84)	1 .41	4 .21	4 .03
Cash Flow per Share	1 .69	(1 .74)	2 .18	4 .83	5 .55
Book Value per Share	12 .99	13 .73	16 .31	15 .50	11 .88
O/S Common Shares	11 ,560	11 ,560	7 ,639	7 ,636	7 ,633
Total Revenue	180 ,984	173 ,517	224 ,071	266 ,698	254 ,359
Income before extra.	(6 ,818)	(15 ,014)	10 ,776	32 ,137	30 ,794
Cash Flow	19 ,594	(16 ,690)	16 ,619	36 ,845	42 ,367
Debt/Equity	0 .54	0 .11	0 .17	0 .20	0 .25
Return on Capital (%)	(4 .26)	(15 .51)	13 .65	43 .34	52 .04
Ret. on Com. Equity (%)	(4 .42)	(10 .60)	8 .87	30 .75	39 .68
% Change Profit	54 .6	(239 .3)	(66 .5)	4 .4	15 .1
% Change Revenue	4 .3	(22 .6)	(16 .0)	4 .9	5 .8
% Change Assets	23 .3	17 .1	2 .7	11 .4	24 .3

Date	EPS	DPS	Tot Rev	Inc Bex
Mar 93	0 .33	0 .15	52 ,115	3 ,836
Dec 92	0 .01	0 .00	59 ,010	84
Sep 92	(0 .10)	0 .00	43 ,244	(1 ,087)
Jun 92	(0 .28)	0 .00	38 ,509	(3 ,288)
Mar 92	(0 .22)	0 .15	39 ,341	(2 ,527)
Dec 91	(0 .79)	0 .00	44 ,530	(7 ,019)
Sep 91	(0 .29)	0 .30	47 ,448	(2 ,161)
Jun 91	(0 .44)	0 .00	42 ,192	(3 ,351)

Preferred Div. Coverage	np	np	np
Total Div. Coverage	0 .0	0 .0	2 .4
Interest Coverage	0 .0	0 .0	9 .9
Current Ratio	2 .6	2 .9	2 .4
Operating Margin	(5 .7)	(20 .0)	7 .1
Asset Turnover	0 .6	0 .7	1 .0
5 YEAR RATIOS (%)			
Return on Capital	17 .9	28 .8	34 .9
Return on Com. Equity	12 .9	24 .0	29 .1
Profit Growth	na	na	38 .9
Revenue Growth	(5 .5)	1 .4	9 .5
Asset Growth	15 .4	12 .2	8 .3
BALANCE SHEET (000)			
Cash	7 ,440	7 ,216	15 ,927
Current Assets	85 ,501	92 ,345	84 ,360
Net Fixed Assets	128 ,457	122 ,385	100 ,012
Invest's & Advances	83 ,937	33 ,208	26 ,700
Total Assets	305 ,914	248 ,048	211 ,754
Short Term Debt	3 ,050	2 ,772	6 ,147
Current Liabilities	32 ,518	31 ,980	34 ,783
Long Term Debt	77 ,335	15 ,255	14 ,632
Total Liabilities	155 ,798	89 ,380	87 ,197
Total Equity	150 ,116	158 ,668	124 ,557
Total Liab. & Equity	305 ,914	248 ,048	211 ,754
CAPITAL (000)			
Total Debt	80 ,385	18 ,027	20 ,779
Preferred Equity	0	0	0
Common Equity	150 ,116	158 ,668	124 ,557

Business:

CRESTBROOK FOREST INDUSTRIES LTD. is a vertically integrated forest products company. The company has operations in British Columbia and Alberta. Products, including lumber and bleached kraft pulp, are sold to markets in the United States, Canada, Japan, Mexico and Europe. Both Honshu Paper Co. Ltd. and Mitsubishi Corp. of Japan each own 26.78% of the company's common shares.

Synopsis:

Crestbrook expects to add some of the best hardwood pulp in the world to its product line with the start-up of its new joint venture pulp facility in northeastern Alberta in September 1993. Crestbrook's 40% equity interest in the Alberta-Pacific joint venture will double the company's current pulp production, bringing its total annual output to 400,000 air dry tonnes. This will make the company far more leveraged to pulp than to lumber. Lumber accounted for 60% of Crestbrook's 1992 net sales, and pulp, 40%.

Equity commitments by the joint venture parties totaled $1-billion for construction and operation of the bleached kraft pulp mill. The company's share totaled $124-million. The mill represents the first phase of the joint venture. Once the mill is fully operational, the viability of the second phase, a world-scale fine paper mill, will be determined. The mill's new technology will virtually eliminate the production of dioxins and furans in the bleaching process.

As part of its asset renewal program, Crestbrook is building a $129-million recovery facility at the Skookumchuck pulp mill, which is expected to be operational in August 1993. The facility will reduce costs for recovering chemicals in the pulping process.

Long-term debt will rise in 1993 to $325-million from $80-million at the end of 1992 because of capital spending. The company expects that no significant capital expenditures related to environmental compliance will be required after 1994. However, the B.C. provincial government proposed regulations in 1992 that would eliminate chlorinated organic compounds from the bleaching process by December 31, 2002. There is currently no known proven technology to accomplish this at mills such as the Skookumchuck pulp mill.

Net sales by geographic region in 1992 (1991) were: United States, 84% (77%); Canada, 2% (6%); Japan, 9% (12%); Mexico, 1% (2%); Korea, 2% (1%); Europe, 2% (1%); and other, - (1%). Because 98% of the sales revenues are in U.S. dollars, Crestbrook's earning are subject to foreign exchange transaction risks.

Relative strength to TSE300

Price

Volume (in 1000's of board lots)

Rank (Profit/Revenue/Assets)
857   289   269

Sakae Hosaka
Chairman & C.E.O.

Stuart A. Lang
President & C.O.O.

Robert H. Langin
Controller & Acting C.F.O.

Address
220 Cranbrook Street North
Cranbrook
BC
V1C 3R2
(604) 426-6241

Fax: (604) 426-3406
C0011687/G/4.2

DOMAN INDUSTRIES LIMITED

Exchanges	Price (Jun24'93)	12.75	Trailing P/E	98.08	Stock Symbol
TV	Trailing Yield (%)	2.20	Trailing EPS	0.13	**DOM.B**

Period Ending	Dec92	Dec91	Dec90	Dec89	Dec88
Yearly Statistics					
Price-Close	8.50	5.75	5.38	9.25	7.00
Price-High	8.50	8.50	11.38	10.50	11.75
Price-Low	5.50	4.50	4.95	5.63	5.00
P/E-Close	10.00	nm	23.37	5.61	7.00
Dividends per Share	0.27	0.30	0.09	0.07	0.05
Dividend Yield (%)	3.18	5.18	5.12	2.16	2.14
Sales per Share	20.17	25.60	10.25	8.71	5.58
EPS before extra. item	0.85	(2.34)	0.08	0.55	0.33
Cash Flow per Share	1.95	(0.95)	1.16	1.85	0.69
Book Value per Share	3.75	1.72	1.49	1.47	0.99
O/S Common Shares	27,316	19,385	57,417	55,814	55,706
Total Revenue	582,061	514,240	615,756	493,820	303,508
Income before extra.	27,213	(46,537)	5,376	31,887	20,231
Cash Flow	53,171	(18,529)	66,032	103,090	37,332
Debt/Equity	3.12	14.45	6.61	6.28	1.15
Return on Capital (%)	11.26	(0.95)	12.84	22.51	29.71
Ret. on Com. Equity (%)	34.44	(80.08)	5.08	44.53	43.65
% Change Profit	158.5	(965.6)	(83.1)	57.6	(17.5)
% Change Revenue	13.2	(16.5)	24.7	62.7	(5.9)
% Change Assets	5.5	(4.0)	0.2	385.1	20.3

Date	EPS	DPS	Tot Rev	Inc Bex
Mar 93	0.35	0.07	177,362	10,975
Dec 92	0.14	0.07	151,538	5,821
Sep 92	(0.10)	0.07	140,891	132
Jun 92	(0.26)	0.07	136,318	(3,323)
Mar 92	1.06	0.07	153,342	24,583
Dec 91	(0.83)	0.07	115,234	(17,153)
Sep 91	(0.16)	0.02	133,577	(8,900)
Jun 91	(0.54)	0.07	143,347	(10,379)

Preferred Div. Coverage	7.1	0.0	4.8
Total Div. Coverage	2.6	0.0	0.8
Interest Coverage	1.6	0.0	1.2
Current Ratio	1.4	1.0	1.4
Operating Margin	11.5	(3.3)	11.5
Asset Turnover	0.5	0.5	0.5
5 YEAR RATIOS (%)			
Return on Capital	15.1	20.3	25.9
Return on Com. Equity	9.5	22.6	66.1
Profit Growth	2.1	na	18.1
Revenue Growth	12.5	13.6	24.4
Asset Growth	42.6	40.5	40.2
BALANCE SHEET (000)			
Cash	0	0	0
Current Assets	257,519	239,703	286,423
Net Fixed Assets	749,415	748,191	750,113
Invest's & Advances	19,889	19,008	24,249
Total Assets	1,079,690	1,023,636	1,066,588
Short Term Debt	104,731	166,985	149,299
Current Liabilities	178,209	229,997	205,344
Long Term Debt	609,917	522,917	509,756
Total Liabilities	850,672	975,874	966,933
Total Equity	229,018	47,762	99,655
Total Liab. & Equity	1,079,690	1,023,636	1,066,588
CAPITAL (000)			
Total Debt	714,648	689,902	659,055
Preferred Equity	126,648	14,339	14,339
Common Equity	102,370	33,423	85,316

Business:

DOMAN INDUSTRIES Ltd. is a forest products company with logging, pulp and sawmill operations along the coast of British Columbia. The main products are kraft pulp, sulphite pulp and lumber, which the company markets worldwide. Doman also sells logs and pulp chips.

Synopsis:

Doman Industries sold four million special warrants on March 5, 1993, which are exchangeable into four million Class B Non-Voting Shares. Gross proceeds from the issue totaled $42-million. Net proceeds will be used to reduce short-term bank indebtedness incurred by the company under its operating line of credit in funding its day-to-day operations. If net proceeds are taken into account on a pro forma basis as at the end of 1992, the shareholders' equity would increase to $270-million and the debt-equity ratio would become 2.3 to 1.

The company completed a $52-million secondary treatment facility for the processing of effluent at the Squamish pulp mill in December 1992. The mill has the capacity to produce 240,000 air dried tonnes (ADT) of softwood kraft pulp per year. Term debt was arranged so that no significant principal payments are due until July 1994. Construction of an $8-million hog fuel dryer to reduce particle emissions is scheduled to commence in 1993 at the Port Alice pulp mill. The mill has an annual production capacity of 160,000 ADT of dissolving sulphite pulp.

Of the $80-million improvement in the 1992 operating earnings before interest expense over the previous year, $60-million is attributed to the forest and wood products segment and $20-million to the pulp segment. Lumber sales in 1992 of $270-million (645 million board feet) increased 29% from 1991 sales of $209-million (565 million board feet). External pulp sales in 1992 of $195-million (314,000 tonnes) fell 8% from 1991 sales of $211-million (359,000 tonnes).

Doman's products were sold in 40 countries around the world in 1992. Percentages of sales by geographic region in 1992 (1991) were: Canada, 31% (28%); the U.S., 32% (28%); Europe, 16% (20%); the Far East, 18% (19%); and other, 3% (5%). Export sales for the year were $381-million in 1992 and $360-million in 1991, including $179-million in 1992 and $140-million in 1991 to the United States.

Relative strength to TSE300 / Price / Volume (in 1000's of board lots)

Rank (Profit/Revenue/Assets)
107 144 149
H.S. Doman — Chairman & President
J.R. Abercrombie — V.P., Fin., Admin. & Treasurer

Address
435 Trunk Road
Duncan
BC
V9L 2P9
(604) 748-3711

Fax: (604) 748-1600
D0001516/G/4.2

DOMTAR INC.

Exchanges	Price (Jun24'93)		7.25	Trailing P/E		nm	Stock Symbol
TMVN	Trailing Yield (%)		0.00	Trailing EPS		(1.20)	**DTC**

Period Ending	Dec92	Dec91	Dec90	Dec89	Dec88
Yearly Statistics					
Price-Close	5.25	7.75	9.50	13.00	14.63
Price-High	8.38	10.00	13.50	18.00	16.50
Price-Low	4.25	7.00	9.00	12.88	12.00
P/E-Close	nm	nm	nm	54.17	12.72
Dividends per Share	0.00	0.21	0.31	0.50	0.50
Dividend Yield (%)	0.00	2.66	3.21	3.85	3.42
Sales per Share	15.56	19.05	26.64	29.06	29.01
EPS before extra. item	(1.36)	(1.69)	(3.44)	0.24	1.15
Cash Flow per Share	(0.59)	(0.48)	(0.14)	2.38	3.55
Book Value per Share	5.58	7.12	8.94	12.78	13.06
O/S Common Shares	126,235	100,892	87,036	86,717	86,315
Total Revenue	1,885,000	1,805,000	2,314,000	2,519,000	2,503,000
Income before extra.	(159,000)	(148,000)	(294,000)	33,000	111,000
Cash Flow	(72,000)	(45,000)	(12,000)	206,000	306,000
Debt/Equity	1.23	1.40	1.17	0.88	0.77
Return on Capital (%)	(7.10)	(6.08)	(15.60)	4.76	9.53
Ret. on Com. Equity (%)	(23.07)	(21.39)	(32.45)	1.88	8.99
% Change Profit	(7.4)	49.7	(990.9)	(70.3)	(31.1)
% Change Revenue	4.4	(22.0)	(8.1)	0.6	(2.8)
% Change Assets	(2.6)	(2.9)	(13.9)	2.9	9.4

Preferred Div. Coverage	0.0	0.0	0.0
Total Div. Coverage	0.0	0.0	0.0
Interest Coverage	0.0	0.0	0.0
Current Ratio	1.3	2.1	1.4
Operating Margin	(5.8)	(6.0)	(1.7)
Asset Turnover	0.7	0.7	0.8
5 YEAR RATIOS (%)			
Return on Capital	(2.9)	1.6	6.5
Return on Com. Equity	(13.2)	(5.7)	1.4
Profit Growth	na	na	na
Revenue Growth	(6.1)	(5.2)	1.5
Asset Growth	(1.8)	3.8	9.4
BALANCE SHEET (000)			
Cash	42,000	115,000	2,000
Current Assets	599,000	632,000	618,000
Net Fixed Assets	1,955,000	2,038,000	2,115,000
Invest's & Advances	19,000	16,000	17,000
Total Assets	2,670,000	2,742,000	2,824,000
Short Term Debt	169,000	25,000	97,000
Current Liabilities	465,000	308,000	447,000
Long Term Debt	976,000	1,181,000	986,000
Total Liabilities	1,741,000	1,878,000	1,900,000
Total Equity	929,000	864,000	924,000
Total Liab. & Equity	2,670,000	2,742,000	2,824,000
CAPITAL (000)			
Total Debt	1,145,000	1,206,000	1,083,000
Preferred Equity	225,000	146,000	146,000
Common Equity	704,000	718,000	778,000

Business:

DOMTAR INC. has operations in pulp and paper, packaging, and construction materials in Canada and the United States. It has customers worldwide and its principal products include fine papers, newsprint, corrugated containers and gypsum board. Two Quebec government partners, Caisse de depot et placement du Quebec and Societe generale de financement own 42% of the common stock.

Date	EPS	DPS	Tot Rev	Inc Bex
Mar 93	(0.28)	0.00	460,000	(35,000)
Dec 92	(0.34)	0.00	469,000	(42,000)
Sep 92	(0.26)	0.00	482,000	(32,000)
Jun 92	(0.32)	0.00	484,000	(39,000)
Mar 92	(0.46)	0.00	450,000	(46,000)
Dec 91	(0.47)	0.21	432,000	(44,000)
Sep 91	(0.43)	0.00	454,000	(39,000)
Jun 91	(0.46)	0.00	469,000	(37,000)

Synopsis:

In an effort to become more competitive, Domtar will concentrate its financial resources on fewer core businesses. The company is considering the possible sale or joint venture of several businesses, but is unlikely to unload its core fine-paper mills.

During the last two years, Domtar cut its workforce to 9,500 from 14,000. In an industry first, total-flexibility union agreements were reached in 1992 with employees at four Quebec mills, two Ontario mills, box plants in Eastern Canada and gypsum plants in California. These agreements allow different trades people to do the job of anyone else in the mill. With its leaner, more flexible workforce and improved productivity at its plants, Domtar hopes to benefit when markets improve. However, because of high debt service charges on its $1.1-billion debt, Domtar does not expect to turn a profit until 1994.

Substantial environment-protection investment will be required over the next several years due to new federal and provincial regulations regarding water and air quality, and the disposal of solid wastes. The estimated direct cost to Domtar could amount to some $370-million in additional capital speding between 1993 and 1996, of which $20-million is expected to be spent in 1993.

In 1992, the company's Canadian facilities had $982-million of sales within Canada ($1,084-million in 1992), $584-million to the United States ($465-million in 1991) and $90-million offshore ($67-million in 1991). Its U.S. facilities had $228-million of sales ($188-million in 1991). 1992 total sales of $1,884-million by product were: fine papers, 36%; newsprint, 14%; market pulp, 9%; packaging, 20%; and construction materials, 21%.

Domtar's research center in Senneville, Quebec, has developed exclusive technology for recycled bleached corrugated cardboard. This will allow tons of old cartons formerly destined for landfill to be turned into writing paper that is indistinguishable from virgin-fibre paper.

Relative strength to TSE300 / Price / Volume (in 1000's of board lots)

Rank (Profit/Revenue/Assets)
980   65   73

Robert Despres
Chairman

Pierre Desjardins
President & C.E.O.

Robert G. Vaux
V.P., Fin., Corp. Dev. & C.F.O

Address
395 De Maisonneuve Blvd. W.
Montreal
PQ
H3A 1L6
(514) 848-5400

Fax: (514) 848-6850
D0002748/G/4.1

DONOHUE INC.

Exchanges	Price (Jun24'93)	19.50	Trailing P/E	nm	Stock Symbol
TM	Trailing Yield (%)	0.00	Trailing EPS	(0.03)	**DHC.A**

Period Ending	Dec92	Dec91	Dec90	Dec89	Dec88
Yearly Statistics					
Price-Close	14.00	12.00	11.50	11.25	13.88
Price-High	14.00	15.25	12.50	16.50	17.00
Price-Low	13.00	10.75	9.50	9.50	13.00
P/E-Close	nm	nm	12.92	8.21	6.28
Dividends per Share	0.00	0.18	0.48	0.48	0.42
Dividend Yield (%)	0.00	1.50	4.17	4.27	3.03
Sales per Share	16.10	14.61	19.01	20.09	21.06
EPS before extra. item	(0.47)	(1.82)	0.89	1.37	2.21
Cash Flow per Share	0.94	1.68	3.20	4.14	5.50
Book Value per Share	10.16	10.31	12.32	11.91	11.02
O/S Common Shares	35,182	32,163	32,163	32,044	31,845
Total Revenue	523,228	482,203	629,744	661,244	671,705
Income before extra.	(14,712)	(58,013)	29,088	44,250	68,691
Cash Flow	30,464	54,114	102,950	132,326	169,152
Debt/Equity	0.64	0.95	0.51	0.67	0.72
Return on Capital (%)	0.49	(8.79)	12.99	17.77	24.73
Ret. on Com. Equity (%)	(4.41)	(16.10)	7.33	11.92	21.66
% Change Profit	74.6	(299.4)	(34.3)	(35.6)	55.2
% Change Revenue	8.5	(23.4)	(4.8)	(1.6)	28.6
% Change Assets	(9.5)	(2.6)	(3.6)	3.2	4.9

Date	EPS	DPS	Tot Rev	Inc Bex
Mar 93	0.18	0.00	135,412	6,349
Dec 92	0.07	0.00	137,223	2,398
Sep 92	(0.18)	0.00	129,378	(5,852)
Jun 92	(0.10)	0.00	139,569	(2,958)
Mar 92	(0.26)	0.00	113,763	(8,300)
Dec 91	(1.20)	0.00	109,983	(38,477)
Sep 91	(0.45)	0.06	103,348	(14,423)
Jun 91	(0.12)	0.06	126,028	(3,773)

Preferred Div. Coverage	0.0	0.0	50.9
Total Div. Coverage	0.0	0.0	1.8
Interest Coverage	0.2	0.0	3.5
Current Ratio	2.1	2.6	3.0
Operating Margin	1.6	0.1	15.1
Asset Turnover	0.7	0.5	0.7
5 YEAR RATIOS (%)			
Return on Capital	9.4	12.8	17.3
Return on Com. Equity	4.1	8.3	13.5
Profit Growth	na	na	7.1
Revenue Growth	0.0	(0.3)	7.7
Asset Growth	(1.7)	1.2	4.8
BALANCE SHEET (000)			
Cash	28,682	45,299	116,437
Current Assets	226,034	287,469	338,376
Net Fixed Assets	545,758	574,573	520,347
Invest's & Advances	3,517	3,517	35,061
Total Assets	795,377	878,834	902,296
Short Term Debt	41,107	46,709	32,948
Current Liabilities	105,625	110,514	113,269
Long Term Debt	191,180	276,073	174,834
Total Liabilities	430,463	538,522	496,912
Total Equity	364,914	340,312	405,384
Total Liab. & Equity	795,377	878,834	902,296
CAPITAL (000)			
Total Debt	232,287	322,782	207,782
Preferred Equity	7,578	8,578	9,295
Common Equity	357,336	331,734	396,089

Business:

DONOHUE INC. is an integrated forest products company. The company produces newsprint, market pulp and lumber at its operations in the province of Quebec. The company markets its products to customers in the United States, Canada, Europe, Asia and South America. Through its subsidiaries, it has arrangements with Normick Perron Inc. and The New York Times Company.

Synopsis:

Donohue is one of the continent's lowest-cost producers of newsprint, woodpulp and lumber. Its gross operating margin has generally been higher than the industry average for the last five years, including each quarter of 1992.

The company increased its overall productivity and reduced manufacturing costs in 1992. The ratio of labor to tonne produced in its newsprint mills remained lower than the industry average: 2.75 personhours per tonne in 1992, compared to 4.2 for the industry in 1991. The company produced 465,000 tonnes of newsprint in 1992 (428,000 in 1991), but the average net selling price was 22% lower than the previous year due to overproduction affecting the entire industry. Newsprint accounted for 39% of 1992 net sales of $520-million.

In 1992, Donohue produced 307,000 tonnes of kraft pulp (257,000 tonnes in 1991), and the average price remained about 2% higher than the previous year. Kraft pulp accounted for 34% of 1992 net sales.

Donohue is the largest lumber producer in eastern Canada. In 1992, it produced 608 million board feet (468 million board feet in 1991). Lumber prices rose significantly throughout the year and continued their upward movement in 1993. During the first quarter ending March 31, 1993, the selling price for lumber increased by more than 50% compared to the first quarter last year. Lumber accounted for 27% of 1992 net sales. Donohue has to renew its timber supply and forest management agreements in the Spring of 1994.

Federal and provincial legislation setting new environmental standards for effluent, atmospheric emissions and sold waste will require Donohue to invest $63-million by 1996.

1992 sales by geographical segment were: the United Sates, 55%; Canada, 27%; and Overseas, 17%.

Rank (Profit/Revenue/Assets)		
907	151	173

Charles-Albert Poissant
Chairman & C.E.O.

Michel Page
President & C.E.O.

Richard Garneau
V.P. Finance

Michel Desbiens
Exec. V.P. & C.O.O.

Address
801 Chemin Saint-Louis
Quebec
PQ
G1S 4W3
(418) 684-7700

Fax: (418) 684-7707
D0004980/G/4.1

FLETCHER CHALLENGE CANADA LIMITED

Exchanges	Price (Jun24'93)	21.75	Trailing P/E	nm	Stock Symbol
TMV	Trailing Yield (%)	0.00	Trailing EPS	(0.67)	**FCC.A**

Period Ending	Jun92	Dec91	Jun91	Dec90	Dec89
Yearly Statistics					
Price-Close	15.38	16.88	18.00	15.63	15.75
Price-High	18.63	18.63	18.50	17.50	20.00
Price-Low	14.00	14.00	12.25	12.25	14.63
P/E-Close	nm	nm	nm	16.98	9.78
Dividends per Share	0.00	0.23	0.40	0.60	0.80
Dividend Yield (%)	0.00	1.36	2.22	3.84	5.08
Sales per Share	15.43	17.27	18.59	19.35	23.48
EPS before extra. item	(0.70)	(0.44)	(0.42)	0.92	1.61
Cash Flow per Share	(0.79)	(0.70)	0.18	1.35	2.96
Book Value per Share	14.30	14.81	14.77	15.39	14.97
O/S Common Shares	77,058	60,186	60,086	59,976	59,961
Total Revenue	1,020,000	1,116,316	1,162,800	1,253,993	1,450,662
Income before extra.	(43,500)	(26,317)	(25,000)	54,892	96,207
Cash Flow	(49,200)	(42,300)	10,700	81,064	176,556
Debt/Equity	0.40	0.69	0.74	0.60	0.58
Return on Capital (%)	(1.57)	0.12	0.13	7.60	12.70
Ret. on Com. Equity (%)	(4.36)	(2.96)	(2.76)	6.03	10.98
% Change Profit	(65.3)	(5.3)	(145.5)	(42.9)	(46.6)
% Change Revenue	(8.6)	(4.0)	(7.3)	(13.6)	(4.7)
% Change Assets	0.5	(4.7)	3.1	2.3	11.0

Preferred Div. Coverage	np	np	np
Total Div. Coverage	na	0.0	0.0
Interest Coverage	0.0	0.0	0.0
Current Ratio	1.6	1.5	1.2
Operating Margin	(9.0)	(7.4)	(4.1)
Asset Turnover	0.5	0.6	0.6
5 YEAR RATIOS (%)			
Return on Capital	3.8	9.5	14.8
Return on Com. Equity	1.4	6.9	12.3
Profit Growth	na	na	na
Revenue Growth	(7.7)	(4.8)	0.9
Asset Growth	2.2	6.9	10.7
BALANCE SHEET (000)			
Cash	4,500	315	25,000
Current Assets	340,500	316,789	359,300
Net Fixed Assets	1,470,200	1,484,650	1,502,500
Invest's & Advances	35,900	35,889	70,600
Total Assets	1,866,100	1,856,913	1,948,600
Short Term Debt	21,300	26,485	65,600
Current Liabilities	213,100	216,287	295,600
Long Term Debt	413,700	591,779	586,400
Total Liabilities	764,200	965,334	1,061,100
Total Equity	1,101,900	891,579	887,500
Total Liab. & Equity	1,866,100	1,856,913	1,948,600
CAPITAL (000)			
Total Debt	435,000	618,264	652,000
Preferred Equity	0	0	0
Common Equity	1,101,900	891,579	887,500

Business:

FLETCHER CHALLENGE CANADA LIMITED, is a forest products company. Its operations are in Western Canada and the United States. Products include lumber, market kraft, pulp, newsprint and ground wood specialties, and lightweight coated paper. The company has markets worldwide. As at April 28, 1993, Fletcher Challenge Ltd. of New Zealand owns a 63% interest, on a fully diluted basis.

Date	EPS	DPS	Tot Rev	Inc Bex
Mar 93	(0.07)	0.00	322,800	(6,700)
Dec 92	(0.06)	0.00	267,700	(4,800)
Sep 92	(0.24)	0.00	207,500	(18,800)
Jun 92	(0.30)	0.00	226,000	(20,100)
Mar 92	(0.40)	0.00	230,000	(24,300)
Dec 91	0.28	0.00	310,500	17,200
Sep 91	(0.27)	0.00	255,800	(16,300)
Jun 91	(0.27)	0.10	276,400	(16,500)

Synopsis:

Fletcher Challenge Canada acquired the Elk Falls pulp, paper and lumber complex in February 1993. This operation has an annual capacity of 500,000 tonnes of newsprint, 200,000 tonnes of market kraft pulp, and other products. The acquisition will more than double the company's newsprint capacity and boost market pulp capacity by 40%.

Fletcher announced in April 1993 that it wants to build a multimillion dollar newsprint recycling mill north of Tuscon, Arizona. Fletcher plans to go ahead with engineering studies and permit applications for the 97-hectare site. If approved, construction could begin in October for completion by the Fall of 1995. The plant would produce 100% recycled newsprint.

For the nine months ending March 31, 1993, the company recorded a net loss of $30-million, compared with a net loss of $24-million for the same period a year ago. However, the previous period's results reflected a non-recurring, after-tax gain of $35-million from the sale of the company's interest in a Quebec forest products company. Excluding the gain from the comparative period, the results represent a $28-million improvement from a year ago.

Sales for the quarter ending March 31, 1993, increased 39% to $319-million from $230-million for the same period of 1992. This increase includes volumes shipped from the Elk Falls complex from the date of its February acquisition.

Sales for the year ended June 30, 1992 (1991) by industry segment were: pulp and paper, $646-million ($739-million); and wood products, $311-million ($376-million). Sales for 1992 (1991) by country of production were: Canada, $643-million ($798-million); and the U.S., $314-million ($317-million).

Effective January 1, 1992, the company changed its fiscal year-end to June 30 from December 31 to coincide with the year-end of its parent, Fletcher Challenge Limited of New Zealand.

Relative strength to TSE300 / Price / Volume (in 1000's of board lots)

Rank (Profit/Revenue/Assets)
951 102 98

Garry Mace
Chairman

Douglas W.G. Whitehead
President & C.E.O.

Keith E. Winrow
Sr. V.P., Finance & Secretary

Address
P.O. Box 10058, Pacific Centre
9th Floor
700 West Georgia Street
Vancouver
BC
V7Y 1J7
(604) 654-4000

B0003889/G/4.2

INTERNATIONAL FOREST PRODUCTS LIMITED

Exchanges	Price (Jun24'93)	15.50	Trailing P/E	20.13	Stock Symbol
T	Trailing Yield (%)	0.00	Trailing EPS	0.77	**IFP.A**

Period Ending	Dec92	Dec91	Dec90	Dec89	Dec88
Yearly Statistics					
Price-Close	10.75	8.50	6.50	7.75	6.38
Price-High	10.88	9.00	9.38	9.38	7.75
Price-Low	7.38	5.50	5.25	5.25	5.00
P/E-Close	97.73	nm	nm	7.38	637.50
Dividends per Share	0.00	0.22	0.23	0.22	0.21
Dividend Yield (%)	0.00	2.55	3.54	2.84	3.29
Sales per Share	14.55	11.05	16.85	21.74	24.96
EPS before extra. item	0.11	(0.94)	(0.69)	1.05	0.01
Cash Flow per Share	1.41	(0.72)	0.21	2.42	1.67
Book Value per Share	5.91	5.47	6.04	6.92	6.19
O/S Common Shares	32,444	29,884	18,972	18,448	16,330
Total Revenue	465,478	254,948	319,159	378,249	403,168
Income before extra.	3,517	(21,672)	(13,031)	19,138	775
Cash Flow	45,101	(16,602)	3,990	42,157	26,859
Debt/Equity	0.58	0.75	0.98	0.64	0.74
Return on Capital (%)	5.11	(10.81)	(4.76)	17.95	7.00
Ret. on Com. Equity (%)	1.98	(15.59)	(10.76)	15.97	(0.09)
% Change Profit	116.2	(66.3)	(168.1)	2,369.4	(96.3)
% Change Revenue	82.6	(20.1)	(15.6)	(6.2)	5.0
% Change Assets	13.3	15.7	1.3	(15.7)	2.2
Preferred Div. Coverage	np	np	np		
Total Div. Coverage	na	0.0	0.0		
Interest Coverage	1.7	0.0	0.0		
Current Ratio	2.2	1.6	1.2		
Operating Margin	4.0	(11.0)	(3.5)		
Asset Turnover	1.3	0.8	1.2		
5 YEAR RATIOS (%)					
Return on Capital	2.9	9.8	18.1		
Return on Com. Equity	(1.7)	3.5	8.7		
Profit Growth	(30.1)	na	na		
Revenue Growth	3.9	(4.8)	4.0		
Asset Growth	2.7	6.3	4.3		
BALANCE SHEET (000)					
Cash	0	0	0		
Current Assets	151,705	98,766	94,136		
Net Fixed Assets	189,920	202,075	165,149		
Invest's & Advances	9,050	8,589	8,441		
Total Assets	351,656	310,298	268,162		
Short Term Debt	28,222	39,473	55,004		
Current Liabilities	69,611	60,242	76,487		
Long Term Debt	83,342	83,670	57,078		
Total Liabilities	160,030	146,775	153,628		
Total Equity	191,626	163,523	114,534		
Total Liab. & Equity	351,656	310,298	268,162		
CAPITAL (000)					
Total Debt	111,564	123,143	112,082		
Preferred Equity	0	0	0		
Common Equity	191,626	163,523	114,534		

Business:

INTERNATIONAL FOREST PRODUCTS LTD. operates seven sawmill and 46 logging operations on the coast and one logging and sawmill operation in the interior of B.C. The company makes a variety of lumber products, including hemlock, balsam fir, western red cedar, cypress and spruce, for markets in North America, Europe and Japan. The firm has secondary markets in China, Africa and Australia.

Date	EPS	DPS	Tot Rev	Inc Bex
Mar 93	0.56	0.00	145,299	18,047
Dec 92	0.18	0.00	142,431	5,799
Sep 92	0.08	0.00	129,963	2,650
Jun 92	(0.05)	0.00	111,216	(1,731)
Mar 92	(0.10)	0.00	82,076	(3,201)
Dec 91	(0.24)	0.21	65,033	(7,130)
Sep 91	(0.23)	0.00	68,972	(5,057)
Jun 91	(0.18)	0.00	62,606	(3,812)

Synopsis:

International Forest Products (Interfor) expects to benefit sooner than the big, integrated companies in the industry when the economy recovers. Unlike the integrated companies it has no pulp-producing operations, and history shows that in an economic recovery lumber companies benefit first.

As a result of the provincial government's decision to reduce timber cutting rights on the British Columbia coast, Interfor closed its Pioneer Lumber division in December 1992. Interfor's annual allowable cut is continually assessed by the government. Since 1991, it has lost 254,000 cubic metres of annual cutting rights under one Tree Farm Licence and four Forest Licences.

Profitability improved throughout 1992 as a result of several factors. During 1992, Interfor integrated into its business two sawmills and twenty logging operations acquired at the end of 1991. This enabled it to increase its lumber production by 62% to 710 million board feet.

Interfor intends to increase its road construction expenditures to $30-million in 1993, and to spend $20-million on logging and sawmill plant and equipment. These expenditures will be financed by cash generated from operations.

Regulations restricting imports of undried lumber are expected to be implemented by the European community in June 1993. Interfor reduced its exports to that market, and renewed the emphasis on higher grade, kiln-dried products.

Percentage contributions to total sales by product line in 1992 (1991) were: lumber, 73% (70%); logs, 18% (20%); wood chips and other byproducts, 6% (9%); sawmill custom cutting revenue, 1% (1%); and contract helicopter logging revenue, 2% (-). Percentages of lumber sales to major markets in 1992 (1991) were: Pacific Rim, 30% (36%); the U.S., 29% (17%); Canada, 22% (18%); U.K. and Europe, 17% (22%); and other, 2% (7%).

Relative strength to TSE300 / Price / Volume (in 1000's of board lots) chart, 1990–1993.

Rank (Profit/Revenue/Assets)
294   164   253

William L. Sauder
Chairman & C.E.O.

R.M. Sitter
President & C.O.O.

G.J. Friesen
V.P., Finance & Secretary

Address
P.O. Box 49114
Bentall Postal Station
3500 - 1055 Dunsmuir Street
Vancouver
BC
V7X 1H7
(604) 681-3221
Fax: (604) 688-0313
W0002647/G/4.2

MACMILLAN BLOEDEL LIMITED

Exchanges	Price (Jun24'93)	23.25	Trailing P/E	nm	Stock Symbol
TMVQ	Trailing Yield (%)	2.58	Trailing EPS	0.00	**MB**

Period Ending	Dec92	Dec91	Dec90	Dec89	Dec88
Yearly Statistics					
Price-Close	16.88	18.50	16.75	18.13	18.00
Price-High	21.13	22.63	18.87	21.38	23.87
Price-Low	15.63	15.50	14.25	16.75	16.50
P/E-Close	nm	nm	45.27	7.99	5.84
Dividends per Share	0.60	0.60	0.80	0.80	0.90
Dividend Yield (%)	3.56	3.24	4.78	4.41	5.00
Sales per Share	27.15	25.48	29.26	31.89	31.91
EPS before extra. item	(0.52)	(0.98)	0.37	2.27	3.08
Cash Flow per Share	1.31	(0.27)	1.75	3.48	4.94
Book Value per Share	12.01	13.37	14.39	14.70	13.41
O/S Common Shares	112,629	111,302	102,650	102,650	102,650
Total Revenue	3,066,600	2,754,600	3,014,500	3,285,200	3,277,800
Income before extra.	(48,800)	(93,400)	50,800	246,700	329,800
Cash Flow	146,600	(29,000)	179,600	357,300	506,600
Debt/Equity	1.24	0.96	0.78	0.57	0.42
Return on Capital (%)	1.92	(3.07)	4.43	18.02	26.13
Ret. on Com. Equity (%)	(4.25)	(7.30)	2.36	16.02	24.34
% Change Profit	47.8	(283.9)	(79.4)	(25.2)	17.5
% Change Revenue	11.3	(8.6)	(8.2)	0.2	4.0
% Change Assets	2.2	6.9	9.2	18.9	9.4

Preferred Div. Coverage	0.0	0.0	3.3
Total Div. Coverage	0.0	0.0	0.5
Interest Coverage	0.4	0.0	1.3
Current Ratio	2.2	2.1	2.1
Operating Margin	2.2	(4.3)	3.0
Asset Turnover	0.8	0.7	0.8
5 YEAR RATIOS (%)			
Return on Capital	9.5	14.6	18.0
Return on Com. Equity	6.2	11.9	15.6
Profit Growth	na	na	3.3
Revenue Growth	(0.6)	1.7	5.0
Asset Growth	9.1	11.6	9.0
BALANCE SHEET (000)			
Cash	139,700	227,600	78,500
Current Assets	1,198,500	1,162,700	992,000
Net Fixed Assets	2,034,600	1,943,300	2,065,800
Invest's & Advances	672,000	713,900	516,800
Total Assets	3,905,100	3,819,900	3,574,600
Short Term Debt	131,400	160,400	79,200
Current Liabilities	539,600	562,100	469,800
Long Term Debt	1,664,900	1,367,600	1,166,000
Total Liabilities	2,456,500	2,220,300	1,977,700
Total Equity	1,448,600	1,599,600	1,596,900
Total Liab. & Equity	3,905,100	3,819,900	3,574,600
CAPITAL (000)			
Total Debt	1,796,300	1,528,000	1,245,200
Preferred Equity	96,200	111,900	119,500
Common Equity	1,352,400	1,487,700	1,477,400

Business:

MACMILLAN BLOEDEL LTD. is one of North America's largest forest products companies, with integrated operations in Canada and the United States as well as major investments in Canada and Europe. Its products, which are marketed throughout the world, include lumber, panelboards, kraft pulp, newsprint, groundwood printing papers, fine papers, and containerboard.

Date	EPS	DPS	Tot Rev	Inc Bex
Mar 93	0.40	0.15	903,600	46,300
Dec 92	(0.17)	0.15	812,700	(16,500)
Sep 92	(0.15)	0.15	755,800	(14,200)
Jun 92	(0.08)	0.15	780,300	(7,100)
Mar 92	(0.12)	0.15	719,500	(11,000)
Dec 91	(0.55)	0.15	658,400	(56,400)
Sep 91	(0.29)	0.15	671,800	(29,500)
Jun 91	(0.13)	0.15	740,500	(11,300)

Synopsis:

MacMillan Bloedel is investigating the possibility of adopting a shareholder rights plan now that the company is widely held. The plan would buy it time in the event of a hostile takeover attempt. MacMillan's main shareholder, Noranda Forest, sold its 49% ownership in the company on February 25, 1993.

MacMillan issued two million common shares for $40-million on April 16, 1993, to acquire an 81% interest in American Cemwood Corp. American Cemwood, which manufactures fire-resistant cement-fibre roofing materials that resemble cedar shakes, had 1992 sales of $25-million (U.S.) and a net profit of $5-million.

One of MacMillan's affiliates, N.V. Koninklijke KNP (KNP), completed a merger with two other companies on March 9, 1993. MacMillan's fully diluted interest in the merged company fell from 30% to 16%. KNP is a major producer of coated and uncoated specialty printing paper in the European Economic Community. The merged company has $7-billion in sales annually.

MacMillan sold its 50% interest in UK Corrugated during the first quarter of 1993, resulting in a non-taxable gain of $39-million. For the period ending March 31, 1993, operating earnings improved $47-million, from a profit of $9-million last year to $56-million this year. The improved earnings are attributed to excellent markets for building materials and cost cutting over the past two years.

1992 sales (contribution to earnings) by segment were: building materials, 54% (105%); pulp and paper, 27% (-10%); containerboard and packaging, 17% (-3%); and other, 2% (8%). Contributions to 1992 (1991) sales by country were: the U.S., 47% (44%); Canada, 21% (44%); Japan and the Orient, 19% (8%); U.K. and Europe, 9% (4%), and other, 4% (-).

Rank (Profit/Revenue/Assets)
954　42　56

Raymond V. Smith
Chairman

Robert B. Findlay
President & C.E.O.

A.N. Grunder
Sr. V.P., Finance & Admin.

R.D Tuckey
Exec. V.P., Operations

Address
925 West Georgia Street
Vancouver
BC
V6C 3L2
(604) 661-8000

M0000374/G/4.2

NORANDA FOREST INC.

Exchanges	Price (Jun24'93)	11.50	Trailing P/E	nm	Stock Symbol
TMV	Trailing Yield (%)	3.48	Trailing EPS	(0.97)	**NF**

Period Ending	Dec92	Dec91	Dec90	Dec89	Dec88
Yearly Statistics					
Price-Close	7.60	8.75	8.00	13.88	14.63
Price-High	9.50	10.50	14.50	16.75	20.50
Price-Low	6.38	6.88	7.13	13.25	13.25
P/E-Close	nm	nm	nm	8.07	5.81
Dividends per Share	0.40	0.40	0.70	0.80	0.70
Dividend Yield (%)	5.26	4.57	8.75	5.76	4.79
Sales per Share	34.59	36.79	45.80	49.34	47.83
EPS before extra. item	(0.77)	(2.01)	(1.16)	1.72	2.52
Cash Flow per Share	1.25	(0.88)	1.06	5.55	7.30
Book Value per Share	7.03	8.31	11.16	13.01	12.18
O/S Common Shares	132,692	127,283	101,964	98,682	98,657
Total Revenue	4,494,000	4,133,000	4,565,000	4,929,000	4,780,000
Income before extra.	(88,000)	(209,000)	(95,000)	189,000	263,000
Cash Flow	162,000	(99,000)	105,000	548,000	720,000
Debt/Equity	2.78	2.31	1.97	1.34	0.86
Return on Capital (%)	2.11	(3.76)	1.80	16.62	24.09
Ret. on Com. Equity (%)	(10.05)	(20.49)	(9.50)	13.68	22.11
% Change Profit	57.9	(120.0)	(150.3)	(28.1)	29.6
% Change Revenue	8.7	(9.5)	(7.4)	3.1	5.8
% Change Assets	0.9	1.1	6.9	23.4	9.4

Preferred Div. Coverage	0.0	0.0	0.0
Total Div. Coverage	0.0	0.0	0.0
Interest Coverage	0.4	0.0	0.3
Current Ratio	1.8	1.3	1.3
Operating Margin	2.2	(4.6)	1.7
Asset Turnover	0.7	0.7	0.8
5 YEAR RATIOS (%)			
Return on Capital	8.2	11.5	na
Return on Com. Equity	(0.8)	5.9	na
Profit Growth	na	na	na
Revenue Growth	(0.1)	2.8	na
Asset Growth	8.0	11.1	na
BALANCE SHEET (000)			
Cash	140,000	238,000	84,000
Current Assets	1,643,000	1,548,000	1,434,000
Net Fixed Assets	3,614,000	3,639,000	3,870,000
Invest's & Advances	766,000	791,000	652,000
Total Assets	6,076,000	6,020,000	5,956,000
Short Term Debt	317,000	596,000	476,000
Current Liabilities	932,000	1,174,000	1,067,000
Long Term Debt	2,835,000	2,311,000	2,159,000
Total Liabilities	4,943,000	4,762,000	4,618,000
Total Equity	1,133,000	1,258,000	1,338,000
Total Liab. & Equity	6,076,000	6,020,000	5,956,000
CAPITAL (000)			
Total Debt	3,152,000	2,907,000	2,635,000
Preferred Equity	200,000	200,000	200,000
Common Equity	933,000	1,058,000	1,138,000

Business:

NORANDA FOREST INC. is one of Canada's largest forest products companies with operations across North America and in the United Kingdom. Products include lumber and building materials, paper and pulp. The company markets its products worldwide. Noranda Inc. of Toronto holds 83% of the company's outstanding common shares.

Date	EPS	DPS	Tot Rev	Inc Bex
Mar 93	(0.41)	0.10	388,000	(52,000)
Dec 92	(0.22)	0.10	1,190,000	(26,000)
Sep 92	(0.16)	0.10	1,124,000	(17,000)
Jun 92	(0.18)	0.10	1,148,000	(21,000)
Mar 92	(0.21)	0.10	1,051,000	(24,000)
Dec 91	(0.67)	0.10	985,000	(78,000)
Sep 91	(0.48)	0.10	1,022,000	(51,000)
Jun 91	(0.45)	0.10	1,096,000	(42,000)

Synopsis:

Noranda Forest expects that the February 1993 sale of its 49% interest in MacMillan Bloedel will enable the company to improve its existing asset base and make profitable new investments for the future. The company is looking at building a new oriented strand board (OSB) mill in the southern United States, which could cost between $70-million (U.S.) and $90-million (U.S.). OSB, which is fast replacing plywood in home flooring and roofing, reached record price levels this year.

Noranda Forest received a $333-million payment in February for the sale of its MacMillan Bloedel stake, and will receive two more payments of $319-million each in 1994 and 1995, for a total of $971-million. The company took a $58-million charge in the first quarter of 1993 to reflect the present value of the future installments. Almost all of the charge will be recovered through amortization as the installments are received.

If the sale of MacMillan Bloedel had occurred on December 31, 1991, Noranda Forests's 1992 net loss, on a pro forma basis, would have been $24-million compared to the reported loss of $88-million. The improved results would be attributable to the elimination of the company's share of MacMillan's 1992 losses, to the saving on interest expense from the first installment of proceeds from the sale, and to imputed interest on the outstanding installment receipts.

Noranda Forest recorded its best quarter in three years as operating earnings in the first three months of 1993 increased to $32-million from $1-million for the same period last year. Strong demand and record high prices for lumber and panel products were the main reasons for the improved results. This segment accounted for 50% of sales during this quarter.

The breakdown of 1992 net sales of $4,478-million by product were: building materials, 50%; communication papers, 28%; pulp, 8%; paperboard packaging, 12%; and other, 2%.

Rank (Profit/Revenue/Assets)		
968	29	38

Alfred Powis
Chairman

K. Linn Macdonald
President & C.E.O.

Ian M. Young
Sr. V.P., Finance & C.F.O.

Address
Suite 4414, P.O. Box 7
Toronto Dominion Bank Tower
Toronto Dominion Centre
Toronto
ON
M5K 1A1
(416) 982-7444
Fax: (416) 982-7396
N0001251/G/4.1

REPAP ENTERPRISES INC.

Exchanges	Price (Jun24'93)	4.85	Trailing P/E	nm	Stock Symbol
TMVQ	Trailing Yield (%)	0.00	Trailing EPS	(2.62)	**RPP**

Period Ending	Dec92	Dec91	Dec90	Dec89	Dec88
Yearly Statistics					
Price-Close	2.10	5.25	5.13	9.88	11.50
Price-High	6.88	8.75	10.00	14.13	16.75
Price-Low	1.51	3.80	4.90	8.50	10.25
P/E-Close	nm	nm	85.42	5.52	6.43
Dividends per Share	0.00	0.00	0.21	0.28	0.22
Dividend Yield (%)	0.00	0.00	4.10	2.84	1.91
Sales per Share	13.40	18.08	21.19	21.28	18.07
EPS before extra. item	(2.77)	(3.47)	0.06	1.79	1.79
Cash Flow per Share	(1.95)	(2.49)	1.89	4.47	4.32
Book Value per Share	3.27	6.20	9.69	9.82	8.42
O/S Common Shares	84,394	51,949	51,949	52,094	51,730
Total Revenue	1,014,100	939,800	1,117,900	1,118,200	947,200
Income before extra.	(209,900)	(180,200)	3,100	93,100	92,800
Cash Flow	(147,800)	(129,500)	98,100	232,100	223,700
Debt/Equity	4.94	3.99	2.62	2.26	2.48
Return on Capital (%)	(5.54)	(5.96)	4.65	10.96	16.30
Ret. on Com. Equity (%)	(70.15)	(43.66)	0.61	19.66	23.03
% Change Profit	(16.5)	(5,912.9)	(96.7)	0.3	63.7
% Change Revenue	7.9	(15.9)	(0.1)	18.1	11.3
% Change Assets	6.8	0.4	10.7	23.0	47.5

Preferred Div. Coverage	na	na	na
Total Div. Coverage	na	na	0.3
Interest Coverage	0.0	0.0	0.5
Current Ratio	1.3	1.3	1.5
Operating Margin	(8.0)	(8.3)	9.4
Asset Turnover	0.3	0.3	0.4
5 YEAR RATIOS (%)			
Return on Capital	4.1	8.5	11.8
Return on Com. Equity	(14.1)	3.7	14.6
Profit Growth	na	na	1.9
Revenue Growth	3.6	11.5	23.4
Asset Growth	16.5	19.6	29.3
BALANCE SHEET (000)			
Cash	26,600	36,500	23,100
Current Assets	422,700	408,600	412,000
Net Fixed Assets	2,461,800	2,457,800	2,545,100
Invest's & Advances	28,400	27,800	30,800
Total Assets	3,308,600	3,097,200	3,085,500
Short Term Debt	29,500	36,500	60,200
Current Liabilities	336,000	307,000	276,800
Long Term Debt	2,016,500	1,799,500	1,618,900
Total Liabilities	2,894,800	2,637,400	2,444,600
Total Equity	413,800	459,800	640,900
Total Liab. & Equity	3,308,600	3,097,200	3,085,500
CAPITAL (000)			
Total Debt	2,046,000	1,836,000	1,679,100
Preferred Equity	137,600	137,600	137,600
Common Equity	276,200	322,200	503,300

Business:

REPAP ENTERPRISES INC. is a forest products company. Its products include high-quality coated paper for magazines, catalogues, inserts, coupons and brochures, and northern bleached softwood kraft pulp used for quality fine papers. Repap has operations in Wisconsin, Manitoba, New Brunswick and British Columbia and markets in North America, Europe and Japan.

Date	EPS	DPS	Tot Rev	Inc Bex
Mar 93	(0.64)	0.00	308,500	(54,200)
Dec 92	(1.13)	0.00	252,200	(95,000)
Sep 92	(0.41)	0.00	270,300	(34,500)
Jun 92	(0.44)	0.00	256,000	(35,800)
Mar 92	(0.86)	0.00	242,700	(44,600)
Dec 91	(1.66)	0.00	214,500	(86,200)
Sep 91	(0.81)	0.00	234,900	(41,900)
Jun 91	(0.67)	0.00	251,100	(34,600)

Synopsis:

Repap Enterprises expects to be cash positive by the third quarter of 1993 owing to a number of restructurings and refinancings that are under way to ease its $1.8-billion debt load. The company has a debt-to-equity ratio of more than four to one. The major portion of its debt is a result of a six-year, $1.6-billion investment to construct three world-class coated paper machines. The company plans to transform the project financings of its coated paper expansion, which have terms of seven to 10 years, to better match the 20 to 25-year life expectancy of these machines.

Repap completed its conversion in 1992 to acid-free paper making at its New Brunswick coated paper mill where the last of the new machines was put in place in 1989. During the first quarter of 1993, coated paper revenues increased 20% to $198-million from the same period last year. Shipments of coated paper totaled 197,000 short tons, up 14% from first quarter 1992 shipments. Repap hopes to realize an 11% price increase for this product in 1993 through increasing list prices and reducing discounts.

Lumber shipments totaled 118 million board feet, up 45% from the 81 million board feet shipped during the first quarter of 1992, largely a result of the $20-million acquisition in 1992 of the Carnaby sawmill in British Columbia which increased annual capacity by 170 million board feet. Pulp shipments fell 21% from first quarter of 1992 to 90,000 metric tons. Even though the demand and supply balance in world pulp markets has begun to stabilize, producer inventories remain high.

Percentage contribution to net sales (operating income) in 1992 by product segment was: pulp and lumber, 30% (-40%); paper, 70% (-42%); corporate, NA (-18%). Contributions to net sales (operating income) in 1992 by geographic region were: Canadian operations, 55% (-105%); and U.S. operations, 45% (5%). Contributions to net sales from Canadian operations by market destination were: the U.S., 34%; Europe, 26%; Asia, 23%; other export sales, 3%; and Canada, 14%.

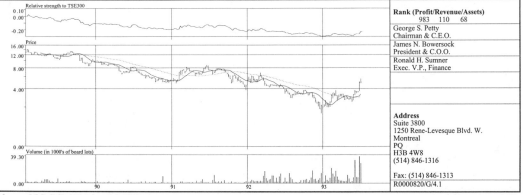

Rank (Profit/Revenue/Assets)		
983	110	68

George S. Petty
Chairman & C.E.O.

James N. Bowersock
President & C.O.O.

Ronald H. Sumner
Exec. V.P., Finance

Address
Suite 3800
1250 Rene-Levesque Blvd. W.
Montreal
PQ
H3B 4W8
(514) 846-1316

Fax: (514) 846-1313
R0000820/G/4.1

ROLLAND INC.

Exchanges	Price (Jun24'93)	6.00	Trailing P/E	nm	Stock Symbol
TM	Trailing Yield (%)	0.00	Trailing EPS	(2.03)	**RL**

Period Ending	Dec92	Dec91	Dec90	Dec89	Dec88
Yearly Statistics					
Price-Close	5.00	7.63	8.38	10.50	12.50
Price-High	8.00	11.50	11.00	16.50	12.50
Price-Low	4.25	7.50	6.75	9.50	9.25
P/E-Close	nm	nm	22.04	nm	7.72
Dividends per Share	0.00	0.05	0.00	0.41	0.54
Dividend Yield (%)	0.00	0.66	0.00	3.86	4.32
Sales per Share	45.86	81.98	108.83	118.77	120.75
EPS before extra. item	(2.60)	(2.09)	0.38	(2.63)	1.62
Cash Flow per Share	(1.24)	(1.89)	(1.10)	0.13	3.89
Book Value per Share	6.59	11.04	13.20	12.94	15.99
O/S Common Shares	7,629	3,695	3,695	3,695	3,687
Total Revenue	259,192	305,692	415,739	441,352	447,768
Income before extra.	(9,877)	(7,726)	1,461	(9,682)	6,021
Cash Flow	(7,020)	(6,994)	(4,052)	484	14,325
Debt/Equity	1.41	1.28	1.11	1.47	1.09
Return on Capital (%)	(7.36)	(3.23)	4.62	(5.99)	13.65
Ret. on Com. Equity (%)	(21.82)	(17.38)	2.90	(18.25)	10.47
% Change Profit	(27.8)	(628.8)	115.1	(260.8)	79.6
% Change Revenue	(15.2)	(26.5)	(5.8)	(1.4)	14.9
% Change Assets	23.9	(15.5)	(9.4)	(6.4)	12.3

Business:

ROLLAND INC. is engaged in the manufacturing and distribution of fine and specialty papers. The company makes well over 100 grades of high quality fine papers from all-cotton to chemical pulp grades and to recycled grades used for commercial printing, reprography, business forms, envelopes and special applications. Rolland has paper distribution operations in Canada and the United States.

Date	EPS	DPS	Tot Rev	Inc Bex
Mar 93	0.02	0.00	72,252	143
Dec 92	(0.94)	0.00	62,992	(3,789)
Sep 92	(0.74)	0.00	62,054	(2,712)
Jun 92	(0.37)	0.00	65,698	(1,348)
Mar 92	(0.55)	0.00	68,448	(2,028)
Dec 91	(1.12)	0.00	70,866	(4,143)
Sep 91	(0.69)	0.00	72,088	(2,536)
Jun 91	(0.36)	0.06	77,512	(1,360)

Preferred Div. Coverage	0.0	0.0	24.8
Total Div. Coverage	0.0	0.0	24.8
Interest Coverage	0.0	0.0	0.6
Current Ratio	0.9	1.0	1.5
Operating Margin	(2.0)	(1.1)	1.0
Asset Turnover	1.8	2.5	2.8
5 YEAR RATIOS (%)			
Return on Capital	0.3	3.8	8.0
Return on Com. Equity	(8.8)	(3.2)	3.2
Profit Growth	na	na	(22.5)
Revenue Growth	(7.9)	(2.5)	6.5
Asset Growth	(0.1)	(2.2)	6.7
BALANCE SHEET (000)			
Cash	0	0	0
Current Assets	68,332	67,963	87,967
Net Fixed Assets	59,957	37,872	41,295
Invest's & Advances	7,189	9,638	9,631
Total Assets	148,141	119,574	141,502
Short Term Debt	55,691	48,532	30,210
Current Liabilities	76,826	67,812	58,542
Long Term Debt	17,241	5,372	25,413
Total Liabilities	96,478	77,367	91,314
Total Equity	51,663	42,207	50,188
Total Liab. & Equity	148,141	119,574	141,502
CAPITAL (000)			
Total Debt	72,932	53,904	55,623
Preferred Equity	1,399	1,399	1,399
Common Equity	50,264	40,808	48,789

Synopsis:

Control of Rolland's voting shares was acquired by Cascades in October 1992. A major reorganization plan was initiated which included the sale of Desencrage Cascades (1988), a subsidiary of Cascades, to Rolland for $29.5-million. The sale was paid through Rolland shares and a $9.8-million promissory note maturing on December 31, 1994. Desencrage is seen as a welcome addition to the company because its plant in Breakeyville, Quebec, produces de-inked kraft pulp. The company believes that this product will help it to meet the growing demand for uncoated fine papers made from recycled fibre, a market that is growing by 10% to 20% a year.

Rolland hopes to become a leader in recycled fine paper. By the introduction of new products in 1992, the company increased the proportion of recycled papers in its total production to 35% compared with 24% in 1991. This proportion is expected to reach 43% in 1993, and to exceed 90% by 1996.

For the 1992 fiscal year ending December 31, 1992, Rolland posted a consolidated net loss of $10-million, largely owing to: a drop in average selling prices; a $2.5-million share in the loss of PWA Rolland Decor; and a non-recurring loss of $600,000 related to the disposal of the business assets of Select Robinson.

First quarter results for 1993 mark a return to profitability. Sales increased 5.6% to $72-million, compared to $68-million for the same period last year. This return to profitability is mainly a result of cost-costing measures that reduced the 1992 cost structure by $13-million, and to the contribution of Desencrage whose earnings have been consolidated with those of the company for this period.

Sales outside Canada are mainly in the U.S. and represent $53-million ($61-million in 1991) of the company's 1992 net sales of $260-million (papers division, $83 million; and distribution division, $177-million).

Relative strength to TSE300

Price

Volume (in 1000's of board lots)

Rank (Profit/Revenue/Assets)
887   238   356

Lucien G. Rolland
Chairman

Roger A. Ashby
President & C.E.O.

Address
2000 McGill College Avenue
Suite 1400
Montreal
PQ
H3A 3H3
(514) 289-1779

Fax: (514) 289-9349
R0002304/G/4.1

SLOCAN FOREST PRODUCTS LTD.

Exchanges	Price (Jun24'93)	23.62	Trailing P/E	17.63	Stock Symbol
T	Trailing Yield (%)	0.66	Trailing EPS	1.34	**SFF**

Period Ending	Dec92	Dec91	Dec90	Dec89	Dec88
Yearly Statistics					
Price-Close	11.88	5.88	4.70	7.25	5.00
Price-High	12.00	7.25	8.50	7.75	5.31
Price-Low	5.88	4.40	4.45	5.00	4.38
P/E-Close	25.27	nm	nm	7.47	4.51
Dividends per Share	0.10	0.09	0.18	0.16	0.13
Dividend Yield (%)	0.84	1.53	3.83	2.21	2.50
Sales per Share	19.04	15.43	18.36	18.48	17.22
EPS before extra. item	0.47	(1.14)	(0.12)	0.97	1.11
Cash Flow per Share	3.54	1.03	1.71	2.46	2.85
Book Value per Share	4.59	4.21	5.46	5.78	4.98
O/S Common Shares	13,534	13,486	10,829	10,761	10,695
Total Revenue	257,574	192,826	199,346	198,570	184,736
Income before extra.	6,369	(14,234)	(1,319)	10,404	11,887
Cash Flow	47,888	12,790	18,591	26,355	30,482
Debt/Equity	1.32	1.91	1.44	0.85	0.25
Return on Capital (%)	15.54	(5.71)	4.48	21.42	32.08
Ret. on Com. Equity (%)	10.71	(24.56)	(2.18)	18.03	24.74
% Change Profit	144.7	(979.2)	(112.7)	(12.5)	0.2
% Change Revenue	33.6	(3.3)	0.4	7.5	23.5
% Change Assets	3.5	9.6	12.4	59.4	8.7

Date	EPS	DPS	Tot Rev	Inc Bex
Mar 93	0.88	0.06	97,386	11,979
Dec 92	0.21	0.05	70,764	2,837
Sep 92	0.08	0.05	68,754	1,090
Jun 92	0.17	0.00	61,330	2,359
Mar 92	0.01	0.00	56,727	83
Dec 91	(0.44)	0.05	46,687	(5,770)
Sep 91	(0.32)	0.05	50,168	(4,215)
Jun 91	(0.01)	0.00	56,028	(133)

Preferred Div. Coverage	np	np	np	
Total Div. Coverage	4.7	0.0	0.0	
Interest Coverage	3.7	0.0	0.8	
Current Ratio	1.0	0.9	1.1	
Operating Margin	12.9	(0.1)	3.1	
Asset Turnover	1.2	0.9	1.0	
5 YEAR RATIOS (%)				
Return on Capital	13.6	19.6	32.8	
Return on Com. Equity	5.3	10.5	26.3	
Profit Growth	(11.7)	na	na	
Revenue Growth	11.4	17.3	28.7	
Asset Growth	17.1	33.4	42.5	
BALANCE SHEET (000)				
Cash	0	0	0	
Current Assets	72,700	62,882	58,294	
Net Fixed Assets	101,012	106,744	111,138	
Invest's & Advances	43,736	40,257	21,664	
Total Assets	218,371	210,996	192,442	
Short Term Debt	33,743	38,833	24,217	
Current Liabilities	74,422	66,308	52,019	
Long Term Debt	48,152	69,860	60,892	
Total Liabilities	156,290	154,176	133,355	
Total Equity	62,081	56,820	59,087	
Total Liab. & Equity	218,371	210,996	192,442	
CAPITAL (000)				
Total Debt	81,895	108,693	85,109	
Preferred Equity	0	0	0	
Common Equity	62,081	56,820	59,087	

Business:

SLOCAN FOREST PRODUCTS LTD., through its subsidiary and affiliated companies, participates in the harvesting, manufacturing and marketing of lumber, pulp, plywood and wood chips which are sold throughout the world. The principal markets for these products are North America, Asia and Europe. Slocan has a 50% interest in a plywood plant in New Westminster, B.C., and an 85.8% interest in a pulp mill in B.C.

Synopsis:

Slocan Forest Products acquired the Plateau sawmill at Vanderhoof, B.C., in May 1993, for cash proceeds of $72-million, including the value of inventories. In order to assist in the financing of the transaction, Slocan completed an issue of three million Special Warrants for a total of $32-million. The balance of the purchase price will be financed with operating and term debt.

Adding the Plateau operation to existing operations will increase Slocan's timber resources and manufacturing capacity by 25%. The Plateau sawmill and woodlands operation produce 275 million board feet annually, and 170,000 bone dry units of wood chips. Slocan will also acquire cutting rights to 619,000 cubic metres of timber in the Prince George, B.C., timber supply area. As a result of the acquisition, Slocan's total assets will increase from $220-million to in excess of $280-million.

Slocan implemented a significant accounting change effective January 1, 1993, driven by its 80% ownership in Fibreco Pulp. Slocan wants to divest down to 50% ownership, but cannot predict when this will be accomplished given adverse pulp market conditions. As a consequence, it elected to consolidate the Fibreco Pulp joint venture financial statements with those of Slocan. On a pro forma basis, had Slocan accounted for its investment in the joint venture on a consolidated basis, the financials for 1992 would have been: assets, $398-million; sales, $305-million; earnings from operations, $31-million; and net earnings, $6-million.

Consolidated net earnings for the first quarter ending March 31, 1993, totaled $12-million. The solid wood segment (lumber and plywood) contributed $15-million, and affiliates, chiefly Fibreco Pulp, lost $3-million. Net consolidated sales of $97-million in the first quarter of 1993 included $12-million from Fibreco. Percentages of sales in 1992 (1991) by geographic market were: the U.S., 56% (40%); Canada, 36% (45%); and other, 8% (15%). All the operations of Slocan are based in British Columbia.

Relative strength to TSE300 / Price / Volume (in 1000's of board lots)

Rank (Profit/Revenue/Assets)
227 239 310

Irving K. Barber
Chairman, President & C.E.O.

Ronald D. Price
Sr. V.P., C.F.O. & Secretary

George A. Edgson
Sr. V.P., Operations

Address
240 - 10451 Shellbridge Way
Richmond
BC
V6X 2W8
(604) 278-7311

01000475/G/4.2

TEMBEC INC.

Exchanges	Price (Jun24'93)	9.37	Trailing P/E	nm	Stock Symbol
TM	Trailing Yield (%)	0.00	Trailing EPS	(1.34)	**TBC.A**

Period Ending	Sep92	Sep91	Sep90	Sep89	Sep88
Yearly Statistics					
Price-Close	10.88	9.25	9.00	11.50	7.75
Price-High	11.25	10.63	10.50	11.63	9.38
Price-Low	8.00	8.75	8.75	7.25	4.00
P/E-Close	nm	nm	8.33	5.13	4.21
Dividends per Share	0.00	0.00	0.00	0.00	0.00
Dividend Yield (%)	0.00	0.00	0.00	0.00	0.00
Sales per Share	15.93	14.52	16.24	18.28	17.95
EPS before extra. item	(1.36)	(1.98)	1.08	2.24	1.84
Cash Flow per Share	0.05	0.98	2.37	3.98	3.26
Book Value per Share	8.75	10.06	12.10	11.02	8.81
O/S Common Shares	28,022	17,767	17,581	15,353	15,249
Total Revenue	343,417	262,790	277,866	287,313	257,835
Income before extra.	(28,821)	(34,997)	18,374	34,214	25,950
Cash Flow	971	17,319	39,104	60,836	46,109
Debt/Equity	1.51	1.22	0.70	0.82	0.91
Return on Capital (%)	(3.70)	(6.23)	10.77	22.91	22.06
Ret. on Com. Equity (%)	(13.64)	(17.88)	9.62	22.54	23.14
% Change Profit	17.6	(290.5)	(46.3)	31.8	224.3
% Change Revenue	30.7	(5.4)	(3.3)	11.4	41.2
% Change Assets	75.3	16.5	17.2	23.0	23.6

Preferred Div. Coverage	0.0	na	na
Total Div. Coverage	0.0	na	na
Interest Coverage	0.0	0.0	2.3
Current Ratio	2.6	2.4	2.1
Operating Margin	(4.4)	3.8	10.6
Asset Turnover	0.3	0.4	0.5
5 YEAR RATIOS (%)			
Return on Capital	9.2	12.3	13.2
Return on Com. Equity	4.8	9.7	11.7
Profit Growth	na	na	37.5
Revenue Growth	13.4	17.5	20.8
Asset Growth	29.4	30.4	27.3
BALANCE SHEET (000)			
Cash	21,466	40,784	24,676
Current Assets	234,476	168,844	144,984
Net Fixed Assets	746,226	406,556	313,705
Invest's & Advances	40,054	17,862	53,341
Total Assets	1,056,622	602,798	517,357
Short Term Debt	30,406	23,117	30,049
Current Liabilities	91,544	71,343	69,387
Long Term Debt	393,783	235,438	133,018
Total Liabilities	776,367	390,739	284,663
Total Equity	280,255	212,059	232,694
Total Liab. & Equity	1,056,622	602,798	517,357
CAPITAL (000)			
Total Debt	424,189	258,555	163,067
Preferred Equity	34,965	33,302	20,000
Common Equity	245,290	178,757	212,694

Business:

TEMBEC INC. is a fully integrated forest products company. Tembec's products are sold in over 50 countries and include softwood and hardwood lumber, market sulfite pulp, high-yield chlorine-free pulp, lignin-derived co-products, paperboard, as well as recycled fine paper.

Date	EPS	DPS	Tot Rev	Inc Bex
Mar 93	(0.59)	0.00	94,718	(16,451)
Dec 92	(0.39)	0.00	92,973	(10,962)
Sep 92	(0.23)	0.00	95,008	(6,058)
Jun 92	(0.13)	0.00	99,913	(4,304)
Mar 92	(0.46)	0.00	82,249	(8,850)
Dec 91	(0.54)	0.00	59,311	(9,609)
Sep 91	(0.29)	0.00	70,902	(5,231)
Jun 91	(1.81)	0.00	65,219	(31,933)

Synopsis:

Tembec wrote off its investment in U.S. subsidiary Patriot Paper, which filed for bankruptcy on March 17, 1993. The company also took a provision for potential liabilities. Patriot operated a 70,000 tonne per year recycled paper mill in Boston, and incurred persistent losses due to poor market conditions and high operating costs associated with the use of post consumer raw material supply. Patriot was Tembec's first involvement in manufacturing recycled products. It was also Tembec's first U.S. operation. All the company's other mills are located in Canada.

Tembec incurred a net loss of $7-million for the second quarter ending March 31, 1993, from discontinued operations at Patriot. The net loss from continuing operations for this period was $9.4-million. Tembec essentially completed its capital program during this period, at a total cost of $17-million, and its focus will now be on asset optimization.

Hydro-Quebec signed a $400-million agreement in January 1993 to purchase electricity under a cogeneration deal with Tembec. Under the 15-year deal, a $150-million power station will be built in Temiscaming, Quebec. Tembec will pay for the natural gas-fired plant, and the electricity produced will be purchased by Hydro-Quebec, while the steam will be used by Tembec's cardboard factory.

During 1992, Tembec initiated a program aimed at producing totally chlorine-free dissolving pulp (TFC). This makes Tembec the first North American producer of TFC dissolving grades.

Percentages of consolidated gross sales (gross profit) by industry segment for 1992 were: pulp, 42% (11%); wood products, 29% (90%); paper products, 7% (3%); paperboard products, 17% (-5%); converted products, 4% (-5); and other products, 1% (6%). Gross sales in 1992 by geographic area were: Canada, 31%; the United States, 39%; Pacific Rim and India, 4%; and United Kingdom, Europe and other, 26%.

Relative strength to TSE300 / Price / Volume (in 1000's of board lots)

Rank (Profit/Revenue/Assets)
935　210　151

Jacques Giasson
Chairman Of The Board

Frank A. Dottori
President & C.E.O.

Thomas W. Laberge
V.P., Finance & C.F.O.

Address
800 Rene-Levesque Blvd. West
27th Floor
Montreal
PQ
H3B 1X9
(514) 871-0137

Fax: (514) 397-0896
T0013617/G/4.1

WELDWOOD OF CANADA LIMITED

Exchanges	Price (Jun24'93)		20.50	Trailing P/E		23.30	Stock Symbol
T	Trailing Yield (%)		0.98	Trailing EPS		0.88	WLW

Period Ending	Dec92	Dec91	Dec90	Dec89	Dec88
Yearly Statistics					
Price-Close	17.50	11.00	16.00	16.00	16.38
Price-High	17.50	16.00	18.50	21.50	18.75
Price-Low	11.00	9.50	13.25	14.50	14.38
P/E-Close	37.23	nm	106.67	8.94	8.40
Dividends per Share	0.20	0.20	0.40	0.40	0.40
Dividend Yield (%)	1.14	1.82	2.50	2.50	2.44
Sales per Share	19.75	18.06	19.29	21.07	25.67
EPS before extra. item	0.47	(0.89)	0.15	1.79	1.95
Cash Flow per Share	2.33	0.14	1.93	3.97	3.75
Book Value per Share	10.94	10.62	11.70	11.94	10.55
O/S Common Shares	37,361	36,844	36,450	36,450	36,435
Total Revenue	737,993	666,467	694,466	781,363	903,659
Income before extra.	17,511	(33,097)	5,396	65,390	68,414
Cash Flow	86,574	5,091	68,389	144,581	130,686
Debt/Equity	0.61	0.75	0.69	0.54	0.24
Return on Capital (%)	7.26	(3.83)	5.19	19.80	31.89
Ret. on Com. Equity (%)	4.38	(8.10)	1.25	15.95	22.48
% Change Profit	152.9	(713.4)	(91.7)	(4.4)	43.8
% Change Revenue	10.7	(4.0)	(11.1)	(13.5)	20.5
% Change Assets	0.5	(5.0)	5.2	29.1	69.6
Preferred Div. Coverage	np	np	np		
Total Div. Coverage	2.4	0.0	0.4		
Interest Coverage	2.7	0.0	1.4		
Current Ratio	2.0	2.1	2.4		
Operating Margin	7.9	(2.8)	5.3		
Asset Turnover	0.8	0.7	0.7		
5 YEAR RATIOS (%)					
Return on Capital	12.1	17.8	23.8		
Return on Com. Equity	7.2	11.0	16.1		
Profit Growth	(18.2)	na	(6.3)		
Revenue Growth	(0.3)	0.0	1.8		
Asset Growth	17.0	22.0	23.6		
BALANCE SHEET (000)					
Cash	4,854	4,667	6,975		
Current Assets	260,233	222,309	257,033		
Net Fixed Assets	596,731	622,651	601,988		
Invest's & Advances	20,588	18,735	17,139		
Total Assets	917,363	912,375	960,130		
Short Term Debt	16,788	18,414	19,614		
Current Liabilities	129,235	107,472	106,488		
Long Term Debt	233,497	275,879	276,003		
Total Liabilities	508,531	521,038	533,505		
Total Equity	408,832	391,337	426,625		
Total Liab. & Equity	917,363	912,375	960,130		
CAPITAL (000)					
Total Debt	250,285	294,293	295,617		
Preferred Equity	0	0	0		
Common Equity	408,832	391,337	426,625		

Business:

WELDWOOD OF CANADA LIMITED is an integrated forest products company with operations in British Columbia, Alberta, and Ontario. Products include plywood, waferboard, lumber, logs, and pulp. It has markets in the United States, Canada, Japan, the United Kingdom, Europe, Australia, New Zealand and South-East Asia.

Date	EPS	DPS	Tot Rev	Inc Bex
Mar 93	0.45	0.05	230,400	16,900
Dec 92	0.14	0.05	187,800	5,200
Sep 92	0.17	0.05	186,300	6,300
Jun 92	0.12	0.05	181,800	4,500
Mar 92	0.04	0.05	180,800	1,500
Dec 91	(0.44)	0.05	150,200	(16,700)
Sep 91	(0.24)	0.05	161,800	(9,000)
Jun 91	0.01	0.05	195,500	100

Synopsis:

Weldwood of Canada accelerated construction of its $70-million sawmill at Hinton, Alberta, during 1992. The sawmill is designed to produce 215 million board feet of lumber annually and will start production in late summer 1993. The sawmill will also be a major source of chips for the pulp mill.

In the South Cariboo region of B.C., Weldwood faces reduced wood availability when special harvesting licences for beetle infested areas end. As a result, the Williams Lake sawmill will be phased out during 1993 and 1994.

The Hinton pulp mill operated near its 385,000 tonne capacity in 1992. The Cariboo mill, a 50% owned joint venture, operated at near capacity. Weldwood's share of production was 136,000 tonnes in 1992. Although revenues from the pulp operations were almost unchanged over 1991 operations, the profitability of these operations improved in 1992 with lower per tonne costs of production. Both the Hinton and Cariboo pulp mills have the ability to manufacture pulp without the use of chlorine gas, and are benefiting from the growing market for this product.

In the solid wood operations, selling prices for all lumber and panelboard increased significantly and most operations returned to normal production levels in 1992. Lumber production rose by 10% to 873 million board feet. Total panelboard production was up by 4% to 546 million square feet. Revenues rose by 18%, but the increased sales returns did not all flow to earnings as the cost of purchased logs and stumpage also increased.

Percentage contributions to net sales for 1992 (1991) by product were: pulp, 34% (37%); lumber, 38% (31%); softwood plywood, 12% (11%); hardwood plywood, 5% (5%); waferboard, 3% (3%); and logs and other, 8% (13%). Net sales in 1992 (1991) by country were: the United States, 46% (48%); Canada, 29%, (32%); and other , 25% (20%).

Rank (Profit/Revenue/Assets)		
131	130	159

Thomas A. Buell
Chairman

Graham I. Bender
President & C.E.O.

Kent T. Williamson
V.P. & Controller

Address
P.O. Box 2179
1055 West Hastings Street
Vancouver
BC
V6B 3V8
(604) 687-7366

Fax: (604) 662-2858
W0001122/G/4.2

WEST FRASER TIMBER CO. LTD.

Exchanges	Price (Jun24'93)	37.75	Trailing P/E	28.60	Stock Symbol
TV	Trailing Yield (%)	1.06	Trailing EPS	1.32	WFT

Period Ending	Dec92	Dec91	Dec90	Dec89	Dec88
Yearly Statistics					
Price-Close	31.50	20.25	16.75	16.63	17.25
Price-High	31.50	22.50	21.00	19.88	23.50
Price-Low	20.00	17.00	16.50	16.50	16.50
P/E-Close	52.50	nm	76.14	9.04	6.61
Dividends per Share	0.40	0.40	0.40	0.37	0.33
Dividend Yield (%)	1.27	1.98	2.39	2.23	1.91
Sales per Share	39.75	32.94	34.90	35.65	30.00
EPS before extra. item	0.60	(1.02)	0.22	1.84	2.61
Cash Flow per Share	4.12	2.38	5.05	5.81	5.41
Book Value per Share	16.20	16.00	17.08	17.26	15.79
O/S Common Shares	17,037	17,037	15,537	15,452	15,452
Total Revenue	677,027	537,730	542,084	551,980	465,813
Income before extra.	10,226	(16,532)	3,407	28,397	40,319
Cash Flow	70,182	38,502	78,212	89,666	83,560
Debt/Equity	1.35	1.33	1.44	1.09	0.67
Return on Capital (%)	6.47	(1.99)	3.52	12.80	22.32
Ret. on Com. Equity (%)	3.73	(6.15)	1.28	11.12	17.82
% Change Profit	161.9	(585.2)	(88.0)	(29.6)	(14.6)
% Change Revenue	25.9	(0.8)	(1.8)	18.5	13.1
% Change Assets	3.8	(1.3)	19.0	32.5	30.7

Date	EPS	DPS	Tot Rev	Inc Bex
Mar 93	0.84	0.10	188,300	15,700
Dec 92	0.13	0.10	171,927	2,226
Sep 92	0.18	0.10	171,200	3,100
Jun 92	0.17	0.10	179,900	2,900
Mar 92	0.10	0.10	154,000	2,000
Dec 91	(0.26)	0.10	138,430	(4,432)
Sep 91	(0.24)	0.10	146,500	(3,900)
Jun 91	0.00	0.10	151,400	0

	Dec92	Dec91	Dec90
Preferred Div. Coverage	np	np	np
Total Div. Coverage	1.5	0.0	0.5
Interest Coverage	1.8	0.0	0.5
Current Ratio	2.1	2.3	1.7
Operating Margin	6.6	(2.3)	3.6
Asset Turnover	0.8	0.7	0.7
5 YEAR RATIOS (%)			
Return on Capital	8.6	14.1	20.1
Return on Com. Equity	5.6	8.8	15.2
Profit Growth	(26.4)	na	(22.2)
Revenue Growth	10.4	6.8	10.0
Asset Growth	16.1	17.3	17.3
BALANCE SHEET (000)			
Cash	63,923	17,914	2,591
Current Assets	273,619	237,071	229,255
Net Fixed Assets	567,187	575,463	594,259
Invest's & Advances	7,120	4,264	4,976
Total Assets	850,422	819,103	829,873
Short Term Debt	39,248	30,692	63,514
Current Liabilities	129,997	102,323	135,945
Long Term Debt	333,387	331,845	318,231
Total Liabilities	574,373	546,465	564,579
Total Equity	276,049	272,638	265,294
Total Liab. & Equity	850,422	819,103	829,873
CAPITAL (000)			
Total Debt	372,635	362,537	381,745
Preferred Equity	0	0	0
Common Equity	276,049	272,638	265,294

Business:

WEST FRASER TIMBER CO. LTD. is a forest products and building supplies company. The company produces lumber, linerboard, kraft paper, newsprint and bleached CTMP pulp at its operations in British Columbia and Alberta. It has markets in North America, Europe, and the Far East. Revelstoke Home Centres Ltd., a 100% subsidiary, operates a chain of building supply stores in Western Canada.

Synopsis:

West Fraser Timber Co. announced its intention in May 1993 to purchase the half-interest of Enso-Gutzeit Oy of Finland in the Eurocan Pulp and Paper Co. joint venture, giving it 100% of the project. Upon closing, West Fraser will pay Enso $95-million in cash and issue to Enso two million common shares. The company will also pre-pay $43-million owing on a note issued by it to Enso.

Eurocan owns and operates a large pulp and paper mill at Kitimat, B.C., having an annual capacity of 345,000 tonnes of unbleached kraft linerboard and 112,000 tonnes of unbleached kraft paper. It also has sawmills and interests in sawmills in both Canada and the U.S. In April 1993, the Kitimat mill began an 18-day shutdown for extensive maintenance work on the recovery boiler. Legal proceedings have been initiated by a native group in respect of the discharge of effluent at the mill, but the amount of potential liability, if any, has not yet been determined.

Capital expenditures in 1992 totaled $42-million, of which $25-million was spent on upgrading and replacing sawmill equipment and building logging roads, $11-million was spent for pulp and paper, and $6-million was spent by Revelstoke Home Centres. Capital expenditures for 1993 are expected to total $50-million.

West Fraser earned $16-million for the first quarter ending March 31, 1993, owing to a number of factors that include an increase in lumber prices, and revenues generated by Revelstoke Home Centres. Operations at all of the company's pulp and paper units suffered from the extreme cold encountered in January 1993. Linerboard and kraft paper prices remained depressed throughout the quarter.

Contributions to net sales in 1992 (1991) by industry segment were: lumber and wood chips, 49% (44%); pulp and paper, 27% (28%); and building supplies, 24% (28%). Contributions to net sales by geographic area in 1992 (1991) were: the U.S., 41% (36%); Canada, 40% (45%); Europe, 7% (7%); the Far East, 10% (9%); and other 2% (3%).

Rank (Profit/Revenue/Assets)
181 132 167

Henry H. Ketcham, Jr.
Chairman Of The Board

Henry H. Ketcham, III
President & C.E.O.

Martti Solin
V.P., Finance & C.F.O.

Gary W. Townsend
V.P., Lumber Operations

Address
Suite 1000
1100 Melville Street
Vancouver
BC
V6E 4A6
(604) 681-8282

Fax: (604) 681-6061
W0000488/G/4.2

Page	Company	$	Latest year end	Earnings per Share Actual	Estimate this year	Estimate next year
155	Andres Wines		9203	1.03	n.a.	n.a.
156	BC Sugar Refinery		9209	0.62	0.81	1.01
157	Canada Malting		9212	0.95	1.23	1.33
158	Coca-Cola Beverages		9212	(1.25)	(0.52)	(0.05)
159	Corby Distillers		9302	4.94	5.26	5.18
160	Corporate Foods		9212	0.80	0.89	1.01
161	Cott Corporation		9301	0.50	1.03	1.55
162	Dover Industries		9212	1.28	n.a.	n.a.
163	FPI Limited		9212	(4.09)	(0.03)	0.10
164	Maple Leaf Foods		9212	0.86	0.96	1.08
165	Molson Companies		9303	1.90	2.14	2.42
166	National Sea Products		9212	(0.43)	(0.15)	0.05
167	Rothmans		9303	10.04	10.27	10.31
168	Schneider Corporation		9210	1.13	1.25	1.50
169	T.G. Bright & Co.		9203	1.11	n.a.	n.a.

Estimates from I/B/E/S Inc., 345 Hudson St., New York, NY 10014 (212) 243-3335. In Canada: 6 Lansing Square, Ste. 235, Willowdale, ON M2J 1T5 (416) 496-0977.

Food, Beverages & Tobacco

Soft Drink Industry - Industry Report [Apr-8-1993]. PAINEWEBBER INC. reported by Goldman, E., et al

Supermarket scanner data for 1992 show soft drink industry volume up 2.9% and prices off 1%, with large differences between companies and between individual brands. Coca-Cola's Coke Classic' gallonage was up 2.6% for 1992, following a 6% gain the prior year. Prices were up modestly in the last three quarters of the year, following a 3% drop in 1Q:92, with the full year ending with flat pricing. Supermarket gallonage for Diet Coke was off in each quarter of 1992 and dropped 2.9% for the year as a whole. By contrast, Diet Pepsi's supermarket gallonage was up nearly 2% for the year. Regular (sugared) Sprite gallonage rose healthy 7.2% for the year, above the 2.2% gain shown by Diet Sprite. [RN 1323088]

Food/Beverage/Tobacco Conference Highlights - Industry Report [Mar-29-1993]. ARGUS RESEARCH CORPORATION reported by Bivens, T.

Unlike the 1980s, when volumes, prices and profits rose dramatically, the '90s appear to offer most domestic industry categories (cereal is a notable exception) steady but uninspiring annual growth of 1-2%. Value is king, as the relentless rise of the warehouse clubs and private labels attest. Companies are adapting well, however, with a new competitive model for the current decade. Powerful brands are the first key element, since top-line growth will depend on leveraging those brands through new products and line extensions. Expansion into faster-growing markets overseas is the second. [RN 1317759]

Food Industry - Industry Report [Apr-13-1993]. MERRILL LYNCH CAPITAL MARKETS reported by Maguire, W.F., et al

Food stocks have not been exempt from the problems caused by Philip Morris's Marlboro price-cutting disclosure on April 2, 1993. Real volume gains throughout the industry are hard to come by. Private label is still inflicting damage in many categories. Price flexibility is equally hard to come by, and private label is a problem in that regard too. Margin improvement is a function of cost controls almost exclusively. Most food companies' bottom-line growth reflects only their top line, and both for the most part are much less than in the 1980's. In these years, A&M spending was not inflationary because price increases were taken so frequently and to such an extent as to eliminate the problem. Often price increases were taken simply in order to justify aggressive A&M spending. For now at least, meaningful price increases are out, and so might meaningful advertising increases in the near future. However, promotional spending to defend market share is not out, and it might be aggressive enough to be an inflationary factor in relation to sales growth looking ahead at least through 1993 and maybe 1994. Promotional spending is over two-thirds of a food company's average A&M budget, and alone it is usually a more significant line item than labor, packaging, energy or commodities. [RN 1322060]

Tobacco Industry - Industry Report [May-18-1993]. DEAN WITTER REYNOLDS reported by Adelman, L., et al

In the case of Wilks Versus American Brands, an unprecedented pretrial decision was made on May 11, 1993 by Judge Bogen. The Judge determined, as a matter of law, that cigarettes are defective and unreasonably dangerous. By making this decision, Judge Bogen removed the issue from those to be considered by the jury. The case is scheduled to begin on June 7, 1993, in the Mississippi state trial court. The defendant cannot use assumption of risk as a defense in this case since Judge Bogen has ruled, as a matter of law, that the plaintiff did not assume the risk associated with smoking. In addition, the judge ruled that, as a matter of law, that the plaintiff was not contributorily negligent because he did not misuse or alter the product and used it as intended. If this decision is not successfully appealed by the industry, the trial will be limited to the issues of whether smoking caused the plaintiff's cancer, and how much damage there was. Under Judge Bogen's ruling, cigarette manufacturers are liable for damages caused by cigarettes as long as the plaintiff can prove that smoking caused his/her disease. [RN 1331614]

Canadian Consumer Products Monthly Digest - Industry Report [May-7-1993]. WOOD GUNDY INC. reported by Holt, S., et al

Ault Foods been spun off by John Labatt Ltd. on the basis of one Ault share for every five Labatt shares held on or before May 7, 1993. With net sales for the year ending April 1993 estimated at $1.2 billion, Ault is the largest fully-integrated dairy operation in Canada. Its major segments include Fluid Milk (39% of sales), Cheese (18% of sales), Butter/margarine (17% of sales), and Packaged Ice Cream & Novelties (14% of sales). Although Ault sells many of its products across Canada and exports some products and technology as well, the main markets for many of Ault's products are Ontario and Quebec. In Fluid Milk, Ault has 31% and 23% of the Ontario and Quebec markets, respectively. Ault is moving away from commodity-like businesses by increasing its presence in branded and private-label products, both by acquisition and new product introductions. CCL Industries Inc. had 1Q:93 EPS of $0.11 versus $0.09 a year ago. Sales rose 17%, but most of the increase was due to the acquisition of Barr Co. and a plant in Memphis. [RN 1329773]

Canadian Consumer Products Monthly Digest - Industry Report [Mar-1-1993]. WOOD GUNDY INC. reported by Holt, S., et al

During 1992, one of the weakest consumer products sectors was brewing, where beer shipments declined 6.8%. The food processing industry continued its decline, although the momentum of the decline lessened. The non-alcoholic beverage industry reported marginal growth in 1992 from a low base. The one sector which maintained a consistent growth trend was household cleaning products. [RN 1308290]

ANDRES WINES LTD.

Exchanges	Price (Jun24'93)	11.00	Trailing P/E	10.78	Stock Symbol
TMV	Trailing Yield (%)	5.45	Trailing EPS	1.02	**ADW.A**

Period Ending	Mar92	Mar91	Mar90	Mar89	Mar88
Yearly Statistics					
Price-Close	14.00	9.63	11.00	12.88	12.25
Price-High	15.00	9.63	12.75	12.88	21.00
Price-Low	9.50	8.00	10.00	10.00	9.75
P/E-Close	13.59	9.63	10.78	14.31	13.76
Dividends per Share	0.60	0.60	0.60	0.60	0.60
Dividend Yield (%)	4.27	6.21	5.44	4.65	4.88
Sales per Share	12.51	11.78	11.95	12.56	12.78
EPS before extra. item	1.03	1.00	1.02	0.90	0.89
Cash Flow per Share	1.26	1.26	1.29	1.20	1.20
Book Value per Share	10.44	9.99	9.57	9.14	8.82
O/S Common Shares	4,462	4,462	4,462	4,462	4,462
Total Revenue	55,803	52,634	53,311	56,042	57,007
Income before extra.	4,616	4,467	4,557	4,021	4,006
Cash Flow	5,623	5,621	5,734	5,333	5,361
Debt/Equity	0.03	0.04	0.04	0.05	0.05
Return on Capital (%)	16.90	17.04	17.65	16.59	17.57
Ret. on Com. Equity (%)	10.09	10.19	10.87	9.99	10.32
% Change Profit	3.3	(2.0)	13.3	0.4	(16.1)
% Change Revenue	6.0	(1.3)	(4.9)	(1.7)	0.5
% Change Assets	2.3	5.4	2.7	4.2	(0.2)

Preferred Div. Coverage	230.9	223.5	228.0
Total Div. Coverage	1.8	1.7	1.7
Interest Coverage	47.9	40.4	36.4
Current Ratio	8.2	7.6	9.0
Operating Margin	14.6	15.0	14.7
Asset Turnover	1.0	1.0	1.0
5 YEAR RATIOS (%)			
Return on Capital	17.2	18.3	19.8
Return on Com. Equity	10.3	10.9	12.0
Profit Growth	(0.7)	(4.0)	(4.1)
Revenue Growth	(0.3)	(1.4)	(1.0)
Asset Growth	2.8	3.3	2.3
BALANCE SHEET (000)			
Cash	21,563	19,437	17,201
Current Assets	44,699	43,127	39,745
Net Fixed Assets	10,699	10,942	11,472
Invest's & Advances	0	0	0
Total Assets	55,501	54,249	51,464
Short Term Debt	175	175	175
Current Liabilities	5,421	5,708	4,423
Long Term Debt	1,309	1,498	1,738
Total Liabilities	8,590	9,346	8,420
Total Equity	46,911	44,903	43,044
Total Liab. & Equity	55,501	54,249	51,464
CAPITAL (000)			
Total Debt	1,484	1,673	1,913
Preferred Equity	333	333	333
Common Equity	46,578	44,570	42,711

Business:

ANDRES WINES LTD. operates wineries in British Columbia, Alberta, Manitoba, Ontario, Quebec and Nova Scotia. The company sells wine across Canada and exports wine to the United States and Japan. To meet the demand for imported wines, the company has three importing agencies, handling a full range of quality wines and spirits.

Date	EPS	DPS	Tot Rev	Inc Bex
Dec 92	0.48	0.15	18,993	2,138
Sep 92	0.24	0.15	14,924	1,076
Jun 92	0.23	0.15	13,817	1,049
Mar 92	0.07	0.15	9,449	332
Dec 91	0.49	0.15	18,626	2,196
Sep 91	0.17	0.15	13,617	734
Jun 91	0.30	0.15	14,111	1,354
Mar 91	0.21	0.15	9,817	915

Synopsis:

In April 1993, Andres Wines Ltd. withdrew its plan to purchase T.G. Bright & Co., Ltd. Andres decided against the purchase after a management group led by a Toronto investor took possession of the 53% control block previously held by the Hatch family. The bid proposed by Andres was allowed to lapse on April 19 since it hadn't acquired the 90% ownership it wanted. The management group currently has control of 80% of the total shares, with 16.1% still controlled by Andres, and 3.9% widely held. Andres has no plans to sell its stake. Control of T.G. Bright would have resulted in Andres gaining control of Canada's wine industry.

The Canadian wine industry, which was destined to collapse in the mid-1980s from less restrictive trade barriers due the Free Trade Agreement, has come around. This is a result of marked improvement in quality and the aggressive marketing of Canadian wines. Sales of Ontario red wines jumped 35% last year, doubling the increase of imported wines, while sales of Canadian white wines remained stable. This a good sign in an industry where the federal and provincial governments are slowly eliminating trade barriers that protected the industry from wines produced in California and Europe. By 1995, all price markups on imported wines will be eliminated.

In addition to this, interprovincial trade barriers may be relaxed resulting in the possible streamlining of the wine industry in Canada. As well, the threat of U.S. sanctions against some European wines may improve the prospects of exports to the U.S. for Canadian wineries. Andres currently has wineries in B.C., Alberta, Manitoba, Quebec, Nova Scotia and California, along with three import agencies that market imported wines.

Relative strength to TSE300

Price

Volume (in 1000's of board lots)

Rank (Profit/Revenue/Assets)		
265	455	514

Joseph A. Peller
Chairman & C.E.O.

John E. Peller
President

N.D. Smith
Sr. Exec. V.P., Sec. & C.F.O.

Address
P.O. Box 550
Winona
ON
L0R 2L0
(416) 643-4131

Fax: (416) 643-4944
A0002263/G/5.3.3

BC SUGAR REFINERY, LIMITED

Exchanges	Price (Jun24'93)		9.25	Trailing P/E		13.03	Stock Symbol
T	Trailing Yield (%)		6.49	Trailing EPS		0.71	**BCS.A**

Period Ending	Sep92	Sep91	Sep90	Sep89	Sep88
Yearly Statistics					
Price-Close	9.00	15.00	14.13	17.00	15.00
Price-High	15.75	16.25	18.38	17.50	15.75
Price-Low	8.13	13.63	13.50	14.25	10.50
P/E-Close	12.68	nm	17.23	10.00	8.07
Dividends per Share	0.60	0.80	0.80	0.80	0.70
Dividend Yield (%)	6.67	5.33	5.66	4.71	4.67
Sales per Share	17.09	11.29	13.04	20.76	20.75
EPS before extra. item	0.71	(0.60)	0.82	1.70	1.86
Cash Flow per Share	0.97	0.66	1.14	2.45	2.78
Book Value per Share	6.73	5.18	6.59	6.24	5.19
O/S Common Shares	22,722	14,271	14,176	13,973	13,869
Total Revenue	281,445	161,187	184,261	289,040	262,086
Income before extra.	11,694	(8,554)	11,603	23,417	23,563
Cash Flow	16,009	9,450	16,091	34,070	35,120
Debt/Equity	1.96	2.27	0.52	0.48	0.45
Return on Capital (%)	9.22	5.81	18.32	38.22	43.78
Ret. on Com. Equity (%)	10.32	(10.32)	12.76	29.33	34.77
% Change Profit	236.7	(173.7)	(50.5)	(0.6)	31.1
% Change Revenue	74.6	(12.5)	(36.3)	10.3	24.1
% Change Assets	102.4	60.6	(11.6)	17.2	(0.6)

Date	EPS	DPS	Tot Rev	Inc Bex
Mar 93	0.12	0.10	158,710	2,720
Dec 92	0.22	0.10	171,336	5,070
Sep 92	0.26	0.10	165,284	5,203
Jun 92	0.11	0.10	40,573	1,679
Mar 92	0.24	0.20	36,306	3,324
Dec 91	0.10	0.20	39,282	1,488
Sep 91	(1.03)	0.20	40,689	(14,629)
Jun 91	0.18	0.20	40,860	2,589

Preferred Div. Coverage	na	0.0	146.9
Total Div. Coverage	1.2	0.0	1.0
Interest Coverage	1.8	0.7	3.6
Current Ratio	2.1	2.1	1.3
Operating Margin	10.8	15.9	13.8
Asset Turnover	0.5	0.6	1.1
5 YEAR RATIOS (%)			
Return on Capital	23.1	28.2	29.5
Return on Com. Equity	15.4	19.5	22.7
Profit Growth	(8.3)	na	7.3
Revenue Growth	5.9	3.1	6.7
Asset Growth	27.3	18.7	1.2
BALANCE SHEET (000)			
Cash	27,779	18,924	0
Current Assets	228,754	91,379	41,072
Net Fixed Assets	140,030	18,007	18,099
Invest's & Advances	2,768	152,537	103,914
Total Assets	530,247	261,923	163,085
Short Term Debt	55,088	31,118	19,783
Current Liabilities	108,440	43,222	31,797
Long Term Debt	247,902	140,000	30,000
Total Liabilities	375,844	186,443	68,043
Total Equity	154,403	75,480	95,042
Total Liab. & Equity	530,247	261,923	163,085
CAPITAL (000)			
Total Debt	302,990	171,118	49,783
Preferred Equity	1,570	1,570	1,570
Common Equity	152,833	73,910	93,472

Business:

BC SUGAR is involved in the production, distribution and marketing of sugar products, and the production and sale of specialty chemicals. With the acquistion of Lanctic Sugar Limited in 1992, BC Sugar now has five sugar facilities in Canada and one in the U.S. BC Sugar supplies more than 80% of Western Canada's sugar, 65% of Eastern Canada's, and about 27% of the northeastern United States sugar market.

Synopsis:

In March 1993, BC Sugar Refinery, Limited issued two million Class A Common shares generating $19.25-million in funds. The proceeds are geared towards reducing bank debt which was incurred to provide a portion of approximately $120-million used by the company to acquire Lantic Sugar Limited in October 1992.

For the quarter ending December 31, 1992, net profit increased 240% on a revenue increase of 336%, compared to the same period last year. The results included the start of BC Sugar's first full year as 100% owner of Lantic Sugar Ltd. and its subsidiary, Refined Sugars Inc.

The company has announced intentions to cut its Vancouver work force by 15%. The reason is linked to intensified competition in the Canadian market due to increased sugar imports. The company has stressed the need to become more efficient due to sugar support programs in other countries resulting in lower production costs in those countries. Canada has a minimal import duty on sugar, creating a perfect opportunity for lower cost foreign sugar producers. The acquisition of Lantic Sugar will aid in the creation of economies of scale and opportunities for additional savings.

In fiscal 1992, 78% of the company's revenues were from Canada with the remaining 22% from the United States. The company has begun a major repositioning program in order to operate more efficiently in the new business climate. This includes improving its cash flow by reducing its dividend to 10 cents from 20 cents a share. Furthermore, in order to become a major North American player in the sugar market, the company sold its interests in the specialty chemicals industry, Chatterton Petrochemical Corp. and Kalama Chemical Inc.

Sugar production in 1992 amounted to 1.14 million tonnes.

Rank (Profit/Revenue/Assets)
161   232   203

Peter A. Cherniavsky
Chairman

William C. Brown
President & C.E.O.

James W. Hudson
V.P., Finance, Secty. & C.F.O.

Address
P.O. Box 2150
Vancouver
BC
V6B 3V2
(604) 253-1131

Fax: (604) 253-2517
B0004142/G/5.1

CANADA MALTING CO. LIMITED

Exchanges	Price (Jun24'93)	14.12	Trailing P/E	17.02	Stock Symbol
TM	Trailing Yield (%)	2.55	Trailing EPS	0.83	**CMG**

Period Ending	Dec92	Dec91	Dec90	Dec89	Dec88
Yearly Statistics					
Price-Close	13.63	15.33	9.67	11.33	6.00
Price-High	17.50	15.33	11.33	12.17	6.50
Price-Low	12.88	8.67	8.67	5.75	4.96
P/E-Close	17.03	12.85	6.84	7.94	5.68
Dividends per Share	0.35	0.33	0.32	0.27	0.21
Dividend Yield (%)	2.57	2.17	3.31	2.35	3.56
Sales per Share	18.86	19.15	22.72	23.31	12.19
EPS before extra. item	0.80	1.19	1.41	1.43	1.06
Cash Flow per Share	1.77	1.73	1.54	1.58	1.46
Book Value per Share	11.41	11.51	10.79	8.65	7.50
O/S Common Shares	19,156	19,105	19,087	14,097	14,091
Total Revenue	361,120	366,147	407,901	332,690	172,381
Income before extra.	15,268	22,781	24,888	20,080	14,880
Cash Flow	33,781	33,100	27,181	22,306	20,500
Debt/Equity	0.72	0.59	0.65	1.63	0.02
Return on Capital (%)	8.40	12.23	15.00	19.48	23.16
Ret. on Com. Equity (%)	6.96	10.70	15.18	17.64	14.92
% Change Profit	(33.0)	(8.5)	23.9	34.9	57.3
% Change Revenue	(1.4)	(10.2)	22.6	93.0	9.5
% Change Assets	6.6	3.8	4.1	197.6	0.7

Business:

CANADA MALTING CO. LTD. is a producer and exporter of barley malt for sale to brewers, distillers and food manufacturers. Export markets include Japan and other Pacific Rim countries. Canada Malting is Canada's leading malt producer and exporter. Subsidiary companies include Great Western Malting Co. in the western United States and Hugh Baird & Sons in England. Leaver Mushrooms grows fresh mushrooms.

Date	EPS	DPS	Tot Rev	Inc Bex
Mar 93	0.26	0.09	84,174	4,993
Dec 92	(0.03)	0.09	87,005	(530)
Sep 92	0.25	0.09	88,802	4,779
Jun 92	0.35	0.09	100,622	6,627
Mar 92	0.23	0.08	84,469	4,392
Dec 91	0.27	0.08	82,793	5,189
Sep 91	0.30	0.09	96,045	5,826
Jun 91	0.37	0.09	100,565	6,981

	Dec92	Dec91	Dec90
Preferred Div. Coverage	np	np	np
Total Div. Coverage	2.3	3.6	4.3
Interest Coverage	2.7	3.5	3.0
Current Ratio	1.4	1.9	1.9
Operating Margin	11.3	11.4	10.4
Asset Turnover	0.8	0.9	1.0
5 YEAR RATIOS (%)			
Return on Capital	15.7	17.5	16.6
Return on Com. Equity	13.1	13.8	12.6
Profit Growth	10.0	41.1	42.9
Revenue Growth	18.0	20.0	21.2
Asset Growth	28.1	28.5	29.2
BALANCE SHEET (000)			
Cash	8,663	536	4,412
Current Assets	154,328	152,258	163,220
Net Fixed Assets	272,210	246,068	214,138
Invest's & Advances	0	0	5,357
Total Assets	434,235	407,182	392,164
Short Term Debt	72,595	42,477	46,452
Current Liabilities	107,772	80,482	85,047
Long Term Debt	84,394	86,377	87,257
Total Liabilities	215,601	187,300	186,241
Total Equity	218,634	219,882	205,923
Total Liab. & Equity	434,235	407,182	392,164
CAPITAL (000)			
Total Debt	156,989	128,854	133,709
Preferred Equity	0	0	0
Common Equity	218,634	219,882	205,923

Synopsis:

In fiscal 1992, net profit at Canada Malting Co. Limited dropped 31% when compared to fiscal 1991, due to two unusual charges which negatively affected its operations. The company was affected by the recession, a damp 1992 summer, and increased competition both domestically and internationally. Revenue for the year remained flat at about $360-million. However, in the first quarter of 1993, net profit rose 13.6% as a result of better prices in the United States.

The unusual charges in 1992 were related to the cost of a mortgage turned sour and the closing of antiquated plants in Western Canada. The company will spend $170-million in a four-year capital expansion program at those plants which is expected to be completed this year. The company opened a $15-million automated grain handling terminal in Thunder Bay and a $43-million malthouse in Calgary. The new facilities will be used to help expand export markets, which are viewed as having great growth potential. The company is eyeing new potential sales in Latin America and China, and will attempt to better improve its existing export markets. Major operations for the company exist in Britain and the United States. Approximately 42% of sales from Canadian operations are exported.

The $20-million Calgary malt handling plant was built to take advantage of new export opportunities in Mexico once the North American Free Trade Agreement is ratified. The plant will have an annual production of 165,000 tonnes of beer malt. The majority of this production currently is allocated to Japan and South Korea. The company will now look toward Mexico, a market that requires about $100-million worth of beer malt annually. A new $40-million tower malting plant in Calgary will further strengthen the company's export potential.

Relative strength to TSE300

Price

Volume (in 1000's of board lots)

Rank (Profit/Revenue/Assets)		
145	202	227

Ronald W. Eden
President & C.E.O.
W. Wesley De Shane
V.P., C.F.O. & Secretary

Address
10 Four Seasons Place
Suite 600
Toronto
ON
M9B 6H7
(416) 620-7575

Fax: (416) 620-4182
C0001506/G/5.1

COCA-COLA BEVERAGES LTD.

Exchanges	Price (Jun24'93)		4.65	Trailing P/E		nm	Stock Symbol
TM	Trailing Yield (%)		1.08	Trailing EPS		(1.26)	**KOC**

Period Ending	Dec92	Dec91	Dec90	Dec89	Dec88
Yearly Statistics					
Price-Close	4.30	7.88	9.25	12.25	7.75
Price-High	8.50	11.38	13.00	13.00	8.13
Price-Low	3.10	6.38	8.63	7.75	5.50
P/E-Close	nm	787.50	44.05	31.41	27.68
Dividends per Share	0.05	0.05	0.05	0.05	0.50
Dividend Yield (%)	1.16	0.64	0.54	0.41	6.45
Sales per Share	22.32	25.10	25.14	23.31	20.51
EPS before extra. item	(1.25)	0.01	0.21	0.39	0.28
Cash Flow per Share	(0.13)	1.03	1.68	1.39	1.17
Book Value per Share	5.04	6.34	6.38	6.22	5.88
O/S Common Shares	40,103	40,103	40,008	40,005	40,000
Total Revenue	894,967	1,005,399	1,005,646	937,636	820,631
Income before extra.	(45,049)	5,300	13,215	15,867	11,263
Cash Flow	(5,360)	41,249	67,167	55,622	46,978
Debt/Equity	1.54	1.10	1.01	0.93	1.14
Return on Capital (%)	(3.90)	8.56	10.76	5.08	5.07
Ret. on Com. Equity (%)	(21.91)	0.14	3.29	6.39	4.88
% Change Profit	(950.0)	(59.9)	(16.7)	40.9	138.3
% Change Revenue	(11.0)	(0.0)	7.3	14.3	13.5
% Change Assets	(4.6)	8.0	5.6	17.1	22.1
Preferred Div. Coverage	0.0	1.1	2.7		
Total Div. Coverage	0.0	0.8	1.9		
Interest Coverage	0.0	1.2	1.6		
Current Ratio	1.5	1.4	1.7		
Operating Margin	(1.7)	6.2	7.3		
Asset Turnover	1.1	1.2	1.3		
5 YEAR RATIOS (%)					
Return on Capital	5.1	6.5	5.8		
Return on Com. Equity	(1.4)	3.5	na		
Profit Growth	na	(2.0)	6.8		
Revenue Growth	4.3	12.2	16.7		
Asset Growth	9.2	15.4	31.5		
BALANCE SHEET (000)					
Cash	13,681	6,318	8,000		
Current Assets	184,117	210,096	185,115		
Net Fixed Assets	393,162	403,361	388,287		
Invest's & Advances	0	0	0		
Total Assets	807,984	847,132	784,612		
Short Term Debt	20,832	11,149	19,477		
Current Liabilities	120,221	147,210	109,111		
Long Term Debt	386,412	336,362	299,941		
Total Liabilities	543,638	530,795	467,338		
Total Equity	264,346	316,337	317,274		
Total Liab. & Equity	807,984	847,132	784,612		
CAPITAL (000)					
Total Debt	407,244	347,511	319,418		
Preferred Equity	62,202	62,202	62,202		
Common Equity	202,144	254,135	255,072		

Business:

COCA-COLA BEVERAGES LTD. is a soft drink beverage company. Through subsidiaries, it produces, packages, distributes, and markets under license Coca Cola trademark beverages as well as Canada Dry, Schweppes and A & W brands. The company has operations in parts of all Canadian provinces. Coca-Cola Company indirectly holds 49% of the company's common shares.

Date	EPS	DPS	Tot Rev	Inc Bex
Apr 93	(0.33)	0.01	185,618	(11,827)
Dec 92	(0.44)	0.01	219,884	(16,258)
Sep 92	(0.25)	0.01	237,446	(8,777)
Jun 92	(0.24)	0.01	258,737	(8,295)
Mar 92	(0.32)	0.01	182,901	(11,719)
Dec 91	(0.16)	0.01	263,670	(5,239)
Sep 92	0.18	0.01	296,946	8,260
Jun 91	0.25	0.01	275,629	11,388

Synopsis:

In April 1993, Coca-Cola Beverages Ltd. made an arrangement for a $440-million credit facility with a group of Canadian and U.S. financial institutions. The facility allows the company to refinance approximately $200-million of debt maturing in the near future, in addition to replacing a $95-million credit line which has expired. The new credit arrangement will aid Coca-Cola, since it has been experiencing problems with its operating cash flow which has declined over the past two years. Operating cash flow in fiscal 1992 dropped 73.3%. Consequently, the company has had to depend more on higher priced financing for its daily cash needs.

In fiscal 1992, the company had a loss of $45-million compared to a gain of $5.3-million the past year. This decline was attributed to poor summer weather along with increased competition from cheaper private label brands. This represents the first loss for the company since going public in 1987. The weak performance resulted in its securities being downgraded to medium-quality investments from good-quality investments by both major Canadian bond rating agencies. The negative adjustments were attributed to the company's negative retained earnings position and increased debt leverage ratio.

The rise of private label brands to 20% of the Canadian soft drink market, from 5% before the recession, has severely affected the company's operating profits. To combat this, the company sold its product to retailers at a loss in order to maintain market share last year. This has since been stopped.

For fiscal 1993, the company has indicated its desire to focus on four specific agenda items: the creation of an integrated customer strategy; the restoration of realistic margins in the soft drink category through strategic pricing and package-mix initiatives; efficiency improvements in human resources and operations; and the development of a more integrated and efficient supply chain that will better meet customer needs.

Relative strength to TSE300 / Price / Volume (in 1000's of board lots)

Rank (Profit/Revenue/Assets)
953   114   172

Ira C. Herbert
Chairman
William P. Casey
President & C.E.O.
Shaun B. Higgins
Sr. V.P. & C.F.O.
William T. Highberger
Sr. V.P. & C.O.O.

Address
42 Overlea Boulevard
Toronto
ON
M4H 1B8
(416) 424-6000

Fax: (416) 424-6079
T0001589/G/5.1

CORBY DISTILLERIES LIMITED

Exchanges		Price (Jun24'93)	52.75	Trailing P/E	10.68	Stock Symbol
TMVZ		Trailing Yield (%)	2.03	Trailing EPS	4.94	**CDL.A**

Period Ending	Feb93	Feb92	Feb91	Feb90	Feb89
Yearly Statistics					
Price-Close	48.25	51.00	36.25	29.25	31.25
Price-High	54.00	56.00	37.00	31.38	31.50
Price-Low	42.00	35.00	28.75	24.00	17.50
P/E-Close	9.77	22.97	11.96	13.00	15.94
Dividends per Share	1.07	0.88	0.76	0.72	0.70
Dividend Yield (%)	2.22	1.73	2.10	2.46	2.24
Sales per Share	12.08	12.67	13.99	15.14	14.46
EPS before extra. item	4.94	2.22	3.03	2.25	1.96
Cash Flow per Share	4.89	2.46	3.37	2.82	2.59
Book Value per Share	24.67	21.01	19.74	17.38	15.09
O/S Common Shares	7,024	7,009	6,968	6,959	6,907
Total Revenue	114,059	109,064	112,325	117,829	110,262
Income before extra.	34,664	15,518	21,111	15,566	13,549
Cash Flow	34,307	17,181	23,443	19,506	17,884
Debt/Equity	0.01	0.01	0.01	0.03	0.03
Return on Capital (%)	35.20	17.55	27.51	22.57	20.80
Ret. on Com. Equity (%)	21.63	10.90	16.33	13.83	14.07
% Change Profit	123.4	(26.5)	35.6	14.9	35.4
% Change Revenue	4.6	(2.9)	(4.7)	6.9	27.6
% Change Assets	14.6	3.0	15.5	4.6	7.2

Preferred Div. Coverage	np	np	np
Total Div. Coverage	4.6	2.5	4.0
Interest Coverage	na	na	na
Current Ratio	9.2	7.4	6.4
Operating Margin	42.6	37.7	26.6
Asset Turnover	0.4	0.5	0.6
5 YEAR RATIOS (%)			
Return on Capital	24.7	20.9	20.9
Return on Com. Equity	15.4	13.3	13.3
Profit Growth	28.2	10.2	16.8
Revenue Growth	5.6	9.1	9.8
Asset Growth	8.8	11.0	11.5
BALANCE SHEET (000)			
Cash	111,447	80,798	65,000
Current Assets	164,769	140,930	135,382
Net Fixed Assets	2,039	5,241	11,118
Invest's & Advances	15,880	14,794	9,361
Total Assets	191,445	167,047	162,191
Short Term Debt	1,525	1,684	1,924
Current Liabilities	17,857	19,082	21,268
Long Term Debt	0	0	0
Total Liabilities	18,155	19,758	24,622
Total Equity	173,290	147,289	137,569
Total Liab. & Equity	191,445	167,047	162,191
CAPITAL (000)			
Total Debt	1,525	1,684	1,924
Preferred Equity	0	0	0
Common Equity	173,290	147,289	137,569

Business:

CORBY DISTILLERIES LTD. markets a full range of domestically produced spirits and liqueurs, as well as imported spirits, liqueurs and wines including Canadian Club, Beefeater, Wiser's Deluxe and Lamb's rums. Subsidiaries include Meaghers Distillery Ltd. and McGuinness Distillers Ltd. Hiram Walker owns 52% of the voting shares.

Date	EPS	DPS	Tot Rev	Inc Bex
Feb 93	0.93	0.28	22,582	6,570
Nov 92	2.09	0.28	41,842	14,634
Aug 92	1.08	0.28	25,917	7,599
May 92	0.84	0.23	23,718	5,861
Feb 92	0.71	0.23	20,971	4,987
Nov 91	1.83	0.23	39,043	12,782
Aug 91	0.80	0.23	24,290	5,576
May 91	(1.12)	0.19	24,760	(7,828)

Synopsis:

For fiscal 1993, Corby Distilleries Limited's net earnings increase was attributed to the full year impact of last year's restructuring, improved results from equity investments (up 270%), and increased investment and other income (up 27%). With short-term investments at $111-million at fiscal year-end, the company will be looking at investment opportunities in the beverage alcohol industry. During the year, the $111-million was invested mainly in Hiram Walker Gooderham & Worts Limited commercial paper. Also during the year, export sales accounted for less than 10% of gross revenue. The company's equity income is derived primarily from European operations.

In the Canadian marketplace, the total traditional spirits market in Canada continued to be concentrated with the top 25 leading brands accounting for 53% of the domestic market. Corby accounts for nine of the top 25 brands, and is the largest marketer of traditional spirits in Canada with 27% of the market. The company had been known in the past as a distiller of spirits, but has now become a marketer and distributor of world renowned brands.

Overall industry sales of traditional spirits declined by 4.5% in fiscal 1993, following on the heels of a 7.6% decline in 1992. As well, provincial liquor boards reduced inventories during the year which affected Corby's shipments. Other negative factors affecting sales included: cross border shopping; high taxation; and consumption patterns towards a healthier lifestyle. Corby as part of its strategy to be a marketer versus a distiller, continues to look for potential purchasers for its distilling site in Corbyville, Ontario. The company plans to increase the market share of its core brands and develop new products targeted to market niches with the most potential.

Rank (Profit/Revenue/Assets)
140 363 340

John Giffen
Chairman

Martin A. Jones
President & C.E.O.

Alastair K. Symers
V.P., Finance & C.F.O.

Address
1201, Rue Sherbrooke Ouest
Montreal
PQ
H3A 1J1
(514) 288-4181

Fax: (514) 288-6310
C0010839/G/5.3.2

CORPORATE FOODS LIMITED

Exchanges	Price (Jun24'93)	14.50	Trailing P/E	18.35	Stock Symbol
T	Trailing Yield (%)	1.66	Trailing EPS	0.79	**CFL**

Period Ending	Dec92	Dec91	Dec90	Dec89	Dec88
Yearly Statistics					
Price-Close	16.50	17.88	11.75	11.50	8.88
Price-High	19.75	19.75	12.00	12.25	8.88
Price-Low	14.75	10.00	8.75	8.13	6.25
P/E-Close	20.63	19.02	14.33	17.16	14.79
Dividends per Share	0.24	0.21	0.20	0.20	0.17
Dividend Yield (%)	1.46	1.18	1.70	1.74	1.92
Sales per Share	10.07	10.83	11.00	10.66	10.59
EPS before extra. item	0.80	0.94	0.82	0.67	0.60
Cash Flow per Share	0.79	0.96	0.92	0.75	0.73
Book Value per Share	6.15	4.84	4.08	3.44	2.91
O/S Common Shares	20,902	19,283	19,144	19,037	18,820
Total Revenue	203,563	209,387	217,018	203,390	198,104
Income before extra.	15,502	18,103	15,700	12,743	11,259
Cash Flow	15,876	18,504	17,621	14,304	13,669
Debt/Equity	0.01	0.01	0.01	0.02	0.10
Return on Capital (%)	19.03	30.02	31.41	29.99	34.47
Ret. on Com. Equity (%)	13.94	21.05	21.79	21.08	25.48
% Change Profit	(14.4)	15.3	23.2	13.2	58.4
% Change Revenue	(2.8)	(3.5)	6.7	2.7	45.6
% Change Assets	35.8	14.2	14.3	12.1	41.3

Preferred Div. Coverage	np	262.4	227.5
Total Div. Coverage	3.3	4.4	4.0
Interest Coverage	na	na	na
Current Ratio	1.7	2.1	1.7
Operating Margin	6.7	8.9	8.1
Asset Turnover	1.2	1.7	2.0
5 YEAR RATIOS (%)			
Return on Capital	29.0	30.3	28.7
Return on Com. Equity	20.7	22.5	22.6
Profit Growth	16.8	25.5	24.0
Revenue Growth	8.3	11.0	15.2
Asset Growth	22.8	16.9	16.6
BALANCE SHEET (000)			
Cash	3,471	5,454	3,416
Current Assets	52,742	44,025	36,198
Net Fixed Assets	58,452	36,204	32,830
Invest's & Advances	43,745	38,505	34,393
Total Assets	165,637	121,997	106,837
Short Term Debt	1,817	672	1,012
Current Liabilities	30,585	21,410	21,275
Long Term Debt	0	0	0
Total Liabilities	37,048	27,493	27,571
Total Equity	128,589	94,504	79,266
Total Liab. & Equity	165,637	121,997	106,837
CAPITAL (000)			
Total Debt	1,817	672	1,012
Preferred Equity	0	1,225	1,225
Common Equity	128,589	93,279	78,041

Business:

CORPORATE FOODS LIMITED is a leading manufacturer and distributor of bakery products in Ontario and through its wholly owned subsidiary, Eastern Bakeries Limited, is the largest wholesale baker in Atlantic Canada. It owns 25% of Multi-Marques, a Quebec bakery, and 49% of Dough Delight Ltd., which supplies in-store bakeries and restaurants.

Date	EPS	DPS	Tot Rev	Inc Bex
Mar 93	0.15	0.06	67,417	3,158
Dec 92	0.27	0.06	62,368	5,231
Sep 92	0.19	0.06	49,485	3,627
Jun 92	0.18	0.06	48,069	3,598
Mar 92	0.16	0.06	43,909	3,046
Dec 91	0.32	0.06	64,174	6,097
Sep 91	0.22	0.06	49,454	4,379
Jun 91	0.23	0.05	48,920	4,340

Synopsis:

For the first quarter of 1993, revenues for Corporate Foods Limited jumped 54% compared to the same period last year. However, net profit rose only 3.7% with net profit per share declining 6.3%. The company attributed the increased sales figure to the acquisition of McGavin Foods Ltd., and the increase in ownership of Circlet Foods Inc. to 60% from 50%. The drop in earnings per share resulted from the issue of additional shares following the McGavin purchase.

For fiscal 1992, sales dropped 2.8% as a result of higher discounts in Ontario and the purchase of a major customer. The company's total fresh bakery unit sales dropped 6.5% during the year. According to the company, "excess retail capacity and the poor economic climate have put pressures on margins in the Ontario retail food sector, and may prompt a period of consolidation and/or store closings." A number of competitors have introduced lower priced basic breads as a result of declining sales volumes, affecting the already competitive nature of the Ontario fresh bakery market.

The company introduced 12 new products in 1992 on a regional basis. As well, the company plans to develop new pasta products in 1993, through its subsidiary, Olivieri Foods Ltd. Olivieri has plans to continue its market expansion down the U.S. West Coast.

Other projects undertaken in 1992 include investing in plants and facilities to remain current technologically, and to improve productivity and product quality. Net additions to fixed assets in the year declined 20% to $6.4-million from 1991. Capital expenditures in 1993 are expected to increase, with the expansion of Olivieri Foods and on the consolidation of McGavin Foods and Circlet Foods. All of these additional expenditures will be financed by the company's cash flow or through credit facilities.

In August 1992, the company's minority shareholders turned down the amalgamation of the company with Maple Leaf Foods, which owns 66% of Corporate Foods. The last offer was $19.90 cash or 1.15 shares of Maple Leaf Food stock per share.

Rank (Profit/Revenue/Assets)
142   272   342

Norman T. Currie
Chairman

R.H. Bonus
President & C.O.O.

D.G. McInnis
V.P., Finance

Address
10 Four Seasons Place
Etobicoke
ON
M9B 6H7
(416) 622-2040

Fax: (416) 622-8954
C0010940/G/5.1

COTT CORPORATION

Exchanges	Price (Jun24'93)	57.25	Trailing P/E	112.25	Stock Symbol
TMQ	Trailing Yield (%)	0.14	Trailing EPS	0.51	**BCB**

Period Ending	Jan93	Jan92	Jan91	Jan90	Jan89
Yearly Statistics					
Price-Close	40.25	9.25	0.67	0.73	0.51
Price-High	40.88	10.44	0.79	0.88	0.88
Price-Low	12.13	0.65	0.67	0.50	0.47
P/E-Close	78.92	22.02	13.33	33.46	nm
Dividends per Share	0.08	0.03	0.02	0.00	0.00
Dividend Yield (%)	0.20	0.76	2.48	0.00	0.00
Sales per Share	13.69	7.22	3.47	2.27	1.62
EPS before extra. item	0.51	0.42	0.05	0.02	(0.03)
Cash Flow per Share	0.82	0.60	0.02	0.06	0.00
Book Value per Share	2.91	1.30	0.56	0.53	0.51
O/S Common Shares	26,128	22,294	18,646	18,833	18,839
Total Revenue	331,551	137,427	68,208	42,842	29,944
Income before extra.	12,796	8,094	958	415	(557)
Cash Flow	19,787	11,509	400	1,099	67
Debt/Equity	0.38	0.71	2.15	1.44	0.10
Return on Capital (%)	31.62	32.08	3.14	6.49	1.37
Ret. on Com. Equity (%)	24.38	40.90	9.33	4.24	(5.56)
% Change Profit	58.1	744.9	130.8	174.5	(71.4)
% Change Revenue	141.3	101.5	59.2	43.1	(5.7)
% Change Assets	153.6	71.9	42.9	101.7	(24.0)

Preferred Div. Coverage	np	np	np		
Total Div. Coverage	6.5	11.6	3.1		
Interest Coverage	10.0	5.0	1.1		
Current Ratio	1.2	1.3	0.8		
Operating Margin	8.0	10.3	2.9		
Asset Turnover	1.6	1.6	1.4		
5 YEAR RATIOS (%)					
Return on Capital	14.9	9.5	7.6		
Return on Com. Equity	14.7	9.2	4.2		
Profit Growth	89.1	51.6	(1.0)		
Revenue Growth	59.8	43.2	27.5		
Asset Growth	57.0	36.2	40.3		
BALANCE SHEET (000)					
Cash	7,894	0	61		
Current Assets	117,073	42,945	19,482		
Net Fixed Assets	48,178	33,595	21,927		
Invest's & Advances	10,303	0	568		
Total Assets	211,870	83,536	48,608		
Short Term Debt	5,727	3,175	9,045		
Current Liabilities	101,183	33,910	23,621		
Long Term Debt	23,145	17,391	13,568		
Total Liabilities	135,955	54,486	38,078		
Total Equity	75,915	29,050	10,530		
Total Liab. & Equity	211,870	83,536	48,608		
CAPITAL (000)					
Total Debt	28,872	20,566	22,613		
Preferred Equity	0	0	0		
Common Equity	75,915	29,050	10,530		

Business:

COTT CORPORATION produces a wide selection of bottled and canned carbonated beverages which are sold under private label, under its own brand names and under licensed brand names.

Date	EPS	DPS	Tot Rev	Inc Bex
Jan 93	0.14	0.02	110,711	3,547
Oct 92	0.12	0.02	80,370	3,061
Jul 92	0.16	0.02	89,408	4,115
Apr 92	0.09	0.02	51,062	2,073
Jan 92	0.04	0.00	36,613	883
Oct 92	0.08	0.03	32,548	1,551
Jul 91	0.20	0.00	46,844	3,774
Apr 91	0.10	0.00	21,422	1,886

Synopsis:

In March 1993, Cott Corporation announced the completion of the sale of 1.2 million common shares for a total contribution before expenses of about $43.6-million (U.S.). The money raised through this equity financing will be earmarked for working capital purposes and the expansion of Cott's bottling beverages capacity.

For the fourth quarter of 1992, net earnings jumped 301% on a revenue increase of 202%, when compared to the same period last year. The big increase in sales was attributed to increased sales to U.S.-based retailers which accounted for 53% of total dollar sales in the quarter. Revenues from Canadian sources for the quarter gained 91% over last year.

In June 1992, Cott made an agreement to purchase a 25% interest in Menu Foods Limited, and has also acquired an option on additional shares. If the option is exercised, it would increase ownership to 43.75%. Menu Foods comprises manufacturing facilities in Mississauga, Ontario, and New Jersey. It is one of North America's leading suppliers of private label canned pet foods. Company officials said "the association with a high quality manufacturer such as Menu Foods will allow us to further capitalize on the knowledge and expertise that have developed in the marketing of upscale retailer branded products."

Rank (Profit/Revenue/Assets)
199 327 447

Gerald N. Pencer
Chairman & C.E.O.

Heather Reisman
President

Paul Henderson
V.P. Fin. & Admin. Sec.

Fraser Latta
Vice Chairman & C.O.O.

Address
1660 Chomedey Boulevard
Laval
PQ
H7V 2X3
(514) 688-3793

Fax: (514) 688-3840
01000795/G/5.1

DOVER INDUSTRIES LIMITED

Exchanges	Price (Jun24'93)	15.50	Trailing P/E	11.74	Stock Symbol
T	Trailing Yield (%)	2.71	Trailing EPS	1.32	**DVI**

Period Ending	Dec92	Dec91	Dec90	Dec89	Dec88
Yearly Statistics					
Price-Close	15.25	18.00	13.38	18.50	14.75
Price-High	18.50	18.50	18.75	21.00	15.63
Price-Low	14.00	13.25	13.00	15.00	13.00
P/E-Close	11.91	12.77	9.29	12.09	10.17
Dividends per Share	0.56	0.56	0.56	0.50	0.44
Dividend Yield (%)	3.67	3.11	4.19	2.70	2.98
Sales per Share	30.46	30.98	31.63	31.76	32.42
EPS before extra. item	1.28	1.41	1.44	1.53	1.45
Cash Flow per Share	2.09	2.09	2.10	2.12	1.95
Book Value per Share	11.74	11.02	10.17	9.29	8.26
O/S Common Shares	3,428	3,428	3,428	3,428	3,428
Total Revenue	104,501	106,313	108,406	108,856	111,948
Income before extra.	4,443	4,882	5,012	5,306	5,020
Cash Flow	7,176	7,147	7,191	7,257	6,684
Debt/Equity	0.05	0.05	0.25	0.10	0.17
Return on Capital (%)	17.33	19.40	21.87	26.61	26.67
Ret. on Com. Equity (%)	11.24	13.27	14.85	17.44	18.66
% Change Profit	(9.0)	(2.6)	(5.5)	5.7	26.9
% Change Revenue	(1.7)	(1.9)	(0.4)	(2.8)	7.9
% Change Assets	2.7	(1.4)	16.3	1.6	3.4

Date	EPS	DPS	Tot Rev	Inc Bex
Mar 93	0.26	0.14	24,881	914
Dec 92	0.50	0.14	25,860	1,722
Sep 92	0.26	0.14	26,087	897
Jun 92	0.30	0.14	27,083	1,052
Mar 92	0.22	0.14	25,486	772
Dec 91	0.39	0.14	23,934	1,328
Sep 91	0.36	0.14	27,106	1,260
Jun 91	0.36	0.14	29,413	1,224

Preferred Div. Coverage	71.7	78.7	80.8
Total Div. Coverage	2.2	2.5	2.5
Interest Coverage	90.2	20.5	10.7
Current Ratio	3.0	2.7	2.2
Operating Margin	6.9	7.7	8.2
Asset Turnover	1.9	2.0	2.0
5 YEAR RATIOS (%)			
Return on Capital	22.4	23.6	24.7
Return on Com. Equity	15.1	16.1	16.9
Profit Growth	2.3	5.5	4.1
Revenue Growth	0.1	1.7	3.3
Asset Growth	4.2	4.8	9.0
BALANCE SHEET (000)			
Cash	0	0	0
Current Assets	30,294	29,026	32,438
Net Fixed Assets	23,506	23,474	20,973
Invest's & Advances	0	0	0
Total Assets	54,559	53,125	53,884
Short Term Debt	2,223	2,035	9,048
Current Liabilities	9,980	10,944	14,454
Long Term Debt	0	0	0
Total Liabilities	13,309	14,337	17,997
Total Equity	41,250	38,788	35,887
Total Liab. & Equity	54,559	53,125	53,884
CAPITAL (000)			
Total Debt	2,223	2,035	9,048
Preferred Equity	1,026	1,026	1,026
Common Equity	40,224	37,762	34,861

Business:

DOVER INDUSTRIES LTD. is a food products and packaging company. Operations and products include flour milling for domestic and export markets, grain elevators in southwestern Ontario, disposable paper food containers, folding cartons, pastic drinking straws and ice cream cones. It has facilities in Ontario and Nova Scotia. Operations include Bondware, Dover Flour Mills, Howell Packaging, Robinson Cone.

Synopsis:

In fiscal 1992, Dover Industries Limited experienced a slight 9% decline in net income, compared to fiscal 1991. Sales volume declined in all business segments except the flour divisions. The poorer results were attributed to the recession and diversification. Dover reduced inventory levels during the year. As a result of the lower interest rate environment, Dover's interest rate expense dropped by 80%. Working capital increased 12.3% as a result of strong fourth quarter sales performance along with the timing of receipts of grain shipments due to the late corn harvest in 1992. Capital expenditures in the year fell 44% from 1991. In terms of capital spending by segment, the food products divisions accounted for 77% of expenditures, with the major allocations to Robinson Cone and the two flour mills. The capital program is geared towards lowering production costs and increasing productivity.

The paper and plastic products segment comprises the Bondware division, Howell Packaging division, and the packaging section of Robinson Cone. This segment had a 24% increase in operating profit to $4.6-million in 1992. During the year, Bondware focused its efforts on market rationalization and product mix in order to improving profits. The Howell division faced stiff foreign and domestic competition in the year. Unit sales declined as some U.S.-based customers transferred production from their Canadian divisions to U.S. plants. However, Howell's return on sales remain constant as a result of improved plant efficiencies and supplier support. The food products segment recorded a 8.5% decline in sales in 1992. The flour and grain operations accounted for 91% of the sales volume. A 40% drop in operating profit was attributed to the loss of two major U.S. accounts at the Robinson Cone division.

For the year ended December 31, 1992, Dover derived 55% of its sales from the food products segment, and 45% from the plastic and paper products segment. However, food products accounted for only 36% of operating profit. Export sales accounted for 6.5% of consolidated sales in 1992.

Relative strength to TSE300 / Price / Volume (in 1000's of board lots)

Rank (Profit/Revenue/Assets)
275   373   520

Mrs. Kenneth L. Campbell
Chairman & President

Brian J. Short
V.P. Finance & Admin.

Address
P.O. Box 10
4350 Harvester Road
Burlington
ON
L7R 3X8
(416) 333-1515

Fax: (416) 333-1584

D0002819/G/5.1

FPI LIMITED

Exchanges	Price (Jun24'93)		4.15	Trailing P/E		nm	Stock Symbol
TM	Trailing Yield (%)		0.00	Trailing EPS		(1.28)	**FPL**

Period Ending	Dec92	Dec91	Dec90	Dec89	Dec88
Yearly Statistics					
Price-Close	3.10	6.38	4.80	5.75	15.00
Price-High	7.38	8.63	7.00	11.25	17.25
Price-Low	2.65	4.85	4.00	5.63	8.00
P/E-Close	nm	nm	6.67	nm	14.29
Dividends per Share	0.00	0.00	0.00	0.00	0.40
Dividend Yield (%)	0.00	0.00	0.00	0.00	2.67
Sales per Share	35.98	33.10	32.63	21.58	22.90
EPS before extra. item	(4.10)	(0.02)	0.72	(1.38)	1.05
Cash Flow per Share	0.75	1.05	1.44	0.01	1.83
Book Value per Share	8.96	13.04	13.07	12.38	13.91
O/S Common Shares	16,411	16,407	16,402	16,392	16,019
Total Revenue	598,667	553,066	552,589	355,391	369,819
Income before extra.	(67,299)	(288)	11,771	(22,202)	16,755
Cash Flow	12,348	17,199	23,584	140	29,275
Debt/Equity	0.69	0.29	0.31	0.34	0.20
Return on Capital (%)	(22.80)	2.34	6.84	(6.05)	7.96
Ret. on Com. Equity (%)	(37.29)	(0.13)	5.64	(10.43)	7.70
% Change Profit	nm	(102.4)	153.0	(232.5)	(46.0)
% Change Revenue	8.2	0.1	55.5	(3.9)	(7.0)
% Change Assets	(3.6)	(1.3)	0.1	6.5	11.1

Preferred Div. Coverage	np	np	np
Total Div. Coverage	na	na	na
Interest Coverage	0.0	1.1	3.0
Current Ratio	1.6	2.2	2.2
Operating Margin	0.6	1.3	1.9
Asset Turnover	1.9	1.7	1.6
5 YEAR RATIOS (%)			
Return on Capital	(2.3)	8.1	13.2
Return on Com. Equity	(6.9)	3.9	7.2
Profit Growth	na	na	na
Revenue Growth	8.5	7.2	12.9
Asset Growth	2.4	7.7	10.4
BALANCE SHEET (000)			
Cash	3,595	3,776	6,190
Current Assets	206,036	165,822	164,548
Net Fixed Assets	95,907	152,403	158,522
Invest's & Advances	872	4,140	2,362
Total Assets	313,391	325,179	329,418
Short Term Debt	64,291	28,372	26,728
Current Liabilities	128,955	76,987	74,510
Long Term Debt	37,414	34,230	40,615
Total Liabilities	166,369	111,217	115,125
Total Equity	147,022	213,962	214,293
Total Liab. & Equity	313,391	325,179	329,418
CAPITAL (000)			
Total Debt	101,705	62,602	67,343
Preferred Equity	0	0	0
Common Equity	147,022	213,962	214,293

Business:

FPI LTD. is an integrated seafood harvesting, processing and marketing company. It operates a fleet of deep sea vessels and processing plants in Newfoundland, Nova Scotia and Massachusetts, and sources seafood products worldwide, particularly through its Clouston Foods division. FPI sells fresh and frozen seafood to food service and retail markets in the U.S., Canada, Europe and Japan.

Date	EPS	DPS	Tot Rev	Inc Bex
Apr 93	(0.02)	0.00	151,695	(312)
Dec 92	(1.14)	0.00	171,401	(18,774)
Sep 92	0.01	0.00	152,483	152
Jun 92	(2.88)	0.00	139,964	(47,149)
Mar 92	(0.09)	0.00	135,207	(1,528)
Dec 91	0.07	0.00	145,475	1,198
Sep 91	(0.13)	0.00	140,410	(2,170)
Jun 91	(0.12)	0.00	133,149	(1,940)

Synopsis:

In fiscal 1992, Fishery Products International's (FPI) results were severely affected by the major decline in Atlantic groundfish stocks, relating to reduced quotas set by the federal government. FPI recorded a $65-million provision to reflect the impact on its assets of the government's two-year ban on cod. Despite record sales in the year, the all time low catch rates negatively affected results. Catches of cod and groundfish fell 38% in the year to 69,000 tonnes, and are expected to drop a further 48% to 36,000 tonnes. To replace reduced quotas, FPI will continue to use external sources for species such as Alaskan pollock. FPI officials attributed increased sales to its Clouston Foods division purchased last year from National Sea Products (NatSea). As a result of the quota problems, FPI has been closing plants, suspending the operation of some trawlers, and cutting staff. So far, nine of FPI's groudfish processing plants in Newfoundland have closed.

Sales for the first quarter of 1993 improved over the 1992 period, with sales in the FPI division up 14.7% reflecting the impact of the new U.S. food service business acquired from NatSea. The Clouston division continues to maintain its strong sales performance with an increase of 12.3% over the same period last year. However in the quarter, performance was negatively affected by the late start in harvesting operations following changes to government regulations. As well, catches were below par. Groundfish sales levels were maintained but with the sourcing of some more expensive groudfish externally, margins declined. The strong results of expanding U.S. food service business partially offset the impact of the reduced fish harvest.

In late 1992, FPI purchased NatSea's U.S. food service business for $4.1-million (U.S.). This business includes the marketing of frozen groundfish, secondary processed products, and shrimp to institutions, restaurants, and club stores in the U.S. FPI also bought NatSea's inventory and accounts receivables related to the business, valued at $23.7-million (U.S.). This is part of FPI's strategy to acquire fish externally and to acquire strategic businesses to offset its losses elsewhere.

Rank (Profit/Revenue/Assets)
963 141 266

Victor L. Young
Chairman & C.E.O.

David G. Norris
Exec. V.P., Fin. & Bus. Dev.

Address
70 O'Leary Avenue
P.O. Box 550
St. John'S
NF
A1C 5L1
(709) 570-0000

Fax: (709) 570-0479
F0001100/G/5.1

MAPLE LEAF FOODS INC.

Exchanges	Price (Jun24'93)	13.62	Trailing P/E	16.22	Stock Symbol
TM	Trailing Yield (%)	2.79	Trailing EPS	0.84	MLF

Period Ending	Dec92	Dec91	Dec90	Mar90	Dec89
Yearly Statistics					
Price-Close	14.63	17.00	10.88	14.13	17.38
Price-High	17.50	17.50	18.50	20.50	20.50
Price-Low	13.13	10.75	9.00	13.13	13.38
P/E-Close	16.25	17.53	17.26	40.36	32.18
Dividends per Share	0.38	0.38	0.38	0.38	0.38
Dividend Yield (%)	2.60	2.24	3.49	2.69	2.19
Sales per Share	34.03	43.89	54.68	85.70	61.45
EPS before extra. item	0.90	0.97	0.63	0.35	0.54
Cash Flow per Share	1.60	1.92	1.27	1.29	1.26
Book Value per Share	11.68	11.12	9.67	10.76	9.38
O/S Common Shares	80,856	80,800	65,621	36,091	65,621
Total Revenue	2,772,112	3,043,311	3,582,008	3,095,511	3,970,903
Income before extra.	72,493	67,228	41,102	12,591	34,744
Cash Flow	129,625	133,035	83,235	46,597	80,895
Debt/Equity	0.05	0.09	0.28	0.51	0.35
Return on Capital (%)	12.40	13.60	15.38	6.40	12.72
Ret. on Com. Equity (%)	7.87	8.77	8.04	2.51	6.92
% Change Profit	7.8	63.6	226.4	(63.8)	37.8
% Change Revenue	(8.9)	(15.0)	15.7	(22.0)	30.3
% Change Assets	(0.8)	13.3	61.7	(41.0)	64.0
Preferred Div. Coverage	np	np	np		
Total Div. Coverage	2.4	2.5	3.3		
Interest Coverage	36.9	14.7	3.7		
Current Ratio	2.0	1.5	1.0		
Operating Margin	4.0	3.8	3.3		
Asset Turnover	1.9	2.1	2.8		
5 YEAR RATIOS (%)					
Return on Capital	12.1	11.3	11.2		
Return on Com. Equity	6.8	6.5	6.7		
Profit Growth	23.5	12.6	1.3		
Revenue Growth	(1.9)	(1.9)	2.2		
Asset Growth	11.9	11.9	13.3		
BALANCE SHEET (000)					
Cash	253,118	228,973	16,137		
Current Assets	678,567	680,054	497,757		
Net Fixed Assets	521,832	573,719	597,419		
Invest's & Advances	58,528	48,729	43,123		
Total Assets	1,419,018	1,431,153	1,262,779		
Short Term Debt	2,299	63,713	76,928		
Current Liabilities	343,066	452,356	489,069		
Long Term Debt	46,089	14,232	97,598		
Total Liabilities	474,390	532,608	628,439		
Total Equity	944,628	898,545	634,340		
Total Liab. & Equity	1,419,018	1,431,153	1,262,779		
CAPITAL (000)					
Total Debt	48,388	77,945	174,526		
Preferred Equity	0	0	0		
Common Equity	944,628	898,545	634,340		

Business:

MAPLE LEAF FOODS INC. operates a diverse portfolio of food businesses. The company has operations in Canada, the United Kingdom and the United States. Its products include fresh and prepared meats, poultry, flour, fresh and frozen bakery products, seafood and animal feeds. Maple Leaf sells to retail, wholesale, industrial and foodservice customers worldwide.

Date	EPS	DPS	Tot Rev	Inc Bex
Mar 93	0.13	0.10	637,491	10,189
Dec 92	0.22	0.10	742,458	17,784
Sep 92	0.24	0.10	697,719	19,390
Jun 92	0.25	0.10	684,647	20,040
Mar 92	0.19	0.10	641,630	15,279
Dec 91	0.29	0.10	742,647	22,878
Sep 91	0.27	0.10	744,081	17,198
Jun 91	0.26	0.10	810,610	17,125

Synopsis:

For the first quarter of 1993, the weaker performance of Maple Leaf Foods versus 1992 was attributed to the recession, the sale of its edible oils division and an equity issue last year.

Maple Leaf strives to be the lowest cost producer in both brand name items and high quality private label goods. Maple Leaf has undergone a major restructuring since the merger of Canada Packers and Maple Leaf Mills in 1990. Staff levels have fallen 37.5% to 10,000 in two years. Its unprofitable beef slaughter houses have been eliminated, and 20 beef, chicken and hog processing plants have been amalgamated. Maple Leaf has formed a joint venture in flour milling with a major U.S. competitor, and made $105-million on the sale of its edible oils division.

Maple Leaf initiated a $226-million share issue and has only $46-million in debt and $253-million in cash. There exists the possibility of U.S. expansion in the near future, but Maple Leaf's attempt to acquire Corporate Foods last year failed.

In fiscal 1992, net earnings from continuing operations increased 16% compared to 1991. Sales for the year dropped 7% due to the company's withdrawal from the beef business. Also in the year, acquisitions cost Maple Leaf $48-million, and it invested nearly $50-million in the company's facilities and ongoing operations. Earnings in the consumer foods group fell 13%. Improvements in grocery products and frozen foods businesses were offset by reduced earnings in prepared meats and food service that were affected by the wet summer and recession. Earnings in the milling and baking group climbed 29%, due to improved earnings resulting from the ConAgra flour milling joint venture and increased profits from acquisitions. This offset poor results at Corporate Foods, which suffered from competition. The earnings of the agribusiness group fell 16%, due to poor returns in the poultry and pork businesses. Also responsible for the poor results was the aquaculture business, which was sold in 1991.

Rank (Profit/Revenue/Assets)
49 50 116

Harry Solomon
Chairman Of The Board

Charles John Bowen
President & C.E.O.

Lewis Norman Rose
Sr. V.P. & C.F.O.

Address
30 St. Clair Avenue West
Suite 1500
Toronto
ON
M4V 3A2
(416) 926-2000

Fax: (416) 926-2018
C0001677/G/5.1

For further company information, call Globe Information Services 1-800-268-9128 or (416)585-5345

MOLSON COMPANIES LIMITED (THE)

Exchanges	Price (Jun24'93)		23 .50	Trailing P/E		8 .51	Stock Symbol
TMV	Trailing Yield (%)		3 .06	Trailing EPS		2 .76	**MOL.A**

Period Ending	Mar93	Mar92	Mar91	Mar90	Mar89
Yearly Statistics					
Price-Close	25 .50	34 .75	28 .83	25 .17	21 .67
Price-High	36 .00	35 .25	29 .09	26 .83	22 .50
Price-Low	25 .38	27 .00	18 .83	21 .08	15 .08
P/E-Close	9 .24	15 .44	nm	11 .62	12 .26
Dividends per Share	0 .72	0 .72	0 .67	0 .61	0 .59
Dividend Yield (%)	2 .82	2 .07	2 .32	2 .44	2 .71
Sales per Share	45 .46	45 .53	39 .78	42 .79	43 .04
EPS before extra. item	2 .76	2 .25	(0 .72)	2 .17	1 .77
Cash Flow per Share	3 .18	4 .08	3 .42	3 .36	3 .04
Book Value per Share	19 .68	16 .32	14 .41	14 .71	12 .87
O/S Common Shares	59 ,382	56 ,588	55 ,637	49 ,333	49 ,262
Total Revenue	2 ,906 ,667	2 ,577 ,840	2 ,053 ,176	2 ,134 ,975	2 ,134 ,286
Income before extra.	164 ,694	126 ,223	(38 ,667)	106 ,696	87 ,119
Cash Flow	190 ,117	229 ,067	183 ,511	165 ,867	149 ,669
Debt/Equity	0 .59	0 .68	1 .16	0 .47	0 .42
Return on Capital (%)	13 .56	15 .59	9 .04	20 .89	18 .40
Ret. on Com. Equity (%)	15 .75	14 .63	(5 .06)	15 .69	14 .22
% Change Profit	30 .5	426 .4	(136 .2)	22 .5	10 .7
% Change Revenue	12 .8	25 .6	(3 .8)	0 .0	5 .4
% Change Assets	14 .7	(8 .0)	39 .7	30 .0	3 .8

Preferred Div. Coverage	np	np	np
Total Div. Coverage	3 .8	3 .1	0 .0
Interest Coverage	3 .9	3 .6	1 .2
Current Ratio	1 .3	1 .3	1 .6
Operating Margin	7 .3	9 .2	9 .7
Asset Turnover	1 .0	1 .1	0 .8
5 YEAR RATIOS (%)			
Return on Capital	15 .5	16 .5	16 .3
Return on Com. Equity	11 .0	10 .7	9 .9
Profit Growth	15 .9	19 .3	na
Revenue Growth	7 .5	6 .7	4 .0
Asset Growth	14 .7	13 .8	17 .7
BALANCE SHEET (000)			
Cash	208 ,590	97 ,559	691 ,996
Current Assets	1 ,130 ,456	881 ,827	1 ,308 ,779
Net Fixed Assets	782 ,601	784 ,337	651 ,055
Invest's & Advances	342 ,415	270 ,861	387 ,509
Total Assets	2 ,715 ,627	2 ,368 ,087	2 ,573 ,147
Short Term Debt	275 ,366	139 ,325	264 ,030
Current Liabilities	901 ,223	676 ,716	827 ,897
Long Term Debt	412 ,415	484 ,250	668 ,222
Total Liabilities	1 ,547 ,292	1 ,444 ,397	1 ,771 ,439
Total Equity	1 ,168 ,335	923 ,690	801 ,708
Total Liab. & Equity	2 ,715 ,627	2 ,368 ,087	2 ,573 ,147
CAPITAL (000)			
Total Debt	687 ,781	623 ,575	932 ,252
Preferred Equity	0	0	0
Common Equity	1 ,168 ,335	923 ,690	801 ,708

Business:

MOLSON COS. LTD. is a diversified corporation operating in the brewing, cleaning and sanitizing, retail merchandising, and sports and entertainment industries in Canada, the U.S., and around the world. Subsidiaries include Molson Breweries, Diversey Corp., Beaver Lumber, Aikenhead's Home Improvement Warehouse, and the Montreal Canadiens. It owns 19.9% of Canada Malting Co. Limited.

Date	EPS	DPS	Tot Rev	Inc Bex
Mar 93	1 .08	0 .18	801 ,062	64 ,592
Dec 92	0 .42	0 .18	678 ,098	25 ,307
Sep 92	0 .60	0 .18	811 ,845	36 ,388
Jun 92	0 .66	0 .18	798 ,921	38 ,407
Mar 92	0 .28	0 .18	581 ,521	15 ,782
Dec 91	0 .59	0 .18	637 ,046	33 ,395
Sep 91	0 .67	0 .18	767 ,169	37 ,706
Jun 91	0 .71	0 .18	762 ,029	39 ,340

Synopsis:

In January 1993, The Molson Companies Limited announced a strategic alliance between Molson Breweries and the Miller Brewing Company. In the deal, Miller will acquire a 20% interest in Molson Breweries, with Molson Companies and Foster's Brewing each owning 40%. The alliance is aimed at making Molson a major national brand name in the United States. Molson Breweries will retain its license to produce and market the Miller brands in Canada. Miller will acquire the U.S. marketing and distribution rights for Molson and Foster's brands. Molson will still export beer into the U.S. from Canada. Miller will also acquire Molson Breweries U.S.A. and will pay a royalty on sales of Molson and Foster's brands. Miller is the second largest brewer in North America with 1991 volumes of about 51 million hectolitres. The four reasons for the alliance are: to establish a competitive Canadian based North American presence; to provide opportunities for major incremental growth; to capitalize on Molson's established presence in the U.S.; and to obtain North American scale synergies.

In fiscal 1993, Molson Breweries and the operations of Diversey Corp. outside of North America experienced increased operating profits. This was offset however by declines in operating profits in Diversey's North American operations and in Beaver Lumber, and by a loss in the first year of operation of the Aikenhead's warehouse chain. Unusual items in fiscal 1993 accounted for $51-million or 86 cents per share, on an after-tax basis. The unusual item included a $174.2-million gain from the sale of part of the company's interest in Molson Breweries to Miller, and $156.6-million in provisions for rationalization and restructuring activities in the company's operating businesses. The provisions will attempt to position these businesses to compete effectively and to increase profitability.

During fiscal 1993, sales were derived as follows: brewing, 38%; cleaning and sanitizing, 42%; retail merchandising, 18%; and other, 2%. Both the brewing and cleaning had returned positive operating profits, while the retail and other sectors had negative returns.

Relative strength to TSE300 / Price / Volume (in 1000's of board lots)

Rank (Profit/Revenue/Assets)		
27	53	85

Eric H. Molson
Chairman Of The Board

Marshall Cohen
President & C.E.O.

S.L. Hartley
Exec. V.P. & C.F.O.

Address
40 King Street West
Suite 3600, Scotia Plaza
Toronto
ON
M5H 3Z5
(416) 360-1786

Fax: (416) 360-4345
M0004536/G/5.3.1

NATIONAL SEA PRODUCTS LIMITED

Exchanges	Price (Jun24'93)	2.00	Trailing P/E	nm	Stock Symbol
TM	Trailing Yield (%)	0.00	Trailing EPS	(1.14)	**NSP**

Period Ending	Jan93	Dec91	Dec90	Dec89	Dec88
Yearly Statistics					
Price-Close	2.15	4.25	5.50	5.00	10.00
Price-High	5.75	7.25	7.50	11.88	18.00
Price-Low	1.50	3.90	4.00	4.85	8.88
P/E-Close	nm	nm	nm	nm	nm
Dividends per Share	0.00	0.00	0.00	0.08	0.10
Dividend Yield (%)	0.00	0.00	0.00	1.50	1.00
Sales per Share	11.97	16.70	24.28	35.04	34.48
EPS before extra. Item	(1.16)	(1.70)	(0.22)	(2.03)	(0.52)
Cash Flow per Share	0.32	0.16	0.32	(1.48)	0.28
Book Value per Share	0.98	2.02	3.05	3.14	3.57
O/S Common Shares	29,404	29,347	19,783	18,822	16,538
Total Revenue	351,492	372,361	467,506	613,145	561,624
Income before extra.	(32,525)	(35,873)	(2,201)	(32,390)	(5,847)
Cash Flow	9,397	3,568	6,111	(25,647)	4,630
Debt/Equity	1.99	1.51	2.14	2.91	2.19
Return on Capital (%)	(11.82)	(9.02)	6.73	(6.56)	2.82
Ret. on Com. Equity (%)	(74.21)	(64.25)	(3.86)	(54.96)	(23.82)
% Change Profit	9.3	(1,529.9)	93.2	(454.0)	(121.2)
% Change Revenue	(5.6)	(20.4)	(23.8)	9.2	2.1
% Change Assets	(21.6)	(20.3)	(18.5)	(6.3)	34.4

Date		EPS	DPS	Tot Rev	Inc Bex
Apr	93	0.09	0.00	79,573	2,936
Jan	93	(0.17)	0.00	74,133	(4,424)
Sep	92	(1.05)	0.00	71,904	(30,602)
Jun	92	(0.01)	0.00	108,316	193
Mar	92	0.07	0.00	117,514	2,308
Dec	91	(0.07)	0.00	78,197	(5,038)
Sep	91	(0.42)	0.00	83,034	(8,797)
Jun	91	(1.22)	0.00	105,451	(26,448)

Preferred Div. Coverage	0.0	0.0	0.0	
Total Div. Coverage	0.0	0.0	0.0	
Interest Coverage	0.0	0.0	0.9	
Current Ratio	1.2	1.4	1.1	
Operating Margin	2.2	2.2	3.5	
Asset Turnover	1.8	1.5	1.5	
5 YEAR RATIOS (%)				
Return on Capital	(3.6)	4.7	13.3	
Return on Com. Equity	(44.2)	(21.1)	1.6	
Profit Growth	na	na	na	
Revenue Growth	(8.6)	(6.4)	0.5	
Asset Growth	(8.5)	(3.1)	4.2	
BALANCE SHEET (000)				
Cash	1,850	984	373	
Current Assets	78,667	117,620	124,446	
Net Fixed Assets	87,907	99,607	118,493	
Invest's & Advances	4,331	3,668	2,899	
Total Assets	193,597	246,827	309,749	
Short Term Debt	21,014	41,315	62,517	
Current Liabilities	63,101	84,611	114,133	
Long Term Debt	79,772	81,134	113,446	
Total Liabilities	142,873	165,745	227,579	
Total Equity	50,724	81,082	82,170	
Total Liab. & Equity	193,597	246,827	309,749	
CAPITAL (000)				
Total Debt	100,786	122,449	175,963	
Preferred Equity	21,929	21,929	21,929	
Common Equity	28,795	59,153	60,241	

Business:

NATIONAL SEA PRODUCTS LTD. is a diversified vertically integrated harvester, procurer, processer and marketer of a full spectrum of fresh and frozen seafoods. It operates a fleet of scallop and ground fish ships and has operations in Canada and the U.S. The company's products include fresh fish, groundfish, shrimp and scallops. The company markets its products principally in North America.

Synopsis:

In 1992, the core businesses of National Sea Products Limited (NatSea) all performed well. The Canadian retail business, specifically its High Liner brand, improved upon its dominant market share. The Canadian food service and fresh food businesses posted a strong year, with higher volumes and profits. Exports also had higher profit margins despite slight sale reductions. The U.S. retail business improved the profitability of its Fisher Boy brand due to improved sales and distribution. NatSea continues to reduce debt.

At the beginning of the 1992, the total North American debt, including the debts related with its former U.S. food service business which was sold to Fishery Products International in September 1992, stood at $149.2-million. At year-end, the debt was reduced to by 32% to $100.8-million. This was achieved through cash flow generated from operations, the disposal of its U.S. food service business, other asset dispositions and reduced working capital requirements within continuing operations. The company said it will focus on value-added, secondary processing, the fresh and export businesses and innovative, aggressive marketing. The sale of its U.S. food service business and the closure of a shrimp plant will allow NatSea to concentrate on its retail and private label businesses. NatSea will allocate funds to core businesses, generating positive cash flow and profitability. To maintain fish supplies, NatSea will procure fish from sources worldwide for both Canadian and U.S. operations.

In early 1993, Pacific Aqua Foods initiated an offer for NatSea to pick up its long-term debt in exchange for its convertible preferred shares. NatSea currently is the majority shareholder of the Vancouver-based fish farm, with about 75% ownership of the shares outstanding. Pacific owes NatSea about $7.2-million in long-term debt, representing 85% of its total long-term debt.

In fiscal 1992, sales by region were: Canada, 35%; the U.S., 51%; and Europe and Pacific Rim, 14%. Exports made up 32% of Canadian sales.

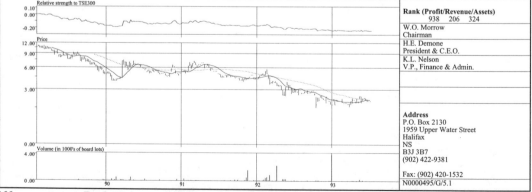

Rank (Profit/Revenue/Assets)		
938	206	324

W.O. Morrow
Chairman

H.E. Demone
President & C.E.O.

K.L. Nelson
V.P., Finance & Admin.

Address
P.O. Box 2130
1959 Upper Water Street
Halifax
NS
B3J 3B7
(902) 422-9381

Fax: (902) 420-1532
N0000495/G/5.1

ROTHMANS INC.

Exchanges	Price (Jun24'93)	102.00	Trailing P/E	10.16	Stock Symbol
TMV	Trailing Yield (%)	3.92	Trailing EPS	10.04	**ROC**

Period Ending	Mar93	Mar92	Mar91	Mar90	Mar89
Yearly Statistics					
Price-Close	101.00	94.00	55.00	68.00	62.50
Price-High	104.00	97.00	69.50	72.00	63.00
Price-Low	85.00	54.00	42.00	58.00	39.50
P/E-Close	10.06	10.86	7.26	9.66	10.74
Dividends per Share	4.00	3.70	18.40	2.00	1.60
Dividend Yield (%)	3.96	3.94	33.46	2.94	2.56
Sales per Share	84.96	80.62	75.74	70.36	75.12
EPS before extra. item	10.04	8.66	7.58	7.04	5.82
Cash Flow per Share	17.57	15.67	13.00	13.23	11.03
Book Value per Share	32.23	26.19	21.24	32.05	26.99
O/S Common Shares	5,511	5,511	5,511	5,511	5,511
Total Revenue	472,453	448,517	428,960	400,553	420,172
Income before extra.	55,327	49,305	43,318	40,394	33,701
Cash Flow	96,824	86,342	71,652	72,890	60,810
Debt/Equity	0.24	0.37	0.39	0.38	0.39
Return on Capital (%)	53.60	50.26	41.22	33.89	38.18
Ret. on Com. Equity (%)	34.37	36.54	28.46	23.85	23.39
% Change Profit	12.2	13.8	7.2	19.9	10.9
% Change Revenue	5.3	4.6	7.1	(4.7)	(0.7)
% Change Assets	4.1	10.0	(17.9)	8.6	(0.2)

Preferred Div. Coverage	np	np	28.4
Total Div. Coverage	2.5	2.2	0.4
Interest Coverage	134.9	71.7	12.5
Current Ratio	2.3	2.0	2.1
Operating Margin	30.7	28.4	26.5
Asset Turnover	1.2	1.1	1.2
5 YEAR RATIOS (%)			
Return on Capital	43.4	38.0	30.6
Return on Com. Equity	29.3	25.0	19.2
Profit Growth	12.7	16.3	66.5
Revenue Growth	2.2	9.4	10.5
Asset Growth	0.3	(7.6)	0.2
BALANCE SHEET (000)			
Cash	86,241	26,601	26,831
Current Assets	343,981	327,599	295,232
Net Fixed Assets	43,718	44,161	46,377
Invest's & Advances	1,179	6,884	6,090
Total Assets	406,358	390,230	354,759
Short Term Debt	42,742	53,258	54,468
Current Liabilities	151,170	167,578	139,595
Long Term Debt	0	0	0
Total Liabilities	228,752	245,908	215,131
Total Equity	177,606	144,322	139,628
Total Liab. & Equity	406,358	390,230	354,759
CAPITAL (000)			
Total Debt	42,742	53,258	54,468
Preferred Equity	0	0	22,589
Common Equity	177,606	144,322	117,039

Business:

ROTHMANS INC. is a holding company. It produces and sells tobacco products through its 60% owned subsidiary Rothmans Bensons & Hedges Inc. Rothmans International plc of the United Kingdom owns 71.2% of the company's common shares.

Date	EPS	DPS	Tot Rev	Inc Bex
Mar 93	2.17	1.00	108,311	11,970
Dec 92	2.75	1.00	112,668	15,157
Sep 92	2.53	1.00	113,283	13,946
Jun 92	2.59	1.00	137,854	14,254
Mar 92	2.29	1.00	110,683	13,055
Dec 91	2.57	1.00	304,232	14,532
Sep 91	1.84	1.00	112,221	10,528
Jun 91	1.96	0.70	111,590	11,190

Synopsis:

Consolidated earnings for Rothmans Inc. for fiscal 1992 increased 12% compared to 1991. Earnings from tobacco operations, after a provision for minority interest, increased 12.7% over last year. This was attributed to the full year impact of industry cigarette selling price increases. Investment income, net of income taxes, was unchanged from 1991 at $1.9-million. Growth in surplus funds was offset by continuing interest rate declines in the year. During the period, demand for exports significantly increased, resulting in major shifts in volume mix.

Overall, the tobacco industry is in decline with new additional taxes on cigarettes and new strict bylaws on smoking rules in public areas. Taxes and trade margins in Canada account for approximately 85% of the price of cigarettes. Governments are also looking at tighter legislative control over tobacco sales.

The importance of the U.S. export market has increased. Rothmans expects this rise in exports to be profitable in the short-term, but warns the flood of cigarettes into the U.S. will annoy the company's major customers - Canadian wholesalers and retailers. An estimated 80% of exports are eventually smuggled back into Canada. The federal government recently dropped a $2-a-pack export tax on Canadian cigarettes.

Rank (Profit/Revenue/Assets)
62   170   241

The Hon. William M. Kelly
Chairman

Joseph J. Heffernan
President & C.E.O.

Dennis Robertson
V.P., Finance

Address
1500 Don Mills Road
North York
ON
M3B 3L1
(416) 449-5525

R0002697/G/5.2

SCHNEIDER CORPORATION

Exchanges	Price (Jun24'93)		15.00	Trailing P/E		14.29	Stock Symbol
T	Trailing Yield (%)		1.67	Trailing EPS		1.05	**SCD.A**

Period Ending	Oct92	Oct91	Oct90	Oct89	Oct88
Yearly Statistics					
Price-Close	14.50	12.13	8.25	13.25	12.25
Price-High	16.44	12.25	13.50	13.50	13.50
Price-Low	11.88	8.00	8.25	12.00	10.44
P/E-Close	12.95	13.04	nm	2,650.00	32.24
Dividends per Share	0.23	0.22	0.22	0.22	0.22
Dividend Yield (%)	1.59	1.81	2.67	1.66	1.80
Sales per Share	116.32	115.88	117.45	116.77	112.77
EPS before extra. item	1.12	0.93	(0.31)	0.01	0.38
Cash Flow per Share	2.77	2.26	1.56	1.56	2.10
Book Value per Share	12.88	11.99	11.28	11.85	12.07
O/S Common Shares	5,585	5,585	5,430	5,302	5,302
Total Revenue	649,877	630,966	627,797	619,168	597,932
Income before extra.	6,279	5,064	(1,677)	20	2,007
Cash Flow	15,445	12,285	8,327	8,291	11,160
Debt/Equity	0.75	0.90	1.06	1.00	0.64
Return on Capital (%)	13.43	12.63	4.76	4.68	7.40
Ret. on Com. Equity (%)	9.04	7.90	(2.70)	0.03	3.16
% Change Profit	24.0	402.0	(8,485.0)	(99.0)	(64.2)
% Change Revenue	3.0	0.5	1.4	3.6	(12.6)
% Change Assets	(2.2)	5.4	(3.0)	19.0	(1.8)

	Date	EPS	DPS	Tot Rev	Inc Bex
	May 93	0.27	0.07	162,197	1,588
	Feb 93	0.23	0.06	210,459	1,318
	Oct 92	0.17	0.06	158,702	951
	Aug 92	0.38	0.06	158,124	2,098
	May 92	0.23	0.06	145,785	1,271
	Feb 92	0.35	0.06	187,266	1,959
	Oct 91	0.31	0.06	142,440	1,681
	Aug 91	0.38	0.06	159,304	2,041

Preferred Div. Coverage	np	np	np		
Total Div. Coverage	4.8	4.2	0.0		
Interest Coverage	2.8	2.3	0.7		
Current Ratio	1.5	1.4	1.2		
Operating Margin	2.6	2.5	1.0		
Asset Turnover	3.8	3.6	3.8		
5 YEAR RATIOS (%)					
Return on Capital	8.6	8.8	7.5		
Return on Com. Equity	3.5	3.5	2.3		
Profit Growth	2.3	35.7	na		
Revenue Growth	(1.1)	(0.6)	(0.7)		
Asset Growth	3.1	5.0	3.0		
BALANCE SHEET (000)					
Cash	0	0	0		
Current Assets	76,352	75,058	78,330		
Net Fixed Assets	83,872	89,352	81,077		
Invest's & Advances	2,666	2,606	1,173		
Total Assets	171,561	175,466	166,520		
Short Term Debt	11,479	15,041	34,653		
Current Liabilities	49,682	54,307	65,762		
Long Term Debt	42,171	44,900	30,490		
Total Liabilities	99,648	108,520	105,297		
Total Equity	71,913	66,946	61,223		
Total Liab. & Equity	171,561	175,466	166,520		
CAPITAL (000)					
Total Debt	53,650	59,941	65,143		
Preferred Equity	0	0	0		
Common Equity	71,913	66,946	61,223		

Business:

SCHNEIDER CORP., through its subsidiaries, J.M. Schneider Inc., Mother Jackson's Open Kitchens Limited, Charcuterie Roy Inc., Horizon Poultry Products Inc., and Fleetwood Sausage Ltd., and its 50% owned joint venture National Meats Inc., produces and distributes meat, poultry, cheese and baked goods across Canada. The companies have retail and food service markets in Canada, the U.S. and Japan.

Synopsis:

For the first quarter of 1993, Schneider Corporation had a 12.4% increase in sales versus the same period last year. However, net earnings declined 33%. About 50% of the increase in sales resulted from the acquisition of businesses. The company's largest operating subsidiary, J. M. Schneider benefited from relatively favorable commodity prices last year, but this trend has reversed itself. As well, the subsidiary has experienced a very competitive environment in its retail and food service markets. The operating results of Charcuterie Roy Inc. were also affected by the adverse market conditions. The company's baked goods subsidiary, Mother Jackson's, had improved earnings over 1991.

Subsequent to year-end, Schneider increased its investment in Horizon Poultry Products from 50% to 75%, maintaining its desire to achieve new business growth in the poultry area. In this quarter, Horizon experienced growth in sales and earnings. Recently, Horizon signed a letter of intent to purchase a poultry slaughter facility located in St. Mary's, Ontario, from Campbell Soup Company. The purchase will allow Schneider to consolidate its poultry slaughter operations.

In the first quarter of 1993, Schneider completed the purchase of 100% of the outstanding shares of Fleetwood Sausage Ltd., of Surrey, British Columbia. Fleetwood manufactures and markets a wide range of delicatessen products under the Fleetwood brand, and a line of Italian meat products under the Fiorentina label. The company has annual sales of over $30-million. The acquisition should strengthen Schneider's processed meat business by providing geographic and product line diversification and a manufacturing presence in the Western Canada.

For fiscal 1993, Schneider expects a very competitive market with very little opportunity to expand margins in its red meat business. The company expects improvement in its poultry and baked goods businesses.

Relative strength to TSE300

Price

Volume (in 1000's of board lots)

Rank (Profit/Revenue/Assets)
230   134   338

Herbert J. Schneider
Chairman

Douglas W. Dodds
President & C.E.O.

Gerald A. Hooper
V.P. & C.F.O.

Address
321 Courtland Avenue East
P.O. Box 130
Kitchener
ON
N2G 3X8
(519) 885-8259

Fax: (519) 885-8918
H0001263/G/5.1

For further company information, call Globe Information Services 1-800-268-9128 or (416)585-5345

T.G. BRIGHT & CO., LIMITED

Exchanges	Price (Jun24'93)	18.00	Trailing P/E	9.63	Stock Symbol
TM	Trailing Yield (%)	1.39	Trailing EPS	1.87	**BRT.A**

Period Ending	Mar92	Mar91	Mar90	Mar89	Mar88
Yearly Statistics					
Price-Close	12.00	15.00	16.25	13.25	8.75
Price-High	15.00	17.00	19.38	14.75	17.00
Price-Low	9.50	7.25	11.88	8.75	8.63
P/E-Close	10.81	26.32	nm	18.40	9.02
Dividends per Share	0.25	0.25	0.25	0.25	0.25
Dividend Yield (%)	2.08	1.67	1.54	1.89	2.86
Sales per Share	36.42	33.96	35.98	39.74	41.05
EPS before extra. item	1.11	0.57	(0.52)	0.72	0.97
Cash Flow per Share	2.01	1.77	(0.65)	1.97	3.39
Book Value per Share	14.92	14.06	13.74	14.80	13.70
O/S Common Shares	2,068	2,068	2,067	2,067	2,067
Total Revenue	75,302	70,226	74,384	82,132	84,827
Income before extra.	2,296	1,179	(1,066)	1,485	2,009
Cash Flow	4,154	3,665	(1,340)	4,074	7,005
Debt/Equity	0.64	0.71	0.70	0.95	1.31
Return on Capital (%)	9.82	7.41	(1.30)	9.63	11.08
Ret. on Com. Equity (%)	7.66	4.10	(3.61)	5.04	7.41
% Change Profit	94.7	210.6	(171.8)	(26.1)	(10.9)
% Change Revenue	7.2	(5.6)	(9.4)	(3.2)	12.5
% Change Assets	0.7	(7.9)	(12.2)	(6.1)	2.4

Preferred Div. Coverage	np	np	np
Total Div. Coverage	4.4	2.3	0.0
Interest Coverage	3.6	2.1	0.0
Current Ratio	2.2	2.2	2.3
Operating Margin	6.5	5.2	4.5
Asset Turnover	1.3	1.2	1.2
5 YEAR RATIOS (%)			
Return on Capital	7.3	8.1	7.9
Return on Com. Equity	4.1	4.4	4.6
Profit Growth	0.3	2.4	na
Revenue Growth	(0.0)	10.5	11.9
Asset Growth	(4.8)	10.5	14.7
BALANCE SHEET (000)			
Cash	108	114	102
Current Assets	34,431	36,722	41,776
Net Fixed Assets	17,020	14,522	13,733
Invest's & Advances	3,779	4,179	5,116
Total Assets	58,466	58,078	63,069
Short Term Debt	11,284	12,217	5,957
Current Liabilities	15,890	16,787	18,302
Long Term Debt	8,488	8,517	14,000
Total Liabilities	27,616	29,011	34,668
Total Equity	30,850	29,067	28,401
Total Liab. & Equity	58,466	58,078	63,069
CAPITAL (000)			
Total Debt	19,772	20,734	19,957
Preferred Equity	0	0	0
Common Equity	30,850	29,067	28,401

Business:

T.G. BRIGHT & CO. LTD. owns and operates wineries, cider operations, research and development facilities, and retail outlets across Canada. It produces a range of wines, ciders, sparkling wine beverages and Canadian champagnes.

Date	EPS	DPS	Tot Rev	Inc Bex
Dec 92	1.30	0.00	25,661	2,699
Sep 92	0.38	0.13	20,809	785
Jun 92	0.15	0.00	19,687	307
Mar 92	0.04	0.13	13,145	88
Dec 91	0.60	0.00	23,462	1,240
Sep 91	0.30	0.13	19,412	611
Jun 91	0.17	0.00	19,412	357
Mar 91	(0.22)	0.13	12,920	(462)

Synopsis:

In May 1993, a management group spearheaded by Toronto investor Leland Verner acquired additional shares of T.G. Bright & Co., raising its stake in Bright to 80%. The purchase basically eliminated chances for Andres Wines Limited to effect a similar takeover of Bright. Andres currently owns 16.1% of Bright and has intention of selling its stake. The remaining 3.9% of Bright shares are widely held. The ownership change at Bright started to take form after Mr. Verner acquired a 53% stake previously owned by the Hatch family. The Hatch family has attempted to sell its stake in Bright for years, but was unable to due to its inability to attract properly financed bids.

For the first nine months of fiscal 1993, revenues at Bright remained flat at $64-million, but profit increased 73%. The results included an after-tax profit of $1.4-million from the sale of land. The revenue increase was attributed to increased cider volumes in Western Canada and higher sale prices for many products across Canada. Bright is the largest winery in Canada with 1992 sales of approximating $99-million, and an estimated 35% share of the domestic wine market. There has been gradual improvement in the Canadian wine industry due to quality improvements and aggressive marketing. Sales of Ontario red wines jumped 35% last year, doubling the increase of imports, while sales of Canadian white wines remain stable.

There are no immediate plans to change current management, nor change the Bright's brand name. Furthermore, most of the wineries in the Niagara region of Ontario and Quebec will remain intact, along with the chain of retail wine stores. The old Bright winery in Niagara Falls will be replaced by a new winery, and the winery in Surrey, B.C., will be closed. There are possibilities of expanding Bright's business beyond the existing markets with an expanded chain of retail wine stores, and possible expansion into the U.S. private label business. Overall, Mr. Verner plans to revive a sluggishly performing company by building a bigger and more aggressive company under the current management team.

Rank (Profit/Revenue/Assets)
346   416   503

Edward S. Arnold
President
Fred J. Karner
V.P., Finance & Secretary

Address
P.O Box 510
Niagara Falls
ON
L2E 6V4
(416) 358-7141

Fax: (416) 358-7750
B0003556/G/5.3.3

Page	Company	$	Latest year end	Earnings per Share		
				Actual	Estimate this year	Estimate next year
173	Camco		9212	0.08	0.45	0.70
174	Canadian Manoir Industries	8M	9208	(0.34)	n.a.	n.a.
175	Canstar Sports		9212	0.81	1.00	1.20
176	Dominion Textile		9206	(0.43)	0.68	0.99
177	International Semi-Tech Microelectronics		9204	4.34	n.a.	n.a.
178	Irwin Toy		9301	0.33	n.a.	n.a.

Estimates from I/B/E/S Inc., 345 Hudson St., New York, NY 10014 (212) 243-3335. In Canada: 6 Lansing Square, Ste. 235, Willowdale, ON M2J 1T5 (416) 496-0977.

Major Appliance Industry - Industry Report [Apr-22-1993]. MERRILL LYNCH CAPITAL MARKETS reported by Goldfarb, J.

In 1992, U.S. major appliance shipments saw a solid uptrend, which persisted in 1Q:93. Shipments of core products are expected to rise by about 6% in 1993. Though smaller, increases should occur during the following few years. [RN 1324196]

Monthly Appliance Shipment Forecast - Industry Report [Apr-12-1993]. SHEARSON LEHMAN BROTHERS, INC. reported by Cornell, R.T., et al

Major home appliance shipments in February 1993 were up 7.5%, the thirteenth consecutive month of increasing appliance shipments, with strength in almost all categories (except for room air conditioners and compactors). Year-to-date, appliance shipments are up 4%. Shipments for 1993 could be up 5%-7%, and shipments for 1994 are forecast to increase 0%-5%. [RN 1322379]

Cosmetics & Household Products Earnings - Industry Report [Apr-6-1993]. THE FIRST BOSTON CORPORATION reported by Hyman, L.R., et al

For the cosmetics and household products industry, consumer demand shows no evidence of a recovery. Notwithstanding the acceleration in domestic consumer spending that began six months or so ago, sales of most consumer staple products have shown no improvement over the past year. Orders picked up somewhat in late December 1992, and the strength carried into January 1993, but by February, shipments had flattened out again and March was even softer. Alberto Culver's 2Q:93 sales and profits are softer than expected due to ongoing industrywide weakness in the United States, bad weather, and unfavorable currency fluctuations. In 1Q:93, Avon Products' revenue growth is expected to be soft, reflecting ongoing weakness in U.S. demand and recessions in Germany and Japan. [RN 1319757]

Major Appliance First Quarter Wrap-Up - Industry Report [Apr-5-1993]. PAINEWEBBER INC. reported by Sprague, J.T.

It is expected that 1Q:93 earnings releases will feature numerous charges and write downs, continuing the current trend. Appliance shipments were slightly stronger than expected, with "core 6" appliances increasing 5.5% through February 1993. On a seasonally adjusted basis, shipments have been about flat for six months. Wholesale prices of appliances increased in February for the first time in 20 months, while retail prices declined. Products and services cited include household appliances, household cooking equipment, household laundry equipment, ranges, microwave ovens, dishwashers, disposals, trash compactors, refrigerators, freezers, air conditioners and dehumidifiers. [RN 1322574]

Clothes Line (The) - Industry Report [Apr-29-1993]. SHEARSON LEHMAN BROTHERS, INC. reported by Esquivel, J.R., et al

March 1993 textile and apparel employment continued lower than a year ago. Apparel shipments remained strong in February (+25.6%), while textile shipments were weaker (+4.1%). Consumer sentiment continued to fall in March to 85.9 from 86.6 in February. Increases in personal income declined slightly in February (from gains of 2.2% in 1992). Retail sales year-to-date were above a yearago, but momentum was slowing. [RN 1328649]

CAMCO INC.

Exchanges	Price (Jun24'93)		6.50	Trailing P/E		46.43	Stock Symbol
T	Trailing Yield (%)		0.46	Trailing EPS		0.14	**COC**

Period Ending	Dec92	Dec91	Dec90	Dec89	Dec88
Yearly Statistics					
Price-Close	6.00	8.75	8.13	8.25	8.25
Price-High	10.38	10.25	9.00	10.00	9.50
Price-Low	4.55	6.25	4.75	7.63	7.00
P/E-Close	75.00	175.00	13.11	8.87	5.43
Dividends per Share	0.02	0.24	0.36	0.83	0.44
Dividend Yield (%)	0.33	2.74	4.43	10.06	5.33
Sales per Share	21.01	20.96	23.39	25.85	27.94
EPS before extra. item	0.08	0.05	0.62	0.93	1.52
Cash Flow per Share	0.55	0.45	0.93	1.30	1.15
Book Value per Share	6.30	6.24	6.43	6.11	6.02
O/S Common Shares	20,000	20,000	20,000	20,000	20,000
Total Revenue	422,527	422,293	469,624	520,247	559,262
Income before extra.	1,518	985	12,461	18,547	30,444
Cash Flow	11,026	9,050	18,553	25,908	22,979
Debt/Equity	0.02	nd	nd	0.02	0.11
Return on Capital (%)	2.26	1.16	16.75	27.30	41.02
Ret. on Com. Equity (%)	1.21	0.78	9.93	15.29	27.80
% Change Profit	54.1	(92.1)	(32.8)	(39.1)	35.4
% Change Revenue	0.1	(10.1)	(9.7)	(7.0)	6.0
% Change Assets	0.3	(3.2)	(6.7)	(10.9)	5.1

Date	EPS	DPS	Tot Rev	Inc Bex
Mar 93	(0.04)	0.03	83,773	(792)
Dec 92	0.08	0.00	125,179	1,498
Sep 92	0.05	0.00	115,608	1,117
Jun 92	0.05	0.00	106,709	901
Mar 92	(0.10)	0.02	75,031	(1,998)
Dec 91	(0.17)	0.06	116,288	(3,391)
Sep 91	0.09	0.06	112,114	1,794
Jun 91	0.11	0.06	110,377	2,118

Preferred Div. Coverage	np	np	np
Total Div. Coverage	3.8	0.2	1.7
Interest Coverage	na	nd	20.9
Current Ratio	2.5	2.3	2.3
Operating Margin	0.1	1.2	4.1
Asset Turnover	2.2	2.2	2.4
5 YEAR RATIOS (%)			
Return on Capital	17.7	24.9	32.8
Return on Com. Equity	11.0	15.7	20.8
Profit Growth	(41.8)	(46.0)	(7.7)
Revenue Growth	(4.4)	(3.9)	1.0
Asset Growth	(3.3)	(2.4)	0.7
BALANCE SHEET (000)			
Cash	50,242	32,766	22,707
Current Assets	139,619	134,581	141,327
Net Fixed Assets	50,087	54,697	54,233
Invest's & Advances	0	0	0
Total Assets	192,129	191,650	197,893
Short Term Debt	0	0	0
Current Liabilities	55,499	58,995	61,503
Long Term Debt	2,900	0	0
Total Liabilities	66,155	66,794	69,222
Total Equity	125,974	124,856	128,671
Total Liab. & Equity	192,129	191,650	197,893
CAPITAL (000)			
Total Debt	2,900	0	0
Preferred Equity	0	0	0
Common Equity	125,974	124,856	128,671

Business:

CAMCO INC. is a manufacturer and distributor of major home appliances in Canada. Its products include such brands as GE, Hotpoint, Moffat and McClary, and private brands for leading department stores. The company produces refrigerators, ranges, dishwashers, and automatic washers and dryers. Its production facilities are in Montreal and Hamilton.

Synopsis:

The higher revenues reported by Camco in the first quarter of 1993, when compared to the first quarter of 1992, were attributed to increased exports of dryers and dishwashers to the United States. The rise in exports was partially offset by a decline in domestic selling prices, as the competitive market conditions continue.

Camco said that the $17-million increase in cash balances during the year was the result of improved inventory and accounts receivable management. With approximately 50% of the manufactured product being shipped directly from Camco's factories to customers, product inventory levels are being substantially reduced.

The benefits from cost reductions that Camco received in 1992 were offset by rising costs for imported material and products, due to the lower value of the Canadian dollar and the drop in selling prices. Appliance prices have fallen due to the intense competition within the industry. Camco lost some market share in the retail segment of the Canadian major appliance market, with sales dipping 2% from 1991 levels. However, the number of units sold climbed as Camco successfully executed programs to export dishwashers and larger capacity dryers to the United States. The company expects exports to reach approximately $40-million in 1993.

The largest minority shareholder of Camco, GSW Inc., initiated legal action against majority shareholder General Electric Canada Inc. and its parent General Electric Company of the United States. GE Canada and GE are defending the action and have brought an action against GSW, which GSW is defending. The actions are scheduled to come to trial in September 1993.

Contributions to total sales by segment in 1992 (1991) were: kitchen products, 62% (61%); laundry products, 28% (28%); and consumer service, 10% (11%). Export revenues in 1992 totalled $30-million, an increase of 64% from 1991 due primarily to increased dryer and dishwasher exports. Export sales are primarily through General Electric Company. In 1991, export sales to GE totalled $26.7-million.

Relative strength to TSE300 / Price / Volume (in 1000's of board lots) chart

Rank (Profit/Revenue/Assets)
384   180   327

R.M. Barford
Chairman

John G. Rice
President & C.E.O.

John L. Theler
V.P., Fin., Info. Tech. & Sec.

Address
2645 Skymark Avenue
Mississauga
ON
L4W 4H2
(416) 629-3000

C0990015/G/5.5.4

CANADIAN MANOIR INDUSTRIES LIMITED

Exchanges	Price (Jun24'93)	0.80	Trailing P/E	nm	Stock Symbol
T	Trailing Yield (%)	0.00	Trailing EPS	(0.16)	**CMQ**

Period Ending	Aug92	Dec91	Dec90	Dec89	Dec88
Yearly Statistics	8M				
Price-Close	0.30	0.25	1.40	2.60	2.70
Price-High	0.45	1.50	2.60	3.10	3.30
Price-Low	0.26	0.20	1.40	2.25	2.50
P/E-Close	nm	nm	nm	nm	nm
Dividends per Share	0.00	0.00	0.00	0.00	0.00
Dividend Yield (%)	0.00	0.00	0.00	0.00	0.00
Sales per Share	5.77	6.40	7.14	10.74	10.95
EPS before extra. item	(0.34)	(0.83)	(1.30)	(0.05)	(0.28)
Cash Flow per Share	(0.32)	(0.47)	(1.02)	(0.15)	(0.15)
Book Value per Share	1.95	2.29	3.12	4.42	4.47
O/S Common Shares	5,092	5,092	5,092	5,092	5,092
Total Revenue	19,576	32,587	36,355	54,714	55,759
Income before extra.	(1,736)	(4,240)	(6,632)	(251)	(1,398)
Cash Flow	(1,073)	(2,399)	(5,207)	(781)	(759)
Debt/Equity	0.63	0.46	0.51	0.50	0.69
Return on Capital (%)	(10.32)	(17.40)	(16.78)	0.70	(2.65)
Ret. on Com. Equity (%)	(24.16)	(30.80)	(34.54)	(1.11)	(5.96)
% Change Profit	38.6	36.1	(2,542.2)	82.0	66.8
% Change Revenue	0.0	(10.4)	(33.6)	(1.9)	(33.6)
% Change Assets	1.2	(27.8)	(24.9)	(9.8)	(4.7)

Preferred Div. Coverage	np np np
Total Div. Coverage	na na na
Interest Coverage	0.0 0.0 0.0
Current Ratio	2.0 2.7 2.2
Operating Margin	(5.8) (7.7) (9.2)
Asset Turnover	1.3 1.5 1.2
5 YEAR RATIOS (%)	
Return on Capital	(9.3) (9.8) (5.6)
Return on Com. Equity	(19.3) (17.7) (11.8)
Profit Growth	na na na
Revenue Growth	(18.9) (15.0) (20.0)
Asset Growth	(14.1) (13.2) (10.7)

BALANCE SHEET (000)

Cash	28	52	648
Current Assets	14,684	14,092	19,870
Net Fixed Assets	7,250	7,588	8,206
Invest's & Advances	0	0	0
Total Assets	21,934	21,680	30,034
Short Term Debt	1,482	491	3,198
Current Liabilities	7,276	5,213	9,215
Long Term Debt	4,747	4,820	4,932
Total Liabilities	12,023	10,033	14,147
Total Equity	9,911	11,647	15,887
Total Liab. & Equity	21,934	21,680	30,034

CAPITAL (000)

Total Debt	6,229	5,311	8,130
Preferred Equity	0	0	0
Common Equity	9,911	11,647	15,887

Business:

CANADIAN MANOIR INDUSTRIES LTD. operates two businesses, DMO Industries and Air Heat Supplies, that manufacture and distribute residential heating, ventilation and cooling equipment. Its markets are in Toronto and Southwestern Ontario, the northeastern United States and Western Canada.

Date	EPS	DPS	Tot Rev	Inc Bex
Feb 93	(0.12)	0.00	6,420	(605)
Nov 92	0.18	0.00	13,635	905
Aug 92	(0.09)	0.00	5,085	(473)
Jun 92	(0.13)	0.00	7,872	(642)
Mar 92	(0.12)	0.00	6,513	(621)
Dec 91	0.03	0.00	11,732	156
Sep 91	(0.01)	0.00	10,240	(55)
Jun 91	(0.47)	0.00	6,273	(2,389)

Synopsis:

The second quarter results for Canadian Manoir Industries Limited reflect the relatively unchanged demand for heating products, when compared to last year. Better utilization of manufacturing capacity at DMO Industries's Wallaceburg plant and a better product and geographic sales mix are the reasons given for the improved first half results by Canadian Manoir. The improvement on the gross margins was partially offset by the increased selling costs required to support existing sales volumes as well as to attract increased demand. The improved first quarter results were mainly due to the increased export shipments of oil furnaces to the United States, when compared to the fourth quarter of last year. The domestic sales for the first quarter were at a reduced rate from one year ago.

DMO Industries continues to search for products which require DMO's expertise in light metal fabrication and are counter-cyclical to the demand for furnaces to better utilize available capacity in the Wallaceburg plant. Canadian Manoir continues to look for opportunities to better utilize its manufacturing and sales facilities during its non-peak periods, during which it incurs losses. Capital expenditures are not expected to exceed $200,000 in fiscal 1993. Capital expenditures during 1992 of $140,000 was limited to expenditures required to maintain a safe and healthy working environment and for tooling to enhance the product offering.

The company changed its year-end to August so that it could track more closely the seasonality of its operations. Approximately 66% of Canadian Manoir's sales are generated during the traditional fall heating season. During the eight-month period ending August 31, 1992, DMO experienced a better product mix with a bigger portion of sales being represented by the higher margin high-efficiency gas and oil furnaces.

Export sales from continuing operations, made primarily to the United States, accounted for 36% of net sales for the eight months ended August 31, 1992, and 33% of net sales for 1991.

Rank (Profit/Revenue/Assets)
779 564 699

Geraldine Clever
Chairman & President

Douglas A. Fraser
Executive Vice President

Address
2 Glengrove Avenue West
Toronto
ON
M4R 1N4
(416) 487-5363

Fax: (416) 487-7290
C0003637/G/5.5.4

CANSTAR SPORTS INC.

Exchanges	Price (Jun24'93)	16.87	Trailing P/E	19.85	Stock Symbol
TM	Trailing Yield (%)	1.18	Trailing EPS	0.85	**HKY**

Period Ending	Dec92	Dec91	Dec90	Dec89	Dec88
Yearly Statistics					
Price-Close	15.88	6.00	3.10	3.30	2.08
Price-High	17.25	6.12	4.10	3.75	12.00
Price-Low	5.87	2.60	2.75	2.25	2.01
P/E-Close	19.60	12.77	6.60	6.11	8.32
Dividends per Share	0.15	0.05	0.00	0.00	0.00
Dividend Yield (%)	0.95	0.83	0.00	0.00	0.00
Sales per Share	9.91	8.54	8.76	6.59	0.00
EPS before extra. item	0.81	0.47	0.47	0.54	0.25
Cash Flow per Share	1.23	0.96	0.76	0.71	2.50
Book Value per Share	2.97	2.40	2.06	1.34	0.76
O/S Common Shares	18,050	17,497	17,406	14,919	14,919
Total Revenue	177,062	149,066	145,373	99,623	90,574
Income before extra.	14,420	8,526	8,412	8,711	3,007
Cash Flow	22,028	16,831	12,543	10,644	7,708
Debt/Equity	0.97	1.20	1.32	1.34	2.05
Return on Capital (%)	29.00	22.32	23.59	26.03	17.33
Ret. on Com. Equity (%)	30.18	20.86	27.81	51.84	335.69
% Change Profit	69.1	1.4	(3.4)	189.7	207.2
% Change Revenue	18.8	2.5	45.9	10.0	11.9
% Change Assets	20.5	(3.2)	51.0	13.3	(16.7)

Preferred Div. Coverage	np	np	13.3
Total Div. Coverage	5.3	3.4	13.3
Interest Coverage	5.9	3.0	2.1
Current Ratio	2.6	2.9	1.7
Operating Margin	16.3	14.5	12.4
Asset Turnover	1.3	1.3	1.2
5 YEAR RATIOS (%)			
Return on Capital	23.7	19.9	14.7
Return on Com. Equity	93.3	na	na
Profit Growth	71.2	78.8	157.7
Revenue Growth	16.9	16.7	16.4
Asset Growth	10.7	(1.2)	2.5
BALANCE SHEET (000)			
Cash	0	0	0
Current Assets	98,397	77,233	81,697
Net Fixed Assets	28,572	28,292	28,696
Invest's & Advances	0	750	750
Total Assets	137,192	113,888	117,687
Short Term Debt	10,733	9,149	31,674
Current Liabilities	37,584	26,332	48,009
Long Term Debt	41,112	41,085	24,998
Total Liabilities	83,617	71,907	74,768
Total Equity	53,575	41,981	42,919
Total Liab. & Equity	137,192	113,888	117,687
CAPITAL (000)			
Total Debt	51,845	50,234	56,672
Preferred Equity	0	0	7,000
Common Equity	53,575	41,981	35,919

Business:

CANSTAR SPORTS INC., through its subsidiaries, makes and markets ice skates under the Bauer, Micron, Daoust, Mega and Lange brands. The company also makes and distributes hockey equipment under the Cooper, Bauer and Flak brands, skate blades, Bauer in-line roller skates and multi-purpose helmets. Canstar has manufacturing facilities in Canada and Europe. Its main markets are the United States, Europe and Canada.

Date	EPS	DPS	Tot Rev	Inc Bex
Mar 93	0.09	0.05	38,648	1,605
Dec 92	0.06	0.05	34,002	1,052
Sep 92	0.36	0.05	59,216	6,463
Jun 92	0.34	0.05	51,361	6,158
Mar 92	0.04	0.00	32,483	747
Dec 91	0.13	0.05	33,386	2,386
Sep 91	0.22	0.00	49,822	3,854
Jun 91	0.22	0.00	45,793	4,045

Synopsis:

Canstar will build a new manufacturing facility in the Czech Republic to produce figure and hockey skates for sale throughout Europe. The plant is expected to cost approximately $6-million and begin production in the Spring of 1994.

Canstar's first quarter sales of hockey equipment in the United States exceeded expectations. No particular reason could be given for the growth but the company felt that the National Hockey League's efforts to raise the sport's profile in the U.S. market may have contributed. Strong demand in all major markets and the ability to ensure delivery on a timely basis contributed to improved first quarter results, compared to the same period last year.

Canstar Sports Inc. and Rollerblade Inc. entered into a cross-licence agreement whereby each party has granted the other certain rights to use their respective patents. The agreement was part of a settlement over a complaint Rollerblade filed with the U.S. International Trade Commission to seek enforcement of certain patents against rival companies.

Canstar purchased the Daoust skate division from A. Lambert International Inc. for $2.8-million. Under the agreement Canstar receives the Daoust name, inventories and plant equipment. Canstar's Cambridge, Ontario, plant will take over production of the skates. The Daoust division has annual sales of $4-million, about 8% of the world skate market and 10% of the Canadian market.

Canstar has a stereolithography unit that allows "quick and cost effective simulation of both product design changes and new product concepts." This allows Canstar to make three-dimensional models in one-sixth of the time required for manual prototypes.

Contributions to 1992 revenue (operating income) by geographic segment were: Canada, 55% (59%); the United States, 31% (28%); and Europe, 14% (13%). Export sales, primarily to Europe, accounted for approximately 13.5% of Canadian sales in 1992 and 16% in 1991.

Rank (Profit/Revenue/Assets)
148   293   370

Icaro Olivieri
Chairman

Donald MacMartin
President & C.O.O.

Robert A. Desrosiers
V.P., Finance & Secretary

Address
5705 Ferrier Street
Suite 200
Mont-Royal
PQ
H4P 1N3
(514) 738-3011

Fax: (514) 738-5178
W0000829/G/5.5.3

DOMINION TEXTILE INC.

Exchanges	Price (Jun24'93)		11.00	Trailing P/E		nm	Stock Symbol
TM	Trailing Yield (%)		0.00	Trailing EPS		(1.28)	**DTX**

Period Ending	Jun92	Jun91	Jun90	Jun89	Jun88
Yearly Statistics					
Price-Close	6.25	7.75	11.88	16.13	16.75
Price-High	9.50	12.00	18.31	17.00	22.00
Price-Low	5.63	5.00	10.79	13.75	14.75
P/E-Close	nm	nm	62.50	115.18	8.77
Dividends per Share	0.00	0.22	0.60	0.60	0.57
Dividend Yield (%)	0.00	2.84	5.05	3.72	3.40
Sales per Share	39.71	38.52	47.33	52.82	61.92
EPS before extra. item	(2.31)	(4.07)	0.19	0.14	1.91
Cash Flow per Share	3.89	1.20	4.05	2.67	4.86
Book Value per Share	8.82	10.51	16.11	16.40	19.57
O/S Common Shares	34,588	34,571	30,524	28,692	24,792
Total Revenue	1,378,763	1,281,000	1,400,155	1,415,160	1,224,963
Income before extra.	(74,823)	(128,827)	11,043	9,280	43,061
Cash Flow	134,462	39,600	118,012	70,960	95,541
Debt/Equity	1.54	1.41	0.97	1.00	1.22
Return on Capital (%)	0.86	(7.85)	6.42	5.89	10.73
Ret. on Com. Equity (%)	(23.94)	(31.39)	1.16	0.79	8.94
% Change Profit	41.9	(1,266.6)	19.0	(78.4)	33.8
% Change Revenue	7.6	(8.5)	(1.1)	15.5	16.2
% Change Assets	(2.6)	(5.5)	5.0	(11.3)	89.3

Date	EPS	DPS	Tot Rev	Inc Bex
Mar 93	0.22	0.00	345,101	9,107
Dec 92	0.14	0.00	338,158	6,402
Sep 92	0.07	0.00	297,010	3,558
Jun 92	(1.71)	0.00	384,079	(57,839)
Mar 92	0.03	0.00	339,302	2,079
Dec 91	(0.23)	0.00	333,122	(6,568)
Sep 91	(0.40)	0.00	321,997	(12,495)
Jun 91	(2.14)	0.00	365,100	(70,306)

	Jun92	Jun91	Jun90
Preferred Div. Coverage	0.0	0.0	2.0
Total Div. Coverage	0.0	0.0	0.5
Interest Coverage	0.1	0.0	1.2
Current Ratio	1.8	1.8	1.9
Operating Margin	6.3	(1.2)	4.7
Asset Turnover	1.0	0.9	1.0
5 YEAR RATIOS (%)			
Return on Capital	3.2	5.6	8.6
Return on Com. Equity	(8.9)	(2.5)	4.4
Profit Growth	na	na	22.4
Revenue Growth	5.5	6.5	12.7
Asset Growth	10.1	12.9	16.3
BALANCE SHEET (000)			
Cash	46,956	39,119	65,784
Current Assets	527,440	496,929	502,669
Net Fixed Assets	627,021	626,814	688,783
Invest's & Advances	28,748	64,282	89,575
Total Assets	1,323,155	1,357,806	1,436,287
Short Term Debt	66,261	85,331	65,288
Current Liabilities	295,364	277,821	257,921
Long Term Debt	517,380	527,853	480,961
Total Liabilities	945,067	921,449	870,439
Total Equity	378,088	436,357	565,848
Total Liab. & Equity	1,323,155	1,357,806	1,436,287
CAPITAL (000)			
Total Debt	583,641	613,184	546,249
Preferred Equity	73,041	73,052	74,052
Common Equity	305,047	363,305	491,796

Business:

DOMINION TEXTILE INC. manufactures textiles and related products. It is engaged in the design, manufacturing, finishing and marketing of denim fabrics, industrial products, yarns, apparel fabrics and interlinings. The company operates 38 manufacturing facilities - 12 in Canada, 10 in the United States, 12 in Europe, two in South America, one in North Africa and one in Hong Kong.

Synopsis:

Dominion Textile has completed most of a restructuring, which involved the closure or sale of several operations to control debt and focus on core products. Domtex sold its subsidiary Wayne-Tex, which manufactures carpetbacking, for approximately $72-million and used the funds to reduce debt. Domtex had ceased operations of its Canadian carpetbacking facility, Fibreworld, in December 1992. After evaluating alternatives concerning the future of the Dominion Yarn Group, Domtex concluded that the best option would be to retain the business.

Domtex has been renegotiating its debt payment schedule which called for debt repayments of more than $300-million in fiscal 1994 and 1995. Domtex hopes to spread payments more evenly over a longer period and feels confident that this will be accepted due to its improving quarterly results.

Dominion Textile attributed the improved third quarter profit for the three months ended March 1993 compared to the third quarter a year ago to the improved business climate and recent restructuring decisions. Higher denim and yarn sales contributed to the improved results. The denim division, the Far East interlinings business, the industrial fabrics operations and the European non-woven business are all performing well.

Domtex issued six million common shares and used the net proceeds of $51.8-million to finance its ongoing capital expenditure program, for working capital and to reduce long-term debt. Domtex will be investing $16.4-million (U.S.), including working capital, in its Swift Textiles denim manufacturing facility in Georgia. To expand and upgrade manufacturing capacity for non-woven fabrics in North America and Europe, Domtex will invest $29-million (U.S.).

The portion of total sales in fiscal 1992 by product was: denim, 30%; yarns, 23%; apparel fabrics, 20%; technical fabrics, 15%; and industrial fabrics, 12%. Sales by geographic segment in 1992 were: Canada, 26%; the United States, 45%; and Europe and Other, 29%.

Relative strength to TSE300 / Price / Volume (in 1000's of board lots)

Rank (Profit/Revenue/Assets)
965   81   126

Charles H. Hantho
Chairman, President & C.E.O.

Address
1950 Sherbrooke Street West
Montreal
PQ
H3H 1E7
(514) 989-6000

Fax: (514) 989-6214
D0002586/G/5.5.2

INTERNATIONAL SEMI-TECH MICROELECTRONICS INC.

Exchanges	Price (Jun24'93)		20.75	Trailing P/E		4.09	Stock Symbol
T	Trailing Yield (%)		0.00	Trailing EPS		5.07	**ISE.A**

Period Ending	Apr92	Jan92	Apr91	Jan91	Jan90
Yearly Statistics					
Price-Close	16.88	16.00	9.50	3.75	7.88
Price-High	17.00	16.50	9.88	8.38	10.38
Price-Low	9.13	3.65	3.25	3.25	6.63
P/E-Close	3.89	3.43	27.14	8.72	7.10
Dividends per Share	0.00	0.00	0.00	0.00	0.00
Dividend Yield (%)	0.00	0.00	0.00	0.00	0.00
Sales per Share	na	na	na	na	na
EPS before extra. item	4.34	4.66	0.35	0.43	1.11
Cash Flow per Share	0.36	0.43	(0.08)	(0.00)	0.14
Book Value per Share	9.15	9.05	3.92	4.01	5.30
O/S Common Shares	16,584	13,147	12,893	12,857	12,854
Total Revenue	52,472	53,504	36,029	35,038	25,162
Income before extra.	60,048	60,463	4,530	5,473	13,381
Cash Flow	4,952	5,602	(1,083)	(57)	1,741
Debt/Equity	0.65	0.88	1.79	1.76	0.81
Return on Capital (%)	25.00	31.43	7.32	8.39	9.94
Ret. on Com. Equity (%)	44.37	71.33	8.87	9.15	25.57
% Change Profit	(0.7)	1,234.7	(17.2)	(59.1)	106.4
% Change Revenue	(1.9)	48.5	2.8	39.3	(93.9)
% Change Assets	9.3	36.6	0.1	26.1	(52.3)
Preferred Div. Coverage	na	na	na		
Total Div. Coverage	na	na	na		
Interest Coverage	12.2	10.2	1.6		
Current Ratio	2.3	0.1	0.2		
Operating Margin	(36.0)	na	(17.6)		
Asset Turnover	na	na	na		
5 YEAR RATIOS (%)					
Return on Capital	16.4	15.8	14.3		
Return on Com. Equity	31.9	26.7	16.8		
Profit Growth	56.2	56.4	(2.9)		
Revenue Growth	(33.6)	16.0	18.7		
Asset Growth	(2.1)	34.1	43.6		
BALANCE SHEET (000)					
Cash	53,978	1,995	185		
Current Assets	57,126	3,954	5,110		
Net Fixed Assets	28,127	28,385	29,171		
Invest's & Advances	208,073	235,769	163,136		
Total Assets	295,863	270,774	198,224		
Short Term Debt	2,570	33,176	1,506		
Current Liabilities	24,439	54,483	24,792		
Long Term Debt	103,755	81,397	110,567		
Total Liabilities	132,254	139,917	135,737		
Total Equity	163,609	130,857	62,487		
Total Liab. & Equity	295,863	270,774	198,224		
CAPITAL (000)					
Total Debt	106,325	114,573	112,073		
Preferred Equity	11,912	11,912	11,912		
Common Equity	151,697	118,945	50,575		

Business:

INTERNATIONAL SEMI-TECH MICROELECTRONICS INC. is a multinational company with interests in the retailing and distribution of consumer durables and sewing related products principally through the company's 39% investment in Semi-Tech (Global). The principal operating units are Singer Co. NV, Consumers Distributing, and an interest in Sansui Electric Co.

Date	EPS	DPS	Tot Rev	Inc Bex
Jan 93	0.24	0.00	9,602	8,084
Oct 92	0.42	0.00	16,839	14,418
Jul 92	2.94	0.00	55,750	51,364
Jan 92	1.47	0.00	23,304	19,212
Oct 91	0.46	0.00	9,496	5,979
Jul 91	2.10	0.00	7,567	27,196
Apr 91	0.38	0.00	9,780	4,914
Jan 91	(0.41)	0.00	14,697	(5,329)

Synopsis:

International Semi-Tech Microelectronics Inc. (ISTM) announced in early June 1993 that its affiliate, Semi-Tech (Global) Co. completed the acquisition of a 51% stake in G.M. Pfaff AG for 449 million Hong Kong dollars, or $28.5-million. Pfaff is the world's largest manufacturer and distributor of industrial sewing machines. Pfaff reported revenues of $600-million (U.S.) in 1992. The acquisition complements ISTM's current sewing machine operations through Singer Co. NV. Singer provides a new distributorship network for Pfaff while Singer receives additional expertise in the industrial sewing machine segment of its operations. Pfaff is expected to shift its focus away from the European markets to the emrging markets of China, Vietnam and Indonesia.

Singer will spend $20-million in a joint venture with Shangai Yah Chong Sewing Machine Co. Ltd., a Chinese state-owned company, to make advanced sewing machines in Shanghai. The partners will create a new manufacturing company, Singer (Shanghai) Sewing Machine Co. Ltd. The joint venture gives Singer a 70% stake in the new company. Singer will supply new technology to the Shanghai plant. Another $100-milion (U.S.) is expected to be spent in China on a variety of projects that include the production of sewing machine needles, the establishment of retail stores and the supplying of credit to customers.

In 1992, a Florida bankruptcy court ruled that Shinwa Co. Ltd. of Hong Kong, a subsidiary of Semi-Tech (Global), owed $45.2-million (U.S.) in royalties to BiCoastal Corp. for the use of the Singer name and trademark from the period April 15, 1989, to April 30, 1991. Semi-Tech is appealing the decision. Semi-Tech has filed a letter of credit with Bankers Trust Co. of New York that authorizes Bankers Trust to pay up to $59.4-million if Semi-Tech loses the appeal. An additional $30-million (U.S.) lawsuit that was filed by BiCoastal to cover the period May 1, 1991 to October 31, 1992, is still pending. Semi-Tech purchased the Singer trademark from BiCoastal in 1989 and since then the companies have disagreed over which products royalties apply to and the method of royalty payment.

Relative strength to TSE300 / Price / Volume (in 1000's of board lots)

Rank (Profit/Revenue/Assets)
55   463   274

James H. Ting
Chairman, President & C.E.O.

Chuck C.H. Tam
Exec. V.P. & C.F.O.

Address
131 McNabb Street
Markham
ON
L3R 5V7
(416) 475-2670

Fax: (416) 475-3652
S0001900/G/5.5.4

IRWIN TOY LIMITED

Exchanges	Price (Jun24'93)		5.75	Trailing P/E		19.83	Stock Symbol
TM	Trailing Yield (%)		3.83	Trailing EPS		0.29	**IWT**

Period Ending	Jan93	Jan92	Jan91	Jan90	Jan89
Yearly Statistics					
Price-Close	5.50	7.50	4.50	5.63	6.75
Price-High	8.25	7.50	7.00	7.50	6.75
Price-Low	5.25	4.50	4.05	5.00	5.00
P/E-Close	16.67	16.67	22.50	12.50	22.50
Dividends per Share	0.22	0.20	0.20	0.20	0.20
Dividend Yield (%)	4.00	2.67	4.44	3.56	2.96
Sales per Share	23.49	20.72	17.91	18.66	18.56
EPS before extra. Item	0.33	0.45	0.20	0.45	0.30
Cash Flow per Share	0.61	0.71	0.46	0.70	0.56
Book Value per Share	4.27	4.16	3.91	3.91	3.66
O/S Common Shares	5,170	5,124	5,105	5,097	5,076
Total Revenue	120,857	105,973	91,333	94,921	93,727
Income before extra.	1,705	2,296	1,015	2,284	1,515
Cash Flow	3,159	3,609	2,338	3,554	2,837
Debt/Equity	0.76	0.64	0.85	0.68	1.01
Return on Capital (%)	14.99	21.35	14.31	20.28	15.14
Ret. on Com. Equity (%)	7.86	11.13	5.09	11.87	8.28
% Change Profit	(25.7)	126.2	(55.6)	50.8	(6.0)
% Change Revenue	14.0	16.0	(3.8)	1.3	14.7
% Change Assets	10.8	4.9	6.7	(2.4)	14.0

Preferred Div. Coverage	np	np	np
Total Div. Coverage	1.5	2.2	1.0
Interest Coverage	2.7	2.4	1.6
Current Ratio	1.9	2.1	2.2
Operating Margin	4.6	7.2	5.5
Asset Turnover	1.9	1.9	1.7
5 YEAR RATIOS (%)			
Return on Capital	17.2	17.1	15.8
Return on Com. Equity	8.8	9.1	9.1
Profit Growth	1.1	4.2	9.8
Revenue Growth	8.1	10.2	6.5
Asset Growth	6.6	5.1	4.5
BALANCE SHEET (000)			
Cash	7,000	5,000	3,500
Current Assets	55,373	48,818	45,709
Net Fixed Assets	7,406	7,830	8,298
Invest's & Advances	0	0	0
Total Assets	62,779	56,648	54,007
Short Term Debt	6,041	2,647	3,965
Current Liabilities	29,384	23,646	20,421
Long Term Debt	10,757	11,065	12,991
Total Liabilities	40,680	35,338	34,056
Total Equity	22,099	21,310	19,951
Total Liab. & Equity	62,779	56,648	54,007
CAPITAL (000)			
Total Debt	16,798	13,712	16,956
Preferred Equity	0	0	0
Common Equity	22,099	21,310	19,951

Business:

IRWIN TOY LTD. manufactures and distributes a broad range of leisure products in Canada. The main business of the company is toys and games. The company also distributes souvenir items, furniture and other leisure goods. It markets Winnwell hockey and Cooper baseball equipment. The company also distributes the products of foreign toy companies and develops its own products.

Date	EPS	DPS	Tot Rev	Inc Bex
Apr 93	(0.02)	0.00	12,691	(113)
Jan 93	0.18	0.11	35,558	935
Oct 92	0.11	0.00	48,750	575
Jul 92	0.02	0.11	19,994	111
Apr 92	0.02	0.00	16,571	84
Jan 92	0.20	0.10	22,676	1,042
Oct 91	0.20	0.00	45,627	1,008
Jul 91	0.04	0.10	21,962	207

Synopsis:

Irwin Toy Limited discontinued its distributor relationship with Japanese video game company Sega Enterprises Ltd. on February 1, 1993. Irwin, which exclusively marketed the Sega product line for seven years, wants to concentrate management efforts and financial resources on toy and sporting goods products. Irwin expects the transfer to have a large impact on 1993 sales but a small effect on earnings, due to the low margin for the products.

Irwin hopes that the Barcode Battler (TM) will help the company crack the $15-billion (U.S.) United States toy market. The Battler is a camera-sized electronic game that turns bar codes on consumer goods into attacking warriors with names like Gummy Bear and Pea Brain. Close to a million of the games were sold in Japan last year by Japanese toy maker Epoch Co. Ltd. Irwin won exclusive rights to sell this product in North America in the fall of 1992 and has test marketed the product in the United States. Irwin estimates that about $100,000 has been spent on marketing, packaging and new tooling equipment to introduce the Battler to North America. Millions more would have to be spent if test sales indicate that the toy could become a big seller. To give its products more exposure in the U.S., Irwin now has a permanent show room in the New York Toy Building. Irwin also exhibited products at the Nuremberg Toy Fair in Germany for the first time and developed many valuable contacts.

Irwin has become the exclusive Canadian distributor of the Meccano (TM) line of metal construction toys on behalf of their French manufacturer. Another addition to the range of products is the Winnwell (R) adjustable hockey shin guard, allowing for a custom fit. The Winnwell (R) products sold out completely for the 1993 fiscal year.

Irwin introduced Roberto Alomar and Dennis Eckersley licensed products to its Cooper (R) baseball line, as well as an adjustable batter's helmet. Irwin expects this line to have a good year, due in part to the introduction of the new products.

Rank (Profit/Revenue/Assets)		
376	339	493

Arnold B. Irwin
Co-Chairman

S. Macdonal Irwin
Co-Chairman

George M. Irwin
President

Address
43 Hanna Avenue
Toronto
ON
M6K 1X6
(416) 533-3521

Fax: (416) 533-3257
I0002152/G/5.5.3

Page	Company	$	Latest year end	Earnings per Share		
				Actual	Estimate this year	Estimate next year
183	Budd Canada		9209	0.95	1.20	2.00
184	Ford Motor Company of Canada		9212	(43.87)	n.a.	n.a.
185	Hayes-Dana		9212	0.01	0.62	1.12
186	Magna International		9207	2.30	2.65	3.18
187	TCG International		9212	1.21	n.a.	n.a.

Estimates from I/B/E/S Inc., 345 Hudson St., New York, NY 10014 (212) 243-3335. In Canada: 6 Lansing Square, Ste. 235, Willowdale, ON M2J 1T5 (416) 496-0977.

Automobile Industry - Industry Report [May-19-1993]. MERRILL LYNCH CAPITAL MARKETS reported by Heinbach, H.E., et al

U.S. new-vehicle sales have been strong recently, with the April 1993 selling rate moving up to the highest level in over three years, at 14.5 million units. The U.S. companies have been enjoying especially strong volume gains, as they are taking market share back from the Japanese for the second consecutive year. This reflects the impact of the stronger yen on Japanese vehicle prices, improvements made in U.S. products, and a continuing shift in consumer demand to the truck sector (which is dominated by the domestic companies). While the daily selling rate for all vehicles increased 7% in the first four months of 1993, GM, Ford and Chrysler's sales rate rose 11%. Chrysler has been the big market-share winner in 1993, reflecting the success of its new LH full-size sedans and the Jeep Grand Cherokee. [RN 1332073]

Automotive Industry - Industry Report [May-7-1993]. MERRILL LYNCH CAPITAL MARKETS reported by Cherry, M.A.

High yield automotive issuers exhibited continued strength in sales and cash flow in 4Q:92. Cost structure reduction during the last recession is now resulting in increased profitability throughout the industry. Sales gains are coming primarily from new product introductions and persistent increases in customer demand for light trucks. Companies that manufacture and supply parts for successful new car and light truck models will show the greatest improvement going forward. Chrysler is planning to increase production of its LH cars to 320,000 annually in September 1993. [RN 1328461]

Auto Trends - Industry Report [Apr-27-1993]. SHEARSON LEHMAN BROTHERS, INC. reported by Phillippi, J.S., et al

Mid-April 1993 light vehicle sales were up by 19.5%, coming in ahead of a lackluster year-ago period, in which all of April 1992 came in quite weak. That gain resulted in an estimated 11.7 million unit seasonally adjusted annual rate, versus the weak 9.8 million unit SAAR of a year ago. While each of the Big Three posted good car numbers, for a combined gain in deliveries of 19.1%, GM and Chrysler's light trucks continued to power their numbers with 31.4% and 32.8% gains, respectively. Light trucks were the strongest segment overall, rising 24%, for a SAAR of 5.1 million units, versus the 4.0 million of last year. Given the fact that overall fleet sales are usually a modest factor at this time of year, the car numbers look positive. [RN 1327049]

Automotive Industry - Industry Report [Apr-15-1993]. PAINEWEBBER INC. reported by Girsky, S.J.

Domestically built vehicles are gaining share. This is positive for the U.S. supply base. March 1993 was a strong month for the Big Three. Industry sales improved to a 13.4 million SAAR

from 13.1 million in February and 13.3 million in January. Sales of domestically made vehicles matched the best seasonally adjusted rates of the 1990s. With inventories in line, 2Q:93 U.S. vehicle production is forecast to increase 8-10%, barring a significant falloff in demand. North American production should show even stronger increases due to GM's ramp up of the Camaro in Canada and Chrysler's continued ramp up of the LH cars. [RN 1325338]

Automotive Parts - Industry Reports [Apr-1-1993]. MERRILL LYNCH CAPITAL MARKETS reported by McGann, F.J., et al

Over the short term, earnings for the group should benefit from strong North American vehicle production, past and on-going cost-reduction efforts, increasing business with transplant manufacturers, and a general improvement in the North American economy. These factors should more than offset the largest risks to earnings over the short run, namely the weak European market and increasing pressure on prices from OEMs, particularly Ford and GM, in North America. For North America, 1993 North American vehicle production should rise a strong 11% to 12.9 million units, with autos rising 10% and trucks 12%. [RN 1318325]

Tire Gauge: Monthly Shipment Update - Industry Report [Apr-21-1993]. SHEARSON LEHMAN BROTHERS, INC. reported by Soffen, S.L., et al

An increase in demand has caused both Cooper Tire and Goodyear Tire to announce plant capacity expansions for late 1993. There will be some weakness in the replacement market in January and February 1993, but tire shipments should regain momentum in 2Q:93 and finish with healthy gains for full year 1993. The recent announcement by Goodyear, Bridgestone/Firestone, and Continental/General of a 3%-5% price increase on replacement tires was encouraging. While recent history has shown that only a portion of this increase will hold, tire makers have abandoned predatory pricing and will act like an oligopoly in 1993. [RN 1325674]

Tire Tracks: February 1993 - Industry Report [Mar-25-1993]. PAINEWEBBER INC. reported by Girsky, S.J.

Spread remains favorable for tire manufacturers, with PPI wholesale prices up 2.1% and crude rubber down 0.7%. Retail tire prices declined in February 1993. Tire industry production and capacity utilization continues to increase. The original equipment tire market is down in response to a sharp decline in new vehicle sales. This would affect Michelin the most due to high OE share (estimated at 40% car share and 75% truck share) and Goodyear the least due to low OE share (estimated at 10-12%). [RN 1319386]

BUDD CANADA INC.

Exchanges	Price (Jun24'93)	29 .50	Trailing P/E	32 .07	Stock Symbol
T	Trailing Yield (%)	11 .86	Trailing EPS	0 .92	**BUD**

Period Ending	Sep92	Sep91	Sep90	Sep89	Sep88
Yearly Statistics					
Price-Close	32 .00	31 .00	29 .00	36 .50	29 .50
Price-High	39 .00	39 .50	37 .00	43 .25	38 .00
Price-Low	29 .75	28 .25	28 .00	29 .00	27 .00
P/E-Close	33 .68	70 .46	5 .89	4 .96	5 .66
Dividends per Share	3 .50	6 .00	6 .00	3 .95	2 .60
Dividend Yield (%)	10 .94	19 .36	20 .69	10 .82	8 .81
Sales per Share	50 .57	46 .54	61 .02	76 .72	65 .39
EPS before extra. item	0 .95	0 .44	4 .92	7 .36	5 .21
Cash Flow per Share	2 .83	2 .34	6 .70	9 .24	7 .31
Book Value per Share	23 .90	26 .45	32 .00	33 .09	29 .69
O/S Common Shares	3 ,767	3 ,767	3 ,767	3 ,763	3 ,748
Total Revenue	194 ,253	191 ,409	250 ,967	298 ,686	260 ,979
Income before extra.	3 ,587	1 ,675	18 ,518	27 ,642	19 ,520
Cash Flow	10 ,669	8 ,802	25 ,233	34 ,722	27 ,392
Debt/Equity	0 .04	0 .00	0 .00	nd	nd
Return on Capital (%)	6 .75	3 .15	25 .84	40 .36	32 .62
Ret. on Com. Equity (%)	3 .78	1 .52	15 .11	23 .45	18 .35
% Change Profit	114 .1	(91 .0)	(33 .0)	41 .6	(25 .0)
% Change Revenue	1 .5	(23 .7)	(16 .0)	14 .4	0 .1
% Change Assets	(11 .1)	(10 .3)	(5 .4)	5 .7	7 .6

Business:

BUDD CANADA INC. is an automotive parts manufacturer, specializing in the production of chassis component parts, light truck frames, and cold weather starting products and accessories. It has production facilities in Kitchener and Winnipeg. Budcan Holdings Inc., a wholly owned subsidiary of The Budd Company of Michigan, owns 77.3% of the outstanding shares of the company.

Date	EPS	DPS	Tot Rev	Inc Bex
Mar 93	0 .46	0 .25	80 ,601	1 ,723
Dec 92	0 .29	0 .25	56 ,363	1 ,091
Sep 92	(0 .02)	2 .75	43 ,555	(84)
Jun 92	0 .19	0 .25	46 ,893	749
Mar 92	0 .25	0 .25	49 ,701	925
Dec 91	0 .53	0 .25	54 ,912	1 ,997
Sep 91	0 .22	5 .25	50 ,669	851
Jun 91	(0 .10)	0 .25	46 ,717	(368)

Preferred Div. Coverage	np	np	np	
Total Div. Coverage	0 .3	0 .1	0 .8	
Interest Coverage	na	526 .5	189 .8	
Current Ratio	3 .0	3 .1	4 .5	
Operating Margin	1 .5	(2 .7)	8 .0	
Asset Turnover	1 .6	1 .3	1 .5	
5 YEAR RATIOS (%)				
Return on Capital	21 .7	29 .8	39 .7	
Return on Com. Equity	12 .4	16 .9	22 .8	
Profit Growth	(32 .9)	(43 .4)	(7 .1)	
Revenue Growth	(5 .8)	(6 .9)	(0 .5)	
Asset Growth	(3 .0)	(0 .9)	1 .1	
BALANCE SHEET (000)				
Cash	26 ,546	44 ,527	58 ,455	
Current Assets	73 ,995	91 ,473	102 ,659	
Net Fixed Assets	43 ,681	43 ,377	48 ,271	
Invest's & Advances	0	0	0	
Total Assets	120 ,433	135 ,407	151 ,031	
Short Term Debt	3 ,698	274	218	
Current Liabilities	25 ,037	29 ,544	22 ,735	
Long Term Debt	0	0	0	
Total Liabilities	30 ,413	35 ,790	30 ,488	
Total Equity	90 ,020	99 ,617	120 ,543	
Total Liab. & Equity	120 ,433	135 ,407	151 ,031	
CAPITAL (000)				
Total Debt	3 ,698	274	218	
Preferred Equity	0	0	0	
Common Equity	90 ,020	99 ,617	120 ,543	

Synopsis:

Budd Canada experienced improved results for the second quarter of 1993, compared to the same period last year and the prior quarter. During the first quarter of 1993, lower manufacturing activity and lower interest income resulted in reduced earnings. The replacement of the main assembly line for GM's sport truck frame was completed. The automotive market continues to remain weak and uncertain.

Sales in fiscal 1992 rose 4.1% over fiscal 1991. Improved product sales by the Kitchener, Ontario, plant were offset by reduced sales of tooling and prototypes. Sales by the Temro operations were down from the prior year primarily due to a decline in demand from the aftermarket. Cash flow from operations at $3.6-million were down 71%. Inventory levels increased 46% in the year, mainly due to the shutdown of Budd's largest assembly line, which produces GM's truck frames. Capital expenditures jumped 119% to $8-million. Budd has said it will continue to meet its business requirements with cash generated from its operations. The company had total dividend payouts of $6 per share in 1991, including a special dividend of $2.50 a share. Special dividends are a function of numerous factors, including the company's cash position. The balance sheet remains strong with cash and short-term investments at $26.5-million and no debt for borrowed funds.

Sales to non-affiliated foreign customers represented approximately 86% of gross sales in fiscal 1992, compared to 82% in 1991. Budd's sales are mainly to the three North American automobile producers, General Motors, Ford and Chrysler.

Budd expects that increased competition resulting from excess capacity in the automotive assembly and parts manufacturing industry and the resulting pressure on prices will continue into the future.

Relative strength to TSE300

Price

Volume (in 1000's of board lots)

Rank (Profit/Revenue/Assets)		
290	278	389

Robert C. Blaine
President & General Manager

Robert H. Hird
Vice President, Finance

Address
P.O. Box 1204
Kitchener
ON
N2G 4G8
(519) 895-1000

Fax: (519) 895-0099
B0004697/G/5.6

FORD MOTOR COMPANY OF CANADA, LIMITED

Exchanges	Price (Jun24'93)	120.00	Trailing P/E	nm	Stock Symbol
TA	Trailing Yield (%)	0.00	Trailing EPS	(28.18)	**FMC**

Period Ending	Dec92	Dec91	Dec90	Dec89	Dec88
Yearly Statistics					
Price-Close	110.00	140.00	120.00	184.00	137.00
Price-High	150.00	146.00	185.00	198.00	151.00
Price-Low	108.00	113.00	110.00	136.00	115.00
P/E-Close	nm	nm	nm	4.86	4.21
Dividends per Share	0.00	0.00	11.00	11.00	4.00
Dividend Yield (%)	0.00	0.00	9.17	5.98	2.92
Sales per Share	1,741.99	1,468.33	1,653.12	1,846.77	1,922.93
EPS before extra. item	(43.87)	(26.67)	(6.89)	37.87	32.54
Cash Flow per Share	10.90	13.48	23.69	84.93	78.44
Book Value per Share	81.61	125.83	172.73	191.33	170.86
O/S Common Shares (mil)	8	8	8	8	8
Total Revenue ($mil)	14,475	12,248	13,798	15,395	16,125
Income before extra. ($mil)	(364)	(221)	(57)	314	270
Cash Flow ($mil)	90	112	196	704	650
Debt/Equity	0.64	0.50	0.34	0.09	0.08
Return on Capital (%)	(38.23)	(12.59)	(1.66)	33.39	32.53
Ret. on Com. Equity (%)	(42.31)	(17.86)	(3.78)	20.91	21.07
% Change Profit	(64.5)	(287.2)	(118.2)	16.4	117.9
% Change Revenue	18.2	(11.2)	(10.4)	(4.5)	14.6
% Change Assets	9.3	(0.3)	1.0	(2.2)	(0.4)

Business:

FORD MOTOR CO. OF CANADA LTD. is a major automotive manufacturer and distributor. The company owns assembly plants in Oakville and St. Thomas, ON, and parts plants in Windsor and Niagara Falls. Cars and trucks are sold through a national network of dealers. The company has subsidiaries in Australia and New Zealand. Ford Motor Co. of Michigan owns 94% of the company's shares.

Date	EPS	DPS	Tot Rev	Inc Bex
Mar 93	1.74	0.00	3,630,700	14,500
Dec 92	(19.36)	0.00	3,880,700	(160,600)
Sep 92	(3.67)	0.00	3,307,500	(30,400)
Jun 92	(6.89)	0.00	4,098,800	(57,100)
Mar 92	(14.33)	0.00	3,158,200	(118,900)
Dec 91	(11.18)	0.00	2,968,100	(92,600)
Sep 91	(3.29)	0.00	3,188,700	(27,400)
Jun 91	(3.39)	0.00	3,595,800	(28,100)

	Dec92	Dec91	Dec90
Preferred Div. Coverage	np	np	np
Total Div. Coverage	na	na	0.0
Interest Coverage	0.0	0.0	0.0
Current Ratio	0.9	0.9	1.0
Operating Margin	(3.1)	(2.2)	(0.9)
Asset Turnover	3.7	3.4	3.8
5 YEAR RATIOS (%)			
Return on Capital	2.7	14.0	20.2
Return on Com. Equity	(4.4)	6.3	11.8
Profit Growth	na	na	na
Revenue Growth	0.5	(3.2)	0.6
Asset Growth	1.3	2.6	3.6
BALANCE SHEET (000)			
Cash	375,500	143,600	261,800
Current Assets	1,690,800	1,372,300	1,655,000
Net Fixed Assets	1,895,600	1,934,600	1,788,600
Invest's & Advances	44,200	41,500	55,600
Total Assets	3,881,900	3,551,900	3,564,200
Short Term Debt	93,100	281,300	477,400
Current Liabilities	1,973,400	1,500,300	1,661,000
Long Term Debt	340,400	236,700	13,800
Total Liabilities	3,205,300	2,508,600	2,132,100
Total Equity	676,600	1,043,300	1,432,100
Total Liab. & Equity	3,881,900	3,551,900	3,564,200
CAPITAL (000)			
Total Debt	433,500	518,000	491,200
Preferred Equity	0	0	0
Common Equity	676,600	1,043,300	1,432,100

Synopsis:

In April 1993, Ford Motor Company of Canada announced plans to shift its parts distribution centre in Edmonton to a newer and larger facility in the same city. The new facility will be Ford's major parts supply depot for Western Canada. The Winnipeg distribution plant in Winnipeg will be consolidated into the newer Edmonton plant. This is part of a major overhaul of Ford's nationwide parts distribution system aimed at improving service to its dealers and customers.

For fiscal 1992, a change in accounting treatment for health and other post-retirement benefits negatively affected earnings. Net income was reduced by about $1.57 a share, and opening equity was reduced by $20.38 a share to reflect the retroactive portion. This change will not affect Ford's cash flow because payments will continue on a pay-as-you-go basis. Working capital dropped to $154-million for a deficit of $282-million at year end. As a result, debt was 64% of shareholder's equity. Operating costs rose 20%. Canadian operating losses rose by $367-million due to a decline in the Canadian dollar, higher product and programs cost, and higher marketing costs. Losses were partially offset by manufacturing efficiencies, increased vehicle production, and a more favorable product mix. Capital expenditures amounted to $323-million, representing a major investment program.

In fiscal 1992, domestic sales accounted for 30% of total sales, sales to Ford Motor (U.S.) were 54%, and overseas sales were 16%. In Canada, Ford garnered 16.1% of the car market and 26.2% of the truck market. Vehicle sales to dealers in Canada were down 9% and sales to Ford U.S. increased 19%. Vehicle production in was Canada up 15%.

Rank (Profit/Revenue/Assets)
993   2   57

James G. O'Connor
President & C.E.O.

Albert E. Matthews, Jr.
V.P., Finance & C.F.O.

Address
The Canadian Road
Oakville
ON
L6J 5E4
(416) 845-2511

Fax: (416) 844-8085
F0001536/G/5.6

HAYES-DANA INC.

Exchanges	Price (Jun24'93)	15.75	Trailing P/E	63.00	Stock Symbol
T	Trailing Yield (%)	3.56	Trailing EPS	0.25	**HAY**

Period Ending	Dec92	Dec91	Dec90	Dec89	Dec88
Yearly Statistics					
Price-Close	12.00	12.50	11.63	14.38	12.62
Price-High	14.00	15.50	14.50	15.50	13.25
Price-Low	10.75	11.25	10.63	12.62	9.38
P/E-Close	1,200.00	nm	11.51	10.97	10.43
Dividends per Share	0.56	0.56	0.56	0.55	0.48
Dividend Yield (%)	4.67	4.48	4.82	3.83	3.80
Sales per Share	32.97	25.10	28.78	31.22	34.09
EPS before extra. item	0.01	(0.94)	1.01	1.31	1.21
Cash Flow per Share	0.85	(0.25)	1.61	1.88	1.98
Book Value per Share	7.50	8.05	9.56	9.15	8.87
O/S Common Shares	15,137	15,133	15,138	15,336	16,617
Total Revenue	503,103	381,251	443,536	499,104	573,031
Income before extra.	92	(14,294)	15,303	20,684	20,317
Cash Flow	12,930	(3,709)	24,484	29,797	33,207
Debt/Equity	0.26	0.40	0.12	0.15	0.13
Return on Capital (%)	2.54	(13.90)	17.06	22.54	23.05
Ret. on Com. Equity (%)	0.08	(10.73)	10.74	14.37	14.37
% Change Profit	100.6	(193.4)	(26.0)	1.8	1.3
% Change Revenue	32.0	(14.0)	(11.1)	(12.9)	13.8
% Change Assets	(11.4)	10.8	(0.3)	(9.5)	0.2

Preferred Div. Coverage	np	np	np
Total Div. Coverage	0.0	0.0	1.8
Interest Coverage	1.1	0.0	15.7
Current Ratio	1.6	1.6	3.4
Operating Margin	0.5	(6.4)	5.1
Asset Turnover	2.5	1.7	2.1
5 YEAR RATIOS (%)			
Return on Capital	10.3	14.5	21.8
Return on Com. Equity	5.8	8.9	13.9
Profit Growth	(66.9)	na	(0.6)
Revenue Growth	(0.1)	(4.2)	0.4
Asset Growth	(2.4)	1.8	(1.7)
BALANCE SHEET (000)			
Cash	5,120	5,513	17,976
Current Assets	99,460	123,102	112,244
Net Fixed Assets	94,011	96,678	85,815
Invest's & Advances	0	0	0
Total Assets	200,585	226,295	204,195
Short Term Debt	21,065	39,030	6,650
Current Liabilities	63,217	79,112	32,551
Long Term Debt	8,075	9,027	9,950
Total Liabilities	87,112	104,491	59,516
Total Equity	113,473	121,804	144,679
Total Liab. & Equity	200,585	226,295	204,195
CAPITAL (000)			
Total Debt	29,140	48,057	16,600
Preferred Equity	0	0	0
Common Equity	113,473	121,804	144,679

Business:

HAYES-DANA INC. is a manufacturer and distributor of both new and replacement components for trucks, automobiles, off-highway vehicles and industrial equipment. The company markets its products to heavy truck and car makers, warehouse distributors, mass merchandisers and industrial distributors and equipment suppliers. The company has facilities in Ontario, Quebec, Manitoba, Alberta and B.C.

Date	EPS	DPS	Tot Rev	Inc Bex
Mar 93	0.15	0.14	145,219	2,256
Dec 92	0.10	0.14	129,826	1,458
Sep 92	(0.02)	0.14	116,889	(309)
Jun 92	0.02	0.14	133,550	376
Mar 92	(0.09)	0.14	122,838	(1,433)
Dec 91	(0.60)	0.14	106,482	(9,195)
Sep 91	(0.40)	0.14	97,461	(5,933)
Jun 91	0.01	0.14	97,024	153

Synopsis:

Fiscal 1992 was a large improvement over 1991 for Hayes Dana Inc., but according to company officials fiscal 1993 will be an even better year. The company expects a 5% to 10% increase in sales in 1993, with the rate of profit growth to exceed sales growth. The expected results will reflect an increase in North American truck production, for which the company supplies frames. Hayes Dana also plans to increase its sales in the aftermarket, replacement parts for vehicles and industrial equipment, to about 50% of its sales. The acquisition of another company according to Hayes Dana will be required to achieve this goal.

About 40% of Hayes' sales are geared to light trucks, a market which is growing. In 1991, the company became the exclusive supplier of frames for Ford Motor Co.'s F-series pickup, the largest player in the market.

For the first quarter of 1993, Hayes continued its strong performance. This was attributed to strength in all Hayes markets. Sales to the company's major market, highway vehicles, were up 20%. Sales to the automotive and truck parts distribution markets were both up 7%. Mobile off-highway and industrial equipment sales also rose during the period. Hayes also said operating improvements at the company's facilities added to the results.

In fiscal 1992, capital expenditures were $11.8-million, down 48% from 1991. 1993 capital additions are expected in the $12-million range. The spending is geared towards a wide variety of productivity and quality related programs.

For 1992, vehicular sales accounted for 91% of net sales compared to 9% for industrial sales. Export sales accounted for 47% of net sales. The company's markets were divided as follows: highway vehicles, 73%; truck parts distribution, 5%; automotive distribution, 14%; mobile off-highway, 5%; and industrial equipment, 3%. Hayes' major customer was Ford Motor Company representing 43% of net sales.

Relative strength to TSE300
Price
Volume (in 1000's of board lots)

Rank (Profit/Revenue/Assets)		
561	154	316

S.J. Morcott
Chairman

Thomas A. Dattilo
President & C.E.O.

A. Glenn Paton
Vice President, Finance

Address
One St. Paul
P.O. Box 3029
St Catharines
ON
L2R 7K9
(416) 687-4200

Fax: (416) 687-4246
H0001001/G/5.6

MAGNA INTERNATIONAL INC.

Exchanges	Price (Jun24'93)	49.50	Trailing P/E	13.16	Stock Symbol
TMQ	Trailing Yield (%)	1.01	Trailing EPS	3.76	**MG.A**

Period Ending	Ju l92	Ju l91	Ju l90	Ju l89	Ju l88
Yearly Statistics					
Price-Close	30.38	12.88	3.60	12.63	13.50
Price-High	35.25	14.25	13.38	16.13	24.38
Price-Low	12.13	2.10	3.15	10.63	9.25
P/E-Close	10.44	21.82	nm	10.43	19.29
Dividends per Share	0.20	0.00	0.24	0.48	0.48
Dividend Yield (%)	0.66	0.00	6.67	3.80	3.56
Sales per Share	70.15	72.50	69.28	69.15	52.40
EPS before extra. item	2.91	0.59	(8.06)	1.21	0.70
Cash Flow per Share	7.30	5.46	2.62	3.12	3.56
Book Value per Share	14.74	9.63	8.31	16.69	16.04
O/S Common Shares	40,044	27,849	27,819	27,819	27,819
Total Revenue	2,358,000	2,014,500	1,930,700	2,002,404	1,474,611
Income before extra.	98,000	16,500	(224,200)	33,611	19,542
Cash Flow	245,300	151,800	72,800	86,830	99,004
Debt/Equity	0.55	2.82	nd	1.99	1.95
Return on Capital (%)	20.37	20.03	(14.21)	9.61	6.95
Ret. on Com. Equity (%)	22.83	6.61	(64.48)	7.38	4.37
% Change Profit	493.9	107.4	(767.0)	72.0	(51.6)
% Change Revenue	17.1	4.3	(3.6)	35.8	26.3
% Change Assets	(4.6)	(18.3)	(3.5)	11.9	29.8

Preferred Div. Coverage	np	np	np
Total Div. Coverage	13.2	na	0.0
Interest Coverage	4.0	1.5	0.0
Current Ratio	1.2	1.0	0.5
Operating Margin	9.1	6.7	2.7
Asset Turnover	1.7	1.4	1.1
5 YEAR RATIOS (%)			
Return on Capital	8.6	6.7	6.1
Return on Com. Equity	(4.7)	(7.2)	(5.6)
Profit Growth	19.4	(19.0)	na
Revenue Growth	15.1	14.2	22.8
Asset Growth	1.7	10.1	23.3
BALANCE SHEET (000)			
Cash	51,600	60,300	100,000
Current Assets	500,200	485,600	740,300
Net Fixed Assets	706,200	777,900	831,300
Invest's & Advances	80,300	71,200	85,700
Total Assets	1,401,400	1,469,000	1,797,400
Short Term Debt	79,700	175,100	0
Current Liabilities	407,100	471,800	1,363,000
Long Term Debt	245,700	581,800	0
Total Liabilities	811,100	1,200,900	1,566,300
Total Equity	590,300	268,100	231,100
Total Liab. & Equity	1,401,400	1,469,000	1,797,400
CAPITAL (000)			
Total Debt	325,400	756,900	0
Preferred Equity	0	0	0
Common Equity	590,300	268,100	231,100

Business:

MAGNA INTERNATIONAL INC. designs and manufactures a broad range of automotive components and systems for the North American facilities of the major automobile manufacturers. The company has plants across North America and also in Europe. Products include engine parts and systems, brake component systems, door systems, body panels and trim, cooling systems, transmission systems, and related components.

Date	EPS	DPS	Tot Rev	Inc Bex
Jan 93	1.33	0.15	1,215,700	56,400
Oct 92	0.76	0.15	618,900	31,700
Jul 92	0.78	0.10	628,900	31,300
Apr 92	0.89	0.10	632,700	30,500
Jan 92	0.33	0.00	480,600	10,700
Oct 91	0.92	0.00	615,800	25,500
Jul 91	0.41	0.00	539,864	11,547
Apr 91	0.16	0.00	494,344	4,414

Synopsis:

For the second quarter of 1993, the improved results of Magna International were attributed primarily to increased car and truck production this year. North American vehicle production increased in the second quarter by 16% to 2.9 million units, and in the first six months by 7% to 5.9 million units. However, despite the improved sales, gross margins remained under pressure. This was attributed to major programs associated with a new customer vehicle, increased customer pricing pressures, and startup costs related to a new operating facility. Magna said North American vehicle production is expected to continue to strengthen in fiscal 1993 and should surpass 1992 levels by 5% to 8%.

Magna's $30-million venture into operating a plant in Mexico to supply parts to a local Volkswagen plant there has so far proved successful. The operation is said to be about 75% as productive as other Magna plants in Canada, the U.S., and Europe. Vehicles and auto parts are the largest segment of Canadian and Mexican exports to each other. Last year, auto parts represented between 20% and 25% of total Canadian shipments values at $770.6-million. More than 50% of the $2.75-billion total of Mexican shipments to Canada in 1992 were vehicles and auto parts. The Mexican plant is currently operating at only 45% capacity, and the site has room for two more plants of similar size. Magna is attempting to make a further deal with Volkswagen to produce additional parts. Magna is also investigating opportunities with the Big Three U.S. auto makers, which have been in Mexico for decades. Sales in its first year of Mexican operations were $13-million.

In late 1992, the Canadian Bond Rating Service upgraded Magna's commercial paper and 7% convertible subordinated debentures due to Magna's improving financial performance. This is the first time since 1989 that its debt instruments have returned to investment grade. The Dominion Bond Rating Service did a similar upgrade to Magna's most senior debt and notes, and both series of convertible subordinated debentures. The reason given was a stronger balance sheet and improved operating cash flow.

Relative strength to TSE300

Price

Volume (in 1000's of board lots)

Rank (Profit/Revenue/Assets)		
37	55	117
Frank Stronach		
Chairman Of The Board		
John Doddridge		
Vice Chairman & C.E.O.		
Don Walker		
President & C.O.O		

Address
36 Apple Creek Boulevard
Markham
ON
L3R 4Y4
(416) 477-7766

Fax: (416) 475-0776
M0000667/G/5.6

TCG INTERNATIONAL INC.

Exchanges	Price (Jun24'93)	3.10	Trailing P/E	2.74	Stock Symbol
TV	Trailing Yield (%)	3.23	Trailing EPS	1.13	**TCG.A**

Period Ending	Dec92	Dec91	Dec90	Dec89	Dec88
Yearly Statistics					
Price-Close	4.15	3.50	3.65	9.63	6.42
Price-High	5.00	5.75	9.75	15.00	7.00
Price-Low	3.30	3.20	3.00	6.38	2.92
P/E-Close	3.43	nm	nm	19.65	20.06
Dividends per Share	0.10	0.10	0.10	0.10	0.25
Dividend Yield (%)	2.41	2.86	2.74	1.04	3.89
Sales per Share	16.09	16.07	21.30	19.24	13.44
EPS before extra. item	1.21	(0.22)	(1.63)	0.49	0.32
Cash Flow per Share	(0.18)	0.16	0.70	0.86	0.69
Book Value per Share	3.10	2.00	2.31	4.01	2.70
O/S Common Shares	23,263	23,253	23,253	23,255	19,955
Total Revenue	387,461	374,735	496,523	416,022	268,394
Income before extra.	28,074	(5,069)	(37,868)	10,437	6,382
Cash Flow	(4,162)	3,835	16,338	18,257	13,810
Debt/Equity	0.85	3.62	3.22	2.08	0.69
Return on Capital (%)	24.10	3.50	(2.55)	17.71	20.48
Ret. on Com. Equity (%)	47.40	(10.11)	(51.48)	14.19	12.91
% Change Profit	653.8	86.6	(462.8)	63.5	31.1
% Change Revenue	3.4	(24.5)	19.4	55.0	21.5
% Change Assets	(29.2)	(6.1)	(20.3)	177.5	20.1

Date	EPS	DPS	Tot Rev	Inc Bex
Mar 93	(0.03)	0.03	85,948	(771)
Dec 92	0.85	0.03	2,249	19,611
Sep 92	0.12	0.03	123,511	2,717
Jun 92	0.19	0.03	142,175	4,408
Mar 92	0.06	0.03	89,102	1,338
Dec 91	(0.04)	0.03	6,670	(867)
Sep 91	0.02	0.03	124,273	423
Jun 91	(0.14)	0.03	130,725	(3,347)

	Dec92	Dec91	Dec90
Preferred Div. Coverage	np	np	np
Total Div. Coverage	11.8	0.0	0.0
Interest Coverage	5.6	0.7	0.0
Current Ratio	2.0	1.8	1.3
Operating Margin	(0.8)	0.4	5.3
Asset Turnover	1.7	1.2	1.5
5 YEAR RATIOS (%)			
Return on Capital	12.6	11.9	15.2
Return on Com. Equity	2.6	(4.6)	(0.5)
Profit Growth	42.0	na	na
Revenue Growth	11.8	13.9	27.3
Asset Growth	12.0	26.2	34.4
BALANCE SHEET (000)			
Cash	9,860	0	0
Current Assets	123,124	158,007	166,822
Net Fixed Assets	68,736	82,825	90,159
Invest's & Advances	18,995	22,003	19,533
Total Assets	224,035	316,537	336,940
Short Term Debt	4,741	9,955	55,371
Current Liabilities	61,893	85,847	133,252
Long Term Debt	56,167	158,368	117,973
Total Liabilities	152,031	270,081	283,148
Total Equity	72,004	46,456	53,792
Total Liab. & Equity	224,035	316,537	336,940
CAPITAL (000)			
Total Debt	60,908	168,323	173,344
Preferred Equity	0	0	0
Common Equity	72,004	46,456	53,792

Business:

TCG INTERNATIONAL INC. is a retail and wholesale distributor of automotive glass in Canada, the United States and the United Kingdom. The company also operates a chain of muffler shops in Quebec and sells, leases and services cellular telephones across Canada. Branch names include Speedy Auto Glass, G. Lebeau, Trans Canada Glass, Speedy Cellular, Monsieur Muffler and Bridgewater Speedy Auto Glass.

Synopsis:

For fiscal 1992, TCG International Inc. had a $34.5-million profit in discontinued operations derived from the sale of subsidiary Glenayre Electronic's manufacturing division in November 1992. In the year, TCG's long-term debt dropped by 65% or just over $100-million. For 1993, the company plans to continuing to focus on growth and diversification of its core businesses, the automotive aftermarket and personal communications.

TCG in 1992 was able to strengthen its position in the North American automotive replacement glass (ARG) market through two major transactions in the year. The company increased its equity interest in Apple Auto Glass Limited , a major franchiser of retail ARG in Canada, to 73% from 40%. This addition will add to the company's presence in the Canadian retail ARG market and improve distribution efficiencies. Furthermore, TCG acquired 70 retail ARG locations from Libbey-Owens-Ford Co. in the U.S. in exchange for 22 of TCG's warehouse distribution centres, operating as Trans America Glass. TCG also received $27.5-million (U.S.). There are now 116 corporate and franchise stores operating in the U.S. TCG plans to concentrate on growth and diversification in its core businesses through new products.

TCG also completed the sale of the manufacturing assets of its subsidiary, Glenayre Electronics for $130.3-million. TCG will retain a 10% interest in the company. Glenayre's remaining business unit, Glenayre Communications, specializes in the sale and service of two-way radios, paging systems and cellular products.

In fiscal 1992, TCG's sales were divided as follows: automotive sector, 92%; and communication sector 8%. Sales in Canada represented 76% of total sales, with 17% in the U.S. and 7% in other countries. There were no significant inter-segment sales.

Relative strength to TSE300
Price
Volume (in 1000's of board lots)

Rank (Profit/Revenue/Assets)
103   192   306

Arthur Skidmore
Chairman Of The Board & C.E.O.

Ronald E. Sowerby
Exec. V.P. Fin., C.F.O. & Sec.

A. Allan Skidmore
Vice Chairman, Operations

Address
28th Floor
4710 Kingsway
Burnaby
BC
V5H 4M2
(604) 431-2300

Fax: (604) 438-7414
T0002435/G/5.6

Page	Company	$	Latest year end	Earnings per Share		
				Actual	Estimate this year	Estimate next year
191	Biochem Pharma		9301	(0.32)	(0.04)	0.15
192	Biomira		9212	(0.80)	(0.99)	0.20
193	Deprenyl Research	$US	9212	0.39	0.19	0.28
194	Quadra Logic Technologies		9212	(0.69)	(0.68)	(0.37)

Estimates from I/B/E/S Inc., 345 Hudson St., New York, NY 10014 (212) 243-3335. In Canada: 6 Lansing Square, Ste. 235, Willowdale, ON M2J 1T5 (416) 496-0977.

Biotechnology & Pharmaceuticals

Health Care Strategies And Positioning - Industry Report [Apr-19-1993]. SHEARSON LEHMAN BROTHERS, INC. reported by Brimeyer, J.R., et al

There is a sales slowdown that is occurring in addition to the effects of the political side of U.S. health care reform. This has already developed throughout the health care system, affecting pharmaceuticals, medical supplies, and devices. This trend toward sluggish demand and weaker pricing probably began in mid-year 1992. What caused health care reform to be such a hot political issue, that health care spending has reached intolerable levels in this economy, is the same force behind the slowdown in health care utilization that has already begun. [RN 1325715]

Biotechnology - Industry Report [Apr-1-1993]. THE FIRST BOSTON CORPORATION report by Swarz, J.R., et al

Competitive pricing of look-alike drugs and price discounting byHMOs are continuing to put pressure on margins, but more fundamentally,the change is occurring at the lab bench, and the dearth of new productsexpected out of the traditional drug companies highlights the problem. Genetic engineering is dominating drug discovery in this country. New significant medical discoveries are now coming at the rate of one per week in biotechnology. Immune cells thought to be crucial in causing multiple sclerosis were identified, and an FDA advisory panel recommended approval for Betaseron (Schering AG and Chiron), the first real therapy for MS in 40 years. [RN 1322485]

Bio-Financials: Executive Summary - Industry Report [Mar-31-1993]. SHEARSON LEHMAN BROTHERS, INC. reported by Lerner, T., et al

Biotechnology companies have high liquidity, and can become exceptional cash generators once product revenue begins to appear. Until product revenue arrives, cash burn is extraordinarily high. [RN 1320777]

Doctor's Orders: New Prescription Trends - Industry Report [May-4-1993]. SHEARSON LEHMAN BROTHERS, INC. reported by Brimeyer, J.R., et al

Calcium anatgonists (drugs for hypertension and angina) continued their relatively strong growth, up 9% in year-over-year comparisons for February 1993. Pfizer continued to gain share with Procardia XL/Procardia (31.6% of new prescriptions in February) and Norvasc (3.3%). Combined, Pfizer drugs captured nearly 35% of the U.S. calcium antagonist new prescription market. New prescriptions for Norvasc have captured 3.3% of the new prescriptions for this class, after three to four months on the market. Norvasc is expected to be one of the most successful new drugs launched in the 1990s, because of its relative safety compared with its competitors. Norvasc is the only calcium antagonist which has been proven safe in congestive heart failure patients. Norvasc is expected to capture 15%-20% of the U.S. calcium antagonist market by 1995 and to double this share by the end of the decade. These estimates should allow the drug to post U.S. sales of $500 million (U.S.) in 1995 and over $1 billion (U.S.) by 2000. Foreign revenues should double these forecasts. [RN 1328636]

Drug Industry - Industry Report [Apr-2-1993]. MERRILL LYNCH CAPITAL MARKETS report by Vietor, R.R., et al

Drug company fundamentals continue to be in a cyclical downtrend and have not reached bottom yet. However the long-term outlook remains favorable. The are current worries surrounding the preparation of health care restructuring proposals by the Clinton Administration. Chief among these fears have been threats of price controls, applied as managed control (subtle) or as price freezes or rollbacks (not subtle). Pressure by the private sector for discounting me-too drugs is mounting. More companies see the need to enter the managed care segment but to knock out those who are already there may require deeper discounts or new contracts with greater concessions. The option of raising prices is gone for good, and the risk of a price-war is rising. Thus, gross margins are likely to decline. There are few important new products pending. The therapeutic segments to be most impacted by innovative drugs include epilepsy, migraine, and possibly Alzheimer's disease. Lack of major new drugs means little stimulus to the market growth for many other large selling therapeutic segments. This will not change for the next couple of years. [RN 1320697]

Japanese Drug Industry - Industry Report [Mar-31-1993]. MERRILL LYNCH CAPITAL MARKETS reported by Onoda, T.

Protease inhibitors aim at preventing the HIV virus from producing the enzyme protease which is related to viral reproduction. International companies which are researching protease inhibitors include Upjohn, Abott, Merck and SmithKline Beecham. TAT inhibitors aim at interfering with the TAT protein which is related to viral replication. The major research is being conducted by Roche. AIDS diagnostics with faster speed and accuracy should be researched by major diagnostic companies, including Fujirebio. [RN 1318341]

BIOCHEM PHARMA INC.

Exchanges	Price (Jun24'93)		12.87	Trailing P/E		nm	Stock Symbol
TM	Trailing Yield (%)		0.00	Trailing EPS		(0.33)	**BCH**

Period Ending	Jan93	Jan92	Jan91	Jan90	Jan89
Yearly Statistics					
Price-Close	19.75	30.50	6.50	5.13	1.44
Price-High	35.50	30.88	7.00	6.94	2.44
Price-Low	12.68	6.38	2.50	2.81	1.01
P/E-Close	nm	82.43	nm	512.50	nm
Dividends per Share	0.00	0.00	0.00	0.00	0.00
Dividend Yield (%)	0.00	0.00	0.00	0.00	0.00
Sales per Share	0.69	0.59	0.31	0.12	0.10
EPS before extra. item	(0.32)	0.37	(0.03)	0.01	(0.04)
Cash Flow per Share	(0.12)	0.05	0.03	0.01	(0.05)
Book Value per Share	2.45	2.12	1.18	0.88	0.60
O/S Common Shares	46,653	39,700	33,599	29,213	24,605
Total Revenue	36,568	47,359	16,461	6,206	3,158
Income before extra.	(13,147)	12,674	(925)	225	(945)
Cash Flow	(4,929)	1,562	863	220	(1,047)
Debt/Equity	0.08	0.14	0.13	0.07	0.08
Return on Capital (%)	(10.50)	18.72	(1.52)	3.12	(6.39)
Ret. on Com. Equity (%)	(13.27)	20.49	(2.83)	1.12	(7.32)
% Change Profit	(203.7)	1,469.9	(510.9)	123.8	10.2
% Change Revenue	(22.8)	187.7	165.2	96.5	97.6
% Change Assets	27.1	109.6	79.3	66.2	34.8

Date	EPS	DPS	Tot Rev	Inc Bex
Jan 93	(0.09)	0.00	7,055	(3,781)
Oct 92	(0.04)	0.00	11,364	(1,812)
Jul 92	(0.07)	0.00	8,432	(2,569)
Apr 92	(0.13)	0.00	9,716	(4,986)
Jan 92	(0.04)	0.00	10,069	(1,328)
Oct 91	0.45	0.00	9,300	15,898
Jul 91	(0.02)	0.00	5,866	(971)
Apr 91	(0.03)	0.00	5,069	(924)

Preferred Div. Coverage	np	np	na
Total Div. Coverage	na	na	na
Interest Coverage	0.0	16.6	0.0
Current Ratio	4.6	3.0	5.0
Operating Margin	(16.8)	(11.6)	(12.5)
Asset Turnover	0.2	0.2	0.2
5 YEAR RATIOS (%)			
Return on Capital	0.7	na	na
Return on Com. Equity	(0.4)	na	na
Profit Growth	na	na	na
Revenue Growth	87.0	na	na
Asset Growth	60.6	na	na
BALANCE SHEET (000)			
Cash	60,248	37,410	26,922
Current Assets	82,350	57,947	34,312
Net Fixed Assets	20,918	15,338	9,148
Invest's & Advances	20,763	22,677	7,462
Total Assets	138,373	108,846	51,939
Short Term Debt	5,776	7,931	70
Current Liabilities	17,759	19,014	6,865
Long Term Debt	2,895	3,926	5,223
Total Liabilities	24,151	24,889	12,088
Total Equity	114,222	83,957	39,851
Total Liab. & Equity	138,373	108,846	51,939
CAPITAL (000)			
Total Debt	8,671	11,857	5,293
Preferred Equity	0	0	100
Common Equity	114,222	83,957	39,751

Business:

BIOCHEM PHARMA INC. is a Canadian-based pharmaceutical company engaged in the research, development and manufacture of high quality products for the diagnosis, treatment and prevention of human disease.

Synopsis:

For fiscal 1992, despite a 21% increase in revenues, BioChem Pharma Inc.'s bottomline was the reverse of fiscal 1991. Increased sales were primarily due to the growth in sales of diagnostic products. The year's loss was attributed to increased R&D expenses, and the decline in Canadian vaccine revenues. BioChem raised its R&D budget by 29% to $12.3-million. The net loss included a $2.5-million charge resulting from a cancelled international share issue and a non-cash charge of $4.9-million, which represents BioChem's share of the loss yielded by its associated company, North American Vaccine Inc. (NAVA).

The prior year's profit was primarily due to a $17-million gain on dilution resulting from a public share offering by NAVA. BioChem's cash on hand on January 31, 1993, was up 61% over the preceeding year. Company officials said "with several therapeutic products in advanced human clinical trials and the successful development of our diagnostic and vaccine businesses, we are optimistic regarding our prospects for 1993." The total revenue for fiscal 1992 was allocated as follows: sales, 77%; royalties, 3%; R&D contracts, 13%; and interest and other revenues, 7%.

Internationally, the Japanese company Nippon Shoji Kaisha has become the exclusive distributor in Japan for the retrovirology product line of BioChem's diagnostic products subsidiary. An Italian subsidairy of BioChem has signed a major sales contract to sell $5-million worth of diagnostic equipment to an Italian company, Sorin Biomedica.

BioChem has begun Phase II and III clinical trials for its AIDS treatment, 3TC. This is the last step before the company submits its request for regulatory approval for the drug. If approved as an AIDS therapy, 3TC could have a market opportunity of $500-million a year. Glaxo Canada exercised its option in January 1993 to increase its holding in BioChem to 17%, for $30-million. Glaxo is betting on the success of 3TC. BioChem is also developing products for cancer, pain control, immune disorders and cardiovascular disease.

Rank (Profit/Revenue/Assets)
903   521   367

Jean-Louis Fontaine
Chairman

Francesco Bellini
President & C.E.O.

Francois Legault
Sr. V.P., Fin. & Treasurer

Philippe Lacaille
Exec. V.P. & C.O.O.

Address
Suite 600
2550, Boul. Daniel-Johnson
Laval
PQ
H7T 2L1
(514) 681-1744

Fax: (514) 681-4207
I0000852/G/5.7

BIOMIRA INC.

Exchanges	Price (Jun24'93)	9.37	Trailing P/E	nm	Stock Symbol
TM	Trailing Yield (%)	0.00	Trailing EPS	(1.37)	**BRA**

Period Ending	Dec92	Dec91	Dec90	Dec89	Dec88
Yearly Statistics					
Price-Close	11.25	13.38	2.10	3.55	3.15
Price-High	31.00	17.38	3.60	5.00	5.68
Price-Low	7.13	2.05	1.30	3.00	2.26
P/E-Close	nm	nm	nm	nm	nm
Dividends per Share	0.00	0.00	0.00	0.00	0.00
Dividend Yield (%)	0.00	0.00	0.00	0.00	0.00
Sales per Share	0.31	0.42	0.18	0.08	0.06
EPS before extra. item	(1.25)	(0.70)	(0.61)	(0.41)	(0.31)
Cash Flow per Share	(0.55)	(0.36)	(0.43)	(0.36)	(0.27)
Book Value per Share	2.38	3.36	0.88	1.11	1.52
O/S Common Shares	18,979	18,001	11,242	9,793	9,810
Total Revenue	17,581	17,524	7,552	2,584	2,087
Income before extra.	(22,674)	(9,240)	(6,004)	(4,038)	(3,043)
Cash Flow	(9,956)	(4,744)	(4,170)	(3,493)	(2,679)
Debt/Equity	0.02	0.01	0.06	0.01	0.01
Return on Capital (%)	(41.99)	(25.49)	(55.75)	(31.08)	(18.37)
Ret. on Com. Equity (%)	(42.93)	(26.38)	(57.86)	(31.31)	(18.51)
% Change Profit	(145.4)	(53.9)	(48.7)	(32.7)	(36.5)
% Change Revenue	0.3	132.0	192.2	23.8	94.5
% Change Assets	(25.5)	324.3	39.5	(23.8)	(16.5)

Preferred Div. Coverage	na	0.0	na
Total Div. Coverage	na	0.0	na
Interest Coverage	0.0	0.0	0.0
Current Ratio	9.3	10.4	2.3
Operating Margin	(137.5)	(42.2)	(85.6)
Asset Turnover	0.1	0.1	0.1

5 YEAR RATIOS (%)			
Return on Capital	(34.5)	(29.7)	(34.4)
Return on Com. Equity	(35.4)	(31.5)	(74.1)
Profit Growth	na	(41.1)	na
Revenue Growth	74.9	136.1	na
Asset Growth	22.9	55.1	277.3

BALANCE SHEET (000)			
Cash	34,995	53,699	3,672
Current Assets	42,184	62,633	8,293
Net Fixed Assets	4,584	3,034	2,109
Invest's & Advances	3,986	2,752	4,174
Total Assets	52,049	69,875	16,469
Short Term Debt	147	203	349
Current Liabilities	4,542	5,998	3,677
Long Term Debt	708	571	203
Total Liabilities	6,875	9,343	6,564
Total Equity	45,174	60,532	9,905
Total Liab. & Equity	52,049	69,875	16,469

CAPITAL (000)			
Total Debt	855	774	552
Preferred Equity	30	30	30
Common Equity	45,144	60,502	9,875

Business:

BIOMIRA is a biotechnology company formed to conduct research and to develop and market products in the fields of cancer diagnostics and therapeutics. The company has developed and continues to develop technology for the production of synthetic carbohydrate antigens. It markets four in-vitro cancer diagnostic kits for gastrointestinal, ovarian and breast cancer under the Truquant label.

Date	EPS	DPS	Tot Rev	Inc Bex
Mar 93	(0.22)	0.00	3,908	(4,130)
Dec 92	(0.66)	0.00	3,375	(12,069)
Sep 92	(0.24)	0.00	4,112	(4,406)
Jun 92	(0.25)	0.00	3,259	(4,543)
Mar 92	(0.09)	0.00	7,495	(1,656)
Dec 91	(0.12)	0.00	5,571	(1,790)
Sep 91	(0.27)	0.00	2,960	(3,610)
Jun 91	(0.24)	0.00	3,261	(2,987)

Synopsis:

For the first quarter of 1993, Biomira Inc.'s poorer results were attributed to aggressive R&D expenditures, and the cost of clinical trials. HealthVision, a hospital information corporation which is 75% owned by Biomira, posted a 52% decline in sales to $2.6-million, due to volatility relating to the high value of each individual contract.

Among Biomira's findings from research into cancer treatment is THERATOPE (R), a vaccine currently in Phase II clinical trials in Canada, and soon to begin trials in the U.K. and the U.S. Biomira is expected to file Investigational New Drug Applications with the U.S. Food and Drug Administration later in 1993. Further, Phase I and II clinical trials for the TRU-SCINT(R) imaging agents to identify carcinomas are underway in Canada and Germany.

In the fourth quarter of 1992, losses included a $6.9-million non-cash item from a shareholder's decision to exercise its rights to acquire 850,000 common shares of Biomira instead of taking all future royalties on products incorporating the company's active specific immunotherapy (ASI) technology. Further in the quarter, HealthVision experienced lower sales in computer hardware and software. Biomira is currently investing heavily in its R&D and clinical trial programs.

In December 1992, Biomira signed an agreement with Ribi ImmunoChem Research Inc. to market Ribi's MELACINE (R) therapeutic cancer vaccines in Canada. Under the agreement, Biomira will have an exclusive license to sell MELACINE (R) in Canada, following regulatory approval. Biomira will be responsible for conducting Canadian clinical trials and applying for regulatory approval. In addition to license fees, Ribi will receive transfer payments for supplies of MELACINE (R) and will be entitled to royalties from Biomira upon commercialization. This is the second agreement between the companies. In 1990, the companies entered into a license agreement for the use of Ribi's DETOX (R)-B adjuvant in Biomira's THERATOPE (R).

Rank (Profit/Revenue/Assets)
930   628   533

Eric E. Baker
Chairman Of The Board

T. Alexander McPherson
President & C.E.O.

James E. Devancy
V.P., Fin., C.F.O. & Secretary

Address
Edmonton Research Park
2011 - 94 Street
Edmonton
AB
T6N 1H1
(403) 450-3761

Fax: (403) 463-0871
01001473/G/5.7

DEPRENYL RESEARCH LIMITED

Exchanges	Price (Jun24'93)		4 .35	Trailing P/E		435 .00	Stock Symbol
TQ	Trailing Yield (%)		0 .00	Trailing EPS		0 .01	**DEP**

Period Ending	Dec92	Dec91	Dec90	Dec89	Dec88
Yearly Statistics					
Price-Close	7 .00	20 .88	5 .94	5 .96	n t
Price-High	23 .50	21 .38	7 .18	6 .25	n t
Price-Low	3 .75	5 .25	4 .75	2 .58	n t
P/E-Close	18 .92	50 .92	22 .84	25 .54	n t
Dividends per Share	0 .46	0 .43	0 .12	0 .05	0 .00
Dividend Yield (%)	6 .57	2 .06	2 .02	0 .84	0 .00
Sales per Share	1 .02	0 .86	0 .77	0 .13	0 .03
EPS before extra. item	0 .37	0 .41	0 .26	0 .23	0 .00
Cash Flow per Share	0 .14	0 .24	0 .26	0 .02	0 .00
Book Value per Share	1 .25	1 .53	2 .09	0 .91	0 .73
O/S Common Shares	17 ,042	17 ,144	7 ,394	13 ,792	12 ,999
Total Revenue	24 ,537	22 ,375	13 ,494	6 ,556	645
Income before extra.	6 ,327	6 ,552	3 ,771	3 ,087	31
Cash Flow	2 ,380	3 ,799	3 ,763	207	49
Debt/Equity	nd	nd	nd	0 .01	0 .02
Return on Capital (%)	44 .68	51 .57	43 .44	35 .14	0 .83
Ret. on Com. Equity (%)	26 .68	31 .44	26 .89	28 .02	0 .65
% Change Profit	(3 .4)	73 .8	22 .2	9 ,834 .8	1 ,941 .1
% Change Revenue	9 .7	65 .8	105 .8	916 .4	na
% Change Assets	(24 .1)	51 .5	67 .6	62 .9	5 ,670 .6

Business:

DEPRENYL RESEARCH LIMITED is engaged in the marketing and sale in Canada of prescription pharmaceutical products discovered, developed, or acquired by Chinion Pharmaceutical Chemical Works Limited, a Hungarian company. Deprenyl received approval from Health and Welfare Canada in January 1989 to sell the drug Eldepryl to the physicians of patients suffering from Parkinson's Disease.

Date	EPS	DPS	Tot Rev	Inc Bex
Mar 93	(0 .15)	0 .00	1 ,190	(2 ,673)
Dec 92	0 .02	0 .17	5 ,705	397
Sep 92	0 .06	0 .10	5 ,553	1 ,054
Jun 92	0 .08	0 .10	5 ,863	1 ,298
Mar 92	0 .22	0 .09	8 ,346	3 ,705
Dec 91	0 .12	0 .11	6 ,740	1 ,991
Sep 91	0 .09	0 .08	4 ,647	1 ,406
Jun 91	0 .06	0 .07	3 ,866	1 ,004

Preferred Div. Coverage	np	np	np
Total Div. Coverage	0 .8	0 .9	2 .1
Interest Coverage	nd	nd	nd
Current Ratio	2 .1	2 .1	1 .9
Operating Margin	20 .0	26 .9	33 .4
Asset Turnover	0 .6	0 .3	0 .4
5 YEAR RATIOS (%)			
Return on Capital	35 .1	na	na
Return on Com. Equity	22 .7	na	na
Profit Growth	429 .2	na	na
Revenue Growth	na	na	na
Asset Growth	182 .8	na	na
BALANCE SHEET (000)			
Cash	8 ,833	18 ,399	16 ,636
Current Assets	15 ,588	24 ,747	20 ,960
Net Fixed Assets	605	284	225
Invest's & Advances	7 ,805	11 ,474	2 ,008
Total Assets	30 ,727	40 ,503	26 ,735
Short Term Debt	0	0	0
Current Liabilities	7 ,341	11 ,523	11 ,242
Long Term Debt	0	0	0
Total Liabilities	9 ,481	14 ,316	11 ,242
Total Equity	21 ,246	26 ,188	15 ,493
Total Liab. & Equity	30 ,727	40 ,503	26 ,735
CAPITAL (000)			
Total Debt	0	0	0
Preferred Equity	0	0	0
Common Equity	21 ,246	26 ,188	15 ,493

Synopsis:

In May 1993, Deprenyl purchased the rights to a sleep-suppressing drug, Modafinil, from a French company as part of its strategy to expand its base from Eldepryl, the drug on which the company was built. Deprenyl currently has almost 20 drugs on its list, up from four a year ago. Eldepryl is said to be the main reason the company expects revenue to escalate this year. However, Deprenyl is faced with generic competition for Eldepryl, and is considering legal action. Currently, Eldepryl will be protected for up to 30 months by regulations pursuant to the recent Patent Act Changes that will strengthened protection for holders of pharmaceutical patents. Eldepryl was added to the Ontario Drug Benefit Formulary in January 1993, and this should increase the sales for the drug in Ontario.

For the first quarter 1993, the results included a $1.42-million loss on pharmaceutical operations, a $1.65-million loss on investments and a $790,000 gain from income tax recoveries. The company attributed the losses to a change in the accounting treatment of its advertising and sales promotion expenses, the write-off of expenses related to the launch of its dermatology products and increased investment in R&D. Deprenyl also plans to divest itself of its securities portfolio which lost $1.65-million in the quarter. Deprenyl reorganized last year to concentrate more on its pharmaceutical business and less on investments and stock markets. This new mandate will involve development, marketing, and forming strategic alliances.

In April 1993, Deprenyl reduced its equity in Wisconsin-based Lunar Corp., a pharmaceutical company, to 2.1%. The company lost about $2-million on its investment in Lunar. In July 1992, Deprenyl purchased a 78% stake in Lipopharm for $1.6-million. The acquired company has total assets of $306,000, shareholder's equity of $43,000, and revenue of $15,000 in for its last fiscal year. Lipopharm has a patent on a liposome drug delivery system that promises improved ways of getting a drug to where it can do the most good in the body with reduced side effects. The patent for the product is the key in the deal.

Relative strength to TSE300 — Price — Volume (in 1000's of board lots)

Rank (Profit/Revenue/Assets)		
228	591	635

Morton P. Shulman
Co-Chairman & C.E.O.

James P. Doherty
President & C.O.O.

Edward L. Foster
V.P. & C.F.O.

Address
378 Roncesvalles Avenue
Toronto
ON
M6R 2M7
(416) 537-4372

D0002642/G/5.7

QUADRA LOGIC TECHNOLOGIES INC.

Exchanges	Price (Jun24'93)		11.25	Trailing P/E		nm	Stock Symbol
TQ	Trailing Yield (%)		0.00	Trailing EPS		(0.69)	**QLT**

Period Ending	Dec92	Dec91	Dec90	Jan90	Dec89
Yearly Statistics					
Price-Close	9.88	8.50	8.00	9.63	9.63
Price-High	10.63	11.75	14.25	13.13	13.13
Price-Low	4.70	5.38	7.00	4.10	4.10
P/E-Close	nm	nm	nm	nm	nm
Dividends per Share	0.00	0.00	0.00	0.00	0.00
Dividend Yield (%)	0.00	0.00	0.00	0.00	0.00
Sales per Share	na	na	0.03	0.03	0.03
EPS before extra. item	(0.69)	(0.88)	(0.81)	(0.87)	(0.94)
Cash Flow per Share	(0.62)	(0.79)	(0.73)	(0.81)	(0.88)
Book Value per Share	1.23	0.91	1.78	2.53	2.53
O/S Common Shares	15,622	12,703	12,667	12,621	12,530
Total Revenue	1,282	1,567	3,463	3,764	3,137
Income before extra.	(9,788)	(11,176)	(10,196)	(8,614)	(9,048)
Cash Flow	(8,825)	(10,019)	(9,222)	(7,988)	(8,495)
Debt/Equity	0.29	0.38	0.11	nd	0.09
Return on Capital (%)	(31.48)	(37.63)	(29.33)	(21.89)	(30.54)
Ret. on Com. Equity (%)	(63.49)	(65.54)	(37.40)	(27.07)	(40.94)
% Change Profit	12.4	(9.6)	(18.4)	4.8	(1.5)
% Change Revenue	(18.2)	(54.7)	(8.0)	20.0	101.0
% Change Assets	33.5	(29.3)	(19.6)	1.4	82.6

Preferred Div. Coverage	na	na	na
Total Div. Coverage	na	na	na
Interest Coverage	0.0	0.0	na
Current Ratio	19.6	8.6	7.1
Operating Margin	na	(10,385.0)	(3,626.0)
Asset Turnover	na	na	0.0
5 YEAR RATIOS (%)			
Return on Capital	(30.2)	(34.6)	(32.8)
Return on Com. Equity	(46.9)	(49.6)	(44.0)
Profit Growth	(3.1)	na	na
Revenue Growth	(4.0)	27.2	50.3
Asset Growth	7.0	10.7	53.5
BALANCE SHEET (000)			
Cash	26,680	17,464	26,410
Current Assets	27,176	18,351	27,252
Net Fixed Assets	1,332	1,350	1,955
Invest's & Advances	0	0	670
Total Assets	33,781	25,314	35,829
Short Term Debt	129	950	0
Current Liabilities	1,386	2,128	3,850
Long Term Debt	7,226	5,719	3,190
Total Liabilities	8,613	7,847	7,390
Total Equity	25,169	17,467	28,439
Total Liab. & Equity	33,781	25,314	35,829
CAPITAL (000)			
Total Debt	7,356	6,669	3,190
Preferred Equity	5,900	5,900	5,900
Common Equity	19,269	11,567	22,539

Business:

QUADRA LOGIC TECHNOLOGIES is a pharmaceutical corporation engaged in the development of new drugs and applications for photodynamic therapy, an emerging medical field that uses photosensitive drugs in the treatment and prevention of cancer and other diseases.

Date	EPS	DPS	Tot Rev	Inc Bex
Mar 93	(0.18)	0.00	375	(2,816)
Dec 92	(0.16)	0.00	344	(2,717)
Sep 92	(0.13)	0.00	401	(2,024)
Jun 92	(0.22)	0.00	169	(2,734)
Mar 92	(0.18)	0.00	367	(2,313)
Dec 91	(0.24)	0.00	265	(2,952)
Sep 91	(0.14)	0.00	677	(1,834)
Jun 91	(0.29)	0.00	164	(3,711)

Synopsis:

Quadra Logic Technologies Inc. has been primarily involved in the research and development of proprietary pharmaceutical products, since its inception in 1981. So far, Quadra has not generated any revenues from the commercial sale of such products. Quadra expects to incur further significant operating losses in the upcoming years until it earns the approval to market its first product, Photofrin.

The company's current products, Photofrin and BFD, are subject to the approval by various health regulatory agencies prior to commercial sales. Product license applications have been filed in Canada, Japan, and seven European countries for the approval to market Photofrin for the treatment of certain forms of cancer. Quadra plans to pursue further regulatory filings for Photofrin in the U.S. and at least two other European countries during 1993. Early clinical trials for using BPD in the treatment of malignant skin lesions and psoriasis are underway in the U.S. and Canada. The trials are expected to take several years. The most significant operating risk to the company is the potential for a delay or denial in the regulatory approval of its products. This would impact planned cash flow from the sale of the products and would lead to increased R&D expenses.

Quadra's strategy for developing and commercializing its products involves forming key alliances and collaborations. Under the terms of its agreements with American Cyanamid Company, Quadra granted Cyanamid the exclusive worldwide distribution rights to market Photofrin and BFD. Under the agreement, Quadra will receive between 26% and 35% of gross proceeds on worldwide product sales. Cyanamid will absorb marketing and distribution costs, with Quadra handling manufacturing costs. Total R&D costs fell 16% to $8.9-million in 1992 due to the impact of the revised cost-sharing arrangement between Quadra and Cyanamid. Quadra finances product development, operations and capital expenditures primarily from the public and private sale of equity securities and through funding arrangements with strategic partners.

Relative strength to TSE300 / Price / Volume (in 1000's of board lots)

Rank (Profit/Revenue/Assets)		
886	878	616

E. Duff Scott
Chairman
William J. Foran
President & C.E.O.
Kenneth H. Galbraith
V.P., Finance & C.F.O.
Randal D. Chase
V.P., Operations & C.O.O.

Address
520 West 6th Avenue
Vancouver
BC
V5Z 4H5
(604) 872-7881

Fax: (604) 875-0001
Q0001711/G/5.7

Page	Company	$	Latest year end	Earnings per Share Actual	Estimate this year	Estimate next year
199	Canam Manac Group		9212	(0.62)	0.00	0.05
200	Co-Steel		9212	0.11	0.84	1.72
201	Dofasco		9212	(2.77)	0.14	1.48
202	Emco		9212	(0.67)	0.30	0.70
203	Harris Steel		9212	(0.03)	0.35	0.60
204	IPSCO		9212	0.98	1.47	1.70
205	Ivaco		9212	(1.71)	(0.27)	0.55
206	Samuel Manu-Tech		9212	0.48	1.55	2.00
207	Slater Industries		9212	(0.72)	n.a.	n.a.
208	Stelco		9212	(1.75)	(1.30)	(0.14)
209	Varity	$US	9301	0.55	1.29	2.39

Estimates from I/B/E/S Inc., 345 Hudson St., New York, NY 10014 (212) 243-3335. In Canada: 6 Lansing Square, Ste. 235, Willowdale, ON M2J 1T5 (416) 496-0977.

The Canadian steel industry, involved in an intense international tit-for-tat trade war, has charged that steel is being dumped into Canada at unfairly low prices and has lobbied for anti-dumping tariffs to be levied against foreign steel. In June 1993, the federal government announced a preliminary decision, to impose anti-dumping duties of up to 87.3% on cold-rolled steel sheet imports from five countries. Revenue Canada reported it had found imports from the five countries were dumped on the Canadian market at unfairly low prices. Italy topped the list with the highest margin of dumping - 87.3% below the fair price. It was followed by Britain at 55.7%, France at 38.1%, Germany at 31.2% and the United States at 25.5%. Duties were set at rates equivalent to the margin of dumping for each country. The Canadian International Trade Tribunal will review the case to determine whether the dumping is causing injury, a decision is expected by July 29, 1993.

In an earlier ruling, U.S. trade regulators sharply boosted provisional duties on Canadian steel, ruling that 19 countries are dumping steel in the United States. The decision by the U.S. Commerce Department affects an estimated $3.2-billion (U.S.) worth of steel entering the country and is a major victory for U.S. steel makers seeking protection from foreign competition. Canadian steel makers hotly deny charges of dumping steel in the United States and have denounced the decisions as irrational and unfair, but few industry observers expect the Canadians to remain unscathed by the ruling.

The European Community steel industry accused U.S. steel makers of launching a full-scale trade war with apparent government support and urged the EC to use all legal and political ways to combat it. The industry lobby group Eurofer is calling for a co-ordinated protest to be made against U.S. trade practices at the July G7 summit in Tokyo in the light of final anti-dumping and countervailing duties imposed against steel imports from a score of countries including seven EC states and Canada.

Canadian primary steel production totaled 284,526 tonnes in the week ended May 22, 1993, down 3.9% from 295,969 tonnes the previous week, but up 3.6% from 274,649 tonnes a year earlier. Statistics Canada said year-to-date production totalled 5,625,274 tonnes, up 4.1% from 5,405,419 tonnes a year earlier.

Steel Gauge (The) - Industry Report [Apr-19-1993]. SHEARSON LEHMAN BROTHERS, INC. reported by Van Leeuwen, T.M., et al

February 1993 orders exceeded the U.S. steel industry's capacity. Producer inventories declined and prices edged higher. Carbon and stainless production rose. Shipments of all steel grades increased, and imports have dropped. April 1993 sheet price increases are sticking in the wake of declining imports. The combination of higher orders and lower steel imports has created an environment in which domestic producers can raise prices and restore profitability. [RN 1325793]

Metal Stock Strategies: European Trip Finds - Industry Report [Mar-30-1993]. PAINEWEBBER INC. reported by Marcus, P.F

Steel prices in Europe continue to rise in early 1993. Production cutbacks and the mills' need for higher prices are contributing to the increase in prices. As of April 1, 1993, major mill product prices will be raised about $30 per metric tonne, with some increases up to $45 per tonne. More increases are planned for the summer 1993. Orders have risen for the integrated companies. [RN 1319378]

Construction Equipment Trends - Industry Report [Apr-20-1993]. MERRILL LYNCH CAPITAL MARKETS reported by McCann, J.R., et al

The 1993 survey of construction machinery dealers produced the most optimistic outlook for construction equipment demand since 1984. 86% of the respondents expect higher revenues this year, up from 80% a year ago, and only 32% in 1991. Only 4% of the dealers contacted forecast a sales decline this year, compared with 10% in the previous survey and 60% in 1991. [RN 1324432]

Metal Stock Strategies - Industry Report [Mar-9-1993]. PAINEWEBBER INC. reported by Marcus, P.F., et al

Orders for steel boomed in February 1993 at about a 110 million ton seasonally adjusted annual rate, versus 82 million tons in 1992. Spot flat-rolled prices are still rising. Inland has just announced a further $20 (U.S.) per ton increase in flat-rolled prices as of July 1993, which would put hot-rolled band up about $50 (U.S.) per ton, or 18%, from 4Q:92 levels. However, current labor negotiations may not work out particularly in the mills' favor, since the union well recognizes the improvement in the outlook. In addition, the companies may be unable to garner sizable price boosts from General Motors and Ford in their current negotiations for 1994 model year cars. In Germany, the price of hot-rolled coil is down from $330 (U.S.) to $260 (U.S.) per ton the past six months, with the U.S. price up from $300 (U.S.) to $320 (U.S.), and on the way to $340 (U.S.). For steel minimills, the 1993 earnings outlook is poor in the first half, but could be promising in the second half if price boosts take effect. Further EPS gains are expected in 1994 and 1995 as shipments continue to recover. [RN 1315780]

CANAM MANAC GROUP INC. (THE)

Exchanges	Price (Jun24'93)	2.75	Trailing P/E	nm	Stock Symbol
TM	Trailing Yield (%)	0.00	Trailing EPS	(0.39)	**CAM.A**

Period Ending	Dec92	Dec91	Dec90	Dec89	Dec88
Yearly Statistics					
Price-Close	1.90	2.80	3.25	5.13	6.25
Price-High	3.00	4.30	5.50	7.25	9.00
Price-Low	1.17	2.00	2.65	4.85	6.13
P/E-Close	nm	nm	nm	nm	6.79
Dividends per Share	0.00	0.13	0.20	0.20	0.46
Dividend Yield (%)	0.00	4.46	6.15	3.90	7.36
Sales per Share	11.32	9.72	10.91	12.89	16.32
EPS before extra. item	(0.60)	(0.73)	(2.05)	(0.09)	0.92
Cash Flow per Share	0.19	(1.28)	(0.20)	(0.25)	0.95
Book Value per Share	2.86	3.51	4.35	6.57	6.88
O/S Common Shares	30,892	23,821	23,820	23,820	23,817
Total Revenue	285,797	246,956	254,656	311,395	384,033
Income before extra.	(14,941)	(17,272)	(48,851)	(1,955)	21,577
Cash Flow	4,743	(30,462)	(4,860)	(5,973)	22,368
Debt/Equity	2.30	2.52	4.31	2.76	2.65
Return on Capital (%)	(1.03)	(1.60)	(7.71)	0.97	8.45
Ret. on Com. Equity (%)	(17.38)	(18.45)	(37.65)	(1.28)	14.02
% Change Profit	13.5	64.6	(2,398.8)	(109.1)	4.7
% Change Revenue	15.7	(3.0)	(18.2)	(18.9)	(16.5)
% Change Assets	(0.2)	(42.5)	(5.5)	(2.9)	62.5

Date	EPS	DPS	Tot Rev	Inc Bex
Mar 93	(0.09)	0.00	70,377	(2,627)
Dec 92	0.09	0.00	88,747	1,393
Sep 92	(0.15)	0.00	77,353	(3,612)
Jun 92	(0.24)	0.00	65,213	(5,751)
Mar 92	(0.29)	0.00	54,174	(6,971)
Dec 91	(0.36)	0.00	60,075	(8,399)
Sep 91	(0.31)	0.03	65,073	(7,311)
Jul 91	(0.21)	0.05	66,195	(4,938)

Preferred Div. Coverage	na	na	0.0
Total Div. Coverage	na	0.0	0.0
Interest Coverage	0.0	0.0	0.0
Current Ratio	1.2	1.5	1.2
Operating Margin	(2.2)	(10.4)	3.7
Asset Turnover	0.8	0.7	0.4
5 YEAR RATIOS (%)			
Return on Capital	(0.2)	4.0	8.6
Return on Com. Equity	(12.1)	(5.5)	1.5
Profit Growth	na	na	na
Revenue Growth	(9.1)	(8.5)	(0.9)
Asset Growth	(3.1)	4.5	28.0
BALANCE SHEET (000)			
Cash	12,508	16,803	6,919
Current Assets	143,940	137,596	149,307
Net Fixed Assets	130,212	137,518	132,403
Invest's & Advances	26,237	31,090	303,024
Total Assets	347,766	348,453	606,524
Short Term Debt	75,076	48,718	84,000
Current Liabilities	121,685	92,100	127,496
Long Term Debt	131,141	165,301	368,474
Total Liabilities	258,158	263,595	501,589
Total Equity	89,608	84,858	104,935
Total Liab. & Equity	347,766	348,453	606,524
CAPITAL (000)			
Total Debt	206,217	214,019	452,474
Preferred Equity	1,270	1,270	1,270
Common Equity	88,338	83,588	103,665

Business:

CANAM MANAC GROUP INC. makes and markets steel products in Canada and the United States. Its main product is open-web steel joists. The company also makes other steel products related to the commercial and industrial construction industry.

Synopsis:

After four consecutive years of losses and the disposition of a number of assets, upgraded operations and a focus on higher value products, Canam Manac is still in a tough environment. There are signs, however, that it has turned the corner. In the first quarter, Canam Manac had a loss of 9 cents a share, compared with 29 cents a year earlier. Sales increased by 30% to $70.2-million. There were 31 million shares outstanding, up 30% from a year earlier.

Many people know the company from seeing the Manac name on tractor-trailers that cruise the highways of Canada. But Canam is first and foremost a steel fabricator - the largest manufacturer in Canada of open-web steel joists, and the second largest in North America. Dependent as it is on the construction and transportation industries, Canam Manac has seen hard times in recent years. Only an economic turnaround is likely to restore it to a reasonable degree of health, and the company believes that this is happening, or is about to happen.

Although the steel construction sector remains weak in Canada where most of the company's sales are made, it is firming in the United States. Major contracts signed during the quarter included $9-million for a building in Mexico, $19.2-million to provide steel for the new Boston Garden and $2.5-million for the new BMW automotive plant in South Carolina. Late in 1992, the Manac trailer division landed major contracts, including a $3-million contract from Canadian Tire Corp. Ltd. for 150 new vans. By the end of the first quarter, Canam Manac held orders for 679 units, up from 266 a year earlier. MRM Steel will also benefit from an order position that is 35% superior to 1992.

About 75% of revenues were derived in Canada in 1992, with the remainder from the United States. In 1992, export sales accounted for 16% of total revenue, most of which was to the U.S.

Relative strength to TSE300 / Price / Volume (in 1000's of board lots)

Rank (Profit/Revenue/Assets)
908   230   256

Marcel Dutil
Chairman, President & C.E.O.
Bernard Gouin
V.P., Finance & Treasurer

Address
11535, 1re Avenue
Bureau 500
Ville De St-Georges
PQ
G5Y 7H5
(418) 228-8031

Fax: (418) 228-1750
C0055041/G/6.2

CO-STEEL INC.

Exchanges	Price (Jun24'93)		24 .25	Trailing P/E		134 .72	Stock Symbol
TM	Trailing Yield (%)		1 .32	Trailing EPS		0 .18	**CEI**

Period Ending	Dec92	Dec91	Dec90	Dec89	Dec88
Yearly Statistics					
Price-Close	17 .50	18 .00	15 .75	16 .00	16 .63
Price-High	19 .38	20 .75	17 .50	19 .25	17 .13
Price-Low	15 .50	15 .75	14 .63	15 .75	13 .00
P/E-Close	159 .09	81 .82	3 .97	8 .60	7 .63
Dividends per Share	0 .32	0 .48	0 .60	0 .54	0 .46
Dividend Yield (%)	1 .83	2 .67	3 .81	3 .38	2 .77
Sales per Share	30 .33	34 .10	35 .99	39 .56	40 .10
EPS before extra. item	0 .11	0 .22	3 .97	1 .86	2 .18
Cash Flow per Share	1 .51	1 .93	2 .94	3 .86	4 .16
Book Value per Share	16 .01	16 .56	16 .78	12 .82	11 .90
O/S Common Shares	30 ,162	24 ,455	24 ,312	24 ,312	24 ,208
Total Revenue	877 ,722	848 ,476	882 ,474	969 ,754	977 ,876
Income before extra.	3 ,153	5 ,461	96 ,470	45 ,139	52 ,687
Cash Flow	43 ,566	47 ,911	71 ,456	93 ,752	100 ,745
Debt/Equity	0 .29	0 .38	0 .40	0 .42	0 .58
Return on Capital (%)	3 .09	4 .50	27 .11	21 .93	25 .52
Ret. on Com. Equity (%)	0 .71	1 .34	26 .81	15 .05	19 .80
% Change Profit	(42 .3)	(94 .3)	113 .7	(14 .3)	81 .6
% Change Revenue	3 .4	(3 .9)	(9 .0)	(0 .8)	19 .2
% Change Assets	7 .0	(2 .0)	16 .6	(0 .6)	5 .2

Period Ending	Dec92	Dec91	Dec90
Preferred Div. Coverage	np	np	np
Total Div. Coverage	0 .3	0 .5	6 .6
Interest Coverage	1 .2	1 .2	4 .6
Current Ratio	1 .8	1 .4	1 .5
Operating Margin	1 .6	2 .7	7 .6
Asset Turnover	1 .1	1 .1	1 .1
5 YEAR RATIOS (%)			
Return on Capital	16 .4	19 .3	21 .9
Return on Com. Equity	12 .7	15 .1	17 .4
Profit Growth	(36 .3)	(24 .4)	92 .7
Revenue Growth	1 .3	2 .1	5 .4
Asset Growth	5 .0	4 .7	6 .9
BALANCE SHEET (000)			
Cash	69 ,006	0	46 ,743
Current Assets	317 ,621	237 ,308	284 ,082
Net Fixed Assets	370 ,730	389 ,680	363 ,652
Invest's & Advances	64 ,905	64 ,905	64 ,905
Total Assets	827 ,035	772 ,846	788 ,827
Short Term Debt	46 ,263	33 ,988	40 ,218
Current Liabilities	175 ,530	167 ,800	192 ,502
Long Term Debt	91 ,911	119 ,978	124 ,361
Total Liabilities	344 ,006	367 ,883	380 ,869
Total Equity	483 ,029	404 ,963	407 ,958
Total Liab. & Equity	827 ,035	772 ,846	788 ,827
CAPITAL (000)			
Total Debt	138 ,174	153 ,966	164 ,579
Preferred Equity	0	0	0
Common Equity	483 ,029	404 ,963	407 ,958

Business:

CO-STEEL INC. manufactures and markets steel products including special quality bar and rod, concrete reinforcing bar and rod and other structural shapes. Its products are used in the construction, automotive, appliance, machinery and equipment industries in North America and Europe. The company has facilities in Ontario, New Jersey and the United Kingdom.

Date	EPS	DPS	Tot Rev	Inc Bex
Mar 93	0 .07	0 .08	244 ,309	2 ,107
Dec 92	0 .07	0 .08	219 ,179	2 ,031
Sep 92	0 .00	0 .08	204 ,890	60
Jun 92	0 .04	0 .08	251 ,182	1 ,003
Mar 92	0 .00	0 .08	203 ,034	59
Dec 91	0 .04	0 .08	196 ,364	1 ,151
Sep 91	0 .02	0 .08	201 ,097	501
Jun 91	0 .06	0 .16	225 ,320	1 ,407

Synopsis:

Co-Steel expects a significant improvement in earnings in the second quarter of 1993 as price increases take effect in most of its markets. Although the Canadian and European economies will likely remain lackluster, earnings should improve, reflecting continuing improvement in the U.S. economy, some strengthening of the U.K. economy, and improved productivity of operations.

The company's results improved in the quarter ended March 31, 1993, as production and shipments reached record highs. Sales rose 20% from 1992 levels to $244-million, as shipments climbed 22% to 644,000 tons. The higher level of shipments was due principally to improving U.S. and overseas markets, particularly in the Far East.

In March 1993, Co-Steel formed a partnership with Dofasco to build a two million ton flat rolled minimill in the central U.S. to serve extensive North American markets with quality hot rolled steel made from scrap and direct reduced iron. Phase one will produce one million tons annually and is estimated to cost $300-million (U.S.), to be shared equally by the partners. Construction is due to begin later in 1993, with production to commence early in 1995. The facility will benefit from the use of the most sophisticated equipment available to maximize cost advantages in the marketplace. Phase two expansion is anticipated to begin in 1997.

While the steel industry posted huge losses in 1992, Co-Steel reported net earnings of more than $3-million, despite a reduction in sales prices, by continuing its 1991 programs of major cost reductions and cash conservation. Shipments were up by 5% to a near record 2.3 million tons while sales grew by 3% to $874-million. Price declines were particularly severe in the U.K. and continental Europe, while the major North American price decreases occurred in 1991.

1992 sales (operating earnings) by country were: Canada, 26% (24); the United States, 34% (45%); and the European Economic Community, 40% (31%). Exports accounted for half of Canadian sales.

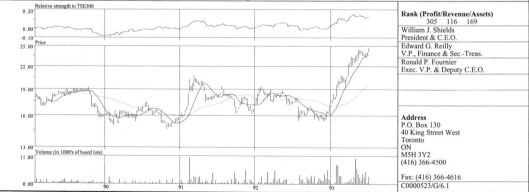

Rank (Profit/Revenue/Assets)
305   116   169

William J. Shields
President & C.E.O.
Edward G. Reilly
V.P., Finance & Sec.-Treas.
Ronald P. Fournier
Exec. V.P. & Deputy C.E.O.

Address
P.O. Box 130
40 King Street West
Toronto
ON
M5H 3Y2
(416) 366-4500

Fax: (416) 366-4616
C0000523/G/6.1

DOFASCO INC.

Exchanges	Price (Jun24'93)	14.62	Trailing P/E	nm	Stock Symbol
TM	Trailing Yield (%)	1.03	Trailing EPS	(2.89)	**DFS**

Period Ending	Dec92	Dec91	Dec90	Dec89	Dec88
Yearly Statistics					
Price-Close	10.25	16.50	16.25	24.50	26.25
Price-High	19.00	23.50	24.75	31.13	30.00
Price-Low	7.25	15.00	16.25	24.00	24.25
P/E-Close	nm	nm	nm	8.31	7.79
Dividends per Share	0.15	0.80	1.28	1.28	1.06
Dividend Yield (%)	1.46	4.85	7.88	5.22	4.04
Sales per Share	24.81	29.03	35.49	60.30	49.84
EPS before extra. item	(2.96)	(0.73)	(10.64)	2.95	3.37
Cash Flow per Share	1.68	1.80	3.92	7.40	8.12
Book Value per Share	12.98	16.19	17.34	29.35	27.71
O/S Common Shares	79,276	78,290	67,018	65,364	64,206
Total Revenue	1,978,800	2,064,200	2,363,100	3,941,900	3,007,300
Income before extra.	(207,100)	(25,000)	(679,200)	217,900	222,000
Cash Flow	132,200	127,300	259,200	479,500	485,600
Debt/Equity	0.70	0.55	0.56	0.53	0.56
Return on Capital (%)	(11.73)	0.53	(18.50)	12.87	14.85
Ret. on Com. Equity (%)	(20.36)	(4.26)	(45.83)	10.34	12.29
% Change Profit	(728.4)	96.3	(411.7)	(1.8)	44.2
% Change Revenue	(4.1)	(12.6)	(40.1)	31.1	37.2
% Change Assets	(5.3)	1.5	(33.2)	4.5	59.2

Preferred Div. Coverage	0.0	0.0	0.0
Total Div. Coverage	0.0	0.0	0.0
Interest Coverage	0.0	0.1	0.0
Current Ratio	2.9	3.5	2.8
Operating Margin	2.1	2.2	11.0
Asset Turnover	0.6	0.6	0.7
5 YEAR RATIOS (%)			
Return on Capital	(0.4)	4.7	7.1
Return on Com. Equity	(9.6)	(3.6)	(1.0)
Profit Growth	na	na	na
Revenue Growth	(2.1)	0.8	3.0
Asset Growth	1.3	4.3	4.9
BALANCE SHEET (000)			
Cash	214,900	102,600	16,900
Current Assets	1,111,200	1,038,700	1,082,300
Net Fixed Assets	2,003,800	2,206,900	2,121,100
Invest's & Advances	139,600	166,900	134,800
Total Assets	3,266,900	3,450,100	3,400,800
Short Term Debt	26,600	3,600	27,900
Current Liabilities	381,600	295,400	383,100
Long Term Debt	927,600	872,300	813,000
Total Liabilities	1,897,900	1,842,900	1,898,400
Total Equity	1,369,000	1,607,200	1,502,400
Total Liab. & Equity	3,266,900	3,450,100	3,400,800
CAPITAL (000)			
Total Debt	954,200	875,900	840,900
Preferred Equity	339,700	340,100	340,200
Common Equity	1,029,300	1,267,100	1,162,200

Business:

DOFASCO INC. is a fully integrated steel maker specializing in a broad range of high quality flat rolled products. These include cold rolled, hot rolled and plate, galvanized, Galvalume, prepainted, tinplate, chromium coated and motor laminated, all in coils and cut lengths. Dofasco has customers in several sectors including the automotive, energy and appliance industries.

Date	EPS	DPS	Tot Rev	Inc Bex
Mar 93	(0.24)	0.00	526,000	(12,500)
Dec 92	(1.46)	0.00	478,500	(108,900)
Sep 92	(0.27)	0.00	485,000	(14,700)
Jun 92	(0.92)	0.15	550,400	(65,900)
Mar 92	(0.31)	0.15	464,900	(17,600)
Dec 91	(0.09)	0.20	502,500	(1,500)
Sep 91	(0.24)	0.20	499,000	(10,100)
Jun 91	(0.47)	0.20	558,400	(24,600)

Synopsis:

Dofasco is refocusing its product mix to take advantage of the capabilities of its modern slab casting and associated No. 2 Stream of production facilities. After the closure of the ingot producing No. 1 Stream facilities in August and September 1993, the product mix will be more focused on higher value-added cold rolled and coated products. These markets include more consumer durable goods, which will likely lead the recovery in spending activity. This strategy will also place Dofasco in markets that are less vulnerable to the competitive threats of mini-mills. Dofasco is continuing to reduce employment levels and to sell non-strategic assets.

In March 1993, Dofasco formed a partnership with Co-Steel Inc. to build a mini-mill in the United States. The facility will serve North American markets with quality hot rolled steel made from scrap and direct reduced iron, utilizing the thin slab casting process. Phase I of the facility, scheduled to be on-stream early in 1995, will have a capacity of one million tons per year. Dofasco's 50% share of the estimated cost of $300-million (U.S.) will be financed through cash on hand. A phase II expansion program, expected to begin in 1997, will result in a total capacity of two million tons per year.

Demand for Dofasco's products in the early months of 1993 has continued to improve and order intake has increased significantly. A strong automotive segment is leading the way, but the improvement is broadly based across all major markets. First quarter shipments of 852,000 tons were 14% ahead of the first quarter of last year, however selling prices were lower.

Dofasco's sales to North American markets were unchanged in 1992, while sales to offshore export markets fell slightly during the year. Flat rolled shipments of 3.419 million tons were marginally higher than last year's level of 3.375 million tons. Selling prices were lower across all flat rolled lines in 1992, with average prices down approximately 3.5% from the already depressed levels of 1991.

Rank (Profit/Revenue/Assets)		
985	64	63

John D. Leitch
Chairman

John T. Mayberry
President & C.E.O.

Bill P. Solski
Sr. V.P., Finance

Address
P.O. Box 2460
Hamilton
ON
L8N 3J5
(416) 544-3761

Fax: (416) 545-3236
D0001405/G/6.1

EMCO LIMITED

Exchanges	Price (Jun24'93)		8.12	Trailing P/E		nm	Stock Symbol
TM	Trailing Yield (%)		0.00	Trailing EPS		(0.36)	**EML**

Period Ending	Dec92	Dec91	Dec90	Dec89	Dec88
Yearly Statistics					
Price-Close	5.38	4.85	4.75	11.38	13.75
Price-High	8.00	8.00	11.25	13.63	14.50
Price-Low	4.25	3.60	4.00	10.75	11.50
P/E-Close	nm	nm	nm	nm	13.35
Dividends per Share	0.00	0.00	0.35	0.40	0.38
Dividend Yield (%)	0.00	0.00	7.37	3.52	2.76
Sales per Share	73.25	70.38	80.68	85.53	83.35
EPS before extra. item	(0.67)	(1.37)	(2.11)	(0.68)	1.03
Cash Flow per Share	0.49	(0.50)	(1.04)	0.06	2.49
Book Value per Share	4.63	5.30	6.36	8.60	10.10
O/S Common Shares	14,167	14,167	14,167	14,167	14,167
Total Revenue	1,038,983	1,004,774	1,139,916	1,211,649	1,180,949
Income before extra.	(9,504)	(19,394)	(29,957)	(9,616)	14,580
Cash Flow	6,945	(7,142)	(14,666)	826	35,300
Debt/Equity	4.71	4.41	3.58	2.87	2.74
Return on Capital (%)	5.92	3.80	(0.15)	5.40	11.73
Ret. on Com. Equity (%)	(13.52)	(23.49)	(28.27)	(7.26)	10.26
% Change Profit	51.0	35.3	(211.5)	(166.0)	(14.6)
% Change Revenue	3.4	(11.9)	(5.9)	2.6	40.8
% Change Assets	(4.6)	1.5	(10.7)	(13.0)	9.4

Business:

EMCO LTD. is a manufacturer and distributer of building and home improvement products, including plumbing products, roofing materials, fibreboard products, vinyl siding and vinyl windows. In addition, Emco manufactures in seven countries and distributes worldwide, fluid handling equipment for the petroleum, petrochemical and other industries.

Date	EPS	DPS	Tot Rev	Inc Bex
Mar 93	(0.37)	0.00	205,110	(7,261)
Dec 92	(0.28)	0.00	242,202	(4,043)
Sep 92	0.27	0.00	298,033	3,807
Jun 92	0.02	0.00	283,520	228
Mar 92	(0.67)	0.00	215,228	(9,496)
Dec 91	(0.46)	0.00	247,113	(6,553)
Sep 91	0.11	0.00	291,169	1,490
Jun 91	0.04	0.00	276,576	538

Preferred Div. Coverage	np	np	np	
Total Div. Coverage	na	na	0.0	
Interest Coverage	0.8	0.4	0.0	
Current Ratio	1.9	2.1	2.3	
Operating Margin	2.2	1.1	1.1	
Asset Turnover	2.0	1.9	2.2	
5 YEAR RATIOS (%)				
Return on Capital	5.3	6.8	8.8	
Return on Com. Equity	(12.5)	(7.2)	(0.6)	
Profit Growth	na	na	na	
Revenue Growth	4.3	8.8	17.5	
Asset Growth	(3.8)	7.9	11.1	
BALANCE SHEET (000)				
Cash	2,749	2,244	6,742	
Current Assets	332,276	340,564	304,390	
Net Fixed Assets	141,605	154,851	175,633	
Invest's & Advances	7,081	7,249	8,334	
Total Assets	506,341	530,550	522,850	
Short Term Debt	41,834	38,176	28,558	
Current Liabilities	171,912	160,043	134,322	
Long Term Debt	266,983	292,779	294,388	
Total Liabilities	440,780	455,496	432,753	
Total Equity	65,561	75,054	90,097	
Total Liab. & Equity	506,341	530,550	522,850	
CAPITAL (000)				
Total Debt	308,817	330,955	322,946	
Preferred Equity	0	0	0	
Common Equity	65,561	75,054	90,097	

Synopsis:

Emco's earnings are affected by the level of interest rates, currency rate fluctuations and the general state of the economy. In particular, Emco's sales depend heavily on the level of activity in the construction industry which tends to be cyclical. About 85% of Emco's business consists of the manufacture and sale of plumbing and related products and the manufacture and sale of building materials. Sales are particularly sensitive to residential construction activity. Repair and renovation represented 44% of total residential construction expenditures in Canada in 1992.

The Canada-U.S. Free Trade Agreement and the North American Free Trade Agreement are expected to benefit Emco. It expects increased sources of supply and reduced prices for the its distribution business, and enhanced export opportunities for its manufacturing businesses. Emco believes these benefits will outweigh the potential adverse effects of increased competition.

Emco is projecting the economy to grow by 3% in 1993 and total housing starts to increase by 6% overall. Particularly strong will be single family starts which are expected to increase by about 14% in Canada and 30% in Ontario. Retail sales data suggests an upturn in the do-it-yourself renovation market, and a recovery in the contractor market is expected in 1993. Emco is forecasting an increase of 4% in home renovation activity.

Despite the difficult economy and low construction activity levels, Emco has been refocusing on its core businesses and improving its financial results by increasing market share and gross margins and reducing operating costs and debt levels.

Emco's debt levels have fallen by $103.2-million during the past three years and dropped an additional $54-million through an equity offering of 8.9 million common shares in February 1993. This issue allowed Emco to pre-pay a loan and establish a more favorable credit agreement. The lowered debt and lower interest rates are significantly reducing interest expenses.

Rank (Profit/Revenue/Assets)		
883	100	209

Wayne B. Lyon
Chairman Of The Board

Frank M. Hennessey
President & C.E.O.

Richard B. Grogan
V.P., Fin., C.F.O. & Secretary

Address
Box 5252
620 Richmond Street
London
ON
N6A 4L6
(519) 645-3900

Fax: (519) 645-3939
E0001142/G/6.2

For further company information, call Globe Information Services 1-800-268-9128 or (416)585-5345

HARRIS STEEL GROUP INC.

Exchanges	Price (Jun24'93)	9.37	Trailing P/E	78.13	Stock Symbol
T	Trailing Yield (%)	1.37	Trailing EPS	0.12	**HSG.A**

Period Ending	Dec92	Dec91	Dec90	Dec89	Dec88
Yearly Statistics					
Price-Close	5.25	6.00	4.30	5.38	8.00
Price-High	7.75	7.00	6.00	9.00	9.75
Price-Low	5.00	4.00	3.80	4.85	7.00
P/E-Close	nm	33.33	9.77	nm	25.81
Dividends per Share	0.13	0.13	0.24	0.24	0.24
Dividend Yield (%)	2.48	2.08	5.58	4.47	3.00
Sales per Share	17.86	17.18	19.53	19.38	17.41
EPS before extra. item	(0.03)	0.18	0.44	0.00	0.31
Cash Flow per Share	0.18	0.47	0.95	1.26	1.34
Book Value per Share	4.67	4.83	4.78	4.54	4.78
O/S Common Shares	11,521	11,568	11,591	12,341	12,341
Total Revenue	206,556	198,777	235,862	239,115	214,822
Income before extra.	(377)	2,092	5,325	(14)	3,855
Cash Flow	2,088	5,473	11,541	15,502	16,598
Debt/Equity	0.33	0.01	0.07	0.16	1.34
Return on Capital (%)	3.11	9.09	21.51	8.71	8.79
Ret. on Com. Equity (%)	(0.69)	3.76	9.56	(0.03)	6.47
% Change Profit	(118.0)	(60.7)	nm	(100.4)	(41.8)
% Change Revenue	3.9	(15.7)	(1.4)	11.3	15.8
% Change Assets	19.8	(11.2)	(7.8)	(40.0)	(11.2)
Preferred Div. Coverage	np	np	np		
Total Div. Coverage	0.0	1.4	1.8		
Interest Coverage	11.5	12.4	14.4		
Current Ratio	1.6	2.1	1.8		
Operating Margin	2.1	3.3	7.4		
Asset Turnover	1.9	2.2	2.4		
5 YEAR RATIOS (%)					
Return on Capital	10.2	11.5	11.7		
Return on Com. Equity	3.8	6.0	6.8		
Profit Growth	na	(14.7)	(10.7)		
Revenue Growth	2.1	3.8	(2.9)		
Asset Growth	(12.2)	(13.5)	(6.6)		
BALANCE SHEET (000)					
Cash	0	2,766	0		
Current Assets	82,380	65,667	74,115		
Net Fixed Assets	22,855	21,958	23,566		
Invest's & Advances	0	0	0		
Total Assets	107,051	89,335	100,654		
Short Term Debt	17,652	525	3,275		
Current Liabilities	51,184	30,999	41,773		
Long Term Debt	0	0	525		
Total Liabilities	53,264	33,429	45,298		
Total Equity	53,786	55,906	55,356		
Total Liab. & Equity	107,051	89,335	100,654		
CAPITAL (000)					
Total Debt	17,652	525	3,799		
Preferred Equity	0	0	0		
Common Equity	53,786	55,906	55,356		

Business:

HARRIS STEEL GROUP INC. is engaged in the fabrication and instalation of concrete reinforcing steel and structural steel. The company also manufactures and distributes wire and wire products, welded wire mesh, cold finished bar and heavy industrial steel and aluminium grating. The company serves Canada and the northeastern, central and western United States.

Date	EPS	DPS	Tot Rev	Inc Bex
Mar 93	0.01	0.03	40,108	94
Dec 92	0.06	0.03	50,394	647
Sep 92	0.06	0.03	64,607	666
Jun 92	(0.01)	0.03	53,939	(98)
Mar 92	(0.14)	0.03	37,640	(1,592)
Dec 91	0.03	0.03	47,388	311
Sep 91	0.13	0.03	60,522	1,561
Jun 91	0.08	0.03	52,663	938

Synopsis:

Harris Steel is focusing on the infrastructure market. Many parts of the North American infrastructure, particularly roads and bridges, are in an advanced state of deterioration. Many billions of dollars need to be spent to patch them up or replace them completely. The company's strong suit is manufacturing epoxy-coated reinforcing steel, an essential ingredient in concrete construction. The epoxy makes the steel resistant to corrosion and can extend the life of bridge decks and parking slabs to 50 years or more, compared with an average life of 18 years for outdoor surfaces built with uncoated steel.

Harris expects a slow but steady growth in the construction and manufacturing sectors in Canada. Large new public works projects will not feed into the marketplace until November 1994. It does not expect a recovery in the commercial construction markets in the foreseeable future, but residential markets are gradually strengthening as cheap interest rates make housing more affordable. In 1992, Harris Steel generated 70% of revenues from Canada, and 30% from the U.S.

Large infrastructure jobs will continue to come to market in the United States. This trend will accelerate later in 1993 when the $156-billion (U.S.) Transportation Act of 1991 will begin to fund actual projects. In anticipation, Harris has expanded its branches in Seattle, Boston and Phoenix. The company also has 14 reinforcing steel manufacturing plants in Canada. It already has a $20-million (U.S.) contract to supply 40,000 tons of rebar for the Boston Central Artery highway expansion. This is the largest single contract in the company's history, to which shipments began in April 1993.

The most significant change in business conditions for Harris Steel, beginning in 1992's fourth quarter, has been the rapid reversal in the steel markets. After losing 9 cents a share in the first nine months of 1992, it made a profit of 6 cents a share in the fourth quarter. The 1992 loss was mainly caused by record low margins which reflected very weak steel and construction markets for most of the year.

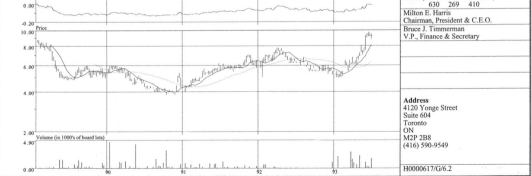

Rank (Profit/Revenue/Assets)
630   269   410

Milton E. Harris
Chairman, President & C.E.O.

Bruce J. Timmerman
V.P., Finance & Secretary

Address
4120 Yonge Street
Suite 604
Toronto
ON
M2P 2B8
(416) 590-9549

H0000617/G/6.2

IPSCO INC.

	Price (Jun24'93)	25.25	Trailing P/E	29.71	Stock Symbol
Exchanges **TZQ**	Trailing Yield (%)	1.90	Trailing EPS	0.85	**ISP**

Period Ending	Dec92	Dec91	Dec90	Dec89	Dec88
Yearly Statistics					
Price-Close	20.25	22.63	18.25	18.50	17.50
Price-High	24.25	25.25	19.00	21.25	19.75
Price-Low	15.88	17.75	13.25	17.00	10.50
P/E-Close	20.66	8.94	nm	13.60	8.49
Dividends per Share	0.48	0.48	0.48	0.48	0.42
Dividend Yield (%)	2.37	2.12	2.63	2.60	2.40
Sales per Share	30.35	37.49	32.92	32.41	30.70
EPS before extra. item	0.98	2.53	(0.34)	1.36	2.06
Cash Flow per Share	1.72	3.96	0.89	2.44	3.18
Book Value per Share	19.01	18.61	16.62	17.44	16.58
O/S Common Shares	16,874	14,464	14,240	14,237	14,182
Total Revenue	480,359	538,657	462,105	460,577	430,809
Income before extra.	15,512	36,348	(4,772)	19,329	28,838
Cash Flow	27,254	56,935	12,506	34,633	44,682
Debt/Equity	0.18	0.21	0.32	0.27	0.33
Return on Capital (%)	8.86	20.75	0.54	12.76	19.98
Ret. on Com. Equity (%)	5.26	14.37	(1.97)	8.00	12.98
% Change Profit	(57.3)	861.7	(124.7)	(33.0)	246.4
% Change Revenue	(10.8)	16.6	0.3	6.9	44.3
% Change Assets	10.4	3.3	0.4	(2.3)	14.9

Preferred Div. Coverage	np	np	np
Total Div. Coverage	2.0	5.3	0.0
Interest Coverage	5.5	10.2	0.2
Current Ratio	3.0	2.5	2.0
Operating Margin	6.5	12.3	7.8
Asset Turnover	1.0	1.2	1.0
5 YEAR RATIOS (%)			
Return on Capital	12.6	12.2	7.8
Return on Com. Equity	7.7	7.5	3.9
Profit Growth	13.3	na	na
Revenue Growth	9.9	20.2	8.7
Asset Growth	5.1	3.6	1.5
BALANCE SHEET (000)			
Cash	66,728	15,509	0
Current Assets	248,268	204,229	205,855
Net Fixed Assets	256,113	252,455	217,602
Invest's & Advances	0	764	1,527
Total Assets	505,415	457,929	443,449
Short Term Debt	0	0	18,728
Current Liabilities	82,317	82,327	104,169
Long Term Debt	57,787	57,704	57,704
Total Liabilities	184,656	188,756	206,766
Total Equity	320,759	269,173	236,683
Total Liab. & Equity	505,415	457,929	443,449
CAPITAL (000)			
Total Debt	57,787	57,704	76,432
Preferred Equity	0	0	0
Common Equity	320,759	269,173	236,683

Business:

IPSCO INC. manufactures a diverse range of steel and steel products. Products include steel coil, sheet, plate, bar, tubular products, and alloy steel and line pipe. It operates facilities in Saskatchewan, Alberta, British Columbia, Iowa, Minnesota, and Nebraska. IPSCO markets its products across Canada and the United States.

Date	EPS	DPS	Tot Rev	Inc Bex
Mar 93	0.54	0.12	156,490	9,085
Dec 92	0.38	0.12	139,310	6,113
Sep 92	0.07	0.12	106,870	1,560
Jun 92	(0.14)	0.12	91,588	(1,840)
Mar 92	0.67	0.12	142,591	9,679
Dec 91	0.76	0.12	145,149	10,851
Sep 91	0.54	0.12	124,935	7,823
Jun 91	0.53	0.12	123,329	7,646

Synopsis:

IPSCO's optimism for 1993 is based on stronger than usual drilling activity in Canada and the still improving demand for steel products in North America. It believes the enhanced level of pipeline construction in North America is not fully played out but the company cannot determine when demand levels for large diameter pipe will increase. IPSCO also foresees continuing higher demand for oil country tubular goods and small diameter line pipe in Canada for the last half of 1993.

IPSCO should also start to benefit from its repositioning towards fabricated products as opposed to steel mill products and energy related tubulars, and with initial work in the development of thin slab casting techniques using IPSCO technology. The first quarter of 1993 showed promise, as sales revenues were 12% higher and shipments of 249,000 tons were 7% higher than the fourth quarter of last year.

IPSCO is at risk from both U.S. trade cases against Canadian steel and pricing pressures. Canada and the United States continue to attract substantial imports, particularly with steel usage declining in the rest of the world. Imports captured 23% of Canadian and 18% of U.S. markets.

Sales in 1992 of 804,300 tons were down 1% from 1991. Steel mill products were static, energy tubulars were down 10%, and fabricated products rose 28%. Contributing to the increased fabricated product sales was the start of standard pipe production in the United States. IPSCO's average unit selling price was off about 10% from 1991, almost entirely due to a change in product mix, as the volume of higher priced large diameter pipe fell.

In 1992, steel mill products remained at 23% of tonnage sales volume. Fabricated products grew from 22% to 27% of overall volume, while energy related tubulars dropped from 55% to 50% (as large diameter pipe fell from 30% to 25%). 64% of sales were to Canadian customers, with 36% to U.S. customers.

Relative strength to TSE300 / Price / Volume (in 1000's of board lots)

Rank (Profit/Revenue/Assets)
141   159   211

W.M. Elliott
Chairman Of The Board
Roger Phillips
President & C.E.O.
Mario J. Dalla-Vicenza
Sr. V.P. & C.F.O.
Milan Kosanovich
Exec. V.P. & C.O.O.

Address
P.O. Box 1670
Regina
SK
S4P 3C7
(306) 924-7700

Fax: (306) 924-7500
I0001728/G/6.1

IVACO INC.

Exchanges	Price (Jun24'93)		4.85	Trailing P/E		nm	Stock Symbol
TM	Trailing Yield (%)		0.00	Trailing EPS		(1.59)	**IVA.A**

Period Ending	Dec92	Dec91	Dec90	Dec89	Dec88
Yearly Statistics					
Price-Close	2.30	3.60	6.75	11.13	11.00
Price-High	5.13	8.00	11.50	14.00	14.25
Price-Low	2.00	3.00	6.13	10.50	8.50
P/E-Close	nm	nm	nm	nm	9.73
Dividends per Share	0.00	0.32	0.60	0.60	0.64
Dividend Yield (%)	0.00	8.89	8.89	5.39	5.82
Sales per Share	51.60	55.06	98.31	108.89	110.05
EPS before extra. item	(1.71)	(3.86)	(0.25)	(0.55)	1.13
Cash Flow per Share	(0.05)	(1.78)	2.67	5.03	8.20
Book Value per Share	9.28	10.32	14.38	15.36	16.87
O/S Common Shares	21,833	20,584	19,950	18,378	18,360
Total Revenue	1,095,244	1,120,592	1,883,878	2,008,723	2,019,618
Income before extra.	(19,565)	(59,396)	16,966	12,851	43,793
Cash Flow	(1,161)	(36,048)	50,707	92,375	149,979
Debt/Equity	1.32	1.36	1.13	1.46	1.28
Return on Capital (%)	1.38	(2.47)	7.47	7.52	11.24
Ret. on Com. Equity (%)	(10.77)	(28.53)	(1.66)	(3.43)	6.63
% Change Profit	67.1	(450.1)	32.0	(70.7)	14.2
% Change Revenue	(2.3)	(40.5)	(6.2)	(0.5)	(5.4)
% Change Assets	(8.8)	(8.2)	(23.2)	(0.8)	4.9

Preferred Div. Coverage	0.0	0.0	0.8	
Total Div. Coverage	0.0	0.0	0.5	
Interest Coverage	0.3	0.0	1.2	
Current Ratio	1.4	1.5	1.7	
Operating Margin	0.3	(1.7)	3.8	
Asset Turnover	0.9	0.9	1.3	
5 YEAR RATIOS (%)				
Return on Capital	5.0	7.0	9.9	
Return on Com. Equity	(7.6)	(4.5)	2.5	
Profit Growth	na	na	(13.6)	
Revenue Growth	(12.5)	(10.5)	6.9	
Asset Growth	(7.7)	(5.3)	1.9	
BALANCE SHEET (000)				
Cash	0	0	5,374	
Current Assets	453,356	533,155	620,701	
Net Fixed Assets	484,661	508,446	532,959	
Invest's & Advances	191,559	194,240	200,482	
Total Assets	1,182,633	1,296,632	1,411,763	
Short Term Debt	153,214	156,532	153,860	
Current Liabilities	325,833	354,922	369,301	
Long Term Debt	404,653	451,941	450,905	
Total Liabilities	760,359	849,759	876,261	
Total Equity	422,274	446,873	535,502	
Total Liab. & Equity	1,182,633	1,296,632	1,411,763	
CAPITAL (000)				
Total Debt	557,867	608,473	604,765	
Preferred Equity	219,724	234,384	248,672	
Common Equity	202,550	212,489	286,830	

Business:

IVACO is a steel producer with annual steelmaking and rolling capacity in excess of two million tons. Ivaco produces steel billets, hot rolled bars and shapes, wire rod, wire, welded wire fabric, nails, fasteners, precision machined components, forgings, and wire ropes, and cables. Ivaco has 55 plants: 38 in Canada, and 17 in the United States.

Date	EPS	DPS	Tot Rev	Inc Bex
Mar 93	(0.57)	0.00	281,433	(8,880)
Dec 92	(1.03)	0.00	271,146	(18,321)
Sep 92	0.62	0.00	269,911	16,698
Jun 92	(0.61)	0.00	330,555	(8,213)
Mar 92	(0.69)	0.00	256,824	(9,729)
Dec 91	(1.20)	0.03	267,353	(20,039)
Sep 91	(0.80)	0.08	277,484	(11,774)
Jun 91	(0.82)	0.08	342,890	(11,833)

Synopsis:

Hit hard by falling steel prices and slumping demand, the cost cutting by Ivaco during the last several years has paid off and the company is finally making money. Ivaco expects that it will post a second-quarter profit and that its financial picture will improve further in the third quarter.

As well, Ivaco has cut its long-term debt to about $300-million from a 1990 level of $550-million. If the sale of its 49.8% interest in St. Louis-based Laclede Steel Co. goes through as expected in 1993, Ivaco's debt will drop to below $250-million. Ivaco also is planning several joint ventures this year with North American manufacturers.

Ivaco, buffeted by the downturn in the steel industry, took stiff measures beginning in 1990 to cut costs by about $40-million a year. It laid off 1,500 people at its Canadian and U.S. operations, and shed non-core businesses, including Florida Wire and Cable Co. for $87-million and railway maintenance equipment company Tamper Corp. for $39-million.

The outlook for steel is improving and demand for wire rods, a major Ivaco product, is particularly strong. Wire rod prices have risen to $30 (U.S.) a ton in the second quarter and another $15 increase is set for July. There is a shortage of wire rods in North America and Ivaco's rod mills are heavily booked into the third quarter. Atlantic Steel expects a substantially reduced loss compared to 1992, mainly because of a dramatic cost cutting program. Canron's structural steel business will continue to operate within the harsh conditions of the construction industry.

1992 sales (operating earnings) by business were: steel, 74% (62%); plastic pipe and fabrication and erection of structural steel, 26% (38%). 1992 sales (operating earnings) by country were: Canada, $731.8-million ($68-million); the U.S., $362.6-million ($20.8-million loss). Canadian sales include $312-million of exports, primarily to the U.S.

Relative strength to TSE300 / Price / Volume (in 1000's of board lots) charts

Rank (Profit/Revenue/Assets)		
919	97	138
Isin Ivanier		
Chairman		
Paul Ivanier		
President & C.E.O.		
Albert A. Kassab		
V.P. & C.F.O.		

Address
Place Mercantile
770, Rue Sherbrooke Ouest
Montreal
PQ
H3A 1G1
(514) 288-4545

Fax: (514) 848-1846
I0002425/G/6.1

SAMUEL MANU-TECH INC.

Exchanges	Price (Jun24'93)	18.25	Trailing P/E	29.44	Stock Symbol
T	Trailing Yield (%)	1.32	Trailing EPS	0.62	**SMT**

Period Ending	Dec92	Dec91	Dec90	Dec89	Dec88
Yearly Statistics					
Price-Close	14.63	14.00	11.50	13.00	17.00
Price-High	16.00	14.00	13.25	17.50	18.00
Price-Low	13.75	11.25	9.50	12.50	13.75
P/E-Close	30.47	21.21	10.55	9.22	9.39
Dividends per Share	0.24	0.33	0.48	0.48	0.44
Dividend Yield (%)	1.64	2.36	4.17	3.69	2.59
Sales per Share	21.90	19.48	22.47	25.51	22.27
EPS before extra. item	0.48	0.66	1.09	1.41	1.81
Cash Flow per Share	1.61	1.17	1.57	2.05	2.45
Book Value per Share	9.72	9.39	9.08	8.47	6.93
O/S Common Shares	8,722	8,722	8,819	8,835	8,009
Total Revenue	191,427	170,705	199,173	220,806	178,847
Income before extra.	4,232	5,759	9,660	12,157	14,511
Cash Flow	14,072	10,233	13,902	17,682	19,588
Debt/Equity	0.17	0.11	0.10	0.15	0.35
Return on Capital (%)	11.30	12.10	20.99	29.14	43.53
Ret. on Com. Equity (%)	5.08	7.11	12.47	18.66	28.65
% Change Profit	(26.5)	(40.4)	(20.5)	(16.2)	29.3
% Change Revenue	12.1	(14.3)	(9.8)	23.5	39.9
% Change Assets	11.0	2.9	(1.7)	9.0	52.7

Preferred Div. Coverage	np	np	np
Total Div. Coverage	2.0	2.0	2.3
Interest Coverage	16.3	15.3	20.0
Current Ratio	2.4	3.0	3.3
Operating Margin	7.7	6.9	8.9
Asset Turnover	1.5	1.5	1.8
5 YEAR RATIOS (%)			
Return on Capital	23.4	30.5	36.4
Return on Com. Equity	14.4	18.7	22.0
Profit Growth	(17.8)	(7.3)	0.2
Revenue Growth	8.4	11.4	17.6
Asset Growth	13.3	16.1	18.6
BALANCE SHEET (000)			
Cash	7,811	6,639	5,246
Current Assets	78,364	66,034	70,525
Net Fixed Assets	49,422	44,128	42,540
Invest's & Advances	0	4,601	0
Total Assets	129,210	116,385	113,065
Short Term Debt	6,760	2,110	2,517
Current Liabilities	32,280	21,846	21,167
Long Term Debt	7,278	7,049	5,168
Total Liabilities	44,437	34,524	32,964
Total Equity	84,774	81,861	80,101
Total Liab. & Equity	129,210	116,385	113,065
CAPITAL (000)			
Total Debt	14,039	9,160	7,685
Preferred Equity	0	0	0
Common Equity	84,774	81,861	80,101

Business:

SAMUEL MANU-TECH INC. processes steel and manufactures steel products. Products include stainless steel pipe and tube, pickled flat rolled coil steel, steel and plastic packaging systems, steel tanks and wire rope and chain. The company markets products to the automotive, urban transit, mining and construction industries in Canada, the United States and Europe.

Date	EPS	DPS	Tot Rev	Inc Bex
Mar 93	0.35	0.06	56,670	3,059
Dec 92	0.22	0.06	49,839	1,926
Sep 92	0.25	0.06	48,749	2,209
Jun 92	(0.20)	0.06	49,347	(1,748)
Mar 92	0.21	0.06	43,492	1,845
Dec 91	0.15	0.06	41,812	1,332
Sep 91	0.18	0.09	41,587	1,544
Jun 91	0.19	0.09	45,547	1,682

Synopsis:

Samuel Manu-Tech seems to be performing well in the recovery from a recession which by most standards will be slower than normal in many of its markets in Canada and the United States. The company's products that depend on construction activity, for example, will not likely return to pre-recession levels for some time. On the other hand, the company is encouraged by increased activity in automotive, rail car building, and resource industries. The company remains concerned that this improving trend could by offset if there is no satisfactory resolution to the steel trade dispute between the United States and Canada.

Sales for the three months to March 31, 1993, were $56.6-million, an increase of 30.4% over the comparable period of last year. All divisions contributed to the higher sales which are attributable to the improved North American economy and a favorable Canadian dollar. The company has also been expanding operations, particularly in the United States. In 1992, Samuel Manu-Tech started looking closely at Mexico as a source of markets and joint ventures.

Samuel Manu-Tech's sales in 1992 were ahead by 12.4% from a year earlier, while operating profit was up 37%. The reduction in interest rates and the lower Canadian dollar in relation to its U.S. counterpart permitted its downsized and lower-cost divisions to post better profits than the year before. 1992 was a year of restructuring and renewal as upgrades and consolidations were completed at several divisions.

The company would have posted a profit of 99 cents a share in 1992, up from 72 cents a year earlier, had it not been for its ill fated investment in Redipac Recycling Corp. It took an after-tax loss of $4.4-million on the Redipac investment, and in the process reduced net profit to 48 cents a share compared with 66 cents a year earlier. Taking into account its original investment in Redipac, subsequent loans and the cost of putting Redipac into receivership, Samuel Manu-Tech lost about $10-million on the venture.

Rank (Profit/Revenue/Assets)
279 280 379

Ernest L. Samuel
Chairman

Wallace H. Rayner
V.P., Finance & Secretary

Address
191 The West Mall
Suite 418
Etobicoke
ON
M9C 5K8
(416) 626-2190

S0000269/G/6.2

For further company information, call Globe Information Services 1-800-268-9128 or (416)585-5345

SLATER INDUSTRIES INC.

Exchanges	Price (Jun24'93)	5.00	Trailing P/E	nm	Stock Symbol
T	Trailing Yield (%)	0.00	Trailing EPS	(0.39)	**SSI.B**

Period Ending	Dec92	Dec91	Dec90	Dec89	Dec88
Yearly Statistics					
Price-Close	3.00	4.00	4.00	6.00	6.00
Price-High	4.45	6.25	6.25	8.00	6.25
Price-Low	2.45	3.90	3.80	5.88	4.60
P/E-Close	nm	nm	25.00	6.32	8.00
Dividends per Share	0.00	0.00	0.00	0.00	0.00
Dividend Yield (%)	0.00	0.00	0.00	0.00	0.00
Sales per Share	45.06	43.34	47.45	47.90	48.02
EPS before extra. item	(0.72)	(1.16)	0.16	0.95	0.75
Cash Flow per Share	0.59	(0.81)	1.04	1.93	2.30
Book Value per Share	14.17	14.71	15.85	15.68	14.82
O/S Common Shares	8,100	8,100	8,100	8,100	8,100
Total Revenue	364,951	351,028	384,347	393,607	386,331
Income before extra.	(5,643)	(9,210)	1,507	7,911	6,264
Cash Flow	4,755	(6,537)	8,427	15,607	18,507
Debt/Equity	0.95	0.92	0.85	0.76	0.72
Return on Capital (%)	(0.47)	(2.53)	4.80	9.95	9.15
Ret. on Com. Equity (%)	(4.99)	(7.61)	1.01	6.22	5.16
% Change Profit	38.7	(711.1)	(81.0)	26.3	27.2
% Change Revenue	4.0	(8.7)	(2.4)	1.9	19.6
% Change Assets	(0.3)	(8.7)	5.2	3.4	12.6
Preferred Div. Coverage	0.0	0.0	6.9		
Total Div. Coverage	0.0	0.0	6.9		
Interest Coverage	0.0	0.0	1.1		
Current Ratio	2.5	3.3	3.4		
Operating Margin	(0.3)	(1.7)	3.7		
Asset Turnover	1.3	1.3	1.3		
5 YEAR RATIOS (%)					
Return on Capital	4.2	5.7	7.7		
Return on Com. Equity	(0.0)	1.8	4.2		
Profit Growth	na	na	(25.9)		
Revenue Growth	2.4	5.0	10.6		
Asset Growth	2.2	4.5	14.8		
BALANCE SHEET (000)					
Cash	0	0	0		
Current Assets	126,906	122,105	145,381		
Net Fixed Assets	116,085	121,343	125,639		
Invest's & Advances	1,267	1,584	1,584		
Total Assets	275,813	276,629	302,862		
Short Term Debt	11,191	4,376	415		
Current Liabilities	51,034	37,545	42,576		
Long Term Debt	99,850	107,626	111,593		
Total Liabilities	158,304	154,668	171,534		
Total Equity	117,509	121,961	131,328		
Total Liab. & Equity	275,813	276,629	302,862		
CAPITAL (000)					
Total Debt	111,041	112,002	112,008		
Preferred Equity	2,750	2,792	2,947		
Common Equity	114,759	119,169	128,381		

Business:

SLATER INDUSTRIES INC. is a steel products and transportation company. The company has operations in Canada and the United States. Steel products include stainless, carbon and low alloy steels, tool and die steels, and custom forgings. The company also makes pole line hardware for the electic power and communications industries. Melburn Truck Lines Inc. hauls from Ontario to the eastern United States.

Date	EPS	DPS	Tot Rev	Inc Bex
Mar 93	0.11	0.00	109,039	958
Dec 92	(0.26)	0.00	93,824	(2,076)
Sep 92	(0.20)	0.00	88,621	(1,608)
Jun 92	(0.04)	0.00	94,931	(296)
Mar 92	(0.21)	0.00	87,573	(1,663)
Dec 91	(0.41)	0.00	81,782	(3,298)
Sep 91	(0.55)	0.00	82,020	(4,428)
Jun 91	(0.11)	0.00	93,966	(809)

Synopsis:

Slater Industries expects to benefit from the extensive restructuring of costs and operations since 1990. Certain benefits were not readily apparent due to the slower economy throughout this period. It expects the competitive conditions in all the company's markets to continue throughout 1993, and that selling prices for its steel products to remain under pressure for most of the year. Profitability is improving in 1993 as both Fort Wayne Specialty Alloys and Hamilton Specialty Bar are benefiting from their strengthening markets.

Capital spending will be limited to essential projects until financial results warrant, and in light of the significant debt reductions of $11.2-million scheduled in 1993. Manufacturing plants remain very competitive due to the significant capital expenditures made in recent years. Improved cash flow is a priority.

Activity levels were high in all operations in the first quarter of 1993, resulting in all operations being profitable and generating the first profitable quarter for the company since 1990. Fort Wayne benefited from strong shipments with the improving U.S. economy and was able to generate a modest profit. Hamilton achieved excellent productivity and enjoyed exceptionally strong shipments in the quarter, predominantly in the automotive sector. Higher raw material costs negatively impacted the full benefit of strong volume. Sorel Forge's improved sales generated a sound profit. The improvement came from North America and a growing market in Asia.

Two-thirds of the loss in 1992 was incurred in the second half of the year with poor results at Fort Wayne and Hamilton. Net sales improved to $365-million from the low of $351-million in 1991. Most of the improvement came from the Hamilton and Renown Steel operations, offset somewhat by the lower sales at the Fort Wayne and Sorel Forge operations. All operations saw improvement in their earnings other than Fort Wayne. At Fort Wayne, shipments fell 7%. Hamilton returned to profitability in 1992 from a 14% jump in shipments over 1991.

Rank (Profit/Revenue/Assets)
842 201 285

J. Paul Fingold
Chairman & C.E.O.

James T. Roddy
President & C.O.O.

Robert J. Armour
V.P., Finance

Address
Yonge Corporate Centre
4100 Yonge Street
Suite 410
Toronto
ON
M2P 2B5
(416) 733-4400

S0003304/G/6.1

Relative strength to TSE300 / Price / Volume (in 1000's of board lots) chart, 1990–1993

STELCO INC.

Exchanges	Price (Jun24'93)	1.88	Trailing P/E	nm	Stock Symbol
TMV	Trailing Yield (%)	0.00	Trailing EPS	(1.81)	**STE.A**

Period Ending	Dec92	Dec91	Dec90	Dec89	Dec88
Yearly Statistics					
Price-Close	1.40	6.38	12.13	21.00	22.00
Price-High	6.63	12.38	21.38	26.25	26.37
Price-Low	0.90	5.00	11.00	20.00	19.62
P/E-Close	nm	nm	nm	9.33	11.00
Dividends per Share	0.00	0.00	0.75	1.00	1.00
Dividend Yield (%)	0.00	0.00	6.18	4.76	4.55
Sales per Share	27.43	44.47	59.25	78.19	78.02
EPS before extra. item	(1.76)	(3.05)	(5.96)	2.25	2.00
Cash Flow per Share	(1.02)	(1.17)	(4.40)	5.56	7.42
Book Value per Share	9.81	11.42	22.71	22.80	28.28
O/S Common Shares	80,436	80,094	35,492	35,288	34,949
Total Revenue	2,221,000	1,959,000	2,092,000	2,759,935	2,738,784
Income before extra.	(127,000)	(136,000)	(197,000)	93,869	98,371
Cash Flow	(82,000)	(52,000)	(156,000)	195,429	257,854
Debt/Equity	1.02	0.81	0.99	0.81	0.76
Return on Capital (%)	(5.13)	(6.76)	(11.90)	10.13	10.58
Ret. on Com. Equity (%)	(14.91)	(15.81)	(26.20)	8.82	7.17
% Change Profit	6.6	31.0	(309.9)	(4.6)	55.2
% Change Revenue	13.4	(6.4)	(24.2)	0.8	6.8
% Change Assets	(2.3)	(1.6)	(18.1)	7.7	1.9

Preferred Div. Coverage	na	na	0.0
Total Div. Coverage	na	na	0.0
Interest Coverage	0.0	0.0	0.0
Current Ratio	1.5	1.8	1.4
Operating Margin	(5.4)	1.5	(0.4)
Asset Turnover	0.9	0.8	0.8
5 YEAR RATIOS (%)			
Return on Capital	(0.6)	1.8	4.4
Return on Com. Equity	(8.2)	(4.7)	(1.5)
Profit Growth	na	na	na
Revenue Growth	(2.9)	(4.3)	(3.3)
Asset Growth	(2.9)	(3.2)	(2.9)
BALANCE SHEET (000)			
Cash	68,000	11,000	6,000
Current Assets	867,000	822,000	734,000
Net Fixed Assets	1,309,000	1,424,000	1,532,000
Invest's & Advances	193,000	204,000	228,000
Total Assets	2,423,000	2,481,000	2,521,000
Short Term Debt	216,000	97,000	157,000
Current Liabilities	588,000	452,000	521,000
Long Term Debt	767,000	796,000	826,000
Total Liabilities	1,456,000	1,383,000	1,530,000
Total Equity	967,000	1,098,000	991,000
Total Liab. & Equity	2,423,000	2,481,000	2,521,000
CAPITAL (000)			
Total Debt	983,000	893,000	983,000
Preferred Equity	178,000	183,000	185,000
Common Equity	789,000	915,000	806,000

Business:

STELCO INC. is a steel producer composed of many different units which are either wholly owned, joint ventures, or partnerships. Steel works are located in Alberta, Quebec, and Ontario. The Ontario plants produce steel from iron ore. The two smaller plants recycle used steel. Stelco wholly owns a number of steel fabricating and manufacturing units.

Date	EPS	DPS	Tot Rev	Inc Bex
Mar 93	(0.51)	0.00	573,000	(38,000)
Dec 92	(0.10)	0.00	550,000	(4,000)
Sep 92	(0.75)	0.00	512,000	(58,000)
Jun 92	(0.45)	0.00	590,000	(33,000)
Mar 92	(0.45)	0.00	569,000	(32,000)
Dec 91	(0.24)	0.00	487,000	(38,000)
Sep 91	(0.50)	0.00	572,000	(19,000)
Jun 91	(0.87)	0.00	535,000	(27,000)

Synopsis:

The international steel trade war is the greatest uncertainty facing Stelco. It started last year when U.S. producers filed unfair-trade complaints against their rivals in Canada and elsewhere, seeking to restrict imports into the United States and force up prices. Stelco is already shifting its product mix and its marketing focus to other countries and companies, in anticipation of being virually shut out of the U.S. market when the U.S. Commerce Department issues its final determination on dumping June 21.

There are signs of increasing demand from certain market sectors and recently announced steel price increases appear to be holding. Much of this increase is derived from U.S.-based activities and there is little indication of the re-appearance of consumer confidence in Canada. North American automobile manufacturers expect to produce 12.7 million units in 1993, up 8% over 1992 levels. While demand from the construction sector is expected to remain weak, there are signs of increased activity in the energy sector, especially with respect to renewed investment in pipelines and distribution systems. Stelco feels it is well positioned to benefit from such market trends.

Strengthening markets, combined with continuing cost containment, were key factors in the strong level of shipments and improved performance that were achieved in the first quarter of 1993. Product shipments were 1,062,000 tons, up 4% over the comparable period of 1992. Revenue, at $541 per ton, although down from the $561 per ton in the first quarter of 1992 continued to recover from the low of $506 per ton in the third quarter of 1992.

Poor results in 1992 were mainly due to depressed prices for steel and low demand for its higher-value products, especially large-diameter pipe. Shipments of this higher-value product fell by 50% during the year. Shipments of steel products recovered by 28% to the more normal level of 4.2 million tons in 1992. Sales rose slightly to $2.2-billion.

Relative strength to TSE300
Price
Volume (in 1000's of board lots)

Rank (Profit/Revenue/Assets)
976   60   83

Frederick H. Telmer
Chairman & C.E.O.
Robert J. Milbourne
President & C.O.O.
R. Eric Rogan
Exec. V.P. & C.F.O.

Address
Stelco Tower
100 King Street West
P.O. Box 2030
Hamilton
ON
L8N 3T1
(416) 528-2511
Fax: (417) 577-4412
S0004667/G/6.1

VARITY CORPORATION

Exchanges	Price (Jun24'93)		30 .50	Trailing P/E		44 .53	Stock Symbol
TMN	Trailing Yield (%)		0 .00	Trailing EPS		0 .55	**VAT**

Period Ending	Jan93	Jan92	Jan91	Jan90	Jan89
Yearly Statistics	US	US	US	US	US
Price-Close	36 .88	17 .75	24 .00	36 .50	33 .00
Price-High	38 .00	33 .50	40 .50	38 .00	46 .00
Price-Low	14 .13	12 .13	19 .00	23 .50	31 .00
P/E-Close	53 .84	nm	6 .73	8 .82	8 .21
Dividends per Share	0 .00	0 .00	0 .00	0 .00	0 .00
Dividend Yield (%)	0 .00	0 .00	0 .00	0 .00	0 .00
Sales per Share	128 .48	126 .99	145 .08	111 .74	113 .32
EPS before extra. item	0 .56	(7 .87)	3 .06	3 .50	3 .30
Cash Flow per Share	6 .10	2 .02	9 .07	6 .51	7 .71
Book Value per Share	10 .53	10 .93	19 .96	17 .94	13 .86
O/S Common Shares	30 ,999	24 ,988	24 ,930	24 ,697	20 ,629
Total Revenue	3 ,403 ,400	3 ,190 ,300	3 ,681 ,600	2 ,440 ,500	2 ,335 ,200
Income before extra.	33 ,400	(178 ,000)	94 ,400	92 ,100	81 ,700
Cash Flow	160 ,200	50 ,500	226 ,000	138 ,800	155 ,500
Debt/Equity	0 .84	2 .56	1 .73	1 .44	0 .73
Return on Capital (%)	14 .08	0 .14	6 .45	16 .95	21 .11
Ret. on Com. Equity (%)	4 .97	(50 .99)	16 .22	20 .27	29 .04
% Change Profit	118 .8	(288 .6)	2 .5	12 .7	61 .5
% Change Revenue	6 .7	(13 .3)	50 .9	4 .5	13 .5
% Change Assets	(34 .4)	(8 .4)	16 .3	83 .2	0 .3

Preferred Div. Coverage	1 .8	0 .0	5 .2
Total Div. Coverage	1 .8	0 .0	5 .2
Interest Coverage	1 .3	0 .0	na
Current Ratio	1 .1	1 .1	1 .2
Operating Margin	5 .7	3 .4	7 .7
Asset Turnover	1 .6	1 .0	1 .0
5 YEAR RATIOS (%)			
Return on Capital	11 .7	12 .6	13 .7
Return on Com. Equity	3 .9	7 .6	13 .6
Profit Growth	(8 .0)	na	89 .1
Revenue Growth	10 .5	17 .7	22 .6
Asset Growth	5 .1	16 .1	22 .6
BALANCE SHEET (000)			
Cash	153 ,600	223 ,800	203 ,500
Current Assets	1 ,008 ,500	1 ,532 ,100	1 ,782 ,300
Net Fixed Assets	597 ,100	933 ,900	953 ,500
Invest's & Advances	130 ,500	227 ,700	229 ,700
Total Assets	2 ,086 ,500	3 ,179 ,800	3 ,469 ,600
Short Term Debt	156 ,800	402 ,300	451 ,300
Current Liabilities	915 ,200	1 ,441 ,100	1 ,510 ,000
Long Term Debt	305 ,200	864 ,200	793 ,100
Total Liabilities	1 ,538 ,000	2 ,684 ,700	2 ,749 ,600
Total Equity	548 ,500	495 ,100	720 ,000
Total Liab. & Equity	2 ,086 ,500	3 ,179 ,800	3 ,469 ,600
CAPITAL (000)			
Total Debt	462 ,000	1 ,266 ,500	1 ,244 ,400
Preferred Equity	222 ,100	222 ,100	222 ,300
Common Equity	326 ,400	273 ,000	497 ,700

Business:

VARITY CORP. is an industrial management company. Its businesses design, manufacture, and distribute farm machinery, diesel engines and automotive and hydraulic components at facilities in North America and Europe. Subsidiaries are Kelsey-Hayes, Massey-Ferguson, Perkins Engines, Dayton Walther and Pacoma. The company markets its product internationally through distributors, dealers and other outlets.

Date		EPS	DPS	Tot Rev	Inc Bex
Jan 93	US	0 .23	0 .00	834 ,200	11 ,200
Oct 92	US	0 .23	0 .00	844 ,400	10 ,500
Jul 92	US	0 .37	0 .00	894 ,700	14 ,100
Apr 92	US	(0 .28)	0 .00	824 ,400	(2 ,400)
Jan 92	US	(4 .80)	0 .00	899 ,600	(115 ,300)
Oct 91	US	(0 .91)	0 .00	761 ,700	(17 ,800)
Jul 91	US	(0 .49)	0 .00	832 ,000	(7 ,600)
Apr 91	US	(1 .67)	0 .00	681 ,500	(37 ,300)

Synopsis:

Varity believes that it is positioned to make further improvements in operating performance in fiscal 1993. The anticipated continuing weakness of the British pound will benefit both the engines and farm equipment segments, although Varity sees no signs of any immediate economic recovery in Europe.

Intensive actions and cost-cutting will position the Massey-Ferguson division (farm equipment segment) to avoid becoming a drain on Varity's resources in what is anticipated to again be a contracting European farm equipment market. Kelsey-Hayes (automotive segment), is expected to benefit from a boom in anti-lock brake sales, while Perkins (engines segment) has signed new contracts with truck manufacturers in Europe and North America.

Sales in fiscal 1992 rose to $3.4-billion (U.S.) from $3.2-billion (U.S.), primarily due to increased sales in its automotive products segment. Operating profit rose 66% from last year and every operating division improved.

The top performer at Varity is clearly the Kelsey-Hayes division. In 1992 operating profit grew 25% to $133-million (U.S.) on sales of $1.5-billion (U.S.). The Perkins diesel engine division also performed better than expected and its operating profit increased 31%. The biggest surprise, however, was the Massey-Ferguson farm equipment division, which had an operating profit of $22-million (U.S.) despite poor markets.

The results for the first quarter of 1993 reflect a one-time charge of $146.1-million (U.S.) to recognize the cost of post-retirement medical and life insurance and post-employment benefits.

Sales in 1992 by market were: North America (mainly the United States) 45.2%; Europe, 40.2%; and the rest of world, 14.6%. Net sales in 1992 by product were: farm equipment (64% of which were tractors), 32.9%; engines, 20.1%; automotive parts, 45.5%; and other components, 1.5%.

Relative strength to TSE300 / Price / Volume (in 1000's of board lots)

Rank (Profit/Revenue/Assets)
43   35   60

Victor Rice
Chairman & C.E.O.
Vincent D. Laurenzo
Vice Chairman & President
Neil D. Arnold
Sr. V.P. & C.F.O.

Address
672 Deleware Avenue
Buffalo
NY
14209
(716) 888-8000

Fax: (716) 888-8010
M0002283/G/6.3

Page	Company	$	Latest year end	Earnings per Share Actual	Estimate this year	Estimate next year
213	Archer Communications		9212	(0.34)	n.a.	n.a.
214	Bombardier		9301	0.85	1.07	1.18
215	CAE Industries		9303	0.31	0.33	0.33
216	Canadian Marconi		9303	1.01	1.17	1.47
217	Circo Craft		9212	0.30	0.36	0.48
218	Develcon Electronics		9208	(0.20)	n.a.	n.a.
219	Fleet Aerospace		9209	(0.46)	n.a.	n.a.
220	Gandalf Technologies		9303	(0.92)	(1.30)	n.a.
221	Gennum		9211	1.02	1.10	1.29
222	Glenayre Electronics		9212	6.12	n.a.	n.a.
223	Haley Industries	15M	9212	(0.24)	n.a.	n.a.
224	Hawker Siddeley Canada		9212	1.78	n.a.	n.a.
225	Helix Circuits		9212	(0.11)	n.a.	n.a.
226	International Verifact		9303	0.10	0.18	0.36
227	Linamar		9206	1.07	1.37	1.74
228	Newbridge Networks	$US	9304	1.46	1.24	1.61
229	Noma		9212	0.04	0.26	0.45
230	SBN Systems		9209	(3.29)	n.a.	n.a.
231	Spar Aerospace		9212	1.25	1.12	1.36
232	TIE/Telecommunications Canada		9212	0.10	0.80	1.14
233	Xerox Canada		9212	1.74	n.a.	n.a.

Estimates from I/B/E/S Inc., 345 Hudson St., New York, NY 10014 (212) 243-3335. In Canada: 6 Lansing Square, Ste. 235, Willowdale, ON M2J 1T5 (416) 496-0977.

Semiconductor Industry-Summer Slowdown - Industry Report [May-11-1993]. MERRILL LYNCH CAPITAL MARKETS reported by Kurlak, T.P

All of the companies in the semiconductor industry are reporting continuing strong orders driven mostly by strong sales of personal computers and communications/networking products. Much more innovation and price adjustments in notebook computers are expected as this product class moves to the 486. A new 100 MHz 486 chip for the high end desk top market is expected in July or August of 1993. [RN 1330471]

Semiconductor Industry - Industry Report. MERRILL LYNCH CAPITAL MARKETS reported by Kurlak, T.P.

Based on the trend of orders in May 1993 to date, the booked-to-billed ratio should rise from the reported April 1993 level of 1.13. Orders and shipments remain healthy and more growth is expected throughout the year. The Semiconductor Industry Association, which supplies the booked-to-billed information, has released actual product line orders and sales through the end of 1Q:93. It shows that U.S. OEM microprocessor orders were up 32% over 4Q:92, which in turn was up 21% over 3Q:92. European orders were up 17% in 1Q:93, after a down 4Q:92. Japanese orders were up 9%, after a flat 4Q:92 comparison. [RN 1330470]

Semiconductors: EPS Calendar - Industry Report [Apr-6-1993]. SHEARSON LEHMAN BROTHERS, INC. reported by Gumport, M.A.

Despite disk drive turmoil and excess 486 concerns, surveys indicate late March 1993 chip demand accelerated. 15%-20+% 1993 world chip industry growth is expected. Intel's 2Q93 X86 price cuts are just 3%-7% (in line with cost cuts), which is not indicative of a chip glut. Hall-Mark Electronic's orders were strong in late March 1993. Pioneer Standard reported a similar trend with strong, end of March 1993 orders likely pushing 4Q:93 sales up. [RN 1320754]

Semiconductors: First Quarter Outlook - Industry Report [Mar-25-1993]. PAINEWEBBER INC. reported by Lazlo, J.J., et al

Semiconductor companies' 1Q:93 results are expected to meet or exceed consensus expectations. February 1993's SIA flash data confirmed another strong month, as orders increased 40% and shipments rose 31%. The B/B ratio was 1.18. 20-25% domestic semiconductor industry growth is expected in 1993, while the global industry increase is expected to be almost 17% to $70 billion (U.S.). The Winchester disk drive is one of the few electronic components that is more of a commodity than a semiconductor device. Lower prices for disk drives force market elasticity and also force drive manufacturers to withdraw from the low end of the market and convert production to higher density drives with higher margin potential. [RN 1318526]

Multi-Protocol Router Market - Industry Report [Apr-15-1993]. PAINEWEBBER INC. reported by Diwan, A.

The multi-protocol router market is expected to grow rapidly over next three years driven by the fundamental shift from the host-terminal architecture to the networked client-server architecture. Multi-protocol routers provide high gross (greater than 60%) and operating (greater than 20%) margins. This is a result of the high software content, barriers to entry and the ability of vendors to lock in customers. [RN 1325348]

Aerospace/Defense Industry (The) - Industry Report [May-12-1993]. ARGUS RESEARCH CORPORATION reported by Abramowitz, W.

The end of the Soviet Union, and the end of a major threat to the security of the United States, has many politicians leaning toward reductions in defense spending. It is inevitable that defense cuts will continue over the next several years, but it is not yet clear which programs will receive the deepest cuts. Aerospace/defense contractors are looking at ways to expand their core defense-related operations, rather than enter unfamiliar territory with questionable growth prospects. Martin Marietta, which acquired General Electric's aerospace division, and Lockheed, which bought General Dynamics' tactical aircraft business, will continue to emphasize the military applications of these operations. [RN 1331447]

Microcomputer Weekly - Industry Report [May-18-1993]. MERRILL LYNCH CAPITAL MARKETS reported by Preston, M.S., et al

Dealer surveys continue to show above average demand for PCs. Major brand vendors, most notably Compaq and IBM, continue to gain share at the expense of third-tier vendors, whose share in March 1993 dropped to 31.3% from 37.6% in 1992. In March, unit sales of the PC hardware industry through the dealer channel increased 41.3%, compared with an increase of 14.2% in February. Revenue continued to show the effect of lower average selling prices, increasing in March by 16.7%, following a decrease of 9% in February. All processors, with the exception of the 80386DX, showed increases versus February, with the 80486DX posting the largest increases. While the 80386 declined versus a year ago, the 80486 processors posted large year to year increases. Notebooks for the industry showed impressive year to year and sequential growth in March. [RN 1331661]

ARCHER COMMUNICATIONS INC.

Exchanges	Price (Jun24'93)		5.25	Trailing P/E		nm	Stock Symbol
TQ	Trailing Yield (%)		0.00	Trailing EPS		(0.30)	**AAZ**

Period Ending	Dec92	Dec91	Dec90	Dec89	Dec88
Yearly Statistics					
Price-Close	2.75	2.35	12.00	22.00	n t
Price-High	3.55	14.50	26.00	25.63	n t
Price-Low	0.75	2.15	10.50	14.00	n t
P/E-Close	nm	nm	nm	nm	n t
Dividends per Share	0.00	0.00	0.00	0.00	0.00
Dividend Yield (%)	0.00	0.00	0.00	0.00	0.00
Sales per Share	0.22	0.22	na	na	na
EPS before extra. item	(0.34)	(0.56)	(0.43)	(0.24)	(0.12)
Cash Flow per Share	(0.23)	(0.50)	(0.18)	(0.24)	(0.12)
Book Value per Share	(0.04)	0.26	0.48	0.57	0.47
O/S Common Shares	12,734	12,516	11,737	11,340	10,304
Total Revenue	2,848	2,742	265	222	23
Income before extra.	(4,270)	(6,775)	(4,976)	(2,628)	(1,068)
Cash Flow	(2,855)	(6,087)	(2,028)	(2,596)	(1,040)
Debt/Equity	na	0.61	0.07	0.10	0.08
Return on Capital (%)	(67.13)	(109.06)	(74.84)	(41.71)	(33.05)
Ret. on Com. Equity (%)	(311.01)	(153.94)	(82.19)	(46.42)	(46.26)
% Change Profit	37.0	(36.2)	(89.3)	(146.1)	(113.4)
% Change Revenue	3.9	935.2	19.5	864.4	2,267.4
% Change Assets	16.5	(15.3)	9.8	60.3	349.9

Preferred Div. Coverage	np	na	np
Total Div. Coverage	na	na	na
Interest Coverage	0.0	0.0	0.0
Current Ratio	0.7	0.2	1.2
Operating Margin	(127.9)	(225.1)	na
Asset Turnover	0.3	0.3	na
5 YEAR RATIOS (%)			
Return on Capital	(65.2)	(66.9)	na
Return on Com. Equity	(128.0)	na	na
Profit Growth	na	na	na
Revenue Growth	393.6	286.6	na
Asset Growth	50.8	128.3	na

BALANCE SHEET (000)			
Cash	234	101	398
Current Assets	1,305	629	1,552
Net Fixed Assets	2,227	2,341	2,490
Invest's & Advances	2,209	455	0
Total Assets	9,715	8,338	9,842
Short Term Debt	869	1,940	7
Current Liabilities	1,788	3,036	1,288
Long Term Debt	5,021	373	382
Total Liabilities	10,176	4,566	4,247
Total Equity	(461)	3,771	5,595
Total Liab. & Equity	9,715	8,338	9,842
CAPITAL (000)			
Total Debt	5,890	2,313	389
Preferred Equity	0	564	0
Common Equity	(461)	3,207	5,595

Business:

ARCHER COMMUNICATIONS INC. has patent pending status for its Q-Sound enhancement and audio imaging system. The music industry, film and television are primary markets for Q-Sound.

Date	EPS	DPS	Tot Rev	Inc Bex
Mar 93	(0.04)	0.00	899	(482)
Dec 92	(0.04)	0.00	1,567	(402)
Sep 92	(0.09)	0.00	363	(1,213)
Jun 92	(0.13)	0.00	406	(1,581)
Mar 92	(0.08)	0.00	431	(1,074)
Dec 91	(0.25)	0.00	69	(3,136)
Sep 91	(0.15)	0.00	125	(1,777)
Jun 91	(0.18)	0.00	151	(2,061)

Synopsis:

In July 1992, Archer Communications was refinanced by Capcom Co., Ltd. of Japan. By early 1993 Capcom had provided loans of $8.2-million (U.S.) to Archer. Capcom is one of the world's most successful video arcade game developers as well as being one of the largest third party licencees of home video games for the Nintendo and Super Nintendo Entertainment Systems. Archer's five-year distribution agreement with Capcom netted the company $1.5-million in 1992. Archer will soon change its name to QSound Labs, Inc.

Capcom advanced Archer $2.025-million (U.S.) in an initial loan repayable in three equal semi-annual installments starting on October 1, 1993. It also advanced a convertible loan of $5.5-million (U.S.), half of which was advanced in early 1993. Three million shares are issuable on the convertible loan, 2.5 million shares are issuable on the warrant held by Capcom, and the quarterly repayments, which begin in 1997, are $160,714 (U.S.). Archer can elect to pay all or part of the interest payable on the convertible loan by issuing common shares, potentially 13 million shares. In early 1993, Capcom advanced Archer $702,000 (U.S.), repayable in 1995. Archer issued a $20-million (U.S.) debenture to Capcom covering substantially all of the assets of the company as security for the Capcom loans. As of December 1992, $4.3-million (U.S.), plus accrued interest, was payable under these loan agreements.

In early 1993 Archer finalized agreements to license other uses of the QSound technology. Virgin Games and Sega will use of the QSound technology on Sega CD-ROM systems for the home video game industry. Analog Devices Inc. and Creative Technology are using QSound on their multimedia platforms. Furthermore, Archer has been actively co-marketing the technology on the MWave platform (a partnership between IBM and Texas Instruments). The company's joint venture (HEAR) with the House Ear Institute has signed a development and licensing agreement with Starkey Laboratories, a major U.S. hearing aid manufacturer and distributor. Archer continues to research and develop headphone algorithms.

Rank (Profit/Revenue/Assets)		
856	839	894

Danny D. Lowe
Chairman

David Gallagher
President & C.E.O.

Bernard Stolar
Sr. V.P., Marketing & Sales

Address
2748 - 37th Avenue N.E.
Calgary
AB
T1Y 5L3
(403) 291-2492

Fax: (403) 250-1521
01000068/G/6.5

BOMBARDIER INC.

Exchanges	Price (Jun24'93)	12.50	Trailing P/E	14.04	Stock Symbol
TM	Trailing Yield (%)	1.65	Trailing EPS	0.89	**BBD.B**

Period Ending	Jan93	Jan92	Jan91	Jan90	Jan89
Yearly Statistics					
Price-Close	11.63	17.13	7.88	7.81	6.69
Price-High	17.25	17.25	10.31	9.00	6.81
Price-Low	10.38	7.75	6.44	5.56	4.06
P/E-Close	13.68	23.46	11.10	11.49	12.99
Dividends per Share	0.21	0.17	0.17	0.14	0.12
Dividend Yield (%)	1.83	1.01	2.18	1.76	1.83
Sales per Share	29.03	21.22	20.84	16.24	11.12
EPS before extra. item	0.85	0.73	0.71	0.68	0.52
Cash Flow per Share	1.37	1.33	1.37	0.99	1.02
Book Value per Share	6.16	5.67	4.64	3.54	2.92
O/S Common Shares	154,280	152,337	141,443	131,398	125,657
Total Revenue	4,445,800	3,054,300	2,894,400	2,099,000	1,416,400
Income before extra.	132,800	107,700	100,100	91,500	68,300
Cash Flow	210,200	191,400	185,800	127,200	128,600
Debt/Equity	1.82	1.35	1.40	0.66	0.19
Return on Capital (%)	9.40	9.21	13.90	18.91	20.15
Ret. on Com. Equity (%)	14.36	13.79	17.13	21.08	18.47
% Change Profit	23.3	7.6	9.4	34.0	31.1
% Change Revenue	45.6	5.5	37.9	48.2	0.6
% Change Assets	39.1	19.8	67.9	75.2	15.7

Period Ending	Jan93	Jan92	Jan91
Preferred Div. Coverage	51.1	37.1	25.0
Total Div. Coverage	3.8	4.0	3.7
Interest Coverage	2.9	3.3	3.3
Current Ratio	1.1	1.1	1.1
Operating Margin	5.3	6.5	6.6
Asset Turnover	1.0	1.0	1.1
5 YEAR RATIOS (%)			
Return on Capital	14.3	17.0	19.8
Return on Com. Equity	17.0	17.2	17.5
Profit Growth	20.5	24.1	44.0
Revenue Growth	25.8	22.2	33.8
Asset Growth	41.4	35.6	43.5
BALANCE SHEET (000)			
Cash	235,100	179,200	87,500
Current Assets	2,438,200	1,768,400	1,503,400
Net Fixed Assets	834,500	626,800	533,500
Invest's & Advances	942,100	640,800	491,300
Total Assets	4,270,000	3,070,700	2,563,500
Short Term Debt	884,900	640,100	558,200
Current Liabilities	2,265,800	1,541,500	1,390,000
Long Term Debt	908,100	575,000	411,300
Total Liabilities	3,285,900	2,171,400	1,869,300
Total Equity	984,100	899,300	694,200
Total Liab. & Equity	4,270,000	3,070,700	2,563,500
CAPITAL (000)			
Total Debt	1,793,000	1,215,100	969,500
Preferred Equity	34,100	35,700	37,400
Common Equity	950,000	863,600	656,800

Business:

BOMBARDIER INC. is engaged in design, development, manufacturing and marketing activities in the fields of transportation equipment, civil and military aerospace, and motorized consumer products. The company operates in Canada, the U.S., Austria, Belgium, France, the U.K., and Finland. More than 90% of the company's sales are made in markets outside Canada.

Date	EPS	DPS	Tot Rev	Inc Bex
Apr 93	0.25	0.05	992,900	39,200
Jan 93	0.27	0.05	1,403,600	42,100
Oct 92	0.18	0.05	1,131,400	28,300
Jul 92	0.19	0.05	974,500	29,700
Apr 92	0.21	0.05	938,500	32,700
Jan 92	0.24	0.04	975,100	36,800
Oct 91	0.15	0.08	734,200	21,500
Jul 91	0.16	0.04	692,100	23,800

Synopsis:

Bombardier increased revenue and profit in its first quarter of 1993 amid a tough economy and the cancellation of an important aircraft order. The 20% profit increase was due mainly to the performance of the motorized consumer products group, which manufactures the Ski-Doo and Sea-Doo vehicles.

In April 1993, de Havilland, which produces the Dash 8 turboprop aircraft, lost an important contract to build 22 planes for GPA Group plc when the huge, financially troubled Irish aircraft leasing firm cancelled those orders. However, in early May, Bombardier delivered the first two of 20 Canadair Regional Jets that it has on order to Comair, a feeder airline for Delta Air Lines. At that time, there were orders and options for 72 Canadair Regional Jets, with eight already delivered.

In addition, Bombardier has not produced trains for the Chunnel project linking Britain and France since March 1992. The company is in a dispute with Trans-Manche Link (TML), the main Chunnel contractor, over cost overruns caused by changes to the design of the cars and new requirements from the client. Bombardier has also twice missed out on contracts to build subway cars in Mexico - in August 1992 and again in April 1993.

In fiscal 1992, consolidated net revenues, which rose by 45%, reflected the start of deliveries of the Canadair Regional Jet, as well as the acquisitions of UTDC, de Havilland and Bombardier S.A. de C.V. (Concarril). Net income rose by 23% due to good performance in all industry segments, except in the transportation equipment segment which recorded a loss. This loss was mainly attributable to the contract dispute for the shuttle-train cars for the English Channel tunnel.

Fiscal 1992 sales by country of destination were: Canada, 10%; United States and Mexico, 38%; Europe, 48%; and other, 4%. Sales by industry segment were: transportation equipment, 28%; motorized consumer products, 12%; aerospace, 50%; defence, 8%; and Bombardier Capital Group, 2%.

Rank (Profit/Revenue/Assets)
26   30   50

Laurent Beaudoin
Chairman & C.E.O.

Raymond Royer
President & C.O.O.

Paul H. Larose
V.P., Finance

Address
Suite 2900
800 Rene-Levesque Blvd. West
Montreal
PQ
H3B 1Y8
(514) 861-9481

Fax: (514) 861-7053
B0002455/G/6.4

CAE INC.

Exchanges	Price (Jun24'93)		4 .90	Trailing P/E		16 .33	Stock Symbol
TM	Trailing Yield (%)		3 .27	Trailing EPS		0 .30	**CAE**

Period Ending	Mar93	Mar92	Mar91	Mar90	Mar89
Yearly Statistics					
Price-Close	4 .90	6 .00	6 .25	7 .63	12 .00
Price-High	6 .63	7 .75	8 .13	15 .50	12 .75
Price-Low	4 .75	5 .75	3 .90	6 .63	7 .13
P/E-Close	16 .33	19 .36	25 .00	254 .17	21 .43
Dividends per Share	0 .16	0 .16	0 .16	0 .16	0 .16
Dividend Yield (%)	3 .27	2 .67	2 .56	2 .10	1 .33
Sales per Share	9 .24	9 .75	11 .40	12 .49	10 .84
EPS before extra. item	0 .30	0 .31	0 .25	0 .03	0 .56
Cash Flow per Share	0 .69	0 .70	0 .62	0 .56	0 .95
Book Value per Share	5 .53	5 .14	4 .74	4 .59	2 .89
O/S Common Shares	108 ,565	108 ,510	96 ,380	96 ,292	77 ,504
Total Revenue	1 ,003 ,237	1 ,045 ,952	1 ,097 ,728	1 ,128 ,300	844 ,419
Income before extra.	32 ,244	32 ,785	24 ,157	2 ,689	43 ,154
Cash Flow	74 ,422	74 ,879	59 ,749	49 ,775	73 ,593
Debt/Equity	0 .38	0 .37	0 .67	0 .74	2 .58
Return on Capital (%)	7 .88	9 .36	8 .78	8 .24	16 .32
Ret. on Com. Equity (%)	5 .57	6 .46	5 .37	0 .81	19 .86
% Change Profit	(1 .7)	35 .7	798 .4	(93 .8)	59 .4
% Change Revenue	(4 .1)	(4 .7)	(2 .7)	33 .6	145 .5
% Change Assets	3 .9	(4 .7)	(4 .4)	9 .9	250 .8

	np	np	np
Preferred Div. Coverage	np	np	np
Total Div. Coverage	1 .9	1 .9	1 .6
Interest Coverage	3 .5	3 .9	2 .2
Current Ratio	0 .9	0 .9	0 .9
Operating Margin	6 .1	6 .8	6 .1
Asset Turnover	0 .8	0 .9	0 .9

5 YEAR RATIOS (%)			
Return on Capital	10 .1	13 .1	17 .6
Return on Com. Equity	7 .6	9 .3	12 .1
Profit Growth	3 .7	0 .3	1 .1
Revenue Growth	23 .8	23 .1	26 .5
Asset Growth	29 .5	22 .1	25 .8

BALANCE SHEET (000)			
Cash	31 ,786	22 ,317	0
Current Assets	339 ,048	343 ,416	429 ,866
Net Fixed Assets	169 ,937	140 ,401	146 ,154
Invest's & Advances	0	0	0
Total Assets	1 ,208 ,142	1 ,163 ,130	1 ,220 ,012
Short Term Debt	19 ,218	4 ,760	7 ,413
Current Liabilities	390 ,848	396 ,439	460 ,769
Long Term Debt	207 ,503	199 ,159	296 ,607
Total Liabilities	608 ,280	605 ,575	762 ,897
Total Equity	599 ,862	557 ,555	457 ,115
Total Liab. & Equity	1 ,208 ,142	1 ,163 ,130	1 ,220 ,012

CAPITAL (000)			
Total Debt	226 ,721	203 ,919	304 ,020
Preferred Equity	0	0	0
Common Equity	599 ,862	557 ,555	457 ,115

Business:

CAE is the world leader in commercial, military and manned space-flight simulation and training. CAE is also engaged in a number of other aerospace, electronics and industrial product activities globally. It has facilities throughout Canada, the United States and Europe. including the Army, Navy, Air Force, Marines and NASA.

Date	EPS	DPS	Tot Rev	Inc Bex
Mar 93	0 .08	0 .04	268 ,197	8 ,619
Dec 92	0 .10	0 .04	253 ,731	10 ,899
Sep 92	0 .07	0 .04	239 ,968	7 ,026
Jun 92	0 .05	0 .04	239 ,658	5 ,700
Mar 92	0 .09	0 .04	259 ,030	9 ,582
Dec 91	0 .09	0 .04	253 ,096	9 ,530
Sep 91	0 .06	0 .04	260 ,633	6 ,945
Jun 91	0 .07	0 .04	273 ,397	6 ,728

Synopsis:

CAE's primary customers in commercial aviation and defence are undergoing radical restructuring. The commercial aviation industry has been shaken by huge debt burdens, a worldwide recession and fierce competition. With the end of the Cold War, military organizations are being forced to rationalize and restructure.

Despite these factors, which reduced revenues and income in fiscal 1993, CAE captured 70% of all global orders for full flight simulators and flight training devices. At year-end, the order backlog at CAE Electronics amounted to $460-million, 17% higher than at March 1992.

CAE is responding in part to defence budget restraints by focusing on cost reductions and process improvement, and by applying the technological expertise it has developed for military applications to commercial applications. In fiscal 1993, CAE-Link entered the air traffic control market. Its Virtual Controller can be customized to match any air traffic system in the world. CAE-Link also opened new markets in the health care industry. It introduced Virtual Anesthesiology, Virtual Heart, and Telemedicine to link medical specialists with patients in remote areas.

Growth and change in commercial aviation will increase training and simulation needs. Passenger traffic throughout the 1990s and beyond is predicted to grow an average of at least 5% annually, particularly in the Asia/Pacific area. There will also be aging flight crews, stricter environmental and noise legislation and the need to modernize or replace aging aircraft. Increased alliances among airlines will affect air traffic patterns, routes and aircraft types. In the military, training and simulation is a cost-effective solution to changing training needs.

Revenues by market in fiscal 1993 were: military and space, 54%; commercial/industrial, 26%; other aerospace and electronics, 11%; and industrial products, 9%. Revenues by geographic distribution were: the United States, 58%; Canada, 15%; Asia/Africa, 12%; Europe, 12%; and other, 3%. R&D spending was $191-million or 19% of revenues.

Relative strength to TSE300 / Price / Volume (in 1000's of board lots) charts

Rank (Profit/Revenue/Assets)
86   104   134

David H. Race
Chairman Of The Board

John E. Caldwell
President & C.E.O.

Address
Suite 3060
P.O. Box 30
Royal Bank Plaza
Toronto
ON
M5J 2J1
(416) 865-0070
Fax: (416) 865-0337
C0000203/G/6.4

CANADIAN MARCONI COMPANY

Exchanges	Price (Jun24'93)	15.50	Trailing P/E	15.35	Stock Symbol
TMA	Trailing Yield (%)	1.81	Trailing EPS	1.01	**CMW**

Period Ending	Mar92	Mar91	Mar90	Mar89	Mar88
Yearly Statistics					
Price-Close	15.88	12.75	10.75	18.00	16.75
Price-High	18.00	13.63	18.13	19.63	23.13
Price-Low	11.75	8.88	10.63	15.25	12.50
P/E-Close	13.45	24.06	13.61	17.65	18.01
Dividends per Share	0.21	0.21	0.28	0.28	0.28
Dividend Yield (%)	1.32	1.65	2.61	1.56	1.67
Sales per Share	13.70	12.21	12.70	12.82	8.72
EPS before extra. item	1.18	0.53	0.79	1.02	0.93
Cash Flow per Share	1.90	1.64	1.55	1.68	1.38
Book Value per Share	12.23	11.20	10.90	10.43	9.77
O/S Common Shares	23,773	23,773	23,773	23,773	23,773
Total Revenue	338,810	303,949	312,870	315,589	222,430
Income before extra.	27,955	12,715	18,827	24,320	22,039
Cash Flow	45,279	39,011	36,907	39,824	32,748
Debt/Equity	0.02	0.02	0.02	0.03	0.00
Return on Capital (%)	10.97	5.49	8.65	10.81	12.25
Ret. on Com. Equity (%)	10.04	4.84	7.43	10.13	9.82
% Change Profit	119.9	(32.5)	(22.6)	10.4	(17.9)
% Change Revenue	11.5	(2.9)	(0.9)	41.9	(2.3)
% Change Assets	4.8	4.8	(3.5)	16.0	9.6

Business:

CANADIAN MARCONI CO. is a designer and manufacturer of electronics systems and components in the fields of avionics, communications and radar. Customers include military and government agencies and commercial companies worldwide. The firm has plants in Quebec, Ontario in addition to subsidiaries in Nova Scotia, New Jersey, Massachusetts, and Ohio. GEC plc of the U.K. owns 51.6% of the company.

Date	EPS	DPS	Tot Rev	Inc Bex
Mar 93	0.24	0.00	86,108	5,738
Dec 92	0.37	0.14	76,696	8,674
Sep 92	0.29	0.14	66,016	6,969
Jun 92	0.11	0.14	76,100	2,590
Mar 92	0.28	0.00	95,767	6,603
Dec 91	0.37	0.15	91,755	8,640
Sep 91	0.33	0.00	74,931	8,016
Jun 91	0.20	0.07	76,357	4,696

Preferred Div. Coverage	np	np	np
Total Div. Coverage	5.6	2.5	2.8
Interest Coverage	56.9	19.4	32.9
Current Ratio	4.1	3.3	3.3
Operating Margin	6.0	3.1	4.0
Asset Turnover	0.9	0.8	0.9
5 YEAR RATIOS (%)			
Return on Capital	9.6	11.1	13.9
Return on Com. Equity	8.4	9.0	10.8
Profit Growth	0.8	(13.3)	(18.4)
Revenue Growth	8.2	6.0	(0.1)
Asset Growth	6.1	6.4	5.5
BALANCE SHEET (000)			
Cash	176,751	129,905	100,535
Current Assets	305,661	266,118	234,347
Net Fixed Assets	54,253	55,626	66,579
Invest's & Advances	6,362	27,134	33,623
Total Assets	375,951	358,798	342,284
Short Term Debt	0	0	0
Current Liabilities	73,932	81,441	70,734
Long Term Debt	6,510	6,214	6,149
Total Liabilities	85,236	92,635	83,223
Total Equity	290,715	266,163	259,061
Total Liab. & Equity	375,951	358,798	342,284
CAPITAL (000)			
Total Debt	6,510	6,214	6,149
Preferred Equity	0	0	0
Common Equity	290,715	266,163	259,061

Synopsis:

In an attempt to cope with the worldwide decline in defence spending, Canadian Marconi intends to bolster sales of its non-military products. The company derives 25% of its $294-million in annual sales from commercial products while the other 75% comes from such military machinery as navigation systems and integrated missions systems. Marconi wants a 50-50 split between military and commercial sales within five years.

In a move to add $10-million more annually in commercial sales, Marconi purchased Northstar Technologies in December 1992. Northstar is a producer of navigational systems serving the general aviation and marine sectors in the U.S. market. Marconi has also been signing defence contracts. For instance, the company stands to make sales of $150-million as a result of the Canadian government's decision to buy a fleet of EH-101 helicopters. The order backlog at March 1993 stood at $260-million, down 10% from last year.

The company is an expert in the two landing systems for airports which are being sought to replace the obsolete generation of runway approach radars. The estimated replacement value globally is about $4-billion (U.S.). Marconi produces ground-based microwave landing systems (MLS) and sells the receivers necessary for satellite tracking by the Global Positioning System (GPS). Marconi's fortunes appear to lie with MLS bids abroad. In March it bid to supply the U.S. Air Force with 2,200 airborne MLS receivers at about $25,000-$30,000 apiece.

In fiscal 1993, income before income taxes and special charges rose 5% to $33.7-million. This improvement occurred in spite of a 10% drop in sales of electronic products to $294-million. Had it not been for the loss of $5.2-million in the disposal of the remainder of the company's holdings of preferred shares, this year's earnings per share would have compared favorably with last year's. Continuing initiatives to reduce costs and improve productivity have contributed to the improvement in income before taxes. The United States accounts for 88% of sales, most of which are exported from Canadian operations.

Rank (Profit/Revenue/Assets)
104   211   247

William I.M. Turner, Jr.
Chairman Of The Board

John H. Simons
President & C.E.O.

Michel P. Salbaing
V.P. & C.F.O.

Address
2442 Trenton Avenue
Montreal
PQ
H3P 1Y9
(514) 341-7630

Fax: (514) 340-3100
C0003728/G/6.5

CIRCO CRAFT CO. INC.

Exchanges	Price (Jun24'93)		6.37	Trailing P/E		18.74	Stock Symbol
TM	Trailing Yield (%)		0.00	Trailing EPS		0.34	CCC

Period Ending	Dec92	Dec91	Dec90	Dec89	Dec88
Yearly Statistics					
Price-Close	6.50	1.75	2.10	3.90	4.60
Price-High	6.75	2.25	4.25	7.63	5.63
Price-Low	1.80	1.45	1.25	3.90	3.25
P/E-Close	26.00	nm	nm	9.07	12.78
Dividends per Share	0.00	0.00	0.00	0.00	0.00
Dividend Yield (%)	0.00	0.00	0.00	0.00	0.00
Sales per Share	7.79	6.63	6.73	7.51	7.57
EPS before extra. item	0.25	(0.49)	(0.19)	0.43	0.36
Cash Flow per Share	0.81	0.12	0.31	0.90	0.94
Book Value per Share	3.55	3.30	3.79	3.90	3.76
O/S Common Shares	12,073	12,073	12,073	12,073	12,073
Total Revenue	94,010	80,068	81,301	90,972	91,374
Income before extra.	3,037	(5,878)	(2,374)	5,219	4,289
Cash Flow	9,758	1,432	3,687	10,919	11,404
Debt/Equity	0.23	0.43	0.18	0.02	0.14
Return on Capital (%)	9.70	(13.14)	(5.98)	17.33	13.92
Ret. on Com. Equity (%)	7.35	(13.75)	(5.12)	11.29	9.92
% Change Profit	151.7	(147.6)	(145.5)	21.7	66.1
% Change Revenue	17.4	(1.5)	(10.6)	(0.4)	30.3
% Change Assets	(1.0)	0.4	9.1	(10.8)	(1.5)
Preferred Div. Coverage	np	np	np		
Total Div. Coverage	na	na	na		
Interest Coverage	6.2	0.0	0.0		
Current Ratio	2.2	1.5	1.9		
Operating Margin	5.7	(9.1)	(3.8)		
Asset Turnover	1.4	1.1	1.2		
5 YEAR RATIOS (%)					
Return on Capital	4.4	4.3	9.9		
Return on Com. Equity	1.9	1.8	6.6		
Profit Growth	3.3	na	na		
Revenue Growth	6.0	7.3	12.0		
Asset Growth	(1.0)	1.3	6.7		
BALANCE SHEET (000)					
Cash	1,083	0	982		
Current Assets	27,505	22,758	20,486		
Net Fixed Assets	41,972	47,412	51,105		
Invest's & Advances	0	0	0		
Total Assets	69,477	70,170	69,915		
Short Term Debt	351	6,709	200		
Current Liabilities	12,572	14,812	10,523		
Long Term Debt	9,467	10,507	8,010		
Total Liabilities	26,615	30,345	24,212		
Total Equity	42,862	39,825	45,703		
Total Liab. & Equity	69,477	70,170	69,915		
CAPITAL (000)					
Total Debt	9,818	17,216	8,210		
Preferred Equity	0	0	0		
Common Equity	42,862	39,825	45,703		

Business:

CIRCO CRAFT CO. INC. is a manufacturer of sophisticated printed circuits for telecommunications, computers and other electronic systems. The company has manufacturing facilities in Kirkland, Granby and Pointe-Claire, PQ. The company supplies its products to telecommunications and computer equipment manufacturers in Canada and the United States.

Date	EPS	DPS	Tot Rev	Inc Bex
Mar 93	0.08	0.00	24,001	1,006
Dec 92	0.13	0.00	28,169	1,537
Sep 92	0.06	0.00	21,383	834
Jun 92	0.07	0.00	22,909	789
Mar 92	(0.01)	0.00	21,549	(123)
Dec 91	(0.05)	0.00	23,410	(479)
Sep 91	(0.08)	0.00	20,628	(957)
Jun 91	(0.12)	0.00	19,668	(1,486)

Synopsis:

Circo Craft ranks sixth by sales in the $6-billion (U.S.) North American printed circuit board industry. After two years of losses, Circo underwent a major strategic change. By investing more than $45-million in equipment and training, Circo has repositioned itself as a supplier of more complex, higher-margin products, used in everything from luxury cars to telephone switching equipment. These moves are paying off. In 1992 Circo was certified as a supplier of two auto parts giants, Delco Electronics Corp. (a subsidiary of General Motors Corp.), and Matsushita Electric Corp. It also renewed its contract with Northern Telecom, worth $45-million in 1993.

In 1992, Circo began to reap the benefits of vastly superior process control. By manufacturing quality products with very high yields, it was able to increase volumes significantly and to achieve better margins in the absence of any tangible firming of selling prices. Gross margin improved by 86%. In the second half of 1992, output reached record levels at all three plants. The resulting increase in efficiency and productivity was evident as sales per employee rose to $121,304 in 1992, against $99,340 in 1991. Also, the manufacturing cycle time was reduced by 29% and international sales, mostly to the United States, accounted for 53% of business volume, up from 47% in 1991.

To complement its new direction, in early 1993 Circo acquired the printed circuit operations of Digital Equipment Corporation in Puerto Rico. It will provide Circo with easy access to the United States and Mexican markets, sales on the island itself, an attractive domestic corporate tax structure, competitive wage rates, and a large pool of highly skilled people.

Circo feels demand is growing in the North American market. The company is accelerating its efforts to enhance flexibility and responsiveness in every facet of its operations, placing special emphasis on manufacturing cycle time with a 50% reduction goal for 1993.

Relative strength to TSE300

Price

Volume (in 1000's of board lots)

Rank (Profit/Revenue/Assets)		
315	392	482

Hans-Karl Muhlegg
President & C.E.O.
Normand Potvin
Director Of Finances

Address
17600 Trans Canada Highway
Kirkland
PQ
H9J 3A3
(514) 694-8000

Fax: (514) 694-8604
C0056940/G/6.5

DEVELCON ELECTRONICS LTD.

Exchanges		Price (Jun24'93)		0.40	Trailing P/E		nm	Stock Symbol
T		Trailing Yield (%)		0.00	Trailing EPS		(0.11)	**DLC**

Period Ending	Aug92	Aug91	Aug90	Aug89	Aug88
Yearly Statistics					
Price-Close	0.11	0.40	0.60	1.20	0.70
Price-High	0.40	0.50	0.90	1.60	3.80
Price-Low	0.10	0.10	0.20	1.00	0.65
P/E-Close	nm	nm	nm	nm	nm
Dividends per Share	0.00	0.00	0.00	0.00	0.00
Dividend Yield (%)	0.00	0.00	0.00	0.00	0.00
Sales per Share	1.12	1.19	1.35	2.49	2.07
EPS before extra. item	(0.20)	(0.17)	(0.36)	(0.80)	(2.48)
Cash Flow per Share	(0.12)	(0.05)	(0.19)	(0.39)	(2.20)
Book Value per Share	0.20	0.40	0.58	0.14	0.81
O/S Common Shares	7,730	7,730	7,678	3,761	3,743
Total Revenue	8,931	10,005	10,671	13,460	9,778
Income before extra.	(1,542)	(1,319)	(2,072)	(2,964)	(9,162)
Cash Flow	(933)	(377)	(1,054)	(1,437)	(8,126)
Debt/Equity	2.86	1.58	0.97	4.00	1.55
Return on Capital (%)	(15.44)	(8.96)	(18.27)	(25.72)	(63.15)
Ret. on Com. Equity (%)	(65.84)	(34.97)	(83.85)	(176.15)	(113.60)
% Change Profit	(16.9)	36.3	30.1	67.6	(17.8)
% Change Revenue	(10.7)	(6.2)	(20.7)	37.7	(43.6)
% Change Assets	0.0	(6.9)	(17.3)	(11.9)	(23.1)

Preferred Div. Coverage	np	np	np
Total Div. Coverage	na	na	na
Interest Coverage	0.0	0.0	0.0
Current Ratio	1.1	1.4	1.7
Operating Margin	(16.0)	(17.5)	(26.8)
Asset Turnover	1.1	1.0	0.8
5 YEAR RATIOS (%)			
Return on Capital	(26.3)	(31.0)	(34.7)
Return on Com. Equity	(94.9)	(90.8)	(89.1)
Profit Growth	15.2	14.4	na
Revenue Growth	(12.4)	(10.4)	(15.8)
Asset Growth	(16.0)	(17.6)	(20.8)
BALANCE SHEET (000)			
Cash	550	405	141
Current Assets	4,562	6,013	6,060
Net Fixed Assets	3,062	3,492	3,908
Invest's & Advances	0	0	0
Total Assets	7,624	9,505	10,214
Short Term Debt	2,729	2,922	2,087
Current Liabilities	4,292	4,397	3,591
Long Term Debt	1,761	1,995	2,192
Total Liabilities	6,053	6,392	5,783
Total Equity	1,571	3,113	4,431
Total Liab. & Equity	7,624	9,505	10,214
CAPITAL (000)			
Total Debt	4,490	4,917	4,279
Preferred Equity	0	0	0
Common Equity	1,571	3,113	4,431

Business:

DEVELCON ELECTRONICS LTD. designs and manufactures sophisticated electronic data communications equipment. Its network products, under the trademark DevelNet, allow for the transmission of information among mainframe computers, minicomputers, microcomputers, terminals and other equipment. The company has operations in Canada and the United States.

Date	EPS	DPS	Tot Rev	Inc Bex
Feb 93	0.00	0.00	2,463	15
Nov 92	0.00	0.00	2,896	24
Aug 92	(0.05)	0.00	2,344	(377)
May 92	(0.06)	0.00	2,113	(450)
Feb 92	(0.03)	0.00	2,422	(221)
Nov 91	(0.06)	0.00	2,034	(494)
Aug 91	0.01	0.00	2,838	26
May 91	(0.04)	0.00	2,235	(305)

Synopsis:

In the year ended August 31, 1992, revenues for Develcon fell 5% from 1991 due to declining markets for its traditional product lines. Sales of its local area network (LAN) bridging products showed significant growth during the fourth quarter of the fiscal year, accounting for in excess of 50% of corporate revenues. In spite of these losses, the company devoted 21% of gross revenues to research and development. Develcon is committed to the expansion of its LAN Internetworking product line to capitalize on this growth market.

During fiscal 1992, Develcon entered into a funding agreement with the Department of Western Economic Diversification under which funds are provided over a two-year period to assist in expanding international markets for Develcon's products. Accordingly, the company continues to expand its distribution channels outside Canada. As at August 1992, Develcon products were offered for sale through over 150 distributors in 16 countries.

In February 1993, Develcon completed a financial restructuring resulting in the issue of 12,140,000 common shares for proceeds of $2,428,000. The proceeds were used to retire long-term debt, resulting in reduced interest costs and extended repayment terms on the balance of the debt. In addition, Develcon entered into a sale/leaseback of its land and building located in Saskatoon for proceeds of $600,000. The proceeds were used to reduce long-term debt, which in turn was replaced by a capital lease obligation on the property. As a result, shares outstanding increased to 19.8 million and an employee-owned company headed by Develcon senior management controls about 50% of the company.

As at February 1993, the reduced carrying cost of debt, combined with increased sales levels and product margins, contributed to a second consecutive profitable quarter for the company. Sales increased in all geographic markets as it continues to gain momentum in the LAN bridging marketplace. Orders booked during the second quarter exceeded product revenues, strengthening the order backlog.

Relative strength to TSE300 / Price / Volume (in 1000's of board lots)

Rank (Profit/Revenue/Assets)
730   712   914

William D. Vancoughnett
President & C.E.O.

Address
856 - 51st Street East
Saskatoon
SK
S7K 5C7
(306) 933-3300

Fax: (306) 931-1377
D0009758/G/6.5

For further company information, call Globe Information Services 1-800-268-9128 or (416)585-5345

FLEET AEROSPACE CORPORATION

Exchanges	Price (Jun24'93)	0.66	Trailing P/E	nm	Stock Symbol
T	Trailing Yield (%)	0.00	Trailing EPS	na	FLT

Period Ending	Sep92	Sep91	Sep90	Sep89	Sep88
Yearly Statistics					
Price-Close	0.32	0.75	1.00	1.30	2.80
Price-High	1.85	2.00	2.90	3.70	10.75
Price-Low	0.30	0.50	0.75	1.20	2.20
P/E-Close	nm	nm	nm	nm	nm
Dividends per Share	0.00	0.00	0.00	0.00	0.00
Dividend Yield (%)	0.00	0.00	0.00	0.00	0.00
Sales per Share	18.69	15.25	17.04	16.88	20.47
EPS before extra. item	(0.46)	(0.65)	(1.42)	(1.07)	(0.38)
Cash Flow per Share	0.12	0.15	(0.37)	0.27	0.46
Book Value per Share	0.56	(4.15)	(3.78)	0.74	2.11
O/S Common Shares	22,314	7,891	7,811	7,893	8,133
Total Revenue	95,273	120,932	134,260	135,274	200,892
Income before extra.	(2,345)	(2,699)	(8,613)	(6,193)	(727)
Cash Flow	636	1,165	(2,876)	2,167	3,732
Debt/Equity	1.14	4.94	4.20	1.56	1.25
Return on Capital (%)	2.54	4.16	(1.96)	(0.73)	4.60
Ret. on Com. Equity (%)	na	na	na	(74.80)	(11.29)
% Change Profit	13.1	68.7	(39.1)	(751.9)	(154.5)
% Change Revenue	(21.2)	(9.9)	(0.8)	(32.7)	28.4
% Change Assets	7.6	(8.6)	(28.7)	(9.7)	4.2

Preferred Div. Coverage	np	na	0.0
Total Div. Coverage	na	na	0.0
Interest Coverage	0.3	0.4	0.0
Current Ratio	1.3	0.9	0.9
Operating Margin	3.4	2.8	(0.1)
Asset Turnover	0.9	1.2	1.2
5 YEAR RATIOS (%)			
Return on Capital	1.7	2.3	3.8
Return on Com. Equity	na	na	na
Profit Growth	na	na	na
Revenue Growth	(9.5)	5.4	18.9
Asset Growth	(8.0)	(5.4)	17.1

BALANCE SHEET (000)

Cash	0	0	0
Current Assets	78,588	72,088	78,531
Net Fixed Assets	13,768	13,388	15,998
Invest's & Advances	402	402	758
Total Assets	108,763	101,087	110,634
Short Term Debt	36,096	60,833	65,372
Current Liabilities	59,131	81,131	88,117
Long Term Debt	6,619	2,277	1,698
Total Liabilities	71,187	88,319	94,681
Total Equity	12,576	12,768	15,953
Total Liab. & Equity	108,763	101,087	110,634
CAPITAL (000)			
Total Debt	42,715	63,110	67,070
Preferred Equity	0	45,478	45,481
Common Equity	12,576	(32,710)	(29,528)

Business:

FLEET AEROSPACE CORP., through its subsidiaries and divisions manufactures products for the commercial aerospace and defence markets. The company has facilities and markets in Canada and the United States. Products include commercial and military aircraft components.

Date	EPS	DPS	Tot Rev	Inc Bex
Mar 93	(0.13)	0.00	25,987	(3,067)
Dec 92	(0.03)	0.00	23,583	(620)
Sep 92	(0.06)	0.00	19,556	(1,340)
Jun 92	nm	0.00	25,776	(552)
Mar 92	(0.12)	0.00	26,386	(307)
Dec 91	(0.09)	0.00	24,800	(146)
Sep 91	(0.24)	0.00	29,327	(1,294)
Jun 91	(0.14)	0.00	31,407	(473)

Synopsis:

Defence sales have declined as governments have generally cut back on aerospace procurement programs. A glut of commercial aircraft has also led to softer demand for Fleet Aerospace's products for new commercial programs. The production of commercial aircraft has slowed due to the financial distress of a number of air carriers and a dramatic rise in the cancellation or deferral of orders for new commercial airplanes. As a result, some of Fleet's principal customers have scaled back production schedules. Any substantial increase in production would be in part through an improvement in economic conditions, and as existing aircraft age to the point where they must be replaced.

Losses in fiscal 1992 were reduced even though sales declined 19%, reflecting cost cutting, financial restructuring, lower interest rates and improvements in operating efficiencies. Workforce reductions were implemented in fiscal 1992 and early fiscal 1993.

On July 21, 1992, a financial reorganization plan was approved by shareholders. The governments of Canada and Ontario provided $19.7-million in loans and loan guarantees to Fleet. The Canadian Imperial Bank of Commerce restructured the company's debt by reducing the interest rate payable and by converting $25-million in debt into term preferred shares. This plan increased the stock outstanding to 22.3 million shares from 8.2 million.

Fleet expects results for the second half of fiscal 1993 to improve as a result of significant reductions in compensation agreed to by all Canadian personnel, expected productivity gains and new business. In May 1993, Fleet was awarded the global mandate to build the rear fuselage section for the EH-101 helicopter. The mandate is worth more than $30-million over 10 years. Increased global orders could push Fleet's program activity to $94-million. In January, Fleet received a contract extension from de Havilland for $56.3-million over the next three years. An option for an additional year could bring the total value of the order to $75-million. Canadian operations generated 47% of sales in fiscal 1992.

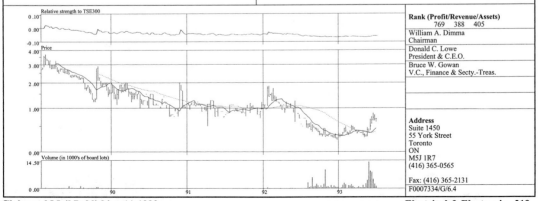

Rank (Profit/Revenue/Assets)
769   388   405

William A. Dimma
Chairman

Donald C. Lowe
President & C.E.O.

Bruce W. Gowan
V.C., Finance & Secty.-Treas.

Address
Suite 1450
55 York Street
Toronto
ON
M5J 1R7
(416) 365-0565

Fax: (416) 365-2131
F0007334/G/6.4

GANDALF TECHNOLOGIES INC.

Exchanges	Price (Jun24'93)		3.90	Trailing P/E		nm	Stock Symbol
TQ	Trailing Yield (%)		0.00	Trailing EPS		(1.24)	**GAN**

Period Ending	Mar92	Ju l91	Ju l90	Ju l89	Ju l88
Yearly Statistics	US /8M				
Price-Close	3.25	2.85	3.50	7.13	8.63
Price-High	3.90	4.30	7.75	8.25	10.75
Price-Low	1.50	2.10	2.90	4.90	6.00
P/E-Close	nm	nm	nm	237.50	15.97
Dividends per Share	0.00	0.00	0.00	0.00	0.00
Dividend Yield (%)	0.00	0.00	0.00	0.00	0.00
Sales per Share	8.46	9.85	11.28	12.16	13.27
EPS before extra. item	(0.63)	(0.55)	(0.87)	0.03	0.54
Cash Flow per Share	(0.43)	(0.12)	0.11	0.39	1.26
Book Value per Share	3.54	5.63	6.40	7.09	7.21
O/S Common Shares	15,672	12,195	12,195	12,154	12,142
Total Revenue	121,450	153,034	164,364	170,681	165,414
Income before extra.	(9,912)	(6,759)	(10,583)	377	6,571
Cash Flow	(4,512)	(1,444)	1,342	4,685	15,268
Debt/Equity	0.83	0.34	0.25	0.24	0.12
Return on Capital (%)	(11.74)	(4.21)	(6.80)	3.66	15.04
Ret. on Com. Equity (%)	(25.49)	(9.21)	(12.89)	0.43	8.78
% Change Profit	(154.1)	36.1	(2,907.2)	(94.3)	5.1
% Change Revenue	37.5	(6.9)	(3.7)	3.2	24.6
% Change Assets	41.8	(7.0)	(4.5)	4.4	28.0

Preferred Div. Coverage	np	np	np
Total Div. Coverage	na	na	na
Interest Coverage	0.0	0.0	0.0
Current Ratio	1.3	1.6	1.9
Operating Margin	(4.9)	(5.7)	(3.3)
Asset Turnover	0.9	1.0	1.1
5 YEAR RATIOS (%)			
Return on Capital	(0.8)	4.9	8.2
Return on Com. Equity	(7.7)	(0.4)	2.7
Profit Growth	na	na	na
Revenue Growth	9.6	6.5	12.7
Asset Growth	10.9	7.9	11.3
BALANCE SHEET (000)			
Cash	3,832	6,144	9,584
Current Assets	81,464	69,259	81,391
Net Fixed Assets	38,416	26,213	31,180
Invest's & Advances	3,019	6,862	1,566
Total Assets	141,408	118,620	127,551
Short Term Debt	22,102	16,794	13,390
Current Liabilities	62,188	43,518	43,414
Long Term Debt	23,729	6,389	6,139
Total Liabilities	85,917	49,907	49,553
Total Equity	55,491	68,713	77,998
Total Liab. & Equity	141,408	118,620	127,551
CAPITAL (000)			
Total Debt	45,831	23,183	19,529
Preferred Equity	0	0	0
Common Equity	55,491	68,713	77,998

Business:

GANDALF TECHNOLOGIES INC. designs, manufactures, markets and services a line of computerized communications systems, software and hardware products that permit users to communicate between computers and terminals of various types in local and wide area networks. The company has operations in North America and Europe and markets its products and services worldwide.

Date		EPS	DPS	Tot Rev	Inc Bex
Mar 93	US	(0.06)	0.00	38,485	(975)
Dec 92	US	0.00	0.00	41,417	8
Sep 92	US	(0.95)	0.00	41,536	(14,948)
Jun 92	US	(0.23)	0.00	40,296	(3,592)
Mar 92	US	0.09	0.00	33,306	1,453
Jan 92		(0.33)	0.00	43,783	(5,204)
Oct 91		(0.39)	0.00	44,361	(6,161)
Jul 91		(0.36)	0.00	37,375	(4,415)

Synopsis:

Since Autumn 1991 Gandalf has been repositioning itself to be a viable and profitable participant in the data communication market. The market for computer-networking products, which connect personal computers into networks, and networks into each other, has been growing at a meteoric pace. In the United States, it is an $800-million (U.S.) market, with annual growth in the 20% range. In Canada, growth has been slower but still dramatic.

Gandalf is focusing on asynchronous transfer mode (ATM) and remote local-area network access technology. Gandalf has spent $60-million on new technology and products and the results are now coming to market. One recent success is the introduction of the Premier LANLine 5220 bridge, which exceeded company expectations.

In the "intelligent hubs" area, Gandalf has a strong product line, but faces stiff competition from larger companies such as SynOptics and Cabletron. And in the booming market for routers, Gandalf licences one from U.S-based Proteon, which is dwarfed by industry leaders Cisco Systems and Wellfleet Communications. In April 1993, Gandalf cut prices on a wide range of products. The cuts were as much as 40% on multiplexers, modems and its intelligent local-area network hub, the Access Hub 132/48. The cuts were to defend against companies that offer cut-rate prices without the full service Gandalf provides, and foreign competitors.

Net losses in fiscal 1993 were $19.5-million (U.S.) or $1.24 (U.S.) per share on revenues of $160.9-million (U.S.), reflecting the restructuring that took place in Autumn 1992. In fiscal 1993 Gandalf cut costs dramatically through down-sizing. In early 1993, a $30-million convertible debenture issue paid down some long-term debt, and $35-million in loans that were in default were restructured.

In the year ended March 1993, product revenue generated 71% of sales and service revenue generated the remainder. Revenues by country in fiscal 1992 were: the U.S., 30%; the U.K., 22%; Canada, 22%; Holland and France, 10%; and other countries, 12%.

Relative strength to TSE300 / Price / Volume (in 1000's of board lots) chart

Rank (Profit/Revenue/Assets)
913   264   339
Desmond Cunningham
Chairman & C.E.O.
James R. Newell
V.P., Finance

Address
130 Colonnade Road South
Nepean
ON
K2E 7M4
(613) 723-6500

Fax: (613) 226-0617
G0000314/G/6.5

GENNUM CORPORATION

Exchanges	Price (Jun24'93)		16 .50	Trailing P/E		16 .34	Stock Symbol
T	Trailing Yield (%)		6 .06	Trailing EPS		1 .01	**GND**

Period Ending	Nov92	Nov91	Nov90	Nov89	Nov88
Yearly Statistics					
Price-Close	13 .75	8 .75	5 .00	9 .25	11 .50
Price-High	13 .75	10 .75	9 .75	12 .00	12 .50
Price-Low	8 .50	4 .38	4 .75	9 .00	7 .88
P/E-Close	13 .48	8 .75	nm	13 .41	12 .78
Dividends per Share	1 .00	3 .00	0 .00	0 .00	0 .00
Dividend Yield (%)	7 .27	34 .29	0 .00	0 .00	0 .00
Sales per Share	6 .61	6 .10	4 .74	4 .73	5 .78
EPS before extra. item	1 .02	1 .00	(0 .59)	0 .69	0 .90
Cash Flow per Share	1 .57	1 .38	0 .93	1 .10	1 .46
Book Value per Share	4 .05	3 .93	5 .88	6 .45	5 .73
O/S Common Shares	3 ,960	3 ,904	3 ,889	3 ,941	3 ,918
Total Revenue	26 ,238	24 ,410	19 ,588	19 ,561	23 ,078
Income before extra.	4 ,018	3 ,907	(2 ,338)	2 ,731	3 ,502
Cash Flow	6 ,195	5 ,391	3 ,642	4 ,336	5 ,677
Debt/Equity	nd	nd	nd	nd	nd
Return on Capital (%)	41 .68	32 .73	(3 .98)	19 .13	29 .83
Ret. on Com. Equity (%)	25 .62	20 .47	(9 .69)	11 .41	17 .12
% Change Profit	2 .8	267 .1	(185 .6)	(22 .0)	27 .4
% Change Revenue	7 .5	24 .6	0 .1	(15 .2)	32 .6
% Change Assets	14 .9	(27 .4)	(7 .0)	1 .6	21 .3

Period			
Preferred Div. Coverage	np	np	np
Total Div. Coverage	1 .0	0 .3	na
Interest Coverage	nd	nd	nd
Current Ratio	2 .3	3 .2	6 .0
Operating Margin	24 .4	22 .8	13 .0
Asset Turnover	1 .1	1 .2	0 .7
5 YEAR RATIOS (%)			
Return on Capital	23 .9	21 .5	19 .3
Return on Com. Equity	13 .0	11 .1	9 .3
Profit Growth	7 .9	18 .1	na
Revenue Growth	8 .5	14 .3	9 .5
Asset Growth	(0 .9)	1 .2	9 .4
BALANCE SHEET (000)			
Cash	3 ,894	1 ,372	8 ,067
Current Assets	13 ,087	10 ,530	17 ,650
Net Fixed Assets	10 ,040	9 ,590	10 ,058
Invest's & Advances	0	0	0
Total Assets	23 ,127	20 ,120	27 ,708
Short Term Debt	0	0	0
Current Liabilities	5 ,657	3 ,335	2 ,960
Long Term Debt	0	0	0
Total Liabilities	7 ,097	4 ,788	4 ,857
Total Equity	16 ,030	15 ,332	22 ,851
Total Liab. & Equity	23 ,127	20 ,120	27 ,708
CAPITAL (000)			
Total Debt	0	0	0
Preferred Equity	0	0	0
Common Equity	16 ,030	15 ,332	22 ,851

Business:

GENNUM CORPORATION is a high-technology company engaged in the design and manufacture of silicon integrated and hybrid circuits. Its operations are in Ontario. The company markets its products to the electronics, telecommunications and instrumentation industries worldwide.

Date	EPS	DPS	Tot Rev	Inc Bex
Feb 93	0.24	0.00	6 ,148	970
Nov 92	0.25	0.00	6 ,625	967
Aug 92	0.24	1.00	6 ,779	940
May 92	0.28	0.00	6 ,945	1 ,146
Feb 92	0.25	0.00	5 ,889	965
Nov 91	0.27	0.00	6 ,644	1 ,109
Aug 91	0.25	3.00	5 ,816	966
May 91	0.24	0.00	6 ,129	898

Synopsis:

Gennum has a 75% share of the global market for its main product. The company designs and manufactures integrated circuits, or miniature amplifiers and related devices, for the hearing aid industry. Growth of hearing aid chips is being driven by an aging population in the developed countries of the world.

In recent years, the company has branched out into a related technology, digital video chips. Television studios around the world are switching to digital systems from analog ones, and they will be needing Gennum's products. The incorporation of Gennum components in the master routing switcher for the 1992 Barcelona Olympics was significant event in achieving market acceptance. Gennum expects sales in this product line to accelerate in 1994. Gennum also designs and manufactures user specific integrated circuits (USIC) for a wide variety of special applications where information is conditioned, transmitted or interpreted.

Revenues in 1992 were $26-million, a gain of 10% over 1991. The increase was directly attributable to a significant contribution by the video and broadcast group (digital video chips) and the USIC communications product group, while sales of the hearing instrument products experienced moderate growth. Hearing instrument products, which are sold throughout the world, accounted for a major part of total revenues. While hearing aids remain a growth opportunity for Gennum, the growth in sales of these products was low in 1992 due to a weak economy worldwide.

The hearing instrument and USIC communications product groups are expected to achieve little growth in 1993. The increase in revenue is expected from the video and broadcast products. The R&D thrust within Gennum is focused on product development, silicon processing technology and packaging technology.

Revenues in 1992 by principal market: Western Europe, 40%; United States, 36%; Canada, 12%; and Pacific Rim, 12%.

Relative strength to TSE300 / Price / Volume (in 1000's of board lots)

Rank (Profit/Revenue/Assets)
282   577   688

H. Patrick Thode
Chairman

H. Douglas Barber
President & C.E.O.

C. Timothy Zahavich
V.P., Fin., Admin. & C.F.O.

Address
P.O. Box 489
Station A
Burlington
ON
L7R 3Y3
(416) 632-2996

Fax: (416) 632-2055
L0003627/G/6.5

GLENAYRE ELECTRONICS LTD.

Exchanges	Price (Jun24'93)	3.35	Trailing P/E	0.58	Stock Symbol
T	Trailing Yield (%)	1.19	Trailing EPS	5.78	GLN

Period Ending	Dec92	Dec91	Dec90	Sep90	Sep89
Yearly Statistics			3M		
Price-Close	1.70	4.85	3.20	5.25	15.50
Price-High	7.00	5.50	5.38	18.50	19.13
Price-Low	1.00	3.00	3.00	4.95	8.50
P/E-Close	0.28	nm	nm	nm	nm
Dividends per Share	0.04	0.05	0.00	na	0.12
Dividend Yield (%)	2.53	0.99	0.00	na	0.77
Sales per Share	2.25	2.83	16.30	19.57	15.89
EPS before extra. item	6.12	(1.63)	(0.47)	(5.29)	(0.78)
Cash Flow per Share	(0.96)	(1.05)	(0.86)	(1.00)	(0.08)
Book Value per Share	4.51	1.67	3.28	3.76	8.85
O/S Common Shares	8,721	8,708	8,507	8,507	8,141
Total Revenue	21,983	21,309	34,669	181,086	100,018
Income before extra.	53,994	(13,581)	(3,964)	(44,942)	(4,869)
Cash Flow	(8,345)	(9,012)	(1,822)	(8,524)	(508)
Debt/Equity	nd	3.71	2.72	2.33	1.23
Return on Capital (%)	83.30	(10.81)	(11.38)	(21.64)	(0.60)
Ret. on Com. Equity (%)	200.44	(63.91)	na	na	na
% Change Profit	497.6	14.3	64.7	(823.0)	(275.3)
% Change Revenue	3.2	(84.6)	(23.4)	81.1	69.0
% Change Assets	(63.7)	(22.0)	(6.2)	(17.4)	151.4

Preferred Div. Coverage	np	na	na
Total Div. Coverage	144.8	0.0	0.0
Interest Coverage	38.7	0.0	0.0
Current Ratio	3.6	1.8	1.5
Operating Margin	(42.5)	(36.5)	(10.9)
Asset Turnover	0.4	0.2	0.9
5 YEAR RATIOS (%)			
Return on Capital	7.8	(6.9)	(1.9)
Return on Com. Equity	na	na	na
Profit Growth	81.0	na	na
Revenue Growth	(18.1)	(9.3)	42.5
Asset Growth	(11.3)	27.0	41.2
BALANCE SHEET (000)			
Cash	9,860	0	3,894
Current Assets	21,944	58,714	79,181
Net Fixed Assets	7,345	21,998	33,025
Invest's & Advances	15,013	2,899	2,069
Total Assets	45,342	125,076	160,286
Short Term Debt	0	4,004	21,322
Current Liabilities	6,033	33,060	52,559
Long Term Debt	0	70,832	69,833
Total Liabilities	6,042	104,911	126,771
Total Equity	39,300	20,165	33,515
Total Liab. & Equity	45,342	125,076	160,286
CAPITAL (000)			
Total Debt	0	74,836	91,155
Preferred Equity	0	5,590	5,590
Common Equity	39,300	14,575	27,925

Business:

GLENAYRE ELECTRONICS LTD. designs, manufactures and sells advanced wireless communications products and systems worldwide for radio paging, voice processing, computer assisted telephone message management, radio telephone, mobile data and transportation communications.

Date	EPS	DPS	Tot Rev	Inc Bex
Mar 93	0.01	0.00	4,954	83
Dec 92	6.09	0.04	(78,763)	53,416
Sep 92	0.41	0.00	32,738	3,710
Jun 92	(0.73)	0.00	32,995	(6,237)
Mar 92	0.34	0.00	11,317	3,105
Dec 91	0.07	0.05	(75,647)	637
Sep 91	(0.34)	0.00	29,916	(2,793)
Jun 91	(1.19)	0.00	32,599	(10,084)

Synopsis:

In October 1992 Glenayre Electronics Ltd. sold its paging terminal and radio transmitter manufacturing business, with sales of $102-million and operating income of $14-million. The business was sold to N-W Group of New York (now known as Glenayre Technologies, Inc.) for net proceeds of $130.3-million and a net gain of $55.7-million. Included in the consideration, the company received about 10% of the outstanding shares of Glenayre Technologies (GTI).

As a condition of the sale, the company must cease the use of its Glenayre name by the end of 1993. The company will change its name from Glenayre Electronics Ltd. to GLENTEL Inc. The remaining mobile business communications unit was renamed Airtel. Airtel is a one stop retail and distribution network serving customer needs for two-way radio, cellular and paging products.

GLENTEL was concerned with its greatly leveraged debt position, the ongoing need for additional financial support from its major shareholder, and the ever increasing need for ongoing research and development moneys required to remain on the leading edge of the technology required in the manufacturing of its paging and transmitter products.

In 1992, Airtel did not make a positive contribution. Sales from continuing operations were $19.6-million, a drop of 19% from 1991 sales of $24.3-million. The company's continuing operations lost $15.7-million or $1.87 a share, similar to the loss in 1991. Included in the loss were special charges of $7.8-million for the write-down of goodwill, licences, and other assets.

In the first quarter of 1993 the mobile communications business showed its first profit. The improvement is the result of better profit margins and streamlining efforts initiated in 1992. The company continues to work towards reducing and controlling operating costs.

Relative strength to TSE300

Price

Volume (in 1000's of board lots)

Rank (Profit/Revenue/Assets)		
59	605	558

Robert M. Franklin
Chairman

Thomas E. Skidmore
C.E.O. & Vice Chairman

John J. Hurley
President & C.O.O.

Ronald E. Sowerby
C.F.O., Secretary-Treasurer

Address
Suite 2600
4710 Kingsway
Burnaby
BC
V5H 4M2
(604) 431-2345

Fax: (604) 431-2259
G0013950/G/6.25

HALEY INDUSTRIES LIMITED

Exchanges	Price (Jun24'93)	1 .55	Trailing P/E	nm	Stock Symbol
T	Trailing Yield (%)	0 .00	Trailing EPS	(0 .21)	HLY

Period Ending	Dec92	Sep91	Sep90	Sep89	Sep88
Yearly Statistics	15M				
Price-Close	1 .50	3 .70	2 .20	6 .25	7 .75
Price-High	3 .60	4 .80	6 .00	7 .88	6 .25
Price-Low	1 .20	2 .10	2 .00	6 .00	4 .75
P/E-Close	nm	11 .94	nm	19 .53	16 .03
Dividends per Share	0 .05	0 .05	0 .10	0 .24	0 .24
Dividend Yield (%)	3 .33	1 .35	4 .55	3 .84	3 .84
Sales per Share	2 .46	4 .01	3 .42	3 .98	3 .96
EPS before extra. item	(0 .24)	0 .31	(0 .76)	0 .32	0 .39
Cash Flow per Share	(0 .01)	0 .47	0 .30	0 .46	0 .62
Book Value per Share	1 .66	1 .84	1 .60	2 .47	2 .36
O/S Common Shares	10 ,334	10 ,334	10 ,300	10 ,300	10 ,300
Total Revenue	32 ,168	41 ,785	36 ,407	41 ,732	40 ,766
Income before extra.	(2 ,429)	3 ,202	(7 ,874)	3 ,253	3 ,966
Cash Flow	(66)	4 ,859	3 ,137	4 ,723	6 ,424
Debt/Equity	1 .10	0 .91	1 .15	0 .75	0 .21
Return on Capital (%)	(5 .17)	17 .00	(12 .79)	16 .19	26 .99
Ret. on Com. Equity (%)	(10 .77)	18 .08	(37 .65)	13 .08	16 .82
% Change Profit	(160 .7)	140 .7	(342 .1)	(18 .0)	20 .1
% Change Revenue	38 .4	14 .8	(12 .8)	2 .4	13 .5
% Change Assets	0 .8	0 .1	(15 .3)	39 .9	18 .1

Date	EPS	DPS	Tot Rev	Inc Bex
Mar 93	0 .00	0 .00	7 ,667	27
Dec 92	(0 .03)	0 .00	6 ,491	(291)
Sep 92	(0 .16)	0 .00	5 ,611	(1 ,564)
Jun 92	(0 .02)	0 .00	6 ,630	(250)
Mar 92	(0 .02)	0 .03	6 ,581	(215)
Dec 91	(0 .01)	0 .03	7 ,007	(109)
Sep 91	0 .06	0 .03	8 ,669	678
Jun 91	0 .10	0 .03	11 ,865	1 ,020

Preferred Div. Coverage	np	np	np
Total Div. Coverage	0 .0	6 .2	0 .0
Interest Coverage	0 .0	3 .5	0 .0
Current Ratio	6 .5	6 .1	3 .6
Operating Margin	(3 .4)	13 .8	14 .3
Asset Turnover	0 .6	1 .0	0 .8
5 YEAR RATIOS (%)			
Return on Capital	8 .4	14 .5	20 .9
Return on Com. Equity	(0 .1)	4 .9	7 .4
Profit Growth	na	(13 .1)	na
Revenue Growth	(6 .5)	0 .2	(2 .2)
Asset Growth	19 .0	6 .4	7 .7
BALANCE SHEET (000)			
Cash	6 ,350	7 ,310	6 ,205
Current Assets	21 ,653	22 ,569	23 ,077
Net Fixed Assets	17 ,053	18 ,149	17 ,775
Invest's & Advances	525	0	0
Total Assets	42 ,639	42 ,962	42 ,901
Short Term Debt	0	0	2 ,015
Current Liabilities	3 ,322	3 ,725	6 ,446
Long Term Debt	18 ,822	17 ,263	16 ,925
Total Liabilities	25 ,531	23 ,979	26 ,455
Total Equity	17 ,108	18 ,983	16 ,446
Total Liab. & Equity	42 ,639	42 ,962	42 ,901
CAPITAL (000)			
Total Debt	18 ,822	17 ,263	18 ,940
Preferred Equity	0	0	0
Common Equity	17 ,108	18 ,983	16 ,446

Business:

HALEY INDUSTRIES LTD. makes and markets light alloy sand castings for the international aerospace industry. The company's main facility is located near Haley, west of Ottawa. The company has an American subsidary, Presto Casting Co. of Arizona, which is a high-tech aerospace industry supplier.

Synopsis:

The sales and loss for the period ending December 1992 reflect the impact on Haley Industries of continuing United States defence budget cutbacks and severe recessionary effects on the commercial aerospace industry. The Haley Renfrew plant and Presto Casting Company were both equally affected.

Haley expects sales for 1993 to be similar to sales recorded in 1992. The company continues to focus on reducing costs in all areas of operations. Productivity improvements are continuing in order to bring costs in line with anticipated sales. Haley is seeking closer integration between itself and its customers. It is also developing new sales opportunities by drawing on its ability to produce high quality magnesium and aluminum castings.

Haley has received casting supplier awards from two of its major customers and has attained Government of Canada national defence quality accreditation. It has also continued to pursue business for new aerospace programs. Pattern inventory levels, which are indicative of early commitments between Haley and its customers for castings for new aircraft or engine programs, are at high levels. Haley expects that this will result in some limited new production orders in 1993, but is important to the long term success of the firm.

Presto Casting has suffered sales declines since the fall of 1991. Despite this, Presto strengthened its market position by acquiring casting patterns due to the closure of smaller competing foundries. This should help Presto to continue supplying quality castings under short lead times. Over the past few years, Presto's technical capabilities have increased substantially through investment in state-of-the-art equipment in the foundry.

For the 15-month period ended December 1992, the Canadian operations accounted for 73% of company sales. About 50% of the Canadian operation sales were denominated in U.S. funds. Sales by destination were: Canada, 29%; United States, 55%; and Europe, 16%.

Relative strength to TSE300

Price

Volume (in 1000's of board lots)

Rank (Profit/Revenue/Assets)
751   582   573

Brian W. Barr
Chairman Of The Board

William B. Ferguson
Vice Chairman & C.E.O.

James C. Lemenchick
V.P., Finance

Address
Haley
ON
K0J 1Y0
(613) 432-8841

Fax: (613) 432-9456
H0000162/G/6.4

HAWKER SIDDELEY CANADA INC.

Exchanges	Price (Jun24'93)	24.00	Trailing P/E	11.94	Stock Symbol
TMV	Trailing Yield (%)	4.50	Trailing EPS	2.01	**HSC**

Period Ending	Dec92	Dec91	Dec90	Dec89	Dec88
Yearly Statistics					
Price-Close	20.25	26.00	22.50	25.63	22.00
Price-High	26.00	28.00	26.50	27.75	25.50
Price-Low	20.00	22.00	20.00	22.00	18.00
P/E-Close	11.38	20.16	8.04	16.22	10.58
Dividends per Share	1.08	1.08	1.08	1.08	1.08
Dividend Yield (%)	5.33	4.15	4.80	4.22	4.91
Sales per Share	45.14	47.89	50.33	44.29	47.67
EPS before extra. item	1.78	1.29	2.80	1.58	2.08
Cash Flow per Share	5.67	4.31	5.84	5.85	4.19
Book Value per Share	29.27	28.67	28.80	26.04	26.46
O/S Common Shares	8,200	8,184	8,157	8,156	8,150
Total Revenue	371,100	392,700	413,000	366,500	395,596
Income before extra.	15,400	11,300	23,700	13,700	17,744
Cash Flow	46,500	35,200	47,600	47,700	34,166
Debt/Equity	0.40	0.47	0.26	0.28	0.32
Return on Capital (%)	10.79	8.46	13.96	11.94	13.01
Ret. on Com. Equity (%)	6.15	4.47	10.24	6.03	7.76
% Change Profit	36.3	(52.3)	73.0	(22.8)	(16.8)
% Change Revenue	(5.5)	(4.9)	12.7	(7.4)	(1.3)
% Change Assets	0.6	12.9	3.7	(3.6)	7.9

Date	EPS	DPS	Tot Rev	Inc Bex
Mar 93	0.35	0.27	92,100	3,100
Dec 92	0.71	0.27	96,500	6,000
Sep 92	0.56	0.27	89,500	4,800
Jun 92	0.39	0.27	93,800	3,400
Mar 92	0.18	0.27	90,200	1,700
Dec 91	0.72	0.27	109,600	6,000
Sep 91	0.03	0.27	90,100	500
Jun 91	0.08	0.27	95,600	800

Preferred Div. Coverage	19.3	14.1	29.6
Total Div. Coverage	1.6	1.2	2.5
Interest Coverage	4.3	4.0	7.5
Current Ratio	1.3	1.7	1.8
Operating Margin	11.7	8.3	10.8
Asset Turnover	0.7	0.7	0.9
5 YEAR RATIOS (%)			
Return on Capital	11.6	12.6	13.8
Return on Com. Equity	6.9	7.7	8.5
Profit Growth	(6.3)	(8.1)	0.0
Revenue Growth	(1.5)	(1.5)	(0.6)
Asset Growth	4.1	5.1	2.5
BALANCE SHEET (000)			
Cash	21,800	38,900	15,400
Current Assets	158,300	196,000	184,800
Net Fixed Assets	332,400	320,900	272,600
Invest's & Advances	0	0	0
Total Assets	532,700	529,500	469,000
Short Term Debt	39,700	37,300	26,700
Current Liabilities	120,700	114,000	101,900
Long Term Debt	61,700	79,500	37,300
Total Liabilities	278,000	280,900	220,100
Total Equity	254,000	248,600	248,900
Total Liab. & Equity	532,700	529,500	469,000
CAPITAL (000)			
Total Debt	101,400	116,800	64,000
Preferred Equity	14,000	14,000	14,000
Common Equity	240,000	234,600	234,900

Business:

HAWKER SIDDELEY CANADA INC. produces steel castings and forgings for the hydro and railway industries and for industrial markets, mining equipment, tunnelling machines, sawmill equipment, and components for jet engines and industrial gas turbines. The company also repairs and overhauls jet engines and leases railcars. BTR plc owns 59% of the company.

Synopsis:

Sales in the first quarter of 1993 for Hawker-Siddeley were $92.1-million compared with $90.2-million in the first quarter of 1992. Operating profit was $10.1-million compared with $7.4-million and net earnings were $3.1-million compared with $1.7-million. Results in the first quarter benefited from the company's staff reduction program in 1992, the costs of which largely impacted the first quarter's results in that year, and operating profit as a percentage of sales improved from 8.2% to 11.0%. In the transportation and industrial products segment, CGTX's leasing revenues and operating profit continued to grow. The sales and operating profits of the aerospace operations dipped slightly, reflecting the difficult market conditions in the aerospace industry. The results of the Canadian Steel Foundries and Canadian Steel Wheel divisions were much lower.

In 1992, the markets served by a number of the company's operations were beset by special problems. In the U.K. coal industry 31 of the industry's 50 mines were threatened with closure. The North American forest products industry began to recover slowly from the 1991 recession, and the aerospace industry faced the twin problems of declining military spending and order cancellations and deferrals by the troubled airline industry. On the positive side, the decline in the value of the Canadian dollar and the British pound during the year brought welcome relief in export markets.

Despite difficult market conditions, the company showed improvement over the previous year. Operating profit increased by 34% from $32.4-million in 1991 to $43.4-million in 1992.

In 1992 the transportation and industrial products segment generated 58% of the $382-million in sales and all the operating profit. The resource industry equipment sector generated the remainder. Canadian operations generated 57% of sales (and basically all operating profit), United States operations, 12% of sales, and European operations, 31%. Canadian export sales were $50-million, primarily to customers in the United States.

Relative strength to TSE300 / Price / Volume (in 1000's of board lots)

Rank (Profit/Revenue/Assets)
144 199 201

Robert F. Faircloth
Chairman
A.M. Gordon Turnbull
V.P., Finance

Address
3 Robert Speck Parkway
#700
Mississauga
ON
L4Z 2G5
(416) 897-7161

Fax: (416) 897-1466
H0000980/G/6.4

For further company information, call Globe Information Services 1-800-268-9128 or (416)585-5345

HELIX CIRCUITS INC.

Exchanges	Price (Jun24'93)	0.45	Trailing P/E	nm	Stock Symbol
TM	Trailing Yield (%)	0.00	Trailing EPS	(0.09)	**HLX**

Period Ending	Dec92	Dec91	Dec90	Dec89	Dec88
Yearly Statistics					
Price-Close	0.38	0.15	0.09	0.24	0.40
Price-High	0.58	0.20	0.25	0.83	1.20
Price-Low	0.14	0.03	0.05	0.15	0.35
P/E-Close	nm	nm	nm	nm	nm
Dividends per Share	0.00	0.00	0.00	0.00	0.00
Dividend Yield (%)	0.00	0.00	0.00	0.00	0.00
Sales per Share	3.74	2.91	3.54	4.49	4.72
EPS before extra. item	(0.11)	(0.42)	(0.99)	(0.40)	(0.04)
Cash Flow per Share	0.16	(0.12)	(0.02)	0.10	0.50
Book Value per Share	(1.76)	(1.75)	(1.43)	(0.53)	(0.92)
O/S Common Shares	10,601	10,601	10,611	10,620	10,645
Total Revenue	39,689	30,838	37,543	47,757	50,973
Income before extra.	39	(3,238)	(9,475)	(3,377)	(448)
Cash Flow	1,729	(1,276)	(181)	1,097	5,432
Debt/Equity	na	na	na	na	na
Return on Capital (%)	20.15	(18.39)	(44.27)	(8.88)	7.68
Ret. on Com. Equity (%)	na	na	na	na	na
% Change Profit	101.2	65.8	(180.6)	(653.8)	95.9
% Change Revenue	28.7	(17.9)	(21.4)	(6.3)	20.3
% Change Assets	21.5	(22.7)	(41.5)	(15.9)	(33.9)

Preferred Div. Coverage	na	na	na
Total Div. Coverage	na	na	na
Interest Coverage	1.0	0.0	0.0
Current Ratio	1.2	1.2	0.9
Operating Margin	3.7	(4.6)	(7.0)
Asset Turnover	2.6	2.4	2.3
5 YEAR RATIOS (%)			
Return on Capital	(8.7)	(17.5)	(18.9)
Return on Com. Equity	na	na	na
Profit Growth	na	na	na
Revenue Growth	(1.3)	(0.2)	(4.5)
Asset Growth	(21.2)	(26.3)	(22.1)
BALANCE SHEET (000)			
Cash	0	60	743
Current Assets	11,578	8,247	9,915
Net Fixed Assets	3,798	4,404	6,259
Invest's & Advances	50	50	344
Total Assets	15,552	12,800	16,559
Short Term Debt	1,139	1,449	5,975
Current Liabilities	9,450	7,066	11,475
Long Term Debt	17,583	17,084	13,079
Total Liabilities	27,033	24,150	24,554
Total Equity	(11,481)	(11,350)	(7,995)
Total Liab. & Equity	15,552	12,800	16,559
CAPITAL (000)			
Total Debt	18,722	18,533	19,054
Preferred Equity	7,164	7,164	7,164
Common Equity	(18,645)	(18,514)	(15,159)

Business:

HELIX CIRCUITS INC. designs and manufactures printed circuit boards. It has operations in Ontario and California. The company markets its products to computer industry, military and telecommunications customers in Canada and the United States. The company's controlling shareholder is Helix Investments, which owns 47 per cent of the common stock.

Date	EPS	DPS	Tot Rev	Inc Bex
Apr 93	(0.01)	0.00	12,969	163
Dec 92	(0.02)	0.00	11,186	77
Oct 92	(0.02)	0.00	10,752	107
Jul 92	(0.04)	0.00	9,360	(99)
Apr 92	(0.03)	0.00	8,391	(46)
Dec 92	(0.13)	0.00	7,170	(1,047)
Sep 91	(0.14)	0.00	7,127	(1,156)
Jun 91	(0.06)	0.00	8,186	(350)

Synopsis:

In 1992, Helix Circuits returned to operating profitability for the first time since 1988. However, the company must contend with its crushing debt load. In 1992, sales of $39.7-million were up 30% over 1991. And in the first quarter of 1993, sales were $13-million, up 55% from the comparable quarter last year. Cash flow also turned positive in 1992, $1.9-million compared to 1991's cash loss of $1.3-million. The $39,000 in profit was obliterated by $1.2-million in cumulative unpaid dividends on preferred shares, all of which are owned by the controlling shareholder Helix Investments.

Helix Circuits has virtually no equity left on its books; it has been more than erased by successive annual losses over the last five years. The company's long-term debt of about $16-million is also greater than the book value of its assets. (And that's not even including the $7.2-million in preferred shares as debt, which they effectively are.) This state of affairs has only worsened over the past three years, despite two rounds of major debt restructuring by the company. Helix has proposed a restructuring to its two major lenders, Helix Investments and Penfund Management Ltd., that would convert their debt into common equity.

In the late 1980s, as the manufacture of printed circuit boards for computers rapidly became a commodity business dominated by low-cost Asian suppliers, Helix cut its margins almost to zero, incurring losses to maintain sales. However, its defect rate started climbing and large clients like Northern Telecom fled. Even as sales shrank, costs remained high. Sales dropped 6% in 1989, 21% in 1990, and 18% in 1991.

Over the last two years, Helix has cut costs, reduced the defect rate from 20% to less than 1%, and signed up new clients like Motorola by stressing high-margin products (high and medium density multilayer circuit boards). More than 80% of sales now come from new clients won over with this approach, but real growth is going to depend on rebuilding its balance sheet.

Relative strength to TSE300 / Price / Volume (in 1000's of board lots)

Rank (Profit/Revenue/Assets)
573   507   759

Donald C. Webster
Chairman

Vahan Kolouan
President & C.E.O.

John Angaritis
Treasurer & C.F.O.

Address
250 Finchdene Square
Scarborough
ON
M1X 1A5
(416) 299-4000

Fax: (416) 299-1140
H0008344/G/6.5

INTERNATIONAL VERIFACT INC.

Exchanges	Price (Jun24'93)	4.25	Trailing P/E	42.50	Stock Symbol
T	Trailing Yield (%)	0.00	Trailing EPS	0.10	**IVI**

Period Ending	Mar92	Mar91	Mar90	Mar89	Mar88
Yearly Statistics					
Price-Close	1.67	0.31	0.41	0.46	0.72
Price-High	1.97	0.47	1.12	0.75	1.53
Price-Low	0.27	0.27	0.35	0.45	0.55
P/E-Close	167.00	nm	nm	nm	nm
Dividends per Share	0.00	0.00	0.00	0.00	0.00
Dividend Yield (%)	0.00	0.00	0.00	0.00	0.00
Sales per Share	0.41	0.45	0.50	0.85	0.17
EPS before extra. item	0.01	(0.06)	(0.14)	(0.09)	(0.57)
Cash Flow per Share	0.03	(0.03)	(0.06)	(0.06)	(0.53)
Book Value per Share	0.27	0.10	(0.21)	(0.42)	(0.33)
O/S Common Shares	31,737	22,455	16,235	11,137	11,137
Total Revenue	11,009	8,928	7,680	9,417	1,598
Income before extra.	433	(934)	(1,837)	(1,010)	(5,091)
Cash Flow	904	(519)	(927)	(711)	(4,715)
Debt/Equity	0.00	0.52	1.50	na	na
Return on Capital (%)	10.61	(11.13)	(26.58)	0.23	(87.93)
Ret. on Com. Equity (%)	8.00	na	na	na	na
% Change Profit	146.4	49.2	(82.0)	80.2	(5.9)
% Change Revenue	23.3	16.2	(18.4)	489.3	(77.5)
% Change Assets	141.3	(35.3)	11.6	43.8	(43.1)

Preferred Div. Coverage	np	np	na
Total Div. Coverage	na	na	0.0
Interest Coverage	3.1	0.0	0.0
Current Ratio	3.4	1.0	1.0
Operating Margin	5.8	(4.9)	(11.3)
Asset Turnover	1.0	2.0	1.2
5 YEAR RATIOS (%)			
Return on Capital	(23.0)	(42.8)	(57.8)
Return on Com. Equity	na	na	na
Profit Growth	2.4	na	na
Revenue Growth	9.1	22.8	60.0
Asset Growth	7.4	(3.0)	36.3
BALANCE SHEET (000)			
Cash	2,025	1	8
Current Assets	8,061	2,336	4,892
Net Fixed Assets	546	559	686
Invest's & Advances	1,116	1,116	1,116
Total Assets	11,026	4,570	7,063
Short Term Debt	21	1,118	3,172
Current Liabilities	2,382	2,338	4,897
Long Term Debt	12	33	33
Total Liabilities	2,394	2,371	4,930
Total Equity	8,632	2,199	2,133
Total Liab. & Equity	11,026	4,570	7,063
CAPITAL (000)			
Total Debt	33	1,151	3,205
Preferred Equity	0	0	5,611
Common Equity	8,632	2,199	(3,478)

Business:

INTERNATIONAL VERIFACT INC. is a publicly-owned corporation engaged in the design, development, manufacture and marketing of terminals and related products for use in electronic funds transfer and point of sale applications (EFT/POS). These applications include credit card authorization and verification, direct debit transactions and electronic draft capture.

Date	EPS	DPS	Tot Rev	Inc Bex
Mar 93	0.03	0.00	8,167	1,213
Dec 92	0.03	0.00	7,121	1,018
Sep 92	0.03	0.00	6,307	867
Jun 92	0.01	0.00	5,000	459
Mar 92	0.11	0.00	3,900	300
Dec 91	0.00	0.00	2,383	24
Sep 91	0.00	0.00	2,279	29
Jun 91	(0.05)	0.00	2,400	80

Synopsis:

International Verifact is a beneficiary of debit cards becoming a reality. They enable card-holders to pay for items by withdrawing funds directly from their bank accounts right at the store counter. The company has been performing very well since December 1991, with the introduction of new electronic funds transfer and point-of-sale (EFT/POS) systems. In the year ended March 31, 1993, the company earned $3.6-million, or 10 cents per share, on sales of $26.6-million. Compared to the previous year, sales were 2.4 times greater, and earnings were eight times greater. The company has no long-term debt, and completed a $6-million private placement in 1992 to bolster working capital.

Verifact has about 70% of the market for debit/credit point-of-sale terminals in Canada, and its customers include most of the major banks in Canada; the most aggressive player, the Royal Bank, is a key client. There have been similar debit card launches in the United States. The U.S. accounts for 30% of Verifact's sales and that proportion is expected to grow to 50% by the end of 1994.

The company expects its C2000 line, introduced in late 1992, to be its strongest selling product line in the United States in the future. These models connect easily to existing cash registers, and can be used to handle not only debit, but also credit and related transactions like frequent-buyer and coupon purchases. Analysts say that of the roughly 500,000 retailers in Canada who accept credit cards, only about 150,000 use such electronic verification units, meaning there is considerable growth to be had in that market as well.

The company's main competition in Canada is SBN Systems, which supplies a couple of the major Canadian banks. The U.S. market is dominated by Verifone Inc., which has annual sales in the $200-million (U.S.) range. In December 1992, BCE Telecom International, International Verifact's largest shareholder, sold its 30% interest in the company, in order to concentrate on the international telecommunications market.

Relative strength to TSE300

Price

Volume (in 1000's of board lots)

Rank (Profit/Revenue/Assets)
502 687 840

George Whitton
Chairman, President & C.E.O.
William N. Kinnear
V.P., Finance & Secretary

Address
79 Torbarrie Road
Downsview
ON
M3L 1G5
(416) 245-6700

Fax: (416) 245-6701
01000241/G/6.5

LINAMAR CORPORATION

Exchanges	Price (Jun24'93)		28 .25	Trailing P/E		21 .73	Stock Symbol
T	Trailing Yield (%)		0 .00	Trailing EPS		1 .30	**LNR**

Period Ending	Jun92	Jun91	Jun90	Jun89	Jun88
Yearly Statistics					
Price-Close	16 .25	7 .13	4 .40	5 .88	7 .75
Price-High	16 .75	7 .50	6 .00	8 .50	14 .13
Price-Low	7 .00	4 .00	3 .80	4 .40	6 .00
P/E-Close	15 .19	11 .13	10 .73	22 .60	13 .14
Dividends per Share	0 .00	0 .00	0 .00	0 .00	0 .00
Dividend Yield (%)	0 .00	0 .00	0 .00	0 .00	0 .00
Sales per Share	21 .89	21 .64	16 .21	14 .51	14 .60
EPS before extra. item	1 .07	0 .64	0 .41	0 .26	0 .59
Cash Flow per Share	1 .98	1 .89	1 .48	1 .19	1 .79
Book Value per Share	6 .51	4 .88	4 .24	3 .83	3 .66
O/S Common Shares	8 ,886	7 ,919	7 ,890	7 ,968	7 ,950
Total Revenue	179 ,998	171 ,007	128 ,936	114 ,614	113 ,862
Income before extra.	8 ,730	5 ,069	3 ,262	2 ,044	4 ,576
Cash Flow	16 ,167	14 ,950	11 ,730	9 ,343	13 ,899
Debt/Equity	0 .60	0 .90	1 .19	1 .05	0 .98
Return on Capital (%)	19 .47	15 .90	14 .60	12 .28	21 .82
Ret. on Com. Equity (%)	18 .10	14 .07	10 .20	6 .86	17 .41
% Change Profit	72 .2	55 .4	59 .6	(55 .3)	0 .8
% Change Revenue	5 .3	32 .6	12 .5	0 .7	40 .6
% Change Assets	21 .7	4 .6	22 .3	(1 .3)	22 .6

Preferred Div. Coverage	np	np	np
Total Div. Coverage	na	na	na
Interest Coverage	5 .5	3 .4	2 .9
Current Ratio	1 .5	1 .4	1 .4
Operating Margin	8 .1	7 .0	8 .4
Asset Turnover	1 .3	1 .6	1 .2
5 YEAR RATIOS (%)			
Return on Capital	16 .8	18 .3	21 .2
Return on Com. Equity	13 .3	14 .1	15 .8
Profit Growth	13 .9	12 .4	14 .0
Revenue Growth	17 .2	31 .7	28 .7
Asset Growth	13 .5	25 .5	33 .7
BALANCE SHEET (000)			
Cash	0	0	0
Current Assets	66 ,368	56 ,497	58 ,024
Net Fixed Assets	66 ,152	51 ,977	44 ,448
Invest's & Advances	0	250	0
Total Assets	133 ,033	109 ,344	104 ,552
Short Term Debt	9 ,223	11 ,869	17 ,825
Current Liabilities	45 ,128	40 ,162	41 ,507
Long Term Debt	25 ,400	22 ,836	22 ,001
Total Liabilities	75 ,172	70 ,725	71 ,137
Total Equity	57 ,861	38 ,619	33 ,415
Total Liab. & Equity	133 ,033	109 ,344	104 ,552
CAPITAL (000)			
Total Debt	34 ,623	34 ,705	39 ,826
Preferred Equity	0	0	0
Common Equity	57 ,861	38 ,619	33 ,415

Business:

LINAMAR CORPORATION operates in two industry segments. The machining segment consists of the manufacturing and assembly of components for the automotive, aerospace, defence and transportation industries. The combines segment consists of the assembly and sale of rotary combines.

Date	EPS	DPS	Tot Rev	Inc Bex
Mar 93	0 .40	0 .00	61 ,954	3 ,630
Dec 92	0 .30	0 .00	60 ,768	2 ,668
Sep 92	0 .24	0 .00	52 ,894	2 ,149
Jun 92	0 .36	0 .00	55 ,866	3 ,044
Mar 92	0 .29	0 .00	44 ,219	2 ,335
Dec 91	0 .22	0 .00	38 ,778	1 ,740
Sep 91	0 .20	0 .00	41 ,135	1 ,611
Jun 91	0 .26	0 .00	47 ,217	2 ,057

Synopsis:

Linamar has continued to achieve record sales and earnings throughout fiscal 1993 and expects earnings for its fiscal year ending in June 1993 to be $1.40 per share. Fundamental to this accomplishment is its continued focus on the high volume automotive sector and the commitment to never ending cost and quality improvements.

Linamar's strategy is to concentrate on product lines mainly for braking systems, steering components and assemblies, oil and water pump assemblies, and vacuum pump components and assemblies as products that will have a 10 to 12 year manufacturing life span.

Sales in fiscal 1992 were $178.6-million, an increase of 4.4% from 1991. Its core business grew by 14% from additional production volumes coming from its automotive sector, while combine sales were $14-million below the 1991 level. Linamar's operating earnings increased from $8.5-million in 1991 to $11.5-million in 1992, due to higher volume production from its automotive plants, and from its many continuous improvement activities. Net earnings rose 71% from 1991, impacted by the gain on the disposal of its Duo-Pact facility. Linamar's net purchases of fixed assets were $19.8-million. It was not able to maintain its capital spending within the cash flow generated from operations due to the timing of two major automotive contracts.

In fiscal 1992, Linamar built on its expertise in Western Combines by acquiring Mezogep, a producer of agricultural components for harvesting equipment, located in Hungary. In January 1993, Linamar continued its European expansion by signing a deal with Russia to build a combine harvester factory in that country.

Sales in fiscal 1992 by business segment were: machining of automotive components, 90%, and combines, 10%. Substantially all automotive sales were to the major North American manufacturers, and 60% of sales were to three customers. Export sales amounted to $161.2-million, or 90% of consolidated sales.

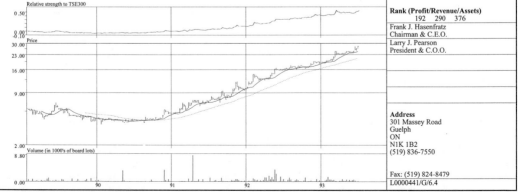

Rank (Profit/Revenue/Assets)
192   290   376

Frank J. Hasenfratz
Chairman & C.E.O.

Larry J. Pearson
President & C.O.O.

Address
301 Massey Road
Guelph
ON
N1K 1B2
(519) 836-7550

Fax: (519) 824-8479
L0000441/G/6.4

NEWBRIDGE NETWORKS CORPORATION

Exchanges	Price (Jun24'93)	54.00	Trailing P/E	66.26	Stock Symbol
TQ	Trailing Yield (%)	0.00	Trailing EPS	0.81	**NNC**

Period Ending	Apr92	Apr91	Apr90	Apr89	Apr88
Yearly Statistics					
Price-Close	8.56	4.19	5.50	nt	nt
Price-High	10.63	5.56	10.69	nt	nt
Price-Low	3.13	1.78	4.00	nt	nt
P/E-Close	61.16	nm	84.61	nt	nt
Dividends per Share	0.00	0.00	0.00	0.00	0.00
Dividend Yield (%)	0.00	0.00	0.00	0.00	0.00
Sales per Share	2.53	2.20	1.94	1.81	0.89
EPS before extra. item	0.14	(0.26)	0.06	0.24	(0.11)
Cash Flow per Share	0.51	(0.09)	0.16	0.32	(0.08)
Book Value per Share	1.56	1.37	1.63	0.87	0.13
O/S Common Shares	70,308	68,290	67,040	44,498	32,926
Total Revenue	179,872	150,280	122,457	67,385	17,636
Income before extra.	9,777	(17,913)	3,889	9,148	(2,156)
Cash Flow	36,947	(6,041)	10,361	11,882	(1,651)
Debt/Equity	0.31	0.40	0.52	0.33	0.43
Return on Capital (%)	14.20	(6.85)	7.59	30.63	na
Ret. on Com. Equity (%)	9.62	(17.65)	5.25	42.29	na
% Change Profit	154.6	(560.6)	(57.5)	524.3	na
% Change Revenue	19.7	22.7	81.7	282.1	na
% Change Assets	9.7	(8.6)	104.7	174.9	na

Date	EPS	DPS	Tot Rev	Inc Bex
Apr 93	0.34	0.00	98,093	25,493
Jan 93	0.23	0.00	85,528	17,692
Oct 92	0.15	0.00	67,787	10,629
Aug 92	0.09	0.00	56,192	6,186
Apr 92	0.06	0.00	51,929	4,723
Feb 92	0.04	0.00	45,950	2,421
Nov 91	0.02	0.00	42,360	1,589
Aug 91	0.02	0.00	41,161	1,067

Preferred Div. Coverage	np	np	np
Total Div. Coverage	na	na	na
Interest Coverage	2.2	0.0	2.2
Current Ratio	2.8	2.8	3.2
Operating Margin	12.6	1.0	7.4
Asset Turnover	1.0	0.9	0.7
5 YEAR RATIOS (%)			
Return on Capital	na	na	na
Return on Com. Equity	na	na	na
Profit Growth	na	na	na
Revenue Growth	na	na	na
Asset Growth	na	na	na
BALANCE SHEET (000)			
Cash	17,019	4,584	15,277
Current Assets	101,012	86,892	111,084
Net Fixed Assets	62,037	62,800	59,484
Invest's & Advances	3,923	3,221	612
Total Assets	178,069	162,395	177,667
Short Term Debt	6,482	6,055	24,287
Current Liabilities	36,040	30,745	34,509
Long Term Debt	27,525	31,446	32,909
Total Liabilities	68,339	68,898	68,227
Total Equity	109,730	93,497	109,440
Total Liab. & Equity	178,069	162,395	177,667
CAPITAL (000)			
Total Debt	34,007	37,501	57,196
Preferred Equity	0	0	0
Common Equity	109,730	93,497	109,440

Business:

NEWBRIDGE NETWORKS CORPORATION designs, manufactures and markets integrated digital networking products. The company distributes and services its products in over 50 countries either through its direct sales force or through authorized dealers, distributors, common carriers, original equipment manufacturers and value added resellers. Products are manufactured in Canada, the U.S., and the U.K.

Synopsis:

Newbridge Networks has been performing very well. In the year ended in April 1993, sales increased by 170% to $308-million, net earnings increased to $60-million from $9.8-million in the previous year, and earnings per share increased to $1.63 from 28 cents. In fiscal 1993, sales to telephone companies accounted for more than 60% of revenues. Newbridge's specialty is in data communications. It designs and makes multiplexers, black-box devices with custom made microchips that contain software to boost the information carrying capacity of telephone lines for private computer networks.

Throughout 1992, Newbridge enhanced its products and developed new ones. It continued to enhance its MainStreet networking product line with advanced technologies. For example, the 36120 MainStreet Packet Transfer Exchange was selected by Pacific Bell to provide Frame Relay service planned for implementation in 1993.

Newbridge unveiled a family of products, 36120 MainStreet ATMnet, based on a new standard for high-speed private networks called asynchronous transfer mode. These networks will save businesses, such as banks, money by allowing them to send more data at dizzying speeds along smaller phone lines. In early 1993, Newbridge Microsystems together with Motorola, was selected by Raytheon to partner on a new initiative to provide next generation computing for the U.S. military. The Microsystems semiconductor product line is expected to fuel significant growth in 1993.

Significant growth in 1993 is expected in its microsystems semiconductor product line, in the areas of open bus components, encryption and open bus communication modules. Newbridge also expects to see major business in Asia, particularly in Japan and China, as well as Germany, France and South America.

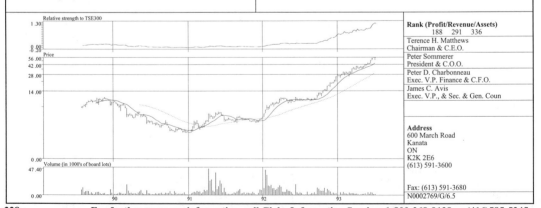

Rank (Profit/Revenue/Assets)
188   291   336

Terence H. Matthews
Chairman & C.E.O.

Peter Sommerer
President & C.O.O.

Peter D. Charbonneau
Exec. V.P. Finance & C.F.O.

James C. Avis
Exec. V.P., & Sec. & Gen. Coun

Address
600 March Road
Kanata
ON
K2K 2E6
(613) 591-3600

Fax: (613) 591-3680
N0002769/G/6.5

For further company information, call Globe Information Services 1-800-268-9128 or (416)585-5345

NOMA INDUSTRIES LIMITED

Exchanges	Price (Jun24'93)		5.50	Trailing P/E		nm	Stock Symbol
T	Trailing Yield (%)		2.18	Trailing EPS		(0.01)	**NMA.A**

Period Ending	Dec92	Dec91	Dec90	Dec89	Dec88
Yearly Statistics					
Price-Close	5.50	5.50	4.65	12.50	16.25
Price-High	7.50	8.50	13.00	18.38	18.63
Price-Low	4.75	4.20	4.10	11.75	9.75
P/E-Close	137.50	nm	nm	50.00	16.58
Dividends per Share	0.12	0.15	0.24	0.24	0.22
Dividend Yield (%)	2.18	2.73	5.16	1.92	1.38
Sales per Share	18.02	17.91	18.25	21.21	20.92
EPS before extra. item	0.04	(0.36)	(0.01)	0.25	0.98
Cash Flow per Share	0.52	0.45	0.67	0.64	1.51
Book Value per Share	4.61	4.36	4.89	5.15	5.18
O/S Common Shares	33,870	30,210	30,210	30,210	30,118
Total Revenue	583,799	541,201	551,191	639,737	628,760
Income before extra.	1,288	(10,837)	(474)	7,434	29,467
Cash Flow	16,838	13,605	20,191	19,236	45,279
Debt/Equity	0.76	0.98	1.17	1.15	0.80
Return on Capital (%)	5.91	(0.10)	6.86	10.95	24.01
Ret. on Com. Equity (%)	0.89	(7.76)	(0.31)	4.77	19.49
% Change Profit	111.9	(2,186.3)	(106.4)	(74.8)	15.6
% Change Revenue	7.9	(1.8)	(13.8)	1.7	19.4
% Change Assets	6.6	(16.0)	(5.7)	10.4	10.0

Preferred Div. Coverage	np	np	np
Total Div. Coverage	0.3	0.0	0.0
Interest Coverage	1.1	0.0	1.0
Current Ratio	2.0	1.8	1.8
Operating Margin	3.1	2.6	5.5
Asset Turnover	1.7	1.7	1.5
5 YEAR RATIOS (%)			
Return on Capital	9.5	13.0	18.7
Return on Com. Equity	3.4	7.0	13.0
Profit Growth	(45.1)	na	na
Revenue Growth	2.0	10.4	18.1
Asset Growth	0.4	3.3	22.3
BALANCE SHEET (000)			
Cash	0	0	0
Current Assets	222,968	207,458	245,584
Net Fixed Assets	101,159	99,631	110,420
Invest's & Advances	0	0	0
Total Assets	339,414	318,320	378,988
Short Term Debt	50,741	55,978	84,992
Current Liabilities	114,327	112,327	134,707
Long Term Debt	68,397	73,293	87,809
Total Liabilities	183,138	186,562	231,258
Total Equity	156,276	131,758	147,730
Total Liab. & Equity	339,414	318,320	378,988
CAPITAL (000)			
Total Debt	119,138	129,271	172,801
Preferred Equity	0	0	0
Common Equity	156,276	131,758	147,730

Business:

NOMA INDUSTRIES LTD. is a group of companies with operations in Canada and the United States that make and distribute a range of electrical and mechanical products for consumer and industrial markets in Canada, the United States and Europe. Products include lawnmowers, snow removal equipment, electrical and non-electrical Christmas decorations, electrical wire, and automotive products.

Date	EPS	DPS	Tot Rev	Inc Bex
Mar 93	0.09	0.03	137,343	3,074
Dec 92	0.01	0.03	179,186	376
Sep 92	(0.04)	0.03	159,237	(1,338)
Jun 92	(0.07)	0.03	100,830	(2,087)
Mar 92	0.14	0.03	144,546	4,337
Dec 91	(0.25)	0.03	161,660	(7,389)
Sep 91	(0.12)	0.03	129,992	(3,861)
Jun 91	(0.04)	0.03	114,249	(1,043)

Synopsis:

The results for Noma Industries in 1992 were good considering the two prior years of losses. In 1990 and 1991, the weather turned against its home and garden equipment lines with cold summers and warm winters. The deepening recession did not help either, particularly in its wire and automotive products business. But 1992 saw some recovery and sales rebounded by 8% to $584-million and profit recovered to $1.3-million from a loss of $10.8-million a year earlier, despite continuing weak residential and commercial lighting markets.

The problems that existed for a couple years at Noma's new manufacturing plant in Tennessee seem over. It is at this plant that Noma builds many of its most expensive products, such as snow blowers and lawn care equipment. The 1992-93 winter weather was more conductive to Noma's business, particularly its Christmas products group. Its sales were helped by the acquisition in 1992 of Hudson Valley Tree of New York, which it merged with its existing artificial tree business, American Tree Co.

Noma has about 50% of the Christmas product market in Canada and is the biggest player in the United States in Christmas lights and trees. It is also the world's biggest consumer snow blower maker and a leading producer of engine block heaters, automotive battery warmers and outdoor electrical extension cords. Noma is also Canada's biggest supplier of wiring and cable to appliance makers, a producer of automotive wire harnesses, and the nation's biggest manufacturer of residential lighting fixtures. As a high-tech manufacturer of low-tech products, Noma is able to challenge low-cost overseas labor with technology, and compete with competitive products from the United States as tariffs under free trade diminish. It also has a knack for controlling its inventories.

Sales in 1992 by product group were: outdoor power equipment, 42%; electrical wire and components, 17%; Christmas products, 33%; and other, 8%. The United States is responsible for 51% of sales with the remainder sold in Canada.

Relative strength to TSE300 / Price / Volume (in 1000's of board lots)

Rank (Profit/Revenue/Assets)		
399	143	258

H. Thomas Beck
Chairman & C.E.O.

Stephen G. Snyder
President & C.O.O.

Norman S. Eckler
V.P., Finance

Address
4211 Yonge Street
Suite 315
Willowdale
ON
M2P 2A9
(416) 222-6662

N0002031/G/6.5

SBN SYSTEMS INC.

Exchanges	Price (Jun24'93)	1.80	Trailing P/E	nm	Stock Symbol
TQ	Trailing Yield (%)	0.00	Trailing EPS	(3.33)	**SBY**

Period Ending	Sep92	Sep91	Sep90	Sep89	Sep88
Yearly Statistics					
Price-Close	2.70	0.43	0.62	6.50	15.20
Price-High	3.70	0.85	7.40	20.40	245.00
Price-Low	0.60	0.43	0.60	6.30	14.00
P/E-Close	nm	nm	nm	nm	nm
Dividends per Share	0.00	0.00	0.00	0.00	0.00
Dividend Yield (%)	0.00	0.00	0.00	0.00	0.00
Sales per Share	73.47	77.95	81.20	80.19	76.17
EPS before extra. item	(3.29)	(12.36)	(28.51)	(23.35)	(46.40)
Cash Flow per Share	3.32	(6.07)	(14.45)	(16.28)	(23.48)
Book Value per Share	(73.26)	(70.26)	(58.01)	(29.50)	(4.59)
O/S Common Shares	1,600	1,600	1,600	1,600	1,600
Total Revenue	117,534	124,708	132,706	126,519	121,164
Income before extra.	(4,808)	(19,601)	(45,602)	(37,347)	(74,423)
Cash Flow	5,317	(9,711)	(23,123)	(26,042)	(37,737)
Debt/Equity	na	na	na	na	na
Return on Capital (%)	27.86	(14.59)	(47.14)	(19.37)	(29.30)
Ret. on Com. Equity (%)	na	na	na	na	(204.64)
% Change Profit	75.5	57.0	(22.1)	49.8	(120.1)
% Change Revenue	(5.8)	(6.0)	4.9	4.4	(15.3)
% Change Assets	(15.3)	(17.2)	(28.9)	(29.1)	(32.9)
Preferred Div. Coverage	na	na	na		
Total Div. Coverage	na	na	na		
Interest Coverage	0.6	0.0	0.0		
Current Ratio	0.6	0.6	0.8		
Operating Margin	7.2	2.0	(2.6)		
Asset Turnover	1.8	1.6	1.4		
5 YEAR RATIOS (%)					
Return on Capital	(16.5)	(24.5)	(19.3)		
Return on Com. Equity	na	na	na		
Profit Growth	na	na	na		
Revenue Growth	(3.9)	2.2	14.7		
Asset Growth	(25.0)	(17.2)	(5.6)		
BALANCE SHEET (000)					
Cash	0	0	0		
Current Assets	40,046	44,467	57,985		
Net Fixed Assets	25,842	33,281	34,440		
Invest's & Advances	0	0	0		
Total Assets	65,888	77,748	93,931		
Short Term Debt	30,761	25,782	22,133		
Current Liabilities	69,931	71,743	70,649		
Long Term Debt	111,178	111,386	113,528		
Total Liabilities	176,501	185,353	185,535		
Total Equity	(110,613)	(107,605)	(91,604)		
Total Liab. & Equity	65,888	77,748	93,931		
CAPITAL (000)					
Total Debt	141,939	137,168	135,661		
Preferred Equity	6,593	4,793	1,193		
Common Equity	(117,206)	(112,398)	(92,797)		

Business:

SBN SYSTEMS INC. supplies equipment and related services to issuers of plastic transcation cards. The company sells card embossers, encoders, imprinters, benefits and credit authorization terminals, and non-impact printers to banks, oil companies, retailers, hospitals, universities, and government agencies.

Date	EPS	DPS	Tot Rev	Inc Bex
Mar 93	(0.51)	0.00	29,702	(689)
Dec 92	(1.76)	0.00	26,037	(2,689)
Sep 92	(1.49)	0.00	32,187	(1,929)
Jun 92	0.43	0.00	30,936	696
Mar 92	(0.19)	0.00	29,117	(305)
Dec 91	(2.04)	0.00	25,294	(3,270)
Sep 91	(3.74)	0.00	27,567	(5,815)
Jun 91	(5.57)	0.00	32,986	(8,902)

Synopsis:

SBN Systems, formerly Consolidated NBS Systems, feels it has successfully withstood both the effects of the recession and the events arising prior to February 1988. For about the last five years, SBN has been one of the Hees-Edper group's workouts. The company has focused largely on recovering from a scandal in 1988, when its $14.2-million profit suddenly changed to a $33.8-million loss. Former C.E.O. Clive Raymond later pleaded guilty to filing a false prospectus. In April 1991, the company launched an action for damages of $135-million against its former accountants, Price Waterhouse and Greenwood Cook, relating to the audits of the company from 1985 to 1987. In another action, SBN is continuing to pursue former management of the company and the surety company that provided a $9.5-million fidelity bond which covered the improper transfer of $10-million of treasury bills to a third party.

SBN continues to improve, recording reduced losses over last year, as a result of higher sales, reduced operating costs and improved gross margins. The point of sales (POS) group is continuing its contribution to the success of the INTERAC national debit card system in Canada. SBN is a major supplier of debit card transaction terminals and software to two Canadian chartered banks. By 1994, citizens throughout Canada will be able to use debit cards for purchases at various retail outlets. The POS Group continues its efforts to identify an investment partner or a merger candidate committed to the telecommunication and transaction processing industry.

The imaging group was awarded a major contract by the British Army to supply a proprietary digitized imaging identification system, in the second quarter of fiscal 1993. There has also been increased demand for products supplied by the embossing group.

Revenues by business segment in 1992 were: card services, 53%; imaging, 24%; point of sale, 17%; and other, 6%. Revenues by country were: Canada, 31%; United States, 55%; and United Kingdom, 14%.

Rank (Profit/Revenue/Assets)
831 346 486

Timothy W. Casgrain
President & C.E.O.

J. Kenneth Rutherford
V.P., C.F.O. & Secretary

Address
3220 Orlando Drive
Mississauga
ON
L4V 1R5
(416) 671-3334

Fax: (416) 671-0690
N0024728/G/6.5

SPAR AEROSPACE LIMITED

Exchanges	Price (Jun24'93)	16.50	Trailing P/E	36.67	Stock Symbol
TM	Trailing Yield (%)	1.45	Trailing EPS	0.45	**SPZ**

Period Ending	Dec92	Dec91	Dec90	Dec89	Dec88
Yearly Statistics					
Price-Close	15.88	16.00	10.88	8.63	17.63
Price-High	20.00	16.25	11.38	17.50	21.50
Price-Low	14.63	10.50	7.88	7.88	13.50
P/E-Close	32.40	16.33	45.31	nm	31.47
Dividends per Share	0.24	0.12	0.12	0.20	0.28
Dividend Yield (%)	1.51	0.75	1.10	2.32	1.59
Sales per Share	38.91	35.01	27.06	18.86	22.28
EPS before extra. item	0.49	0.98	0.24	(1.05)	0.56
Cash Flow per Share	3.32	2.20	1.31	(0.39)	1.02
Book Value per Share	8.44	8.17	7.29	7.15	8.03
O/S Common Shares	12,497	12,394	12,420	12,395	12,329
Total Revenue	485,500	434,339	335,691	233,163	270,668
Income before extra.	5,684	11,245	2,715	(11,818)	6,189
Cash Flow	41,322	27,252	16,257	(4,770)	12,355
Debt/Equity	0.83	0.11	0.24	1.02	0.70
Return on Capital (%)	9.88	17.03	3.34	(10.80)	6.32
Ret. on Com. Equity (%)	5.50	11.72	3.03	(12.60)	6.55
% Change Profit	(49.5)	314.2	123.0	(291.0)	53.3
% Change Revenue	11.8	29.4	44.0	(13.9)	13.9
% Change Assets	49.7	17.9	(22.5)	0.6	12.5

Business:

SPAR AEROSPACE LTD. is engaged in the design, development, manufacture and servicing of systems for the space, robotics, communications, remote sensing, electro-optics and aviation markets. Products include satellites and satellite subsystems, and the Shuttle Remote Manipulator System. The company markets its products in Canada and internationally.

Date	EPS	DPS	Tot Rev	Inc Bex
Mar 93	0.22	0.06	116,423	2,880
Dec 92	(0.43)	0.06	113,156	(4,866)
Sep 92	0.37	0.06	129,852	4,197
Jun 92	0.29	0.06	128,219	3,326
Mar 92	0.26	0.06	104,044	3,027
Dec 91	0.38	0.03	101,276	4,410
Sep 91	0.26	0.03	115,807	2,895
Jun 91	0.17	0.03	111,109	1,948

Preferred Div. Coverage	np	np	np	
Total Div. Coverage	2.1	8.2	2.0	
Interest Coverage	na	na	na	
Current Ratio	1.0	1.1	1.1	
Operating Margin	5.0	5.2	2.6	
Asset Turnover	1.4	1.8	1.7	
5 YEAR RATIOS (%)				
Return on Capital	5.2	4.1	2.0	
Return on Com. Equity	2.8	2.6	1.2	
Profit Growth	7.1	20.7	(27.0)	
Revenue Growth	15.3	17.7	8.2	
Asset Growth	9.1	(0.8)	3.3	
BALANCE SHEET (000)				
Cash	0	2,148	0	
Current Assets	183,700	137,611	111,852	
Net Fixed Assets	72,178	63,332	51,820	
Invest's & Advances	9,869	2,151	2,032	
Total Assets	353,062	235,874	199,988	
Short Term Debt	23,722	100	14,556	
Current Liabilities	182,434	123,385	102,234	
Long Term Debt	63,566	11,213	7,204	
Total Liabilities	247,622	134,598	109,438	
Total Equity	105,440	101,276	90,550	
Total Liab. & Equity	353,062	235,874	199,988	
CAPITAL (000)				
Total Debt	87,288	11,313	21,760	
Preferred Equity	0	0	0	
Common Equity	105,440	101,276	90,550	

Synopsis:

Spar Aerospace wants to reduce its dependence on government related business and transform itself into a fully integrated communications and information company. Spar could make higher profit margins in commercially related businesses by taking advantage of its strength in satellite-based communications and remote sensing. Spar hopes its restructuring process will result in space-related activities generating less than 50% of its revenues by 1996. At present, 60% of Spar's revenue comes from designing and manufacturing satellites, robotics and aviation systems, mostly for government-funded projects. Spar also wants to increase the revenue stream from software operations to 40%. In 1992, exports accounted for 40% of revenues.

Spar has made a series of acquisitions since the beginning of 1992 to expand its presence in communications and software, while selling off its gears and transmission division. Recently acquired operations in the satellite and communications systems group include Comtel and ComStream Corp., both based in San Diego, and Prior Data Sciences Ltd. of Kanata, Ontario. ComStream is a world leader in digital compression technology. Prior Data is real-time systems software firm. Spar also joined Canada's telephone companies to form Alouette Telecom, which purchased Telesat Canada. This gives Spar preferred access to the domestic commercial satellite and ground terminal market.

The U.S. space station program, Freedom, is undergoing cost cutting. However, Spar feels there is a significant role for space robotics, the vital piece of the $40-billion space station for which Spar is responsible. In the past two years, the space station project has contributed 30% of Spar's total revenues. The space station project is expected to contribute a steady stream of earnings, an estimated 50 cents to 70 cents per share until 1996.

Telesat Mobile Inc., Spar's Canadian customer for the Mobile Satellite program, has filed for restructuring under the Bankruptcy and Insolvency Act. Spar expects work on the two satellite program to continue.

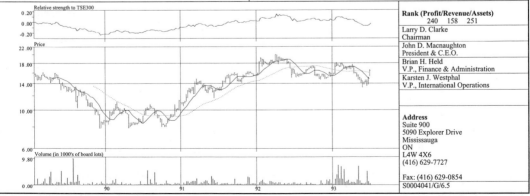

Rank (Profit/Revenue/Assets)
240   158   251

Larry D. Clarke
Chairman

John D. Macnaughton
President & C.E.O.

Brian H. Held
V.P., Finance & Administration

Karsten J. Westphal
V.P., International Operations

Address
Suite 900
5090 Explorer Drive
Mississauga
ON
L4W 4X6
(416) 629-7727

Fax: (416) 629-0854
S0004041/G/6.5

TIE/TELECOMMUNICATIONS CANADA LIMITED

Exchanges	Price (Jun24'93)	1.32	Trailing P/E	9.43	Stock Symbol
TM	Trailing Yield (%)	0.00	Trailing EPS	0.14	**TTI**

Period Ending	Dec92	Dec91	Dec90	Dec89	Dec88	Business:
Yearly Statistics						TIE/TELECOMMUNICATIONS CANADA
Price-Close	0.90	1.20	0.30	0.90	1.60	LTD. designs, sells, services and repairs
Price-High	1.55	1.75	1.00	2.40	3.10	advanced telecommunications equipment.
Price-Low	0.75	0.25	0.25	0.85	1.40	Products include business telephone systems
P/E-Close	7.50	10.00	nm	nm	nm	and telecommunications equipment for
Dividends per Share	0.00	0.00	0.00	0.00	0.00	financial traders. The company operates in
Dividend Yield (%)	0.00	0.00	0.00	0.00	0.00	Canada and the United States and markets its
Sales per Share	3.82	4.21	2.86	4.22	8.13	products across North America and worldwide.
EPS before extra. item	0.12	0.12	(0.12)	(3.04)	(0.08)	
Cash Flow per Share	0.18	0.27	0.02	(0.69)	0.08	
Book Value per Share	1.09	0.98	0.86	0.98	4.01	
O/S Common Shares	8,252	8,214	8,201	8,201	8,201	
Total Revenue	31,905	35,914	23,826	34,653	67,185	
Income before extra.	951	1,009	(990)	(24,898)	(654)	

Date	EPS	DPS	Tot Rev	Inc Bex
Mar 93	0.01	0.00	7,373	87
Dec 92	0.06	0.00	8,287	446
Sep 92	0.04	0.00	7,922	320
Jun 92	0.03	0.00	8,732	235
Mar 92	(0.01)	0.00	7,893	(50)
Dec 91	0.02	0.00	8,609	148
Sep 91	0.03	0.00	8,912	277
Jun 91	0.05	0.00	10,219	388

	Dec92	Dec91	Dec90	Dec89	Dec88
Cash Flow	1,478	2,255	157	(5,662)	617
Debt/Equity	0.02	0.03	0.13	0.58	0.19
Return on Capital (%)	10.96	12.51	(5.89)	(93.88)	(0.65)
Ret. on Com. Equity (%)	11.17	13.41	(13.18)	(121.71)	(1.97)
% Change Profit	(5.7)	201.9	96.0	(3,707.0)	(140.1)
% Change Revenue	(11.2)	50.7	(31.2)	(48.4)	(8.1)
% Change Assets	(12.1)	(11.3)	12.2	(54.8)	(4.1)

						Synopsis:
Preferred Div. Coverage	np	np	np			TIE/Telecommunications Canada aims to become the premier supplier of
Total Div. Coverage	na	na	na			business communications products and services to small and medium sized
Interest Coverage	na	na	0.0			businesses. Its products are competitively priced, reliable and feature rich. The
Current Ratio	1.8	1.6	1.4			balance sheet is debt free and the company has a presence in every metropolitan
Operating Margin	2.5	(0.9)	(2.1)			market within Canada. Over the past two years, the company has changed from a
Asset Turnover	1.7	1.6	1.0			distribution company to a direct sales and service company. It is changing its

approach to the market place by adding higher margin products, services and

5 YEAR RATIOS (%)				software. This should make the company less dependent on key systems by
Return on Capital	(15.4)	(16.2)	(16.8)	offering more PBX, voice response, video conferencing, long distance and other
Return on Com. Equity	(22.5)	(23.8)	(25.6)	network services.
Profit Growth	(10.3)	(8.7)	na	
Revenue Growth	(15.3)	(17.0)	(25.4)	Sales dipped by 9% in 1992 from 1991, and by 6% in the first quarter of 1993
Asset Growth	(17.6)	(19.5)	(17.0)	over the comparable period in 1992. This decline was attributable to the continued

poor economic conditions within Canada, which has adversely affected the sales

BALANCE SHEET (000)				of the direct sales and service division. The division's sales decline was partially
Cash	4,729	4,179	7,067	offset by an increase in sales of refurbished, Caller ID and peripheral products
Current Assets	14,442	16,300	18,885	from the company's telecommunications accessories (TAI) division. The TAI
Net Fixed Assets	755	1,043	1,058	group contributed 80% of the company's net income in 1992.
Invest's & Advances	623	746	723	
Total Assets	18,801	21,400	24,126	The company's gross margins declined from 44.4% in 1991 to 43% in the first
Short Term Debt	133	200	883	quarter of 1993. This reduction was mainly due to a change in product mix and
Current Liabilities	7,966	10,504	13,679	increased competition causing lower pricing in the repair business of the TAI
Long Term Debt	0	0	0	division. Profitability over the past two years has been a result of the company's
Total Liabilities	9,810	13,369	17,108	cost reduction and market share improvement programs, implemented in an effort
Total Equity	8,991	8,031	7,018	to offset the negative performance of the Canadian economy.
Total Liab. & Equity	18,801	21,400	24,126	

In May 1993, the company's parent, TIE/Communications Inc. of Shelton,
Connecticut, purchased 804,000 of its common shares from an unidentified

CAPITAL (000)				shareholder at $1.25. The purchase raised its stake in TIE/Telecommunications
Total Debt	133	200	883	Canada to about six million shares or 73%. In August 1992, the company sold its
Preferred Equity	0	0	0	Canadian key system distribution business to Nitsuko America Corporation.
Common Equity	8,991	8,031	7,018	

Rank (Profit/Revenue/Assets)
430   547   726

George N. Benjamin, III
President & C.E.O.

Gordon R. Tingets
V.P., Finance & Asst. Secty.

Address
7550 Birchmount Road
Markham
ON
L3R 6C6
(416) 475-5577

Fax: (416) 479-4201
T0014849/G/6.5

XEROX CANADA INC.

Exchanges	Price (Jun24'93)	33.50	Trailing P/E	19.94	Stock Symbol
TM	Trailing Yield (%)	3.88	Trailing EPS	1.68	XXC.B

Period Ending	Dec92	Dec91	Dec90	Dec89	Dec88
Yearly Statistics					
Price-Close	33.38	25.75	13.50	22.00	17.50
Price-High	34.00	25.75	22.50	23.13	20.00
Price-Low	25.00	14.50	12.00	17.50	15.38
P/E-Close	19.18	23.62	13.92	13.50	9.07
Dividends per Share	1.21	1.14	1.17	1.01	0.72
Dividend Yield (%)	3.63	4.43	8.67	4.59	4.11
Sales per Share	19.06	18.64	18.15	18.22	19.47
EPS before extra. item	1.74	1.09	0.97	1.63	1.93
Cash Flow per Share	2.62	2.14	2.11	2.79	3.87
Book Value per Share	17.44	16.16	15.67	14.92	13.95
O/S Common Shares	34,115	34,777	35,313	35,525	37,938
Total Revenue	1,079,301	1,051,390	1,040,681	1,064,059	1,131,942
Income before extra.	61,125	39,504	35,664	63,340	74,597
Cash Flow	90,122	74,796	74,610	105,213	146,855
Debt/Equity	0.97	0.97	1.44	1.61	1.65
Return on Capital (%)	11.61	8.65	8.34	10.64	16.61
Ret. on Com. Equity (%)	10.35	6.85	6.35	11.66	14.80
% Change Profit	54.7	10.8	(43.7)	(15.1)	15.8
% Change Revenue	2.7	1.0	(2.2)	(6.0)	13.1
% Change Assets	1.5	(11.4)	(2.1)	3.9	16.9
Preferred Div. Coverage	47.8	30.9	27.9		
Total Div. Coverage	9.2	2.1	4.7		
Interest Coverage	5.2	3.3	2.4		
Current Ratio	0.7	1.1	0.8		
Operating Margin	2.2	0.3	(1.4)		
Asset Turnover	0.4	0.4	0.3		
5 YEAR RATIOS (%)					
Return on Capital	11.2	12.3	14.3		
Return on Com. Equity	10.0	10.8	12.5		
Profit Growth	(1.0)	(7.4)	(7.6)		
Revenue Growth	1.5	3.9	6.2		
Asset Growth	1.3	6.1	17.9		
BALANCE SHEET (000)					
Cash	6,397	332	13,453		
Current Assets	238,496	203,434	247,893		
Net Fixed Assets	115,998	100,268	77,057		
Invest's & Advances	740,080	714,642	740,105		
Total Assets	1,711,335	1,686,869	1,904,837		
Short Term Debt	187,602	28,466	199,792		
Current Liabilities	333,592	181,054	307,060		
Long Term Debt	403,132	530,424	617,780		
Total Liabilities	1,100,427	1,108,819	1,335,536		
Total Equity	610,908	578,050	569,301		
Total Liab. & Equity	1,711,335	1,686,869	1,904,837		
CAPITAL (000)					
Total Debt	590,734	558,890	817,572		
Preferred Equity	16,000	16,000	16,000		
Common Equity	594,908	562,050	553,301		

Business:

XEROX CANADA INC. operates in the document services industry. Its primary operations being the development, manufacture, marketing, financing, servicing, distribution and administration of Xerox equipment, the providing of supplies for office systems and the providing of related professional consulting services in document management.

Date	EPS	DPS	Tot Rev	Inc Bex
Mar 93	0.23	0.32	243,913	8,241
Dec 92	0.64	0.30	313,733	22,042
Sep 92	0.39	0.39	259,125	13,538
Jun 92	0.42	0.29	267,297	14,848
Mar 92	0.30	0.28	239,677	10,697
Dec 91	0.41	0.29	310,152	14,743
Sep 91	0.28	0.28	238,868	9,963
Jun 91	0.26	0.29	266,621	9,639

Synopsis:

Xerox Canada's profit growth of 55% to $61-million on flat sales of $1-billion has come largely from domestic sales of equipment (61% of sales), better cost controls, and lower interest charges on borrowings. The DocuTech Production Publisher has been a high volume seller.

However, it will take more than cost controls to transform Xerox from an office equipment manufacturer into a major service organization offering computer consulting, systems integration, network management, and hardware and software repairs. Xerox wants to take services from less than 30% of revenues to more than half of its business in two years. Xerox is facing stiff competition in the service market from companies like Andersen Consulting, EDS and Systemhouse, and smaller firms like DMR Group, LGS and CGL. IBM and mainframe maker Unisys also want to be major players. There are forecasts of 20% growth over the next five years in this market.

Xerox has expanded the scope of its Xerox Service Centres. The chain now services products from a range of manufacturers like Sun Microsystems, AST, Compaq, Samsung and Wyse. This third-party maintenance market is already well populated by established competitors like Bull HN Information Systems, and ComputerLand, not to mention many smaller companies. Software support has been offered by resellers like ComputerLand for years.

Xerox has been losing ground in its core copier business for almost a decade to Canon, Toshiba and Sharp. Where it once had more than 80% of the copier market, Xerox now sells about 20% of all machines shipped in Canada and the United States. It dominates the high-end market, which gives it about 40% of total industry sales.

Xerox Canada shares are a surrogate for its parent company. They are perpetually exchangeable on the basis of three class B shares for one share of Xerox Corp. In addition, the Canadian class B shares are entitled to at least one-third of the dividend paid on Xerox Corp. shares.

Rank (Profit/Revenue/Assets)
54 98 103

Richard S. Barton
President, Chairman & C.E.O.
Richard Ragazzo
V.P. & Controller

Address
5650 Yonge Street
North York
ON
M2M 4G7
(416) 229-3769

X0000213/G/6.5

Page	Company	$	Latest year end	Actual	Estimate this year	Estimate next year
				Earnings per Share		
237	Celanese Canada		9212	3.35	3.83	4.60
238	Du Pont Canada		9212	2.16	2.80	3.38
239	Methanex		9212	(0.25)	0.35	1.20
240	Sico		9212	1.18	1.30	1.45

Estimates from I/B/E/S Inc., 345 Hudson St., New York, NY 10014 (212) 243-3335. In Canada: 6 Lansing Square, Ste. 235, Willowdale, ON M2J 1T5 (416) 496-0977.

Chemicals

U.S. Industrial Gases (Transcript) - Industry Report [May-14-1993]. MERRILL LYNCH CAPITAL MARKETS reported by Hardiman, R.D., et al

For the United States industrial gases industry, above average volume growth is projected, particularly for on-site gases. Environmental factors are expected to be the single most important factor driving demand growth in the next several years. The proposed BTU tax could be readily passed through to onsite customers. [RN 1331328]

Chemical Industry Fundamentals - Industry Report [Apr-29-1993]. PAINEWEBBER INC. reported by Cash, A.W.

U.S. capacity utilization was 81.9% for February 1993, an increase over the restated rate of 81.5% for January 1993 and above the restated rate of 81.3% for December 1992. As the recovery continues and begins to take hold overseas, rates should continue to register positive comparisons. Rail shipments are 0.2% ahead of a year ago, in spite of generally poor weather throughout 1Q:93. Several categories of fiber inventories show marked improvement compared to year ago levels, but two areas were down more than 30%. Plastic resin inventories are down. Commodity margins weakened slightly on price weakness and feedstock cost stability. [RN 1328945]

International: Chemical Notes #303 - Industry Report [Apr-19-1993]. SHEARSON LEHMAN BROTHERS, INC. reported by Semegran, T.S., et al

Ethylene oversupply is expected to continue for several more years. Propylene availability could be enhanced by the new fuel reformulation needs. Methanol excesses are possible, based upon current MTBE demand outlooks. Far East demands for PVC and VCM will likely require significant exports of EDC, since that region is experiencing a shortage of chlorine which is likely to continue. [RN 1323460]

Fertilizer Monthly - Industry Report [Apr-13-1993]. MERRILL LYNCH CAPITAL MARKETS reported by Groh, D.B.

Not only has the planting season gotten off to a slow start in 1993, but the fertilizer stocks have been dragged down by a slump in fertilizer demand. In spite of the temporary stall in demand, several of the companies in the group are improving their cost position and market share. Vigoro completed the refinancing of its 12.75% senior subordinated notes, which will save the company an estimated $0.05 (U.S.) per share. Terra Industries announced the completion of the acquisition of ICI's nitrogen facility in Canada. The acquisition adds to Terra's distribution base through exposure of 32 outlets in Canada. IMC Fertilizer Group and Freeport McMoRan Resource Partners have reached a definitive agreement regarding the formation of their joint venture that was announced in January 1993. In particular, the announcement is an indication that despite IMC's recent setback from a suit which was settled for a net of $109 million (U.S.), the two companies will go forward with their plans to reduce costs by $80 million (U.S.) and form the largest integrated phosphate chemical operations in the world. [RN 1322058]

Fertilizer Industry - Industry Report [Apr-1-1993]. MERRILL LYNCH CAPITAL MARKETS reported by Groh, D.B.

There is no doubt that the ever expanding world population will continue to rely on more efficient food production from a limited land base and that world fertilizer consumption will increase. The major opportunities for the fertilizer industry are in Asia and Latin America, which are relatively low in fertilizer use and low on the agricultural productivity curve. Fertilizer application rates for countries in these regions are where the U.S. was thirty to forty years ago. The U.S. is a mature agricultural market with regard to fertilizer use, and North American fertilizer producers will need to continue to lower their cost and increase their international market share in order to improve their profit growth prospects Opportunities will arise in the U.S. as environmental issues and concerns require more intensive agronomic management and comprehensive services from ag-input providers and distributors. Market share will go to those distributors that are current with environmental compliance and can offer value added service along with ag-input products. [RN 1320601]

Chemical Industry - Industry Report [Mar-30-1993]. KIDDER, PEABODY & COMPANY, INCORPORATED reported by Leming, P.T.

All the chemical companies, except for Union Carbide, have underperformed the S&P 500 since the end of April 1992. While the market moved up 8% during the same time-frame, over half of the chemcial group declined more than 10% in absolute price. Total nylon shipments increased in January 1993 by 5%, with all of the upswing from the carpet market. The noncarpet nylon market continued its long-term decline. The polyester market was weaker after two years of relatively strong shipments, with all three polyester segments down about 10% from the prior month. [RN 1317814]

Chemicals—Specialty - Industry Report [Mar-29-1993] . MERRILL LYNCH CAPITAL MARKETS reported by Hardiman, R.D., et al

Despite the upturn in economic activity suggested by the macro statistics, recent contacts with specialty chemical company managements indicate that these companies are experiencing little improvement in their business. Earnings could be flat to down versus year earlier 1Q:93 for slightly more than half the group. Domestic sales are showing modest improvement, at best. Industrial gas producers Air Products and Praxair suggest that March 1993 quarter liquid oxygen and nitrogen volumes are running about flat year-to-year. Industrial water treatment suppliers Nalco and Betz also reported slow U.S. sales. [RN 1318086]

CELANESE CANADA INC.

Exchanges		Price (Jun24'93)	47 .00	Trailing P/E	15 .46	Stock Symbol
TM		Trailing Yield (%)	3 .40	Trailing EPS	3 .04	**CCL**

Period Ending	Dec92	Dec91	Dec90	Dec89	Dec88
Yearly Statistics					
Price-Close	40 .00	41 .25	32 .25	29 .75	28 .50
Price-High	47 .75	42 .00	32 .75	37 .25	29 .75
Price-Low	38 .00	30 .75	26 .75	26 .25	17 .50
P/E-Close	15 .21	16 .91	10 .86	8 .52	8 .07
Dividends per Share	1 .50	1 .50	1 .85	2 .00	2 .00
Dividend Yield (%)	3 .75	3 .64	5 .74	6 .72	7 .02
Sales per Share	33 .03	31 .00	26 .86	29 .21	29 .99
EPS before extra. item	2 .63	2 .44	2 .97	3 .49	3 .53
Cash Flow per Share	5 .78	4 .57	4 .74	4 .75	5 .15
Book Value per Share	17 .21	16 .07	15 .13	14 .01	12 .52
O/S Common Shares	13 ,578	13 ,578	13 ,578	13 ,577	13 ,575
Total Revenue	456 ,006	421 ,701	379 ,509	410 ,385	412 ,269
Income before extra.	36 ,720	34 ,142	41 ,273	48 ,343	48 ,904
Cash Flow	78 ,465	62 ,055	64 ,294	64 ,541	69 ,915
Debt/Equity	nd	nd	nd	nd	nd
Return on Capital (%)	26 .82	24 .07	31 .34	39 .07	45 .01
Ret. on Com. Equity (%)	15 .82	15 .66	20 .37	26 .30	30 .04
% Change Profit	7 .6	(17 .3)	(14 .6)	(1 .1)	72 .5
% Change Revenue	8 .1	11 .1	(7 .5)	(0 .5)	15 .3
% Change Assets	(0 .0)	19 .3	0 .6	(3 .7)	18 .1

Preferred Div. Coverage	37 .6	34 .9	42 .2
Total Div. Coverage	1 .7	1 .6	1 .6
Interest Coverage	nd	nd	nd
Current Ratio	2 .8	2 .4	2 .8
Operating Margin	14 .5	13 .1	14 .1
Asset Turnover	1 .3	1 .2	1 .2

5 YEAR RATIOS (%)			
Return on Capital	33 .3	33 .8	32 .8
Return on Com. Equity	21 .6	22 .3	21 .8
Profit Growth	5 .3	12 .7	26 .8
Revenue Growth	4 .9	3 .9	2 .1
Asset Growth	6 .3	7 .3	1 .7

BALANCE SHEET (000)			
Cash	122 ,192	74 ,381	72 ,017
Current Assets	231 ,195	206 ,418	181 ,402
Net Fixed Assets	118 ,514	142 ,065	109 ,434
Invest's & Advances	0	0	0
Total Assets	352 ,534	352 ,553	295 ,553
Short Term Debt	0	0	0
Current Liabilities	84 ,004	85 ,754	65 ,543
Long Term Debt	0	0	0
Total Liabilities	106 ,560	121 ,955	77 ,761
Total Equity	245 ,974	230 ,598	217 ,792
Total Liab. & Equity	352 ,534	352 ,553	295 ,553

CAPITAL (000)			
Total Debt	0	0	0
Preferred Equity	12 ,363	12 ,363	12 ,363
Common Equity	233 ,611	218 ,235	205 ,429

Business:

CELANESE CANADA INC. is a diversified manufacturer of fibres, chemicals and industrial products. The company's textile group makes polyester and acetate yarns. The chemicals group makes petrochemicals and cellulose products. The company serves Canadian and international markets. Hoechst AG of Frankfurt, Germany, through a subsidiary, controls the majority of the company's common shares.

Date	EPS	DPS	Tot Rev	Inc Bex
Mar 93	0.92	0.35	104 ,510	12 ,748
Dec 92	1.20	0.75	130 ,292	16 ,478
Sep 92	1.00	0.25	114 ,913	12 ,936
Jun 92	(0.08)	0.25	112 ,432	(879)
Mar 92	0.58	0.25	92 ,837	8 ,185
Dec 91	0.77	0.75	116 ,516	10 ,787
Sep 91	0.69	0.25	100 ,110	9 ,592
Jun 91	0.31	0.25	102 ,170	4 ,326

Synopsis:

Celanese Canada's improved first quarter earnings were primarily due to results in polyester and cellulosics, as well as lower depreciation in its methanol unit. Net income and income from continuing operations for the first quarter were $12.7-million or 92 cents per common share on net sales of $101.7-million. This compared favorably with the same period in 1992, when net income was $8.2-million or 58 cents per common share on net sales of $89.9-million.

The company ended 1992 free of both long-term and short-term debt. It will finance future working capital requirements and any capital investment needs through internally generated funds, and external sources, if appropriate. Operating lines of credit available at Canadian chartered banks totaled $63-million on December 31, 1992. Cash and short-term investments were $122.2-million, an increase of $47.8-million, which came from net income and lower capital spending.

In 1993 the company plans to spend approximately $25-million on capital projects, of which $4.1-million was committed at year-end. Further plans are for expenditures of about $28-million in 1994.

The lower Canadian dollar in 1992 boosted export sales in all product areas with the exception of chemicals. Sales of methanol were redirected from export markets to the growing domestic market to satisfy the requirements of Alberta Envirofuels which uses the product in the manufacture of MTBE, an octane enhancer in gasoline.

The pending elimination of all tariffs on the company's textile products between Canada and the U.S. in 1993, will positively affect earnings. As well, the North American Free Trade Agreement will mark the initiation of a "rules of origin" concept which stipulates that textile and apparel goods must be produced from yarn and fibre made in a NAFTA country to qualify for preferential treatment.

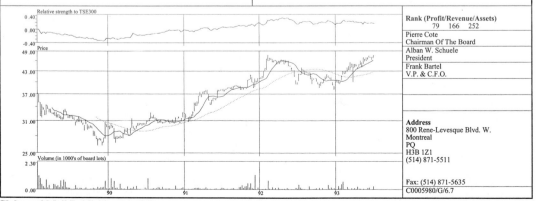

Rank (Profit/Revenue/Assets)
79   166   252

Pierre Cote
Chairman Of The Board
Alban W. Schuele
President
Frank Bartel
V.P. & C.F.O.

Address
800 Rene-Levesque Blvd. W.
Montreal
PQ
H3B 1Z1
(514) 871-5511

Fax: (514) 871-5635
C0005980/G/6.7

DU PONT CANADA INC.

Exchanges	Price (Jun24'93)	45.50	Trailing P/E	19.44	Stock Symbol
TM	Trailing Yield (%)	1.54	Trailing EPS	2.34	**DUP.A**

Period Ending	Dec92	Dec91	Dec90	Dec89	Dec88
Yearly Statistics					
Price-Close	41.00	40.50	24.50	25.25	24.00
Price-High	48.00	41.50	30.00	31.00	31.00
Price-Low	40.00	23.75	21.75	23.00	23.63
P/E-Close	15.53	22.38	12.13	9.08	7.57
Dividends per Share	0.70	0.70	0.70	0.68	0.50
Dividend Yield (%)	1.71	1.73	2.86	2.67	2.08
Sales per Share	45.87	42.92	45.78	45.62	43.80
EPS before extra. item	2.64	1.81	2.02	2.78	3.17
Cash Flow per Share	6.00	4.68	4.49	4.75	4.93
Book Value per Share	21.83	20.23	19.14	17.84	15.91
O/S Common Shares	30,739	30,982	30,784	30,767	31,216
Total Revenue	1,453,019	1,341,153	1,439,063	1,432,083	1,391,917
Income before extra.	81,779	56,165	62,433	86,517	99,910
Cash Flow	185,434	144,531	138,351	147,497	155,182
Debt/Equity	0.17	0.21	0.29	0.29	0.05
Return on Capital (%)	18.32	14.16	15.79	22.14	34.87
Ret. on Com. Equity (%)	12.58	9.21	10.94	16.52	21.94
% Change Profit	45.6	(10.0)	(27.8)	(13.4)	10.3
% Change Revenue	8.3	(6.8)	0.5	2.9	3.0
% Change Assets	9.4	1.5	8.0	27.3	(1.8)

Preferred Div. Coverage	470.0	322.8	358.8
Total Div. Coverage	3.8	2.6	2.9
Interest Coverage	8.6	5.5	6.0
Current Ratio	1.7	2.0	2.2
Operating Margin	8.4	7.7	7.5
Asset Turnover	1.2	1.2	1.3

5 YEAR RATIOS (%)			
Return on Capital	21.1	24.1	26.4
Return on Com. Equity	14.2	16.5	18.5
Profit Growth	(2.0)	(1.5)	24.8
Revenue Growth	1.4	1.3	3.7
Asset Growth	8.4	6.8	7.5

BALANCE SHEET (000)			
Cash	88,559	40,486	66,558
Current Assets	442,846	366,830	426,531
Net Fixed Assets	660,786	630,317	555,531
Invest's & Advances	45,663	56,359	43,216
Total Assets	1,166,431	1,065,719	1,049,587
Short Term Debt	10,743	4,581	27,941
Current Liabilities	261,764	182,278	189,773
Long Term Debt	105,885	128,033	142,143
Total Liabilities	493,129	436,696	458,048
Total Equity	673,302	629,023	591,539
Total Liab. & Equity	1,166,431	1,065,719	1,049,587

CAPITAL (000)			
Total Debt	116,628	132,614	170,084
Preferred Equity	2,325	2,325	2,325
Common Equity	670,977	626,698	589,214

Business:

DU PONT CANADA INC. makes and markets specialty products and chemicals for use by customers in the manufacturing, resource and service sectors in over 60 countries. Products include synthetic fibres and intermediate chemicals used in nylon production, specialty chemicals, plastic resins and packaging systems. The company is about 75% owned by E.I. du Pont de Nemours & Company of Delaware.

Date	EPS	DPS	Tot Rev	Inc Bex
Mar 93	0.61	0.18	381,226	18,660
Dec 92	0.38	0.18	340,900	11,618
Sep 92	0.41	0.18	335,952	12,858
Jun 92	0.94	0.18	424,201	29,177
Mar 92	0.91	0.18	352,121	28,126
Dec 91	0.46	0.18	320,045	14,274
Sep 91	0.50	0.18	320,176	15,668
Jun 91	0.57	0.18	374,893	17,490

Synopsis:

Exports will continue to be an essential element in the Canadian recovery at Du Pont, and a cornerstone of the company's strategy. However, the strong advances in revenues reported in the first quarter of 1993, with earnings of $18.7-million or 61 cents per share, up 8% from underlying earnings of $17.3-million or 56 cents per share for the same period last year, may be hard to sustain.

The company is coming out of a five year trough of low prices and over capacity and it is taking advantage of better conditions to put some of its polyethylene business up for sale. Company revenue increases were spread across all three of its industry segments, fibre revenue up 19%, plastics and films revenue up by 14% and chemicals revenue up by 9%. Flooring systems, nylon industrial specialties, engineering polymers and modified polymers each delivered substantially higher revenues in this quarter.

In January 1993, Du Pont announced a $7-million spending program to upgrade its Lycra spandex facility at Maitland, Ontario. In March 1993, it announced the acceleration of its phase-out of CFC production.

On April 12, 1993, the company sought offers for the SCLAIR Polyethylene business unit and its related licensing operations. The two represented 1992 revenue of $224.6-million, including sales of $26.4-million to other Du Pont Canada business units. To date it has licenced the SCLAIR process to 12 companies around the world and is currently constructing plants in Nigeria and Venezuela. The sale of the Sarnia plant is part of a strategic plan to concentrate on core applications. The division makes 225,000 tonnes of polyethylene a year (most of it sold in Canada) and has annual revenues of about $250-million.

Du Pont is to focus on other elements in its chemical business, including strengths in such areas as fibres and textiles, nylon and lycra, expanding its hydrogen peroxide facilities and focusing in other areas such as manufacturing automobile finishes.

Relative strength to TSE300

Price

Volume (in 1000's of board lots)

Rank (Profit/Revenue/Assets)	41 80 139
Arthur R. Sawchuk	President & C.E.O.
William B. Barley	V.P. & C.F.O.

Address
Box 2200, Streetsville
Mississauga
ON
L5M 2H3
(416) 821-3300

Fax: (416) 821-5110
D0003465/G/6.7

METHANEX CORPORATION

Exchanges	Price (Jun24'93)	9.00	Trailing P/E	nm	Stock Symbol
TM	Trailing Yield (%)	0.00	Trailing EPS	(0.20)	**MX**

Period Ending	Dec92	Dec91	Dec90	Dec89	Dec88
Yearly Statistics	US	US	US		
Price-Close	9.50	8.63	6.00	10.25	8.63
Price-High	14.88	8.75	10.50	14.25	12.00
Price-Low	7.50	4.50	5.25	8.00	6.75
P/E-Close	nm	62.96	nm	nm	34.50
Dividends per Share	0.00	0.00	0.00	0.00	0.00
Dividend Yield (%)	0.00	0.00	0.00	0.00	0.00
Sales per Share	2.69	3.62	3.44	10.68	15.08
EPS before extra. item	(0.20)	0.12	(1.95)	(2.20)	0.25
Cash Flow per Share	(0.09)	0.30	(1.14)	1.37	1.62
Book Value per Share	1.53	(0.93)	(4.71)	(3.24)	(1.18)
O/S Common Shares	54,033	35,367	16,320	16,270	16,022
Total Revenue	121,853	75,266	55,762	173,501	246,037
Income before extra.	(8,579)	2,505	(31,734)	(35,555)	3,892
Cash Flow	(3,837)	6,076	(18,601)	(22,144)	25,246
Debt/Equity	1.33	na	na	na	na
Return on Capital (%)	(3.11)	17.39	(35.95)	(2.47)	23.05
Ret. on Com. Equity (%)	(34.41)	na	na	na	na
% Change Profit	(442.5)	107.9	(4.2)	(1,013.5)	106.4
% Change Revenue	61.9	35.0	(62.5)	(29.5)	96.4
% Change Assets	58.6	(25.2)	(7.6)	(11.3)	(38.5)

Preferred Div. Coverage	np	np	np
Total Div. Coverage	na	na	na
Interest Coverage	0.0	2.4	0.0
Current Ratio	1.7	0.8	0.3
Operating Margin	(4.6)	17.5	(2.1)
Asset Turnover	0.5	0.5	0.3
5 YEAR RATIOS (%)			
Return on Capital	(0.2)	0.9	(1.4)
Return on Com. Equity	na	na	na
Profit Growth	na	na	na
Revenue Growth	2.6	(12.7)	(25.5)
Asset Growth	(9.7)	(21.7)	(22.9)
BALANCE SHEET (000)			
Cash	10,057	5,724	0
Current Assets	48,857	26,589	23,321
Net Fixed Assets	126,172	85,417	63,840
Invest's & Advances	18,207	0	8,334
Total Assets	223,014	140,586	188,003
Short Term Debt	292	3,267	25,073
Current Liabilities	29,239	33,273	78,254
Long Term Debt	109,856	135,965	110
Total Liabilities	140,166	173,577	264,886
Total Equity	82,848	(32,991)	(76,883)
Total Liab. & Equity	223,014	140,586	188,003
CAPITAL (000)			
Total Debt	110,148	139,232	25,183
Preferred Equity	0	0	0
Common Equity	82,848	(32,991)	(76,883)

Business:

METHANEX CORPORATION is engaged in the production and marketing of methanol. The company operates a methanol production facility at Kitimat, British Columbia. The company markets its products worldwide.

Date		EPS	DPS	Tot Rev	Inc Bex
Mar 93	US	0.02	0.00	117,442	2,650
Dec 92	US	(0.05)	0.00	45,139	(2,565)
Sep 92	US	(0.09)	0.00	23,008	(3,672)
Jun 92	US	(0.08)	0.00	24,704	(2,920)
Mar 92	US	0.07	0.00	101,143	11,337
Dec 91	US	(0.09)	0.00	19,165	(970)
Sep 91	US	0.13	0.00	19,466	2,147
Jun 91	US	(0.11)	0.00	18,995	(1,798)

Synopsis:

In the face of a $8.6-million (U.S.) loss for 1992, which included $7-million (U.S.) for discontinued operations, Methanex has made a number of acquisitions that will boost its production levels of methanol. In 1992 the total revenues for the company's two business segments, methanol and ammonia operations, amounted to $116.2-million (U.S.), up $42.7-million (U.S.) from 1991 revenues.

During 1992, Methanex completed a number of transactions with Metallgesellschaft Corp. (MG) and its affiliates acquiring a 10% equity interest in Caribbean Methanol Co. Ltd., representing approximately 55,000 tonnes of methanol per year. MG is in the process of constructing a methanol plant in Trinidad, and has exclusive marketing rights to the additional production capacity representing approximately 500,000 tonnes of methanol per year from this plant in exchange for 3,929,256 shares.

As well, Methanex acquired MG's 70% interest in a joint venture to redesign and convert an idle ammonia plant into a methanol plant capable of producing approximately 570,000 tonnes of methanol per year along with MG's methanol marketing and trading operations located in Frankfurt, Germany. As a consideration for this acquisition, Methanex issued 2,912,043 common shares, made a cash payment of $11.7-million and granted MG an option to purchase one million common shares at $9 per share until September 30, 1993.

Methanex is committed to fund $90-million for the conversion of an idle ammonia plant into a methanol plant, and the company has entered into specific purchase commitments, with respect to this obligation, amounting to $25.5-million. Methanex is currently in the process of arranging non-recourse financing for $68-million of its total commitment. Through its ammonia partnership Methanex is currently upgrading its 51% owned facility in Kitimat, B.C., at an estimated cost of $19-million. Methanex also entered into an arrangement with MG for the purchase of approximately 38 million gallons of methanol at MG's holding cost, currently valued at $13.7-million.

Relative strength to TSE300 / Price / Volume (in 1000's of board lots)

Rank (Profit/Revenue/Assets)
889   315   282

Siegfried K. Hodapp
Chairman
Brooke N. Wade
President & C.E.O.
Ken E. Vidalin
Exec. V.P. & C.O.O.

Address
Suite 1000
1055 West Hastings Street
Vancouver
BC
V6E 2E9
(604) 684-7500

Fax: (604) 684-6103
O0000405/G/6.7

SICO INC.

Exchanges	Price (Jun24'93)		13.50	Trailing P/E		11.16	Stock Symbol
TM	Trailing Yield (%)		2.33	Trailing EPS		1.21	**SIC**

Period Ending	Dec92	Dec91	Dec90	Dec89	Dec88
Yearly Statistics					
Price-Close	13.75	9.00	7.50	13.63	10.88
Price-High	14.00	9.63	12.00	16.25	12.75
Price-Low	8.75	7.25	6.50	10.50	9.75
P/E-Close	11.65	nm	18.29	13.49	7.45
Dividends per Share	0.30	0.28	0.44	0.44	0.40
Dividend Yield (%)	2.18	3.11	5.87	3.23	3.68
Sales per Share	30.77	31.76	29.91	41.60	42.44
EPS before extra. item	1.18	(0.85)	0.41	1.01	1.46
Cash Flow per Share	1.68	1.23	1.25	1.89	2.13
Book Value per Share	6.24	5.31	6.10	6.14	5.59
O/S Common Shares	5,027	4,961	4,936	4,911	4,889
Total Revenue	152,959	156,799	146,915	203,446	206,600
Income before extra.	6,239	(3,832)	2,404	5,321	7,462
Cash Flow	8,352	6,082	6,137	9,220	10,385
Debt/Equity	0.54	0.89	1.28	1.38	1.64
Return on Capital (%)	20.89	1.25	9.27	14.68	18.38
Ret. on Com. Equity (%)	20.30	(14.91)	6.72	17.20	28.15
% Change Profit	262.8	(259.4)	(54.8)	(28.7)	10.8
% Change Revenue	(2.4)	6.7	(27.8)	(1.5)	13.8
% Change Assets	(8.5)	(14.0)	(9.1)	(0.7)	11.7

Preferred Div. Coverage	16.4	0.0	6.3
Total Div. Coverage	3.3	0.0	0.9
Interest Coverage	6.3	0.4	2.8
Current Ratio	1.9	1.8	1.8
Operating Margin	7.7	5.5	6.4
Asset Turnover	2.0	1.8	1.5
5 YEAR RATIOS (%)			
Return on Capital	12.9	12.8	17.7
Return on Com. Equity	11.5	13.5	23.1
Profit Growth	(1.5)	na	(17.2)
Revenue Growth	(3.4)	2.5	6.2
Asset Growth	(4.5)	3.7	15.7
BALANCE SHEET (000)			
Cash	216	177	343
Current Assets	50,534	54,472	65,411
Net Fixed Assets	24,039	28,481	30,827
Invest's & Advances	193	0	593
Total Assets	77,906	85,137	98,976
Short Term Debt	7,106	5,054	19,056
Current Liabilities	27,347	29,591	35,765
Long Term Debt	12,000	21,869	24,295
Total Liabilities	42,739	54,974	65,046
Total Equity	35,167	30,163	33,930
Total Liab. & Equity	77,906	85,137	98,976
CAPITAL (000)			
Total Debt	19,106	26,923	43,351
Preferred Equity	3,800	3,800	3,800
Common Equity	31,367	26,363	30,130

Business:

SICO INC. manufactures and distributes trade, industrial, and specialty paints and coatings across Canada. Products include paint, varnish, and stains under the brand names Sico, Crown Diamond, and Mulco. The company has operations in Quebec and Ontario.

Date	EPS	DPS	Tot Rev	Inc Bex
Apr 93	(0.12)	0.08	30,375	(486)
Dec 92	(0.23)	0.08	27,059	(1,043)
Sep 92	0.44	0.08	40,983	2,302
Jun 92	1.12	0.08	54,772	5,654
Mar 92	(0.15)	0.07	30,145	(674)
Dec 91	(1.49)	0.07	27,406	(7,290)
Sep 91	0.31	0.07	42,369	1,636
Jun 91	0.77	0.07	59,182	3,896

Synopsis:

A significant increase in net earnings of $6.2-million for the Sico Group in 1992, up from a net loss of $3.8-million in 1991, was overshadowed by a number of adverse market factors. The recession dampened sales and the liberalization of trade in North America has driven prices down and continues to do so. Benefits came from lower interest rates and the divestiture of operations that did not fit in with Sico Group's core business and did not meet profitability or growth objectives.

The year was one of consolidation and rationalization with the discontinuation of operations that did not fit in with the core business. Gone were Mulco's admixtures operations, the Sterling Group, and the powder paint operations of the Industrial Products Division. Sico will be on the lookout for acquisitions, both in Canada and the U.S. as long as the companies meet its rigorous criteria established with respect to return on equity and market leadership, and fit in with Sico's core business.

Sico expects a very slow market recovery during 1993 and it plans to achieve gains by becoming one of the leading Canadian manufacturers in advanced technology sectors in which they have a definite edge. The best growth potential is expected in Ontario and Sico intends to strengthen its position in industrial sectors where the company enjoys a competitive edge.

The first quarterly figures of 1993 confirmed the gradual pace of growth as sales increased to $30.4-million, slightly higher than the 1992 figures for the same period and a net loss of $486,000 or 12 cents per common share, compared with a net loss of $674,000 or 15 cents per common share, a 28% improvement.

In 1993 Sico began a three-year process to implement the Management Information Systems strategic plan to improve the management of daily operations and enhance customer service.

Relative strength to TSE300 / Price / Volume (in 1000's of board lots)

Rank (Profit/Revenue/Assets)
232 311 462

Jean-Paul Lortie
Chairman Of The Board
Gilles Beauchamp
President & C.E.O.
Gilles Laurin
V.P., Fin., Admin. & Treasurer

Address
2505, De La Metropole
Longueuil
PQ
J4G 1E5
(514) 527-5111

Fax: (514) 651-1257
S0000449/G/6.7

Page	Company	$	Latest year end	Earnings per Share		
				Actual	Estimate this year	Estimate next year
245	Bonar		9212	(1.49)	n.a.	n.a.
246	CCL Industries		9212	0.38	0.49	0.67
247	Consumers Packaging		9212	(0.76)	0.00	0.15
248	International Innopac		9212	(2.50)	0.20	n.a.
249	Lawson Mardon Group		9212	0.58	0.73	0.97

Estimates from I/B/E/S Inc., 345 Hudson St., New York, NY 10014 (212) 243-3335. In Canada: 6 Lansing Square, Ste. 235, Willowdale, ON M2J 1T5 (416) 496-0977.

Packaging & Containers

Canadian soft-drink makers have cut their packaging waste by 53% in the past four years, surpassing the target set out under the National Packaging Protocol. The protocol - an agreement between the federal government and Canadian packaging industries - requires the companies to reduce the amount of packaging sent for disposal to half of 1988 levels by the year 2000. The Canadian Soft Drink Association said the industry used 234 kilograms of packaging, including such things as pallets, trays and cans, for every 1,000 litres of soft drinks produced last year, compared with 453 kilograms for 1,000 litres in 1988. Almost 60% of the reduction is a result of the shift in sales to recyclable containers such as metal cans and polyethylene terephalate (PET) bottles from refillable glass containers.

The Grocery Products Manufacturers of Canada, an association representing 165 manufacturers, is proposing to have industry members pay a levy, based on weight, for the packaging they use. Under a "conceptual model" developed by the association, levies would be collected by a newly created industry organization that would use the money to encourage municipal multimaterial recycling programs and the development of markets for recyclable materials.

Representatives of the 700 Canadian packaging manufacturers announced the adoption of a voluntary code that will reduce the amount of packaging going into landfills to half the current amount - about nine million tonnes - by the year 2000. If packaging is not reduced by that amount, manufacturers will see improperly packaged products banned from the marketplace or face heavy fines The adoption of the Canadian Code of Preferred Packaging Practices comes as manufacturers are trying to retool plants to make new, slimmed-down packages and use recycled materials.

Containers & Packaging - Industry Report [Apr-13-1993]. MER-RILL LYNCH CAPITAL MARKETS reported by Palm, R.S
Ball's 1993 beverage can segment profits are under pressure from prices that are an estimated 10% below the year ago level. The cost of aluminum can sheet has declined, and Ball is reducing the weight of its cans and streamlining its operations. However, the cost reductions are not enough to fully offset lower realizations. Aerospace profits have been reduced by an extremely competitive environment as defense contractors compete for less business. Bemis' profits in Europe have declined, reflecting poor general economic trends and currency fluctuations. The company's businesses in the U.S. and Canada, which accounted for 90% of 1992's operating profit, are benefiting from better general economic trends. Sonoco's 1Q:93 earnings should be strong despite poor general economic trends in Europe. Profits should benefit from continued general economic growth in North America while the recent sale of the European plastic bag operations eliminates a business that had been running at a loss. [RN 1322057]

Packaging Wrap-Up - Industry Report [Apr-13-1993]. PAINEWEBBER INC. reported by Staphos, G.L.
Continental Can Co. reported a better 4Q:92 and obtained needed catalysts from the Bundesbank's interest rate cuts. Ball Corporation is expected to see a slow 1Q:93. First, Ball's furnace expansion at its Ruston, LA glass plant is slow to come on line. The expansion, required to produce glass containers efficiently under a recently awarded, but competitively-priced food glass contract, will not get desired efficiency levels until 2H:93. [RN 1323093]

Packaging Wrap Up: Conference Highlights - Industry Report [Mar-29-1993]. PAINEWEBBER INC. reported by Staphos, G.L.
The packaging life cycle favors different materials at different stages of economic developments. International markets: PET still appears to be the globally hot beverage package, followed by cans. Glass' share increasingly eroded, but "upscale" packaging still an opportunity. Products and services cited include glass containers, and plastic containers. [RN 1319368]

BONAR INC.

Exchanges	Price (Jun24'93)		23.75	Trailing P/E		nm	Stock Symbol
T	Trailing Yield (%)		0.84	Trailing EPS		(1.27)	**BON**

Period Ending	Nov92	Nov91	Dec90	Dec89	Dec88
Yearly Statistics					
Price-Close	20.00	22.00	23.50	24.00	24.25
Price-High	26.00	26.13	24.50	26.00	26.00
Price-Low	20.00	22.00	22.00	23.00	16.00
P/E-Close	nm	21.78	11.41	15.09	10.54
Dividends per Share	0.20	0.35	0.40	0.52	0.52
Dividend Yield (%)	1.00	1.59	1.70	2.17	2.14
Sales per Share	39.63	41.84	41.54	47.56	46.62
EPS before extra. item	(1.49)	1.01	2.06	1.59	2.30
Cash Flow per Share	(0.94)	2.89	3.28	2.92	3.64
Book Value per Share	18.31	19.64	19.08	17.37	16.40
O/S Common Shares	4,898	4,898	4,898	4,898	4,898
Total Revenue	194,081	204,942	203,460	232,922	228,362
Income before extra.	(7,301)	4,916	10,074	7,769	11,257
Cash Flow	(4,595)	14,165	16,071	14,304	17,842
Debt/Equity	0.35	0.13	0.11	0.23	0.31
Return on Capital (%)	(7.33)	9.03	17.01	14.37	21.35
Ret. on Com. Equity (%)	(7.86)	5.18	11.29	9.39	14.66
% Change Profit	(248.5)	(51.2)	29.7	(31.0)	20.4
% Change Revenue	(5.3)	0.7	(12.6)	2.0	13.9
% Change Assets	13.5	6.4	1.7	(6.0)	22.0

Date	EPS	DPS	Tot Rev	Inc Bex
Feb 93	0.36	0.05	45,357	1,742
Nov 92	(2.12)	0.05	47,861	(10,364)
Aug 92	0.14	0.05	47,862	648
May 92	0.35	0.05	51,959	1,737
Feb 92	0.14	0.05	46,399	678
Nov 91	0.00	0.09	50,968	(38)
Aug 91	0.16	0.10	49,184	773
Jun 91	0.45	0.10	53,235	2,240

Preferred Div. Coverage	np	np	np
Total Div. Coverage	0.0	2.9	5.1
Interest Coverage	na	na	14.6
Current Ratio	1.2	1.8	2.1
Operating Margin	5.0	6.7	8.7
Asset Turnover	1.2	1.4	1.5
5 YEAR RATIOS (%)			
Return on Capital	10.9	16.4	18.7
Return on Com. Equity	6.5	10.9	12.8
Profit Growth	na	(9.0)	6.5
Revenue Growth	(0.7)	4.3	7.8
Asset Growth	7.0	5.1	11.5
BALANCE SHEET (000)			
Cash	12,768	1,379	0
Current Assets	81,748	73,575	67,492
Net Fixed Assets	79,629	67,552	64,799
Invest's & Advances	0	0	1,276
Total Assets	166,172	146,374	137,596
Short Term Debt	31,119	11,931	9,901
Current Liabilities	68,120	40,196	32,177
Long Term Debt	0	50	171
Total Liabilities	76,495	50,181	44,146
Total Equity	89,677	96,193	93,450
Total Liab. & Equity	166,172	146,374	137,596
CAPITAL (000)			
Total Debt	31,119	11,981	10,072
Preferred Equity	0	0	0
Common Equity	89,677	96,193	93,450

Business:

BONAR INC. is a manufacturer of flexible packaging, plastic films and bags and rotationally molded plastics. The company operates in Canada and the United States. It supplies products to many industries in the United States and Canada, including food processing, fishing, chemicals, construction, and agribusiness.

Synopsis:

Economic activity for Bonar Inc. remained sluggish although there were signs that its expansion into the U.S. market has been effective in increasing demand, and there is a ongoing attempt to creatively market products.

Although Bonar remains cautious about the general economic environment throughout North America and the effects of free trade, the company is confident the significant cost reductions and restructuring programs put into effect during the last quarter of 1992 will continue to provide a solid base for future profit improvement. As part of that new program Bonar is planning to close the Fredericton, New Brunswick, manufacturing facility.

Results for the three months ended February 27, 1993, show sales of $45.4-million, a drop of 2% from the equivalent period last year, but 14% higher for ongoing business. Operating income of almost $3-million was jump of 143%. Profit before income taxes soared by 152%, to $2.9-million. Earnings per share was 36 cents and an unchanged dividend of five cents per share was declared payable on May 15, 1993.

In 1992 a major restructuring was undertaken to achieve a more competitive cost base and improve on Bonar's responsiveness to the demands of a competitive market. The financial impact of the restructuring program is a pre-tax charge of $17.5-million against income to cover losses on disposal of assets, the write-off of redundant assets, employee severance and plant closure costs associated with the consolidation and restructuring of facilities.

Technical expertise in the design and manufacture of rigid plastics has created a diverse product group, ranging from garden composters to recycled plastics, to double-walled, insulated containers for temperature sensitive products.

Relative strength to TSE300
Price
Volume (in 1000's of board lots)

Rank (Profit/Revenue/Assets)
858 279 341

J.W. Leng
Chairman

J.L. Heilig
C.E.O. & President

Todd D.G. Eby
V.P., Finance & C.F.O.

Address
2380 McDowell Road
Burlington
ON
L7R 4A1
(416) 637-5611

Fax: (416) 637-9954
B0021687/G/6.8

CCL INDUSTRIES INC.

Exchanges	Price (Jun24'93)	8 .25	Trailing P/E	6 .02	Stock Symbol
TM	Trailing Yield (%)	3 .39	Trailing EPS	1 .37	**CCQ.B**

Period Ending	Dec92	Dec91	Dec90	Dec89	Dec88
Yearly Statistics					
Price-Close	9 .38	9 .50	8 .00	9 .50	10 .75
Price-High	10 .38	11 .88	10 .13	14 .25	11 .50
Price-Low	7 .50	8 .00	7 .00	9 .25	6 .50
P/E-Close	6 .84	950 .00	13 .56	3 .86	15 .14
Dividends per Share	0 .28	0 .28	0 .28	0 .26	0 .24
Dividend Yield (%)	2 .99	2 .95	3 .50	2 .74	2 .23
Sales per Share	21 .58	18 .19	14 .52	12 .07	11 .38
EPS before extra. item	1 .37	0 .01	0 .59	2 .46	0 .71
Cash Flow per Share	1 .28	0 .97	1 .46	1 .05	0 .81
Book Value per Share	9 .21	7 .82	8 .13	7 .70	5 .52
O/S Common Shares	32 ,907	32 ,870	32 ,695	32 ,475	31 ,819
Total Revenue	758 ,854	621 ,711	476 ,678	385 ,920	357 ,851
Income before extra.	44 ,708	185	18 ,982	78 ,495	22 ,083
Cash Flow	41 ,958	31 ,674	47 ,714	33 ,628	25 ,345
Debt/Equity	0 .82	0 .77	0 .75	0 .78	1 .23
Return on Capital (%)	16 .59	4 .81	8 .95	19 .50	9 .10
Ret. on Com. Equity (%)	15 .96	0 .07	7 .36	36 .87	13 .13
% Change Profit	nm	(99 .0)	(75 .8)	255 .5	174 .5
% Change Revenue	22 .1	30 .4	23 .5	7 .8	(52 .3)
% Change Assets	23 .3	5 .2	(5 .2)	30 .9	(23 .0)

Business:

CCL INDUSTRIES INC. is active in three major business segments. The Custom Manufacturing Division produces many of the household, personal care, and cosmetic products. The Container Division manufactures aluminum spray containers and tubes. The Label Division produces the labels used in a broad spectrum of products. Based in Canada, CCL operates 33 facilities throughout North America, Europe and Australia.

Date	EPS	DPS	Tot Rev	Inc Bex
Mar 93	0 .09	0 .07	203 ,823	2 ,888
Dec 92	0 .09	0 .07	188 ,802	2 ,915
Sep 92	1 .09	0 .07	225 ,830	35 ,762
Jun 92	0 .10	0 .07	168 ,921	3 ,278
Mar 92	0 .09	0 .07	174 ,233	2 ,753
Dec 91	(0 .04)	0 .07	147 ,581	(1 ,121)
Sep 91	(0 .13)	0 .07	175 ,294	(4 ,331)
Jun 91	0 .10	0 .07	159 ,305	3 ,232

	Dec92	Dec91	Dec90
Preferred Div. Coverage	np	np	np
Total Div. Coverage	5 .0	0 .0	2 .2
Interest Coverage	5 .0	1 .0	2 .6
Current Ratio	1 .3	1 .1	1 .2
Operating Margin	5 .6	5 .2	6 .4
Asset Turnover	1 .0	1 .0	0 .8
5 YEAR RATIOS (%)			
Return on Capital	11 .8	8 .9	11 .0
Return on Com. Equity	14 .7	8 .2	10 .5
Profit Growth	na	(61 .9)	(10 .5)
Revenue Growth	0 .2	(2 .3)	(6 .2)
Asset Growth	4 .4	1 .0	2 .7
BALANCE SHEET (000)			
Cash	0	0	0
Current Assets	314 ,651	164 ,742	137 ,352
Net Fixed Assets	248 ,227	214 ,381	182 ,467
Invest's & Advances	50 ,000	100 ,000	150 ,000
Total Assets	737 ,442	598 ,211	568 ,422
Short Term Debt	60 ,670	12 ,551	13 ,930
Current Liabilities	239 ,583	155 ,267	116 ,171
Long Term Debt	188 ,122	185 ,766	186 ,495
Total Liabilities	434 ,517	341 ,033	302 ,666
Total Equity	302 ,925	257 ,178	265 ,756
Total Liab. & Equity	737 ,442	598 ,211	568 ,422
CAPITAL (000)			
Total Debt	248 ,792	198 ,317	200 ,425
Preferred Equity	0	0	0
Common Equity	302 ,925	257 ,178	265 ,756

Synopsis:

CCL Industries Inc. has capped off four years of growth, consolidation and expansion that has left it in a solid position and it is now poised for another phase of international expansion. However, an attempt to purchase a major European consumer goods manufacturer, believed to be British Petroleum Co. plc's Robert McBride unit which makes private label domestic cleaning products, was withdrawn, costing the company $1.1-million.

After acquiring 11 companies in the past three years, all of which are located outside of Canada, and becoming the largest custom product manufacturer in North America, CCL is slowing the pace in an effort to strengthen its existing businesses.

In 1992 CCL purchased the former Shulton plant in Memphis, Tennessee, manufacturer of Old Spice products, for $1.8-million. CCL also sold more than 2.5 million shares of Crown Cork and Seal for $102.4-million, for a gain of $48.2-million, and may sell its remaining stake in the company which would bring in about $100-million after tax. CCL acquired the assets of The Barr Company of Niles, Illinois, the second largest North American custom manufacturer of aerosols and liquids for $13.2-million, and also acquired the assets of the pressure sensitive label business of Kimball Aim in Toronto for $2.1-million.

CCL's continuous improvement programs have enhanced profits from improved service, better and constant quality and reduced costs through the elimination of non value-added activities.

In 1989, 65% of $385.7-million worth of sales were in Canada. By 1992, only 25% per cent of the $709.6-million in sales were in Canada with 61% in the U.S., 12% in the U.K., and 2% in Mexico. In the first quarter of 1993, sales increased by 17% to $203.8-million from $174.2-million the previous year. Net income increased to $2.9-million from $2.8-million. Earnings were reduced from 11 cents per share to nine cents per share because of the special projects expense of $1.1-million.

Relative strength to TSE300

Price

Volume (in 1000's of board lots)

Rank (Profit/Revenue/Assets)
65 125 177

Gordon S. Lang
Chairman

Wayne M.E. McLeod
President & C.E.O.

Mel H. Snider
Sr. V.P., Finance & Admin.

Gary W. Ullman
C.E.O., CCL Custom Manufacture

Address
105 Gordon Baker Road
Suite 800
Willowdale
ON
M2H 3P8
(416) 756-8500

Fax: (416) 756-8555
C0005879/G/6.8

CONSUMERS PACKAGING INC.

Exchanges	Price (Jun24'93)		1 .60	Trailing P/E		nm	Stock Symbol
T	Trailing Yield (%)		0 .00	Trailing EPS		(0 .88)	**CGC**

Period Ending	Dec92	Dec91	Dec90	Dec89	Dec88
Yearly Statistics					
Price-Close	1 .90	2 .90	4 .00	17 .00	22 .00
Price-High	4 .50	5 .25	18 .00	25 .50	23 .50
Price-Low	0 .40	1 .95	3 .90	16 .00	12 .00
P/E-Close	nm	nm	nm	nm	nm
Dividends per Share	0 .00	0 .00	0 .38	0 .90	0 .90
Dividend Yield (%)	0 .00	0 .00	9 .50	5 .29	4 .09
Sales per Share	15 .81	15 .73	25 .20	31 .14	30 .01
EPS before extra. item	(1 .35)	(2 .76)	(3 .01)	(0 .66)	(3 .43)
Cash Flow per Share	0 .16	(0 .69)	(0 .80)	1 .18	1 .04
Book Value per Share	2 .20	3 .55	6 .31	9 .47	4 .40
O/S Common Shares	25 ,948	25 ,948	25 ,948	20 ,758	12 ,942
Total Revenue	414 ,236	419 ,417	579 ,642	573 ,870	391 ,623
Income before extra.	(35 ,149)	(71 ,563)	(69 ,037)	(10 ,960)	(42 ,743)
Cash Flow	4 ,022	(17 ,851)	(18 ,481)	21 ,297	13 ,405
Debt/Equity	4 .57	2 .85	1 .73	1 .27	1 .43
Return on Capital (%)	(4 .48)	(12 .20)	(7 .15)	0 .56	(22 .30)
Ret. on Com. Equity (%)	(47 .19)	(55 .95)	na	(9 .06)	(51 .89)
% Change Profit	50 .9	(3 .7)	(529 .9)	74 .4	(384 .4)
% Change Revenue	(1 .2)	(27 .6)	1 .0	46 .5	(3 .3)
% Change Assets	(11 .3)	(16 .6)	(3 .8)	67 .8	19 .8

Period Ending	Dec92	Dec91	Dec90
Preferred Div. Coverage	0 .0	0 .0	na
Total Div. Coverage	0 .0	0 .0	0 .0
Interest Coverage	0 .0	0 .0	0 .0
Current Ratio	0 .8	1 .3	1 .0
Operating Margin	(1 .0)	(4 .7)	(5 .4)
Asset Turnover	1 .0	0 .9	1 .1
5 YEAR RATIOS (%)			
Return on Capital	(9 .1)	(4 .7)	1 .9
Return on Com. Equity	na	na	na
Profit Growth	na	na	na
Revenue Growth	0 .5	2 .0	10 .3
Asset Growth	7 .4	9 .8	16 .4
BALANCE SHEET (000)			
Cash	0	0	37 ,374
Current Assets	169 ,223	191 ,433	194 ,764
Net Fixed Assets	231 ,467	257 ,444	346 ,886
Invest's & Advances	0	0	0
Total Assets	401 ,435	452 ,520	542 ,440
Short Term Debt	138 ,450	58 ,523	101 ,720
Current Liabilities	212 ,003	144 ,924	187 ,196
Long Term Debt	124 ,325	205 ,487	182 ,365
Total Liabilities	343 ,923	359 ,831	378 ,086
Total Equity	57 ,512	92 ,689	164 ,354
Total Liab. & Equity	401 ,435	452 ,520	542 ,440
CAPITAL (000)			
Total Debt	262 ,775	264 ,010	284 ,085
Preferred Equity	558	558	558
Common Equity	56 ,954	92 ,131	163 ,796

Business:

CONSUMERS PACKAGING INC. makes and markets glass containers. Customers include the food, beverage, dairy, pharmaceutical, household product, toiletries and cosmetics industries in Canada and the United States. Consolidated Enfield Corp. has a 57.6% equity interest in the company.

Date	EPS	DPS	Tot Rev	Inc Bex
Mar 93	(0.02)	0.00	85 ,994	(421)
Dec 92	(0.61)	0.00	101 ,878	(15 ,925)
Sep 92	(0.29)	0.00	127 ,624	(7 ,570)
Jun 92	0.04	0.00	157 ,510	1 ,157
Mar 92	(0.49)	0.00	85 ,732	(12 ,811)
Dec 91	(2.21)	0.00	95 ,606	(57 ,262)
Sep 91	(0.23)	0.00	135 ,032	(5 ,916)
Jun 91	0.04	0.00	162 ,020	869

Synopsis:

In the first quarter of 1993, Consumers Packaging sold two divisions in an effort to reduce debt and concentrate on the company's core business of making glass containers. In 1992, Consumers Packaging's glass container business accounted for 77% of total sales.

In April 1993, Consumers sold its custom plastic bottles unit to Graham Packaging Co. Plax Inc., Canada's largest producer of custom plastic bottles. The company operates two plants in Burlington and Mississauga, Ontario. Terms of the deal were not disclosed.

In January 1993, Consumers sold its Portion Packaging division to Winipak Ltd. Portion Packaging was sold for $57-million and the price could increase to $61-million depending on how much the division makes in 1993. The Portion Packaging division is one of North America's largest makers of individual semi-rigid plastic packaging for creamers, margarine blends and condiments. The proceeds from the sale will be used to pay debts, including a $27.7-million principal payment due November 1, 1992, and to improve working capital.

Besides the overdue debt payable November 1, 1992, Consumers Packaging defaulted on its interest payments to debenture holders on June 1, 1993. The debenture holders were expected to receive their interest payment on May 1, 1993, but a grace period of 30 days extended the deadline to June 1, 1993. It is now up to the debenture holders to decide if any action will be taken to petition the company into receivership.

In late 1992, Consumers Packaging was delisted from the TSE 300 share composite index. A Toronto Stock Exchange official said the move reflects the reduced market capitalization of the publicly held shares of Consumers.

Relative strength to TSE300

Price

Volume (in 1000's of board lots)

Rank (Profit/Revenue/Assets)
940   182   238

R. Bryan McJannet
Chairman Of The Board

James C. Bacon
President & C.E.O.

Brian K. Higgins
V.P., Finance

Address
401 The West Mall
Suite 900
Etobicoke
ON
M9C 5J7
(416) 232-3309

Fax: (416) 232-3314
C0009364/G/6.8

INTERNATIONAL INNOPAC INC.

Exchanges	Price (Jun24'93)	14.00	Trailing P/E	nm	Stock Symbol
TM	Trailing Yield (%)	0.00	Trailing EPS	(1.95)	**INO**

Period Ending	Dec92	Dec91	Dec90	Aug90	Aug89
Yearly Statistics			16M		
Price-Close	13.00	10.63	6.75	22.50	52.50
Price-High	13.63	11.13	23.00	54.38	62.50
Price-Low	10.25	5.00	6.75	22.50	48.75
P/E-Close	nm	nm	nm	nm	52.50
Dividends per Share	0.00	0.00	1.20	1.20	1.20
Dividend Yield (%)	0.00	0.00	17.78	5.33	2.29
Sales per Share	69.21	89.79	104.90	105.51	105.77
EPS before extra. item	(2.50)	(4.16)	(6.11)	(4.55)	1.00
Cash Flow per Share	4.20	4.45	4.36	4.79	7.77
Book Value per Share	23.73	24.19	32.94	34.30	41.08
O/S Common Shares	3,449	3,449	2,759	2,759	2,759
Total Revenue	238,681	260,949	386,175	282,709	292,932
Income before extra.	(8,609)	(12,081)	(16,881)	(12,564)	2,730
Cash Flow	14,477	12,912	16,026	13,202	21,424
Debt/Equity	0.93	1.23	1.34	1.31	1.07
Return on Capital (%)	1.54	0.49	(0.07)	0.09	5.95
Ret. on Com. Equity (%)	(10.42)	(13.86)	(13.65)	(12.08)	2.35
% Change Profit	28.7	4.6	(0.8)	(560.2)	(73.3)
% Change Revenue	(8.5)	(9.9)	2.4	(3.5)	15.4
% Change Assets	(10.5)	(11.2)	(3.1)	(8.1)	22.8

Preferred Div. Coverage	np	np	np
Total Div. Coverage	na	na	0.0
Interest Coverage	0.3	0.1	0.0
Current Ratio	1.8	2.2	1.7
Operating Margin	1.7	1.6	2.1
Asset Turnover	1.2	1.2	1.2

5 YEAR RATIOS (%)			
Return on Capital	1.6	3.3	4.8
Return on Com. Equity	(9.5)	(5.8)	(1.8)
Profit Growth	na	na	na
Revenue Growth	(1.3)	3.4	6.4
Asset Growth	(2.7)	1.6	2.5

BALANCE SHEET (000)			
Cash	2,972	2,028	556
Current Assets	61,211	64,463	75,480
Net Fixed Assets	101,177	117,391	127,234
Invest's & Advances	0	0	0
Total Assets	192,207	214,649	241,691
Short Term Debt	2,790	4,893	20,795
Current Liabilities	33,820	28,941	45,497
Long Term Debt	73,126	97,966	100,912
Total Liabilities	110,367	131,247	150,795
Total Equity	81,840	83,402	90,896
Total Liab. & Equity	192,207	214,649	241,691

CAPITAL (000)			
Total Debt	75,916	102,859	121,707
Preferred Equity	0	0	0
Common Equity	81,840	83,402	90,896

Date	EPS	DPS	Tot Rev	Inc Bex
Mar 93	(0.61)	0.00	60,533	(2,090)
Dec 92	(0.62)	0.00	61,417	(2,137)
Sep 92	(0.69)	0.00	58,375	(2,367)
Jun 92	(0.03)	0.00	59,929	(105)
Mar 92	(1.16)	0.00	59,018	(4,000)
Dec 91	(2.19)	0.00	62,959	(6,636)
Sep 91	(0.79)	0.00	63,988	(2,176)
Jun 91	(0.38)	0.00	67,506	(1,107)

Business:

INTERNATIONAL INNOPAC is a group of companies providing packaging products and systems to food service, pharmaceutical and industrial customers in North America. Company operations in Ontario, Quebec and the eastern United States produce foam products, injection molded containers, flexible packaging, corrugated plastics, rigid packaging systems and extruded, collapsible aluminum tubes.

Synopsis:

Jim Pattison Industries Ltd. increased its hold on International Innopac Inc. by purchasing 53,200 common shares to bring its total to more than 1.5 million common shares, or 43.68% of the outstanding shares of Innopac.

Innopac's sales for the first quarter of 1993 increased 8% over the same period in 1992. However, half of this increase is a result of the effect of a stronger U.S. dollar and the conversion of U.S. sales of the company into Canadian dollars.

Nevertheless after provision for income taxes, Innopac recorded a net loss of $2-million, or 61 cents per share as compared to a net loss of $4-million, or $1.16 per share in the first quarter of 1992. In 1992, sales from continuing operations improved slightly over 1991, when reported in Canadian dollars. Innopac recorded a net loss of $8.6-million for 1992, compared to a net loss of $12.1-million for 1991 after providing for the losses on the disposal of the assets of Mammoth Containers. The $5.1-million in 1991 and 1992 loss on the sale of certain assets and the operations of Mammoth arises from the write-off of goodwill of $3.1-million and other costs of $2.3-million offset by a gain on sale of net assets of $300,000. Including the debt assumed on the sale of Mammoth, term debt has been reduced by $27-million to $75.9-million in 1992, in addition to the reduction of $18.8-million to $102.9-million in 1991.

Innopac is planning to maintain the status quo, referring to the slow recovery from the recession as keeping a cap on sales, and it is planning no material change in operations. No major acquisitions or changes in operations are anticipated, but Innopac continues to work to resolve operating problems in certain divisions.

Free trade is effecting Innopac through the loss of customers transferring their operations to the U.S. The Canadian operations are offsetting this loss of sales volume by pursuing sales in U.S. markets.

Relative strength to TSE300

Rank (Profit/Revenue/Assets)
872 247 326

Jim Pattison
Chairman, President & C.E.O.

Address
Suite 1600
1055 West Hastings Street
Vancouver
BC
V6E 2H2
(604) 688-6764

Fax: (604) 687-2601
I0010637/G/6.8

LAWSON MARDON GROUP LIMITED

Exchanges		Price (Jun24'93)	9.37	Trailing P/E		18.75	Stock Symbol
TMA		Trailing Yield (%)	4.27	Trailing EPS		0.50	**LMP.A**

Period Ending	Dec92	Dec91	Dec90	Dec89	Dec88
Yearly Statistics					
Price-Close	9.25	9.75	8.25	10.75	12.63
Price-High	10.88	10.13	10.75	13.13	15.25
Price-Low	8.38	7.63	7.50	10.25	11.13
P/E-Close	15.95	nm	9.27	11.69	8.71
Dividends per Share	0.40	0.40	0.40	0.40	0.30
Dividend Yield (%)	4.32	4.10	4.85	3.72	2.38
Sales per Share	42.45	41.80	37.59	34.60	38.51
EPS before extra. item	0.58	(0.38)	0.89	0.92	1.45
Cash Flow per Share	1.71	2.32	2.21	1.50	2.10
Book Value per Share	11.25	12.36	13.19	11.60	11.31
O/S Common Shares	39,661	28,609	28,609	28,826	28,837
Total Revenue	1,297,636	1,199,290	1,084,049	1,004,847	1,119,186
Income before extra.	17,397	(10,840)	25,472	26,418	41,948
Cash Flow	51,677	66,301	63,482	43,305	60,670
Debt/Equity	0.86	0.99	0.96	0.70	0.76
Return on Capital (%)	9.67	5.73	11.22	11.92	15.79
Ret. on Com. Equity (%)	4.35	(2.97)	7.16	8.00	13.48
% Change Profit	260.5	(142.6)	(3.6)	(37.0)	51.7
% Change Revenue	8.2	10.6	7.9	(10.2)	7.9
% Change Assets	13.8	(1.4)	25.3	(4.6)	(0.2)

Preferred Div. Coverage	np	np	np
Total Div. Coverage	1.4	0.0	2.2
Interest Coverage	1.6	0.9	1.8
Current Ratio	1.3	1.1	1.3
Operating Margin	6.5	6.7	7.6
Asset Turnover	1.2	1.2	1.1
5 YEAR RATIOS (%)			
Return on Capital	10.9	12.1	14.0
Return on Com. Equity	6.0	8.2	14.0
Profit Growth	(8.9)	na	12.1
Revenue Growth	4.5	6.0	5.1
Asset Growth	6.0	7.6	7.5
BALANCE SHEET (000)			
Cash	36,110	110	164
Current Assets	429,664	329,717	341,703
Net Fixed Assets	425,873	364,076	351,506
Invest's & Advances	6,534	23,722	26,130
Total Assets	1,113,787	978,356	991,870
Short Term Debt	95,317	51,925	51,330
Current Liabilities	339,206	294,092	268,816
Long Term Debt	289,598	296,684	309,162
Total Liabilities	667,431	624,847	614,530
Total Equity	446,356	353,509	377,340
Total Liab. & Equity	1,113,787	978,356	991,870
CAPITAL (000)			
Total Debt	384,915	348,609	360,492
Preferred Equity	0	0	0
Common Equity	446,356	353,509	377,340

Business:

LAWSON MARDON GROUP LTD. is a packaging company with operations in Canada, the United States, Britain, Ireland, Germany and France. The company produces folding cartons, flexible packaging, blow-molded plastic containers, open-top cans, decorated tinware and composite containers and paper labels.

Date	EPS	DPS	Tot Rev	Inc Bex
Mar 93	0.13	0.10	304,278	5,284
Dec 92	0.41	0.10	339,466	12,500
Sep 92	0.13	0.10	328,502	3,771
Jun 92	(0.17)	0.10	320,390	(4,963)
Mar 92	0.21	0.10	309,278	6,089
Dec 91	(0.88)	0.10	303,069	(25,141)
Sep 91	0.01	0.10	285,400	416
Jun 91	0.29	0.10	294,978	8,278

Synopsis:

Deteriorating economic performances in Germany, France and Spain, flat economies in the U.K. and Italy, and hesitant growth in North America did not prevent Lawson Mardon Group from maintaining strong earnings for the first quarter of 1993. Net income of $5.3-million (13 cents per share) on sales of $303.8-million was slightly lower than the $6.1-million (21 cents per share) on sales of $308.6-million in 1992.

Earnings from trading, exclusive of the impact resulting from the weakness of the British pound against the Canadian dollar, and after removing the effects of acquisitions and divestments, rose by approximately $2.1-million during the first quarter. In 1992 trading increased to $80.1-million from $77.7- million in 1991.

Lawson Mardon has taken aggressive action to cut costs, increase productivity and improve on its ability to make profit. It is positioning Lawson Mardon to become a global packaging company and to successfully manage the most fundamental change the industry has ever experienced.

Lawson Mardon took advantage of the soft market to purchase Suner in Spain in 1992 and Seleprint, a flexible packaging company near Milan in northern Italy in 1993. The moves were critical steps in its strategy to increase its continental presence, and to achieve pan-European levels of service to global customers. Lawson Mardon is carrying a debt load of $207-million. It will pay $37-million this year and expects to retire most of the debt by 1997.

In 1992 the North America group entered the Latin American marketplace to take advantage of possible North American Free Trade advantages. In an effort to cut down on costs and streamline operations, more stringent quality standards are being implemented on every facility. By the end of 1993, most of the Lawson Mardon companies will be ISO 9000 quality certified and maintaining high quality levels in production.

Rank (Profit/Revenue/Assets)		
132	90	145

William Blundel
Chairman

Andrea Mattiussi
President & C.E.O.

John B. Lanaway
Sr. V.P., North America

Marcel Pilon
C.O.O., North America

Sergio Marchionne
Group V.P., C.F.O. & Secty.

Address
Suite 700
6733 Mississauga Rd.
Mississauga
ON
L5N 6P6
(416) 821-9711

L0001139/G/6.8

Page	Company	$	Latest year end	Earnings per Share		
				Actual	Estimate this year	Estimate next year
253	BF Realty Holdings		9112	(0.23)	n.a.	n.a.
254	Bramalea		9210	(9.72)	(0.10)	0.02
255	Cambridge Shopping Centres		9203	0.66	0.50	0.48
256	Camdev		9301	(2.16)	n.a.	n.a.
257	Carena Developments		9210	0.23	0.15	0.15
258	Consolidated Carma		9212	0.61	0.40	0.40
259	Consolidated HCI Holdings		9209	(0.95)	n.a.	n.a.
260	Coscan Development		9212	0.02	0.23	0.31
261	Intrawest		9209	1.03	0.50	0.55
262	Markborough Properties		9301	0.15	0.10	0.11
263	Melcor Developments		9212	1.68	0.55	0.50
264	Revenue Properties Company		9212	(0.27)	0.03	0.04
265	Royal LePage		9212	(1.04)	(1.23)	(0.55)
266	Trizec		9210	0.28	0.03	0.03

Estimates from I/B/E/S Inc., 345 Hudson St., New York, NY 10014 (212) 243-3335. In Canada: 6 Lansing Square, Ste. 235, Willowdale, ON M2J 1T5 (416) 496-0977.

According to Royal LePage's national survey of vacancy rates, Canada's national office vacancy rate will fall slightly in 1993 with larger declines expected in 1994 and 1995. Canada's office vacancy rate stood at 19.5% at the end of 1992. Hamilton had the highest office vacancy rate at 27.4%. Metro Toronto had the second highest vacancy rate with 24.6% of office space unoccupied. In Toronto's downtown core, the vacancy rate stood at 21.8% in 1992. The vacancy rate in downtown Toronto is expected to be 21.0% in 1993, 19% in 1994 and drop to about 16% by 1995. Office vacancy rates at the end of 1992 for Montreal and Vancouver were 21.7% and 16.9%, respectively.

Royal LePage's national survey of housing prices, which was released on in July 1993, states low interest rates and stable house prices have failed to spark a recovery in the housing market in Eastern Canada. The quarterly survey suggests the market in British Columbia continues to outpace the rest of the country. Prices in the Vancouver area for a large four or five bedroom house have risen by as much as 34% since July 1992. The prices of these homes range from $255,000 in the Maple Ridge area to $810,000 in Vancouver's Westside. In Toronto, the oversupplied condominium market continues to take a beating. The median price of a two-bedroom condo has fallen 10% to $115,000 since July 1992.

Canada Mortgage and Housing Corp. reported that national housing starts for May 1993 declined compared to last year. Two years ago, CMHC predicted that Canada would require almost 200,000 new homes a year from 1991 until 1996. In contrast, only 156,000 units were built in 1991 and only 168,000 units in 1992. Figures for the first five months of 1993 suggest even fewer units will be built this year. The construction of houses was hurt by an oversupply in the market, particularly from condominiums. CMHC expects housing starts to increase to 190,400 units in 1994 with Vancouver and Victoria leading the way.

The market in Greater Toronto has been weak for three years now with the supply of new housing starts running at about half the level shown in demographic demand forecasts released by CMHC. CMHC statistics for Greater Toronto show 20,770 housing starts for 1992, with a forecast of 21,300 for 1993. Housing starts in Toronto totaled 46,522 in 1987, 38,741 in 1988, 35,184 in 1989 and 18,723 in 1990.

While new home construction has been slow, activity in the resale market is picking up. The Canadian Real Estate Association says 20,461 existing homes traded hands in May, 1993, up 5.5% compared to the same period last year. This marks the first time this year that Canada's 25 major markets posted an overall sales increase. Calgary had the most activity.

Lower residential real estate prices across some markets in Canada have forced lenders of mortgages on these properties to repossess thousands of houses. This has added to the oversupply presently being experienced in the residential housing market in Canada. The totalfigure held in mortgages by lenders is estimated to be several billion dollars.

BF REALTY HOLDINGS LIMITED

Exchanges	Price (Jun24'93)	0.06	Trailing P/E	nm	Stock Symbol
TZ	Trailing Yield (%)	0.00	Trailing EPS	(0.19)	BFR

Period Ending	Dec91	Dec90	Dec89	Dec88	Dec87
Yearly Statistics					
Price-Close	0.03	0.13	1.21	3.10	2.35
Price-High	0.17	1.24	3.85	4.10	5.00
Price-Low	0.03	0.10	1.10	2.45	1.90
P/E-Close	nm	nm	nm	nm	78.33
Dividends per Share	0.00	0.00	0.00	0.00	0.00
Dividend Yield (%)	0.00	0.00	0.00	0.00	0.00
Sales per Share	0.64	0.94	0.83	5.08	2.31
EPS before extra. item	(0.23)	(1.64)	(4.33)	(0.06)	0.03
Cash Flow per Share	(0.03)	(0.20)	(0.39)	0.04	0.15
Book Value per Share	(2.85)	(2.68)	(1.08)	2.96	3.48
O/S Common Shares	166,015	166,012	166,012	165,967	165,880
Total Revenue	122,637	191,313	168,439	882,688	453,683
Income before extra.	(28,336)	(262,679)	(709,763)	44	12,727
Cash Flow	(4,509)	(32,497)	(65,039)	6,817	24,313
Debt/Equity	na	na	na	2.88	2.82
Return on Capital (%)	1.78	(6.68)	(28.43)	3.14	3.67
Ret. on Com. Equity (%)	na	na	(455.96)	(1.80)	0.88
% Change Profit	89.2	63.0	nm	(99.7)	158.9
% Change Revenue	(35.9)	13.6	(80.9)	94.6	45.2
% Change Assets	2.8	4.2	(16.0)	(9.6)	13.9
Preferred Div. Coverage	na	na	0.0		
Total Div. Coverage	na	na	0.0		
Income prop.(% tot. prop.)	29.0	36.2	47.0		
Develop. prop.(% tot. prop.)	71.0	63.8	53.0		
5 YEAR RATIOS (%)					
Return on Capital	(5.3)	(5.3)	(3.4)		
Return on Com. Equity	na	na	(91.8)		
Profit Growth	na	na	na		
Revenue Growth	(17.1)	(9.0)	(18.0)		
Asset Growth	(1.5)	(1.6)	14.5		
BALANCE SHEET (000)					
Cash	41,000	56,304	54,511		
Total Real Estate Assets	2,245,220	2,148,265	2,013,211		
Invest's & Advances	193,734	204,149	212,670		
Total Assets	2,499,845	2,430,722	2,332,312		
Bank Indebtedness	139,477	135,211	92,505		
Long Term Debt	2,161,506	2,065,474	1,857,774		
Total Liabilities	2,866,584	2,768,892	2,404,008		
Total Equity	(366,739)	(338,170)	(71,696)		
Total Liab. & Equity	2,499,845	2,430,722	2,332,312		
CAPITAL (000)					
Total Debt	2,300,983	2,200,685	1,950,279		
Preferred Equity	106,859	106,859	106,859		
Common Equity	(473,598)	(445,029)	(178,555)		

Business:

BF REALTY HOLDINGS LIMITED is a commercial, industrial and residential real estate development company. The company has commercial office projects in Toronto, Montreal, Chicago, Minneapolis and other North American cities. It also owns industrial parks and residental land in Southern California. The company is currently being restructured.

Date	EPS	DPS	Tot Rev	Inc Bex
Mar 92	(0.05)	0.00	25,418	(6,241)
Dec 91	0.04	0.00	28,043	9,667
Sep 91	(0.09)	0.00	28,582	(12,301)
Jun 91	(0.09)	0.00	31,601	(12,662)
Mar 91	(0.09)	0.00	34,411	(13,040)
Dec 90	(1.27)	0.00	45,821	(207,954)
Sep 91	(0.11)	0.00	52,645	(16,642)
Jun 90	(0.13)	0.00	45,669	(18,183)

Synopsis:

In May 1993, BF Realty Holdings Ltd. was hounded by the holders of its 10.75% debentures to start bankruptcy proceedings. BF Realty management had told debenture holders that their paper is worthless. But it is not clear whether forcing a bankruptcy will provide them anything since the company's primary asset is its wholly owned operating subsidiary, Brookfield Development Corp., which was pledged as collateral to a $915-million loan from its 67% shareholder, BCE Inc., and from Carena Development Ltd.

The possibility of pushing BF Realty into bankruptcy comes more than three years after National Trust Co. launched a lawsuit against the company on behalf of BF Realty's other class of debenture holders. While the 10.75% debenture holders have counted on riding the coattails of National Trust, the lawsuit filed for the 8% debenture holders has been dogged by financial difficulties. Moreover, a BF Realty restructuring plan intended to exchange the BCE-Carena loan for Brookfield shares and to provide some financial return for debenture holders has been delayed indefinitely. There is a chance that the two classes of debenture holders will join forces in a combined legal battle against BF Realty, BCE and Carena.

Despite increasing its leased space by more than 500,000 square feet over the past year, rental revenues at BF Realty fell by almost $15-million in the first months of 1992. Rental revenue was $67.1-million for the nine months ended September 30, 1992, compared with $82.4-million a year earlier. Interest income raised total revenue to $75.4-million, compared with $94.6-million. Brookfield said business in its projects in Orange County, California, and Denver, Colorado, was particularly good, but progress in Toronto is the poorest of all the company's markets.

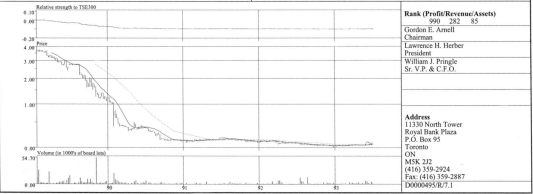

Rank (Profit/Revenue/Assets)		
990	282	85

Gordon E. Arnell
Chairman

Lawrence H. Herber
President

William J. Pringle
Sr. V.P. & C.F.O.

Address
11330 North Tower
Royal Bank Plaza
P.O. Box 95
Toronto
ON
M5K 2J2
(416) 359-2924
Fax: (416) 359-2887
D0000495/R/7.1

BRAMALEA LIMITED

Exchanges	Price (Jun24'93)		0.18	Trailing P/E		nm	Stock Symbol
T	Trailing Yield (%)		0.00	Trailing EPS		(10.16)	**BCD**

Period Ending	Oct 92	Oct 91	Oct 90	Oct 89	Oct 88
Yearly Statistics					
Price-Close	0.48	5.63	5.88	22.13	26.75
Price-High	6.00	9.75	22.75	23.63	28.38
Price-Low	0.28	4.15	5.50	15.38	19.25
P/E-Close	nm	187.50	nm	25.14	41.80
Dividends per Share	0.19	0.37	0.37	0.33	0.29
Dividend Yield (%)	38.54	6.58	6.30	1.49	1.08
Sales per Share	8.67	10.95	13.57	16.76	12.00
EPS before extra. item	(9.72)	0.03	(0.95)	0.88	0.64
Cash Flow per Share	(0.69)	(2.57)	1.84	2.41	1.83
Book Value per Share	0.32	9.98	10.86	12.19	11.10
O/S Common Shares	105,121	84,131	71,629	71,596	66,635
Total Revenue	854,900	908,600	1,030,900	1,181,200	814,900
Income before extra.	(937,300)	5,500	(63,700)	64,800	47,400
Cash Flow	(66,900)	(197,400)	132,000	164,300	121,800
Debt/Equity	60.81	5.42	5.80	4.22	3.72
Return on Capital (%)	(15.89)	4.39	3.89	7.65	7.36
Ret. on Com. Equity (%)	(214.81)	0.26	(8.29)	7.46	5.87
% Change Profit	nm	108.6	(198.3)	36.7	15.0
% Change Revenue	(5.9)	(11.9)	(12.7)	45.0	3.8
% Change Assets	(17.6)	1.9	13.5	28.9	9.6

Preferred Div. Coverage	0.0	1.6	0.0
Total Div. Coverage	0.0	0.2	0.0
Income prop.(% tot. prop.)	67.6	57.1	54.7
Develop. prop.(% tot. prop.)	32.4	42.9	45.3
5 YEAR RATIOS (%)			
Return on Capital	1.5	6.2	6.5
Return on Com. Equity	(41.9)	2.1	3.0
Profit Growth	na	(26.7)	na
Revenue Growth	1.6	6.0	17.4
Asset Growth	6.0	12.4	19.5
BALANCE SHEET (000)			
Cash	1,100	0	5,000
Total Real Estate Assets	4,581,100	5,509,400	5,271,500
Invest's & Advances	333,600	480,400	517,500
Total Assets	5,062,800	6,147,700	6,034,900
Bank Indebtedness	0	0	0
Long Term Debt	4,676,200	4,795,500	4,780,700
Total Liabilities	4,985,900	5,263,400	5,211,000
Total Equity	76,900	884,300	823,900
Total Liab. & Equity	5,062,800	6,147,700	6,034,900
CAPITAL (000)			
Total Debt	4,676,200	4,795,500	4,780,700
Preferred Equity	43,200	44,300	45,900
Common Equity	33,700	840,000	778,000

Business:

BRAMALEA LTD. is a North American property and real estate developer. The company owns office properties, shopping centres, hotels and business parks across North America. The company also develops residential housing properties in Ontario and California. Trizec Corp. Ltd. will have a 24% interest in the company on completion of the issue of common shares.

Date	EPS	DPS	Tot Rev	Inc Bex
Apr 93	(0.16)	0.00	211,200	(14,100)
Jan 93	(0.26)	0.00	196,900	(27,000)
Oct 92	(9.34)	0.00	244,600	(903,300)
Jul 92	(0.40)	0.00	203,100	(37,800)
Apr 92	(0.16)	0.00	216,500	(14,100)
Jan 92	(0.06)	0.19	211,300	(4,500)
Oct 91	0.01	0.00	254,100	1,200
Jul 91	(0.48)	0.19	109,100	(34,100)

Synopsis:

Bramalea Limited initiated debt restructuring discussions with major lenders in May 1992, and with debenture holders in July 1992. By December 1992, agreement in principle was reached with the majority of lenders on the restructuring of Bramalea's debt obligations and five-year business plan. Common and preference shareholders approved the plan at a meeting on October 27, 1992.

The risk remains, however, that a few lenders with whom the company was unable to reach complete agreement could take actions against Bramalea that would undo the consensual plan and possibly force the liquidation of assets.

On December 22, 1992, following consultations with principal lenders, Bramalea filed a business plan with the Ontario Court of Justice (General Division) under the Companies' Creditors Arrangement Act. The purpose of the filing was to seek court supervision of a final vote on the plan by all lenders to formalize and confirm the restructuring of Bramalea's debt and capital base. For purposes of approving the plan, stakeholders were divided into six credit classes, each of which voted approval at meetings held from February 17 to 19, 1993.

The business plan approved by lenders has five elements. Firstly, the company's major lenders along with largest shareholder, Trizec Corp. Ltd., are to provide $67-million of new funds. Secondly, interest will be deferred on senior debentures, unsecured loans, a convertible debenture owned by Trizec, and land and construction loans. Thirdly, Bramalea's debt must be reduced through asset sales. In 1992, it sold $704-million worth of assets. In the first quarter of 1993, Bramalea realized $68-million from asset sales, with a further $285-million under contract to close later in 1993. Bramalea is on its way to meeting the business plan target of selling $2.7-billion of assets by end of 1997. A fourth element of the business plan is the conversion of $685-million of debt and preference shares into common shares. The final element is an agreement with seven lenders to exchange a portion of the debt for $682-million of distress preference shares.

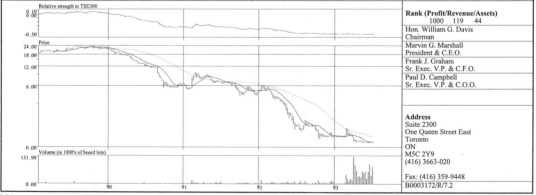

Rank (Profit/Revenue/Assets)
1000   119   44

Hon. William G. Davis
Chairman

Marvin G. Marshall
President & C.E.O.

Frank J. Graham
Sr. Exec. V.P. & C.F.O.

Paul D. Campbell
Sr. Exec. V.P. & C.O.O.

Address
Suite 2300
One Queen Street East
Toronto
ON
M5C 2Y9
(416) 3663-020

Fax: (416) 359-9448
B0003172/R/7.2

CAMBRIDGE SHOPPING CENTRES LIMITED

Exchanges	Price (Jun24'93)	16.87	Trailing P/E	nm	Stock Symbol
TM	Trailing Yield (%)	2.93	Trailing EPS	(2.42)	**CBG**

Period Ending	Mar93	Mar92	Mar91	Mar90	Mar89
Yearly Statistics					
Price-Close	15.75	18.50	27.75	28.63	31.50
Price-High	19.25	28.50	29.75	37.50	32.75
Price-Low	10.13	18.25	20.25	28.63	25.50
P/E-Close	nm	28.03	396.43	29.51	37.50
Dividends per Share	0.46	0.60	0.60	0.60	0.56
Dividend Yield (%)	2.92	3.24	2.16	2.10	1.78
Sales per Share	10.04	10.84	10.59	9.61	9.97
EPS before extra. item	(2.42)	0.66	0.07	0.97	0.84
Cash Flow per Share	1.67	2.06	2.16	2.46	2.53
Book Value per Share	15.09	18.43	14.23	17.31	16.94
O/S Common Shares	27,643	27,932	25,833	25,833	25,807
Total Revenue	354,659	308,421	280,364	255,227	225,269
Income before extra.	(77,547)	18,483	1,701	24,927	23,434
Cash Flow	53,488	57,278	55,730	63,409	55,887
Debt/Equity	3.95	3.27	3.54	3.17	2.94
Return on Capital (%)	1.41	7.43	7.00	8.22	8.29
Ret. on Com. Equity (%)	(16.64)	4.19	0.42	5.64	4.87
% Change Profit	(519.6)	986.6	(93.2)	6.4	20.7
% Change Revenue	15.0	10.0	9.8	13.3	14.1
% Change Assets	(3.7)	24.4	6.0	9.3	14.2

Preferred Div. Coverage	na	na	na	
Total Div. Coverage	0.0	1.1	0.1	
Income prop.(% tot. prop.)	92.4	87.7	87.6	
Develop. prop.(% tot. prop.)	7.6	12.3	12.4	
5 YEAR RATIOS (%)				
Return on Capital	6.5	7.9	8.2	
Return on Com. Equity	(0.3)	3.8	4.0	
Profit Growth	na	(1.3)	(24.1)	
Revenue Growth	12.3	11.7	16.6	
Asset Growth	9.6	13.6	10.3	
BALANCE SHEET (000)				
Cash	101,451	67,882	65,700	
Total Real Estate Assets	2,396,955	2,506,656	1,983,894	
Invest's & Advances	19,302	63,158	62,876	
Total Assets	2,577,445	2,677,617	2,152,430	
Bank Indebtedness	213,962	264,181	121,666	
Long Term Debt	1,693,900	1,631,809	1,413,382	
Total Liabilities	2,094,777	2,097,088	1,719,176	
Total Equity	482,668	580,529	433,254	
Total Liab. & Equity	2,577,445	2,677,617	2,152,430	
CAPITAL (000)				
Total Debt	1,907,862	1,895,990	1,535,048	
Preferred Equity	65,665	65,665	65,665	
Common Equity	417,003	514,864	367,589	

Business:

CAMBRIDGE SHOPPING CENTRES LTD. is a developer and manager of commercial real estate across Canada and the southwestern United States. The company acquires, develops and manages shopping centres (over 26 million square feet), urban mixed-use properties with a significant retail component, and self-storage facilities.

Date	EPS	DPS	Tot Rev	Inc Bex
Mar 93	0.09	0.12	84,520	3,017
Dec 92	(2.70)	0.08	81,461	(86,522)
Sep 92	0.16	0.15	104,482	4,992
Jun 92	0.03	0.15	84,196	966
Mar 92	0.18	0.15	84,325	5,909
Dec 91	0.17	0.15	77,381	4,467
Sep 91	0.13	0.15	75,616	3,449
Jun 91	0.18	0.15	71,099	4,658

Synopsis:

In May 1993, Cambridge Shopping Centres Limited announced that Cambridge Leaseholds Limited, a wholly owned subsidiary, intends to offer for sale a 4.82 acre site bounded by Dundas Street, Ridout Street, King Street and Talbot Street that it owns London, Ontario. The company said that building the $400-million office-retail-hotel complex slated for the area no longer makes financial sense. The property will be listed for sale at about $25-million.

In March 1993, Cambridge Leaseholds Ltd. sold $105-million of debentures to a handful of institutional investors in a debt refinancing scheme unrelated to its exposure to the Woodward's Ltd. department store chain. The debentures will be secured by mortgages on three shopping malls and backed by a corporate guarantee of Cambridge Leaseholds Ltd. Proceeds from deal will be used to retire mortgages and reduce the Toronto-based developer's floating-rate debt. Cambridge has remained loyal to a policy of holding this category of debt to 25% of its total, and this deal is expected to leave the company with 16% of its debt at a floating rate.

During early 1993, Cambridge planned to sell the Woodward's Ltd. store in downtown Vancouver to Wall Financial Corp. for about $24-million. However, the deal was turned down by Wall Financial in March 1993. Only a week after the deal was turned down, Woodward's unveiled its merger with Hudson's Bay Co. Cambridge, whose $50-million investment in Woodward's was written down to almost nothing in December 1992, stands to pocket $30-million from a deal that nearly eliminates the company's most serious financial worry. Because of the write-down of its Woodward's investment, it appears that Cambridge will now have to account for a $20-million gain. In December 1992, Woodward's filed for court protection from its creditors when it build up a $65-million debt load with its suppliers that it was unable to pay.

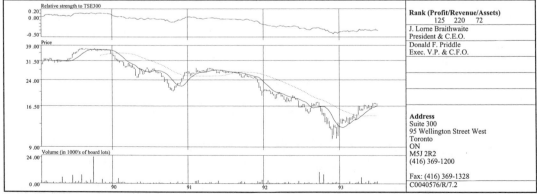

Rank (Profit/Revenue/Assets)
125   220   72

J. Lorne Braithwaite
President & C.E.O.

Donald F. Priddle
Exec. V.P. & C.F.O.

Address
Suite 300
95 Wellington Street West
Toronto
ON
M5J 2R2
(416) 369-1200

Fax: (416) 369-1328
C0040576/R/7.2

CAMDEV CORPORATION

Exchanges	Price (Jun24'93)	2.85	Trailing P/E	nm	Stock Symbol
TM	Trailing Yield (%)	0.00	Trailing EPS	(1.79)	**CVO**

Period Ending	Jan93	Jan92	Jan91	Jan90	Jan89
Yearly Statistics					US
Price-Close	2.80	24.00	21.50	122.50	787.50
Price-High	18.75	72.50	150.00	1,112.50	1,275.00
Price-Low	2.40	18.50	17.50	112.50	700.00
P/E-Close	nm	nm	nm	nm	nm
Dividends per Share	0.00	0.00	0.00	4.50	18.00
Dividend Yield (%)	0.00	0.00	0.00	3.67	2.29
Sales per Share	13.21	32.43	288.75	263.90	315.85
EPS before extra. item	(2.16)	na	(605.71)	(2,299.00)	(52.00)
Cash Flow per Share	(0.45)	(13.06)	(103.77)	51.85	185.00
Book Value per Share	20.57	22.67	(2,959.72)	(2,342.75)	(14.85)
O/S Common Shares	6,353	6,353	887	887	886
Total Revenue	83,937	465,000	312,000	(1,593,000)	9,159,000
Income before extra.	(13,693)	2,470,000	(525,000)	(2,021,000)	(34,000)
Cash Flow	(2,890)	(83,000)	(92,000)	46,000	164,000
Debt/Equity	3.50	3.29	na	na	128.91
Return on Capital (%)	4.48	1,720.52	na	(27.01)	12.05
Ret. on Com. Equity (%)	(9.97)	na	na	na	(383.33)
% Change Profit	(100.6)	570.5	74.0	(4,778.2)	8,120.7
% Change Revenue	(81.9)	49.0	119.6	(114.3)	180.4
% Change Assets	(5.4)	(49.3)	(14.0)	(91.3)	147.3

Date	EPS	DPS	Tot Rev	Inc Bex
Apr 93	(0.03)	0.00	19,414	(211)
Jan 93	(0.98)	0.00	19,178	(6,192)
Oct 92	(0.43)	0.00	24,042	(2,716)
Jul 92	(0.35)	0.00	20,581	(2,219)
Apr 92	(0.40)	0.00	20,136	(2,566)
Jan 92	na	0.00	45,000	2321,000
Oct 91	31.00	0.00	73,429	30,463
Jul 91	65.70	0.00	148,114	58,249

Preferred Div. Coverage	np	np	0.0
Total Div. Coverage	na	205.8	0.0
Income prop.(% tot. prop.)	93.5	91.3	100.0
Develop. prop.(% tot. prop.)	6.5	8.7	na
5 YEAR RATIOS (%)			
Return on Capital	na	na	na
Return on Com. Equity	na	na	na
Profit Growth	na	181.7	na
Revenue Growth	(54.7)	(19.5)	6.7
Asset Growth	(38.5)	(40.3)	(9.2)
BALANCE SHEET (000)			
Cash	13,247	14,000	13,000
Total Real Estate Assets	493,518	504,000	1,151,000
Invest's & Advances	93,990	121,000	53,000
Total Assets	608,956	644,000	1,269,000
Bank Indebtedness	0	11,000	1,565,000
Long Term Debt	457,935	462,000	609,000
Total Liabilities	478,276	500,000	3,753,000
Total Equity	130,680	144,000	(2,484,000)
Total Liab. & Equity	608,956	644,000	1,269,000
CAPITAL (000)			
Total Debt	457,935	473,000	2,174,000
Preferred Equity	0	0	140,000
Common Equity	130,680	144,000	(2,624,000)

Business:

CAMDEV CORPORATION owns and manager real estate properties, which includes more than 3.1 million square feet of commercial and retail space, of which approximately 2.3 million square feet is located in the National Capital Region.

Synopsis:

With high vacancy rates and reduced cash flow, Camdev Corporation, formerly Campeau Corp., continues to focus on its restructuring plan, implemented February 11, 1993, by aggressively seeking new leasing contracts and selling non-core assets. The 12.8% owned California supermarket chain, Ralph Grocery Company, with 159 stores, is to play an important role in Camdev's future development.

Camdev signed several long lease contracts in Ottawa. The Journal Towers were leased for 11 years to the federal government, the Citadel Inn was leased for a 10-year term, and Camdev extended the lease for the Radisson Hotel with its operators, Commonwealth Hospitality Limited, until 1998. Camdev received a five-year extension on leases at two Place de Ville Towers. Camdev plans a $25-million upgrade on the Journal Towers. On March, 29, 80% of the Pinecrest office was under lease to Public Works Canada for five years. Camdev owns more than 3.1 million square feet of commercial and retail space, with 2.3 million square feet in Ottawa alone.

The poor economic climate brought on a decline in rents and reduced operating profits for Camdev. It received rents of $79.2-million, mostly from Ottawa properties. Camdev has had a net loss $13.7-million since restructuring. It's total debt as of January 31, 1993, was $457.9-million. The liquidation of Federated Stores Inc. was finalized. Land sales in 1992 generated $4.8-million that went towards reducing debt.

On May 28, 1993, Camdev sought Revenue Canada's approval to issue distress preferred shares in exchange for the debt secured by its Galleria London Shopping Centre.

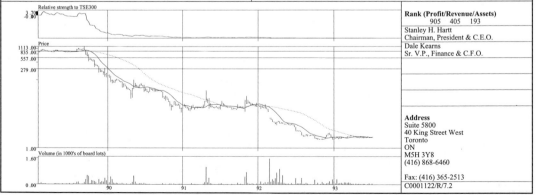

Rank (Profit/Revenue/Assets)
905   405   193

Stanley H. Hartt
Chairman, President & C.E.O.

Dale Kearns
Sr. V.P., Finance & C.F.O.

Address
Suite 5800
40 King Street West
Toronto
ON
M5H 3Y8
(416) 868-6460

Fax: (416) 365-2513
C0001122/R/7.2

CARENA DEVELOPMENTS

Exchanges	Price (Jun24'93)		1.52	Trailing P/E		nm	Stock Symbol
TM	Trailing Yield (%)		30.26	Trailing EPS		(4.61)	**CDN**

Period Ending	Oct92	Oct91	Oct90	Oct89	Oct88
Yearly Statistics					
Price-Close	3.10	10.75	10.38	28.25	22.67
Price-High	12.00	15.63	28.25	30.00	22.83
Price-Low	3.00	9.00	10.38	21.00	14.50
P/E-Close	nm	17.62	18.86	34.45	30.91
Dividends per Share	0.42	0.50	0.50	0.40	0.27
Dividend Yield (%)	13.55	4.65	4.82	1.42	1.18
Sales per Share	22.00	38.85	44.23	50.25	26.44
EPS before extra. item	(4.55)	0.61	0.55	0.82	0.73
Cash Flow per Share	8.61	16.42	22.18	7.65	7.33
Book Value per Share	5.42	10.27	9.93	9.90	8.14
O/S Common Shares	56,732	56,149	50,844	50,844	47,231
Total Revenue	1,343,984	2,269,181	2,447,440	2,537,067	1,267,913
Income before extra.	(245,468)	45,000	42,052	54,025	47,118
Cash Flow	487,934	883,829	1,127,627	367,477	328,858
Debt/Equity	12.47	15.17	16.04	12.85	12.96
Return on Capital (%)	0.84	5.73	6.47	6.65	6.74
Ret. on Com. Equity (%)	(58.33)	6.02	5.55	8.82	9.38
% Change Profit	(645.5)	7.0	(22.2)	14.7	19.5
% Change Revenue	(40.8)	(7.3)	(3.5)	100.1	7.6
% Change Assets	(40.8)	3.2	15.3	19.9	17.0

Preferred Div. Coverage	0.0	3.6	3.0		
Total Div. Coverage	0.0	1.1	1.1		
Income prop.(% tot. prop.)	74.2	65.3	60.7		
Develop. prop.(% tot. prop.)	25.8	34.7	39.3		
5 YEAR RATIOS (%)					
Return on Capital	5.3	7.6	8.1		
Return on Com. Equity	(5.7)	7.6	8.4		
Profit Growth	na	4.0	6.1		
Revenue Growth	2.7	113.9	108.7		
Asset Growth	(0.3)	84.7	96.8		
BALANCE SHEET (mil)					
Cash	181	177	180		
Total Real Estate Assets	6,380	11,430	11,049		
Invest's & Advances	1,093	1,236	1,129		
Total Assets	8,362	14,129	13,684		
Bank Indebtedness	251	240	513		
Long Term Debt	6,274	10,640	10,007		
Total Liabilities	7,839	13,411	13,029		
Total Equity	523	717	656		
Total Liab. & Equity	8,362	14,129	13,684		
CAPITAL (mil)					
Total Debt	6,525	10,881	10,520		
Preferred Equity	216	141	151		
Common Equity	307	577	505		

Business:

CARENA DEVELOPMENTS LTD. is a diversified North American real estate development company owning rental properties concentrated in major urban centres in the United States and Canada. Its activites are conducted directly and through subsidiaries. The company has equity interests in Trizec Corp., 40%; Coscan Development Corp., 51%; and Consolidated Carma Corp., 42%.

Date	EPS	DPS	Tot Rev	Inc Bex
Jan 93	0.06	0.00	379,772	7,564
Oct 92	(4.68)	0.17	(265,070)	(260,748)
Jul 92	0.01	0.00	526,672	3,223
Apr 92	0.00	0.25	520,693	2,358
Jan 92	0.12	0.00	561,689	9,699
Oct 91	0.15	0.25	570,764	10,937
Jul 91	0.13	0.00	591,197	10,742
Apr 91	0.19	0.25	516,680	12,709

Synopsis:

In April 1993, Carena Developments Ltd. agreed to extend the deadline for its massive loans to ailing Brookfield Development Corp. Carena could have called its $348-million loan to Brookfield at the end April, sparking the real estate developer into bankruptcy courts and sparking a fight with the banks and hundreds of debenture holders over the spoils. The extension marked the third time Carena has postponed plans to swap its loan for a major stake in Brookfield since it first began pouring money into the company in 1989.

During 1992, Carena subscribed for $50-million in a Trizec public issue of common shares which enabled Trizec to complete a $275-million common share issue. Early in 1992, the corporation also purchased an additional 1.1 million Trizec shares for $5.8-million. The drop in the book value of Carena's investment in Trizec is due to the equity accounted loss resulting from the write-down by Trizec of its investment in Bramalea and other provisions recorded by Trizec.

Carena's common share investment in Coscan dropped during 1992 due to Carena reflecting Coscan's provision for a diminution in the value of its assets. As of October 31, 1992 Carena had advanced $109-million to Coscan under a $145-million credit facility.

On December 31, 1991, Consolidated Carma Corp. redeemed a $75-million preferred share held by Carena which was converted into a note receivable. During 1992, $50-million of this note was sold for cash proceeds. The increase in common and participating equity relates to Carena's share of Carma's earnings during 1992.

The Carena group issued $350-million of new equity in 1992 which, combined with the $363-million raised in 1991, brought the total equity raised by Carena and its affiliates to $713-million over the two-year period. Of the total, $542-million was subscribed for by institutional and retail investors. For Carena alone, the company raised $75-million through the issue of three million preferred shares during 1992.

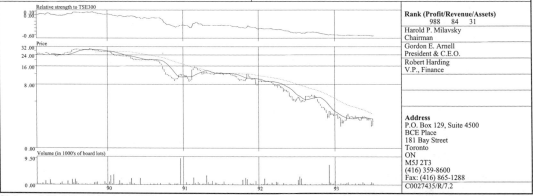

Rank (Profit/Revenue/Assets)		
988	84	31
Harold P. Milavsky		
Chairman		
Gordon E. Arnell		
President & C.E.O.		
Robert Harding		
V.P., Finance		

Address
P.O. Box 129, Suite 4500
BCE Place
181 Bay Street
Toronto
ON
M5J 2T3
(416) 359-8600
Fax: (416) 865-1288
C0027435/R/7.2

CONSOLIDATED CARMA CORPORATION

Exchanges	Price (Jun24'93)		2.60	Trailing P/E		4.91	Stock Symbol
TZ	Trailing Yield (%)		0.00	Trailing EPS		0.53	**CVP.A**

Period Ending	Dec92	Dec91	Dec90	Dec89	Dec88
Yearly Statistics					
Price-Close	1.95	2.10	1.80	2.65	2.00
Price-High	2.70	2.55	2.70	2.70	2.15
Price-Low	1.65	1.67	1.55	1.90	1.50
P/E-Close	3.20	4.38	4.00	7.79	15.39
Dividends per Share	0.00	0.00	0.00	0.00	0.00
Dividend Yield (%)	0.00	0.00	0.00	0.00	0.00
Sales per Share	5.88	3.66	4.79	5.54	2.01
EPS before extra. item	0.61	0.48	0.45	0.34	0.13
Cash Flow per Share	1.95	1.81	1.74	1.05	0.62
Book Value per Share	5.32	3.85	2.80	1.88	1.53
O/S Common Shares	20,797	20,797	20,797	20,797	20,755
Total Revenue	142,675	110,552	143,608	142,005	53,075
Income before extra.	39,905	37,082	35,643	20,597	11,461
Cash Flow	40,589	37,654	36,164	21,820	12,223
Debt/Equity	0.06	0.51	0.78	1.02	0.16
Return on Capital (%)	17.21	14.16	12.60	8.60	9.01
Ret. on Com. Equity (%)	31.88	31.66	0.73	20.18	8.82
% Change Profit	7.6	4.0	73.0	79.7	163.0
% Change Revenue	29.1	(23.0)	1.1	167.6	58.7
% Change Assets	(13.1)	(32.5)	2.9	112.9	127.8

Preferred Div. Coverage	4.2	2.4	2.2
Total Div. Coverage	4.2	2.4	2.2
Income prop.(% tot. prop.)	13.5	12.7	11.7
Develop. prop.(% tot. prop.)	86.5	87.3	88.3
5 YEAR RATIOS (%)			
Return on Capital	12.3	6.6	2.3
Return on Com. Equity	18.7	(7.8)	na
Profit Growth	55.7	na	na
Revenue Growth	33.6	34.6	169.2
Asset Growth	24.0	20.3	110.8
BALANCE SHEET (000)			
Cash	14,991	32,845	54,344
Total Real Estate Assets	143,948	152,802	154,752
Invest's & Advances	82,352	79,566	197,158
Total Assets	301,130	346,361	513,009
Bank Indebtedness	0	10,000	14,679
Long Term Debt	14,156	90,358	182,368
Total Liabilities	71,996	147,626	261,258
Total Equity	229,134	198,735	251,751
Total Liab. & Equity	301,130	346,361	513,009
CAPITAL (000)			
Total Debt	14,156	100,358	197,047
Preferred Equity	118,575	118,575	193,500
Common Equity	110,559	80,160	58,251

Business:

CONSOLIDATED CARMA CORP. is a real estate company active in the development of master-planned residential communities, primarily in Edmonton and Calgary. The company also develops retail and commercial income properties that are held for investment or for sale. The company maintains offices in Calgary, Edmonton, Regina, Saskatoon, and Winnipeg. It often operates with third parties.

Date	EPS	DPS	Tot Rev	Inc Bex
Mar 93	0.17	0.00	25,098	5,873
Dec 92	0.13	0.00	34,249	10,912
Sep 92	0.11	0.00	40,837	9,326
Jun 92	0.12	0.00	36,419	10,725
Mar 92	0.25	0.00	31,170	8,942
Dec 91	0.04	0.00	12,860	6,040
Sep 91	0.14	0.00	41,926	13,373
Jun 91	0.06	0.00	31,164	7,269

Synopsis:

The demand for single-family homes improved significantly in each of Consolidated Carma Corp.'s markets during 1992. This improvement was due primarily to lower interest rates as well as government programs to encourage new home purchases. In Calgary, Carma maintained a 22% market share as single-family lot sales increased by 40%. Its housing operation more than doubled its volume and delivered in excess of 200 homes in middle and middle markets.

In Edmonton, lot sales more than tripled and the company's market share increased from 4% to 6%. Unlike Calgary, Carma is positioned more in middle and upper markets in Edmonton. This somewhat limited the company's ability to capitalize on the strong lower-priced markets during 1992.

In Regina, Carma consistently accounted for approximately 50% of single-family lot sales markets. In 1992, Carma's lot sales more than tripled in volume. The Regina residential market received a boost in late 1991 when the Farm Credit Corporation and Crown Life Insurance Company both announced they would be relocating their operations to Regina. These two relocations will add approximately 1,300 new jobs in Regina. In late 1992, Sears Canada Inc. announced that they would be adding 900 new positions to its distribution facility in Regina. The announcement of these new job initiatives had a positive influence on Regina's new-home market in 1992.

In Winnipeg, Carma increased its single-family lot sales by over 40% while market share remained at 8%.

Carma sold the balance of its developed lot and housing inventory in Saskatoon during 1992. The Saskatoon market remains very slow, and although Carma has developable land in the city, the company has decided not to begin development until market conditions improve. Concurrent with this decision, it closed the Saskatoon office at the end of the first quarter of 1993.

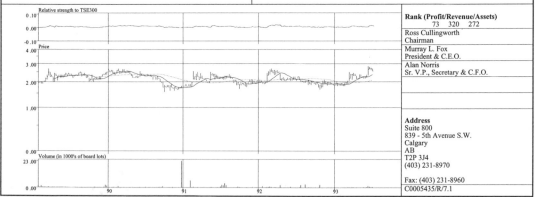

Rank (Profit/Revenue/Assets)
73   320   272

Ross Cullingworth
Chairman

Murray L. Fox
President & C.E.O.

Alan Norris
Sr. V.P., Secretary & C.F.O.

Address
Suite 800
839 - 5th Avenue S.W.
Calgary
AB
T2P 3J4
(403) 231-8970

Fax: (403) 231-8960
C0005435/R/7.1

CONSOLIDATED HCI HOLDINGS CORPORATION

Exchanges	Price (Jun24'93)	0.65	Trailing P/E	nm	Stock Symbol
T	Trailing Yield (%)	0.00	Trailing EPS	(0.96)	**CXA.A**

Period Ending	Sep92	Sep91	Sep90	Sep89	Sep88
Yearly Statistics					
Price-Close	0.86	3.80	7.00	9.63	8.38
Price-High	4.00	8.50	13.50	10.75	9.75
Price-Low	0.55	3.80	7.00	8.50	6.00
P/E-Close	nm	nm	nm	10.82	6.81
Dividends per Share	0.00	0.00	0.00	0.00	0.00
Dividend Yield (%)	0.00	0.00	0.00	0.00	0.00
Sales per Share	1.86	4.31	3.68	5.72	6.68
EPS before extra. item	(0.95)	(1.82)	(1.35)	0.89	1.23
Cash Flow per Share	0.04	0.09	(0.83)	1.01	2.58
Book Value per Share	2.33	3.27	4.89	6.24	5.35
O/S Common Shares	19,368	19,368	16,766	16,766	16,766
Total Revenue	38,101	83,095	64,033	97,154	111,651
Income before extra.	(18,385)	(34,079)	(22,599)	14,942	20,657
Cash Flow	725	1,618	(13,970)	16,895	43,330
Debt/Equity	4.05	2.85	3.33	2.10	1.97
Return on Capital (%)	(9.62)	(16.85)	(7.81)	11.41	17.93
Ret. on Com. Equity (%)	(33.91)	(46.86)	(24.21)	15.38	25.99
% Change Profit	46.1	(50.8)	(251.2)	(27.7)	5.2
% Change Revenue	(54.1)	29.8	(34.1)	(13.0)	18.3
% Change Assets	(4.5)	(31.5)	0.0	17.0	15.6

Preferred Div. Coverage	np	np	np		
Total Div. Coverage	na	na	na		
Income prop.(% tot. prop.)	29.4	32.3	27.0		
Develop. prop.(% tot. prop.)	70.6	67.7	73.0		
5 YEAR RATIOS (%)					
Return on Capital	(1.0)	5.2	14.9		
Return on Com. Equity	(12.7)	0.6	18.9		
Profit Growth	na	na	na		
Revenue Growth	(16.6)	5.0	122.7		
Asset Growth	(2.5)	6.6	87.2		
BALANCE SHEET (000)					
Cash	8,084	8,118	8,500		
Total Real Estate Assets	237,179	208,392	378,337		
Invest's & Advances	1,654	0	4,348		
Total Assets	278,625	291,617	425,474		
Bank Indebtedness	69,352	90,349	92,595		
Long Term Debt	113,140	90,461	180,862		
Total Liabilities	233,594	228,201	343,429		
Total Equity	45,031	63,416	82,045		
Total Liab. & Equity	278,625	291,617	425,474		
CAPITAL (000)					
Total Debt	182,492	180,810	273,457		
Preferred Equity	0	0	0		
Common Equity	45,031	63,416	82,045		

Business:

CONSOLIDATED HCI HOLDINGS CORP. is a real estate company based in Ontario. The company develops residential, industrial and commercial land in the Greater Toronto Area. In addition it both builds and leases industrial and commercial properties. Through various joint ventures, Cosolidated HCI is involved in housing sales. The company maintains significant land holdings in the Toronto area.

Date	EPS	DPS	Tot Rev	Inc Bex
Mar 93	0.00	0.00	4,751	(35)
Dec 92	0.03	0.00	7,294	661
Sep 92	(1.01)	0.00	8,921	(19,579)
Jun 92	0.02	0.00	7,701	336
Mar 92	(0.02)	0.00	5,857	(318)
Dec 91	0.06	0.00	15,622	1,176
Sep 91	(1.28)	0.00	2,238	(24,161)
Jun 91	(1.29)	0.00	(27,089)	(23,524)

Synopsis:

In March 1993, Consolidated HCI Holdings Corporation announced the sale of the real estate assets of the Mont-Royal Partnership, in which the company had an 83% equity interest, at a sheriff's sale in Montreal for approximately $32-million. The Bank of Montreal and Toronto-Dominion Bank together paid $25-million for the two office towers and condominiums of Les Cours Mont-Royal and another parcel of land. Mutual Life of Canada and Confederation Life Insurance Co., who held the first mortgage on the shopping mall, paid $7-million for the retail segment. The price is roughly one-third of the property's debt. The banks intend to sell the property, and it appears the complex's former owners will be responsible for the probable shortfall between the eventual sale price and the mortgage.

Expected to begin in the summer of 1993, HCI has a major project that it is preparing based on an offer to purchase 450 building lots of a planned 476 lots in Markham, Ontario. According to HCI, its principal bankers have indicated they are prepared to supply a credit facility to fully service the lands. The project will last five years.

HCI sold 39 building lots in the Greater Toronto Area, of which 18 closed in the first quarter of 1993 with full payment. The remainder are scheduled for closing in the summer of 1993 with final payment to be received upon sale to the end user.

HCI is attempting to rezone certain lands in Woodbridge, Ontario, which would allow it to develop the lands as residential townhouses. If successful, the zoning change from industrial commercial would mean that revenue from the land can be achieved in late 1993 or 1994.

For the year ended September 30, 1992, real estate sales of HCI fell over 60% from a year earlier, representing 69% of total revenue. The $29.4-million loss before income taxes includes a $29.1-million provision for the loss in value of the Mont-Royal Partnership.

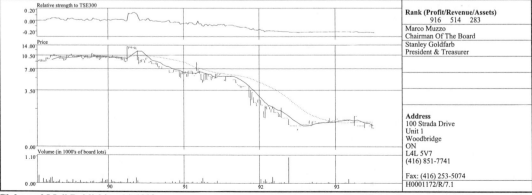

Rank (Profit/Revenue/Assets)
916 514 283

Marco Muzzo
Chairman Of The Board

Stanley Goldfarb
President & Treasurer

Address
100 Strada Drive
Unit 1
Woodbridge
ON
L4L 5V7
(416) 851-7741

Fax: (416) 253-5074
H0001172/R/7.1

COSCAN DEVELOPMENT CORPORATION

Exchanges	Price (Jun24'93)		1.30	Trailing P/E		nm	Stock Symbol
T	Trailing Yield (%)		0.00	Trailing EPS		(4.81)	**COT**

Period Ending	Dec92	Dec91	Dec90	Dec89	Dec88
Yearly Statistics					
Price-Close	1.50	8.50	5.00	11.75	11.25
Price-High	9.00	9.38	12.25	13.50	11.63
Price-Low	1.40	4.75	5.00	10.63	8.50
P/E-Close	nm	13.93	4.43	7.68	8.40
Dividends per Share	0.00	0.30	0.30	0.30	0.25
Dividend Yield (%)	0.00	3.53	6.00	2.55	2.22
Sales per Share	10.41	15.59	18.62	26.11	41.74
EPS before extra. item	(4.78)	0.61	1.13	1.53	1.34
Cash Flow per Share	8.54	13.96	16.46	2.60	2.27
Book Value per Share	7.82	12.11	13.69	12.85	11.68
O/S Common Shares	20,489	20,449	14,772	14,772	13,722
Total Revenue	249,455	319,097	331,017	413,002	466,790
Income before extra.	(94,747)	15,038	22,813	27,505	19,025
Cash Flow	174,991	240,335	243,160	36,995	24,496
Debt/Equity	3.04	2.85	3.49	3.40	2.19
Return on Capital (%)	(10.89)	5.27	7.86	10.79	9.48
Ret. on Com. Equity (%)	(48.07)	4.66	8.51	12.44	11.02
% Change Profit	(730.1)	(34.1)	(17.1)	44.6	26.6
% Change Revenue	(21.8)	(3.6)	(19.9)	(11.5)	36.6
% Change Assets	(3.4)	(0.1)	5.7	50.1	3.7

Preferred Div. Coverage	0.0	3.3	3.7
Total Div. Coverage	0.0	1.4	2.2
Income prop.(% tot. prop.)	32.2	30.3	27.5
Develop. prop.(% tot. prop.)	67.8	69.7	72.5
5 YEAR RATIOS (%)			
Return on Capital	4.5	7.6	7.5
Return on Com. Equity	(2.3)	9.5	10.3
Profit Growth	na	3.1	27.0
Revenue Growth	(6.2)	(1.0)	8.1
Asset Growth	9.7	13.0	18.2
BALANCE SHEET (000)			
Cash	0	0	0
Total Real Estate Assets	681,403	704,864	750,518
Invest's & Advances	399,876	417,770	363,074
Total Assets	1,226,109	1,269,687	1,270,787
Bank Indebtedness	219,047	272,357	0
Long Term Debt	663,752	591,777	899,189
Total Liabilities	935,337	966,435	1,012,988
Total Equity	290,772	303,252	257,799
Total Liab. & Equity	1,226,109	1,269,687	1,270,787
CAPITAL (000)			
Total Debt	882,799	864,134	899,189
Preferred Equity	130,574	55,574	55,574
Common Equity	160,198	247,678	202,225

Business:

COSCAN DEVELOPMENT CORP. is a real estate development company that operates in major market areas of North America. The company acquires, develops and manages commercial properties, develops land for sale and builds and markets single family homes and condominium units. Coscan and its partners are involved in Ontario, Alberta, British Columbia, the Washington D.C. area, Florida, Colorado and California.

Date	EPS	DPS	Tot Rev	Inc Bex
Mar 93	(0.02)	0.00	60,908	1,042
Dec 92	(4.76)	0.00	77,098	(96,852)
Sep 92	(0.04)	0.00	59,316	18
Jun 92	0.01	0.00	69,877	1,090
Mar 92	0.01	0.00	43,164	997
Dec 91	0.23	0.30	103,317	5,386
Sep 91	0.27	0.00	63,159	5,498
Jun 91	0.09	0.00	90,034	2,524

Synopsis:

Coscan Development Corp. told shareholders in May 1993 that the company had sold 970 homes in 1993, compared with 1,100 closings for all of last year. Coscan believes it is on track to sell 1,350 homes by the end of the year. The company is pinning its hopes on government-fed markets in Ottawa and Washington D.C., and new demand for housing spurred by immigration into California markets. If all goes well, the company expects to post a profit this year, unlike in 1992, when a $170-million pretax write-down led to a $94.7-million loss.

More than $200-million of debt falls due this year and the company is relying on its 56% shareholder, Carena Developments Ltd., to help it foot the bill. Coscan has put land purchases on hold, refinanced part of its debt and made plans to sell pieces of its real estate portfolio.

In an effort to pare debt, Coscan issued $75-million of preferred shares last December to replace the same amount of debt owed to Carena. Support from Hees-Edper has also come in the shape of $125-million in credit lines that are tapped to repay portions of $235.2-million(U.S.) in loans with a syndicate of 13 banks each quarter. About $185-million of these bank lines are drawn. In a clear sign of the mass movement by banks to slash their real estate exposure, the bank syndicate exacted stiff terms when the loans were renewed last year, requiring Coscan to repay almost $30-million every three months until it matures in September 1993.

Coscan will be juggling other debt that matures in September 1993. A $17-million letter of credit with a bank that fell due in April 1993 was extended until September 1993.

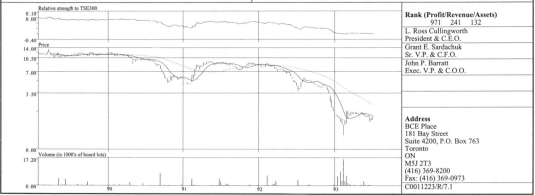

Rank (Profit/Revenue/Assets)
971   241   132

L. Ross Cullingworth
President & C.E.O.

Grant E. Sardachuk
Sr. V.P. & C.F.O.

John P. Barratt
Exec. V.P. & C.O.O.

Address
BCE Place
181 Bay Street
Suite 4200, P.O. Box 763
Toronto
ON
M5J 2T3
(416) 369-8200
Fax: (416) 369-0973
C0011223/R/7.1

INTRAWEST CORPORATION

Exchanges	Price (Jun24'93)	11.37	Trailing P/E	11.04	Stock Symbol
TMV	Trailing Yield (%)	2.11	Trailing EPS	1.03	**ITW**

Period Ending	Sep92	Sep91	Sep90	Sep89	Sep88
Yearly Statistics					
Price-Close	10.88	10.50	6.38	n t	n t
Price-High	11.50	12.00	10.00	n t	n t
Price-Low	9.50	6.00	6.38	n t	n t
P/E-Close	nm	nm	9.24	n t	n t
Dividends per Share	0.16	0.16	0.00	0.49	0.00
Dividend Yield (%)	1.47	1.52	0.00	n t	0.00
Sales per Share	2.46	2.31	7.02	3.65	2.23
EPS before extra. item	(1.03)	(0.20)	0.69	1.18	na
Cash Flow per Share	0.91	0.67	1.89	2.22	1.15
Book Value per Share	10.00	9.00	9.34	8.75	7.98
O/S Common Shares	20,016	17,281	14,111	10,321	10,118
Total Revenue	122,271	76,915	118,992	63,549	49,482
Income before extra.	19,631	(3,186)	8,504	12,118	6,517
Cash Flow	17,405	10,561	23,310	22,770	11,611
Debt/Equity	1.27	1.41	1.27	1.75	1.46
Return on Capital (%)	6.95	0.86	6.33	9.84	na
Ret. on Com. Equity (%)	11.04	(2.22)	7.66	14.16	na
% Change Profit	716.2	(137.5)	(29.8)	85.9	na
% Change Revenue	59.0	(35.4)	87.2	28.4	na
% Change Assets	21.2	21.6	27.1	27.0	na

Preferred Div. Coverage	np	np	np
Total Div. Coverage	6.6	0.0	na
Income prop.(% tot. prop.)	26.2	8.0	11.1
Develop. prop.(% tot. prop.)	73.8	92.0	88.9
5 YEAR RATIOS (%)			
Return on Capital	na	na	na
Return on Com. Equity	na	na	na
Profit Growth	na	na	na
Revenue Growth	na	na	na
Asset Growth	na	na	na
BALANCE SHEET (000)			
Cash	43,240	14,005	17,716
Total Real Estate Assets	304,775	241,262	178,936
Invest's & Advances	26,678	26,012	32,153
Total Assets	501,618	413,971	340,436
Bank Indebtedness	254,714	218,903	167,292
Long Term Debt	0	0	0
Total Liabilities	301,505	258,457	208,641
Total Equity	200,113	155,514	131,795
Total Liab. & Equity	501,618	413,971	340,436
CAPITAL (000)			
Total Debt	254,714	218,903	167,292
Preferred Equity	0	0	0
Common Equity	200,113	155,514	131,795

Business:

INTRAWEST CORPORATION operates in two businesses: resorts and real estate. The company is the owner and operator of ski resorts at Blackcomb in Whistler, B.C. and Mont Tremblant in Quebec. Real estate activities focus on residential multi-family developments and niche industrial and commercial markets in Vancouver, Calgary and Seattle.

Date	EPS	DPS	Tot Rev	Inc Bex
Mar 93	0.20	0.08	55,235	4,144
Dec 92	0.19	0.08	47,041	3,749
Sep 92	0.65	0.00	30,990	12,433
Jun 92	(0.01)	0.00	20,053	146
Mar 92	0.18	0.08	47,110	3,349
Dec 92	0.21	0.08	27,260	3,703
Sep 91	(0.04)	0.00	20,056	(6,783)
Jun 91	(0.04)	0.08	15,028	(359)

Synopsis:

Intrawest Development announced revenues of $102.3-million for the six months ended March 31, 1993, compared with $74.4-million in 1992. The increase was primarily attributable to real estate sales which more than doubled to $47.7-million from $22.6-million in 1992. Real estate gross profit rose from $2.3-million to $6.8-million, and ski and resort operation profit was $13.9-million, up slightly from $13.8-million last year.

Real estate sales during the second quarter principally comprised units of Ashlea Gate in Surrey, British Columbia, Painted Cliff at Blackcomb, B.C., and La Chouette at Mont Tremblant, Quebec.

Ski and resort operations revenue was $47-million compared with $44.3-million in 1992. Skier visits at Blackcomb and Mont Tremblant exceeded last year's levels despite poor weather conditions early in the ski season.

In March 1993 Intrawest announced that IW Resorts Limited Partnership, in which an Intrawest unit is general partner, acquired Panorama Resort, a ski resort in southeastern B.C. Panorama will be managed by Blackcomb Skiing Enterprises Ltd., an 87% owned Intrawest subsidiary that also owns the Blackcomb ski resort in Whistler, B.C.

In February 1993, Intrawest said it will spend $413-million over the next five years to make Mont Tremblant into a world class ski resort. The Quebec and federal governments will contribute about $20-million to phase one of the project and may provide an additional $14-million in the form of refundable contributions or loan guarantees. The renovation aims to boost the number of tourists from outside Quebec using the resort north of Montreal.

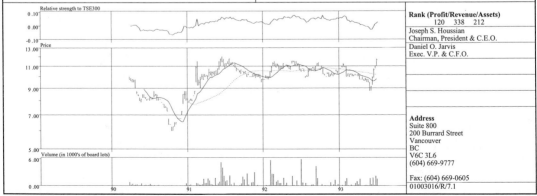

Rank (Profit/Revenue/Assets)
120   338   212

Joseph S. Houssian
Chairman, President & C.E.O.

Daniel O. Jarvis
Exec. V.P. & C.F.O.

Address
Suite 800
200 Burrard Street
Vancouver
BC
V6C 3L6
(604) 669-9777

Fax: (604) 669-0605
01003016/R/7.1

MARKBOROUGH PROPERTIES INC.

Exchanges	Price (Jun24'93)	3.35	Trailing P/E	nm	Stock Symbol
TM	Trailing Yield (%)	0.00	Trailing EPS	(6.99)	**MKP**

Period Ending	Jan93	Jan92	Jan91	Jan90	Jan89
Yearly Statistics					
Price-Close	2.50	7.38	7.50	na	na
Price-High	8.00	10.50	9.75	na	na
Price-Low	2.25	6.13	5.75	na	na
P/E-Close	nm	49.17	24.19	nt	nt
Dividends per Share	0.00	0.00	0.00	0.00	0.00
Dividend Yield (%)	0.00	0.00	0.00	0.00	0.00
Sales per Share	2.89	3.07	9.27	25.89	25.43
EPS before extra. item	(6.98)	0.15	0.31	0.59	1.36
Cash Flow per Share	0.79	0.82	4.37	6.00	11.65
Book Value per Share	2.04	8.38	8.43	35.84	33.02
O/S Common Shares	153,248	72,018	45,011	10,186	10,258
Total Revenue	220,854	209,139	260,852	271,916	258,746
Income before extra.	(507,522)	10,031	14,021	26,441	13,477
Cash Flow	57,337	54,424	120,679	61,074	115,284
Debt/Equity	4.84	2.52	4.67	3.90	3.36
Return on Capital (%)	(22.17)	3.77	4.92	7.89	7.61
Ret. on Com. Equity (%)	(110.86)	2.04	3.77	7.51	4.55
% Change Profit	(5,159.5)	(28.5)	(47.0)	96.2	115.3
% Change Revenue	5.6	(19.8)	(4.1)	5.1	1.4
% Change Assets	(14.3)	8.0	20.3	21.8	5.7

Business:
MARKBOROUGH PROPERTIES INC. is a real estate development company that carries on business primarily in Canada and also in the U.S. and the U.K. The company's principal business is the development, ownership and management of income producing properties. The company also develops land for sale for residential, retail, office and industrial uses.

Date	EPS	DPS	Tot Rev	Inc Bex
Apr 93	0.01	0.00	56,400	2,400
Jan 93	(7.08)	0.00	69,289	(514,905)
Oct 92	0.04	0.00	73,601	3,255
Jul 92	0.04	0.00	67,325	2,431
Apr 92	0.02	0.00	65,600	1,700
Jan 92	0.04	0.00	61,362	3,181
Oct 91	0.05	0.00	65,575	3,496
Jul 91	0.03	0.00	59,179	2,037

	Jan93	Jan92	Jan91
Preferred Div. Coverage	np	np	np
Total Div. Coverage	na	na	na
Income prop.(% tot. prop.)	54.5	53.5	40.0
Develop. prop.(% tot. prop.)	45.5	46.5	60.0
5 YEAR RATIOS (%)			
Return on Capital	0.4	3.3	4.3
Return on Com. Equity	(18.6)	(2.3)	0.1
Profit Growth	na	(26.9)	(17.8)
Revenue Growth	(2.9)	(13.7)	(4.9)
Asset Growth	7.4	8.7	6.8
BALANCE SHEET (000)			
Cash	0	0	0
Total Real Estate Assets	1,870,261	1,752,686	2,162,725
Invest's & Advances	17,923	22,353	43,144
Total Assets	2,125,251	2,479,277	2,295,384
Bank Indebtedness	178,501	199,408	325,179
Long Term Debt	1,332,709	1,318,539	1,446,075
Total Liabilities	1,813,147	1,875,786	1,916,185
Total Equity	312,104	603,491	379,199
Total Liab. & Equity	2,125,251	2,479,277	2,295,384
CAPITAL (000)			
Total Debt	1,511,210	1,517,947	1,771,254
Preferred Equity	0	0	0
Common Equity	312,104	603,491	379,199

Synopsis:

In March 1993, Markborough Properties Inc. said its rights offering was 94.6% subscribed to, resulting in proceeds of about $238.4-million. Shareholders received rights to purchase an additional seven shares for every share held at an exercise price of $2.50 a share. Markborough parent Woodbridge Co. Ltd., controlled by Kenneth Thomson, said Woodbridge and its affiliates increased their combined holdings to 129,250,811 Markborough common shares (83.9% of the common shares outstanding) from 58,021,173 (80.6%). Mr. Thomson personally holds 400,000 Markborough common shares.

In early 1993, Markborough sold its U.S. community land business to Woodbridge Co. Ltd. for a nominal sum plus the assumption of approximately $160-million in related debt. The deal marked the third time in less than two years that Woodbridge has relieved its real estate subsidiary's debt burden, and it shows the depth of commitment to the company. The deal surprised the investment community, where rumors that Markborough would take an enormous write-down on its troubled U.S. land holdings had swirled for several weeks after Markborough raised that possibility with analysts.

On January 21, 1993, despite the enormous loss to Markborough's balance sheet, Dominion Bond Rating Service Ltd. confirmed its single-A (low) rating on Markborough's senior debt, predicting that shedding the money-losing U.S. land operation will turn a cash flow shortfall expected next year into a surplus.

On January 14, 1993, Markborough and Cadillac Fairview Corporation announced plans for an $18-million renovation program at Les Galeries d'Anjou in Ville d'Anjou, Quebec. Located at the interchange of Boulevard Metropolitain and Autoroute 25, the one million square foot shopping centre has 175 stores anchored by La Baie, Eaton, Sears and Maxi.

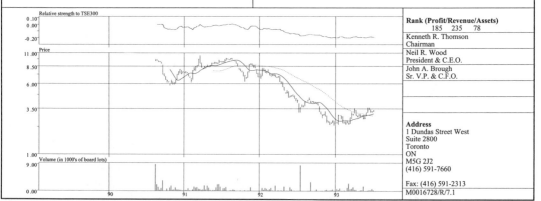

Rank (Profit/Revenue/Assets)
185   235   78

Kenneth R. Thomson
Chairman

Neil R. Wood
President & C.E.O.

John A. Brough
Sr. V.P. & C.F.O.

Address
1 Dundas Street West
Suite 2800
Toronto
ON
M5G 2J2
(416) 591-7660

Fax: (416) 591-2313
M0016728/R/7.1

MELCOR DEVELOPMENTS LTD.

Exchanges	Price (Jun24'93)	10 .00	Trailing P/E	6 .41	Stock Symbol
T	Trailing Yield (%)	2 .00	Trailing EPS	1 .56	**MRD**

Period Ending	Dec92	Dec91	Dec90	Dec89	Dec88
Yearly Statistics					
Price-Close	11 .00	11 .25	9 .25	9 .75	7 .50
Price-High	11 .50	12 .75	10 .50	9 .75	8 .75
Price-Low	9 .75	9 .00	7 .88	5 .50	5 .75
P/E-Close	6 .55	18 .44	2 .96	3 .13	9 .26
Dividends per Share	0 .25	0 .20	0 .10	0 .10	0 .00
Dividend Yield (%)	2 .27	1 .78	1 .08	1 .03	0 .00
Sales per Share	16 .95	12 .78	14 .26	27 .63	20 .87
EPS before extra. item	1 .68	0 .61	3 .13	3 .12	0 .81
Cash Flow per Share	3 .65	1 .94	2 .38	3 .47	0 .80
Book Value per Share	16 .19	14 .68	14 .38	11 .02	8 .11
O/S Common Shares	3 ,016	2 ,996	2 ,958	2 ,950	2 ,950
Total Revenue	54 ,297	42 ,091	57 ,413	88 ,157	67 ,337
Income before extra.	4 ,945	1 ,854	9 ,279	9 ,238	2 ,396
Cash Flow	10 ,977	5 ,823	7 ,043	10 ,247	2 ,360
Debt/Equity	0 .84	0 .87	1 .02	2 .51	4 .30
Return on Capital (%)	12 .87	7 .64	18 .09	15 .10	9 .02
Ret. on Com. Equity (%)	10 .57	4 .19	24 .66	32 .65	10 .31
% Change Profit	166 .7	(80 .0)	0 .4	285 .6	117 .7
% Change Revenue	29 .0	(26 .7)	(34 .9)	30 .9	(18 .7)
% Change Assets	9 .8	2 .4	(21 .9)	(8 .1)	(10 .8)

Business:

MELCOR DEVELOPMENTS LTD. is a real estate development company. It acquires land for the development and sale of residential and industrial subdivisions. It also builds and markets single-family housing and develops and acquires income-producing properties. Current activities are located in Alberta.

Date	EPS	DPS	Tot Rev	Inc Bex
Mar 93	0 .06	0 .00	7 ,324	171
Dec 92	1 .04	0 .10	20 ,828	2 ,998
Sep 92	0 .22	0 .00	13 ,330	663
Jun 92	0 .24	0 .10	10 ,748	742
Mar 92	0 .18	0 .00	9 ,391	542
Dec 91	0 .29	0 .10	17 ,112	907
Sep 91	0 .16	0 .00	10 ,682	460
Jun 91	0 .28	0 .10	10 ,569	843

Preferred Div. Coverage	123 .6	46 .4	386 .6	
Total Div. Coverage	6 .3	2 .9	29 .0	
Income prop.(% tot. prop.)	23 .0	24 .8	22 .2	
Develop. prop.(% tot. prop.)	77 .0	75 .2	77 .8	
5 YEAR RATIOS (%)				
Return on Capital	12 .5	9 .4	8 .1	
Return on Com. Equity	16 .5	5 .3	2 .6	
Profit Growth	35 .0	na	na	
Revenue Growth	(8 .1)	(3 .6)	5 .5	
Asset Growth	(6 .4)	(10 .0)	(9 .4)	
BALANCE SHEET (000)				
Cash	1 ,558	1 ,570	10 ,400	
Total Real Estate Assets	97 ,523	91 ,877	75 ,220	
Invest's & Advances	1 ,542	1 ,253	10 ,069	
Total Assets	123 ,577	112 ,531	109 ,848	
Bank Indebtedness	0	0	0	
Long Term Debt	42 ,417	39 ,337	44 ,974	
Total Liabilities	73 ,116	67 ,255	65 ,767	
Total Equity	50 ,461	45 ,276	44 ,081	
Total Liab. & Equity	123 ,577	112 ,531	109 ,848	
CAPITAL (000)				
Total Debt	42 ,417	39 ,337	44 ,974	
Preferred Equity	1 ,618	1 ,292	1 ,536	
Common Equity	48 ,843	43 ,984	42 ,545	

Synopsis:

For the 1992 fiscal year, Melcor Developments Ltd.'s land development activities continued to be its primary business with revenue of $30.2-million, compared with $23.48-million in 1991. A total of 636 single family residential lots were sold in subdivisions located in Edmonton, Spruce Grove, Red Deer and Calgary which represents an increase of 125 over the prior year.

In 1992, through a joint venture it manages, Melcor acquired a 40% interest in three parcels of land for residential development, totaling 339 acres. Development began on two of the parcels with sales recorded during the year.

Melcor Homes, the company's house construction division, recorded revenues of $16.9-million in 1992, compared with $11-million in the prior year. Improved performance in this division stems partly from management's strategy of concentrating on the construction of housing projects that target specific markets. In 1993, the company will be entering into a partnership with senior management of the division who will purchase a one-third interest. The company anticipates that this partnership will optimize its return on investment, reduce its risk and provide greater incentive for performance.

During 1992, Melcor reduced $3,536,000 of the bank term loan to $10,205,000 at year-end. Bank debt reduction continues to be a company priority. As at December 31, 1992, the loan payments for 1993 have been paid. It is the company's goal to maintain adequate cash reserves. The company also plans to: increase dividend payments to shareholders; selectively and prudently acquire lands for future development; and to accelerate the payment of the bank term loan.

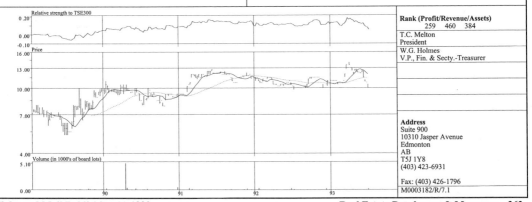

Rank (Profit/Revenue/Assets)
259   460   384

T.C. Melton
President

W.G. Holmes
V.P., Fin. & Secty.-Treasurer

Address
Suite 900
10310 Jasper Avenue
Edmonton
AB
T5J 1Y8
(403) 423-6931

Fax: (403) 426-1796
M0003182/R/7.1

REVENUE PROPERTIES COMPANY LIMITED

Exchanges	Price (Jun24'93)	3.40	Trailing P/E	nm	Stock Symbol
T	Trailing Yield (%)	0.00	Trailing EPS	(0.61)	RPC

Period Ending	Dec92	Dec91	Dec90	Dec89	Dec88
Yearly Statistics					
Price-Close	2.85	3.95	3.75	5.63	3.70
Price-High	4.00	4.55	6.38	6.00	3.85
Price-Low	2.50	3.50	3.25	3.40	2.30
P/E-Close	nm	197.50	9.38	22.50	18.50
Dividends per Share	0.00	0.00	0.00	0.00	0.00
Dividend Yield (%)	0.00	0.00	0.00	0.00	0.00
Sales per Share	2.49	1.19	2.49	1.57	1.75
EPS before extra. item	(0.62)	0.02	0.40	0.25	0.20
Cash Flow per Share	(0.04)	0.10	0.41	0.40	0.33
Book Value per Share	1.51	1.64	1.67	1.08	0.93
O/S Common Shares	44,022	37,074	37,162	16,063	15,013
Total Revenue	106,297	46,499	103,104	27,386	31,043
Income before extra.	(26,545)	773	14,819	4,028	3,307
Cash Flow	(1,797)	3,670	15,095	6,435	5,460
Debt/Equity	5.94	1.93	1.66	4.48	5.18
Return on Capital (%)	(0.77)	6.50	23.35	11.63	11.92
Ret. on Com. Equity (%)	(41.71)	1.26	37.28	25.74	23.76
% Change Profit	(3,534.0)	(94.8)	267.9	21.8	50.7
% Change Revenue	128.6	(54.9)	276.5	(11.8)	(20.4)
% Change Assets	154.0	4.5	99.8	8.1	11.2
Preferred Div. Coverage	na	na	na		
Total Div. Coverage	na	na	na		
Income prop.(% tot. prop.)	91.8	72.2	74.8		
Develop. prop.(% tot. prop.)	8.2	27.8	25.2		
5 YEAR RATIOS (%)					
Return on Capital	10.5	13.2	13.3		
Return on Com. Equity	9.3	20.8	18.9		
Profit Growth	na	6.8	113.1		
Revenue Growth	22.2	(3.6)	4.8		
Asset Growth	44.7	15.2	16.1		
BALANCE SHEET (000)					
Cash	15,123	3,127	2,199		
Total Real Estate Assets	490,610	168,459	164,121		
Invest's & Advances	17,593	19,605	28,914		
Total Assets	534,718	210,554	201,511		
Bank Indebtedness	28,695	14,765	11,344		
Long Term Debt	384,743	113,347	105,347		
Total Liabilities	465,157	144,319	131,346		
Total Equity	69,561	66,235	70,165		
Total Liab. & Equity	534,718	210,554	201,511		
CAPITAL (000)					
Total Debt	413,438	128,112	116,691		
Preferred Equity	3,095	5,425	8,000		
Common Equity	66,466	60,810	62,165		

Business:

REVENUE PROPERTIES COMPANY LIMITED operates in various segments of the real estate industry. On April 2, 1992, it acquired a controlling interest in Pan Pacific Development Corp. On a consolidated basis, the company earns 75% of rental revenues from retail properties, and over one-third of rental revenues from the United States. The company has properties in Toronto, Seattle, Las Vegas, and Los Angeles.

Date	EPS	DPS	Tot Rev	Inc Bex
Mar 93	(0.01)	0.00	28,028	(583)
Dec 92	(0.54)	0.00	19,692	(23,282)
Sep 92	(0.06)	0.00	29,172	(2,732)
Jun 92	0.00	0.00	47,026	(66)
Mar 92	(0.01)	0.00	16,163	(465)
Dec 91	(0.01)	0.00	12,254	(395)
Sep 91	0.00	0.00	13,257	54
Jun 91	0.02	0.00	17,971	834

Synopsis:

In April 1993, the boards of Revenue Properties Co. Ltd. and Pan Pacific Development Corp. approved a plan that will see Revenue acquire all the shares and warrants of Pan Pacific not owned by Revenue. Revenue currently owns about 59% of Pan Pacific. It will issue one of its own shares for each 2.7 common shares of Pan Pacific and one share-purchase warrant for each warrant of Pan Pacific. Each Revenue warrant would let the holder buy one share for $3.60 until December 31, 1994.

In 1992, Revenue Properties recorded a cash deficiency from continuing operations of $1.8-million or 4 cents per share compared to cash flow of $3.7-million or 10 cents per share in 1991. This change is primarily due to the loss on sale of real estate in 1992 of $1.8-million as compared to a profit on sale of real estate during 1991 of $1.4-million.

During 1992, the company spent approximately $50-million on the acquisition and development of real estate. In addition, the company spent $30-million, net of cash acquired, for the acquisition of a 59% interest in Pan Pacific Development Company. These investments were financed by additional long-term debt and by the issue of 7,181,250 treasury shares of Revenue Properties to The Toronto-Dominion Bank and Citibank Canada as part of the investment transaction at $4.13 per share.

At 1992 year-end, the company's total portfolio of income producing properties had an occupancy rate of approximately 94%. In April 1992, there was an 89% occupancy rate in Pan Pacific's portfolio; however, subsequent to the acquisition, the company reorganized Pan Pacific's management and leasing operations. Weak tenants were terminated and leasing efforts have increased the level of occupancy for Pan Pacific's properties to 94% at year-end. Total rental operations in Metropolitan Toronto had an occupancy rate of about 95% with the vacancies existing primarily in the residential sector. Shopping centers are virtually fully leased.

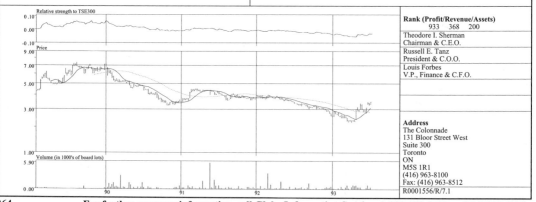

Rank (Profit/Revenue/Assets)
933   368   200

Theodore I. Sherman
Chairman & C.E.O.

Russell E. Tanz
President & C.O.O.

Louis Forbes
V.P., Finance & C.F.O.

Address
The Colonnade
131 Bloor Street West
Suite 300
Toronto
ON
M5S 1R1
(416) 963-8100
Fax: (416) 963-8512
R0001556/R/7.1

ROYAL LEPAGE LIMITED

Exchanges	Price (Jun24'93)	2.60	Trailing P/E	nm	Stock Symbol
TMV	Trailing Yield (%)	11.54	Trailing EPS	(1.40)	**RLG**

Period Ending	Dec92	Dec91	Dec90	Dec89	Dec88
Yearly Statistics					
Price-Close	5.00	8.00	7.63	12.25	8.75
Price-High	10.50	10.13	12.13	14.25	10.13
Price-Low	4.25	6.75	6.00	9.00	7.50
P/E-Close	nm	160.00	nm	5.95	4.44
Dividends per Share	0.55	0.70	0.70	0.64	0.48
Dividend Yield (%)	7.50	8.75	9.18	5.22	5.49
Sales per Share	na	na	na	na	na
EPS before extra. item	(1.04)	0.05	(0.50)	2.06	1.97
Cash Flow per Share	(0.68)	0.97	(0.95)	2.15	2.44
Book Value per Share	3.99	5.43	6.71	7.82	6.32
O/S Common Shares	15,944	15,242	14,220	13,797	13,372
Total Revenue	480,274	498,963	466,877	639,703	652,415
Income before extra.	(16,275)	756	(6,988)	28,053	26,319
Cash Flow	(10,543)	14,638	(13,248)	29,298	32,532
Debt/Equity	1.76	2.11	2.30	2.92	3.02
Return on Capital (%)	(4.62)	4.21	1.72	16.28	21.57
Ret. on Com. Equity (%)	(22.23)	0.85	(6.88)	29.17	35.47
% Change Profit	(2,252.8)	110.8	(124.9)	6.6	32.3
% Change Revenue	(3.7)	6.9	(27.0)	(1.9)	14.4
% Change Assets	(27.2)	(13.9)	(30.6)	15.4	45.8

Period Ending	Dec92	Dec91	Dec90
Preferred Div. Coverage	np	np	np
Total Div. Coverage	0.0	0.1	0.0
Income prop.(% tot. prop.)	na	na	na
Develop. prop.(% tot. prop.)	na	na	na
5 YEAR RATIOS (%)			
Return on Capital	7.8	13.8	19.6
Return on Com. Equity	7.3	19.5	28.3
Profit Growth	na	(44.4)	na
Revenue Growth	(3.4)	(0.5)	0.2
Asset Growth	(6.1)	3.3	24.0
BALANCE SHEET (000)			
Cash	0	0	35,815
Total Real Estate Assets	0	0	0
Invest's & Advances	110,091	180,543	197,869
Total Assets	240,067	329,603	382,978
Bank Indebtedness	111,823	174,454	76,000
Long Term Debt	0	0	142,991
Total Liabilities	176,433	246,790	287,608
Total Equity	63,634	82,813	95,370
Total Liab. & Equity	240,067	329,603	382,978
CAPITAL (000)			
Total Debt	111,823	174,454	218,991
Preferred Equity	0	0	0
Common Equity	63,634	82,813	95,370

Business:

ROYAL LEPAGE LIMITED is a diversified real estate services company. It has residential, commercial and professional services offices Canada. International affiliates further augment the company's service network. Trilon Financial Corp. of Toronto is a major shareholder of the company.

Date	EPS	DPS	Tot Rev	Inc Bex
Mar 93	(0.51)	0.00	90,202	(8,151)
Dec 92	(0.54)	0.10	97,326	(8,462)
Sep 92	(0.11)	0.10	124,658	(1,752)
Jun 92	(0.24)	0.18	134,911	(3,752)
Mar 92	(0.15)	0.18	123,379	(2,309)
Dec 91	(0.20)	0.18	96,860	(2,958)
Sep 91	0.01	0.18	116,612	163
Jun 91	0.16	0.18	162,096	2,468

Synopsis:

Royal LePage management was disappointed and concerned with the company's 1992 results. Gross commission and other revenue of $481.3-million produced a loss of $16.3-million. This compared with revenue of $500.5-million and net income of $800,000 in 1991.

The company attributed the poor performance in 1992 to five factors. Weak consumer confidence, a poor fourth quarter following interest rate increases and uncertainty associated with the October 1992 Referendum reduced market share in several geographic areas. Secondly, the development of new technology initiatives related to residential and commercial market information and agent sales support systems cost $6.7-million. Thirdly, re-aligning Royal LePage's residential branch network cost $1-million, and closing commercial offices in Chicago and Atlanta cost $600,000. Fourthly, tax recovery levels were reduced, $2.8-million compared to $6-million in 1991. And finally, operating costs were ahead of 1991 levels due to increased legal costs and increased costs to support the residential listings inventory.

Royal LePage has taken three immediate actions to halt the erosion of its profitability and increase its ability to generate revenue. It has accelerated its cost reduction effort. The company is committed to reducing all costs by $10-million in 1993. Secondly, the company has taken steps to improve liquidity. In late 1992, Royal LePage accelerated its disposition of the preferred share portfolio maintained by the Investment Group to further pay down debt. In 1992, holdings in preferred shares were reduced by $23.6-million. A further $12-million is expected to be sold in early 1993 and will be applied to the repayment of debt. As well, dividends will be suspended. This will preserve $3-million on an annual basis. Finally, Royal LePage has implemented strategies that will strengthen its ability to build revenues. For example, the company has invested about $25-million in the past three years in new technology. It is also rethinking a decades-old commission structure that could see the company take a smaller slice from the sale price of a home to stem the tide of departing salespeople.

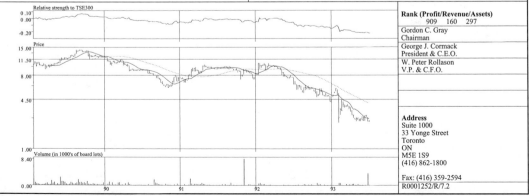

Rank (Profit/Revenue/Assets)
909   160   297

Gordon C. Gray
Chairman

George J. Cormack
President & C.E.O.

W. Peter Rollason
V.P. & C.F.O.

Address
Suite 1000
33 Yonge Street
Toronto
ON
M5E 1S9
(416) 862-1800

Fax: (416) 359-2594
R0001252/R/7.2

TRIZEC CORPORATION LTD.

Exchanges	Price (Jun24'93)		1.14	Trailing P/E		nm	Stock Symbol
TM	Trailing Yield (%)		14.91	Trailing EPS		(3.33)	**TZC.A**

Period Ending	Oct 92	Oct 91	Oct 90	Oct 89	Oct 88
Yearly Statistics					
Price-Close	3.00	12.13	10.63	26.75	33.00
Price-High	13.38	17.25	26.75	29.00	33.00
Price-Low	2.90	10.00	10.25	26.00	32.13
P/E-Close	nm	73.49	442.71	53.82	73.83
Dividends per Share	0.30	0.36	0.36	0.34	0.28
Dividend Yield (%)	10.00	2.97	3.39	1.27	0.85
Sales per Share	5.23	11.56	12.40	13.80	8.62
EPS before extra. item	(3.28)	0.17	0.02	0.50	0.45
Cash Flow per Share	0.84	1.49	5.19	2.26	2.03
Book Value per Share	2.36	5.42	5.24	5.57	4.25
O/S Common Shares	214,039	152,928	144,305	144,139	135,946
Total Revenue	894,100	1,761,600	1,829,900	1,945,600	1,192,600
Income before extra.	(544,100)	62,100	49,400	112,200	101,200
Cash Flow	146,800	222,000	748,700	312,100	274,700
Debt/Equity	5.43	7.34	7.08	5.73	5.86
Return on Capital (%)	(6.78)	4.79	5.37	6.94	7.04
Ret. on Com. Equity (%)	(85.71)	2.98	0.46	9.97	10.58
% Change Profit	(976.2)	25.7	(56.0)	10.9	12.4
% Change Revenue	(49.2)	(3.7)	(5.9)	63.1	4.6
% Change Assets	(46.1)	4.0	12.7	17.8	8.2

Date		EPS	DPS	Tot Rev	Inc Bex
Jan	93	(0.01)	0.05	261,500	5,400
Oct	92	(3.21)	0.00	230,500	(554,500)
Jul	92	(0.06)	0.12	350,500	(1,600)
Apr	92	(0.06)	0.00	343,900	(1,600)
Jan	92	0.04	0.18	363,000	13,600
Oct	91	0.06	0.00	352,500	16,500
Jul	91	0.03	0.18	354,500	13,800
Apr	91	0.03	0.00	356,800	14,300

Preferred Div. Coverage	0.0	1.6	1.1
Total Div. Coverage	0.0	0.7	0.5
Income prop.(% tot. prop.)	80.9	67.9	63.8
Develop. prop.(% tot. prop.)	19.1	32.1	36.2
5 YEAR RATIOS (%)			
Return on Capital	3.5	6.6	7.1
Return on Com. Equity	(12.3)	6.9	8.7
Profit Growth	na	(4.7)	(5.9)
Revenue Growth	(4.8)	19.6	24.9
Asset Growth	(4.3)	19.6	22.7
BALANCE SHEET (mil)			
Cash	0	0	0
Total Real Estate Assets	5,560	10,472	9,970
Invest's & Advances	401	599	619
Total Assets	6,409	11,899	11,440
Bank Indebtedness	24	9	37
Long Term Debt	5,122	9,390	8,985
Total Liabilities	5,461	10,618	10,166
Total Equity	948	1,281	1,274
Total Liab. & Equity	6,409	11,899	11,440
CAPITAL (mil)			
Total Debt	5,145	9,399	9,022
Preferred Equity	443	452	518
Common Equity	505	829	756

Business:

TRIZEC CORP. LTD. is a North American real estate development company. It owns office and mixed-use buildings and retail centres across North America. It also owns and operates retirement and nursing homes.

Synopsis:

In April 1993, Trizec Corp. sold $25-million (U.S.) of convertible debentures in Rouse Co., moving closer to eliminating its stake in the U.S. shopping mall developer. Trizec, which once owned a 25% interest in Rouse, based in Columbia, Maryland, has whittled that down to raise cash and reduce a heavy debt. Since September 1992, Trizec has sold 11 million shares to U.S. institutions for a total proceeds of about $138-million. The latest sale leaves Trizec with $60-million of debentures convertible into 2.1 million Rouse shares and warrants for 500,000 shares. Trizec said it intends to sell the remainder of its Rouse holdings by the end of 1993.

The company chairman told the annual meeting, held in April 1993, that a refinancing plan to help troubled Trizec would be considered by its board of directors in a month or two. Over the next three and one-half years, $2.39-billion of Trizec loans are maturing, $180-million in preferred shares are due for redemption, and $698.4-million of senior debentures must be repaid. And the climate for such financial negotiations is not too friendly. Trizec said lenders are anxious to reduce their overall exposure to real estate. However, Trizec does not expect to have a difficult time in its meetings with bankers. The Trizec property portfolio of office buildings, shopping centres and retirement homes is strong. Many of the mortgages that are up for renewal will be easily replaced.

In February 1993, Dominion Bond Rating Services Ltd. cut the rating on Trizec's senior debentures to triple-B (low), just above junk bond status, from single-A the top rating in the beleaguered real estate industry. DBRS also cut Trizec's commercial paper grade to pfd-4 from pfd-2. The move will raise Trizec's cost of borrowing.

During 1992, Trizec deconsolidated the results of its subsidiary Bramalea and wrote down $669-million in the carried value of its investment in Bramalea. Trizec's share of Bramalea's operating losses to the date of deconsolidation reduced net income by a further $27-million. The loss sustained from Bramalea resulted in a net loss for the year of $544-million or $3.28 per share.

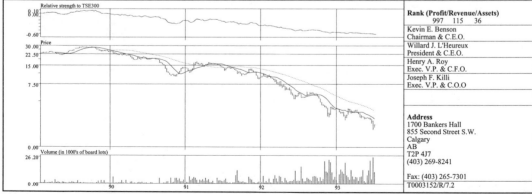

Rank (Profit/Revenue/Assets)
997   115   36

Kevin E. Benson
Chairman & C.E.O.

Willard J. L'Heureux
President & C.E.O.

Henry A. Roy
Exec. V.P. & C.F.O.

Joseph F. Killi
Exec. V.P. & C.O.O

Address
1700 Bankers Hall
855 Second Street S.W.
Calgary
AB
T2P 4J7
(403) 269-8241

Fax: (403) 265-7301
T0003152/R/7.2

Page	Company	$	Latest year end	Earnings per Share		
				Actual	Estimate this year	Estimate next year
271	Air Canada		9212	(6.13)	(2.99)	(0.34)
272	Algoma Central		9212	1.85	n.a.	n.a.
273	Greyhound Lines of Canada		9212	2.04	n.a.	n.a.
274	Newfoundland Capital		9212	(1.27)	4.90	5.20
275	PWA Corporation		9212	(4.40)	(2.84)	(0.81)
276	Trimac		9212	0.37	0.54	0.65
277	Westar Group		9212	(0.58)	n.a.	n.a.

Estimates from I/B/E/S Inc., 345 Hudson St., New York, NY 10014 (212) 243-3335. In Canada: 6 Lansing Square, Ste. 235, Willowdale, ON M2J 1T5 (416) 496-0977.

Transportation

The International Air Transport Association (IATA) reported passenger traffic on international scheduled services for member airlines rose 4% in February 1993, down from 11% in January. Passenger seat supply, as measured in available seat miles, rose 7% from a year earlier. The passenger load factor for the month was 63%. The February drop in traffic growth was described as disturbing particularly in view of the signs of a slowdown in the dynamic Far Eastern travel market

Canadian National Railways has teamed up with U.S. trucking giant J.B. Hunt Transport Services Inc. in a deal that the railway hopes will help it regain lost traffic. CN and J.B. Hunt, the largest publicly traded truckload carrier in the U.S., announced an intermodal agreement to join forces to transport freight on either side of the border. The deal will provide clients with truck and rail services throughout Ontario, Quebec and the United States. J.B. Hunt has similar deals with seven other freight railways in the U.S.

The two major airlines, Air Canada and Canadian Airlines International Ltd., reported that they are losing about $2-million a day, but according to the president of the Air Transport Association of Canada all the other airlines are either close to being profitable or are actually posting modest profits. Air Nova, Air Transit and Bearskin Lake Air Service Ltd. are a few of the more profitable companies. The share value of Air Canada and Canadian Airlines International Ltd.'s parent, PWA Corporation, has shrunk by $1.2-billion in the past few years. Passenger volume for the first nine months of 1992 for all the airline industry was down 19% compared with pre-recession 1989. Revenue is off 3% when compared with 1989, while expenses during the same period have risen by the same amount.

World airlines are expected to lose $2.5-billion (U.S.) in 1993, bringing the total losses in the last three years to more than $9-billion. Combined losses in 1990 and 1991 were $2.7-billion and $4-billion respectively. The airlines are largely to blame for the high losses as few major carriers were willing to cut back on costs as the economy fell into recession in 1990. Trying to maintain market share airlines were forced to cut prices. Since then, traffic and yields have remained too low, with capacity and unit costs too high. These economic difficulties have forced the airlines to try to put their houses in order, particularly in the areas of controlling expenses and raising productivity. According to IATA figures, member airlines cut staff by 1.45 million or 3.4% last year, with productivity per employee increasing by 1.7%.

Airlines Monthly Traffic: March 1993 - Industry Report [Apr-27-1993]. SHEARSON LEHMAN BROTHERS, INC. reported by Becker, H.
British Airways is one of the fastest growing airlines in the world. The company has one of the strongest balance sheets of all worldwide airline companies. British Air's major growth over the next few years is expected to be in international markets, primarily Asia. The airline has invested $300 million (U.S.) in USAir. Delta Air Lines' growth in 1993 is expected to be primarily in Europe. Management has retired its DC9 fleet. Further capacity adjustments will follow. [RN 1327467]

Airline Industry (Transcript) - Industry Report [Apr-1-1993]. SHEARSON LEHMAN BROTHERS, INC. reported by Becker, H.
To address the slow recovery in the U.S., and the ongoing recessions in Europe and Japan, U.S. airlines have announced sharp cutbacks in their proposed capital spending plans. The three largest U.S. airlines have reduced planned capital spending, collectively, by $27 billion (U.S.) over the next five years. [RN 1318685]

Railroad/Trucking Quarterly Earnings Estimates-Industry Report [Mar-30-1993]. SHEARSON LEHMAN BROTHERS, INC. reported by Strauss, B., Jr.
Despite poor weather and major declines in coal and grain traffic, the continuing reduction in costs at Burlington Northern should enable 1Q:93 earnings to approach 1992's figure. CSX Corp.'s poor coal traffic caused by miners' strike and weak export demand combined with slow shipping volume will cause earnings to approximate 1992. Canadian Pacific Limited's continuing weakness in forest products and slow rail traffic cannot be made up by strong energy earnings, although losses will be less. Consolidated Rail's traffic is up a bit with better mix of commodities likely to enhance profits over 1992. Norfolk Southern saw a slow 1Q:93 hurt by poor export coal demand and weather problems. [RN 1318684]

Trucking Market Segmentation: Part III - Industry Report [May-5-1993]. ALEX. BROWN & SONS, INC. reported by Boyle, H.P., Jr.
As the business environment becomes more competitive, manufacturers and retailers are locating closer to their customers and cutting costs. For the trucking industry in general and the LTL segment in particular, this translates into regionalization. Shippers, in an attempt to minimize inventory costs and to conform to their customers' just-in-time requirement are increasingly focusing on regional distribution strategies that reduce delivery times from two or more days to two days or less. This is fueling tonnage growth in the regional LTL sector, while tonnage growth in the national LTL sector is essentially flat. [RN 1330542]

AIR CANADA

Exchanges	Price (Jun24'93)	3.55	Trailing P/E	nm	Stock Symbol
TMVZW	Trailing Yield (%)	0.00	Trailing EPS	(7.87)	**AC**

Period Ending	Dec92	Dec91	Dec90	Dec89	Dec88	Business:
Yearly Statistics						AIR CANADA is an international air carrier
Price-Close	2.75	8.00	8.50	12.88	7.50	providing scheduled and chartered air
Price-High	8.38	10.38	11.38	14.88	8.25	transportation for passengers and cargo. The
Price-Low	2.20	6.63	7.25	7.25	7.00	company also provides computer services,
P/E-Close	nm	nm	nm	6.07	4.03	maintenance and other ground services to other
Dividends per Share	0.00	0.00	0.00	0.00	0.00	airlines. It holds equity interest in five Canadian
Dividend Yield (%)	0.00	0.00	0.00	0.00	0.00	regional airlines. The airline's diversification
Sales per Share	42.62	42.81	48.38	45.61	64.68	includes Air Canada Vacations, a tour operator.
EPS before extra. item	(6.13)	(2.94)	(1.01)	2.12	1.86	
Cash Flow per Share	(2.74)	(1.81)	1.32	1.97	2.61	
Book Value per Share	4.27	10.40	13.35	14.55	12.70	

O/S Common Shares	74,034	74,034	74,027	72,990	71,896
Total Revenue	3,501,000	3,529,000	4,032,000	3,921,000	3,552,000
Income before extra.	(454,000)	(218,000)	(74,000)	149,000	89,000
Cash Flow	(203,000)	(134,000)	97,000	143,000	125,000

Date	EPS	DPS	Tot Rev	Inc Bex
Mar 93	(3.96)	0.00	811,000	(293,000)
Dec 92	(1.99)	0.00	786,000	(147,000)
Sep 92	(0.19)	0.00	1,013,000	(14,000)
Jun 92	(1.73)	0.00	910,000	(129,000)
Mar 92	(2.23)	0.00	809,000	(164,000)
Dec 91	(1.24)	0.00	776,000	(92,000)
Sep 91	0.06	0.00	974,000	4,000
Jun 91	(0.41)	0.00	921,000	(30,000)

	Dec92	Dec91	Dec90	Dec89	Dec88
Debt/Equity	10.68	3.92	2.25	1.70	1.57
Return on Capital (%)	(6.34)	(5.43)	0.72	12.00	10.57
Ret. on Com. Equity (%)	(83.61)	(24.80)	(7.22)	15.09	11.77
% Change Profit	(108.3)	(194.6)	(149.7)	67.4	93.5
% Change Revenue	(0.8)	(12.5)	2.8	10.4	10.6
% Change Assets	(2.3)	7.5	11.1	19.9	11.4

				Synopsis:
Preferred Div. Coverage	np	np	np	
Total Div. Coverage	na	na	na	
Interest Coverage	0.0	0.0	0.2	
Current Ratio	1.1	1.2	1.5	
Operating Margin	(5.6)	(5.7)	(0.3)	
Asset Turnover	0.7	0.6	0.8	
5 YEAR RATIOS (%)				
Return on Capital	2.3	5.4	8.3	
Return on Com. Equity	(17.8)	0.6	6.9	
Profit Growth	na	na	na	
Revenue Growth	1.7	3.6	7.6	
Asset Growth	9.3	10.9	12.3	
BALANCE SHEET (000)				
Cash	418,000	128,000	436,000	
Current Assets	925,000	978,000	1,311,000	
Net Fixed Assets	2,949,000	2,954,000	2,557,000	
Invest's & Advances	206,000	203,000	231,000	
Total Assets	4,810,000	4,921,000	4,579,000	
Short Term Debt	45,000	47,000	34,000	
Current Liabilities	851,000	850,000	890,000	
Long Term Debt	3,330,000	2,970,000	2,184,000	
Total Liabilities	4,494,000	4,151,000	3,591,000	
Total Equity	316,000	770,000	988,000	
Total Liab. & Equity	4,810,000	4,921,000	4,579,000	
CAPITAL (000)				
Total Debt	3,375,000	3,017,000	2,218,000	
Preferred Equity	0	0	0	
Common Equity	316,000	770,000	988,000	

Synopsis:

In April 1993, Air Canada and Air Partners of Fort Worth became partners with beleaguered Continental Airlines Inc. of Houston which came out of its second bankruptcy protection with more than $600-million in cash from debt restructuring. Continental now ranks as the fourth largest airline in North America. Air Canada received a 25% voting interest in Continental in exchange for buying $235-million of the airline's notes and stock. The combined destinations of both airlines could boost annual revenues for both carriers by $400-million annually when and if a broader bilateral airlines pact is negotiated.

Air Canada is aggressively pursuing programs to help reduce debt, increase revenue and position itself to take a larger market share in North America as airlines compete globally in a shrinking market. Air Canada maintains that Canada cannot support two national carriers and that re-regulation and U.S. airline support might be the answer if a merger with Canadian Airlines International cannot be achieved. A restructuring of $5-billion in various long-term debt obligations is being considered. Other remaining issues are the maintenance and survival of the Gemini reservation system and the sale or merger of CAI with American Airlines.

The $293-million loss in first quarter of 1993 was the biggest ever for Air Canada, and further management shakeups are planned. A year ago management was trimmed, and another 1,000 to 1,500 of 18,700 jobs will be cut. Nevertheless the company is still projecting an operating profit for 1993, with a final loss of between $200 to $300-million. In the past 3 1/2 years Air Canada has lost more than $1-billion.

In 1992 revenue fell slightly to $801-million from $802-million as system capacity and usage shrunk. As an example of its restructuring efforts, Air Canada raised $190-million (U.S.) through the sale of five Airbus A320 aircraft to a consortium of international banks. Part of the deal involved the signing of long-term agreements to lease the five aircraft from the consortium. Air Canada has similar plans for its three Boeing 747-400s, which would boost its cash and available credit position to close to $1-billion.

Rank (Profit/Revenue/Assets)		
994	38	46

Hollis L. Harris
Chairman, President & C.E.O.

J.F. Ricketts
Exec. V.P., Finance & C.F.O.

Address
Air Canada Centre
P.O. Box 14000
Postal Station St-Laurent
Montreal
PQ
H4Y 1H4
(514) 422-5000

A0015425/G/8.0

ALGOMA CENTRAL CORPORATION

Exchanges	Price (Jun24'93)	10 .00	Trailing P/E	4 .27	Stock Symbol
T	Trailing Yield (%)	0 .00	Trailing EPS	2 .34	**ALC**

Period Ending	Dec92	Dec91	Dec90	Dec89	Dec88
Yearly Statistics					
Price-Close	12 .50	8 .38	10 .00	14 .00	20 .75
Price-High	12 .68	8 .38	15 .25	43 .00	25 .00
Price-Low	8 .00	7 .75	7 .00	14 .00	22 .00
P/E-Close	6 .76	9 .74	7 .81	11 .67	10 .53
Dividends per Share	0 .00	0 .00	0 .15	20 .65	0 .65
Dividend Yield (%)	0 .00	0 .00	1 .50	147 .50	3 .13
Sales per Share	40 .81	42 .60	41 .68	39 .26	36 .96
EPS before extra. item	1 .85	0 .86	1 .28	1 .20	1 .97
Cash Flow per Share	5 .75	5 .63	5 .98	6 .00	5 .10
Book Value per Share	15 .08	13 .17	12 .29	11 .16	30 .68
O/S Common Shares	3 ,891	3 ,891	3 ,891	3 ,887	3 ,879
Total Revenue	161 ,416	166 ,342	167 ,804	155 ,555	145 ,501
Income before extra.	7 ,181	3 ,346	4 ,982	4 ,672	7 ,619
Cash Flow	22 ,358	21 ,918	23 ,268	23 ,321	19 ,753
Debt/Equity	1 .30	1 .69	3 .48	3 .73	0 .58
Return on Capital (%)	13 .04	10 .80	14 .15	8 .69	11 .12
Ret. on Com. Equity (%)	13 .07	6 .76	10 .93	5 .76	6 .66
% Change Profit	114 .6	(32 .8)	6 .6	(38 .7)	7 .1
% Change Revenue	(3 .0)	(0 .9)	7 .9	6 .9	(19 .9)
% Change Assets	(5 .4)	(22 .1)	3 .3	4 .4	5 .3

Preferred Div. Coverage	np	np	np
Total Div. Coverage	na	na	8 .5
Interest Coverage	2 .3	1 .6	1 .4
Current Ratio	0 .8	0 .7	1 .1
Operating Margin	12 .8	11 .1	14 .8
Asset Turnover	0 .7	0 .7	0 .5
5 YEAR RATIOS (%)			
Return on Capital	11 .6	11 .6	11 .4
Return on Com. Equity	8 .6	7 .4	6 .5
Profit Growth	0 .2	4 .5	2 .5
Revenue Growth	(2 .3)	(4 .4)	(3 .5)
Asset Growth	(3 .6)	(4 .5)	1 .1
BALANCE SHEET (000)			
Cash	3 ,649	1 ,273	57 ,259
Current Assets	33 ,609	33 ,010	90 ,181
Net Fixed Assets	204 ,925	218 ,986	233 ,281
Invest's & Advances	469	782	1 ,091
Total Assets	239 ,003	252 ,778	324 ,553
Short Term Debt	14 ,796	15 ,337	60 ,548
Current Liabilities	43 ,529	44 ,817	84 ,212
Long Term Debt	61 ,317	71 ,132	105 ,630
Total Liabilities	180 ,328	201 ,551	276 ,746
Total Equity	58 ,675	51 ,227	47 ,807
Total Liab. & Equity	239 ,003	252 ,778	324 ,553
CAPITAL (000)			
Total Debt	76 ,113	86 ,469	166 ,178
Preferred Equity	0	0	0
Common Equity	58 ,675	51 ,227	47 ,807

Business:

ALGOMA CENTRAL CORPORATION is a diversified transportation company moving cargo by water and rail. It operates a fleet of vessels on the Great Lakes and the St. Lawrence Seaway. Its main railway line serves the Algoma region of Northern Ontario. It has commercial real estate complexes in Sault St. Marie and Elliot Lake, Ont., and owns land including timber and mineral rights, in the Algoma region.

Date	EPS	DPS	Tot Rev	Inc Bex
Mar 93	(0 .03)	0 .00	14 ,223	(100)
Dec 92	0 .60	0 .00	47 ,256	2 ,303
Sep 92	0 .82	0 .00	51 ,272	3 ,196
Jun 92	0 .95	0 .00	48 ,700	3 ,703
Mar 92	(0 .52)	0 .00	14 ,188	(2 ,021)
Dec 91	0 .71	0 .00	47 ,550	2 ,781
Sep 91	0 .22	0 .00	49 ,243	849
Jun 91	0 .49	0 .00	53 ,980	1 ,895

Synopsis:

Negotiations have begun to restructure Algoma Central Corporation as a prerequisite for the Illinois-based Wisconsin Central Ltd. to consider purchasing the operation. The president of the U.S. company said that Algoma Central must be overhauled, and that may include a drastic reduction in its workforce of 1,500 workers if the company is to become profitable.

Net loss for the first quarter of 1993 went from $2-million in 1992 to $100,000 in 1993, however the change was primarily due to a timing difference in the receipt of non-passenger operating grants to the railway from the Ontario government. Algoma has not paid out any dividends to shareholders since 1990.

Algoma's railway is under-used and not profitable at the volumes of traffic available to it and could not continue operating without government support which provided $5.6-million in the first half of 1993, $2.8-million in 1992. Discussions are underway to set up long-term arrangements for maintaining the rail operation.

Because of better earnings from self-unloader ships and reduced interest expense, net income rose from $3.3-million in 1991 to $7.1-million in 1992. Algoma's primary business and future strength is in marine shipping, and the company's strategy is to promote the industry on the Great Lakes and explore ocean shipping opportunities.

However, bulk shipping is down because grain exports through the St. Lawrence Seaway have collapsed, partly because the Canadian Wheat Board now prefers ports on the West Coast due to more vibrant Far East markets and federal subsidies towards the costs of moving grain by rail.

Real estate investments in Elliot Lake, Ontario, were written down by $5.1-million in 1992 because of flat growth. As well, Algoma has discontinued land development in Florida and is in the final stage of liquidation, providing an accounting gain of $2.6-million.

Relative strength to TSE300

Price

Volume (in 1000's of board lots)

Rank (Profit/Revenue/Assets)
212   303   300

Frank S. Miller
Chairman

Peter R. Cresswell
President & C.E.O.

Robert G. Topp
V.P., Finance

Address
289 Bay Street
P.O. Box 7000
Sault Ste. Marie
ON
P6A 5P6
(705) 949-2113

A0001475/G/8.0

GREYHOUND LINES OF CANADA LTD.

Exchanges	Price (Jun24'93)	18.25	Trailing P/E	8.65	Stock Symbol
T	Trailing Yield (%)	6.58	Trailing EPS	2.11	**GHL**

Period Ending	Dec92	Dec91	Dec90	Dec89	Dec88
Yearly Statistics					
Price-Close	27.25	34.00	31.50	29.00	24.00
Price-High	36.25	37.38	33.50	32.75	25.50
Price-Low	25.25	31.25	28.75	23.50	19.50
P/E-Close	13.36	17.71	11.05	11.11	8.99
Dividends per Share	1.20	1.20	1.20	1.20	1.20
Dividend Yield (%)	4.40	3.53	3.81	4.14	5.00
Sales per Share	22.08	23.27	35.45	31.91	31.08
EPS before extra. item	2.04	1.92	2.85	2.61	2.67
Cash Flow per Share	2.13	2.31	3.86	3.43	3.58
Book Value per Share	21.32	20.48	19.73	18.31	16.88
O/S Common Shares	8,398	8,392	8,349	8,493	8,474
Total Revenue	185,507	194,626	305,345	276,479	268,366
Income before extra.	17,091	16,106	24,066	22,102	22,598
Cash Flow	17,862	19,278	32,623	29,087	30,350
Debt/Equity	0.00	0.01	0.00	0.04	0.03
Return on Capital (%)	14.19	14.34	26.08	25.74	29.24
Ret. on Com. Equity (%)	9.74	9.57	15.03	14.81	16.52
% Change Profit	6.1	(33.1)	8.9	(2.2)	28.0
% Change Revenue	(4.7)	(36.3)	10.4	3.0	8.9
% Change Assets	2.8	1.5	2.7	11.9	5.2

Preferred Div. Coverage	np	np	np
Total Div. Coverage	1.7	1.6	2.4
Interest Coverage	65.2	63.6	na
Current Ratio	1.9	2.0	1.7
Operating Margin	8.6	9.0	12.3
Asset Turnover	0.8	0.8	1.3
5 YEAR RATIOS (%)			
Return on Capital	21.9	24.2	25.5
Return on Com. Equity	13.1	14.0	14.5
Profit Growth	(0.7)	1.4	4.6
Revenue Growth	(5.5)	(2.3)	5.9
Asset Growth	4.7	5.8	5.0
BALANCE SHEET (000)			
Cash	86	1,398	2,227
Current Assets	75,808	75,878	71,465
Net Fixed Assets	152,191	143,192	135,294
Invest's & Advances	6,337	10,703	19,547
Total Assets	240,024	233,544	230,159
Short Term Debt	458	1,853	631
Current Liabilities	40,932	38,111	42,830
Long Term Debt	0	0	0
Total Liabilities	61,012	61,715	65,448
Total Equity	179,012	171,829	164,711
Total Liab. & Equity	240,024	233,544	230,159
CAPITAL (000)			
Total Debt	458	1,853	631
Preferred Equity	0	0	0
Common Equity	179,012	171,829	164,711

Business:

GREYHOUND LINES OF CANADA LTD. is a motor coach transportation and bus manufacturing company. The company operates a scheduled and charter transportation service covering western and northern Canada and Ontario. It also offers package courier service. Motor Coach Industries Ltd., a wholly owned subsidiary, makes motor coaches at facilities in Winnipeg for the North American market.

Date	EPS	DPS	Tot Rev	Inc Bex
Mar 93	0.04	0.30	40,402	324
Dec 92	0.57	0.30	(42,755)	4,774
Sep 92	1.06	0.30	81,512	8,907
Jun 92	0.44	0.30	80,167	3,643
Mar 92	(0.03)	0.30	66,583	(233)
Dec 91	0.36	0.30	(23,422)	3,018
Sep 91	0.96	0.30	77,988	8,042
Jun 91	0.38	0.30	77,479	3,194

Synopsis:

Two major changes at Greyhound Lines of Canada were completed in 1992. Shareholders voted on February 8, 1993, to set up Motor Coach Industries Ltd. (MCI) of Winnipeg, a wholly-owned coach shell manufacturing subsidiary of Greyhound, as a separate, publicly traded company with The Dial Corp., of Phoenix, Arizona, as its major shareholder. Common shares of MCI were distributed to Greyhound shareholders on a one-for-one basis. Dividends of the parent company were maintained with the first quarterly dividend of the new company at 12.5 cents while Greyhound declared a quarterly divided of 17.5 cents. Prior to separation Greyhound was paying 30 cents a quarter.

The second major change was the December 1992 completion of the purchase of Gray Coach Lines Inc. (Gray Coach) of Toronto, which was insolvent and reorganizing. Gray Coach is expected to contribute approximately $18-million to revenues in 1993. The acquisition adds three major routes moving one million passengers a year in Southern Ontario.

In spite of lower ridership Greyhound had first quarter revenues of $40.4-million, an increase of 7.6% from $37.5-million for the same period a year ago. Net losses were $1.3-million or 15 cents per share, compared to net losses of $1.9 million or 23 cents per share, for the corresponding period last year, an improvement of 35.6%.

In 1993 Greyhound will be negotiating various labor agreements but does not expect any disruptions. As well MCI's income tax returns for the fiscal years 1981 to 1986 are under review by Revenue Canada. Revenue Canada is considering assessing higher rates of income related to transactions between MCI and a U.S. based affiliate. A judgment could add additional income taxes of $19-million plus interest. As well, taxation years subsequent to 1986 may be subject to reassessment on the same basis, resulting in further income tax of as much as $11-million plus interest through to December 31, 1992.

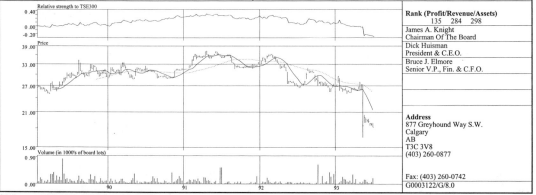

Rank (Profit/Revenue/Assets)		
135	284	298
James A. Knight		
Chairman Of The Board		
Dick Huisman		
President & C.E.O.		
Bruce J. Elmore		
Senior V.P., Fin. & C.F.O.		

Address
877 Greyhound Way S.W.
Calgary
AB
T3C 3V8
(403) 260-0877

Fax: (403) 260-0742
G0003122/G/8.0

NEWFOUNDLAND CAPITAL CORPORATION LIMITED

Exchanges	Price (Jun24'93)	2.60	Trailing P/E		nm	Stock Symbol
TM	Trailing Yield (%)	0.00	Trailing EPS		(0.96)	**NCC.A**

Period Ending	Dec92	Dec91	Dec90	Dec89	Dec88
Yearly Statistics					
Price-Close	1.25	2.50	3.60	6.50	9.25
Price-High	2.65	4.00	6.75	9.25	10.88
Price-Low	1.00	2.10	3.25	6.25	7.00
P/E-Close	nm	nm	nm	15.48	9.16
Dividends per Share	0.00	0.00	0.00	0.15	0.30
Dividend Yield (%)	0.00	0.00	0.00	2.31	3.24
Sales per Share	41.94	42.15	37.52	35.53	38.68
EPS before extra. item	(1.27)	(0.90)	(4.69)	0.42	1.01
Cash Flow per Share	1.08	1.00	(1.08)	0.92	1.96
Book Value per Share	2.56	3.83	4.73	9.42	9.57
O/S Common Shares	4,953	4,953	4,953	4,953	4,953
Total Revenue	208,114	210,233	187,639	184,658	196,448
Income before extra.	(6,305)	(4,458)	(23,229)	13	5,021
Cash Flow	5,357	4,949	(5,343)	4,546	9,706
Debt/Equity	7.46	5.62	4.85	1.97	1.59
Return on Capital (%)	1.30	5.26	(8.28)	8.39	14.18
Ret. on Com. Equity (%)	(39.82)	(21.01)	(66.26)	0.03	11.03
% Change Profit	(41.4)	80.8	nm	(99.7)	141.5
% Change Revenue	(1.0)	12.0	1.6	(6.0)	19.2
% Change Assets	(14.1)	(3.7)	(0.8)	4.3	41.4

Date	EPS	DPS	Tot Rev	Inc Bex
Mar 93	(0.31)	0.00	48,769	(1,539)
Dec 92	(0.81)	0.00	54,294	(4,039)
Sep 92	0.08	0.00	52,522	426
Jun 92	0.08	0.00	54,523	382
Mar 92	(0.62)	0.00	46,775	(3,074)
Dec 91	0.02	0.00	51,315	119
Sep 91	0.06	0.00	57,370	303
Jun 91	(0.20)	0.00	52,758	(974)

Preferred Div. Coverage	np	np	np
Total Div. Coverage	na	na	na
Interest Coverage	0.2	0.6	0.0
Current Ratio	0.6	0.7	0.8
Operating Margin	2.4	2.8	1.6
Asset Turnover	1.6	1.3	1.1
5 YEAR RATIOS (%)			
Return on Capital	4.2	6.7	8.4
Return on Com. Equity	(23.2)	(14.3)	(8.7)
Profit Growth	na	na	na
Revenue Growth	4.7	10.1	8.3
Asset Growth	3.9	16.5	19.3
BALANCE SHEET (000)			
Cash	336	3,363	3,400
Current Assets	37,426	49,675	42,077
Net Fixed Assets	53,780	59,772	57,488
Invest's & Advances	0	0	14,823
Total Assets	134,010	156,023	161,999
Short Term Debt	34,406	41,532	28,669
Current Liabilities	60,752	70,436	52,545
Long Term Debt	60,230	65,236	85,033
Total Liabilities	121,328	137,036	138,554
Total Equity	12,682	18,987	23,445
Total Liab. & Equity	134,010	156,023	161,999
CAPITAL (000)			
Total Debt	94,636	106,768	113,702
Preferred Equity	0	0	0
Common Equity	12,682	18,987	23,445

Business:

NEWFOUNDLAND CAPITAL CORP. LTD. is a transportation and communications company. Operating transportation divisions include rail pool cars, trucking, container shipping and marine container terminal services and a vehicle and passenger ferry service. Communications operations include radio stations across Canada, The Daily News of Halifax, and commercial printing businesses.

Synopsis:

Concern about Newfoundland Capital Corp. Ltd.'s $60.2-million debt load, which had placed severe constraints on its operations over the past three years, was eased by a new deal with its debenture holders extending the date of maturity by five years. This added in excess of $22-million to its equity base and resulted in interest savings of $1.8-million annually. The long-term debt will be offset by a corresponding amount, bringing it down to $38-million.

Earnings strengthened on first quarter consolidated revenue of $48-million, a loss of $1.5-million (31 cents per share), compared to 1992's quarterly loss of $3-million (62 cents per share) on revenue of $46.7-million.

Losses for 1992 were inflated by the write-down of carrying values of intangible assets pertaining to communication holdings which continue to be weak and had losses of $2.3-million in 1992. This one time charge of $3.4-million was the main reason for the net loss of $6.3-million ($1.27 per share). Last year's comparable loss was $4.5-million (90 cents per share).

Cash flow from the transportation group provides the company with its underlying strength. On revenue of $149.6-million, the transportation group generated $14.6-million in cash before interest and taxes, with the corresponding profit of $10.3-million. This generated a return of 19% on average capital employed, one of the highest in the industry. The company is expected to pick up additional sea transportation business with the development of Hibernia oil. And Clarke Railfast, which operates the largest freight consolidation and rail forwarding business in Canada, established Clark International to capitalize on the freer flow of goods between Canada, the U.S. and Mexico.

Over the last four years the company invested more than $45-million in new and improved facilities and plans a capital program of $2-million for 1993, including its proportionate share ($700,000) of joint venture expenditures.

Relative strength to TSE300 / Price / Volume (in 1000's of board lots)

Rank (Profit/Revenue/Assets)
853   267   374

John J. Fleming
Chairman

Harry R. Steele
President & C.E.O.

Address
Suite 302
800 Windmill Road
Dartmouth
NS
B3B 1L1
(902) 468-7557

Fax: (902) 468-7558
N0001132/G/8.0

For further company information, call Globe Information Services 1-800-268-9128 or (416)585-5345

PWA CORPORATION

Exchanges	Price (Jun24'93)		0.80	Trailing P/E		nm	Stock Symbol
TZV	Trailing Yield (%)		0.00	Trailing EPS		(12.05)	**PWA**

Period Ending	Dec92	Dec91	Dec90	Dec89	Dec88
Yearly Statistics					
Price-Close	0.80	5.63	7.50	13.75	15.63
Price-High	6.25	9.38	13.00	19.38	22.25
Price-Low	0.54	4.00	6.75	12.88	13.63
P/E-Close	nm	nm	nm	nm	12.50
Dividends per Share	0.00	0.00	0.00	0.00	0.00
Dividend Yield (%)	0.00	0.00	0.00	0.00	0.00
Sales per Share	58.51	61.93	87.07	92.39	124.54
EPS before extra. item	(11.37)	(3.66)	(0.60)	(2.18)	1.25
Cash Flow per Share	(3.94)	(2.74)	(1.36)	(2.48)	4.89
Book Value per Share	(0.35)	10.99	17.67	18.37	22.75
O/S Common Shares	48,248	48,009	31,815	31,425	18,504
Total Revenue	2,901,286	2,904,200	2,831,400	2,717,300	2,339,306
Income before extra.	(543,300)	(161,700)	(14,600)	(56,000)	30,322
Cash Flow	(189,800)	(124,000)	(43,000)	(71,200)	90,351
Debt/Equity	67.40	2.71	2.56	2.34	1.91
Return on Capital (%)	(21.81)	(3.72)	3.50	(0.89)	8.04
Ret. on Com. Equity (%)	(214.38)	(30.44)	(3.32)	(12.52)	5.64
% Change Profit	(236.0)	(1,007.5)	73.9	(284.7)	(47.7)
% Change Revenue	(0.1)	2.6	4.2	16.2	23.4
% Change Assets	(12.4)	(5.2)	1.8	37.0	6.8

Date	EPS	DPS	Tot Rev	Inc Bex
Mar 93	(2.24)	0.00	674,800	(107,100)
Dec 92	(9.11)	0.00	668,300	(437,700)
Sep 92	0.04	0.00	834,500	2,700
Jun 92	(0.74)	0.00	702,000	(34,400)
Mar 92	(1.56)	0.00	684,200	(73,900)
Dec 91	(1.56)	0.00	704,500	(71,800)
Sep 91	0.14	0.00	826,000	7,500
Jun 91	(0.75)	0.00	706,000	(34,700)

	Dec92	Dec91	Dec90
Preferred Div. Coverage	0.0	0.0	0.0
Total Div. Coverage	0.0	0.0	0.0
Interest Coverage	0.0	0.0	0.7
Current Ratio	0.7	0.8	0.7
Operating Margin	(3.8)	(3.1)	(0.4)
Asset Turnover	1.1	1.0	0.9
5 YEAR RATIOS (%)			
Return on Capital	(3.0)	4.7	7.1
Return on Com. Equity	(51.0)	(5.0)	3.9
Profit Growth	na	na	na
Revenue Growth	8.8	49.4	50.9
Asset Growth	4.3	24.3	45.5
BALANCE SHEET (000)			
Cash	107,600	185,800	179,600
Current Assets	510,600	622,200	678,800
Net Fixed Assets	1,783,700	1,926,000	2,043,500
Invest's & Advances	20,200	109,500	130,500
Total Assets	2,461,900	2,811,100	2,964,400
Short Term Debt	9,700	97,900	157,800
Current Liabilities	739,600	783,100	913,600
Long Term Debt	1,675,200	1,445,200	1,394,600
Total Liabilities	2,436,900	2,241,100	2,359,000
Total Equity	25,000	570,000	605,400
Total Liab. & Equity	2,461,900	2,811,100	2,964,400
CAPITAL (000)			
Total Debt	1,684,900	1,543,100	1,552,400
Preferred Equity	41,800	42,600	43,400
Common Equity	(16,800)	527,400	562,000

Business:

PWA CORP. is a holding company with investments in the airline industry. PWA owns 100% of both Canadian Airlines International Ltd. (CAI) and Canadian Holidays. PWA also has significant investments in regional air carriers. CAI provides scheduled transportation for passengers and cargo to cities in Canada, the United States, Europe, South America and the Pacific.

Synopsis:

It has been a turbulent time for the PWA Corporation, which owns cash-strapped Canadian Airlines International Ltd. PWA faces $3.2-billion worth of debts, reduced revenues and restructuring hurdles. PWA posted a record $543.3-million loss for 1992. The loss included a $33.2-million charge for 1992 to cover the cost of its restructuring, which included investment write-offs and the cost of canceling and deferring the delivery of new aircraft. Air Canada, PWA's major domestic competitor, reported a $454-million loss for 1992.

PWA lost $107-million or $2.24 a share in the first quarter of 1993, compared to $73.9-million or $1.56 a year earlier. Revenues were $673.3-million, down from $680.4-million in 1992.

On November 30, 1992, PWA stopped paying its creditors, including aircraft lessors and airport operators, while it undertook voluntary restructuring. One plan suggested adding more than one billion new shares to the 48 million outstanding, and adding $246-million worth of share investment of from AMR Corp., the parent of American Airlines Inc. In May 1993, one of the largest creditors, Tokyo Leasing Co. holder of $109-million in loans, rejected the proposed restructuring plan and declared PWA's loans due and payable.

One stumbling block in this plan was PWA's partnership in the Toronto-based Gemini Group reservation computer system, which AMR wanted Canadian Airlines to dump in favor of American's Sabre system. In April, PWA failed to break up the Gemini partnership.

In spite of the uncertainty, PWA's traffic volumes were stronger than expected. PWA had $175-million in cash and available credit, and in May 1993 began paying its $35-million monthly bill to creditors.

Rank (Profit/Revenue/Assets)		
996	45	80

Rhys T. Eyton
Chairman, President & C.E.O.
D.R. Murphy
Senior V.P. Finance

Address
Suite 2800
700 - 2nd Street S.W.
Calgary
AB
T2P 2W2
(403) 294-2000

P0014192/G/8.0

TRIMAC LIMITED

Exchanges	Price (Jun24'93)		16 .50	Trailing P/E		21 .15	Stock Symbol
TM	Trailing Yield (%)		0 .73	Trailing EPS		0 .78	**TMA**

Period Ending	Dec92	Dec91	Dec90	Dec89	Dec88
Yearly Statistics					
Price-Close	9 .38	8 .50	6 .63	6 .00	3 .50
Price-High	9 .38	9 .88	8 .63	6 .88	4 .50
Price-Low	7 .25	6 .13	6 .13	3 .50	2 .90
P/E-Close	13 .02	13 .93	19 .50	31 .58	35 .00
Dividends per Share	0 .12	0 .10	0 .20	0 .00	0 .10
Dividend Yield (%)	1 .28	1 .18	3 .02	0 .00	2 .83
Sales per Share	13 .01	12 .21	13 .04	11 .14	9 .90
EPS before extra. item	0 .72	0 .61	0 .34	0 .19	0 .10
Cash Flow per Share	1 .53	1 .32	1 .38	1 .25	1 .08
Book Value per Share	5 .66	4 .97	4 .63	4 .34	3 .08
O/S Common Shares	36 ,683	36 ,515	36 ,177	30 ,464	30 ,333
Total Revenue	503 ,837	473 ,759	459 ,798	359 ,258	335 ,481
Income before extra.	26 ,823	22 ,715	13 ,183	8 ,646	3 ,793
Cash Flow	56 ,039	48 ,576	47 ,284	38 ,134	35 ,086
Debt/Equity	1 .01	0 .76	0 .91	0 .96	1 .64
Return on Capital (%)	11 .99	12 .93	11 .17	11 .99	8 .76
Ret. on Com. Equity (%)	13 .63	12 .83	7 .75	5 .23	3 .09
% Change Profit	18 .1	72 .3	52 .5	127 .9	(52 .3)
% Change Revenue	6 .3	3 .0	28 .0	7 .1	13 .1
% Change Assets	33 .6	1 .4	4 .3	(3 .9)	(5 .6)
Preferred Div. Coverage	81 .0	64 .0	8 .4		
Total Div. Coverage	5 .7	5 .7	1 .7		
Interest Coverage	3 .8	3 .1	1 .9		
Current Ratio	1 .0	1 .0	1 .2		
Operating Margin	3 .7	4 .0	5 .1		
Asset Turnover	0 .9	1 .1	1 .1		
5 YEAR RATIOS (%)					
Return on Capital	11 .4	10 .8	9 .8		
Return on Com. Equity	8 .5	7 .1	4 .8		
Profit Growth	27 .5	64 .9	39 .7		
Revenue Growth	11 .1	9 .7	5 .3		
Asset Growth	5 .0	2 .1	1 .3		
BALANCE SHEET (000)					
Cash	10 ,143	9 ,057	6 ,263		
Current Assets	138 ,686	88 ,429	96 ,791		
Net Fixed Assets	310 ,582	219 ,383	208 ,713		
Invest's & Advances	70 ,778	78 ,740	74 ,101		
Total Assets	531 ,005	397 ,556	392 ,072		
Short Term Debt	36 ,860	17 ,846	16 ,735		
Current Liabilities	133 ,918	85 ,016	79 ,438		
Long Term Debt	176 ,777	122 ,634	139 ,481		
Total Liabilities	319 ,951	212 ,438	220 ,619		
Total Equity	211 ,054	185 ,118	171 ,453		
Total Liab. & Equity	531 ,005	397 ,556	392 ,072		
CAPITAL (000)					
Total Debt	213 ,637	140 ,480	156 ,216		
Preferred Equity	3 ,612	3 ,775	4 ,095		
Common Equity	207 ,442	181 ,343	167 ,358		

Business:

TRIMAC LIMITED is involved in transportation, contract drilling, truck leasing and rentals, and environmental services. Its core businesses are carried on through wholly owned business units such as: Trimac Transportation System; Kenting Energy Services; Rentway; and TriWaste Reduction Services. Trimac owns 58% of BOVAR Inc., a waste management services company.

Date	EPS	DPS	Tot Rev	Inc Bex
Mar 93	0 .07	0 .12	145 ,104	2 ,837
Dec 92	0 .14	0 .00	145 ,330	5 ,212
Sep 92	0 .52	0 .00	141 ,142	19 ,363
Jun 92	0 .05	0 .00	110 ,141	1 ,908
Mar 92	0 .01	0 .12	107 ,224	340
Dec 91	0 .02	0 .00	111 ,066	1 ,175
Sep 91	0 .13	0 .00	118 ,150	4 ,742
Jun 91	0 .41	0 .00	121 ,638	14 ,854

Synopsis:

Trimac Company president Jeffrey McCaig expects that 1993 net income will be close to analysts' estimates of 70 cents a share. This comes after a strong showing in 1992 when revenue amounted to $476.1-million. Net income was $27.2-million or 73 cents a share after a small loss from discontinued operations.

McCaig predicts that 1993 trucking revenue will total about $330-million to $350-million, up 10% to 15% from 1992 level, and that there will be more investment in infrastructure in Canada and the U.S. this year. The first quarter results confirm that optimism as overall profit rose to $2.9-million or 7 cents a share, from $340,000 or 1 cent a year earlier. Revenues were up 38% at $142.4-million.

The Financial Times on March 2, 1993, recommended purchasing Trimac stock. It said trucking operations will continue to grow in the next five years, earnings should double by 1996 and truck leasing revenues should increase by 17% annually. As well a recovery in the drilling industry combined with new pipeline expansion, should raise Trimac's net asset value per share to $18 by 1996.

In March 1993, Trimac issued 3.5 million common shares at $12.87 a share for gross proceeds of $45-million, which is to be used to reduce short and long-term debt for general corporate purposes.

Trimac is considering the acquisition of a small trucking company preferably located along the U.S.-Mexico border in advance of the finalization of the North American Free Trade Agreement. Its size would match that of Pacific Trucking of Seattle, with annual revenue of about $4-million (U.S.), which Trimac acquired in April 1993.

Losses are expected in Tri Waste Reduction Services Inc. in 1993. Tri Waste has been operating at a break even level, but staff levels are being increased and the operation should be profitable by 1994.

Rank (Profit/Revenue/Assets)
108   153   202

J.R. McCaig
Chairman & C.E.O.

J.J. McCaig
President & C.O.O.

T.J. Jackson
V.P., Finance & C.F.O.

Address
P.O. Box 3500
Ste. 2100
800 - 5th Avenue S.W.
Calgary
AB
T2P 2P9
(403) 298-5100
Fax: (403) 298-5258
T0002980/G/8.0

WESTAR GROUP LTD.

Exchanges					Stock Symbol
TV	Price (Jun24'93)	0.13	Trailing P/E	nm	**WGL**
	Trailing Yield (%)	0.00	Trailing EPS	(0.62)	

Period Ending	Dec92	Dec91	Dec90	Dec89	Dec88
Yearly Statistics					
Price-Close	0.18	0.53	0.60	0.93	1.16
Price-High	0.72	0.88	1.15	1.40	1.26
Price-Low	0.08	0.41	0.50	0.82	0.80
P/E-Close	nm	nm	nm	3.88	9.67
Dividends per Share	0.00	0.00	0.00	0.00	0.00
Dividend Yield (%)	0.00	0.00	0.00	0.00	0.00
Sales per Share	0.38	0.57	0.69	3.80	3.52
EPS before extra. item	(0.58)	(0.04)	(0.11)	0.24	0.12
Cash Flow per Share	(0.04)	0.33	0.39	0.88	0.29
Book Value per Share	(1.18)	(0.61)	(0.57)	(1.83)	(2.07)
O/S Common Shares	192,994	192,994	192,994	96,497	96,409
Total Revenue	72,700	110,700	99,600	391,000	350,800
Income before extra.	(110,300)	(7,800)	(19,200)	26,200	17,300
Cash Flow	(8,600)	63,600	57,100	84,400	28,100
Debt/Equity	na	na	na	na	na
Return on Capital (%)	(17.91)	16.02	12.71	29.82	21.62
Ret. on Com. Equity (%)	na	na	na	na	na
% Change Profit	(1,314.1)	59.4	(173.3)	51.4	1,335.7
% Change Revenue	(34.3)	11.1	(74.5)	11.5	24.4
% Change Assets	(29.5)	(10.7)	(21.7)	(4.0)	3.0

Preferred Div. Coverage	np	np	np
Total Div. Coverage	na	na	0.0
Interest Coverage	0.0	0.9	0.6
Current Ratio	0.1	0.9	0.9
Operating Margin	14.8	50.0	48.9
Asset Turnover	0.3	0.3	0.3
5 YEAR RATIOS (%)			
Return on Capital	12.5	18.3	15.9
Return on Com. Equity	na	na	na
Profit Growth	na	na	na
Revenue Growth	(23.9)	(22.8)	(37.9)
Asset Growth	(13.4)	(16.5)	(28.8)
BALANCE SHEET (000)			
Cash	15,300	1,500	7,200
Current Assets	57,800	133,500	19,700
Net Fixed Assets	167,800	177,700	161,500
Invest's & Advances	0	6,000	46,400
Total Assets	225,600	319,900	358,300
Short Term Debt	406,500	127,500	11,700
Current Liabilities	425,200	141,500	22,900
Long Term Debt	0	258,400	369,200
Total Liabilities	454,200	438,200	468,800
Total Equity	(228,600)	(118,300)	(110,500)
Total Liab. & Equity	225,600	319,900	358,300
CAPITAL (000)			
Total Debt	406,500	385,900	380,900
Preferred Equity	0	0	0
Common Equity	(228,600)	(118,300)	(110,500)

Business:

WESTAR GROUP LTD. primarily operates a shipping terminal near Vancouver serving coal producers in Western Canada and the United States, through Westshore Terminals. Westar Petroleum produces oil and gas in Western Canada.

Date	EPS	DPS	Tot Rev	Inc Bex
Mar 93	(0.03)	0.00	16,200	(4,900)
Dec 92	(0.24)	0.00	10,600	(44,600)
Sep 92	(0.26)	0.00	11,400	(50,600)
Jun 92	(0.09)	0.00	22,900	(17,300)
Mar 92	0.01	0.00	27,600	2,200
Dec 91	0.00	0.00	27,300	400
Sep 91	0.01	0.00	26,300	900
Jun 91	(0.01)	0.00	29,100	(2,300)

Synopsis:

The future of Westar Group Ltd. will depend on the completion of a successful restructuring of bank debts of $406.5-million currently owned, a recovery in the volumes of coal handled at Westshore Terminals Ltd., and the achievement of operating efficiencies at the terminal facilities.

The difficulties experienced in 1992 continued to have an effect. The operating income for the first quarter was $2.6-million, compared to $12.8-million in the comparable period of 1992. A major part of the decline came from the reduced activity of its Westshore Terminals, with 2.9 million tonnes being handled in the first three months of 1993 as compared to 5.2 million tonnes in the first three months of 1992. Much of that loss came from the lack of product from the Balmar and Greenhills mines which were previously owned and operated by Westar Mining Ltd. The Balmar mine was sold for $37-million by bankrupt Westar Mining Ltd. to Teck Corp. An earlier $33-million sale of the Greenhills mine to Fording Coal Ltd. of Calgary was contested in the courts in February 1993.

In April 1993, Westar Timber Ltd. sold the Kitwanga sawmill to C Ged Forest Products Ltd., a company owned by the Gitwangak Indian Band. In January 1993, Westar completed the sale of the Plateau sawmill at Vanderhoof, B.C., to a unit of Slocan Forest Products Ltd., of Richmond, B.C., for cash proceeds of about $72-million, including the value of inventories.

The sale of the company's forest product operations is anticipated to be completed in the second quarter of 1993, which will leave Westar Group Ltd. much leaner, with only the operations of its subsidiary, Westshore Terminals Ltd., and Westar Petroleum Ltd., which was deconsolidated in 1986, remaining.

Relative strength to TSE300

Price

Volume (in 1000's of board lots)

Rank (Profit/Revenue/Assets)		
973	422	305

Nicholas Geer
Chairman & President

Robert F. Chase
Sr. V.P., Finance & C.F.O.

Address
Suite 1600
1055 West Hastings Street
Vancouver
BC
V6E 2H2
(604) 687-2600

Fax: (604) 681-9537
B0004071/G/8.0

Page	Company	$	Latest year end	Earnings per Share		
				Actual	Estimate this year	Estimate next year
281	Interprovincial Pipe Line System		9212	2.62	1.99	2.28
282	Nova Corporation		9212	0.39	0.52	0.77
283	Trans Mountain Pipe Line		9212	1.82	1.76	1.83
284	TransCanada PipeLines		9212	1.56	1.58	1.69
285	Westcoast Energy		9212	1.27	1.57	1.77

Estimates from I/B/E/S Inc., 345 Hudson St., New York, NY 10014 (212) 243-3335. In Canada: 6 Lansing Square, Ste. 235, Willowdale, ON M2J 1T5 (416) 496-0977.

Pipelines

TransCanada PipeLines Ltd. has submitted an application to the National Energy Board to build $637.3-million worth of new facilities. Under the plan, TransCanada would build 290.3 kilometres of new pipe in Saskatchewan, Manitoba and Ontario. The facilities would be in place by December 1995. The company also announced that it was in talks with partners to build a new pipeline in the southeastern United States and that it was joining two new U.S. pipeline ventures - the $130-million (U.S.) Oregon to Nevada Tuscarora pipeline and the $360-million New York to Boston Mayflower line. TransCanada already has major stakes in three major U.S. pipelines - Great Lakes Gas Transmission System (Manitoba to Michigan), Iroquois Gas Transmission System (Ontario to New York City) and Northern Border Pipeline Co. (Alberta to Indiana).

Robert Anderson, chief executive of Hondo Gas and Oil Co., wants to build a 1,200-kilometre pipeline to bring natural gas from the fields of the Mackenzie Delta to southern Alaska where it would be sent to the Pacific Rim to generate electricity and for household use. The proposed $12-billion (U.S.) project, to be built by Mackenzie Porcupine Pipeline Co., follows a similar Alaska proposal that has an 11-year head start. Since the early 1980s, Yukon Pacific Corp. has pushed for a natural gas pipeline along the same route as the trans-Alaska pipeline. Mackenzie Porcupine Pipeline Co. hopes to begin laying pipe in 1994 and start the gas flow by 1998. Despite ambitious construction programs for both coal and nuclear plants, Japan, South Korea and Taiwan all have said they will sharply increase their use of natural gas for power generation. Asian countries are expecting to spend at least $500-billion in the next decade building new power plants and transmission lines.

According to the July 1993 *Report on Business 1000* magazine, the pipeline industry has had an average one year return on capital of 12.79%. The average five year return on capital is 15.6%

Natural Gas Industry Storage Market - Industry Report [May-13-1993]. MERRILL LYNCH CAPITAL MARKETS reported by Olson, J.E., et al

The situation is good for domestic producers, pipelines and gatherers, and for integrated LDC's. The gas group has substantially outperformed the market over 1992. Pipelines and gatherers have done five times better than the market and LDC's over three times better. The storage situation should serve to keep gas prices higher for a longer period than previously anticipated. [RN 1331026]

Weekly Natural Gas Monitor - Industry Report [May-4-1993] . MERRILL LYNCH CAPITAL MARKETS reported by Olson, J.E., et al

In 1Q:93, earnings were strong, with few shortfalls. Natural gas stocks have done about five time better than the market over the past year, with not much distinction among producers, pipelines and LDC's. The Williams Companies' operating earnings rose to $1.38 (U.S.) per share from a "clean" $0.72 (U.S.) per share a year ago. Both interstate pipelines benefited from major weather turnarounds. Williams Field Services saw a 80% earnings surge. The product pipeline NOI rose 55%. [RN 1331067]

Natural Gas: Industry Review - Industry Report [Apr-26-1993]. MORGAN STANLEY & CO. INC. reported by Helm, M.

Pipeline construction activity has begun to decelerate. The outlook for natural gas prices over the remainder of 1993 is considerably more bullish than it has been in the past two years, due to the need to refill storage. The increase in natural gas consumption that occurred in 1Q:93 relative to 1992 should have reduced natural gas storage levels to 14-year lows at the end of March 1993. Storage levels at the beginning of the 1992/93 winter were 3,222 bcf, or 4.4% below the year-ago level. The removal of 4-5% of productive capacity for a six-week period in the summer of 1992, when Hurricane Andrew disrupted Gulf of Mexico supplies, was the primary reason for the lower storage levels at October 31, 1992. With the return of normal weather in the winter, storage levels have been drawn down substantially. [RN 1326731]

Monthly Natural Gas Monitor - Industry Report [Apr-12-1993]. MERRILL LYNCH CAPITAL MARKETS reported by Olson, J.E., et al

Natural gas stocks outperformed the stock and bond markets in 1Q:93. Producers rose 23%, gatherers rose 18.1%, pipelines were 18.2% higher, and LDC's rose 13.8% in a 3.7% higher stock market. Over the past five quarters, the pipeline group has risen from 86% of the market (S&P 500) multiple with a 33% yield premium to 121% of the market and no yield premium. Since year end 1992, the long bond has dropped from 7.39% to 6.89%. T-bills have moved from 3.08% to 2.96%. Weather degree days in the Northeast ran 8% colder year to year and 1% colder than normal. In the past three months, the Gulf Coast wellhead price forecast has moved from $1.71 (U.S.) to $1.85 (U.S.) per MCF. [RN1322199]

INTERPROVINCIAL PIPE LINE SYSTEM INC.

Exchanges	Price (Jun24'93)	28.25	Trailing P/E	16.24	Stock Symbol
TMN	Trailing Yield (%)	7.08	Trailing EPS	1.74	**IPL**

Period Ending	Dec92	Dec91	Dec90	Dec89	Dec88
Yearly Statistics					
Price-Close	23.00	32.38	47.75	44.00	42.88
Price-High	34.25	49.50	50.50	50.50	48.75
Price-Low	21.88	28.50	42.75	41.75	41.00
P/E-Close	12.11	3.81	13.12	15.02	16.49
Dividends per Share	2.00	9.00	2.00	2.00	2.00
Dividend Yield (%)	8.70	27.80	4.19	4.55	4.67
Sales per Share	9.86	15.80	15.70	15.17	15.61
EPS before extra. item	1.90	8.50	3.64	2.93	2.60
Cash Flow per Share	2.96	4.57	5.05	8.84	8.54
Book Value per Share	11.53	11.55	27.89	26.23	25.06
O/S Common Shares	39,816	39,699	39,637	39,621	39,581
Total Revenue	436,300	1,010,200	625,100	881,900	870,000
Income before extra.	75,500	337,200	144,000	116,200	103,100
Cash Flow	117,900	181,200	200,200	349,900	338,000
Debt/Equity	1.66	1.52	0.55	1.09	1.16
Return on Capital (%)	14.94	41.86	15.13	14.59	14.66
Ret. on Com. Equity (%)	16.46	43.12	13.43	11.44	10.57
% Change Profit	(77.6)	134.2	23.9	12.7	(15.8)
% Change Revenue	(56.8)	61.6	(29.1)	1.4	1.4
% Change Assets	(12.2)	(8.9)	(33.2)	4.0	1.6

Preferred Div. Coverage	np	np	np
Total Div. Coverage	0.9	0.9	1.8
Interest Coverage	2.4	7.9	4.3
Current Ratio	2.5	1.8	0.5
Operating Margin	34.0	35.7	40.5
Asset Turnover	0.2	0.3	0.3
5 YEAR RATIOS (%)			
Return on Capital	20.2	20.7	15.9
Return on Com. Equity	19.0	18.3	12.7
Profit Growth	(9.2)	20.8	0.7
Revenue Growth	(12.7)	11.3	2.9
Asset Growth	(10.9)	(8.5)	3.6
BALANCE SHEET (000)			
Cash	358,300	625,600	5,500
Current Assets	395,000	685,200	66,700
Net Fixed Assets	1,113,400	1,062,600	1,361,900
Invest's & Advances	138,600	130,700	0
Total Assets	1,663,900	1,895,400	2,081,300
Short Term Debt	103,000	26,600	45,700
Current Liabilities	160,100	388,500	143,000
Long Term Debt	660,400	668,200	559,700
Total Liabilities	1,205,000	1,436,700	975,800
Total Equity	458,900	458,700	1,105,500
Total Liab. & Equity	1,663,900	1,895,400	2,081,300
CAPITAL (000)			
Total Debt	763,400	694,800	605,400
Preferred Equity	0	0	0
Common Equity	458,900	458,700	1,105,500

Business:

INTERPROVINCIAL PIPE LINE SYSTEM transports crude oil and other liquid hydrocarbons through a pipeline extending about 2,300 miles from Edmonton through Superior, Wisconsin, and Chicago, Illinois, to Sarnia and Montreal. Another 540 mile pipeline carries crude oil from Norman Wells in the Northwest Territories to Zama, Alberta, where it enters a connecting pipeline for delivery to Edmonton.

Date	EPS	DPS	Tot Rev	Inc Bex
Mar 93	0.42	0.50	108,400	16,500
Dec 92	0.30	0.50	102,700	11,700
Sep 92	0.57	0.50	110,800	22,700
Jun 92	0.45	0.50	105,900	18,000
Mar 92	0.58	0.50	116,900	23,100
Dec 91	6.91	7.50	530,100	274,000
Sep 91	0.47	0.50	154,400	18,800
Jun 91	0.54	0.50	163,900	21,200

Synopsis:

Interprovincial Pipe Line System Inc. has a $275-million capacity expansion program planned to meet increased deliveries of Western Canadian crude oil to Eastern Canada and the Midwest United States. The system has been operating at capacity for more than two and one-half years, resulting in the apportionment of volumes. The earliest the expansion could be completed would be 1994.

Interprovincial retained a portion of the proceeds from its sale of 80% of the U.S. pipeline business. The retained funds, totaling more than $300-million, are placed in highly liquid marketable securities while the company evaluates a number of investment opportunities.

Interprovincial has proposed an intercoastal pipeline to transport natural gas across the U.S. border at Sarnia to a point near Toronto. The construction phase of the pipeline will cost about $40-million and will be completed by November 1994. The second phase, building a compressor station to increase pipeline capacity, is estimated to cost $27-million and is scheduled for completion by November 1996. The St. Lawrence Pipeline project, connecting Ultramar Canada Inc.'s refinery near Quebec City with a product terminal in Montreal, is proceeding on schedule and on budget at an estimated cost of $117-million.

The Sarnia-Montreal pipeline was reactivated in July 1992 in response to demand for west-to-east crude oil delivery. Interprovincial is investigating economic alternatives for this line. The company planned to use the Sarnia-Toronto pipeline in the construction of the intercoastal pipeline but a more cost effective method was found. After a detailed evaluation, the company found that the most efficient use for the line in the long term is to reverse its flow and deliver offshore oil to Ontario refineries. The cost of this project is estimated at $45-million.

Deliveries of oil, in cubic metres per day, during 1992 (1991) were: 231,167 (229,418).

Relative strength to TSE300 / Price / Volume (in 1000's of board lots) chart

Rank (Profit/Revenue/Assets)		
46	175	107

H. Gordon MacNeill
Chairman

Brian F. MacNeill
President & C.E.O.

Derek P. Truswell
V.P., Finance

Address
P.O. Box 398
Edmonton
AB
T5J 2J9
(403) 420-5210

Fax: (403) 420-5389
I0001637/G/9.1

NOVA CORPORATION OF ALBERTA

Exchanges	Price (Jun24'93)	10 .00	Trailing P/E	22 .22	Stock Symbol
TMZN	Trailing Yield (%)	2 .40	Trailing EPS	0 .45	**NVA**

Period Ending	Dec92	Dec91	Dec90	Dec89	Dec88
Yearly Statistics					
Price-Close	8 .75	7 .25	8 .63	8 .63	12 .00
Price-High	9 .13	9 .50	9 .38	14 .00	14 .75
Price-Low	6 .88	6 .38	6 .63	8 .38	8 .75
P/E-Close	22 .44	nm	15 .40	13 .48	7 .36
Dividends per Share	0 .24	0 .45	0 .52	0 .50	0 .42
Dividend Yield (%)	2 .74	6 .21	6 .03	5 .80	3 .50
Sales per Share	7 .80	9 .82	13 .31	18 .54	17 .21
EPS before extra. item	0 .39	(2 .99)	0 .56	0 .64	1 .63
Cash Flow per Share	1 .16	0 .71	1 .70	2 .30	3 .77
Book Value per Share	4 .98	4 .18	7 .40	7 .40	6 .95
O/S Common Shares	406 ,280	325 ,661	299 ,625	298 ,704	245 ,323
Total Revenue	3 ,085 ,000	3 ,161 ,000	4 ,098 ,000	4 ,848 ,000	3 ,976 ,000
Income before extra.	164 ,000	(923 ,000)	185 ,000	186 ,000	396 ,000
Cash Flow	451 ,000	223 ,000	509 ,000	600 ,000	863 ,000
Debt/Equity	1 .48	2 .30	1 .40	1 .73	2 .43
Return on Capital (%)	10 .31	(11 .37)	11 .20	11 .90	18 .31
Ret. on Com. Equity (%)	8 .98	(52 .35)	7 .55	8 .59	26 .17
% Change Profit	117 .8	(598 .9)	(0 .5)	(53 .0)	121 .2
% Change Revenue	(2 .4)	(22 .9)	(15 .5)	21 .9	70 .6
% Change Assets	6 .7	(13 .2)	(15 .5)	(2 .7)	73 .3
Preferred Div. Coverage	13 .7	0 .0	10 .3		
Total Div. Coverage	1 .5	0 .0	1 .1		
Interest Coverage	1 .6	0 .0	1 .6		
Current Ratio	0 .9	0 .7	0 .8		
Operating Margin	16 .1	10 .9	14 .9		
Asset Turnover	0 .5	0 .5	0 .6		
5 YEAR RATIOS (%)					
Return on Capital	8 .1	8 .5	13 .0		
Return on Com. Equity	(0 .2)	0 .9	12 .1		
Profit Growth	(1 .7)	na	6 .6		
Revenue Growth	5 .8	3 .5	4 .0		
Asset Growth	5 .7	4 .0	1 .4		
BALANCE SHEET (000)					
Cash	17 ,000	2 ,000	3 ,000		
Current Assets	750 ,000	676 ,000	798 ,000		
Net Fixed Assets	5 ,096 ,000	4 ,846 ,000	4 ,734 ,000		
Invest's & Advances	306 ,000	248 ,000	466 ,000		
Total Assets	6 ,189 ,000	5 ,802 ,000	6 ,681 ,000		
Short Term Debt	303 ,000	368 ,000	334 ,000		
Current Liabilities	841 ,000	903 ,000	962 ,000		
Long Term Debt	2 ,956 ,000	3 ,206 ,000	3 ,050 ,000		
Total Liabilities	3 ,985 ,000	4 ,251 ,000	4 ,268 ,000		
Total Equity	2 ,204 ,000	1 ,551 ,000	2 ,413 ,000		
Total Liab. & Equity	6 ,189 ,000	5 ,802 ,000	6 ,681 ,000		
CAPITAL (000)					
Total Debt	3 ,259 ,000	3 ,574 ,000	3 ,384 ,000		
Preferred Equity	182 ,000	189 ,000	195 ,000		
Common Equity	2 ,022 ,000	1 ,362 ,000	2 ,218 ,000		

Business:

NOVA CORP. is a widely held company operating internationally. Nova operates pipelines, and is engaged in the manufacturing and marketing of chemicals processed primarily from Alberta natural resources.

Date	EPS	DPS	Tot Rev	Inc Bex
Mar 93	0 .12	0 .06	814 ,000	50 ,000
Dec 92	0 .12	0 .06	810 ,000	53 ,000
Sep 92	0 .11	0 .06	769 ,000	47 ,000
Jun 92	0 .10	0 .06	763 ,000	41 ,000
Mar 92	0 .07	0 .06	750 ,000	27 ,000
Dec 91	(2 .14)	0 .06	749 ,000	(673 ,000)
Sep 91	(0 .82)	0 .13	718 ,000	(258 ,000)
Jun 91	(0 .08)	0 .13	794 ,000	(18 ,000)

Synopsis:

During the first quarter of 1993, NOVA's Alberta Gas Transmission Division (AGTD) transported record volumes through its system. Natural gas shipments increased 13% to 959 billion cubic feet (bcf) in the first quarter of 1993 from 848 bcf in the first quarter of 1992. All destinations that the system transports natural gas to experienced increases. Gas used within Alberta increased 23.2% to 174 bcf, while gas destined for Central Canada and the eastern United States increased by 68 bcf to 509 bcf. Unaudited net income from NOVA's chemical business was $6-million, compared to a $12-million in the first quarter of 1992. Lower interest expense, a lower-valued Canadian dollar and reduced feedstock costs contributed to the improved performance, although weak market conditions continue to exist for this segment.

NOVA issued in the U.S. $200-million (U.S.) of its 7 7/8% Debentures due April 1, 2023. The proceeds will be used to finance a portion of the 1993 capital spending for the AGTD pipeline system and to repay debt incurred to finance the system's expansion.

Capital expenditures for AGTD's pipeline system are expected to average approximately $500-million per year through 1995. The increasing demand for natural gas in North America combined with the record volumes being transported by AGTD supports the need for a continued expansion of the pipeline system. Nova will spend $85-million on low capital cost expansion opportunities at three of its plants. Nova's capital expenditures are expected to total between $750-million and $800-million in 1993. At December 1992, Nova had unutilized credit facilities totaling approximately $1.2-billion.

In 1991, Nova transported a record 3.4 trillion cubic feet of natural gas, marking the sixth consecutive year that a new record was set. Revenue percentages (operating income) in 1992 by segment were: chemicals, 71% (24%); and pipelines, 29% (76%). Revenue percentages (operating income) in 1991 by segment were: chemicals, 73% (7%); and pipelines, 27% (93%).

Rank (Profit/Revenue/Assets)		
21	41	37

S. Robert Blair
Chairman

J.E. Newall
President & C.E.O.

William G. Wilson
Exec. V.P. & C.F.O.

Address
P.O. Box 2535
Postal Station M
Calgary
AB
T2P 2N6
(403) 290-6000

Fax: (403) 290-6379
N0003576/G/9.2

TRANS MOUNTAIN PIPE LINE COMPANY LTD.

Exchanges	Price (Jun24'93)	19 .50	Trailing P/E	9 .61	Stock Symbol
TVMZ	Trailing Yield (%)	4 .51	Trailing EPS	2 .03	**TMP**

Period Ending	Dec92	Dec91	Dec90	Dec89	Dec88
Yearly Statistics					
Price-Close	15 .50	16 .25	14 .75	17 .38	14 .25
Price-High	17 .00	16 .63	17 .63	18 .63	15 .50
Price-Low	14 .00	12 .50	12 .50	14 .00	10 .75
P/E-Close	20 .67	9 .13	11 .35	10 .53	nm
Dividends per Share	0 .86	0 .80	0 .78	0 .69	0 .60
Dividend Yield (%)	5 .55	4 .92	5 .29	3 .97	4 .21
Sales per Share	11 .19	10 .51	9 .08	8 .66	8 .20
EPS before extra. item	0 .75	1 .78	1 .30	1 .65	(0 .27)
Cash Flow per Share	4 .41	3 .88	3 .06	2 .95	2 .52
Book Value per Share	11 .31	11 .41	10 .43	9 .91	8 .12
O/S Common Shares	8 ,582	8 ,581	8 ,581	8 ,581	7 ,581
Total Revenue	103 ,717	97 ,740	86 ,205	76 ,082	66 ,514
Income before extra.	6 ,471	15 ,330	11 ,120	12 ,994	(2 ,033)
Cash Flow	37 ,822	33 ,256	26 ,291	23 ,336	19 ,126
Debt/Equity	1 .63	1 .58	1 .67	1 .60	1 .70
Return on Capital (%)	11 .97	15 .94	13 .96	15 .59	7 .50
Ret. on Com. Equity (%)	6 .64	16 .36	12 .74	17 .73	(3 .14)
% Change Profit	(57 .8)	37 .9	(14 .4)	739 .2	(123 .2)
% Change Revenue	6 .1	13 .4	13 .3	14 .4	22 .9
% Change Assets	2 .2	9 .7	8 .3	33 .7	2 .7
Preferred Div. Coverage	np	np	np		
Total Div. Coverage	0 .9	2 .2	1 .7		
Interest Coverage	2 .1	2 .6	2 .0		
Current Ratio	0 .2	0 .2	0 .3		
Operating Margin	34 .9	36 .8	32 .7		
Asset Turnover	0 .3	0 .3	0 .3		
5 YEAR RATIOS (%)					
Return on Capital	13 .0	13 .2	12 .3		
Return on Com. Equity	10 .1	11 .4	10 .3		
Profit Growth	(5 .9)	17 .6	5 .4		
Revenue Growth	13 .8	14 .7	11 .2		
Asset Growth	10 .7	13 .6	16 .0		
BALANCE SHEET (000)					
Cash	0	0	266		
Current Assets	13 ,229	13 ,002	11 ,826		
Net Fixed Assets	224 ,786	210 ,183	199 ,956		
Invest's & Advances	48 ,431	48 ,431	48 ,431		
Total Assets	294 ,021	287 ,806	262 ,478		
Short Term Debt	47 ,827	44 ,227	39 ,300		
Current Liabilities	58 ,676	55 ,024	47 ,031		
Long Term Debt	110 ,000	110 ,000	110 ,000		
Total Liabilities	196 ,971	189 ,863	173 ,000		
Total Equity	97 ,050	97 ,943	89 ,478		
Total Liab. & Equity	294 ,021	287 ,806	262 ,478		
CAPITAL (000)					
Total Debt	157 ,827	154 ,227	149 ,300		
Preferred Equity	0	0	0		
Common Equity	97 ,050	97 ,943	89 ,478		

Business:

TRANS MOUNTAIN PIPE LINE CO. LTD. operates a pipeline system transporting petroleum from Alberta to its terminal in Burnaby, B.C. The pipeline also joins the pipeline of the company's wholly owned subsidiary, Trans Mountain Oil Pipe Line Corp., which delivers Canadian petroleum to Washington State. BC Gas Inc. of Vancouver is the company's major shareholder.

Date	EPS	DPS	Tot Rev	Inc Bex
Mar 93	0 .67	0 .22	29 ,495	5 ,777
Dec 92	0 .41	0 .22	27 ,177	3 ,544
Sep 92	0 .47	0 .22	25 ,735	4 ,059
Jun 92	0 .48	0 .22	26 ,199	4 ,123
Mar 92	(0 .61)	0 .20	24 ,606	(5 ,255)
Dec 91	0 .49	0 .20	25 ,579	4 ,246
Sep 91	0 .52	0 .20	25 ,220	4 ,470
Jun 91	0 .23	0 .20	20 ,712	2 ,007

Synopsis:

Trans Mountain Pipe Line Company Ltd. (TMPL) has benefited from an allocation of capacity on the Interprovincial Pipe Line Company Inc. system. The allocation, at a time when crude oil production was higher than expected, caused shippers to use TMPL's system to move the additional volumes to export markets. Forecasts for 1993 indicate that the higher export volumes to the United States will likely continue.

The primary focus of the 1993 capital expenditure program for TMPL is the construction of facilities to deliver refined petroleum products from Edmonton to terminals in the lower mainland of B.C. Petro-Canada announced in 1992 that its Lower Mainland refinery would be converted to a products-handling facility. Shell Canada Limited made a similar announcement in 1992. TMPL worked with the two companies to develop the plan to construct the facilities, at an estimated cost of $24.5-million. TMPL views the project as a trend towards more finished product shipments on its pipeline. Should Imperial Oil Limited begin shipping finished products from Edmonton, which it has considered doing, then total finished products and semi-refined products could account for 50% of pipeline volumes. In the future TMPL would like to construct a separate refined product pipeline. TMPL estimates that routine capital expenditures will total $11.5-million for 1993.

The construction of facilities to transport methyl tertiary butyl ether from the Alberta Envirofuels plant near Edmonton to Chevron Canada Limited's refinery in Burnaby was completed before the middle of 1993.

The capital and operating requirements are being funded from internally generated funds combined with a $110-million bank line of credit. The facility supports TMPL's commercial paper program. The paper carries a rating of R-1(low) and A-1(low).

Deliveries, in cubic metres per day, during 1992 (1991) were: petroleum, 32,340 (28,753); and jet fuel, 2,306 (2,208).

Relative strength to TSE300 / Price / Volume (in 1000's of board lots) chart 1990–1993

Rank (Profit/Revenue/Assets)
224   374   275

Ronald L. Cliff
Chairman

Stephen T. Bellringer
President & C.E.O.

Barry E. Harper
Sr. V.P. Fin., C.F.O. & Treas.

Thomas D. Doyle
Exec. V.P. & C.O.O.

Address
Suite 900
1333 West Broadway
Vancouver
BC
V6H 4C2
(604) 739-5000

Fax: (604) 739-5001
T0002708/G/9.1

TRANSCANADA PIPELINES LIMITED

Exchanges	Price (Jun24'93)	19.75	Trailing P/E	12.58	Stock Symbol
TMZVN	Trailing Yield (%)	4.05	Trailing EPS	1.57	**TRP**

Period Ending	Dec92	Dec91	Dec90	Dec89	Dec88
Yearly Statistics					
Price-Close	17.63	17.50	17.00	17.00	15.00
Price-High	18.50	18.00	18.00	17.75	16.25
Price-Low	16.00	16.00	14.38	13.88	12.50
P/E-Close	11.30	13.06	13.82	15.60	nm
Dividends per Share	0.78	0.73	0.69	0.68	0.68
Dividend Yield (%)	4.43	4.17	4.06	4.00	4.53
Sales per Share	20.17	18.40	19.17	20.32	22.34
EPS before extra. item	1.56	1.34	1.23	1.09	(0.31)
Cash Flow per Share	2.69	2.06	1.97	1.91	1.96
Book Value per Share	11.13	9.68	8.30	7.66	11.73
O/S Common Shares	188,512	171,377	154,187	152,642	150,540
Total Revenue	4,007,600	3,308,100	3,242,800	3,255,800	3,388,000
Income before extra.	328,700	251,200	214,900	196,700	(8,600)
Cash Flow	486,900	337,100	302,300	289,700	286,500
Debt/Equity	1.78	1.66	1.81	1.69	1.03
Return on Capital (%)	13.77	14.26	14.64	13.35	9.28
Ret. on Com. Equity (%)	14.91	14.93	15.47	11.30	(2.67)
% Change Profit	30.9	16.9	9.3	2,387.2	(105.4)
% Change Revenue	21.1	2.0	(0.4)	(3.9)	2.8
% Change Assets	24.7	26.0	13.3	(8.0)	(6.2)
Preferred Div. Coverage	6.8	7.9	8.5		
Total Div. Coverage	1.7	1.6	1.6		
Interest Coverage	2.0	1.9	1.8		
Current Ratio	0.8	1.1	1.5		
Operating Margin	18.2	17.9	14.9		
Asset Turnover	0.4	0.5	0.6		
5 YEAR RATIOS (%)					
Return on Capital	13.1	12.6	11.8		
Return on Com. Equity	10.8	9.3	6.4		
Profit Growth	15.5	36.9	5.7		
Revenue Growth	3.9	(5.0)	(7.8)		
Asset Growth	9.0	2.1	(3.7)		
BALANCE SHEET (000)					
Cash	598,900	520,500	638,200		
Current Assets	1,180,200	955,700	959,600		
Net Fixed Assets	6,000,600	4,846,900	3,570,100		
Invest's & Advances	879,500	652,000	439,200		
Total Assets	8,236,600	6,604,700	5,239,800		
Short Term Debt	741,500	134,200	163,300		
Current Liabilities	1,409,100	854,400	633,100		
Long Term Debt	4,044,800	3,519,600	2,859,300		
Total Liabilities	5,550,100	4,406,400	3,570,100		
Total Equity	2,686,500	2,198,300	1,669,700		
Total Liab. & Equity	8,236,600	6,604,700	5,239,800		
CAPITAL (000)					
Total Debt	4,786,300	3,653,800	3,022,600		
Preferred Equity	588,300	539,000	389,300		
Common Equity	2,098,200	1,659,300	1,280,400		

Business:

TRANSCANADA PIPELINES LTD. transports and markets natural gas. The company owns and manages a pipeline system from Alberta to Quebec, and has investments in other pipeline systems in Canada and the United States. Its subsidiary, Western Gas Marketing Ltd., buys and sells natural gas from Western Canada.

Date	EPS	DPS	Tot Rev	Inc Bex
Mar 93	0.40	0.21	1,162,600	87,300
Dec 92	0.39	0.21	1,182,200	84,300
Sep 92	0.39	0.19	912,400	83,900
Jun 92	0.39	0.19	903,600	81,000
Mar 92	0.39	0.19	979,300	79,500
Dec 91	0.34	0.19	891,700	66,700
Sep 91	0.34	0.18	733,300	64,500
Jun 91	0.33	0.18	765,800	61,500

Synopsis:

TransCanada PipeLines (TCPL) acquired a 30% interest in the proposed 960 kilometre SunShine Pipeline Project. The $600-million project would link markets in Florida with gas supplies from Mobile Bay, the Gulf Coast and other supply basins. Service is expected to begin in 1995, provided all regulatory approvals are received in a timely fashion. TCPL is involved in a joint venture with ANR Pipeline Company and Brooklyn Union Gas Company. The proposed Mayflower Gas Transmission System pipeline will extend 320 kilometres east from the Iroquois Gas Transmission System in New York to Boston. The cost of the project is estimated from between $340-million (U.S.) to $360-million (U.S.). TCPL and a partner plan to build a $130-million natural gas pipeline system that will serve markets in Reno, northern Nevada and northeastern California. The 322 kilometre pipeline will extend from the Pacific Gas Transmission System in Oregon through California and Nevada to a location near Reno.

The percentage of funds provided to finance the capital program and other activities in 1992 were: internally generated, 14%; new common and preferred equity, 21%; debentures, 30%; medium-term notes, 27%; and notes payable, 8%. TCPL continues to maintain a single A credit rating. TCPL's 1993 expenditures are expected to be financed mainly from a mixture of internally generated funds and new debt. After 1993, TCPL expects its requirement for outside funding to be reduced as returns from its capital investment programs are realized and a major part of expenditures for the current expansion are completed. Capital expenditures are expected to total about $637.3-million for 1993, with the majority being spent on the expansion of the mainline system. The size and timing of the investment will depend on economic conditions and firm shipping requirements.

Annual gas transmission volumes for 1992 (1991) in billions of cubic feet were: domestic, 1136 (1043.8); and export, 835.3 (611.3). 1992 revenue percentages (operating income) by segment were: gas transmission, 39% (98%); and gas sales, marketing and other, 61% (2%).

Relative strength to TSE300 / Price / Volume (in 1000's of board lots)

Rank (Profit/Revenue/Assets)
9   32   34

Gerald J. Maier
Chairman & C.E.O.

George W. Watson
President & C.F.O.

George M. Hugh
Chief Operating Officer

Address
111 - Fifth Avenue S.W.
P.O. Box 1000
Station M
Calgary
AB
T2P 4K5
(403) 267-6100
Fax: (403) 267-8538
T0002546/G/9.2

284

WESTCOAST ENERGY INC.

Exchanges	Price (Jun24'93)		20.12	Trailing P/E		nm	Stock Symbol
TMVN	Trailing Yield (%)		3.98	Trailing EPS		(0.76)	**W**

Period Ending	Dec92	Dec91	Dec90	Dec89	Dec88
Yearly Statistics					
Price-Close	17.25	20.63	21.50	20.38	15.88
Price-High	21.13	21.50	22.25	21.88	18.00
Price-Low	15.00	19.00	19.63	15.75	15.50
P/E-Close	nm	15.17	15.25	16.17	14.17
Dividends per Share	0.80	0.80	0.80	0.80	0.80
Dividend Yield (%)	4.64	3.88	3.72	3.93	5.04
Sales per Share	21.50	20.26	24.82	12.96	14.50
EPS before extra. item	(1.31)	1.36	1.41	1.26	1.12
Cash Flow per Share	3.65	3.11	4.23	3.33	3.23
Book Value per Share	14.05	15.78	15.18	13.91	13.46
O/S Common Shares	72,679	57,255	56,487	49,489	48,329
Total Revenue	1,825,949	1,499,273	1,648,599	844,000	846,333
Income before extra.	(64,272)	86,028	86,250	70,249	61,969
Cash Flow	219,277	176,777	232,104	162,027	153,750
Debt/Equity	3.01	2.07	1.92	1.11	1.17
Return on Capital (%)	4.59	9.52	13.69	10.75	11.74
Ret. on Com. Equity (%)	(8.15)	8.76	10.01	9.17	8.38
% Change Profit	(174.7)	(0.3)	22.8	13.4	(2.3)
% Change Revenue	21.8	(9.1)	95.3	(0.3)	(1.8)
% Change Assets	68.5	8.3	66.8	0.0	(0.8)

Preferred Div. Coverage	0.0	9.7	9.7	
Total Div. Coverage	0.0	1.6	1.6	
Interest Coverage	0.9	1.5	1.6	
Current Ratio	0.6	0.4	0.6	
Operating Margin	18.6	16.4	17.5	
Asset Turnover	0.2	0.3	0.4	
5 YEAR RATIOS (%)				
Return on Capital	10.1	11.8	12.3	
Return on Com. Equity	5.6	9.2	9.1	
Profit Growth	na	11.0	7.7	
Revenue Growth	16.2	9.4	6.3	
Asset Growth	24.7	15.3	12.7	
BALANCE SHEET (000)				
Cash	0	0	0	
Current Assets	845,738	333,127	335,601	
Net Fixed Assets	5,517,620	3,388,954	3,006,093	
Invest's & Advances	169,351	155,951	237,668	
Total Assets	6,594,924	3,912,967	3,612,839	
Short Term Debt	783,578	523,748	349,210	
Current Liabilities	1,326,292	764,591	593,431	
Long Term Debt	2,977,684	1,572,665	1,510,077	
Total Liabilities	5,344,037	2,899,585	2,645,585	
Total Equity	1,250,887	1,013,382	967,254	
Total Liab. & Equity	6,594,924	3,912,967	3,612,839	
CAPITAL (000)				
Total Debt	3,761,262	2,096,413	1,859,287	
Preferred Equity	229,969	109,969	109,989	
Common Equity	1,020,918	903,413	857,265	

Business:

WESTCOAST ENERGY INC. operates in Canada's natural gas industry. Company interests include natural gas transportation pipelines, distribution systems, power generation and marketing. Subsidiaries include Union Gas Limited, Centra Gas Inc., Pacific Northern Gas Ltd., Unigas Corporation and Canadian Hydrocarbons Marketing Inc. Joint ventures include 50% owned Foothills Pipe Lines Ltd.

Date	EPS	DPS	Tot Rev	Inc Bex
Mar 93	1.26	0.20	1,140,639	96,358
Dec 92	(1.97)	0.20	735,921	(111,696)
Sep 92	(0.20)	0.20	283,985	(6,507)
Jun 92	0.15	0.20	327,222	11,094
Mar 92	0.71	0.20	452,712	42,837
Dec 91	0.62	0.20	340,239	37,370
Sep 91	(0.21)	0.20	254,076	(9,631)
Jun 91	0.10	0.20	356,311	8,206

Synopsis:

Westcoast Energy Inc. completed the purchase of Union Energy Inc., whose principal investment is Union Gas Limited, in November 1992. Through the acquisition, Westcoast was following its strategy of expanding the distribution side of its business and growing in natural gas storage, transportation and marketing. Westcoast had offered $16 or one common share of Westcoast for each share of Union Energy Inc. The purchase price was $618-million, of which $381-million was paid in cash and $237-million was through the issue of common shares of Westcoast. Westcoast used bridge financing to finance the cash portion.

Westcoast sold its oil and gas subsidiary, Westcoast Petroleum Ltd., to five private investors from Hong Kong; the price was $247.5-million. The net proceeds will be used to reduce the amount owing through the bridge financing. Westcoast plans to repay the remainder of the financing through the issue of its common shares as market conditions permit.

Through its subsidiary Westcoast Power Inc., the company is actively pursuing cogeneration opportunities. Westcoast uses its gas distribution subsidiaries to work with customers in finding the benefits of cogeneration within their operations. Westcoast currently has one 100% owned plant in operation with two 50% owned plants expected to come online in 1993.

Capital expenditures over the next five years are expected to total $1.2-billion on the pipeline system, expansion capital expenditures of $985-million are planned, $172-million is forecast for replacement and upgrading, and $2.2-billion will be spent by the distribution companies.

1992 revenues (operating income) by segment as a percentage of total revenue (operating income) were: pipeline, 20% (41%); gas distribution, 65% (58%); and other (includes cogeneration), 15% (1%).

Rank (Profit/Revenue/Assets)
962 67 35

Arthur H. Willms
President & C.O.O.

Graham M. Wilson
Exec. V.P. & C.F.O.

Address
1333 West Georgia Street
Vancouver
BC
V6E 3K9
(604) 691-5500

Fax: (604) 691-5702
W0001495/G/9.2

Page	Company	$	Latest year end	Earnings per Share		
				Actual	Estimate this year	Estimate next year
289	Anglo-Canadian Telephone		9212	93.42	n.a.	n.a.
290	BC Gas		9212	0.48	1.34	1.52
291	BCE Inc.		9212	4.21	3.95	4.23
292	British Columbia Telephone		9212	1.84	1.72	1.85
293	Bruncor		9212	1.76	1.78	1.86
294	Canadian Utilities		9212	2.00	1.98	2.07
295	Canadian Western Natural Gas		9212	5.51	n.a.	n.a.
296	Centra Gas Ontario		9212	1.94	n.a.	n.a.
297	Consumers' Gas Company		9209	1.50	n.a.	n.a.
298	Fortis		9212	2.55	2.59	2.69
299	Island Telephone		9212	1.97	1.91	2.02
300	Maritime Electric		9212	1.85	1.88	1.93
301	Maritime Telegraph and Telephone		9212	2.03	1.99	2.07
302	Newfoundland Light & Power		9212	2.73	n.a.	n.a.
303	Newtel Enterprises		9212	1.73	1.81	1.88
304	Nortwestern Utilities		9212	8.58	n.a.	n.a.
305	Nova Scotia Power		9112	n.a.	1.07	1.11
306	Pacific Northern Gas		9212	3.10	n.a.	n.a.
307	Quebec-Telephone		9212	1.70	1.71	1.76
308	Telus Corporation		9212	1.28	1.23	1.36
309	TransAlta Utilities		9212	1.18	1.17	1.21
310	Unicorp Energy		9212	0.60	n.a.	n.a.

Estimates from I/B/E/S Inc., 345 Hudson St., New York, NY 10014 (212) 243-3335. In Canada: 6 Lansing Square, Ste. 235, Willowdale, ON M2J 1T5 (416) 496-0977.

Facing $36-billion in debt and a projected electricity surplus into the next century, Ontario Hydro is reviewing 66 cogeneration projects called NUGs (non-utility generation). Ontario Hydro's freeze on new privately owned power stations, however, is threatening expansion at Chrysler Canada Ltd.'s operations in Windsor, Ontario. Chrysler and partner TransAlta Utilities Corp. of Calgary have already invested about $10-million in a $140-million cogeneration project. The 135-megawatt Windsor plant, financed and owned by TransAlta, would produce enough electricity to supply a city of 60,000 people. Chrysler said cancellation would eliminate the huge energy saving the company counted on and without question it would go to court over the issue. The power plant is scheduled to open in January 1995. A long delay could result in TransAlta loosing the favorable deal it negotiated for Alberta natural gas to fuel the plant.

Canadian Utilities Ltd. of Edmonton and Suncor Inc. of Toronto have signed an agreement to jointly develop, own and operate a new cogeneration plant to provide steam and electric power to Suncor's oil sands operation near Fort McMurray, Alberta. The venture will be owned and operated equally by the two companies. The plant, with an estimated total construction cost of $270-million, will replace Suncor's existing steam and electric facility.

Utility Monthly: Regulation And Structure - Industry Report [Apr-8-1993]. MERRILL LYNCH CAPITAL MARKETS reported by Hyman, L.S., et al

Over the past ten years, the margins between the regulated limit on earnings, what the utilities actually earn, and what the utilities pay out as dividends have narrowed. Years ago, utilities performed a wider range of functions than they do currently. In the gas business, the pipelines no longer provide all the services they used to give to the local gas distribution companies. TransAlta, Canada's largest investor-owned electric utility, has filed with its regulators an unbundled tariff. That means that TransAlta will charge for the distribution (local lines), transmission (long distance high voltage lines) and generation (the actual electricity) separately. Customers (and others) will be able to use TransAlta's lines as a pipeline for electricity they have purchased elsewhere, or take the entire package from TransAlta. American Electric Power, which has one of the largest transmission networks in the U.S., has proposed to open its lines for use by other utilities. [RN 1319705]

Utility Industry - Industry Report [Apr-1-1993] MERRILL LYNCH CAPITAL MARKETS reported by Hyman, L.S., et al

U.S. Utility stocks performed well in 1992, reflecting falling interest rates. The dividend yield on the stocks followed bond yields. Utility earnings are expected to improve from the 1992 trough, but dividends are not expected to advance at much, due to high payout ratios. Utilities usually produce returns on equity investment of about 11%, while the utilities' diversified business and investments typically return about 8% on assets. [RN 1324431]

Utility Industry - Industry Report [Apr-1-1993]. MERRILL LYNCH CAPITAL MARKETS reported by Hyman, L.S., et al

Competition in the electric industry is increasing. Non-utility generators are expected to have a larger role in meeting the electric requirements of the United States. Currently accounting for about 6.1% of electric requirements, non-utility generators are expected to provide about 10.9% of the country's electric demand by the year 2000. Annual electric sales growth is expected to average 1.9% through 2000. Average annual growth for the first decade of the next century is estimated at 1.7%. With limited sales growth, companies will be looking elsewhere for earnings potential. One area they are likely to consider is foreign investment. Utilities are no longer prohibited from building power plants abroad or holding interests in foreign utilities. U.S. utilities may also find it profitable to market their industry expertise to foreign utilities. [RN 1317817]

Canada: Regulated Industries - Industry Report [Mar-17-1993. BBN JAMES CAPEL INC. reported by Cunningham, D.

The Canadian Radio-television and Telecommunications Commission (CRTC) enacted long-distance competition in June 1992. Less than eight months later, Bell Canada applied for local rate increases of up to 60%. The telco's decision to drop WATS rates for low- and medium-volume subscribers will have a negative effect upon many resellers. Cam-Net Communications Network and Smart Talk Network will be affected to a greater extent than Call-Net Enterprises. Call-Net acquired two competitors in March 1993, doubling its sales volume to more than $170 million per annum. An affiliation with Sprint could further enhance Call-Net's fundamentals. [RN 1317396]

ANGLO-CANADIAN TELEPHONE COMPANY

Exchanges	Price (Jun24'93)		39 .50	Trailing P/E		nc	Stock Symbol
TM	Trailing Yield (%)		nc	Trailing EPS		92 .04	**ACT.PR.C**

Period Ending	Dec92	Dec91	Dec90	Dec89	Dec88
Yearly Statistics					
Price-Close	38 .00	35 .25	29 .75	31 .63	31 .00
Price-High	40 .50	36 .00	32 .25	33 .50	35 .50
Price-Low	33 .00	30 .25	28 .75	30 .50	30 .50
P/E-Close	nc	nc	nc	nc	nc
Dividends per Share	nc	nc	nc	nc	nc
Dividend Yield (%)	nc	nc	nc	nc	nc
Sales per Share	1 ,480 .81	1 ,422 .14	1 ,603 .59	1 ,252 .10	1 ,224 .22
EPS before extra. item	93 .42	91 .53	83 .24	88 .83	125 .18
Cash Flow per Share	396 .41	391 .18	358 .14	265 .95	273 .94
Book Value per Share	721 .33	669 .79	612 .16	467 .03	474 .23
O/S Common Shares	1 ,284	1 ,284	1 ,284	1 ,527	1 ,527
Total Revenue	2 ,302 ,456	2 ,223 ,351	2 ,106 ,112	1 ,913 ,813	1 ,872 ,626
Income before extra.	119 ,926	117 ,500	108 ,541	137 ,677	193 ,157
Cash Flow	508 ,859	502 ,142	466 ,992	406 ,018	418 ,212
Debt/Equity	1 .81	1 .84	1 .98	2 .02	1 .83
Return on Capital (%)	18 .47	18 .28	11 .10	19 .24	23 .82
Ret. on Com. Equity (%)	13 .20	14 .03	14 .04	18 .88	28 .47
% Change Profit	2 .1	8 .3	(21 .2)	(28 .7)	79 .1
% Change Revenue	3 .6	5 .6	10 .0	2 .2	4 .1
% Change Assets	4 .8	4 .3	4 .1	6 .2	4 .7

Date	EPS	DPS	Tot Rev	Inc Bex
Mar 93	16 .50	nc	581 ,849	21 ,185
Dec 92	28 .74	nc	575 ,525	36 ,897
Sep 92	24 .38	nc	587 ,059	31 ,308
Jun 92	22 .42	nc	581 ,250	28 ,775
Mar 92	17 .87	nc	551 ,735	22 ,946
Dec 91	28 .76	nc	574 ,289	36 ,923
Sep 91	22 .32	nc	548 ,669	28 ,657
Jun 91	22 .31	nc	569 ,905	28 ,633

Preferred Div. Coverage	58 .3	57 .1	32 .9
Total Div. Coverage	2 .2	2 .7	3 .0
Interest Coverage	3 .0	2 .8	na
Current Ratio	0 .6	0 .6	0 .7
Operating Margin	25 .9	25 .2	24 .7
Asset Turnover	0 .4	0 .4	0 .5
5 YEAR RATIOS (%)			
Return on Capital	18 .2	18 .9	19 .5
Return on Com. Equity	17 .7	18 .7	19 .3
Profit Growth	2 .1	4 .3	4 .6
Revenue Growth	5 .0	5 .0	5 .6
Asset Growth	4 .7	3 .9	3 .7
BALANCE SHEET (000)			
Cash	35 ,993	29 ,835	26 ,542
Current Assets	457 ,231	420 ,177	409 ,794
Net Fixed Assets	3 ,861 ,426	3 ,715 ,955	3 ,587 ,099
Invest's & Advances	103 ,255	81 ,161	71 ,776
Total Assets	4 ,485 ,137	4 ,279 ,068	4 ,103 ,024
Short Term Debt	368 ,134	334 ,021	238 ,537
Current Liabilities	762 ,577	712 ,833	599 ,087
Long Term Debt	1 ,372 ,820	1 ,319 ,268	1 ,391 ,354
Total Liabilities	3 ,521 ,692	3 ,381 ,784	3 ,279 ,706
Total Equity	963 ,445	897 ,284	823 ,318
Total Liab. & Equity	4 ,485 ,137	4 ,279 ,068	4 ,103 ,024
CAPITAL (000)			
Total Debt	1 ,740 ,954	1 ,653 ,289	1 ,629 ,891
Preferred Equity	37 ,500	37 ,500	37 ,500
Common Equity	925 ,945	859 ,784	785 ,818

Business:

ANGLO-CANADIAN TELEPHONE CO. operates, through subsidiaries, telecommunications services in British Columbia and Quebec. The company owns 50.27% of British Columbia Telephone Co. and 50.30% of Quebec-Telephone. Dominion Directories is an operating division. GTE Corp. of Stamford, Conn., is the major shareholder of the company.

Synopsis:

Anglo-Canadian Telephone Company reported operating earnings increased by 6.6% in fiscal 1992 over the same period last year. The improvement in operating earnings reflect relatively strong performances from all of the company's operations. The growth in net income was only 2% representing the impact of higher provincial income tax rates in both British Columbia and Quebec.

Long distance service revenues increased by $1.3-million in 1992 to a level of $1.054-billion. The total number of long distance calls completed by the company's operating units increased by 7.25% over last year to reach 475 million calls. The growth in long distance service revenues was offset by the decline in the subsidiaries' portion of long distance revenues shared with other Canadian telephone companies and by price reductions and the loss of some customers to more competitively priced services.

Local service revenues increased by $74-million to $846.8-million in 1992. The main factors attributed to the increase are a 4.3% growth rate in the number of customer access lines, the increased customer base in the cellular business and the expansion of customer calling features.

Anglo-Canadian's planned capital expenditures for fiscal 1993 total $564-million. Capital expenditures for the 1994 through 1998 period are expected to range from $539-million to $589-million annually.

Revenues from long distance services in 1993 are expected to decline from 1992 levels. The main factor for the lower levels is the continuing loss of market share to resellers. Growth in the number of customer access lines in 1993 is expected to be near 1992 levels.

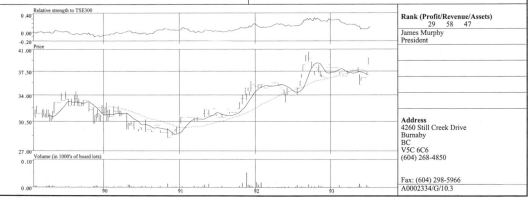

Rank (Profit/Revenue/Assets)
        29   58   47
James Murphy
President

Address
4260 Still Creek Drive
Burnaby
BC
V5C 6C6
(604) 268-4850

Fax: (604) 298-5966
A0002334/G/10.3

BC GAS INC.

Period Ending	Dec92	Dec91	Dec90	Dec89	Dec88
Yearly Statistics					
Price-Close	14.75	17.13	14.75	15.25	12.88
Price-High	17.88	17.38	15.75	15.38	13.88
Price-Low	13.88	14.25	13.75	12.75	11.25
P/E-Close	42.14	8.83	8.24	8.20	14.97
Dividends per Share	0.90	0.90	0.82	0.74	0.68
Dividend Yield (%)	6.10	5.26	5.56	4.85	5.28
Sales per Share	16.21	31.37	35.96	35.35	29.22
EPS before extra. item	0.35	1.94	1.79	1.86	0.86
Cash Flow per Share	2.80	5.52	5.51	5.14	4.91
Book Value per Share	11.42	11.85	11.42	10.43	9.42
O/S Common Shares	39,388	38,495	16,338	16,041	15,528
Total Revenue	699,006	707,746	690,944	660,639	339,079
Income before extra.	26,153	50,882	42,547	35,263	9,075
Cash Flow	97,178	103,538	89,725	81,942	44,719
Debt/Equity	1.61	1.34	3.07	3.41	5.70
Return on Capital (%)	8.23	11.98	11.94	12.22	8.85
Ret. on Com. Equity (%)	3.48	12.60	18.62	19.23	7.52
% Change Profit	(48.6)	0.0	20.7	288.6	198.1
% Change Revenue	(1.2)	2.4	4.6	94.8	62.7
% Change Assets	9.7	7.3	7.9	10.0	215.3

Date	EPS	DPS	Tot Rev	Inc Bex
Mar 93	1.10	0.23	278,370	40,587
Dec 92	1.46	0.23	246,941	53,527
Sep 92	(1.21)	0.23	107,650	(38,169)
Jun 92	(0.89)	0.23	117,385	(26,660)
Mar 92	0.29	0.23	221,232	13,517
Dec 91	1.86	0.23	218,778	38,700
Sep 91	(1.75)	0.23	101,916	(25,200)
Jun 91	(0.83)	0.23	133,863	(9,912)

Preferred Div. Coverage	2.5	4.9	4.4
Total Div. Coverage	0.6	1.8	1.9
Interest Coverage	1.5	1.6	1.5
Current Ratio	0.3	0.4	0.4
Operating Margin	18.0	22.4	21.7
Asset Turnover	0.3	0.4	0.4
5 YEAR RATIOS (%)			
Return on Capital	10.6	11.1	11.7
Return on Com. Equity	12.3	12.1	13.0
Profit Growth	53.7	37.2	38.3
Revenue Growth	27.3	26.4	20.5
Asset Growth	34.4	35.5	37.6
BALANCE SHEET (000)			
Cash	0	0	0
Current Assets	138,541	118,296	127,228
Net Fixed Assets	1,515,448	1,376,120	1,281,154
Invest's & Advances	14,246	10,917	7,424
Total Assets	1,687,386	1,538,240	1,432,975
Short Term Debt	332,279	213,522	229,551
Current Liabilities	463,642	333,027	355,687
Long Term Debt	583,154	560,841	712,519
Total Liabilities	1,117,713	962,088	1,126,410
Total Equity	569,673	576,152	306,565
Total Liab. & Equity	1,687,386	1,538,240	1,432,975
CAPITAL (000)			
Total Debt	915,433	774,363	942,070
Preferred Equity	120,000	120,000	120,000
Common Equity	449,673	456,152	186,565

Business:

BC GAS INC., formerly Inland Natural Gas Co. Ltd., is a natural gas distributor. It operates a natural gas transmission pipeline and distribution network in British Columbia. An affiliate, Trans Mountain Pipe Line Co. Ltd. of Vancouver, operates an oil pipeline between northern Alberta and the Vancouver area.

Synopsis:

In May 1993, BC Gas Inc. said it will refund to customers the full amount of a 4.1% interim rate increase collected since January 1. The company said the refund results from the B.C. Utilities Commission's approval of a BC Gas request to withdraw its 1993 revenue requirement application. It said this will be the seventh year that the company's cost service charges to natural gas customers have been unchanged. BC Gas said it withdrew its application as a result of utility revenue being greater than forecast, due to the much colder than normal temperatures during the 1993 first quarter. It said it also withdrew the application "to avoid a lengthy and time consuming hearing and associated costs."

In March 1993, the board of directors of BC Gas approved a corporate reorganization, subject to regulatory approvals. The reorganization will separate the operations of BC Gas into two groups - those regulated by the British Columbia Utilities Commission (BCUC) and those not regulated by the BCUC. The company said it is responding to a request from the BCUC to isolate its utility assets so that a clearer picture of its structure is available for the next regulatory hearing. If the plan receives necessary approvals, common shareholders would become investors in a new parent company called BC Gas Inc. Preferred shareholders would remain investors in the utility, to be renamed BC Gas Utility Ltd. The company expects the changes to become effective around July 1, 1993.

BC Gas attributed reduced 1992 earnings to three unforeseen circumstances. The largest contributor to the decline in earnings was unseasonably warm weather which reduced earnings per share by $0.72 during 1992. Trans Mountain's write-off of its Low Point project accounted for $0.17 of the per share decline. Finally, the denial of a requested 2.9% rate increase contained in an August 1992 decision from the BCUC reduced anticipated earnings per share by $0.51.

Relative strength to TSE300 / Price / Volume (in 1000's of board lots)

Rank (Profit/Revenue/Assets)		
109	131	106

Ronald L. Cliff
Chairman Of The Board

Robert E. Kadlec
President & C.E.O.

Michael C. Burns
Exec. V.P., Finance & Admin.

Address
1066 West Hastings Street
Vancouver
BC
V6E 3G3
(604) 443-6559

Fax: (604) 443-6614
I0001011/G/10.1

BCE INC.

Exchanges	Price (Jun24'93)	45 .75	Trailing P/E	11 .49	Stock Symbol
TMVN	Trailing Yield (%)	5 .73	Trailing EPS	3 .98	**B**

Period Ending	Dec92	Dec91	Dec90	Dec89	Dec88
Yearly Statistics					
Price-Close	41 .50	47 .63	39 .50	45 .63	37 .25
Price-High	50 .00	48 .25	46 .50	45 .63	39 .63
Price-Low	40 .88	38 .25	34 .75	36 .38	36 .13
P/E-Close	9 .86	11 .88	11 .29	18 .78	12 .63
Dividends per Share	2 .61	2 .57	2 .53	2 .49	2 .45
Dividend Yield (%)	6 .29	5 .40	6 .41	5 .46	6 .58
Sales per Share	62 .94	59 .42	53 .71	51 .00	47 .96
EPS before extra. item	4 .21	4 .01	3 .50	2 .43	2 .95
Cash Flow per Share	13 .22	13 .12	11 .72	10 .83	9 .54
Book Value per Share	36 .28	34 .57	33 .04	31 .61	31 .82
O/S Common Shares (mil)	305	310	305	302	290
Total Revenue ($mil)	21 ,270	20 ,194	18 ,846	17 ,087	14 ,775
Income before extra. ($mil)	1 ,390	1 ,329	1 ,147	761	846
Cash Flow ($mil)	4 ,065	4 ,036	3 ,562	3 ,221	2 ,723
Debt/Equity	0 .93	0 .85	0 .82	0 .90	0 .91
Return on Capital (%)	14 .34	14 .94	13 .50	12 .65	12 .32
Ret. on Com. Equity (%)	11 .88	11 .87	10 .82	7 .72	9 .22
% Change Profit	4 .6	15 .9	50 .7	(10 .0)	(22 .2)
% Change Revenue	5 .3	7 .2	10 .3	15 .6	(1 .6)
% Change Assets	5 .7	8 .9	6 .9	51 .1	(0 .8)

Business:

BCE INC. is Canada's largest telecommunications company. Its subsidiaries and affiliated companies, including wholly owned Bell Canada, provide telecommunications services to some 70% of the Canadian population. Its subsidiary Northern Telecom Limited, 52.4% owned, is a world leader in the manufacture of telecommunications equipment. BCE also has a major interest in financial services.

Date	EPS	DPS	Tot Rev	Inc Bex
Mar 93	0.65	0.66	5,072,000	221,000
Dec 92	1.65	0.66	6,256,000	528,000
Sep 92	0.96	0.65	5,093,000	318,000
Jun 92	0.72	0.65	5,053,000	246,000
Mar 92	0.88	0.65	4,891,000	298,000
Dec 91	1.11	0.65	5,400,000	368,000
Sep 91	1.10	0.64	4,936,000	361,000
Jun 91	0.92	0.64	5,101,000	307,000

	Dec92	Dec91	Dec90
Preferred Div. Coverage	14 .6	14 .1	13 .5
Total Div. Coverage	1 .6	1 .5	1 .3
Interest Coverage	3 .0	3 .0	2 .9
Current Ratio	0 .8	0 .8	1 .1
Operating Margin	15 .5	16 .4	16 .6
Asset Turnover	0 .4	0 .4	0 .4
5 YEAR RATIOS (%)			
Return on Capital	13 .6	13 .7	14 .1
Return on Com. Equity	10 .3	10 .3	10 .5
Profit Growth	5 .0	5 .3	1 .8
Revenue Growth	7 .1	7 .3	6 .8
Asset Growth	13 .0	14 .0	15 .3
BALANCE SHEET (mil)			
Cash	237	300	308
Current Assets	6 ,753	5 ,762	5 ,761
Net Fixed Assets	21 ,384	19 ,995	18 ,574
Invest's & Advances	16 ,874	16 ,520	16 ,582
Total Assets	48 ,312	45 ,704	41 ,987
Short Term Debt	2 ,832	2 ,247	1 ,878
Current Liabilities	8 ,700	7 ,248	5 ,414
Long Term Debt	8 ,613	7 ,971	7 ,431
Total Liabilities	36 ,005	33 ,745	30 ,662
Total Equity	12 ,307	11 ,959	11 ,325
Total Liab. & Equity	48 ,312	45 ,704	41 ,987
CAPITAL (mil)			
Total Debt	11 ,445	10 ,218	9 ,309
Preferred Equity	1 ,229	1 ,232	1 ,235
Common Equity	11 ,078	10 ,727	10 ,090

Synopsis:

In April 1993, Bell Canada, a wholly owned subsidiary of BCE Inc., joined five of its Stentor partners and submitted a proposal on how the CRTC should regulate the telecommunications industry. The six telecommunication companies proposed industry changes to the regulatory framework to make the telecommunication industry less restrictive towards new and existing competition. The submission followed the CRTC's decision in 1992 to allow long distance competition in Canada. The joint submission calls for a fully competitive environment where all suppliers, either telephone, cable or cellular companies, are able to enter businesses and make decisions for themselves. The group feels that a regulatory process that better adapts to changes in technologies and competition will benefit customers through cheaper rates and better services.

In early June 1993, Bell Canada applied to the CRTC for rate increases which would apply to both residential and business customers. If approved by the CRTC, residential rates would increase $1.10 a month and business rates would increase $3.30 a month. Bell Canada expects approval of the application by August 4, 1993.

In March 1993, BCE sold its remaining interest in TransCanada PipeLines. The 4.5% stake in the natural gas pipeline company was sold to two investment dealers at $18 per share.

In January 1993, BCE announced it intends to sell its interest in SHL Systemhouse. The $83-million stake represents approximately 25% of the total outstanding shares of SHL Systemhouse. The sale will be underwritten by Gordon Capital. After the sale is complete, BCE will no longer hold any investments relating to SHL Systemhouse.

As of December 31, 1992, BCE's telecommunication assets accounted for almost 72% of the company's total assets. Revenues from the telecommunication segment accounted for over 93% of BCE's total revenues in 1992. The remaining revenues were generated from the financial services sector and other corporate investments.

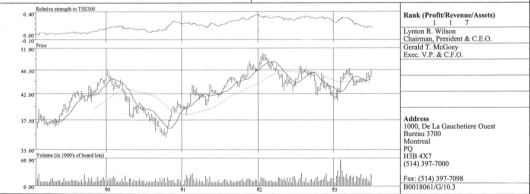

Rank (Profit/Revenue/Assets)
1   1   7

Lynton R. Wilson
Chairman, President & C.E.O.

Gerald T. McGoey
Exec. V.P. & C.F.O.

Address
1000, De La Gauchetiere Ouest
Bureau 3700
Montreal
PQ
H3B 4X7
(514) 397-7000

Fax: (514) 397-7098
B0018061/G/10.3

BRITISH COLUMBIA TELEPHONE COMPANY

Exchanges	Price (Jun24'93)	21 .25	Trailing P/E	11.81	Stock Symbol
TMV	Trailing Yield (%)	5 .46	Trailing EPS	1 .80	**BCT**

Period Ending	Dec92	Dec91	Dec90	Dec89	Dec88
Yearly Statistics					
Price-Close	19 .63	23 .00	19 .25	18 .00	14 .06
Price-High	23 .88	23 .00	19 .50	18 .75	14 .75
Price-Low	18 .75	18 .63	16 .25	14 .00	13 .13
P/E-Close	11 .03	12 .92	11 .19	11 .39	9 .70
Dividends per Share	1 .15	1 .10	1 .02	0 .95	0 .91
Dividend Yield (%)	5 .86	4 .78	5 .30	5 .28	6 .47
Sales per Share	18 .44	17 .99	17 .67	16 .55	16 .37
EPS before extra. item	1 .78	1 .78	1 .72	1 .58	1 .45
Cash Flow per Share	4 .61	4 .53	4 .45	4 .44	4 .34
Book Value per Share	14 .22	13 .42	12 .59	11 .80	11 .09
O/S Common Shares	111 ,596	108 ,746	105 ,698	103 ,504	100 ,568
Total Revenue	2 ,063 ,400	1 ,969 ,700	1 ,877 ,700	1 ,700 ,700	1 ,643 ,600
Income before extra.	205 ,700	201 ,000	193 ,200	177 ,500	160 ,600
Cash Flow	509 ,900	487 ,900	466 ,400	453 ,300	433 ,800
Debt/Equity	0 .89	0 .91	0 .97	0 .94	0 .94
Return on Capital (%)	17 .05	17 .08	16 .77	16 .54	17 .16
Ret. on Com. Equity (%)	12 .91	13 .71	14 .15	13 .84	13 .44
% Change Profit	2 .3	4 .0	8 .8	10 .5	9 .1
% Change Revenue	4 .8	4 .9	10 .4	3 .5	0 .6
% Change Assets	5 .0	4 .6	4 .1	8 .3	2 .2

Preferred Div. Coverage	22 .9	20 .5	15 .3
Total Div. Coverage	1 .5	1 .6	1 .6
Interest Coverage	3 .5	3 .3	3 .2
Current Ratio	0 .6	0 .5	0 .6
Operating Margin	25 .7	25 .3	24 .5
Asset Turnover	0 .5	0 .5	0 .5
5 YEAR RATIOS (%)			
Return on Capital	16 .9	17 .1	17 .2
Return on Com. Equity	13 .6	13 .6	13 .4
Profit Growth	6 .9	8 .9	10 .7
Revenue Growth	4 .7	5 .1	5 .8
Asset Growth	4 .7	3 .7	3 .4
BALANCE SHEET (000)			
Cash	0	0	0
Current Assets	379 ,700	349 ,300	345 ,600
Net Fixed Assets	3 ,398 ,900	3 ,261 ,000	3 ,079 ,000
Invest's & Advances	94 ,300	78 ,000	67 ,400
Total Assets	3 ,934 ,900	3 ,747 ,900	3 ,584 ,800
Short Term Debt	312 ,600	308 ,700	216 ,800
Current Liabilities	673 ,300	648 ,700	543 ,500
Long Term Debt	1 ,221 ,900	1 ,160 ,600	1 ,226 ,000
Total Liabilities	2 ,201 ,800	2 ,133 ,700	2 ,094 ,900
Total Equity	1 ,733 ,100	1 ,614 ,200	1 ,489 ,900
Total Liab. & Equity	3 ,934 ,900	3 ,747 ,900	3 ,584 ,800
CAPITAL (000)			
Total Debt	1 ,534 ,500	1 ,468 ,800	1 ,442 ,800
Preferred Equity	146 ,400	154 ,400	159 ,400
Common Equity	1 ,586 ,700	1 ,459 ,800	1 ,330 ,500

Business:

BRITISH COLUMBIA TELEPHONE COMPANY provides telephone and cellular telephone service, and telecommunications services within British Columbia, and through interconnecting agreements, worldwide. Through subsidiary companies comprising the B.C. Tel Group, the company also designs, makes and markets a range of telecommunications products and services. Anglo-Canadian Telephone Co. owns 50.2% of the company.

Date	EPS	DPS	Tot Rev	Inc Bex
Mar 93	0 .30	0 .29	521 ,900	35 ,800
Dec 92	0 .57	0 .29	539 ,000	65 ,600
Sep 92	0 .49	0 .29	511 ,300	56 ,400
Jun 92	0 .38	0 .29	510 ,000	44 ,500
Mar 92	0 .34	0 .28	491 ,500	39 ,200
Dec 91	0 .54	0 .28	507 ,700	60 ,800
Sep 91	0 .50	0 .28	493 ,900	55 ,600
Jun 91	0 .38	0 .28	487 ,200	43 ,900

Synopsis:

Effective May 1, 1993, British Columbia Telephone changed its name to BC Telecom Inc. and also reorganized the company to better reflect the nature of its operations. BC Telecom will be structured like a holding company. The new structure simplifies the regulation process by segregating BC Telecom's regulated telecommunications services and systems from largely non-regulated subsidiaries. BC Telecom's new structure is not expected to change the focus of its efforts on the telecommunications industry. Shareholders overwhelmingly approved the plan.

In an attempt to become more competitive in the eyes of the CRTC, BC Telecom announced in April 1993 that it cut staff by 3.3% last year with an additional 4% cut expected in 1993. BC Telecom hopes that being more competitive and efficient will help the company when it applies for rate increases, and also when it bids with the Stentor telephone alliance for wide-open competition.

In early April, BC Telecom applied for two rate increases in 1993. The first rate increase, which the CRTC says can take place no earlier than June 1, 1993, would raise the monthly average rate for individual residence lines by 30% and individual business lines by an average of 7.8%. The first rate increase would raise $52-million in 1993. A second rate increase would be scheduled for December 1, 1993, and would raise an additional $9-million. BC Telecom says it needs the increases to offset new long distance competition in the Canadian market.

Revenues by segment in 1992 (1991) were: long distance service, 45% (47%); local services, 38% (36%); and directory advertising, equipment sales and other, 17% (17%).

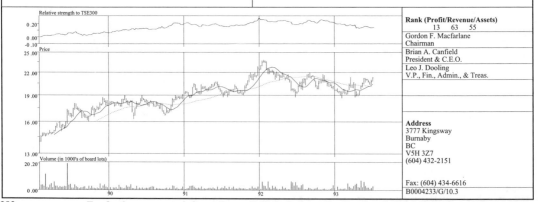

Rank (Profit/Revenue/Assets)
13   63   55

Gordon F. Macfarlane
Chairman

Brian A. Canfield
President & C.E.O.

Leo J. Dooling
V.P., Fin., Admin., & Treas.

Address
3777 Kingsway
Burnaby
BC
V5H 3Z7
(604) 432-2151

Fax: (604) 434-6616
B0004233/G/10.3

BRUNCOR INC.

Exchanges	Price (Jun24'93)	21.87	Trailing P/E	12.57	Stock Symbol
TM	Trailing Yield (%)	5.85	Trailing EPS	1.74	**BRR**

Period Ending	Dec92	Dec91	Dec90	Dec89	Dec88
Yearly Statistics					
Price-Close	20.25	18.63	17.88	17.50	17.38
Price-High	21.00	19.00	18.13	18.63	18.63
Price-Low	18.00	16.63	15.25	16.63	16.25
P/E-Close	11.51	11.36	11.53	92.11	11.07
Dividends per Share	1.27	1.24	1.21	1.20	1.20
Dividend Yield (%)	6.27	6.66	6.77	6.86	6.90
Sales per Share	18.36	18.66	18.13	16.86	14.59
EPS before extra. item	1.76	1.64	1.55	0.19	1.57
Cash Flow per Share	5.65	5.06	5.26	5.07	4.51
Book Value per Share	14.83	14.02	13.48	13.15	14.05
O/S Common Shares	21,374	20,138	19,282	19,282	19,114
Total Revenue	392,339	373,739	354,888	329,440	297,379
Income before extra.	38,494	34,017	31,643	5,464	31,708
Cash Flow	117,740	99,543	101,462	97,465	86,034
Debt/Equity	1.23	1.38	1.37	1.16	0.89
Return on Capital (%)	15.63	15.27	15.73	11.32	13.60
Ret. on Com. Equity (%)	12.24	11.88	11.62	1.40	11.31
% Change Profit	13.2	7.5	479.1	(82.8)	(1.2)
% Change Revenue	5.0	5.3	7.7	10.8	(13.1)
% Change Assets	3.9	6.6	10.7	7.4	(25.4)

Preferred Div. Coverage	21.2	18.8	17.5
Total Div. Coverage	1.4	1.3	1.3
Interest Coverage	2.5	2.3	2.3
Current Ratio	0.8	0.6	0.7
Operating Margin	28.1	27.6	27.4
Asset Turnover	0.4	0.4	0.4
5 YEAR RATIOS (%)			
Return on Capital	14.3	14.4	14.4
Return on Com. Equity	9.7	9.7	9.8
Profit Growth	3.8	2.9	3.7
Revenue Growth	2.7	6.9	7.5
Asset Growth	(0.4)	0.7	8.2
BALANCE SHEET (000)			
Cash	0	0	0
Current Assets	115,244	116,760	100,410
Net Fixed Assets	677,887	649,001	614,923
Invest's & Advances	99,131	88,385	85,975
Total Assets	904,106	869,815	816,242
Short Term Debt	86,559	133,319	78,592
Current Liabilities	147,895	192,818	133,989
Long Term Debt	335,584	290,024	312,917
Total Liabilities	562,095	562,507	531,295
Total Equity	342,011	307,308	284,947
Total Liab. & Equity	904,106	869,815	816,242
CAPITAL (000)			
Total Debt	422,143	423,343	391,509
Preferred Equity	25,000	25,000	25,000
Common Equity	317,011	282,308	259,947

Business:

BRUNCOR INC. is a diversified management holding company. Its main interests are in telecommunications, financial services and real estate. The bulk of the company's business is in New Brunswick. The company's principal subsidiary is wholly owned New Brunswick Telephone Co. Ltd. Bruncor owns commercial real estate in Saint John, Moncton, Fredericton, Toronto and Boston.

Date	EPS	DPS	Tot Rev	Inc Bex
Mar 93	0.41	0.32	96,119	9,263
Dec 92	0.49	0.32	103,973	10,767
Sep 92	0.39	0.32	96,196	8,796
Jun 92	0.45	0.32	97,022	9,737
Mar 92	0.43	0.31	95,148	9,194
Dec 91	0.44	0.31	95,936	9,190
Sep 91	0.37	0.31	93,266	7,843
Jun 91	0.44	0.31	94,057	9,100

Synopsis:

In the first quarter of 1993, New Brunswick Telephone Company, Limited (NB Tel), a wholly owned subsidiary of Bruncor Inc., joined five of its Stentor partners and submitted a proposal on how the CRTC should regulate the telecommunications industry. The six telecommunication companies propose changes to the regulatory framework to make the telecommunication industry less restrictive towards new competition. The submission follows the CRTC's decision to allow long distance competition in Canada. The joint submission calls for a fully competitive environment where all suppliers, either telephone, cable or cellular companies, are able to enter any line of business that they wish to. The group feels a regulatory process that better adapts to changes in technologies and competition will benefit customers through cheaper rates and better services.

Bruncor announced at its annual meeting held in April 1992 that NB Tel would be reducing prices and increasing services due to competition and regulation. The price decreases relate to long distance calls which in the past have been subsidizing local call revenues. NB Tel will also be 100% digital by the end of the year, which means everyone in New Brunswick will have access to services such as Call Display and TalkMail. It would also mean New Brunswick would be the first all-digital province in Canada. Because of the new services, NB Tel reported an 8.2% increase in local service revenues in the first quarter of 1993.

As of March 31, 1993, NB Tel had 465,378 network access services, compared with 449,889 on March 31, 1992. Almost 54% of revenues in the first quarter of 1993 were generated from long distances calls. Local service calls made up over 43% of revenues in the quarter. In the first quarter of 1992, long distance revenues made up over 57% of total operating revenues.

The telecommunications industry accounts for 80% of Bruncor's assets. Real estate accounts for 11% of Bruncor's assets with financial services making up the rest.

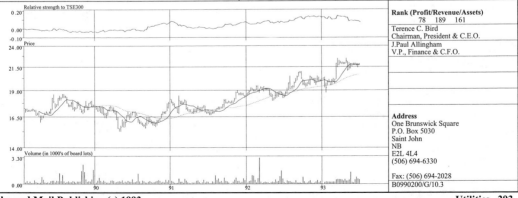

Rank (Profit/Revenue/Assets)
78   189   161

Terence C. Bird
Chairman, President & C.E.O.
J.Paul Allingham
V.P., Finance & C.F.O.

Address
One Brunswick Square
P.O. Box 5030
Saint John
NB
E2L 4L4
(506) 694-6330

Fax: (506) 694-2028
B0990200/G/10.3

CANADIAN UTILITIES LIMITED

Exchanges	Price (Jun24'93)		23 .00	Trailing P/E		10 .90	Stock Symbol
TMZ	Trailing Yield (%)		6.11	Trailing EPS		2.11	**CU**

Period Ending	Dec92	Dec91	Dec90	Dec89	Dec88
Yearly Statistics					
Price-Close	20 .50	21.38	20.38	21.88	19 .63
Price-High	23 .00	21.75	22 .00	22.38	20 .38
Price-Low	18 .75	18 .63	18.25	18.75	18 .00
P/E-Close	10.25	11 .94	11 .71	12.29	10 .44
Dividends per Share	1 .40	1 .38	1 .37	1 .35	1 .33
Dividend Yield (%)	6 .83	6 .46	6 .70	6 .15	6 .75
Sales per Share	19 .91	18 .87	20 .27	19 .97	21 .11
EPS before extra. item	2 .00	1 .79	1 .74	1 .78	1 .88
Cash Flow per Share	3 .96	3 .59	3 .66	4 .38	3 .90
Book Value per Share	15 .18	14 .48	14 .08	14 .81	14 .37
O/S Common Shares	62 ,091	60 ,825	60 ,818	59 ,519	59 ,433
Total Revenue	1 ,256 ,636	1 ,192 ,621	1 ,243 ,832	1 ,220 ,812	1 ,181 ,742
Income before extra.	175 ,077	157 ,388	145 ,412	148 ,078	144 ,898
Cash Flow	241 ,114	218 ,244	218 ,290	260 ,725	213 ,703
Debt/Equity	0 .80	0 .76	0 .87	0 .74	0 .64
Return on Capital (%)	14 .67	13 .89	14 .52	14 .64	15 .85
Ret. on Com. Equity (%)	13 .34	12 .51	11 .91	12 .20	13 .02
% Change Profit	11 .2	8 .2	(1 .8)	2 .2	(5 .5)
% Change Revenue	5 .4	(4 .1)	1 .9	3 .3	(0 .6)
% Change Assets	5 .2	(1 .7)	2 .4	8 .4	4 .6
Preferred Div. Coverage	3 .3	3 .2	3 .5		
Total Div. Coverage	1 .3	1 .2	0 .8		
Interest Coverage	3 .1	2 .8	2 .9		
Current Ratio	1 .2	1 .1	1 .0		
Operating Margin	31 .3	28 .9	27 .6		
Asset Turnover	0 .4	0 .4	0 .4		
5 YEAR RATIOS (%)					
Return on Capital	14 .7	15 .1	15 .8		
Return on Com. Equity	12 .6	12 .6	13 .6		
Profit Growth	2 .6	(1 .5)	(0 .6)		
Revenue Growth	1 .1	(1 .8)	(2 .1)		
Asset Growth	3 .6	1 .7	3 .6		
BALANCE SHEET (000)					
Cash	18 ,099	17 ,597	545		
Current Assets	262 ,401	233 ,679	213 ,517		
Net Fixed Assets	2 ,767 ,981	2 ,641 ,551	2 ,731 ,080		
Invest's & Advances	96 ,637	94 ,185	79 ,003		
Total Assets	3 ,148 ,257	2 ,992 ,756	3 ,045 ,189		
Short Term Debt	34 ,263	59 ,722	40 ,873		
Current Liabilities	216 ,469	213 ,431	204 ,697		
Long Term Debt	1 ,273 ,825	1 ,154 ,087	1 ,168 ,074		
Total Liabilities	1 ,506 ,603	1 ,385 ,784	1 ,652 ,878		
Total Equity	1 ,641 ,654	1 ,606 ,972	1 ,392 ,311		
Total Liab. & Equity	3 ,148 ,257	2 ,992 ,756	3 ,045 ,189		
CAPITAL (000)					
Total Debt	1 ,308 ,088	1 ,213 ,809	1 ,208 ,947		
Preferred Equity	699 ,277	726 ,340	536 ,203		
Common Equity	942 ,377	880 ,632	856 ,108		

Business:

CANADIAN UTILITIES LTD., through subsidiaries, is primarily in the business of generating, transmitting, distributing and selling electric power and natural gas. Utilities operations are carried out mainly in Western Canada.

Date	EPS	DPS	Tot Rev	Inc Bex
Mar 93	0.81	0.36	433 ,797	63 ,361
Dec 92	0.69	0.35	379 ,568	55 ,280
Sep 92	0.26	0.35	243 ,987	28 ,974
Jun 92	0.35	0.35	262 ,997	34 ,886
Mar 92	0.70	0.35	370 ,084	55 ,937
Dec 91	0.81	0.35	346 ,751	63 ,190
Sep 91	0.19	0.35	216 ,832	24 ,799
Jun 91	0.20	0.35	245 ,592	23 ,261

Synopsis:

For the first quarter of 1993, Canadian Utilities Limited's (CU) natural gas throughput increased 16% compared to the first quarter of 1992. The higher throughput resulted from increased sales due to cooler weather, as well as an increase in the volume of natural gas transported for others by Northwestern Utilities, a subsidiary of CU. Firm electric energy retail sales also rose over the corresponding period last year.

Regulatory hearings regarding CU's purchase of Centra Power Inc. and Northwestern Utilities' sale of Northland Utilities (B.C.) Ltd. were scheduled in May 1993. Centra Power Inc. owns and operates the electric distribution system serving Yellowknife, Northwest Territories. Northland Utilities (B.C.) Ltd. owns and operates natural gas distribution systems in the Dawson Creek area and the town of Tumbler Ridge in northeastern British Columbia. Pacific Northern Gas Ltd. has agreed to purchase all the outstanding shares of Northland at a price of approximately $2.5-million.

Construction of the 120-megawatt McMahon cogeneration project at Taylor, B.C., is ahead of schedule. The $115-million plant, a joint venture between CU Power Canada Ltd. (CUPCAN) and Westcoast Power Inc., will begin commercial operation in October 1993.

Preliminary work is under way for a cogeneration plant to provide steam and electric power to Suncor Inc.'s oil sands operation near Fort McMurray, Alberta. The plant will be jointly developed, owned and operated by CUPCAN and Suncor. Construction is scheduled to begin in early 1994 and be completed by mid-1996.

Alberta Public Utilities Board hearings on Alberta Power Limited's 1993 rate application were held in April 1993. Alberta Power, also a subsidiary of CU, is currently operating on interim refundable rates.

Rank (Profit/Revenue/Assets)
19 92 67

R.D. Southern
Chairman
J.D. Wood
President & C.E.O.
C.S. Richardson
Deputy Chairman & C.F.O.

Address
10035 - 105 Street
Edmonton
AB
T5J 2V6
(403) 420-7757

Fax: (403) 420-7400
C0004425/G/10.2

CANADIAN WESTERN NATURAL GAS COMPANY LIMITED

Exchanges	Price (Jun24'93)		11.50	Trailing P/E		nm	Stock Symbol
TZ	Trailing Yield (%)		nm	Trailing EPS		nm	**CWN.PR.A**

Period Ending	Dec92	Dec91	Dec90	Dec89	Dec88
Yearly Statistics					
Price-Close	10.00	9.50	8.50	9.00	9.50
Price-High	11.00	9.50	9.25	9.75	10.38
Price-Low	9.00	8.25	8.50	8.75	8.63
P/E-Close	nc	nc	nc	nc	nc
Dividends per Share	nc	nc	nc	nc	nc
Dividend Yield (%)	nc	nc	nc	nc	nc
Sales per Share	120.38	119.64	127.36	130.25	134.41
EPS before extra. item	5.51	6.08	6.43	5.48	6.92
Cash Flow per Share	13.87	13.56	13.04	12.26	13.21
Book Value per Share	50.49	47.02	45.13	42.79	41.89
O/S Common Shares	2,456	2,456	2,456	2,216	2,216
Total Revenue	297,138	296,585	297,448	290,758	298,555
Income before extra.	19,268	19,929	19,271	16,467	19,656
Cash Flow	34,075	33,313	30,361	27,177	29,276
Debt/Equity	0.96	0.73	0.82	0.81	0.83
Return on Capital (%)	13.74	14.68	16.51	15.09	18.07
Ret. on Com. Equity (%)	11.30	13.20	14.56	12.95	16.85
% Change Profit	(3.3)	3.4	17.0	(16.2)	5.4
% Change Revenue	0.2	(0.3)	2.3	(2.6)	(3.7)
% Change Assets	13.4	(12.1)	8.1	2.8	5.2

Date	EPS	DPS	Tot Rev	Inc Bex
Mar 93	4.76	nc	124,066	13,110
Dec 92	4.01	nc	104,324	11,279
Sep 92	(0.81)	nc	44,136	(562)
Jun 92	(0.27)	nc	52,204	774
Mar 92	2.58	nc	96,474	7,777
Dec 91	2.55	nc	94,053	7,737
Sep 91	(0.53)	nc	35,801	83
Jun 91	0.17	nc	52,658	1,453

Preferred Div. Coverage	3.4	4.0	4.5
Total Div. Coverage	1.8	1.3	1.3
Interest Coverage	2.8	2.8	3.2
Current Ratio	1.2	0.8	0.8
Operating Margin	16.7	15.4	16.3
Asset Turnover	0.7	0.8	0.7
5 YEAR RATIOS (%)			
Return on Capital	15.6	16.5	18.4
Return on Com. Equity	13.8	14.7	16.6
Profit Growth	0.6	(4.6)	(4.6)
Revenue Growth	(0.9)	(5.8)	(6.6)
Asset Growth	3.0	1.1	4.9
BALANCE SHEET (000)			
Cash	0	0	0
Current Assets	73,643	45,853	54,619
Net Fixed Assets	365,559	341,394	386,000
Invest's & Advances	0	0	0
Total Assets	441,605	389,294	442,792
Short Term Debt	21,382	12,477	10,877
Current Liabilities	62,635	58,355	69,779
Long Term Debt	173,759	131,533	129,765
Total Liabilities	238,330	192,726	270,728
Total Equity	203,275	196,568	172,064
Total Liab. & Equity	441,605	389,294	442,792
CAPITAL (000)			
Total Debt	195,141	144,010	140,642
Preferred Equity	79,265	81,075	61,219
Common Equity	124,010	115,493	110,845

Business:

CANADIAN WESTERN NATURAL GAS CO. LTD. distributes natural gas to 115 communities in southern Alberta. The company serves industrial, commercial and residential customers. Canadian Utilities Ltd. is the corporation's parent company.

Synopsis:

In February 1993, the Alberta Public Utilities Board (PUB) issued a decision on the general rate application of Canadian Western Natural Gas Company Limited, approving a 12.25% rate of return on that portion of the rate base considered to be financed by common equity. The PUB approved an increase to 1992 revenues of $9.9-million, and a further increase of $7.8-million to 1993 revenues than would have been the case under existing rate.

For the fiscal 1992, capital expenditures to provide for customer growth and to meet the needs of existing customers amounted to $51.9-million compared to $47.5-million in 1991. The largest individual project was the replacement of bare steel mains originally installed in urban areas in the 1920s on which the company spent $6.1-million in the third year of a 10-year program. At year-end, property, plant and equipment required to service customers, net of accumulated depreciation, totaled $442.5-million. During 1992, the company used the net proceeds of a $45-million 9.4% debenture issue to partially finance its capital expenditure program.

Taking advantage of lower interest rates to reduce financing costs, Canadian Western issued $5.5-million of 8.82% long term notes to redeem $4.2-million of 11.48% debentures and $1.2-million of 11.74% debentures in 1992.

Relative strength to TSE300 / Price / Volume (in 1000's of board lots)

Rank (Profit/Revenue/Assets)
122 224 225

J.D. Wood
Chairman & C.E.O.
R.G. Lock
President
B.M. Andrews
V.P. & Controller

Address
909 - 11th Avenue S.W.
Calgary
AB
T2R 1L8
(403) 245-7110

Fax: (403) 245-7488
C0004536/G/10.1

CENTRA GAS ONTARIO INC.

Exchanges	Price (Jun24'93)		25 .37	Trailing P/E		nm	Stock Symbol
TM	Trailing Yield (%)		nm	Trailing EPS		nm	**CGE.PR.C**

Period Ending	Dec92	Dec91	Dec90	Dec89	Dec88
Yearly Statistics					
Price-Close	23 .75	23 .13	19 .00	22 .75	22 .50
Price-High	25 .00	23 .13	23 .88	24 .00	25 .00
Price-Low	22 .00	20 .00	19 .00	22 .00	22 .00
P/E-Close	nc	nc	nc	nc	nc
Dividends per Share	nc	nc	nc	nc	nc
Dividend Yield (%)	nc	nc	nc	nc	nc
Sales per Share	34 .72	32 .28	32 .54	30 .58	23 .89
EPS before extra. item	1 .94	1 .54	1 .74	2 .21	1 .91
Cash Flow per Share	4 .44	4 .46	4 .27	3 .51	2 .72
Book Value per Share	16 .27	15 .94	15 .65	15 .35	14 .76
O/S Common Shares	14 ,283	14 ,283	14 ,283	14 ,283	17 ,861
Total Revenue	557 ,708	513 ,303	491 ,098	517 ,090	458 ,029
Income before extra.	29 ,343	23 ,704	26 ,792	37 ,561	36 ,503
Cash Flow	63 ,365	63 ,772	61 ,025	56 ,270	48 ,565
Debt/Equity	1 .57	1 .61	1 .75	1 .39	1 .15
Return on Capital (%)	12 .72	10 .39	11 .04	14 .13	13 .69
Ret. on Com. Equity (%)	12 .08	9 .76	11 .24	14 .68	13 .40
% Change Profit	23 .8	(11 .5)	(28 .7)	2 .9	39 .2
% Change Revenue	8 .7	4 .5	(5 .0)	12 .9	(25 .8)
% Change Assets	2 .3	(2 .0)	15 .8	(4 .4)	(4 .5)

Preferred Div. Coverage	18 .7	14 .0	14 .1
Total Div. Coverage	1 .2	1 .2	1 .2
Interest Coverage	2 .2	1 .9	1 .7
Current Ratio	0 .9	0 .7	0 .7
Operating Margin	14 .4	12 .2	12 .6
Asset Turnover	0 .6	0 .6	0 .6
5 YEAR RATIOS (%)			
Return on Capital	12 .4	12 .2	12 .6
Return on Com. Equity	12 .2	11 .8	12 .2
Profit Growth	2 .2	(4 .8)	(0 .2)
Revenue Growth	(2 .1)	(6 .4)	(9 .2)
Asset Growth	1 .2	0 .8	(0 .6)
BALANCE SHEET (000)			
Cash	0	0	0
Current Assets	119 ,016	119 ,570	129 ,224
Net Fixed Assets	602 ,121	569 ,899	543 ,163
Invest's & Advances	45 ,682	56 ,226	95 ,480
Total Assets	781 ,438	763 ,582	779 ,453
Short Term Debt	36 ,430	96 ,354	108 ,781
Current Liabilities	130 ,836	171 ,838	183 ,698
Long Term Debt	361 ,621	306 ,977	325 ,300
Total Liabilities	528 ,302	513 ,478	531 ,906
Total Equity	253 ,136	250 ,104	247 ,547
Total Liab. & Equity	781 ,438	763 ,582	779 ,453
CAPITAL (000)			
Total Debt	398 ,051	403 ,331	434 ,081
Preferred Equity	20 ,807	22 ,412	24 ,017
Common Equity	232 ,329	227 ,692	223 ,530

Business:

CENTRA GAS ONTARIO INC. owns and operates natural gas distribution facilities in Ontario, serving about 140 communities in northwestern, northern and eastern Ontario. It sells to industrial, commercial and and residential customers. The company's common shares are held by Westcoast Energy Inc.

Date	EPS	DPS	Tot Rev	Inc Bex
Mar 93	1 .93	nc	214 ,011	27 ,873
Dec 92	0 .84	nc	168 ,713	12 ,378
Sep 92	(0 .52)	nc	84 ,243	(6 ,960)
Jun 92	0 .13	nc	108 ,492	2 ,208
Mar 92	1 .49	nc	196 ,260	21 ,717
Dec 91	0 .89	nc	155 ,782	13 ,196
Sep 91	(0 .38)	nc	80 ,946	(5 ,052)
Jun 91	(0 .14)	nc	99 ,082	(1 ,539)

Synopsis:

In February 1993, the Ontario Energy Board (OEB) said that Centra Gas Ontario's 1993 rate will be reviewed at a public hearing with the date and time to be determined. The company has proposed that the 1993 review be combined with the 1994 rate application with an expected hearing in September 1993.

On October 27, 1992, the company filed an application with the OEB to approve for inclusion in its rates, a restructured cost of gas agreement as negotiated between Centra Gas and Western Gas Marketing Ltd. (WGML). The OEB indicated that it the expected the company to reopen gas price negotiations with WGML. After discussions with WGML and other producers, the company has been unable to further reduce the contracted price of $1.98 per gigajoule. The company, however, has contracted for an incremental short-term source of supply with North Canadian Marketing Inc. and has submitted to the OEB, for approval, a weighted price of the WGML and NCMI contracts of $1.89 per gigajoule.

Rank (Profit/Revenue/Assets)		
98	148	175

Richard D. Walker
Chairman & President
Wayne M. Bingham
V.P., Finance & Reg. Affairs
Mark A. Wolnik
V.P., Operations

Address
200 Yorkland Boulevard
North York
ON
M2J 5C6
(416) 491-1880

Fax: (416) 496-5218
N0003021/G/10.1

CONSUMERS' GAS COMPANY LTD. (THE)

Exchanges	Price (Jun24'93)	16 .62	Trailing P/E	8 .66	Stock Symbol
T	Trailing Yield (%)	5 .65	Trailing EPS	1 .92	CGT

Period Ending	Sep92	Sep91	Sep90	Sep89	Sep88
Yearly Statistics					
Price-Close	n t	n t	n t	n t	n t
Price-High	n t	n t	n t	n t	n t
Price-Low	n t	n t	n t	n t	n t
P/E-Close	n t	n t	n t	n t	n t
Dividends per Share	0 .94	0 .94	0 .94	0 .91	0 .82
Dividend Yield (%)	n t	n t	n t	n t	n t
Sales per Share	25 .61	23 .63	24 .73	25 .23	25 .69
EPS before extra. item	1 .50	1 .12	0 .91	1 .41	1 .38
Cash Flow per Share	2 .92	2 .49	2 .69	2 .71	2 .58
Book Value per Share	10 .59	9 .37	9 .13	9 .18	8 .63
O/S Common Shares	66 ,124	66 ,124	65 ,218	65 ,082	64 ,776
Total Revenue	1 ,801 ,349	1 ,692 ,472	1 ,771 ,963	1 ,801 ,083	1 ,813 ,746
Income before extra.	107 ,501	81 ,990	67 ,487	102 ,807	100 ,766
Cash Flow	192 ,945	164 ,569	175 ,120	176 ,247	166 ,620
Debt/Equity	1 .62	1 .99	1 .79	1 .56	1 .59
Return on Capital (%)	13 .09	12 .09	12 .62	15 .61	15 .74
Ret. on Com. Equity (%)	15 .07	12 .17	9 .96	15 .85	16 .33
% Change Profit	31 .1	21 .5	(34 .4)	2 .0	21 .8
% Change Revenue	6 .4	(4 .5)	(1 .6)	(0 .7)	8 .8
% Change Assets	(4 .0)	9 .9	8 .6	1 .7	8 .4

Date	EPS	DPS	Tot Rev	Inc Bex
Mar 93	1 .42	0 .24	793 ,768	95 ,783
Dec 92	0 .43	0 .24	452 ,921	30 ,536
Sep 92	(0 .13)	0 .24	188 ,858	(6 ,191)
Jun 92	0 .20	0 .24	367 ,917	14 ,967
Mar 92	1 .04	0 .24	780 ,725	71 ,052
Dec 91	0 .39	0 .24	463 ,903	27 ,673
Sep 91	(0 .17)	0 .24	193 ,262	(9 ,061)
Jun 91	0 .11	0 .24	341 ,115	8 ,996

	Sep92	Sep91	Sep90
Preferred Div. Coverage	13 .4	10 .2	8 .4
Total Div. Coverage	1 .5	1 .2	1 .0
Interest Coverage	2 .2	1 .8	1 .8
Current Ratio	0 .8	0 .8	0 .8
Operating Margin	10 .5	7 .7	7 .0
Asset Turnover	0 .7	0 .6	0 .7
5 YEAR RATIOS (%)			
Return on Capital	13 .8	14 .1	14 .9
Return on Com. Equity	13 .9	13 .6	14 .2
Profit Growth	5 .3	(2 .4)	(6 .7)
Revenue Growth	1 .6	(0 .8)	(0 .2)
Asset Growth	4 .7	7 .3	6 .4
BALANCE SHEET (000)			
Cash	1 ,844	59 ,841	126 ,435
Current Assets	441 ,286	558 ,869	585 ,827
Net Fixed Assets	1 ,872 ,927	1 ,807 ,902	1 ,561 ,034
Invest's & Advances	0	0	40 ,031
Total Assets	2 ,364 ,638	2 ,462 ,008	2 ,240 ,943
Short Term Debt	319 ,235	431 ,619	497 ,205
Current Liabilities	567 ,037	684 ,941	741 ,014
Long Term Debt	987 ,826	1 ,013 ,864	763 ,968
Total Liabilities	1 ,557 ,738	1 ,734 ,951	1 ,538 ,068
Total Equity	806 ,900	727 ,057	702 ,875
Total Liab. & Equity	2 ,364 ,638	2 ,462 ,008	2 ,240 ,943
CAPITAL (000)			
Total Debt	1 ,307 ,061	1 ,445 ,483	1 ,261 ,173
Preferred Equity	106 ,867	107 ,293	107 ,651
Common Equity	700 ,033	619 ,764	595 ,224

Business:

CONSUMERS' GAS CO. LTD. is a natural gas distribution utility serving over one million residential, commercial and industrial customers in south-central and eastern Ontario, western Quebec and northern New York State. British Gas plc owns 85% of the company's common shares.

Synopsis:

On March 3, 1993, The Consumers' Gas Company Ltd., for the 1993 fiscal year, received approval from the Ontario Energy Board (OEB) for a rate base of $2,069.5-million, a rate of return on rate base of 10.86% ($1,842.4-million and 11.58% for 1992), and a rate of return on common equity of 12.3% on a deem common equity component of 35% (13.125% and 35% for 1992). As a result, the OEB found a gross revenue deficiency shortfall of expected revenues from existing rates over the forecast costs of $26-million, which will be recovered from customers on consumption since October 1, 1992. The impact of this decision on the annual gas bill of a typical residential customer, in combination with the OEB's decision on August 21, 1992, would be a $3 (or less than 1%) increase.

During February 1993, Consumers' Gas was planned to issue $100-million of new equity, possibly this fall. However, it is not likely to be in form of instalment receipts. The company's instalment receipts, issued at $17, have been suffering from a sharp drop in price. Instalment receipts are partly paid shares allowing investors to buy stock with only a down payment, with a further payment due later. Consumers' attributed the market weakness in the receipts to short-term investors who are now selling their positions before the second payment comes due.

In January 1993, Consumers' Gas agreed be a major customer of the proposed InterCoastal pipeline. Consumers' Gas currently buys about 370 billion cubic feet of Alberta natural gas a year, making it one of Alberta's bigger customers. Once the new pipeline is in operation in 1994, the company will pick up between 10 billion and 12 billion cubic feet a year from American producers. Most of that gas will be put into storage to serve the Toronto market.

On November 26, 1992, Canadian Bond Rating service Ltd. assigned an A rating to Consumer's Gas proposed medium-term notes. CBRS said Consumers' plans to issue unsecured medium-term notes with maturities of one to 10 years, which will rank equally with all other unsecured debt and will not exceed $300-million in total.

Relative strength to TSE300

Price

Volume (in 1000's of board lots)

Rank (Profit/Revenue/Assets)
34   68   86

R.S.K. Welch
Chairman
C.F. Safrance
President & C.E.O.
J.L. Aiken
Sr. V.P. & C.F.O.
R.D. Munkley
Sr. V.P. & C.O.O.

Address
100 Simcoe Street
Toronto
ON
M5H 3G2
(416) 591-6611

Fax: (416) 868-0221
C0027980/G/10.1

FORTIS INC.

Exchanges	Price (Jun24'93)	25 .25	Trailing P/E	9 .90	Stock Symbol
TM	Trailing Yield (%)	5 .94	Trailing EPS	2 .55	**FTS**

Period Ending	Dec92	Dec91	Dec90	Dec89	Dec88
Yearly Statistics					
Price-Close	24 .50	23 .88	21 .63	22 .38	20 .00
Price-High	25 .38	24 .25	22 .75	22 .50	20 .75
Price-Low	21 .38	21 .00	19 .38	19 .75	17 .25
P/E-Close	9 .61	9 .91	8 .79	9 .52	8 .89
Dividends per Share	1 .49	1 .48	1 .45	1 .39	1 .32
Dividend Yield (%)	6 .08	6 .20	6 .71	6 .21	6 .60
Sales per Share	34 .69	33 .75	33 .35	30 .56	31 .16
EPS before extra. item	2 .55	2 .41	2 .46	2 .35	2 .25
Cash Flow per Share	5 .64	5 .62	5 .44	4 .71	4 .70
Book Value per Share	21 .10	20 .04	18 .82	17 .78	16 .63
O/S Common Shares	10 ,191	10 ,071	9 ,291	9 ,172	8 ,666
Total Revenue	353 ,250	335 ,902	310 ,409	279 ,288	268 ,333
Income before extra.	30 ,162	28 ,192	23 ,998	21 ,392	19 ,278
Cash Flow	57 ,184	55 ,674	50 ,313	42 ,780	40 ,320
Debt/Equity	0 .91	0 .87	0 .97	1 .26	1 .21
Return on Capital (%)	14 .88	14 .96	15 .48	14 .97	16 .62
Ret. on Com. Equity (%)	12 .39	12 .66	13 .49	13 .93	13 .88
% Change Profit	7 .0	17 .5	12 .2	11 .0	8 .9
% Change Revenue	5 .2	8 .2	11 .1	4 .1	6 .9
% Change Assets	6 .4	9 .2	16 .2	13 .1	7 .9

Preferred Div. Coverage	6 .9	6 .5	19 .9
Total Div. Coverage	1 .5	1 .5	1 .6
Interest Coverage	2 .8	2 .7	2 .4
Current Ratio	0 .6	0 .4	0 .4
Operating Margin	20 .0	20 .0	20 .8
Asset Turnover	0 .5	0 .6	0 .6
5 YEAR RATIOS (%)			
Return on Capital	15 .4	15 .6	na
Return on Com. Equity	13 .3	13 .5	na
Profit Growth	11 .2	10 .5	na
Revenue Growth	7 .0	6 .4	na
Asset Growth	10 .4	10 .4	na
BALANCE SHEET (000)			
Cash	9 ,465	1 ,819	49
Current Assets	62 ,176	53 ,095	46 ,775
Net Fixed Assets	493 ,631	474 ,831	456 ,536
Invest's & Advances	73 ,696	66 ,411	42 ,551
Total Assets	642 ,220	603 ,828	552 ,775
Short Term Debt	21 ,275	60 ,406	59 ,420
Current Liabilities	96 ,638	125 ,134	108 ,533
Long Term Debt	218 ,906	157 ,312	157 ,881
Total Liabilities	377 ,177	352 ,028	327 ,917
Total Equity	265 ,043	251 ,800	224 ,858
Total Liab. & Equity	642 ,220	603 ,828	552 ,775
CAPITAL (000)			
Total Debt	240 ,181	217 ,718	217 ,301
Preferred Equity	50 ,000	50 ,000	50 ,000
Common Equity	215 ,043	201 ,800	174 ,858

Business:

FORTIS INC. is a management holding company. Its main subsidiary is Newfoundland Light and Power Co. Ltd., the main electrical utility in Newfoundland. Its other subsidiaries are Fortis Trust Corporation, dealing principally in residential mortgages, and Fortis Properties Corporation, a commercial real estate company. The company holds a 33% investment in the common equity of Maritime Electric.

Date	EPS	DPS	Tot Rev	Inc Bex
Mar 93	1 .03	0 .38	114 ,196	11 ,639
Dec 92	0 .30	0 .38	87 ,029	4 ,100
Sep 92	0 .31	0 .37	65 ,314	4 ,251
Jun 92	0 .91	0 .37	85 ,852	10 ,329
Mar 92	1 .03	0 .37	113 ,162	11 ,482
Dec 91	0 .27	0 .37	81 ,712	3 ,801
Sep 91	0 .27	0 .37	62 ,686	3 ,841
Jun 91	0 .94	0 .37	84 ,062	10 ,538

Synopsis:

Fortis Inc.'s principal subsidiary, Newfoundland Power, had initially forecast a 4.8% increase in electricity sales for 1992. The closure of the Northern Cod fishery and the slowdown of Hibernia development activity forced management to revise its estimates and reduce both operating costs and capital expenditures. While weather adjusted sales grew by only 1.1%, the controls put into place, coupled with a 2.2% increase in rates approved in late 1991, enabled the company to earn 13.46%, well within the range of rate of return on equity permitted by the Public Utilities Board of Newfoundland. Capital expenditures for Newfoundland Power in 1992 totaled $40.3-million, compared to $42.5-million in 1991, $67.3-million in 1990 and $56.5-million in 1989. As in the past, the greatest portion of expenditures was comprised of numerous small projects related to the upgrading of the power distribution system.

During 1992, Fortis Properties continued the redevelopment of its properties in downtown St. John's and expanded its holdings in this area with the acquisition of another property. The company also made its first real estate acquisition outside St. John's with the purchase of the Herald Tower property in Corner Brook, Newfoundland. This 70,000 square foot building is the premier office tower in the city and is fully leased. In addition to property acquisitions, the company expanded its property management activity with an 18-month contract to manage four shopping centres located throughout the island.

In 1992, operations of the company's 50% owned Unitel Newfoundland reached several milestones in the organization's development. On April 1, 1993, the trans-island digital microwave system was commissioned and operations began. During the the year, existing Unitel customers were transferred to the new system and several new Unitel products were introduced to customers. In June 1992, the CRTC approved Unitel's application to open long distance services to full competition. The decision, subsequently upheld by the Federal Court of Appeal, has fundamentally changed the telecommunications industry in Canada.

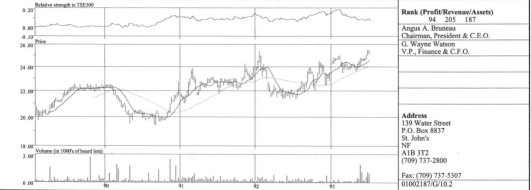

Rank (Profit/Revenue/Assets)
94   205   187

Angus A. Bruneau
Chairman, President & C.E.O.

G. Wayne Watson
V.P., Finance & C.F.O.

Address
139 Water Street
P.O. Box 8837
St. John's
NF
A1B 3T2
(709) 737-2800

Fax: (709) 737-5307
01002187/G/10.2

ISLAND TELEPHONE COMPANY LIMITED (THE)

Exchanges	Price (Jun24'93)	21 .50	Trailing P/E	11 .26	Stock Symbol
TM	Trailing Yield (%)	5 .26	Trailing EPS	1 .91	**IT**

Period Ending	Dec92	Dec91	Dec90	Dec89	Dec88
Yearly Statistics					
Price-Close	18 .75	20 .25	15 .00	16 .00	16 .88
Price-High	20 .25	20 .50	16 .75	17 .50	17 .00
Price-Low	17 .00	14 .50	14 .00	15 .50	14 .25
P/E-Close	9 .52	10 .60	8 .52	9 .30	10 .23
Dividends per Share	1 .13	1 .09	1 .05	1 .02	0 .96
Dividend Yield (%)	6 .03	5 .38	7 .00	6 .38	5 .69
Sales per Share	15 .09	14 .78	16 .11	15 .87	14 .99
EPS before extra. item	1 .97	1 .91	1 .76	1 .72	1 .65
Cash Flow per Share	5 .62	5 .28	5 .55	6 .46	5 .53
Book Value per Share	15 .82	14 .99	14 .07	13 .29	12 .49
O/S Common Shares	3 ,469	3 ,466	3 ,144	2 ,977	2 ,881
Total Revenue	55 ,746	53 ,029	51 ,998	48 ,471	44 ,840
Income before extra.	7 ,246	6 ,922	5 ,814	5 ,468	5 ,190
Cash Flow	19 ,234	17 ,760	16 ,788	18 ,659	15 ,739
Debt/Equity	0 .87	0 .87	1 .05	1 .08	1 .02
Return on Capital (%)	16 .72	15 .64	15 .67	17 .07	17 .54
Ret. on Com. Equity (%)	12 .66	13 .39	12 .73	13 .20	13 .55
% Change Profit	4 .7	19 .1	6 .3	5 .4	6 .8
% Change Revenue	5 .1	2 .0	7 .3	8 .1	10 .3
% Change Assets	3 .8	3 .5	7 .0	9 .3	10 .8

Business:

ISLAND TELEPHONE COMPANY LTD. is the telecommunications company serving Prince Edward Island. It provides telephone and telecommunications services. Maritime Telephone and Telegraph Co. Ltd. of Halifax has a 52% interest in the company.

Date	EPS	DPS	Tot Rev	Inc Bex
Mar 93	0.34	0.29	13 ,027	1 ,309
Dec 92	0.45	0.28	13 ,939	1 ,676
Sep 92	0.56	0.28	13 ,911	2 ,032
Jun 92	0.56	0.28	15 ,018	2 ,019
Mar 92	0.40	0.28	12 ,877	1 ,519
Dec 91	0.41	0.27	13 ,067	1 ,553
Sep 91	0.56	0.28	13 ,667	1 ,998
Jun 91	0.43	0.27	13 ,256	1 ,597

	Dec92	Dec91	Dec90
Preferred Div. Coverage	15 .0	14 .3	12 .0
Total Div. Coverage	1 .7	1 .6	1 .6
Interest Coverage	3 .4	2 .9	2 .7
Current Ratio	0 .6	0 .8	0 .6
Operating Margin	32 .9	30 .7	29 .3
Asset Turnover	0 .4	0 .4	0 .4
5 YEAR RATIOS (%)			
Return on Capital	16 .5	17 .0	17 .5
Return on Com. Equity	13 .1	13 .3	13 .4
Profit Growth	8 .2	8 .5	5 .5
Revenue Growth	6 .4	7 .7	9 .2
Asset Growth	6 .7	7 .9	9 .4
BALANCE SHEET (000)			
Cash	44	237	61
Current Assets	9 ,783	8 ,984	8 ,961
Net Fixed Assets	120 ,885	117 ,003	112 ,534
Invest's & Advances	474	60	60
Total Assets	134 ,395	129 ,443	125 ,112
Short Term Debt	10 ,099	3 ,526	5 ,849
Current Liabilities	17 ,281	11 ,506	14 ,191
Long Term Debt	43 ,000	47 ,100	47 ,100
Total Liabilities	73 ,271	71 ,251	74 ,636
Total Equity	61 ,123	58 ,192	50 ,476
Total Liab. & Equity	134 ,395	129 ,443	125 ,112
CAPITAL (000)			
Total Debt	53 ,099	50 ,626	52 ,949
Preferred Equity	6 ,250	6 ,250	6 ,250
Common Equity	54 ,873	51 ,942	44 ,226

Synopsis:

In April 1993, Island Telephone, joined five of its Stentor partners and submitted a proposal on how the CRTC should regulate the telecommunications industry. The six companies proposed changes to the regulatory framework to make the telecommunication industry less restrictive towards new and existing competition. The submission follows the CRTC's decision in 1992 to allow long distance competition in Canada. The industry submission calls for a fully competitive environment where all suppliers, either telephone, cable or cellular companies, are able to enter businesses and make decisions for themselves. The group feels a regulatory process that better adapts to changes in technologies and competition will benefit customers through cheaper rates and better services.

In February 1993, Island Telephone applied to the CRTC for an increase in its present customer service charges. Island Telephone wants to apply a directory assistance charge for each requested long distance call whether it be for a number in Canada or in the United States. The proposed long distance directory assistance charge would be 95 cents for requests in Canada and the United States. Island Telephone also wants to raise its local directory assistance charge from 80 cents to 95 cents for numbers listed in the current directory.

For 1992, Island Telephone recorded local service revenues up over 10% compared to the same time last year. Long distance revenues, however, were off by almost 2% in the year. The company had 71,049 network lines in 1992, representing an increase of 4% over last year. Of this amount, 70% of the network lines relate to residential customers with business customers making up the rest.

In February 1993, Island Telephone arranged for the issue and sale of $5-million of series V First Mortgage Bonds bearing an interest rate of 9.77% and maturing on March 1, 2018. The placement is set to close on March 1, 1993.

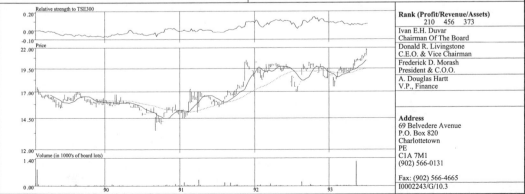

Rank (Profit/Revenue/Assets)
210   456   373

Ivan E.H. Duvar
Chairman Of The Board
Donald R. Livingstone
C.E.O. & Vice Chairman
Frederick D. Morash
President & C.O.O.
A. Douglas Hartt
V.P., Finance

Address
69 Belvedere Avenue
P.O. Box 820
Charlottetown
PE
C1A 7M1
(902) 566-0131

Fax: (902) 566-4665
I0002243/G/10.3

MARITIME ELECTRIC COMPANY, LIMITED

Exchanges	Price (Jun24'93)	18.12	Trailing P/E	9.54	Stock Symbol
TM	Trailing Yield (%)	5.08	Trailing EPS	1.90	**MEC**

Period Ending	Dec92	Dec91	Dec90	Dec89	Dec88
Yearly Statistics					
Price-Close	15.25	15.63	12.75	14.38	13.25
Price-High	17.50	16.00	14.88	14.50	13.25
Price-Low	14.75	12.25	12.00	13.00	11.50
P/E-Close	8.24	8.73	7.92	9.52	9.33
Dividends per Share	0.92	0.88	0.84	0.82	0.80
Dividend Yield (%)	6.03	5.63	6.59	5.70	6.04
Sales per Share	28.16	21.75	22.32	20.45	18.80
EPS before extra. item	1.85	1.79	1.61	1.51	1.42
Cash Flow per Share	5.44	4.03	3.86	3.37	3.19
Book Value per Share	13.95	12.98	12.13	11.35	10.65
O/S Common Shares	3,613	3,560	3,250	3,221	3,194
Total Revenue	82,142	74,678	72,567	65,981	60,025
Income before extra.	7,939	7,274	6,236	5,538	5,275
Cash Flow	15,704	13,719	12,496	10,814	10,145
Debt/Equity	0.75	0.79	0.76	0.87	0.90
Return on Capital (%)	17.80	17.39	17.38	17.92	19.46
Ret. on Com. Equity (%)	13.75	13.75	13.75	13.75	13.75
% Change Profit	9.1	16.6	12.6	5.0	3.0
% Change Revenue	10.0	2.9	10.0	9.9	(2.1)
% Change Assets	3.2	11.1	11.7	12.4	7.6

Preferred Div. Coverage	6.1	5.2	6.2
Total Div. Coverage	1.7	1.7	1.7
Interest Coverage	3.7	3.2	3.0
Current Ratio	0.9	1.3	0.8
Operating Margin	23.6	23.9	22.1
Asset Turnover	0.6	0.5	0.6
5 YEAR RATIOS (%)			
Return on Capital	18.0	18.6	19.4
Return on Com. Equity	13.8	13.8	14.1
Profit Growth	0.0	6.4	4.3
Revenue Growth	5.9	6.4	2.5
Asset Growth	9.1	9.0	7.9
BALANCE SHEET (000)			
Cash	0	3,849	0
Current Assets	11,851	14,961	11,873
Net Fixed Assets	129,928	122,987	112,677
Invest's & Advances	0	0	0
Total Assets	144,269	139,756	125,744
Short Term Debt	3,243	125	6,826
Current Liabilities	13,450	11,310	15,000
Long Term Debt	45,788	48,403	36,463
Total Liabilities	78,878	77,943	68,719
Total Equity	65,390	61,813	57,025
Total Liab. & Equity	144,269	139,756	125,744
CAPITAL (000)			
Total Debt	49,031	48,528	43,289
Preferred Equity	15,000	15,600	17,600
Common Equity	50,390	46,213	39,425

Business:

MARITIME ELECTRIC CO. LTD. is an investor-owned utility serving Prince Edward Island. The company owns and operates a fully integrated electric utility system providing for the generation, transmission and distribution of electricity. The company operates two generating plants at Charlottetown and Borden and has an equity interest in N.B. Power's No. 2 Unit located in Dalhousie, N.B.

Date	EPS	DPS	Tot Rev	Inc Bex
Mar 93	0.58	0.23	22,048	2,427
Dec 92	0.40	0.23	21,343	1,770
Sep 92	0.54	0.23	20,181	2,259
Jun 92	0.38	0.23	19,429	1,696
Mar 92	0.53	0.23	20,386	2,214
Dec 91	0.20	0.23	19,104	1,041
Sep 91	0.53	0.23	18,675	2,067
Jun 91	0.48	0.21	17,083	1,885

Synopsis:

The December 1992 decision of the Prince Edward Island Regulatory and Appeals Commission (IRAC) allows Maritime Electric Company, Limited to earn up to a 13% return on average common equity during 1993. This allowed return, while down from the 13.75% allowed in 1992, will still afford the company the opportunity to increase earnings per share during 1993.

In July 1992, company directors, based on the recommendation of management, revised the company's long-term plan which had been filed with IRAC in December 1991. This revision reduced the planned level of capital investment for new generation over the next seven years and increased the company's reliance on power contracts with its neighboring utilities. This decision reflects the company's concern over the slow recovery of the provincial and Canadian economies together with a recognition of the opportunities available because of surplus capacity in the whole North East Canada/United States region. These surpluses are expected to continue for the next 10 years. This decision will result in lower rate increases than would otherwise be the case.

The company generated or purchased 772 million kilowatt hours (kWh) of electricity in 1992 to supply its customers' energy needs. Company owned sources located on Prince Edward Island and in New Brunswick provided 18% of the requirements amounting to 137 million kWh. Contract energy amounting to 349 million kWh and 286 million kWh interruptible energy were purchased from the New Brunswick Power Corp. The Charlottetown generating plant produced 51% less energy than in 1991. The increased use of off Island energy sources reflects the greater availability of lower-cost interruptible energy and improved access to that market due to the upgrading of the interconnection. The transfer capability of the interconnection was doubled from 100 to 200 megawatts late in 1991.

Net capital expenditures for 1992 were $13.7-million, compared to net capital expenditures of $16.7-million in 1991. The capital budget for 1993 is $13-million.

Rank (Profit/Revenue/Assets)
201 406 359

R.W. Smith
Chairman

J.H. Reynolds
President & C.E.O.

P.G. Hughes
V.P., Fin., Admin. & C.F.O.

Address
P.O. Box 1328
Charlottetown
PE
C1A 7N2
(902) 566-1599

Fax: (902) 566-2692
M0001768/G/10.2

For further company information, call Globe Information Services 1-800-268-9128 or (416)585-5345

MARITIME TELEGRAPH AND TELEPHONE COMPANY, LIMITED

Exchanges	Price (Jun24'93)	21 .62	Trailing P/E	11 .09	Stock Symbol
TM	Trailing Yield (%)	5 .64	Trailing EPS	1 .95	MTT

Period Ending	Dec92	Dec91	Dec90	Dec89	Dec88
Yearly Statistics					
Price-Close	21 .13	21 .00	18 .25	18 .88	15 .25
Price-High	22 .38	21 .75	19 .00	19 .25	16 .63
Price-Low	18 .50	17 .88	16 .00	15 .38	14 .38
P/E-Close	10 .41	11 .23	9 .61	10 .66	9 .08
Dividends per Share	1 .21	1 .17	1 .12	1 .06	1 .02
Dividend Yield (%)	5 .73	5 .57	6 .14	5 .62	6 .69
Sales per Share	18 .21	18 .07	17 .58	16 .87	15 .06
EPS before extra. item	2 .03	1 .87	1 .90	1 .77	1 .68
Cash Flow per Share	6 .44	6 .23	5 .80	5 .57	5 .22
Book Value per Share	16 .54	15 .72	14 .89	14 .00	13 .14
O/S Common Shares	28 ,040	27 ,929	27 ,060	26 ,005	24 ,780
Total Revenue	548 ,397	533 ,440	501 ,023	457 ,925	389 ,411
Income before extra.	64 ,028	59 ,259	57 ,114	48 ,960	42 ,061
Cash Flow	178 ,325	170 ,050	152 ,893	140 ,698	125 ,110
Debt/Equity	0 .98	0 .94	0 .96	1 .08	1 .06
Return on Capital (%)	16 .27	16 .12	15 .25	17 .19	17 .15
Ret. on Com. Equity (%)	12 .43	12 .11	13 .06	12 .98	13 .04
% Change Profit	8 .0	3 .8	16 .7	16 .4	7 .2
% Change Revenue	2 .8	6 .5	9 .4	17 .6	7 .1
% Change Assets	4 .6	5 .0	9 .1	23 .2	11 .7

Preferred Div. Coverage	8 .1	7 .2	8 .2
Total Div. Coverage	1 .5	1 .5	1 .6
Interest Coverage	3 .3	3 .0	2 .7
Current Ratio	0 .7	0 .7	0 .9
Operating Margin	31 .8	30 .4	27 .8
Asset Turnover	0 .4	0 .4	0 .4
5 YEAR RATIOS (%)			
Return on Capital	16 .4	16 .8	17 .3
Return on Com. Equity	12 .7	12 .9	13 .1
Profit Growth	10 .2	11 .6	10 .8
Revenue Growth	8 .5	9 .3	9 .7
Asset Growth	10 .4	11 .2	12 .2
BALANCE SHEET (000)			
Cash	1 ,361	921	858
Current Assets	125 ,116	109 ,008	101 ,885
Net Fixed Assets	1 ,214 ,772	1 ,175 ,915	1 ,116 ,089
Invest's & Advances	12 ,602	8 ,863	12 ,983
Total Assets	1 ,364 ,088	1 ,304 ,655	1 ,242 ,707
Short Term Debt	99 ,571	81 ,877	35 ,022
Current Liabilities	173 ,018	160 ,840	112 ,716
Long Term Debt	447 ,351	423 ,286	449 ,306
Total Liabilities	804 ,487	764 ,845	738 ,099
Total Equity	559 ,601	539 ,810	504 ,608
Total Liab. & Equity	1 ,364 ,088	1 ,304 ,655	1 ,242 ,707
CAPITAL (000)			
Total Debt	546 ,922	505 ,163	484 ,328
Preferred Equity	95 ,884	100 ,871	101 ,608
Common Equity	463 ,717	438 ,939	403 ,000

Business:

MARITIME TELEGRAPH AND TELEPHONE CO. LTD. is a telecommunications company providing services throughout Nova Scotia. The company offers telephone and a wide range of telecommunications services including data, audio and video transmission. The company owns 51% of The Island Telephone Co. Ltd. of Prince Edward Island.

Date	EPS	DPS	Tot Rev	Inc Bex
Mar 93	0.31	0.31	129 ,747	10 ,435
Dec 92	0.54	0.31	136 ,424	16 ,774
Sep 92	0.56	0.30	137 ,263	17 ,378
Jun 92	0.54	0.30	143 ,082	16 ,999
Mar 92	0.39	0.30	131 ,628	12 ,877
Dec 91	0.48	0.30	133 ,242	15 ,176
Sep 91	0.51	0.29	133 ,564	16 ,067
Jun 91	0.48	0.29	135 ,527	15 ,131

Synopsis:

In the first quarter of 1993, Maritime Telegraph and Telephone Co. Ltd. (MT&T) joined five of its Stentor partners and submitted a proposal on how the CRTC should regulate the telecommunications industry. The six telecommunication companies proposed changes to the regulatory framework to make the telecommunication industry less restrictive towards new and existing competition. The submission followed the CRTC's decision in 1992 to allow long distance competition in Canada. The joint submission calls for a fully competitive environment where all suppliers, either telephone, cable or cellular companies, are able to enter businesses and make decisions for themselves. The group feels a regulatory process that better adapts to changes in technologies and competition will benefit customers through cheaper rates and better services.

In February 1993, MT&T applied to the CRTC for an increase in its present customer service charges. MT&T wants to apply a directory assistance charge for each requested long distance call whether it be for a number in Canada or in the United States. The proposed long distance directory assistance charge will be 95 cents for requests in Canada and the United States. Island Telephone also wants to increase its local directory assistance charge from 80 cents to 95 cents for numbers listed in the current directory.

MT&T reported that it had strong increases in demand for both cellular services and long distance calls in the first quarter of 1993. A total of 5,913 new lines were added in the first quarter, up from the 3,928 lines added in the first quarter of 1992. Growth from the cellular network accounted for 43 % of these new lines. As of March 31, 1993, MT&T had 609,052 total lines in service, an increase of 4.3% over a year ago. Long distance volume was also up in the quarter. MT&T reported that long distance messages increased 8.8 % compared to last year to a level of 31.5 million calls.

Rank (Profit/Revenue/Assets)
53 149 122

Ivan E.H. Duvar
Chairman, President & C.E.O.
Ronald E. Smith
V.P., Finance
Donald F. Farmer
V.P., Operations

Address
Maritime Centre
1505 Barrington Street
P.O. Box 880
Halifax
NS
B3J 2W3
(902) 421-4311
Fax: (902) 429-8755
M0001839/G/10.3

NEWFOUNDLAND LIGHT & POWER CO. LIMITED

Exchanges	Price (Jun24'93)	10.25	Trailing P/E	nc	Stock Symbol
M	Trailing Yield (%)	nc	Trailing EPS	2.35	**NFL.PR.J**

Period Ending	Dec92	Dec91	Dec90	Dec89	Dec88
Yearly Statistics					
Price-Close	10.13	9.50	9.88	9.63	9.88
Price-High	10.38	10.00	9.88	9.88	10.25
Price-Low	9.88	9.50	9.00	9.25	9.50
P/E-Close	nc	nc	nc	nc	nc
Dividends per Share	nc	nc	nc	nc	nc
Dividend Yield (%)	nc	nc	nc	nc	nc
Sales per Share	33.88	32.56	31.71	30.08	31.02
EPS before extra. item	2.73	2.52	2.36	2.37	2.27
Cash Flow per Share	5.42	5.32	5.29	4.67	4.77
Book Value per Share	20.87	19.67	18.65	17.58	16.60
O/S Common Shares	10,200	10,121	10,071	9,222	9,188
Total Revenue	346,431	330,271	307,632	278,295	268,337
Income before extra.	29,662	27,799	26,235	24,448	22,232
Cash Flow	55,105	53,683	51,055	43,014	41,091
Debt/Equity	0.98	0.95	0.95	0.98	0.88
Return on Capital (%)	15.07	14.99	15.49	14.62	15.85
Ret. on Com. Equity (%)	13.46	13.17	13.59	13.92	13.66
% Change Profit	6.7	6.0	7.3	10.0	8.5
% Change Revenue	4.9	7.4	10.5	3.7	6.9
% Change Assets	4.6	4.4	9.8	8.6	7.6

Preferred Div. Coverage	15.4	12.0	10.7
Total Div. Coverage	1.7	1.6	1.6
Interest Coverage	2.9	2.8	2.7
Current Ratio	0.9	0.5	0.5
Operating Margin	19.3	19.5	20.4
Asset Turnover	0.6	0.6	0.6
5 YEAR RATIOS (%)			
Return on Capital	15.2	15.2	15.6
Return on Com. Equity	13.6	13.6	13.8
Profit Growth	7.6	6.4	4.6
Revenue Growth	6.6	6.0	4.7
Asset Growth	6.9	7.2	7.1
BALANCE SHEET (000)			
Cash	7,610	465	21
Current Assets	57,127	49,578	46,117
Net Fixed Assets	477,711	464,900	448,785
Invest's & Advances	0	0	0
Total Assets	545,843	522,075	500,025
Short Term Debt	11,275	60,374	48,898
Current Liabilities	66,133	109,312	97,709
Long Term Debt	218,906	157,312	157,881
Total Liabilities	310,643	293,104	281,273
Total Equity	235,200	228,971	218,752
Total Liab. & Equity	545,843	522,075	500,025
CAPITAL (000)			
Total Debt	230,181	217,686	206,779
Preferred Equity	22,296	29,889	30,938
Common Equity	212,904	199,082	187,814

Business:

NEWFOUNDLAND LIGHT & POWER CO. LTD. is an electrical utility serving the province of Newfoundland. Fortis Inc. of St. John's is the company's major shareholder.

Date	EPS	DPS	Tot Rev	Inc Bex
Mar 93	1.00	0.38	112,367	11,406
Dec 92	(0.03)	0.40	5,823	77
Sep 92	0.35	0.38	63,430	4,020
Jun 92	1.03	0.38	84,175	10,418
Mar 92	1.03	0.38	111,038	10,993
Dec 91	0.29	0.38	79,827	4,154
Sep 91	0.34	0.38	61,310	3,452
Jun 91	0.97	0.38	82,916	10,350

Synopsis:

During 1992, Newfoundland Light & Power Co. Limited did not see the 4.8% growth in sales it expected. The fishery did not recover as anticipated due to low cod stocks. As well there were difficulties with the Hibernia Offshore Project, and the general recession continued. These events indicated there would be little or no sales growth in 1992, leading to a reduction of $12-million in planned revenue for the year.

The company took several steps to deal with the effects of lower sales growth. These measures including controls on operating and capital expenditures, a reduction in the number of temporary employees, and a restriction on hiring of regular staff, made a substantial contribution to the 8.8% growth on 1992 earnings.

The company is projecting 1993 sales to remain at 1992 levels, with no net growth. Accordingly, further measures took effect early in 1993 including the large scale deferral of capital projects and strict limits on operating expenses. There was also a further cut in temporary staff levels, 36 layoffs of regular employees, and a 2% to 5% reduction in managerial salaries.

Energy produced and purchased for resale increased by 1.9% from 4,538 million kilowatt hours (kWh) in 1991 to 4,624 million kWh in 1992. On a weather adjusted basis the increase was 1.3%. Approximately 8.2% of energy supplied was generated in the 22 small hydro plants owned and operated by the company, with the balance purchased from Newfoundland and Labrador Hydro Corporation.

Capital expenditures in 1992 totaled $40.3-million, compared to $42.5-million in 1991, $67.3-million in 1990, and $56.5-million in 1989. Two new substations were completed in 1992, one at North West Brook in the company's Eastern Region and the other at Colliers in its Avalon Region. In addition, the company completed a transmission line project in the Heart's Content area, improving reliability of service.

Rank (Profit/Revenue/Assets)		
97	209	198

Angus A. Bruneau
Chairman
Aidan F. Ryan
President & C.E.O.
Kevin S. Warr
V.P., Fin. & Treas. & C.F.O.

Address
P.O. Box 8910
St. John's
NF
A1B 3P6
(709) 737-5862

Fax: (709) 737-5832
N0001223/G/10.2

NEWTEL ENTERPRISES LIMITED

Exchanges	Price (Jun24'93)		21.25	Trailing P/E		12.01	Stock Symbol
TM	Trailing Yield (%)		6.40	Trailing EPS		1.77	**NEL**

Period Ending	Dec92	Dec91	Dec90	Dec89	Dec88
Yearly Statistics					
Price-Close	19.38	19.50	17.38	19.38	16.50
Price-High	20.88	20.25	19.50	20.25	18.25
Price-Low	17.25	17.00	14.50	16.50	15.63
P/E-Close	11.20	12.04	13.37	10.42	9.27
Dividends per Share	1.36	1.36	1.36	1.30	1.22
Dividend Yield (%)	7.02	6.97	7.83	6.71	7.39
Sales per Share	17.21	19.29	19.77	20.43	16.14
EPS before extra. item	1.73	1.62	1.30	1.86	1.78
Cash Flow per Share	6.36	7.28	7.06	7.40	5.37
Book Value per Share	16.56	16.11	15.41	15.37	14.64
O/S Common Shares	16,187	15,464	13,321	12,559	11,774
Total Revenue	288,014	280,242	268,294	258,759	194,577
Income before extra.	30,958	25,817	20,366	25,599	20,452
Cash Flow	100,804	100,203	91,786	90,344	61,600
Debt/Equity	0.94	1.00	1.34	1.34	1.92
Return on Capital (%)	14.72	14.60	13.89	15.52	14.99
Ret. on Com. Equity (%)	10.60	9.80	8.45	12.43	12.53
% Change Profit	19.9	26.8	(20.4)	25.2	6.7
% Change Revenue	2.8	4.5	3.7	33.0	16.1
% Change Assets	4.6	3.3	6.1	7.8	52.3
Preferred Div. Coverage	8.7	7.3	5.7
Total Div. Coverage	1.2	1.1	1.0
Interest Coverage	3.0	2.6	2.3
Current Ratio	0.7	0.8	1.2
Operating Margin	30.2	30.8	30.2
Asset Turnover	0.4	0.4	0.4
5 YEAR RATIOS (%)			
Return on Capital	14.7	15.7	16.8
Return on Com. Equity	10.8	11.3	12.0
Profit Growth	10.0	7.8	(0.2)
Revenue Growth	11.4	12.8	14.0
Asset Growth	13.4	13.7	16.3
BALANCE SHEET (000)			
Cash	1,423	2,442	2,414
Current Assets	51,442	58,756	59,151
Net Fixed Assets	631,399	603,941	576,435
Invest's & Advances	24,901	13,992	19,639
Total Assets	723,660	691,868	669,537
Short Term Debt	37,777	37,620	22,517
Current Liabilities	76,474	69,966	51,225
Long Term Debt	257,052	255,800	311,865
Total Liabilities	410,613	397,771	419,277
Total Equity	313,047	294,097	250,260
Total Liab. & Equity	723,660	691,868	669,537
CAPITAL (000)			
Total Debt	294,829	293,420	334,382
Preferred Equity	45,000	45,000	45,000
Common Equity	268,047	249,097	205,260

Business:

NEWTEL ENTERPRISES LTD. is an investment holding company with principal operations in telecommunications. The company's wholly owned subsidiary, Newfoundland Telephone Co. Ltd., supplies telecommunications and information handling services to Newfoundland and Labrador. Subsidiaries have operations in office automation, electronic engineering, manufacturing and financial services.

Date	EPS	DPS	Tot Rev	Inc Bex
Mar 93	0.33	0.34	71,454	6,211
Dec 92	0.52	0.34	70,259	9,780
Sep 92	0.54	0.34	72,890	9,409
Jun 92	0.38	0.34	72,721	6,842
Mar 92	0.28	0.34	72,144	4,926
Dec 91	0.35	0.34	67,076	6,040
Sep 91	0.50	0.34	70,579	7,923
Jun 91	0.43	0.34	70,331	6,661

Synopsis:

In the first quarter of 1993, Newfoundland Telephone Co., a wholly owned subsidiary of NewTel Enterprises Ltd., joined five of its Stentor partners and submitted a proposal on how the CRTC should regulate the telecommunications industry. The six telecommunication companies proposed industry changes to the regulation process after the CRTC allowed long distance competition in Canada. The joint submission calls for a fully competitive environment where all suppliers, either telephone, cable or cellular companies, are able to enter any businesses they wish to. The group feels a regulatory process that better adapts to changes in technologies and competition will benefit customers through cheaper rates and better services.

In late August 1992, Newfoundland Telephone was granted approval from the CRTC to increase basic local service rates by an average of 8%, effective January 1, 1993. The CRTC also granted the company a rate of return in the range of 12% to 13%. The company also received approval to reduce long distance rates for calls placed within the province by an average of 2%.

As of December 31, 1992, Newfoundland Telephone had 255,787 network access services, an increase of 2.5% from the number of lines at the end of 1991. About 70% of these lines were served by digital technology. Newfoundland Telephone expects to achieve 100% digital in toll switching and 80% digital in local switching by the end of 1993.

Long distance messages during 1992 totaled 71,059, up 8.5% compared to the 1991 level. Long distance revenues accounted for almost 60% of revenues in 1992.

As of December 31, 1992, 96% of the total assets of NewTel Enterprises were invested in its wholly owned subsidiary, Newfoundland Telephone Co.

Relative strength to TSE300 / Price / Volume (in 1000's of board lots)

Rank (Profit/Revenue/Assets)
89   228   181

Anthony A. Brait
Chairman

Vincent G. Withers
President & C.E.O.

Robert H. Benson
V.P., Finance & Administration

Address
Fort William Building
Factory Lane, P.O. Box 12110
St. John's
NF
A1C 6J7
(709) 739-3310

Fax: (709) 739-3155
01000328/G/10.3

NORTHWESTERN UTILITIES LIMITED

Exchanges	Price (Jun24'93)	55.00	Trailing P/E	nc	Stock Symbol
TZ	Trailing Yield (%)	nc	Trailing EPS	9.29	**NWT.PR.A**

Period Ending	Dec92	Dec91	Dec90	Dec89	Dec88
Yearly Statistics					
Price-Close	49.00	42.75	40.50	45.00	45.38
Price-High	50.00	42.88	45.00	46.00	49.00
Price-Low	43.25	39.00	40.50	44.00	44.50
P/E-Close	nc	nc	nc	nc	nc
Dividends per Share	nc	nc	nc	nc	nc
Dividend Yield (%)	nc	nc	nc	nc	nc
Sales per Share	114.83	123.59	123.26	123.96	113.06
EPS before extra. item	8.58	8.55	7.66	8.90	11.34
Cash Flow per Share	19.46	18.16	15.96	20.40	16.88
Book Value per Share	67.72	63.63	62.72	59.41	57.12
O/S Common Shares	3,167	2,941	2,901	2,901	2,901
Total Revenue	353,985	366,357	363,902	362,742	331,130
Income before extra.	36,625	34,579	30,607	34,236	32,887
Cash Flow	59,552	53,396	46,612	59,161	48,970
Debt/Equity	0.73	0.76	0.79	0.76	0.71
Return on Capital (%)	14.64	14.90	15.12	16.65	17.11
Ret. on Com. Equity (%)	13.07	13.64	12.54	15.28	15.21
% Change Profit	5.9	13.0	(10.6)	4.1	25.4
% Change Revenue	(3.4)	0.7	0.3	9.5	0.7
% Change Assets	6.2	(6.2)	5.5	4.9	(0.0)

	Dec92	Dec91	Dec90
Preferred Div. Coverage	3.5	3.7	3.6
Total Div. Coverage	1.3	1.2	1.3
Interest Coverage	3.1	3.1	3.1
Current Ratio	1.0	1.1	1.1
Operating Margin	24.1	21.9	20.6
Asset Turnover	0.5	0.6	0.5
5 YEAR RATIOS (%)			
Return on Capital	15.7	15.9	17.1
Return on Com. Equity	13.9	13.6	14.7
Profit Growth	6.8	(1.5)	(7.5)
Revenue Growth	1.4	(1.4)	(5.1)
Asset Growth	1.9	1.2	3.6
BALANCE SHEET (000)			
Cash	0	0	0
Current Assets	69,347	72,438	71,086
Net Fixed Assets	590,201	549,432	593,578
Invest's & Advances	0	0	0
Total Assets	666,599	627,697	669,486
Short Term Debt	22,780	23,000	18,661
Current Liabilities	72,428	68,835	66,694
Long Term Debt	237,382	226,732	214,484
Total Liabilities	312,371	298,150	372,984
Total Equity	354,228	329,547	296,502
Total Liab. & Equity	666,599	627,697	669,486
CAPITAL (000)			
Total Debt	260,162	249,732	233,145
Preferred Equity	139,719	142,431	114,573
Common Equity	214,509	187,116	181,929

Business:

NORTHWESTERN UTILITIES LIMITED is a natural gas utility, serving customers in central and northern Alberta and northeastern British Columbia. The company is a subsidiary of Canadian Utilities Limited of Edmonton.

Date	EPS	DPS	Tot Rev	Inc Bex
Mar 93	5.24	nc	149,903	19,192
Dec 92	4.52	nc	117,213	16,916
Sep 92	(0.53)	nc	53,201	1,002
Jun 92	0.06	nc	60,994	2,760
Mar 92	4.53	nc	122,577	15,947
Dec 91	4.50	nc	118,669	15,900
Sep 91	0.29	nc	50,275	3,421
Jun 91	(0.54)	nc	59,610	508

Synopsis:

In February 1993, Northwestern Utilities Ltd. entered into an agreement with Pacific Northern Gas Ltd. to sell the outstanding shares of Northland Utilities (B.C.) Ltd. for about $2.5-million. Regulatory hearings were scheduled in May. Northern Utilities owns and operates natural gas distribution systems in the Dawson Creek area and the town of Tumbler Ridge in northeastern B.C.

For 1992, capital expenditures to provide for customer growth and to meet the needs of existing customers amounted to $78.4-million compared to $73.7-million in 1991. The largest individual projects were the 90 kilometres of transmission line built from Ranfurly to Lloydminster, Alberta, to serve the Bi Provincial Upgrader and the replacement of bare steel mains originally installed in urban areas in the 1920s. Expenditures on the Upgrader pipeline amounted to $10-million while $9.8-million was spent on the bare mains replacement in 1992, the sixth year of a 10-year program. At year-end, property plant and equipment required to serve customers, net of accumulated depreciation, was $685.9-million

During 1992, the company used the net proceeds of a $20-million common share issue and a $15-million 9.4% debenture issue to partially finance its capital expenditure program.

Taking the advantage of lower interest rates to reduce financing costs, Northwestern issued $5.1-million of 8.82% and $3.5-million of 6.53% long-term notes to redeem $3.4-million of 9.75% bonds, $900,000 of 11.74% debentures and $4.2-million of 11.48% debentures.

On December 30, 1992, the Alberta Public Utilities Board (PUB) issued a decision which set final rates for 1991 and 1992. On January 6, 1993, Northwestern filed a general rate application with the PUB for an increase in the cost of service. The last application for cost of service was filed in 1991.

Relative strength to TSE300 / Price / Volume (in 1000's of board lots)

Rank (Profit/Revenue/Assets)
80   204   186

J.D. Wood
Chairman & C.E.O.

R.G. Lock
President

D.M. Ellard
Sr. V.P. & General Manager

Address
10035 - 105 Street
Edmonton
AB
T5J 2V6
(403) 420-7211

Fax: (403) 420-7400
N0003465/G/10.1

NOVA SCOTIA POWER INC.

Exchanges	Price (Jun24'93)		11 .75	Trailing P/E		na		Stock Symbol
TM	Trailing Yield (%)		na	Trailing EPS		na		**NSI**

Period Ending	Dec92	Mar92	Mar91	Mar90	Mar89
Yearly Statistics	9M				
Price-Close	10 .75	n t	n t	n t	n t
Price-High	11 .63	n t	n t	n t	n t
Price-Low	10 .50	n t	n t	n t	n t
P/E-Close	17 .92	n t	n t	n t	n t
Dividends per Share	0 .19	nc	nc	nc	nc
Dividend Yield (%)	1 .74	nc	nc	nc	nc
Sales per Share	7 .70	nc	nc	nc	nc
EPS before extra. item	0 .45	nc	nc	nc	nc
Cash Flow per Share	1 .55	nc	nc	nc	nc
Book Value per Share	8 .80	nc	nc	nc	nc
O/S Common Shares	85 ,135	0	0	0	0
Total Revenue	573 ,200	770 ,600	677 ,200	645 ,500	582 ,901
Income before extra.	38 ,000	46 ,300	24 ,000	21 ,000	(11 ,443)
Cash Flow	99 ,000	125 ,000	98 ,200	84 ,000	28 ,219
Debt/Equity	2 .14	18 .11	27 .40	37 .83	72 .58
Return on Capital (%)	12 .86	15 .23	12 .71	13 .65	11 .26
Ret. on Com. Equity (%)	11 .78	52 .47	45 .20	68 .56	(44 .21)
% Change Profit	9 .4	92 .9	14 .3	283 .5	58 .8
% Change Revenue	(0 .8)	13 .8	4 .9	10 .7	8 .1
% Change Assets	7 .7	17 .0	15 .7	7 .6	5 .6

Preferred Div. Coverage	np	np	np
Total Div. Coverage	2 .4	na	na
Interest Coverage	1 .2	1 .2	1 .0
Current Ratio	0 .9	0 .4	0 .5
Operating Margin	29 .3	31 .5	30 .0
Asset Turnover	0 .3	0 .3	0 .3
5 YEAR RATIOS (%)			
Return on Capital	13 .1	12 .5	11 .5
Return on Com. Equity	26 .8	12 .2	(1 .2)
Profit Growth	71 .1	na	na
Revenue Growth	7 .1	8 .6	5 .5
Asset Growth	10 .5	9 .4	6 .9
BALANCE SHEET (000)			
Cash	0	0	200
Current Assets	201 ,100	185 ,300	182 ,300
Net Fixed Assets	2 ,208 ,700	2 ,101 ,100	1 ,779 ,700
Invest's & Advances	0	0	0
Total Assets	2 ,500 ,700	2 ,322 ,600	1 ,984 ,600
Short Term Debt	67 ,800	260 ,600	217 ,300
Current Liabilities	213 ,900	454 ,000	352 ,000
Long Term Debt	1 ,537 ,700	1 ,757 ,200	1 ,566 ,100
Total Liabilities	1 ,751 ,600	2 ,211 ,200	1 ,919 ,500
Total Equity	749 ,100	111 ,400	65 ,100
Total Liab. & Equity	2 ,500 ,700	2 ,322 ,600	1 ,984 ,600
CAPITAL (000)			
Total Debt	1 ,605 ,500	2 ,017 ,800	1 ,783 ,400
Preferred Equity	0	0	0
Common Equity	749 ,100	111 ,400	65 ,100

Business:

NOVA SCOTIA POWER INC. generates, transmits and distributes electricity in Nova Scotia.

Date	EPS	DPS	Tot Rev	Inc Bex

Synopsis:

During 1992, the Province of Nova Scotia passed legislation to facilitate the reorganization and privatization of the business of Nova Scotia Power Corporation (NSPC). On August 10, 1992, NSPC transferred all of its existing assets, liabilities and retained earnings except for long-term debt and sinking fund assets to Nova Scotia Power Inc. (NSPI) in exchange for: matching notes receivable equivalent to outstanding long-term debt, net of matching notes payable equivalent to sinking fund assets; and 20,134,666 fully paid common shares of NSPI, which were subsequently sold on August 12, 1992, by the Province of Nova Scotia as a secondary offering. Concurrently, the $13.3-million of contributed surplus of NSPC was transferred to the retained earnings of NSPI.

Subsequent to the reorganization and privatization, the business activities of NSPC continued under NSPI. NSPC changed its name to Nova Scotia Power Financial Corporation (NSPF) which continues to hold the long term debt and sinking fund assets.

Nova Scotia Power Inc.'s singular business is electricity production and distribution. Most of its power is thermally produced by burning Nova Scotia coal (approximately 65%) and heavy fuel oil (around 23%). Most of the remaining 12% comes from 33 hydroelectric stations. Between April 1 and December 31, 1992, the company produced 6,274,590,832 kilowatt hours (kWh) of power for 404,866 customers. An annual estimate based on this amount plus budgeted sales for January to March 1993 totals 8,850,000 kWh.

In March 1993, in the first rate case decision since the privatization of NSPI, the Utilities Review Board (URB) granted the company an average rate increase of 1.8%, to take effect April 1, 1993. This will allow a return on equity in the range of 11.5% to 12.0%, less than the company's request of 12.5% to 13.0%. The URB also approved three other requests: a debt retirement program; a new capital structure for the company; and the deferral of costs associated with the construction of new generating capacity at Point Aconi.

Relative strength to TSE300

Price

Volume (in 1000's of board lots)

Rank (Profit/Revenue/Assets)
61   124   77

Louis R. Comeau
President & C.E.O.

Gary Kendall Oickle
Vice President & C.F.O.

Address
P.O. Box 910
Halifax
NS
B3J 2W5
(902) 428-6224

Fax: (902) 428-6112
N0990033/G/10.2

PACIFIC NORTHERN GAS LTD.

Exchanges	Price (Jun24'93)		34 .00	Trailing P/E		9 .77	Stock Symbol
TV	Trailing Yield (%)		4 .82	Trailing EPS		3 .48	PNG.A

Period Ending	Dec92	Dec91	Dec90	Dec89	Dec88
Yearly Statistics					
Price-Close	33 .00	27 .25	22 .50	23 .50	22 .75
Price-High	33 .00	29 .13	25 .00	24 .38	23 .25
Price-Low	26 .00	21 .50	21 .25	20 .25	19 .38
P/E-Close	10 .65	8 .39	7 .01	8 .13	8 .49
Dividends per Share	1 .60	1 .55	1 .50	1 .50	1 .50
Dividend Yield (%)	4 .85	5 .69	6 .67	6 .38	6 .59
Sales per Share	28 .83	40 .37	45 .28	44 .32	46 .00
EPS before extra. item	3 .10	3 .25	3 .21	2 .89	2 .68
Cash Flow per Share	5 .60	5 .91	6 .43	5 .06	5 .34
Book Value per Share	24 .59	23 .16	21 .51	19 .85	18 .59
O/S Common Shares	1 ,719	1 ,701	1 ,680	1 ,671	1 ,654
Total Revenue	49 ,459	68 ,529	76 ,380	74 ,264	76 ,738
Income before extra.	5 ,633	5 ,828	5 ,726	5 ,149	4 ,797
Cash Flow	9 ,569	9 ,996	10 ,781	8 ,415	8 ,828
Debt/Equity	1 .49	1 .50	1 .70	1 .54	1 .65
Return on Capital (%)	13 .06	15 .14	15 .14	15 .46	15 .24
Ret. on Com. Equity (%)	12 .97	14 .54	15 .55	15 .06	14 .73
% Change Profit	(3 .3)	1 .8	11 .2	7 .4	3 .8
% Change Revenue	(27 .8)	(10 .3)	2 .9	(3 .2)	1 .9
% Change Assets	4 .4	2 .7	7 .6	0 .8	2 .1
Preferred Div. Coverage	16 .7	17 .3	17 .0		
Total Div. Coverage	1 .8	2 .0	2 .0		
Interest Coverage	2 .0	2 .2	2 .0		
Current Ratio	0 .5	0 .6	0 .3		
Operating Margin	30 .0	24 .3	20 .4		
Asset Turnover	0 .3	0 .5	0 .6		
5 YEAR RATIOS (%)					
Return on Capital	14 .8	15 .3	16 .0		
Return on Com. Equity	14 .6	15 .0	14 .7		
Profit Growth	4 .0	8 .3	5 .9		
Revenue Growth	(8 .1)	(3 .5)	(4 .4)		
Asset Growth	3 .4	2 .5	3 .0		
BALANCE SHEET (000)					
Cash	0	0	0		
Current Assets	12 ,185	10 ,666	10 ,649		
Net Fixed Assets	127 ,640	124 ,089	120 ,833		
Invest's & Advances	0	0	252		
Total Assets	143 ,439	137 ,443	133 ,874		
Short Term Debt	18 ,535	10 ,644	27 ,164		
Current Liabilities	25 ,796	18 ,594	32 ,526		
Long Term Debt	51 ,875	55 ,817	42 ,763		
Total Liabilities	96 ,161	93 ,058	92 ,723		
Total Equity	47 ,278	44 ,385	41 ,151		
Total Liab. & Equity	143 ,439	137 ,443	133 ,874		
CAPITAL (000)					
Total Debt	70 ,410	66 ,461	69 ,927		
Preferred Equity	5 ,000	5 ,000	5 ,000		
Common Equity	42 ,278	39 ,385	36 ,151		

Business:

PACIFIC NORTHERN GAS LTD. is a natural gas utility. It supplies natural gas to industry in Prince Rupert, Kitimat, and northwestern B.C. The company's east-west pipeline connects with the north-south pipeline of its parent company, Westcoast Energy Inc. of Vancouver.

Date	EPS	DPS	Tot Rev	Inc Bex
Mar 93	1 .52	0 .44	16 ,221	2 ,703
Dec 92	1 .20	0 .40	13 ,244	2 ,138
Sep 92	0 .15	0 .40	10 ,360	340
Jun 92	0 .61	0 .40	11 ,513	1 ,123
Mar 92	1 .14	0 .40	14 ,396	2 ,032
Dec 91	0 .59	0 .39	14 ,786	1 ,083
Sep 91	0 .55	0 .40	15 ,516	1 ,029
Jun 91	0 .75	0 .40	17 ,296	1 ,341

Synopsis:

In February 1993, Pacific Northern Gas Ltd. entered into an agreement in principle with Northwestern Utilities Ltd. to purchase the outstanding shares of Northland Utilities (B.C.) Ltd. for about $2.5-million. Northland Utilities owns and operates natural gas distribution systems in Dawson Creek and Tumbler Ridge, B.C.

Pacific Northern's operating revenues in 1992 fell to $49-million from $68-million in the preceding year. The drop in operating revenues was largely offset by lower gas purchase costs, as a greater number of industrial customers now purchase gas directly from producers and contract with the company for transportation services. Under the current method of regulation, the conversion of industrial gas sales to transportation service has no effect on the company's net income. Labor disputes in the B.C. forest industry, together with a planned maintenance shutdown at the petrochemical complex at Kitimat also contributed to the reduction in operating revenues in 1992.

During 1992, Methanex Corporation, the largest customer of Pacific Northern accounting for 67% of the company's delivery, announced its intention to acquire all of the methanol facilities of Fletcher Challenge. That acquisition would make Methanex the largest producer and marketer of methanol in the world. Although there are no immediate plans to expand the methanol plant in Kitimat, plans are under way to expand the existing ammonia plant. The current proposal would see an existing plant in the United States moved to Kitimat for tie-in to the current plant and start-up early in 1994. The new plant is expected to use 198,300 square metres of gas per day. Pacific Northern intends to install looping facilities in the summer of 1994 to begin providing additional service to the ammonia plant in the fall of 1994.

In 1994, new looping will also likely be required to serve the new Orenda Forest Products Ltd. paper mill located between Terrace and Kitimat. This paper mill is expected to use 141,600 square metres of gas per day.

Rank (Profit/Revenue/Assets)
243 475 360

Robert F. O'Shaughnessy
Chairman Of The Board

Address
Suite 1400
1185 West Georgia Street
Vancouver
BC
V6E 4E6
(604) 664-5680

Fax: (604) 691-5863
P0000304/G/10.1

QUEBEC-TELEPHONE

Exchanges	Price (Jun24'93)		18 .75	Trailing P/E		11 .09	Stock Symbol
TM	Trailing Yield (%)		6 .29	Trailing EPS		1 .69	**QT**

Period Ending	Dec92	Dec91	Dec90	Dec89	Dec88
Yearly Statistics					
Price-Close	16 .75	18 .50	14 .38	15 .81	13 .88
Price-High	19 .38	18 .75	16 .00	16 .00	14 .50
Price-Low	16 .00	14 .13	13 .75	13 .25	13 .00
P/E-Close	9 .85	11 .64	9 .91	11 .46	10 .52
Dividends per Share	1 .17	1 .12	1 .06	1 .01	0 .97
Dividend Yield (%)	6 .99	6 .03	7 .34	6 .39	6 .99
Sales per Share	12 .72	12 .51	12 .17	11 .81	12 .74
EPS before extra. item	1 .70	1 .59	1 .45	1 .38	1 .32
Cash Flow per Share	4 .24	4 .02	3 .69	3 .95	3 .58
Book Value per Share	11 .97	11 .40	10 .90	10 .49	10 .01
O/S Common Shares	16 ,700	16 ,525	16 ,364	16 ,188	15 ,795
Total Revenue	245 ,091	235 ,577	226 ,544	215 ,526	203 ,515
Income before extra.	28 ,849	26 ,716	24 ,072	22 ,625	21 ,372
Cash Flow	70 ,469	66 ,198	60 ,052	63 ,002	56 ,389
Debt/Equity	0 .79	0 .83	0 .88	0 .89	0 .86
Return on Capital (%)	17 .51	16 .64	16 .13	16 .32	16 .46
Ret. on Com. Equity (%)	14 .57	14 .26	13 .50	13 .46	13 .44
% Change Profit	8 .0	11 .0	6 .4	5 .9	4 .4
% Change Revenue	4 .0	4 .0	5 .1	5 .9	7 .6
% Change Assets	0 .8	1 .6	1 .5	5 .8	8 .4
Preferred Div. Coverage	51 .6	47 .6	42 .9		
Total Div. Coverage	1 .4	1 .4	1 .4		
Interest Coverage	3 .7	3 .3	3 .1		
Current Ratio	0 .5	0 .7	0 .8		
Operating Margin	25 .7	24 .5	23 .8		
Asset Turnover	0 .5	0 .5	0 .4		
5 YEAR RATIOS (%)					
Return on Capital	16 .6	16 .5	16 .5		
Return on Com. Equity	13 .8	13 .6	13 .4		
Profit Growth	7 .0	5 .9	2 .0		
Revenue Growth	5 .2	4 .8	4 .8		
Asset Growth	3 .6	4 .9	5 .5		
BALANCE SHEET (000)					
Cash	0	6 ,088	6 ,179		
Current Assets	26 ,686	33 ,278	34 ,300		
Net Fixed Assets	415 ,972	410 ,710	401 ,550		
Invest's & Advances	7 ,028	2 ,070	2 ,633		
Total Assets	453 ,060	449 ,430	442 ,148		
Short Term Debt	15 ,688	7 ,500	358		
Current Liabilities	55 ,690	51 ,040	40 ,502		
Long Term Debt	150 ,000	157 ,575	165 ,142		
Total Liabilities	242 ,798	250 ,458	253 ,176		
Total Equity	210 ,262	198 ,972	188 ,972		
Total Liab. & Equity	453 ,060	449 ,430	442 ,148		
CAPITAL (000)					
Total Debt	165 ,688	165 ,075	165 ,500		
Preferred Equity	10 ,380	10 ,540	10 ,541		
Common Equity	199 ,882	188 ,432	178 ,431		

Business:

QUEBEC-TELEPHONE is a telecommunications company. Its network serves clients on the outskirts of Quebec City and in the Lower St. Lawrence, Gaspe and North Shore regions of Quebec. The company provides voice, data, image and cellular transmission services. Anglo Canadian Telephone Co. of Montreal holds 50.4% of the company's outstanding common shares.

Date	EPS	DPS	Tot Rev	Inc Bex
Mar 93	0.35	0.30	58 ,973	5 ,985
Dec 92	0.47	0.30	62 ,503	8 ,115
Sep 92	0.44	0.29	60 ,673	7 ,447
Jun 92	0.43	0.29	61 ,993	7 ,249
Mar 92	0.36	0.29	59 ,922	6 ,038
Dec 91	0.42	0.29	60 ,477	7 ,035
Sep 91	0.41	0.28	59 ,447	7 ,001
Jun 91	0.42	0.28	59 ,634	6 ,981

Synopsis:

Quebec-Telephone reported that first quarter revenues for 1993 were down 1.5% compared to last year. Quebec-Telephone attributes this decline to a 5% drop in long distance revenues. Long distance revenues were lower because of rate reductions granted to customers in the last 12 months. However, this was partially offset by a 2.4% increase in the volume of long distance messages. Also, local service revenues rose by 5.9% in the year, with the major factor being the improved market penetration of new services.

On February 18, 1993, the Regie des telecommunications approved Quebec-Telephone's request for an increase in local basic rates. The rate increases, which take effect March 1, 1993, are 3.9% for residential customers and 6.7% for business customers. Proceeds from the increases will be use to lower long distance rates in the face of new competition. The re-balancing of rates is intended to reduce the cross-subsidization of local basic service by long distance revenues.

In April 1993, Quebec-Telephone announced the creation of a distinct management unit called Quebec Tel Mobilite. The unit is intended to group together the company's mobile services to allow customers one stop shopping for all their mobile communication needs.

The breakdown of revenues for 1992 (1991) was: long distance service, 58% (60%); local service, 29.5% (29%); and equipment sales and rentals 12.5% (11%).

In 1992, Quebec-Telephone spent over $52-million on additions to telecommunications property. Over half of this amount was spent on extending basic telephone services. Quebec-Telephone expects to spend $320-million in the next five years on new telecommunication property.

Rank (Profit/Revenue/Assets)		
99	244	222

Raymond Sirois
Chairman Of The Board

Gilles Laroche
President & C.E.O.

Yvon Gendron
V.P., Finance & Treasurer

Address
6, Rue Jules-A-Brillant
Rimouski
PQ
G5L 7E4
(418) 723-2271

Fax: (418) 722-2059
Q0000536/G/10.3

TELUS CORPORATION

Exchanges	Price (Jun24'93)	13.37	Trailing P/E	11.73	Stock Symbol
TMZ	Trailing Yield (%)	6.88	Trailing EPS	1.14	**AGT**

Period Ending	Dec92	Dec91	Dec90
Yearly Statistics			3M
Price-Close	13.00	15.75	13.25
Price-High	16.38	15.75	13.50
Price-Low	13.00	12.88	11.88
P/E-Close	10.16	11.84	6.37
Dividends per Share	0.92	0.89	0.22
Dividend Yield (%)	7.08	5.65	1.66
Sales per Share	7.92	8.34	8.05
EPS before extra. item	1.28	1.33	0.52
Cash Flow per Share	2.63	2.56	2.67
Book Value per Share	11.61	11.31	10.93
O/S Common Shares	139,195	138,416	137,626
Total Revenue	1,241,151	1,289,730	298,690
Income before extra.	177,768	183,379	71,718
Cash Flow	363,926	353,380	91,954
Debt/Equity	0.63	0.61	0.74
Return on Capital (%)	11.67	12.33	na
Ret. on Com. Equity (%)	11.18	11.95	na
% Change Profit	(3.1)	(36.1)	na
% Change Revenue	(3.8)	7.9	na
% Change Assets	5.3	(2.8)	na

Date	EPS	DPS	Tot Rev	Inc Bex
Mar 93	0.21	0.23	295,307	28,704
Dec 92	0.35	0.23	288,857	48,943
Sep 92	0.27	0.23	296,395	36,960
Jun 92	0.31	0.23	300,986	43,313
Mar 92	0.35	0.23	300,375	48,552
Dec 91	0.27	0.23	296,452	36,876
Sep 91	0.37	0.23	307,505	51,239
Jun 91	0.36	0.22	316,945	50,050

Preferred Div. Coverage	np	np	np
Total Div. Coverage	1.4	1.5	2.4
Interest Coverage	2.5	2.5	3.9
Current Ratio	0.9	1.1	1.1
Operating Margin	20.0	21.7	23.2
Asset Turnover	0.3	0.4	0.4
5 YEAR RATIOS (%)			
Return on Capital	na	na	na
Return on Com. Equity	na	na	na
Profit Growth	na	na	na
Revenue Growth	na	na	na
Asset Growth	na	na	na
BALANCE SHEET (000)			
Cash	114,247	89,202	5,418
Current Assets	361,154	358,512	489,077
Net Fixed Assets	2,728,588	2,638,493	2,577,404
Invest's & Advances	41,241	29,116	46,873
Total Assets	3,195,164	3,033,940	3,122,004
Short Term Debt	0	0	154,850
Current Liabilities	402,877	329,163	465,304
Long Term Debt	1,009,863	957,506	963,095
Total Liabilities	1,579,602	1,468,650	1,617,432
Total Equity	1,615,562	1,565,290	1,504,572
Total Liab. & Equity	3,195,164	3,033,940	3,122,004
CAPITAL (000)			
Total Debt	1,009,863	957,506	1,117,945
Preferred Equity	0	0	0
Common Equity	1,615,562	1,565,290	1,504,572

Business:

TELUS CORPORATION is a management holding company serving as a corporate umbrella for AGT Limited, AGT Mobility and AGT Directory. AGT Limited, an Alberta telephone company, contributes about 95% of Telus's revenues.

Synopsis:

In May 1993, AGT Limited, a wholly owned subsidiary of Telus Corporation, announced it had signed an agreement with Bell Atlantic to jointly research, plan and develop advanced intelligent network (AIN) services. As a member of the Stentor alliance, AGT is planning Canada's first AIN service through a trial in May with further trials set for the summer. The AIN services are made possible by the Integrated Services Control Points software developed by Bellcore. AGT and the other nine phone companies making up the Stentor alliance, will pay a licensing fee of up to $17-million for the use of the software. The key benefit of AIN services is the ability to customize telecommunication services. This will provide the phone companies and their customers the opportunity to conceive, create, test and introduce new services in a cost-efficient and timely fashion.

In early May 1993, Telus completed an agreement with CUC Broadcasting Ltd. to enter the cable television and local telephone market in Britain. The two companies plan to invest $126-million over five years towards the project.

In April 1993, the CRTC approved AGT's request for an increase in local residential telephone rates. Effective May 1, 1993, AGT will increase local rates by $1.80. AGT had been asking for a $3.50 increase. In another request, AGT requested charges be placed on long distance directory request in Canada. It also wants to eliminate a policy that allows customers 50 free directory assistance calls to the United States each month. The CRTC will rule on the requests after submission have been received.

Telus says in its 1993 annual report that it expects capital spending in 1993 to fall to $360-million from $368.1-million in 1992. Telus also said it expects to see a decline in revenues from long distance calls in 1993. Telus cites increased competition in the long distance market as a major factor for the decline. An increase in local rates is expected to offset the decline in long distance revenues.

Rank (Profit/Revenue/Assets)
18   93   65

Neil Webber
Chairman
Hal Neldner
President & C.E.O.
Frank Parrotta
Exec. V.P., Finance
Don Lowry
President & C.O.O., AGT Ltd.

Address
10020 - 100th Street
Edmonton
AB
T5J 0N5
(403) 498-7300

Fax: (403) 498-7399
T0003086/G/10.3

TRANSALTA UTILITIES CORPORATION

Price (Jun24'93)	25.75		Trailing P/E	nm	**Stock Symbol**
Trailing Yield (%)	nm		Trailing EPS	nm	**TAU.PR.T**

Period Ending	Dec92	Dec91	Dec90	Dec89	Dec88
Yearly Statistics					
Price-Close	26.13	25.25	24.88	25.13	25.25
Price-High	28.00	26.00	26.00	25.88	26.50
Price-Low	24.75	24.75	24.25	25.00	25.00
P/E-Close	nc	nc	nc	nc	nc
Dividends per Share	nc	nc	nc	nc	nc
Dividend Yield (%)	nc	nc	nc	nc	nc
Sales per Share	8.23	8.21	7.83	7.06	6.72
EPS before extra. item	1.12	1.16	0.26	1.01	0.86
Cash Flow per Share	2.45	2.46	2.35	2.30	2.31
Book Value per Share	8.65	8.47	8.42	9.10	9.04
O/S Common Shares	158,500	144,000	137,300	135,300	135,300
Total Revenue	1,305,200	1,208,600	1,111,500	997,600	959,400
Income before extra.	233,100	220,800	87,300	189,400	176,200
Cash Flow	379,600	348,100	319,700	310,800	313,000
Debt/Equity	0.64	0.75	0.88	0.81	0.74
Return on Capital (%)	15.85	15.20	11.85	14.80	15.51
Ret. on Com. Equity (%)	13.44	13.78	2.96	11.16	9.08
% Change Profit	5.6	152.9	(53.9)	7.5	(28.8)
% Change Revenue	8.0	8.7	11.4	4.0	(1.4)
% Change Assets	1.4	1.1	(1.2)	4.9	0.7

Preferred Div. Coverage	4.0	3.9	1.7
Total Div. Coverage	1.0	1.1	0.5
Interest Coverage	3.8	3.2	2.3
Current Ratio	0.5	0.5	0.7
Operating Margin	40.9	41.0	44.1
Asset Turnover	0.3	0.3	0.3
5 YEAR RATIOS (%)			
Return on Capital	14.6	15.1	15.0
Return on Com. Equity	10.1	10.1	8.2
Profit Growth	(1.3)	12.0	(19.4)
Revenue Growth	6.0	4.3	4.0
Asset Growth	1.3	0.9	0.6
BALANCE SHEET (000)			
Cash	0	0	0
Current Assets	230,200	242,000	227,900
Net Fixed Assets	3,683,200	3,609,800	3,538,700
Invest's & Advances	0	0	15,800
Total Assets	3,939,000	3,884,800	3,844,200
Short Term Debt	208,300	245,200	136,000
Current Liabilities	440,100	441,300	337,600
Long Term Debt	1,148,000	1,242,400	1,469,700
Total Liabilities	1,814,000	1,902,400	2,020,200
Total Equity	2,125,000	1,982,400	1,824,000
Total Liab. & Equity	3,939,000	3,884,800	3,844,200
CAPITAL (000)			
Total Debt	1,356,300	1,487,600	1,605,700
Preferred Equity	754,400	763,000	668,200
Common Equity	1,370,600	1,219,400	1,155,800

Business:

TRANSALTA UTILITIES CORP., the largest investor-owned electric utility in Canada, supplies more than two-thirds of all the electricity used by utility customers in the province of Alberta.

Date	EPS	DPS	Tot Rev	Inc Bex
Mar 93	0.34	0.25	342,100	68,700
Dec 92	0.24	0.25	330,500	52,600
Sep 92	0.25	0.25	324,700	55,300
Jun 92	0.26	0.25	315,800	56,200
Mar 92	0.36	0.25	322,200	67,800
Dec 91	0.36	0.25	293,100	65,900
Sep 91	0.24	0.25	301,300	50,000
Jun 91	0.27	0.25	301,200	51,900

Synopsis:

In late March 1993, TransAlta Utilities, along with Alberta's other large utility companies, requested and received an extension for comments on proposed changes to the Electric Energy Marketing Act (EEMA). A letter jointly written to the Alberta Minister of Energy stated that the four utilities (TransAlta, Alberta Power, Edmonton Power, and the City of Calgary) should be able to reach a consensus on the proposed changes to the EEMA by July 15, 1993.

In February 1993, an Alberta government review panel recommended certain changes to the EEMA. One of the panel's key findings is that while EEMA has been effective in reducing rate disparity throughout the province, there is an element of unfairness in the current pricing formula. The government panel recommended that the equalization pricing formula be adjusted to provide transfer payments to utility companies only when their generation and transmission costs exceed the average provincial wholesale cost by 6%.

In late 1992, TransAlta Utilities filed an application with the Alberta Public Utilities Board to approve rates that would provide open access to the company's transmission and distribution systems as early as 1994. This will enable customers to buy electricity from sources other than TransAlta, while protecting the interests of customers who are unable to pursue self-generation or to purchase electricity from independent power producers.

For the year ended December 1992, TransAlta's electric energy sales totaled 25,247 million kilowatt hours, an increase of 4.1% from 1991. Energy sales reflect higher spot market sales to Alberta's gas processing sector and slower growth in the wholesale and commercial sectors. Energy sales for fiscal 1993 are forecast to increase by 1.5%.

Relative strength to TSE300 / Price / Volume (in 1000's of board lots)

Rank (Profit/Revenue/Assets)		
	10 88 54	

H.G. Schaefer
Chairman & C.F.O.

K.F. McCready
President & C.E.O.

W. Saponja
Sr. V.P., Operations

Address
P.O. Box 1900
110 - 12th Avenue S.W.
Calgary
AB
T2P 2M1
(403) 267-7110

Fax: (403) 267-3630
T0002324/G/10.2

UNICORP ENERGY CORPORATION

Exchanges	Price (Jun24'93)	0.57	Trailing P/E	nm	Stock Symbol
T	Trailing Yield (%)	0.00	Trailing EPS	(0.63)	UNI.A

Period Ending	Dec92	Dec91	Dec90	Dec89	Dec88	Business:
Yearly Statistics						UNICORP ENERGY CORPORATION is a
Price-Close	0.26	0.46	2.55	14.40	24.00	Canadian-owned management company.
Price-High	2.30	0.87	15.00	23.63	25.13	
Price-Low	0.26	0.25	2.25	13.95	15.38	
P/E-Close	0.43	nm	nm	nm	8.33	
Dividends per Share	0.00	0.00	0.15	1.20	1.20	
Dividend Yield (%)	0.00	0.00	5.88	8.33	5.00	
Sales per Share	125.65	164.34	166.58	254.79	258.61	
EPS before extra. item	0.60	(2.80)	(1.62)	(23.82)	2.88	
Cash Flow per Share	(1.30)	17.21	18.28	20.86	21.72	
Book Value per Share	0.69	0.10	2.91	(0.49)	24.08	
O/S Common Shares	10,735	10,735	10,735	7,157	7,109	

Date	EPS	DPS	Tot Rev	Inc Bex
Mar 93	0.02	0.00	206	191
Dec 92	1.06	0.00	16,043	11,457
Sep 92	(1.20)	0.00	347,200	(13,000)
Jun 92	(0.51)	0.00	400,900	(5,400)
Mar 92	1.25	0.00	24,716	17,979
Dec 91	(1.83)	0.00	509,454	(15,190)
Sep 91	(3.33)	0.00	295,500	(10,300)
Jun 91	(0.72)	0.00	369,500	(3,200)

	Dec92	Dec91	Dec90	Dec89	Dec88
Total Revenue	1,365,143	1,764,154	1,759,700	1,832,400	1,719,200
Income before extra.	11,057	(11,890)	1,000	(151,200)	36,900
Cash Flow	(13,972)	184,776	193,000	148,600	139,400
Debt/Equity	nd	0.58	5.69	6.65	3.18
Return on Capital (%)	22.05	(0.08)	11.49	1.75	11.87
Ret. on Com. Equity (%)	151.06	(186.53)	(124.19)	(202.27)	12.20
% Change Profit	193.0	(1,289.0)	100.7	(509.8)	12.8
% Change Revenue	(22.6)	0.3	(4.0)	6.6	19.3
% Change Assets	(98.0)	2.0	4.8	2.1	(57.2)

				Synopsis:
Preferred Div. Coverage	np	0.0	0.1	
Total Div. Coverage	2.4	0.0	0.1	
Interest Coverage	1.4	0.0	1.3	
Current Ratio	8.3	1.1	0.6	
Operating Margin	1.5	0.0	11.8	
Asset Turnover	24.0	0.6	0.6	
5 YEAR RATIOS (%)				
Return on Capital	9.4	7.4	10.4	
Return on Com. Equity	(69.9)	(97.9)	(60.2)	
Profit Growth	(19.5)	na	(46.2)	
Revenue Growth	(1.1)	3.5	10.1	
Asset Growth	(61.0)	4.0	2.2	

BALANCE SHEET (000)

	Dec92	Dec91	Dec90
Cash	13,206	0	0
Current Assets	13,206	2,759,829	356,500
Net Fixed Assets	0	0	2,145,000
Invest's & Advances	0	0	57,500
Total Assets	56,300	2,765,510	2,710,300
Short Term Debt	0	116,626	323,800
Current Liabilities	1,584	2,546,910	574,400
Long Term Debt	0	0	1,001,800
Total Liabilities	48,849	2,562,704	2,477,300
Total Equity	7,451	202,806	233,000
Total Liab. & Equity	56,300	2,765,510	2,710,300

CAPITAL (000)

Total Debt	0	116,626	1,325,600
Preferred Equity	0	201,737	201,800
Common Equity	7,451	1,069	31,200

Synopsis:

In March 1992, Unicorp Energy Corporation announced the refinancing of its bank debt and the redemption of its preferred shares. The bank debt maturity was extended to September 30, 1992, and $120-million of senior notes and $100-million of junior notes were issued to permit the redemption of the retracted preferred. BrasPower Limited, an affiliate of Brascan Limited and Hees International Bancorp Inc., subscribed for the junior notes. This refinancing was completed by Union Holdings Inc., a wholly owned subsidiary of Unicorp and provided Unicorp the time to examine various alternatives to realize maximum value for its investment in Union Energy Inc.

In the fall of 1992, Unicorp announced the sale of its investment in Union Energy Inc. realizing a net proceeds of approximately $355-million which was used to repay the short-term bank debt as well as senior and junior notes.

In January 1993, regulatory authorities in the United States cleared the way for Unicorp's sale of Lincoln Savings Bank. The agreement with the authorities involved an infusion of capital into Lincoln and the settlement of a dispute arising out of the assertion by the regulators that Unicorp had an obligation to maintain the capital of Lincoln at specified regulatory levels. Unicorp decided it was in the company's best interests to enter into the agreement settling the capital maintenance dispute and making Lincoln more salable with the regulatory approval of its new capital plan.

Unicorp's challenges for 1993 are to seek out investment opportunities, to continue to work towards minimizing the risk associated with discontinued operations, and when opportunities arise, to dispose of these assets.

Relative strength to TSE300 / Price / Volume (in 1000's of board lots)

Rank (Profit/Revenue/Assets)
170   83   513

Robert A. Dunford
Chairman

Address
21 St. Clair Avenue East
Toronto
ON
M4T 2T7
(416) 961-1200

Fax: (416) 923-3299
U0000465/G/10.1

Page	Company	$	Latest year end	Earnings per Share		
				Actual	Estimate this year	Estimate next year
315	Baton Broadcasting		9208	0.00	0.08	0.23
316	BCE Mobile Communications		9212	(0.07)	0.12	0.46
317	Canadian Satellite		9208	0.68	0.64	0.68
318	CanWest Global Communications		9208	0.86	1.06	1.29
319	CFCF Inc.		9208	0.24	0.51	0.79
320	CHUM Limited		9208	1.40	1.51	1.71
321	G.T.C. Transcontinental Group		9210	0.43	0.59	0.79
322	Groupe Videotron		9208	0.05	0.26	0.49
323	Hollinger		9212	1.19	0.63	0.72
324	Maclean Hunter		9212	0.47	0.62	0.74
325	Mitel		9303	(0.01)	0.10	0.27
326	Moffat Communications		9208	0.57	0.98	1.36
327	Northern Telecom	$US	9212	2.17	2.27	2.60
328	Quebecor Inc.		9212	0.88	1.20	1.39
329	Quebecor Printing		9212	1.08	1.43	1.56
330	Rogers Cantel Mobile		9212	(1.86)	(0.93)	(0.53)
331	Rogers Communications		9212	(1.30)	(0.96)	(0.79)
332	Shaw Cablesystems		9208	0.78	0.86	0.99
333	Southam		9212	(0.44)	0.34	0.71
334	Tele-Metropole		9208	0.20	0.68	1.08
335	Thomson Corporation		9212	0.30	0.87	1.01
336	Toronto Sun Publishing		9212	0.10	0.44	0.61
337	Torstar		9212	1.21	0.89	1.26
338	WIC Western International		9208	0.19	0.40	0.58

Estimates from I/B/E/S Inc., 345 Hudson St., New York, NY 10014 (212) 243-3335. In Canada: 6 Lansing Square, Ste. 235, Willowdale, ON M2J 1T5 (416) 496-0977.

Communications & Media

Leased Commercial Access - Industry Report [May-13-1993]. MACDONALD GRIPPO RIELY INC. reported by Riley, M.A.
The FCC is attempting to encourage use of leased access channels by adopting guidelines for maximum rates. A reading of the current rules and formulas suggests moderate to heavy usage by video retailers, selective usage for pay-per-view that could reduce event related income to system operators, and negligible usage by others, unless the FCC introduces some flexibility for users who rely on more than one revenue source. Longer term, the issue of leased access may be of importance to system operators, since a significant amount of capacity is mandated for this use. [RN 1331630]

Cable Rate Regulation - Industry Report [May-13-1993]. MACDONALD GRIPPO RIELY INC. reported by Riely, M.A.
Investors and cable operators have found the full text of the FCC's cable rate regulation report to be complex and confusing. System operators who offer more than 40 channels of basic in the low $20 (U.S.) range are expected to experience minimal impact from the new rules. Those who currently price above the benchmark will find it difficult to bring pricing back into line by expanding the basic package rather than rolling back prices. The FCC pricing grid allows cable operators little upside rate flexibility for the addition of incremental channels to the basic package. After netting out affiliation fees for services other than shoppingnetworks, the incremental revenue will be even more modest. Channel capacity may not exist, due to implementation of must carry and to increased demand for leased access channels. [RN 1331632]

Cable TV/Broadcasting Industry - Industry Report [Apr-1-1993]. MERRILL LYNCH CAPITAL MARKETS reported by Falco, P.A., et al
With each passing month it becomes increasingly clear that a geometric increase in video distribution capacity is at hand. It could happen within a five to ten year time frame, although it still seems likely that ten years plus or minus a few years might be required to actually get expanded capability into most cable households. Established programming services that do not take advantage of the enhanced distribution capability could lose ground to those who can. It is also likely that the market power and profitability associated with cable systems that remain simple broadband distribution pipelines for entertainment television will be eroded. Products and services cited include cable television, telephone systems, television productions, and television broadcasting. [RN 1319624]

Canadian Communications & Media - Industry Report [Apr-6-1993]. BBN JAMES CAPEL INC. reported by Godwin, M.
1993 is failing to deliver a recovery in linage for Canadian publishers. The publishers saw linage declines in February 1993. March linage may be weak year-over-year as well. Canadian advertising linage trends pale in comparison to the improving trend for U.S. publishers. [RN 1321224]

Telecom Services: Part III - Industry Report [Apr-6-1993]. MERRILL LYNCH CAPITAL MARKETS reported by Reingold, D.P., et al
AT&T, MCI and Sprint should see improved results as the long distance business benefits from improving trends in the U.S. and, over the longer term, from global privatization and deregulatory trends. All three major long distance carriers should be positively impacted by price pressures subsiding, access expenses declining, and privatizations which should stimulate international demand. Global long distance volume should accelerate as more and more phone bureaucracies are privatized and worldwide phone penetration expands. Deregulation should open new markets outside the U.S. [RN 1320596]

Cellular Industry Update - Industry Report [Mar-29-1993]. MORGAN STANLEY & CO. INC. reported by Runyon, L.J.
The Cellular Telecommunications Industry Association reported the results of its semiannual survey on March 2, 1993, and two big positives emerged: subscriber growth beat expectations, while declines in revenue per subscriber were more moderate than anticipated. Estimated total subscribers as of December 1992 were 11.033 million, a 46% rise from 1991. The number of subscribers grew 43% in 1991. The average monthly bill for the six months ending December 1992 was $68.68 (U.S.), up from $68.51 (U.S.) at the end of June, and the first increase since 1989. The December number dropped 5.6% from the year-earlier period versus a 10.1% decline in December 1991. [RN 1318016]

BATON BROADCASTING INCORPORATED

Exchanges	Price (Jun24'93)		6.12	Trailing P/E		266.30	Stock Symbol
TM	Trailing Yield (%)		0.00	Trailing EPS		0.02	BNB

Period Ending	Aug92	Aug91	Aug90	Aug89	Aug88
Yearly Statistics					
Price-Close	7.00	6.13	7.13	14.25	13.50
Price-High	9.00	7.25	15.25	14.75	15.00
Price-Low	5.25	5.25	7.00	11.38	10.00
P/E-Close	700.00	nm	64.77	21.92	19.01
Dividends per Share	0.00	0.00	0.24	0.24	0.22
Dividend Yield (%)	0.00	0.00	3.37	1.68	1.63
Sales per Share	7.13	6.56	6.27	6.34	5.33
EPS before extra. item	0.01	(1.25)	0.11	0.65	0.71
Cash Flow per Share	0.51	0.21	0.44	1.07	0.88
Book Value per Share	3.98	3.97	5.43	5.54	5.03
O/S Common Shares	28,122	28,122	28,122	27,811	27,678
Total Revenue	200,439	184,426	175,719	175,680	147,430
Income before extra.	290	(35,062)	3,131	17,951	19,543
Cash Flow	14,268	5,879	12,332	29,733	24,374
Debt/Equity	1.22	1.32	0.57	0.51	0.88
Return on Capital (%)	6.62	(12.86)	7.10	16.42	19.08
Ret. on Com. Equity (%)	0.26	(26.53)	2.04	12.25	14.77
% Change Profit	100.8	(1,219.8)	(82.6)	(8.1)	13.7
% Change Revenue	8.7	5.0	0.0	19.2	(34.1)
% Change Assets	(2.5)	7.5	1.2	(8.8)	42.2

Preferred Div. Coverage	np	np	np
Total Div. Coverage	na	na	0.5
Interest Coverage	1.1	0.0	1.5
Current Ratio	1.7	1.0	2.0
Operating Margin	8.4	3.1	9.5
Asset Turnover	0.7	0.7	0.7
5 YEAR RATIOS (%)			
Return on Capital	7.3	10.9	18.7
Return on Com. Equity	0.6	3.4	12.0
Profit Growth	(56.3)	na	(29.1)
Revenue Growth	(2.2)	(0.5)	0.5
Asset Growth	6.5	8.5	15.4
BALANCE SHEET (000)			
Cash	0	0	0
Current Assets	56,687	63,725	63,876
Net Fixed Assets	74,774	73,205	70,122
Invest's & Advances	7,287	6,575	7,911
Total Assets	275,281	282,367	262,743
Short Term Debt	6,773	37,502	17,296
Current Liabilities	33,431	60,807	32,214
Long Term Debt	130,000	110,000	70,000
Total Liabilities	163,431	170,807	110,021
Total Equity	111,850	111,560	152,722
Total Liab. & Equity	275,281	282,367	262,743
CAPITAL (000)			
Total Debt	136,773	147,502	87,296
Preferred Equity	0	0	0
Common Equity	111,850	111,560	152,722

Business:

BATON BROADCASTING INC. is a communications company with broadcasting subsidiaries holding TV licenses for CTV network affiliates in 11 cities in Ontario and Saskatchewan, including Toronto and Ottawa, and CBC affiliates in six cities in Ontario and Saskatchewan. Baton has extensive television programming production facilities in Toronto and Ottawa.

Date	EPS	DPS	Tot Rev	Inc Bex
May 93	0.06	0.00	62,099	1,736
Feb 93	(0.14)	0.00	43,865	(3,874)
Nov 92	0.21	0.00	65,831	5,876
Aug 92	(0.11)	0.00	43,692	(3,009)
May 92	0.08	0.00	57,084	2,351
Feb 92	(0.12)	0.00	41,337	(3,322)
Nov 91	0.15	0.00	58,326	4,271
Aug 91	(1.28)	0.00	41,324	(35,751)

Synopsis:

A new agreement concluded between the seven shareholders of the CTV Television Network Ltd., in January 1993, calls for each company to subscribe to $2-million of convertible debentures, totaling $14-million in additional financing. The seven shareholders are Baton Broadcasting Inc. (CFTO-TV Limited), CFCF Inc. (CFCF 12), CHUM Limited, Electrohome Limited, Maclean Hunter (CFCN Communications Limited), Moffat Communications Limited and WIC Western International Communications (Westcom TV Group Ltd.). The new shareholder agreement and previously negotiated new affiliation agreements clearly define Baton's shareholder and affiliation responsibilities to the network. The new affiliation agreement, which is effective for one year from September 1992, has a key component. It guarantees a minimum payment to Baton for airtime provided to the network.

The terms of a new CBC affiliation agreement call for approximately 45% of affiliate programming to be supplied by the network. In excess of 70% of these hours represent available inventory for the CBC to program and sell, for which Baton receives compensation from the network. The 30% remaining airtime is supplied at no cost, but the company can sell related airtime and preempt and reschedule this portion of CBC programming as desired.

Baton received permission from the CRTC for the purchase of two television stations in Southwestern Ontario owned by the Blackburn Group Inc. for $28.6-million. The CRTC also granted Baton a license for a new television station in Wheatley, Ontario. Both approvals carried a warning that the CRTC will monitor the company for its hiring and promotion practices. The new stations will add to Baton's coverage of the province through its ONT network. ONT, which allows Baton to sell television advertising on a regional basis in Ontario, will expand its hours of programming in 1994.

Rank (Profit/Revenue/Assets)
524   274   286

Allan L. Beattie
Chairman

Douglas G. Bassett
President & C.E.O.

Robin A. Fillingham
Sr. V.P., Fin., C.F.O. & Secty

Joseph J. Garwood
Exec. V.P. & C.O.O.

Address
9 Channel Nine Court
Scarborough
ON
M1S 4B5
(416) 299-2000

Fax: (416) 299-2220
B0001041/G/11.1

BCE MOBILE COMMUNICATIONS INC.

Exchanges	Price (Jun24'93)		38 .00	Trailing P/E		nm	Stock Symbol
TM	Trailing Yield (%)		0 .00	Trailing EPS		(0 .01)	**BCX**

Period Ending	Dec92	Dec91	Dec90	Dec89	Dec88
Yearly Statistics					
Price-Close	32 .00	29 .63	18 .38	33 .00	20 .75
Price-High	33 .25	30 .00	34 .00	39 .00	22 .75
Price-Low	24 .25	18 .00	14 .75	20 .38	8 .50
P/E-Close	nm	nm	nm	nm	691 .67
Dividends per Share	0 .00	0 .00	0 .00	0 .00	0 .00
Dividend Yield (%)	0 .00	0 .00	0 .00	0 .00	0 .00
Sales per Share	6 .50	5 .67	5 .34	3 .93	2 .91
EPS before extra. item	(0 .06)	(0 .27)	(0 .34)	(0 .11)	0 .03
Cash Flow per Share	1 .44	0 .89	0 .83	0 .75	0 .55
Book Value per Share	5 .60	5 .65	4 .95	4 .48	3 .87
O/S Common Shares	69 ,153	69 ,106	64 ,994	61 ,992	59 ,884
Total Revenue	449 ,744	391 ,433	337 ,027	241 ,704	175 ,843
Income before extra.	(3 ,873)	(17 ,901)	(21 ,320)	(6 ,930)	2 ,021
Cash Flow	99 ,469	59 ,341	52 ,460	45 ,795	32 ,098
Debt/Equity	0 .87	0 .86	1 .24	0 .98	0 .46
Return on Capital (%)	5 .62	3 .60	3 .29	2 .74	5 .09
Ret. on Com. Equity (%)	(1 .00)	(5 .03)	(7 .11)	(2 .72)	1 .00
% Change Profit	78 .4	16 .0	(207 .6)	(442 .9)	118 .4
% Change Revenue	14 .9	16 .1	39 .4	37 .5	42 .0
% Change Assets	1 .5	1 .5	30 .8	57 .6	33 .6

Preferred Div. Coverage	np	np	np
Total Div. Coverage	na	na	na
Interest Coverage	1 .0	0 .6	0 .5
Current Ratio	1 .1	1 .0	1 .0
Operating Margin	10 .4	4 .3	7 .8
Asset Turnover	0 .5	0 .5	0 .4
5 YEAR RATIOS (%)			
Return on Capital	4 .1	1 .7	(3 .4)
Return on Com. Equity	(3 .0)	(4 .3)	(8 .4)
Profit Growth	na	na	na
Revenue Growth	29 .4	42 .6	136 .5
Asset Growth	23 .1	30 .8	75 .3
BALANCE SHEET (000)			
Cash	1 ,052	174	2 ,679
Current Assets	103 ,468	86 ,812	91 ,424
Net Fixed Assets	592 ,205	592 ,353	549 ,870
Invest's & Advances	38 ,414	35 ,961	34 ,994
Total Assets	822 ,515	810 ,308	798 ,638
Short Term Debt	19 ,951	20 ,205	27 ,238
Current Liabilities	94 ,279	89 ,997	89 ,103
Long Term Debt	318 ,517	315 ,296	371 ,385
Total Liabilities	434 ,969	419 ,779	476 ,842
Total Equity	387 ,546	390 ,529	321 ,796
Total Liab. & Equity	822 ,515	810 ,308	798 ,638
CAPITAL (000)			
Total Debt	338 ,468	335 ,501	398 ,623
Preferred Equity	0	0	0
Common Equity	387 ,546	390 ,529	321 ,796

Business:

BCE MOBILE COMMUNICATIONS INC. is a mobile communications holding company. It provides cellular telecommunications in Ontario and Quebec through Bell Cellular Inc., national paging and messaging services through National Pagette Ltd. and two-way radio communication services in Ontario and Quebec through Bell Radiocommunications Inc. BCE Inc. of Montreal owns 67.7% of the company.

Date	EPS	DPS	Tot Rev	Inc Bex
Mar 93	(0 .03)	0 .00	111 ,651	(2 ,324)
Dec 92	0 .00	0 .00	122 ,245	142
Sep 92	0 .00	0 .00	116 ,361	66
Jun 92	0 .02	0 .00	114 ,380	1 ,544
Mar 92	(0 .07)	0 .00	98 ,222	(4 ,942)
Dec 91	(0 .02)	0 .00	109 ,742	(1 ,159)
Sep 91	(0 .07)	0 .00	99 ,811	(4 ,968)
Jun 91	(0 .08)	0 .00	96 ,740	(5 ,360)

Synopsis:

In September 1992, BCE Mobile Communications and the mobile telephone arms of Canada's major telephone companies formed Mobility Canada, to provide a national common wireless service. BCE Mobile will have the largest share of the new identity with a 66% ownership, which is based on revenue size. Mobility Canada's business goals are to accelerate the introduction of new products and nationally branded services, and to improve joint research and business planning. In December, Mobility Canada was granted one of four national licences to offer a personal cordless telephone service. The new telephone service will allow the use of pocket-sized digital telephones at home, at the office and within 150 to 200 metres of a public PCT antenna.

During 1992, BCE Mobile launched its new Bell Mobility campaign. An $83-million agreement was reached with Motorola-Nortel Communications for new cell site radios and network control architecture, which will give the company Canada's most flexible digital platform. The company's paging division set up a new service, PagePlus International, a partnership with Mobility Canada and MobileComm, which allows customers to select their preferred region of paging coverage within the continental United States. Skytel Communications received a full commercial licence to operate an air-to-ground public telephone service.

In February 1993, Mobility Canada and 14 leading U.S. mobile communication companies introduced a new service, MobiLink (TM), which allows subscribers to make or receive calls using a standard dialing code in major metropolitan areas in North America. The service should be available to customers in the early fall.

1992 revenues (operating profit before depreciation and administration) by segment were: cellular service, 75% (89%); paging and telephone answering services, 8% (9%); and product sales, private radio and other operations, 17% (2%). Capital spending is expected to increase during 1993 as the company expands the capacity of its cellular telephone system.

Relative strength to TSE300

Price

Volume (in 1000's of board lots)

Rank (Profit/Revenue/Assets)
816   168   170

W. Brian Hewat
Chairman

John T. McLennan
President & C.E.O.

Pierre N. Lessard
V.P., Finance & Corp. Serv.

Address
Suite 200
6505 Trans Canada Highway
St-Laurent
PQ
H4T 1S3
(514) 748-3200

Fax: (514) 748-0347
01001728/G/11.4

CANADIAN SATELLITE COMMUNICATIONS INC.

Exchanges	Price (Jun24'93)	9 .50	Trailing P/E	25 .68	Stock Symbol
TM	Trailing Yield (%)	2 .11	Trailing EPS	0 .37	SAT

Period Ending	Aug92	Aug91	Aug90	Aug89	Aug88
Yearly Statistics					
Price-Close	13 .25	11 .63	13 .50	16 .00	13 .75
Price-High	14 .50	13 .75	17 .00	16 .50	17 .00
Price-Low	10 .50	11 .00	12 .25	11 .25	9 .00
P/E-Close	19 .49	15 .50	16 .88	41 .03	80 .88
Dividends per Share	0 .20	0 .10	0 .00	0 .00	0 .00
Dividend Yield (%)	1 .51	0 .86	0 .00	0 .00	0 .00
Sales per Share	4 .67	4 .16	3 .90	3 .57	3 .02
EPS before extra. item	0 .68	0 .75	0 .80	0 .39	0 .17
Cash Flow per Share	1 .26	1 .16	1 .20	0 .83	0 .55
Book Value per Share	3 .36	2 .88	2 .22	1 .41	0 .87
O/S Common Shares	10 ,317	10 ,318	10 ,305	10 ,275	10 ,159
Total Revenue	48 ,135	42 ,662	40 ,082	36 ,431	30 ,545
Income before extra.	7 ,034	7 ,708	8 ,193	3 ,981	1 ,732
Cash Flow	13 ,036	11 ,910	12 ,330	8 ,450	5 ,583
Debt/Equity	0 .01	0 .02	0 .37	1 .34	2 .59
Return on Capital (%)	25 .58	26 .28	30 .05	25 .19	18 .71
Ret. on Com. Equity (%)	21 .87	29 .32	43 .79	34 .05	23 .76
% Change Profit	(8 .7)	(5 .9)	105 .8	129 .8	22 .3
% Change Revenue	12 .8	6 .4	10 .0	19 .3	23 .9
% Change Assets	24 .3	3 .4	(7 .2)	5 .7	0 .9

Preferred Div. Coverage	np	np	np
Total Div. Coverage	3 .4	7 .6	na
Interest Coverage	na	20 .7	6 .1
Current Ratio	3 .1	2 .7	3 .6
Operating Margin	17 .5	19 .5	24 .6
Asset Turnover	1 .1	1 .2	1 .2
5 YEAR RATIOS (%)			
Return on Capital	25 .2	24 .6	19 .9
Return on Com. Equity	30 .6	53 .6	na
Profit Growth	37 .7	76 .4	100 .0
Revenue Growth	14 .3	14 .8	25 .3
Asset Growth	4 .8	11 .2	18 .7
BALANCE SHEET (000)			
Cash	5 ,493	7 ,156	4 ,976
Current Assets	18 ,235	10 ,757	7 ,365
Net Fixed Assets	21 ,111	19 ,637	21 ,684
Invest's & Advances	3 ,480	4 ,072	4 ,132
Total Assets	43 ,742	35 ,194	34 ,023
Short Term Debt	175	225	175
Current Liabilities	5 ,950	3 ,952	2 ,044
Long Term Debt	0	458	8 ,196
Total Liabilities	9 ,090	5 ,519	11 ,121
Total Equity	34 ,652	29 ,675	22 ,901
Total Liab. & Equity	43 ,742	35 ,194	34 ,023
CAPITAL (000)			
Total Debt	175	683	8 ,371
Preferred Equity	0	0	0
Common Equity	34 ,652	29 ,675	22 ,901

Business:

CANADIAN SATELLITE COMMUNICATIONS INC. (Cancom) provides radio and television signals to Canadian households, through cable companies and direct to home services, via satellite. It also offers businesses its commercial satellite network for the transmittal of interactive digital data, audio video services, mobile messaging and tracking service for the transportation industry, and video conferencing.

Date	EPS	DPS	Tot Rev	Inc Bex
Feb 93	(0 .07)	0 .10	15 ,295	(732)
Nov 92	0 .13	0 .00	14 ,826	1 ,384
Aug 92	0 .12	0 .10	12 ,714	1 ,229
May 92	0 .19	0 .00	12 ,420	2 ,026
Feb 92	0 .20	0 .10	11 ,581	2 ,072
Nov 91	0 .17	0 .00	11 ,355	1 ,707
Aug 91	0 .21	0 .10	11 ,120	2 ,171
May 91	0 .22	0 .00	11 ,013	2 ,199

Synopsis:

In March 1993, Canadian Satellite Communications (Cancom) announced that it was writing down a development project carried on by its wholly owned U.S. subsidiary Amcom Inc. Amcom decided to cease distribution of the North American Bar Network signal because the market for the service did not meet expectations. The write-down was approximately $3.5-million.

Cancom introduced a new satellite fax service, Faxcast, in January 1993. The service can deliver a fax message to an unlimited number of recipients simultaneously. Faxcast is part of a common satellite based fax network capable of serving the greater part of the North American continent. The technology was developed by Faxcast Broadcast Corporation of Britain, which also has licencing agreements in Europe, Asia, Australia and New Zealand as part of its objective of a seamless global network for information delivery. Cancom was granted an exclusive licence for Canada and the two companies have a joint venture in a U.S.-based enterprise to market the service in the United States, Mexico and parts of Central and South America.

Cancom acquired a new operations centre and satellite uplink facilities in Mississauga, Ontario, in January 1993. The broadcast group is expected to move into the new building in February.

The cable market services unit distributed television and radio signals to 2,330 affiliated systems as of February 28, 1993. Cable households receiving one or more satellite signals reached 3,005,067 an increase of 107,160, channel subscribers (number of households multiplied by number of signals taken) reached 8,677,603 an increase of 461,555, and U.S. superstation signals to some of its cable affiliates and to cable companies that buy only the superstations from Cancom increased 225,057 to 1,352,388. The direct-to-home unit added 8,536 subscribers, ending the February 1993 period with 22,659 subscribers. The business services division, Satlink/Mobile, continued to add contracts for its Qualcomm OmniTRACS service, increasing these contracts by 335 units, to 1,422 at the end of February.

Rank (Profit/Revenue/Assets)
215   478   568

Douglas M. Holtby
Chairman Of The Board

Sheelagh D. Whittaker
President & C.E.O.

Louise Tremblay
V.P. & C.F.O.

Address
50 Burnhamthorpe Road West
10th Floor
Mississauga
ON
L5B 3C2
(416) 272-4960

Fax: (416) 272-3399
C0039192/G/11.4

CANWEST GLOBAL COMMUNICATIONS CORP.

Exchanges	Price (Jun24'93)	19.12	Trailing P/E	20.13	Stock Symbol
TM	Trailing Yield (%)	0.52	Trailing EPS	0.95	CWW

Period Ending	Aug92	Aug91	Aug90	Aug89
Yearly Statistics				
Price-Close	13.00	nt	nt	nt
Price-High	14.75	nt	nt	nt
Price-Low	10.75	nt	nt	nt
P/E-Close	15.12	nt	nt	nt
Dividends per Share	0.10	0.30	2.61	0.00
Dividend Yield (%)	0.77	nt	nt	nt
Sales per Share	13.57	17.12	14.91	10.52
EPS before extra. item	0.86	0.69	0.39	0.37
Cash Flow per Share	1.88	1.84	0.81	0.66
Book Value per Share	4.42	0.48	0.53	2.75
O/S Common Shares	17,896	13,160	13,160	13,160
Total Revenue	235,162	225,872	196,181	138,381
Income before extra.	14,860	9,023	6,024	7,648
Cash Flow	32,513	24,173	10,633	8,745
Debt/Equity	2.22	40.20	39.66	1.34
Return on Capital (%)	20.28	18.05	16.28	na
Ret. on Com. Equity (%)	34.80	136.26	23.77	na
% Change Profit	64.7	49.8	(21.2)	na
% Change Revenue	4.1	15.1	41.8	na
% Change Assets	3.7	1.9	68.6	na
Preferred Div. Coverage	np	np	np	
Total Div. Coverage	8.3	2.3	0.2	
Interest Coverage	2.7	1.7	1.5	
Current Ratio	1.0	1.0	1.1	
Operating Margin	25.1	23.7	19.0	
Asset Turnover	0.6	0.5	0.5	
5 YEAR RATIOS (%)				
Return on Capital	na	na	na	
Return on Com. Equity	na	na	na	
Profit Growth	na	na	na	
Revenue Growth	na	na	na	
Asset Growth	na	na	na	
BALANCE SHEET (000)				
Cash	809	637	5,215	
Current Assets	145,970	132,900	125,397	
Net Fixed Assets	39,853	41,426	42,935	
Invest's & Advances	32,681	21,812	6,999	
Total Assets	427,524	412,314	404,789	
Short Term Debt	7,268	11,987	9,554	
Current Liabilities	146,005	130,537	114,813	
Long Term Debt	167,907	241,547	265,597	
Total Liabilities	348,431	406,007	397,852	
Total Equity	79,093	6,307	6,937	
Total Liab. & Equity	427,524	412,314	404,789	
CAPITAL (000)				
Total Debt	175,175	253,534	275,151	
Preferred Equity	0	0	0	
Common Equity	79,093	6,307	6,937	

Business:

CANWEST GLOBAL COMMUNICATIONS CORP. through its principal broadcasting subsidiaries, is licensed to provide over-the-air English language television broadcasting services through independent television stations with signals originating in Toronto, Winnipeg, Regina, Saskatoon and Vancouver. CanWest Global owns 20% of New Zealand's TV3 network, and 57.5% of Australia's Channel Ten television network.

Date	EPS	DPS	Tot Rev	Inc Bex
Feb 93	0.16	0.00	58,574	2,842
Nov 92	0.45	0.00	70,141	8,056
Aug 92	0.02	0.10	49,020	523
May 92	0.32	0.00	67,223	5,594
Feb 92	0.10	0.00	53,187	2,035
Nov 91	0.42	0.00	65,732	6,708
Aug 91	(0.01)	0.19	52,600	(584)
May 91	0.31	0.00	58,344	4,002

Synopsis:

CanWest Global Communications in its first year as a public company began by expanding into the South Pacific. In May 1993, CanWest joined a consortium, through its subsidiary Ten Television Network, seeking a pay television licence in Australia. The consortium, which includes Australia's other commercial television networks, is bidding on two pay television licences, to provide up to four channels to subscribers. A third licence will be issued to the state-owned Australian Broadcasting Corp.

In December 1992, CanWest acquired a 57.5% economic interest and 15% voting equity, in Channel Ten Television Network of Australia. CanWest paid $45.8-million of the $202.4-million paid by a consortium lead by CanWest for Ten Television. The consortium also includes Sheldon Berney of Toronto, with a 4% equity interest, and Telecasters North Queensland of Australia, with a 40% equity interest. The consortium is called Oltec Limited. Currently, foreign ownership laws in Australia only allow for 20% foreign ownership, however CanWest has acquired convertible debt of Oltec. Should future laws permit, the debt would be converted to voting equity increasing the company's interest to 57.5%.

In December 1991, CanWest acquired a 20% interest in New Zealand's TV3 Television Network. The company, which has an option to increase ownership interest to 50%, assumed responsibility for management of TV3. CanWest believes the strategic investments made in the South Pacific will further strengthen the company.

The company's objectives in 1993 are: to submit an application with the CRTC for television licences to broadcast in much of Alberta; to expand ownership of the TV3 Television Network; to search for opportunities to acquire additional non-Canadian television operations; to monitor opportunities to bring more of CanWest programming to Montreal and Atlantic Canada; and to pursue licences for new specialty television services should the CRTC decide to licence such additional services.

Relative strength to TSE300

Price

Volume (in 1000's of board lots)

Rank (Profit/Revenue/Assets)
147   251   229

I.H. Asper
Chairman & C.E.O.

Stephen Gross
President & C.O.O.

Thomas C. Strike
V.P., Finance & C.F.O.

Address
600 Richardson Building
One Lombard Place
Winnipeg
MB
R3B 0X3
(204) 956-2025

Fax: (204) 947-9841
01003215/G/11.1

For further company information, call Globe Information Services 1-800-268-9128 or (416)585-5345

CFCF INC.

Exchanges	Price (Jun24'93)	13.75	Trailing P/E	12.97	Stock Symbol
TM	Trailing Yield (%)	0.18	Trailing EPS	1.06	**CF**

Period Ending	Aug92	Aug91	Aug90	Aug89	Aug88
Yearly Statistics					
Price-Close	8.75	6.50	9.50	16.25	19.88
Price-High	10.50	11.00	18.13	22.50	21.00
Price-Low	7.63	6.25	8.13	16.00	13.50
P/E-Close	36.46	nm	nm	56.03	16.70
Dividends per Share	0.00	0.00	0.15	0.20	0.20
Dividend Yield (%)	0.00	0.00	1.58	1.23	1.01
Sales per Share	13.97	14.63	14.73	11.44	9.43
EPS before extra. item	0.24	(2.13)	(1.54)	0.29	1.19
Cash Flow per Share	2.10	(1.02)	(0.31)	1.59	2.86
Book Value per Share	4.54	4.30	6.36	8.13	7.52
O/S Common Shares	11,040	11,040	11,040	11,040	11,040
Total Revenue	154,252	161,521	162,572	125,185	104,156
Income before extra.	2,668	(23,566)	(16,987)	3,173	13,151
Cash Flow	23,193	(11,212)	(3,454)	17,414	31,614
Debt/Equity	2.33	2.84	1.75	1.04	0.94
Return on Capital (%)	10.96	(6.54)	(3.60)	7.85	17.30
Ret. on Com. Equity (%)	5.47	(40.06)	(21.23)	3.67	16.96
% Change Profit	111.3	(38.7)	(635.4)	(75.9)	33.8
% Change Revenue	(4.5)	(0.6)	29.9	20.2	13.0
% Change Assets	(4.8)	(12.6)	10.4	15.1	19.3

Business:

CFCF INC. is a diversified communications company active in television broadcasting, cable television and production. It owns and operates the Montreal affiliate of the CTV network and the Four Seasons Television Network Inc., a Quebec based French language network. CF Cable is a cable television company serving the Montreal region. Champlain Productions Inc. is a TV production company.

Date	EPS	DPS	Tot Rev	Inc Bex
May 93	0.55	0.00	45,800	6,200
Feb 93	0.03	0.03	36,799	279
Nov 92	0.61	0.00	45,545	6,752
Aug 92	(0.13)	0.00	28,730	(1,472)
May 92	0.35	0.00	47,549	3,871
Feb 92	(0.24)	0.00	34,084	(2,573)
Nov 91	0.26	0.00	43,896	2,842
Aug 91	(0.37)	0.00	32,118	(4,092)

	Aug92	Aug91	Aug90
Preferred Div. Coverage	np	np	np
Total Div. Coverage	na	na	0.0
Interest Coverage	1.3	0.0	0.0
Current Ratio	0.9	0.6	0.9
Operating Margin	14.2	(2.8)	(4.2)
Asset Turnover	0.6	0.6	0.6
5 YEAR RATIOS (%)			
Return on Capital	5.2	6.8	13.1
Return on Com. Equity	(7.0)	(5.2)	6.5
Profit Growth	(23.0)	na	na
Revenue Growth	10.8	13.1	14.3
Asset Growth	4.7	13.6	24.3
BALANCE SHEET (000)			
Cash	0	4,286	0
Current Assets	57,162	58,906	87,144
Net Fixed Assets	86,386	94,104	101,135
Invest's & Advances	931	1,008	596
Total Assets	242,366	254,525	291,111
Short Term Debt	803	35,000	8,997
Current Liabilities	62,597	96,201	93,860
Long Term Debt	116,152	99,899	114,000
Total Liabilities	192,234	207,061	220,906
Total Equity	50,132	47,464	70,205
Total Liab. & Equity	242,366	254,525	291,111
CAPITAL (000)			
Total Debt	116,955	134,899	122,997
Preferred Equity	0	0	0
Common Equity	50,132	47,464	70,205

Synopsis:

A new agreement concluded in January 1993 among the seven shareholders of the CTV Television Network Ltd. calls for each company to subscribe for $2-million of convertible debentures, totaling $14-million in additional financing. The agreement effectively converts the network from a cooperative to a one-share/one-vote for-profit corporation. The seven shareholders are CFCF Inc. (CFCF 12), Baton Broadcasting Inc. (CFTO-TV Limited), CHUM Limited, Electrohome Limited, Maclean Hunter (CFCN Communications Limited), Moffat Communications Limited and Westcom TV Group Ltd. (a division of WIC Western International Communications).

CFCF has agreed to purchase Telecable Laurentien Inc. from Slaight Communications Inc. for cash considerations of $63.5-million, subject to adjustments at the closing in September 1993. The deal is subject to a definitive purchase agreement and to regulatory approval. Telecable Laurentien serves approximately 67,000 subscribers in the Hull, Quebec area. This acquisition is in keeping with the development objectives of CF Cable TV, CFCF's cable subsidiary. CF Cable's goals for 1993 are: to provide increasingly personalized service; to expand services with the addition of pay-per-view; to pursue the upgrade of the network through fibre optics and modernization; and to investigate new business development opportunities.

CFCF 12's application to change the condition of its licence regarding minimum Canadian programming expenditures was denied by the CRTC in December 1992, and an alternative requirement was proposed by the CRTC. CFCF 12 had fallen short of the minimum in fiscal 1991 and 1992 by $3.9-million and expected to have a $2.6-million shortfall in 1993. All other conditions of the licence were met. CFCF television's operations plan to strengthen their market position and renew contact with their audience.

The breakdown of 1992 (1991) revenues by business in was: broadcasting and related revenues, 68% (71%); and cable television, 32% (29%).

Relative strength to TSE300

Price

Volume (in 1000's of board lots)

Rank (Profit/Revenue/Assets)
330 309 296

Jean A. Pouliot
Chairman & C.E.O.

Adrien D. Pouliot
President & C.O.O.

G.R. Price
V.P., Finance & Secretary

Address
405 Ogilvy Avenue
Montreal
PQ
H3N 1M4
(514) 273-6311

Fax: (514) 276-9399
C0000044/G/11.1

CHUM LIMITED

Exchanges	Price (Jun24'93)		18.87	Trailing P/E		13.98	Stock Symbol
T	Trailing Yield (%)		0.90	Trailing EPS		1.35	**CHM.B**

Period Ending	Aug92	Aug91	Aug90	Aug89	Aug88
Yearly Statistics					
Price-Close	25.13	21.38	19.00	23.50	17.25
Price-High	26.25	27.50	26.75	24.50	19.00
Price-Low	20.50	17.00	16.88	17.25	13.75
P/E-Close	17.50	17.81	13.87	18.22	16.59
Dividends per Share	0.17	0.17	0.17	0.17	0.12
Dividend Yield (%)	0.68	0.80	0.90	0.72	0.70
Sales per Share	15.57	14.63	14.10	13.05	12.23
EPS before extra. item	1.40	1.20	1.37	1.29	1.04
Cash Flow per Share	2.03	1.80	1.97	1.86	1.66
Book Value per Share	12.77	11.60	10.57	9.44	8.40
O/S Common Shares	12,815	12,878	12,878	12,946	13,022
Total Revenue	203,047	192,150	183,564	171,069	159,980
Income before extra.	18,013	15,504	17,683	16,734	13,589
Cash Flow	26,089	23,222	25,412	24,258	21,585
Debt/Equity	nd	0.00	0.00	0.00	0.00
Return on Capital (%)	21.18	20.70	25.20	26.78	28.21
Ret. on Com. Equity (%)	11.51	10.86	13.69	14.45	13.14
% Change Profit	16.2	(12.3)	5.7	23.1	39.3
% Change Revenue	5.7	4.7	7.3	6.9	10.9
% Change Assets	10.4	8.9	10.7	5.8	11.7

Preferred Div. Coverage	np	np	np
Total Div. Coverage	8.2	7.1	8.1
Interest Coverage	352.7	26.9	693.4
Current Ratio	4.7	4.2	4.4
Operating Margin	15.8	14.2	17.3
Asset Turnover	1.1	1.1	1.2
5 YEAR RATIOS (%)			
Return on Capital	24.4	24.8	25.9
Return on Com. Equity	12.7	12.5	12.8
Profit Growth	13.0	8.2	10.7
Revenue Growth	7.0	7.2	9.2
Asset Growth	9.4	8.1	10.4
BALANCE SHEET (000)			
Cash	38,116	13,618	19,175
Current Assets	82,217	61,682	60,251
Net Fixed Assets	53,851	55,834	56,381
Invest's & Advances	1,351	1,553	1,764
Total Assets	182,674	165,397	151,882
Short Term Debt	0	0	0
Current Liabilities	17,559	14,670	13,848
Long Term Debt	0	37	142
Total Liabilities	19,050	16,000	15,800
Total Equity	163,624	149,397	136,082
Total Liab. & Equity	182,674	165,397	151,882
CAPITAL (000)			
Total Debt	0	37	142
Preferred Equity	0	0	0
Common Equity	163,624	149,397	136,082

Business:

CHUM LTD. is a radio and television broadcasting company. It operates television stations in the Toronto area and the Maritime provinces. The company also operates radio stations across Canada. CHUM operates the MuchMusic network across Canada. A division of the company operates an environmental music distribution business. CHUM has a 50% interest in MusiquePlus Inc.

Date	EPS	DPS	Tot Rev	Inc Bex
Feb 93	0.00	0.02	41,689	36
Nov 92	0.42	0.02	58,208	5,415
Aug 92	0.56	0.11	49,643	7,153
May 92	0.37	0.02	54,310	4,808
Feb 92	0.04	0.02	41,148	502
Nov 91	0.43	0.02	57,946	5,550
Aug 91	0.52	0.11	47,649	6,731
May 91	0.30	0.02	50,489	3,866

Synopsis:

A new agreement concluded in January 1993 among the seven shareholders of the CTV Television Network Ltd. calls for each company to subscribe for $2-million of convertible debentures, totaling $14-million in additional financing. The agreement converts the network from a cooperative to a one-share/one-vote for-profit corporation. The seven shareholders are CHUM Limited (The Atlantic Television System Group), Baton Broadcasting Inc. (CFTO-TV Limited), CFCF Inc. (CFCF 12), Electrohome Limited, Maclean Hunter (CFCN Communications Limited), Moffat Communications Limited and Westcom TV Group Ltd. (a division of WIC Western International Communications).

CHUM received CRTC approval in February 1993 for the purchase of Windsor radio stations CKLW-AM and CKLW-FM. The purchase between CHUM and Amicus Communications was announced in April 1992. CHUM currently operates two radio stations in Windsor, and will integrate the operation of the four stations.

An agreement has been reached with a group of Vancouver investors to buy CHQM-AM in Vancouver. The sale requires CRTC approval and is in response to a CRTC directive that CHUM sell one of its Vancouver stations. CHUM still owns CHQM-FM and CFUN-AM.

CHUM has agreed to purchase the assets of Electrohome Limited's Kitchener radio stations, CKKW-AM and CFCA-FM, for about $5.5-million. The deal is subject to CRTC approval, with a hearing scheduled for June 1993.

CHUM believes the industry is faced with changing advertiser needs, a changing regulatory environment and new sources of competition. CHUM expects changes to copyright legislation in the next few years, and The Society of Authors, Composers and Publishers is seeking increases to royalty payments. The Canadian Association of Broadcasters is opposed to both these possible changes and is requesting a reduction in copyright rates. CHUM is also working with the industry to establish a permanent, experimental digital radio transmitting facility in Toronto.

Relative strength to TSE300

Price

Volume (in 1000's of board lots)

Rank (Profit/Revenue/Assets)
129   273   332

Allan Waters
President

Taylor C. Baiden
V.P., Finance & Asst. Secty.

Address
1331 Yonge Street
Toronto
ON
M4T 1Y1
(416) 925-6666

C0007071/G/11.1

320   **For further company information, call Globe Information Services 1-800-268-9128 or (416)585-5345**

G.T.C. TRANSCONTINENTAL GROUP LTD.

Exchanges	Price (Jun24'93)	10.50	Trailing P/E	20.59	Stock Symbol
TM	Trailing Yield (%)	0.48	Trailing EPS	0.51	**GRT.B**

Period Ending	Oct92	Oct91	Oct90	Oct89	Oct88
Yearly Statistics					
Price-Close	8.63	3.80	2.80	5.88	4.45
Price-High	9.00	4.90	5.25	7.13	7.50
Price-Low	4.85	3.45	2.50	4.20	5.25
P/E-Close	20.07	190.00	23.33	15.88	14.83
Dividends per Share	0.00	0.00	0.00	0.00	0.00
Dividend Yield (%)	0.00	0.00	0.00	0.00	0.00
Sales per Share	42.91	20.28	20.45	18.08	16.18
EPS before extra. item	0.43	0.02	0.12	0.37	0.30
Cash Flow per Share	3.34	1.58	1.31	1.35	1.23
Book Value per Share	5.60	4.89	4.92	4.83	4.48
O/S Common Shares	23,432	20,257	20,324	20,324	20,197
Total Revenue	544,566	411,901	415,631	366,382	326,010
Income before extra.	11,466	1,987	2,750	7,455	6,004
Cash Flow	42,421	32,163	26,677	27,383	24,764
Debt/Equity	0.64	0.92	0.70	1.16	0.69
Return on Capital (%)	13.26	6.64	8.73	11.01	10.32
Ret. on Com. Equity (%)	8.08	0.33	2.36	7.90	6.88
% Change Profit	477.1	(27.7)	(63.1)	24.2	(45.7)
% Change Revenue	32.2	(0.9)	13.4	12.4	24.8
% Change Assets	35.0	8.1	0.0	30.8	2.2

Date		EPS	DPS	Tot Rev	Inc Bex
Apr	93	0.18	0.05	152,667	4,851
Jan	93	0.05	0.00	144,661	1,575
Oct	92	0.25	0.00	172,211	6,191
Jul	92	0.03	0.00	136,918	1,329
Apr	92	0.12	0.00	123,977	2,937
Jan	92	0.03	0.00	111,460	1,009
Oct	91	0.18	0.00	112,999	4,019
Jul	91	(0.01)	0.00	96,037	205

	Oct92	Oct91	Oct90
Preferred Div. Coverage	5.3	1.2	6.6
Total Div. Coverage	5.3	1.2	6.6
Interest Coverage	2.6	1.4	1.5
Current Ratio	1.2	1.4	1.3
Operating Margin	6.4	3.8	4.6
Asset Turnover	1.3	1.3	1.4
5 YEAR RATIOS (%)			
Return on Capital	10.0	11.2	15.8
Return on Com. Equity	5.1	6.5	10.7
Profit Growth	0.7	(27.8)	(14.4)
Revenue Growth	15.8	19.6	30.9
Asset Growth	14.3	18.1	30.4
BALANCE SHEET (000)			
Cash	0	14,379	0
Current Assets	142,556	115,630	97,862
Net Fixed Assets	239,331	153,633	145,892
Invest's & Advances	617	1,383	2,961
Total Assets	420,771	311,623	288,192
Short Term Debt	13,204	21,872	11,807
Current Liabilities	116,075	83,007	73,285
Long Term Debt	95,450	86,224	71,804
Total Liabilities	250,638	193,593	169,296
Total Equity	170,133	118,030	118,896
Total Liab. & Equity	420,771	311,623	288,192
CAPITAL (000)			
Total Debt	108,654	108,096	83,611
Preferred Equity	39,000	19,000	19,000
Common Equity	131,133	99,030	99,896

Business:

G.T.C. TRANSCONTINENTAL GROUP LTD. is a management holding company which, through its subsidiaries and a joint venture, carries on business in the printed communications industry.

Synopsis:

G.T.C. Transcontinental Group began a thorough review of the performance and strategic fit of its businesses in 1989. As a result certain operations were reorganized, sold or discontinued. This had a direct effect on 1992 results. In accordance with this plan, the company completed a major expansion project in March 1992, with the acquisition of the commercial printing operations of Southam Inc. G.T.C.'s desire to expand and diversify its range of products for retail customers and publishers were a key reason behind the acquisition.

Significant progress was made by the G.T.C.'s printing sector, in achieving three of its five strategic goals during 1992. The achieved goals were: to maintain its leadership in advertising inserts; to increase its commitment to commercial printing; and to improve operating margins.

The distribution sector made an important contribution to the overall profitability of the company. Publi-Sac network, the company's primary distribution vehicle, continues to expand outside of Quebec. In Manitoba, the addition of two specialty newspapers has increased the selection of advertising vehicles and enhanced the company's integrated approach to publishing, printing and distribution.

The publishing sector maintained market share despite the recession. The development of related products such as telemarketing, Teleservice, business conferences and the Transcript division also offer additional opportunities.

The company's priorities for 1993 are: to seek new business opportunities, which provide added-value; to remain committed to markets it knows well; to maintain a low cost structure; and to emphasize continuous improvement and training.

Revenues (operating income) in 1992 by segment were: printing, 85% (80%); distribution, 8% (12%); and publishing, 7% (8%).

Rank (Profit/Revenue/Assets)
163   150   231

Remi Marcoux
Chairman President & C.E.O.

Christian M. Paupe
V.P. Finance & Treasurer

Address
375, Boulevard Lebeau
Saint-Laurent
PQ
H4N 1S2
(514) 337-8560

Fax: (514) 334-1361
G0025506/G/11.3

GROUPE VIDEOTRON LTEE (LE)

Exchanges	Price (Jun24'93)	23.62	Trailing P/E	90.86	Stock Symbol
TM	Trailing Yield (%)	0.51	Trailing EPS	0.26	**VDO**

Period Ending	Aug92	Aug91	Aug90	Aug89	Aug88
Yearly Statistics					
Price-Close	16.25	13.88	9.75	19.00	11.88
Price-High	18.00	15.00	19.50	20.25	15.38
Price-Low	12.25	9.50	9.63	11.50	7.00
P/E-Close	325.00	nm	34.82	31.67	21.99
Dividends per Share	0.12	0.12	0.12	0.12	0.12
Dividend Yield (%)	0.74	0.87	1.23	0.63	1.01
Sales per Share	10.59	10.63	10.94	8.98	7.86
EPS before extra. item	0.05	(0.12)	0.28	0.60	0.54
Cash Flow per Share	2.28	1.54	1.62	2.08	1.71
Book Value per Share	7.39	4.76	5.19	5.05	4.05
O/S Common Shares	47,294	38,422	38,364	38,824	38,912
Total Revenue	563,730	481,950	431,306	347,001	308,373
Income before extra.	12,594	5,341	18,070	24,597	21,022
Cash Flow	98,003	58,983	62,317	80,589	66,750
Debt/Equity	1.70	2.29	1.63	1.70	1.41
Return on Capital (%)	7.45	6.45	0.00	13.43	14.76
Ret. on Com. Equity (%)	0.76	(2.48)	5.16	13.08	13.98
% Change Profit	135.8	(70.4)	(26.5)	17.0	15.8
% Change Revenue	17.0	11.7	24.3	12.5	5.2
% Change Assets	27.6	22.6	35.6	34.6	11.1

Preferred Div. Coverage	1.2	0.5	2.3
Total Div. Coverage	0.8	0.4	1.4
Interest Coverage	1.2	0.9	1.4
Current Ratio	1.2	0.6	0.5
Operating Margin	13.7	9.0	12.0
Asset Turnover	0.3	0.3	0.4
5 YEAR RATIOS (%)			
Return on Capital	10.4	13.2	16.9
Return on Com. Equity	6.1	9.4	16.2
Profit Growth	(7.1)	(19.9)	10.7
Revenue Growth	13.9	29.9	31.8
Asset Growth	25.9	40.3	45.3
BALANCE SHEET (000)			
Cash	141,856	17,806	17,318
Current Assets	267,122	136,060	101,317
Net Fixed Assets	923,470	715,464	480,583
Invest's & Advances	35,893	38,344	141,173
Total Assets	1,639,894	1,284,749	1,047,835
Short Term Debt	44,627	52,910	55,139
Current Liabilities	219,323	215,779	189,124
Long Term Debt	719,644	596,138	432,977
Total Liabilities	1,190,294	1,001,833	748,844
Total Equity	449,600	282,916	298,991
Total Liab. & Equity	1,639,894	1,284,749	1,047,835
CAPITAL (000)			
Total Debt	764,271	649,048	488,116
Preferred Equity	100,003	100,003	100,003
Common Equity	349,597	182,913	198,988

Business:

GROUPE VIDEOTRON LTEE is a broadcasting holding company. It owns 100% of the voting rights of Videotron Ltee, a cable television operator in Quebec and Alberta. The company also holds 99.7% of the voting rights and 40.8% of participating shares of Tele-Metropole Inc. Tele-Metropole operates French-language TV stations in Montreal and Chicoutimi, Quebec.

Date	EPS	DPS	Tot Rev	Inc Bex
May 93	0.15	0.03	154,600	9,900
Feb 93	0.02	0.03	140,985	3,611
Nov 92	0.13	0.03	154,599	8,553
Aug 92	(0.04)	0.03	131,594	1,020
May 92	0.14	0.03	147,200	8,468
Feb 92	(0.04)	0.03	126,385	1,031
Nov 91	(0.01)	0.03	139,700	2,075
Aug 91	(0.20)	0.03	113,014	(5,868)

Synopsis:

Groupe Videotron hopes to reach break-even with its Videoway technology in 1994. The technology provides a range of videotex services, video games and interactive broadcasts. As of February 1993, there were 202,000 Videoway subscribers. Videoway is a growing source of revenue for Videotron, and the revenue is not regulated by the CRTC. Revenue is currently derived from subscribers, but in the future is expected to come increasingly from advertisers and service providers. Videoway has helped the company reduce the churn rate among its basic cable service subscribers. In addition, through multiplexing, a technique whereby three movies are shown at the same time on the same channel, and an effective anti-pirating system, Videoway has been a contributing factor in the 29.2% increase in pay-television subscriptions in Quebec.

In June 1993, the CRTC announced new regulatory changes, but some of the required amendments to cable television rules may take months to complete. Developers of new specialty, pay and pay-per-view services won't get new channels on the air until December 1994. However, the cable television industry will see the elimination of its guaranteed return of 23% of net assets, and loses its automatic rate increases tied to the consumer price index. One of the principal objectives of the changes is to direct more money to Canadian programming. The CRTC has created a production fund that will generate up to $300-million over five years. The industry has been given the option of paying rebates to customers or contributing to the fund.

Groupe Videotron and Unitel Communications have an agreement that will expand their Quebec fibre-optic networks without spending a cent. The agreement is a swap of services, whereby each company gains access to the other's fibre-optic network.

The breakdown of 1992 revenues (operating income before inter segment items) by segment was: cable television, 53% (76%); broadcasting and related activities, 29% (16%); and other services, 18% (8%). Other services include Videoway and Telecash technology.

Relative strength to TSE300 / Price / Volume (in 1000's of board lots)

Rank (Profit/Revenue/Assets)		
158	147	108

Andre Chagnon
Chairman & C.E.O.

Serge Gouin
President & C.O.O.

Alain Michel
V.P., Finance & Treasurer

Address
2000, Rue Berri
Montreal
PQ
H2L 4V7
(514) 281-1232

Fax: (514) 985-8840
G0000447/G/11.2

For further company information, call Globe Information Services 1-800-268-9128 or (416)585-5345

HOLLINGER INC.

Exchanges	Price (Jun24'93)	13.75	Trailing P/E	6.98	Stock Symbol
TMV	Trailing Yield (%)	5.09	Trailing EPS	1.97	**HLG**

Period Ending	Dec92	Dec91	Dec90	Dec89	Dec88
Yearly Statistics					
Price-Close	10.63	11.63	11.38	12.50	14.50
Price-High	13.50	14.50	14.00	15.25	15.50
Price-Low	9.75	9.88	10.00	10.75	9.50
P/E-Close	9.32	38.75	47.40	11.91	23.02
Dividends per Share	0.70	0.40	0.70	0.20	0.20
Dividend Yield (%)	6.59	3.44	6.15	1.60	1.38
Sales per Share	15.50	13.84	14.05	13.45	12.42
EPS before extra. item	1.14	0.30	0.24	1.05	0.63
Cash Flow per Share	2.07	1.89	1.43	1.94	1.80
Book Value per Share	3.96	4.15	4.38	3.94	3.67
O/S Common Shares	54,892	55,353	55,158	55,093	54,968
Total Revenue	922,560	808,888	809,999	754,867	695,518
Income before extra.	73,971	31,427	34,201	73,087	40,173
Cash Flow	114,401	104,463	79,077	106,513	99,062
Debt/Equity	1.31	1.94	1.58	1.29	2.05
Return on Capital (%)	14.98	9.56	10.02	13.36	12.19
Ret. on Com. Equity (%)	28.27	7.01	5.87	27.53	17.00
% Change Profit	135.4	(8.1)	(53.2)	81.9	207.7
% Change Revenue	14.1	(0.1)	7.3	8.5	32.6
% Change Assets	(6.2)	8.8	19.1	9.0	18.0

Business:

HOLLINGER INC., through its subsidiaries, is engaged in the printing, publishing, and distribution of newspapers and magazines in Canada, the U.K., and the U.S. Publications include Saturday Night, The Daily Telegraph and Sunday Telegraph, and The Jerusalem Post in Israel. The company has an interest in Southam Inc.

Date	EPS	DPS	Tot Rev	Inc Bex
Mar 93	0.20	0.10	224,142	13,695
Dec 92	0.14	0.40	227,819	10,790
Sep 92	0.13	0.10	216,121	9,109
Jun 92	1.50	0.10	294,955	85,796
Mar 92	(0.63)	0.10	209,031	(31,724)
Dec 91	0.12	0.10	210,234	9,510
Sep 91	(0.21)	0.10	175,021	(7,748)
Jun 91	0.15	0.10	207,924	12,278

Preferred Div. Coverage	6.9	2.1	1.6
Total Div. Coverage	1.5	0.9	0.6
Interest Coverage	3.3	1.8	1.7
Current Ratio	1.2	0.4	0.7
Operating Margin	15.6	13.7	14.6
Asset Turnover	0.6	0.5	0.5
5 YEAR RATIOS (%)			
Return on Capital	12.0	10.4	7.9
Return on Com. Equity	17.1	12.3	7.8
Profit Growth	41.4	41.8	143.6
Revenue Growth	11.9	24.0	374.1
Asset Growth	9.3	14.2	20.5
BALANCE SHEET (000)			
Cash	70,523	42,122	97,733
Current Assets	220,427	193,673	308,078
Net Fixed Assets	715,130	753,948	176,419
Invest's & Advances	404,231	501,691	389,758
Total Assets	1,465,409	1,561,552	1,435,436
Short Term Debt	55,602	349,637	296,474
Current Liabilities	180,063	492,335	429,201
Long Term Debt	509,226	502,473	418,778
Total Liabilities	1,034,664	1,122,324	982,888
Total Equity	430,745	439,228	452,548
Total Liab. & Equity	1,465,409	1,561,552	1,435,436
CAPITAL (000)			
Total Debt	564,828	852,110	715,252
Preferred Equity	213,381	209,381	211,133
Common Equity	217,364	229,847	241,415

Synopsis:

Hollinger's U.K. subsidiary Telegraph plc was listed on the London Stock Exchange in 1992. The sale required Hollinger to sell approximately 26 million Telegraph shares and produced a capital gain of over $100-million. At the same time, at the request of the London Stock Exchange, both companies entered into a cooperation agreement, which divided the world for the purposes of acquiring and operating newspapers. North America and Israel are run by Hollinger and Europe and Australasia come under the Telegraph. Joint ventures are permitted between the companies. As part of this, Hollinger transferred shares of Trinity International Holdings plc to Telegraph; these shares were sold in February 1993.

In November 1992, Hollinger purchased from Torstar Corporation $259-million worth of common shares of Southam Inc., which represented 22.5% of Southam shares. An agreement reached between Hollinger and Southam allows Hollinger to have representation on the Southam board in proportion to its holdings. This was followed in March 1993 with the purchase by Power Corporation of Southam common shares. Power's purchase resulted in Hollinger and Power both holding approximately 18.7% in Southam, and both companies agreed on voting parity, notwithstanding the number of Southam shares held by each other. Hollinger offered a 50% participation in its Southam investment to Telegraph at one-half of Hollinger's acquisition cost. Telegraph's independent directors unanimously recommended the joint venture. In April 1993, Telegraph's minority shareholders approved the deal.

The Australian government gave Telegraph approval in April 1993 to increase its holdings in John Fairfax Group Pty Ltd., from 15% to 25%. In May 1993, Telegraph purchased additional options for $27.4-million, which on a fully diluted basis represents just over 21%, when exercised with other options by the end of the year.

The breakdown of 1992 sales (operating income) by country was: Canada, 17% (1%); the United States, 22% (19%); the United Kingdom, 59% (82%); and other, 2% (-2%).

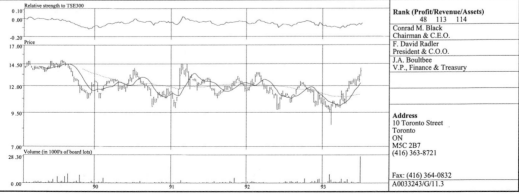

Rank (Profit/Revenue/Assets)
48   113   114

Conrad M. Black
Chairman & C.E.O.

F. David Radler
President & C.O.O.

J.A. Boultbee
V.P., Finance & Treasury

Address
10 Toronto Street
Toronto
ON
M5C 2B7
(416) 363-8721

Fax: (416) 364-0832
A0033243/G/11.3

MACLEAN HUNTER LIMITED

Exchanges	Price (Jun24'93)		11.50	Trailing P/E		23.47	Stock Symbol
TM	Trailing Yield (%)		2.17	Trailing EPS		0.49	**MHP**

Period Ending	Dec92	Dec91	Dec90	Dec89	Dec88
Yearly Statistics					
Price-Close	12.13	11.50	9.63	12.13	13.25
Price-High	13.00	11.75	12.38	14.25	14.88
Price-Low	11.00	9.13	7.88	11.50	9.88
P/E-Close	25.80	35.94	87.55	20.56	20.70
Dividends per Share	0.25	0.25	0.25	0.24	0.21
Dividend Yield (%)	2.06	2.17	2.60	2.00	1.59
Sales per Share	9.78	9.86	9.92	9.25	8.71
EPS before extra. item	0.47	0.32	0.11	0.59	0.64
Cash Flow per Share	1.20	1.09	1.04	1.31	1.16
Book Value per Share	4.80	3.87	3.80	3.97	2.96
O/S Common Shares	171,616	155,713	154,803	153,937	183,879
Total Revenue	1,645,400	1,538,400	1,539,400	1,438,700	1,317,100
Income before extra.	81,200	50,600	15,300	92,200	96,000
Cash Flow	199,900	170,300	160,900	202,000	173,300
Debt/Equity	0.56	0.99	1.19	1.18	1.48
Return on Capital (%)	14.25	12.05	9.27	14.41	19.76
Ret. on Com. Equity (%)	11.01	8.07	2.10	15.92	18.80
% Change Profit	60.5	230.7	(83.4)	(4.0)	13.2
% Change Revenue	7.0	(0.1)	7.0	9.2	16.3
% Change Assets	6.7	(4.2)	2.9	(2.1)	68.7
Preferred Div. Coverage	30.6	19.7	5.6		
Total Div. Coverage	1.8	1.2	0.4		
Interest Coverage	6.1	2.7	1.5		
Current Ratio	0.8	0.4	0.5		
Operating Margin	11.9	11.1	12.3		
Asset Turnover	0.9	0.9	0.8		
5 YEAR RATIOS (%)					
Return on Capital	13.9	16.9	19.9		
Return on Com. Equity	11.2	12.9	15.2		
Profit Growth	(0.9)	(6.2)	(24.0)		
Revenue Growth	7.7	9.2	9.3		
Asset Growth	11.7	12.7	15.6		
BALANCE SHEET (000)					
Cash	87,700	36,700	41,900		
Current Assets	438,300	302,200	352,200		
Net Fixed Assets	658,400	632,400	628,700		
Invest's & Advances	80,500	79,900	77,900		
Total Assets	1,871,900	1,753,600	1,830,900		
Short Term Debt	301,200	449,700	508,100		
Current Liabilities	556,400	675,300	719,500		
Long Term Debt	188,100	189,500	241,700		
Total Liabilities	1,006,600	1,110,000	1,200,400		
Total Equity	865,300	643,600	630,500		
Total Liab. & Equity	1,871,900	1,753,600	1,830,900		
CAPITAL (000)					
Total Debt	489,300	639,200	749,800		
Preferred Equity	40,800	40,800	42,300		
Common Equity	824,500	602,800	588,200		

Business:

MACLEAN HUNTER LTD. is a diversified communications company with operations in Canada, the United States and Europe. The company is involved in the publishing of periodicals and newspapers, business forms and commercial printing, radio broadcasting, cable television and communications services. The company owns a 62% interest in Toronto Sun Publishing Corp.

Date	EPS	DPS	Tot Rev	Inc Bex
Mar 93	0.10	0.06	419,800	17,900
Dec 92	0.15	0.06	454,300	26,100
Sep 92	0.10	0.06	397,900	17,000
Jun 92	0.14	0.06	407,900	24,500
Mar 92	0.08	0.06	386,000	13,600
Dec 91	0.12	0.06	413,000	19,300
Sep 91	0.07	0.06	367,600	10,300
Jun 91	0.08	0.06	381,900	13,000

Synopsis:

Maclean Hunter is going to be faced with technological competition in the future from Direct Broadcast Satellite services in North America. The company believes that this service will be successful in rural and non-cabled areas, but will have little impact on urban areas served by cable television systems. Regulatory changes in Canada and the United States are expected to have a greater impact.

In June 1993, the CRTC announced new regulatory changes. Some of the required amendments to cable television rules, may take months to complete and the developers of new specialty, pay and pay-per-view services being allowed won't get new channels on the air until December 1994. The cable industry will see the elimination of its guaranteed return of 23% of net assets, and loses its automatic rate increases tied to the consumer price index. The CRTC also created a Canadian programming production fund that will generate up to $300-million over five years, with money that will come from the cable industry, which has been given the option of paying rebates to customers or contributing to the fund.

The Cable Television Consumer Protection Act of 1992 was passed by the U.S. Congress on October 5, 1992. Major provisions of the law include enforcement of rate regulations, the right by franchising authorities and subscribers to file a complaint with the Federal Communications Commission (FCC) concerning unreasonable rates for programming services (excluding pay-per-view or pay services), and the right of broadcast stations to negotiate with cable operators for re-transmission consent rights, or invoke "must carry" rights to require carriage.

The broadcast division will have to contribute $2-million to the CTV Network as part of a new shareholders agreement.

1992 revenues (operating profit) by segment were: cable TV, 24% (72%); periodicals, 22% (8%); business forms and commercial printing, 25% (16%); newspapers, 20% (2%); broadcasting, 5% (3%); and communications services, 4% (-1%).

Relative strength to TSE300

Price

Volume (in 1000's of board lots)

Rank (Profit/Revenue/Assets)		
42	73	97

Donald G. Campbell
Chairman

Ronald W. Osborne
President & C.E.O.

J. Robert Furse
V.P., Finance & C.F.O.

Address
Maclean Hunter Bldg.
777 Bay Street
Toronto
ON
M5W 1A7
(416) 596-5000

Fax: (416) 593-3175
M0000203/G/11.3

MITEL CORPORATION

Exchanges	Price (Jun24'93)		5.12	Trailing P/E		nm		Stock Symbol
TMN	Trailing Yield (%)		0.00	Trailing EPS		(0.01)		**MLT**

Period Ending	Mar93	Mar92	Mar91	Mar90	Mar89
Yearly Statistics					
Price-Close	2.78	1.55	1.55	2.55	3.00
Price-High	2.98	2.24	2.83	4.25	3.80
Price-Low	1.35	0.70	0.98	2.20	2.55
P/E-Close	nm	nm	nm	28.33	14.29
Dividends per Share	0.00	0.00	0.00	0.00	0.00
Dividend Yield (%)	0.00	0.00	0.00	0.00	0.00
Sales per Share	5.28	5.14	5.46	5.41	5.47
EPS before extra. item	(0.01)	(0.12)	(1.41)	0.09	0.21
Cash Flow per Share	0.30	0.21	(0.62)	0.44	0.49
Book Value per Share	1.55	1.50	1.60	2.98	2.92
O/S Common Shares	104,478	79,019	79,019	79,019	78,951
Total Revenue	426,200	411,000	441,500	441,300	449,700
Income before extra.	2,600	(5,700)	(107,000)	12,100	22,200
Cash Flow	23,800	16,700	(49,300)	34,400	38,300
Debt/Equity	0.13	0.11	0.03	0.04	0.05
Return on Capital (%)	0.88	(1.78)	(44.37)	5.12	8.26
Ret. on Com. Equity (%)	(0.86)	(7.92)	(61.40)	3.00	7.23
% Change Profit	145.6	94.7	(984.3)	(45.5)	168.1
% Change Revenue	3.7	(6.9)	0.0	(1.9)	1.8
% Change Assets	5.0	(3.6)	(19.9)	(8.4)	(2.4)

Date	EPS	DPS	Tot Rev	Inc Bex
Mar 93	0.14	0.00	118,600	11,900
Dec 92	0.01	0.00	112,900	1,400
Sep 92	(0.06)	0.00	98,700	(3,700)
Jun 92	(0.10)	0.00	96,000	(7,000)
Mar 92	0.05	0.00	122,800	5,000
Dec 91	(0.06)	0.00	98,200	(3,400)
Sep 91	(0.04)	0.00	100,500	(1,900)
Jun 91	(0.08)	0.00	89,500	(5,400)

Preferred Div. Coverage	0.7	0.0	0.0
Total Div. Coverage	0.7	0.0	0.0
Interest Coverage	3.0	0.0	0.0
Current Ratio	2.4	1.6	1.5
Operating Margin	(0.2)	(2.0)	(26.7)
Asset Turnover	1.3	1.3	1.3
5 YEAR RATIOS (%)			
Return on Capital	(6.4)	(7.2)	(7.1)
Return on Com. Equity	(12.0)	(15.0)	(16.5)
Profit Growth	na	na	na
Revenue Growth	(0.8)	(3.4)	0.5
Asset Growth	(6.3)	(13.7)	(16.9)
BALANCE SHEET (000)			
Cash	82,800	49,900	61,400
Current Assets	232,700	206,700	209,200
Net Fixed Assets	78,700	90,100	103,300
Invest's & Advances	2,700	2,800	500
Total Assets	323,400	308,000	319,600
Short Term Debt	2,800	4,000	700
Current Liabilities	95,900	131,000	141,400
Long Term Debt	23,200	13,400	5,100
Total Liabilities	119,100	144,400	146,500
Total Equity	204,300	163,600	173,100
Total Liab. & Equity	323,400	308,000	319,600
CAPITAL (000)			
Total Debt	26,000	17,400	5,800
Preferred Equity	42,800	44,800	46,900
Common Equity	161,500	118,800	126,200

Business:

MITEL CORP. makes and markets telecommunications products. The company has operations in Canada, the U.S., the U.K. and Europe. Products include telephone switching systems, data communications systems, public switching products, and semiconductor devices. It serves markets in over 80 countries. Schroders & Partners Ltd. owns 51% of the company.

Synopsis:

Mitel Corporation's results for fiscal 1993 were attributed to a significant improvements in profit margins and expense reductions. The expense reductions were from downsizing and a federal government grant received in the fourth quarter, which partly offset research and development expenses. Mitel is cautious about these results and feels the fourth quarter results may not be sustained during the first half of fiscal 1994, due to the cyclical nature of its business.

Mitel received a $20-million loan from the Ontario government in December 1992, to help pay for the development of new products for a three-year period beginning March 25, 1992. A condition of the loan was a promise by Schroder Ventures to infuse an additional $10-million into Mitel.

In March 1993, Mitel completed a public offering of 25.2 million shares, including the full exercise of an underwriters' over allotment option, at $2.05 a share. Four entities advised by Schroder Ventures, an affiliate of Britain's Schroder Ventures plc, have agreed to purchase 4,878,049 of the common shares for $10-million. The Canadian affiliate of Schroder Ventures, Schroders & Partners Ltd., purchased 51% of Mitel from British Telecommunications plc in 1992.

In January 1993, Mitel announced 125 job cuts, which are being done to increase operating efficiency. This is the result of improved methods and procedures over the past several years and an increased focus on select programs.

1992 sales by product were: PBXs, 40%; other telecommunications, 51%; and semiconductors, 9%. Sales by geographic destination were: the United States, 41%; Canada, 11%; the United Kingdom, 25%; and Europe and other countries, 23%.

Relative strength to TSE300

Price

Volume (in 1000's of board lots)

Rank (Profit/Revenue/Assets)
843 183 268

Anthony F. Griffiths
Chairman, President & C.E.O.

John Millard
President & C.E.O.

James D. Ellis
Sr. V.P., Finance

Anthony P. Crisalli
C.O.O., Systems Division

Address
350 Legget Drive
P.O. Box 13089
Kanata
ON
K2K 1X3
(613) 592-2122

Fax: (613) 592-4784
M0004314/G/11.4

MOFFAT COMMUNICATIONS LIMITED

Exchanges	Price (Jun24'93)	17.87	Trailing P/E	6.72	Stock Symbol
T	Trailing Yield (%)	0.28	Trailing EPS	2.66	**MOF**

Period Ending	Aug92	Aug91	Aug90	Aug89	Aug88
Yearly Statistics					
Price-Close	15.50	11.63	10.50	25.50	20.00
Price-High	15.88	12.00	25.50	26.50	23.00
Price-Low	11.00	8.25	9.50	16.25	11.50
P/E-Close	29.25	55.36	23.33	28.65	19.23
Dividends per Share	0.00	0.11	0.42	0.42	0.42
Dividend Yield (%)	0.00	0.90	4.00	1.65	2.10
Sales per Share	11.94	10.77	15.58	14.51	13.96
EPS before extra. item	0.53	0.21	0.45	0.89	1.04
Cash Flow per Share	2.55	2.03	2.17	2.52	2.44
Book Value per Share	11.32	10.79	10.68	10.65	10.15
O/S Common Shares	4,862	4,862	4,862	4,862	4,850
Total Revenue	58,051	52,367	75,742	70,472	67,688
Income before extra.	2,577	1,021	2,188	4,328	5,045
Cash Flow	12,377	9,865	10,532	12,226	11,814
Debt/Equity	1.08	1.06	1.06	0.59	0.53
Return on Capital (%)	10.14	7.54	10.20	14.17	18.52
Ret. on Com. Equity (%)	4.80	1.96	4.22	8.57	10.55
% Change Profit	152.4	(53.3)	(49.4)	(14.2)	(1.8)
% Change Revenue	10.9	(30.9)	7.5	4.1	6.1
% Change Assets	6.3	0.9	28.2	9.8	10.2

Preferred Div. Coverage	np	np	np
Total Div. Coverage	na	2.0	1.1
Interest Coverage	2.1	1.3	1.8
Current Ratio	0.8	1.1	0.2
Operating Margin	22.1	15.8	13.7
Asset Turnover	0.4	0.4	0.6
5 YEAR RATIOS (%)			
Return on Capital	12.1	14.2	17.5
Return on Com. Equity	6.0	7.3	9.5
Profit Growth	(12.9)	(28.5)	(12.7)
Revenue Growth	(2.0)	(3.1)	6.3
Asset Growth	10.6	12.0	12.9
BALANCE SHEET (000)			
Cash	0	0	0
Current Assets	13,887	14,546	14,463
Net Fixed Assets	76,974	74,142	73,018
Invest's & Advances	824	1,006	1,050
Total Assets	135,525	127,550	126,451
Short Term Debt	8,411	5,693	50,218
Current Liabilities	17,483	13,626	58,698
Long Term Debt	51,132	50,114	5,000
Total Liabilities	80,489	75,091	74,501
Total Equity	55,036	52,459	51,950
Total Liab. & Equity	135,525	127,550	126,451
CAPITAL (000)			
Total Debt	59,543	55,807	55,218
Preferred Equity	0	0	0
Common Equity	55,036	52,459	51,950

Business:

MOFFAT COMMUNICATIONS LTD. is a communications company with television and cable television operations in Canada and the United States. It has cable operations in Winnipeg, Houston and Tampa. It owns the Winnipeg CTV affiliate. Moffat has a 10% interest in the Winnipeg Jets Hockey Club.

Date	EPS	DPS	Tot Rev	Inc Bex
Feb 93	0.31	0.05	17,419	1,507
Nov 92	2.01	0.00	17,099	9,750
Aug 92	0.06	0.00	(4,102)	292
May 92	0.28	0.00	21,633	1,361
Feb 92	0.02	0.00	14,443	98
Nov 91	0.17	0.00	14,077	826
Aug 91	0.04	0.00	(6,387)	195
May 91	0.05	0.00	19,781	241

Synopsis:

In June 1993, the CRTC announced new regulatory changes, but some of the required amendments to cable television rules, may take months to complete. Developers of new specialty, pay and pay-per-view services won't get new channels on the air until December 1994. However, the cable industry will see the elimination of its guaranteed return of 23% of net assets, and loses its automatic rate increases tied to the consumer price index. One of the CRTC's principal objectives is to direct more money to Canadian programming. The CRTC has created a production fund that will generate up to $300-million over five years. The money will come from the cable industry, which has been given the option of paying rebates to customers or contributing to the fund.

The Cable Television Consumer Protection Act of 1992 was passed by the United States Congress on October 5, 1992. Major provisions of the law include the enforcement by local authorities of rate regulations, the right by franchising authorities and subscribers to file a complaint with the Federal Communications Commission (FCC) concerning unreasonable rates for programming services (excluding pay-per-view or pay services), and the right of broadcast stations to negotiate with cable operators for retransmission consent rights. The impact on Moffat is not clear, because it is dependent upon bench-mark rates that are not available.

Moffat's subsidiary Winnipeg Videon acquired the cable television systems serving the communities of Fort Frances and Atikokan, Ontario, and Thompson, Flin Flon and Snow Lake, Manitoba, for $6.5-million in August 1992. Two of Moffat's U.S. cable television subsidiaries, Florida Satellite Network and Moffat Communications Corp., entered into a joint venture partnership with another operating in Pasco County, Florida, in October 1992. The partnership calls for the existing systems to be merged into a new system called Florida Satellite Network, Ltd.

Fiscal 1992 revenues (operating profit after depreciation) by country were: Canada, 74% (81%); and the U.S., 26% (19%).

Relative strength to TSE300

Price

Volume (in 1000's of board lots)

Rank (Profit/Revenue/Assets)
333   452   371

Randall L. Moffat
President & Chairman

William A. Davis
V.P., Finance & Treasurer

Address
CKY Building
Polo Park
Winnipeg
MB
R3G 0L7
(204) 788-3440

Fax: (204) 956-2710
M0004425/G/11.2

NORTHERN TELECOM LIMITED

Exchanges	Price (Jun24'93)	47.12	Trailing P/E	22.88	Stock Symbol
TMVN	Trailing Yield (%)	0.74	Trailing EPS	2.06	**NTL**

Period Ending	Dec92	Dec91	Dec90	Dec89	Dec88
Yearly Statistics	US	US	US	US	US
Price-Close	55.00	52.00	32.50	26.88	19.75
Price-High	58.50	52.50	34.63	27.88	25.25
Price-Low	37.88	30.25	25.63	16.88	18.63
P/E-Close	20.87	22.37	15.47	15.46	23.02
Dividends per Share	0.34	0.32	0.30	0.28	0.26
Dividend Yield (%)	0.62	0.62	0.92	1.04	1.32
Sales per Share	34.03	33.45	27.91	25.34	22.76
EPS before extra. item	2.17	2.03	1.80	1.47	0.70
Cash Flow per Share	4.07	4.13	3.52	2.60	2.02
Book Value per Share	15.97	14.97	13.24	11.14	10.16
O/S Common Shares	248,414	245,619	243,516	241,885	239,253
Total Revenue	8,521,100	8,284,400	6,835,400	6,191,900	5,519,500
Income before extra.	548,300	514,900	460,200	376,500	183,200
Cash Flow	1,006,900	1,011,200	853,500	627,400	480,500
Debt/Equity	0.47	0.53	0.38	0.50	0.51
Return on Capital (%)	16.15	17.30	15.20	14.48	8.09
Ret. on Com. Equity (%)	14.04	14.39	14.73	13.82	6.95
% Change Profit	6.5	11.9	22.2	105.5	(47.2)
% Change Revenue	2.9	21.2	10.4	12.2	11.2
% Change Assets	(1.6)	39.3	8.4	7.3	17.4

Preferred Div. Coverage	46.1	28.0	19.0
Total Div. Coverage	5.7	5.3	4.7
Interest Coverage	4.5	4.2	8.7
Current Ratio	1.2	1.0	1.6
Operating Margin	10.9	10.7	9.8
Asset Turnover	0.9	0.9	1.0
5 YEAR RATIOS (%)			
Return on Capital	14.2	14.4	14.9
Return on Com. Equity	12.8	13.1	13.5
Profit Growth	9.5	10.4	8.9
Revenue Growth	11.3	13.1	9.5
Asset Growth	13.3	19.1	14.3
BALANCE SHEET (000)			
Cash	89,900	182,600	105,000
Current Assets	4,155,100	3,779,200	3,224,000
Net Fixed Assets	1,929,600	1,986,600	1,552,000
Invest's & Advances	1,148,800	1,135,200	1,529,500
Total Assets	9,379,300	9,534,200	6,842,300
Short Term Debt	794,500	914,000	504,800
Current Liabilities	3,409,300	3,606,900	1,987,300
Long Term Debt	1,146,800	1,161,400	797,700
Total Liabilities	5,257,900	5,615,400	3,374,800
Total Equity	4,121,400	3,918,800	3,467,500
Total Liab. & Equity	9,379,300	9,534,200	6,842,300
CAPITAL (000)			
Total Debt	1,941,300	2,075,400	1,302,500
Preferred Equity	154,100	243,100	243,100
Common Equity	3,967,300	3,675,700	3,224,400

Business:

NORTHERN TELECOM LTD. is a global supplier of fully digital telecommunications systems. The company has a presence in more than 90 countries and operates 52 manufacturing facilities worldwide. It conducts research principally through its subsidiary Bell-Northern Research Ltd. in Canada, the United States, the United Kingdom and Japan. BCE Inc. is the company's major shareholder.

Date		EPS	DPS	Tot Rev	Inc Bex
Mar 93	US	0.30	0.09	1,942,100	75,900
Dec 92	US	1.02	0.09	2,592,200	255,600
Sep 92	US	0.46	0.09	2,038,900	116,200
Jun 92	US	0.28	0.08	1,986,600	72,300
Mar 92	US	0.41	0.08	1,903,400	104,200
Dec 91	US	0.83	0.08	2,355,600	208,000
Sep 91	US	0.42	0.08	1,921,400	106,700
Jun 91	US	0.42	0.08	2,130,900	106,500

Synopsis:

Northern Telecom reported in its first quarter that it is not immune to the global recession and that there is mounting pressure on prices and profit margins. The company believes its challenge is to keep focused on future growth. The building of markets outside North America will receive special attention as they become an increasingly important and growing part of Northern's revenue base. Northern's goal is to increase its global market share from 7.5% to 12% by 1997. Most of the international growth is expected to come from partnerships with companies located in the markets Northern wants to develop. Current partnerships include Matra Communications in France, Netas in Turkey and China Tong Guang Electronics Corp. in China.

Northern's strategy for long-term growth also requires its continued investment in research and development. This is to stimulate the evolution of its core technologies and to ensure that new products are delivered to market in a timely fashion, to capture market share.

Northern's contracts in early 1993 include: a substantial portion of a $650-million (U.S.) contract from Pacific Bell of San Francisco to install equipment for a high-speed, fibre-optic network; two additional contracts in Russia for Synchronous Digital Hierarchy transmission equipment; and a contract to design and install the nation-wide voice and data network for ENERGIS of the U.K.

Revenues by geographical segment in 1992 (% change from 1991) were: United States, 51% (up 4%); Canada, 23% (up 1%); Europe (including Africa, C.I.S. and the Middle East), 15% (down 10%); and other international, 11% (up 30%). 1992 revenues by product line (% change over 1991) were: central office switching, 50% (down 1%); business communications systems and terminals, 25% (up 11%); transmission, 11% (up 5%); cable and outside plant, 8% (up 21%); and other, 6% (down 24%). Research and development expenses in 1992 were $931-million or 11% of total revenues.

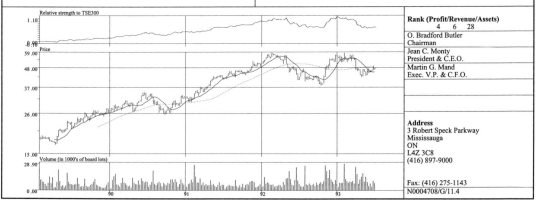

Rank (Profit/Revenue/Assets)
4   6   28

O. Bradford Butler
Chairman

Jean C. Monty
President & C.E.O.

Martin G. Mand
Exec. V.P. & C.F.O.

Address
3 Robert Speck Parkway
Mississauga
ON
L4Z 3C8
(416) 897-9000

Fax: (416) 275-1143
N0004708/G/11.4

QUEBECOR INC.

Exchanges	Price (Jun24'93)	20.25	Trailing P/E	12.27	Stock Symbol
TMA	Trailing Yield (%)	0.74	Trailing EPS	1.65	**QBR.A**

Period Ending	Dec92	Dec91	Dec90	Dec89	Sep88
Yearly Statistics					
Price-Close	16.63	10.87	7.62	7.44	10.00
Price-High	17.00	10.87	7.75	10.81	10.44
Price-Low	10.50	7.62	5.50	7.19	6.25
P/E-Close	11.63	27.89	4.61	18.83	11.30
Dividends per Share	0.15	0.13	0.12	0.12	0.10
Dividend Yield (%)	0.90	1.20	1.57	1.61	1.00
Sales per Share	41.38	49.34	51.63	37.24	34.58
EPS before extra. item	1.43	0.39	1.65	0.39	0.88
Cash Flow per Share	3.92	4.32	4.92	4.30	5.50
Book Value per Share	10.01	7.76	7.22	5.76	4.71
O/S Common Shares	64,282	53,581	47,133	47,140	37,138
Total Revenue	2,612,196	2,390,312	2,521,196	1,778,780	1,304,608
Income before extra.	87,339	18,516	77,945	18,542	32,887
Cash Flow	240,254	207,668	232,000	202,741	204,387
Debt/Equity	1.12	2.88	3.45	2.72	3.17
Return on Capital (%)	16.33	8.97	21.59	17.12	19.31
Ret. on Com. Equity (%)	16.49	4.90	25.47	8.31	20.28
% Change Profit	371.7	(76.2)	320.4	(43.6)	41.5
% Change Revenue	9.3	(5.2)	41.7	36.3	89.7
% Change Assets	(0.5)	(3.3)	45.1	30.4	5.7

Preferred Div. Coverage	np	np	np
Total Div. Coverage	9.5	2.8	13.8
Interest Coverage	2.9	1.4	2.3
Current Ratio	1.6	1.7	2.2
Operating Margin	8.0	7.0	10.3
Asset Turnover	1.0	0.9	0.9
5 YEAR RATIOS (%)			
Return on Capital	16.7	16.2	18.6
Return on Com. Equity	15.1	15.7	18.6
Profit Growth	30.3	2.8	42.6
Revenue Growth	30.5	39.9	49.0
Asset Growth	14.0	59.8	67.2
BALANCE SHEET (000)			
Cash	51,341	77,792	182,326
Current Assets	669,320	704,889	832,229
Net Fixed Assets	1,593,377	1,511,419	1,480,903
Invest's & Advances	15,147	15,497	42,496
Total Assets	2,623,869	2,636,261	2,725,884
Short Term Debt	48,593	90,512	51,642
Current Liabilities	413,699	406,719	378,866
Long Term Debt	671,624	1,108,927	1,123,926
Total Liabilities	1,980,260	2,220,368	2,385,415
Total Equity	643,609	415,893	340,469
Total Liab. & Equity	2,623,869	2,636,261	2,725,884
CAPITAL (000)			
Total Debt	720,217	1,199,439	1,175,568
Preferred Equity	0	0	0
Common Equity	643,609	415,893	340,469

Business:

QUEBECOR INC. is a publishing and distribution, printing, and forest products company. It publishes four daily newspapers including Le Journal de Montreal. It also publishes weekly newspapers in Quebec, New Brunswick, and Manitoba, and several French language magaines. It has commercial printing plants across North America, and owns an interest in Donohue Inc. of Quebec City, a forest products company.

Date	EPS	DPS	Tot Rev	Inc Bex
Mar 93	0.24	0.00	671,492	15,407
Dec 92	0.01	0.08	697,302	2,015
Sep 92	0.27	0.00	623,404	16,102
Jun 92	1.13	0.07	688,041	64,019
Mar 92	0.08	0.00	594,863	5,203
Dec 91	0.03	0.07	632,069	1,318
Sep 91	0.13	0.00	572,908	6,079
Jun 91	0.18	0.07	593,077	8,778

Synopsis:

Quebecor Inc.'s most important and successful event in 1992 was the initial public offering by its printing division Quebecor Printing Inc. The offering raised $236.3-million that was used to reduce debt. The strategy for Quebecor Printing includes: the diversification and vertical integration of its services; the strategic positioning of its manufacturing locations; emphasis on its state-of-the-art equipment; and quality and on going investment activity.

In 1992, The Quebecor Group continued to pursue its goal of expanding its publishing sector outside Quebec. The group acquired three weekly newspapers in Manitoba during the year.

Quebecor's forest products subsidiary, Donohue Inc., pursued its objectives in 1992 through the combined effort of its newsprint, market pulp and lumber sectors. This resulted in a general increase in productivity and lower production costs. Donohue also made major investments in the environment through pollution control equipment, reforestation programs and a new de-inking plant. A share swap of Donohue shares in November 1992 resulted in Quebecor acquiring the Mirror Group Newspapers plc's stake in Donohue. After the restructuring Quebecor will have a 65% interest in Donohue.

1992 revenues before inter-segment eliminations (operating income) by segment were: publishing and distribution, 13% (16%); printing, 67% (83%); and forest products, 20% (1%). 1992 revenues (operating income) by country were: Canada, 56% (44%); and the United States, 44% (56%). About 35% of Canadian revenues are exports to the United States, Europe, and other countries.

Relative strength to TSE300
Price
Volume (in 1000's of board lots)

Rank (Profit/Revenue/Assets)
40   51   75

Pierre Peladeau
Chairman, President & C.E.O.

Francois R. Roy
V.P., Finance & Treasurer

Address
612, Rue St-Jacques
Montreal
PQ
H3C 4M8
(514) 877-9777

Q0001162/G/11.3

QUEBECOR PRINTING INC.

Exchanges	Price (Jun24'93)	26.00	Trailing P/E	22.22	Stock Symbol
TM	Trailing Yield (%)	0.00	Trailing EPS	1.17	**IQI**

Period Ending	Dec92	Dec91	Dec90	Dec89
Yearly Statistics	US	US	US	
Price-Close	21.88	n t	n t	n t
Price-High	22.13	n t	n t	n t
Price-Low	15.75	n t	n t	n t
P/E-Close	16.67	n t	n t	n t
Dividends per Share	0.24	0.14	0.17	0.10
Dividend Yield (%)	1.10	n t	n t	n t
Sales per Share	28.75	34.70	33.03	26.35
EPS before extra. item	1.08	0.82	0.57	0.30
Cash Flow per Share	3.11	2.96	2.47	1.67
Book Value per Share	8.69	6.09	5.33	3.74
O/S Common Shares	54,965	39,250	38,750	28,750
Total Revenue	1,444,426	1,386,852	1,264,937	757,687
Income before extra.	54,491	33,223	21,643	8,510
Cash Flow	156,206	118,206	94,510	48,073
Debt/Equity	0.79	2.51	3.07	2.77
Return on Capital (%)	15.11	13.28	16.83	na
Ret. on Com. Equity (%)	15.14	14.67	14.56	na
% Change Profit	64.0	53.5	196.9	na
% Change Revenue	4.2	9.6	94.9	na
% Change Assets	3.6	(1.2)	151.1	na

Preferred Div. Coverage	np	61.0	na
Total Div. Coverage	4.4	5.6	3.4
Interest Coverage	3.8	2.1	1.6
Current Ratio	1.4	1.5	1.8
Operating Margin	9.8	9.0	8.8
Asset Turnover	1.2	1.2	1.1

5 YEAR RATIOS (%)			
Return on Capital	na	na	na
Return on Com. Equity	na	na	na
Profit Growth	na	na	na
Revenue Growth	na	na	na
Asset Growth	na	na	na

BALANCE SHEET (000)			
Cash	0	0	0
Current Assets	290,419	286,083	297,528
Net Fixed Assets	771,772	729,097	730,812
Invest's & Advances	0	0	0
Total Assets	1,219,512	1,177,170	1,192,026
Short Term Debt	7,232	20,264	8,865
Current Liabilities	203,908	189,222	168,102
Long Term Debt	369,184	592,486	655,999
Total Liabilities	742,067	933,355	975,355
Total Equity	477,445	243,815	216,671
Total Liab. & Equity	1,219,512	1,177,170	1,192,026

CAPITAL (000)			
Total Debt	376,416	612,750	664,864
Preferred Equity	0	4,621	10,269
Common Equity	477,445	239,194	206,402

Business:

QUEBECOR PRINTING INC. offers a range of printed products and distribution in the industry. It offers printing, typesetting, colour separation, computerized page composition, stripping and binding. It is a subsidiary of Quebecor Inc.

Date		EPS	DPS	Tot Rev	Inc Bex
Mar 93	US	0.27	0.00	377,900	14,800
Dec 92	US	0.34	0.00	390,284	18,475
Sep 92	US	0.32	0.00	360,199	16,866
Jun 92	US	0.24	0.00	340,898	11,937
Mar 92	US	0.18	0.00	353,045	7,213
Dec 91	US	0.30	0.00	389,291	12,233
Sep 91	US	0.29	0.00	346,361	11,385
Jun 91	US	0.18	0.00	334,204	7,284

Synopsis:

In 1992, the initial public offering of Quebecor Printing Inc. was made by its parent Quebecor Inc. This offering raised $236.3-million for Quebecor, which was used to reduce debt. Quebecor Printing was established in 1989. Its strategy is: to be prepared for North American free trade by strengthening its Canadian base and expanding into the U.S. and Mexico; to build a diverse product within its core business; to provide earnings stability; to become a major supplier in every market its services; to ensure market strength and competitiveness; to become a low-cost supplier in all its key markets by optimizing the benefits of its economies of scale, asset utilization and technology transfer; and to be a customer-driven company.

Quebecor Printing will buy Sears Canada's 44% stake in catalogue printer Photo Engravers and Electrotypers Ltd. (PE&E) for $29-million as part of a takeover bid for PE&E launched in April 1993. The offer is $37.875 each for all 767,000 outstanding shares of Toronto-based PE&E. A special committee of PE&E's board was established to recommend acceptance of the $37.875 a share bid. Quebecor Printing feels PE&E can generate more profit as part of its group of plants than as a one plant, stand-alone entity. Other acquisitions during 1992 and early 1993 include: Haughton Graphics Inc.; Arcata Graphics San Jose; Nadco Directory Management Corporation; and Graphique-Couler Ltee. The company also divided its U.S. operations into two parts: Quebecor Book Printing; and Quebecor Printing (USA) Corp., which will oversee the commercial printing operations in the United States.

1992 revenues (operating income) by country were: Canada, 36% (32%); United States, 64% (68%). The company has also established operations in Mexico. About 18% of Canadian revenues are exports to the United States and other countries. The breakdown of revenue in 1992 by type was: inserts and circulars, 34.8%; magazines, 25.8%; catalogues, 10.8%; directories, 6.6%; books, 6.3%; cheques, bonds and bank notes, 6.2%; specialty printing, 5.5%; newspapers, 1.3%; and related services, 2.7%.

Relative strength to TSE300

Price

Volume (in 1000's of board lots)

Rank (Profit/Revenue/Assets)		
52	69	110

Jean Neveu
Chairman & C.E.O.

Charles G. Cavell
President & C.O.O.

Gaetan Lussier
V.P. Finance

Address
612, St-Jacques Ouest
Montreal
PQ
H3C 4M8
(514) 954-0101

01003273/G/11.3

ROGERS CANTEL MOBILE COMMUNICATIONS INC.

Exchanges	Price (Jun24'93)		28.37	Trailing P/E		nm	Stock Symbol
TMVZQ	Trailing Yield (%)		0.00	Trailing EPS		(2.06)	**RCM.B**

Period Ending	Dec92	Dec91	Dec90	Aug90	Aug89
Yearly Statistics			4M		
Price-Close	24.50	26.38	n t	n t	n t
Price-High	30.00	26.38	n t	n t	n t
Price-Low	19.75	18.13	n t	n t	n t
P/E-Close	nm	nm	n t	n t	n t
Dividends per Share	0.00	0.00	0.00	0.00	0.00
Dividend Yield (%)	0.00	0.00	0.00	0.00	0.00
Sales per Share	5.26	4.24	3.99	3.05	1.84
EPS before extra. item	(1.86)	(0.45)	(0.46)	(1.06)	(0.36)
Cash Flow per Share	0.41	0.28	(0.40)	(0.42)	(0.04)
Book Value per Share	0.96	2.81	1.77	0.06	0.09
O/S Common Shares	93,894	93,894	93,851	93,851	93,851
Total Revenue	494,797	439,764	125,956	286,279	172,358
Income before extra.	(174,279)	(42,022)	(43,152)	(99,421)	(33,589)
Cash Flow	38,523	25,991	(12,380)	(39,522)	(3,969)
Debt/Equity	10.51	2.58	3.76	121.91	44.14
Return on Capital (%)	(9.07)	3.11	(1.81)	(3.86)	na
Ret. on Com. Equity (%)	(98.48)	(19.55)	(150.93)	(1,448.23)	na
% Change Profit	(314.7)	67.5	(30.2)	(196.0)	na
% Change Revenue	12.5	16.4	32.0	66.1	na
% Change Assets	13.4	18.0	11.3	78.1	na

Business:

ROGERS CANTEL MOBILE COMMUNICATIONS INC. through its subsidiaries Rogers Cantel Mobile Inc. and Rogers Cantel Inc., operates the largest integrated cellular telephone network in Canada and is the only company authorized to provide cellular telephone service on a nation-wide basis. Cantel also operates retail service centres, a national paging system, and a mobile data communications service.

Date	EPS	DPS	Tot Rev	Inc Bex
Mar 93	(0.36)	0.00	130,712	(34,261)
Dec 92	(0.65)	0.00	137,384	(60,509)
Sep 92	(0.24)	0.00	130,924	(22,439)
Jun 92	(0.81)	0.00	126,267	(76,280)
Mar 92	(0.16)	0.00	112,881	(15,051)
Dec 91	0.05	0.00	112,344	4,854
Sep 91	(0.06)	0.00	115,817	(5,307)
Jun 91	(0.07)	0.00	110,087	(6,318)

	Dec92	Dec91	Dec90
Preferred Div. Coverage	np	np	np
Total Div. Coverage	na	na	na
Interest Coverage	0.0	0.4	0.0
Current Ratio	0.7	0.6	0.6
Operating Margin	(4.6)	(3.7)	(4.5)
Asset Turnover	0.4	0.4	0.4
5 YEAR RATIOS (%)			
Return on Capital	na	na	na
Return on Com. Equity	na	na	na
Profit Growth	na	na	na
Revenue Growth	na	na	na
Asset Growth	na	na	na
BALANCE SHEET (000)			
Cash	34,901	0	0
Current Assets	117,976	84,306	78,976
Net Fixed Assets	930,034	826,800	774,665
Invest's & Advances	11,420	5,901	1,053
Total Assets	1,198,804	1,056,994	895,951
Short Term Debt	6,710	24,317	20,221
Current Liabilities	163,214	131,736	126,641
Long Term Debt	937,122	658,168	603,414
Total Liabilities	1,108,967	792,878	730,055
Total Equity	89,837	264,116	165,896
Total Liab. & Equity	1,198,804	1,056,994	895,951
CAPITAL (000)			
Total Debt	943,832	682,485	623,635
Preferred Equity	0	0	0
Common Equity	89,837	264,116	165,896

Synopsis:

During 1992, Rogers Cantel began to add digital transmission capacity coast-to-coast in its network. The company believes the digital cellular technology will reduce capital costs, due to reduced purchases of radio channels and reduced requirements to split existing cells. In 1992, the company joined with McCaw and other U.S. cellular companies to form the North American Cellular Network. This service allows callers to reach Cantel subscribers anywhere in the network, by using the subscriber's Cantel number.

In June 1992, the CRTC opened up the monopoly public switched long distance market to competition. Rogers Cantel believes as wireline long distance rates drop it is likely that cellular long distance rates will drop by corresponding amounts. This means that even with expected increases in long distance usage, long distance revenue per subscriber will likely continue to drop in the future.

In December 1992, Rogers Cantel was awarded one of four national licences to operate a public digital cordless telephone service (DCT). The company is currently reassessing its DCT plan, given the terms and conditions of the licence, and the plans of the other licensees. The company expects the cost of DCT development will be approximately $25-million over the next three years. Extensive development of DCT service is not expected until 1994, and the company does not expect it to be a significant source of revenues or expenses in the near future.

Rogers Cantel believes one of its challenges for 1993 will be to continue to improve operating efficiency. The company recently began development of a new customer information and billing system. Another challenge in 1993 and ensuing years will be to translate high growth into steadily improving financial performance.

As at March 1993, cellular subscribers totaled 483,265 and paging service subscribers totaled 96,688. In 1992 of revenues by business segment were: cellular, 77%; Cantel service centres, 19%; and paging and other, 4%.

Rank (Profit/Revenue/Assets)
982   156   136

George A. Fierheller
Chairman & C.E.O.
James F. Sward
President & C.O.O
William W. Linton
V.P., Finance & C.F.O.

Address
10 York Mills Road
North York
ON
M2P 2C9
(416) 229-1400

01003181/G/11.4

ROGERS COMMUNICATIONS INC.

Exchanges	Price (Jun24'93)	19.00	Trailing P/E	nm	Stock Symbol
TMZV	Trailing Yield (%)	0.00	Trailing EPS	(1.59)	**RCI.B**

Period Ending	Dec92	Dec91	Dec90	Aug89	Aug88
Yearly Statistics			16M		
Price-Close	14.50	14.00	5.88	16.80	7.50
Price-High	15.13	14.38	16.86	19.07	8.25
Price-Low	11.75	5.86	5.25	7.54	2.07
P/E-Close	nm	nm	nm	nm	nm
Dividends per Share	0.00	0.00	0.00	0.00	0.00
Dividend Yield (%)	0.00	0.00	0.00	0.00	0.00
Sales per Share	9.35	7.64	7.30	5.88	2.56
EPS before extra. item	(1.30)	(0.76)	(1.51)	(0.49)	(0.11)
Cash Flow per Share	0.91	0.77	0.68	1.14	0.62
Book Value per Share	1.07	0.93	2.28	4.10	(1.19)
O/S Common Shares	265,331	242,322	128,232	103,403	193,021
Total Revenue	1,199,497	1,115,153	1,130,779	625,945	366,462
Income before extra.	(180,317)	(59,994)	(113,122)	(25,839)	1,452
Cash Flow	111,240	99,890	105,534	116,763	86,530
Debt/Equity	3.91	2.96	2.38	1.02	na
Return on Capital (%)	2.90	7.35	3.46	7.14	12.92
Ret. on Com. Equity (%)	(79.00)	(36.03)	(35.14)	(51.67)	na
% Change Profit	(200.6)	29.3	(228.3)	(1,879.5)	117.2
% Change Revenue	7.6	31.5	35.5	70.8	32.5
% Change Assets	22.5	4.3	60.3	80.0	70.3
Preferred Div. Coverage	0.0	0.0	0.0		
Total Div. Coverage	0.0	0.0	0.0		
Interest Coverage	0.3	0.9	0.5		
Current Ratio	1.7	0.6	0.5		
Operating Margin	6.5	8.1	8.7		
Asset Turnover	0.3	0.3	0.3		
5 YEAR RATIOS (%)					
Return on Capital	6.8	7.7	7.4		
Return on Com. Equity	na	na	na		
Profit Growth	na	na	na		
Revenue Growth	34.0	21.7	18.7		
Asset Growth	44.3	24.7	27.3		
BALANCE SHEET (000)					
Cash	419,840	0	0		
Current Assets	613,073	169,264	140,900		
Net Fixed Assets	1,835,005	1,646,511	1,510,014		
Invest's & Advances	520,946	450,501	556,205		
Total Assets	4,100,755	3,348,749	3,210,741		
Short Term Debt	0	39,599	49,965		
Current Liabilities	364,027	295,468	284,297		
Long Term Debt	2,696,286	2,000,832	1,871,795		
Total Liabilities	3,410,629	2,659,826	2,404,154		
Total Equity	690,126	688,923	806,587		
Total Liab. & Equity	4,100,755	3,348,749	3,210,741		
CAPITAL (000)					
Total Debt	2,696,286	2,040,431	1,921,760		
Preferred Equity	406,723	463,533	514,860		
Common Equity	283,403	225,390	291,727		

Business:

ROGERS COMMUNICATIONS has operations in cable television, broadcasting, mobile communications and telecommunications. Rogers operates cable systems across Canada. It owns radio stations and a TV station in Toronto, in B.C. and Alberta. It has interests in the YTV and CHSN cable channels. It owns 40% of Unitel Communications Inc. Rogers Cantel Mobile Communications operates a celluar phone network.

Date	EPS	DPS	Tot Rev	Inc Bex
Mar 93	0.25	0.00	303,031	44,393
Dec 92	(1.02)	0.00	907,726	(142,798)
Sep 92	(0.28)	0.00	291,771	(37,519)
Jun 92	(0.54)	0.00	288,065	(76,515)
Mar 92	(0.01)	0.00	314,609	3,904
Dec 91	(0.34)	0.00	253,276	(37,753)
Sep 91	0.14	0.00	344,876	27,218
Jun 91	(0.21)	0.00	258,256	(16,402)

Synopsis:

Rogers Cablesystems is planning the implementation of video-on-demand with digital compression technology. The technology will enable a cable system carrying 50 channels to offer up to 300 channels. The technology is in response to high-powered satellites that deliver programming directly to viewers. Rogers is also attempting to take the 96% owned Canadian Home Shopping Network (CHSN) private. The offer for CHSN is 87.5 cents a share, or minority shareholders can choose Rogers class B non-voting shares in lieu of cash for every $19.25 of CHSN shares. The choice must be made before September 1, 1993.

In June 1993, the CRTC announced new regulatory changes, but some of the required amendments to cable television rules, may take months to complete, and any new specialty, pay and pay-per-view services allowed won't get new channels on the air until December 1994. The cable television industry will see the elimination of its guaranteed return of 23% of net assets, and loses its automatic rate increases tied to the consumer price index. One of the principal objectives is to direct more money to Canadian programming. The CRTC has created a production fund that will generate up to $300-million over five years. The money will come from the cable industry, which has been given the option of paying rebates to customers or contributing to the fund.

The Wireless Communications division added nearly 114,000 cellular subscribers to bring the 1992 year-end total to 460,000. It also took steps towards a fully digital network and began adding digital transmission capacity to its national network. In December 1992, Rogers Cantel was awarded a national licence to operate a public digital cordless telephone service, which allows customers to use cordless handsets with conventional service and allows access to a new public cordless telephone network.

1992 revenue by segment was: cable television, 49%; mobile communications, 43%; and broadcasting, 8%.

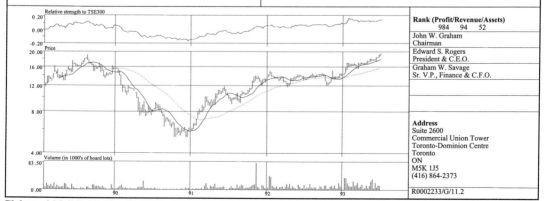

Rank (Profit/Revenue/Assets)		
984	94	52

John W. Graham
Chairman

Edward S. Rogers
President & C.E.O.

Graham W. Savage
Sr. V.P., Finance & C.F.O.

Address
Suite 2600
Commercial Union Tower
Toronto-Dominion Centre
Toronto
ON
M5K 1J5
(416) 864-2373

R0002233/G/11.2

SHAW COMMUNICATIONS INC.

Exchanges	Price (Jun24'93)	19.12	Trailing P/E	22.93	Stock Symbol
TZ	Trailing Yield (%)	0.53	Trailing EPS	0.83	**SCL.B**

Period Ending	Aug92	Aug91	Aug90	Aug89	Aug88
Yearly Statistics					
Price-Close	16.75	13.00	8.75	13.50	9.75
Price-High	18.50	14.25	13.50	14.75	10.25
Price-Low	12.25	8.00	8.38	8.75	5.88
P/E-Close	20.43	20.00	7.96	31.40	22.16
Dividends per Share	0.09	0.10	0.10	0.10	0.10
Dividend Yield (%)	0.51	0.77	1.14	0.74	1.03
Sales per Share	7.61	6.60	5.09	3.83	2.94
EPS before extra. item	0.82	0.65	1.10	0.43	0.44
Cash Flow per Share	1.99	1.67	1.30	1.10	0.90
Book Value per Share	7.75	5.20	4.72	4.04	3.89
O/S Common Shares	25,576	21,186	21,615	22,641	22,641
Total Revenue	166,088	143,959	134,740	87,485	69,052
Income before extra.	18,754	15,086	24,853	9,930	10,124
Cash Flow	42,912	35,414	28,522	25,066	20,489
Debt/Equity	0.65	1.32	1.18	1.33	0.64
Return on Capital (%)	16.63	17.14	22.93	13.65	18.73
Ret. on Com. Equity (%)	11.49	12.76	24.80	10.73	12.07
% Change Profit	24.3	(39.3)	150.3	(1.9)	25.9
% Change Revenue	15.4	6.8	54.0	26.7	27.4
% Change Assets	18.0	25.1	7.2	51.1	29.7
Preferred Div. Coverage	18.2	12.5	36.9		
Total Div. Coverage	5.7	4.7	9.0		
Interest Coverage	2.9	2.7	3.7		
Current Ratio	0.8	0.2	1.1		
Operating Margin	32.0	31.4	27.5		
Asset Turnover	0.4	0.4	0.4		
5 YEAR RATIOS (%)					
Return on Capital	17.8	18.1	18.3		
Return on Com. Equity	14.4	14.2	13.4		
Profit Growth	18.5	29.2	63.0		
Revenue Growth	25.0	24.9	26.6		
Asset Growth	25.3	25.6	26.2		
BALANCE SHEET (000)					
Cash	47,289	0	36,587		
Current Assets	56,104	7,998	42,761		
Net Fixed Assets	168,356	163,072	138,818		
Invest's & Advances	8,357	787	4,866		
Total Assets	409,351	346,930	277,298		
Short Term Debt	47,515	19,051	13,616		
Current Liabilities	73,946	43,860	37,688		
Long Term Debt	89,125	154,499	115,116		
Total Liabilities	198,800	215,860	168,412		
Total Equity	210,551	131,070	108,886		
Total Liab. & Equity	409,351	346,930	277,298		
CAPITAL (000)					
Total Debt	136,640	173,550	128,732		
Preferred Equity	12,385	20,813	6,797		
Common Equity	198,166	110,257	102,089		

Business:

SHAW COMMUNICATIONS INC. currently operates cable television systems in British Columbia, Alberta, Saskatchewan, Manitoba, Ontario and Nova Scotia, serving approximately 890,000 subscribers. Shaw operates two radio stations in B.C., four in Alberta, and two in Ontario.

Date	EPS	DPS	Tot Rev	Inc Bex
Feb 93	0.20	0.06	52,409	5,298
Nov 92	0.22	0.00	45,876	5,822
Aug 92	0.22	0.04	43,147	5,327
May 92	0.19	0.00	42,043	4,285
Feb 92	0.23	0.05	40,629	5,138
Nov 91	0.17	0.00	40,299	4,004
Aug 91	0.16	0.05	39,317	3,538
May 91	0.13	0.00	37,091	3,189

Synopsis:

The pending launch of high powered direct broadcast satellites within the next two years represents a potentially significant threat to the Canadian broadcasting systems. This and the new regulations will require Shaw Cablesystems and the industry to develop new technology, like digital video compression, which will enable a cable system carrying 50 channels to offer up to 300 channels.

In June 1993 the CRTC announced new regulatory changes, but some of the required amendments to cable television rules may take months to complete. Developers of the new specialty, pay and pay-per-view services being allowed won't get new channels on the air until December 1994. The cable television industry will see the elimination of its guaranteed return of 23% of net assets, and loses its automatic rate increases tied to the consumer price index. The CRTC has also created a Canadian programming production fund that will generate up to $300-million over five years, with money that will come from the cable industry, which has been given the option of paying rebates to customers or contributing to the fund. Finally, cable systems must also match each foreign satellite channel with a Canadian specialty channel.

Shaw has filed an application with the CRTC to operate a national satellite to cable digital music service called Digital Music Express (DMX) developed by International Cablecasting Technologies of Los Angeles. The service will be delivered through a special decoder attached to home stereo receiver units.

In December 1992, Shaw received CRTC approval for the purchase of CL Systems Limited for $308-million, the sale became effective February 1, 1993. Through its subsidiary Cablecasting Limited, CL Systems operates cable television systems in Calgary, Winnipeg, Toronto, St. Thomas and a number of other communities in Ontario.

1992 revenues by segment were: cable television, 92.5%; radio broadcasting and other, 7.5%.

Rank (Profit/Revenue/Assets)
123   299   235

James R. Shaw, Sr.
Chairman & President
Michael G. Ostopowich
Sr. V.P., Finance
Jim Shaw, Jr.
Sr. V.P., Operations

Address
7605 - 50 Street
Edmonton
AB
T6B 2W9
(403) 468-1230

Fax: (403) 466-4544
C0013738/G/11.2

SOUTHAM INC.

Exchanges	Price (Jun24'93)		17.62	Trailing P/E		nm	Stock Symbol
TM	Trailing Yield (%)		1.99	Trailing EPS		(4.11)	**STM**

Period Ending	Dec92	Dec91	Dec90	Dec89	Dec88
Yearly Statistics					
Price-Close	15.38	16.38	18.75	32.88	31.13
Price-High	20.38	20.88	32.88	35.25	32.00
Price-Low	14.75	14.75	17.25	29.50	16.13
P/E-Close	nm	nm	625.00	21.92	25.31
Dividends per Share	0.40	0.40	0.80	0.76	0.62
Dividend Yield (%)	2.60	2.44	4.27	2.31	1.99
Sales per Share	19.20	20.01	21.35	28.55	26.46
EPS before extra. item	(4.26)	(2.60)	0.03	1.50	1.23
Cash Flow per Share	0.85	0.28	1.13	2.40	1.76
Book Value per Share	3.74	7.11	9.85	10.48	10.39
O/S Common Shares	63,503	63,278	62,892	61,867	63,616
Total Revenue	1,171,385	1,179,021	1,227,000	1,677,709	1,572,729
Income before extra.	(262,851)	(153,157)	1,403	88,100	72,870
Cash Flow	52,625	16,628	64,885	140,753	104,435
Debt/Equity	1.32	1.48	0.93	0.69	0.41
Return on Capital (%)	(32.01)	(11.09)	4.50	17.07	17.08
Ret. on Com. Equity (%)	(76.44)	(28.65)	0.22	13.46	12.51
% Change Profit	(71.6)	nm	(98.4)	20.9	(6.9)
% Change Revenue	(0.6)	(3.9)	(26.9)	6.7	8.3
% Change Assets	(35.3)	(9.7)	8.6	13.3	8.6

Date	EPS	DPS	Tot Rev	Inc Bex
Mar 93	(0.11)	0.05	272,528	(7,167)
Dec 92	(1.21)	0.10	340,566	(76,909)
Sep 92	(0.66)	0.10	271,524	(42,749)
Jun 92	(2.13)	0.10	300,410	(127,901)
Mar 92	(0.26)	0.10	278,589	(15,292)
Dec 91	(1.94)	0.10	341,827	(114,337)
Sep 91	(0.37)	0.10	271,996	(21,545)
Jun 91	(0.06)	0.10	291,583	(3,868)

Preferred Div. Coverage	np	np	np	
Total Div. Coverage	0.0	0.0	0.0	
Interest Coverage	0.0	0.0	1.2	
Current Ratio	1.2	1.6	1.3	
Operating Margin	3.1	1.4	7.0	
Asset Turnover	1.3	0.9	0.8	
5 YEAR RATIOS (%)				
Return on Capital	(0.9)	9.3	15.4	
Return on Com. Equity	(15.8)	2.8	11.9	
Profit Growth	na	na	(51.8)	
Revenue Growth	(4.2)	(1.7)	0.7	
Asset Growth	(4.9)	7.3	10.9	
BALANCE SHEET (000)				
Cash	20,823	0	0	
Current Assets	307,078	407,476	382,584	
Net Fixed Assets	316,542	470,613	547,567	
Invest's & Advances	10,811	235,962	245,609	
Total Assets	894,359	1,381,567	1,530,133	
Short Term Debt	0	11,800	38,583	
Current Liabilities	262,749	252,349	299,703	
Long Term Debt	312,883	652,781	538,407	
Total Liabilities	656,639	931,561	910,916	
Total Equity	237,720	450,006	619,217	
Total Liab. & Equity	894,359	1,381,567	1,530,133	
CAPITAL (000)				
Total Debt	312,883	664,581	576,990	
Preferred Equity	0	0	0	
Common Equity	237,720	450,006	619,217	

Business:

SOUTHAM INC. is a leading Canadian information company. It operates daily newspapers in major cities across Canada. Through Coles Book Stores Ltd., the company operates a chain of bookstores across Canada. Southam also publishes business information in print and electronic formats, and produces and manages trade and consumer shows in Canada and the United States.

Synopsis:

During 1992 Southam's objectives were: to rationalize its non-core businesses; reduce debt; restore the profitability of its newspaper division; develop an appropriate plan for Pacific Press; and further reorganize and exploit its business communications division. The targets for 1993 call for continued focus on achieving the 1992 objectives and to look beyond for new growth initiatives and strategic alliances.

In November 1992, Hollinger Inc. purchased from Torstar Corporation $259-million worth of common shares of Southam Inc., which represented 22.5% of total shares. An agreement between Hollinger and Southam allows Hollinger representation on the Southam board in proportion to its share holdings and to abide by Southam's Shareholder Rights Protection Plan, pending a planned review by minority shareholders in 1995. Any major transactions between Southam and Hollinger will require independent director and/or minority shareholder approval. The purchase was followed in March 1993, with a purchase by Power Corporation, from treasury, of Southam common shares for $180-million, which will being used to retire debt. The purchase by Power resulted in Hollinger and Power both holding approximately 18.7% of Southam. Both companies agreed on voting parity, despite the number of shares held by each other. Following these two transactions Southam's new debt to equity ratio is 1:4 and the company is assured of an excellent relationship between its two major shareholders.

Southam will cut about 400 newspaper jobs as part of a three-year cost reduction program. This follows a staff reduction of about 250 jobs in 1992. Southam hopes to cut labor overhead to $75-million a year by 1994, when the program is completed. The company has disposed of must of its graphics properties and its principal remaining graphics asset, Dittler Brothers, will be retained until the industry and operating results improve.

Revenues (operating income) by in 1992 segment were: newspapers, 68% (82%); business communications, 15% (5%); and book retailing, 17% (13%).

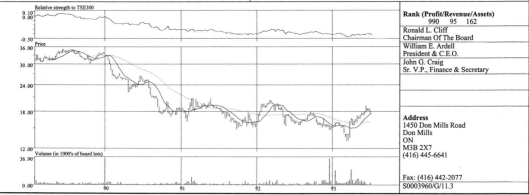

Rank (Profit/Revenue/Assets)
990   95   162

Ronald L. Cliff
Chairman Of The Board

William E. Ardell
President & C.E.O.

John G. Craig
Sr. V.P., Finance & Secretary

Address
1450 Don Mills Road
Don Mills
ON
M3B 2X7
(416) 445-6641

Fax: (416) 442-2077
S0003960/G/11.3

TELE-METROPOLE INC.

Exchanges	Price (Jun24'93)		11.50	Trailing P/E		17.97	Stock Symbol
TM	Trailing Yield (%)		0.00	Trailing EPS		0.64	**TM.B**

Period Ending	Aug92	Aug91	Aug90	Aug89	Aug88
Yearly Statistics					
Price-Close	12.50	11.25	12.75	21.00	16.75
Price-High	14.00	11.75	24.00	23.00	27.50
Price-Low	12.00	8.50	12.00	15.00	13.00
P/E-Close	65.79	nm	nm	131.25	335.00
Dividends per Share	0.00	0.00	0.00	0.00	0.20
Dividend Yield (%)	0.00	0.00	0.00	0.00	1.19
Sales per Share	21.26	19.74	17.53	14.38	12.92
EPS before extra. item	0.19	(1.75)	(1.33)	0.16	0.05
Cash Flow per Share	1.44	(1.50)	(1.38)	0.46	0.70
Book Value per Share	9.14	8.93	10.69	12.02	11.87
O/S Common Shares	7,877	7,835	7,804	7,804	7,804
Total Revenue	167,504	154,901	137,725	112,931	102,985
Income before extra.	1,502	(13,729)	(10,415)	1,212	381
Cash Flow	11,286	(11,692)	(10,737)	3,557	5,498
Debt/Equity	1.64	1.79	1.35	0.58	nd
Return on Capital (%)	8.51	(3.29)	(4.13)	3.66	0.69
Ret. on Com. Equity (%)	2.12	(17.90)	(11.75)	1.30	0.40
% Change Profit	110.9	(31.8)	(959.3)	218.1	(95.3)
% Change Revenue	8.1	12.5	22.0	9.7	5.6
% Change Assets	(2.0)	(1.9)	28.3	46.0	(3.3)

Preferred Div. Coverage	np	np	np
Total Div. Coverage	na	na	na
Interest Coverage	1.2	0.0	0.0
Current Ratio	1.2	1.2	1.4
Operating Margin	9.4	(4.6)	(7.4)
Asset Turnover	0.7	0.7	0.6
5 YEAR RATIOS (%)			
Return on Capital	1.1	2.1	7.0
Return on Com. Equity	(5.2)	(4.0)	2.3
Profit Growth	(28.7)	na	na
Revenue Growth	11.4	6.9	5.9
Asset Growth	11.7	12.2	11.4
BALANCE SHEET (000)			
Cash	0	0	279
Current Assets	61,712	60,364	62,822
Net Fixed Assets	62,628	68,138	71,237
Invest's & Advances	3,191	2,994	2,932
Total Assets	226,806	231,432	235,801
Short Term Debt	17,990	16,587	13,910
Current Liabilities	53,579	51,316	46,052
Long Term Debt	99,864	108,609	98,648
Total Liabilities	154,832	161,445	152,380
Total Equity	71,974	69,987	83,421
Total Liab. & Equity	226,806	231,432	235,801
CAPITAL (000)			
Total Debt	117,854	125,196	112,558
Preferred Equity	0	0	0
Common Equity	71,974	69,987	83,421

Business:

TELE-METROPOLE INC. is a television broadcasting and production company. It operates French-language television stations in Montreal, Quebec City, Sherbrooke, Rimouski, Trois-Rivieres, and Chicoutimi, Quebec. Through subsidiaries, it supplies production services to advertising agencies, producers, and film makers. Groupe Videotron is the company's major shareholder.

Date	EPS	DPS	Tot Rev	Inc Bex
May 93	0.74	0.00	50,272	5,815
Feb 93	(0.12)	0.00	38,835	(923)
Nov 92	0.74	0.00	50,506	5,836
Aug 92	(0.72)	0.00	32,349	(5,642)
May 92	0.58	0.00	51,767	4,524
Feb 92	(0.12)	0.00	36,350	(976)
Nov 91	0.46	0.00	46,706	3,596
Aug 91	(0.96)	0.00	27,474	(7,547)

Synopsis:

During fiscal 1992, Tele-Metropole reduced its operating costs by 12% through the elimination of 321 jobs, 200 of these jobs were outright layoffs. Cost cutting programs and productivity improvements are being pursued to continue the company's turnaround.

The CRTC awarded Tele-Metropole authorization to acquire control of TVA Television Network Inc., and renewed all of Tele-Metropole's broadcasting licences, which confirms the company's specific nature as a Quebec television network.

Tele-Metropole believes it has to deal with both the recession and fragmentation of the television market. This shows up in the proliferation of signals brought by satellite technology, the introduction of specialty channels, and through new ways of distributing television, such as through the telephone. One way the company is responding is by using the Videoway interactive TV technology belonging to its largest shareholder, Groupe Videotron. This technology allows viewers to select different viewing angles of programs, and lets them choose from three different shows, all on the same channel.

The changes in technology used by broadcasters will require Tele-Metropole to renew some of its equipment in the coming years. A return to profitability should provide the funds to modernize equipment, retire long-term debt, and allow the company to meet the challenges of the future.

Tele-Metropole operates five French language stations through its wholly-owned subsidiary, TM Multi-Regions Inc. (formerly Pathonic Network Inc.). TM Multi-Regions accounted for 41% of total revenue and 39% of income before depreciation and financial expenses in fiscal 1992.

Rank (Profit/Revenue/Assets)		
385	297	304

Mario Bertrand
President & C.E.O.

Address
1600 De Maisonneuve Blvd. E.
Montreal
PQ
H2L 4P2
(514) 526-9251

Fax: (514) 526-4857
T0000899/G/11.1

334   **For further company information, call Globe Information Services 1-800-268-9128 or (416)585-5345**

THOMSON CORPORATION (THE)

Exchanges	Price (Jun24'93)		15 .62	Trailing P/E		53 .88	Stock Symbol
TM	Trailing Yield (%)		2 .89	Trailing EPS		0 .29	**TOC**

Period Ending	Dec92	Dec91	Dec90	Dec89	Dec88
Yearly Statistics	US	US	US	US	US
Price-Close	14 .50	16 .00	17 .00	16 .63	15 .00
Price-High	17 .63	18 .25	17 .00	20 .13	15 .75
Price-Low	12 .13	14 .00	12 .50	15 .00	11 .25
P/E-Close	39 .84	26 .36	20 .81	18 .03	15 .31
Dividends per Share	0 .45	0 .45	0 .44	0 .41	0 .22
Dividend Yield (%)	3 .12	2 .83	2 .59	2 .48	1 .47
Sales per Share	10 .63	10 .06	9 .80	9 .44	8 .74
EPS before extra. item	0 .30	0 .53	0 .70	0 .78	0 .80
Cash Flow per Share	1 .34	1 .24	1 .10	1 .23	1 .01
Book Value per Share	4 .91	5 .36	5 .24	4 .78	3 .62
O/S Common Shares	567 ,250	559 ,459	552 ,843	543 ,565	540 ,765
Total Revenue	6 ,033 ,000	5 ,654 ,000	5 ,461 ,000	5 ,240 ,000	4 ,809 ,000
Income before extra.	182 ,000	320 ,000	420 ,000	454 ,000	466 ,000
Cash Flow	756 ,000	688 ,000	604 ,000	666 ,000	544 ,000
Debt/Equity	0 .76	0 .69	0 .61	0 .64	0 .55
Return on Capital (%)	7 .56	11 .30	14 .62	15 .97	25 .45
Ret. on Com. Equity (%)	5 .74	9 .91	14 .02	18 .45	28 .87
% Change Profit	(43 .1)	(23 .8)	(7 .5)	(2 .6)	123 .0
% Change Revenue	6 .7	3 .5	4 .2	9 .0	53 .0
% Change Assets	(3 .2)	3 .9	13 .0	31 .2	55 .0

Business:

THOMSON CORP. is a diversified communications and travel company. Its principal activites are newspaper publishing, specialized information and publishing, and leisure travel. Thomson operates primarily in the United Kingdom, the United States, and Canada.

Date		EPS	DPS	Tot Rev	Inc Bex
Mar 93	US	(0.10)	0.11	1 ,069 ,000	(55 ,000)
Dec 92	US	(0.11)	0.11	1 ,363 ,000	(62 ,000)
Sep 92	US	0.38	0.11	1 ,944 ,000	221 ,000
Jun 92	US	0.12	0.11	1 ,535 ,000	70 ,000
Mar 92	US	(0.09)	0.11	1 ,141 ,000	(47 ,000)
Dec 91	US	0.15	0.11	1 ,348 ,000	87 ,000
Sep 91	US	0.35	0.11	1 ,758 ,000	202 ,000
Jun 91	US	0.13	0.11	1 ,412 ,000	79 ,000

Preferred Div. Coverage	11 .4	11 .4	12 .0
Total Div. Coverage	0 .7	1 .1	1 .5
Interest Coverage	2 .2	2 .7	2 .8
Current Ratio	1 .1	1 .0	1 .1
Operating Margin	8 .3	12 .4	13 .5
Asset Turnover	0 .8	0 .7	0 .7
5 YEAR RATIOS (%)			
Return on Capital	15 .0	16 .8	18 .1
Return on Com. Equity	15 .4	18 .4	20 .5
Profit Growth	(2 .8)	17 .3	23 .8
Revenue Growth	13 .9	17 .1	18 .6
Asset Growth	18 .2	24 .6	31 .8
BALANCE SHEET (000)			
Cash	315 ,000	382 ,000	442 ,000
Current Assets	1 ,491 ,000	1 ,576 ,000	1 ,601 ,000
Net Fixed Assets	1 ,940 ,000	2 ,101 ,000	1 ,881 ,000
Invest's & Advances	0	0	0
Total Assets	7 ,907 ,000	8 ,166 ,000	7 ,860 ,000
Short Term Debt	70 ,000	211 ,000	129 ,000
Current Liabilities	1 ,381 ,000	1 ,635 ,000	1 ,451 ,000
Long Term Debt	2 ,227 ,000	1 ,996 ,000	1 ,852 ,000
Total Liabilities	4 ,900 ,000	4 ,944 ,000	4 ,594 ,000
Total Equity	3 ,007 ,000	3 ,222 ,000	3 ,266 ,000
Total Liab. & Equity	7 ,907 ,000	8 ,166 ,000	7 ,860 ,000
CAPITAL (000)			
Total Debt	2 ,297 ,000	2 ,207 ,000	1 ,981 ,000
Preferred Equity	223 ,000	223 ,000	370 ,000
Common Equity	2 ,784 ,000	2 ,999 ,000	2 ,896 ,000

Synopsis:

Thomson Corp. took a $170-million charge to earnings for the impairment of circulation and goodwill in 1992. This was following a comprehensive review of its operations in North America and the United Kingdom.

Thomson Information/Publishing Group (TIPG) had a successful year in 1992, including the acquisition of the Institute for Scientific Information, a commercial provider of library research information to the scientific and academic communities. TIPG will continue to consider high quality acquisition prospects in 1993, but its primary focus will be on internally generated growth. In early 1993, the restructuring of the U.K. free newspaper group was completed with the disposal of most of its titles.

Thomson's newspaper division (TN) continues to control costs and identify and develop new revenue opportunities as well as seeking to build circulation. In 1992, non-productive costs were further reduced with a number of operations being divested or down scaled. In both the U.S. and Canada, community divisions were merged with daily divisions. In 1993, TN will continue to improve the quality of its established titles, develop viable new products and implement aggressive marketing programs. Michael Johnston, President and C.E.O. of Thomson Newspapers, resigned in early 1993.

Thomson Travel Group's policy remains the same, to be the market leader in all sectors in which it operates. Thomson Tour expects to sell a similar number of holidays in 1993 as in 1992. Britannia Airways will continue upgrading its fleet and implementing its new operating systems in 1993.

1992 sales (operating profit before amortization and impairment) by business segment were: information/publishing, 44% (56%); newspapers, 19% (28%); and travel, 37% (16%). 1992 sales (operating profit before amortization and impairment) by geographic location were: the U.K., 50% (27%); the U.S., 38% (59%); Canada, 9% (11%); and other, 3% (3%).

Rank (Profit/Revenue/Assets)
11   16   29

Kenneth R. Thomson
Chairman

John A. Tory
Deputy Chairman

W. Michael Brown
President

Nigel R. Harrison
Exec. V.P. & C.F.O.

Richard Harrington
President, Thomson Newspapers

Address
Suite 2706
Box 24, TD Bank Tower
Toronto-Dominion Centre
Toronto
ON
M5K 1A1
(416) 360-8700
Fax: (416) 360-8812
I0001455/G/11.3

TORONTO SUN PUBLISHING CORPORATION

Exchanges	Price (Jun24'93)	13.00	Trailing P/E	260.00	Stock Symbol
T	Trailing Yield (%)	1.54	Trailing EPS	0.05	**TSP**

Period Ending	Dec92	Dec91	Dec90	Dec89	Dec88
Yearly Statistics					
Price-Close	12.00	14.00	16.75	24.75	24.25
Price-High	17.00	18.50	26.13	27.25	24.25
Price-Low	12.00	12.87	16.50	21.63	19.00
P/E-Close	120.00	466.67	nm	26.61	24.01
Dividends per Share	0.20	0.20	0.20	0.20	0.20
Dividend Yield (%)	1.67	1.43	1.19	0.81	0.83
Sales per Share	12.35	12.34	12.69	12.44	11.15
EPS before extra. item	0.10	0.03	(0.95)	0.93	1.01
Cash Flow per Share	0.89	0.67	0.69	1.03	0.89
Book Value per Share	11.82	11.73	11.87	12.96	12.17
O/S Common Shares	23,811	23,418	23,078	22,778	22,535
Total Revenue	330,510	322,462	323,298	324,386	286,470
Income before extra.	2,358	593	(21,637)	21,043	22,526
Cash Flow	21,001	15,440	15,728	23,279	20,017
Debt/Equity	0.06	0.11	0.12	0.10	nd
Return on Capital (%)	2.34	2.05	(9.96)	9.82	18.60
Ret. on Com. Equity (%)	0.85	0.22	(7.60)	7.39	9.39
% Change Profit	297.6	102.7	(202.8)	(6.6)	23.0
% Change Revenue	2.5	(0.3)	(0.3)	13.2	53.5
% Change Assets	(1.3)	0.2	(7.9)	6.8	45.1

Date	EPS	DPS	Tot Rev	Inc Bex
Mar 93	(0.08)	0.00	75,655	(1,982)
Dec 92	0.03	0.10	88,859	723
Sep 92	(0.04)	0.00	77,813	(988)
Jun 92	0.14	0.10	87,641	3,423
Mar 92	(0.03)	0.00	76,061	(800)
Dec 91	0.14	0.10	90,317	3,238
Sep 91	(0.05)	0.00	75,663	(1,147)
Jun 91	0.05	0.10	82,282	1,051

	Dec92	Dec91	Dec90
Preferred Div. Coverage	np	np	np
Total Div. Coverage	0.5	0.1	0.0
Interest Coverage	7.0	3.0	0.0
Current Ratio	1.1	1.0	0.9
Operating Margin	1.6	1.2	1.6
Asset Turnover	0.8	0.8	0.8
5 YEAR RATIOS (%)			
Return on Capital	4.6	7.5	9.9
Return on Com. Equity	2.0	3.9	6.1
Profit Growth	(33.7)	(48.3)	na
Revenue Growth	12.0	14.8	(0.3)
Asset Growth	7.1	7.7	5.7
BALANCE SHEET (000)			
Cash	6,790	3,938	8,342
Current Assets	62,572	62,331	64,139
Net Fixed Assets	151,076	155,045	150,282
Invest's & Advances	34,098	33,493	33,996
Total Assets	355,115	359,650	359,010
Short Term Debt	16,442	24,160	29,000
Current Liabilities	56,882	64,189	68,616
Long Term Debt	0	5,850	3,249
Total Liabilities	73,772	85,007	85,015
Total Equity	281,343	274,643	273,995
Total Liab. & Equity	355,115	359,650	359,010
CAPITAL (000)			
Total Debt	16,442	30,010	32,249
Preferred Equity	0	0	0
Common Equity	281,343	274,643	273,995

Business:

TORONTO SUN PUBLISHING CORP. is a newspaper publishing company. It operates daily newspapers in Toronto, Ottawa, Calgary, and Edmonton. It owns a 60% interest in Financial Post Co., and a 100% interest in Bowes Publishing, which publishes newspapers and magazines in smaller cities across Canada. The company owns community newspapers in Florida, and commercial printing operations near Washington, D.C.

Synopsis:

Toronto Sun Publishing had a good year editorially, but like most in the publishing companies it was affected by the economic conditions of its markets. Retail and classified advertising markets were particularly soft in 1992. Cost savings in 1992 were a direct result of lower newsprint costs. Cost control will remain a high priority in 1993. The Calgary Sun and Bowes Publishers both had good results in 1992, while the Financial Post and The Ottawa Sun reduced their losses.

In late 1992, the company formed a management committee of publishers and senior corporate officers to plan for the future of newspapers. The committee will be looking at technological change, reviewing industry trends, developing strategic and operational plans, and promoting staff development and management training. The company believes that its challenge to improve profitability throughout the 1990s will require an increase in readership base, expanded advertising appeal and the continued exercise of cost control measures.

Toronto Sun Publishing's outlook for 1993 is uncertain as the economy is forecast to recover from the recession. An improvement in the overall economy should produce increased advertising revenues and improved company performance. This is expected for the second half of 1993. Newsprint prices are expected to increase in 1993, which will have a negative impact on the company's results.

In 1992, Canada accounted for 91% of total revenue and 136% of operating profit. The remainder was from U.S. operations.

In November 1992, Douglas Creighton was removed from his position as Chairman and Chief Executive Officer by the Sun board of directors.

Rank (Profit/Revenue/Assets)
342 214 250

Paul V. Godfrey
President & C.E.O.

Bruce L. Jackson
V.P., Finance & C.F.O.

Address
333 King Street East
Toronto
ON
M5A 3X5
(416) 947-2222

Fax: (416) 947-3119
T0001910/G/11.3

Relative strength to TSE300

Price

Volume (in 1000's of board lots)

For further company information, call Globe Information Services 1-800-268-9128 or (416)585-5345

TORSTAR CORPORATION

Exchanges	Price (Jun24'93)	22.50	Trailing P/E	19.40	Stock Symbol
TM	Trailing Yield (%)	3.73	Trailing EPS	1.16	**TS.B**

Period Ending	Dec92	Dec91	Dec90	Dec89	Dec88
Yearly Statistics					
Price-Close	22.75	22.00	24.00	35.00	31.25
Price-High	25.88	27.25	35.00	37.75	33.75
Price-Low	20.00	20.00	20.00	29.50	23.75
P/E-Close	18.80	nm	22.02	14.71	15.24
Dividends per Share	0.84	0.84	0.84	0.76	0.72
Dividend Yield (%)	3.69	3.82	3.50	2.17	2.30
Sales per Share	22.86	23.06	24.29	23.74	22.76
EPS before extra. item	1.21	(0.09)	1.09	2.38	2.05
Cash Flow per Share	1.95	1.99	2.40	2.80	2.75
Book Value per Share	14.84	13.32	14.13	13.87	13.07
O/S Common Shares	40,762	41,607	41,481	41,674	43,066
Total Revenue	982,606	893,513	938,861	945,506	958,195
Income before extra.	48,828	(3,425)	42,212	94,587	86,465
Cash Flow	78,762	76,971	92,430	111,460	115,402
Debt/Equity	0.72	0.60	0.29	0.22	0.16
Return on Capital (%)	8.68	3.06	12.28	23.85	23.13
Ret. on Com. Equity (%)	8.42	(0.61)	7.24	16.57	16.99
% Change Profit	1,525.6	(108.1)	(55.4)	9.4	7.2
% Change Revenue	10.0	(4.8)	(0.7)	(1.3)	5.6
% Change Assets	17.5	17.1	6.0	3.7	1.8

Preferred Div. Coverage	1,220.7	0.0	1,172.6
Total Div. Coverage	1.4	0.0	1.2
Interest Coverage	2.9	1.1	6.6
Current Ratio	3.1	1.5	1.7
Operating Margin	8.1	9.5	11.6
Asset Turnover	0.7	0.8	1.0
5 YEAR RATIOS (%)			
Return on Capital	14.2	17.2	20.6
Return on Com. Equity	9.7	11.8	15.4
Profit Growth	(9.6)	na	(3.5)
Revenue Growth	1.6	2.2	5.9
Asset Growth	9.0	6.2	3.3
BALANCE SHEET (000)			
Cash	40,004	20,909	21,491
Current Assets	550,356	246,827	239,898
Net Fixed Assets	470,081	399,249	199,429
Invest's & Advances	22,691	205,536	252,999
Total Assets	1,250,328	1,063,804	908,114
Short Term Debt	13,133	26,482	17,553
Current Liabilities	180,072	167,799	141,124
Long Term Debt	424,465	309,578	151,446
Total Liabilities	641,700	506,694	319,394
Total Equity	608,628	557,110	588,720
Total Liab. & Equity	1,250,328	1,063,804	908,114
CAPITAL (000)			
Total Debt	437,598	336,060	168,999
Preferred Equity	3,786	3,096	2,451
Common Equity	604,842	554,014	586,269

Business:

TORSTAR CORP. is a broadly based information and entertainment communications company. Its operations include The Toronto Star newspaper, Metroland Printing, commercial printers, publishers of community newspapers and distributors of advertising materials, Harlequin Enterprises, and Miles Kimball, a direct catalogue marketer. Torstar owns 50% of Hebdo Mag Inc.

Date	EPS	DPS	Tot Rev	Inc Bex
Mar 93	0.13	0.21	230,499	5,469
Dec 92	1.51	0.21	256,214	60,681
Sep 92	0.02	0.21	230,745	735
Jun 92	(0.50)	0.21	219,121	(19,749)
Mar 92	0.18	0.21	215,070	7,161
Dec 91	(0.44)	0.21	247,284	(16,889)
Sep 91	0.03	0.21	217,298	1,239
Jun 91	0.16	0.21	216,264	6,149

Synopsis:

In November 1992, Hollinger Inc. purchased from Torstar Corporation $259-million worth of common shares of Southam Inc. The proceeds were $70-million in cash and a $189-million note receivable, which was repaid in April 1993. Torstar used $140-million to reduce debt and the rest will be used for future investment. Torstar and Southam expect to continue working together in areas of mutual interest such as the SOUTHAMSTAR Network.

Advertising lineage was down 11% at the Toronto Star, and 1% at Metroland community newspapers in 1992. Profit in newspapers and printing was down due to the recession and a 31-day strike at the Toronto Star. In the first half 1993, results at the Toronto Star will be adversely affected by the start-up costs of its new printing plant, these costs should decline in the second half of the year. The Toronto Star also plans to contract out all distribution of the newspaper by the end of 1993, resulting in a reduction of 235 jobs and a $5-million a year drop in distribution costs.

Harlequin had its best year ever in 1992 as the division continued to show steady growth in Eastern Europe. A full year reflecting 1991 price increases for the North American direct marketing division, profits from new Eastern European markets and favorable exchange rates contributed to Harlequin's results. These trends continued into the first quarter of 1993 and are expected to continue the rest of the year. As well, 1993 price increases for the North American retail and overseas businesses and increased volumes from new markets are expected to offset normal operating cost increases and the continued effects of the worldwide recession.

1992 revenues (operating profit) by segment were: newspapers and printing, 46% (12%); book publishing, 45% (83%); catalogue marketing, 9% (11%); and corporate administration, - (-6%). In 1992 revenues (operating profit) by region were: Canada, 48% (14%); the United States, 31% (61%); and other and corporate administration, 21% (25%).

Relative strength to TSE300

Price

Volume (in 1000's of board lots)

Rank (Profit/Revenue/Assets)		
63	105	131

Beland H. Honderich
Chairman

David R. Jolley
Office Of The Chief Executive

David A. Galloway
Office Of The Chief Executive

Robert J. Steacy
Vice President, Finance

Address
1 Yonge Street
Toronto
ON
M5E 1P9
(416) 367-4595

Fax: (416) 869-4183
T0002091/G/11.3

WIC WESTERN INTERNATIONAL COMMUNICATIONS LTD.

Exchanges	Price (Jun24'93)	16.50	Trailing P/E	126.92	Stock Symbol
TV	Trailing Yield (%)	3.18	Trailing EPS	0.13	**WIC.B**

Period Ending	Aug92	Aug91	Aug90	Aug89	Aug88
Yearly Statistics					
Price-Close	14.25	12.63	11.25	15.50	12.62
Price-High	15.00	14.88	15.75	17.13	13.50
Price-Low	10.00	10.63	10.25	12.38	7.63
P/E-Close	71.25	20.04	12.78	6.20	13.15
Dividends per Share	0.50	0.50	0.50	0.50	0.46
Dividend Yield (%)	3.51	3.96	4.44	3.23	3.65
Sales per Share	15.31	15.49	18.26	21.73	15.71
EPS before extra. item	0.20	0.63	0.88	2.50	0.96
Cash Flow per Share	2.44	2.28	2.45	2.93	2.37
Book Value per Share	12.22	12.64	12.46	13.89	11.99
O/S Common Shares	19,581	17,483	13,598	7,080	6,709
Total Revenue	298,181	240,116	207,463	164,833	110,134
Income before extra.	3,775	9,675	9,810	17,235	6,609
Cash Flow	47,183	34,928	27,390	20,207	16,291
Debt/Equity	1.19	1.52	1.36	0.96	1.32
Return on Capital (%)	8.60	9.98	14.08	19.85	12.87
Ret. on Com. Equity (%)	1.64	4.96	7.33	19.28	8.23
% Change Profit	(61.0)	(1.4)	(43.1)	160.8	56.4
% Change Revenue	24.2	15.7	25.9	49.7	13.9
% Change Assets	(3.2)	40.9	94.7	6.8	15.1

Business:

WIC WESTERN INTERNATIONAL COMMUNICATIONS LTD. is a broadcasting company. It owns radio stations in Western Canada and Ontario, and has seven television stations in Western Canada. The company owns 51% of Canadian Satellite Communications Inc. (Cancom), 100% of Allarcom Pay Television Ltd., known as Superchannel, and 50% of the Family Channel.

Date	EPS	DPS	Tot Rev	Inc Bex
Feb 93	(0.28)	0.14	77,471	(5,508)
Nov 92	0.30	0.14	90,286	5,849
Aug 92	(0.19)	0.13	65,489	(3,731)
May 92	0.30	0.13	83,581	5,858
Feb 92	(0.11)	0.13	68,625	(1,987)
Nov 91	0.20	0.13	80,486	3,635
Aug 91	(0.04)	0.13	62,953	(128)
May 91	0.33	0.13	68,547	5,136

Preferred Div. Coverage	np	np	np
Total Div. Coverage	0.4	1.2	1.7
Interest Coverage	1.4	1.5	1.4
Current Ratio	1.0	1.0	0.8
Operating Margin	19.6	20.6	21.0
Asset Turnover	0.5	0.4	0.4
5 YEAR RATIOS (%)			
Return on Capital	13.1	13.6	14.0
Return on Com. Equity	8.3	9.0	9.1
Profit Growth	(2.3)	17.4	17.3
Revenue Growth	25.2	20.6	20.0
Asset Growth	26.6	26.9	26.1
BALANCE SHEET (000)			
Cash	0	5,255	0
Current Assets	78,971	86,799	57,162
Net Fixed Assets	109,761	108,579	78,094
Invest's & Advances	27,456	33,186	30,926
Total Assets	630,499	651,479	462,524
Short Term Debt	19,223	27,586	32,765
Current Liabilities	77,516	83,061	67,735
Long Term Debt	265,161	308,423	197,307
Total Liabilities	391,198	430,422	293,155
Total Equity	239,301	221,057	169,369
Total Liab. & Equity	630,499	651,479	462,524
CAPITAL (000)			
Total Debt	284,384	336,009	230,072
Preferred Equity	0	0	0
Common Equity	239,301	221,057	169,369

Synopsis:

WIC Western International Communications received CRTC approval to purchase CHCH-TV in Hamilton, Ontario, from Maclean Hunter Ltd. The sale is effective January 1, 1993, and will cost $40.5-million plus or minus working capital. The approval did not require WIC to sell one of its British Columbia stations, CHAN-TV Vancouver or CHEK-TV Victoria, which had been a previous condition for approval. The CRTC does require WIC to implement adequate employment equity practices at the station both on and off the air.

WIC has entered into an agreement with Suite 12 Group of New Jersey for the option to acquire the Canadian rights to the technology known as CellularVision. CellularVision is a new, two-way, patented television and data microwave distribution technology that is capable of delivering up to 200 conventional analog television signals.

A new agreement concluded among the seven shareholders of the CTV Television Network Ltd. in January 1993, calls for each company to subscribe for $2-million of convertible debentures. The agreement converts the network from a cooperative to a one-share/one-vote for-profit corporation. WIC is a founding CTV shareholder through its subsidiary Westcom TV Group Ltd. As CTV Network affiliates, the company's BCTV and CHEK stations benefit from strong programming, however, CTV revenues represent less than 1% of WIC's total revenues.

WIC expects modest improvements in economic conditions in the near future, however, it plans to continue to improve the ratings of its television and radio stations, and to enhance services offered by its pay television and satellite services segments. This is expected to improve performance and revenue growth. 1992 revenues (operating income before amortization of licences and rights) by business segment were: television, 61% (74%); pay-television, 7% (9%); radio, 16% (3%); and satellite network services, 16% (14%). WIC also earned $2.4-million from investment income in fiscal 1992.

Relative strength to TSE300 / Price / Volume (in 1000's of board lots)

Rank (Profit/Revenue/Assets)		
287	223	189

Frank A. Griffiths
Chairman

Douglas M. Holtby
President & C.E.O.

William F. Ramsey
V.P., Finance & C.F.O.

Address
Suite 1960
One Bentall Centre
505 Burrard St.
Vancouver
BC
V7X 1M6
(604) 687-2844
Fax: (604) 687-4118
W0007859/G/11.1

For further company information, call Globe Information Services 1-800-268-9128 or (416)585-5345

Page	Company	$	Latest year end	Earnings per Share		
				Actual	Estimate this year	Estimate next year
343	Acklands		9301	0.37	n.a.	n.a.
344	Finning		9212	0.05	0.52	1.09
345	Marshall Steel		9212	(0.92)	n.a.	n.a.
346	UAP Inc.		9212	1.11	1.24	1.36
347	United Westburne		9212	(0.23)	0.35	0.75
348	Wajax		9212	0.07	0.46	0.98

Estimates from I/B/E/S Inc., 345 Hudson St., New York, NY 10014 (212) 243-3335. In Canada: 6 Lansing Square, Ste. 235, Willowdale, ON M2J 1T5 (416) 496-0977.

Wholesale Distibutors

Canadian wholesalers had seasonally adjusted sales of $16.24-billion in April 1993, off 2.3% from March, but up 4.8% from a year earlier, according to Statistics Canada. The median forecast of economists surveyed by the Technical Data division called for an April rise of 0.5% from March. The April figure is the first drop since last September.

Within the group, wholesalers of lumber and building materials recorded a 4.2% decline in April sales after four consecutive months of growth. Sales of machinery, equipment and supplies fell by 3.9%.

Wholesalers' inventories at April 30, 1993, totaled a seasonally adjusted $25.99-billion, up 1.3% from a month earlier and up 6.3% from a year ago.

For the month ended June 30, 1993, the wholesale distributors sub-index of the TSE 300 Compositerose 4.3% from a month earlier or 32.1% from a year earlier. This has been the seventh consecutive month of increases, for a total increase of 65.5% since the ended of November 1992.

According to the July 1993 *Report on Business 1000*, the wholesale industry had an average one year return on capital of 8.59%. The average five year return on capital for the industry was 17%. The current inventory turnover was 16.4 for the year, versus 17.7 for the previous year.

ACKLANDS LIMITED

Exchanges	Price (Jun24'93)	8 .50	Trailing P/E	18 .89	Stock Symbol
TW	Trailing Yield (%)	0 .00	Trailing EPS	0 .45	**ACK**

Period Ending	Jan93	Jan92	Jan91	Jan90	Jan89
Yearly Statistics					14M
Price-Close	5 .00	4 .80	5 .88	10 .25	14 .88
Price-High	6 .00	6 .00	12 .00	15 .25	16 .88
Price-Low	4 .50	4 .00	4 .90	10 .13	14 .25
P/E-Close	13 .51	21 .82	nm	nm	nm
Dividends per Share	0 .00	0 .00	0 .00	0 .00	0 .60
Dividend Yield (%)	0 .00	0 .00	0 .00	0 .00	4 .03
Sales per Share	23 .27	22 .77	36 .98	71 .87	70 .19
EPS before extra. item	0 .37	0 .22	(1 .04)	(1 .73)	(3 .13)
Cash Flow per Share	0 .73	0 .61	(0 .44)	(0 .70)	(1 .73)
Book Value per Share	8 .20	7 .85	7 .62	14 .00	16 .21
O/S Common Shares	13 ,690	13 ,630	13 ,630	4 ,949	4 ,949
Total Revenue	315 ,654	310 ,713	344 ,288	357 ,455	406 ,223
Income before extra.	5 ,012	3 ,048	(9 ,024)	(8 ,561)	(15 ,478)
Cash Flow	9 ,895	8 ,330	(4 ,050)	(3 ,474)	(9 ,978)
Debt/Equity	0 .29	0 .20	0 .24	1 .13	1 .01
Return on Capital (%)	5 .02	4 .25	(1 .33)	0 .45	(4 .56)
Ret. on Com. Equity (%)	4 .57	2 .89	(10 .42)	(11 .45)	(14 .83)
% Change Profit	64 .4	133 .8	(5 .4)	35 .5	(520 .1)
% Change Revenue	1 .6	(9 .8)	(3 .7)	2 .7	(12 .3)
% Change Assets	14 .6	(0 .4)	(11 .2)	(7 .7)	(9 .7)

Preferred Div. Coverage	np	np	np
Total Div. Coverage	na	na	na
Interest Coverage	2 .9	2 .3	0 .0
Current Ratio	2 .0	2 .3	2 .3
Operating Margin	2 .0	1 .6	0 .5
Asset Turnover	1 .6	1 .8	2 .0
5 YEAR RATIOS (%)			
Return on Capital	0 .8	1 .5	2 .4
Return on Com. Equity	(5 .8)	(6 .1)	(6 .1)
Profit Growth	9 .7	3 .4	na
Revenue Growth	(4 .5)	(4 .3)	(1 .9)
Asset Growth	(3 .3)	(4 .9)	(4 .1)
BALANCE SHEET (000)			
Cash	0	0	0
Current Assets	149 ,388	135 ,533	134 ,590
Net Fixed Assets	38 ,468	30 ,501	32 ,641
Invest's & Advances	1 ,660	1 ,726	1 ,496
Total Assets	194 ,595	169 ,808	170 ,470
Short Term Debt	24 ,976	19 ,582	20 ,187
Current Liabilities	73 ,260	59 ,006	59 ,584
Long Term Debt	7 ,358	1 ,894	4 ,791
Total Liabilities	82 ,368	62 ,878	66 ,588
Total Equity	112 ,227	106 ,930	103 ,882
Total Liab. & Equity	194 ,595	169 ,808	170 ,470
CAPITAL (000)			
Total Debt	32 ,334	21 ,476	24 ,978
Preferred Equity	0	0	0
Common Equity	112 ,227	106 ,930	103 ,882

Business:

ACKLANDS LTD. distributes automotive after-market parts and industrial supplies and equipment, and occupational health and safety supplies. It supplies wholesalers and industrial, commericial and retail customers across Canada through 163 branches and warehouses. Some stores it distributes to are: Bumper to Bumper; Western Automotive Rebuilders; and Accruate Door and Hardware.

Date	EPS	DPS	Tot Rev	Inc Bex
Apr 93	0.14	0.00	105 ,202	1 ,860
Jan 93	0.15	0.00	74 ,802	1 ,995
Oct 92	0.08	0.00	78 ,196	1 ,094
Jul 92	0.08	0.00	80 ,715	1 ,133
Apr 92	0.06	0.00	81 ,941	790
Jan 92	0.06	0.00	72 ,859	896
Oct 91	0.06	0.00	78 ,906	757
Jul 91	0.08	0.00	81 ,079	1 ,090

Synopsis:

Acklands Limited attributed its performance in 1992 to its ability to maintain gross margin percentages with only a slight improvement in overall sales. The company also improved its operating cost structure through solid financial planning, continued cost controls and the commitment and dedication of its employees. Acklands' acquisition program continued in 1992 and will be an important aspect of its activities in 1993.

In January 1993, Acklands acquired Safety Supply Canada Ltd. Safety Supply Canada is a national distributor of occupational health, safety, fire and environmental products. The purchase will increase the company's sales by approximately $100-million.

Acklands has also completed the acquisition of J.B. Reid Industrial Sales Limited, effective April 1993. J.B. Reid is an industrial distributor in Southern Ontario, with sales of approximately $25-million. The acquisition is an important step in building its industrial customer base in Ontario.

In May 1993, Acklands announced the acquisition of McKerlie-Millen Inc., a distributor of automotive after-market parts and accessories, from M&M Inc. With this purchase and previous acquisitions Acklands should have annual sales of $550-million.

As part of its overall strategy Acklands plans to operate its automotive and industrial businesses separately. The company believes that each segment is now large enough to require its own focus and management team.

Relative strength to TSE300 / Price / Volume (in 1000's of board lots) chart, 1990–1993

Rank (Profit/Revenue/Assets)
256   218   321

Joe Pal
Chairman

K. (Rai) Sahi
President & C.E.O.

Richard W. Clegg
V.P., Finance

Address
945 Wilson Avenue
Downsview
ON
M3K 1E8
(416) 631-5200

Fax: (416) 635-9549
A0000283/G/12.1

FINNING LTD.

Exchanges	Price (Jun24'93)		17.25	Trailing P/E		156.82	Stock Symbol
TMV	Trailing Yield (%)		0.87	Trailing EPS		0.11	**FTT**

Period Ending	Dec92	Dec91	Dec90	Dec89	Dec88
Yearly Statistics					
Price-Close	12.00	13.50	12.25	13.63	11.00
Price-High	14.50	15.63	17.00	15.75	12.13
Price-Low	10.50	11.75	10.25	10.00	9.00
P/E-Close	200.00	135.00	13.92	9.73	8.43
Dividends per Share	0.15	0.21	0.46	0.40	0.32
Dividend Yield (%)	1.25	1.52	3.76	2.94	2.87
Sales per Share	24.78	25.47	32.84	30.55	28.35
EPS before extra. item	0.06	0.10	0.88	1.40	1.31
Cash Flow per Share	2.81	3.06	3.44	3.80	3.14
Book Value per Share	8.78	9.11	9.28	8.64	6.75
O/S Common Shares	33,685	33,528	33,320	33,098	28,237
Total Revenue	832,737	851,370	1,091,217	903,965	796,519
Income before extra.	2,878	4,612	30,283	42,197	37,067
Cash Flow	94,546	102,180	114,467	112,541	88,346
Debt/Equity	1.59	1.47	1.63	1.41	1.53
Return on Capital (%)	5.91	6.77	13.48	18.22	18.64
Ret. on Com. Equity (%)	0.67	1.12	9.80	17.33	22.62
% Change Profit	(37.6)	(84.8)	(28.2)	13.8	39.3
% Change Revenue	(2.2)	(22.0)	20.7	13.5	20.7
% Change Assets	(1.6)	(3.2)	10.8	39.9	8.6

Business:

FINNING LTD. sells, services and finances Caterpillar heavy equipment and complementary equipment in western and northern Canada and through a wholly owned subsidiary, Finning Limited, in the southwest and Industrial Midlands of England, Wales, Scotland and Poland.

Date	EPS	DPS	Tot Rev	Inc Bex
Mar 93	0.09	0.03	217,981	3,324
Dec 92	(0.09)	0.06	177,424	(2,738)
Sep 92	0.03	0.03	225,441	1,239
Jun 92	0.08	0.03	226,084	2,840
Mar 92	0.04	0.03	190,033	1,537
Dec 91	(0.05)	0.03	163,126	(1,325)
Sep 91	0.03	0.03	223,884	1,327
Jun 91	0.08	0.03	252,851	2,982

	Dec92	Dec91	Dec90
Preferred Div. Coverage	3.3	3.9	26.9
Total Div. Coverage	0.5	0.6	1.8
Interest Coverage	1.0	1.1	1.7
Current Ratio	1.3	1.4	1.3
Operating Margin	5.6	6.5	9.6
Asset Turnover	0.9	0.9	1.1
5 YEAR RATIOS (%)			
Return on Capital	12.6	14.5	16.2
Return on Com. Equity	10.3	14.5	17.6
Profit Growth	(36.0)	(26.1)	9.4
Revenue Growth	4.7	8.7	15.3
Asset Growth	9.8	15.2	17.2
BALANCE SHEET (000)			
Cash	0	0	0
Current Assets	587,329	596,977	670,614
Net Fixed Assets	123,505	132,572	255,015
Invest's & Advances	223,001	218,633	54,446
Total Assets	970,007	985,339	1,018,216
Short Term Debt	314,805	267,448	386,802
Current Liabilities	452,414	423,240	535,920
Long Term Debt	175,458	203,034	132,836
Total Liabilities	661,295	664,108	698,853
Total Equity	308,712	321,231	319,363
Total Liab. & Equity	970,007	985,339	1,018,216
CAPITAL (000)			
Total Debt	490,263	470,482	519,638
Preferred Equity	13,050	15,716	10,060
Common Equity	295,662	305,515	309,303

Synopsis:

Finning believes 1993 will be a promising year with the recovery presently underway in North America strengthening the company's position. Improved results are also anticipated in Europe through cost savings from downsizing and restructuring. As part of this process, Finning announced in March 1993 that it had sold its lift truck operation in Holland. As of the first quarter, all revenue components were up in Canada, and in Europe the plant hire sector was up with all other sectors comparable to 1992.

Part of the sales decline over the past two years is due to the company leasing more equipment. This results in revenue from the transactions not being reflected in current results, but spread over a number of years.

Finning's performance is affected by two forms of currency risk. The first relates to the importing of inventory product for Canadian operations from the United States. Finning can generally realize the cost of exchange rate movements in its transaction price. The second risk is that the company's financial results are reported in Canadian dollars, while the European operations conduct business primarily in British currency.

Total revenue (net income) in 1992 by geographic segment was: Canada, 69% (320%); and Europe, 31% (-220%). This breakdown of revenue has averaged around 70% for Canada and 30% for Europe since the end of 1989. In fiscal 1992 (1991), 56% (57%) of revenue came from equipment with the remainder from product support. 1992 Canadian new prime product deliveries by market segment were: forestry, 36%; mining, 22%; construction, 20%; government, 9%; petroleum, 5%; and other, 8%. European new prime product deliveries by market segment were: quarrying, 33%; mining, 24%; plant hire, 22%; construction, 10%; and other, 11%. Approximately 90% of Finning's sales, parts and service involve Caterpillar products.

Rank (Profit/Revenue/Assets)
318   120   154

Donald W. Lord
Chairman
James F. Shepard
President & C.E.O.
Richard T. Mahler
V.P., Finance & C.F.O.

Address
555 Great Northern Way
Vancouver
BC
V5T 1E2
(604) 872-4444

Fax: (604) 872-2994
F0000788/G/12.1

For further company information, call Globe Information Services 1-800-268-9128 or (416)585-5345

MARSHALL STEEL LIMITED

Exchanges	Price (Jun24'93)	2.00	Trailing P/E	nm	Stock Symbol
TM	Trailing Yield (%)	0.00	Trailing EPS	(0.82)	**MS.A**

Period Ending	Dec92	Dec91	Dec90	Dec89	Dec88
Yearly Statistics					
Price-Close	0.75	1.65	2.65	3.00	5.38
Price-High	1.65	2.50	3.70	5.88	5.75
Price-Low	0.75	1.50	2.20	2.90	4.75
P/E-Close	nm	nm	nm	nm	14.15
Dividends per Share	0.00	0.08	0.15	0.15	0.29
Dividend Yield (%)	0.00	4.55	5.66	5.00	5.34
Sales per Share	5.13	8.38	14.05	15.40	16.64
EPS before extra. item	(0.92)	(1.99)	(0.12)	(0.32)	0.38
Cash Flow per Share	(0.12)	(1.37)	1.09	(0.30)	0.49
Book Value per Share	2.70	3.35	5.42	5.80	5.15
O/S Common Shares	8,536	8,536	8,530	8,523	8,523
Total Revenue	43,760	71,933	121,761	133,062	144,850
Income before extra.	(7,878)	(16,981)	(1,053)	(2,732)	3,662
Cash Flow	(1,009)	(11,699)	9,332	(2,535)	4,231
Debt/Equity	nd	0.36	0.25	0.60	0.70
Return on Capital (%)	(35.34)	(48.07)	3.76	0.40	13.74
Ret. on Com. Equity (%)	(35.35)	(45.41)	(2.20)	(5.86)	7.80
% Change Profit	53.6	(1,512.6)	61.5	(174.6)	(76.0)
% Change Revenue	(39.2)	(40.9)	(8.5)	(8.1)	18.7
% Change Assets	(36.1)	(40.4)	(18.1)	20.3	30.0

Business:			

MARSHALL STEEL LTD. operates as a distributor, processor, fabricator and erector of structural steel products primarily in Canada and the United States. It has operations in Ontario, Quebec, Massachusetts, and Tennessee.

Date	EPS	DPS	Tot Rev	Inc Bex
Mar 93	0.09	0.00	7,270	782
Dec 92	0.03	0.00	9,863	230
Sep 92	0.05	0.00	9,831	414
Jun 92	(0.99)	0.00	12,184	(8,471)
Mar 92	(0.01)	0.00	12,014	(51)
Dec 91	(1.55)	0.00	10,060	(13,228)
Sep 91	(0.07)	0.00	13,060	(601)
Jun 91	(0.11)	0.08	22,378	(931)

Period Ending	Dec92	Dec91	Dec90
Preferred Div. Coverage	na	na	na
Total Div. Coverage	0.0	0.0	0.0
Interest Coverage	0.0	0.0	0.8
Current Ratio	1.9	1.6	1.7
Operating Margin	1.1	(15.1)	1.9
Asset Turnover	1.3	1.4	1.4
5 YEAR RATIOS (%)			
Return on Capital	(13.1)	4.0	14.9
Return on Com. Equity	(16.2)	(2.7)	6.5
Profit Growth	na	na	na
Revenue Growth	(18.7)	(5.6)	(16.4)
Asset Growth	(13.4)	(0.1)	(9.2)
BALANCE SHEET (000)			
Cash	4,077	0	0
Current Assets	18,549	31,258	56,165
Net Fixed Assets	11,932	18,326	29,483
Invest's & Advances	0	0	0
Total Assets	33,628	52,626	88,278
Short Term Debt	0	7,457	5,557
Current Liabilities	9,930	19,841	32,249
Long Term Debt	0	2,700	5,811
Total Liabilities	10,617	24,064	41,986
Total Equity	23,011	28,562	46,292
Total Liab. & Equity	33,628	52,626	88,278
CAPITAL (000)			
Total Debt	0	10,157	11,368
Preferred Equity	10	10	47
Common Equity	23,001	28,552	46,245

Synopsis:

Marshall Steel was acquired in May 1992 by Canadian Erectors Limited, which operates businesses in the metal fabrication and construction industry. The company presently has two businesses, one in Laval, Quebec, and the other in Sept-Iles, Quebec. The Quebec construction scene remains very depressed, thus the outlook for the near future is minimal operating earnings. The company believes at the present it is unduly reliant on the Quebec structural steel market, and plans to expand its geographic and product reach.

The continuing decline in construction activity forced the 1992 closure of the company's distribution facilities in Milton, Ontario, and Palmer, Massachusetts. The severity of market conditions in Quebec resulted in the Laval plant operating at less than 35% capacity throughout 1992.

On December 30, 1992, Marshall acquired from the ultimate parent corporation of its majority shareholder, all the outstanding shares of Norsteel Ltd., a steel distributor in Northern Quebec. The consideration paid for Norsteel was $1.6-million. This was followed in April 1993, with the sale of its U.S. operations in Memphis, Tennessee, for proceeds of $4.6-million. Also in April, the company disposed of a surplus facility located in Richmond, British Columbia, for proceeds of $4.1-million.

Relative strength to TSE300 / Price / Volume (in 1000's of board lots) chart

Rank (Profit/Revenue/Assets)
912   423   528

Derek A. Drummond
Chairman

Jeffrey G. Marshall
President

David M. Carr
Exec.V.P., Finance & Secretary

Address
R.R. #3 Highway 25 North
Milton
ON
L9T 4B6
(416) 684-9421

Fax: (416) 875-2454
M0021233/G/12.1

UAP INC.

Exchanges	Price (Jun24'93)	19.00	Trailing P/E	16.24	Stock Symbol
TM	Trailing Yield (%)	2.42	Trailing EPS	1.17	**UAP.A**

Period Ending	Dec92	Dec91	Dec90	Dec89	Dec88
Yearly Statistics					
Price-Close	18.00	16.50	16.00	18.63	14.50
Price-High	18.25	18.25	19.00	19.00	16.00
Price-Low	15.00	15.25	14.13	14.00	12.13
P/E-Close	16.36	16.02	14.68	13.30	11.89
Dividends per Share	0.46	0.46	0.46	0.40	0.40
Dividend Yield (%)	2.56	2.79	2.88	2.15	2.76
Sales per Share	49.35	48.52	43.99	43.46	46.89
EPS before extra. item	1.10	1.03	1.09	1.40	1.22
Cash Flow per Share	1.96	2.02	1.89	2.27	1.86
Book Value per Share	15.93	15.30	14.73	14.09	12.35
O/S Common Shares	9,516	9,386	9,383	9,383	7,507
Total Revenue	464,435	455,391	412,761	407,789	351,988
Income before extra.	10,208	9,560	10,126	13,011	9,078
Cash Flow	18,449	18,947	17,699	21,290	13,946
Debt/Equity	0.35	0.37	0.39	0.33	0.72
Return on Capital (%)	11.79	12.43	14.15	16.56	14.22
Ret. on Com. Equity (%)	6.92	6.79	7.49	11.57	10.07
% Change Profit	6.8	(5.6)	(22.2)	43.3	13.0
% Change Revenue	2.0	10.3	1.2	15.9	9.0
% Change Assets	6.0	11.7	2.9	20.3	12.6

Preferred Div. Coverage	np	np	np
Total Div. Coverage	2.4	2.3	2.4
Interest Coverage	4.4	3.7	3.5
Current Ratio	3.6	3.8	2.8
Operating Margin	5.2	5.7	6.7
Asset Turnover	1.6	1.7	1.7
5 YEAR RATIOS (%)			
Return on Capital	13.8	14.3	14.7
Return on Com. Equity	8.6	9.3	10.1
Profit Growth	4.9	8.4	7.2
Revenue Growth	7.4	9.6	10.6
Asset Growth	10.4	12.3	14.8
BALANCE SHEET (000)			
Cash	3,379	2,404	4,819
Current Assets	216,144	202,801	183,045
Net Fixed Assets	63,012	59,323	52,375
Invest's & Advances	1,458	1,878	3,128
Total Assets	287,400	271,042	242,721
Short Term Debt	10,924	10,405	34,438
Current Liabilities	60,789	53,338	64,309
Long Term Debt	41,394	42,203	18,757
Total Liabilities	135,778	127,470	104,542
Total Equity	151,622	143,572	138,179
Total Liab. & Equity	287,400	271,042	242,721
CAPITAL (000)			
Total Debt	52,318	52,608	53,195
Preferred Equity	0	0	0
Common Equity	151,622	143,572	138,179

Business:

UAP INC. is a manufacturer and wholesaler of automotive parts and accessories. It imports, sells and distributes auto parts and accessories and rebuilds all parts, accessories and equipment vital to maintenance and repair of vehicles. It operates 14 distribution centres and 215 corporate stores across Canada, and also serves 405 UAP and NAPA associated wholesalers throughout Canada.

Date	EPS	DPS	Tot Rev	Inc Bex
Mar 93	0.14	0.12	109,505	1,262
Dec 92	0.23	0.12	113,754	2,134
Sep 92	0.33	0.12	123,126	3,024
Jun 92	0.48	0.12	124,623	4,464
Mar 92	0.65	0.12	102,932	586
Dec 91	0.26	0.12	106,087	2,386
Sep 91	0.29	0.12	120,452	2,638
Jun 91	0.47	0.12	125,745	4,421

Synopsis:

UAP, in the last decade between 1982 and 1992, concentrated on its cross Canada development, making over 160 acquisitions and entering into a strategic alliance with Genuine Parts Company of the United States, which owns the NAPA network of distributors in Western Canada. This alliance resulted in the creation of the UAP/NAPA Automotive Western Partnership, majority owned by UAP. Also, during this period, UAP's sales increased from $161.4-million to $464.4-million.

During 1992, UAP continued to intensify its marketing efforts with regard to the UAP/NAPA, ULTRAPRO, VERDIC and BODYPRO private brands. Three acquisitions were made in 1992, which were financed directly from working capital. The first acquisition was an automotive wholesaler. The other two acquisitions are being integrated into the company's industrial division. Premier Industrial Sales specializes in the distribution of power transmission products for material handling equipment and industrial bearings, and will give UAP penetration into this highly specialized sector of the industrial market. Les Equipements Industriels Flexco, which specializes in hard chrome electroplating for hydraulic cylinders, as well as the repair, installation and servicing of hydraulic cylinders, will contribute to developing UAP's activities in the hydraulic field in which it has operated since 1989.

UAP plans to focus on internal factors in 1993, including more aggressive marketing programs, sustained development of private brands, the improvement of results in Western Canada, further streamlining of its operations, and reassessment of certain operations whose performance is not in line with UAP standards. Acquisitions should continue in 1993 at a moderate rate in order to take advantage of strategic opportunities.

Sales percentages per region in 1992 (1982) were: Quebec, 39% (52%); Ontario, 21% (28%); Western Provinces, 32% (10%); and Maritime Provinces, 8% (10%).

Rank (Profit/Revenue/Assets)
182   165   279

Claude Ducharme
Chairman Of The Board

Jean Douville
President & C.E.O.

Robert Martin
V.P., Finance & Secretary

Address
7025 Ontario Street East
Montreal
PQ
H1N 2B3
(514) 256-5031

Fax: (514) 256-8469
U0000192/G/12.1

UNITED WESTBURNE INC.

Exchanges	Price (Jun24'93)		6.00	Trailing P/E		nm	Stock Symbol
TM	Trailing Yield (%)		1.33	Trailing EPS		(0.26)	**UWB**

Period Ending	Dec92	Dec91	Dec90	Dec89	Dec88
Yearly Statistics					
Price-Close	4.30	7.13	7.50	9.75	nt
Price-High	9.13	9.63	10.38	14.25	nt
Price-Low	4.00	6.88	5.50	9.50	nt
P/E-Close	nm	nm	15.31	7.62	nt
Dividends per Share	0.12	0.26	0.26	0.26	0.26
Dividend Yield (%)	2.79	3.65	3.47	2.67	na
Sales per Share	56.62	57.17	63.23	84.82	109.32
EPS before extra. item	(0.29)	(0.73)	0.49	1.28	1.87
Cash Flow per Share	0.37	0.12	1.15	1.80	2.49
Book Value per Share	9.45	9.76	10.71	10.56	9.66
O/S Common Shares	37,403	37,367	37,331	37,309	23,417
Total Revenue	2,130,914	2,152,441	2,371,653	2,672,481	2,272,087
Income before extra.	(10,828)	(27,350)	18,197	40,139	38,795
Cash Flow	13,668	4,339	42,836	56,385	51,546
Debt/Equity	1.42	1.43	1.46	1.51	3.03
Return on Capital (%)	3.81	2.17	10.72	15.53	16.25
Ret. on Com. Equity (%)	(3.02)	(7.16)	4.59	12.94	19.13
% Change Profit	60.4	(250.3)	(54.7)	3.5	41.8
% Change Revenue	(1.0)	(9.2)	(11.3)	17.6	30.8
% Change Assets	(1.9)	(5.7)	(5.1)	7.3	46.6

Preferred Div. Coverage	np	np	np
Total Div. Coverage	0.0	0.0	1.9
Interest Coverage	0.7	0.4	1.5
Current Ratio	2.2	2.4	1.9
Operating Margin	1.5	1.7	4.4
Asset Turnover	1.9	1.9	2.0
5 YEAR RATIOS (%)			
Return on Capital	9.7	12.6	15.4
Return on Com. Equity	5.3	9.4	13.7
Profit Growth	na	na	5.6
Revenue Growth	4.1	11.2	15.8
Asset Growth	6.7	18.2	22.0
BALANCE SHEET (000)			
Cash	17,140	20,373	17,780
Current Assets	776,491	814,509	875,415
Net Fixed Assets	113,832	112,981	119,193
Invest's & Advances	2,405	0	1,933
Total Assets	1,095,077	1,116,551	1,184,144
Short Term Debt	113,448	117,927	252,302
Current Liabilities	348,936	341,814	452,063
Long Term Debt	386,645	405,000	330,374
Total Liabilities	741,710	751,819	784,447
Total Equity	353,367	364,732	399,697
Total Liab. & Equity	1,095,077	1,116,551	1,184,144
CAPITAL (000)			
Total Debt	500,093	522,927	582,676
Preferred Equity	0	0	0
Common Equity	353,367	364,732	399,697

Business:

UNITED WESTBURNE INDUSTRIES LIMITED devotes its resources to the wholesale distribution of plumbing, heating, water works, PVF air conditioning, refrigeration, electrical and electronic supplies. Its major markets are the residential, commercial and industrial building and renovation industry, engineering construction, and the replacement market for electrical and mechanical machinery.

Date	EPS	DPS	Tot Rev	Inc Bex
Mar 93	(0.18)	0.00	467,257	(6,721)
Dec 92	(0.08)	0.00	530,858	(2,909)
Sep 92	(0.01)	0.04	582,322	(330)
Jun 92	0.01	0.04	540,678	130
Mar 92	(0.21)	0.04	477,056	(7,719)
Dec 91	(0.62)	0.07	526,567	(23,304)
Sep 91	0.07	0.07	603,495	2,713
Jun 91	0.04	0.07	549,429	1,408

Synopsis:

United Westburne believes that like the industry as a whole it has been seriously effected since the start of the 1990s by the impact of the North American recession, the globalization of markets and the various consequences of the Canada-U.S. Free Trade Agreement. The company has tried to minimize the effects through its decentralization policy, knowledge of local markets, product diversity, the value it adds through the experience of its employees, and the scope of its network.

In early 1992, Westburne announced that it will discontinue its Memphis division. The division took longer to be disposed than anticipated and resulted in an additional after tax cost of $2-million.

Through tighter management controls, Westburne was able to improve its balance sheet during 1992. Inventories, which were fell by 6.6% in 1991, were further reduced by 7.4%, resulting in a decline in working capital requirements of $45-million. The effect of more favorable interest rates helped reduce interest charges by $6-million. Total debt was reduced by $22-million.

Westburne has chosen to concentrate on cost control, productivity and other operation initiatives, as the basis for financial performance in the near term.

Revenues by type of supplies and equipment in 1992 were: plumbing, heating, ventilation and air conditioning, 49%; electrical, 47%; and electronics, 4%. The geographic breakdown of 1992 revenues was: Ontario, 31%; Western Provinces, 25%; Quebec and Atlantic Canada, 20%; California, 15%; and the United States (excluding California), 9%. Types of clients in 1992 were: industrial and commercial, 53%; residential construction, 34%; and other services, 13%. Earnings contributions by country in 1992 were: Canada, -153%; and the United States, 53%.

Relative strength to TSE300

Price

Volume (in 1000's of board lots)

Rank (Profit/Revenue/Assets)
893 61 147

Michel Belanger
Chairman Of The Board

Michel Vennat
Vice Chairman & C.E.O.

Howard F. Campbell
President & C.O.O.

John A. Hanna
Sr. V.P. Fin., Admin. & C.F.O.

Address
6333 Decarie Boulevard
Suite 400
Montreal
PQ
H3W 3E1
(514) 342-5181

Fax: (514) 342-9838
U0001657/G/12.1

WAJAX LIMITED

Exchanges	Price (Jun24'93)	7.37	Trailing P/E	92.19	Stock Symbol
TM	Trailing Yield (%)	0.00	Trailing EPS	0.08	**WJX.A**

Period Ending	Dec92	Dec91	Dec90	Dec89	Dec88	Business:
Yearly Statistics						WAJAX LTD. is the controlling entity in a
Price-Close	6.38	7.00	6.75	11.75	12.75	family of subsidiary companies engaged in the
Price-High	7.75	8.75	11.50	14.25	15.00	manufacture, distribution and servicing of
Price-Low	5.50	6.00	6.25	11.75	9.63	industrial equipment and heavy machinery in
P/E-Close	91.07	50.00	51.92	167.86	nm	the forestry, mining, steel, construction, oil and
Dividends per Share	0.00	0.28	0.50	0.56	0.56	gas, and utility sectors. It operates a
Dividend Yield (%)	0.00	4.00	7.41	4.77	4.39	coast-to-coast network of sales and service
Sales per Share	28.91	30.13	34.61	36.79	34.64	branches. exchangers, bearings and power
EPS before extra. item	0.07	0.14	0.13	0.07	(0.17)	transmission products.
Cash Flow per Share	0.56	0.72	0.37	1.50	1.47	
Book Value per Share	7.56	7.47	7.61	7.97	8.46	
O/S Common Shares	8,545	8,573	8,571	8,580	8,579	
Total Revenue	247,865	258,266	296,913	315,613	297,151	

Date	EPS	DPS	Tot Rev	Inc Bex
Mar 93	(0.04)	0.00	58,996	(376)
Dec 92	0.03	0.00	65,937	238
Sep 92	0.04	0.00	58,325	301
Jun 92	0.05	0.00	66,689	470
Mar 92	(0.05)	0.00	56,914	(435)
Dec 91	(0.04)	0.07	58,424	(343)
Sep 91	0.03	0.07	58,663	266
Jun 91	0.12	0.07	72,133	1,010

Period Ending	Dec92	Dec91	Dec90	Dec89	Dec88
Income before extra.	574	1,170	1,083	640	(1,501)
Cash Flow	4,827	6,169	3,170	12,884	12,593
Debt/Equity	0.95	1.01	1.24	1.21	0.94
Return on Capital (%)	5.87	6.60	8.95	9.36	8.47
Ret. on Com. Equity (%)	0.89	1.81	1.62	0.91	(1.98)
% Change Profit	(50.9)	8.0	69.2	142.6	(122.5)
% Change Revenue	(4.0)	(13.0)	(5.9)	6.2	11.7
% Change Assets	(0.1)	(12.7)	(11.1)	10.6	3.2

Synopsis:

Wajax's 1992 results were lower primarily due to reduced sales volumes combined with the impact of continued pressure on margins from a competitive market and one time costs associate with new cost and efficiency controls. The restructuring and reorganization are finished and Wajax believes it is now in a better position to move ahead. A new strategic plan is in the final stage of development and will provide for the expansion of the equipment distribution business through acquisitions.

During 1992, Wajax bought the assets of Dynesco Inc., a manufacturer and distributor of fluid power equipment. Wajax merged Dynesco with its Affiliated Engineering to form a new entity, Affiliated Dynesco. This business markets its products to industrial, chemical and process customers in Eastern Canada. The company also relocated its Niedner hose operation from Coaticook, Quebec, to new premises nearby in December.

At the beginning of April 1993, Wajax announced that it had reached an agreement in principle for the purchase of the distribution business of Cypress Equipment Co. Limited. This is to be an asset purchase involving primarily inventories and fixed assets at five branch locations throughout British Columbia and should double the company's business within the province.

Gross revenues in 1992 by segment were: parts, accessories and service, 60.2%; equipment distribution, 35.2%; and rentals and other, 4.6%. Gross revenues by end use market in 1992 were: industrial/commercial, 31.7%; mining, petroleum and gas, 25.3%; forest industries, 13%; transportation, 10.4%; construction, 9%; utilities, 9.3%; and military, 1.3%. Gross revenue by geographical destination in 1992 were: Quebec, 25%; Alberta, 27.4%; Ontario, 16.1%; B.C. & Yukon, 14.1%; Saskatchewan/Manitoba, 2.1%; Maritimes, 7.1%; and foreign, 8.2%.

	Dec92	Dec91	Dec90
Preferred Div. Coverage	np	np	np
Total Div. Coverage	na	0.5	0.3
Interest Coverage	1.3	1.3	1.6
Current Ratio	2.1	2.1	1.9
Operating Margin	3.0	3.5	5.8
Asset Turnover	1.5	1.6	1.6
5 YEAR RATIOS (%)			
Return on Capital	7.8	9.0	10.5
Return on Com. Equity	0.7	2.2	3.7
Profit Growth	(38.9)	(29.4)	(35.3)
Revenue Growth	(1.4)	(1.5)	0.5
Asset Growth	(2.5)	(1.8)	0.5
BALANCE SHEET (000)			
Cash	0	0	0
Current Assets	135,761	132,519	157,424
Net Fixed Assets	20,065	21,653	22,962
Invest's & Advances	0	0	0
Total Assets	163,858	163,974	187,878
Short Term Debt	27,167	27,057	40,757
Current Liabilities	65,228	62,181	82,478
Long Term Debt	34,064	37,801	40,188
Total Liabilities	99,292	99,982	122,666
Total Equity	64,566	63,992	65,212
Total Liab. & Equity	163,858	163,974	187,878
CAPITAL (000)			
Total Debt	61,231	64,858	80,945
Preferred Equity	0	0	0
Common Equity	64,566	63,992	65,212

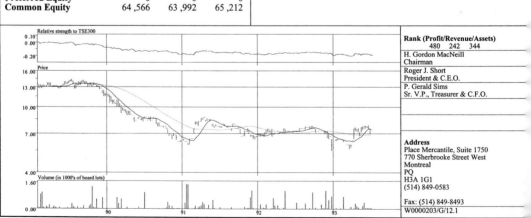

Rank (Profit/Revenue/Assets)
480 242 344

H. Gordon MacNeill
Chairman

Roger J. Short
President & C.E.O.

P. Gerald Sims
Sr. V.P., Treasurer & C.F.O.

Address
Place Mercantile, Suite 1750
770 Sherbrooke Street West
Montreal
PQ
H3A 1G1
(514) 849-0583

Fax: (514) 849-8493

W0000203/G/12.1

Page	Company	$	Latest year end	Earnings per Share		
				Actual	Estimate this year	Estimate next year
353	Canadian Tire		9212	0.80	0.98	1.16
354	Cara Operations		9303	0.25	0.29	0.34
355	Chateau Stores		9301	1.04	1.55	1.85
356	Dalmys Canada		9302	0.30	n.a.	n.a.
357	Dylex		9301	(0.36)	(0.02)	0.16
358	Empire Company		9204	0.33	0.84	1.00
359	Gendis		9301	0.79	1.07	1.34
360	George Weston		9212	0.85	1.99	2.89
361	Hudson's Bay Company		9301	2.32	2.60	3.05
362	Jean Coutu Group		9205	0.69	0.82	0.95
363	Loblaw Companies		9212	0.88	1.22	1.45
364	North West Company		9301	1.05	1.15	1.38
365	Oshawa Group		9301	1.14	1.57	1.83
366	Pennington's Stores		9301	(0.15)	0.13	0.25
367	Peoples Jewellers		9203	(13.06)	n.a.	n.a.
368	Reitmans (Canada)		9301	1.54	1.62	1.95
369	Sears Canada		9212	(1.02)	0.05	0.34
370	Silcorp		9212	(22.21)	n.a.	n.a.
371	Univa		9301	0.20	0.46	0.62
372	Versa Services		9209	0.40	n.a.	n.a

Estimates from I/B/E/S Inc., 345 Hudson St., New York, NY 10014 (212) 243-3335. In Canada: 6 Lansing Square, Ste. 235, Willowdale, ON M2J 1T5 (416) 496-0977.

Retailing

Supermarket Roundup - Industry Report [Apr-5-1993].
SHEARSON LEHMAN BROTHERS, INC. reported by
Comeau, E.F., et al
Sales trends began to show an improving trend in the third and
fourth quarters of 1992, which has continued into 1Q:93 for
most food retailers. As the overall economy has gained some
strength and food deflation has abated, most food retailers
have experienced a gradual recovery from the low point
reached in mid-1992. Looking back over the past several
years, the correlation of same store sales with food inflation is
fairly consistent, with same store sales rates tracking closely
with the rate of food inflation. Food deflation appears to have
stabilized, and modest levels of inflation are expected to
continue, particularly in the important produce category. [RN
1321726]

Retailing Forecaster - Industry Report [Apr-1-1993]. MERRILL
LYNCH CAPITAL MARKETS reported by Barry, D.D., et al
Strong retail sales gains are expected in the Spring and Summer of 1993 against weather depressed 1992 results, which
hurt sales of seasonal merchandise to a significant extent.
1Q:93 retail earnings gains have been hurt by the severe winter
weather in February and March. [RN 1323246]

Retail Stock Monitor - Industry Report [Apr-1-1993]. SHEAR-
SON LEHMAN BROTHERS, INC. reported by Comeau, E.F.,
et al
After a sluggish performance in February 1993, retail stocks
fared a little better in March, despite ongoing concerns over
proposed legislation for income taxes and health care reforms,
and despite the brutal weather experienced for most of the
month. The S&P Retail Index increased 1.9% in March, which
equalled the S&P 500's 1.9% rise and a 1.9% gain in the Dow
Jones Industrials. Most of the individual retail sectors outperformed the market in March, with the best performances
posted by the S&P Food Stores (up 6.5%), and the S&P
Department Stores (up 6.2%). Other indices that outperformed
the market included the S&P Specialty Index, which rose
3.5%, and the S&P Drug Store Index, which gained 2.1%.
Underperforming the market's 1.9% monthly rise was the
S&P Apparel Index and the S&P General Merchandise Index,
the former posting a flat performance and the latter declining
0.6%. [RN 1323476]

Retail: Department Store Stocks - Industry Report [Mar-30-
1993]. SHEARSON LEHMAN BROTHERS, INC. reported by
Walin, K.K.
Consumers and retailers have been concerned with the harsh
winter of 1993, the toughest in several years, as well as
potential tax increases. Yet, while consumer momentum has
slowed after the highlevels starting in the fall of 1992 through
January 1993, further improvement in job growth, gains in
personal income, and further mortgage refinancings are expected to support better spending trends over the next few
months, especially versus the still weak numbers retailers were
seeing in March through July of 1992. Department stores
should continue to benefit from the consumer recovery, with
shoppers looking for more fashion-forward merchandise. Department stores are providing this with more current inventories that emphasize freshness and exclusivity. [RN 1319204]

Canada: Retail Industry - Industry Report [Mar-17-1993. BBN
JAMES CAPEL INC. reported by Hartman, G.
Aikenhead Stores' initial three warehouse outlets are estimated to be generating annualized volumes of about $70
million, about twice the average Home Depot volume. Aikenhead is expected to be profitable in the year ending March 31,
1994. In addition to the two outlets in the Toronto market and
three outlets in the Montreal market in 1993, the company is
aiming to open ten new outlets in calendar 1994. These will
probably include its first stores in the major western Canadian
markets. Chateau Stores reported strong results for FY:93. The
company was profitable in three of the past four years in a
generally weak apparel retailing environment in Canada. [RN
1317395]

CANADIAN TIRE CORPORATION, LIMITED

Exchanges	Price (Jun24'93)		13.37	Trailing P/E		17.37	Stock Symbol
TM	Trailing Yield (%)		2.99	Trailing EPS		0.77	**CTR.A**

Period Ending	Jan93	Dec91	Dec90	Dec89	Dec88
Yearly Statistics					
Price-Close	15.75	22.38	20.50	24.38	16.88
Price-High	23.38	27.50	24.88	26.38	17.88
Price-Low	14.75	22.25	19.25	17.75	13.00
P/E-Close	19.69	15.87	12.81	14.77	12.32
Dividends per Share	0.40	0.40	0.38	0.30	0.24
Dividend Yield (%)	2.54	1.79	1.85	1.23	1.42
Sales per Share	35.14	33.10	33.88	32.58	28.99
EPS before extra. item	0.80	1.41	1.60	1.65	1.37
Cash Flow per Share	1.72	1.96	2.05	1.92	1.69
Book Value per Share	12.61	12.15	11.44	10.23	9.09
O/S Common Shares	91,674	91,674	89,793	90,015	90,722
Total Revenue	3,232,836	3,008,050	3,091,214	2,977,424	2,657,893
Income before extra.	72,293	127,076	144,366	149,616	124,873
Cash Flow	157,666	176,690	185,025	174,576	153,911
Debt/Equity	0.50	0.47	0.44	0.36	0.41
Return on Capital (%)	10.86	16.78	20.97	24.37	24.29
Ret. on Com. Equity (%)	6.37	11.87	14.82	17.15	16.12
% Change Profit	(43.1)	(12.0)	(3.5)	19.8	26.4
% Change Revenue	7.5	(2.7)	3.8	12.0	7.5
% Change Assets	5.6	11.8	14.7	13.0	8.3

Preferred Div. Coverage	np	np	np
Total Div. Coverage	2.0	3.5	4.0
Interest Coverage	2.8	3.9	4.7
Current Ratio	1.9	1.9	2.2
Operating Margin	5.3	8.1	8.3
Asset Turnover	1.4	1.3	1.5
5 YEAR RATIOS (%)			
Return on Capital	19.5	21.9	23.2
Return on Com. Equity	13.3	15.0	15.8
Profit Growth	(6.1)	7.6	28.7
Revenue Growth	5.5	5.1	8.0
Asset Growth	10.6	11.3	10.2
BALANCE SHEET (000)			
Cash	163,624	158,173	157,687
Current Assets	1,308,082	1,225,266	1,148,711
Net Fixed Assets	1,009,046	970,680	821,723
Invest's & Advances	15,054	12,424	9,533
Total Assets	2,345,230	2,220,115	1,984,918
Short Term Debt	125,243	93,733	34,175
Current Liabilities	698,755	653,298	522,881
Long Term Debt	449,331	428,447	421,123
Total Liabilities	1,189,490	1,105,925	957,661
Total Equity	1,155,740	1,114,190	1,027,257
Total Liab. & Equity	2,345,230	2,220,115	1,984,918
CAPITAL (000)			
Total Debt	574,574	522,180	455,298
Preferred Equity	0	0	0
Common Equity	1,155,740	1,114,190	1,027,257

Business:

CANADIAN TIRE CORP. LTD. is engaged in the retail merchandising of automotive products, sporting goods, housewares and hardware products. Its stores, auto parts depots and gas bars are located across Canada. The company's financial services division operates the Canadian Tire credit card and auto club. It also operates a national emergency road service.

Date	EPS	DPS	Tot Rev	Inc Bex
Apr 93	0.18	0.10	778,306	16,536
Jan 93	0.03	0.10	856,979	3,072
Sep 92	0.29	0.10	807,921	26,104
Jun 92	0.27	0.10	885,941	23,867
Mar 92	0.21	0.10	681,995	19,250
Dec 91	0.29	0.10	794,951	26,321
Sep 91	0.36	0.10	749,895	32,295
Jun 91	0.40	0.10	822,332	36,330

Synopsis:

Canadian Tire Corporation Limited continues to brave the depressed retail market by implementing new marketing and management measures throughout its system. Like other retailers it is cutting down on capital expenditures, monitoring the competition and being extra cautious about new acquisitions.

Faced with competition from U.S. chain stores and warehouse outlets, Canadian Tire will introduce its own superstores in the near future to meet with customer demands. Extra push will be placed on customer service and expanding product mix to keep sales up, but the company says survival also means accepting lower margins. Its key message to consumers, delivered through slick TV advertising, will continue to be service and low prices.

This reorganization comes on the heels of another poor year. For the year ending January 2, 1993, profits fell 43% to $72.3-million, while revenue improved to $3.22-billion. The weak numbers were brought on in part by the sluggish economy. About 48% of its fiscal 1993 revenue came from Ontario. Cash generated from operations fell by 10.8% to $157.7-million. The sharp decline in profits is accounted in part by the December 1991 startup of the $213-million distribution center in Brampton. Profits were hurt also by a $9.8-million loss at the petroleum division, and a $15.4-million operating loss at its U.S Auto Source retail chain, where losses are expected to continue. Its U.S. operation is loosing an estimated $2-million a year. This operation will be monitored closely in 1993 and expansion decisions put on hold. Canadian Tire spent $107-million on capital projects in fiscal 1993, a 44.9% drop from 1992, which included $20-million to develop Auto Source.

First-quarter results in fiscal 1994 showed revenues were up but net profit was down by 14%. Net income fell to $16.5-million despite record first quarter sales of $775.6-million.

Rank (Profit/Revenue/Assets)
50 39 87

Hugh L. Macaulay
Chairman Of The Board

Stephen E. Bachand
President & C.E.O.

Gerald S. Kishner
Exec. V.P., Finance & Admin.

James F. Ryan
Sr. V.P., Dealer Operations

Address
2180 Yonge Street
P.O. Box 770
Station K
Toronto
ON
M4P 2V8
(416) 480-3000
Fax: (416) 480-3746
C0004314/G/12.5

CARA OPERATIONS LIMITED

Exchanges	**Price (Jun24'93)**	3.80	**Trailing P/E**	14.67	**Stock Symbol**
TM	**Trailing Yield (%)**	2.08	**Trailing EPS**	0.26	**CAO.A**

Period Ending	Mar93	Mar92	Mar91	Apr90	Apr89
Yearly Statistics					
Price-Close	4.45	5.50	5.50	5.33	5.58
Price-High	5.38	6.63	6.00	6.67	5.83
Price-Low	4.15	5.25	4.50	5.08	3.88
P/E-Close	17.12	20.91	17.74	16.00	19.48
Dividends per Share	0.08	0.08	0.08	0.08	0.07
Dividend Yield (%)	1.80	1.51	1.52	1.44	1.19
Sales per Share	6.65	6.51	4.88	2.81	2.74
EPS before extra. item	0.26	0.26	0.31	0.33	0.29
Cash Flow per Share	0.43	0.44	0.46	0.42	0.37
Book Value per Share	2.15	1.97	1.79	1.49	1.23
O/S Common Shares	117,432	117,432	117,430	114,430	114,430
Total Revenue	783,229	765,904	567,834	324,406	309,688
Income before extra.	30,492	30,835	35,624	38,174	32,272
Cash Flow	50,908	51,571	53,724	48,386	41,879
Debt/Equity	0.37	0.60	0.70	0.03	0.03
Return on Capital (%)	18.01	17.89	27.29	39.52	42.60
Ret. on Com. Equity (%)	12.60	13.96	18.72	24.54	25.48
% Change Profit	(1.1)	(13.4)	(6.7)	18.3	21.1
% Change Revenue	2.3	34.9	75.0	4.8	7.9
% Change Assets	(4.4)	4.3	96.7	14.8	3.4

Preferred Div. Coverage	np	np	np
Total Div. Coverage	3.2	3.2	3.7
Interest Coverage	6.1	5.1	5.9
Current Ratio	1.2	1.1	1.1
Operating Margin	8.4	8.7	12.9
Asset Turnover	1.7	1.6	1.3
5 YEAR RATIOS (%)			
Return on Capital	29.1	33.7	37.5
Return on Com. Equity	19.1	21.8	24.4
Profit Growth	2.7	7.1	14.7
Revenue Growth	22.1	22.8	17.5
Asset Growth	18.4	21.0	21.5
BALANCE SHEET (000)			
Cash	10,355	26,042	9,249
Current Assets	115,080	133,428	116,872
Net Fixed Assets	200,577	199,676	197,134
Invest's & Advances	24,335	24,773	23,099
Total Assets	448,256	469,025	449,613
Short Term Debt	1,690	33,825	26,510
Current Liabilities	93,048	119,781	104,714
Long Term Debt	90,787	105,535	120,061
Total Liabilities	195,747	237,613	239,250
Total Equity	252,509	231,412	210,363
Total Liab. & Equity	448,256	469,025	449,613
CAPITAL (000)			
Total Debt	92,477	139,360	146,571
Preferred Equity	0	0	0
Common Equity	252,509	231,412	210,363

Business:

CARA OPERATIONS LTD. is in the food services and office products industries. It operates and is the franchisor of Swiss Chalet, Harvey's and Steak & Burger restaurants. Catering and support services are provided to educational and health institutions through Beaver Foods and to major airlines through the Airport Services Division. Cara distributes office products through Grand & Toy.

Date	EPS	DPS	Tot Rev	Inc Bex
Mar 93	0.08	0.00	247,682	9,706
Dec 92	0.07	0.04	192,960	8,481
Sep 92	0.06	0.00	271,277	7,514
Jun 92	0.04	0.04	272,141	4,791
Mar 92	0.09	0.00	234,022	10,677
Dec 91	0.07	0.04	191,728	8,302
Sep 91	0.06	0.00	278,464	7,509
Jun 91	0.04	0.04	269,865	4,347

Synopsis:

Cara Operations Limited acquired 17 stores from Willson Stationers in 1993, and all of Willson's commercial business. Previously, Cara bought 24 Willson stores in Ontario in October 1992. In September 1992, the first Harvey's opened at the University of Toronto as part of Cara's expansion into non-traditional locations. Other plans include launching a Harvey's or Swiss Chalet in the Czech republic by 1994. Swiss Chalet will expand its home delivery service in 1993.

Airport services and Beaver Foods were the only divisions that did not experience growth in fiscal 1993, resulting from a downturn in airline business and cutbacks on student purchases. Several food and beverage contracts at Vancouver International Airport were negotiated for an additional five-year term.

Sales and profits were marginally lower in fiscal 1993. Total system sales were $1.19-billion, down 1.2%. Cash flow was $59-million compared to $60.4-million in fiscal 1992. Capital spending was $18.7-million. Cara will spend $26-million on capital initiatives in the coming fiscal year, more than half going to Swiss Chalet and Harvey's. Capital initiatives include opening six new Harvey's locations and renovating 12 Swiss Chalet restaurants. Grand & Toy sales increased by 3%, but Beaver Foods sales dropped for by 4%. In the past year, $52-million of debt was repaid.

Cara donates 1% of pre-tax profits to charity.

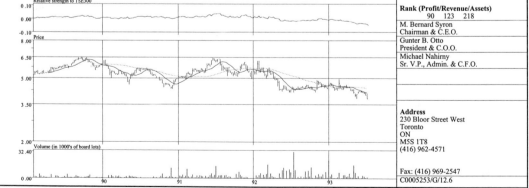

Rank (Profit/Revenue/Assets)	90 123 218
M. Bernard Syron	Chairman & C.E.O.
Gunter B. Otto	President & C.O.O.
Michael Nahirny	Sr. V.P., Admin. & C.F.O.

Address
230 Bloor Street West
Toronto
ON
M5S 1T8
(416) 962-4571

Fax: (416) 969-2547
C0005253/G/12.6

CHATEAU STORES OF CANADA LTD.

Exchanges	Price (Jun24'93)	14.25	Trailing P/E	13.70	Stock Symbol
TM	Trailing Yield (%)	0.00	Trailing EPS	1.04	**CTU.A**

Period Ending	Jan93	Jan92	Jan91	Jan90	Jan89
Yearly Statistics					
Price-Close	7.25	3.05	5.38	3.75	2.00
Price-High	7.75	10.50	10.25	4.50	4.25
Price-Low	2.15	2.90	2.05	1.80	1.60
P/E-Close	6.97	nm	5.43	12.10	nm
Dividends per Share	0.00	0.00	0.00	0.00	0.00
Dividend Yield (%)	0.00	0.00	0.00	0.00	0.00
Sales per Share	36.24	35.22	34.83	29.84	27.54
EPS before extra. item	1.04	(1.25)	0.99	0.31	(0.93)
Cash Flow per Share	2.25	(0.13)	2.20	1.50	0.18
Book Value per Share	5.83	4.81	6.09	5.34	4.65
O/S Common Shares	4,382	4,312	4,234	4,234	4,234
Total Revenue	156,900	150,775	147,456	126,325	116,602
Income before extra.	4,509	(5,349)	4,199	1,332	(3,927)
Cash Flow	9,761	(567)	9,298	6,357	775
Debt/Equity	0.02	0.33	0.12	0.36	0.77
Return on Capital (%)	36.39	(16.93)	31.29	14.92	(5.50)
Ret. on Com. Equity (%)	19.48	(22.99)	17.36	6.30	(18.00)
% Change Profit	184.3	(227.4)	215.2	133.9	(306.1)
% Change Revenue	4.1	2.3	16.7	8.3	(3.3)
% Change Assets	(8.6)	4.7	13.6	(8.9)	(3.6)

Business:

CHATEAU STORES OF CANADA LTD. operates retail stores across Canada and the United States under the name Le Chateau. The stores sell full lines of men's and women's fashionable clothing, footwear and accessories at medium prices. The company designs and manufactures many of the products sold.

Date	EPS	DPS	Tot Rev	Inc Bex
Jan 93	1.25	0.00	49,859	5,411
Oct 92	0.65	0.00	39,461	2,820
Jul 92	(0.58)	0.00	35,846	(2,495)
Apr 92	(0.28)	0.00	31,700	(1,200)
Jan 92	(0.43)	0.00	45,575	(1,779)
Oct 91	(0.29)	0.00	36,685	(1,251)
Jul 91	(0.39)	0.00	37,059	(1,649)
Apr 91	(0.15)	0.00	31,481	(621)

Preferred Div. Coverage	np	np	np
Total Div. Coverage	na	na	na
Interest Coverage	8.0	0.0	6.0
Current Ratio	1.8	1.1	1.4
Operating Margin	8.3	(3.2)	6.3
Asset Turnover	3.9	3.4	3.5
5 YEAR RATIOS (%)			
Return on Capital	12.0	4.6	6.9
Return on Com. Equity	0.4	(4.3)	(1.7)
Profit Growth	na	na	11.8
Revenue Growth	5.4	3.9	5.2
Asset Growth	(1.0)	(2.0)	0.7
BALANCE SHEET (000)			
Cash	10,751	1,914	3,004
Current Assets	24,978	24,374	22,221
Net Fixed Assets	14,071	18,816	19,107
Invest's & Advances	881	516	284
Total Assets	39,930	43,706	41,761
Short Term Debt	187	6,318	2,874
Current Liabilities	13,967	22,345	15,685
Long Term Debt	422	609	302
Total Liabilities	14,389	22,954	15,987
Total Equity	25,541	20,752	25,774
Total Liab. & Equity	39,930	43,706	41,761
CAPITAL (000)			
Total Debt	609	6,927	3,176
Preferred Equity	0	0	0
Common Equity	25,541	20,752	25,774

Synopsis:

Chateau Stores of Canada Limited made a dramatic turnaround in fiscal 1993 reporting $4.5-million in profits compared to a net loss of $5.3-million in 1992. The positive change came about by closing down 11 U.S. stores and eight in Canada during the year, with further closures planned for the coming fiscal year. Profit gain is also a result of Le Chateau's new merchandising strategy to appeal to a broader range of customers by providing "functional clothing. In fiscal 1993, it managed to cut losses by reducing inventory by 36%, lowering its manufacturing production and slashing operating costs.

Sales from Canadian operations increased 8.2% to $147.3-million in fiscal 1993 and accounted for 93.9% of total sales. U.S. sales fell 34.2% to $9.6-million. Le Chateau's U.S. operations lost $2.2-million in fiscal 1993, mainly due to the write-off of fixed assets related to store closures. Total sales figures were also helped by the success of Le Chateau's in-store boutiques now operating at more than 40 Sears outlets across Canada.

Earnings before taxes were $8.6-million. Cash provided by operations was $9.8-million in fiscal 1993. Capital expenditures were reduced to a low-level of $559,000 and working capital increased to $11-million from $2-million in 1992. Le Chateau suffered a one-time charge of $3.2-million in fiscal 1993, comprised of lease cancellation payments, the write-off of fixed assets and other costs. Its inventory was $12.8-million at year-end. Capital expenditure commitments for fiscal 1994 are $2-million.

First quarter results show sales increasing with an improvement in margins compared with the same period last year.

Relative strength to TSE300 / Price / Volume (in 1000's of board lots)

Rank (Profit/Revenue/Assets)
837   313   569

Herschel H. Segal
Chairman, President & C.E.O.
Serge Lanthier
V.P., Finance & Secretary
Joseph Kolatacz
Exec. V.P., & C.O.O.

Address
5695 Ferrier Street
Mont-Royal
PQ
H4P 1N1
(514) 738-7000

Fax: (514) 738-3670
C0038677/G/12.4

DALMYS (CANADA) LIMITED

Exchanges	Price (Jun24'93)	3.00	Trailing P/E	10.00	Stock Symbol
TM	Trailing Yield (%)	0.00	Trailing EPS	0.30	**DYC**

Period Ending	Feb93	Feb92	Feb91	Feb90	Feb89
Yearly Statistics					
Price-Close	3.00	1.25	6.25	7.75	9.00
Price-High	4.00	4.25	8.38	9.50	10.75
Price-Low	1.00	1.10	5.50	7.75	8.88
P/E-Close	10.00	nm	nm	258.33	90.00
Dividends per Share	0.00	0.00	0.06	0.06	0.06
Dividend Yield (%)	0.00	0.00	0.96	0.77	0.67
Sales per Share	27.80	25.53	29.04	37.70	36.71
EPS before extra. item	0.30	(3.95)	(0.63)	0.03	0.10
Cash Flow per Share	1.17	(0.98)	1.09	1.36	1.41
Book Value per Share	3.02	2.71	6.66	7.35	7.38
O/S Common Shares	4,180	4,180	4,180	4,180	4,180
Total Revenue	116,209	106,735	121,383	157,604	153,465
Income before extra.	1,271	(16,495)	(2,627)	111	426
Cash Flow	4,890	(4,108)	4,544	5,681	5,882
Debt/Equity	0.10	1.06	0.36	0.34	0.34
Return on Capital (%)	9.53	(50.41)	(3.99)	4.31	4.76
Ret. on Com. Equity (%)	10.62	(84.22)	(8.97)	0.36	1.39
% Change Profit	107.7	(527.9)	(2,474.2)	(74.0)	(21.7)
% Change Revenue	8.9	(12.1)	(23.0)	2.7	4.9
% Change Assets	(16.9)	(25.4)	(13.0)	(7.0)	0.0

Date	EPS	DPS	Tot Rev	Inc Bex
Feb 93	0.13	0.00	30,318	552
Nov 92	0.40	0.00	30,852	1,694
Aug 92	(0.21)	0.00	28,392	(887)
May 92	(0.02)	0.00	26,680	(88)
Feb 92	(1.65)	0.00	30,330	(6,885)
Nov 91	(0.48)	0.00	27,637	(1,997)
Aug 91	(1.12)	0.00	24,651	(4,671)
May 91	(0.70)	0.00	24,127	(2,942)

	Feb93	Feb92	Feb91
Preferred Div. Coverage	np	np	np
Total Div. Coverage	na	na	0.0
Interest Coverage	3.5	0.0	0.0
Current Ratio	1.0	0.8	1.2
Operating Margin	1.5	(7.1)	0.3
Asset Turnover	3.7	2.8	2.4
5 YEAR RATIOS (%)			
Return on Capital	(7.2)	(7.6)	4.6
Return on Com. Equity	(16.2)	(17.9)	0.1
Profit Growth	18.5	na	na
Revenue Growth	(4.5)	(4.6)	(1.6)
Asset Growth	(12.9)	(9.2)	(2.0)
BALANCE SHEET (000)			
Cash	5,111	0	1,306
Current Assets	16,947	20,690	25,103
Net Fixed Assets	14,033	16,819	25,381
Invest's & Advances	0	0	0
Total Assets	31,278	37,656	50,484
Short Term Debt	204	10,709	8,524
Current Liabilities	17,574	25,017	21,078
Long Term Debt	1,095	1,300	1,573
Total Liabilities	18,669	26,317	22,651
Total Equity	12,609	11,339	27,834
Total Liab. & Equity	31,278	37,656	50,484
CAPITAL (000)			
Total Debt	1,299	12,009	10,097
Preferred Equity	0	0	0
Common Equity	12,609	11,339	27,834

Business:

DALMYS (CANADA) LTD. is in the business of marketing women's apparel through company-operated retail stores in Canada. Serving a wide range of market types, the Canadian stores operate under the names Dalmys, Gazebo, Cactus and Antels. The stores offer dresses, outerwear, sportswear and accessories.

Synopsis:

Hard hit by the recession in fiscal 1992, Dalmys (Canada) Limited is bouncing back with improved sales and restored profitability in fiscal 1993. Since closing its U.S. operations in fiscal 1992, Dalmys has continued with its restructuring plan, concentrating primarily on new merchandising strategies to attract new consumers.

With 10 fewer stores in its network, Dalmys restored its financial position in fiscal 1993 with sales of $116.2-million, compared to $106.7-million in 1992, attributed primarily to new merchandising strategies. The positive numbers are also a result of reduced expenses in occupancy costs and wages. Earnings came to $1.3-million compared to a loss of $8.6-million in fiscal 1992.

Dalmys's year end cash resources amounted to $5.1-million with no bank indebtedness, compared to a bank indebtedness of $10.5-million and no cash in February 1992. Dalmys's improved cash position resulted in part from a $4.9-million cash flow generated from operations and $7.3-million from the May 1992 sale of the accounts receivable related to its credit card operation.

Relative strength to TSE300

Price

Volume (in 1000's of board lots)

Rank (Profit/Revenue/Assets)
911 365 596

Fred Perlman
President

Fred Hutchinson
V.P. Finance

Address
9475 Meilleur Street
Montreal
PQ
H2N 2C6
(514) 384-1030

D0000384/G/12.4

For further company information, call Globe Information Services 1-800-268-9128 or (416)585-5345

DYLEX LIMITED

Exchanges	Price (Jun24'93)	1.51	Trailing P/E	nm	Stock Symbol
TM	Trailing Yield (%)	0.00	Trailing EPS	(0.33)	**DLX.A**

Period Ending	Jan93	Feb92	Feb91	Feb90	Jan89
Yearly Statistics					
Price-Close	1.20	4.50	4.15	6.50	10.88
Price-High	4.60	5.38	7.00	12.38	11.50
Price-Low	1.02	3.00	2.05	5.75	7.13
P/E-Close	nm	nm	nm	nm	17.26
Dividends per Share	0.01	0.01	0.10	0.20	0.20
Dividend Yield (%)	0.46	0.22	2.41	3.08	1.84
Sales per Share	27.44	35.36	36.83	36.27	30.56
EPS before extra. item	(0.35)	(1.07)	(0.07)	(1.28)	0.63
Cash Flow per Share	0.13	(0.09)	0.61	1.21	1.74
Book Value per Share	1.36	1.31	1.93	2.15	3.49
O/S Common Shares	71,380	63,379	47,378	47,378	47,378
Total Revenue	1,940,627	1,840,391	1,757,109	1,729,619	1,455,341
Income before extra.	(21,945)	(55,430)	(3,223)	(60,701)	29,785
Cash Flow	8,854	(4,801)	28,876	57,414	82,225
Debt/Equity	1.94	2.49	2.80	2.56	1.58
Return on Capital (%)	0.38	(6.25)	5.59	0.62	18.50
Ret. on Com. Equity (%)	(27.21)	(63.49)	(3.33)	(45.43)	18.73
% Change Profit	60.4	(1,619.8)	94.7	(303.8)	125.3
% Change Revenue	5.4	4.7	1.6	18.8	10.8
% Change Assets	(3.3)	0.3	5.3	(0.2)	5.6

Preferred Div. Coverage	0.0	na	na
Total Div. Coverage	0.0	0.0	0.0
Interest Coverage	0.0	0.0	0.7
Current Ratio	1.5	1.6	2.5
Operating Margin	0.3	(0.9)	0.9
Asset Turnover	2.6	2.3	2.2
5 YEAR RATIOS (%)			
Return on Capital	3.8	1.9	6.6
Return on Com. Equity	(24.1)	(29.5)	(15.0)
Profit Growth	na	na	na
Revenue Growth	8.0	8.5	10.0
Asset Growth	1.4	2.9	6.9
BALANCE SHEET (000)			
Cash	111,579	117,327	152,539
Current Assets	401,159	461,804	490,028
Net Fixed Assets	215,118	213,056	206,371
Invest's & Advances	16,028	14,411	15,507
Total Assets	756,793	782,712	780,551
Short Term Debt	47,162	54,913	25,160
Current Liabilities	265,789	283,905	199,539
Long Term Debt	240,735	279,586	375,025
Total Liabilities	608,175	648,099	637,549
Total Equity	148,618	134,613	143,002
Total Liab. & Equity	756,793	782,712	780,551
CAPITAL (000)			
Total Debt	287,897	334,499	400,185
Preferred Equity	51,495	51,495	51,495
Common Equity	97,123	83,118	91,507

Business:

DYLEX Ltd. is a specialty fashion retailer and manufacturer. The company is represented in major markets through chains of women's, men's and family clothing stores across North America. Store names in Canada include Fairweather, Suzy Shier, Braemar, TipTop, Harry Rosen, La Senza, Steel, BiWay, Thriftys, Club Monaco and Drug World. U.S. stores include NBO and Club Monaco U.S.A.

Date	EPS	DPS	Tot Rev	Inc Bex
May 93	(0.25)	0.00	399,760	(17,402)
Jan 93	0.04	0.00	602,041	3,819
Oct 92	(0.01)	0.00	501,419	(2,998)
Aug 92	(0.11)	0.00	442,829	(6,972)
May 92	(0.24)	0.00	389,311	(15,794)
Feb 92	(0.13)	0.00	546,901	(10,691)
Nov 91	(0.16)	0.00	474,111	(7,126)
Aug 91	(0.33)	0.00	417,503	(15,949)

Synopsis:

Dylex Limited had agreed to sell its $50.1% stake in Suzy Shier for $60.5-million in June 1993 to raise desperately needed cash to fund working capital requirements. This public offering would cut about $175-million from Dylex's annual revenue and 262 stores from its network. A new company investment includes Pacific Linen Inc. in Washington.

Dylex's consolidated sales for the year ending January 30, 1993, totaled $1.93-billion, up considerably from fiscal 1992, despite poor performance from its Family Stores Group, the BiWay in particular. Its operations loss for the year came down to about $21.9-million from $35.4-million in fiscal 1992. A $29.5-million equity issue reduced the company's long-term debt and obligations under capital leases by $47.7-million to just over $181-million. Manufacturing sales dropped in fiscal 1993 as a result of downsizing and store closures.

Sales in the Canadian men's wear group rose 6%, with Steel and Tip Top Tailors ahead. Canadian women's wear sales jumped by 15.2% led by the Suzy Shier and La Senza chains. Family Stores in Canada reported a 2.6% sales drop, drained away by BiWay. U.S. retail sales rose by 13.3%.

The percentage of sales for fiscal 1993 by segment were: men's Canada, 18%; women's Canada 25%; family Canada 41%; and U.S. operations, 16%. Wet Seal achieved the largest improvement in sales among the U.S. operations.

Relative strength to TSE300 / Price / Volume (in 1000's of board lots)

Rank (Profit/Revenue/Assets)
958 66 174

Wilfred Posluns
Chairman & C.E.O.

Lionel Robins
President & C.O.O.

David Posluns
C.F.O., Sr. V.P. & Sec.-Treas.

Address
637 Lake Shore Boulevard West
Toronto
ON
M5V 1A8
(416) 586-7000

Fax: (416) 586-7056
D0003576/G/12.4

EMPIRE COMPANY LIMITED

Exchanges	Price (Jun24'93)	12.50	Trailing P/E	19.84	Stock Symbol
TM	Trailing Yield (%)	1.36	Trailing EPS	0.63	**EMP.A**

Period Ending	Apr92	Apr91	Apr90	Apr89	Apr88
Yearly Statistics					
Price-Close	12.63	11.88	12.50	14.75	12.00
Price-High	13.75	13.50	17.50	16.00	17.50
Price-Low	11.00	8.75	12.25	10.75	9.00
P/E-Close	45.09	1,187.50	nm	19.41	13.64
Dividends per Share	0.16	0.16	0.16	0.16	0.14
Dividend Yield (%)	1.27	1.35	1.28	1.09	1.17
Sales per Share	65.24	60.66	53.68	50.36	44.49
EPS before extra. item	0.28	0.01	(0.17)	0.76	0.88
Cash Flow per Share	1.87	1.73	1.60	1.75	1.47
Book Value per Share	7.56	7.41	7.42	7.28	6.41
O/S Common Shares	34,461	34,484	34,434	32,243	31,604
Total Revenue	2,248,300	2,092,935	1,809,280	1,596,036	1,403,267
Income before extra.	20,950	14,425	8,568	37,359	36,993
Cash Flow	64,608	59,783	54,078	55,574	46,485
Debt/Equity	1.85	1.70	1.46	1.43	1.12
Return on Capital (%)	9.58	9.73	8.76	11.96	13.80
Ret. on Com. Equity (%)	3.70	0.10	(2.33)	10.85	17.28
% Change Profit	45.2	68.4	(77.1)	1.0	9.8
% Change Revenue	7.4	15.7	13.4	13.7	17.6
% Change Assets	2.9	8.6	5.4	18.3	32.5

Preferred Div. Coverage	1.8	1.0	0.6
Total Div. Coverage	1.4	0.8	0.5
Interest Coverage	1.4	1.3	1.3
Current Ratio	0.7	0.8	0.8
Operating Margin	4.3	4.7	5.0
Asset Turnover	1.6	1.5	1.4

5 YEAR RATIOS (%)			
Return on Capital	10.8	12.2	13.3
Return on Com. Equity	5.9	12.0	15.7
Profit Growth	(9.1)	3.1	0.1
Revenue Growth	13.4	14.9	14.7
Asset Growth	13.0	21.2	23.4

BALANCE SHEET (000)			
Cash	127,323	122,514	123,339
Current Assets	343,216	355,903	308,423
Net Fixed Assets	720,298	673,392	583,739
Invest's & Advances	366,651	363,411	388,979
Total Assets	1,443,249	1,401,989	1,291,382
Short Term Debt	277,002	257,580	223,713
Current Liabilities	490,601	474,815	402,349
Long Term Debt	472,635	430,740	386,684
Total Liabilities	1,037,211	997,689	873,614
Total Equity	406,038	404,300	417,768
Total Liab. & Equity	1,443,249	1,401,989	1,291,382

CAPITAL (000)			
Total Debt	749,637	688,320	610,397
Preferred Equity	145,458	148,781	162,135
Common Equity	260,580	255,519	255,633

Business:

EMPIRE CO. LTD. is a food distribution and real estate company. Sobeys Inc., a supermarket chain, operates in Atlantic Canada, Ontario and Quebec. Sobeys has wholesale operations in Atlantic Canada, Ontario and New England. Empire owns Atlantic Shopping Centres Ltd. and Sobey Leasing. It also owns 36% of Halifax Developments Ltd., 25% of Univa Inc., 16% of Jannock Limited and 46% of Wajax Limited.

Date	EPS	DPS	Tot Rev	Inc Bex
Jan 93	0.19	0.05	603,550	9,052
Oct 92	0.21	0.04	586,956	10,231
Jul 92	0.17	0.04	594,728	8,420
Apr 92	0.06	0.04	549,536	4,632
Jan 92	0.01	0.04	544,479	3,066
Oct 91	0.06	0.04	561,656	4,946
Jul 91	0.15	0.04	576,994	8,306
Apr 91	0.11	0.04	537,874	7,159

Synopsis:

Empire is continuing to pursue opportunities in Atlantic Canada and to strengthen its existing operations, but feels it must expand the boundaries in which it operates in order to grow. The company's current strategies are: to maintain and strengthen its Atlantic base of operations; to expand retail operations in Central Canada, while continuing to grow its Hannaford investment in the northeastern United States; to expand its real estate portfolio; and to maintain its equity investment philosophy of participating in the growth of other enterprises, whose leadership is for long-term growth and profitability.

In February 1993, Empire announced the purchase of Scotia Investments Limited's interest in Halifax Developments Limited. The final purchase price will be determined by an independent valuation and is expected later in the year. This will increase Empire's fully diluted interest from 56% to 84%. Empire also decided to discontinue its underwriting operations in the United Kingdom at the end of 1992.

During fiscal 1992, seven new stores were opened, while plans call for further expansion during fiscal 1993, but at a reduced rate. Two new units are to be built, and major expansion and remodeling are scheduled to be completed at 13 Sobeys locations and 1 Lo-food location.

Empire's wholesale group currently has over 1,000 stores operating under the banners Foodland, Needs, Green Gables, Kwikway, Riteway and Clover Farm. The Foodland program continued to expand Sobey's presence in rural areas of Atlantic Canada and Ontario; there are now 92 franchised and associated stores.

Empire's revenue (earnings) by segment in fiscal 1992 was: food distribution, 88% (46%); real estate, 4% (51%); and corporate and other, 7% (3%).

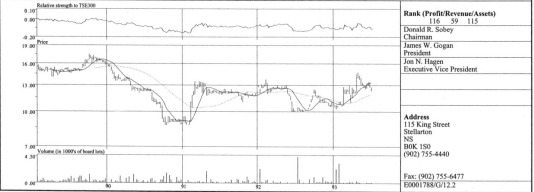

Rank (Profit/Revenue/Assets)
116   59   115

Donald R. Sobey
Chairman

James W. Gogan
President

Jon N. Hagen
Executive Vice President

Address
115 King Street
Stellarton
NS
B0K 1S0
(902) 755-4440

Fax: (902) 755-6477
E0001788/G/12.2

GENDIS INC.

| Exchanges | Price (Jun24'93) | 19.50 | Trailing P/E | 20.53 | Stock Symbol |
| T | Trailing Yield (%) | 2.77 | Trailing EPS | 0.95 | GDS.A |

Period Ending	Jan93	Jan92	Jan91	Jan90	Jan89	Business:
Yearly Statistics						GENDIS INC. is a holding company with
Price-Close	17.00	22.50	19.50	21.50	20.25	interests in merchandising, electronics, real
Price-High	23.25	25.50	22.63	25.63	20.38	estate and oil and gas. The company wholly
Price-Low	16.00	18.25	18.88	19.50	14.13	owns Metropolitan Stores of Canada Ltd.,
P/E-Close	21.52	24.46	11.82	14.33	14.36	which operates junior department and clothing
Dividends per Share	0.54	0.54	0.52	0.50	0.48	stores under the names Greenberg, Saan and
Dividend Yield (%)	3.18	2.40	2.67	2.33	2.37	Metropolitan. It also owns 51% of Sony of
Sales per Share	47.10	44.89	46.18	44.58	36.51	Canada Ltd., a joint venture with Sony
EPS before extra. item	0.79	0.92	1.65	1.50	1.41	Corporation, Japan, and 32% of Chauvco
Cash Flow per Share	1.12	1.40	1.97	2.06	1.94	Resources Ltd.
Book Value per Share	11.28	11.03	10.65	9.50	8.42	
O/S Common Shares	16,838	16,835	16,825	16,842	16,625	
Total Revenue	793,126	755,561	776,962	748,157	676,837	

Date	EPS	DPS	Tot Rev	Inc Bex
May 93	(0.02)	0.14	160,958	(263)
Jan 93	0.53	0.14	251,023	8,992
Oct 92	0.36	0.14	207,753	6,029
Jul 92	0.08	0.14	179,477	1,355
Apr 92	(0.18)	0.14	154,873	(3,097)
Jan 92	0.40	0.14	234,749	6,649
Oct 91	0.37	0.14	200,574	6,260
Jul 91	0.18	0.14	172,772	2,997

Period Ending	Jan93	Jan92	Jan91	Jan90	Jan89
Income before extra.	13,279	15,436	27,757	25,175	26,140
Cash Flow	18,928	23,516	33,083	34,625	35,974
Debt/Equity	0.68	0.62	0.58	0.82	0.70
Return on Capital (%)	9.56	12.26	22.29	22.93	25.77
Ret. on Com. Equity (%)	7.07	8.46	16.36	16.77	17.90
% Change Profit	(14.0)	(44.4)	10.3	(3.7)	16.6
% Change Revenue	5.0	(2.8)	3.9	10.5	11.4
% Change Assets	5.6	6.9	(4.5)	15.4	14.1

Preferred Div. Coverage	np	np	2,135.2
Total Div. Coverage	1.5	1.7	3.2
Interest Coverage	2.4	2.9	2.9
Current Ratio	1.3	1.4	1.7
Operating Margin	2.7	4.0	7.2
Asset Turnover	2.0	2.0	2.2
5 YEAR RATIOS (%)			
Return on Capital	18.6	22.0	25.4
Return on Com. Equity	13.3	15.0	16.6
Profit Growth	(10.0)	(7.3)	1.6
Revenue Growth	5.4	5.0	8.2
Asset Growth	7.2	7.1	6.8
BALANCE SHEET (000)			
Cash	7,927	2,742	2,683
Current Assets	187,943	186,487	189,080
Net Fixed Assets	111,357	109,968	110,537
Invest's & Advances	85,858	68,069	41,629
Total Assets	391,253	370,466	346,504
Short Term Debt	84,344	69,881	57,582
Current Liabilities	147,967	130,547	112,266
Long Term Debt	45,000	45,000	45,675
Total Liabilities	201,329	184,778	167,195
Total Equity	189,924	185,688	179,309
Total Liab. & Equity	391,253	370,466	346,504
CAPITAL (000)			
Total Debt	129,344	114,881	103,257
Preferred Equity	0	0	209
Common Equity	189,924	185,688	179,100

Synopsis:

Gendis Inc. experienced a drop in earnings in fiscal 1993 due largely to a decline in its general merchandising and real estate operations, brought on by reduced consumer spending and depressed real estate prices.

In fiscal 1993, 62% of Gendis's revenue came from its 460 outlet retail operation. Sales at its Metropolitan chain declined, as well as sales at Saan for Kids. Sale at Greenberg stores were down 6%. Saan Stores had a growth in excess of 8% because of strong marketing and advertising campaigns. Gendis closed down several non-profitable stores and opened 29 new stores. Electronic sales held up despite tough economic times, because of the increased sales of video cassette recorders and compact disc players. However, electronics sales did experience a decline in operating margins. Real estate revenues came down, but Gendis's 32% holding in Chauvco Resources Ltd. increased earning contributions by 58% to $8.2-million.

About $21-million in net capital expenditures are planned for fiscal 1994. The money is to be spent on store upgrades.

Rank (Profit/Revenue/Assets)
154   122   240

Albert D. Cohen
Chairman & C.E.O.

G. Allan Mackenzie
President & C.O.O.

Patrick J. Matthews
Vice President, Finance

Address
P.O. Box 9400
Winnipeg
MB
R3C 3C3
(204) 474-5200

Fax: (204) 474-5216
G0000607/G/12.3

GEORGE WESTON LIMITED

Exchanges	Price (Jun24'93)		Trailing P/E		Stock Symbol
TMV	Trailing Yield (%)	45.25	Trailing EPS	45.25	**WN**
		1.54		1.00	

Period Ending	Dec92	Dec91	Dec90	Dec89	Dec88
Yearly Statistics					
Price-Close	36.75	36.75	41.75	43.25	35.00
Price-High	40.00	46.50	43.75	45.50	36.80
Price-Low	33.00	35.50	36.75	35.00	30.00
P/E-Close	43.24	20.30	16.57	14.42	12.96
Dividends per Share	0.70	0.70	0.70	0.66	0.61
Dividend Yield (%)	1.91	1.91	1.68	1.53	1.74
Sales per Share	248.86	232.09	234.84	226.62	234.97
EPS before extra. item	0.85	1.81	2.52	3.00	2.70
Cash Flow per Share	6.69	6.21	7.70	7.97	7.57
Book Value per Share	27.08	26.24	25.35	23.46	20.59
O/S Common Shares (mil)	47	47	46	46	46
Total Revenue ($mil)	11,610	10,782	10,869	10,472	10,831
Income before extra. ($mil)	48	92	125	150	137
Cash Flow ($mil)	312	288	356	368	349
Debt/Equity	0.69	0.63	0.63	0.68	0.77
Return on Capital (%)	8.73	11.93	15.99	18.60	16.35
Ret. on Com. Equity (%)	3.22	7.02	10.37	13.67	13.91
% Change Profit	(47.8)	(26.4)	(16.7)	9.2	2.5
% Change Revenue	7.7	(0.8)	3.8	(3.3)	(1.8)
% Change Assets	3.6	3.3	4.4	2.2	(2.0)

Preferred Div. Coverage	6.0	11.5	15.6
Total Div. Coverage	1.2	2.2	3.0
Interest Coverage	1.8	2.2	2.7
Current Ratio	1.1	1.3	1.2
Operating Margin	1.8	2.4	3.3
Asset Turnover	2.9	2.8	2.9

5 YEAR RATIOS (%)			
Return on Capital	14.3	16.1	17.2
Return on Com. Equity	9.6	12.0	13.5
Profit Growth	(18.6)	(5.0)	4.3
Revenue Growth	1.0	1.4	4.0
Asset Growth	2.2	3.8	7.1

BALANCE SHEET (mil)			
Cash	211,000	274,000	89,000
Current Assets	1,564,000	1,553,000	1,437,000
Net Fixed Assets	2,129,000	1,996,000	1,968,000
Invest's & Advances	125,000	145,000	160,000
Total Assets	3,965,000	3,829,000	3,707,000
Short Term Debt	148,000	102,000	76,000
Current Liabilities	1,388,000	1,215,000	1,193,000
Long Term Debt	730,000	734,000	724,000
Total Liabilities	2,699,000	2,503,000	2,429,000
Total Equity	1,266,000	1,326,000	1,278,000
Total Liab. & Equity	3,965,000	3,829,000	3,707,000

CAPITAL (mil)			
Total Debt	878,000	836,000	800,000
Preferred Equity	4,000	104,000	106,000
Common Equity	1,262,000	1,222,000	1,172,000

Business:

GEORGE WESTON LTD. is a diversified company with interests in food processing, food distribution and resources in North America. Operating groups include Weston Foods Ltd., which makes baked goods, Loblaw Cos. Ltd. a wholesale and retail food distributor, and Weston Resources Ltd., a forest products and fisheries company.

Date	EPS	DPS	Tot Rev	Inc Bex
Mar 93	0.24	0.17	2,714,500	11,100
Dec 92	0.46	0.18	3,028,600	23,900
Sep 92	0.27	0.18	3,389,400	14,200
Jun 92	0.03	0.18	2,680,000	3,800
Mar 92	0.09	0.18	2,501,000	6,100
Dec 91	0.33	0.18	2,551,800	17,200
Sep 91	0.22	0.18	3,182,700	12,200
Jun 91	1.06	0.18	2,600,200	51,300

Synopsis:

Weston feels it is now in a position for a substantial recovery in earnings even in a slow or no growth economy. The significant cost of restructuring has been completed. In 1993, Weston Foods's results will improve as the baking segment improves. Loblaw Companies should have steady growth in sales and modest margin recovery, and Weston Resources earnings should improve along with the economy.

Weston Foods had a good start to 1992, but deflationary pricing, restructuring of key customers and partners, high costs of raw materials and plant start ups and closings resulted in year-end results being depressed. The collapse of the Quebec grocery market and other smaller accounts also affected Canadian results. In the U.S., the failure of Neilson Cadbury's U.S. distribution partner and other retail restructurings caused losses. In early 1993, Weston reorganized its bakeries into one North American division.

Loblaw made market share gains in 1992 in a highly competitive, negative inflation environment, while maintaining its trading profit. Loblaw was able to increase sales by 8.5% and tonnage by 7% by reducing its cost structure, reinvesting in its most efficient formats and increasing concentration on its private label products. Continued control of costs is believed to be the fundamental way for success by Loblaw.

Weston Resources' results improved in 1992 after the poor results of 1991. However, increased economic activity failed to materialize as expected at the beginning of the year. With pessimism still remaining in various markets that are important to its resource operations, Weston continues to temper its prospects in the near term.

The breakdown of 1992 sales (operating income) by business unit was: Weston Foods, 14% (6%); Loblaw Companies, 78% (87%); and Weston Resources, 8% (7%). Sales (operating income) by country were: Canada, 79% (74%); and the U.S., 21% (26%).

Relative strength to TSE300 / Price / Volume (in 1000's of board lots)

Rank (Profit/Revenue/Assets)
64 4 53

W. Galen Weston
Chairman & President
Robert H. Kidd
Sr. V.P. & C.F.O.

Address
22 St. Clair Avenue East
Suite 1901
Toronto
ON
M4T 2S7
(416) 922-2500

Fax: (416) 922-4395
W0002354/G/12.2

HUDSON'S BAY COMPANY

Exchanges	Price (Jun24'93)	36.12	Trailing P/E	15.57	Stock Symbol
TM	Trailing Yield (%)	2.21	Trailing EPS	2.32	**HBC**

Period Ending	Jan93	Jan92	Jan91	Jan90	Jan89
Yearly Statistics					
Price-Close	29.38	29.25	24.00	28.50	25.00
Price-High	32.25	37.00	34.00	38.00	26.25
Price-Low	25.50	23.88	16.00	24.75	18.50
P/E-Close	12.66	18.17	6.94	6.52	34.25
Dividends per Share	0.80	0.80	0.80	0.60	0.60
Dividend Yield (%)	2.72	2.74	3.33	2.11	2.40
Sales per Share	102.51	102.79	110.19	137.64	147.98
EPS before extra. item	2.32	1.61	3.46	4.37	0.73
Cash Flow per Share	4.57	3.46	4.51	5.68	4.42
Book Value per Share	25.92	24.43	23.56	21.12	22.82
O/S Common Shares	50,756	49,828	45,598	44,609	30,993
Total Revenue	5,164,482	5,049,963	4,969,978	4,603,673	4,671,740
Income before extra.	116,723	82,780	163,282	168,189	49,172
Cash Flow	229,803	169,548	203,227	190,005	134,063
Debt/Equity	0.99	1.13	1.10	1.14	1.88
Return on Capital (%)	12.43	11.28	13.73	12.92	9.18
Ret. on Com. Equity (%)	9.19	6.79	15.42	17.72	3.11
% Change Profit	41.0	(49.3)	(2.9)	242.0	162.7
% Change Revenue	2.3	1.6	8.0	(1.5)	(3.6)
% Change Assets	0.2	5.6	12.3	(20.9)	(3.5)

Preferred Div. Coverage	np	16.5	20.8
Total Div. Coverage	2.9	1.9	0.5
Interest Coverage	2.6	1.9	2.0
Current Ratio	2.2	2.0	1.6
Operating Margin	6.4	5.6	6.4
Asset Turnover	1.6	1.5	1.6
5 YEAR RATIOS (%)			
Return on Capital	11.9	9.6	9.2
Return on Com. Equity	10.4	5.9	4.7
Profit Growth	44.1	20.2	na
Revenue Growth	1.3	(2.4)	(1.1)
Asset Growth	(2.0)	(5.3)	(6.7)
BALANCE SHEET (000)			
Cash	14,620	11,952	19,329
Current Assets	2,170,593	2,220,191	2,117,099
Net Fixed Assets	705,571	665,400	624,904
Invest's & Advances	83,843	84,079	67,494
Total Assets	3,279,679	3,274,118	3,100,289
Short Term Debt	426,514	484,019	701,748
Current Liabilities	1,007,462	1,116,850	1,335,581
Long Term Debt	874,792	904,533	592,661
Total Liabilities	1,964,226	2,048,093	1,928,242
Total Equity	1,315,453	1,226,025	1,172,047
Total Liab. & Equity	3,279,679	3,274,118	3,100,289
CAPITAL (000)			
Total Debt	1,301,306	1,388,552	1,294,409
Preferred Equity	0	8,699	97,919
Common Equity	1,315,453	1,217,326	1,074,128

Business:

HUDSON'S BAY CO. is a merchandising company. Through its three operating divisions, The Bay, Zellers, and Fields, the company covers the Canadian retail market across all price zones and from coast to coast. On a combined basis, it accounts for about 7.5% of Canadian retail sales, excluding food and automobiles. The Thomson family holds 25% of the company's common shares.

Date		EPS	DPS	Tot Rev	Inc Bex
Jan	93	1.83	0.20	1,719,651	92,219
Oct	92	0.44	0.20	1,263,955	21,677
Jul	92	0.14	0.20	1,140,500	7,338
Apr	92	(0.09)	0.20	1,028,110	(4,511)
Jan	92	1.43	0.20	1,588,546	70,475
Oct	91	0.50	0.20	1,215,779	25,087
Jul	91	0.20	0.20	1,176,322	10,315
Apr	91	(0.51)	0.20	1,051,596	(23,097)

Synopsis:

Sales for the Hudson's Bay Company (HBC) continued to climb in fiscal 1993 despite the recession and less retail traffic. HBC's healthy position should continue to grow in fiscal 1994 resulting from a June 1993 merger with Woodward's Limited. Under this agreement, 21 out of 25 Woodward's stores would continue operating as either The Bay or Zellers.

A strong performance by Zellers and a recovery at The Bay saw fiscal 1993 company earnings increase from last year and operating profit rise to $315-million. HBC sales totaled $5.2-billion, up from 1992.

Operating profit from Zellers rose by $11.1-million to $229.1-million in fiscal 1993, principally because of an 8.3% sales gain, to $3-billion. Strategic marketing, advertising and Club Z helped increase sales as well. The largest market share gains were recorded in Quebec and Ontario. Over 75% of all purchaes at Zellers are made by Club Z cardholders. Zellers initiated a $40-million program to replace all point-of-sale systems over a three year period. It opened six stores in fiscal 1993.

At The Bay, operating profit rose by $32.1-million to $91.5-million from fiscal 1992, due to a higher gross profit rate, lower expenses and better credit results. The recession is blamed for a decline in sales and revenue, amounting to $2-billion. The Bay opened five new stores in fiscal 1993. In fiscal 1993, The Bay upgraded its 4,500 cash registers with a system that will reduce operating costs.

Fields, HBC's western subsidiary, recorded an operating loss of $1.3-million in fiscal 1993, with sales down by 3.3%, also affected by the slump in consumer spending. Sales totaled $84-million. A hard-sell advertising campaign is planned to increase sales.

On July 10, 1992, the Woodbridge Company Limited completed the sale of 3.5 million common shares of HBC and sold a further 20 million on November 26, 1992. These transactions reduced its holdings from about 72% to around 25% of the outstanding common shares.

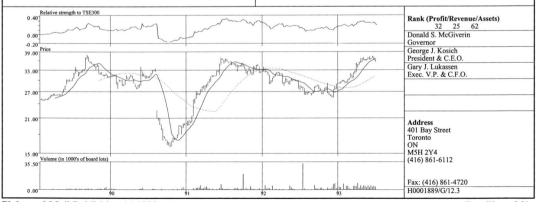

Rank (Profit/Revenue/Assets)		
32	25	62

Donald S. McGiverin
Governor

George J. Kosich
President & C.E.O.

Gary J. Lukassen
Exec. V.P. & C.F.O.

Address
401 Bay Street
Toronto
ON
M5H 2Y4
(416) 861-6112

Fax: (416) 861-4720
H0001889/G/12.3

JEAN COUTU GROUP (PJC) INC. (THE)

Exchanges	Price (Jun24'93)	15.37	Trailing P/E	20.77	Stock Symbol
TM	Trailing Yield (%)	0.78	Trailing EPS	0.74	**PJC.A**

Period Ending	May92	May91	May90	May89	May88
Yearly Statistics					
Price-Close	14.00	11.31	6.56	6.13	4.38
Price-High	15.25	11.88	7.25	6.13	4.75
Price-Low	11.31	6.56	5.88	4.31	2.50
P/E-Close	20.29	nm	12.15	17.25	14.83
Dividends per Share	0.10	0.10	0.07	0.06	0.04
Dividend Yield (%)	0.71	0.88	0.99	0.98	0.91
Sales per Share	12.59	10.78	8.68	7.79	6.41
EPS before extra. item	0.69	(0.58)	0.54	0.36	0.30
Cash Flow per Share	0.89	0.73	0.62	0.46	0.40
Book Value per Share	3.69	3.06	2.59	2.13	1.83
O/S Common Shares	52,464	52,411	52,111	52,070	52,000
Total Revenue	755,002	644,718	522,678	471,690	389,638
Income before extra.	35,945	30,410	28,028	18,495	15,467
Cash Flow	46,645	38,300	32,206	24,153	20,860
Debt/Equity	0.34	0.32	0.03	0.08	0.13
Return on Capital (%)	25.96	29.22	33.88	27.43	30.71
Ret. on Com. Equity (%)	20.31	20.56	22.80	17.97	17.41
% Change Profit	18.2	8.5	51.5	19.6	39.2
% Change Revenue	17.1	23.3	10.8	21.1	40.9
% Change Assets	13.0	53.6	18.3	11.6	30.4

Business:

JEAN COUTU GROUP (PJC) INC. oversees the operation of 210 retail franchises in Canada and 21 company stores in the United States. The drug stores sell pharmaceuticals, health products, cosmetics, snacks and other products. It operates under the names PJC Jean Coutu, Super Escomptes Jean Coutu, Pharmacie Jean Coutu Pharmacy, Maxi Drug, and Douglas Maxi Drug.

Date	EPS	DPS	Tot Rev	Inc Bex
Feb 93	0.19	0.03	185,014	9,941
Nov 92	0.18	0.03	216,563	9,666
Aug 92	0.17	0.03	193,818	8,929
May 92	0.20	0.03	198,447	9,883
Feb 92	0.18	0.03	182,237	9,412
Nov 91	0.16	0.03	195,494	8,058
Aug 91	0.17	0.03	178,824	8,592
May 91	0.13	0.03	181,569	6,614

Preferred Div. Coverage	np	np	na
Total Div. Coverage	6.9	5.8	8.3
Interest Coverage	9.6	17.9	57.0
Current Ratio	1.5	1.4	2.4
Operating Margin	7.4	6.8	6.8
Asset Turnover	2.0	2.0	2.4
5 YEAR RATIOS (%)			
Return on Capital	29.4	31.1	35.1
Return on Com. Equity	19.8	19.9	23.9
Profit Growth	26.4	28.4	34.8
Revenue Growth	22.2	27.1	24.1
Asset Growth	24.4	39.2	35.7
BALANCE SHEET (000)			
Cash	0	0	19,019
Current Assets	152,255	142,550	114,013
Net Fixed Assets	121,661	96,025	36,898
Invest's & Advances	16,244	16,933	20,431
Total Assets	325,172	287,702	187,298
Short Term Debt	33,422	24,416	1,418
Current Liabilities	99,091	100,019	48,445
Long Term Debt	31,803	26,331	3,005
Total Liabilities	131,811	127,111	52,114
Total Equity	193,361	160,591	135,184
Total Liab. & Equity	325,172	287,702	187,298
CAPITAL (000)			
Total Debt	65,225	50,747	4,423
Preferred Equity	0	0	2
Common Equity	193,361	160,591	135,182

Synopsis:

Despite difficult economic times, The Jean Coutu Group is one of the few Canadian retailers that remains profitable and eager to expand, as it seeks new ventures in New England and Ontario. The commune is even considering expanding operations in Europe.

For the nine month period ending February 28, 1993, the Jean Coutu Group posted net earnings of $28.5-million compared to $26-million for the same period last year. Earnings before income taxes and minority interests increased by 15.8% and net earnings by 9.5% due to an increase in the company's tax rate. Consolidated revenue totaled $595.4-million, up from $556.6-million a year earlier. Cash flow was $36.5-million, used to repay a $3.3-million debt. The group's real estate portfolio was $14.8-million in investments.

Retail sales and other revenue for the U.S. Douglas Maxi Drug network amounted to $75.8-million and the group's Canadian operations generated revenue of $519.6-million during this nine-month period. The franchise network posed an increase of almost 10% in retail sales which totaled $941.4-million. Working capital totaled $63.3-million as of February 28, 1993.

Rank (Profit/Revenue/Assets)		
83	128	265

Jean Coutu
Chairman & C.E.O.

Francois Jean Coutu
President & C.O.O.

Carole Bouthillette
V.P., Finance

Address
530, Rue Beriault
Longueuil
PQ
J4G 1S8
(514) 646-9760

Fax: (514) 646-5649
J0000729/G/12.3

LOBLAW COMPANIES LIMITED

Exchanges	Price (Jun24'93)	23.75	Trailing P/E	26.10	Stock Symbol
TMV	Trailing Yield (%)	0.67	Trailing EPS	0.91	**L**

Period Ending	Jan93	Dec91	Dec90	Dec89	Dec88
Yearly Statistics					
Price-Close	19.50	17.88	18.38	14.50	10.50
Price-High	20.50	22.50	18.88	15.25	13.13
Price-Low	16.38	16.38	13.63	10.25	9.88
P/E-Close	22.16	15.28	16.71	18.13	25.61
Dividends per Share	0.24	0.24	0.20	0.20	0.20
Dividend Yield (%)	1.23	1.34	1.09	1.38	1.91
Sales per Share	117.75	112.55	116.19	109.91	114.95
EPS before extra. item	0.88	1.17	1.10	0.80	0.41
Cash Flow per Share	2.61	2.72	2.73	2.46	1.97
Book Value per Share	10.67	9.63	8.11	7.22	6.74
O/S Common Shares	78,932	78,381	72,621	72,255	72,111
Total Revenue	9,266,100	8,539,400	8,416,600	7,933,900	8,307,600
Income before extra.	79,800	104,700	96,000	70,200	40,800
Cash Flow	205,200	206,100	198,000	177,600	142,500
Debt/Equity	0.59	0.63	0.58	0.74	0.96
Return on Capital (%)	12.16	16.00	16.62	14.66	10.14
Ret. on Com. Equity (%)	8.65	13.20	14.35	11.51	5.84
% Change Profit	(23.8)	9.1	36.8	72.1	(44.6)
% Change Revenue	8.5	1.5	6.1	(4.5)	(3.7)
% Change Assets	4.8	12.3	3.1	1.8	(9.5)
Preferred Div. Coverage	7.5	6.5	5.9		
Total Div. Coverage	2.7	3.1	3.1		
Interest Coverage	3.0	3.6	3.3		
Current Ratio	1.2	1.3	1.1		
Operating Margin	2.1	2.6	2.5		
Asset Turnover	3.7	3.6	4.0		
5 YEAR RATIOS (%)					
Return on Capital	13.9	14.3	14.1		
Return on Com. Equity	10.7	11.4	11.7		
Profit Growth	1.6	7.3	7.4		
Revenue Growth	1.4	1.7	3.9		
Asset Growth	2.2	3.5	6.5		
BALANCE SHEET (000)					
Cash	208,000	253,400	31,200		
Current Assets	1,051,900	1,050,100	807,100		
Net Fixed Assets	1,231,400	1,115,100	1,077,700		
Invest's & Advances	94,100	106,800	123,500		
Total Assets	2,474,100	2,361,600	2,102,300		
Short Term Debt	5,600	33,100	4,200		
Current Liabilities	868,400	787,300	756,500		
Long Term Debt	572,000	560,600	469,200		
Total Liabilities	1,501,900	1,420,600	1,290,000		
Total Equity	972,200	941,000	812,300		
Total Liab. & Equity	2,474,100	2,361,600	2,102,300		
CAPITAL (000)					
Total Debt	577,600	593,700	473,400		
Preferred Equity	129,700	185,900	223,500		
Common Equity	842,500	755,100	588,800		

Business:

LOBLAW COS. LTD. is a food distribution company. The company operates grocery stores in all provinces in Canada and in the St. Louis and New Orleans areas of the United States, under various names, including Loblaws, Zehrs, SuperCentre and Real Canadian Superstore. The company also has operations as a food wholesaler across Canada. George Weston Ltd. of Toronto owns 77% of the company's common shares.

Date	EPS	DPS	Tot Rev	Inc Bex
Mar 93	0.21	0.00	2,115,000	18,600
Jan 93	0.33	0.06	2,391,000	28,800
Oct 92	0.26	0.06	2,814,200	23,700
Jun 92	0.11	0.04	2,121,200	10,800
Mar 92	0.18	0.06	1,940,100	16,500
Dec 91	0.33	0.06	2,009,200	29,500
Oct 91	0.34	0.06	2,651,600	31,500
Jun 91	0.30	0.05	2,009,500	25,400

Synopsis:

Loblaw Companies's strong sales growth in fiscal 1993 and strengthening fourth quarter sales and earnings are indications that the company's strategy of maintaining or improving market share or market share per store and being patient for income growth is working. Loblaw expects to see reasonable growth in fiscal 1994, perhaps to record levels. Loblaw will continue to find ways to run its businesses more efficiently, to make even better use of its corporate brands and business systems, and to expand.

In the first quarter Loblaw had growth in both sales and tonnage. The company increased its market share during the recession despite increased competition from warehouse operators. Margins in the grocery business are being squeezed by competition and slack consumer spending, but Loblaw is entirely willing to sacrifice some profit to generate solid sales and tonnage growth. Loblaw is also responding to this with its introduction of innovative products under the President's Choice and generic house labels.

During fiscal 1993, Loblaw spend more than $200-million to open new stores in an effort to further boost its share of Canada's retail food market. Loblaw does not expect any major acquisitions over the next three years, unless the perfect opportunity arises. Loblaw plans to augment growth in its existing business by increasing the level of new store openings as fiscal 1994 progresses.

The company's former U.S. subsidiary, Peter J. Schmitt Co., filed under Chapter 11 of the U.S. Bankruptcy Code in 1992, resulting in a $10-million pre-tax charge to earnings. Loblaw sold the business in a 1988 leveraged buyout, but it retained a preferred share investment and granted certain loan guarantees.

In fiscal 1993 (1992), 69% (63%) of the company's sales were retail, and 31% (37%) were wholesale to franchised independent dealers. Sales (operating income) by geographic region were: Eastern Canada, 52.3% (34.2%); Western Canada, 32.3% (48.6%); and the United States, 15.4% (17.2%).

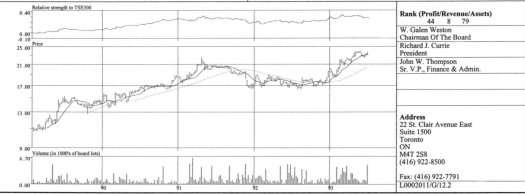

Rank (Profit/Revenue/Assets)		
44	8	79

W. Galen Weston
Chairman Of The Board

Richard J. Currie
President

John W. Thompson
Sr. V.P., Finance & Admin.

Address
22 St. Clair Avenue East
Suite 1500
Toronto
ON
M4T 2S8
(416) 922-8500

Fax: (416) 922-7791
L0002011/G/12.2

NORTH WEST COMPANY INC. (THE)

Exchanges	Price (Jun24'93)	19.50	Trailing P/E	18.40	Stock Symbol
TW	Trailing Yield (%)	1.85	Trailing EPS	1.06	**NWC**

Period Ending	Jan93	Jan92	Jan91	Jan90	Jan89
Yearly Statistics					
Price-Close	15.00	16.13	7.00	nt	nt
Price-High	16.00	16.50	8.75	nt	nt
Price-Low	12.38	5.25	6.13	nt	nt
P/E-Close	14.15	16.62	20.00	nt	nt
Dividends per Share	0.36	0.30	0.32	0.30	0.30
Dividend Yield (%)	2.40	1.86	4.57	nt	nt
Sales per Share	32.20	28.90	28.87	30.03	52.71
EPS before extra. item	1.06	0.97	0.35	1.17	1.25
Cash Flow per Share	1.77	1.47	1.46	1.58	2.02
Book Value per Share	8.41	6.89	6.29	6.27	5.96
O/S Common Shares	16,097	13,673	13,290	13,004	9,711
Total Revenue	452,185	390,446	377,413	368,346	425,257
Income before extra.	14,954	12,923	4,575	12,022	10,088
Cash Flow	24,789	19,841	19,071	19,405	16,314
Debt/Equity	0.79	1.05	1.63	1.37	2.24
Return on Capital (%)	15.31	16.06	12.03	17.58	17.65
Ret. on Com. Equity (%)	13.03	14.54	5.54	17.25	21.66
% Change Profit	15.7	182.5	(61.9)	19.2	61.7
% Change Revenue	15.8	3.5	2.5	(13.4)	6.4
% Change Assets	23.2	(5.4)	10.4	2.5	2.8
Preferred Div. Coverage	np	np	np		
Total Div. Coverage	2.9	3.0	1.1		
Interest Coverage	3.8	3.1	1.8		
Current Ratio	2.1	1.6	1.7		
Operating Margin	7.4	8.3	7.6		
Asset Turnover	1.5	1.6	1.5		
5 YEAR RATIOS (%)					
Return on Capital	15.7	na	na		
Return on Com. Equity	14.4	na	na		
Profit Growth	19.1	na	na		
Revenue Growth	2.5	na	na		
Asset Growth	6.2	na	na		
BALANCE SHEET (000)					
Cash	13,385	4,621	6,701		
Current Assets	179,880	154,945	172,403		
Net Fixed Assets	118,503	87,269	83,691		
Invest's & Advances	0	0	0		
Total Assets	298,383	242,214	256,094		
Short Term Debt	40,933	53,694	74,867		
Current Liabilities	87,113	94,772	104,103		
Long Term Debt	66,382	45,000	61,000		
Total Liabilities	163,037	148,082	172,509		
Total Equity	135,346	94,132	83,585		
Total Liab. & Equity	298,383	242,214	256,094		
CAPITAL (000)					
Total Debt	107,315	98,694	135,867		
Preferred Equity	0	0	0		
Common Equity	135,346	94,132	83,585		

Business:

THE NORTHWEST COMPANY INC., operating under its trading names NORTHERN and ALASKA COMMERCIAL COMPANY, is the leading retailer of food, family apparel and general merchandise in small, northern communities. It also operates complementary businesses which applies its unique heritage and knowledge of the North.

Date	EPS	DPS	Tot Rev	Inc Bex
May 93	0.08	0.09	123,549	1,267
Jan 93	0.46	0.09	155,700	6,727
Oct 92	0.30	0.09	103,995	4,139
Jul 92	0.22	0.09	99,290	2,950
Apr 92	0.08	0.09	97,102	1,138
Jan 92	0.40	0.08	111,591	5,401
Oct 91	0.31	0.08	99,131	4,067
Jul 91	0.22	0.08	93,481	2,933

Synopsis:

The North West Company continued its aggressive expansion into Alaska in fiscal 1993 and opened up a potential new market in Greenland through a joint venture project. On November 20, 1992, it purchased the Alaska Commercial Company and Frontier Expeditors Inc., adding 90 stores and $90-million in sales. In December 1992, North West entered an agreement to launch its NORTHERN Selections catalogue in Greenland, hoping to increase sales by $2-million in fiscal 1994. It spent $11.5-million on the new Winnipeg distribution centre, opened April 2, 1993, and expects to reduce costs by $2-million in fiscal 1994.

North West's sales and revenue jumped to $452-million in fiscal 1993, primarily from an expansion of its customer base through new ventures and growth in the NORTHERN stores. Food sales increased 9.2% in its Canadian operations and general merchandise improved by 10.6%. NORTHERN stores accounted for 91.7% of total revenue while Alaskan operations contributed 5.6%. Capital expenditures totaled $25.3-million in fiscal 1993: $10.6-million on store replacements and extensions; $1.6-million on new stores; and $1.4 million on systems. The discontinued junior department stores lost $2.7-million in fiscal 1993.

North West's plans include opening 42 NORTHERN stores over the next three years at a cost of about $40-million. This will affect about 35% of the company's current base of Canadian revenue.

First quarter results in fiscal 1994 show earnings up by 11.3% and revenues up by 27.2%. Food products and general merchandising sales were up while fur sales were down.

Rank (Profit/Revenue/Assets)
146 167 273

J. Derek Riley
Chairman

Ralph E. Trott
President & C.E.O.

Gary Eggertson
V.P., Finance & Admin.

Dave M. Brears
V.P., Retail Operations

Address
77 Main Street
Winnipeg
MB
R3C 2R1
(204) 943-0881

Fax: (204) 934-1455
N0002766/G/12.3

OSHAWA GROUP LIMITED (THE)

Exchanges	Price (Jun24'93)	22.75	Trailing P/E	19.12	Stock Symbol
TM	Trailing Yield (%)	2.02	Trailing EPS	1.19	**OSH.A**

Period Ending	Jan93	Jan92	Jan91	Jan90	Jan89
Yearly Statistics					
Price-Close	21.63	18.88	33.75	28.25	24.25
Price-High	24.13	35.63	33.75	33.88	25.25
Price-Low	17.00	19.25	27.25	23.13	19.00
P/E-Close	18.97	19.66	20.09	13.39	13.62
Dividends per Share	0.46	0.46	0.43	0.39	0.35
Dividend Yield (%)	2.13	2.41	1.27	1.38	1.44
Sales per Share	136.18	126.57	127.64	133.14	133.43
EPS before extra. item	1.14	0.96	1.68	2.11	1.78
Cash Flow per Share	2.29	2.03	3.09	2.80	2.70
Book Value per Share	17.98	17.29	16.70	15.42	12.13
O/S Common Shares	36,987	36,618	36,346	35,844	32,114
Total Revenue	5,021,900	4,635,600	4,609,500	4,389,135	4,279,309
Income before extra.	41,800	35,100	60,400	69,570	56,870
Cash Flow	84,400	74,000	111,500	92,049	86,414
Debt/Equity	0.16	0.07	0.10	0.11	0.25
Return on Capital (%)	9.62	8.90	17.05	22.04	23.48
Ret. on Com. Equity (%)	6.44	5.66	10.42	14.76	15.56
% Change Profit	19.1	(41.9)	(13.2)	22.3	14.0
% Change Revenue	8.3	0.6	5.0	2.6	12.3
% Change Assets	15.1	1.2	9.8	13.8	18.2

Business:

OSHAWA GROUP LTD. is engaged in marketing groceries and pharmaceuticals through a network of distribution centres and retail stores in nine provinces. The company supplies IGA markets across Canada, and operates Food City and IGA supermarkets, and Pharma Plus drug stores. The company also has real estate holdings.

Date	EPS	DPS	Tot Rev	Inc Bex
Apr 93	0.21	0.12	1,271,900	7,600
Jan 93	0.33	0.12	1,321,900	12,100
Oct 92	0.23	0.12	1,221,000	8,500
Aug 92	0.42	0.12	1,450,200	15,500
Apr 92	0.16	0.12	1,028,800	5,700
Jan 92	0.22	0.11	1,056,600	8,300
Nov 91	0.10	0.12	1,078,869	3,491
Aug 91	0.29	0.12	1,482,225	10,750

	Jan93	Jan92	Jan91
Preferred Div. Coverage	np	np	np
Total Div. Coverage	2.5	2.1	3.9
Interest Coverage	13.1	11.7	17.3
Current Ratio	1.4	2.0	2.0
Operating Margin	1.2	1.3	2.4
Asset Turnover	4.3	4.6	4.6
5 YEAR RATIOS (%)			
Return on Capital	16.2	19.3	22.4
Return on Com. Equity	10.6	12.4	14.3
Profit Growth	(3.5)	(4.1)	8.1
Revenue Growth	5.6	5.5	8.2
Asset Growth	11.4	10.1	11.8
BALANCE SHEET (000)			
Cash	5,200	94,800	112,400
Current Assets	566,100	588,200	605,700
Net Fixed Assets	466,500	350,200	346,500
Invest's & Advances	34,700	33,300	24,500
Total Assets	1,158,100	1,006,400	994,000
Short Term Debt	82,100	17,800	32,700
Current Liabilities	411,000	290,800	303,200
Long Term Debt	23,700	23,200	25,300
Total Liabilities	493,200	373,200	387,000
Total Equity	664,900	633,200	607,000
Total Liab. & Equity	1,158,100	1,006,400	994,000
CAPITAL (000)			
Total Debt	105,800	41,000	58,000
Preferred Equity	0	0	0
Common Equity	664,900	633,200	607,000

Synopsis:

The most significant marketing and production change implemented at the Oshawa Group Limited in fiscal 1993 was the introduction of its own up-scale private label brand to be sold at IGA and Food City stores, to grab a share of the market now focused on the Loblaw Companies President's Choice brand.

Other significant changes include a September 19, 1992, $35-million purchase of 23 Steinberg stores, and four warehouses and seven Cash & Carry facilities from Aligro, a medium-sized wholesaler. In 1992, Oshawa gained control of IGA Canada Limited and the IGA franchise rights in Central Canada. It also bought IGA Alberta supplier, Horne & Pitfield. Oshawa believes this move improves regional balance and reduces dependency upon any individual province.

Oshawa supplies 670 IGA stores in Canada and operates 100 corporate stores under the Food City, Price Choppers and Dutch Boy names.

First quarter results in fiscal 1994 show food distribution sales increasing in all regions except Atlantic Canada. A reduction in tobacco sales affected its Pharma Plus drugstore operations.

Despite weak consumer spending and high unemployment Oshawa's net earnings in fiscal 1993 were up to $41.8-million, due largely to new acquisitions, the elimination of unprofitable stores and the absence of restructuring and strike costs that affected 1992 figures. Profits were up 19% for largely the same reasons, mainly in food distribution and drugstore operations. For the first time sales surpassed the $5-billion mark.

Sales in fiscal 1993 by segment were : food distribution, $4.6-billion; drug store sales, $415-million; and real estate, $22.7-million. Ontario was the only market where the total market for retail food actually fell in fiscal 1993.

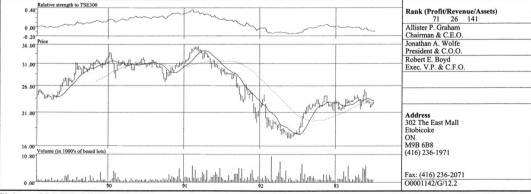

Rank (Profit/Revenue/Assets)
71   26   141

Allister P. Graham
Chairman & C.E.O.

Jonathan A. Wolfe
President & C.O.O.

Robert E. Boyd
Exec. V.P. & C.F.O.

Address
302 The East Mall
Etobicoke
ON
M9B 6B8
(416) 236-1971

Fax: (416) 236-2071
O0001142/G/12.2

PENNINGTON'S STORES LIMITED

Exchanges	Price (Jun24'93)	2.50	Trailing P/E	nm	Stock Symbol
T	Trailing Yield (%)	0.00	Trailing EPS	(0.40)	**PNS**

Period Ending	Jan93	Feb92	Feb91	Feb90	Jan89
Yearly Statistics					
Price-Close	2.75	4.20	5.00	6.63	13.50
Price-High	4.75	6.00	7.75	14.00	15.13
Price-Low	2.45	3.50	3.50	5.75	10.38
P/E-Close	nm	nm	nm	nm	15.52
Dividends per Share	0.01	0.01	0.05	0.30	0.40
Dividend Yield (%)	0.18	0.12	1.00	4.53	2.96
Sales per Share	18.10	18.17	19.27	20.11	19.97
EPS before extra. item	(0.26)	(0.27)	(0.01)	(0.68)	0.87
Cash Flow per Share	0.18	0.51	0.46	0.98	1.66
Book Value per Share	7.18	7.45	7.72	7.76	8.80
O/S Common Shares	4,050	4,050	4,050	4,133	4,133
Total Revenue	73,307	73,580	78,630	83,127	82,637
Income before extra.	(1,059)	(1,079)	(66)	(2,819)	3,581
Cash Flow	739	2,074	1,884	4,040	6,852
Debt/Equity	0.55	0.23	0.33	0.26	0.19
Return on Capital (%)	(2.36)	(2.57)	2.39	(0.58)	18.89
Ret. on Com. Equity (%)	(3.58)	(3.51)	(0.21)	(8.24)	10.11
% Change Profit	1.9	(1,526.8)	97.6	(178.7)	(26.1)
% Change Revenue	(0.4)	(6.4)	(5.4)	0.6	(14.3)
% Change Assets	(4.7)	(6.4)	4.5	(6.6)	17.2

Date	EPS	DPS	Tot Rev	Inc Bex
May 93	(0.33)	0.00	16,285	(1,362)
Jan 93	0.11	0.00	20,467	458
Oct 92	(0.09)	0.00	18,694	(379)
Aug 92	(0.09)	0.00	18,243	(367)
May 92	(0.19)	0.00	15,903	(771)
Feb 92	0.02	0.01	20,409	97
Nov 91	(0.05)	0.00	18,660	(196)
Aug 91	(0.03)	0.00	18,457	(128)

	Jan93	Feb92	Feb91
Preferred Div. Coverage	np	np	np
Total Div. Coverage	0.0	0.0	0.0
Interest Coverage	0.0	0.0	0.6
Current Ratio	1.9	1.9	1.0
Operating Margin	(1.3)	(1.4)	0.3
Asset Turnover	1.6	1.6	1.6
5 YEAR RATIOS (%)			
Return on Capital	3.2	9.4	20.3
Return on Com. Equity	(1.1)	2.6	8.3
Profit Growth	na	na	na
Revenue Growth	(5.4)	(5.4)	(2.0)
Asset Growth	0.4	2.4	5.2
BALANCE SHEET (000)			
Cash	4,564	0	0
Current Assets	17,941	18,130	19,710
Net Fixed Assets	26,170	28,211	29,842
Invest's & Advances	0	0	0
Total Assets	45,058	47,288	50,498
Short Term Debt	9,320	220	10,425
Current Liabilities	9,320	9,633	18,973
Long Term Debt	6,666	6,708	0
Total Liabilities	15,986	17,137	19,248
Total Equity	29,072	30,151	31,251
Total Liab. & Equity	45,058	47,288	50,498
CAPITAL (000)			
Total Debt	15,986	6,929	10,425
Preferred Equity	0	0	0
Common Equity	29,072	30,151	31,251

Business:

PENNINGTON'S STORES LTD. operates retail women's wear stores. The stores operate under the names Pennington's, Liz Porter, and Pennington's Wearhouse in nine provinces.

Synopsis:

The recession and reduced consumer spending have affected Pennington's Stores Limited's revenues for the past three years. The company continues to reduce borrowing and cut overhead to increase its working capital. Sales for the year ending January 30, 1993, totaled $73,307,221 compared with $73,579,738 for the previous year. Working capital at year end amounted to $8.62-million compared to $8.49 in fiscal 1992.

Relative strength to TSE300 / Price / Volume (in 1000's of board lots)

Rank (Profit/Revenue/Assets)
702   420   551

William Drevnig
Chairman Emeritus

Sol Armel
President & C.E.O.

William Farewell
V.P., Finance & Treasurer

Address
5101 Orbitor Dr.
Mississauga
ON
L4W 4V1
(416) 629-3500

Fax: (416) 629-9665
P0002051/G/12.4

For further company information, call Globe Information Services 1-800-268-9128 or (416)585-5345

PEOPLES JEWELLERS LIMITED

Exchanges	Price (Jun24'93)	0.18	Trailing P/E	nm	Stock Symbol
TM	Trailing Yield (%)	61.11	Trailing EPS	(6.86)	**PCJ.A**

Period Ending	Mar92	Mar91	Mar90	Mar89	Mar88
Yearly Statistics					
Price-Close	1.45	8.00	13.75	15.88	13.25
Price-High	8.00	14.00	22.50	18.50	14.50
Price-Low	1.06	4.25	12.25	13.75	13.00
P/E-Close	nm	nm	6.46	9.07	22.46
Dividends per Share	0.23	0.23	0.44	0.40	0.30
Dividend Yield (%)	2.88	2.14	3.20	2.52	2.26
Sales per Share	17.10	18.43	22.33	19.64	19.48
EPS before extra. item	(13.06)	(0.28)	2.13	1.75	0.59
Cash Flow per Share	0.96	1.96	2.41	1.88	1.17
Book Value per Share	(1.55)	12.42	15.51	13.97	12.39
O/S Common Shares	11,513	11,513	9,008	9,301	9,820
Total Revenue	196,855	212,143	216,631	201,810	200,021
Income before extra.	(159,174)	(3,314)	20,647	17,974	6,042
Cash Flow	11,076	22,593	23,432	19,363	12,042
Debt/Equity	na	1.12	0.92	0.92	0.81
Return on Capital (%)	(64.63)	2.48	12.44	11.94	7.24
Ret. on Com. Equity (%)	(254.76)	(2.56)	15.11	14.11	5.07
% Change Profit	(4,703.1)	(116.1)	14.9	197.5	133.4
% Change Revenue	(7.2)	(2.1)	7.3	0.9	2.4
% Change Assets	(45.6)	11.1	9.1	9.3	3.4

Date	EPS	DPS	Tot Rev	Inc Bex
Dec 92	(3.48)	0.00	69,006	(46,819)
Sep 92	(0.98)	0.11	37,456	(12,006)
Jun 92	(0.26)	0.00	38,221	(3,145)
Mar 92	(2.14)	0.00	27,863	(26,288)
Dec 91	(7.29)	0.00	88,886	(88,834)
Sep 91	(2.62)	0.11	42,724	(31,769)
Jun 91	(1.01)	0.11	42,251	(12,283)
Mar 91	(2.51)	0.11	29,219	(29,428)

	Mar92	Mar91	Mar90
Preferred Div. Coverage	0.0	0.0	74.0
Total Div. Coverage	0.0	0.0	4.9
Interest Coverage	0.0	1.3	5.6
Current Ratio	1.0	1.4	2.1
Operating Margin	5.4	10.8	11.0
Asset Turnover	1.1	0.6	0.7
5 YEAR RATIOS (%)			
Return on Capital	(6.1)	6.0	6.8
Return on Com. Equity	(44.6)	3.3	3.9
Profit Growth	na	na	21.7
Revenue Growth	0.1	2.6	3.7
Asset Growth	(5.7)	4.9	3.1
BALANCE SHEET (000)			
Cash	70	126	70
Current Assets	130,971	145,577	154,627
Net Fixed Assets	40,447	44,758	44,458
Invest's & Advances	1,791	134,424	92,761
Total Assets	180,791	332,096	298,862
Short Term Debt	105,913	90,585	64,385
Current Liabilities	130,879	101,188	73,224
Long Term Debt	58,315	78,924	74,863
Total Liabilities	189,194	180,112	148,087
Total Equity	(8,403)	151,984	150,775
Total Liab. & Equity	180,791	332,096	298,862
CAPITAL (000)			
Total Debt	164,228	169,509	139,248
Preferred Equity	9,478	9,022	11,063
Common Equity	(17,881)	142,962	139,712

Business:

PEOPLES JEWELLERS LTD. is a specialty retailer. It owns jewelry stores under the names Peoples Jewellers and Mappins across Canada. Peoples holds an investment in Jewelers Holding Corp. of Dallas which controls Zale Corporation, the largest jewellery in the U.S. Zale is currently undergoing voluntary reorganization under Chapter 11 of the U.S. Bankruptcy Code.

Synopsis:

Crippled by the recession, weak demand for jewelry and reduced selling margins, Peoples Jewellers Limited expects to climb out of its $217-million debt by operating a leaner company. This will be done by cutting expenses and offering quality products at reasonable prices to stimulate demand. Peoples filed for court protection on December 29, 1992. It owes the Bank of Nova Scotia $106.5-million. Peoples filed its restructuring plan on April 21, 1993 for approval.

One option requires converting $70-million of the bank's debt into distressed preferred shares and the balance into preferred shares convertible into 80% of the voting equity, which in effect means the Bank of Nova Scotia could end up owning 80% of Peoples. Under this plan 5% of the restructured company would go to creditors of bankrupt Zale Corp., a U.S. jewelry operation which People' bought into in 1986. Zale went under bankruptcy protection in January 1993. Its restructuring plan was confirmed in U.S. Bankruptcy Court on May 21,1993. It was expected to emerge from bankruptcy protection by mid-1993. Peoples wrote off its $133-million equity in Zale in 1993.

Since filing for protection, Peoples has closed 40 stores across Canada and was in desperate need for a potential investor. In February 1993, while preparing its restructuring plan, Peoples discovered some irregularities in its books.

Total sales for the nine-month period ending Dec. 26, 1992 fell to $144.7-million from $169-million in 1991. Peoples posted a nine-month loss of $57.6-million loss compared to $132.9-million in 1991, brought on by losses at Zale.

Relative strength to TSE300

Rank (Profit/Revenue/Assets)
981 276 335

E. Duff Scott
Acting Chairman
Roman Doroniuk
Exec. Vice President & C.F.O.

Address
1440 Don Mills Road
Don Mills
ON
M3B 3M1
(416) 441-1515

Fax: (416) 441-1363
P0002213/G/12.5

REITMANS (CANADA) LIMITED

Exchanges	Price (Jun24'93)	20 .25	Trailing P/E	10 .60	Stock Symbol
TM	Trailing Yield (%)	2 .57	Trailing EPS	1 .91	**RET.A**

Period Ending	Jan93	Feb92	Feb91	Feb90	Jan89
Yearly Statistics					
Price-Close	18 .75	20 .00	13 .25	16 .13	17 .50
Price-High	19 .50	20 .00	17 .25	23 .00	19 .00
Price-Low	15 .00	14 .00	11 .25	13 .00	15 .25
P/E-Close	9 .57	18 .18	nm	21 .50	20 .12
Dividends per Share	0 .52	0 .52	0 .52	0 .52	0 .52
Dividend Yield (%)	2 .77	2 .60	3 .93	3 .23	2 .97
Sales per Share	34 .07	32 .01	32 .29	30 .70	37 .96
EPS before extra. item	1 .96	1 .10	(3 .18)	0 .75	0 .87
Cash Flow per Share	2 .33	2 .00	0 .87	1 .48	1 .12
Book Value per Share	13 .41	11 .97	11 .38	15 .19	14 .85
O/S Common Shares	9 ,330	9 ,324	9 ,314	9 ,314	9 ,314
Total Revenue	324 ,150	303 ,651	308 ,176	293 ,250	360 ,702
Income before extra.	18 ,273	10 ,260	(29 ,647)	6 ,976	8 ,103
Cash Flow	21 ,699	18 ,661	8 ,059	13 ,820	10 ,477
Debt/Equity	0 .00	0 .03	0 .04	0 .04	0 .04
Return on Capital (%)	19 .80	13 .47	(19 .59)	10 .55	7 .03
Ret. on Com. Equity (%)	15 .44	9 .43	(23 .96)	4 .99	5 .89
% Change Profit	78 .1	134 .6	(525 .0)	(13 .9)	(14 .2)
% Change Revenue	6 .8	(1 .5)	5 .1	(18 .7)	0 .8
% Change Assets	11 .7	(1 .6)	(21 .0)	6 .7	0 .7

Preferred Div. Coverage	np	np	np
Total Div. Coverage	3 .8	2 .1	0 .0
Interest Coverage	90 .9	32 .7	0 .0
Current Ratio	1 .8	1 .8	1 .6
Operating Margin	4 .5	3 .4	2 .8
Asset Turnover	2 .0	2 .1	2 .0
5 YEAR RATIOS (%)			
Return on Capital	6 .3	4 .0	4 .8
Return on Com. Equity	2 .4	0 .7	1 .1
Profit Growth	14 .1	(7 .2)	na
Revenue Growth	1 .8	(3 .2)	(2 .2)
Asset Growth	1 .3	(3 .1)	(1 .8)
BALANCE SHEET (000)			
Cash	29 ,679	21 ,037	22 ,472
Current Assets	60 ,409	52 ,631	58 ,747
Net Fixed Assets	22 ,978	23 ,902	25 ,949
Invest's & Advances	74 ,931	65 ,246	56 ,271
Total Assets	161 ,788	144 ,862	147 ,169
Short Term Debt	0	638	638
Current Liabilities	33 ,811	30 ,079	37 ,307
Long Term Debt	0	3 ,189	3 ,827
Total Liabilities	36 ,684	33 ,268	41 ,134
Total Equity	125 ,104	111 ,594	106 ,035
Total Liab. & Equity	161 ,788	144 ,862	147 ,169
CAPITAL (000)			
Total Debt	0	3 ,827	4 ,465
Preferred Equity	0	0	0
Common Equity	125 ,104	111 ,594	106 ,035

Business:

REITMANS (CANADA) LTD. operates a network of clothing stores specializing in women's fashions and accessories. The company operates stores under the names Reitmans, Smart Set, Un-Deux-Trois, and Kookai.

Date	EPS	DPS	Tot Rev	Inc Bex
May 93	0 .01	0 .13	65 ,667	136
Jan 93	0 .77	0 .13	102 ,830	7 ,145
Oct 92	0 .35	0 .13	75 ,717	3 ,298
Aug 92	0 .78	0 .13	86 ,113	7 ,317
May 92	0 .06	0 .13	63 ,385	513
Feb 92	0 .39	0 .13	91 ,499	3 ,619
Nov 91	0 .18	0 .13	72 ,018	1 ,716
Aug 91	0 .39	0 .13	76 ,620	3 ,578

Synopsis:

Since selling its capital stock in Worth Stores Corp. on May 31, 1992, and a distribution center for a net gain of $3,895,000, Reitmans Limited plans to focus its attention and capital on improving its money-making operations, Smart Set and Reitmans department stores.

In fiscal 1993, the company opened seven new Reitmans and three Smart Set stores, but it also closed 20 others, bringing the total number of outlets to 587. Its Un-Deux-Trois and Kookai operations have not been successful and might be converted to other uses.

Capital expenditures during fiscal 1993 came to $8.69-million, the majority spent on a new point-of-sale cash register system. For fiscal 1994, Reitmans plans to open 15 new stores, close down non-profitable ones and spend $6-million on capital expenditures on store development and a further $1.3-million on its new point-of-sale cash register system.

Sales for the year ending January 30, 1992, climbed 6.5% to $317,890,000 as compared to $298,568,000 in 1991. Earnings from continuing operations jumped 40%, which included a pretax amount of $942,00. These earnings include a 6% increase in comparable store sales and a reduction in expenses. Investment income increased by $1.17-million.

Relative strength to TSE300

Price

Volume (in 1000's of board lots)

Rank (Profit/Revenue/Assets)
127   216   346

Jack Reitman
Chairman Of The Board

Jeremy H. Reitman
President

Eric Williams
V.P. & Comptroller

Address
250 Sauve Street West
Montreal
PQ
H3L 1Z2
(514) 384-1140

R0001263/G/12.4

SEARS CANADA INC.

Exchanges	Price (Jun24'93)	8.00	Trailing P/E	nm	Stock Symbol
TM	Trailing Yield (%)	3.00	Trailing EPS	(0.85)	**SCC**

Period Ending	Dec92	Dec91	Dec90	Dec89	Dec88
Yearly Statistics					
Price-Close	7.00	10.88	10.00	13.25	13.13
Price-High	10.50	14.25	12.50	15.38	13.88
Price-Low	5.50	9.38	10.00	12.25	9.50
P/E-Close	nm	nm	40.00	10.77	11.82
Dividends per Share	0.24	0.24	0.24	0.24	0.24
Dividend Yield (%)	3.43	2.21	2.40	1.81	1.83
Sales per Share	45.23	48.51	53.84	53.00	49.90
EPS before extra. item	(1.04)	(0.34)	0.25	1.23	1.11
Cash Flow per Share	(1.26)	0.16	0.66	1.61	1.65
Book Value per Share	9.10	10.67	11.25	11.26	10.27
O/S Common Shares	94,866	84,383	84,260	86,156	86,022
Total Revenue	3,974,600	4,089,200	4,590,000	4,562,300	4,327,200
Income before extra.	(90,900)	(28,800)	21,300	106,100	95,700
Cash Flow	(110,500)	13,500	55,800	138,500	143,100
Debt/Equity	1.06	1.18	1.77	1.63	1.66
Return on Capital (%)	(1.62)	5.16	8.03	14.33	14.45
Ret. on Com. Equity (%)	(10.31)	(3.12)	2.22	11.45	11.21
% Change Profit	(215.6)	(235.2)	(79.9)	10.9	16.6
% Change Revenue	(2.8)	(10.9)	0.6	5.4	7.2
% Change Assets	(9.2)	(17.7)	2.6	10.6	9.2

Preferred Div. Coverage	np	np	np
Total Div. Coverage	0.0	0.0	1.0
Interest Coverage	0.0	0.7	1.1
Current Ratio	2.1	2.5	2.2
Operating Margin	0.2	2.9	5.0
Asset Turnover	1.6	1.5	1.4
5 YEAR RATIOS (%)			
Return on Capital	8.1	11.2	13.1
Return on Com. Equity	2.3	6.5	9.3
Profit Growth	na	na	(22.3)
Revenue Growth	(0.3)	0.9	3.9
Asset Growth	(1.5)	1.1	6.8
BALANCE SHEET (000)			
Cash	57,600	5,200	5,200
Current Assets	1,704,800	1,927,300	2,676,500
Net Fixed Assets	565,100	595,500	450,900
Invest's & Advances	35,100	35,800	23,100
Total Assets	2,431,400	2,676,900	3,251,000
Short Term Debt	183,700	158,400	669,500
Current Liabilities	806,800	780,800	1,218,600
Long Term Debt	732,400	906,600	1,004,200
Total Liabilities	1,568,300	1,776,400	2,302,700
Total Equity	863,100	900,500	948,300
Total Liab. & Equity	2,431,400	2,676,900	3,251,000
CAPITAL (000)			
Total Debt	916,100	1,065,000	1,673,700
Preferred Equity	0	0	0
Common Equity	863,100	900,500	948,300

Business:

SEARS CANADA INC. is a retailer of general merchandise. It operates department stores across Canada. The company also operates a Canada-wide network of catalogue sales offices. Sears, Roebuck and Co. of Chicago is the company's major shareholder.

Date	EPS	DPS	Tot Rev	Inc Bex
Mar 93	(0.23)	0.06	772,465	(21,762)
Dec 92	(0.01)	0.06	1,303,579	(3,702)
Sep 92	(0.26)	0.06	944,959	(22,370)
Jun 92	(0.35)	0.06	934,088	(29,229)
Mar 92	(0.42)	0.06	775,074	(35,599)
Dec 91	0.17	0.06	1,332,903	14,127
Sep 91	(0.17)	0.06	967,155	(14,110)
Jun 91	(0.03)	0.06	972,276	(3,028)

Synopsis:

The recession and weak consumer demand in 1992 yielded Sears Canada Inc. a $90.9-million net earnings loss, a huge jump from 1991.

Sears continued to bleed in the first-quarter of 1993, reporting a $21.8-million net earnings loss, and weak sales, brought on by a slow economic recovery, bad weather and losses in its catalogue operations. Despite the early figures, Sears hopes to report a profit by year-end. One way it expects to get out of the red is by reducing inventories of big-ticket merchandise and expanding its fashion merchandise.

Sears sells more merchandise than any other retailer in Canada. In a cost-cutting measure, it laid off 1,400 full time staff in 1992 and implemented a one-year salary freeze on February 1, 1992. Sears's 1992 losses included severance payments and restructuring costs.

In 1992, weak consumer demand, especially in the Metro Toronto area, pushed revenue down to $3.96-billion.

Relative strength to TSE300 / Price / Volume (in 1000's of board lots)

Rank (Profit/Revenue/Assets)
969   33   82

C. Richard Sharpe
Chairman

G. Joseph Reddington
President & C.E.O.

Larry E. Ginther
V.P., C.F.O. & Treasurer

Address
222 Jarvis Street
Toronto
ON
M5B 2B8
(416) 362-1711

Fax: (416) 941-4793
S0003142/G/12.3

SILCORP LIMITED

Exchanges	Price (Jun24'93)		0.80	Trailing P/E		nm	Stock Symbol
TM	Trailing Yield (%)		0.00	Trailing EPS		(20.07)	**SIL**

Period Ending	Dec92	Dec91	Dec90	Dec89	Dec88
Yearly Statistics					
Price-Close	0.25	2.40	2.50	12.50	16.50
Price-High	2.75	2.50	12.75	18.25	19.75
Price-Low	0.10	1.75	2.50	11.00	14.88
P/E-Close	nm	nm	nm	nm	22.60
Dividends per Share	0.00	0.00	0.14	0.40	0.38
Dividend Yield (%)	0.00	0.00	5.60	3.20	2.27
Sales per Share	232.98	263.08	272.78	300.44	253.33
EPS before extra. item	(22.21)	(10.56)	(2.59)	(2.02)	0.73
Cash Flow per Share	1.11	1.82	1.59	3.07	5.60
Book Value per Share	3.80	(1.57)	8.96	11.66	17.28
O/S Common Shares	2,870	2,870	2,870	2,870	2,870
Total Revenue	671,767	755,732	783,618	853,247	723,272
Income before extra.	(63,739)	(30,312)	(7,428)	(5,728)	2,084
Cash Flow	3,199	5,227	4,552	8,700	15,979
Debt/Equity	3.77	na	4.21	3.30	2.01
Return on Capital (%)	(72.37)	(17.64)	0.35	3.70	8.52
Ret. on Com. Equity (%)	(1,993.40)	(286.17)	(25.11)	(13.79)	4.19
% Change Profit	(110.3)	(308.1)	(29.7)	(374.9)	(51.0)
% Change Revenue	(11.1)	(3.6)	(8.2)	18.0	7.4
% Change Assets	(38.1)	(14.5)	(12.1)	2.5	22.9

Preferred Div. Coverage	np	np	np
Total Div. Coverage	na	na	0.0
Interest Coverage	0.0	0.0	0.0
Current Ratio	0.9	0.7	0.7
Operating Margin	(0.3)	(0.1)	0.1
Asset Turnover	6.0	4.2	3.7
5 YEAR RATIOS (%)			
Return on Capital	(15.5)	1.5	7.6
Return on Com. Equity	(462.9)	(62.4)	(4.1)
Profit Growth	na	na	na
Revenue Growth	(0.1)	2.9	7.1
Asset Growth	(10.2)	0.4	6.7
BALANCE SHEET (000)			
Cash	0	0	0
Current Assets	53,008	74,731	80,417
Net Fixed Assets	41,051	73,555	93,190
Invest's & Advances	7,055	8,128	8,589
Total Assets	112,170	181,146	211,923
Short Term Debt	4,977	42,661	47,829
Current Liabilities	58,326	112,105	121,387
Long Term Debt	36,187	66,995	60,446
Total Liabilities	101,258	185,663	186,221
Total Equity	10,912	(4,517)	25,702
Total Liab. & Equity	112,170	181,146	211,923
CAPITAL (000)			
Total Debt	41,164	109,656	108,275
Preferred Equity	0	0	0
Common Equity	10,912	(4,517)	25,702

Business:

SILCORP LTD. operates convenience stores, gas bars and fast food outlets in Canada and the United States. Convenience stores include Mac's, La Maisonnee, and Mike's Mart in Canada and Hop-In Food Stores in the United States.

Date	EPS	DPS	Tot Rev	Inc Bex
Mar 93	(0.27)	0.00	124,150	(783)
Dec 92	(2.15)	0.00	190,658	(6,146)
Sep 92	0.68	0.00	156,443	1,941
Jun 92	(18.33)	0.00	167,275	(52,595)
Mar 92	(2.41)	0.00	154,225	(6,939)
Dec 91	(9.35)	0.00	224,510	(26,851)
Sep 91	1.07	0.00	195,385	3,097
Jun 91	(0.30)	0.00	178,112	(883)

Synopsis:

Silcorp Limited's approved restructuring plan took effect on June 21, 1993, and provided for the issuance of shares and making certain payments by Silcorp to its creditors. Class A non-voting shares and Class B shares were changed into New Common Shares. The plan is in effect until June 21, 1996. Silcorp filed for court protection on June 11, 1992.

In 1992 Silcorp closed 228 stores, more than 25% of the network, downsized five office/warehouse locations, redistributed $8-million of closed store inventory, achieved rent reductions in excess of $2.5-million in remaining stores, and in December 1992 sold 199 Baskin-Robbins outlets. Silcorp now operates over 615 convenience stores across Canada with an approximate 15% national market share.

Silcorp's new management scheme includes increasing individual store focus, improving distribution of management information and selling non-strategic business units.

Silcorp's 1992 sales totaled $668.6-million, a drop of 11.4% from 1991, primarily due to a 16.7% reduction in the number of four-week store periods, Sunday shopping and the cool summer. First quarter results for fiscal 1993 showed sales at $124.2-million, or 19.5% lower than 1992, as a result of fewer stores.

Rank (Profit/Revenue/Assets)
937   127   334

Eric F. Findlay
Chairman

Derek M. Ridout
President & C.E.O.

Dale A. Pettit
V.P., C.F.O. & Treasurer

Address
10 Connander Blvd.
Scarborough
ON
M1S 3T2
(416) 291-4441

Fax: (416) 678-0793
S0002970/G/12.2

UNIVA INC.

Exchanges	Price (Jun24'93)	7.12	Trailing P/E	26.39	Stock Symbol
TM	Trailing Yield (%)	3.93	Trailing EPS	0.27	**UVA**

Period Ending	Jan93	Jan92	Jan91	Jan90	Jan89
Yearly Statistics					
Price-Close	7.75	8.38	10.40	8.75	10.75
Price-High	9.63	13.00	10.50	11.25	12.25
Price-Low	6.50	8.13	8.25	8.63	8.25
P/E-Close	25.83	14.69	1,040.00	nm	15.14
Dividends per Share	0.28	0.25	0.24	0.24	0.23
Dividend Yield (%)	3.61	2.97	2.31	2.75	2.15
Sales per Share	77.51	77.64	76.01	71.87	63.05
EPS before extra. item	0.30	0.57	0.01	(0.60)	0.71
Cash Flow per Share	0.58	1.55	1.38	0.87	1.18
Book Value per Share	4.02	3.94	3.59	3.87	4.66
O/S Common Shares	86,538	86,442	86,024	86,154	85,109
Total Revenue	6,764,100	6,714,600	6,540,700	6,153,800	5,367,700
Income before extra.	32,500	49,300	700	(51,400)	60,200
Cash Flow	50,200	134,100	118,200	74,300	100,100
Debt/Equity	1.38	2.10	2.22	2.02	1.37
Return on Capital (%)	11.27	13.80	11.31	4.56	15.27
Ret. on Com. Equity (%)	7.76	15.19	0.22	(14.09)	15.85
% Change Profit	(34.1)	6,942.9	101.4	(185.4)	(10.4)
% Change Revenue	0.7	2.7	6.3	14.6	(14.7)
% Change Assets	(4.1)	2.3	3.4	7.8	(9.3)

Date	EPS	DPS	Tot Rev	Inc Bex
Apr 93	0.02	0.07	1,413,700	3,500
Jan 93	(0.04)	0.07	1,593,100	(1,000)
Oct 92	0.08	0.07	1,491,900	9,000
Aug 92	0.21	0.07	2,161,200	19,600
Apr 92	0.05	0.07	1,502,800	4,900
Jan 92	0.07	0.06	1,521,900	6,200
Nov 91	0.11	0.07	1,551,400	9,400
Aug 91	0.24	0.06	2,121,900	21,000

	Jan93	Jan92	Jan91
Preferred Div. Coverage	5.6	np	na
Total Div. Coverage	1.1	2.3	0.0
Interest Coverage	1.9	2.1	1.4
Current Ratio	1.2	1.0	1.3
Operating Margin	1.5	2.2	2.2
Asset Turnover	4.6	4.4	4.4
5 YEAR RATIOS (%)			
Return on Capital	11.2	13.4	15.6
Return on Com. Equity	5.0	7.4	8.4
Profit Growth	(13.5)	(4.0)	(57.4)
Revenue Growth	1.4	4.3	6.5
Asset Growth	(0.2)	8.7	11.5
BALANCE SHEET (000)			
Cash	27,000	7,000	1,600
Current Assets	602,100	677,700	759,400
Net Fixed Assets	557,200	534,900	505,100
Invest's & Advances	169,000	170,000	141,500
Total Assets	1,465,600	1,528,900	1,494,700
Short Term Debt	92,300	257,500	112,200
Current Liabilities	516,500	706,200	586,000
Long Term Debt	500,300	456,300	573,100
Total Liabilities	1,035,600	1,188,500	1,186,000
Total Equity	430,000	340,400	308,700
Total Liab. & Equity	1,465,600	1,528,900	1,494,700
CAPITAL (000)			
Total Debt	592,600	713,800	685,300
Preferred Equity	82,400	0	100
Common Equity	347,600	340,400	308,600

Business:

UNIVA INC. is a food distribution company. It has retail and wholesale operations in Quebec, Ontario, Alberta, and California under such names as Provigo, Maxi, Heritage, LOEB, Petrini's, and Cost Less. It has, under the names Provi-soir, Winks, Top Valu, and Red Rooster, convenience store operations in Quebec, Ontario, and Alberta.

Synopsis:

Unigesco Inc., a majority shareholder of grocery chain Univa Inc., tried twice in 1993 to sell its 26% stake in the company, but both times its efforts collapsed. In March 1993, its $250-million deal with New York investor the Blackstone Group fell through. On June 7, Unigesco's $200-million deal to sell its stake to another U.S. investor also collapsed. Unigesco is in a cash crunch situation and needs to sell its stake to reduce its debt.

Unigesco needed $45-million to redeem a series of debentures, but asked shareholders if it could defer redemption until October 29, 1993, instead of on June 16. Debenture holders threatened to force Unigesco into default unless it paid. Industry observers say the collapsed deals reflect negatively on Univa and paint a shaky future for the chain. In mid-year, the Canadian Bond Rating Service had Univa on credit watch. Empire Co. Ltd. owns roughly 24% of Univa and Caisse de depot et placement du Quebec owns 13.5%.

In fiscal 1993, Univa sold Horne & Pitfield Foods Limited in Western Canada, acquired Steinberg's Quebec network, reorganized Provigo Distribution, and disposed of LOEB Inc.'s shareholder interest in IGA Canada and its trademark and franchise rights. Economic conditions were not favorable to dispose of Sports Experts Inc.

Fiscal 1994 first quarter net sales were $1.4-billion, operating income improved to $19.9-million as a result of the Steinberg buy, and U.S. operations showed an operating loss of $1.9-million (U.S.) as a result of the soft economy in Northern California and an aggressive retail environment. Net income for the quarter was $3.5-million, compared with $4.9-million last year.

Net sales in fiscal 1994 totaled $6.7-billion, with Canadian sales amounting to $5.8 billion. Operating income was $87.7 million compared with $133.7 million in fiscal 1993. Gross interest expense amounted to $64.1-million. Income from continuing operations came to $38.5-million.

Rank (Profit/Revenue/Assets)
85   17   113

Bertin F. Nadeau
Chairman

Yvan Bussieres
President

Germain Lecours
Exec. V.P., C.F.O. & Treasurer

Address
1250 Rene-Levesque Blvd. W.
41st Floor
Montreal
PQ
H3B 4X1
(514) 938-1250

Fax: (514) 938-8054
P0004273/G/12.2

VERSA SERVICES LTD.

Exchanges	Price (Jun24'93)	7.25	Trailing P/E	16.48	Stock Symbol
TM	Trailing Yield (%)	3.03	Trailing EPS	0.44	**VSL**

Period Ending	Sep92	Sep91	Sep90	Sep89	Sep88
Yearly Statistics					
Price-Close	9.00	9.00	8.00	9.75	7.94
Price-High	10.00	10.00	10.00	9.88	8.50
Price-Low	8.13	8.00	7.00	7.88	6.00
P/E-Close	22.50	30.00	15.09	17.11	15.88
Dividends per Share	0.22	0.22	0.22	0.20	0.18
Dividend Yield (%)	2.44	2.44	2.75	2.05	2.27
Sales per Share	33.77	33.75	34.36	28.48	27.73
EPS before extra. item	0.40	0.30	0.53	0.57	0.50
Cash Flow per Share	1.13	1.01	1.29	1.23	1.15
Book Value per Share	5.57	5.41	5.31	4.98	4.67
O/S Common Shares	12,616	12,651	12,385	12,191	12,248
Total Revenue	424,963	423,996	424,595	350,280	340,338
Income before extra.	5,161	3,869	6,699	7,068	6,255
Cash Flow	14,219	12,639	15,890	14,983	14,080
Debt/Equity	nd	nd	nd	nd	nd
Return on Capital (%)	14.48	11.85	19.44	21.89	21.77
Ret. on Com. Equity (%)	7.23	5.55	10.36	11.74	11.10
% Change Profit	33.4	(42.2)	(5.2)	13.0	7.1
% Change Revenue	0.2	(0.1)	21.2	2.9	4.4
% Change Assets	4.5	7.7	4.8	6.2	(0.1)

Business:

VERSA SERVICES LTD. is a diversified management company providing dietary, food service, vending, office coffee systems, laundry, housekeeping, and maintenance and material management to clients in health care, business, education, and public markets. Its businesses operate across Canada. Subsidiaries include: Major Foods Ltd.; Modern Building Cleaning Inc.; Versabec Inc.; and Parnell.

Date	EPS	DPS	Tot Rev	Inc Bex
Mar 93	0.11	0.06	101,370	1,419
Dec 92	0.11	0.06	100,058	1,427
Sep 92	0.13	0.06	106,833	1,696
Jun 92	0.09	0.06	104,190	1,176
Mar 92	0.08	0.06	104,583	1,035
Dec 91	0.10	0.06	109,357	1,254
Sep 91	0.02	0.06	101,477	254
Jun 91	0.07	0.06	104,564	912

Preferred Div. Coverage	35.6	26.9	44.7	
Total Div. Coverage	1.8	1.3	2.4	
Interest Coverage	nd	nd	nd	
Current Ratio	1.7	1.6	1.8	
Operating Margin	2.3	1.8	2.6	
Asset Turnover	3.7	3.9	4.2	
5 YEAR RATIOS (%)				
Return on Capital	17.9	19.5	21.0	
Return on Com. Equity	9.2	10.0	11.2	
Profit Growth	(2.5)	(6.5)	2.5	
Revenue Growth	5.4	5.9	8.4	
Asset Growth	4.5	4.8	4.7	
BALANCE SHEET (000)				
Cash	30,671	13,634	14,310	
Current Assets	71,915	62,617	58,454	
Net Fixed Assets	23,614	28,104	30,427	
Invest's & Advances	1,353	6,064	883	
Total Assets	113,818	108,946	101,147	
Short Term Debt	0	0	0	
Current Liabilities	42,483	39,430	32,779	
Long Term Debt	0	0	0	
Total Liabilities	43,104	40,165	35,087	
Total Equity	70,714	68,781	66,060	
Total Liab. & Equity	113,818	108,946	101,147	
CAPITAL (000)				
Total Debt	0	0	0	
Preferred Equity	429	369	338	
Common Equity	70,285	68,412	65,722	

Synopsis:

During the last half of fiscal 1992, Versa Services Ltd. improved its net income by 24% over the prior year. Income from operations was up by 30%, in spite of decline in revenues due to reduced government funding, the GST and the recession.

During fiscal 1992, Versa served fewer airport clients as a result of a decline in airline travel, but it also signed a contract with Hydro-Quebec's James Bay Project construction camp site to provide food, housekeeping and retail services. Versa still has a similar account with the Hibernia oil camp.

Versa's food management segment proved profitable in fiscal 1992 as a result of company downsizing, new contracts and increased concession sales at Montreal's Olympic Stadium. Revenues in cleaning services dipped 1.7% from fiscal 1991, because of the elimination of non-profitable accounts and high vacancy in the real estate market.

Total revenues increased in fiscal 1992 by 0.2% from 1991 to $423.4-million, through gains in food services, new dining accounts in Toronto and increased service to the health care and education markets. The revenue gains were offset by client plant closures and layoffs.

Versa's outlook for fiscal 1993 shows increased concession sales at Olympic Stadium, further restructuring of low profit accounts and taking on new education accounts.

Rank (Profit/Revenue/Assets)
252 179 394

Dixon S. Chant
Chairman

James E. Graham
President & C.E.O.

Hugh N. Macdonald
Corp. V.P. & C.F.O.

Address
Box 950
Station "U"
Etobicoke
ON
M8Z 5Y7
(416) 255-1331

Fax: (416) 255-4706
V0000748/G/12.6

Page	Company	$	Latest year end	Earnings per Share Actual	Estimate this year	Estimate next year
377	B.C. Bancorp		9210	0.12	n.a.	n.a.
378	Bank of Montreal		9210	2.38	2.41	2.73
379	Bank of Nova Scotia		9210	2.94	2.90	3.20
380	Canada Trustco Mortgage		9212	3.48	n.a.	n.a.
381	Canadian Imperial Bank of Commerce		9210	(0.60)	2.98	3.50
382	Central Guaranty Trustco		9212	(12.29)	n.a.	n.a.
383	General Trustco of Canada		9212	(3.90)	n.a.	n.a.
384	Gentra Inc.		9212	(6.25)	(0.44)	0.00
385	Laurentian Bank of Canada		9210	2.04	1.70	2.14
386	Montreal Trustco		9212	(1.98)	n.a.	n.a.
387	National Bank of Canada		9210	(0.29)	1.01	1.22
388	National Trustco		9210	1.14	1.35	1.65
389	Royal Bank of Canada		9210	(0.05)	2.42	3.04
390	Toronto-Dominion Bank		9210	1.25	0.98	1.68

Estimates from I/B/E/S Inc., 345 Hudson St., New York, NY 10014 (212) 243-3335. In Canada: 6 Lansing Square, Ste. 235, Willowdale, ON M2J 1T5 (416) 496-0977.

Banks & Trusts

Many of the same factors affecting the bank and trust sectors in 1991 were still evident in 1992. The expected recovery in the economy has yet to surface. In relation to the banking sector, this has had a negative effect on non-performing loans and loan loss provisions. Despite this, the bank rate continues to drop, and should aid operating margins through the stimulation of loan demand. For fiscal 1992, total revenue for the seven largest chartered banks dropped 11.52% while profits plummeted 49.6%, when compared to fiscal 1991.

The Bank Index, which measures the performance of the seven major banks, was up 1% for fiscal 1992 compared to 1991, and up 20% for the six months ended June 1993. This compares to a 5% drop in the TSE Composite 300 Index for the banks' fiscal year; however, for the six months ended June 1993, the TSE Index gained 20%. Revenue growth for the bank industry was down 11.6% for 1992, and earnings growth fell by 49.7% in the same period. The average bank price-earnings ratio (P/E) increased slightly to 12.2 in June 1993, up from 10.9 a year earlier. The Trust, Savings & Loan Index after experiencing a 40.9% decline for the year ended June 1992, continues to experience poor results with a further 48% drop for the year ended June 1993. Furthermore, revenue growth in the trust sector declined by 26% and earnings growth fell by 637% in 1992.

A study by the Royal Bank reported that the recent mergers and acquisitions activitiy in the sector is expected to increase over the next five years. A likely scenario might find a small concentrated industry with the key players controlling prices in a quasi-monopoly structure or oligopoly. The doors to increase consolidation opened last year when revisions to federal financial service's laws changed, allowing banks to buy trust and insurance companies and vice versa. Over the past year, transactions of significance in this sector included: Toronto-Dominion Bank's purchase of the assets of Central Guaranty Trust; National Bank's purchase of three of General Trustco's subsidiaries; Laurantian Bank's purchase of General Trustco's Ontario subsidiary; and Royal Bank's purchase of Royal Trustco's key assets.

The stagnant economy continues to affect the quality and collection of loans. As at January 31, 1993, non-performing loans of key banks climbed 13% to $2.48-billion from a year earlier. In general, banks try to keep loan losses to a minimum of 0.5% to 1% of their total loan portfolio. Currently, non-performing loans as a percentage of total loans and acceptances range from 2.28% to 3.4% for the six major banks, and this is expected to continue. At the moment, loan volumes have remained flat, with personal lending up 0.4% and business loans down slightly. Retail banking, however, has benefited from the strong growth in residential mortgages, RRSPs and mutual funds.

Overall, further major changes affecting the operating environment of the financial services industry may be just around the corner. The larger banks should dominate the industry of the future, with the eventual disappearance or rationalization of the trust industry, leaving behind only the largest and most efficient players.

B.C. BANCORP

Exchanges	Price (Jun24'93)	1.42	Trailing P/E	20.29	Stock Symbol
TV	Trailing Yield (%)	0.00	Trailing EPS	0.07	**BBC**

Period Ending	Oc t92	Oc t91	Oc t90	Oc t89	Oc t88
Yearly Statistics					
Price-Close	1.25	2.02	1.71	1.71	0.98
Price-High	2.34	2.20	1.80	1.45	1.04
Price-Low	1.22	1.69	1.37	0.95	0.56
P/E-Close	10.42	10.10	6.58	8.55	98.00
Dividends per Share	0.00	0.00	0.00	0.00	0.00
Dividend Yield (%)	0.00	0.00	0.00	0.00	0.00
Sales per Share	0.21	0.30	0.31	0.27	0.22
EPS before extra. item	0.12	0.20	0.26	0.20	0.01
Cash Flow per Share	0.19	0.30	0.36	0.30	0.11
Book Value per Share	1.02	1.92	1.74	1.74	1.44
O/S Common Shares	33,964	33,964	33,964	33,964	33,964
Total Revenue	7,207	10,662	12,870	9,286	7,933
Income before extra.	6,412	10,089	12,077	10,064	3,568
Cash Flow	6,412	10,089	12,077	10,064	3,568
Debt/Equity	nd	nd	nd	nd	nd
Return on Capital (%)	9.82	10.43	12.80	11.19	8.76
Ret. on Com. Equity (%)	6.75	8.32	(2.57)	(0.48)	(0.41)
% Change Profit	(36.4)	(16.5)	20.0	182.1	68.7
% Change Revenue	(32.4)	(17.2)	38.6	17.1	51.4
% Change Assets	(65.5)	5.7	(2.0)	6.4	9.7

Date	EPS	DPS	Tot Rev	Inc Bex
Apr 93	0.01	0.00	597	400
Jan 93	0.02	0.00	712	517
Oct 92	0.01	0.00	641	455
Jul 92	0.03	0.00	1,810	1,573
Apr 92	0.04	0.00	2,266	2,117
Jan 92	0.04	0.00	2,415	2,267
Oct 91	0.06	0.00	3,062	2,928
Jul 91	0.05	0.00	2,451	2,309

Preferred Div. Coverage	np	2.5	1.0		
Total Div. Coverage	2.1	2.5	1.0		
Capital Ratio	1.0	1.0	1.0		
Operat. Costs/$100 of Assets	1.3	0.4	0.7		
5 YEAR RATIOS					
Return on Capital	10.6	9.4	11.2		
Return on Com. Equity	2.3	0.4	(2.5)		
Profit Growth	24.8	63.9	9.9		
Revenue Growth	6.5	(49.8)	(48.9)		
Asset Growth	(16.1)	(48.0)	(50.7)		
BALANCE SHEET (000)					
Cash	11,505	20,373	9,910		
Total Loans	4,307	5,578	5,748		
Net Fixed Assets	0	1,127	2,497		
Total Assets	35,549	102,950	97,423		
Total Deposits	0	0	0		
Subordinated Debt	0	0	0		
Total Liabilities	1,085	1,409	1,874		
Total Equity	34,464	101,541	95,549		
Total Liab. & Equity	35,549	102,950	97,423		
CAPITAL (000)					
Total External Debt	0	0	0		
Preferred Equity	0	36,470	36,470		
Common Equity	34,464	65,071	59,079		

Business:

B.C. BANCORP, formerly the Bank of British Columbia, has since Nov. 27, 1986, restricted its activities to those incidental to the winding-up of its affairs.

Synopsis:

B.C. Bancorp, formed to wind up the Bank of British Columbia in 1986, continues the long, deliberate process of winding down affairs and distributing the remaining assets to shareholders.

Net income for the first quarter ended January 31, 1993, was $517,000 up from $445,000 in the prior quarter and down from $2.3-million in the first quarter of 1992.

In its second quarter ended April 30, the company posted a profit of $400,000, down from $2.1-million a year earlier. Its six-month profit was $917,000, compared with $4.4-million.

The estimate of future distribution to common shareholders, excluding future earnings, in April was $1.04 or $1.05 a share. This will be increased further by $1.10 per share if the full pension surplus is obtained.

Only one legal action, the issue of the disposal of the surplus in the bank's pension fund, will be heard by the Supreme Court of British Columbia in March 1993. It is expected that any decision by the court will be appealed.

A special meeting of shareholders is to be held in August 1993 to approve of an interim distribution of 50 cents a share.

Rank (Profit/Revenue/Assets)
225   738   607

Peter H. Stafford
Chairman & C.E.O.
William J. Bryden
Pres., Chief Gen. Mgr. & Acct.

Address
Suite 610
1130 West Pender Street
Vancouver
BC
V6E 4A4
(604) 681-3911

Fax: (604) 681-2172
B0000475/B/13.1

BANK OF MONTREAL

Exchanges	Price (Jun24'93)		25.75	Trailing P/E		10.60	Stock Symbol
TMVZW	Trailing Yield (%)		4.27	Trailing EPS		2.43	**BMO**

Period Ending	Oct 92	Oct 91	Oct 90	Oct 89	Oct 88
Yearly Statistics					
Price-Close	23.57	18.69	13.50	17.00	14.25
Price-High	24.13	19.19	17.25	17.63	14.88
Price-Low	18.51	13.25	12.25	13.32	12.32
P/E-Close	9.90	8.07	6.43	nm	5.83
Dividends per Share	1.06	1.06	1.06	1.06	1.00
Dividend Yield (%)	4.50	5.67	7.85	6.24	7.02
Sales per Share	30.91	37.18	42.18	43.82	38.35
EPS before extra. item	2.38	2.32	2.10	(0.40)	2.45
Cash Flow per Share	2.65	2.53	2.34	(0.18)	5.22
Book Value per Share	17.70	16.05	15.00	13.98	15.62
O/S Common Shares (mil)	245	239	230	222	214
Total Revenue ($mil)	8,847	9,960	10,581	10,672	9,180
Income before extra. ($mil)	640	595	522	(39)	553
Cash Flow ($mil)	640	595	529	(39)	1,095
Debt/Equity	0.53	0.51	0.55	0.63	0.54
Return on Capital (%)	18.50	19.89	20.68	4.98	19.92
Ret. on Com. Equity (%)	14.11	14.94	14.49	(2.67)	16.15
% Change Profit	7.6	13.9	1,453.5	(107.0)	357.2
% Change Revenue	(11.2)	(5.9)	(0.9)	16.3	14.5
% Change Assets	10.4	13.0	10.7	0.0	(6.3)
Preferred Div. Coverage	10.0	11.7	10.9		
Total Div. Coverage	2.0	2.0	1.8		
Capital Ratio	21.1	21.7	22.3		
Operat. Costs/$100 of Assets	2.5	2.6	2.8		
5 YEAR RATIOS					
Return on Capital	16.8	14.0	12.3		
Return on Com. Equity	11.4	6.8	5.9		
Profit Growth	na	11.0	9.0		
Revenue Growth	2.0	3.6	4.3		
Asset Growth	5.3	2.5	1.2		
BALANCE SHEET (mil)					
Cash	11,288	13,607	12,502		
Total Loans	68,251	60,172	55,106		
Net Fixed Assets	1,327	1,300	1,330		
Total Assets	109,035	98,725	87,370		
Total Deposits	90,747	82,789	73,321		
Subordinated Debt	1,666	1,570	1,473		
Total Liabilities	103,871	94,175	83,444		
Total Equity	5,164	4,550	3,926		
Total Liab. & Equity	109,035	98,725	87,370		
CAPITAL (mil)					
Total External Debt	2,733	2,307	2,161		
Preferred Equity	832	718	475		
Common Equity	4,332	3,832	3,451		

Business:

BANK OF MONTREAL is chartered under the Bank Act of Canada. The bank provides a full range of banking services to individuals, small business, corporations and governments through its network of branches and offices across Canada and around the world. Subsidiaries of the bank include Harris Bankcorp Inc., a Chicago-area bank, and Nesbitt Thomson Corporation Ltd., a full-service investment dealer.

Date	EPS	DPS	Tot Rev	Inc Bex
Apr 93	0.63	0.28	2,174,000	173,000
Jan 93	0.56	0.28	2,241,000	155,000
Oct 92	0.59	0.27	2,132,093	160,059
Jul 92	0.65	0.27	2,219,548	172,831
Apr 92	0.53	0.27	2,181,000	143,000
Jan 92	0.62	0.27	2,314,000	164,000
Oct 91	0.68	0.27	2,346,702	175,901
Jul 91	0.59	0.27	2,418,996	152,124

Synopsis:

The Bank of Montreal credits continuing growth in business volumes and improvements in productivity for its second quarter earnings of $173-million, up $30-million or 21% from a year earlier. Revenues grew 13%, with business volume growth augmented by before tax income of $24-million from the sale of Brazilian past due interest bonds.

The bank's return on investment has been 11.3% since the beginning of the fiscal year on November 1, 1992. During the quarter the price of common shares closed at an all-time high of $25 and one-eighth (after an adjustment for stock distribution that was effectively a two-for-one stock split). Share prices in general have responded favorably to lower interest rates and other indications of economic recovery.

Loan volumes were up 7%, with strong growth in residential mortgages, loans to small and mid-sized businesses in Canada, and large corporate loans in the U.S., all of which are low risk and well diversified. Increased securities trading activity by the bank's investment dealer subsidiary, Nesbitt Thomson, and higher revenues from Treasury services contributed to 15% growth in other income.

Ongoing productivity initiatives held expense growth from normal operations to less than 3% which, combined with increased sales commissions paid as a result of higher trading volumes by the Bank's investment dealer, the effects of a lower Canadian dollar relative to the U.S. dollar and higher government levies, resulted in total expense growth of 6%.

In light of the continued weak economic recovery, the bank's forecast provision for credit losses for fiscal 1993 remains at $650-million. Net non-performing loans at April 30, 1993, were $2-billion, down 14% from the first quarter. Total assets as of April 30, 1993, were $109-billion, up by $5-billion over the year.

Rank (Profit/Revenue/Assets)		
5	11	3

Matthew W. Barrett
Chairman & C.E.O.

F. Anthony Comper
President & C.O.O.

Robert B. Wells
Exec. V.P. & C.F.O.

Address
1 First Canadian Place
First Bank Tower
Toronto
ON
M5X 1A1
(416) 867-6656

Fax: (416) 867-7193
B0000586/B/13.1

BANK OF NOVA SCOTIA (THE)

Exchanges	Price (Jun24'93)		24 .87	Trailing P/E		8 .76	Stock Symbol
TMZVW	Trailing Yield (%)		4 .34	Trailing EPS		2 .84	**BNS**

Period Ending	Oc t92	Oc t91	Oc t90	Oc t89	Oc t88
Yearly Statistics					
Price-Close	24 .00	19 .75	11 .00	17 .25	15 .00
Price-High	24 .75	20 .00	18 .13	19 .25	16 .00
Price-Low	19 .00	10 .50	11 .00	13 .63	11 .50
P/E-Close	8 .16	7 .03	4 .72	17 .08	5 .47
Dividends per Share	1 .04	1 .00	1 .00	0 .88	0 .76
Dividend Yield (%)	4 .33	5 .06	9 .09	5 .10	5 .07
Sales per Share	36 .55	42 .71	43 .76	42 .40	36 .30
EPS before extra. item	2 .94	2 .81	2 .33	1 .01	2 .74
Cash Flow per Share	4 .27	7 .77	4 .34	5 .62	2 .89
Book Value per Share	19 .78	17 .59	16 .94	15 .41	15 .37
O/S Common Shares	206 ,187	201 ,061	190 ,198	187 ,694	183 ,625
Total Revenue	8 ,420 ,179	9 ,315 ,176	9 ,353 ,990	8 ,700 ,640	7 ,032 ,561
Income before extra.	676 ,224	633 ,015	511 ,989	221 ,817	506 ,647
Cash Flow	867 ,927	1 ,534 ,395	845 ,104	1 ,040 ,205	506 ,647
Debt/Equity	0 .66	0 .68	0 .77	0 .65	0 .86
Return on Capital (%)	20 .58	22 .55	22 .68	14 .71	22 .72
Ret. on Com. Equity (%)	15 .69	16 .42	14 .49	6 .55	18 .20
% Change Profit	6 .8	23 .6	130 .8	(56 .2)	337 .1
% Change Revenue	(9 .6)	(0 .4)	7 .5	23 .7	15 .9
% Change Assets	10 .1	1 .7	7 .7	8 .5	4 .5

Date		EPS	DPS	Tot Rev	Inc Bex
Apr	93	0.71	0.28	2 ,020 ,000	172 ,000
Jan	93	0.70	0.28	2 ,117 ,636	165 ,168
Oct	92	0.72	0.26	2 ,070 ,910	166 ,336
Jul	92	0.71	0.26	2 ,133 ,689	164 ,678
Apr	92	0.75	0.26	2 ,094 ,000	171 ,000
Jan	92	0.76	0.26	2 ,137 ,406	174 ,168
Oct	91	0.72	0.25	2 ,261 ,485	164 ,956
Jul	91	0.73	0.25	2 ,229 ,481	164 ,562

Preferred Div. Coverage	8 .6	8 .1	7 .4
Total Div. Coverage	2 .3	2 .3	2 .0
Capital Ratio	19 .2	19 .6	22 .0
Operat. Costs/$100 of Assets	2 .2	2 .2	2 .0
5 YEAR RATIOS			
Return on Capital	20 .6	17 .9	16 .7
Return on Com. Equity	14 .3	9 .3	8 .5
Profit Growth	42 .3	13 .5	11 .0
Revenue Growth	6 .7	8 .4	8 .6
Asset Growth	6 .3	6 .7	7 .3
BALANCE SHEET (mil)			
Cash	8 ,263	7 ,022	7 ,844
Total Loans	67 ,644	62 ,131	59 ,822
Net Fixed Assets	1 ,071	1 ,043	999
Total Assets	97 ,661	88 ,715	87 ,227
Total Deposits	76 ,153	67 ,833	65 ,000
Subordinated Debt	2 ,128	1 ,979	1 ,832
Total Liabilities	92 ,582	84 ,178	83 ,256
Total Equity	5 ,079	4 ,536	3 ,971
Total Liab. & Equity	97 ,661	88 ,715	87 ,227
CAPITAL (mil)			
Total External Debt	3 ,368	3 ,100	3 ,043
Preferred Equity	1 ,000	1 ,000	750
Common Equity	4 ,079	3 ,536	3 ,221

Business:

THE BANK OF NOVA SCOTIA is chartered under the Bank Act (Canada). The bank offers a full range of retail, commercial, corporate, investment and wholesale banking and other related financial services through its network of branches and offices across Canada and around the world. SociaMcLeod, a 100% owned subsidiary of the bank, provides full service brokerage and underwriting services.

Synopsis:

In June 1993, the Canadian Bond Rating Service Ltd. upgraded its ratings on the Bank of Nova Scotia, citing the bank's solid financial performance throughout the economic recession. CBRS upgraded long term deposits to A-plus from A-plus low, subordinated debentures to A-plus low from A high, cumulative preferred shares to P-1 from P-2, and non-cumulative preferred shares to P-2 from P-2 low.

The six months to April 30, 1992, results of the country's fourth largest bank saw revenues reduced by $90-million, falling from $4.24-billion to $4.15-billion this year. The net profit was $337-million, or $1.41 per share, compared with $345-million and $1.51 per share the year previous.

Assets, however, increased for the year, totaling $99.7-billion, compared with $95.8-billion, and a return on assets of 72 cents for each $100, compared with 74 cents. The economic environment continued to have an adverse effect on business and personal borrowers and there was no appreciable decline in non-performing loans in the second quarter. They remained at $2.15-billion, almost unchanged from the end of the first quarter. A further threat to bank revenues was seen in the recent increases in the Ontario and Quebec taxes which will affect the amount of disposable income people have and may spill over into their ability to pay their bank loans.

The bank moved further into the Mexican market late in 1992 acquiring a 5% interest in Grupo Financiero Inverlat, a major financial group in Mexico for $75-million (U.S.). Inverlat controls Mexico's second largest investment bank, Casa de Bolsa Inverlat, as well as Multibanco Comermex, Mexico's fourth largest commercial bank. Because of a recognition of the significantly improved economic performance in Mexico by the Superintendent of Financial Institutions in 1992, the bank was able to reverse into income $300-million from its country risk provision

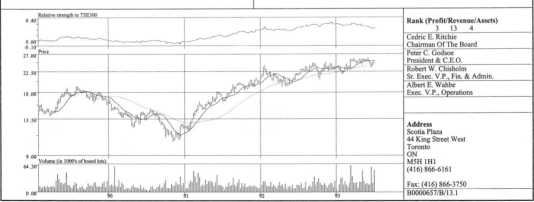

Rank (Profit/Revenue/Assets)
  3   13   4

Cedric E. Ritchie
Chairman Of The Board

Peter C. Godsoe
President & C.E.O.

Robert W. Chisholm
Sr. Exec. V.P., Fin. & Admin.

Albert E. Wahbe
Exec. V.P., Operations

Address
Scotia Plaza
44 King Street West
Toronto
ON
M5H 1H1
(416) 866-6161

Fax: (416) 866-3750
B0000657/B/13.1

CANADA TRUSTCO MORTGAGE COMPANY

Exchanges	Price (Jun24'93)		17.25	Trailing P/E		nc	Stock Symbol
T	Trailing Yield (%)		nc	Trailing EPS		2.73	**CT.PR.C**

Period Ending	Dec92	Dec91	Dec90	Dec89	Dec88
Yearly Statistics					
Price–Close	17.00	16.50	18.75	19.13	19.00
Price–High	18.75	19.50	20.50	19.88	21.00
Price–Low	15.00	16.25	17.50	18.00	18.75
P/E–Close	nc	nc	nc	nc	nc
Dividends per Share	nc	nc	nc	nc	nc
Dividend Yield (%)	nc	nc	nc	nc	nc
Sales per Share	90.07	102.22	108.48	99.99	82.35
EPS before extra. item	3.48	4.75	4.89	6.20	5.77
Cash Flow per Share	10.71	9.53	7.73	8.07	6.45
Book Value per Share	35.17	40.47	35.57	31.81	25.38
O/S Common Shares	39,287	39,287	39,287	39,287	39,287
Total Revenue	3,548,425	4,018,115	4,267,666	3,951,957	3,258,734
Income before extra.	155,437	196,403	205,155	243,612	242,751
Cash Flow	420,906	374,517	303,776	316,858	253,446
Debt/Equity	0.30	0.27	0.30	0.37	0.25
Return on Capital (%)	10.44	13.91	15.89	20.72	25.01
Ret. on Com. Equity (%)	9.21	12.50	14.52	20.23	22.95
% Change Profit	(20.9)	(4.3)	(15.8)	0.4	12.4
% Change Revenue	(11.7)	(5.8)	8.0	21.3	12.0
% Change Assets	3.2	3.6	6.5	11.8	13.8

Preferred Div. Coverage	8.4	20.1	15.8
Total Div. Coverage	0.7	1.9	1.9

5 YEAR RATIOS (%)			
Return on Capital	17.2	20.9	19.4
Return on Com. Equity	15.9	19.0	17.6
Profit Growth	(6.4)	31.4	8.6
Revenue Growth	4.0	17.5	10.9
Asset Growth	7.7	13.6	9.9

BALANCE SHEET (mil)			
Cash	2,680	2,153	2,471
Total Loans	6,740	27,019	25,518
Net Fixed Assets	1,250	1,116	960
Invest's & Advances	26,288	5,527	5,617
Total Assets	36,984	35,828	34,593
Total Deposits	34,582	33,501	32,475
Insurance Liability	0	0	0
Long Term Debt	500	469	458
Total Liabilities	35,323	34,106	33,061
Total Equity	1,661	1,721	1,532
Total Liab. & Equity	36,984	35,828	34,593

CAPITAL (mil)			
Total Debt	500	469	458
Preferred Equity	279	131	134
Common Equity	1,382	1,590	1,398

Business:

CANADA TRUSTCO MORTGAGE CO. and its wholly owned subsidiary, Canada Trust Co., are completely integrated for operating purposes. The companies offer a range of savings, loans and trust services through a Canada-wide branch network. Residential real estate brokerage services are also available. Imasco Ltd. of Montreal, has a major interest in the company, through CT Financial Services Inc.

Date	EPS	DPS	Tot Rev	Inc Bex
Mar 93	0.53	nc	822,990	25,596
Dec 92	0.40	nc	844,832	20,638
Sep 92	0.76	nc	866,272	34,314
Jun 92	1.04	nc	885,956	45,943
Mar 92	1.28	nc	904,858	54,542
Dec 91	0.99	nc	947,382	40,913
Sep 91	1.27	nc	967,211	52,407
Jun 91	1.28	nc	1,013,248	52,802

Synopsis:

Net earnings of Canada Trustco continued to decline in 1993, with first quarter figures coming in at $25.5-million, 53% below the $54.5-million for the same period last year. For 1992, net earnings fell by 21% to $155-million, reflecting the depressed economy. Net investment income increased as the interest spread widened, with lower interest rates causing customers to shift funds from term deposits to higher yielding investments such as mutual funds. Canada Trustco's provision for investment losses charged to earnings was $190-million, compared to $103-million in 1991, with the increase primarily due to non-performing commercial mortgages and commercial real estate loans which came about thorough deflation.

The company continues to be a conservative lender, with more than 89% of its loan portfolio owned by individual borrowers, of which 65% is secured by residential properties. The fewer write-offs of the residential mortgage portfolio were evidence of a tighter lending policy and the company's strength was reflected in its strong credit rating, which for Canada Trustco and The Canada Trust Company (its principal wholly owned subsidiary) is ahead of all of the six largest Canadian Banks.

Canada Trust will continue to focus on retail banking, meeting needs for wealth management services, and pension asset management while expanding retail market share. In January 1993, EasyLine telephone banking service was launched to allow individuals to access banking services by phone.

In December, the company's operation in the Netherlands, where it has been since 1983 as The Canada Trust Company B.V., was granted full banking status . This will enable Canada Trustco to broaden its future options in Europe and provide banking services throughout the European Community without the need for additional local licencing. New Canadian legislation requires controlling shareholder, Imasco Ltd., to reduce its voting shares of from 97.8% to a maximum of 65% by 1997.

Relative strength to TSE300 / Price / Volume (in 1000's of board lots)

Rank (Profit/Revenue/Assets)		
23	37	11

Peter C. Maurice
President & C.E.O.

G. Tom Gunn
Sr. V.P., Cap. Funds & C.F.O.

W. Edmund Clark
Vice Chairman & C.O.O.

Address
P.O. Box 5703
London
ON
N6A 4S4
(519) 663-1619

Fax: (519) 663-5114
C0002283/F/13.2

CANADIAN IMPERIAL BANK OF COMMERCE

Exchanges	Price (Jun24'93)	31.75	Trailing P/E	13.01	Stock Symbol
TMVZ	Trailing Yield (%)	4.16	Trailing EPS	2.44	**CM**

Period Ending	Oc t92	Oc t91	Oc t90	Oc t89	Oc t88
Yearly Statistics					
Price-Close	28.75	30.88	22.25	31.63	25.13
Price-High	37.00	33.00	33.63	32.50	25.88
Price-Low	25.13	21.63	21.63	22.75	16.88
P/E-Close	nm	7.86	5.52	13.87	7.52
Dividends per Share	1.32	1.32	1.32	1.24	1.14
Dividend Yield (%)	4.59	4.28	5.93	3.92	4.54
Sales per Share	51.96	62.64	66.01	58.35	50.05
EPS before extra. item	(0.59)	3.93	4.03	2.28	3.34
Cash Flow per Share	5.97	8.77	4.55	2.60	3.61
Book Value per Share	27.44	29.41	26.90	24.31	23.35
O/S Common Shares (mil)	189	184	179	175	172
Total Revenue ($mil)	11,388	12,912	13,005	11,285	9,158
Income before extra. ($mil)	12	811	802	450	591
Cash Flow ($mil)	1,107	1,587	1,605	(0)	(0)
Debt/Equity	0.43	0.37	0.46	0.52	0.74
Return on Capital (%)	2.06	17.67	19.70	13.32	17.96
Ret. on Com. Equity (%)	(2.04)	13.89	15.66	9.56	14.27
% Change Profit	(98.5)	1.1	78.3	(23.9)	3,439.2
% Change Revenue	(11.8)	(0.7)	15.2	23.2	14.2
% Change Assets	9.2	6.0	14.0	5.8	7.1

Preferred Div. Coverage	0.1	8.0	8.6
Total Div. Coverage	0.0	2.4	2.5
Capital Ratio	19.9	18.1	19.5
Operat. Costs/$100 of Assets	2.6	2.5	2.5
5 YEAR RATIOS			
Return on Capital	14.1	15.2	14.1
Return on Com. Equity	10.3	10.3	9.4
Profit Growth	(7.6)	18.9	17.3
Revenue Growth	7.2	10.3	10.6
Asset Growth	8.3	8.3	8.5
BALANCE SHEET (mil)			
Cash	6,245	7,465	6,751
Total Loans	94,927	86,361	83,331
Net Fixed Assets	1,754	1,605	1,380
Total Assets	132,212	121,025	114,196
Total Deposits	107,018	95,471	90,110
Subordinated Debt	2,848	2,485	2,026
Total Liabilities	125,574	114,322	108,328
Total Equity	6,638	6,703	5,869
Total Liab. & Equity	132,212	121,025	114,196
CAPITAL (mil)			
Total External Debt	2,848	2,485	2,684
Preferred Equity	1,460	1,300	1,050
Common Equity	5,178	5,403	4,819

Business:

CANADIAN IMPERIAL BANK OF COMMERCE is chartered under the Bank Act of Canada. The bank is comprised of five busiess units: Individual Bank; Corporate Bank; Investment Bank; Administative Bank; and CIBC Development Corp. The CIBC group provides banking and financial services around the world. CIBC owns a majority of CIBC Wood Gundy Corp., a full service investment dealer.

Date	EPS	DPS	Tot Rev	Inc Bex
Apr 93	0.75	0.33	2,692,000	180,000
Jan 93	0.74	0.33	2,827,000	169,000
Oct 92	0.10	0.33	2,735,890	45,307
Jul 92	0.85	0.33	2,874,020	186,231
Apr 92	(2.55)	0.33	2,787,000	(440,000)
Jan 92	1.01	0.33	2,992,000	221,000
Oct 91	1.09	0.33	3,077,585	224,774
Jul 91	0.96	0.33	3,150,484	200,998

Synopsis:

The results of the Canadian Imperial Bank of Commerce's strong revenue growth and restructuring program emphasizing retail banking were evident in the second quarter of 1993. Net income climbed to $180-million from $169-million in the first quarter, bringing the total for six months to $349-million, or $1.49 a share, up from a loss of $219-million, or $1.53 a share, a year earlier.

This compares favorably with a losses of $440-million, or $2.54 a share, and $219-million for the second quarter and six month period last year, which resulted from soured loans to commercial real estate companies, primarily Olympia & York Developments Ltd.

Loans still remained a problem although the total of non-performing loans slipped to 2.9% of all the outstanding loans at April 30, 1993, from 3.1% at the end of the first quarter, with most of that coming from U.S. accounts. The Canadian component of those non-performers climbed to $2.48-billion from $2.35-billion at January 31, 1993, primarily due to a reassessment.

CIBC maintained its first quarter forecast for 1993 of $880-million in provisions against potential loan losses and took a $220-million hit against profit in the second quarter as it did in the first.

The good quarterly showing was powered in part by CIBC's investment dealer, Wood Gundy Inc., which appears to have more than doubled its profit since the first quarter to about $20-million.

Net interest margin climbed seven basis points to 2.81% during the quarter, reflecting strong performances in securities trading operations and domestic retail banking business. The issuing of additional capital during the quarter also boosted the margin. Total assets at April 30, 1993, stood at $137.9-billion, compared with $136.2-billion at the end of the previous quarter and up significantly from $128.2-billion a year ago.

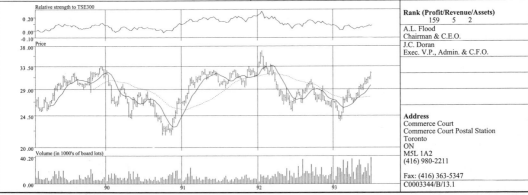

Rank (Profit/Revenue/Assets)
159 5 2

A.L. Flood
Chairman & C.E.O.
J.C. Doran
Exec. V.P., Admin. & C.F.O.

Address
Commerce Court
Commerce Court Postal Station
Toronto
ON
M5L 1A2
(416) 980-2211

Fax: (416) 363-5347
C0003344/B/13.1

CENTRAL GUARANTY TRUSTCO LIMITED

Exchanges
TMVZ

Price (Jun24'93) 0.06
Trailing Yield (%) 0.00

Trailing P/E nm
Trailing EPS (11.98)

Stock Symbol
CGA

Period Ending	Dec91	Dec90	Dec89	Dec88	Dec87
Yearly Statistics					
Price-Close	1.15	5.88	10.25	19.38	9.00
Price-High	9.25	10.25	12.50	22.50	15.88
Price-Low	0.90	5.25	7.88	18.63	8.25
P/E-Close	nm	12.77	7.82	13.18	6.72
Dividends per Share	0.38	0.50	0.49	0.41	0.38
Dividend Yield (%)	32.61	8.51	4.73	2.12	4.22
Sales per Share	28.51	31.63	29.81	26.83	25.90
EPS before extra. item	(12.29)	0.46	1.31	1.47	1.34
Cash Flow per Share	(0.12)	1.61	1.98	1.01	1.40
Book Value per Share	(2.86)	9.78	9.82	9.23	8.23
O/S Common Shares	59,482	59,229	59,060	57,688	40,827
Total Revenue	1,645,001	1,879,481	1,745,981	1,359,185	1,011,743
Income before extra.	(728,671)	27,524	76,727	75,037	54,921
Cash Flow	(7,043)	95,317	115,036	50,060	53,763
Debt/Equity	na	0.93	0.91	1.29	1.37
Return on Capital (%)	(94.96)	1.32	5.78	4.57	7.40
Ret. on Com. Equity (%)	(355.93)	4.71	13.67	16.80	16.98
% Change Profit	(2,747.4)	(64.1)	2.3	36.6	35.6
% Change Revenue	(12.5)	7.6	28.5	34.3	1.1
% Change Assets	(13.9)	2.7	6.1	36.5	23.3
Preferred Div. Coverage	0.0	112.3	111.0		
Total Div. Coverage	0.0	0.9	2.7		

5 YEAR RATIOS (%)			
Return on Capital	(15.2)	6.0	8.2
Return on Com. Equity	(60.8)	14.4	18.9
Profit Growth	na	10.0	10.0
Revenue Growth	10.4	31.9	1,230.1
Asset Growth	9.5	31.0	1,242.3

BALANCE SHEET (mil)			
Cash	651	1,137	854
Total Loans	10,962	11,903	11,920
Net Fixed Assets	159	110	105
Invest's & Advances	761	1,137	1,038
Total Assets	12,726	14,776	14,387
Total Deposits	11,710	12,843	12,389
Insurance Liability	0	0	0
Long Term Debt	431	543	22
Total Liabilities	12,893	14,194	13,804
Total Equity	(167)	582	583
Total Liab. & Equity	12,726	14,776	14,387

CAPITAL (mil)			
Total Debt	431	543	532
Preferred Equity	3	3	3
Common Equity	(170)	579	580

Business:

CENTRAL GUARANTY TRUSTCO LTD. is a financial services holding company.

Date	EPS	DPS	Tot Rev	Inc Bex
Sep 92	(0.65)	0.00	421,800	(38,964)
Jun 92	(1.20)	0.00	317,127	(71,739)
Mar 92	(0.50)	0.00	356,267	(29,529)
Dec 91	(9.63)	0.00	343,740	(571,231)
Sep 91	(2.55)	0.13	355,039	(150,979)
Jun 91	(0.06)	0.13	439,710	(3,652)
Mar 91	(0.05)	0.13	456,719	(2,809)
Dec 90	(0.05)	0.13	488,449	(2,594)

Synopsis:

In June 1993, Central Guaranty Trustco said the Ontario Court's General Division sanctioned its plan of arrangement proposed under the Companies' Creditors Arrangement Act. Central Guaranty's creditors also approved the plan of arrangement at a meeting held on April 30, 1993. The plan states all actions against Central Guaranty will be stayed for five years. The plan may be extended to 10 years during which Central will be managed by receiver Ernst & Young. As of December 31, 1992, there was a deficiency in Central Guaranty's shareholders' equity account of $328.7-million, compared to a deficiency of $167.1-million at the end of 1991.

In late 1992, shareholders of Central Guaranty Trustco's major subsidiary, Central Guaranty Trust, agreed to sell most of the company's assets to the Toronto-Dominion Bank. The deal is expected to leave shareholders with nothing. The purchase, which was overwhelmingly approved by shareholders, relates to Central Guaranty's 154 retail branches worth about $9-billion, as well as all deposit liability. Although investors saw their investments in the company drop to zero, many approved the deal because they have more at stake as depositors in the company. In February 1993, publicly traded preferred shares of Central Guaranty Trust Co. were delisted from the Toronto, Montreal and Vancouver stock exchanges.

In November 1992, Central Guaranty Trustco also completed the sale of its consumer finance arm, Trans Canada Credit Corp., to Norwest Corp. Under the terms of the agreement, 129 Trans Canada branches across Canada and $500-million in assets will be transferred to Norwest. In October 1992, Trans Canada Credit Corp. was granted court protection from its creditors, who are owed $410-million.

Relative strength to TSE300

Price

Volume (in 1000's of board lots)

Rank (Profit/Revenue/Assets)
998   74   26

Robert G. Graham
Chairman
W.T. Hodgson
President & C.E.O.
G.R. Paton-Ash
Sr. V.P. & C.F.O.

Address
105 Adelaide Street West
3rd Floor
Toronto
ON
M5H 4A4
(416) 345-4880

Fax: (416) 345-5346
C0000047/F/13.2

GENERAL TRUSTCO OF CANADA INC.

Exchanges	Price (Jun24'93)	0.30	Trailing P/E	nm	Stock Symbol
TM	Trailing Yield (%)	0.00	Trailing EPS	(3.73)	**TTG**

Period Ending	Dec92	Dec91	Dec90	Dec89	Dec88
Yearly Statistics					
Price-Close	2.50	2.75	5.13	7.25	6.63
Price-High	3.00	5.75	7.63	9.25	8.63
Price-Low	2.00	2.75	4.85	5.88	6.00
P/E-Close	nm	nm	256.25	11.51	11.04
Dividends per Share	0.00	0.13	0.32	0.36	0.36
Dividend Yield (%)	0.00	4.55	6.24	4.97	5.43
Sales per Share	0.28	0.82	20.61	18.48	15.61
EPS before extra. item	(3.90)	(1.84)	0.02	0.63	0.60
Cash Flow per Share	(0.32)	(0.27)	0.60	1.18	0.71
Book Value per Share	(0.35)	3.28	5.24	5.50	5.23
O/S Common Shares	45,073	35,012	34,893	34,893	34,893
Total Revenue	(563)	16,233	719,241	644,865	544,846
Income before extra.	(157,781)	(59,946)	5,473	26,684	24,937
Cash Flow	(12,837)	(9,520)	21,019	41,199	24,937
Debt/Equity	7.96	1.55	1.04	0.95	0.78
Return on Capital (%)	(43.38)	(13.35)	0.09	6.13	7.20
Ret. on Com. Equity (%)	(325.05)	(43.09)	0.29	11.79	11.67
% Change Profit	(163.2)	(1,195.3)	0.0	7.0	(19.0)
% Change Revenue	(103.5)	(97.7)	11.5	18.4	15.3
% Change Assets	(34.0)	(5.3)	4.3	14.9	19.5

Preferred Div. Coverage	0.0	0.0	1.1
Total Div. Coverage	0.0	0.0	0.4

Business:

GENERAL TRUSTCO OF CANADA INC. is a trust company with operations in Quebec and Ontario. The company, with its subsidiaries, provides individual and corporate clients with such services as RRSPs, savings and deposits services, mortgage financing, stock transfer, and corporate financial services. Alliance-Industrial Financial Corp. of Montreal owns 63% of the company's common shares.

Date	EPS	DPS	Tot Rev	Inc Bex
Mar 93	(0.08)	0.00	808	(3,301)
Dec 92	(3.48)	0.00	(56,283)	(143,363)
Sep 92	(0.05)	0.00	130,036	(2,189)
Jun 92	(0.12)	0.00	130,110	(4,470)
Mar 92	(0.25)	0.00	1,518	(7,922)
Dec 91	(1.72)	0.03	(60,103)	(58,769)
Sep 91	(0.18)	0.03	158,818	(5,270)
Jun 91	0.01	0.05	171,929	1,356

5 YEAR RATIOS (%)			
Return on Capital	(8.7)	2.6	7.5
Return on Com. Equity	(68.9)	(0.5)	11.5
Profit Growth	na	na	(21.5)
Revenue Growth	na	(48.3)	14.1
Asset Growth	(2.3)	9.6	14.2

BALANCE SHEET (000)			
Cash	300,508	405,567	455,979
Total Loans	2,618,714	4,275,802	4,639,639
Net Fixed Assets	191,109	238,847	209,780
Invest's & Advances	509,930	601,597	575,818
Total Assets	3,701,992	5,608,971	5,925,897
Total Deposits	3,369,227	5,163,821	5,417,685
Insurance Liability	0	0	0
Long Term Debt	271,714	255,559	241,416
Total Liabilities	3,667,835	5,444,179	5,693,216
Total Equity	34,157	164,792	232,681
Total Liab. & Equity	3,701,992	5,608,971	5,925,897

CAPITAL (000)			
Total Debt	271,714	255,559	241,416
Preferred Equity	50,000	50,000	50,000
Common Equity	(15,843)	114,792	182,681

Synopsis:

In June 1993, General Trustco of Canada released consolidated results for the year ended 1992 and the first quarter of 1993. During fiscal 1992, General Trustco continued to record heavy losses in its trust and real estate subsidiaries. Because of this, the company continued to seek out additional funds necessary to meet its debt obligations, some of which matured on March 23, 1993. During the period, General Trustco also had to generate liquid assets required to meet the capitalization norms of Quebec regulatory authorities. General Trustco must find a way to satisfy its creditors or the company will be forced into bankruptcy during 1993.

In March 1993, General Trustco concluded an agreement in principal whereby the National Bank of Canada would acquire three of the company's subsidiaries: General Trust, Sherbrooke Trust and Gentrust Investment Counsellors. The proposal is subject to a number of conditions before the sale can be completed. A main stumbling block is the approval by holders of General Trustco debentures. General Trustco is in default with these creditors and some want to force the company into bankruptcy.

Since March 22, 1993, when General Trustco's debentures became due, the company has met several times with all parties involved the transaction with the National Bank. General Trustco is trying to develop a financial arrangement satisfactory to all debenture holders. General Trustco expects to send an arrangement proposal to debenture holders on June 18, 1993. The future for General Trustco depends on the acceptance of this proposal by debenture holders as well as the approval by common shareholders of General Trustco, for the sale of General Trustco's Quebec subsidiaries to the National Bank.

In another move to generate additional funds, General Trustco completed the sale of its Ontario subsidiary subsequent to the 1992 year end. Laurentian Bank purchased the assets for $82-million.

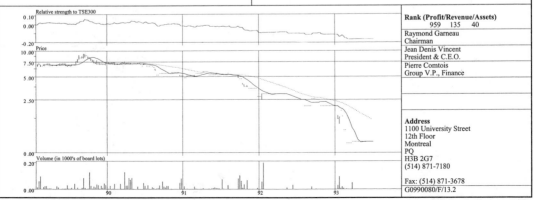

Rank (Profit/Revenue/Assets)
959   135   40

Raymond Garneau
Chairman

Jean Denis Vincent
President & C.E.O.

Pierre Comtois
Group V.P., Finance

Address
1100 University Street
12th Floor
Montreal
PQ
H3B 2G7
(514) 871-7180

Fax: (514) 871-3678
G0990080/F/13.2

GENTRA INC.

Exchanges	Price (Jun24'93)	0.36	Trailing P/E	nm	Stock Symbol
TMZV	Trailing Yield (%)	66.67	Trailing EPS	(6.72)	**GTA**

Period Ending	Dec92	Dec91	Dec90	Dec89	Dec88
Yearly Statistics					
Price-Close	2.94	8.00	9.50	17.88	16.38
Price-High	9.38	11.25	18.25	19.38	17.63
Price-Low	2.40	6.38	8.13	15.88	12.75
P/E-Close	nm	32.00	nm	10.52	11.06
Dividends per Share	0.52	0.74	0.74	0.70	0.62
Dividend Yield (%)	17.69	9.25	7.79	3.92	3.79
Sales per Share	18.47	25.44	40.02	33.63	26.87
EPS before extra. item	(5.93)	0.25	(1.20)	1.70	1.48
Cash Flow per Share	0.95	1.89	1.87	2.40	2.23
Book Value per Share	1.32	7.74	8.87	10.40	8.61
O/S Common Shares	153,446	152,667	125,982	124,519	105,733
Total Revenue	2,827,000	3,706,000	5,025,000	3,763,000	2,830,000
Income before extra.	(852,000)	107,000	(65,000)	265,000	212,000
Cash Flow	146,000	274,000	235,000	269,000	235,000
Debt/Equity	2.95	2.96	3.05	0.40	0.40
Return on Capital (%)	(11.04)	1.63	(2.47)	8.36	9.73
Ret. on Com. Equity (%)	(131.16)	2.96	(10.94)	17.05	17.74
% Change Profit	(896.3)	264.6	(124.5)	25.0	12.8
% Change Revenue	(23.7)	(26.2)	33.5	33.0	24.7
% Change Assets	(33.1)	(8.4)	2.8	39.7	16.3

Preferred Div. Coverage	0.0	1.5	0.0
Total Div. Coverage	0.0	0.6	0.0

5 YEAR RATIOS (%)			
Return on Capital	1.2	5.7	7.8
Return on Com. Equity	(20.9)	9.1	12.3
Profit Growth	na	(7.0)	na
Revenue Growth	4.5	14.8	20.9
Asset Growth	0.4	14.1	24.9

BALANCE SHEET (mil)			
Cash	3,131	3,715	4,958
Total Loans	17,614	20,146	29,067
Net Fixed Assets	236	243	471
Invest's & Advances	2,974	5,435	5,568
Total Assets	25,114	37,526	40,946
Total Deposits	21,048	29,490	32,991
Insurance Liability	0	0	0
Long Term Debt	2,855	5,794	5,775
Total Liabilities	24,146	35,570	39,053
Total Equity	968	1,956	1,893
Total Liab. & Equity	25,114	37,526	40,946

CAPITAL (mil)			
Total Debt	2,855	5,794	5,775
Preferred Equity	766	775	775
Common Equity	202	1,181	1,118

Business:

GENTRA INC., parent of the Royal Trust Group, is 47% owned by Trilon Financial Corporation.

Date	EPS	DPS	Tot Rev	Inc Bex
Mar 93	(0.57)	0.00	557,000	(75,000)
Dec 92	(4.17)	0.05	602,000	(625,000)
Sep 92	(1.84)	0.10	333,000	(243,000)
Jun 92	(0.14)	0.19	942,000	(8,000)
Mar 92	0.06	0.19	763,000	24,000
Dec 91	(0.17)	0.19	870,000	(8,000)
Sep 91	0.10	0.19	443,000	33,000
Jun 91	0.17	0.19	1,151,000	43,000

Synopsis:

Gentra Inc., formerly Royal Trustco Limited, got a reprieve on March 18, 1993, when the Royal Bank of Canada purchased the shares and subordinated debt of certain of the company's Canadian and international operating subsidiaries. The Royal Bank purchase included the two principal trust company subsidiaries, The Royal Trust Company and Royal Trust Corporation of Canada, and the Royal Trustco's banking and trust company subsidiaries internationally. Based on the assets and liabilities of the business at December, 31, 1992, the purchase price would be $1.645-billion. The book value of the operations which are proposed to be sold to Royal Bank was approximately $1.38-billion at December 31, 1992.

Excluded from the agreement are allowances for loan losses of $700-billion, a Canadian commercial loan portfolio of $2-billion and loan portfolios of $900-million in Canada, and $1.4-billion in the U.S. and the U.K. Of the $4.3-billion of net loans, 24% were non-performing at year end.

Client assets under administration at December 31, 1992 totaled approximately $124.3-billion. Trilon Financial Corp. is expected to provide financial assistance of about $100-million.

Preliminary financial estimates showed the company had lost $850-million last year, compared with profits of $107-million in 1991, this the legacy of aggressive expansion into the U.S. and U.K. commercial real estate market in the late 1980s. Royal Trustco was battered by the global real estate losses as well as troubles that were compounded by problems at Hees-Edper group.

In June 1993, the Canadian Bond Rating Service Ltd. added a sour note to shareholders, saying preferred shareholders owed $766-million will likely receive little or nothing after the proposed sale. As for senior lenders owed $1.3-billion, the likelihood of being paid out in full is reasonable, while subordinate debt holders owed $1.3-billion will potentially recover a good part of their investment.

Relative strength to TSE300 / Price / Volume (in 1000's of board lots) chart

Rank (Profit/Revenue/Assets)		
999	48	14

Hartland M. MacDougall
Chairman

James W. Miller
President & C.E.O.

Anthony Flynn
Treasurer & C.F.O.

William J. Inwood
Exec. V.P. & C.O.O.

Address
Royal Trust Tower
Suite 3900
Toronto
ON
M5W 1P9
(416) 981-7000

Fax: (416) 864-9021
R0002960/F/13.2

For further company information, call Globe Information Services 1-800-268-9128 or (416)585-5345

LAURENTIAN BANK OF CANADA

Exchanges	Price (Jun24'93)		17.87	Trailing P/E		10.04	Stock Symbol
TM	Trailing Yield (%)		4.03	Trailing EPS		1.78	**LB**

Period Ending	Oct 92	Oct 91	Oct 90	Oct 89	Oct 88
Yearly Statistics					
Price-Close	18.00	20.25	13.63	16.00	12.13
Price-High	22.75	20.63	17.00	16.50	13.00
Price-Low	17.00	13.38	13.00	11.75	10.75
P/E-Close	8.82	9.88	6.71	8.79	11.55
Dividends per Share	0.60	0.68	0.60	0.54	0.54
Dividend Yield (%)	3.33	3.36	4.40	3.38	4.45
Sales per Share	52.31	46.21	42.27	34.56	29.94
EPS before extra. item	2.04	2.05	2.03	1.82	1.05
Cash Flow per Share	5.53	4.05	2.27	2.45	1.35
Book Value per Share	18.66	17.39	16.11	14.78	13.51
O/S Common Shares	15,500	15,500	15,500	15,500	15,500
Total Revenue	865,014	758,665	693,952	582,058	500,258
Income before extra.	38,675	34,159	35,154	34,426	22,466
Cash Flow	85,780	62,773	35,154	37,899	20,926
Debt/Equity	0.20	0.21	nd	nd	nd
Return on Capital (%)	13.55	12.83	16.42	14.98	8.81
Ret. on Com. Equity (%)	11.35	12.22	13.12	12.90	8.07
% Change Profit	13.2	(2.8)	2.1	53.2	(5.9)
% Change Revenue	14.0	9.3	19.2	16.4	25.7
% Change Assets	18.9	15.4	15.2	8.6	23.3

Preferred Div. Coverage	5.5	14.0	9.4
Total Div. Coverage	2.1	2.6	2.7
Capital Ratio	21.9	19.4	21.7
Operat. Costs/$100 of Assets	2.6	2.4	2.5
5 YEAR RATIOS			
Return on Capital	13.3	12.3	11.5
Return on Com. Equity	11.5	11.2	10.3
Profit Growth	10.1	10.9	10.0
Revenue Growth	16.8	15.0	13.7
Asset Growth	16.1	12.6	11.7
BALANCE SHEET (000)			
Cash	296,246	349,768	450,846
Total Loans	6,730,448	5,765,566	4,798,447
Net Fixed Assets	91,435	67,584	54,183
Total Assets	8,307,784	6,989,723	6,059,190
Total Deposits	7,570,106	6,330,666	5,564,073
Subordinated Debt	75,000	75,000	0
Total Liabilities	7,928,637	6,630,165	5,779,463
Total Equity	379,147	359,558	279,727
Total Liab. & Equity	8,307,784	6,989,723	6,059,190
CAPITAL (000)			
Total External Debt	75,000	75,000	0
Preferred Equity	90,000	90,000	30,000
Common Equity	289,147	269,558	249,727

Business:

LAURENTIAN BANK OF CANADA is chartered under the Bank Act of Canada. The bank offers a full range of banking and financial services responding to the needs of individuals and small and medium-sized businesses through branches across Quebec, Ontario, Manitoba, Alberta, Saskatchewan and British Columbia. The bank is a member of the Laurentian Group of companies.

Date	EPS	DPS	Tot Rev	Inc Bex
Apr 93	0.38	0.19	216,390	8,258
Jan 93	0.36	0.19	200,293	7,505
Oct 92	0.51	0.15	207,354	9,780
Jul 92	0.53	0.19	219,673	10,140
Apr 92	0.47	0.19	215,567	9,037
Jan 92	0.53	0.19	222,420	9,718
Oct 91	0.53	0.17	194,388	8,731
Jul 91	0.56	0.17	192,818	9,241

Synopsis:

The second quarter of 1993 was marked by the Laurentian Bank's acquisition of General Trust, increasing assets to $9.7-billion, a $1.4-billion or 17% rise since the beginning of the fiscal year.

The bank has been particularly active in acquisitions over the past two years. In 1991 Laurentian bought La Financiere-Cooperants Prets-Epargne Inc. and La Financiere-Cooperants Credit-Bail Inc. for $99-million. As well the bank concluded an agreement with Canada Deposit Insurance Corporation for the winding down of the business of Standard Trust Company and Standard Loan Company which the bank purchased in liquidation. In 1992 Laurentian purchased the shares of Guardian Trust and Guardcor Loans Inc., and in 1992 the bank acquired a 51% interest in BLC Rousseau Inc.

The acquisitions carry out the bank's strategy of focusing on personal trust and banking services with residential mortgages representing close to 60% of total loans while about 90% of deposits came from individuals at the end of 1992, up from 85% in 1991. As well the acquisitions strongly established the bank's presence in Ontario and Quebec and enhanced the geographic distribution of its loan portfolio.

Net income for the second quarter of 1993 was $8.3-million, down from $9-million in the corresponding quarter of 1992 but higher than the first quarter of 1993. The results were adversely affected by provision of $3-million, established in respect of certain marketable securities, including Royal Trustco.

The bank's objectives for 1993 include: increasing assets by 5%, excluding growth from acquisitions; maintaining an efficiency ratio of 70 cents per dollar of revenue; obtaining an 11% return on common shareholders' equity; and adding 25 new automated banking machines. Laurentian Bank believes that lower interest rates and debt loads, as well as stronger exports, will improve business conditions in 1993, with consumer and business credit growth remaining soft.

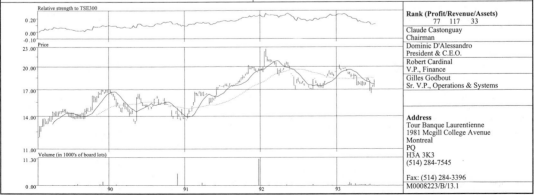

Rank (Profit/Revenue/Assets)
77 117 33
Claude Castonguay
Chairman
Dominic D'Alessandro
President & C.E.O.
Robert Cardinal
V.P., Finance
Gilles Godbout
Sr. V.P., Operations & Systems

Address
Tour Banque Laurentienne
1981 Mcgill College Avenue
Montreal
PQ
H3A 3K3
(514) 284-7545

Fax: (514) 284-3396
M0008223/B/13.1

MONTREAL TRUSTCO INC.

Exchanges	Price (Jun24'93)		14.12	Trailing P/E		nc	Stock Symbol
TM	Trailing Yield (%)		nc	Trailing EPS		(2.18)	**MTU.PR.A**

Period Ending	Dec92	Dec91	Dec90	Dec89	Dec88
Yearly Statistics					
Price-Close	15.50	20.25	19.50	22.25	22.25
Price-High	20.38	22.00	23.00	23.00	23.63
Price-Low	15.00	18.13	18.00	20.50	20.50
P/E-Close	nc	nc	nc	nc	nc
Dividends per Share	nc	nc	nc	nc	nc
Dividend Yield (%)	nc	nc	nc	nc	nc
Sales per Share	30.71	37.86	42.25	37.55	33.29
EPS before extra. item	(1.98)	0.87	1.50	1.69	1.62
Cash Flow per Share	0.88	2.12	2.52	2.37	1.99
Book Value per Share	11.74	12.54	11.83	11.04	9.98
O/S Common Shares	45,240	39,675	37,327	37,327	36,474
Total Revenue	1,306,016	1,491,251	1,577,248	1,391,713	1,106,832
Income before extra.	(78,867)	41,580	64,760	71,224	61,595
Cash Flow	37,386	83,309	93,938	87,675	66,227
Debt/Equity	16.30	17.92	19.78	18.28	18.75
Return on Capital (%)	7.30	10.46	12.03	11.70	17.94
Ret. on Com. Equity (%)	(16.35)	7.26	13.08	16.13	16.71
% Change Profit	(289.7)	(35.8)	(9.1)	15.6	18.1
% Change Revenue	(12.4)	(5.5)	13.3	25.7	23.1
% Change Assets	(2.9)	1.3	12.3	8.0	33.2

Preferred Div. Coverage	0.0	5.6	7.2
Total Div. Coverage	0.0	1.2	1.8

5 YEAR RATIOS (%)			
Return on Capital	11.9	32.3	31.2
Return on Com. Equity	7.4	14.0	15.1
Profit Growth	na	9.0	28.6
Revenue Growth	7.7	18.7	30.9
Asset Growth	9.7	12.1	31.8
BALANCE SHEET (mil)			
Cash	1,073	772	1,135
Total Loans	9,480	9,732	9,442
Net Fixed Assets	119	122	127
Invest's & Advances	1,177	1,671	1,438
Total Assets	12,187	12,549	12,383
Total Deposits	1,184	1,189	1,071
Insurance Liability	0	0	0
Long Term Debt	10,287	10,711	10,711
Total Liabilities	11,555	11,952	11,842
Total Equity	631	598	542
Total Liab. & Equity	12,187	12,549	12,383
CAPITAL (mil)			
Total Debt	10,287	10,711	10,711
Preferred Equity	100	100	100
Common Equity	531	498	442

Business:

MONTREAL TRUSTCO INC. is a diversified marketer of financial and trust services to individuals, businesses and other types of organizations. Incorporated in 1889, the company operates throughout Canada from more than 140 branches and offices. Montreal Trustco Inc. is a wholly owned subsidiary of BCE Inc.

Date	EPS	DPS	Tot Rev	Inc Bex
Mar 93	(0.01)	nc	303,822	616
Dec 92	(0.67)	nc	315,006	(27,982)
Sep 92	0.01	nc	317,477	1,587
Jun 92	(1.51)	nc	333,301	(58,515)
Mar 92	0.12	nc	338,248	6,043
Dec 91	0.00	nc	353,959	1,518
Sep 91	0.22	nc	366,731	10,908
Jun 91	0.31	nc	379,128	14,097

Synopsis:

The Canadian Bond Rating Service Ltd. downgraded Montreal Trustco Ltd. and its two principal operating subsidiaries in June 1993 noting its concern about the deterioration in their loan quality. The companies had been forced to set aside large provisions to cover losses, mainly from commercial real estate loans, and exposure to Olympia & York Developments Ltd. and Bramalea Ltd.

It was felt that the $30-million set aside at the end of 1992 did not provide a strong enough buffer to protect against unforeseen increases in non performers. Loan portfolios continued to deteriorate with net non performing loans accounting for 4.3%, up from 4.1% at year-end and 3.9% a year ago. In an effort to reduce exposure the company revised its lending criteria and rationalized some of its branch network in order to reduce costs. Special teams have been set up to monitor all non-accrual loans, and to ensure a swift resolution.

The net loss for 1992 was $78.9-million, or $1.98 per share. These figures reflect the high loan loss provisions of $178-million, compared to $33.1-million in 1991. The total net non-performing loans were $386.9-million. The first quarter net loss in 1993 was $616,000 compared with $6-million a year ago, and up from a loss of $28-million during the last quarter of 1992.

A 9.1% increase in the fee income from 1992, rising to $154.3-million from the previous year's $141.4-million resulted from the acquisition of the corporate trust operations of Central Guaranty Trust. The net investment and loan income was $163.4-million, down from $184.1-million in 1991.

Assets declined marginally to $12.2-billion. Mortgages remained stable at $7.7-billion. Corporate and commercial loans dropped to $1.7-billion from $1.9-billion a year ago. In spite of the losses, shareholders were taken care of as equity increased to $631.3-million, from $597.6-million in 1991 as a result of a $125-million capital injection in June 1992, from parent company BCE Inc.

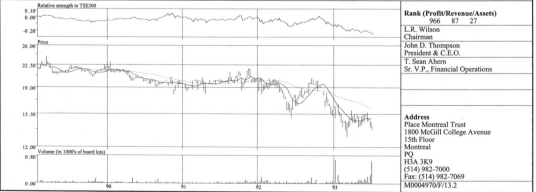

Rank (Profit/Revenue/Assets)
966   87   27

L.R. Wilson
Chairman

John D. Thompson
President & C.E.O.

T. Sean Ahern
Sr. V.P., Financial Operations

Address
Place Montreal Trust
1800 McGill College Avenue
15th Floor
Montreal
PQ
H3A 3K9
(514) 982-7000
Fax: (514) 982-7069
M0004970/F/13.2

386

NATIONAL BANK OF CANADA

Exchanges	Price (Jun24'93)	10.50	Trailing P/E	nm	Stock Symbol
TMV	Trailing Yield (%)	4.76	Trailing EPS	(0.26)	**NA**

Period Ending	Oct 92	Oct 91	Oct 90	Oct 89	Oct 88
Yearly Statistics					
Price-Close	8.13	11.13	7.13	14.00	12.00
Price-High	12.75	11.38	14.00	15.13	12.63
Price-Low	7.38	7.00	7.13	11.00	8.75
P/E-Close	nm	9.27	6.36	233.33	6.42
Dividends per Share	0.70	0.80	0.80	0.72	0.64
Dividend Yield (%)	8.62	7.19	11.23	5.14	5.33
Sales per Share	24.97	29.13	32.90	28.97	26.06
EPS before extra. item	(0.29)	1.20	1.12	0.06	1.87
Cash Flow per Share	3.90	4.07	4.00	4.04	4.21
Book Value per Share	10.26	11.18	10.78	10.64	11.30
O/S Common Shares	127,152	127,031	126,875	118,200	114,725
Total Revenue	3,713,168	4,170,559	4,382,345	3,775,053	3,139,576
Income before extra.	1,016	185,971	170,323	31,738	226,298
Cash Flow	494,881	517,273	479,142	473,561	458,144
Debt/Equity	0.79	0.85	0.78	0.94	0.93
Return on Capital (%)	2.96	11.74	11.88	7.59	16.88
Ret. on Com. Equity (%)	(2.67)	10.95	10.19	0.53	16.69
% Change Profit	(99.5)	9.2	436.7	(86.0)	594.7
% Change Revenue	(11.0)	(4.8)	16.1	20.2	12.8
% Change Assets	9.8	1.5	5.9	9.7	3.2

Date		EPS	DPS	Tot Rev	Inc Bex
Apr	93	0.23	0.10	837,612	40,090
Jan	93	0.28	0.10	889,612	45,000
Oct	92	0.23	0.10	895,317	38,924
Jul	92	(1.00)	0.20	934,855	(117,549)
Apr	92	0.16	0.20	911,417	29,845
Jan	92	0.32	0.20	971,579	49,796
Oct	91	0.26	0.20	1,010,149	41,274
Jul	91	0.25	0.20	1,011,170	39,122

	Oct 92	Oct 91	Oct 90
Preferred Div. Coverage	0.0	5.6	4.7
Total Div. Coverage	0.0	1.4	1.3
Capital Ratio	22.6	20.2	20.5
Operat. Costs/$100 of Assets	2.5	2.5	2.4
5 YEAR RATIOS			
Return on Capital	10.2	11.2	12.4
Return on Com. Equity	7.1	6.5	7.2
Profit Growth	(51.4)	1.2	2.1
Revenue Growth	5.9	8.4	12.7
Asset Growth	5.9	5.4	8.9
BALANCE SHEET (mil)			
Cash	3,693	1,883	2,216
Total Loans	30,003	28,360	27,420
Net Fixed Assets	374	378	367
Total Assets	40,045	36,457	35,922
Total Deposits	33,433	29,987	28,929
Subordinated Debt	969	806	727
Total Liabilities	38,272	34,651	34,167
Total Equity	1,773	1,806	1,755
Total Liab. & Equity	40,045	36,457	35,922
CAPITAL (mil)			
Total External Debt	1,392	1,527	1,369
Preferred Equity	468	385	387
Common Equity	1,305	1,421	1,368

Business:

NATIONAL BANK OF CANADA is chartered under the Bank Act of Canada. The bank offers retail, commercial, corporate, international and treasury banking services through its branches and offices in Canada and around the world. Levesque Beaubien Geoffrion of Montreal, a subsidiary of the bank, is an investment dealer.

Synopsis:

Actions taken by the National Bank of Canada to lower lending limits for single borrowers or group of borrowers from 10% to 8% of shareholders' equity and impose even stricter limits for the real estate sector seem to have paid of in 1993. The net earnings of $40-million or 23 cents per share for the second quarter were up by more than 30% over the $30-million or 16 cents per share for the same period in 1992, bringing the total for the first six months of the fiscal year to $85-million.

The figures did not include the gain of $23-million from the sale of the bank's leasing operations which it directed towards loan losses of an additional $25-million for the quarter. The loan loss provisions for the quarter were $100-million of the total of $ 300-million in losses projected for fiscal 1993. In 1992, $570-million was set aside in loan loss provisions. Of that amount, $396-million involved real estate and $350-million loans to the Olympia & York group.

Bank operations showed strength in several sectors. Higher volumes generated by Levesque Beaubien Geoffrion were fueled by lower interest rates. The bank's U.S. subsidiary, National Canada Finance Corporation which lends to mid-market businesses, also showed higher activity.

Because of loan securitization changes, however, loans were down $1.7-billion. As well, assets for the second quarter were down by $1.3-billion from the previous quarter to $40.3-billion. On the plus side, personal deposits rose $400-million, partially because of an increased market share in Quebec from the decentralization of operations.

In 1992, National Bank instituted new and novel programs to preserve capital and pursue growth in less risky markets. The bank cut its dividend in half to 10 cents per share and is offering a dividend reinvestment and share purchase plan to encourage reinvestment of shares.

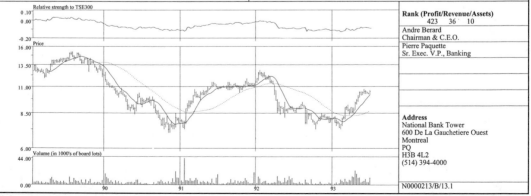

Rank (Profit/Revenue/Assets)
423 36 10

Andre Berard
Chairman & C.E.O.

Pierre Paquette
Sr. Exec. V.P., Banking

Address
National Bank Tower
600 De La Gauchetiere Ouest
Montreal
PQ
H3B 4L2
(514) 394-4000

N0000213/B/13.1

NATIONAL TRUSTCO INC.

Exchanges	Price (Jun24'93)	19.87	Trailing P/E	18.57	Stock Symbol
T	Trailing Yield (%)	4.43	Trailing EPS	1.07	NT

Period Ending	Oct 92	Oct 91	Oct 90	Oct 89	Oct 88
Yearly Statistics					
Price-Close	15.25	23.00	20.25	27.38	24.75
Price-High	24.00	24.75	27.50	28.25	28.00
Price-Low	15.25	19.38	19.00	21.63	16.50
P/E-Close	13.38	11.50	9.60	11.90	12.19
Dividends per Share	0.88	0.88	0.88	0.80	0.80
Dividend Yield (%)	5.77	3.83	4.35	2.92	3.23
Sales per Share	48.47	54.84	53.20	44.65	37.12
EPS before extra. item	1.14	2.00	2.11	2.30	2.03
Cash Flow per Share	2.63	5.30	5.10	4.57	2.46
Book Value per Share	20.58	20.34	19.20	17.97	16.47
O/S Common Shares	34,763	34,338	33,926	33,926	33,926
Total Revenue	1,684,608	1,871,224	1,795,859	1,514,984	1,259,400
Income before extra.	39,287	68,109	71,688	78,163	68,743
Cash Flow	90,853	180,532	172,871	155,096	83,516
Debt/Equity	0.26	0.27	0.17	0.18	0.39
Return on Capital (%)	6.53	11.81	12.65	12.28	12.72
Ret. on Com. Equity (%)	5.56	10.09	11.37	13.38	12.79
% Change Profit	(42.3)	(5.0)	(8.3)	13.7	1.2
% Change Revenue	(10.0)	4.2	18.5	20.3	12.4
% Change Assets	(0.2)	6.0	11.4	15.3	11.5

Business:

NATIONAL TRUSTCO INC. is a public holding company for a group of trust and loan corporations. National Trust Company is the principal operating subsidiary of National Trustco. National Trust provides personal trust and investment management services, retail banking, custody and pension investment services and commercial lending through more than 185 branches across Canada.

Date	EPS	DPS	Tot Rev	Inc Bex
Apr 93	0.35	0.22	375,332	12,467
Jan 93	0.36	0.22	394,524	12,358
Oct 92	0.12	0.22	393,769	4,108
Jul 92	0.24	0.22	425,242	8,372
Apr 92	0.28	0.22	419,064	9,441
Jan 92	0.50	0.22	446,207	17,366
Oct 91	0.24	0.22	457,244	8,238
Jul 91	0.60	0.22	468,107	20,598

Preferred Div. Coverage	np	np	np
Total Div. Coverage	1.3	2.3	2.4

Synopsis:

A stronger financial showing in the second quarter for National Trustco has some believing that the consortium of trust companies has turned the corner, but its January 1993 call for a partner willing to take a large stake in the cash strapped financial service conglomerate signals caution. National Trust held talks with financial institutions interested in pumping cash into the parent company and replacing the Edper-Bronfman group's Trilon Financial Corp. as controlling shareholder. The figure could be up to $300-million and although investors greeted the news positively the Dominion Bond Rating Service Ltd. announced a rating alert with potential negative implications because of the eroding asset quality.

5 YEAR RATIOS (%)			
Return on Capital	11.2	13.3	13.9
Return on Com. Equity	10.6	12.3	12.9
Profit Growth	(10.4)	2.3	2.9
Revenue Growth	8.4	11.9	11.4
Asset Growth	8.6	11.3	12.4

The second quarter in 1993 showed net income for three months at $12.5-million or 35 cents per share, up from the $9.4-million or 28 cents a share the year earlier. The total capital funds grew to $915.5-million at April 30, 1993, versus $904.2-million for the corresponding period. The improvement reflects continued attention to the fundamentals of the company's business, controlling costs and concentrating on profitable core businesses.

BALANCE SHEET (mil)			
Cash	1,672	1,609	1,526
Total Loans	13,957	13,900	13,046
Net Fixed Assets	101	106	81
Invest's & Advances	760	907	925
Total Assets	16,567	16,600	15,653
Total Deposits	15,619	15,639	14,827
Insurance Liability	0	0	0
Long Term Debt	188	188	110
Total Liabilities	15,851	15,901	15,002
Total Equity	715	699	651
Total Liab. & Equity	16,567	16,600	15,653

Losses continue to dog the corporation and provisions for possible losses on loans for the six month period were $31-million versus $28.3-million a year earlier. Net non-performing loans stood at $269.7-million or 1.97% of the total loans outstanding. For the corresponding period a year ago, net non-performing loans were $283.6-million or 2.05% of total loans outstanding.

CAPITAL (mil)			
Total Debt	188	188	110
Preferred Equity	0	0	0
Common Equity	715	699	651

Corporate assets were $16.2-billion at April 30, 1993, down from $16.9-billion a year ago and reflecting a lack of attractive lending opportunities. Nevertheless, National has shown itself to be capable of being aggressive in drumming up business when it led the pack by trimming its prime rate in May 1993 to put some life into loan demand. However the president of the company said that it would take five to seven or more years for the commercial real estate industry to recover.

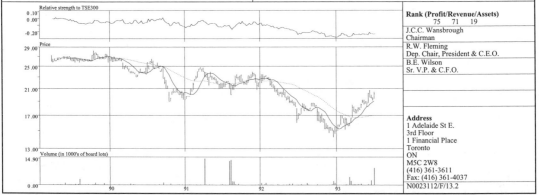

Rank (Profit/Revenue/Assets)
75   71   19

J.C.C. Wansbrough
Chairman

R.W. Fleming
Dep. Chair, President & C.E.O.

B.E. Wilson
Sr. V.P. & C.F.O.

Address
1 Adelaide St E.
3rd Floor
1 Financial Place
Toronto
ON
M5C 2W8
(416) 361-3611
Fax: (416) 361-4037
N0023112/F/13.2

ROYAL BANK OF CANADA

Exchanges	Price (Jun24'93)	27.00	Trailing P/E	nm	Stock Symbol
TMVZW	Trailing Yield (%)	4.30	Trailing EPS	(0.02)	**RY**

Period Ending	Oct92	Oct91	Oct90	Oct89	Oct88
Yearly Statistics					
Price-Close	24.13	27.00	20.75	24.25	18.00
Price-High	29.00	27.50	25.69	24.38	18.25
Price-Low	21.50	20.50	19.75	16.88	13.07
P/E-Close	nm	9.25	6.92	14.79	7.13
Dividends per Share	1.16	1.16	1.16	1.10	1.04
Dividend Yield (%)	4.81	4.30	5.59	4.54	5.78
Sales per Share	33.03	40.44	44.70	41.38	37.20
EPS before extra. item	(0.05)	2.92	3.00	1.64	2.53
Cash Flow per Share	4.01	6.64	3.32	7.02	2.84
Book Value per Share	18.82	19.91	18.10	16.16	15.58
O/S Common Shares (mil)	314	306	293	287	265
Total Revenue ($mil)	12,199	13,954	14,628	13,231	10,595
Income before extra. ($mil)	107	983	965	529	712
Cash Flow ($mil)	1,246	2,004	965	1,984	712
Debt/Equity	0.42	0.40	0.48	0.56	0.63
Return on Capital (%)	3.52	17.72	19.45	13.07	19.52
Ret. on Com. Equity (%)	(0.27)	15.43	17.49	10.60	16.91
% Change Profit	(89.1)	1.9	82.4	(25.7)	347.6
% Change Revenue	(12.6)	(4.6)	10.6	24.9	11.5
% Change Assets	4.5	5.1	9.8	4.2	7.7

Preferred Div. Coverage	0.9	9.5	10.1
Total Div. Coverage	0.2	2.2	2.2
Capital Ratio	18.4	17.1	19.5
Operat. Costs/$100 of Assets	2.8	2.7	2.6
5 YEAR RATIOS			
Return on Capital	14.7	14.4	13.5
Return on Com. Equity	12.0	10.0	9.3
Profit Growth	(7.9)	15.0	14.6
Revenue Growth	5.1	7.2	7.9
Asset Growth	6.2	5.8	5.5
BALANCE SHEET (mil)			
Cash	10,938	8,820	8,763
Total Loans	99,528	98,344	92,694
Net Fixed Assets	1,914	1,921	1,800
Total Assets	138,293	132,352	125,938
Total Deposits	112,222	105,022	99,168
Subordinated Debt	3,127	3,076	2,299
Total Liabilities	130,787	124,590	119,485
Total Equity	7,506	7,762	6,453
Total Liab. & Equity	138,293	132,352	125,938
CAPITAL (mil)			
Total External Debt	3,127	3,076	3,116
Preferred Equity	1,594	1,661	1,146
Common Equity	5,912	6,101	5,308

Business:

THE ROYAL BANK OF CANADA is chartered under the Bank Act of Canada. The Royal provides a full range of banking services for individuals, businesses and communities through its Canada-wide branch network. It also offers corporate, investment and treasury banking through its offices around the world. The bank has a 74% interest in RBC Dominion Securities Ltd., an investment dealer.

Date	EPS	DPS	Tot Rev	Inc Bex
Apr 93	0.64	0.29	2,802,000	243,000
Jan 93	0.71	0.29	3,054,000	254,000
Oct 92	(1.63)	0.29	2,922,000	(474,000)
Jul 92	0.26	0.29	3,001,885	112,375
Apr 92	0.59	0.29	3,024,356	212,321
Jan 92	0.73	0.29	3,250,000	256,000
Oct 91	0.76	0.29	3,320,000	260,000
Jul 91	0.77	0.29	3,398,558	261,321

Synopsis:

The market swing has been slower than expected for the Royal Bank of Canada. With only half of fiscal 1993 behind it, the bank has exhausted its entire $325-million cushion against additional loan losses set aside for the whole year. The bank continues to have difficulty in commercial real estate lending, particularly in the Toronto area. The Royal is expected to prop up earnings with the remaining cushion it still has at its disposal, about $300-million in excess reserves taken against past loans to less developed countries and about $80-million in bonds it expects to collect from Argentina.

The bank reported a profit of $243-million or 64 cents a share for the second quarter. This was up from $212-million or 59 cents a year earlier, but down from the $254-million or 71 cents in the 1993 first quarter. Profit for the first half was $497-million or $1.35 a share, up 6% from a year ago. Second quarter assets totaled $143.1-billion, up $6.1-billion or 4% from the last quarter. Holdings of securities increased by $6.6-billion or 43%.

The key drivers of year-over-year improvement were among the banks more variable sources of profit, its investment dealer subsidiary, RBC Dominion Securities Inc., and capital gains on the sale of securities, such as government bonds. Significant increases in securities and RBC gains largely offset relatively weak core banking results and high loan losses.

Encouraging signs came from non-performing loans, which fell in the second quarter for the first time since the recession began, slipping $15-million from the end of the first quarter to $3.49-billion. Non-performing commercial loans to U.S. borrowers fell 33% from the first quarter to $166-million, while in Canada those to consumers, agriculture and small business fell to $3.44-million from $364-million. Non-performing residential mortgage loans in Canada rose $4-million to $205-million, while those in domestic, commercial real estate rose $141-million to $1.12-billion.

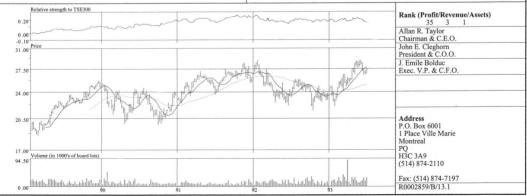

Rank (Profit/Revenue/Assets)		
35	3	1

Allan R. Taylor
Chairman & C.E.O.

John E. Cleghorn
President & C.O.O.

J. Emile Bolduc
Exec. V.P. & C.F.O.

Address
P.O. Box 6001
1 Place Ville Marie
Montreal
PQ
H3C 3A9
(514) 874-2110

Fax: (514) 874-7197
R0002859/B/13.1

TORONTO-DOMINION BANK (THE)

Exchanges	Price (Jun24'93)	18.37	Trailing P/E	20.19	Stock Symbol
TMVZ	Trailing Yield (%)	4.14	Trailing EPS	0.91	**TD**

Period Ending	Oct92	Oct91	Oct90	Oct89	Oct88
Yearly Statistics					
Price-Close	18.13	18.50	15.38	21.38	18.44
Price-High	19.75	19.75	21.63	23.13	19.13
Price-Low	15.75	14.88	14.50	17.25	11.57
P/E-Close	14.50	12.25	8.54	9.72	8.60
Dividends per Share	0.76	0.76	0.76	0.71	0.51
Dividend Yield (%)	4.19	4.11	4.94	3.32	2.77
Sales per Share	17.37	21.06	22.80	21.60	17.38
EPS before extra. item	1.25	1.51	1.80	2.20	2.15
Cash Flow per Share	3.64	3.77	3.45	3.08	5.08
Book Value per Share	15.14	14.55	13.82	12.76	11.33
O/S Common Shares	301,090	301,090	301,090	301,090	300,997
Total Revenue	6,138,000	7,214,000	7,756,198	7,285,390	5,862,035
Income before extra.	408,000	497,000	595,674	694,657	667,776
Cash Flow	1,096,000	1,135,000	1,038,867	927,382	1,519,485
Debt/Equity	0.34	0.21	0.21	0.16	0.11
Return on Capital (%)	11.94	14.52	17.84	23.34	28.69
Ret. on Com. Equity (%)	8.43	10.63	13.57	18.21	19.83
% Change Profit	(17.9)	(16.6)	(14.2)	4.0	357.9
% Change Revenue	(14.9)	(7.0)	6.5	24.3	14.0
% Change Assets	7.6	3.0	6.1	6.4	8.7
Preferred Div. Coverage	13.2	11.6	11.3		
Total Div. Coverage	1.6	1.8	2.1		
Capital Ratio	14.8	14.1	14.2		
Operat. Costs/$100 of Assets	2.5	2.5	2.4		
5 YEAR RATIOS					
Return on Capital	19.3	20.2	21.1		
Return on Com. Equity	14.1	13.2	13.9		
Profit Growth	22.8	4.3	7.5		
Revenue Growth	3.6	6.6	7.6		
Asset Growth	6.2	5.9	5.8		
BALANCE SHEET (mil)					
Cash	2,523	2,129	1,149		
Total Loans	54,236	52,168	52,108		
Net Fixed Assets	845	597	562		
Total Assets	74,133	68,905	66,900		
Total Deposits	59,691	54,673	52,083		
Subordinated Debt	1,560	825	853		
Total Liabilities	69,118	64,027	62,187		
Total Equity	5,015	4,878	4,714		
Total Liab. & Equity	74,133	68,905	66,900		
CAPITAL (mil)					
Total External Debt	1,723	999	966		
Preferred Equity	456	496	552		
Common Equity	4,559	4,382	4,162		

Business:

THE TORONTO-DOMINION BANK is a chartered bank, serving individuals, businesses, financial institutions and governments through its network of Canadian branches. The bank also offers a range of credit, non-credit and financial advisory services to businesses, governments and correspondent banks through offices worldwide. Subsidiaries offer discount brokerage services and a full range of trust services.

Date	EPS	DPS	Tot Rev	Inc Bex
Apr 93	0.27	0.19	1,609,000	90,000
Jan 93	(0.02)	0.19	1,560,000	1,000
Oct 92	0.35	0.19	1,509,000	113,000
Jul 92	0.31	0.19	1,539,000	101,000
Apr 92	0.24	0.19	1,472,000	79,000
Jan 92	0.35	0.19	1,609,000	115,000
Oct 91	0.37	0.19	1,680,000	120,000
Jul 91	0.37	0.19	1,735,400	120,055

Synopsis:

In spite of the Toronto-Dominion Bank's second quarter $11-million increase to net income year over year (at 27 cents a share up from 24 cents a year earlier), results continue to be reigned in by high levels of non-performing loans, loan loss provisions and losses on securities.

Earnings for the first half of 1993 totaled $170-million before the first quarter after tax restructuring costs of $79-million, related to merging Central Guaranty Trust Company with the bank. Consequently these earnings were down by $24-million from the $194-million earned in the first half of 1992. In January, the bank acquired the $7-billion of loans, $10-billion of deposits, 154 branches and the mutual fund, VISA and trust business from Central Guaranty.

Total assets for the second quarter were $82.6-billion, an increase of $1.6-billion from the prior quarter. This reflects an increase in cash and securities, while lending assets were unchanged. Return on assets was 45 cents for each $100, compared with 47 cents one year earlier.

Net non-performing loans of $1.5-billion, amounted to 2.38% of total loans and acceptances outstanding at April 30, 1993. Loan loss provisions were on target with the figure for the second quarter at $150-million, and unchanged from the first quarter, reflecting the continuation of the forecast of $600-million for the year. Net losses on investment securities in the second quarter were $18-million.

In April 1993, TD's U.S. Division acquired $5.5-billion (U.S.) in credit commitments to major U.S. corporations, originally committed to major U.S. banking operations of Australia-based Westpac Banking Corporation. The bank stepped out of traditional roles in 1993 with the GM Card, a no-fee VISA credit card with a unique rebate feature allowing customers a discount of up to $3,500 on the purchase or lease of a new GM car or truck.

Relative strength to TSE300 / Price / Volume (in 1000's of board lots)

Rank (Profit/Revenue/Assets)
7   20   5

Richard M. Thomson
Chairman & C.E.O.

Robert W. Korthals
President

Robert P. Kelly
Sr. V.P., Finance & Control

Address
P.O. Box 1
Toronto-Dominion Centre
55 King Street West
Toronto
ON
M5K 1A2
(416) 982-8222
Fax: (416) 982-5671
T0001809/B/13.1

Page	Company	$	Latest year end	Earnings per Share Actual	Estimate this year	Estimate next year
395	BGR Precious Metals		9301	0.35	n.a.	n.a.
396	Canada Trust Income Investments		9212	0.70	n.a.	n.a.
397	Canadian General Investments		9212	0.91	n.a.	n.a.
398	Central Capital		9212	117.39	n.a.	n.a.
399	Central Fund of Canada		9210	(0.04)	n.a.	n.a.
400	Consolidated Canadian Express		9212	(2.35)	n.a.	n.a.
401	Dundee Bancorp		9212	(0.06)	n.a.	n.a.
402	Fahnestock Viner Holdings		9212	1.19	n.a.	n.a.
403	First Marathon		9212	0.90	n.a.	n.a.
404	Greyvest Financial Services		9212	0.31	n.a.	n.a.
405	Harrowston		9212	(1.03)	n.a.	n.a.
406	Hees International Bancorp		9212	0.10	1.25	1.50
407	Investors Group		9212	1.14	1.28	1.48
408	Laurentian Group		9212	0.60	n.a.	n.a.
409	Mackenzie Financial		9303	0.31	0.50	0.63
410	Midland Walwyn		9212	0.88	n.a.	n.a.
411	Municipal Financial		9210	0.08	0.10	0.30
412	Pagurian		9212	0.33	0.40	0.50
413	Power Corporation		9212	1.28	1.17	1.23
414	Power Financial		9212	2.09	1.95	2.23
415	Traders Group		9212	3.48	n.a.	n.a.
416	Trilon Financial		9212	(3.90)	0.55	0.33
417	United Corporations		9303	1.03	n.a.	n.a.

Estimates from I/B/E/S Inc., 345 Hudson St., New York, NY 10014 (212) 243-3335. In Canada: 6 Lansing Square, Ste. 235, Willowdale, ON M2J 1T5 (416) 496-0977.

The Canadian mutual fund industry recorded net sales of $2.1-billion in May 1993. The Investment Funds Institute of Canada reported that, excluding money market funds, net sales of mutual funds for the same month rose 26.7% to $1.9-billion from $1.5-billion in April. Net sales of Canadian stock funds registered a $716-million gain in May, while money market funds rose $182-million down from $313-million in April. Total mutual fund assets under management as of May 31, 1993, were $82.9-billion, up 4.3% from $79.5-billion a month earlier and 38% from $60-billion a year earlier.

Despite the Canadian mutual fund industry's recent strong growth, the industry still lags well behind the U.S. with respect to the amount of assets under management. The U.S. mutual fund industry has over $1.6-trillion in assets while the Canadian industry manages $83-billion in assets. Representing approximately one-tenth of the U.S. market, Canadian mutual fund companies should have over $160-billion in fund assets. Compared to the U.S., it appears as if the Canadian mutual fund industry is under represented in the market by approximately 50%.

Financial Services Companies - Industry Report [Mar-31-1993] SHEARSON LEHMAN BROTHERS, INC. reported by Rosenberg, J.M., et al
Low rates help banks, asset management firms, and brokers. The insurance cycle is beginning to turn. Bank results should continue in the positive trend seen in 1992, due to a modest pick up in consumer loan growth in the stronger regions and more margin expansion overall than contraction. The asset management, securities brokerage and diversified consumer finance should benefit as the economy continues to rebound, while short-term rates remain low. [RN 1321707]

Financial Services - Industry Report [May-14-1993]. SHEARSON LEHMAN BROTHERS, INC. reported by Eberling, D.P., et al
U.S. households currently hold more than $4.0 trillion (U.S.) in mutual fund and time and saving deposit balances. Since the end of 1990, these balances have increased by more than 11% and have grown at an annual compound rate of 8.6% since 1980. During this period, the growth rates among the various components have changed, as the slope of the yield curve has shifted. Mutual fund assets grew at an annual rate of 23.6% over the 12-year period, while savings and time deposit balances grew at 4.6% annually. Mutual fund balances have grown to represent 40% of the $4.0 trillion (U.S.) total in mutual fund and saving and time deposit balances, up from less than 9.0% at the end of 1980. Mutual fund balances are expected to continue to increase as a percentage of the total, given the moves by banks into the mutual fund business. [RN 1332680]

Canadian Investment Management Companies - Industry Report [May-4-1993]. WOOD GUNDY INC. reported by O'Reilly, R., et al
The mutual funds industry grew by another 6.3% in March 1993 to $76.2 billion (7.7% excluding money market funds to $61.9 billion) for a year-over-year gain of 34.8% (44.3% excluding MMF's). The largest market share improvements in the month were shown by Altamira (+0.6% to 3.2%) and Trimark (+0.3% to 6.2%). Mackenzie's market share also increased (0.1% to 7.3%). [RN 1328995]

Wkly Economic & Financial Commentary - Topical Report [May-3-1993]. MERRILL LYNCH CAPITAL MARKETS reported by Straszheim, D., et al
Households are engaged in a massive asset reallocation process, shifting funds out of low-yielding banks deposits into equity and bond mutual funds. That vast source of liquidity for the financial markets shows no sign of abating. The asset reallocation process is likely to persist as long as short-term rates remain low and the yield curve is steep. [RN 1326705]

Real Estate Securities - Industry Report [Apr-19-1993]. PAINEWEBBER INC. reported by Raiman, L.
REIT (real estate investment trust) shares in the U.S. have been rising since 1991. Over the last two years, equity REITs have posted total returns in excess of 60%. In 1993, equity REITs are up about 15%. REITs are benefiting from high current yield, good cash flow, professional management, and conservative capitalization. Near-term momentum is being generated by two primary sources — yield and the opportunity to buy good real estate at bargain prices. Aided by a tax break, equity REITs now pay high and fairly predictable current yields of about 6-7%. In turn, REITs are investing in properties that, on average, provide cash-on-cash returns of about 10%. The market capitalization of the major equity REITs is now almost $10 billion (U.S.), twice that of two years ago. [RN 1325417]

BGR PRECIOUS METALS INC.

Exchanges	Price (Jun24'93)	11.62	Trailing P/E	33.21	Stock Symbol
TM	Trailing Yield (%)	0.00	Trailing EPS	0.35	**BPT.A**

Period Ending	Jan93	Jan92	Jan91	Jan90	Jan89
Yearly Statistics					
Price-Close	5.88	7.63	7.38	11.25	9.13
Price-High	8.00	8.63	11.75	12.00	12.13
Price-Low	5.25	7.00	7.00	9.00	8.63
P/E-Close	16.79	40.13	32.07	nm	nm
Dividends per Share	0.00	1.00	1.00	1.00	1.00
Dividend Yield (%)	0.00	13.12	13.55	8.89	10.96
Sales per Share	0.16	0.14	0.15	0.50	0.53
EPS before extra. item	0.35	0.19	0.23	(1.20)	(0.54)
Cash Flow per Share	(0.16)	(0.22)	(0.13)	0.56	0.43
Book Value per Share	8.21	8.25	8.42	12.35	11.85
O/S Common Shares	5,604,538	5,957,038	5,957,038	5,960,038	5,957,038
Total Revenue	3,886,000	3,286,000	3,030,000	(7,488,000	(2,624,000)
Income before extra.	2,045,000	1,130,000	1,382,000	(7,172,000	(3,218,000)
Cash Flow	(910,000	(1,306,000)	(771,000)	3,313,000	2,615,000
Debt/Equity	nd	nd	nd	nd	nd
Return on Capital (%)	6.25	2.88	3.13	(13.20)	(4.93)
Ret. on Com. Equity (%)	4.30	2.28	2.23	(9.95)	(4.14)
% Change Profit	81.0	(18.2)	119.3	(122.9)	(113.1)
% Change Revenue	18.3	8.4	140.5	(185.4)	(107.6)
% Change Assets	(5.0)	0.5	(35.9)	10.9	(23.8)
Preferred Div. Coverage	np	np	np		
Total Div. Coverage	na	0.2	0.2		

5 YEAR RATIOS (%)			
Return on Capital	(1.2)	5.4	7.3
Return on Com. Equity	(1.1)	4.0	5.4
Profit Growth	(39.4)	(29.0)	20.1
Revenue Growth	(35.5)	(20.3)	4.2
Asset Growth	(12.4)	(9.3)	(0.9)

BALANCE SHEET (000)			
Cash	2,148	2,708	215
Total Loans	0	0	0
Net Fixed Assets	0	0	0
Invest's & Advances	43,768	46,071	47,116
Total Assets	48,043	50,565	50,289
Total Deposits	0	0	0
Insurance Liability	0	0	0
Long Term Debt	0	0	0
Total Liabilities	2,040	1,421	127
Total Equity	46,003	49,144	50,162
Total Liab. & Equity	48,043	50,565	50,289

CAPITAL (000)			
Total Debt	0	0	0
Preferred Equity	0	0	0
Common Equity	46,003	49,144	50,162

Business:

BGR PRECIOUS METALS INC. is a closed-end investment company that invests primarily in precious metals and shares of precious metals companies. The company invests in North American and overseas equities and precious metals using a flexible asset-mix policy. The company may make use of options and futures contracts but will not make uncovered sales or deal in put options.

Date	EPS	DPS	Tot Rev	Inc Bex
Apr 93	0.15	0.00	1,736	837
Jan 93	(0.04)	0.00	(262)	(283)
Oct 92	0.12	0.00	1,237	700
Jul 92	0.12	0.00	1,362	739
Apr 92	0.15	0.00	1,549	889
Jan 92	(0.15)	0.25	(581)	(910)
Oct 91	(0.07)	0.25	(311)	(392)
Jul 91	(0.07)	0.25	(411)	(427)

Synopsis:

BGR Precious Metals remains positive about the outlook for gold and gold mining shares, in particular. BGR believes the gold market has little downside risk at current levels and substantial potential for gain. World consumption, primarily for jewelry fabrication, continues to exceed new mine production. These views were reflected in the company's portfolio in May 1993, when it held about 90% of the portfolio's assets in equities and the remainder in gold bullion.

On April 19, 1993, BGR began a further normal course issuer bid for up to 559,468 of its 5,594,688 Class A shares currently issued and outstanding. The bid will terminate by April 18, 1994. This will allow BGR to acquire its own shares when the market price falls significantly below the company's net asset value per share. BGR's net asset value per share was $8.21 at January 31, 1993, compared with $8.25 a year earlier. At June 17, the net asset value per share had climbed to $12.46.

Jewelry demand has outpaced gold mining production for four consecutive years. If net sales from central bankers are excluded, global demand for gold for all purposes exceeds supplies from all sources. The market's performance for the year ended January 1993 indicates that there is enough underlying demand to absorb some central bank sales without much difficulty. Should central bank sales drop, the price of gold bullion will almost certainly rise.

BGR feels the shares of gold producers will perform much better than bullion during 1993, and has structured its portfolio accordingly, on a global basis. While about 70% of the portfolio was invested in North American issues in May 1993, almost one-third of those North American companies had a significant exposure in Latin America. During 1993 BGR intends to increase the Australian component of the fund to 25% from its present 10%, with a corresponding reduction in North American holdings to 55%. BGR will maintain a South African component at about 10%. The bullion component will remain at about 10%.

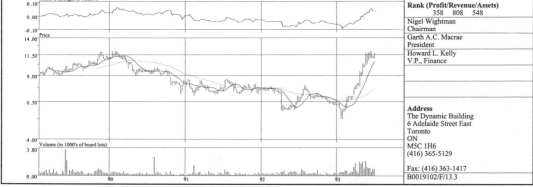

Rank (Profit/Revenue/Assets)
358   808   548

Nigel Wightman
Chairman

Garth A.C. Macrae
President

Howard L. Kelly
V.P., Finance

Address
The Dynamic Building
6 Adelaide Street East
Toronto
ON
M5C 1H6
(416) 365-5129

Fax: (416) 363-1417
B0019102/F/13.3

CANADA TRUST INCOME INVESTMENTS

Exchanges	Price (Jun24'93)	8.37	Trailing P/E	11.95	Stock Symbol
TM	Trailing Yield (%)	7.32	Trailing EPS	0.70	**CNN.UN**

Period Ending	Dec92	Dec91	Dec90	Dec89	Dec88
Yearly Statistics					
Price-Close	8.13	9.13	7.63	8.25	8.00
Price-High	9.38	9.50	8.63	9.13	9.25
Price-Low	8.13	8.13	7.00	7.50	7.75
P/E-Close	11.67	11.14	8.85	9.45	9.48
Dividends per Share	0.70	0.82	0.86	0.87	0.84
Dividend Yield (%)	8.57	8.98	11.31	10.58	10.55
Sales per Share	0.80	0.92	0.96	0.97	0.94
EPS before extra. item	0.70	0.82	0.86	0.87	0.84
Cash Flow per Share	0.70	0.82	0.86	0.87	0.84
Book Value per Share	9.08	9.40	8.53	8.82	8.77
O/S Common Shares	4,435,300	4,435,300	4,423,154	4,423,154	4,423,154
Total Revenue	3,533,115	4,085,341	4,225,904	4,290,519	4,161,126
Income before extra.	3,085,175	3,631,728	3,814,895	3,862,022	3,728,883
Cash Flow	3,085,175	3,631,728	3,814,895	3,862,022	3,728,883
Debt/Equity	nd	nd	nd	nd	nd
Return on Capital (%)	7.53	9.15	9.94	9.93	9.57
Ret. on Com. Equity (%)	7.53	9.15	9.94	9.93	9.57
% Change Profit	(15.0)	(4.8)	(1.2)	3.6	0.7
% Change Revenue	(13.5)	(3.3)	(1.5)	3.1	0.6
% Change Assets	(3.5)	10.2	(8.0)	5.5	(1.0)
Preferred Div. Coverage	np	np	np		
Total Div. Coverage	1.0	1.0	1.0		
5 YEAR RATIOS (%)					
Return on Capital	9.2	9.6	9.7		
Return on Com. Equity	9.2	9.6	9.7		
Profit Growth	(3.7)	(2.1)	(2.8)		
Revenue Growth	(3.2)	(1.7)	(2.4)		
Asset Growth	0.4	(4.2)	(1.4)		
BALANCE SHEET (000)					
Cash	4,459	391	597		
Total Loans	0	0	0		
Net Fixed Assets	0	0	0		
Invest's & Advances	35,563	40,993	36,918		
Total Assets	40,565	42,025	38,129		
Total Deposits	0	0	0		
Insurance Liability	0	0	0		
Long Term Debt	0	0	0		
Total Liabilities	297	341	383		
Total Equity	40,267	41,684	37,746		
Total Liab. & Equity	40,565	42,025	38,129		
CAPITAL (000)					
Total Debt	0	0	0		
Preferred Equity	0	0	0		
Common Equity	40,267	41,684	37,746		

Business:

CANADA TRUST INCOME INVESTMENTS is a closed-end investment trust. Its portfolio contains fixed-income securities. Income from the trust is paid to unit holders on a monthly basis.

Date	EPS	DPS	Tot Rev	Inc Bex
Mar 93	0.20	0.11	1,019	907
Dec 92	0.17	0.16	870	758
Sep 92	0.18	0.17	899	788
Jun 92	0.15	0.19	771	660
Mar 92	0.20	0.19	993	879
Dec 91	0.20	0.20	1,007	893
Sep 91	0.21	0.20	1,038	923
Jun 91	0.20	0.21	1,026	913

Synopsis:

For the first quarter of 1993, Canada Trust Income Investments produced a rate of return of 3.42%, compared to a gain of 8.27% for the Toronto Stock Exchange. The average term of the portfolio was extended from 6.8 years to eight years in the wake of declining interest rates. The term extension is meant to lock into the higher rates available for longer term maturities. However, the term was subsequently lowered back to 6.8 years after concern was raised regarding the exchange rate of the Canadian dollar.

In fiscal 1992, the recession and subsequent slow recovery negatively affected commercial real estate. The company's holdings of Olympia & York First Canadian Place bonds dropped from $102.80 per bond to $55 per bond during fiscal 1992.

Relative strength to TSE300

Price

Volume (in 1000's of board lots)

Rank (Profit/Revenue/Assets)
311   820   580

Peter C. Maurice
President & Trustee

Address
161 Bay Street
3rd Floor
Toronto
ON
M5J 2T2
(416) 361-8256

Fax: (416) 361-4646
C0001839/F/13.3

For further company information, call Globe Information Services 1-800-268-9128 or (416)585-5345

CANADIAN GENERAL INVESTMENTS LIMITED

Exchanges	Price (Jun24'93)	30.00	Trailing P/E	34.88	Stock Symbol
T	Trailing Yield (%)	3.42	Trailing EPS	0.86	**CGI**

Period Ending	Dec92	Dec91	Dec90	Dec89	Dec88
Yearly Statistics					
Price-Close	27.50	21.50	19.50	23.00	19.50
Price-High	32.00	23.75	23.50	24.50	21.00
Price-Low	21.50	18.00	17.57	19.63	19.00
P/E-Close	30.22	19.11	15.29	16.67	17.89
Dividends per Share	1.03	1.03	1.03	1.03	1.00
Dividend Yield (%)	3.73	4.77	5.26	4.46	5.13
Sales per Share	1.35	1.33	1.46	1.57	1.35
EPS before extra. item	0.91	1.13	1.28	1.38	1.09
Cash Flow per Share	0.91	1.12	1.27	1.38	1.09
Book Value per Share	33.34	34.25	31.12	34.48	31.42
O/S Common Shares	7,561	7,561	7,561	7,571	7,667
Total Revenue	10,231	10,080	11,012	11,887	10,380
Income before extra.	6,905	8,496	9,631	10,476	8,380
Cash Flow	6,905	8,496	9,631	10,476	8,380
Debt/Equity	nd	nd	0.01	nd	nd
Return on Capital (%)	2.39	3.45	3.78	4.15	3.80
Ret. on Com. Equity (%)	2.70	3.44	3.88	4.17	3.54
% Change Profit	(18.7)	(11.8)	(8.1)	25.0	13.8
% Change Revenue	1.5	(8.5)	(7.4)	14.5	7.1
% Change Assets	(2.2)	13.6	(12.6)	11.5	4.3
Preferred Div. Coverage	np	np	np		
Total Div. Coverage	0.9	1.1	1.2		

5 YEAR RATIOS (%)			
Return on Capital	3.5	3.7	3.7
Return on Com. Equity	3.5	3.6	3.6
Profit Growth	(1.3)	0.8	3.1
Revenue Growth	1.0	(0.4)	0.7
Asset Growth	2.4	0.2	(2.3)
BALANCE SHEET (000)			
Cash	2,071	1,097	12,647
Total Loans	0	0	369
Net Fixed Assets	0	0	0
Invest's & Advances	272,640	280,189	235,386
Total Assets	278,418	284,689	250,625
Total Deposits	0	0	0
Insurance Liability	0	0	0
Long Term Debt	0	0	1,200
Total Liabilities	26,336	25,724	15,357
Total Equity	252,082	258,965	235,268
Total Liab. & Equity	278,418	284,689	250,625
CAPITAL (000)			
Total Debt	0	0	1,200
Preferred Equity	0	0	0
Common Equity	252,082	258,965	235,268

Business:

CANADIAN GENERAL INVESTMENTS LTD. is a closed-end investment trust. Its portfolio of investments includes securities from Canada and the United States. Industries in the portfolio include beverages, finance, energy, communications, manufacturing, forest products, steel, metals and minerals, real estate, transportation, business forms, merchandising, insurance and venture capital.

Date	EPS	DPS	Tot Rev	Inc Bex
Mar 93	0.21	0.23	2,261	1,565
Dec 92	0.15	0.35	2,720	1,123
Sep 92	0.25	0.23	2,514	1,949
Jun 92	0.25	0.23	2,423	1,858
Mar 92	0.26	0.23	2,573	1,974
Dec 91	0.28	0.04	2,592	2,058
Sep 91	0.28	0.23	2,427	2,086
Jun 91	0.28	0.23	2,464	2,093

Synopsis:

In the first quarter 1993, Canadian General Investments Limited's portfolio increase by 5.5% on a time-weighted rate of return, compared to a 8.3% gain by the TSE 300 Total Return Index, and a 3.7% gain by the Standard & Poor's 500 Index. All major areas in the company's portfolio produced positive results, except the U.S. holdings which yielded a 3.9% decline. The key change in the portfolio during the period was the reduction in the holdings of The Seagram Company from 23% to 17.4% as at December 31, 1992.

In fiscal 1992, net assets per share dropped 2.7% and total return on a time-weighted basis was -0.3%, versus the TSE 300 Total Return Index of -1.4%. These performances reflect weak equity markets. U.S. holdings had an 11.7% total return, and other foreign stocks 15.6%. Non-Canadian securities formed 24.4% of the portfolio at year end.

During the year, revenues increased only 1.5% versus fiscal 1991. The majority of the income was generated by the company in the form of dividends received from Canadian corporations. A greater proportion of the funds were allocated to industry groups with relatively high yields (i.e. pipelines, utilities, and financial services). Expenses soared 73% in the year. Approximately 57% of this increase resulted from $1.5-million of legal and advisory fees and other costs incurred in the discharge of legal obligations. Prior to January 1, 1993, steps were taken to qualify CGI as an investment corporation under the Income Tax Act, resulting in improved tax treatment.

Relative strength to TSE300

Price

Volume (in 1000's of board lots)

Rank (Profit/Revenue/Assets)
218   695   284

Michael A. Meighen
Chairman
Michael A. Smedley
President

Address
Suite 1601
110 Yonge Street
Toronto
ON
M5C 1T4
(416) 366-2931

Fax: (416) 366-2729
C0003182/F/13.3

CENTRAL CAPITAL CORPORATION

Exchanges	Price (Jun24'93)	0.33	Trailing P/E	0.01	Stock Symbol
TM	Trailing Yield (%)	0.00	Trailing EPS	139.10	CEH

Period Ending	Dec92	Dec91	Dec90	Dec89	Dec88
Yearly Statistics					
Price-Close	1.89	28.38	433.67	725.41	709.64
Price-High	31.54	75.69	717.52	835.80	851.57
Price-Low	0.63	17.66	354.82	630.79	615.02
P/E-Close	0.02	nm	nm	9.58	.14.61
Dividends per Share	0.00	15.77	44.15	37.85	31.54
Dividend Yield (%)	0.00	55.56	10.18	5.22	4.44
Sales per Share	3.85	23.56	28.80	2,070.70	1,582.28
EPS before extra. item	117.39	(1,578.24)	(58.03)	75.69	48.57
Cash Flow per Share	(0.21)	(156.19)	(144.68)	419.18	270.99
Book Value per Share	0.78	(925.05)	661.95	756.98	692.34
O/S Common Shares	1,000	1,040	998	1,040	1,049
Total Revenue	208,951	(1,077,978)	146,066	2,221,057	1,758,071
Income before extra.	117,374	(1,561,482)	(43,786)	92,151	63,301
Cash Flow	(13,229)	(156,068)	(146,804)	437,852	292,383
Debt/Equity	1.02	na	1.19	2.08	2.21
Return on Capital (%)	56.51	(130.92)	(4.74)	2.08	3.09
Ret. on Com. Equity (%)	na	na	(8.16)	10.33	7.08
% Change Profit	107.5	(3,466.2)	(147.5)	45.6	25.9
% Change Revenue	119.4	(838.0)	(93.4)	26.3	69.2
% Change Assets	(89.7)	(75.2)	(89.0)	8.9	27.8

Preferred Div. Coverage	np	0.0	0.0
Total Div. Coverage	na	0.0	0.0

5 YEAR RATIOS (%)			
Return on Capital	(14.8)	(25.0)	3.4
Return on Com. Equity	na	na	5.5
Profit Growth	18.5	na	na
Revenue Growth	(27.5)	na	(15.9)
Asset Growth	(71.1)	(36.0)	(8.3)

BALANCE SHEET (000)			
Cash	5,554	7,021	46,702
Total Loans	23,964	44,912	114,879
Net Fixed Assets	4,890	6,063	8,196
Invest's & Advances	12,065	413,027	1,626,274
Total Assets	49,260	478,232	1,924,635
Total Deposits	0	0	0
Insurance Liability	0	0	0
Long Term Debt	21,000	1,107,777	1,012,273
Total Liabilities	28,760	1,213,458	1,072,267
Total Equity	20,500	(735,226)	852,368
Total Liab. & Equity	49,260	478,232	1,924,635

CAPITAL (000)			
Total Debt	21,000	1,107,777	1,012,273
Preferred Equity	0	189,510	191,592
Common Equity	20,500	(924,736)	660,776

Business:

CENTRAL CAPITAL CORP is a financial services industry holding company. On July 9, 1992, an Order in the Ontario Court of Justice was made under which some assets of the company are to be transferred to a new company owned by the company's creditors. The company is authorized to file with the Court a Plan of Arrangement under the Companies' Creditors Arrangment Act and the Canada Business Corporations Act.

Date	EPS	DPS	Tot Rev	Inc Bex
Mar 93	(0.31)	0.00	712	(2,186)
Dec 92	244.75	0.00	249,763	233,052
Sep 92	(39.74)	0.00	(29,265)	(35,873)
Jun 92	(65.60)	0.00	(19,130)	(61,635)
Mar 92	(22.08)	0.00	7,583	(18,170)
Dec 91	(1265.00)	0.00	(967,047)	(1260248)
Sep 91	(257.90)	0.00	(154,852)	(254,072)
Jun 91	(35.95)	0.01	8,242	(32,113)

Synopsis:

On June 12, 1992, the steering committee on behalf of certain unsecured lenders of Central Capital Corporation, applied to the Ontario Court of Justice under the Company's Creditors Arrangement Act (CCAA). On June 15, 1992, Central Capital consented to the issue of an order by the court staying all proceedings against Central and requiring it to comply with conditions restricting the sale of assets and restricting payments to creditors for obligations incurred prior to June 15, 1992.

On October 1, 1992, Central's major operating subsidiaries, MICC Investment Ltd. (excluding MICC Properties Inc.), the Canadian General Insurance Group of Companies, United Financial Management Ltd., the United Kingdom operations, and the operations of holding company Traders Group Ltd., were transferred to The Canadian Insurance Group Limited (CIGL), a company owned by some of the Central's creditors. The consideration for these assets was the reduction by $603-million in the claims against Central by its creditors and certain future participation by Central in CIGL.

On November 24, 1992, Central Capital's creditors approved a plan of arrangement which converted the remaining unsecured debt of Central into a new series of secured debt and new common shares. The result is that Central now carries $21-million of debt in the form of first and second secured notes and, upon full implementation of the plan, will have about 20 million new common shares outstanding. Approximately 18 million of the new common shares will be issued to Central's creditors and two million will be issued to the holders of all common, class A subordinated voting and preferred shares.

As part of the restructuring, Central Capital's 85% ownership interest in Central Guaranty Trustco Limited was reduced to 44.8%. Substantially all of the assets of Central Guaranty Trustco's principal subsidiary, Central Guaranty Trust Company, were sold to The Toronto-Dominion Bank on December 31, 1992. Central Guaranty Trustco is currently subject to a CCAA filing.

Rank (Profit/Revenue/Assets)		
30	265	542

Robert G. Graham
Chairman & C.E.O.

Leonard Ellen
President

David A. Rattee
Exec. V.P. & C.F.O.

Address
20 Queen Street West
35th Floor
Toronto
ON
M5H 3C8
(416) 408-4750

C0000635/F/13.6

CENTRAL FUND OF CANADA LIMITED

Exchanges	Price (Jun24'93)	6.37	Trailing P/E	nm	Stock Symbol
TA	Trailing Yield (%)	0.16	Trailing EPS	(0.04)	**CEF.A**

Period Ending	Oct92	Oct91	Oct90	Oct89	Oct88
Yearly Statistics					
Price-Close	4.80	4.40	5.13	5.63	6.13
Price-High	5.25	5.50	7.25	6.38	8.88
Price-Low	4.25	4.30	4.80	5.25	6.00
P/E-Close	nm	nm	nm	nm	nm
Dividends per Share	0.01	0.01	0.01	0.01	0.10
Dividend Yield (%)	0.21	0.23	0.20	0.18	1.63
Sales per Share	0.01	0.01	0.02	0.02	0.03
EPS before extra. item	(0.04)	(0.05)	(0.06)	(0.06)	(0.07)
Cash Flow per Share	(0.05)	(0.05)	(0.05)	(0.05)	(0.04)
Book Value per Share	5.05	4.94	5.45	5.99	7.11
O/S Common Shares	16,864	16,864	16,864	16,824	16,888
Total Revenue	154	188	162	361	333
Income before extra.	(759)	(823)	(939)	(994)	(1,233)
Cash Flow	(826)	(773)	(803)	(904)	(681)
Debt/Equity	nd	nd	nd	nd	nd
Return on Capital (%)	(0.73)	(0.78)	(0.83)	(0.86)	(0.86)
Ret. on Com. Equity (%)	(0.90)	(0.94)	(0.98)	(0.90)	(0.92)
% Change Profit	7.8	12.4	5.5	19.4	(1,225.0)
% Change Revenue	(18.0)	16.1	(55.2)	8.5	(51.4)
% Change Assets	2.3	(9.3)	(8.9)	(17.0)	(19.2)

Preferred Div. Coverage	np	np	np
Total Div. Coverage	0.0	0.0	0.0

5 YEAR RATIOS (%)			
Return on Capital	(0.8)	(0.7)	(0.6)
Return on Com. Equity	(0.9)	(0.8)	(0.7)
Profit Growth	na	na	na
Revenue Growth	(25.9)	(14.9)	(27.4)
Asset Growth	(10.8)	0.7	4.2

BALANCE SHEET (000)			
Cash	805	1,726	2,650
Total Loans	0	0	0
Net Fixed Assets	0	0	0
Invest's & Advances	84,685	81,841	89,233
Total Assets	85,490	83,568	92,153
Total Deposits	0	0	0
Insurance Liability	0	0	0
Long Term Debt	0	0	0
Total Liabilities	310	327	334
Total Equity	85,181	83,240	91,820
Total Liab. & Equity	85,490	83,568	92,153

CAPITAL (000)			
Total Debt	0	0	0
Preferred Equity	0	0	0
Common Equity	85,181	83,240	91,820

Business:

CENTRAL FUND OF CANADA LTD. is a closed-end investment holding company. The company provides a vehicle for investors interested in holding marketable gold and silver related investments. The company invests primarily in long-term holdings of gold and silver bullion. It holds a minimum of 90% of its non-cash assets in gold and silver bullion, primarily in bar form.

Date	EPS	DPS	Tot Rev	Inc Bex
Jan 93	(0.01)	0.00	23	(225)
Oct 92	(0.01)	0.01	32	(173)
Jul 92	(0.01)	0.00	23	(186)
Apr 92	(0.01)	0.00	40	(227)
Jan 92	(0.01)	0.00	65	(172)
Oct 91	(0.01)	0.01	38	(179)
Jul 91	(0.01)	0.00	38	(184)
Apr 91	(0.01)	0.00	48	(252)

Synopsis:

For the first quarter of 1993, the Central Fund of Canada Limited's total revenue dropped by 50% compared to the same quarter in 1992, primarily as a result of reduced cash reserves and lower interest rates during the quarter. Net asset value changed slightly. The small declines in the prices of gold and silver were offset by the strengthening of the U.S. dollar versus the Canadian dollar. At quarter-end, 64.4% of Central's portfolio was invested in gold bullion, 34.5% in silver bullion, and 1.1% in cash and other.

In fiscal 1992, the 7.8% reduction in losses was primarily attributed to a 19.8% decline in operating expenses. The majority of this 19.8% decline was due to the 10.4% increase in the value of the U.S. dollar against the Canadian dollar during the year, resulting in a foreign currency exchange loss. The change in net assets over time is affected by the changing market prices of gold and silver. Furthermore, since gold and silver are quoted in U.S. dollars, changes in the U.S. dollar against the Canadian dollar will impact net assets which are reported in Canadian dollars. During the year, net assets grew despite declines in the U.S. dollar prices of gold and silver, due to the U.S. dollar increasing by 10.4% relative to the Canadian dollar during the year.

Central's liquidity objective is to hold cash reserves primarily for the generation of cash flow to pay operating expenses. The articles of the company state that at least 75% of its non-cash assets be in gold and silver related investments, and this ratio cannot be altered without shareholder approval. The current stated investment policy requires Central to maintain a minimum of 90% of its net assets in gold and silver bullion, and at least 85% in the form of physical bullion holdings.

Relative strength to TSE300 / Price / Volume (in 1000's of board lots)

Rank (Profit/Revenue/Assets)
680   933   441

Philip M. Spicer
President

Michael A. Parente
V.P., Finance

Address
P.O. Box 7319
Ancaster
ON
L9G 3N6
(416) 648-7878

Fax: (416) 648-5422
C0006172/F/13.3

CONSOLIDATED CANADIAN EXPRESS LIMITED

Exchanges	Price (Jun24'93)	0.95	Trailing P/E	nm	Stock Symbol
T	Trailing Yield (%)	0.00	Trailing EPS	(2.15)	**CXE**

Period Ending	Dec92	Dec91	Dec90	Dec89	Dec88
Yearly Statistics					
Price-Close	0.69	1.80	2.10	14.00	17.60
Price-High	2.40	3.75	14.40	22.40	23.40
Price-Low	0.40	1.20	1.60	13.60	15.80
P/E-Close	nm	nm	nm	nm	nm
Dividends per Share	0.00	0.00	0.00	0.40	0.40
Dividend Yield (%)	0.00	0.00	0.00	2.86	2.27
Sales per Share	2.85	3.06	4.16	2.78	1.30
EPS before extra. item	(2.35)	(9.82)	(2.07)	(9.20)	(28.00)
Cash Flow per Share	2.17	1.61	2.55	0.09	0.42
Book Value per Share	2.60	4.95	14.77	16.84	20.58
O/S Common Shares	8,829	8,829	8,829	8,829	7,167
Total Revenue	7,819	(26,434)	13,490	38,170	20,188
Income before extra.	1,854	(62,452)	7,950	(35,810)	(147,032)
Cash Flow	19,177	14,227	22,544	532	2,442
Debt/Equity	0.18	0.17	nd	nd	0.62
Return on Capital (%)	2.12	(16.61)	2.59	(3.23)	(34.59)
Ret. on Com. Equity (%)	(62.20)	(99.60)	(13.09)	(38.12)	(74.51)
% Change Profit	103.0	(885.6)	122.2	75.6	(901.5)
% Change Revenue	129.6	(296.0)	(64.7)	89.1	(21.9)
% Change Assets	(5.3)	(16.4)	(8.3)	(3.7)	2.0

	Date	EPS	DPS	Tot Rev	Inc Bex
	Mar 93	(0.40)	0.00	3,283	2,108
	Dec 92	(1.04)	0.00	(1,391)	(3,542)
	Sep 92	(0.38)	0.00	3,358	2,273
	Jun 92	(0.33)	0.00	3,992	2,777
	Mar 92	(0.60)	0.00	1,860	346
	Dec 91	(8.38)	0.00	(34,753)	(68,246)
	Sep 91	(0.80)	0.00	(615)	(1,261)
	Jun 91	(0.12)	0.00	6,353	5,267

Preferred Div. Coverage	0.1	0.0	0.3
Total Div. Coverage	0.1	0.0	0.3

5 YEAR RATIOS (%)			
Return on Capital	(9.9)	(9.3)	(5.6)
Return on Com. Equity	(57.5)	(44.5)	(24.4)
Profit Growth	(36.8)	na	na
Revenue Growth	(21.3)	na	na
Asset Growth	(6.6)	(3.7)	10.6

BALANCE SHEET (000)			
Cash	130,808	90,934	97,817
Total Loans	17,731	59,231	38,073
Net Fixed Assets	0	0	0
Invest's & Advances	189,405	206,728	291,155
Total Assets	337,944	356,893	427,045
Total Deposits	0	0	0
Insurance Liability	0	0	0
Long Term Debt	0	0	0
Total Liabilities	71,479	69,694	53,137
Total Equity	266,465	287,199	373,908
Total Liab. & Equity	337,944	356,893	427,045

CAPITAL (000)			
Total Debt	48,986	48,853	0
Preferred Equity	243,500	243,500	243,500
Common Equity	22,965	43,699	130,408

Business:

CONSOLIDATED CANADIAN EXPRESS has investment interests in the manufacturing and financial resources industries.

Synopsis:

The increase in Consolidated Canadian Express Limited's net income, from $300,000 in the first quarter of 1992 compared to $2.1-million in the first quarter of 1993, was attributed to reduced losses from the company's investment in Consolidated Enfield Corporation.

The improved results for the first quarter of 1993 for Consolidated Enfield were attributed to the performance of Consumers Packaging's glass operations. Consumers Packaging decided to focus resources on its core glass container business and to sell its plastics businesses to reduce debt. The company sold the plastic businesses, in two separate transactions, in the first quarter of 1993 for net proceeds of $63-million, and a potential $4-million dependent on the 1993 earnings of the Portion Packaging operations. The proceeds will be used to reduce long-term debt. At the end of the first quarter Consumers had $27.7-million worth of long-term debt that was past due. Consumers continues to look for an equity partner to provide assistance in the consolidation of its position in the North American market.

Planned capital expenditures for 1993 for Consumers Packaging amount to $32.8-million, but only $3.2-million was committed to at the end of 1992. Further capital expenditure commitments will be made as the funding becomes available.

Consolidated Canadian Express Limited's affiliate Complax Corporation closed its $22-million auto parts plant in December 1992. The plant, located in Windsor, Ontario, made polyester glass automotive parts. The Tarxien Corporation purchased Complax Components Corporation from Complax in February 1993. Complax Components is located in Cobourg, Ontario, and manufactures auto parts. Its main assets are machinery and equipment, and contracts for the supply of auto parts. The purchase price was not disclosed. In June 1992, the auto parts plant in Cobourg was listed with a real estate agent at $2.7-million. Complax contributed $43,000 to the revenues recorded by Consolidated Canadian Express in the first quarter of 1993.

Relative strength to TSE300 / Price / Volume (in 1000's of board lots)

Rank (Profit/Revenue/Assets)		
960	999	249

Manfred J. Walt
Chairman

Brian D. Lawson
President & Secretary

Address
Suite 4501
BCE Place
181 Bay Street
Toronto
ON
M5J 2T3
(416) 359-8620
Fax: (416) 865-1288
C0000761/F/13.3

DUNDEE BANCORP INC.

Exchanges	Price (Jun24'93)	6.00	Trailing P/E	na	Stock Symbol
T	Trailing Yield (%)	na	Trailing EPS	na	DBC.A

Period Ending	Dec92	Dec91		**Business:**
Yearly Statistics		3M		DUNDEE BANCORP INC. is involved in the
Price-Close	3.15	3.05		non-precious metals business previously
Price-High	3.55	6.50		conducted and managed by International
Price-Low	2.25	2.90		Corona including the industrial minerals assets,
P/E-Close	nm	nm		oil and gas assets, base metal assets, and
Dividends per Share	0.00	0.00		financial services.
Dividend Yield (%)	0.00	0.00		
Sales per Share	2.45	1.10		
EPS before extra. item	(0.06)	(6.76)		
Cash Flow per Share	(0.39)	0.12		
Book Value per Share	7.70	7.80		
O/S Common Shares	25,412	25,057		
Total Revenue	62,833	7,790		
Income before extra.	626	(168,949)		
Cash Flow	(9,815)	774		

Date	EPS	DPS	Tot Rev	Inc Bex
Mar 93	0.19	0.00	14,849	5,071

	Dec92	Dec91
Debt/Equity	0.22	0.60
Return on Capital (%)	4.79	na
Ret. on Com. Equity (%)	(0.78)	na
% Change Profit	100.1	na
% Change Revenue	101.6	na
% Change Assets	(27.7)	na

Preferred Div. Coverage	0.3	0.0
Total Div. Coverage	0.3	0.0

5 YEAR RATIOS (%)		
Return on Capital	na	na
Return on Com. Equity	na	na
Profit Growth	na	na
Revenue Growth	na	na
Asset Growth	na	na

BALANCE SHEET (000)		
Cash	27,451	6,687
Total Loans	15,035	46,819
Net Fixed Assets	44,977	61,042
Invest's & Advances	224,285	325,093
Total Assets	325,462	450,342
Total Deposits	0	0
Insurance Liability	0	0
Long Term Debt	49,008	130,510
Total Liabilities	106,597	231,557
Total Equity	218,865	218,785
Total Liab. & Equity	325,462	450,342

CAPITAL (000)		
Total Debt	49,008	130,510
Preferred Equity	23,279	23,279
Common Equity	195,586	195,506

Synopsis:

In April 1993, a buyout offer by Dundee Bancorp was accepted by more than 98% of the shareholders of Dundee Capital Inc. of Toronto. Dundee Capital said it will cancel all shares tendered, giving Dundee Bancorp 99.8% of its outstanding shares. Dundee Bancorp intends to acquire 100% of Dundee Capital pursuant to mandatory acquisition.

Also in April 1993, the company sold 12.1% of its share in Baja Gold and 16.9% of its share in Yorbeau Resources to 1021105 Ontario. Dundee received shares in 1021105 Ontario, which is a 50% partnership with Placer Dome Inc.

In March 1993, CMP Resources Ltd., Plexus Resources Corp. and 1021105 Ontario planned to amalgamate by way of a share exchange. The companies said the merger will result in the formation of a new public natural resources company with an initial market capitalization of about $150-million. Principal assets will be stakes in the Denton-Rawhide gold mine in Nevada, the QR Gold Project in British Columbia, and CS Resources Ltd.

In January 1993, Dundee, in connection with an issuer bid by its DCC Equities Ltd. subsidiary to its minority shareholders, said it intends to reduce its direct and indirect investments in Black Hawk Mining Inc., Breakwater Resources Ltd., CS Resources Ltd. and Devran Petroleum Ltd. As a result, Dundee said it will hold 8.4% of Black Hawk, 21.7% of Breakwater, 5.6% of CS Resources and none of Devran. The closing of the transaction is dependent on the completion of a takeover bid by Dundee for the shares of Dundee Capital, and will occur at the same time as the closing of that transaction.

In January 1993, the company's subsidiary DCC Equities was planning to acquire 37.6% of its own shares held by institutional investors. DCC Equities said it will transfer the shares of several companies in its investment portfolio to those institutional investors as payment for their shares of DCC.

Relative strength to TSE300

Rank (Profit/Revenue/Assets)		
467	443	264

Ned Goodman
Chairman & C.E.O.

Garth A.C. MacRae
President & C.O.O.

Address
9th Floor
6 Adelaide Street East
Toronto
ON
M5C 1H6
(416) 863-6990

01003229/F/13.6

FAHNESTOCK VINER HOLDINGS INC.

Exchanges	Price (Jun24'93)	9.00	Trailing P/E	7.44	Stock Symbol
T	Trailing Yield (%)	1.11	Trailing EPS	1.21	FHV.A

Period Ending	Dec92	Dec91	Dec90	Dec89	Dec88
Yearly Statistics	US	US	US	US	US
Price-Close	9.00	8.13	1.63	1.90	1.66
Price-High	12.13	8.75	2.45	2.75	3.05
Price-Low	6.75	1.42	1.40	1.60	1.60
P/E-Close	5.12	7.47	7.98	6.18	21.83
Dividends per Share	0.00	0.00	0.00	0.00	0.00
Dividend Yield (%)	0.00	0.00	0.00	0.00	0.00
Sales per Share	12.00	10.29	7.47	7.39	7.07
EPS before extra. item	1.19	0.83	0.15	0.22	0.05
Cash Flow per Share	1.24	0.90	0.26	0.37	0.20
Book Value per Share	5.06	3.88	3.05	2.90	2.48
O/S Common Shares	11,828	11,441	11,251	11,251	11,251
Total Revenue	139,156	116,176	84,036	83,145	79,582
Income before extra.	13,823	9,401	1,668	2,470	575
Cash Flow	14,344	10,132	2,879	4,185	2,236
Debt/Equity	2.37	0.50	0.20	5.18	7.60
Return on Capital (%)	21.73	39.55	10.83	8.39	6.72
Ret. on Com. Equity (%)	26.54	23.92	4.99	8.17	2.11
% Change Profit	47.0	463.6	(32.5)	329.6	120.6
% Change Revenue	19.8	38.2	1.1	4.5	120.0
% Change Assets	34.7	13.1	(2.5)	(15.9)	88.1

Preferred Div. Coverage	np	np	np
Total Div. Coverage	na	na	na

Business:

FAHNESTOCK VINER HOLDINGS INC. is engaged in the stock brokerage business. Substantially all of the company's revenues and identifiable assets are derived from or applicable to operations in the United States.

Date		EPS	DPS	Tot Rev	Inc Bex
Mar 93	US	0.48	0.10	40,870	5,760
Dec 92	US	0.23	0.00	34,217	2,637
Sep 92	US	0.17	0.00	29,801	2,052
Jun 92	US	0.33	0.00	33,968	3,840
Mar 92	US	0.46	0.00	41,170	5,294
Dec 91	US	0.27	0.00	33,370	3,063
Sep 91	US	0.18	0.00	29,405	2,090
Jun 91	US	0.21	0.00	29,379	2,393

5 YEAR RATIOS (%)			
Return on Capital	17.4	12.5	6.2
Return on Com. Equity	13.1	5.8	2.6
Profit Growth	121.3	40.0	na
Revenue Growth	30.8	38.5	41.0
Asset Growth	18.6	6.9	16.6

BALANCE SHEET (000)			
Cash	5,628	6,341	4,987
Total Loans	0	0	0
Net Fixed Assets	877	342	1,890
Invest's & Advances	31,345	21,401	14,827
Total Assets	318,799	236,745	209,355
Total Deposits	0	0	0
Insurance Liability	0	0	0
Long Term Debt	118,038	2,226	30
Total Liabilities	258,982	192,410	175,080
Total Equity	59,817	44,335	34,275
Total Liab. & Equity	318,799	236,745	209,355

CAPITAL (000)			
Total Debt	141,660	22,061	6,703
Preferred Equity	0	0	0
Common Equity	59,817	44,335	34,275

Synopsis:

Fahnestock Viner Holdings Inc.'s profit levels of $5.8-million (U.S.) for the first-quarter of 1993 rose from the same period last year due in part to the consolidation of several branch offices, growth in assets under management and growth in its investment banking business.

In 1992 its revenues grew 20% over the previous year reflecting gains in commission revenue, profits from principal transactions and increases in underwriting activities

Its retail sales force grew to 389 investment consultants and their average production was $180,000 (U.S.), a 17% increase from 1991. Offerings from corporate and public finance raised over $1.460-billion (U.S.). At year's end investors had deposited assets of more than $5-billion (U.S.) at Fahnestock. The acquisition of Hopper Soliday Corporation in April 1991 added 10 branches to the company's operations base.

Commission income, the largest single component of revenue, increased by 10% in 1992 to $57-million (U.S.) primarily due to a general increase in market related volume. Investment income increased 31% to $47.7-million (U.S.) as the result of growth in retail and institutional transactions in over-the-counter equity securities and retail purchases of mutual funds. Interest income increased 8% to $13.6-million (U.S.) in 1992 and underwriting fees increased 49% to $7-million (U.S.).

Fahnestock is licensed to offer brokerage and other financial services in all 50 of the United States of America.

Relative strength to TSE300

Rank (Profit/Revenue/Assets)
136   296   236

A.G. Lowenthal
Chairman & C.E.O.

E.K. Roberts
President & Treasurer

Address
P.O. Box 16
Suite 1204
181 University Avenue
Toronto
ON
M5H 3M7
(416) 364-3397

G0001708/F/13.7

FIRST MARATHON INC.

Exchanges	Price (Jun24'93)		14.37	Trailing P/E		13.82	Stock Symbol
TV	Trailing Yield (%)		3.06	Trailing EPS		1.04	**FMS.A**

Period Ending	Dec92	Dec91	Dec90	Dec89	Dec88
Yearly Statistics					
Price-Close	10.75	11.00	6.25	8.75	7.00
Price-High	12.88	11.00	9.00	10.50	8.75
Price-Low	9.13	6.00	6.13	7.38	6.50
P/E-Close	11.94	13.75	10.78	10.94	7.87
Dividends per Share	0.45	0.40	0.40	0.40	0.51
Dividend Yield (%)	4.19	3.64	6.40	4.57	7.29
Sales per Share	4.43	3.55	2.76	3.36	3.85
EPS before extra. item	0.90	0.80	0.58	0.80	0.89
Cash Flow per Share	0.38	(0.79)	0.80	0.87	1.27
Book Value per Share	7.90	7.42	6.78	6.58	6.18
O/S Common Shares	23,745	23,466	21,462	20,975	20,616
Total Revenue	106,100	78,866	59,874	69,946	74,936
Income before extra.	21,178	17,385	12,328	16,678	17,328
Cash Flow	9,010	(17,163)	17,016	18,085	24,637
Debt/Equity	1.68	1.49	1.44	1.07	0.96
Return on Capital (%)	6.22	5.67	5.40	8.94	13.65
Ret. on Com. Equity (%)	11.71	10.88	8.70	12.57	14.10
% Change Profit	21.8	41.0	(26.1)	(3.8)	(25.5)
% Change Revenue	34.5	31.7	(14.4)	(6.7)	(21.2)
% Change Assets	55.4	16.7	39.7	41.1	(23.9)

Preferred Div. Coverage	np	np	np
Total Div. Coverage	2.0	2.1	1.4

5 YEAR RATIOS (%)			
Return on Capital	8.0	9.8	10.6
Return on Com. Equity	11.6	14.8	18.3
Profit Growth	(1.8)	13.3	32.4
Revenue Growth	2.2	10.9	20.1
Asset Growth	22.1	21.7	45.0

BALANCE SHEET (000)			
Cash	1,421	1,371	22,524
Total Loans	0	0	0
Net Fixed Assets	4,158	4,424	3,943
Invest's & Advances	580,478	568,682	505,713
Total Assets	1,211,870	779,699	668,263
Total Deposits	0	0	0
Insurance Liability	0	0	0
Long Term Debt	314,058	200,352	207,611
Total Liabilities	1,024,277	605,489	522,785
Total Equity	187,593	174,209	145,478
Total Liab. & Equity	1,211,870	779,699	668,263

CAPITAL (000)			
Total Debt	314,285	259,783	209,585
Preferred Equity	0	0	0
Common Equity	187,593	174,209	145,478

Business:

FIRST MARATHON INC. is a financial services company. Its principal subsidiary is First Marathon Securities Limited, a securities dealer and member of the Toronto, Montreal, Vancouver and Alberta stock exchanges. Marathon Brokerage, a discount brokerage firm, is wholly owned by First Marathon Securities Limited.

Date	EPS	DPS	Tot Rev	Inc Bex
Mar 93	0.37	0.07	44,315	8,837
Dec 92	0.26	0.07	30,619	6,123
Sep 92	0.21	0.07	26,141	5,028
Jun 92	0.20	0.23	23,469	4,512
Mar 92	0.23	0.06	25,870	5,516
Dec 91	0.23	0.06	24,948	5,044
Sep 91	0.18	0.06	18,820	4,006
Jun 91	0.19	0.05	17,515	4,051

Synopsis:

First Marathon Inc.'s first quarter results show business strong in all subsidiaries. Revenue was up to $44.3-million and net profit totaled $8.8-million in this period. The strong early showing was a continuation of the company's healthy financial situation during 1992.

First Marathon's increased 1992 revenues are due in part to its 100% ownership of Marathon Brokerage, a discount broker. This transaction took place in October 1991. 1992 earnings rose as a result of increased trading volumes and increased investment banking activity. Equity capital in the company stood at $188-million as of December, 31, 1992. Year-end assets also grew by 55% to $1.2-billion, reflecting business growth and a wider range of activities. First Marathon's institutional commission revenues grew by approximately 14%.

Each subsidiary showed a profit during the year. Marathon Funding, which deals with placement services, participated in five transactions in 1992. The Correspondent Network, a brokerage and administrative service which began in 1991 exceeded $2.7-billion of total value traded by correspondents in 1992. Marathon Brokerage, showed a 19% increase in commission revenues.

Commission revenues climbed $15.9-million in 1992 to $51.4-million, with the increased ownership in Marathon Brokerage accounting for $4.8-million, and an additional $2.7-million coming from the Correspondent Network. 1992 revenues by sector were: commissions, $51.4-million; corporate finance, $24.3-million; and investment income, $30.4-million.

During 1992, First Marathon financed a variety of companies including Laidlaw Transportation, Magna International, Rogers Cantel and Westcoast Energy.

Rank (Profit/Revenue/Assets)
115   369   133

Thomas A. Kierans
Chairman

Lawrence S. Bloomberg
President & C.E.O.

Stuart W. Henry
V.P., Finance & Secretary

Address
The Exchange Tower
2 First Canadian Place
Suite 3100, P.O. Box 21
Toronto
ON
M5X 1J9
(416) 869-3707
Fax: (416) 869-3319
F0007263/F/13.7

GREYVEST FINANCIAL SERVICES INC.

Exchanges	Price (Jun24'93)	3 .10	Trailing P/E	12 .40	Stock Symbol
T	Trailing Yield (%)	4 .52	Trailing EPS	0 .25	GFI

Period Ending	Dec92	Dec91	Dec90	Dec89	Dec88
Yearly Statistics					
Price-Close	3 .30	2 .90	3 .00	4 .90	4 .10
Price-High	3 .50	3 .50	4 .75	5 .38	5 .25
Price-Low	2 .65	2 .70	3 .00	4 .15	3 .40
P/E-Close	10 .65	12 .61	10 .00	11 .95	11 .39
Dividends per Share	0 .14	0 .14	0 .17	0 .15	0 .14
Dividend Yield (%)	4 .24	4 .83	5 .67	3 .06	3 .42
Sales per Share	2 .92	2 .89	2 .88	2 .98	2 .06
EPS before extra. item	0 .31	0 .23	0 .30	0 .41	0 .36
Cash Flow per Share	0 .90	0 .73	0 .69	0 .78	0 .76
Book Value per Share	3 .13	2 .96	2 .85	2 .72	2 .47
O/S Common Shares	14 ,672	14 ,854	14 ,553	14 ,600	14 ,558
Total Revenue	43 ,127	42 ,206	42 ,020	43 ,475	29 ,963
Income before extra.	4 ,531	3 ,364	4 ,433	5 ,912	5 ,210
Cash Flow	13 ,363	10 ,684	10 ,026	11 ,416	11 ,062
Debt/Equity	3 .28	3 .99	4 .34	5 .43	5 .73
Return on Capital (%)	9 .84	10 .21	11 .65	12 .96	13 .77
Ret. on Com. Equity (%)	10 .07	7 .87	10 .92	15 .63	15 .04
% Change Profit	34 .7	(24 .1)	(25 .0)	13 .5	36 .9
% Change Revenue	2 .2	0 .4	(3 .3)	45 .1	50 .3
% Change Assets	(9 .6)	(0 .0)	(12 .2)	5 .0	165 .1

Date	EPS	DPS	Tot Rev	Inc Bex
Mar 93	0.06	0.00	9 ,466	924
Dec 92	0.05	0.07	11 ,067	757
Sep 92	0.06	0.00	9 ,984	934
Jun 92	0.08	0.07	10 ,885	1 ,228
Mar 92	0.11	0.00	11 ,013	1 ,613
Dec 91	0.10	0.07	10 ,967	1 ,504
Sep 91	0.05	0.00	10 ,139	671
Jun 91	0.05	0.07	10 ,566	686

	Dec92	Dec91	Dec90
Preferred Div. Coverage	np	np	np
Total Div. Coverage	2 .2	1 .7	1 .8
5 YEAR RATIOS (%)			
Return on Capital	11 .7	13 .0	13 .5
Return on Com. Equity	11 .9	12 .2	12 .1
Profit Growth	3 .5	15 .2	24 .4
Revenue Growth	16 .6	21 .3	24 .8
Asset Growth	17 .2	19 .5	22 .7
BALANCE SHEET (000)			
Cash	1 ,311	1 ,821	4
Total Loans	162 ,049	189 ,809	198 ,057
Net Fixed Assets	30 ,564	20 ,490	11 ,324
Invest's & Advances	25 ,144	30 ,144	32 ,144
Total Assets	232 ,602	257 ,290	257 ,360
Total Deposits	0	0	0
Insurance Liability	0	0	0
Long Term Debt	150 ,910	175 ,405	180 ,057
Total Liabilities	186 ,639	213 ,273	215 ,864
Total Equity	45 ,963	44 ,016	41 ,496
Total Liab. & Equity	232 ,602	257 ,290	257 ,360
CAPITAL (000)			
Total Debt	150 ,910	175 ,405	180 ,057
Preferred Equity	0	0	0
Common Equity	45 ,963	44 ,016	41 ,496

Business:

GREYVEST FINANCIAL SERVICES INC. and its subsidiaries provide commercial equipment financing through direct finance leases, conditional sales contracts and secured loans. The company is also actively engaged in the short and long-term rental of PCs and microcomputer systems. Greyvest has branch offices across Canada and in the northeastern United States.

Synopsis:

Major cost reduction measures implemented in 1992 and early 1993 will result in substantially lower operating costs for the current and future years. Greyvest Financial is optimistic about the U.S. expansion plans of Vernon Computer Leasing Inc. for 1993. The U.S. computer rental and leasing market provides the company with opportunities for low-risk new business growth and geographical diversification. In 1992, the company generated 88% of revenues from Canada. The company wants to significantly increase revenues and earnings from the faster growing U.S. market. In 1991 Greyvest recognized a strong micro-computer rental niche in the northeastern United States through the acquisition of Vernon. The company will further develop this segment in 1993 through internal growth and acquisitions.

Margins in the capital leasing business continue to be under pressure from the lack of significant quality business. In 1992, for the third consecutive year, new business levels were at less than half the 1988-1989 levels. Strong competition developed for superior credits and as a result, interest rate spreads and profit margins declined. To focus only on stronger credits, Greyvest gradually reduced its capital financing portfolio, from $189-million in 1991 to $162-million in 1992. Further reductions in the range of $20-million are planned for 1993.

In 1992 revenues rose from 1991, reflecting the acquisition of Meridian Leasing Canada, Inc. and Bottom Line Computer Associates Ltd. as well as, higher revenues generated by Vernon Computer Leasing Inc. (U.S.). This 54% increase in revenues from operating leases and rentals was countered by a significant decline in revenues from direct finance leases. The decrease is primarily due to the $27.7-million reduction in the capital equipment portfolio.

In 1993, Greyvest expects finance lease revenues to decline further while computer rental and leasing revenues continue to rise. Furthermore, the U.S. rental revenues are also expected to climb sharply in 1993.

Relative strength to TSE300

Price

Volume (in 1000's of board lots)

Rank (Profit/Revenue/Assets)
271   496   302

Lou Elmaleh
Chairman, President & C.E.O.

Address
Suite 1300
20 Adelaide Street East
Toronto
ON
M5C 2T6
(416) 366-1513

Fax: (416) 366-2021
G0003051/F/13.6

HARROWSTON INC.

Exchanges	Price (Jun24'93)	0.14	Trailing P/E	0.19	Stock Symbol
T	Trailing Yield (%)	0.00	Trailing EPS	0.74	**HRW.A**

Period Ending	Dec92	Dec91	Dec90	Dec89	Dec88
Yearly Statistics					
Price-Close	0.10	1.70	45.00	116.25	77.50
Price-High	1.75	47.00	115.00	161.25	77.50
Price-Low	0.04	1.00	36.00	75.00	55.00
P/E-Close	nm	nm	nm	10.29	11.07
Dividends per Share	0.00	0.10	1.40	1.08	1.00
Dividend Yield (%)	0.00	5.88	3.11	0.93	1.29
Sales per Share	1.09	10.11	19.86	171.15	144.32
EPS before extra. item	(1.03)	(61.38)	(43.48)	11.30	7.00
Cash Flow per Share	0.56	40.47	75.86	21.13	3.36
Book Value per Share	(2.07)	(0.76)	49.43	76.63	54.00
O/S Common Shares	18,913	22,086	5,240	6,070	6,064
Total Revenue	23,867	(186,492)	(130,771)	970,352	842,620
Income before extra.	(22,428)	(324,495)	(228,064)	61,031	39,060
Cash Flow	12,112	213,941	397,873	114,125	18,773
Debt/Equity	na	na	2.14	3.57	4.65
Return on Capital (%)	(4.80)	(51.44)	(12.23)	9.99	6.91
Ret. on Com. Equity (%)	na	(267.89)	(62.99)	15.40	11.64
% Change Profit	93.1	(42.3)	(473.7)	56.2	134.1
% Change Revenue	112.8	(42.6)	(113.5)	15.2	15.8
% Change Assets	(29.7)	(77.6)	(85.0)	15.4	9.8
Preferred Div. Coverage	np	np	np		
Total Div. Coverage	na	0.0	0.0		

Business:

HARROWSTON INC. is a holding and investment company with interests in real estate development, merchant banking and manufacturing.

Date	EPS	DPS	Tot Rev	Inc Bex
Mar 93	1.54	0.00	36,344	29,959
Dec 92	0.27	0.00	8,896	6,177
Sep 92	(0.29)	0.00	6,420	(6,307)
Jun 92	(0.78)	0.00	1,875	(17,239)
Mar 92	(0.23)	0.00	6,054	(5,059)
Dec 91	4.92	0.00	(234,004)	22,784
Sep 91	(5.23)	0.00	12,825	(26,686)
Jun 91	(53.00)	0.00	(13,137)	(281,175)

5 YEAR RATIOS (%)			
Return on Capital	(10.3)	(8.7)	2.8
Return on Com. Equity	na	(59.7)	(4.8)
Profit Growth	na	na	na
Revenue Growth	(49.8)	na	na
Asset Growth	(51.1)	(47.0)	(25.0)

BALANCE SHEET (000)			
Cash	33,503	38,751	18,534
Total Loans	0	0	0
Net Fixed Assets	39,285	103,911	147,015
Invest's & Advances	63,531	42,709	655,444
Total Assets	142,230	202,230	901,919
Total Deposits	0	0	0
Insurance Liability	0	0	0
Long Term Debt	137,343	163,529	438,149
Total Liabilities	181,421	218,993	642,895
Total Equity	(39,191)	(16,763)	259,024
Total Liab. & Equity	142,230	202,230	901,919

CAPITAL (000)			
Total Debt	160,868	186,950	553,514
Preferred Equity	0	0	0
Common Equity	(39,191)	(16,763)	259,024

Synopsis:

Harrowston Corporation received approval in March 1993 from holders of its Zurich notes, which are due Dec. 31, 1999, for a recapitalization plan. A new holding company, Harrowston Inc., was formed as the principal public company of the Harrowston group. Harrowston Corporation will be a unit of Harrowston Inc. Shareholders will exchange their Harrowston Corp. shares for Harrowston Inc. shares on a share-for-share basis. Harrowston Corp.'s outstanding $81.5-million notes (including accrued interest) will be exchanged at the option of each note holder for either a cash payment equal to $18 or 180 common shares of Harrowston Inc. for each $100 face value. The company believes the plan should reduce debt and improve shareholders' equity from a deficit of $39.2-million at December 31, 1992.

The company also plans to raise between $20-million and $40-million of common equity through the issuance of special warrants to be sold through a private placement. Each warrant will be issued at $2 and can be swapped for 20 Harrowston common shares. A rights offering is also planned for up to $5-million worth of common shares to be offered at 10 cents a share, the same effective price as the special warrants.

Harrowston Inc. reported a net gain of $30.9-million realized on the elimination of certain indebtedness to third parties in connection with its recapitalization plan. First quarter result also includes a $1.7-million gain on the disposal of certain non-consolidated subsidiaries. This was offset by an operating loss of $2.6-million.

In May 1993, the board of American Eagle Petroleums Ltd. agreed to merge with CS Resources Ltd. The proposal offers $12.50, two common shares of the new company and 1.6 warrants for each 100 American Eagle shares. Harrowston indirectly holds a 16%, fully diluted interest in American Eagle. Harrowston expects to get approximately $4.4-million in cash, 708,154 common shares and 566,524 common share warrants of CS.

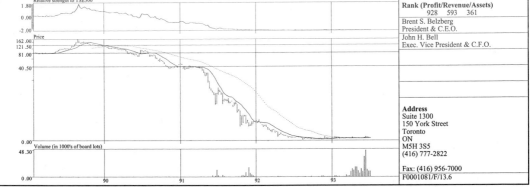

Rank (Profit/Revenue/Assets)		
928	593	361

Brent S. Belzberg
President & C.E.O.

John H. Bell
Exec. Vice President & C.F.O.

Address
Suite 1300
150 York Street
Toronto
ON
M5H 3S5
(416) 777-2822

Fax: (416) 956-7000
F0001081/F/13.6

HEES INTERNATIONAL BANCORP INC.

Exchanges	Price (Jun24'93)		11.87	Trailing P/E		49.48	Stock Symbol
TM	Trailing Yield (%)		8.25	Trailing EPS		0.24	**HIL**

Period Ending	Dec92	Dec91	Dec90	Dec89	Dec88
Yearly Statistics					
Price-Close	8.00	14.88	16.63	29.75	25.00
Price-High	18.13	20.38	30.38	31.83	27.50
Price-Low	7.75	13.75	13.25	24.75	18.38
P/E-Close	80.00	8.60	7.26	11.02	10.87
Dividends per Share	0.98	0.98	0.94	0.82	0.70
Dividend Yield (%)	12.25	6.59	5.65	2.76	2.80
Sales per Share	5.04	6.02	7.31	5.46	5.28
EPS before extra. item	0.10	1.73	2.29	2.70	2.30
Cash Flow per Share	2.63	2.60	3.10	3.46	3.26
Book Value per Share	20.13	21.01	20.49	19.12	15.78
O/S Common Shares	80,436	80,363	79,901	79,251	69,695
Total Revenue	405,011	482,984	667,717	609,229	477,654
Income before extra.	36,255	178,358	232,828	248,804	190,959
Cash Flow	211,451	208,471	246,497	257,450	214,279
Debt/Equity	1.23	1.16	1.29	1.33	1.21
Return on Capital (%)	4.73	8.62	11.25	11.13	10.23
Ret. on Com. Equity (%)	0.50	8.35	11.55	15.38	15.38
% Change Profit	(79.7)	(23.4)	(6.4)	30.3	25.8
% Change Revenue	(16.1)	(27.7)	9.6	27.5	77.5
% Change Assets	0.8	(4.4)	0.7	26.5	13.3

Preferred Div. Coverage	1.3	4.5	4.6
Total Div. Coverage	0.3	1.5	1.9

5 YEAR RATIOS (%)			
Return on Capital	9.2	10.1	10.4
Return on Com. Equity	10.2	13.1	14.5
Profit Growth	(24.9)	8.7	22.6
Revenue Growth	8.5	23.0	39.6
Asset Growth	6.7	21.3	31.5

BALANCE SHEET (000)			
Cash	960,145	1,021,286	868,441
Total Loans	1,458,642	1,413,489	2,095,123
Net Fixed Assets	643,667	633,718	458,383
Invest's & Advances	2,253,735	2,205,253	2,094,966
Total Assets	5,316,189	5,273,746	5,516,913
Total Deposits	0	0	0
Insurance Liability	0	0	0
Long Term Debt	2,580,900	2,518,326	2,052,201
Total Liabilities	3,211,712	3,099,918	3,394,288
Total Equity	2,104,477	2,173,828	2,122,625
Total Liab. & Equity	5,316,189	5,273,746	5,516,913

CAPITAL (000)			
Total Debt	2,580,900	2,518,326	2,736,321
Preferred Equity	485,500	485,500	485,500
Common Equity	1,618,977	1,688,328	1,637,125

Business:

HEES INTERNATIONAL BANCORP INC. is a North American merchant bank. The company provides management, financial and asset management services to a select group of clients. It also owns major interests in a number of North American companies. These companies include Brascan Ltd., Trilon Financial Corp., Noranda Inc., Carena Developments Ltd. and Great Lakes Group Inc.

Date	EPS	DPS	Tot Rev	Inc Bex
Mar 93	0.63	0.25	129,647	57,723
Dec 92	(1.04)	0.25	58,109	(77,814)
Sep 92	0.24	0.25	103,556	26,805
Jun 92	0.41	0.25	118,759	40,776
Mar 92	0.49	0.25	124,587	46,488
Dec 91	0.33	0.25	110,298	34,931
Sep 91	0.39	0.25	126,709	40,452
Jun 91	0.46	0.25	138,804	47,064

Synopsis:

Simplification is the key factor in the Edper Group's effort to get shareholder's confidence. During the first quarter of 1993, the first step was taken in that process. Hees International Bancorp reached an agreement with Edper Enterprises Ltd. to change the provisions governing the ownership of Brascan Holdings Inc. This would clear the way for the elimination of Brascan Holdings as a private company in the event Edper exercises certain rights which it acquired in the transaction to sell Edper's common share investment Brascan Holdings to Hees over the next five years. Meanwhile the focus of the management of the group's operating companies will be on productivity improvements and cost reductions. Emphasis will be placed on core areas of operations. Progress also continues on diversifying the group's borrowing base, such as Great Lakes Power Inc.'s $132-million issue of five-year debentures.

For the first quarter of 1993, Hees had a net income of $57.7-million, compared with $46.5-million recorded in the first quarter of 1992. Cash flow from operations continued to be strong and increased marginally to $49-million, up from $48.5-million in the first quarter of 1992. A big boost to Hees' bottom line came from the $40.9-million contribution from corporate investments compared to $14.8-million in 1992. This was largely due to Brascan's increased earnings in the quarter from the sale of its interest in John Labatt Ltd. The sale of Labatt and MacMillan Bloedel have raised about $2-billion.

Hees is working through two major setbacks in 1992 that saw net income decline to $36.3-million. In one case the decline in real estate values adversely affected Carena and its affiliates, requiring them to record large asset valuation provisions, in particular Trizec's write-down on its investment in Bramalea. And late in 1992, Royal Trustco's new management team decided to establish a strategic alliance with the Royal Bank of Canada to bail it out of losses.

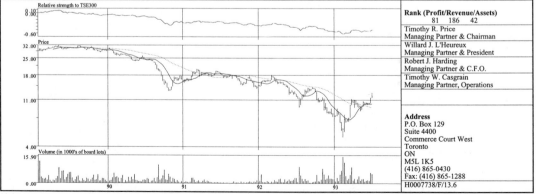

Rank (Profit/Revenue/Assets)		
81	186	42

Timothy R. Price
Managing Partner & Chairman

Willard J. L'Heureux
Managing Partner & President

Robert J. Harding
Managing Partner & C.F.O.

Timothy W. Casgrain
Managing Partner, Operations

Address
P.O. Box 129
Suite 4400
Commerce Court West
Toronto
ON
M5L 1K5
(416) 865-0430
Fax: (416) 865-1288
H0007738/F/13.6

INVESTORS GROUP INC.

Exchanges	Price (Jun24'93)	32 .75	Trailing P/E	28 .48	Stock Symbol
TMW	Trailing Yield (%)	1 .34	Trailing EPS	1 .15	**IGI**

Period Ending	Dec92	Dec91	Dec90	Dec89	Dec88
Yearly Statistics					
Price-Close	25 .88	21 .31	12 .75	12 .06	7 .25
Price-High	28 .00	21 .31	12 .81	12 .19	8 .81
Price-Low	20 .75	12 .63	10 .50	7 .44	6 .13
P/E-Close	22 .70	20 .11	12 .88	11 .83	8 .63
Dividends per Share	0 .44	0 .41	0 .40	0 .35	0 .34
Dividend Yield (%)	1 .70	1 .92	3 .14	2 .90	4 .66
Sales per Share	9 .17	9 .03	8 .06	7 .28	5 .98
EPS before extra. item	1 .14	1 .06	0 .99	1 .02	0 .84
Cash Flow per Share	1 .82	1 .73	1 .77	1 .25	1 .12
Book Value per Share	8 .40	6 .03	5 .40	4 .88	4 .36
O/S Common Shares	52 ,842	47 ,842	47 ,914	48 ,447	49 ,600
Total Revenue	468 ,103	432 ,486	387 ,095	358 ,845	296 ,433
Income before extra.	58 ,333	50 ,715	47 ,620	50 ,319	41 ,765
Cash Flow	93 ,128	82 ,728	85 ,089	61 ,632	55 ,756
Debt/Equity	0 .34	0 .53	0 .59	0 .74	0 .52
Return on Capital (%)	18 .02	18 .61	13 .02	16 .87	17 .85
Ret. on Com. Equity (%)	15 .93	18 .53	19 .23	22 .24	20 .48
% Change Profit	15 .0	6 .5	(5 .4)	20 .5	(9 .5)
% Change Revenue	8 .2	11 .7	7 .9	21 .1	(1 .3)
% Change Assets	(1 .7)	(4 .0)	2 .4	15 .3	26 .4

Business:

INVESTORS GROUP INC. is a financial services holding company. Through subsidiaries, it offers mutual funds, investment certificates, insurance programs, pension plans, annuities and tax-shelter plans. Subsidiaries include Investors Group Financial Services Inc. and Investors Group Trust Co. Ltd. Power Financial Corp. of Montreal owns 67% of the company.

Date	EPS	DPS	Tot Rev	Inc Bex
Mar 93	0 .26	0 .11	119 ,777	13 ,655
Dec 92	0 .34	0 .11	125 ,537	17 ,892
Sep 92	0 .29	0 .11	112 ,624	15 ,440
Jun 92	0 .26	0 .11	111 ,974	12 ,992
Mar 92	0 .25	0 .11	117 ,968	12 ,009
Dec 91	0 .31	0 .11	109 ,944	14 ,536
Sep 91	0 .26	0 .10	107 ,305	12 ,216
Jun 91	0 .25	0 .10	107 ,249	12 ,111

Preferred Div. Coverage	np	np	np
Total Div. Coverage	2 .6	2 .6	2 .5

Synopsis:

Mutual funds are hot and the Investors Group is one of the hottest players in the field. Mutual fund assets in Canada now total $76.7-billion, up by 35.8% from the quarter ended March 31, 1992. President and CEO, H. Sanford Riley, said this is due to the continuing low rates of interest and improving economic indicators, strong Canadian equity markets and the increased involvement of new participants in the Canadian Mutual fund industry.

5 YEAR RATIOS (%)			
Return on Capital	16 .9	19 .1	na
Return on Com. Equity	19 .3	21 .7	na
Profit Growth	4 .8	38 .4	na
Revenue Growth	9 .2	8 .6	na
Asset Growth	7 .0	8 .7	na

Investors Group was the recipient of some of the largesse with a 19% increase in first quarter sales to a record level of $1.29-billion, producing $13.7-million on net income of 26 cents per share for the three months ending March 31, 1993. Mutual fund sales of $1.03-billion for the quarter were 13% above the comparative 1992 quarter level and net cash inflow of $701-million reflected a 9.3% increase over the prior year's quarter. In fact the Investors Group's share price has significantly outperformed the TSE 300 Composite Index during the period from 1988 to 1992 as it increased at an average annual compound rate of 32.9%. During the same period, the TSE composite 300 Index increased 4.9%.

BALANCE SHEET (000)			
Cash	78 ,722	96 ,581	179 ,917
Total Loans	1 ,139 ,469	1 ,280 ,266	1 ,327 ,698
Net Fixed Assets	78 ,680	67 ,217	67 ,719
Invest's & Advances	724 ,800	623 ,297	571 ,092
Total Assets	2 ,102 ,367	2 ,138 ,670	2 ,227 ,519
Total Deposits	1 ,435 ,993	1 ,624 ,241	1 ,748 ,202
Insurance Liability	0	0	0
Long Term Debt	150 ,381	152 ,851	153 ,464
Total Liabilities	1 ,658 ,451	1 ,850 ,142	1 ,968 ,790
Total Equity	443 ,916	288 ,528	258 ,729
Total Liab. & Equity	2 ,102 ,367	2 ,138 ,670	2 ,227 ,519

The mutual fund market is facing increased pressure from the banking industry. This has resulted in a drop in the Investor Group's share of mutual fund assets under administration from 17.9% to 16.3% during 1992. Although the percentages may be hit, the pie is going to get much larger. Mutual fund assets under administration by members of the Investment Funds Institute of Canada, increased by $17.4-billion or 35% to $67.3-billion during the year, and analysts predict mutual fund assets under administration will exceed $300-billion by year 2000.

CAPITAL (000)			
Total Debt	150 ,381	152 ,851	153 ,464
Preferred Equity	0	0	0
Common Equity	443 ,916	288 ,528	258 ,729

In 1992, Investors Group completed the issue of five million additional common shares at a price per share of $24.50. Net proceeds of the issue to the corporation were $23.52 per share or $117.6-million. This contributed to the increase in shareholders' equity during the year from $288.5-million in 1991 to $443.9-million at year end 1992, an increase of 53.85%.

Relative strength to TSE300 / Price / Volume (in 1000's of board lots)

Rank (Profit/Revenue/Assets)
57   162   90

Arthur V. Mauro
Chairman

H. Sanford Riley
President & C.E.O.

Dale A.G. Parkinson
Exec. V.P., Finance & Admin.

Sterling J. McLeod
Exec. V.P., Sales & Marketing

Richard E. Archer
Exec. V.P., Invest. & Trust

Address
One Canada Centre
447 Portage Avenue
Winnipeg
MB
R3C 3B6
(204) 943-0361

Fax: (204) 942-9469
I0000745/F/13.3

LAURENTIAN GROUP CORPORATION (THE)

Exchanges	Price (Jun24'93)	6.62	Trailing P/E	11.04	Stock Symbol
TM	Trailing Yield (%)	4.23	Trailing EPS	0.60	**LGC.B**

Period Ending	Dec92	Dec91	Dec90	Dec89	Dec88
Yearly Statistics					
Price-Close	4.90	6.25	6.13	8.75	6.88
Price-High	6.88	8.00	8.63	9.63	10.00
Price-Low	4.80	5.63	5.00	6.13	6.75
P/E-Close	8.17	9.62	7.21	12.50	16.38
Dividends per Share	0.28	0.28	0.28	0.28	0.28
Dividend Yield (%)	5.71	4.48	4.57	3.20	4.07
Sales per Share	52.40	50.87	50.55	47.26	48.87
EPS before extra. item	0.60	0.65	0.85	0.70	0.42
Cash Flow per Share	7.28	5.85	8.47	3.44	4.99
Book Value per Share	12.79	13.02	13.09	11.86	11.87
O/S Common Shares	52,027	50,146	44,225	44,225	42,841
Total Revenue	2,807,100	2,613,000	2,393,800	2,154,300	2,152,800
Income before extra.	36,100	37,500	43,650	35,800	22,872
Cash Flow	373,304	289,690	381,355	150,218	211,626
Debt/Equity	0.38	0.36	0.26	0.51	0.68
Return on Capital (%)	7.25	5.94	8.25	4.36	2.77
Ret. on Com. Equity (%)	4.68	5.16	6.85	5.92	3.48
% Change Profit	(3.7)	(14.1)	21.9	56.5	(34.7)
% Change Revenue	7.4	9.2	11.1	0.1	29.7
% Change Assets	3.6	23.3	9.2	3.9	1.3

Preferred Div. Coverage	6.9	7.1	8.3
Total Div. Coverage	1.8	2.0	2.4

5 YEAR RATIOS (%)			
Return on Capital	5.7	5.5	5.8
Return on Com. Equity	5.2	5.7	6.0
Profit Growth	0.6	8.6	31.5
Revenue Growth	11.0	17.0	15.1
Asset Growth	7.9	23.7	20.0

BALANCE SHEET (mil)			
Cash	660	707	1,037
Total Loans	8,564	8,509	6,337
Net Fixed Assets	538	483	421
Invest's & Advances	3,852	3,358	2,731
Total Assets	14,246	13,749	11,147
Total Deposits	7,570	7,307	5,564
Insurance Liability	4,298	4,031	3,487
Long Term Debt	277	262	170
Total Liabilities	13,511	13,026	10,480
Total Equity	735	723	667
Total Liab. & Equity	14,246	13,749	11,147

CAPITAL (mil)			
Total Debt	277	262	170
Preferred Equity	70	70	70
Common Equity	665	653	597

Business:

LAURENTIAN GROUP CORP. is a financial services holding company. The company has operations in Canada, the United States, and the United Kingdom. Services include life insurance, general insurance, banking and trust services, and investment management. Subsidiaries include Imperial Life Insurance Co., Laurentian General Insurance Co. and Laurentian Bank of Canada.

Date	EPS	DPS	Tot Rev	Inc Bex
Mar 93	0.13	0.07	727,138	8,065
Dec 92	0.21	0.07	709,223	12,268
Sep 92	0.16	0.07	706,069	9,520
Jun 92	0.10	0.07	666,696	6,323
Mar 92	0.13	0.07	725,112	7,989
Dec 91	0.20	0.07	659,016	11,365
Sep 91	0.14	0.07	608,588	8,364
Jun 91	0.13	0.07	634,392	7,709

Synopsis:

The Laurentian Group announced in early 1993 that it is searching for partners to join forces with to expand in the banking and insurance industries. Its plan is to strengthen its capital base. The search is currently in the exploratory stage and the deal could be in the form of a joint venture, but would not include selling control of Laurentian Group. Laurentian Group has repositioned itself to focus activities on banking and insurance in Canada. The company has expanded out of Quebec into the rest of Canada and internationally in both the United States and the United Kingdom.

New federal legislation governing banks, insurance and trusts companies introduced in June 1992, is intended to increase competition within the financial services sector. The legislation will allow insurance companies to own a bank or trust company, but the industry expects the restrictions to be removed at the next review in 1997. Laurentian Group feels that it is years ahead of the competition, because of the structure it has adopted, in the operation of both insurance companies and Laurentian Bank of Canada.

In 1993, Laurentian Group plans to expand Laurentian Bank's network in Canada. In its life insurance sector, Laurentian Group wants to obtain a competitive return on capital, through repositioning and cost control, mainly in the U.K. The company wants to reinforce its position in the general insurance market and reduce operating expenses in conjunction with its brokers, who are the only distributors of the company's general insurance.

1992 revenues (contribution to net earnings) by segment were: life insurance, 56% (44%); general insurance, 13% (17%); banking, 31% (55%); and corporate and other, (-16%). All operations of Laurentian Group are in Canada, except for 25% of life insurance revenues and 68% of life insurance earnings generated in the United States and the United Kingdom.

Rank (Profit/Revenue/Assets)
82 49 22

Jacques A. Drouin
Chairman & C.E.O.

Guy Rivard
Senior V.P., Finance

Address
The Laurentian Building
1100 Rene-Levesque Blvd. W.
25th Floor
Montreal
PQ
H3B 4N4
(514) 392-6392
Fax: (514) 392-6396
01000329/F/13.6

MACKENZIE FINANCIAL CORPORATION

Exchanges	Price (Jun24'93)	9.00	Trailing P/E	23.68	Stock Symbol
T	Trailing Yield (%)	1.67	Trailing EPS	0.38	**MKF**

Period Ending	Mar92	Mar91	Mar90	Mar89	Mar88
Yearly Statistics					
Price-Close	5.88	8.13	7.88	5.50	4.70
Price-High	8.38	8.63	9.25	6.13	7.38
Price-Low	5.25	5.50	5.13	4.00	3.05
P/E-Close	11.30	14.77	10.79	12.79	14.24
Dividends per Share	0.09	0.08	0.07	0.05	0.04
Dividend Yield (%)	1.53	0.99	0.89	0.91	0.79
Sales per Share	2.51	2.75	2.79	1.99	1.79
EPS before extra. item	0.52	0.55	0.73	0.43	0.33
Cash Flow per Share	0.68	0.73	1.00	0.59	0.39
Book Value per Share	3.18	2.73	1.99	1.33	0.94
O/S Common Shares	57,872	57,100	54,075	53,647	52,290
Total Revenue	145,295	151,515	150,888	105,437	86,499
Income before extra.	30,026	30,630	39,434	23,022	16,049
Cash Flow	39,169	40,050	54,220	31,140	18,774
Debt/Equity	nd	nd	nd	nd	nd
Return on Capital (%)	34.17	46.35	84.24	80.04	84.77
Ret. on Com. Equity (%)	17.67	23.22	44.04	38.28	38.92
% Change Profit	(2.0)	(22.3)	71.3	43.5	36.1
% Change Revenue	(4.1)	0.4	43.1	21.9	40.2
% Change Assets	22.2	23.7	62.4	52.4	24.5

Date	EPS	DPS	Tot Rev	Inc Bex
Mar 93	0.06	0.01	34,402	3,325
Dec 92	0.04	0.10	33,590	2,589
Sep 92	0.11	0.00	34,280	6,091
Jun 92	0.10	0.05	33,994	5,858
Mar 92	0.13	0.00	38,146	7,366
Dec 91	0.14	0.05	35,907	8,214
Sep 91	0.08	0.00	32,871	4,897
Jun 91	0.17	0.04	38,371	9,549

	Mar92	Mar91	Mar90
Preferred Div. Coverage	np	np	np
Total Div. Coverage	5.8	6.9	10.4

5 YEAR RATIOS (%)			
Return on Capital	65.9	77.6	81.9
Return on Com. Equity	32.4	37.3	38.7
Profit Growth	20.5	38.5	55.6
Revenue Growth	18.6	31.7	47.9
Asset Growth	36.0	50.1	61.0

BALANCE SHEET (000)			
Cash	3,047	5,708	6,832
Total Loans	122,098	89,161	72,166
Net Fixed Assets	13,401	13,222	11,420
Invest's & Advances	135,848	113,141	69,412
Total Assets	331,974	271,734	219,650
Total Deposits	121,541	87,951	78,232
Insurance Liability	0	0	0
Long Term Debt	0	0	0
Total Liabilities	148,071	115,684	111,899
Total Equity	183,903	156,050	107,751
Total Liab. & Equity	331,974	271,734	219,650

CAPITAL (000)			
Total Debt	0	0	0
Preferred Equity	0	0	0
Common Equity	183,903	156,050	107,751

Business:

MACKENZIE FINANCIAL CORPORATION is engaged in the management of common stock and bond portfolios. Clients include public mutual funds, pension funds, national associations, and high net worth individuals and estates. The company markets and sponsors mutual funds in Canada and the United States. The company owns 22.6% of brokerage house Midland Walwyn Inc.

Synopsis:

The turnaround hoped for in 1993 has failed to materialize at Mackenzie Financial, resulting in revenue declines for the year ended March 31, 1993. Revenues were $10.8-million below the 1992 figure of $144.2-million. Net earnings were almost halved to $17.8-million, compared with $30-million in 1992. Figures for the fourth quarter alone show some stability, $34.4-million versus $35.8-million. However, net earnings fell into pattern, 55% lower at $3.3-million versus $7.4-million.

The decline for the year was attributed to planned increases in advertising and promotion expenditures, increases in variable expenditures to support the current high levels of mutual fund sales, lower redemption fees on the corporation's portfolio of deferred sales charge financed securities, a decline in average assets under administration and increased real estate and loan loss provisions in relation to Mackenzie's trust company operations. The decline was partially offset by an increase in Mackenzie's share of the earnings of Midland Walwyn Inc., and a reduction in the loss reported by a Mackenzie's subsidiary.

Assets continue to grow to $8.8-billion at March 31, 1993, versus $8.4-billion a year earlier. Canadian mutual fund assets under administration ended the year at $5.9-billion, up from $5.3-billion in March 1992. Positive investment results have led to improvements in net mutual fund sales.

Mackenzie blames bad press for some of its reduced earnings, saying that while it manages 20 mutual funds with widely varied results, only poor results dominate the press coverage. The company has found that Canadian investors prefer mutual funds which are offered without an initial sales charge. To accommodate this growing preference for back-end load investments, virtually all of Mackenzie's Canadian mutual funds were made available with optional loads. New government policies affecting increased RRSP contribution limits and increased RRSP foreign content rules are expected to have a beneficial effect on Mackenzie's business.

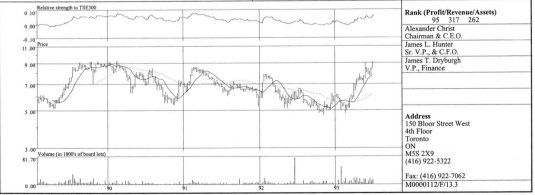

Rank (Profit/Revenue/Assets)
95   317   262

Alexander Christ
Chairman & C.E.O.

James L. Hunter
Sr. V.P., & C.F.O.

James T. Dryburgh
V.P., Finance

Address
150 Bloor Street West
4th Floor
Toronto
ON
M5S 2X9
(416) 922-5322

Fax: (416) 922-7062
M0000112/F/13.3

MIDLAND WALWYN INC.

Exchanges	Price (Jun24'93)	9.25	Trailing P/E	9.34	Stock Symbol
TM	Trailing Yield (%)	0.00	Trailing EPS	0.99	**MWI**

Period Ending	Dec92	Dec91	Dec90	Dec89
Yearly Statistics				
Price-Close	7.25	5.75	2.25	nt
Price-High	9.25	7.50	6.50	nt
Price-Low	5.25	2.00	2.00	nt
P/E-Close	8.24	287.50	nm	nt
Dividends per Share	0.00	0.00	0.00	0.00
Dividend Yield (%)	0.00	0.00	0.00	0.00
Sales per Share	10.68	13.14	24.28	27.51
EPS before extra. item	0.88	0.02	(7.11)	(1.93)
Cash Flow per Share	1.15	0.29	(6.44)	(1.10)
Book Value per Share	3.12	2.22	1.00	7.20
O/S Common Shares	31,178	30,998	7,580	2,781
Total Revenue	332,069	242,840	135,500	76,150
Income before extra.	27,518	370	(39,685)	(5,343)
Cash Flow	35,652	5,381	(35,962)	(3,049)
Debt/Equity	6.05	7.50	16.67	7.17
Return on Capital (%)	7.06	5.89	(26.73)	na
Ret. on Com. Equity (%)	33.15	0.97	(287.95)	na
% Change Profit	7,337.3	100.9	(642.7)	na
% Change Revenue	36.7	79.2	77.9	na
% Change Assets	39.7	41.4	156.4	na

Preferred Div. Coverage	np	np	np
Total Div. Coverage	na	na	na

5 YEAR RATIOS (%)			
Return on Capital	na	na	na
Return on Com. Equity	na	na	na
Profit Growth	na	na	na
Revenue Growth	na	na	na
Asset Growth	na	na	na

BALANCE SHEET (000)			
Cash	5,003	5,856	10,575
Total Loans	16,515	49,317	0
Net Fixed Assets	24,954	19,675	16,649
Invest's & Advances	281,400	202,362	92,596
Total Assets	933,037	667,887	472,309
Total Deposits	0	0	254,346
Insurance Liability	0	0	0
Long Term Debt	587,898	516,478	125,882
Total Liabilities	835,849	599,047	464,758
Total Equity	97,188	68,840	7,551
Total Liab. & Equity	933,037	667,887	472,309

CAPITAL (000)			
Total Debt	587,898	516,478	125,882
Preferred Equity	0	0	0
Common Equity	97,188	68,840	7,551

Business:

MIDLAND WALWYN INC. is a financial services holding company. Its principal operating subsidiary, Midland Walwyn Capital Inc., is Canada's largest financial services organization serving the individual investor, through 72 offices in all 10 provinces. Midland Walwyn Capital is a full-service investment dealer providing investment advice to individuals and institutions.

Date	EPS	DPS	Tot Rev	Inc Bex
Mar 93	0.48	0.00	112,257	15,013
Dec 92	0.17	0.00	79,779	5,431
Sep 92	0.21	0.00	83,874	6,635
Jun 92	0.13	0.00	74,108	4,046
Mar 92	0.37	0.00	94,308	11,406
Dec 91	0.26	0.00	72,619	5,320
Sep 91	(0.41)	0.00	57,055	(10,989)
Jun 91	0.13	0.00	57,117	2,513

Synopsis:

On April 20, 1993, Midland Walwyn Inc. announced it had formed an alliance with U.S. investment dealer Pipper Jaffray Inc. to develop and market a group of international mutual funds, to attract more investors from a market potential of $1.4-trillion. In May 1993, Confederation Life Insurance Co. sold a 9.8% stake in Midland to an undisclosed Canadian investor for approximately $24.8-million.

In 1992, Midland accomplished several financial coups. It was the lead underwriter for Brascan Ltd.'s completed $250-million convertible debenture installment receipt financing and it also participated in a number of corporate financing projects, including the $850-million privatization of Nova Scotia Power Corp. in July 1992.

In 1992 Midland increased total client assets under administration by 25% to $11.6-billion. Managed money products account for $600-million in client assets. Midland has a capital base of $177-million. RRSP accounts grew by 10%.

Midland expects costs relating to its related mergers will drop by $8-million in 1994, and a further $6-million in 1995. Its goals for 1993 include increasing assets by $2.7-billion, $1.2-billion of which had already been realized in the first quarter. First quarter results in 1993 show revenue up to $112.3-million from $94.3-million for the same period in 1992.

1992 revenues by category were: commissions, 45%; principal transactions, 26%; investment banking, 11%; interest, 10%; and other, 8%.

Relative strength to TSE300 / Price / Volume (in 1000's of board lots)

Rank (Profit/Revenue/Assets)		
105	213	158

John A. Rhind
Chairman

Robert B. Schultz
President & C.E.O.

William R.J. Fulton
Chief Financial Officer

Address
Suite 3300
40 King Street West
Toronto
ON
M5H 4A1
(416) 369-7400

Fax: (416) 369-7766
01003046/F/13.7

For further company information, call Globe Information Services 1-800-268-9128 or (416)585-5345

MUNICIPAL FINANCIAL CORPORATION

Exchanges	Price (Jun 24'93)	2.65	Trailing P/E	nm	Stock Symbol
T	Trailing Yield (%)	0.00	Trailing EPS	(0.20)	**MFC.A**

Period Ending	Oc t92	Oc t91	Oc t90	Oc t89	Oc t88
Yearly Statistics					
Price-Close	3.10	8.00	7.50	16.75	9.00
Price-High	8.13	10.50	17.88	18.00	9.50
Price-Low	3.10	4.90	7.00	8.88	6.50
P/E-Close	38.75	15.39	11.72	7.86	5.52
Dividends per Share	0.23	0.60	0.60	0.60	0.48
Dividend Yield (%)	7.42	7.50	8.00	3.58	5.33
Sales per Share	25.07	30.73	32.26	25.84	18.39
EPS before extra. item	0.08	0.52	0.64	2.13	1.63
Cash Flow per Share	4.81	3.40	3.98	3.00	2.23
Book Value per Share	9.69	9.82	9.78	9.73	8.11
O/S Common Shares	5,573	5,569	5,569	5,569	5,277
Total Revenue	144,671	177,201	173,637	149,806	110,447
Income before extra.	693	3,055	4,351	12,038	9,246
Cash Flow	26,790	18,915	22,139	16,727	12,671
Debt/Equity	2.27	2.20	2.15	1.29	1.13
Return on Capital (%)	4.67	6.73	6.31	18.19	19.41
Ret. on Com. Equity (%)	0.82	5.14	6.44	23.05	21.07
% Change Profit	(77.3)	(29.8)	(63.9)	30.2	51.2
% Change Revenue	(18.4)	2.1	15.9	35.6	29.9
% Change Assets	(0.5)	(7.6)	14.7	34.0	19.5
Preferred Div. Coverage	2.8	12.4	5.1		
Total Div. Coverage	0.5	0.9	1.1		

5 YEAR RATIOS (%)			
Return on Capital	11.1	14.6	16.8
Return on Com. Equity	11.3	15.1	18.3
Profit Growth	(35.6)	(5.1)	9.7
Revenue Growth	11.2	20.9	24.6
Asset Growth	11.0	18.5	25.1

BALANCE SHEET (000)			
Cash	81,258	177,136	144,009
Total Loans	991,672	951,938	1,056,157
Net Fixed Assets	43,239	43,734	28,770
Invest's & Advances	181,780	144,794	197,055
Total Assets	1,328,596	1,335,510	1,446,051
Total Deposits	1,118,076	1,128,208	1,219,888
Insurance Liability	0	0	0
Long Term Debt	47,295	52,183	56,375
Total Liabilities	1,272,377	1,278,467	1,383,185
Total Equity	56,219	57,043	62,866
Total Liab. & Equity	1,328,596	1,335,510	1,446,051

CAPITAL (000)			
Total Debt	127,755	125,413	134,840
Preferred Equity	2,219	2,333	8,392
Common Equity	54,000	54,710	54,474

Business:

MUNICIPAL FINANCIAL CORP. provides a broad range of financial and real estate services in communities across Ontario through five subsidiaries. Municipal Savings & Loan and Municipal Trust offer deposit and lending services; Municipal Financial Leasing finances office equipment and cars; MSL Properties develops and operates real estate holdings; and Municor Mortgage Service administers mortgages.

Date	EPS	DPS	Tot Rev	Inc Bex
Apr 93	(0.23)	0.00	32,715	(1,302)
Jan 93	0.01	0.00	31,383	102
Oct 92	(0.02)	0.00	35,301	(55)
Jul 92	0.04	0.00	35,701	283
Apr 92	(0.06)	0.08	33,428	(250)
Jan 92	0.12	0.15	37,074	715
Oct 91	(0.08)	0.15	40,060	(391)
Jul 91	0.27	0.15	41,949	784

Synopsis:

During fiscal 1992 and 1993, Municipal Financial has been affected by the impact of recession on its market, the smaller cities and towns beyond the large urban centres of Ontario. The company would not have shown a profit in the past two years without credits from income tax recoveries. The credit in fiscal 1993 will not be as large as in 1992, when a pretax loss of $4.1-million became a $700,000 profit after a $4.9-million income tax recovery.

Municipal has made specific provisions for potential loan losses, in addition to its general provisions for losses, since its main business is based upon residential first mortgages in Southern Ontario. Specific provisions for potential future loan losses totaled $11.3-million as at April 30, 1993, versus $10-million at October 31, 1992, and $5.4-million one year ago. Write-offs in the first half of fiscal 1993 totaled $7.5-million, compared to $4.9-million in the first half of fiscal 1992. The provision for loan losses in fiscal 1992 were $15.7-million, compared to $10.7-million.

Economic recovery has been hampered by high personal, business and government debt loads, a lack of consumer confidence and spending, and business restructuring and cost control. Despite the low interest rates and housing prices, demand for residential mortgages and residential housing development has remained low.

In the financial services sector, interest rate spreads on retail financial products have narrowed from historical norms as all financial institutions are aggressively competing for limited business. Despite the competitive market, Municipal Trust continues to show growth in its consumer lending and leasing portfolios.

As at April 30, 1993, the leasing portfolio (mostly on motor vehicles) grew to $216-million versus $188-million at October 31, 1992, and $167-million in April 1992. In the fourth quarter of 1992, consumer loans grew 31.1% year-over-year.

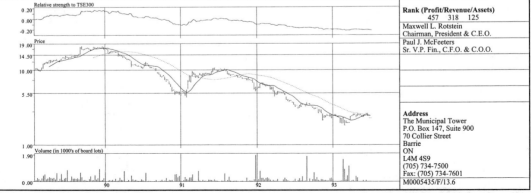

Rank (Profit/Revenue/Assets)
457   318   125

Maxwell L. Rotstein
Chairman, President & C.E.O.

Paul J. McFeeters
Sr. V.P. Fin., C.F.O. & C.O.O.

Address
The Municipal Tower
P.O. Box 147, Suite 900
70 Collier Street
Barrie
ON
L4M 4S9
(705) 734-7500
Fax: (705) 734-7601
M0005435/F/13.6

PAGURIAN CORPORATION LIMITED (THE)

Exchanges	Price (Jun24'93)	2.42	Trailing P/E	5.90	Stock Symbol
T	Trailing Yield (%)	27.89	Trailing EPS	0.41	**PGC.A**

Period Ending	Dec92	Dec91	Dec90	Dec89	Dec88
Yearly Statistics					
Price-Close	2.30	5.25	6.00	8.63	8.50
Price-High	5.63	7.25	8.75	9.38	10.25
Price-Low	2.22	4.10	5.75	7.75	7.25
P/E-Close	6.97	10.29	9.68	11.06	4.70
Dividends per Share	0.60	0.60	0.60	0.60	0.60
Dividend Yield (%)	26.09	11.43	10.00	6.96	7.06
Sales per Share	0.08	0.17	0.29	0.33	0.37
EPS before extra. item	0.33	0.51	0.62	0.78	1.81
Cash Flow per Share	0.37	0.50	0.59	0.78	0.67
Book Value per Share	8.43	8.71	8.80	8.78	8.86
O/S Common Shares	91,395	91,307	91,307	91,307	50,338
Total Revenue	37,203	56,485	68,875	71,558	53,049
Income before extra.	30,190	46,535	56,597	47,277	89,171
Cash Flow	33,543	45,504	53,892	47,081	33,901
Debt/Equity	0.12	0.12	0.12	0.13	nd
Return on Capital (%)	4.18	6.27	7.57	10.25	23.62
Ret. on Com. Equity (%)	3.86	5.82	7.06	7.58	21.39
% Change Profit	(35.1)	(17.8)	19.7	(47.0)	0.8
% Change Revenue	(34.1)	(18.0)	(3.7)	34.9	(47.0)
% Change Assets	(2.5)	(0.9)	(2.7)	103.7	16.8

Business:
PAGURIAN CORP. LTD. is an investment company with significant shareholdings in Edper Enterprises Ltd. and Hees International Bancorp Inc.

Date	EPS	DPS	Tot Rev	Inc Bex
Mar 93	0.19	0.08	19,397	17,718
Dec 92	(0.01)	0.15	26	(1,229)
Sep 92	0.10	0.15	11,456	9,773
Jun 92	0.13	0.30	14,065	12,015
Mar 92	0.11	0.00	11,656	9,631
Dec 91	0.10	0.30	11,208	9,293
Sep 91	0.13	0.00	13,386	11,282
Jun 91	0.14	0.30	15,831	12,803

Preferred Div. Coverage	np	np	np
Total Div. Coverage	0.6	0.8	1.0

5 YEAR RATIOS (%)			
Return on Capital	10.4	15.1	20.2
Return on Com. Equity	9.1	13.6	18.3
Profit Growth	(19.4)	(6.4)	14.4
Revenue Growth	(18.0)	(5.1)	14.4
Asset Growth	17.5	24.6	43.3

BALANCE SHEET (000)			
Cash	0	0	0
Total Loans	77,984	93,233	211,224
Net Fixed Assets	0	0	0
Invest's & Advances	789,348	791,201	686,848
Total Assets	875,563	897,867	906,323
Total Deposits	0	0	0
Insurance Liability	0	0	0
Long Term Debt	0	0	0
Total Liabilities	105,017	102,988	103,195
Total Equity	770,546	794,879	803,128
Total Liab. & Equity	875,563	897,867	906,323

CAPITAL (000)			
Total Debt	94,186	94,310	93,983
Preferred Equity	0	0	0
Common Equity	770,546	794,879	803,128

Synopsis:

Nailing down the financial picture of Pagurian Corp. is difficult because of its multi-layered interconnections with the Hees-Edper group. Consolidation through sales seems to be the key, however, as Edper Enterprises Ltd. had improved results because of the gain realized by Brascan Ltd. from the sale of John Labatt. Net income for the three months ended March 31, 1993, was $17.7-million, compared with $9.6-million for the same period in 1992. Without such a similar boost in 1992, earnings were $30.2-million compared with $46.5-million in the previous year and earnings per share were 33 cents compared with 51 cents in 1991.

The profits benefit from productivity improvements, a lower Canadian dollar and lower interest rates. However, a weak economic environment and low commodity prices which affected natural resources affiliates had a dampening effect on the company.

Some attempt to clean up the web of interconnections, in part to appease investor uncertainty, has been planned by simplifying both the structure and operation of Brascan Holdings Inc. and to relieve Edper and Hees of their contingent financing obligations. Ultimately the proposed Hees Holdings deal will see Hees, Brascan, Edper and Pagurian merged.

Some of Pagurian's financial services were sold. In March 1993, Royal Trustco reached an agreement in principle to sell its operating subsidiaries to the Royal Bank of Canada. This restructuring will allow Trilon Financial to focus on its other businesses which together contributed more than $90-million to Trilon's net income in each of the past three years. This includes the London Insurance Group, which achieved record earnings in 1992.

In an effort to reduce debt, Edper Holdings (49.9% owned by Pagurian) is planning to issue $571-million of equity, more than three times its loans of $174-million. Edper Holdings also sold $25-million of its $27-million securities portfolio of related party stocks in the first quarter and applied the proceeds to debt.

Relative strength to TSE300

Price

Volume (in 1000's of board lots)

Rank (Profit/Revenue/Assets)
93   519   164
Willard J. L'Heureux
Chairman
Manfred Walt
President
Brian D. Lawson
V.P., Finance & Secretary

Address
Suite 4500
BCE Place
Toronto
ON
M5J 2T3
(416) 359-8615

Fax: (416) 865-1288
P0000526/F/13.3

POWER CORPORATION OF CANADA

Exchanges	Price (Jun24'93)	17.00	Trailing P/E	15.60	Stock Symbol
TMV	Trailing Yield (%)	4.12	Trailing EPS	1.09	**POW**

Period Ending	Dec92	Dec91	Dec90	Dec89	Dec88
Yearly Statistics					
Price-Close	15.50	15.00	16.00	15.75	12.88
Price-High	16.25	18.13	16.50	17.00	14.50
Price-Low	13.88	13.38	14.00	13.50	11.75
P/E-Close	13.36	14.71	11.43	9.38	7.80
Dividends per Share	0.70	0.70	0.68	1.60	0.60
Dividend Yield (%)	4.52	4.67	4.22	10.16	4.66
Sales per Share	49.51	46.52	0.66	0.81	0.08
EPS before extra. item	1.16	1.02	1.40	1.68	1.65
Cash Flow per Share	8.41	11.96	0.82	1.38	0.59
Book Value per Share	16.92	15.93	15.89	14.81	11.79
O/S Common Shares	124,892	126,919	126,904	127,024	126,870
Total Revenue	6,379,209	5,987,301	217,433	268,300	230,116
Income before extra.	152,258	136,275	186,293	221,253	217,902
Cash Flow	1,059,344	1,518,094	104,670	174,806	74,738
Debt/Equity	0.29	0.32	nd	nd	nd
Return on Capital (%)	8.58	7.79	9.68	13.89	13.80
Ret. on Com. Equity (%)	7.12	6.39	9.13	12.61	14.40
% Change Profit	11.7	(26.8)	(15.8)	1.5	19.9
% Change Revenue	6.5	2,653.6	(19.0)	16.6	17.3
% Change Assets	9.0	1,055.0	(4.7)	40.6	5.1

Preferred Div. Coverage	29.5	18.7	22.5
Total Div. Coverage	1.6	1.4	2.0

5 YEAR RATIOS (%)			
Return on Capital	10.8	11.6	12.5
Return on Com. Equity	9.9	11.1	12.2
Profit Growth	(3.5)	(0.1)	10.9
Revenue Growth	100.6	108.1	11.6
Asset Growth	77.7	79.7	15.9
BALANCE SHEET (mil)			
Cash	999	1,343	639
Total Loans	8,929	9,016	0
Net Fixed Assets	829	772	89
Invest's & Advances	15,614	13,056	1,416
Total Assets	27,217	24,972	2,162
Total Deposits	1,989	2,172	0
Insurance Liability	19,606	17,657	0
Long Term Debt	654	688	0
Total Liabilities	24,981	22,822	40
Total Equity	2,237	2,150	2,122
Total Liab. & Equity	27,217	24,972	2,162
CAPITAL (mil)			
Total Debt	654	688	0
Preferred Equity	123	129	106
Common Equity	2,113	2,021	2,016

Business:

POWER CORP. OF CANADA is a management holding company. Its principal subsidiaries are Power Financial Corp., Gesca Ltee and Power Broadcasting Inc. Subsidiaries of Power Financial include Great-West Lifeco Inc. and Investors Group Inc., both of Winnipeg, and Pargesa Holdings SA of Switzerland.

Date	EPS	DPS	Tot Rev	Inc Bex
Mar 93	0.23	0.18	1,612,953	29,688
Dec 92	0.13	0.18	1,685,577	17,225
Sep 92	0.24	0.18	1,469,610	32,329
Jun 92	0.49	0.18	1,509,603	63,481
Mar 92	0.30	0.18	1,531,291	39,223
Dec 91	0.25	0.18	1,397,324	32,336
Sep 91	0.21	0.18	1,441,929	28,890
Jun 91	0.33	0.18	1,471,378	43,751

Synopsis:

Questions about Power Corp.'s direction were raised in May 1993 following its purchase of three million shares of Time Warner Inc., a 1% stake, for nearly $100-million (U.S.). This followed on the actions of Seagram Corp., which earlier paid $702-million (U.S.) for a 5.7% stake. The Power purchase was made through Margriette Communications Corp., a wholly owned subsidiary of Power. The parallel investments raise questions about the intentions of the two Montreal-based giants. The deal has already been a good one for Power, which has in a few months realized a profit of more than $10-million on the purchase.

Power had already purchased an 18% stake in Southam Inc., the newspaper chain and bookstore owner. The nature of both purchases seemed to confirm that the company was maintaining a very conservative outlook on spending its massive cash reserves of more than $2.5-billion. That cash surplus came from sales of Consolidated-Bathurst unit to Stone Container Corp. of Chicago for $1.02-billion in 1989, and sale of Montreal Trust to BCE Inc. for $547-million that same year.

Subsidiary Power Broadcasting Inc., in partnership with the CBC, agreed to supply two channels of international news, drama, arts and entertainment to DirecTV. Inc. of Los Angeles, a unit of GM Hughes Electronics. This is to be a part of a digital compression, small dish satellite system slated for operation in late 1994.

Power's consolidated net earnings for 1992 remain strong at $152.3-million or $1.16 per participating share, versus $136.3-million or $1.02 per share in 1991. Earnings from operations, which include Power's investment income, were $132.9-million compared with $120.8-million in the previous year. Shareholders benefited as the book value per share increased by $1 to $17.14 at the end of 1992, and Power paid almost $90-million in dividends to participating shareholders.

Rank (Profit/Revenue/Assets)		
24	18	12

Paul Desmarais
Chairman & C.E.O.

Andre Desmarais
President & C.O.O.

Michel Plessis-Belair
Executive V.P. & C.F.O.

Address
751 Square Victoria
Montreal
PQ
H2Y 2J3
(514) 286-7400

Fax: (514) 286-7424
P0003758/F/13.6

POWER FINANCIAL CORPORATION

Exchanges	Price (Jun24'93)	23.37	Trailing P/E	11.51	Stock Symbol
TMW	Trailing Yield (%)	2.99	Trailing EPS	2.03	**PWF**

Period Ending	Dec92	Dec91	Dec90	Dec89	Dec88
Yearly Statistics					
Price-Close	20.88	20.00	18.25	21.13	14.63
Price-High	22.25	23.13	21.50	21.50	17.13
Price-Low	18.00	17.50	16.25	14.50	12.00
P/E-Close	9.99	11.30	9.04	9.43	8.22
Dividends per Share	0.70	0.70	0.68	1.60	0.60
Dividend Yield (%)	3.35	3.50	3.70	7.57	4.10
Sales per Share	70.10	66.71	0.69	0.81	0.19
EPS before extra. item	2.09	1.77	2.02	2.24	1.78
Cash Flow per Share	12.10	17.49	0.88	0.93	0.72
Book Value per Share	20.27	17.80	16.89	14.77	13.03
O/S Common Shares	84,552	84,341	84,253	84,193	84,095
Total Revenue	6,066,074	5,707,472	241,061	257,127	190,111
Income before extra.	184,884	159,695	184,653	202,194	161,770
Cash Flow	1,021,768	1,474,765	74,232	78,616	60,536
Debt/Equity	0.35	0.41	0.33	0.35	0.14
Return on Capital (%)	10.51	8.95	9.10	12.49	11.39
Ret. on Com. Equity (%)	10.99	10.19	12.78	16.11	13.90
% Change Profit	15.8	(13.5)	(8.7)	25.0	11.7
% Change Revenue	6.3	2,267.6	(6.2)	35.3	10.2
% Change Assets	0.0	966.5	8.1	41.0	(0.2)

Preferred Div. Coverage	22.6	14.9	12.9
Total Div. Coverage	2.7	2.3	2.6

5 YEAR RATIOS (%)		
Return on Capital	10.5	10.6	11.3
Return on Com. Equity	12.8	13.3	14.5
Profit Growth	4.9	3.7	9.9
Revenue Growth	103.8	107.7	15.0
Asset Growth	77.8	79.2	21.4

BALANCE SHEET (mil)		
Cash	420	736	141
Total Loans	8,929	9,016	0
Net Fixed Assets	676	620	9
Invest's & Advances	15,326	12,759	2,053
Total Assets	26,094	23,789	2,231
Total Deposits	1,989	2,172	0
Insurance Liability	19,606	17,657	0
Long Term Debt	646	672	516
Total Liabilities	24,226	22,129	645
Total Equity	1,868	1,660	1,586
Total Liab. & Equity	26,094	23,789	2,231

CAPITAL (mil)		
Total Debt	646	672	516
Preferred Equity	154	159	163
Common Equity	1,714	1,502	1,423

Business:

POWER FINANCIAL CORP. is a holding and management company. Its operations provide a range of individual and corporate financial and fiduciary services in North America and Europe. Subsidiaries include Great-West Lifeco Inc. and Investors Group Inc., both of Winnipeg, and major affiliate, Pargesa Holding SA of Switzerland. Power Corp. of Canada is the company's main shareholder.

Date	EPS	DPS	Tot Rev	Inc Bex
Mar 93	0.45	0.18	1,551,584	39,564
Dec 92	0.22	0.18	1,596,455	21,096
Sep 92	0.31	0.18	1,391,859	28,044
Jun 92	1.05	0.18	1,434,454	90,709
Mar 92	0.51	0.18	1,459,955	45,035
Dec 91	0.34	0.18	1,310,063	30,702
Sep 91	0.41	0.18	1,382,143	37,044
Jun 91	0.62	0.17	1,403,886	55,383

Synopsis:

Cash rich Power Corp. is in the enviable position of sitting on a surplus of $2.5-billion. The company is waiting patiently for the right investment to appear, while indicating that any eventual investments would likely be in North America. Power has $200-million in its 69% owned Power Financial Corp., and $1.5-billion through Pargesa, Power Financial's European subsidiary.

In March 1993, Power Corp. bought 16.8% of Southam Inc. and three seats on the board for $180-million, with the chairman Paul Desmarais saying that newspaper publishers should not be losing money and should be operating more efficiently. Southam lost $262.9-million last year on revenues of $1.18-billion. Power shares the control of Southam with Conrad Black's Hollinger Inc., which bought 22.5% of Southam for $259-million in January 1993.

The profit picture of the Power Financial remained secure as second quarter earnings in March went up to $46.8-million compared with $42.5-million a year earlier. Other income, consisting mostly of its share of non-recurring gains on the sale of long-term holdings by companies in the Pargesa group, fell to $300,000 from $4.5-million. In 1992, the consolidated net earnings of Power Financial were $184.9-million or $2.09 per share, as against $159.7-million or $1.77 per share in 1991. However, Power Financial's share of earnings from its subsidiaries and affiliates fell to $147.7-million from $160.8-million in 1991, primarily due to the its $22.2-million share of a restructuring charge recorded by Great-West Lifeco.

Nevertheless Great-West's net income before restructuring was $110-million in 1992, as against $116.2-million in the previous year. And despite unfavorable business conditions, a sharp increase in sales was experienced in 1992, reflecting the implementation of an array of strategic initiatives. The increase in the total assets of Power Financial came primarily from Great-West Lifeco's increased assets of $2,333-million, boosting the total assets to $26,094-million at year end as against $23,789-million in 1991.

Relative strength to TSE300

Rank (Profit/Revenue/Assets)
16 21 13
Paul Desmarais, Jr. Chairman
Robert Gratton President & C.E.O.
Michel Plessis-Belair Sr. V.P., Finance

Address
751 Square Victoria
Montreal
PQ
H2Y 2J3
(514) 286-7430

Fax: (514) 286-7424
P0024920/F/13.3

TRADERS GROUP LIMITED

Exchanges	Price (Jun24'93)		6.25	Trailing P/E		nc	Stock Symbol
T	Trailing Yield (%)		nc	Trailing EPS		1.01	**TG.PR.G**

Period Ending	Dec92	Dec91	Dec90	Dec89	Dec88
Yearly Statistics					
Price-Close	6.75	2.00	9.50	10.50	10.25
Price-High	6.88	9.88	11.00	10.75	10.88
Price-Low	1.75	2.00	8.75	9.25	10.00
P/E-Close	nc	nc	nc	nc	nc
Dividends per Share	nc	nc	nc	nc	nc
Dividend Yield (%)	nc	nc	nc	nc	nc
Sales per Share	84.11	81.28	86.98	47.89	40.06
EPS before extra. item	3.48	(49.54)	3.78	9.98	6.85
Cash Flow per Share	3.73	2.37	1.71	3.64	2.26
Book Value per Share	17.04	13.16	62.99	59.61	51.07
O/S Common Shares	4,538	4,538	4,538	4,538	4,538
Total Revenue	386,829	367,720	386,149	221,617	187,294
Income before extra.	17,814	(223,277)	19,216	47,437	33,258
Cash Flow	16,917	10,734	7,771	16,537	10,244
Debt/Equity	0.58	0.72	0.30	0.18	0.26
Return on Capital (%)	12.78	(77.95)	4.29	12.85	14.30
Ret. on Com. Equity (%)	25.75	(130.12)	6.16	18.04	15.20
% Change Profit	108.0	(1,261.9)	(59.5)	42.6	168.7
% Change Revenue	5.2	(4.8)	74.2	18.3	(7.6)
% Change Assets	6.0	(23.9)	30.8	60.2	1.7

Preferred Div. Coverage	105.4	0.0	9.3
Total Div. Coverage	105.4	0.0	4.9

5 YEAR RATIOS (%)			
Return on Capital	(6.7)	(8.0)	9.1
Return on Com. Equity	(13.0)	(17.0)	10.4
Profit Growth	7.6	na	8.8
Revenue Growth	13.7	13.7	(11.6)
Asset Growth	11.4	11.6	(22.6)

BALANCE SHEET (000)			
Cash	88,430	164,281	143,001
Total Loans	5,678	21,160	38,005
Net Fixed Assets	69,667	70,541	71,016
Invest's & Advances	571,523	441,706	728,692
Total Assets	954,415	900,467	1,183,452
Total Deposits	0	0	0
Insurance Liability	459,987	437,019	455,954
Long Term Debt	59,967	62,332	93,713
Total Liabilities	850,140	813,837	870,548
Total Equity	104,275	86,630	312,904
Total Liab. & Equity	954,415	900,467	1,183,452

CAPITAL (000)			
Total Debt	59,967	62,332	93,713
Preferred Equity	26,933	26,933	27,065
Common Equity	77,342	59,697	285,839

Business:

TRADERS GROUP LTD. is a financial services holding company. Its subsidiaries offer insurance services. They include Canadian General Insurance Co., Toronto General Insurance Co., Traders General Insurance Co. and the Scottish and York group of insurance companies. The company also holds an interest in Central Guaranty Trustco Ltd. of Toronto.

Date	EPS	DPS	Tot Rev	Inc Bex
Mar 93	(1.35)	nc	103,033	(5,630)
Dec 92	0.09	nc	101,630	907
Sep 92	1.48	nc	103,700	7,209
Jun 92	0.79	nc	90,415	4,608
Mar 92	1.12	nc	91,084	5,090
Dec 91	(37.62)	nc	89,757	(170,731)
Sep 91	(13.17)	nc	26,120	(59,222)
Jun 91	0.35	nc	91,057	2,099

Synopsis:

Traders Group Limited reported a net loss for the first quarter of 1993 compared to a net profit for the first quarter of 1992. The loss was attributed to the results of its subsidiary Canadian General Insurance Group. The insurance group had a net loss of $3.9-million in the first quarter of 1993 compared to a $6.8-million profit a year earlier. The loss reflected an increase in claims on damages from severe weather in Eastern Canada.

The increase in earnings from a net loss in 1991 to a net income of $17.8-million was attributed mainly to the non-recurrence of the provision that reduced the carrying value in Central Guaranty Trustco Limited to $1. Canadian General Insurance Group contributed $19.1-million to earnings in 1992 compared to $21.6-million in 1991. The decrease in contributions was due to decreasing underwriting results, from a loss of $24.1-million in 1991 to $28.8-million in 1992. The results were due to the increase in the frequency and severity of claims, especially in the fourth quarter of 1992 where it was the highest it had been over the past three years. Investment income fell because of lower interest rates and the company expects the decline to continue into 1994. A computer system to process premiums and claims is completed and policies are being converted to the new system. The system is expected to reduce processing costs and improve operating efficiencies.

Canadian Insurance Shares Limited (CIS) has debt of $14.5-million, which is obtained in late 1991, that is payable on demand and that restricts the payment of dividends by CIS until repayment of the debt. Traders and CIS are negotiating with the lenders to allow CIS to pay dividends before the debt is repaid and to change the debt from a demand to a term basis.

With the exception of the 4.5% preferred shares, the company did not pay dividends on its shares in 1992. The January 1993 preferred share dividends were not paid, leaving dividends in arrears at $2,375,000.

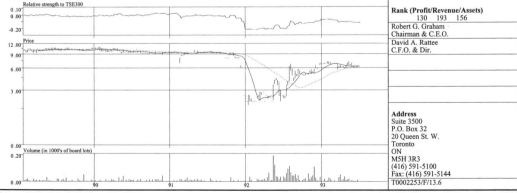

Rank (Profit/Revenue/Assets)
130   193   156

Robert G. Graham
Chairman & C.E.O.

David A. Rattee
C.F.O. & Dir.

Address
Suite 3500
P.O. Box 32
20 Queen St. W.
Toronto
ON
M5H 3R3
(416) 591-5100
Fax: (416) 591-5144
T0002253/F/13.6

TRILON FINANCIAL CORPORATION

Exchanges	Price (Jun24'93)		1.86	Trailing P/E		nm	Stock Symbol
TMV	Trailing Yield (%)		33.60	Trailing EPS		(4.41)	**TFC.A**

Period Ending	Dec92	Dec91	Dec90	Dec89	Dec88
Yearly Statistics					
Price-Close	4.40	10.75	12.38	20.63	17.75
Price-High	11.13	13.12	21.00	22.38	19.00
Price-Low	3.15	9.12	11.00	17.50	14.63
P/E-Close	nm	14.93	176.79	8.78	7.82
Dividends per Share	0.76	0.90	0.90	0.85	0.76
Dividend Yield (%)	17.27	8.37	7.27	4.12	4.28
Sales per Share	46.42	48.82	76.54	66.50	60.21
EPS before extra. item	(3.90)	0.72	0.07	2.35	2.27
Cash Flow per Share	12.03	16.68	4.71	5.71	6.32
Book Value per Share	9.56	14.22	15.21	16.08	16.68
O/S Common Shares	93,643	93,300	80,281	77,247	64,151
Total Revenue	4,345,000	4,264,000	6,223,000	5,060,000	3,883,000
Income before extra.	(331,000)	107,000	59,000	218,000	169,000
Cash Flow	1,126,000	1,457,000	378,000	428,000	400,000
Debt/Equity	0.09	0.87	0.93	0.57	nd
Return on Capital (%)	(12.47)	4.55	(0.67)	8.98	13.59
Ret. on Com. Equity (%)	(32.85)	4.87	0.41	15.23	14.10
% Change Profit	(409.3)	81.4	(72.9)	29.0	12.7
% Change Revenue	1.9	(31.5)	23.0	30.3	23.9
% Change Assets	(66.7)	19.9	1.3	39.6	16.8

Preferred Div. Coverage	0.0	2.4	1.1
Total Div. Coverage	0.0	0.9	0.5

5 YEAR RATIOS (%)			
Return on Capital	2.8	7.9	10.2
Return on Com. Equity	0.3	9.8	11.8
Profit Growth	na	(3.6)	(9.6)
Revenue Growth	6.7	9.1	22.6
Asset Growth	(8.1)	19.9	24.3

BALANCE SHEET (mil)			
Cash	690	4,397	5,137
Total Loans	7,130	34,164	30,375
Net Fixed Assets	1,466	1,629	334
Invest's & Advances	7,806	11,675	7,813
Total Assets	17,987	53,946	44,985
Total Deposits	1,892	35,690	38,988
Insurance Liability	12,370	11,225	358
Long Term Debt	125	1,486	1,490
Total Liabilities	16,609	52,236	43,381
Total Equity	1,378	1,710	1,604
Total Liab. & Equity	17,987	53,946	44,985

CAPITAL (mil)			
Total Debt	125	1,486	1,490
Preferred Equity	483	383	383
Common Equity	895	1,327	1,221

Business:

TRILON FINANCIAL CORP. is a diversified financial services company. It provides investment banking and brokerage, commercial lending and leasing, trust, financial and insurance services. Subsidiaries include London Insurance Group Inc., Royal LePage Ltd. and Trilon Securities Corp. of Toronto. It also has a 47% interest in Gentra Inc. of Toronto, formerly Royal Truscto Ltd.

Date	EPS	DPS	Tot Rev	Inc Bex
Mar 93	(0.33)	0.08	1,089,000	(21,000)
Dec 92	(3.03)	0.14	(1170,000)	(275,000)
Sep 92	(1.09)	0.18	1,356,000	(94,000)
Jun 92	0.04	0.23	2,000,000	12,000
Mar 92	0.18	0.23	2,159,000	26,000
Dec 91	(0.09)	0.23	(1205,000)	7,000
Sep 91	0.29	0.18	1,435,000	34,000
Jun 91	0.28	0.23	2,249,000	34,000

Synopsis:

Trilon Financial Corporation's loss for the first quarter of 1993 was attributed to its share of Royal Trustco's losses. Excluding Royal Trustco, Trilon reported a net income of $17-million for the first quarter of 1993 compared to $21-million last year. Insurance operations increased their contribution by $1-million, to $14-million. Commercial lending and leasing contributed $10-million, an increase of $2-million, due to the investment of proceeds from a subordinated notes issue late in 1992. The investment banking and brokerage activities contributed $6-million, down from $12-million a year ago. The decline was due in part to the loss reported by Royal LePage, which was $8.2-million for the 1993 first quarter compared to a loss in 1992 of $2.3-million.

Trilon has not written down its investment in Royal Trustco, which totaled $339-million at March 31, 1993, consisting of common shares valued at $113-million and preferred shares valued at $226-million. Royal Trustco has a deal to sell its operations to Royal Bank of Canada but Royal Trustco has to buy back the loans the bank does not want. Royal Trustco will have $2.1-billion in cash after the sale but has to buy back $3.1-billion worth of loans. The bank will provide a $200-million loan and Trilon will lend $100-million but Royal Trustco will still be at least $700-million short. Royal Trustco will have to liquidate some of the loans it buys back to raise the extra funds.

Trilon sold its interest in 20/20 Financial Corporation, which distributes and administers mutual funds in Canada, during the secondary public offering of 20/20 Financial Corporation's shares.

Trilon will focus on operations that can provide a significant competitive advantage in carefully selected markets. Steady growth from existing insurance and commercial banking operations is expected to help the group build a high quality, stable earnings base. Selective expansion of investment banking operations and cost reductions and agent training in the real estate brokerage operations are also expected to assist in accomplishing this goal.

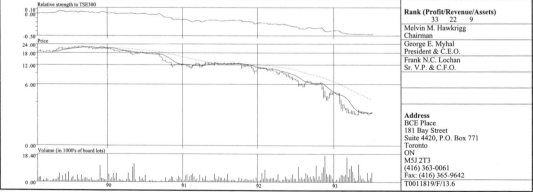

Rank (Profit/Revenue/Assets)		
33	22	9

Melvin M. Hawkrigg
Chairman

George E. Myhal
President & C.E.O.

Frank N.C. Lochan
Sr. V.P. & C.F.O.

Address
BCE Place
181 Bay Street
Suite 4420, P.O. Box 771
Toronto
ON
M5J 2T3
(416) 363-0061
Fax: (416) 365-9642
T0011819/F/13.6

UNITED CORPORATIONS LIMITED

Exchanges	Price (Jun24'93)		32.12	Trailing P/E		31.19	Stock Symbol
TM	Trailing Yield (%)		6.38	Trailing EPS		1.03	**UNC**

Period Ending	Mar93	Mar92	Mar91	Mar90	Mar89
Yearly Statistics					
Price-Close	30.00	27.75	33.50	32.75	34.88
Price-High	30.00	33.00	34.00	36.50	47.00
Price-Low	25.50	25.50	25.13	31.00	31.00
P/E-Close	29.13	25.23	25.77	13.05	26.83
Dividends per Share	2.05	1.02	1.35	2.20	11.13
Dividend Yield (%)	6.83	3.78	4.03	6.72	31.91
Sales per Share	1.28	1.41	1.87	2.91	1.93
EPS before extra. item	1.03	1.10	1.30	2.51	1.30
Cash Flow per Share	1.10	1.15	1.39	2.56	1.44
Book Value per Share	41.78	41.99	42.46	49.45	47.69
O/S Common Shares	7,384	7,195	7,195	6,772	6,772
Total Revenue	9,300	10,164	13,058	19,713	12,253
Income before extra.	7,995	8,258	9,717	17,368	9,156
Cash Flow	7,995	8,258	9,717	17,368	9,156
Debt/Equity	nd	nd	nd	nd	0.01
Return on Capital (%)	2.66	2.91	3.58	5.48	3.44
Ret. on Com. Equity (%)	2.50	2.59	2.92	5.17	2.77
% Change Profit	(3.2)	(15.0)	(44.1)	89.7	27.8
% Change Revenue	(8.5)	(22.2)	(33.8)	60.9	14.1
% Change Assets	2.6	(2.0)	(9.7)	5.3	(0.6)

Date	EPS	DPS	Tot Rev	Inc Bex
Mar 93	0.21	1.45	2,233	1,827
Dec 92	0.29	0.20	2,587	2,240
Sep 92	0.31	0.20	2,507	2,231
Jun 92	0.22	0.20	1,973	1,697
Mar 92	0.23	0.41	2,069	1,657
Dec 91	0.29	0.21	2,595	2,228
Sep 91	0.26	0.21	2,543	1,999
Jun 91	0.32	0.21	2,957	2,374

	Mar93	Mar92	Mar91
Preferred Div. Coverage	21.2	21.8	25.7
Total Div. Coverage	0.5	1.0	1.0

5 YEAR RATIOS (%)			
Return on Capital	3.6	3.6	3.4
Return on Com. Equity	3.2	3.1	2.9
Profit Growth	2.2	9.6	13.3
Revenue Growth	(2.9)	7.7	12.7
Asset Growth	(1.0)	(4.5)	(1.2)

BALANCE SHEET (000)			
Cash	11,949	8,670	43,426
Total Loans	0	0	0
Net Fixed Assets	0	0	0
Invest's & Advances	304,019	299,322	272,217
Total Assets	318,913	310,903	317,143
Total Deposits	0	0	0
Insurance Liability	0	0	0
Long Term Debt	0	0	0
Total Liabilities	4,310	2,666	5,557
Total Equity	314,603	308,237	311,586
Total Liab. & Equity	318,913	310,903	317,143

CAPITAL (000)			
Total Debt	0	0	0
Preferred Equity	6,119	6,119	6,119
Common Equity	308,484	302,118	305,467

Business:

UNITED CORPORATIONS LTD. is an investment company. Its portfolio includes companies in a wide range of Canadian businesses including financial services, precious metals mining, real estate and construction, communications, transportation, and consumer and industrial goods manufacturing.

Synopsis:

In fiscal 1993, United Corporations Limited's Canadian dividend income increased by 1% from $6,990,000 in 1992, to $7,054,000. Foreign dividend income increased by 50% from $664,000 in 1992 to $998,000 in 1993. The increase in foreign dividends is primarily due to an increase in foreign investments which occurred during the previous fiscal year. Interest income amounted to $1,248,000 in 1993, a drop of 50% from 1992 due to reduced holdings of fixed income securities and lower interest rates.

During the year ended March 31, 1993, U-Corp realized net gains on investments of $20,135,000 as compared to the gain of $7,163,000 during the previous year. During the year, U-Corp disposed of its significant investment in Canadian (Refuge) Holdings Limited for a gain of $8,350,000.

The investment portfolio of U-Corp is comprised of a mix of high income yielding Canadian and foreign investments. Total revenue and net income per share will vary significantly from period to period depending on the investment mix of the portfolio.

U-Corp continues to retain National Trust Company and The Empire Life Insurance Company to manage certain investments of the corporation. National Trust Company and The Empire Life Insurance Company each received fees of 0.15% per annum of the market value of their managed portions of U-Corp's portfolio calculated at the close of each calendar month. Excluded from these managed portions are U-Corp's holdings in National Trustco Inc. (1,751,851 shares) and Algoma Central Corporation (362,568 shares). These investments are managed directly by U-Corp.

E-L Financial Corporation Limited has continued to provide clerical, statistical and accounting services to U-Corp. E-L receives in consideration for services, a monthly management fee equal to 0.05% per annum of the market value of the new assets of U-Corp at the close of each calendar month.

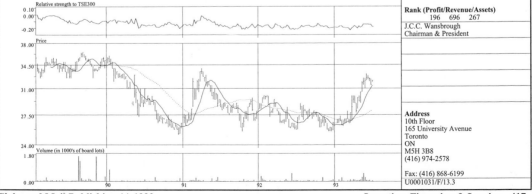

Rank (Profit/Revenue/Assets)
196   696   267

J.C.C. Wansbrough
Chairman & President

Address
10th Floor
165 University Avenue
Toronto
ON
M5H 3B8
(416) 974-2578

Fax: (416) 868-6199
U0001031/F/13.3

Page	Company	$	Latest year end	Earnings per Share		
				Actual	Estimate this year	Estimate next year
421	Crown Life Insurance		9212	(19.59)	n.a.	n.a.
422	E-L Financial Corp		9212	4.87	n.a.	n.a.
423	Fairfax Financial		9212	1.76	2.00	2.50
424	FT Capital		9212	(4.26)	n.a.	n.a.
425	Great-West Life Assurance		9212	43.60	n.a.	n.a.
426	Great-West Lifeco		9212	1.33	1.67	1.84
427	Imperial Life Assurance		9212	8.04	n.a.	n.a.
428	London Insurance Group		9212	2.66	2.74	2.96
429	MICC Investments		9212	(3.27)	n.a.	n.a.
430	Simcoe Erie Investors		9212	0.07	n.a.	n.a.

Estimates from I/B/E/S Inc., 345 Hudson St., New York, NY 10014 (212) 243-3335. In Canada: 6 Lansing Square, Ste. 235, Willowdale, ON M2J 1T5 (416) 496-0977.

Insurance

The capacity of Lloyd's of London is down by close to 15% in Canada because large losses in fiscal 1990 frightened off investment capital. Lloyd's of London reported a record 2.92 British pounds ($5.53-billion) loss for 1990 - its latest reporting year. Lloyd's reports three years in arrears to account for outstanding claims. In 1988 and 1989 the company posted deficits of 2.06 billion British pounds and 510 million British pounds, respectively. The huge shortfall threatens the survival of Lloyd's as well as the future of many of its more than 30,000 members who pledge unlimited liability. The losses in 1990 resulted from a series of natural and industrial disasters in the late 1980s, including Hurricane Hugo and the Exxon Valdez oil spill off Alaska, combined with claims from storms in Europe in 1990.

The Canadian Insurance industry is rapidly changing. In addition to reduced demand for life products and lower profits because of the slumping economy, the industry must now contend with the chartered banks entry into the market place under deregulation. The Toronto-Dominion Bank, Canada's fifth-biggest bank, launched the first volley in the insurance battle with a pilot vending machine project to sell insurance through five "Green Planner" machines. Through the "Green Planner" machines, TD Bank can sell travel and accidental death policies and insurance on Visa credit card balances. The Canadian Imperial Bank of Commerce has applied for insurance company licences in both the life and property-and-casualty sectors, and hopes to be up and running by the fall. Other banks are gearing up for entry into the insurance market as well.

Insurance - Industry Report [Jun-7-1993]. SHEARSON LEHMAN BROTHERS, INC. reported by Smith, M.A., et al
Despite operating income that fell 40% to $2.7 billion (U.S.) in 1Q:93 and a combined ratio of 108.4% (compared to 106.5% in 1Q:92), statutory surplus in the property/casualty industry increased by $5.6 billion (U.S.) in 1Q:93 from year-end 1992, a 3.4% improvement. Most of the improvement was a direct result of strong stock and bond markets in the quarter, as the industry recorded $2.8 billion (U.S.) of realized investment gains and showed unrealized gains of $2.1 billion (U.S.). Written premiums grew 3.6% in the quarter over a year ago. Investment income for the industry fell 4.5%. Paid losses grew 2.3%, and the paid/incurred ratio stood at 90.5%, static with results shown over the past two years. [RN 1336853]

Insurance: Annual Survey - Industry Report [Jun-3-1993]. SHEARSON LEHMAN BROTHERS, INC. reported by Smith, M.A., et al
An extraordinary level of catastrophe losses was recorded by the industry in 1992. Losses incurred grew 11% during the year. The increase in catastrophe claims - $23.5 billion (U.S.) versus $4.7 billion (U.S.) in 1991 - accounted for all of the increase. Excluding the extraordinary increase in catastrophe claims, losses incurred were flat with 1992. This was the fourth year out of the past five during which losses have grown more slowly than nominal GDP. The ratio of paid claims to incurred has risen over the past few years. The paid-to-incurred ratio for the multiline companies dropped in 1992, while the property-casualty companies and reinsurers reported increases. Property-casualty insurers with a more diverse spread of business showed a drop in the ratio, possibly reflecting increases to reserves, at year end, for catastrophe losses. [RN 1336861]

Insurance Summary - Industry Report [Apr-12-1993]. MORGAN STANLEY & CO. INC. reported by Rosenthal, N.L., et al
The Clinton administration is considering folding the health insurance component of workers' compensation and auto insurance coverage into the basic health benefits package that it wants to make available to everyone under its health reform plan. Officials hope that this proposal will soften the opposition of many business groups to another expected Clinton proposal — mandating that all employers contribute to the cost of health insurance for their workers. Any proposal to include workers' compensation medical claims in the package would exclude wages paid to injured employees and legal costs (combined, these two components of workers' compensation obligations account for 60% of the total). [RN 1324412]

1992 Insurance Composite - Industry Report [Apr-7-1993] SHEARSON LEHMAN BROTHERS, INC. reported by Smith, M.A., et al
More positive signs have been seen of the enormous pressures building for an upturn in the property-casualty underwriting cycle. The most important one is that operating cash flow in the industry was negative in 1992. According to the Insurance Services Office, written premiums grew 2.3% in 1992, the fifth consecutive year that growth has been below 5%, while claims paid and incurred grew 11%. [RN 1321589]

Life Insurance Quarterly Update - Industry Report [Apr-1-1993]. SHEARSON LEHMAN BROTHERS, INC. reported by Smith, M.A.
The gradual improvement in the economy is having a positive effect on the life insurance industry. The negatives that face life insurers in 1993 are mostly on the regulatory front. The other major issue lies with the uncertainty regarding changes in the U.S. health care system that the Clinton Administration has promised to bring about. Two decades ago the life insurance industry began a shift away from mortality risk underwriting and toward the marketing of savings oriented products. The population is growing older. [RN 1324575]

CROWN LIFE INSURANCE COMPANY

Exchanges	Price (Jun24'93)	55.00	Trailing P/E	nm	Stock Symbol
TM	Trailing Yield (%)	0.00	Trailing EPS	(20.40)	**CLA**

Period Ending	Dec92	Dec91	Dec90	Dec89	Dec88
Yearly Statistics					
Price-Close	60.00	60.00	100.00	185.00	180.00
Price-High	60.00	90.13	180.00	186.00	180.00
Price-Low	31.00	60.00	100.00	160.00	160.00
P/E-Close	nm	nm	222.22	11.65	44.44
Dividends per Share	0.00	0.00	6.40	6.40	6.40
Dividend Yield (%)	0.00	0.00	6.40	3.46	3.56
Sales per Share	839.52	982.35	1,235.89	1,346.74	1,354.32
EPS before extra. item	(19.59)	(86.66)	0.45	15.88	4.05
Cash Flow per Share	(196.13)	36.20	271.67	319.21	292.20
Book Value per Share	10.46	136.16	178.71	191.71	194.02
O/S Common Shares	2,000	2,000	2,000	2,000	2,000
Total Revenue	1,679,039	1,964,707	2,471,771	3,067,091	2,917,988
Income before extra.	(44,098)	(170,550)	18,788	50,439	20,205
Cash Flow	(392,268)	72,402	543,346	638,419	584,390
Debt/Equity	0.18	0.13	0.43	0.61	0.47
Return on Capital (%)	(5.69)	(24.16)	2.09	5.90	2.30
Ret. on Com. Equity (%)	(36.66)	(58.54)	0.24	8.23	1.90
% Change Profit	74.1	(1,007.8)	(62.8)	149.6	(28.6)
% Change Revenue	(14.5)	(20.5)	(19.4)	5.1	(9.5)
% Change Assets	0.9	(18.4)	5.0	7.3	0.9

Preferred Div. Coverage	0.0	0.0	1.1	
Total Div. Coverage	0.0	0.0	0.6	

Date	EPS	DPS	Tot Rev	Inc Bex
Mar 93	0.61	0.00	414,587	4,405
Dec 92	(22.28)	0.00	435,501	(58,286)
Sep 92	0.59	0.00	398,698	20,662
Jun 92	0.68	0.00	393,541	4,223
Mar 92	1.42	0.00	411,902	5,886
Dec 91	(4.53)	0.00	443,906	(15,608)
Sep 91	(71.05)	0.00	456,887	(145,221)
Jun 91	(5.16)	0.00	505,391	(5,938)

5 YEAR RATIOS (%)			
Return on Capital	(3.9)	(2.2)	3.6
Return on Com. Equity	(17.0)	(8.9)	4.0
Profit Growth	na	na	(23.6)
Revenue Growth	(12.3)	(9.1)	1.5
Asset Growth	(1.4)	2.0	11.2

BALANCE SHEET (mil)			
Cash	174	230	140
Total Loans	3,624	3,693	3,937
Net Fixed Assets	555	474	441
Invest's & Advances	3,400	3,179	3,124
Total Assets	8,338	8,263	10,123
Total Deposits	0	0	194
Insurance Liability	7,299	7,169	6,817
Long Term Debt	0	0	229
Total Liabilities	7,931	7,810	9,590
Total Equity	407	453	533
Total Liab. & Equity	8,338	8,263	10,123

CAPITAL (mil)			
Total Debt	73	59	229
Preferred Equity	387	181	176
Common Equity	21	272	357

Business:

CROWN LIFE INSURANCE CO. offers a range of life and health insurance to individuals and groups. It also offers reinsurance services to other insurance companies. Offices are located in Canada, the United States, the United Kingdom, the Caribbean and Hong Kong. Crownx Inc. of Toronto owns 54.1% of the company's common shares and Haro Financial owns 42%.

Synopsis:

Crown Life's results in 1993 will reflect expense reductions related to its relocation and restructuring programs, which should have a full impact in 1994. The company also believes that asset defaults peaked in mid-1992. The focus will be on profitable sales to its core markets for annuities, life and health insurance. Crown Life will be introducing new universal life products in the United States, and a new variable insurance product in Canada.

The second phase of the relocation of its head office operations to Regina is on schedule. The new building will be available to staff in August 1993. In December 1992, the Saskatchewan government announced it was reducing its commitment to the relocation from $355-million to $275-million.

New laws regulating Canadian financial institutions will result in more direct competition from other financial sectors. Crown Life plans to concentrate on markets where it has a strong competitive position. The relocation of head office operations will help lower cost structures, which will make Crown Life more competitive in the future.

In Canadian operations, the company is working to control claims experience and reduce its exposure to these risks, which tend to be unfavorable in economic recessions. Also, in Canada, Crown Life is continuing to reduce operating expenses. In response to highly competitive U.S. pension and individual life markets, Crown Life shifted from a high-end brokerage market for individual life products to middle-income, narrowed its range of life products, downsized its head office support areas and pension division's sales operations and withdrew from the U.S. GIC market. The U.S. pension division's emphasis is now on the sale of pooled funds.

The company's share of the reinsurance market in North America is approximately 3%. 1992 premium, investment and other income by geographic segment were: the United States, 64%; Canada, 32%; and international, 4%.

Relative strength to TSE300

Price

Volume (in 1000's of board lots)

Rank (Profit/Revenue/Assets)		
952	72	32

H. Michael Burns
Chairman

R. Fred Richardson
President & C.E.O.

Alan M. Rowe
V.P., Finance

Address
1901 Scarth Street
P.O. Box 827
Regina
SK
S4P 3B1
(306) 751-6000

Fax: (306) 751-6001
C0011778/F/13.5.2

E-L FINANCIAL CORPORATION LIMITED

| Exchanges | Price (Jun24'93) | 56.37 | Trailing P/E | 10.40 | Stock Symbol |
| T | Trailing Yield (%) | 0.89 | Trailing EPS | 5.42 | ELF |

Period Ending	Dec92	Dec91	Dec90	Dec89	Dec88
Yearly Statistics					
Price-Close	38.00	54.38	50.00	75.00	53.00
Price-High	57.00	54.50	75.00	77.75	56.00
Price-Low	35.00	45.00	43.00	50.00	45.00
P/E-Close	7.80	6.35	26.60	7.16	4.85
Dividends per Share	0.50	0.50	0.50	1.65	0.10
Dividend Yield (%)	1.32	0.92	1.00	2.20	0.19
Sales per Share	237.67	232.07	169.10	195.67	186.22
EPS before extra. item	4.87	8.56	1.88	10.48	10.92
Cash Flow per Share	4.87	8.56	16.85	22.54	13.89
Book Value per Share	84.04	79.47	64.24	65.15	67.81
O/S Common Shares	3,840	3,840	3,840	3,840	3,284
Total Revenue	933,083	908,680	649,325	696,924	610,928
Income before extra.	18,700	32,875	7,208	40,258	36,097
Cash Flow	18,700	32,875	64,689	80,270	45,556
Debt/Equity	0.09	0.14	nd	nd	nd
Return on Capital (%)	4.85	12.84	2.28	16.46	16.26
Ret. on Com. Equity (%)	5.96	11.92	2.90	17.03	17.48
% Change Profit	(43.1)	356.1	(82.1)	11.5	65.2
% Change Revenue	2.7	39.9	(6.8)	14.1	1.4
% Change Assets	6.7	35.4	2.5	12.8	7.8

Preferred Div. Coverage	na	na	na
Total Div. Coverage	9.7	17.1	3.8

5 YEAR RATIOS (%)			
Return on Capital	10.5	11.8	10.9
Return on Com. Equity	11.1	12.2	12.0
Profit Growth	(3.0)	12.3	8.8
Revenue Growth	9.1	11.0	8.0
Asset Growth	12.4	13.2	11.4

BALANCE SHEET (000)			
Cash	172,074	66,554	60,390
Total Loans	301,819	308,945	228,607
Net Fixed Assets	31,901	29,723	14,586
Invest's & Advances	1,563,222	1,548,498	1,148,997
Total Assets	2,783,297	2,608,529	1,926,790
Total Deposits	0	0	19,711
Insurance Liability	1,615,482	1,498,905	1,094,135
Long Term Debt	0	0	0
Total Liabilities	2,460,591	2,303,393	1,680,131
Total Equity	322,706	305,136	246,659
Total Liab. & Equity	2,783,297	2,608,529	1,926,790

CAPITAL (000)			
Total Debt	29,042	41,403	0
Preferred Equity	1	1	1
Common Equity	322,705	305,135	246,658

Business:

E-L FINANCIAL CORP. LTD. is a financial services holding company. Its subsidiaries are engaged in underwriting all types of insurance. Subsidiaries include Dominion of Canada General Insurance Co., E-L Financial Services Ltd. and Empire Life Insurance Co.

Date	EPS	DPS	Tot Rev	Inc Bex
Mar 93	2.76	0.13	234,161	10,587
Dec 92	2.09	0.13	290,021	8,024
Sep 92	1.98	0.13	219,900	7,603
Jun 92	(1.41)	0.13	199,139	(5,395)
Mar 92	2.67	0.13	240,434	10,271
Dec 91	2.37	0.13	293,009	9,106
Sep 91	0.44	0.13	224,542	1,668
Jun 91	2.55	0.13	218,457	9,803

Synopsis:

E-L Financial feels that all sectors of the insurance industry in Canada suffer from over-capacity and fragmentation, and some face additional regulatory changes. The company is responding by consolidating the SAFECO acquisition (made in 1991), streamlining operations to give better service at lower costs, acquiring blocks of attractive business from companies leaving the industry or vacating certain markets, expanding sales of segregated funds and participating in industry discussions to improve draft legislation.

The company's general insurance operation faces an industry where consolidation is likely, whether through mergers, acquisitions, or withdrawals. New competition from non-traditional players such as banks is expected under deregulation

Based on 1992 accident-year results, E-L's general insurance operation is optimistic about future profitability. Improved shareholder return is expected through increased focus on the marketplace, improved underwriting, appropriate rate action and effective cost management. Interest rates, government initiatives, and further losses in general liability business are not predictable and may have an adverse impact on results. Lower return on investments in the next year is expected based on forecasted economic conditions. However, the focus in 1993 and beyond will be on improved underwriting results.

During 1992, E-L's life insurance operation strengthened its personal and group distribution networks, resulting in increased sales of segregated funds and employee benefits. E-L plans to pursue acquisitions in 1992, which it feels is possible because of its strong capitalization.

1992 life insurance premium income of $201.6-million by line of insurance was: individual insurance, 42%; individual annuities, 24%; individual health, 1%; group insurance, 4%; group annuities, 8%; and group health, 21%. 1992 general insurance premiums written of $523.4-million by line of insurance was: automobile, 64%; casualty, 4%; and property, 32%.

Relative strength to TSE300

Price

Volume (in 1000's of board lots)

Rank (Profit/Revenue/Assets)
124 112 71

E. Kendall Cork
Chairman & President

Address
10th Floor
165 University Avenue
Toronto
ON
M5H 3B8
(416) 947-2578

Fax: (416) 868-6199
E0000950/F/13.5.1

FAIRFAX FINANCIAL HOLDINGS LIMITED

Exchanges	Price (Jun24'93)	34.00	Trailing P/E	17.89	Stock Symbol
T	Trailing Yield (%)	0.00	Trailing EPS	1.90	**FFH**

Period Ending	Dec92	Dec91	Dec90	Dec89	Dec88
Yearly Statistics					
Price-Close	25.00	21.25	11.00	18.75	15.00
Price-High	30.00	22.50	21.63	21.63	15.13
Price-Low	21.75	10.75	8.88	8.88	11.75
P/E-Close	14.21	5.17	3.68	8.19	7.65
Dividends per Share	0.00	0.00	0.00	0.00	0.00
Dividend Yield (%)	0.00	0.00	0.00	0.00	0.00
Sales per Share	49.13	43.79	22.09	13.12	17.45
EPS before extra. item	1.76	4.11	2.99	2.29	1.96
Cash Flow per Share	2.29	6.10	(1.80)	(0.30)	0.49
Book Value per Share	23.75	21.41	17.29	12.42	10.13
O/S Common Shares	6,055	5,455	5,477	7,316	7,323
Total Revenue	286,830	250,353	195,430	125,754	133,649
Income before extra.	10,045	22,515	21,306	16,741	14,357
Cash Flow	13,172	33,417	(12,791)	(2,303)	3,297
Debt/Equity	0.61	0.62	1.02	0.29	0.45
Return on Capital (%)	4.17	16.99	14.18	15.97	22.42
Ret. on Com. Equity (%)	7.71	21.30	22.97	20.29	21.14
% Change Profit	(55.4)	5.7	27.3	16.6	0.3
% Change Revenue	14.6	28.1	55.4	(5.9)	18.3
% Change Assets	14.3	(3.6)	116.1	0.5	33.1

Preferred Div. Coverage	np	np	np
Total Div. Coverage	na	na	na

Date	EPS	DPS	Tot Rev	Inc Bex
Mar 93	0.70	0.00	74,915	4,173
Dec 92	0.61	0.00	74,269	3,535
Sep 92	0.02	0.00	77,203	120
Jun 92	0.57	0.00	69,326	3,249
Mar 92	0.56	0.00	66,032	3,141
Dec 91	1.12	0.00	53,509	5,458
Sep 91	2.12	0.00	74,739	11,622
Jun 91	0.43	0.00	63,780	2,373

5 YEAR RATIOS (%)			
Return on Capital	14.7	21.0	23.9
Return on Com. Equity	18.7	23.5	23.8
Profit Growth	(6.9)	35.9	100.2
Revenue Growth	20.4	36.0	61.7
Asset Growth	26.0	31.8	66.8

BALANCE SHEET (000)			
Cash	83,495	72,362	47,835
Total Loans	0	0	0
Net Fixed Assets	21,882	19,238	23,502
Invest's & Advances	312,482	278,078	306,953
Total Assets	590,548	516,564	535,987
Total Deposits	5,844	3,993	9,513
Insurance Liability	208,816	202,120	220,602
Long Term Debt	81,937	62,467	75,688
Total Liabilities	446,730	399,789	441,311
Total Equity	143,818	116,775	94,676
Total Liab. & Equity	590,548	516,564	535,987

CAPITAL (000)			
Total Debt	88,261	72,754	96,656
Preferred Equity	0	0	0
Common Equity	143,818	116,775	94,676

Business:

FAIRFAX FINANCIAL HOLDINGS LIMITED is engaged in the insurance of long haul trucking, commercial property, oil and gas, casualty and life risks and the provision of claims adjusting and appraisal and loss management services in Canada, the United States and Europe. Its main subsidiaries are Commonwealth Insurance, Federated Insurance, Federated Life Insurance, Markel Insurance and Lindsey Morden Services.

Synopsis:

In 1992 Fairfax Financial Holdings simplified its corporate relationships and focus with the purchase of Hamblin Watsa Investment Counsel Ltd. (HWIC) for $14-million, and the acquisition of the remaining 49.9% interest in The Sixty Two Investment Company Limited (Sixty Two) from Prem Watsa, in exchange for subordinate voting shares of Fairfax. Sixty Two is the controlling shareholder of Fairfax.

HWIC is an investment counseling firm that manages approximately $1-billion in pension, corporate and individual funds. Approximately $240-million are funds that originate from Fairfax's insurance subsidiaries. HWIC will continue to be run as a separate subsidiary with Tony Hamblin as president.

The purchase of the 49.9% interest in Sixty-Two is to provide liquidity to the original investors, on terms attractive to Fairfax. Sixty Two's only asset is the Fairfax shares, and it has no liabilities. Sixty Two will continue to be controlled by V. Prem Watsa.

Fairfax believed the insurance cycle was turning in 1992, but Hurricane Andrew cost the company approximately $11-million. The company has a long-term objective of earning in excess of 20% on shareholders' equity by running Fairfax and its subsidiaries for the long-term benefit of customers, employees and shareholders.

The breakdown of revenues in 1992 by segment was: insurance, 50%; claims adjusting, 49%; and other, 1%. The breakdown of insurance premiums earned in 1992 by operational area was: commercial auto and general liability, 20%; farm and reinsurance run off, 8%; direct commercial lines, 33%; and commercial property and casualty, 39%. Revenues (earnings before taxes) in 1992 by geographic region were: Canada, 62% (95%); United States, 38% (5%). Almost 72% of Fairfax's assets are in Canada with the rest in the United States.

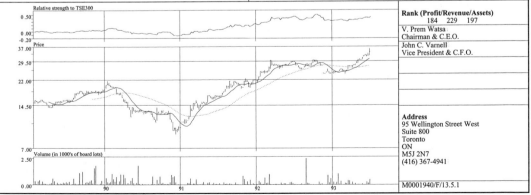

Rank (Profit/Revenue/Assets)		
184	229	197

V. Prem Watsa
Chairman & C.E.O.

John C. Varnell
Vice President & C.F.O.

Address
95 Wellington Street West
Suite 800
Toronto
ON
M5J 2N7
(416) 367-4941

M0001940/F/13.5.1

FT CAPITAL LTD.

Exchanges	Price (Jun24'93)	0.16	Trailing P/E	nm	Stock Symbol
TZ	Trailing Yield (%)	0.00	Trailing EPS	(3.18)	**FTC**

Period Ending	Dec92	Dec91	Dec90	Dec89	Dec88
Yearly Statistics					
Price-Close	0.02	0.03	0.04	0.08	0.60
Price-High	0.08	0.06	0.20	0.90	10.00
Price-Low	0.02	0.02	0.02	0.06	0.50
P/E-Close	nm	nm	nm	nm	nm
Dividends per Share	0.00	0.00	0.00	0.00	0.32
Dividend Yield (%)	0.00	0.00	0.00	0.00	53.33
Sales per Share	8.30	12.02	9.15	7.53	3.95
EPS before extra. item	(4.26)	(2.12)	(3.21)	(3.69)	(22.96)
Cash Flow per Share	(1.31)	3.12	0.58	(1.21)	(3.68)
Book Value per Share	(25.01)	(21.06)	(19.16)	(16.27)	(12.89)
O/S Common Shares	10,199	10,199	10,199	10,199	10,199
Total Revenue	94,952	132,619	95,349	81,285	24,007
Income before extra.	(40,288)	(18,477)	(29,514)	(34,459)	(234,024)
Cash Flow	(13,377)	31,862	5,870	(12,321)	(38,032)
Debt/Equity	na	na	na	na	na
Return on Capital (%)	na	na	na	(15.19)	(92.65)
Ret. on Com. Equity (%)	na	na	na	na	na
% Change Profit	(118.0)	37.4	14.4	85.3	(1,626.7)
% Change Revenue	(28.4)	39.1	17.3	238.6	(84.0)
% Change Assets	18.2	35.4	7.1	(15.2)	(69.8)

Date	EPS	DPS	Tot Rev	Inc Bex
Mar 93	0.05	0.00	37,771	1,428
Dec 92	(1.61)	0.00	34,389	(10,838)
Sep 92	(1.00)	0.00	17,861	(14,277)
Jun 92	(0.62)	0.00	21,204	(5,606)
Mar 92	(1.02)	0.00	23,192	(9,567)
Dec 91	(0.90)	0.00	32,261	(8,415)
Sep 91	(0.44)	0.00	33,494	(2,871)
Jun 91	(0.35)	0.00	39,406	(2,746)

Preferred Div. Coverage	na	na	na
Total Div. Coverage	na	na	na

5 YEAR RATIOS (%)			
Return on Capital	na	na	na
Return on Com. Equity	na	na	na
Profit Growth	na	na	na
Revenue Growth	(8.7)	(8.4)	(0.2)
Asset Growth	(15.1)	(29.0)	(24.2)

BALANCE SHEET (000)			
Cash	112,016	66,826	75,973
Total Loans	49,803	1,883	13,666
Net Fixed Assets	1,534	1,537	2,530
Invest's & Advances	174,685	203,368	98,490
Total Assets	362,966	307,010	226,743
Total Deposits	0	0	0
Insurance Liability	213,509	174,340	106,376
Long Term Debt	139,514	127,116	145,211
Total Liabilities	587,030	490,786	391,131
Total Equity	(224,064)	(183,776)	(164,388)
Total Liab. & Equity	362,966	307,010	226,743

CAPITAL (000)			
Total Debt	207,034	166,502	145,211
Preferred Equity	31,039	31,039	31,039
Common Equity	(255,103)	(214,815)	(195,427)

Business:

FT CAPITAL LTD., formerly Financial Trustco Ltd., is an insurance holding company. Its subsidiary, Morgan Financial Corp. of Toronto, operates Westbury Canadian Life Insurance Co. and MECI Properties Inc.

Synopsis:

FT Capital's increased loss in 1992 was the result of an interest expense accrual on the company's U.S. subordinated debt, a foreign exchange loss on this debt due to the declining Canadian dollar and FT Capital's share of the loss at Morgan Financial. FT Capital over the last year has placed its emphasis on the realization of non-strategic assets, in particular the liquidation of its real estate operation of MECI Properties Inc.

Morgan's improved profitability before a goodwill write-off was due to its Westbury Canadian Life Insurance Company, which increased its profit by approximately 23%. Annuity revenues fell in 1992, but sales rose in both life and health insurance. Westbury plans future growth in Ontario and Western Canada, where during 1992 sales grew by 41% to reach 26% of total sales.

FT Capital expects its life insurance business to grow. And with the restructuring or disposition of non-strategic assets mostly complete, the company will concentrate on the rebuilding and refinancing of its core financial operations. Alternatives are being explored for the development of a refinancing plan and opportunities for controlled and profitable investments.

FT Capital's gross premiums in 1992 (1991) by type were: individual life and health, 52% (35%); group life and health, 40% (30%); and annuities, 8% (35%).

Relative strength to TSE300

Price

Volume (in 1000's of board lots)

Rank (Profit/Revenue/Assets)
947   389   248

Terrence A. Lyons
President & C.E.O.

Address
1632 - 1055 West Georgia St.
P.O. Box 11179 Royal Centre
Vancouver
BC
V6E 3R5
(604) 669-3141

Fax: (604) 687-3419
F0005910/F/13.5.2

GREAT-WEST LIFE ASSURANCE COMPANY (THE)

Exchanges	Price (Jun24'93)		25 .00	Trailing P/E		nc	Stock Symbol
TMW	Trailing Yield (%)		nc	Trailing EPS		46 .43	**GWL.PR.A**

Period Ending	Dec92	Dec91	Dec90	Dec89	Dec88
Yearly Statistics					
Price-Close	25 .50	25 .00	24 .50	24 .75	24 .75
Price-High	26 .00	25 .00	25 .25	25 .38	25 .63
Price-Low	24 .00	21 .50	24 .13	24 .63	24 .50
P/E-Close	nc	nc	nc	nc	nc
Dividends per Share	nc	nc	nc	nc	nc
Dividend Yield (%)	nc	nc	nc	nc	nc
Sales per Share	2 ,677 .30	2 ,560 .09	2 ,849 .90	2 ,593 .32	2 ,465 .11
EPS before extra. item	43 .60	58 .40	58 .58	55 .15	48 .96
Cash Flow per Share	535 .04	723 .26	1 ,005 .72	1 ,027 .00	1 ,131 .28
Book Value per Share	722 .08	659 .11	612 .45	565 .83	526 .67
O/S Common Shares	2 ,000	2 ,000	2 ,000	2 ,000	2 ,000
Total Revenue	5 ,354 ,592	5 ,120 ,173	5 ,596 ,174	5 ,298 ,372	4 ,966 ,459
Income before extra.	116 ,850	139 ,588	155 ,936	151 ,424	127 ,365
Cash Flow	1 ,070 ,079	1 ,446 ,517	2 ,011 ,447	2 ,053 ,997	2 ,262 ,562
Debt/Equity	0 .02	0 .04	0 .04	0 .07	0 .13
Return on Capital (%)	9 .51	10 .46	11 .52	13 .47	10 .28
Ret. on Com. Equity (%)	6 .32	9 .19	11 .59	12 .06	11 .19
% Change Profit	(16 .3)	(10 .5)	3 .0	18 .9	38 .5
% Change Revenue	4 .6	(8 .5)	5 .6	6 .7	2 .6
% Change Assets	11 .3	(2 .6)	10 .7	9 .6	11 .2

Date	EPS	DPS	Tot Rev	Inc Bex
Mar 93	17 .28	nc	1 ,414 ,967	42 ,581
Dec 92	0 .54	nc	1 ,459 ,904	9 ,816
Sep 92	15 .50	nc	1 ,267 ,247	34 ,016
Jun 92	13 .11	nc	1 ,312 ,226	32 ,983
Mar 92	14 .45	nc	1 ,315 ,215	35 ,525
Dec 91	17 .86	nc	1 ,187 ,580	50 ,654
Sep 91	13 .74	nc	1 ,268 ,576	36 ,744
Jun 91	15 .09	nc	1 ,288 ,978	40 ,494

Preferred Div. Coverage	3 .9	6 .1	8 .1
Total Div. Coverage	1 .7	2 .2	2 .6

5 YEAR RATIOS (%)			
Return on Capital	11 .0	10 .8	10 .7
Return on Com. Equity	10 .1	10 .4	10 .9
Profit Growth	4 .8	3 .0	5 .2
Revenue Growth	2 .0	2 .7	10 .2
Asset Growth	7 .8	9 .4	14 .1

BALANCE SHEET (mil)			
Cash	136	499	411
Total Loans	7 ,789	7 ,736	7 ,990
Net Fixed Assets	588	542	634
Invest's & Advances	13 ,552	11 ,047	9 ,205
Total Assets	22 ,698	20 ,392	20 ,929
Total Deposits	0	0	0
Insurance Liability	20 ,159	18 ,205	16 ,958
Long Term Debt	36	61	65
Total Liabilities	20 ,853	18 ,723	19 ,428
Total Equity	1 ,845	1 ,669	1 ,501
Total Liab. & Equity	22 ,698	20 ,392	20 ,929

CAPITAL (mil)			
Total Debt	36	61	65
Preferred Equity	401	351	276
Common Equity	1 ,444	1 ,318	1 ,225

Business:

GREAT-WEST LIFE ASSURANCE CO. offers a range of insurance, retirement and investment products and services for individuals, businesses and organizations. The company has marketing, benefit payment and property investment offices across the United States and Canada. The company is a subsidiary of Great-West Lifeco Inc. of Winnipeg.

Synopsis:

Great-West Life Assurance's results in 1992 were favorably affected by Individual disability income experience in Canada and strong Group life and health results in the United States. The results were offset by the deterioration of Individual mortality experience in the U.S., and in both countries, weakened margins on investment related business and association assessments resulting from insurance company failures.

Great-West, to strengthen its U.S. operation, began in the early 1980s to set up separate autonomous operations in both countries. This was completed with the final transfer of business in 1992 to Great-West Life & Annuity Insurance Company, which will conduct all U.S. activities. Great-West Life & Annuity has established two growth markets. The Employee Benefits Division distributes products to employee groups, and the Financial Services Division primarily distributes products to individuals. The company is continuing to restructure a third market, Individual Life insurance, which is subject to over capacity and severe price competition.

Great-West Life Canada believes the new federal Insurance Companies Act will provide it with greater business powers and new opportunities for the provision of financial products and services. The company feels that in the future there will be fewer, larger and more efficient companies in the industry. These companies will identify their core businesses, shed unprofitable lines and rethink their approach to profitable ones. The Canadian operations during 1992 made progress in developing strategic plans, which are to be finalized in 1993, to put their focus on the markets and product lines that offer the most profit growth. The key will be to achieve superior customer service and lower costs.

In 1992, 61% of total revenues were from U.S. operations and 39% from Canada. Revenues by type of business in 1992: life insurance and annuity Canada, 14%; life insurance and annuity U.S., 29%; accident and health Canada, 11%; accident and health U.S., 12%; net investment income Canada, 14%; net investment income U.S., 20%.

Relative strength to TSE300 / Price / Volume (in 1000's of board lots) charts

Rank (Profit/Revenue/Assets)
31   24   16

James W. Burns
Chairman Of The Board

Raymond L. McFeetors
President & C.E.O. (Canada)

Orest T. Dackow
President

Mitchell T.G. Graye
Sr. V.P. & C.F.O.

Address
100 Osborne Street North
Winnipeg
MB
R3C 3A5
(204) 946-1190

Fax: (204) 946-2961
G0002778/F/13.5.2

GREAT-WEST LIFECO INC.

Exchanges	Price (Jun24'93)	16.75	Trailing P/E	14.88	Stock Symbol
TMW	Trailing Yield (%)	2.99	Trailing EPS	1.13	**GWO**

Period Ending	Dec92	Dec91	Dec90	Dec89	Dec88
Yearly Statistics					
Price-Close	14.75	14.00	12.25	16.25	12.00
Price-High	15.25	16.38	17.13	17.00	13.88
Price-Low	13.00	11.25	9.75	12.13	10.75
P/E-Close	13.80	9.50	8.28	11.68	9.72
Dividends per Share	0.50	0.50	0.50	0.50	0.50
Dividend Yield (%)	3.39	3.57	4.08	3.08	4.17
Sales per Share	67.94	64.93	72.30	66.41	63.68
EPS before extra. item	1.07	1.47	1.48	1.39	1.23
Cash Flow per Share	13.00	18.34	25.51	26.30	29.22
Book Value per Share	12.68	11.02	10.03	9.10	8.21
O/S Common Shares	78,834	78,826	78,813	78,943	77,340
Total Revenue	5,356,045	5,120,725	5,597,004	5,299,215	4,967,191
Income before extra.	89,822	116,173	116,682	108,727	95,578
Cash Flow	1,024,609	1,446,616	2,011,675	2,054,155	2,262,233
Debt/Equity	0.03	0.07	0.08	0.14	0.28
Return on Capital (%)	13.43	16.72	16.32	19.28	14.20
Ret. on Com. Equity (%)	9.02	14.01	15.47	16.07	15.35
% Change Profit	(22.7)	(0.4)	7.3	13.8	49.5
% Change Revenue	4.6	(8.5)	5.6	6.7	2.6
% Change Assets	11.5	(2.6)	10.7	9.7	11.2
Preferred Div. Coverage	16.2	np	np		
Total Div. Coverage	2.0	2.9	3.0		
5 YEAR RATIOS (%)					
Return on Capital	16.0	15.3	13.5		
Return on Com. Equity	14.0	14.3	13.3		
Profit Growth	7.0	16.8	6.2		
Revenue Growth	2.0	2.7	10.2		
Asset Growth	7.9	9.2	14.0		
BALANCE SHEET (mil)					
Cash	137	499	411		
Total Loans	7,789	7,736	7,990		
Net Fixed Assets	588	542	634		
Invest's & Advances	13,555	11,050	9,208		
Total Assets	22,701	20,368	20,904		
Total Deposits	0	0	0		
Insurance Liability	20,159	18,205	16,958		
Long Term Debt	36	61	65		
Total Liabilities	21,501	19,499	20,114		
Total Equity	1,199	868	790		
Total Liab. & Equity	22,701	20,368	20,904		
CAPITAL (mil)					
Total Debt	36	61	65		
Preferred Equity	200	0	0		
Common Equity	999	868	790		

Business:

GREAT-WEST LIFECO INC. is a holding company. It owns 99.4% of the outstanding common shares of Great-West Life Assurance Co. of Winnipeg. In turn, Power Financial Corp. of Montreal owns 86.4% of Great-West Lifeco Inc.'s issued and outstanding common shares.

Date	EPS	DPS	Tot Rev	Inc Bex
Mar 93	0.42	0.13	1,415,058	37,456
Dec 92	0.00	0.13	1,460,209	3,863
Sep 92	0.37	0.13	1,268,173	31,206
Jun 92	0.33	0.13	1,312,331	26,061
Mar 92	0.36	0.13	1,315,332	28,692
Dec 91	0.45	0.13	1,187,710	35,553
Sep 91	0.35	0.13	1,268,716	27,354
Jun 91	0.38	0.13	1,289,108	29,948

Synopsis:

Great-West Lifeco's results in 1992 were favorably affected by Individual disability income experience in Canada and strong Group life and health results in the United States. The results were offset by a deterioration of Individual mortality experience in the U.S., and weakened margins on investment related business and association assessments resulting from insurance company failures in both countries.

Great-West Lifeco owns 99.4% of the outstanding common shares of Great-West Life Assurance Company. Lifeco is not restricted to investing in Great-West Life and may make other investments in the future.

The breakdown of revenue in 1992 by type was: premium income Canada, 25%; premium income U.S., 41%; net investment income Canada, 14%; net investment income U.S., 20%.

Relative strength to TSE300 / Price / Volume (in 1000's of board lots) chart

Rank (Profit/Revenue/Assets)		
39	23	15

James W. Burns
Chairman Of The Board

Orest T. Dackow
President & C.E.O.

Jack A. Miller
Vice President, Finance

Address
100 Osborne Street North
Winnipeg
MB
R3C 3A5
(204) 946-1190

Fax: (204) 946-2961
01000550/F/13.5.2

For further company information, call Globe Information Services 1-800-268-9128 or (416)585-5345

IMPERIAL LIFE ASSURANCE COMPANY OF CANADA (THE)

Exchanges	Price (Jun24'93)		25.00	Trailing P/E		nc	Stock Symbol
TM	Trailing Yield (%)		nc	Trailing EPS		7.82	**IL.PR.C**

Period Ending	Dec92	Dec91	Dec90	Dec89	Dec88
Yearly Statistics					
Price-Close	24.75	24.00	22.25	23.00	23.25
Price-High	25.25	24.38	23.88	24.13	24.88
Price-Low	23.25	21.75	21.00	22.88	23.25
P/E-Close	nc	nc	nc	nc	nc
Dividends per Share	nc	nc	nc	nc	nc
Dividend Yield (%)	nc	nc	nc	nc	nc
Sales per Share	691.84	695.79	786.17	768.96	834.12
EPS before extra. item	8.04	16.31	2.77	11.98	0.00
Cash Flow per Share	74.05	150.23	116.44	115.02	215.81
Book Value per Share	159.29	163.68	116.62	105.32	150.52
O/S Common Shares	1,634	1,634	1,634	1,433	1,433
Total Revenue	1,130,303	1,136,757	1,157,686	1,101,809	1,195,178
Income before extra.	18,393	32,394	11,346	25,517	21,351
Cash Flow	120,978	245,443	171,460	164,805	309,226
Debt/Equity	0.43	0.45	0.69	1.03	1.06
Return on Capital (%)	6.73	7.27	3.38	4.30	4.16
Ret. on Com. Equity (%)	4.98	11.64	2.39	9.36	5.92
% Change Profit	(43.2)	185.5	(55.5)	19.5	(52.1)
% Change Revenue	(0.6)	(1.8)	5.1	(7.8)	13.7
% Change Assets	3.2	(33.1)	5.1	2.1	(0.2)

Preferred Div. Coverage	3.5	5.6	1.6
Total Div. Coverage	1.9	1.5	1.0

5 YEAR RATIOS (%)			
Return on Capital	5.2	5.8	7.2
Return on Com. Equity	6.9	9.6	10.3
Profit Growth	(16.3)	0.0	(7.7)
Revenue Growth	1.4	4.6	4.4
Asset Growth	(5.9)	(3.4)	13.3

BALANCE SHEET (000)			
Cash	2,331,061	210,469	283,495
Total Loans	1,602,278	1,563,360	1,482,412
Net Fixed Assets	310,453	309,923	298,972
Invest's & Advances	0	2,010,511	1,856,404
Total Assets	4,442,623	4,305,669	6,439,801
Total Deposits	0	0	0
Insurance Liability	3,440,994	3,316,791	3,402,471
Long Term Debt	158,581	155,847	32,313
Total Liabilities	4,070,789	3,961,656	6,172,674
Total Equity	371,834	344,013	267,127
Total Liab. & Equity	4,442,623	4,305,669	6,439,801

CAPITAL (000)			
Total Debt	158,581	155,847	183,515
Preferred Equity	111,600	76,600	76,600
Common Equity	260,234	267,413	190,527

Business:

IMPERIAL LIFE ASSURANCE CO. OF CANADA issues a comprehensive line of life insurance and other financial products designed to meet the complex needs of individuals and businesses. It is a member of the Laurentian Group of companies, based in Montreal. Through subsidiaries the company has offices across Canada and in the United States, the Bahamas, the United Kingdom and Hong Kong.

Date	EPS	DPS	Tot Rev	Inc Bex
Mar 93	1.70	nc	300,892	5,624
Dec 92	3.38	nc	283,906	6,834
Sep 92	1.75	nc	284,912	4,129
Jun 92	0.99	nc	259,001	2,956
Mar 92	1.92	nc	296,860	4,474
Dec 91	8.84	nc	287,815	15,817
Sep 91	2.34	nc	252,501	5,249
Jun 91	2.05	nc	274,837	4,802

Synopsis:

The new Insurance Companies Act (ICA), which introduced the prudent person concept for investments replaces a prescribed list of investments. The ICA also allows insurance companies to own a bank or trust company. The Imperial Life Insurance Company has no current plans to enter the banking or trust business.

Imperial Life does not expect head-on competition with the banking sector, because its corporate strategy is to target higher-end life insurance, which it believes is outside the bank's insurance market. The company also feels it is uniquely positioned to adapt to the potential new market, because it is part of the Laurentian Group of companies, which owns 64% of the Laurentian Bank.

Imperial Life purchased Laurentian Life Insurance Company of Canada in January 1993 for $18-million. Laurentian Life will continue as a separate division of Imperial and will operate the mass marketing life insurance operation of Imperial Life. The merger will allow the company to utilize unused tax deductions.

The company's operations in all countries have been effected by the economic recession and increased loan loss provisions were required in 1992. Imperial is responding by instituting cost reduction initiatives. In March 1993, Imperial announced staff layoffs designed to reduce 1993 operating costs by $7-million. A $2.5-million charge will be taken related to the staff reduction program.

In fiscal 1991, Imperial earned 64% of its revenues from life insurance premiums and the remainder from investment income. The 1992 breakdown of total revenue (net operating income) by geographic segment was: Canada, 66% (29%); the United States, 14% (35%); and the United Kingdom, 20% (36%). The results for Canada include operations in the Bahamas and Hong Kong.

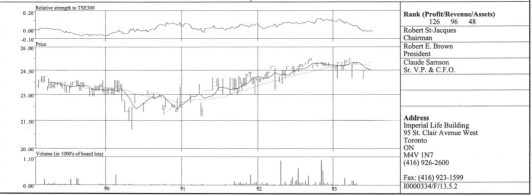

Rank (Profit/Revenue/Assets)		
126	96	48

Robert St-Jacques
Chairman
Robert E. Brown
President
Claude Samson
Sr. V.P. & C.F.O.

Address
Imperial Life Building
95 St. Clair Avenue West
Toronto
ON
M4V 1N7
(416) 926-2600

Fax: (416) 923-1599
I0000334/F/13.5.2

LONDON INSURANCE GROUP INC.

Exchanges	Price (Jun24'93)		24.50	Trailing P/E		9.14	Stock Symbol
TMV	Trailing Yield (%)		5.18	Trailing EPS		2.68	**LON**

Period Ending	Dec92	Dec91	Dec90	Dec89	Dec88
Yearly Statistics					
Price-Close	21.25	25.00	19.63	22.63	17.50
Price-High	26.25	25.50	22.88	24.25	19.13
Price-Low	18.50	19.25	18.00	17.25	15.13
P/E-Close	7.99	10.25	8.08	9.97	8.45
Dividends per Share	1.26	1.20	1.10	1.00	0.90
Dividend Yield (%)	5.93	4.80	5.61	4.42	5.14
Sales per Share	90.15	90.29	97.40	94.86	89.80
EPS before extra. item	2.66	2.44	2.43	2.27	2.07
Cash Flow per Share	31.12	26.47	26.12	31.28	31.57
Book Value per Share	23.09	21.74	20.20	18.92	17.68
O/S Common Shares	41,834	41,730	36,432	35,148	34,501
Total Revenue	3,769,000	3,605,000	3,487,000	3,312,000	3,075,000
Income before extra.	126,000	116,000	114,000	97,000	86,000
Cash Flow	1,301,000	1,057,000	935,000	1,092,000	1,081,000
Debt/Equity	0.56	0.57	0.56	0.74	1.42
Return on Capital (%)	8.48	8.79	8.98	8.42	10.87
Ret. on Com. Equity (%)	11.85	11.81	12.42	12.39	12.16
% Change Profit	8.6	1.8	17.5	12.8	12.7
% Change Revenue	4.5	3.4	5.3	7.7	14.4
% Change Assets	10.3	8.9	5.8	6.3	10.5
Preferred Div. Coverage	8.4	6.1	4.2		
Total Div. Coverage	1.9	1.7	1.7		

Business:

LONDON INSURANCE GROUP INC. is a life and general insurance company. It offers a full line of insurance products to individuals and groups in Canada and the United States. Operations include London Life Insurance Co., Holden Group Inc., Wellington Insurance, Meloche Monnex Inc. and Trivest Insurance Network. Trilon Financial Corp. owns 60% of the company.

Date	EPS	DPS	Tot Rev	Inc Bex
Mar 93	0.59	0.33	987,000	30,000
Dec 92	0.54	0.32	914,000	28,000
Sep 92	0.78	0.32	891,000	35,000
Jun 92	0.77	0.32	909,000	36,000
Mar 92	0.57	0.32	1,055,000	27,000
Dec 91	0.52	0.30	922,000	26,000
Sep 91	0.72	0.30	855,000	34,000
Jun 91	0.70	0.30	888,000	31,000

5 YEAR RATIOS (%)			
Return on Capital	9.1	10.0	10.4
Return on Com. Equity	12.1	12.1	12.1
Profit Growth	10.5	11.3	18.2
Revenue Growth	6.9	12.1	15.4
Asset Growth	8.2	9.7	13.3
BALANCE SHEET (mil)			
Cash	505	615	312
Total Loans	6,339	6,098	5,661
Net Fixed Assets	1,399	1,250	1,109
Invest's & Advances	6,612	5,467	5,196
Total Assets	15,585	14,136	12,981
Total Deposits	0	0	0
Insurance Liability	12,370	11,225	10,332
Long Term Debt	331	228	219
Total Liabilities	14,244	12,979	11,945
Total Equity	1,341	1,157	1,036
Total Liab. & Equity	15,585	14,136	12,981
CAPITAL (mil)			
Total Debt	756	659	585
Preferred Equity	375	250	300
Common Equity	966	907	736

Synopsis:

Trilon Financial Corp. said in April 1993 that London Insurance Group would remain as part of the Edper family. This was to stop speculation about a possible sale of additional assets by Trilon, following the sale of the bulk of its trust operations to the Royal Bank.

Both the federal and the Ontario governments have made changes to insurance laws that govern London Insurance's subsidiaries. The Ontario government is also considering further changes to its automobile and labor legislation.

London Insurance Group plans to continue in 1993 the objectives it put in place in 1992. These objectives are: to continue to expand its domestic base, with particular focus on market share of individual life insurance; to improve the results of all its businesses; and to look for opportunities to expand both in Canada and in the international marketplace.

London Life continued its emphasis on managing every line of its business to ensure ongoing profitability. The company forecasts continued profitability for the life insurance business. The long term nature of the underlying products and the size of the book of business permits earnings to be forcasted with reasonable confidence. The employee benefit business will be impacted by the timing and pace of economic recovery. Business growth will reflect business confidence and employment and wage levels. General insurance underwriting is not significantly impacted by economic factors. The uncertainty created by proposed legislative changes to the Ontario Motorist Protection Plan may have an impact on prices and profitability of the general insurance operation.

Percentages of 1992 revenues (net income) by business were: life insurance, 88% (69%); general insurance, 11% (10%); and investment, 1% (21%). Percentages of 1992 revenues (net income) by geographical distribution were: Canada, 83% (75%); the United States, 16% (5%); and other, 1% (20%).

Relative strength to TSE300 / Price / Volume (in 1000's of board lots)

Rank (Profit/Revenue/Assets)
28 35 20

Earl H. Orser
Chairman.
Gordon R. Cunningham
President & C.E.O.
Douglas S. Alexander
V.P. & C.F.O.

Address
255 Dufferin Avenue
London
ON
N6A 4K1
(416) 432-5281

Fax: (519) 661-0479
L0000064/F/13.5.2

Page	Company	$	Latest year end	Earnings per Share Actual	Estimate this year	Estimate next year
435	Alberta Natural Gas		9212	0.77	1.08	1.35
436	Atco Ltd.		9212	1.43	1.47	1.59
437	B.C. Pacific Capital		9212	0.04	n.a.	n.a.
438	Brascade Resources		9212	(1.15)	n.a.	n.a.
439	Brascan		9212	n.a.	0.25	0.90
440	BRL Enterprises		9212	0.35	n.a.	n.a.
441	Canadian Pacific Limited		9212	(0.65)	0.46	1.16
442	CanCapital		9212	(0.10)	n.a.	n.a.
443	Consolidated Enfield		9212	(3.71)	n.a.	n.a.
444	Counsel Corporation		9212	(6.78)	n.a.	n.a.
445	Crownx		9212	(0.49)	0.48	0.72
446	Federal Industries		9212	(1.49)	0.15	0.58
447	Great Lakes Power		9212	1.88	n.a.	n.a.
448	Imasco		9212	2.97	3.31	3.85
449	Jannock		9212	1.32	0.57	1.24
450	John Labatt		9304	1.64	1.99	2.15
451	Laidlaw	$US	9208	0.52	0.56	0.66
452	Noranda Inc.		9212	0.10	0.24	0.97
453	Onex Corporation		9212	0.36	0.59	1.03
454	Roman Corporation		9212	0.22	n.a.	n.a.
455	Scott's Hospitality		9204	0.70	0.54	0.67
456	Seagram	$US	9301	1.70	2.17	2.37
457	Sherrit Gordon		9212	0.06	0.21	0.71
458	Unigesco		9203	(0.03)	(0.28)	(0.23)
459	United Dominion Industries	$US	9212	0.46	0.91	1.39

Estimates from I/B/E/S Inc., 345 Hudson St., New York, NY 10014 (212) 243-3335. In Canada: 6 Lansing Square, Ste. 235, Willowdale, ON M2J 1T5 (416) 496-0977.

Management Companies

A Report on Business quarterly survey of 181 major reporting Canadian companies shows that after-tax earnings increased 8% in the first quarter of 1993 from a year ago. Moreover, 65% of the companies in the survey reported an increase in profits in the quarter. Profits are still very low, however.

The natural resource sector, fueled by rising natural gas and softwood lumber prices led the way with a 243% improvement from this time last year. This sector is not expected to continue to rise at this rate but the industry could see a 25% to 30% profit improvement for 1993.

Manufacturing profits soared 71% in the first quarter of 1993 compared with the same period last year, reflecting belt-tightening by many companies in the industry. Some analysts feel that the manufacturing sector, especially hard hit during the recession, could outperform other sectors this year. Among manufacturers, Imasco Ltd. of Montreal posted first-quarter profit of $66.5-million or 50 cents a share, up from $63.5-million or 48 cents a year earlier.

Merchandising profits in the first quarter jumped 101% compared with the same period last year. With consumer confidence improving the industry is experiencing a rebound in retail advertising.

In the service category, which includes telecommunications and publishers, profits fell 30% in the quarter.

According to the July 1993 *Report on Business 1000* magazine, management companies had an average one year return on capital of 0.74%. The average five year return on capital was 4.61%.

Multi-Industry Issues - Industry Report [Apr-13-1993]. PAINEWEBBER INC. reported by Modzelewski, J.

In 1992, multi-industry stocks were up 18% versus a 5% increase in the S&P 500. This multi-industry outperformance comes despite somewhat weak EPS in 1992 — EPS were down 5% on average versus a 25% increase in EPS for the S&P 500 universe. A modest U.S. economic rebound is expected, with real GDP increasing about 3.2% in 1993 and 2.8% in 1994, and operating EPS for the S&P 500 increasing about 12% in each year. Multi-industry companies that survived the "break-up 80s" emerged as leaner, stronger organizations with strong management teams. Many of the multi-industry companies have developed a strategy of growth through niche acquisitions in their core businesses. In addition, multi-industry companies with defense exposures are likely to use the cash flow from their defense businesses to fund other operations, and could even be sellers as consolidation continues in the defense business. [RN 1323092]

Industrial Companies - Industry Report [Apr-13-1993]. PAINEWEBBER INC. reported by Lustgarten, E.S.

Most industrial stocks have had a seasonal trading pattern during most years - strength in the early part and underperformance by and during the third calendar quarter. Unfolding fundamentals point to a repeat of that pattern in 1993. [RN 1323159]

Diversified Companies First Quarter '93 - Industry Report [Apr-2-1993] SHEARSON LEHMAN BROTHERS, INC. reported by Young, P.K.

In 1Q:93, the majority of a group of diversified companies should see good EPS gains. Seven of the 11 companies in the group are expected to report positive EPS comparisons that should also outpace the S&P 400's assumed 6% rise for the March 1993 quarter. [RN 1319538]

ALBERTA NATURAL GAS COMPANY LTD

Exchanges	Price (Jun24'93)	16.00	Trailing P/E	533.33	Stock Symbol
TMZV	Trailing Yield (%)	4.25	Trailing EPS	0.03	**ANG**

Period Ending	Dec92	Dec91	Dec90	Dec89	Dec88
Yearly Statistics					
Price-Close	15.75	13.88	12.88	19.00	14.50
Price-High	16.00	17.25	19.50	19.13	16.25
Price-Low	12.00	12.38	11.50	14.25	12.87
P/E-Close	nm	nm	10.64	17.12	17.06
Dividends per Share	0.68	0.68	0.68	0.68	0.68
Dividend Yield (%)	4.32	4.90	5.28	3.58	4.69
Sales per Share	22.11	21.39	17.70	17.14	16.89
EPS before extra. item	(0.10)	(2.00)	1.21	1.11	0.85
Cash Flow per Share	1.87	1.81	2.97	2.61	2.31
Book Value per Share	6.61	5.02	7.94	7.15	6.81
O/S Common Shares	25,654	20,990	21,233	21,359	21,332
Total Revenue	487,403	453,383	382,594	367,830	344,306
Income before extra.	(2,276)	(42,130)	25,728	23,623	17,025
Cash Flow	40,837	38,020	63,166	55,736	46,365
Debt/Equity	1.14	2.36	1.16	1.02	1.16
Return on Capital (%)	9.07	(2.62)	18.57	18.44	13.76
Ret. on Com. Equity (%)	(1.66)	(30.76)	16.02	15.86	12.18
% Change Profit	94.6	(263.8)	8.9	38.8	14.3
% Change Revenue	7.5	18.5	4.0	6.8	6.0
% Change Assets	15.2	(3.1)	18.1	2.5	(2.5)
Preferred Div. Coverage	np	np	np		
Total Div. Coverage	0.0	0.0	1.8		
Interest Coverage	1.7	0.0	3.5		
Current Ratio	1.0	0.9	2.1		
Operating Margin	9.9	9.9	16.0		
Asset Turnover	0.9	1.0	0.8		
5 YEAR RATIOS (%)					
Return on Capital	11.4	12.7	16.7		
Return on Com. Equity	2.3	4.9	13.6		
Profit Growth	na	na	0.6		
Revenue Growth	8.4	7.5	0.2		
Asset Growth	5.6	4.1	5.9		
BALANCE SHEET (000)					
Cash	39,501	10,508	15,152		
Current Assets	179,010	111,411	143,684		
Net Fixed Assets	289,752	211,169	206,902		
Invest's & Advances	18,489	20,655	21,359		
Total Assets	509,272	441,919	455,886		
Short Term Debt	82,009	49,879	16,258		
Current Liabilities	184,833	119,123	67,334		
Long Term Debt	111,813	198,725	178,364		
Total Liabilities	339,796	336,527	287,358		
Total Equity	169,476	105,392	168,528		
Total Liab. & Equity	509,272	441,919	455,886		
CAPITAL (000)					
Total Debt	193,822	248,604	194,622		
Preferred Equity	0	0	0		
Common Equity	169,476	105,392	168,528		

Business:

ALBERTA NATURAL GAS CO. LTD. (ANG) operates in four business segments: pipelines; extraction; marketing; and chemicals. ANG owns and operates gas pipelines in Alberta and British Columbia. The extaction plant is located near Cochrane, AB. Subsidiary Angus Chemical Company makes and markets nitroparrafin products. TransCanada PipeLines Limited owns 49.98% of the of ANG's shares.

Date	EPS	DPS	Tot Rev	Inc Bex
Mar 93	0.20	0.17	142,556	5,026
Dec 92	(0.03)	0.17	154,550	(885)
Sep 92	0.23	0.17	111,118	4,952
Jun 92	(0.37)	0.17	107,730	(7,849)
Mar 92	0.07	0.17	119,281	1,506
Dec 91	0.50	0.17	109,344	10,387
Sep 91	0.00	0.17	100,565	150
Jun 91	0.37	0.17	112,023	7,957

Synopsis:

Alberta Natural Gas Company Ltd. (ANG) has established three priorities for 1993: to complete its pipeline expansion project, to begin the Cochrane extraction plant recommissioning project, and to reacquire markets that subsidiary Angus Chemical Co. had lost. ANG and Foothills Pipe Lines (South B.C.) Ltd., a company in which ANG holds a 49% interest, co-sponsored the pipeline expansion project. Of the total capital cost of $224-million, $96-million is for compression equipment belonging to ANG, and $128-million is for pipeline segments belonging to Foothills. The expansion will increase the capacity of the ANG and Foothills pipeline system by more than 50%, allowing the delivery of an additional 24.7 million cubic metres a day.

The recommission and upgrade of the Cochrane plant will allow it to process the larger volume of natural gas that will come from the pipeline expansion. Angus Chemical rebuilt its plant in Louisiana during 1992 and is regaining markets which suffered from shortages while the plant was closed.

ANG sold Angus Fine Chemicals Ltd. in 1992. The wholly owned subsidiary, located in Ireland, was sold for approximately $43-million (U.S.). The sale resulted in a $16.5-million loss on the sale and an operating loss up to the date of the sale of $3.6-million. Angus Chemical management can now focus on growth within its core nitroparaffins business with the sale of the fine chemicals operation.

Contributions to operating revenue (operating income) for fiscal 1992 by industry segment were: natural gas processing, 28% (56%); natural gas and natural gas liquids (NGL) marketing, 43% (30%); pipeline transport, 6% (14%); chemicals, 24% (19%); and eliminations and other, -1% (-19%). Contributions to operating revenue (operating income) for fiscal 1991 by industry segment were: natural gas processing, 32% (72%); natural gas and NGL marketing, 41% (11%); pipeline transport, 7% (12%); chemicals, 22% (26%); and eliminations and other, -2% (-21%).

Relative strength to TSE300 / Price / Volume (in 1000's of board lots)

Rank (Profit/Revenue/Assets)
767   157   208

Norman E. Wagner
Chairman
John M. Beddome
President & C.E.O.
Wayne E. Lunt
Sr. V.P., C.F.O. & Treasurer

Address
Suite 2900
240 - 4th Avenue S.W.
Calgary
AB
T2P 4L7
(403) 691-7777

Fax: (403) 691-7893
A0004223/G/14.0

ATCO LTD.

Exchanges	Price (Jun24'93)	13.37	Trailing P/E	8.41	Stock Symbol
TMZ	Trailing Yield (%)	1.79	Trailing EPS	1.59	**ACO.X**

Period Ending	Dec92	Dec91	Dec90	Dec89	Dec88
Yearly Statistics					
Price-Close	12.25	12.00	12.00	10.63	7.63
Price-High	12.63	14.25	12.25	11.13	10.38
Price-Low	10.50	11.00	9.38	7.75	7.50
P/E-Close	8.57	9.16	10.00	10.63	nm
Dividends per Share	0.24	0.24	0.24	0.20	0.20
Dividend Yield (%)	1.96	2.00	2.00	1.88	2.62
Sales per Share	51.51	47.99	47.63	45.10	44.21
EPS before extra. item	1.43	1.31	1.20	1.00	(0.96)
Cash Flow per Share	11.67	10.02	9.49	9.04	8.59
Book Value per Share	13.03	11.80	10.78	9.93	9.12
O/S Common Shares	30,297	30,297	30,275	30,261	30,259
Total Revenue	1,595,327	1,497,968	1,489,698	1,414,507	1,383,936
Income before extra.	43,386	39,738	41,542	58,017	(2,492)
Cash Flow	353,580	303,676	287,351	273,488	259,841
Debt/Equity	3.67	3.79	4.08	3.40	3.23
Return on Capital (%)	17.21	16.09	17.32	19.09	15.84
Ret. on Com. Equity (%)	11.53	11.57	11.63	10.44	(10.80)
% Change Profit	9.2	(4.3)	(28.4)	2,428.1	71.9
% Change Revenue	6.5	0.6	5.3	2.2	(0.7)
% Change Assets	5.0	(1.5)	4.5	7.9	3.0
Preferred Div. Coverage	np	np	8.1		
Total Div. Coverage	6.0	5.3	3.4		
Interest Coverage	2.1	1.8	2.0		
Current Ratio	1.1	1.1	1.1		
Operating Margin	26.8	25.1	24.8		
Asset Turnover	0.4	0.4	0.4		
5 YEAR RATIOS (%)					
Return on Capital	17.1	17.2	18.3		
Return on Com. Equity	6.9	2.0	1.6		
Profit Growth	100.6	(5.3)	(2.7)		
Revenue Growth	2.7	(0.9)	(1.4)		
Asset Growth	3.6	1.4	1.4		
BALANCE SHEET (000)					
Cash	14,437	26,544	5,246		
Current Assets	329,702	297,274	301,768		
Net Fixed Assets	3,125,540	2,968,341	3,018,372		
Invest's & Advances	38,749	45,055	39,629		
Total Assets	3,632,325	3,460,009	3,512,956		
Short Term Debt	44,074	71,016	49,264		
Current Liabilities	289,028	280,676	286,098		
Long Term Debt	1,402,852	1,283,639	1,302,942		
Total Liabilities	3,237,478	3,102,419	3,181,669		
Total Equity	394,847	357,590	331,287		
Total Liab. & Equity	3,632,325	3,460,009	3,512,956		
CAPITAL (000)					
Total Debt	1,446,926	1,354,655	1,352,206		
Preferred Equity	0	0	5,000		
Common Equity	394,847	357,590	326,287		

Business:

ATCO LTD. is a diversified company with three operating groups. Atco Enterprises Ltd. of Calgary makes relocatable shelters for lease or sale and offers contract drilling services. Atcor Ltd. of Calgary engages in oil and gas exploration and production in Western Canada and the Canadian North. Canadian Utilities Ltd. of Edmonton, in which the company has a 50.1% interest, is a gas and electric utility.

Date	EPS	DPS	Tot Rev	Inc Bex
Mar 93	0.70	0.06	535,077	26,926
Dec 92	0.59	0.06	462,713	17,874
Sep 92	0.14	0.06	333,159	10,223
Jun 92	0.16	0.06	347,241	10,583
Mar 92	0.54	0.06	443,346	22,145
Dec 91	0.64	0.06	397,799	19,367
Sep 91	0.14	0.06	308,529	9,904
Jun 91	0.04	0.06	324,905	7,120

Synopsis:

ATCO Ltd. continues to spend more time and effort on foreign projects. A manufacturing plant in Hungary, which started production in May 1993, will supply Atco-built housing units to North American companies operating in the former Soviet Union. As well, ATCO continues to look for new project opportunities in Mexico. It is scouting for sites for a manufacturing plant in Mexico. The plant would produce industrial housing products that could be exported to South America. ATCO is also evaluating the market for technical expertise in water and natural gas distribution and independent power generation.

ATCOR Resources Ltd. acquired all of the issued and outstanding shares of Altex Resources Ltd. The approximately 15.7 million shares of Altex were exchanged on the basis of 0.404 Class A Non-Voting shares of ATCOR for each Altex share. Altex is involved in oil and gas exploration and production. The acquisition is expected to add approximately 750 barrels a day of crude oil and natural gas liquids and approximately 255 thousand cubic metres a day of natural gas to ATCOR's 1993 production, and $6-million to its cash flow. ATCOR's production of crude oil and natural gas liquids was 2,617 barrels per day in 1992 and natural gas production was approximately 785,000 cubic metres a day in 1992.

1993 capital expenditures are expected to total $346-million, with financing being provided from four sources. Internal sources are expected to provide $235-million, with $85-million from external sources, $23-million from contributions in aid of construction and $3-million from other sources.

ATCO distributed the shares of Akita Drilling Ltd., formerly ATCO Drilling Ltd., to the shareholders of ATCO Ltd. effective January 1, 1993.

Contributions to revenues (operating profit) in 1992 by industry were: electric power, 36% (60%); natural gas, 41% (30%); manufacturing and leasing, 7% (5%); oil and gas, 9% (4%); and other, 7% (1%).

Relative strength to TSE300 / Price / Volume (in 1000's of board lots)

Rank (Profit/Revenue/Assets)		
68	76	58

R.D. Southern
Chairman, President & C.E.O.
C.S. Richardson
Sr. V.P., Finance & C.F.O.

Address
1600 Canadian Western Centre
909 - 11th Avenue S.W.
Calgary
AB
T2R 1N6
(403) 292-7500

Fax: (403) 292-7507
A0015607/G/14.0

B.C. PACIFIC CAPITAL CORPORATION

Exchanges	Price (Jun24'93)	0.14	Trailing P/E	3.33	Stock Symbol
V	Trailing Yield (%)	0.00	Trailing EPS	0.04	**BPQ.A**

Period Ending	Dec92	Dec91	Dec90	Dec89	Dec88
Yearly Statistics					
Price-Close	0.18	0.35	0.26	1.20	0.66
Price-High	0.39	0.45	1.24	1.89	1.75
Price-Low	0.04	0.19	0.20	0.60	0.50
P/E-Close	4.39	8.33	4.91	21.05	6.00
Dividends per Share	0.00	0.00	0.00	0.00	0.00
Dividend Yield (%)	0.00	0.00	0.00	0.00	0.00
Sales per Share	2.64	0.23	0.29	0.24	0.76
EPS before extra. item	0.04	0.04	0.05	0.06	0.11
Cash Flow per Share	1.21	0.07	0.08	0.08	0.16
Book Value per Share	(5.47)	(5.52)	(5.53)	(5.72)	(5.93)
O/S Common Shares	13,487	13,474	13,634	13,634	13,634
Total Revenue	35,598	44,648	56,228	40,345	21,705
Income before extra.	16,259	16,973	14,625	13,391	4,499
Cash Flow	16,375	13,986	14,625	13,391	4,499
Debt/Equity	1.09	1.47	4.22	3.60	na
Return on Capital (%)	10.15	11.52	15.47	12.95	13.62
Ret. on Com. Equity (%)	na	na	na	na	na
% Change Profit	(4.2)	16.1	9.2	197.6	120.6
% Change Revenue	(20.3)	(20.6)	39.4	85.9	6,083.8
% Change Assets	2.5	(4.2)	15.3	15.8	1,036.4
Preferred Div. Coverage	1.0	1.1	1.2		
Total Div. Coverage	1.0	1.1	1.2		
Interest Coverage	1.9	1.6	1.4		
Current Ratio	0.0	0.0	0.0		
Operating Margin	98.1	98.3	99.2		
Asset Turnover	0.1	0.1	0.1		
5 YEAR RATIOS (%)					
Return on Capital	12.7	7.2	(6.8)		
Return on Com. Equity	na	na	na		
Profit Growth	51.4	73.4	na		
Revenue Growth	151.9	203.0	(38.6)		
Asset Growth	71.6	29.6	(11.4)		
BALANCE SHEET (000)					
Cash	165	176	278		
Current Assets	165	176	7,110		
Net Fixed Assets	0	2,207	13,207		
Invest's & Advances	380,321	370,513	368,950		
Total Assets	382,389	372,896	389,267		
Short Term Debt	0	67,834	174,401		
Current Liabilities	66,849	68,133	174,409		
Long Term Debt	164,291	154,171	140,213		
Total Liabilities	231,140	222,304	314,622		
Total Equity	151,249	150,592	74,645		
Total Liab. & Equity	382,389	372,896	389,267		
CAPITAL (000)					
Total Debt	164,291	222,005	314,614		
Preferred Equity	225,000	225,000	150,000		
Common Equity	(73,751)	(74,408)	(75,355)		

Business:

B.C. PACIFIC CAPITAL CORP. is a British Columbia based financial and investment corporation providing management services to corporations encountering financial difficulties, considering merger or acquisition initiatives or requiring operational evaluations. The company also owns a 49% interest in BRL Enterprises Inc. of Calgary, an oil and gas exploration and investment company.

Date	EPS	DPS	Tot Rev	Inc Bex
Mar 93	0.01	0.00	6,660	3,988
Dec 92	0.02	0.00	10,180	4,303
Sep 92	0.01	0.00	9,272	3,958
Jun 92	0.00	0.00	6,424	3,920
Mar 92	0.01	0.00	9,722	4,078
Dec 91	0.01	0.00	11,386	4,501
Sep 91	0.01	0.00	8,176	4,243
Jun 91	0.02	0.00	13,528	5,160

Synopsis:

B.C. Pacific Capital Corporation will continue to focus on providing management and financial advice to businesses encountering financial difficulties and helping clients repay debt obligations through new capital issues or divestiture of assets. In 1992, B.C. Pacific helped a mining company develop a reorganization and restructuring plan and advised a United States based savings bank on alternative capital structures that meet the regulatory requirements.

MGS Partnership, in which B.C. Pacific has a 50% interest, is managed by Graywood Developments Limited and is involved in four real estate projects. MGS has two condominium projects, Number One York Quay has 812 units while Landmark of Thornhill involves 946 units. Stoneridge Manor is a 240 unit residential development project in suburban Toronto, and Westminster Pier a 880 unit project in suburban Vancouver.

The holder of B.C. Pacific Capital's secured debt has agreed to defer repayment of principal and interest until February 1994. The secured debt totaled approximately $151.8-million at the end of the first quarter of 1993. The average effective interest rate on the secured debt in effect at 1992 year-end was 6.75% compared to 10.85% at December 31, 1992. Loans and other payables were about $12.2-million at March 31, 1993.

The lower net income in the first quarter of 1993, compared to the same period in 1992, reflects lower revenues only partially offset by lower interest costs. The lower revenue is due to a reduction in investments of approximately $68-million from $227.6-million at 1992 year-end, to $159.7-million at the end of the first quarter of 1993.

Allocation of total assets at December 31, 1992, by category was: banking and financial assets (net), 24.7%; mining, 21.6%; forest products, 9.6%; oil and gas, 7.2%; real estate, 19.3%; financial services, 8.3%; utility and other, 8.2%; and insurance, 1.1%.

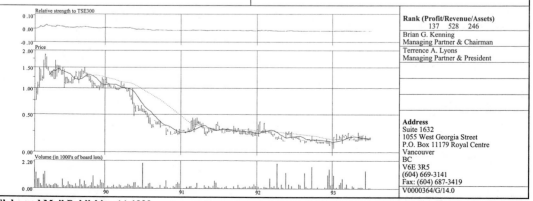

Rank (Profit/Revenue/Assets)
137   528   246

Brian G. Kenning
Managing Partner & Chairman

Terrence A. Lyons
Managing Partner & President

Address
Suite 1632
1055 West Georgia Street
P.O. Box 11179 Royal Centre
Vancouver
BC
V6E 3R5
(604) 669-3141
Fax: (604) 687-3419

V0000364/G/14.0

BRASCADE RESOURCES INC.

Exchanges	Price (Jun24'93)	34.00	Trailing P/E	nc	Stock Symbol
TV	Trailing Yield (%)	nc	Trailing EPS	(1.48)	BCA.PR.A

Period Ending	Dec92	Dec91	Dec90	Dec89	Dec88
Yearly Statistics					
Price-Close	35.00	36.00	38.00	38.25	39.25
Price-High	37.38	39.13	40.50	40.00	40.38
Price-Low	30.00	29.00	32.00	38.25	38.50
P/E-Close	nc	nc	nc	nc	nc
Dividends per Share	nc	nc	nc	nc	nc
Dividend Yield (%)	nc	nc	nc	nc	nc
Sales per Share	1.30	1.66	2.19	3.41	3.62
EPS before extra. item	(1.15)	(3.34)	(1.89)	1.33	0.21
Cash Flow per Share	1.39	1.03	1.79	2.09	2.24
Book Value per Share	11.64	12.78	17.24	19.14	17.81
O/S Common Shares	66,998	66,999	51,407	51,407	51,407
Total Revenue	120,200	83,400	183,000	378,200	404,700
Income before extra.	(20,500)	(123,500)	(36,300)	127,300	63,900
Cash Flow	93,000	60,800	92,200	107,600	115,200
Debt/Equity	0.13	0.33	0.27	0.21	0.26
Return on Capital (%)	0.20	(3.15)	(0.78)	8.27	4.89
Ret. on Com. Equity (%)	(9.38)	(20.67)	(10.41)	7.17	1.18
% Change Profit	83.4	(240.2)	(128.5)	99.2	(41.2)
% Change Revenue	44.1	(54.4)	(51.6)	(6.5)	26.9
% Change Assets	(23.7)	(0.3)	(8.8)	(1.7)	6.1

Preferred Div. Coverage	0.0	0.0	0.0
Total Div. Coverage	0.0	0.0	0.0
Interest Coverage	0.2	0.0	0.0
Current Ratio	1.0	3.3	9.1
Operating Margin	(26.2)	(37.2)	(15.2)
Asset Turnover	0.0	0.0	0.0
5 YEAR RATIOS (%)			
Return on Capital	1.9	3.4	3.0
Return on Com. Equity	(6.4)	(3.1)	(2.7)
Profit Growth	na	na	na
Revenue Growth	(17.8)	(1.0)	36.9
Asset Growth	(6.3)	(0.7)	(0.6)
BALANCE SHEET (000)			
Cash	45,400	299,000	144,200
Current Assets	83,600	324,000	166,300
Net Fixed Assets	173,700	186,400	210,300
Invest's & Advances	1,585,500	1,905,100	2,046,900
Total Assets	1,842,800	2,415,500	2,423,500
Short Term Debt	65,000	87,200	2,300
Current Liabilities	86,600	98,300	18,300
Long Term Debt	125,700	420,900	421,000
Total Liabilities	377,800	870,900	842,900
Total Equity	1,465,000	1,544,600	1,580,600
Total Liab. & Equity	1,842,800	2,415,500	2,423,500
CAPITAL (000)			
Total Debt	190,700	508,100	423,300
Preferred Equity	685,400	688,300	694,200
Common Equity	779,600	856,300	886,400

Business:

BRASCADE RESOURCES INC. is a management company. It has a 36% equity interest in Noranda Inc. of Toronto, a natural resources company, and a 74% interest in Westmin Resources Ltd. of Vancouver, a mining company.

Date	EPS	DPS	Tot Rev	Inc Bex
Mar 93	(0.60)	nc	2,600	(26,600)
Dec 92	(0.48)	nc	16,200	(18,100)
Sep 92	(0.48)	nc	11,900	(17,700)
Jun 92	0.08	nc	57,900	19,700
Mar 92	(0.27)	nc	35,100	(4,400)
Dec 91	(1.11)	nc	(5,000)	(51,200)
Sep 91	(1.12)	nc	10,300	(43,600)
Jun 91	(0.60)	nc	37,700	(16,300)

Synopsis:

Brascade Resources' first quarter results were affected by the loss recorded by Noranda Forests Inc.'s sale of MacMillan Bloedel Limited. Prices for building products and natural gas rose, but prices for other commodities declined. Brascade is benefiting from low interest and exchange rates.

Westmin Resources Limited received $250-million on the sale of the Noranda Series E preferred shares it previously received in exchange for its energy assets. Proceeds from the sale along with the cash flow from operations were used to acquire $9-million of new plant and equipment, repurchase $3-million of Brascade's own preferred shares as part of its redemption obligations, and to reduce minority interests by $188-million. Westmin was also able to reduce its debt by $295-million with the funds. In 1992 Brascade reinvested three quarterly dividends in Westmin to acquire $5-million worth of common shares.

Brascade's share of Noranda Inc.'s income was $18.5-million for purposes of the 1992 income statement. The equity investment in Noranda totaled approximately $1.52-billion on the 1992 balance sheet.

Relative strength to TSE300

Price

Volume (in 1000's of board lots)

Rank (Profit/Revenue/Assets)
924   341   99

Paul M. Marshall
Chairman & President

Edward C. Kress
Vice President, Finance

Address
BCE Place
181 Bay Street
Suite 4400, P.O. Box 762
Toronto
ON
M5J 2T3
(416) 363-9491
Fax: (416) 363-2856
B0003263/G/14.0

For further company information, call Globe Information Services 1-800-268-9128 or (416)585-5345

BRASCAN LIMITED

Exchanges	Price (Jun24'93)	12.25	Trailing P/E	nm	Stock Symbol
TMA	Trailing Yield (%)	8.49	Trailing EPS	(0.09)	**BL.A**

Period Ending	Dec92	Dec91	Dec90	Dec89	Dec88
Yearly Statistics					
Price-Close	13.75	18.25	15.63	27.00	27.00
Price-High	20.00	20.38	26.25	32.38	29.00
Price-Low	12.50	14.25	14.00	26.38	23.50
P/E-Close	nm	nm	39.06	9.31	9.82
Dividends per Share	1.04	1.04	1.04	1.00	0.94
Dividend Yield (%)	7.56	5.70	6.66	3.70	3.48
Sales per Share	na	na	na	na	na
EPS before extra. item	(1.56)	(0.60)	0.40	2.90	2.75
Cash Flow per Share	2.30	2.06	2.77	2.96	2.85
Book Value per Share	18.51	21.20	23.08	23.72	21.84
O/S Common Shares	87,773	87,658	81,213	80,913	80,743
Total Revenue	114,400	249,200	373,100	617,900	628,200
Income before extra.	(113,400)	(17,700)	80,300	280,800	262,800
Cash Flow	201,700	173,700	225,200	238,800	230,300
Debt/Equity	0.67	0.60	0.58	0.43	0.21
Return on Capital (%)	(1.15)	2.78	5.48	11.40	11.22
Ret. on Com. Equity (%)	(7.86)	(2.74)	1.69	12.70	13.11
% Change Profit	(540.7)	(122.0)	(71.4)	6.8	50.6
% Change Revenue	(54.1)	(33.2)	(39.6)	(1.6)	40.7
% Change Assets	(6.2)	(8.3)	(4.6)	23.5	(5.9)

Preferred Div. Coverage	0.0	0.0	1.7
Total Div. Coverage	0.0	0.0	0.6
Interest Coverage	0.0	0.9	1.7
Current Ratio	6.3	8.4	12.9
Operating Margin	na	na	na
Asset Turnover	na	na	na
5 YEAR RATIOS (%)			
Return on Capital	5.9	7.9	8.8
Return on Com. Equity	3.4	6.9	9.1
Profit Growth	na	na	(6.7)
Revenue Growth	(23.9)	(2.8)	5.5
Asset Growth	(0.9)	4.2	8.9
BALANCE SHEET (000)			
Cash	323,800	459,900	456,500
Current Assets	346,800	470,800	840,400
Net Fixed Assets	173,800	187,000	210,800
Invest's & Advances	4,383,300	4,565,800	4,637,300
Total Assets	4,920,300	5,242,700	5,718,200
Short Term Debt	1,700	3,100	18,100
Current Liabilities	54,800	55,800	65,400
Long Term Debt	1,340,600	1,345,500	1,384,300
Total Liabilities	2,918,500	3,005,700	3,307,300
Total Equity	2,001,800	2,237,000	2,410,900
Total Liab. & Equity	4,920,300	5,242,700	5,718,200
CAPITAL (000)			
Total Debt	1,342,300	1,348,600	1,402,400
Preferred Equity	377,300	378,600	536,900
Common Equity	1,624,500	1,858,400	1,874,000

Business:

BRASCAN LTD. is a diversified management company with operating companies in the natural resources, financial services and utility sectors. The company has equity interests in Noranda Inc., Westmin Resources Ltd., Trilon Financial Corp. and Great Lakes Power Inc.

Date	EPS	DPS	Tot Rev	Inc Bex
Mar 93	1.49	0.26	372,900	136,700
Dec 92	(0.99)	0.26	(28,800)	(80,700)
Sep 92	(0.61)	0.26	56,600	(48,300)
Jun 92	0.02	0.26	66,800	8,300
Mar 92	0.02	0.26	68,100	7,300
Dec 91	(0.57)	0.26	24,000	(42,600)
Sep 91	(0.05)	0.26	63,500	3,500
Jun 91	0.01	0.26	71,600	9,800

Synopsis:

Brascan has sold its 38% interest in John Labatt for $993-million, recording a pre-tax gain of approximately $385-million. Noranda Forest sold its 49% interest in MacMillan Bloedel for $971-million. Royal Trustco reached an agreement in principle to sell its operating subsidiaries to The Royal Bank of Canada. Brascan and its affiliates continue to pursue three key operating priorities established in 1991: simplify operations through the sale of non-core assets; strengthen financial position; and improve productivity. The consolidation of corporate structure is being achieved through reducing the number of public companies in the group.

Brascan's natural resource operations intend to reduce unit costs through research and development and by best utilizing available technology. The operations are also placing emphasis on increasing long-life reserves of viable resource products through exploration, development and acquisition. The Trilon group will focus on those operations that can provide a significant competitive advantage in carefully selected markets. The steady growth from existing insurance and commercial banking operations is expected to help the group build a high quality, stable earnings base. The selective expansion of investment banking operations and cost reductions and agent training in the real estate brokerage operations are also expected to assist in accomplishing this goal. Brascan plans to increase its utility investments through expansion and acquisition to capitalize on its historical strengths in this segment and to increase the stable portion of its earning base.

Brascan's unaudited share of group revenues (proportional share of income before unallocated expenses) by industry segment in 1992 was: natural resources, 54% (37%); consumer products, 19% (25%); financial services, 25% (28%); utilities and other operations, 2% (10%). Brascan's unaudited share of group revenues (proportional share of income before unallocated expenses) by industry segment in 1991 was: natural resources, 54% (30%); consumer products, 18% (27%); financial services, 27% (28%); utilities and other operations net, 1% (15%).

Relative strength to TSE300
Price
Volume (in 1000's of board lots)

Rank (Profit/Revenue/Assets)
974   353   45

J. Trevor Eyton
Chairman

Jack L. Cockwell
President

Edward C. Kress
Exec. V.P. & C.F.O.

Address
BCE Place
181 Bay Street
Suite 4400, P.O. Box 762
Toronto
ON
M5J 2T3
(416) 363-9491
Fax: (416) 363-2856
B0003334/G/14.0

BRL ENTERPRISES INC.

Exchanges	Price (Jun24'93)	3.15	Trailing P/E	14.32	Stock Symbol
TQ	Trailing Yield (%)	0.00	Trailing EPS	0.22	BRL

Period Ending	Dec92	Dec91	Dec90	Dec89	Dec88
Yearly Statistics					
Price-Close	2.60	2.85	3.00	11.50	12.50
Price-High	3.10	3.25	12.50	12.75	41.25
Price-Low	2.45	2.50	1.75	6.25	5.00
P/E-Close	7.43	9.83	nm	nm	nm
Dividends per Share	0.00	0.00	0.00	0.00	0.00
Dividend Yield (%)	0.00	0.00	0.00	0.00	0.00
Sales per Share	na	na	1.49	2.27	10.40
EPS before extra. item	0.35	0.29	(1.83)	(0.32)	(32.00)
Cash Flow per Share	0.25	0.38	1.23	1.37	2.85
Book Value per Share	5.38	5.03	4.73	5.03	(37.90)
O/S Common Shares	5,806	5,806	5,809	4,627	978
Total Revenue	2,799	3,081	741	13,453	10,189
Income before extra.	2,054	2,212	(8,661)	(221)	(28,465)
Cash Flow	1,441	2,212	6,668	6,459	2,811
Debt/Equity	nd	nd	nd	0.17	na
Return on Capital (%)	7.10	5.42	(13.09)	0.84	(29.18)
Ret. on Com. Equity (%)	6.80	6.04	(41.99)	na	na
% Change Profit	(7.1)	125.5	(3,819.0)	99.2	21.1
% Change Revenue	(9.2)	315.8	(94.5)	32.0	(15.2)
% Change Assets	6.0	(44.3)	(33.2)	(24.5)	(34.1)

Preferred Div. Coverage	np	np	0.0	
Total Div. Coverage	na	4.4	0.0	
Interest Coverage	nd	nd	0.0	
Current Ratio	5.3	1.1	1.7	
Operating Margin	na	na	(11.9)	
Asset Turnover	na	na	0.1	
5 YEAR RATIOS (%)				
Return on Capital	(5.8)	(12.0)	(15.9)	
Return on Com. Equity	na	na	na	
Profit Growth	na	na	na	
Revenue Growth	(25.1)	(50.7)	(68.7)	
Asset Growth	(27.8)	(31.0)	(28.9)	
BALANCE SHEET (000)				
Cash	2,248	418	1,787	
Current Assets	2,611	839	2,217	
Net Fixed Assets	0	0	0	
Invest's & Advances	29,009	29,009	50,450	
Total Assets	31,747	29,964	53,783	
Short Term Debt	0	0	0	
Current Liabilities	497	768	1,286	
Long Term Debt	0	0	0	
Total Liabilities	497	768	1,286	
Total Equity	31,250	29,196	52,497	
Total Liab. & Equity	31,747	29,964	53,783	
CAPITAL (000)				
Total Debt	0	0	0	
Preferred Equity	0	0	25,000	
Common Equity	31,250	29,196	27,497	

Business:

BRL ENTERPRISES INC., formerly Bralorne Resources Ltd., is primarily an investment company. The company's major shareholder is B.C. Pacific Capital Corp. of Vancouver.

Date	EPS	DPS	Tot Rev	Inc Bex
Mar 93	0.08	0.00	530	451
Dec 92	0.03	0.00	535	218
Sep 92	0.05	0.00	463	276
Jun 92	0.06	0.00	497	328
Mar 92	0.21	0.00	1,304	1,232
Dec 91	0.01	0.00	418	74
Sep 91	0.10	0.00	712	598
Jun 91	0.10	0.00	803	579

Synopsis:

BRL reviewed a number of new investment opportunities in 1992, but found that it was not appropriate to pursue them at this time. The company continues to take a conservative approach with its capital and continues to maintain its portfolio of preferred shares.

BRL held an investment portfolio at December 31, 1992, that consisted of 800,000 Noranda Forest Class A Series 1 Preferred Shares, 73,000 Canadian Imperial Bank of Commerce Class A Series 4 Preferred Shares and 72,000 Brascade Resources Class B Retractable Preferred Shares.

BRL completed a successful Small Shareholder Selling Program during 1992. The program enabled eligible shareholders owning 99 or fewer common shares as at the April 16, 1992 record date, to sell their odd-lot holdings without incurring brokerage fees. The sale of the shares was executed in the open market through a Toronto Stock Exchange member firm. The Proxy Solicitation Company Ltd. was retained to manage the program and to handle share transactions and payments for BRL. The program had a participation rate of 40% of eligible registered shareholders by the time it expired on September 30, 1992.

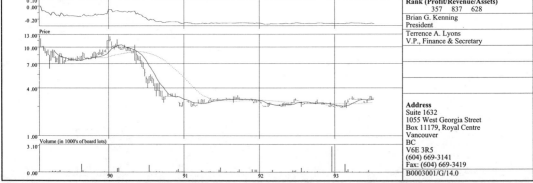

Rank (Profit/Revenue/Assets)
357 837 628

Brian G. Kenning
President

Terrence A. Lyons
V.P., Finance & Secretary

Address
Suite 1632
1055 West Georgia Street
Box 11179, Royal Centre
Vancouver
BC
V6E 3R5
(604) 669-3141
Fax: (604) 669-3419
B0003001/G/14.0

CANADIAN PACIFIC LIMITED

Exchanges	Price (Jun24'93)	21.00	Trailing P/E		nm	Stock Symbol
TMVZN	Trailing Yield (%)	1.52	Trailing EPS		(1.31)	CP

Period Ending	Dec92	Dec91	Dec90	Dec89	Dec88
Yearly Statistics					
Price-Close	16.13	18.00	19.75	25.75	22.00
Price-High	19.38	23.25	26.63	28.63	24.88
Price-Low	13.50	16.38	17.25	21.38	19.50
P/E-Close	nm	nm	17.79	10.96	8.30
Dividends per Share	0.32	0.63	0.92	0.84	0.68
Dividend Yield (%)	1.98	3.50	4.66	3.26	3.09
Sales per Share	28.12	31.62	32.75	34.32	35.35
EPS before extra. item	(1.50)	(2.87)	1.11	2.35	2.65
Cash Flow per Share	1.42	2.36	3.95	4.54	5.02
Book Value per Share	19.66	21.02	24.55	24.46	23.00
O/S Common Shares (mil)	319	319	318	318	317
Total Revenue ($mil)	9,054	10,370	10,620	11,205	10,969
Income before extra. ($mil)	(478)	(914)	355	745	820
Cash Flow ($mil)	452	752	1,259	1,442	1,551
Debt/Equity	1.28	1.16	0.78	0.64	0.57
Return on Capital (%)	(0.43)	(3.67)	8.75	13.28	14.96
Ret. on Com. Equity (%)	(7.38)	(12.60)	4.55	9.88	11.96
% Change Profit	47.7	(357.2)	(52.3)	(9.1)	28.8
% Change Revenue	(12.7)	(2.4)	(5.2)	2.2	(10.2)
% Change Assets	(1.8)	1.8	6.2	7.9	(1.9)

Preferred Div. Coverage	0.0	0.0	710.6		
Total Div. Coverage	0.0	0.0	1.2		
Interest Coverage	0.0	0.0	1.7		
Current Ratio	1.1	1.4	1.0		
Operating Margin	(1.7)	(5.6)	9.9		
Asset Turnover	0.4	0.5	0.5		
5 YEAR RATIOS (%)					
Return on Capital	6.6	9.7	12.3		
Return on Com. Equity	1.3	4.8	7.9		
Profit Growth	na	na	7.0		
Revenue Growth	(5.8)	(7.3)	(3.6)		
Asset Growth	2.3	3.0	(1.1)		
BALANCE SHEET (mil)					
Cash	1,387	1,603	849		
Current Assets	3,090	4,088	3,482		
Net Fixed Assets	15,042	14,807	14,814		
Invest's & Advances	1,271	999	1,335		
Total Assets	20,224	20,587	20,224		
Short Term Debt	844	766	1,498		
Current Liabilities	2,824	2,874	3,548		
Long Term Debt	7,194	6,986	4,606		
Total Liabilities	13,938	13,873	12,396		
Total Equity	6,286	6,714	7,827		
Total Liab. & Equity	20,224	20,587	20,224		
CAPITAL (mil)					
Total Debt	8,038	7,752	6,104		
Preferred Equity	15	15	15		
Common Equity	6,271	6,699	7,813		

Business:

CANADIAN PACIFIC Ltd. is a diversified company. It is active in transportation (CP Rail, CP Ships, CP Trucks); energy (PanCanadian Petroleum and Fording Coal); forestry (Canadian Pacific Forest); real estate and hotels (Marathon Realty and Canadian Pacific Hotels); telecommunications and manufacturing (Unitel and United Dominion Industries); and waste services (Laidlaw Inc.).

Date	EPS	DPS	Tot Rev	Inc Bex
Mar 93	0.07	0.08	1,964,600	21,700
Dec 92	(0.80)	0.08	2,059,700	(254,000)
Sep 92	(0.64)	0.08	2,023,900	(205,600)
Jun 92	0.06	0.08	2,469,200	21,000
Mar 92	(0.12)	0.08	2,426,900	(39,700)
Dec 91	(2.79)	0.16	2,522,600	(887,600)
Sep 91	(0.16)	0.16	2,608,600	(51,800)
Jun 91	0.10	0.23	2,612,300	30,900

Synopsis:

Canadian Pacific Limited declined participation in a share issue by Canadian Pacific Forest Products Limited causing its ownership in CP Forest to dip from 70% to 60.7%. CP Forest used the net proceeds to repay short-term debt, and to fund operations and capital expenditures. CP Limited's ownership in Unitel was reduced from 60% to 48% following AT&T's purchase of a 20% equity interest in Unitel Communications in January. CP Limited's ownership in United Dominion dipped from 55.4% to 45.4% following a share issue by United Dominion in which CP Limited did not participate. CP Limited increased its ownership of Canadian Maritime Limited to 100% in February 1993.

During the first quarter of 1993, CP Rail System's operating income dropped to $32.8-million from $73.5-million in the corresponding period last year. A 9% drop in freight, especially of coal and grain, led to lower revenues. The drop in coal shipments was mainly due to the bankruptcy of one of CP Rail's major customers, Westar Mining. Fording Coal purchased an 80% interest in the Greenhills metallurgical coal mine in December. The mine had been closed following the bankruptcy of Westar Mining, the former owner. Improvements in the operating performance of Fording and CP Rail are projected due to the resumption of coal traffic following the acquisitions and the end of the strike at Fording in December 1992.

CP Trucks recorded a loss of $6-million for the first quarter, $1.2-million less than the first quarter of 1992, due mainly to the divestiture of divisions. CP Trucks sold its U.S.-based truckload operations during 1992 and its Canpar parcel delivery division in early 1993. The divestitures allow CP Trucks to focus exclusively on its truckload and less than truckload operations. CP Ships showed improved results due to better trade conditions and expanded operations.

1992 revenues (operating profit of -$106.3-million) by business were: transportation, 43% (-400%); energy, 13% (303%); forest products, 20% (-253%); real estate and hotels, 11% (238%); and telecommunications and manufacturing, 13% (12%).

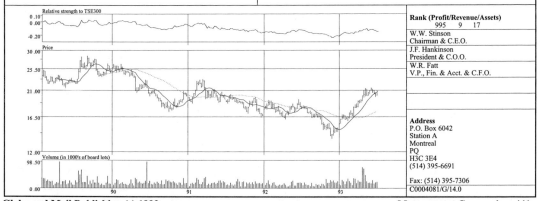

Rank (Profit/Revenue/Assets)		
995	9	17

W.W. Stinson
Chairman & C.E.O.

J.F. Hankinson
President & C.O.O.

W.R. Fatt
V.P., Fin. & Acct. & C.F.O.

Address
P.O. Box 6042
Station A
Montreal
PQ
H3C 3E4
(514) 395-6691

Fax: (514) 395-7306
C0004081/G/14.0

CANCAPITAL CORPORATION

Exchanges					Stock Symbol
T	Price (Jun24'93)	0 .35	Trailing P/E	nm	**CJC**
	Trailing Yield (%)	0 .00	Trailing EPS	(0 .27)	

Period Ending	Dec92	Dec91	Dec90	Dec89	Dec88
Yearly Statistics					
Price-Close	0 .26	0 .02	1 .50	4 .20	5 .00
Price-High	0 .35	1 .75	4 .50	5 .25	6 .00
Price-Low	0 .03	0 .01	1 .25	4 .00	3 .15
P/E-Close	nm	nm	nm	nm	10 .87
Dividends per Share	0 .00	0 .00	0 .00	0 .20	0 .30
Dividend Yield (%)	0 .00	0 .00	0 .00	4 .76	6 .00
Sales per Share	na	na	na	na	na
EPS before extra. item	(0 .10)	(0 .78)	(7 .20)	(0 .02)	0 .46
Cash Flow per Share	0 .42	(0 .50)	(1 .00)	0 .15	0 .31
Book Value per Share	(1 .08)	(0 .98)	(0 .26)	7 .04	7 .23
O/S Common Shares	10 ,554	10 ,554	10 ,143	10 ,143	10 ,334
Total Revenue	7 ,453	5 ,933	(47 ,961)	6 ,100	9 ,744
Income before extra.	4 ,350	(7 ,912)	(73 ,043)	(181)	4 ,835
Cash Flow	4 ,406	(5 ,090)	(10 ,105)	1 ,552	3 ,270
Debt/Equity	na	na	na	0 .79	0 .27
Return on Capital (%)	31 .65	(7 .12)	(63 .98)	2 .27	7 .89
Ret. on Com. Equity (%)	na	na	(212 .29)	(0 .25)	6 .51
% Change Profit	155 .0	89 .2	nm	(103 .7)	(75 .8)
% Change Revenue	25 .6	112 .4	(886 .2)	(37 .4)	(73 .4)
% Change Assets	72 .2	(75 .0)	(46 .4)	42 .2	(0 .8)
Preferred Div. Coverage	na	np	np		
Total Div. Coverage	na	na	na		
Interest Coverage	3 .1	0 .0	0 .0		
Current Ratio	2 .2	0 .5	1 .1		
Operating Margin	82 .3	na	(3 ,974 .0)		
Asset Turnover	na	na	na		
5 YEAR RATIOS (%)					
Return on Capital	(5 .9)	(4 .1)	(7 .3)		
Return on Com. Equity	na	na	(42 .1)		
Profit Growth	(26 .3)	na	na		
Revenue Growth	(27 .3)	(16 .8)	na		
Asset Growth	(20 .2)	(18 .8)	(19 .4)		
BALANCE SHEET (000)					
Cash	31	259	15 ,791		
Current Assets	11 ,713	710	59 ,048		
Net Fixed Assets	0	0	0		
Invest's & Advances	19 ,593	17 ,350	13 ,769		
Total Assets	31 ,451	18 ,262	73 ,075		
Short Term Debt	2 ,272	1 ,286	50 ,202		
Current Liabilities	5 ,229	1 ,562	55 ,714		
Long Term Debt	25 ,898	26 ,486	20 ,000		
Total Liabilities	36 ,527	28 ,613	75 ,714		
Total Equity	(5 ,076)	(10 ,351)	(2 ,639)		
Total Liab. & Equity	31 ,451	18 ,262	73 ,075		
CAPITAL (000)					
Total Debt	28 ,170	27 ,772	70 ,202		
Preferred Equity	6 ,325	0	0		
Common Equity	(11 ,401)	(10 ,351)	(2 ,639)		

Business:

CANCAPITAL CORP. is an investment and merchant banking company. It earns interest and dividends on investment activities. The company also earns fees from corporate finance activities relating to mergers and acquisitions, takeovers and the purchase or sale of assets. The company holds a 38% interest in Trical Resources Ltd. of Calgary, an oil and gas company.

Date	EPS	DPS	Tot Rev	Inc Bex
Mar 93	(0 .13)	0 .00	540	(36)
Dec 92	(0 .01)	0 .00	6 ,323	5 ,229
Sep 92	(0 .04)	0 .00	541	(323)
Jun 92	(0 .09)	0 .00	(727)	(943)
Mar 92	(0 .07)	0 .00	971	387
Dec 91	(0 .64)	0 .00	1 ,995	(6 ,526)
Sep 91	(0 .03)	0 .00	1 ,115	(232)
Jun 91	(0 .01)	0 .00	796	(138)

Synopsis:

In March 1993, CanCapital Corporation announced that it had agreed to acquire the interest of a related party in an assignment agreement under which it will receive royalty payments. CanCapital will issue non-voting 6% preferred shares with a value equal to the actual royalty proceeds to be received by the company. The actual proceeds are estimated to be up to $4-million.

In December 1992, a majority of the minority shareholders approved an agreement between CanCapital and Nalcap Holdings Inc. that transferred an iron mine's royalty rights to CanCapital from Nalcap. The company planned to issue Non-Voting Cumulative Redeemable Retractable Preferred Shares in an amount equal to the fair market value, which had been estimated at approximately $30-million.

Relative strength to TSE300 / Price / Volume (in 1000's of board lots)

Rank (Profit/Revenue/Assets)
863   763   731

John J. Fleming
Chairman & C.E.O.
Wesley G. Ismond
C.F.O. & Secretary

Address
Suite 1250
400 Burrard Street
Vancouver
BC
V6C 3A6
(604) 683-8286

B0020213/G/14.0

CONSOLIDATED ENFIELD CORP. LTD.

Exchanges	Price (Jun24'93)	0.60	Trailing P/E	nm	Stock Symbol
T	Trailing Yield (%)	0.00	Trailing EPS	(2.84)	CEZ

Period Ending	Dec92	Dec91	Dec90	Dec89	Dec88
Yearly Statistics					
Price-Close	0.41	1.10	2.30	26.90	30.63
Price-High	1.50	3.30	25.50	46.25	43.75
Price-Low	0.15	0.81	1.90	26.25	28.75
P/E-Close	nm	nm	nm	nm	nm
Dividends per Share	0.00	0.00	0.00	0.40	2.00
Dividend Yield (%)	0.00	0.00	0.00	1.49	6.53
Sales per Share	40.38	40.81	62.70	70.83	74.37
EPS before extra. item	(3.71)	(14.53)	(1.78)	(3.91)	(2.65)
Cash Flow per Share	0.30	(3.08)	(2.22)	2.16	5.66
Book Value per Share	(3.08)	0.36	14.84	na	21.44
O/S Common Shares	10,926	10,926	10,926	0	7,853
Total Revenue	441,239	445,863	636,035	637,283	611,666
Income before extra.	(37,608)	(155,856)	(14,864)	(31,184)	(17,714)
Cash Flow	3,261	(33,627)	(22,224)	18,839	44,448
Debt/Equity	38.51	8.54	2.18	2.29	1.93
Return on Capital (%)	(4.88)	(23.05)	4.43	(1.13)	(0.40)
Ret. on Com. Equity (%)	na	(190.36)	(11.27)	(21.19)	(11.05)
% Change Profit	75.9	(948.5)	52.3	(76.0)	(143.8)
% Change Revenue	(1.0)	(29.9)	(0.2)	4.2	33.8
% Change Assets	(25.0)	(29.0)	(4.8)	6.3	(5.8)

Business:

CONSOLIDATED ENFIELD CORP. LTD. is a holding company with interests in the packaging and automotive industries. Subsidiaries include 58% owned Consumers Packaging Inc. and 51% owned The Complax Corp.

Date	EPS	DPS	Tot Rev	Inc Bex
Mar 93	(0.10)	0.00	93,012	(343)
Dec 92	(2.40)	0.00	17,805	(25,455)
Sep 92	(0.35)	0.00	134,382	(3,099)
Jun 92	0.01	0.00	167,340	828
Mar 92	(0.97)	0.00	93,021	(9,882)
Dec 91	(12.22)	0.00	4,624	(132,829)
Sep 91	(0.92)	0.00	141,815	(9,311)
Jun 91	(0.27)	0.00	172,501	(2,250)

	Dec92	Dec91	Dec90
Preferred Div. Coverage	na	0.0	0.0
Total Div. Coverage	na	0.0	0.0
Interest Coverage	0.0	0.0	0.5
Current Ratio	0.8	1.1	1.2
Operating Margin	(2.1)	(7.3)	(6.9)
Asset Turnover	0.9	0.7	0.7
5 YEAR RATIOS (%)			
Return on Capital	(5.0)	(1.4)	9.7
Return on Com. Equity	na	na	na
Profit Growth	na	na	na
Revenue Growth	(0.8)	5.2	55.3
Asset Growth	(12.7)	3.1	26.9
BALANCE SHEET (000)			
Cash	40,254	38,509	128,655
Current Assets	219,952	321,107	445,503
Net Fixed Assets	248,817	298,065	432,757
Invest's & Advances	1,212	2,913	2,796
Total Assets	470,726	628,018	884,143
Short Term Debt	169,724	160,353	232,263
Current Liabilities	269,749	281,776	362,678
Long Term Debt	149,144	231,377	212,885
Total Liabilities	462,446	582,130	680,124
Total Equity	8,280	45,888	204,019
Total Liab. & Equity	470,726	628,018	884,143
CAPITAL (000)			
Total Debt	318,868	391,730	445,148
Preferred Equity	41,924	41,924	41,924
Common Equity	(33,644)	3,964	162,095

Synopsis:

Consolidated Enfield Corp. Ltd.'s affiliate, Complax Corp., closed its $22-million auto parts plant in Windsor, Ontario, in December 1992. Complax consolidated operations with another plant near Toronto. The plant made polyester glass automotive parts. The Tarxien Corporation purchased Complax Components Corporation from Complax in February 1993. Complax Components is located in Cobourg, Ontario, and manufactures auto parts. Its main assets are machinery and equipment, and contracts for the supply of auto parts. The purchase price was not disclosed. In June 1992, the auto parts plant in Cobourg was listed with a real estate agent at $2.7-million.

The improved results for the first quarter of 1993 for Consolidated Enfield was attributed to the performance the glass operations of Consumers Packaging. Consumers Packaging decided to focus resources on its core glass container business and to sell its plastics businesses to reduce debt. The company sold the plastic businesses in two separate transactions in the first quarter of 1993, for net proceeds of $63-million, and a potential $4-million dependent on the 1993 earnings of the portion packaging operations. The proceeds will be used to reduce long-term debt. At the end of the first quarter, Consumers had $27.7-million worth of long-term debt that was past due. Consumers continues to look for an equity partner to provide assistance in the consolidation of its position in the North American market.

Planned capital expenditures for 1993 for Consumers Packaging amount to $32.8-million, but only $3.2-million was committed to at the end of 1992. Further capital expenditure commitments will be made as the funding becomes available.

Consolidated Enfield will begin to show improved results when its operating affiliates, most importantly Consumers Packaging, begin to report improved results.

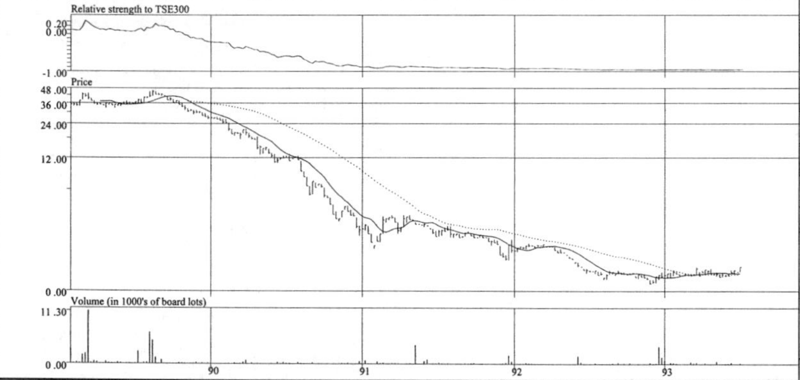

Relative strength to TSE300
0.20
0.00
-1.00
Price
48.00
36.00
24.00
12.00
0.00
Volume (in 1000's of board lots)
11.30
0.00
90
91
92
93

Rank (Profit/Revenue/Assets)
979 142 190

Manfred J. Walt
Chairman

Brian D. Lawson
President & Secretary

Address
Suite 4501, BCE Place
181 Bay Street
Toronto
ON
M5J 2T3
(416) 359-8625

Fax: (416) 865-1288

E0000495/G/14.0

COUNSEL CORPORATION

Exchanges	Price (Jun24'93)		2.43	Trailing P/E		nm	Stock Symbol
T	Trailing Yield (%)		5.35	Trailing EPS		(6.88)	**CXS**

Period Ending	Dec92	Dec91	Dec90	Dec89	Dec88
Yearly Statistics					
Price-Close	4.05	7.00	5.63	10.75	9.50
Price-High	7.75	8.38	12.50	14.50	10.13
Price-Low	3.30	4.60	5.38	8.00	7.00
P/E-Close	nm	6.48	2.25	7.90	10.80
Dividends per Share	0.13	0.26	0.24	0.20	0.18
Dividend Yield (%)	3.21	3.71	4.27	1.86	1.90
Sales per Share	9.65	6.81	13.13	22.37	19.28
EPS before extra. item	(6.78)	1.08	2.50	1.36	0.88
Cash Flow per Share	0.42	1.60	0.46	1.91	3.21
Book Value per Share	3.54	10.25	12.58	10.60	9.76
O/S Common Shares	15,138	14,952	14,952	13,510	10,682
Total Revenue	172,136	135,976	267,763	267,259	350,734
Income before extra.	(98,921)	20,318	36,334	16,087	9,973
Cash Flow	6,381	23,897	6,586	21,048	32,213
Debt/Equity	1.46	1.04	2.69	3.18	3.59
Return on Capital (%)	(27.60)	7.29	10.97	9.93	37.52
Ret. on Com. Equity (%)	(99.47)	9.46	21.63	12.11	9.18
% Change Profit	(586.9)	(44.1)	125.9	61.3	(10.7)
% Change Revenue	26.6	(49.2)	0.2	(23.8)	80.2
% Change Assets	(35.5)	(42.7)	7.6	(63.4)	44.7

Date	EPS	DPS	Tot Rev	Inc Bex
Mar 93	0.05	0.00	51,075	1,808
Dec 92	(5.33)	0.00	45,470	(79,894)
Sep 92	(0.05)	0.00	46,698	207
Jun 92	(1.55)	0.13	40,531	(22,522)
Mar 92	0.15	0.00	41,151	3,288
Dec 91	0.59	0.13	18,165	9,796
Sep 91	0.08	0.00	50,855	2,255
Jun 91	0.20	0.13	35,096	4,015

Preferred Div. Coverage	0.0	4.9	72.5	
Total Div. Coverage	0.0	0.4	9.3	
Interest Coverage	0.0	2.5	0.9	
Current Ratio	0.6	1.8	0.4	
Operating Margin	6.4	10.4	10.0	
Asset Turnover	0.5	0.2	0.2	
5 YEAR RATIOS (%)				
Return on Capital	7.6	21.0	27.9	
Return on Com. Equity	(9.4)	13.2	14.0	
Profit Growth	na	28.2	74.5	
Revenue Growth	(2.5)	(0.8)	23.5	
Asset Growth	(26.9)	(13.0)	7.8	
BALANCE SHEET (000)				
Cash	14,033	18,963	5,707	
Current Assets	52,776	54,848	60,463	
Net Fixed Assets	78,483	125,796	509,379	
Invest's & Advances	106,154	132,056	163,165	
Total Assets	278,251	431,195	753,144	
Short Term Debt	69,360	15,436	121,934	
Current Liabilities	91,202	30,759	163,763	
Long Term Debt	74,328	189,573	384,802	
Total Liabilities	179,825	233,025	564,807	
Total Equity	98,426	198,170	188,337	
Total Liab. & Equity	278,251	431,195	753,144	
CAPITAL (000)				
Total Debt	143,688	205,009	506,736	
Preferred Equity	44,855	44,960	180	
Common Equity	53,571	153,210	188,157	

Business:

COUNSEL CORPORATION operates in two areas of business: asset management through Counsel Asset Management Services Inc.; and health care though Diversicare Incorporated.

Synopsis:

Counsel Corporation wrote off its real estate division. The real estate subsidiary has debts of approximately $334.7-million that are non-recourse to Counsel. Write-downs were also taken on the loans and mortgages held by subsidiaries, Counsel Financial Corporation and Terracan Capital Corporation. Counsel's real estate development and investment holdings are expected to be disposed of over the next five years.

Counsel sold $15-million of five-year 6% convertible debentures to International Capital Partners, a Connecticut-based investment manager acting for a group of U.S. institutions. The debentures are convertible into Counsel shares at a price between $3 and $3.50 a share. The proceeds will be used to repay the $15-million loan to Counsel Financial that the Royal Bank of Canada refused to roll over. The loan had no recourse to Counsel. Counsel and a group of Canadian pension funds and insurance companies agreed to extend the $13-million subordinate debentures until June 30, 1995.

Counsel formed Counsel Management Services Inc. to consolidate all of Counsel's real estate asset management operations. Counsel Management Services manages Counsel's pooled real estate funds, limited partnerships and syndications but does not own any real estate assets for its own account.

Diversicare arranged a $15-million line of credit with NationsBank to fund acquisitions. Diversicare will focus on growth by acquisition and by introducing new products and services. Diversicare's American HomePatient division expanded its home health care business by more than doubling the number of locations to 53 and expanding in six states that previously did not have branches.

Contribution to revenues (earnings from operations) for 1992 by business segment were: asset management, 11% (-17%); health care, 89% (117%). Contributions for 1991 were: ssset management, 21% (72%); sealth care, 79% (28%).

Relative strength to TSE300

Price

Volume (in 1000's of board lots)

Rank (Profit/Revenue/Assets)
118   282   176

Allan Silber
Chairman, President & C.E.O.

Steven Waxman
V.P., Finance

Address
36 Toronto Street
Suite 1200
Toronto
ON
M5C 2C5
(416) 866-3000

Fax: (416) 866-3061
01000547/G/14.0

CROWNX INC.

Exchanges	Price (Jun24'93)	3.50	Trailing P/E	nm	Stock Symbol
TM	Trailing Yield (%)	0.00	Trailing EPS	(0.80)	**CRX.A**

Period Ending	Dec92	Dec91	Dec90	Dec89	Dec88
Yearly Statistics					
Price-Close	2.90	0.76	2.80	7.25	5.68
Price-High	3.15	3.85	6.88	7.75	6.50
Price-Low	0.63	0.50	1.65	5.50	4.75
P/E-Close	nm	25.33	5.83	10.99	nm
Dividends per Share	0.00	0.23	0.30	0.30	0.30
Dividend Yield (%)	0.00	29.61	10.71	4.14	5.28
Sales per Share	62.95	66.92	25.23	23.84	22.46
EPS before extra. item	(0.88)	0.03	0.48	0.66	(0.05)
Cash Flow per Share	(7.84)	3.26	2.55	2.13	1.70
Book Value per Share	2.16	4.74	8.32	8.29	8.03
O/S Common Shares	40,856	40,840	40,811	40,733	40,703
Total Revenue	2,580,454	2,907,217	758,945	746,693	681,161
Income before extra.	(19,598)	19,152	43,362	52,586	15,018
Cash Flow	(320,122)	132,997	73,023	60,422	48,388
Debt/Equity	1.60	0.90	0.72	0.86	0.93
Return on Capital (%)	1.76	6.92	4.57	9.08	3.99
Ret. on Com. Equity (%)	(36.10)	1.48	6.75	9.77	(1.26)
% Change Profit	(202.3)	(55.8)	(17.5)	250.2	(60.4)
% Change Revenue	(11.2)	283.1	1.6	9.6	(6.2)
% Change Assets	0.2	686.6	(6.6)	(1.0)	(33.3)

Preferred Div. Coverage	0.0	1.3	2.1
Total Div. Coverage	0.0	0.8	1.3
Interest Coverage	0.5	1.9	na
Current Ratio	4.9	7.0	1.2
Operating Margin	5.3	4.8	6.8
Asset Turnover	0.3	0.3	0.6
5 YEAR RATIOS (%)			
Return on Capital	5.3	6.0	5.7
Return on Com. Equity	(3.9)	4.0	4.8
Profit Growth	na	(17.0)	(9.6)
Revenue Growth	28.9	36.3	(0.2)
Asset Growth	37.3	38.9	(4.7)
BALANCE SHEET (000)			
Cash	179,634	236,630	33,377
Current Assets	803,479	933,460	143,413
Net Fixed Assets	447,239	402,521	421,716
Invest's & Advances	7,673,647	7,437,829	549,584
Total Assets	9,044,144	9,025,772	1,147,398
Short Term Debt	29,003	16,741	11,221
Current Liabilities	165,534	134,189	119,402
Long Term Debt	427,565	383,684	414,016
Total Liabilities	8,758,268	8,581,113	556,007
Total Equity	285,876	444,659	591,391
Total Liab. & Equity	9,044,144	9,025,772	1,147,398
CAPITAL (000)			
Total Debt	456,568	400,425	425,237
Preferred Equity	197,774	251,290	251,750
Common Equity	88,102	193,369	339,641

Business:

CROWNX INC. operates in two broad segments: health care, principally through 100% owned Extendicare Health Services Inc.; and life insurance through 54.6% owned Crown Life Insurance Company. Health care operations include: nursing and retirement centres; home care services; and hospital management. Crown Life provides life and health insurance and pension programs to individuals and groups.

Date	EPS	DPS	Tot Rev	Inc Bex
Mar 93	0.10	0.00	669,261	8,882
Dec 92	(0.53)	0.00	686,519	(22,525)
Sep 92	(0.39)	0.00	636,291	(13,922)
Jun 92	0.02	0.00	622,224	9,001
Mar 92	0.01	0.00	631,873	7,848
Dec 91	(0.22)	0.00	653,608	(7,315)
Sep 91	0.58	0.08	669,683	35,199
Jun 91	(0.33)	0.08	708,152	(3,199)

Synopsis:

In February 1993, Crownx Inc. completed a $133.4-million mortgage financing. Crownx sold 20-year mortgages on 24 nursing centres in Canada from its Extendicare Group. The mortgages bear interest at 9.81%, have amortization periods of 25 and 30 years and were sold to the Canadian Imperial Bank of Commerce. In October 1992, Crownx sold its 49% stake in Lancaster Financial Inc. for $110-million. The proceeds and other financing were used to pay dividend arrears on the preferred shares totaling $31-million and to repurchase $125-million worth of the preferred shares outstanding. The cancellation of the preferred shares reduces the preferred dividend requirements by approximately $15-million annually based on current interest rates. In July 1992, Crownx reduced overhead expenses by approximately $1.5-million annually by consolidating its corporate offices with those of Extendicare in Markham, Ontario.

The results for the first quarter of 1993 include a $1-million gain on the sale of a nursing home and interest costs of $5.7-million. During the first quarter,Crownx resumed its payment of preferred share dividends after it had suspended payments in December 1992. Crownx announced in April 1993 that it would pay all current and arrears of dividends on its preferred shares. Health care earnings from operations increased to $15.2-million for the first quarter of 1993, from $11.8-million for the same period in 1992. The performance of the United States nursing centres improved due to the development of special care units and therapy services expansion and this was reflected in the earnings. Crownx will focus its management skills and direct investment funds on its health care operations.

Contributions to revenue by business segment in 1991 (1990) were: health care, 36% (30%); life insurance, 64% (70%). Contributions to the health care segment revenues in 1992 (1991) by geographic segment were: Canada and other, 31% (34%); the United States, 69% (66%). Contributions to life insurance segment revenues in 1992 (1991) by geographic segment: Canada, 33% (29%); the United States, 63% (68%); and International, 4% (3%).

Relative strength to TSE300
Price
Volume (in 1000's of board lots)

Rank (Profit/Revenue/Assets)
921   52   30

David J. Hennigar
Chairman

Frederick B. Ladly
President & C.E.O.

Barry L. Stephens
Vice President, Finance

Address
3000 Steeles Avenue East
Suite 700
Markham
ON
L3R 9W2
(416) 470-4000

Fax: (416) 470-4003
C0038384/G/14.0

FEDERAL INDUSTRIES LTD.

Exchanges	Price (Jun24'93)		6 .25	Trailing P/E		nm	Stock Symbol
TW	Trailing Yield (%)		0 .80	Trailing EPS		(1 .40)	**FIL.A**

Period Ending	Dec92	Dec91	Dec90	Dec89	Dec88
Yearly Statistics					
Price-Close	4 .10	7 .50	6 .38	13 .38	16 .50
Price-High	8 .75	10 .50	14 .25	18 .00	18 .00
Price-Low	3 .15	6 .00	5 .75	13 .13	13 .00
P/E-Close	nm	nm	79 .69	8 .06	8 .38
Dividends per Share	0 .10	0 .20	0 .35	0 .40	0 .40
Dividend Yield (%)	2 .44	2 .67	5 .49	2 .99	2 .42
Sales per Share	38 .99	47 .53	64 .80	96 .83	81 .32
EPS before extra. item	(2 .08)	(4 .86)	0 .08	1 .66	1 .97
Cash Flow per Share	(0 .47)	0 .06	1 .83	3 .58	3 .18
Book Value per Share	5 .15	7 .10	14 .04	14 .23	6 .75
O/S Common Shares	33 ,263	33 ,134	23 ,372	23 ,700	23 ,477
Total Revenue	1 ,297 ,987	1 ,390 ,626	1 ,540 ,169	2 ,291 ,759	1 ,916 ,553
Income before extra.	(62 ,714)	(134 ,277)	8 ,372	45 ,647	48 ,820
Cash Flow	(15 ,550)	1 ,681	43 ,087	84 ,311	74 ,603
Debt/Equity	1 .20	0 .98	1 .12	1 .10	1 .10
Return on Capital (%)	(7 .26)	(16 .01)	5 .79	16 .97	18 .61
Ret. on Com. Equity (%)	(34 .00)	(49 .98)	0 .57	15 .84	21 .18
% Change Profit	53 .3	(1 ,703 .9)	(81 .7)	(6 .5)	27 .3
% Change Revenue	(6 .7)	(9 .7)	(32 .8)	19 .6	17 .1
% Change Assets	(8 .5)	(16 .8)	(9 .7)	28 .7	3 .8

Preferred Div. Coverage	0 .0	0 .0	1 .3
Total Div. Coverage	0 .0	0 .0	0 .6
Interest Coverage	0 .0	0 .0	2 .0
Current Ratio	1 .1	1 .4	2 .2
Operating Margin	1 .0	0 .9	3 .3
Asset Turnover	1 .5	1 .5	1 .4

5 YEAR RATIOS (%)			
Return on Capital	3 .6	8 .2	14 .3
Return on Com. Equity	(9 .3)	0 .2	12 .6
Profit Growth	na	na	(14 .3)
Revenue Growth	(4 .6)	3 .2	16 .3
Asset Growth	(1 .7)	0 .7	15 .8

BALANCE SHEET (000)			
Cash	0	0	0
Current Assets	433 ,619	464 ,418	757 ,712
Net Fixed Assets	191 ,193	207 ,617	232 ,770
Invest's & Advances	23 ,737	20 ,938	34 ,212
Total Assets	840 ,740	919 ,187	1 ,104 ,123
Short Term Debt	117 ,124	54 ,161	156 ,537
Current Liabilities	393 ,563	337 ,482	349 ,942
Long Term Debt	190 ,735	260 ,623	311 ,496
Total Liabilities	584 ,298	598 ,105	684 ,971
Total Equity	256 ,442	321 ,082	419 ,152
Total Liab. & Equity	840 ,740	919 ,187	1 ,104 ,123

CAPITAL (000)			
Total Debt	307 ,859	314 ,784	468 ,033
Preferred Equity	85 ,000	85 ,997	90 ,997
Common Equity	171 ,442	235 ,085	328 ,155

Business:

FEDERAL INDUSTRIES LTD. is a diversified management company with operations in Canada and the United States. Company activities are organized into three groups: metals-distribution of general line and flat rolled steel and international steel trading; consumer sales of retail products like lumber and stationary; and transport, petroluem distribution, and terminal facilities.

Date	EPS	DPS	Tot Rev	Inc Bex
Mar 93	(0 .24)	0 .00	280 ,595	(6 ,263)
Dec 92	(0 .91)	0 .00	338 ,198	(48 ,120)
Sep 92	(0 .09)	0 .00	340 ,560	(1 ,595)
Jun 92	(0 .16)	0 .05	346 ,201	(3 ,752)
Mar 92	(0 .33)	0 .05	275 ,928	(9 ,247)
Dec 91	(1 .13)	0 .05	338 ,078	(37 ,905)
Sep 91	(0 .09)	0 .10	351 ,257	(719)
Jun 91	(0 .03)	0 .05	390 ,268	(377)

Synopsis:

Federal Industries is selling a portion of the British Columbia operations of Willson Stationers to Grand & Toy Ltd. for an undisclosed price. Grand & Toy will buy up to 17 Willson stores as well as all of Willson's commercial business in B.C. In October 1992, Willson sold the majority of its Ontario retail operations, 23 stores, and its commercial operations to Grand & Toy.

In May 1993, Federal Industries filed a Registration Statement with the United States Security and Exchange Commission relating to a proposed public offering in the United States of $125-million (U.S.) of senior unsecured notes due in the year 2000. The proceeds would be used principally to repay outstanding bank indebtedness. Federal filed a preliminary prospectus in April 1993 for the secondary public offering of all its interest in Regal Greetings. The proceeds would be used to repay short-term debt.

Federal said that it intends to focus on North American-based industrial products and services, represented by metals distribution, processing and trading through its metals group. Federal's product lines were not materially affected by the U.S. Commerce Department's January 1993 finding of dumping by Canadian steel companies.

Federal entered into an amended and restated Credit Agreement with its bankers providing loan availability totaling $195-million. The facility, which matures December 31, 1993, provides a revolving demand credit facility of $145-million and a non-revolving demand facility of $50-million. Cash requirements for 1993 are to be met through internally generated funds and existing lines of credit.

Contributions to total sales and services for 1992 (1991) by business segment were: consumer, 42% (40%); metals, 49% (52%); and transport, 9% (8%). Segment margin for 1992 (1991) by business segment was: consumer, -13% (12%); metals, 11% (20%); and transport, 102% (68%). In 1992 the metals segment had a positive contribution to its segment margin from U.S. operations and a negative contribution from Canadian operations.

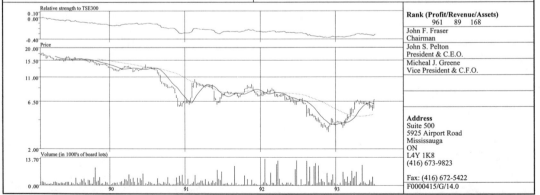

Rank (Profit/Revenue/Assets)
961   89   168

John F. Fraser
Chairman

John S. Pelton
President & C.E.O.

Micheal J. Greene
Vice President & C.F.O.

Address
Suite 500
5925 Airport Road
Mississauga
ON
L4Y 1K8
(416) 673-9823

Fax: (416) 672-5422
F0000415/G/14.0

GREAT LAKES POWER INC.

Exchanges	Price (Jun24'93)		14 .00	Trailing P/E		7.41	Stock Symbol
T	Trailing Yield (%)		6.43	Trailing EPS		1 .89	**GLZ**

Period Ending	Dec92	Dec91	Dec90	Dec89	Dec88
Yearly Statistics					
Price-Close	18 .38	22 .75	21 .75	20 .13	18 .00
Price-High	21 .50	22 .75	22 .00	20 .50	18 .25
Price-Low	14 .75	19 .00	16 .00	17 .75	15 .25
P/E-Close	9 .77	12 .30	11 .45	9 .82	9 .47
Dividends per Share	0 .88	0 .84	0 .84	0 .84	0 .82
Dividend Yield (%)	4 .79	3 .69	3 .86	4 .17	4 .56
Sales per Share	2 .17	2 .21	1 .89	1 .94	1 .68
EPS before extra. item	1 .88	1 .85	1 .90	2 .05	1 .90
Cash Flow per Share	2 .33	2 .36	2 .92	2 .34	1 .92
Book Value per Share	19 .80	18 .79	17 .79	16 .73	15 .51
O/S Common Shares	49 ,889	49 ,889	49 ,889	49 ,889	49 ,889
Total Revenue	226 ,400	255 ,800	278 ,000	269 ,700	219 ,800
Income before extra.	93 ,900	92 ,900	97 ,100	103 ,800	96 ,100
Cash Flow	116 ,200	117 ,500	145 ,900	116 ,900	95 ,700
Debt/Equity	0 .90	0 .86	0 .89	0 .81	1 .00
Return on Capital (%)	9 .07	10 .16	11 .54	12 .26	10 .98
Ret. on Com. Equity (%)	9 .75	10 .09	11 .02	12 .66	12 .65
% Change Profit	1 .1	(4 .3)	(6 .5)	8 .0	15 .4
% Change Revenue	(11 .5)	(8 .0)	3 .1	22 .7	10 .6
% Change Assets	2 .6	(3 .4)	7 .0	18 .5	21 .8

Preferred Div. Coverage	np	np	44 .1
Total Div. Coverage	2 .1	2 .2	2 .2
Interest Coverage	2 .8	2 .5	2 .3
Current Ratio	4 .7	25 .1	31 .0
Operating Margin	53 .8	50 .3	47 .3
Asset Turnover	0 .1	0 .1	0 .0
5 YEAR RATIOS (%)			
Return on Capital	10 .8	11 .3	11 .5
Return on Com. Equity	11 .2	12 .0	12 .5
Profit Growth	2 .4	10 .0	16 .2
Revenue Growth	2 .6	11 .5	17 .3
Asset Growth	8 .8	11 .2	22 .3
BALANCE SHEET (000)			
Cash	680 ,600	482 ,700	547 ,600
Current Assets	713 ,200	503 ,600	582 ,500
Net Fixed Assets	532 ,300	484 ,700	340 ,300
Invest's & Advances	854 ,600	1 ,058 ,600	1 ,195 ,700
Total Assets	2 ,100 ,100	2 ,046 ,900	2 ,118 ,500
Short Term Debt	129 ,000	0	0
Current Liabilities	153 ,100	20 ,100	18 ,800
Long Term Debt	762 ,800	804 ,800	815 ,300
Total Liabilities	1 ,112 ,300	1 ,109 ,300	1 ,206 ,100
Total Equity	987 ,800	937 ,600	912 ,400
Total Liab. & Equity	2 ,100 ,100	2 ,046 ,900	2 ,118 ,500
CAPITAL (000)			
Total Debt	891 ,800	804 ,800	815 ,300
Preferred Equity	0	0	25 ,000
Common Equity	987 ,800	937 ,600	887 ,400

Business:

GREAT LAKES POWER INC. is a holding company. The company's main asset is Great Lakes Power Ltd. of Sault Ste. Marie, ON. The utility has generating stations in Northern Ontario and serves the city of Sault Ste. Marie and the surrounding area. The company also holds a portfolio of securities and other investments.

Date	EPS	DPS	Tot Rev	Inc Bex
Mar 93	0 .47	0 .23	62 ,400	23 ,400
Dec 92	0 .47	0 .23	50 ,400	23 ,600
Sep 92	0 .48	0 .23	54 ,000	23 ,700
Jun 92	0 .47	0 .21	60 ,300	23 ,400
Mar 92	0 .46	0 .21	61 ,700	23 ,200
Dec 91	0 .45	0 .21	61 ,600	22 ,400
Sep 91	0 .49	0 .21	63 ,100	24 ,300
Jun 91	0 .46	0 .21	62 ,500	23 ,300

Synopsis:

For the first quarter of 1993, utility and investment income were stable for Great Lakes Power Inc. Operating earnings improved, even with a slight decline in kilowatt hour sales volumes, as the company generated 75% of electricity in the first quarter of 1993 compared with 72% in 1992. The Louisiana hydroelectric generating facility produced 295.9 million kilowatt hours of energy in the first quarter, which was 65% more than in the same period of 1992. The increase was due to the return to more seasonal weather and precipitation patterns. In April 1993, Great Lakes issued $105-million (U.S.) of 7.56% First Mortgage Bonds Series 2 due in 1998. The net proceeds will be used to reduce bank debt.

Lake Superior Power is building a 95 megawatt cogeneration plant in Sault Ste. Marie, Ontario. The power plant is a joint development between Westcoast Energy and Great Lakes. The electricity from the plant will be supplied to Ontario Hydro and the process steam will be supplied to St. Marys Paper Inc. The cost of the project has been estimated at $125-million and is expected to be in service in early 1994. The design permits a doubling of plant capacity, but expansion plans will not be considered until the first phase is operational. Great Lakes is looking at ways to link its Northern Ontario electrical power plants to U.S. distributors so that it can sell surplus electrical capacity in Michigan, Wisconsin and other northern states.

Sales volumes dipped by 9%, from 2,247.3 million kilowatt hours to 2,044.7 million kilowatt hours in 1992. Internal generation accounted for a record 70.8% of the power sold in 1992 compared to 66.1% of the power sold in 1991. The increase in internal generation resulted from good reservoir levels at the beginning of 1992 and a combination of full operations at the generating plants and reduced overall sales demand.

Contributions to total income in 1992 (1991) were: utility operations, 48% (43%); investment income, 34% (35%); and equity income, 18% (22%).

Rank (Profit/Revenue/Assets)		
38	254	91

Robert A. Dunford
Chairman

Edward C. Kress
President

Address
BCE Place
181 Bay Street
Suite 4400, P.O. Box 762
Toronto
ON
M5J 2T3
(416) 363-9491
Fax: (416) 363-2856
G0001006/G/14.0

IMASCO LIMITED

Exchanges	Price (Jun24'93)	35.00	Trailing P/E	11.71	Stock Symbol
TMV	Trailing Yield (%)	3.97	Trailing EPS	2.99	**IMS**

Period Ending	Dec92	Dec91	Dec90	Dec89	Dec88
Yearly Statistics					
Price-Close	41.25	36.50	27.63	37.75	28.00
Price-High	41.38	36.75	38.25	40.50	29.50
Price-Low	31.50	26.63	25.50	27.63	23.75
P/E-Close	13.89	14.26	12.28	13.15	11.16
Dividends per Share	1.36	1.28	1.28	1.12	1.04
Dividend Yield (%)	3.30	3.51	4.63	2.97	3.71
Sales per Share	67.06	66.80	66.22	25.40	40.64
EPS before extra. item	2.97	2.56	2.25	2.87	2.51
Cash Flow per Share	8.02	6.01	4.83	3.30	3.11
Book Value per Share	22.69	20.63	19.50	18.91	17.24
O/S Common Shares	119,099	119,114	119,113	119,247	119,191
Total Revenue	7,989,800	7,957,700	7,902,000	3,191,200	4,986,600
Income before extra.	380,400	331,600	295,100	366,100	314,300
Cash Flow	955,300	716,000	575,800	393,800	371,000
Debt/Equity	14.39	14.99	13.28	0.79	1.00
Return on Capital (%)	7.21	9.10	18.19	14.53	12.99
Ret. on Com. Equity (%)	13.70	12.75	11.72	15.86	14.58
% Change Profit	14.7	12.4	(19.4)	16.5	(3.8)
% Change Revenue	0.4	0.7	147.6	(36.0)	(3.2)
% Change Assets	4.5	17.3	635.8	1.3	(6.1)

Date	EPS	DPS	Tot Rev	Inc Bex
Mar 93	0.50	0.37	1,904,300	66,500
Dec 92	0.88	0.34	2,024,600	110,700
Sep 92	0.88	0.34	2,027,200	111,500
Jun 92	0.73	0.34	2,019,400	94,600
Mar 92	0.48	0.34	1,918,600	63,600
Dec 91	0.74	0.32	1,993,200	94,400
Sep 91	0.78	0.32	2,051,800	99,800
Jun 91	0.66	0.32	2,056,800	85,500

Preferred Div. Coverage	14.1	12.3	10.9
Total Div. Coverage	2.0	1.8	1.6
Interest Coverage	1.2	1.2	1.1
Current Ratio	1.5	1.5	1.7
Operating Margin	42.6	48.6	50.6
Asset Turnover	0.2	0.2	0.2
5 YEAR RATIOS (%)			
Return on Capital	12.4	13.5	14.0
Return on Com. Equity	13.7	14.1	14.0
Profit Growth	3.1	9.3	2.4
Revenue Growth	9.2	11.3	12.8
Asset Growth	53.6	53.8	67.6
BALANCE SHEET (mil)			
Cash	111	89	169
Current Assets	1,241	1,196	1,280
Net Fixed Assets	1,567	1,476	1,444
Invest's & Advances	43,890	41,891	35,006
Total Assets	48,519	46,420	39,574
Short Term Debt	27	30	65
Current Liabilities	814	813	762
Long Term Debt	43,985	42,148	35,493
Total Liabilities	45,461	43,606	36,896
Total Equity	3,058	2,813	2,678
Total Liab. & Equity	48,519	46,420	39,574
CAPITAL (mil)			
Total Debt	44,012	42,177	35,558
Preferred Equity	356	356	356
Common Equity	2,702	2,457	2,322

Business:

IMASCO LTD. is a diversified consumer products and services company with operations in Canada and the United States. Operations include Imperial Tobacco, Shoppers Drug Mart/Pharmaprix, Hardee's and The UCS Group. Imasco operates in the financial services sector through ownership of 98% of CT Financial Services Inc. of London, Ontario, the holding company of Canada Trustco Mortgage Company.

Synopsis:

Imasco's subsidiary Imperial Tobacco Ltd. reached an agreement with Philip Morris Cos. to market Canadian-made Player's cigarettes in the United States. Imperial hopes to regain market share in the export market, where Imperial's share fell to 31% in 1992 from 57% in 1991. Imperial's exports dropped by about 1.2 billion cigarettes in 1992, a reduction in order to comply with the federal government's attempts to reduce smuggling. Imperial felt that other companies had moved in to fill the gap and decided to allow export sales to rise. Philip Morris owns the Player's brand name in the United States which, until the agreement, prevented Imperial from selling its brand in the United States. The deal currently has Philip Morris buying Canadian-made Player's from Imperial and marketing them in the United States. Imperial may eventually set up its own sales force.

For the first quarter of 1993, only The UCS Group provided a negative contribution to the operating earnings of Imasco. The UCS Group still managed to reduce first quarter loss from operations from $3.9-million last year to $2-million in 1993. CT Financial Services' contribution to earnings dropped from $84-million in the first quarter of 1992 to $59.2-million in the first quarter of 1993. All other segments provided a positive contribution with Hardee's Food Systems showing the most improvement in moving from reporting a loss in the 1992 first quarter to a profit for the first quarter of 1993.

Imasco announced in February 1993 its intention to redeem its eight million outstanding 7.375% retractable First Preference Shares Series C at $25.00 per share plus accrued dividends from June 30 to July 17, 1993. Financing for the total cost of the redemption was still to be determined.

Contributions to total revenues (operating earnings) in 1992 by industry segment were: tobacco, 30% (49%); financial services, 41% (28%); restaurant, 24% (9%); drug store, 2% (11%); land development, 1% (4%); and other retail operations, 3% (-1%).

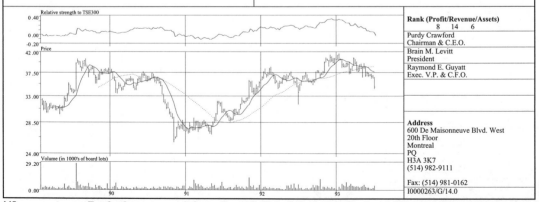

Rank (Profit/Revenue/Assets)
8   14   6

Purdy Crawford
Chairman & C.E.O.

Brain M. Levitt
President

Raymond E. Guyatt
Exec. V.P. & C.F.O.

Address
600 De Maisonneuve Blvd. West
20th Floor
Montreal
PQ
H3A 3K7
(514) 982-9111

Fax: (514) 981-0162
I0000263/G/14.0

JANNOCK LIMITED

Exchanges	Price (Jun24'93)	15.62	Trailing P/E	14.07	Stock Symbol
TM	Trailing Yield (%)	5.12	Trailing EPS	1.11	**JN**

Period Ending	Dec92	Dec91	Dec90	Dec89	Dec88
Yearly Statistics					
Price-Close	14.00	17.00	13.00	19.13	19.63
Price-High	18.50	17.88	19.75	22.00	23.50
Price-Low	12.13	12.50	11.38	17.38	15.25
P/E-Close	13.21	nm	30.95	10.93	10.55
Dividends per Share	0.80	0.80	0.80	0.80	0.74
Dividend Yield (%)	5.71	4.71	6.15	4.18	3.77
Sales per Share	11.85	10.52	11.55	13.52	11.61
EPS before extra. item	1.06	(1.25)	0.42	1.75	1.86
Cash Flow per Share	0.26	0.12	1.26	2.31	3.11
Book Value per Share	9.51	9.00	11.02	11.39	10.54
O/S Common Shares	27,258	27,258	27,158	27,171	27,014
Total Revenue	370,700	279,100	319,100	376,100	334,442
Income before extra.	30,300	(32,400)	13,100	49,000	52,339
Cash Flow	7,100	3,300	34,300	62,600	83,984
Debt/Equity	0.21	0.42	0.64	0.12	0.03
Return on Capital (%)	14.26	(6.18)	7.63	23.15	27.39
Ret. on Com. Equity (%)	11.38	(12.49)	3.78	15.96	18.31
% Change Profit	193.5	(347.3)	(73.3)	(6.4)	(23.1)
% Change Revenue	32.8	(12.5)	(15.2)	12.5	(21.4)
% Change Assets	(6.5)	(28.1)	31.0	15.7	(1.9)

Date	EPS	DPS	Tot Rev	Inc Bex
Mar 93	(0.23)	0.20	66,200	(6,000)
Dec 92	(0.22)	0.20	73,700	(5,800)
Sep 92	1.51	0.20	151,300	41,400
Jun 92	0.05	0.20	87,300	1,800
Mar 92	(0.28)	0.20	59,500	(7,100)
Dec 91	(0.35)	0.20	65,900	(9,000)
Sep 91	(0.39)	0.20	90,100	(10,400)
Jun 91	(0.02)	0.20	80,800	(1,800)

	Dec92	Dec91	Dec90
Preferred Div. Coverage	18.9	0.0	8.2
Total Div. Coverage	1.3	0.0	0.6
Interest Coverage	8.0	0.0	2.1
Current Ratio	2.8	1.0	1.2
Operating Margin	3.7	(1.5)	6.8
Asset Turnover	0.8	0.7	0.5
5 YEAR RATIOS (%)			
Return on Capital	13.2	17.6	24.9
Return on Com. Equity	7.4	11.1	19.3
Profit Growth	(15.0)	na	(14.1)
Revenue Growth	(2.7)	(7.0)	4.3
Asset Growth	(0.1)	3.2	18.6
BALANCE SHEET (000)			
Cash	29,200	0	33,600
Current Assets	170,700	122,500	270,800
Net Fixed Assets	171,300	166,500	168,600
Invest's & Advances	55,300	137,200	156,200
Total Assets	404,900	432,900	602,400
Short Term Debt	1,700	73,700	178,100
Current Liabilities	62,000	121,100	226,100
Long Term Debt	57,800	37,100	27,300
Total Liabilities	126,100	168,000	283,300
Total Equity	278,800	264,900	319,100
Total Liab. & Equity	404,900	432,900	602,400
CAPITAL (000)			
Total Debt	59,500	110,800	205,400
Preferred Equity	19,500	19,600	19,900
Common Equity	259,300	245,300	299,200

Business:

JANNOCK LTD. manufactures clay brick and other construction materials including vinyl siding and extruded polystyrene insulation board. The company has partnerships in steel related businesses, manufactures electrical and electronic products, and has interests in the graphics and security businesses. It operates in Canada and the United States.

Synopsis:

Jannock purchased Norandex's Master Shield business of Weatherford, Texas, for approximately $25-million (U.S.). Master Shield produces vinyl siding and accessories. Master Shield had sales of about $40-million in 1992 and Jannock expects it to boost the company's earnings capacity in the building products industry. Norandex will continue to make vinyl siding at a new facility in North Carolina.

Jannock has discontinued its graphics operations and expects to sell the graphics and electrical businesses in 1993. The estimated proceeds of $25.8-million from the sale of these businesses will be used to reduce debt in the United States and to fund operations in Canada. Jannock wants to focus primarily on building products. Jannock supplemented its operations in 1992 with the purchase of a small brick plant in Saskatchewan and a Montreal business that manufactures fibre-reinforced cement building panels.

Jannock is considering expanding by acquisition, possibly by entering a new sector of its industry. It plans to spend between $200-million and $300-million on acquisitions over the next few years. Jannock will continue to look for opportunities in the United States. Jannock will dismantle its brick plant in Streetsville, Ontario, and plans to invest $7.5-million in 1993 to develop the 108 hectares of land for residential and commercial purposes. Proceeds from the property sale will be used to fund new acquisitions.

Contributions to sales in 1992 (1991) by geographic segment were: Canada, 43% (48%); and the U.S., 57% (52%). Contributions to earnings from operations before corporate expenses in 1992 (1991) by geographic segment were: Canada, 4% (29%); the U.S., 96% (71%). Contributions to sales in 1992 (1991) by industry segment were: brick and other construction materials, 93% (89%); and other, 7% (11%). Other operations includes the electrical operations. Other operations had a loss from operations before corporate expenses, while the brick division's earnings went from $4-million in 1991 to $21.2-million in 1992.

Rank (Profit/Revenue/Assets)		
92	200	237

H. Gordon Macneill
Chairman

R. Jay Atkinson
President & C.E.O.

Brian W. Jamieson
V.P., Finance & C.F.O.

Address
Suite 5203, 52nd Floor
TD Bank Tower
Toronto-Dominion Centre
Toronto
ON
M5K 1B7
(416) 364-8586
Fax: (416) 364-9342
J0000182/G/14.0

JOHN LABATT LIMITED

Exchanges	Price (Jun24'93)	22.75	Trailing P/E	nm	Stock Symbol
TMV	Trailing Yield (%)	3.69	Trailing EPS	(1.12)	**LBT**

Period Ending	Apr92	Apr91	Apr90	Apr89	Apr88
Yearly Statistics					
Price-Close	25.75	23.13	20.63	22.75	23.88
Price-High	27.88	26.00	27.50	24.38	29.75
Price-Low	22.25	18.38	20.50	20.83	20.13
P/E-Close	24.76	21.02	10.31	12.64	12.44
Dividends per Share	0.80	0.77	0.73	0.69	0.62
Dividend Yield (%)	3.09	3.33	3.54	3.01	2.60
Sales per Share	49.47	47.23	62.34	65.64	62.94
EPS before extra. item	1.04	1.10	2.00	1.80	1.92
Cash Flow per Share	3.00	3.10	3.73	3.78	3.94
Book Value per Share	15.23	14.42	14.30	12.85	11.76
O/S Common Shares	78,350	76,560	74,630	74,630	73,790
Total Revenue	3,867,000	3,626,000	4,718,000	4,877,000	4,611,000
Income before extra.	101,000	109,000	169,000	135,000	140,600
Cash Flow	233,000	236,000	280,000	280,000	288,800
Debt/Equity	0.63	0.75	0.65	0.90	1.24
Return on Capital (%)	7.77	8.10	14.26	13.91	15.76
Ret. on Com. Equity (%)	6.97	7.74	14.91	14.78	17.16
% Change Profit	(7.3)	(35.5)	25.2	(4.0)	12.3
% Change Revenue	6.6	(23.1)	(3.3)	5.8	21.2
% Change Assets	9.0	3.4	6.9	8.6	7.8

Preferred Div. Coverage	4.8	4.4	9.4
Total Div. Coverage	1.2	1.3	2.3
Interest Coverage	3.7	5.5	4.4
Current Ratio	2.0	1.2	1.9
Operating Margin	7.7	5.9	5.6
Asset Turnover	1.2	1.2	1.6

5 YEAR RATIOS (%)

Return on Capital	12.0	13.9	16.3
Return on Com. Equity	12.3	14.4	16.2
Profit Growth	(4.3)	1.4	15.6
Revenue Growth	0.3	2.7	14.1
Asset Growth	7.0	11.2	13.7

BALANCE SHEET (000)

Cash	766,000	300,000	300,000
Current Assets	1,634,000	991,000	1,184,000
Net Fixed Assets	1,027,000	933,000	1,181,000
Invest's & Advances	210,000	219,000	186,000
Total Assets	3,320,000	3,046,000	2,946,000
Short Term Debt	41,000	367,000	71,000
Current Liabilities	836,000	822,000	628,000
Long Term Debt	901,000	687,000	821,000
Total Liabilities	1,827,000	1,642,000	1,579,000
Total Equity	1,493,000	1,404,000	1,367,000
Total Liab. & Equity	3,320,000	3,046,000	2,946,000

CAPITAL (000)

Total Debt	942,000	1,054,000	892,000
Preferred Equity	300,000	300,000	300,000
Common Equity	1,193,000	1,104,000	1,067,000

Business:

JOHN LABATT LTD. is principally in the brewing and entertainment industries in Canada, the United States and Europe. Subsidiaries include Labatt Breweries of Canada and BCL Entertainment. The company owns TSN, The Sports Network and 90% of the Toronto Blue Jays Baseball Club.

Date	EPS	DPS	Tot Rev	Inc Bex
Apr 93	(2.64)	0.21	594,000	(204,000)
Jan 93	0.31	0.21	953,000	30,000
Oct 92	0.60	0.21	1,180,000	52,000
Jul 92	0.61	0.21	1,123,000	52,000
Apr 92	(0.36)	0.20	506,000	(23,000)
Jan 92	0.40	0.20	959,000	35,000
Oct 91	0.49	0.20	963,000	45,000
Jul 91	0.51	0.20	1,000,000	44,000

Synopsis:

Brascan Limited sold its stake in John Labatt Limited for $993-million. The shares were sold to a group of underwriters who in turn sold them to the public. John Labatt distributed its Canadian dairy business to its shareholders as a new public company, Ault Foods Ltd. Shareholders and installment receipt holders received one Ault share for each five Labatt common shares held. Holders of Labatt convertible debentures received Ault shares on the same basis as if they converted the debentures into common shares. John Labatt has been considering offers for all or part of Johanna Dairies, its U.S. dairy interest. Labatt estimates that it will lose $160-million on sale of the U.S. dairy unit. In May 1993, Tuscan Dairy Farms Inc., a milk-product processor owned by Johanna, was sold for an undisclosed price.

In May 1993, Labatt Breweries invested $1.5-million in Britain's first national commercial rock station, Virgin radio. Labatt Breweries will be lending its name to two rock concert halls in London and Manchester, under a deal worth approximately $3.9-million. Under the agreement the company receives the exclusive right to sell its beer brands at the two halls.

Effective May 1992, Labatt's ownership in BCL Entertainment increased from 45% to 75% and BCL's results will now be consolidated. Labatt purchased the remaining 30% of Le Reseau des Sports, the French language sports cable channel, to bring its total ownership to 100%. In 1992 Labatt purchased 11% of Supercorp, a company that provides services to the advertising industry, increasing its ownership 80%.

Labatt recorded charges in fiscal 1993 relating to the rationalization of brewing capacity, which included the closing of its Saskatoon brewery. The restructuring charge by the end of the third quarter of 1993 was $16-million. At the end of the third quarter, Labatt's year-to-date national market share stood at 44%, or two percentage points above last year's level. Both the brewing and entertainment segments had improved earnings for the nine months.

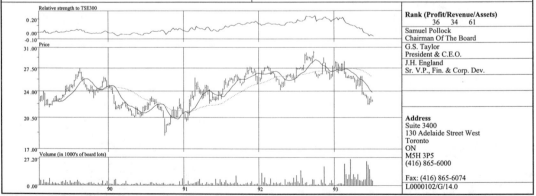

Rank (Profit/Revenue/Assets)
36 34 61

Samuel Pollock
Chairman Of The Board

G.S. Taylor
President & C.E.O.

J.H. England
Sr. V.P., Fin. & Corp. Dev.

Address
Suite 3400
130 Adelaide Street West
Toronto
ON
M5H 3P5
(416) 865-6000

Fax: (416) 865-6074
L0000102/G/14.0

LAIDLAW INC.

Exchanges	Price (Jun24'93)		10.25	Trailing P/E		41.00	Stock Symbol
TMQ	Trailing Yield (%)		1.56	Trailing EPS		0.25	**LDM.B**

Period Ending	Aug92	Aug91	Aug90	Aug89	Aug88
Yearly Statistics	US	US	US	US	US
Price-Close	10.00	13.13	21.25	19.25	15.50
Price-High	13.25	23.50	28.38	20.25	22.25
Price-Low	8.25	11.25	19.00	15.00	13.38
P/E-Close	17.07	nm	17.83	16.12	16.18
Dividends per Share	0.16	0.27	0.23	0.19	0.15
Dividend Yield (%)	1.60	2.04	1.09	1.00	0.95
Sales per Share	7.24	7.63	7.44	6.61	6.68
EPS before extra. item	0.50	(1.41)	1.02	1.00	0.76
Cash Flow per Share	1.32	1.64	1.75	1.59	1.56
Book Value per Share	7.04	6.60	7.98	6.02	3.99
O/S Common Shares	277,188	253,336	239,056	218,340	189,488
Total Revenue	1,978,927	1,925,890	1,868,158	1,426,977	1,204,919
Income before extra.	138,492	(344,361)	247,928	210,785	147,406
Cash Flow	351,341	404,488	409,440	322,413	275,438
Debt/Equity	0.67	0.92	0.72	0.65	0.58
Return on Capital (%)	8.96	(5.50)	13.60	16.61	18.08
Ret. on Com. Equity (%)	7.62	(19.50)	14.86	19.56	19.30
% Change Profit	140.2	(238.9)	17.6	43.0	59.8
% Change Revenue	2.8	3.1	30.9	18.4	31.4
% Change Assets	1.8	(7.7)	46.9	62.0	30.5

Preferred Div. Coverage	248.2	0.0	29.0
Total Div. Coverage	3.8	0.0	4.0
Interest Coverage	2.4	0.0	3.6
Current Ratio	1.5	1.6	1.7
Operating Margin	12.3	13.1	16.8
Asset Turnover	0.5	0.5	0.4

5 YEAR RATIOS (%)			
Return on Capital	10.4	12.6	17.8
Return on Com. Equity	8.4	10.4	18.0
Profit Growth	8.4	na	49.4
Revenue Growth	16.6	28.2	34.6
Asset Growth	23.8	39.3	51.2

BALANCE SHEET (000)			
Cash	131,712	125,226	208,416
Current Assets	523,695	519,948	540,443
Net Fixed Assets	1,795,073	1,833,764	1,701,648
Invest's & Advances	869,905	776,369	1,224,334
Total Assets	3,658,935	3,595,316	3,894,939
Short Term Debt	45,878	36,767	48,721
Current Liabilities	349,289	315,920	317,912
Long Term Debt	1,260,892	1,507,552	1,434,543
Total Liabilities	1,698,981	1,913,253	1,841,072
Total Equity	1,959,954	1,682,063	2,053,867
Total Liab. & Equity	3,658,935	3,595,316	3,894,939

CAPITAL (000)			
Total Debt	1,306,770	1,544,319	1,483,264
Preferred Equity	9,609	9,609	147,042
Common Equity	1,950,345	1,672,454	1,906,825

Business:

LAIDLAW INC. is a waste disposal and passenger services company. The company provides chemical waste services and solid waste services to residential, commercial and industrial customers in the United States and Canada. Laidlaw also operates a fleet of school buses across North America, and maintains a number of public transit systems.

Date		EPS	DPS	Tot Rev	Inc Bex
May 93	US	(0.12)	0.04	543,772	(33,601)
Feb 93	US	0.10	0.04	482,065	24,083
Nov 92	US	0.18	0.04	527,904	48,892
Aug 92	US	0.09	0.04	443,654	24,882
May 92	US	0.14	0.04	517,418	38,774
Feb 92	US	0.11	0.04	474,444	28,159
Nov 91	US	0.16	0.04	532,396	40,577
Aug 91	US	(1.89)	0.07	413,804	(465,596)

Synopsis:

Laidlaw Inc. issued $200-million (U.S.) of notes and debentures in the United States, consisting of $100-million (U.S.) of 7.05% notes due May 15, 2003, and $100-million (U.S.) of debentures due May 15, 2023. The net proceeds from the issue will be used to repay existing indebtedness. In August 1992, Laidlaw issued in the United States 7.7% debentures due August 15, 2002, for proceeds of $200-million. Laidlaw Waste Systems Ltd. has been contracted to handle bulk garbage collection at about 300 apartment buildings throughout the City of Toronto.

The North American hazardous waste operations were unified into a single continental organization. The new structure is expected to allow Laidlaw to better serve markets in Canada, the United States and Mexico. Laidlaw has a repositioning program for its U.S. solid waste business of acquisitions and divestitures to improve its competitive position. Laidlaw sold four hauling operations that had a combined income of $6-million, but operating losses that totaled approximately $300,000. The sales were made at a break even to book value. Three small hauling companies were acquired to strengthen its market presence in Maryland, Illinois and Massachusetts.

Second quarter results for the hazardous waste operations reflect the positive results of the U.S. operations being offset by soft Canadian results. Revenues and operating profit were greater for the second quarter of fiscal 1993 than the same period last year. Canadian operations reflected the start-up losses of operations in Western and Atlantic Canada and the increased volume but lower prices in the Ontario and Quebec markets.

Contributions to total revenues (income from operations) for fiscal 1992 by segment were: solid waste services, 42% (35%); hazardous waste services, 24% (28%); and passenger services, 34% (37%). Contributions to revenue (income from operations) for fiscal 1992 by geographic segment were: United States, 69% (62%); Canada, 31% (38%).

Relative strength to TSE300

Price

Volume (in 1000's of board lots)

Rank (Profit/Revenue/Assets)
22 56 49
Peter N.T. Widdrington
Chairman
Donald K. Jackson
President & C.E.O.
Leslie W. Haworth
Sr. V.P. & C.F.O.

Address
3221 North Service Road
P.O. Box 5028
Burlington
ON
L7R 3Y8
(416) 336-1800

Fax: (416) 336-3976
L0000475/G/14.0

NORANDA INC.

Exchanges	Price (Jun24'93)	21.87	Trailing P/E	nm	Stock Symbol
TMV	Trailing Yield (%)	4.57	Trailing EPS	(0.16)	**NOR**

Period Ending	Dec92	Dec91	Dec90	Dec89	Dec88
Yearly Statistics					
Price-Close	18.50	18.63	16.75	24.25	24.13
Price-High	20.75	20.38	24.50	28.38	27.13
Price-Low	16.38	15.50	14.13	21.38	20.13
P/E-Close	185.00	nm	46.53	11.07	7.69
Dividends per Share	1.00	1.00	1.00	1.00	0.90
Dividend Yield (%)	5.41	5.37	5.97	4.12	3.73
Sales per Share	45.44	44.05	50.86	50.53	48.35
EPS before extra. item	0.10	(1.04)	0.36	2.19	3.14
Cash Flow per Share	4.64	2.72	5.41	6.94	8.47
Book Value per Share	17.39	18.29	20.12	20.61	19.52
O/S Common Shares	188,604	187,166	190,292	187,265	183,619
Total Revenue	8,666,000	8,476,000	9,565,000	9,366,000	8,926,000
Income before extra.	79,000	(133,000)	120,000	442,000	603,000
Cash Flow	872,000	509,000	1,003,000	1,258,000	1,521,000
Debt/Equity	1.36	1.29	1.15	1.00	0.60
Return on Capital (%)	4.93	1.74	2.13	14.72	23.61
Ret. on Com. Equity (%)	0.54	(5.35)	1.72	10.64	16.71
% Change Profit	159.4	(210.8)	(72.9)	(26.7)	75.8
% Change Revenue	2.2	(11.4)	2.1	4.9	21.2
% Change Assets	(1.0)	(2.7)	6.2	26.0	16.1
Preferred Div. Coverage	1.3	0.0	2.2		
Total Div. Coverage	0.3	0.0	0.5		
Interest Coverage	1.2	0.4	7.8		
Current Ratio	1.9	1.8	1.9		
Operating Margin	4.4	(1.7)	6.6		
Asset Turnover	0.6	0.6	0.6		
5 YEAR RATIOS (%)					
Return on Capital	9.4	11.1	11.1		
Return on Com. Equity	4.9	7.0	8.1		
Profit Growth	(25.5)	na	43.1		
Revenue Growth	3.3	6.4	22.5		
Asset Growth	8.4	13.4	19.0		
BALANCE SHEET (mil)					
Cash	501	884	795		
Current Assets	3,719	4,056	4,240		
Net Fixed Assets	8,557	8,528	8,851		
Invest's & Advances	2,027	1,869	1,763		
Total Assets	14,370	14,517	14,917		
Short Term Debt	521	821	712		
Current Liabilities	1,987	2,273	2,226		
Long Term Debt	5,070	4,691	4,672		
Total Liabilities	10,247	10,249	10,244		
Total Equity	4,123	4,268	4,673		
Total Liab. & Equity	14,370	14,517	14,917		
CAPITAL (mil)					
Total Debt	5,591	5,512	5,384		
Preferred Equity	844	844	844		
Common Equity	3,279	3,424	3,829		

Business:

NORANDA INC. is a diversified natural resources company operating in three groups: mining and metals, forest products, and oil and gas. Major assets are in North American, but Noranda operates worldwide. Metals include copper, zinc, nickel, aluminum and gold. Noranda has significant interests in Brunswick Mining & Smelting, Hemlo Gold, Falconbridge, Kerr Addison, Noranda Forest, and Norcen Energy.

Date	EPS	DPS	Tot Rev	Inc Bex
Mar 93	(0.25)	0.25	1,253,000	(31,000)
Dec 92	(0.06)	0.25	2,147,000	4,000
Sep 92	0.06	0.25	2,175,000	26,000
Jun 92	0.09	0.25	2,222,000	32,000
Mar 92	0.01	0.25	2,107,000	17,000
Dec 91	(0.67)	0.25	1,990,000	(109,000)
Sep 91	(0.39)	0.25	2,000,000	(57,000)
Jun 91	0.02	0.25	2,282,000	18,000

Synopsis:

Noranda Inc. sold its common share interest in North Canadian Oils Limited to Norcen Energy Resources Limited in exchange for subordinate voting ordinary shares of Norcen. The transaction increased Noranda's equity interest in Norcen to 44.2%, or 49.6% on a fully diluted basis. Noranda sold its interest in MacMillan Bloedel for $971-million. Noranda received $333-million on closing of the agreement, the second installment of $319-million will be paid on August 25, 1994, and the third installment of $319-million will be paid on or before February 24, 1995. Noranda Forest will use the proceeds from the sale to reduce debt, improve existing assets, and fund new investment opportunities available in the forest industry. Noranda Inc. has stated an interest in acquiring all of Kerr Addison Mines Ltd. by issuing Noranda shares.

Noranda's mines were shutdown during the summer in order to slash zinc production by 13%, from 573,000 tonnes in 1992 to about 500,000 for 1993. The amount of zinc being mined over the last three years has outpaced demand in the automobile and construction industries. The production drop is expected to return the group's zinc concentrate inventories to normal levels by year end. Noranda Inc. has set a priority of adding to its mineral base, especially its copper reserves. Noranda refined 415,000 tonnes of copper and mined 152,000 tonnes in 1992. Falconbridge Ltd., 50% owned by Noranda, has a one-third interest in the $800-million Collahausi project in Chile that is expected to increase Noranda's copper ore reserves by more than 2.5 times.

Contributions to total sales (segment earnings) for the first quarter of 1992 by industry segment were: mining and metals, 64% (-15%); forest products, 30% (80%); oil and gas, 6% (55%); and corporate and inter-segment, -% (-20%). Contributions to segment earnings in 1992 by industry segment were: mining and minerals, 70%; forest products (includes MacMillan Bloedel), 10%; oil and gas, 27%; and corporate and inter-segment, -7%. Canadian operations had export sales of $3.5-billion and sales from U.S. operations were $3.4-billion.

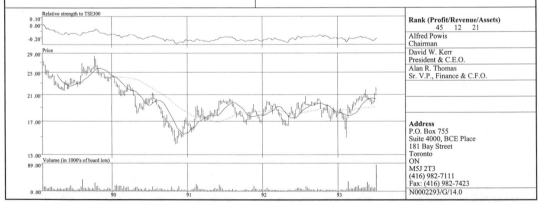

Rank (Profit/Revenue/Assets)
45   12   21

Alfred Powis
Chairman

David W. Kerr
President & C.E.O.

Alan R. Thomas
Sr. V.P., Finance & C.F.O.

Address
P.O. Box 755
Suite 4000, BCE Place
181 Bay Street
Toronto
ON
M5J 2T3
(416) 982-7111
Fax: (416) 982-7423
N0002293/G/14.0

ONEX CORPORATION

Exchanges					Stock Symbol
TM	**Price (Jun24'93)**	11.75	**Trailing P/E**	18.36	**OCX**
	Trailing Yield (%)	3.40	**Trailing EPS**	0.64	

Period Ending	Dec92	Dec91	Dec90	Dec89	Dec88
Yearly Statistics					
Price-Close	7.88	7.00	6.38	14.38	11.75
Price-High	8.88	13.25	14.50	16.63	14.38
Price-Low	5.63	5.88	4.75	12.13	8.63
P/E-Close	17.90	3.54	nm	13.44	7.58
Dividends per Share	0.40	3.89	0.34	0.29	1.74
Dividend Yield (%)	5.08	55.57	5.33	2.02	14.81
Sales per Share	116.71	78.58	58.61	74.67	67.27
EPS before extra. item	0.44	1.98	(1.69)	1.07	1.55
Cash Flow per Share	3.92	3.42	1.27	4.52	4.35
Book Value per Share	11.57	12.74	15.06	16.86	15.85
O/S Common Shares	28,485	22,139	23,257	22,846	22,479
Total Revenue	2,832,938	1,680,182	1,355,547	1,707,560	1,515,738
Income before extra.	13,538	63,410	(19,310)	36,583	35,819
Cash Flow	94,664	72,591	29,024	102,174	97,277
Debt/Equity	1.93	1.91	2.21	3.50	3.25
Return on Capital (%)	11.33	13.96	2.51	7.38	11.95
Ret. on Com. Equity (%)	4.43	20.06	(5.25)	9.87	9.76
% Change Profit	(78.7)	428.4	(152.8)	2.1	44.4
% Change Revenue	68.6	23.9	(20.6)	12.7	25.5
% Change Assets	26.3	(22.1)	(22.0)	12.1	(9.1)

Preferred Div. Coverage	np	np	np
Total Div. Coverage	1.0	0.6	0.0
Interest Coverage	1.6	2.3	0.7
Current Ratio	1.0	1.0	1.2
Operating Margin	4.0	5.7	3.2
Asset Turnover	1.7	1.3	0.8
5 YEAR RATIOS (%)			
Return on Capital	9.4	9.5	10.2
Return on Com. Equity	7.8	8.8	11.0
Profit Growth	(11.4)	19.0	na
Revenue Growth	18.5	19.7	27.5
Asset Growth	(4.8)	11.1	38.8
BALANCE SHEET (000)			
Cash	83,550	90,983	117,469
Current Assets	575,546	362,689	475,914
Net Fixed Assets	450,501	366,229	403,396
Invest's & Advances	0	0	16,000
Total Assets	1,613,729	1,277,505	1,638,989
Short Term Debt	129,834	65,560	55,561
Current Liabilities	570,310	372,989	401,604
Long Term Debt	507,584	471,539	716,829
Total Liabilities	1,284,170	995,535	1,288,819
Total Equity	329,559	281,970	350,170
Total Liab. & Equity	1,613,729	1,277,505	1,638,989
CAPITAL (000)			
Total Debt	637,418	537,099	772,390
Preferred Equity	0	0	0
Common Equity	329,559	281,970	350,170

Business:

ONEX CORP. is a diversified holding company. Its companies operate as autonomous businesses in the airline catering, foodservice distribution, automotive products, foodservice equipment and industrial manufacturing industries. Operating companies include Sky Chefs Inc., ProSource Distribution Services Inc., Automotive Industries, and The Delfield Company.

Date	EPS	DPS	Tot Rev	Inc Bex
Mar 93	0.13	0.10	957,200	3,800
Dec 92	(0.20)	0.10	951,438	(3,462)
Sep 92	0.01	0.10	901,400	700
Jun 92	0.70	0.10	517,200	17,000
Mar 92	(0.07)	0.10	462,900	(700)
Dec 91	1.60	3.60	472,782	53,210
Sep 91	0.18	0.10	441,600	4,700
Jun 91	0.26	0.10	415,700	6,300

Synopsis:

Onex Corporation is planning a simplified share structure that would entail a stock issue worth about $85-million to a company controlled by Onex president and chairman Gerald Schwartz. OMIL Holdings Ltd., the single holder of Onex's multiple voting stock, is entitled to two kinds of dividends. It receives dividends equal to 20% of all dividends paid by the company and gets 20% of any increase in fair value of net assets, subject to certain conditions, paid in subordinate voting stock. The most recent payment of the performance dividend was for 1989 performance, the last time the conditions were met. OMIL, which has 60% of the votes in Onex, would give up the rights to the two dividends in return for 7.1 million new subordinate voting shares.

In June 1993, Onex reported that it was negotiating with Canada Post Corp. regarding the possible sale of Purolator Courier Ltd. Neither party would say what was at stake but a Bay Street analyst said the discussions involved the whole 78% ownership. Onex bought Purolator in a $238-million leveraged buyout in 1986.

Onex plans to add to its existing operations through acquisitions in 1993 rather than starting large new ventures that are unrelated to any of the operations currently owned. With one exception, all of the acquisitions being considered by Onex are in the United States. ProSource, formerly Burger King Distribution Services Inc., acquired Valley Food Services Inc. of Kansas City for $70-million. Valley Food Services is a mid-west U.S. foodservice distributor serving over 400 restaurants with annual revenues of $85-million. ProSource formed a joint venture with a restaurant distributor in Mexico during the first quarter of 1993. The two transactions are part of a plan to expand business beyond the Burger King network.

1992 revenues (operating earnings) by business were: airline catering, 20% (17%); courier services, 20% (-19%); foodservice distribution, 27% (8%); automotive products, 17% (74%); foodservice equipment, 4% (24%); industrial manufacturing, 12% (-15%); and parent company, (less than 1%) (11%).

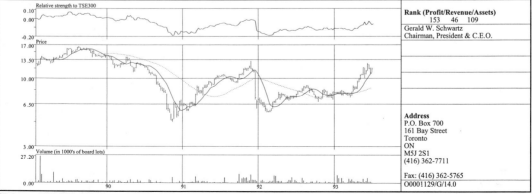

Rank (Profit/Revenue/Assets)
153 46 109

Gerald W. Schwartz
Chairman, President & C.E.O.

Address
P.O. Box 700
161 Bay Street
Toronto
ON
M5J 2S1
(416) 362-7711

Fax: (416) 362-5765
O0001129/G/14.0

ROMAN CORPORATION LIMITED

Exchanges	Price (Jun24'93)	2.53	Trailing P/E	10.12	Stock Symbol
T	Trailing Yield (%)	3.95	Trailing EPS	0.25	**RMN**

Period Ending	Dec92	Dec91	Dec90	Dec89	Dec88	Business:
Yearly Statistics						ROMAN CORP. LTD. is a management
Price-Close	1.75	1.70	2.50	9.75	10.63	company. Its main investment is in 100%
Price-High	2.55	4.60	9.63	13.50	14.75	owned Strathcona Paper Co. Strathcona is a
Price-Low	1.25	1.00	2.00	8.75	9.50	paper recycling company.
P/E-Close	7.96	6.80	nm	12.34	nm	
Dividends per Share	0.10	0.00	0.00	0.00	0.00	
Dividend Yield (%)	5.71	0.00	0.00	0.00	0.00	
Sales per Share	4.52	4.34	4.27	4.20	4.18	
EPS before extra. item	0.22	0.25	(14.41)	0.79	(0.17)	
Cash Flow per Share	0.43	0.69	0.45	0.44	0.30	
Book Value per Share	0.86	0.74	0.48	14.33	13.57	
O/S Common Shares	10,306	10,306	10,306	10,306	10,306	
Total Revenue	46,532	44,709	43,957	43,294	43,495	
Income before extra.	2,506	4,052	(142,471)	2,353	(1,711)	
Cash Flow	4,420	7,076	4,677	4,507	3,107	

Date	EPS	DPS	Tot Rev	Inc Bex
Mar 93	0.04	0.00	11,824	347
Dec 92	0.09	0.10	15,551	924
Sep 92	0.07	0.00	10,331	644
Jun 92	0.05	0.00	10,469	503
Mar 92	0.01	0.00	10,181	435
Dec 91	(0.02)	0.00	13,979	132
Sep 91	0.07	0.00	9,125	1,133
Jun 91	0.04	0.00	10,403	812

Debt/Equity	1.22	0.09	4.81	0.56	0.59
Return on Capital (%)	26.59	11.53	(87.14)	2.46	2.14
Ret. on Com. Equity (%)	27.33	45.40	(187.04)	1.64	(1.22)
% Change Profit	(38.2)	102.8	(6,154.2)	237.5	(120.0)
% Change Revenue	4.1	1.7	1.5	(0.5)	(10.7)
% Change Assets	4.5	(72.6)	(60.4)	2.1	41.4

				Synopsis:
Preferred Div. Coverage	np	3.4	0.0	The restructuring of Roman Corporation Limited, which saw the company selling
Total Div. Coverage	1.9	3.4	0.0	one investment and writing down the value of others to zero, has left the company
Interest Coverage	5.0	11.9	0.0	with a stronger balance sheet and a profitable operating subsidiary. Although
Current Ratio	2.0	1.4	1.0	Roman will remain focused on Strathcona, it plans to use its current position of
Operating Margin	11.3	14.0	12.3	stability to pursue other growth opportunities. Roman Corporation is looking at
Asset Turnover	1.7	1.8	0.5	investing in businesses that complement its activities as well as looking at
5 YEAR RATIOS (%)				acquiring a business that could be integrated with Strathcona.
Return on Capital	(8.9)	(12.4)	(13.6)	The drop in profit in 1992, compared to 1991, reflects the accounting treatment of
Return on Com. Equity	(22.8)	(26.8)	(35.9)	long-term debt financing costs. Long-term debt proceeds were used to redeem the
Profit Growth	(21.8)	na	na	preferred shares. Preferred share dividends are not deducted in calculating profit,
Revenue Growth	(1.0)	1.3	28.5	but interest expense on the long-term debt is. Earnings per common share is more
Asset Growth	(30.5)	(32.2)	(9.0)	comparable as it accounts for the cost of long-term obligations, whether it be debt
BALANCE SHEET (000)				or preferred shares.
Cash	90	0	0	Although net profit for the first quarter of 1993 was down over the comparable
Current Assets	8,785	7,905	76,127	period in 1992, earnings per share was up. The profit reflects the difference in
Net Fixed Assets	16,694	16,809	16,315	accounting for long-term obligations. The increase in earnings per share was
Invest's & Advances	0	0	0	attributed to the increased production and productivity at Strathcona, where the
Total Assets	26,637	25,495	93,058	ongoing focus is on increasing productivity and production capacity.
Short Term Debt	625	1,607	73,164	Exall Resources Limited, a company in which Roman has an equity interest, took
Current Liabilities	4,434	5,613	77,861	over a local Mexican company which has options on three separate copper
Long Term Debt	10,125	0	0	properties. Two of these properties have proven potential while the third would
Total Liabilities	17,827	7,184	77,861	have to be explored. If Exall decides to go into production at one of the properties
Total Equity	8,810	18,311	15,197	with proven potential then it is estimated that it would take 12 to 18 months to
Total Liab. & Equity	26,637	25,495	93,058	install the required facilities.
CAPITAL (000)				
Total Debt	10,750	1,607	73,164	
Preferred Equity	0	10,667	10,285	
Common Equity	8,810	7,644	4,912	

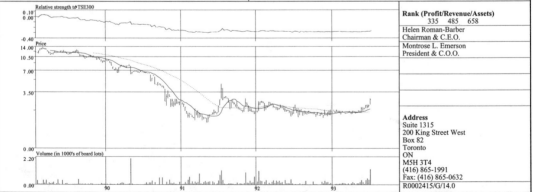

Rank (Profit/Revenue/Assets)
335   485   658

Helen Roman-Barber
Chairman & C.E.O.

Montrose L. Emerson
President & C.O.O.

Address
Suite 1315
200 King Street West
Box 82
Toronto
ON
M5H 3T4
(416) 865-1991
Fax: (416) 865-0632
R0002415/G/14.0

SCOTT'S HOSPITALITY INC.

Exchanges	Price (Jun24'93)	9 .50	Trailing P/E	17 .59	Stock Symbol
TM	Trailing Yield (%)	2 .74	Trailing EPS	0 .54	**SRC.C**

Period Ending	Apr92	Apr91	Apr90	Apr89	Apr88
Yearly Statistics					
Price-Close	15 .00	18 .75	15 .00	17 .25	12 .50
Price-High	19 .88	19 .50	21 .50	18 .00	15 .38
Price-Low	15 .00	13 .00	13 .38	11 .88	9 .50
P/E-Close	16 .67	18 .56	14 .42	19 .17	16 .03
Dividends per Share	0 .26	0 .26	3 .25	0 .22	0 .19
Dividend Yield (%)	1 .73	1 .39	21 .67	1 .28	1 .52
Sales per Share	14 .91	14 .27	15 .60	14 .42	18 .02
EPS before extra. item	0 .90	1 .01	1 .04	0 .90	0 .78
Cash Flow per Share	1 .82	2 .18	2 .06	1 .84	2 .05
Book Value per Share	6 .64	5 .80	5 .09	5 .78	5 .42
O/S Common Shares	59 ,730	59 ,717	59 ,697	59 ,442	59 ,213
Total Revenue	954 ,861	1 ,017 ,550	943 ,488	861 ,302	1 ,070 ,098
Income before extra.	53 ,530	60 ,308	61 ,933	53 ,436	46 ,198
Cash Flow	108 ,931	129 ,923	122 ,577	109 ,018	121 ,242
Debt/Equity	1 .10	1 .27	0 .97	0 .91	1 .14
Return on Capital (%)	13 .26	17 .21	19 .14	16 .61	17 .75
Ret. on Com. Equity (%)	14 .41	18 .54	19 .12	16 .07	15 .10
% Change Profit	(11 .2)	(2 .6)	15 .9	15 .7	18 .1
% Change Revenue	(6 .2)	7 .9	9 .5	(19 .5)	22 .1
% Change Assets	3 .7	15 .7	2 .4	(9 .2)	13 .8

Preferred Div. Coverage	np	np	np
Total Div. Coverage	3 .4	3 .9	0 .3
Interest Coverage	2 .5	3 .3	4 .3
Current Ratio	1 .7	1 .3	0 .9
Operating Margin	9 .6	12 .3	12 .1
Asset Turnover	0 .9	0 .9	1 .2
5 YEAR RATIOS (%)			
Return on Capital	16 .8	17 .5	18 .1
Return on Com. Equity	16 .6	17 .0	17 .4
Profit Growth	6 .4	11 .0	17 .6
Revenue Growth	1 .7	5 .6	9 .7
Asset Growth	4 .8	6 .2	9 .2
BALANCE SHEET (000)			
Cash	12 ,582	43 ,520	81 ,224
Current Assets	152 ,763	134 ,601	159 ,020
Net Fixed Assets	622 ,178	601 ,676	488 ,489
Invest's & Advances	23 ,768	10 ,560	7 ,528
Total Assets	956 ,291	922 ,131	796 ,758
Short Term Debt	137	2 ,196	3 ,161
Current Liabilities	91 ,390	100 ,770	169 ,915
Long Term Debt	436 ,441	437 ,570	291 ,852
Total Liabilities	559 ,713	575 ,636	492 ,727
Total Equity	396 ,578	346 ,495	304 ,031
Total Liab. & Equity	956 ,291	922 ,131	796 ,758
CAPITAL (000)			
Total Debt	436 ,578	439 ,766	295 ,013
Preferred Equity	0	0	0
Common Equity	396 ,578	346 ,495	304 ,031

Business:

SCOTT'S HOSPITALITY INC. is an international consumer service company with interests in the food service, lodging, and transportation industries. The company operates in Canada, the United States, and the United Kingdom. Subsidiaries of the company include Scott's Food Services, Scott's Hotels Limited, and Charterways Transportation Ltd.

Date	EPS	DPS	Tot Rev	Inc Bex
Jan 93	0.12	0.13	244 ,100	7 ,293
Oct 92	0.14	0.00	220 ,563	8 ,328
Jul 92	0.15	0.13	227 ,607	8 ,775
Apr 92	0.13	0.00	239 ,452	7 ,748
Jan 92	0.21	0.13	231 ,861	12 ,630
Oct 92	0.24	0.00	215 ,016	14 ,096
Jul 91	0.32	0.13	252 ,311	19 ,056
Apr 91	0.24	0.00	268 ,508	14 ,573

Synopsis:

Scott's Hospitality Inc. sold its 210-store Black's Photography chain to Fuji Photo Film Canada Inc. for $65-million. Since Scott's acquired Black's in 1985 the number of stores in Canada doubled to 210, with operations in 42 cities in eight provinces. An attempt to expand into the United States ended with the sale of Black's 48 U.S. stores in November 1991.

Scott's attributed the lower earnings for the third quarter ending January 31, 1993, compared to the third quarter last year, to the recession and tougher competition. The transportation division improved third quarter operating earnings over the last year, but the food services and hotels operations reported a decline in operating earnings.

In March 1993, Dominion Bond Rating Services lowered its rating on Scott's senior unsecured debentures to A (low) from A. DBRS said the downgrade reflects the expected decline in Scott's profitability for 1993 and 1994 compared to previous years. In 1992 Scott's issued $100-million of 8.5% unsecured Series B Debentures maturing December 16, 2002. The proceeds were used to pay down commercial paper debt.

In 1992 Perfect Pizza Limited, a subsidiary of Scott's, purchased the assets and business of Gino's Dial a Pizza in Great Britain. The acquisition made Perfect Pizza the largest operator of take-away and home delivery pizza in the market. Manchu Wok purchased 12 restaurants in the United States, from its competitor Magic Wok. Manchu Wok is test marketing home delivery in the Metropolitan Toronto area during 1993. KFC introduced home delivery service throughout Metropolitan Toronto and is looking for ways to provide the service to its other markets.

Sales (operating earnings) by geographic segment in fiscal 1992 were: Canada, 71% (71%); United States, 17% (27%); and Great Britain, 12% (2%). The food services and transportation segments accounted for almost 89% of segmented operating earnings in fiscal 1992.

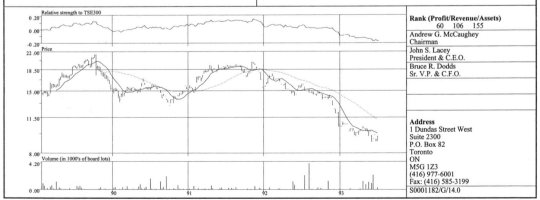

Rank (Profit/Revenue/Assets)
60 106 155

Andrew G. McCaughey
Chairman

John S. Lacey
President & C.E.O.

Bruce R. Dodds
Sr. V.P. & C.F.O.

Address
1 Dundas Street West
Suite 2300
P.O. Box 82
Toronto
ON
M5G 1Z3
(416) 977-6001
Fax: (416) 585-3199
S0001182/G/14.0

SEAGRAM COMPANY LTD. (THE)

Exchanges	Price (Jun24'93)		34.87	Trailing P/E		27.90	Stock Symbol
TMVN	Trailing Yield (%)		1.61	Trailing EPS		1.25	**VO**

Period Ending	Jan93	Jan92	Jan91	Jan90	Jan89
Yearly Statistics	US	US	US	US	US
Price-Close	32.00	35.06	25.81	22.22	21.12
Price-High	36.50	36.25	26.06	27.25	21.12
Price-Low	31.25	25.50	21.12	19.75	15.50
P/E-Close	16.45	13.75	9.46	8.62	9.30
Dividends per Share	0.55	0.50	0.46	0.35	0.29
Dividend Yield (%)	2.08	1.64	2.09	1.86	1.69
Sales per Share	13.84	13.82	13.35	11.62	10.26
EPS before extra. item	1.30	1.94	2.01	1.84	1.53
Cash Flow per Share	1.81	2.61	1.73	1.45	1.18
Book Value per Share	13.19	17.11	15.87	14.03	12.66
O/S Common Shares	373,690	378,841	374,972	381,822	392,859
Total Revenue	5,206,000	5,448,000	5,029,000	4,489,798	3,973,849
Income before extra.	474,000	727,000	756,000	710,578	589,460
Cash Flow	680,000	992,000	650,000	558,614	455,943
Debt/Equity	0.69	0.55	0.65	0.62	0.63
Return on Capital (%)	10.45	12.80	13.39	13.59	12.99
Ret. on Com. Equity (%)	8.31	11.69	13.37	13.76	12.50
% Change Profit	(34.8)	(3.8)	6.4	20.5	13.1
% Change Revenue	(4.4)	8.3	12.0	13.0	38.9
% Change Revenue	(14.9)	3.5	12.4	5.3	28.5

Preferred Div. Coverage	np	np	np
Total Div. Coverage	2.3	3.8	4.3
Interest Coverage	2.9	3.6	3.5
Current Ratio	1.9	2.3	1.3
Operating Margin	15.5	15.3	14.9
Asset Turnover	0.5	0.4	0.4

5 YEAR RATIOS (%)			
Return on Capital	12.6	13.0	12.7
Return on Com. Equity	11.9	12.7	12.7
Profit Growth	(1.9)	11.4	18.7
Revenue Growth	12.7	17.3	18.9
Asset Growth	5.9	11.4	12.9

BALANCE SHEET (mil)			
Cash	116	266	131
Current Assets	3,836	4,327	3,970
Net Fixed Assets	1,215	1,214	1,209
Invest's & Advances	3,315	4,566	4,504
Total Assets	10,104	11,876	11,477
Short Term Debt	851	568	1,838
Current Liabilities	2,003	1,896	3,130
Long Term Debt	2,559	3,013	2,038
Total Liabilities	5,174	5,393	5,525
Total Equity	4,930	6,483	5,952
Total Liab. & Equity	10,104	11,876	11,477

CAPITAL (mil)			
Total Debt	3,410	3,581	3,876
Preferred Equity	0	0	0
Common Equity	4,930	6,483	5,952

Business:

SEAGRAM CO. LTD. makes and markets distilled spirits, wines, soft drinks and fruit juices. Brand names include Chivas, Martell, Glenlivet, Barton & Guestier, Crown Royal, Paul Masson, and Tropicana. The company owns 24 per cent of the outstanding common shares of chemical firm E.I. du Pont de Nemours and Co.

Date		EPS	DPS	Tot Rev	Inc Bex
Apr 93	US	0.43	0.14	1,267,000	162,000
Jan 93	US	(0.06)	0.14	2,079,000	(23,000)
Oct 92	US	0.47	0.14	1,518,000	178,000
Jul 92	US	0.41	0.14	1,483,000	152,000
Apr 92	US	0.41	0.14	1,307,000	153,000
Jan 92	US	0.52	0.12	2,334,000	197,000
Oct 91	US	0.50	0.12	1,570,000	193,000
Jul 91	US	0.39	0.12	1,452,000	149,000

Synopsis:

The Seagram Company Ltd. purchased a 5.7% stake in Time Warner Inc. for $702-million (U.S.). The company intends to buy another 9.3%, bringing its total ownership to 15%, at a cost of roughly $1.3-billion (U.S.). The purchase will be funded through bank credit lines. Seagram plans to use part of its own cash flow to pay financing costs, as the annual dividend from Time Warner will not cover the interest on the bank lines. Time Warner is involved in the entertainment and publishing industries.

Seagram redeemed its $100-million (U.S.) worth of 8.5% Eurodollar Bonds due April 15,1996, at par plus a premium of one percentage point. The company also paid the interest due on the bonds with the surrender of the bonds.

The improvement in net income for the first quarter ended April 30, 1993, compared to the same period last year, reflects the improved performance of E.I. du Pont de Nemours and Company. Equity in unremitted DuPont earnings increased from $36-million to $47-million (U.S.). Operating income for the first quarter fell from $163-million (U.S.) to $148-million (U.S.). The decline reflected the difficult economic conditions in Europe, the spirit and wine group's biggest market, and in Japan and Brazil. The decline was partially offset by strong performances from Tropicana and the North American spirits and wine operations.

Contributions to sales and other income (operating income) for the year ended January 31, 1993, by business segment were: spirits and wines, 77% (90%); fruit juices, coolers and mixers, 23% (12%); and corporate expenses, - (-2%). Contributions to sales and other income (operating income) by geographic segment for the year ended January 31, 1993, were: the United States, 42% (13%); Europe, 39% (56%); Asia Pacific and Latin America, 16% (14%); and Canada, 3% (17%). Seagram recorded a $1.4-billion (U.S.) non-cash charge in its U.S. GAAP statements as a result of new accounting standards in the United States for the treatment of post retirement benefits and deferred taxes.

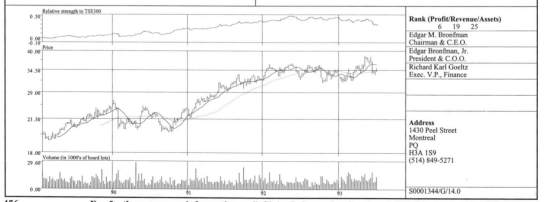

Rank (Profit/Revenue/Assets)
6   19   25

Edgar M. Bronfman
Chairman & C.E.O.

Edgar Bronfman, Jr.
President & C.O.O.

Richard Karl Goeltz
Exec. V.P., Finance

Address
1430 Peel Street
Montreal
PQ
H3A 1S9
(514) 849-5271

S0001344/G/14.0

SHERRITT GORDON LIMITED

Exchanges	Price (Jun24'93)	8.62	Trailing P/E	nm	Stock Symbol
T	Trailing Yield (%)	0.00	Trailing EPS	(0.22)	SE

Period Ending	Dec92	Dec91	Dec90	Dec89	Dec88
Yearly Statistics					
Price-Close	6.63	7.50	6.50	10.00	11.50
Price-High	9.38	8.38	11.00	16.00	11.63
Price-Low	5.88	5.75	5.25	9.75	5.25
P/E-Close	110.42	187.50	nm	8.40	5.07
Dividends per Share	0.00	0.14	0.13	0.30	0.30
Dividend Yield (%)	0.00	1.87	2.00	3.00	2.61
Sales per Share	11.85	12.77	13.76	21.81	23.44
EPS before extra. item	0.06	0.04	(1.29)	1.19	2.27
Cash Flow per Share	1.74	1.34	0.78	3.12	4.21
Book Value per Share	7.82	7.76	8.14	9.57	8.69
O/S Common Shares	42,625	35,033	25,118	25,064	24,963
Total Revenue	439,929	389,160	345,250	545,899	545,409
Income before extra.	2,274	1,150	(32,387)	32,181	56,491
Cash Flow	63,965	40,232	19,600	78,112	97,923
Debt/Equity	0.90	1.22	0.79	0.59	0.65
Return on Capital (%)	3.25	4.01	(10.32)	14.52	21.63
Ret. on Com. Equity (%)	0.75	0.48	(14.58)	13.08	29.09
% Change Profit	97.7	103.6	(200.6)	(43.0)	859.9
% Change Revenue	13.0	12.7	(36.8)	0.1	78.3
% Change Assets	3.1	53.3	(6.6)	(8.6)	12.2
Preferred Div. Coverage	np	np	np		
Total Div. Coverage	na	0.2	0.0		
Interest Coverage	1.1	1.5	0.0		
Current Ratio	1.3	1.3	1.4		
Operating Margin	5.1	3.8	(0.1)		
Asset Turnover	0.5	0.5	0.6		
5 YEAR RATIOS (%)					
Return on Capital	6.6	7.3	6.5		
Return on Com. Equity	5.8	5.9	1.8		
Profit Growth	(17.3)	na	na		
Revenue Growth	7.5	4.7	(5.0)		
Asset Growth	8.6	12.6	(3.4)		
BALANCE SHEET (000)					
Cash	62,595	47,741	3,610		
Current Assets	300,991	280,763	177,374		
Net Fixed Assets	540,203	542,668	353,326		
Invest's & Advances	24,842	16,828	17,357		
Total Assets	866,036	840,259	548,057		
Short Term Debt	139,500	112,124	70,922		
Current Liabilities	239,789	210,621	126,369		
Long Term Debt	160,059	218,922	90,230		
Total Liabilities	532,764	568,292	343,544		
Total Equity	333,272	271,967	204,513		
Total Liab. & Equity	866,036	840,259	548,057		
CAPITAL (000)					
Total Debt	299,559	331,046	161,152		
Preferred Equity	0	0	0		
Common Equity	333,272	271,967	204,513		

Business:

SHERRITT GORDON LTD. is engaged in the refining and sale of nickel and cobalt, the development and marketing of advanced industrial materials and metallurgical technologies, the production and marketing of fertilizers and chemicals, and the production and sale of oil and natural gas.

Date	EPS	DPS	Tot Rev	Inc Bex
Mar 93	(0.28)	0.00	95,190	(11,924)
Dec 92	(0.15)	0.00	100,589	(5,066)
Sep 92	0.01	0.00	86,194	284
Jun 92	0.20	0.00	149,930	7,039
Mar 92	0.00	0.00	103,216	17
Dec 91	(0.08)	0.14	114,552	(2,283)
Sep 91	(0.06)	0.00	69,693	(1,577)
Jun 91	0.15	0.00	117,728	4,290

Synopsis:

Sherrit Gordon Limited issued $200-million (U.S.) worth of 9.75% notes due April 1, 2003. The proceeds were used to repay long-term debt and for general corporate purposes, which may include an acquisition. The transaction strengthens its cash position and enhances its financial flexibility during the next decade. During 1992 7.59 million common shares and 3.75 million share purchase warrants were issued for net proceeds $59-million.

The first quarter results for 1993 includes an $8.1-million foreign exchange loss related to the repayment of long-term debt. The loss recorded in the first quarter could mainly be attributed to the lower nickel and cobalt prices. The metals division reported a loss for the first quarter due to the lower prices, which was partially offset by increased volumes, and higher costs for the refinery expansion. The fertilizers segment increased operating earnings due in part to higher prices for nitrogen fertilizers, which more than offset decreased sales volumes. The oil and gas segment's higher operating earnings was attributed to the combination of higher natural gas prices and an increase in oil and gas production.

Sherrit Gordon's plans to acquire additional gas reserves during 1993, complete the expansion of the metals plant and begin to commercialize some of the technologies that resulted from Westaim's research and development activities. Production at the metals plant is expected to be below capacity for 1993 because of the shutdowns required to allow for the installation of equipment.

Contributions to revenues (operating earnings) for 1992 by segment were: metals, 42% (-9%); fertilizers and chemicals, 36% (41%); technologies, 7% (22%); and oil and gas, 15% (46%). Contributions to revenues (operating earnings) for 1991 by segment were: metals, 50% (7%); fertilizers and chemicals, 36% (53%); technologies, 9% (31%); and oil and gas, 5% (9%). Direct export shipments from Canada, principally to customers in the United States and Europe, accounted for approximately 38% of revenues in 1992 and 35% in 1991.

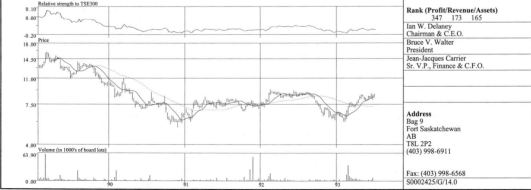

Rank (Profit/Revenue/Assets)		
347	173	165

Ian W. Delaney
Chairman & C.E.O.

Bruce V. Walter
President

Jean-Jacques Carrier
Sr. V.P., Finance & C.F.O.

Address
Bag 9
Fort Saskatchewan
AB
T8L 2P2
(403) 998-6911

Fax: (403) 998-6568
S0002425/G/14.0

UNIGESCO INC.

Exchanges	Price (Jun24'93)	1.00	Trailing P/E	nm	Stock Symbol
TM	Trailing Yield (%)	0.00	Trailing EPS	(0.14)	**UGO.B**

Period Ending	Mar92	Mar91	Mar90	Mar89	Mar88
Yearly Statistics					
Price-Close	2.11	3.25	3.70	3.70	3.65
Price-High	3.30	3.75	5.00	4.35	6.00
Price-Low	2.02	1.90	3.25	3.50	3.05
P/E-Close	nm	nm	nm	14.23	10.74
Dividends per Share	0.14	0.14	0.14	0.14	0.13
Dividend Yield (%)	6.64	4.31	3.78	3.78	3.56
Sales per Share	14.56	13.95	18.61	3.89	1.08
EPS before extra. item	(0.10)	(0.82)	(0.30)	0.26	0.34
Cash Flow per Share	(0.08)	(0.20)	0.23	0.17	0.13
Book Value per Share	3.19	3.43	4.42	4.84	4.84
O/S Common Shares	26,200	26,157	26,099	26,039	26,026
Total Revenue	395,955	380,237	497,134	121,890	42,442
Income before extra.	(899)	(19,726)	(5,988)	8,393	10,019
Cash Flow	(2,176)	(5,298)	5,968	4,469	3,055
Debt/Equity	3.04	2.63	2.05	0.87	0.39
Return on Capital (%)	5.32	0.37	6.89	6.24	5.50
Ret. on Com. Equity (%)	(3.02)	(20.64)	(5.67)	5.30	6.48
% Change Profit	95.4	(229.4)	(171.3)	(16.2)	(25.8)
% Change Revenue	4.1	(23.5)	307.9	187.2	44.0
% Change Assets	7.4	(4.9)	67.0	37.5	(8.9)

Date	EPS	DPS	Tot Rev	Inc Bex
Dec 92	0.02	0.00	89,539	568
Sep 92	0.00	0.00	115,843	70
Jun 92	(0.02)	0.00	132,396	(494)
Mar 92	(0.14)	0.00	(6,435)	(3,327)
Dec 91	(0.07)	0.07	87,557	(1,381)
Sep 91	0.06	0.00	106,392	1,979
Jun 91	0.05	0.07	119,895	1,830
Mar 91	(0.30)	0.00	(35,148)	(7,330)

Preferred Div. Coverage	0.0	0.0	0.0
Total Div. Coverage	0.0	0.0	0.0
Interest Coverage	0.8	0.1	0.8
Current Ratio	1.2	1.2	1.5
Operating Margin	4.5	4.1	5.0
Asset Turnover	0.7	0.8	1.0
5 YEAR RATIOS (%)			
Return on Capital	4.9	5.4	6.3
Return on Com. Equity	(3.5)	(0.6)	4.5
Profit Growth	na	na	na
Revenue Growth	68.1	79.3	98.8
Asset Growth	16.4	23.5	69.2
BALANCE SHEET (000)			
Cash	0	0	0
Current Assets	127,931	109,338	135,093
Net Fixed Assets	71,616	62,070	56,519
Invest's & Advances	198,269	193,701	203,660
Total Assets	513,665	478,228	502,991
Short Term Debt	41,176	32,381	27,902
Current Liabilities	108,610	88,041	92,986
Long Term Debt	293,936	272,936	263,351
Total Liabilities	403,520	361,960	361,098
Total Equity	110,145	116,268	141,893
Total Liab. & Equity	513,665	478,228	502,991
CAPITAL (000)			
Total Debt	335,112	305,317	291,253
Preferred Equity	26,476	26,476	26,476
Common Equity	83,669	89,792	115,417

Business:

UNIGESCO INC. is a Canadian company active in the distribution of food, convenience, hardware and renovation products. Its Excelco Foods division is active in the distribution of specialty foods throughout Canada. Its Sodisco Group subsidiary is a Canadian leader in the distribution and sale of hardware and renovation products.

Synopsis:

Unigesco sold its 26% interest in Univa for a total of $196-million. The Caisse de depot et placement du Quebec will buy 20,117,705 shares of Univa from Unigesco for $8.50 each or $171-million in cash. The purchase will leave the Caisse owning about 36% of the stock. By law the Caisse can own no more than 30% of a company except in certain instances but it must still return to 30% ownership later. Univa operates the Provigo supermarket chain in Quebec and Loeb stores in Ontario. The Teachers' Pension Plan Board of Ontario (TPPB) exercised its exchange privilege provided for in the $25-million debenture, issued to the Board by Unigesco, and exchangeable for Univa shares. The TPPB converted its $25-million debenture into 2,247,250 Univa shares, representing approximately 2.5% of Univa.

Unigesco made two unsuccessful attempts to sell its Univa shares before the deal with the Caisse was made. An offer from New York investment banker E.M. Warburg Pincus & Co. Inc. would have had Unigesco receiving $197.8-million or $8.85 a share for its stake in Univa. The deal fell through for unexplained reasons. The Blackstone Group L.P. withdrew an offer to purchase Univa for $11 a share through a leveraged buyout, after finding that the debt after closing would be higher than expected, and following strong opposition from the Caisse to the proposal.

Unigesco made an offer to debenture holders owed roughly $45-million. The holders would receive 40% of the face value of the debentures plus an 18.75% premium and all interest accrued up to June 16, 1993, within seven days of the completion of the sale of Univa to the Caisse. The remaining 60% would be received after Unigesco's planned United States junk bond issue. Unigesco plans to issue $115-million (U.S.) worth of junk bonds in the United States. The remaining 60% would be convertible at $1.75 a share from the current $7 a share.

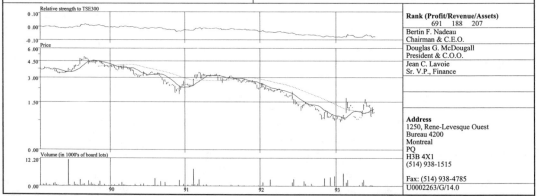

Rank (Profit/Revenue/Assets)
691   188   207

Bertin F. Nadeau
Chairman & C.E.O.

Douglas G. McDougall
President & C.O.O.

Jean C. Lavoie
Sr. V.P., Finance

Address
1250, Rene-Levesque Ouest
Bureau 4200
Montreal
PQ
H3B 4X1
(514) 938-1515

Fax: (514) 938-4785
U0002263/G/14.0

UNITED DOMINION INDUSTRIES LIMITED

Exchanges	Price (Jun24'93)	17.00	Trailing P/E	24.64	Stock Symbol
TMN	Trailing Yield (%)	1.18	Trailing EPS	0.69	**UDI**

Period Ending	Dec92	Dec91	Dec90	Dec89	Dec88
Yearly Statistics	US	US	US	US	US
Price-Close	10.50	10.50	10.00	20.75	19.50
Price-High	13.00	14.00	21.25	24.75	46.88
Price-Low	9.75	9.25	7.75	18.50	16.25
P/E-Close	11.66	10.13	30.59	8.68	265.04
Dividends per Share	0.20	0.51	0.58	0.75	0.63
Dividend Yield (%)	2.31	5.56	6.77	4.28	3.93
Sales per Share	51.47	46.05	50.46	49.22	81.63
EPS before extra. item	0.61	0.79	0.24	1.71	0.05
Cash Flow per Share	1.71	0.88	1.77	1.98	4.30
Book Value per Share	11.12	11.54	11.38	11.49	11.11
O/S Common Shares	35,826	29,325	28,489	28,489	27,096
Total Revenue	1,717,624	1,391,862	1,448,624	1,421,147	1,296,943
Income before extra.	25,684	37,010	26,381	73,219	25,426
Cash Flow	56,668	25,687	50,333	56,511	67,850
Debt/Equity	0.55	0.58	0.46	0.35	0.61
Return on Capital (%)	8.63	9.40	7.97	14.35	8.85
Ret. on Com. Equity (%)	5.50	6.99	2.14	15.50	0.69
% Change Profit	(30.6)	40.3	(64.0)	188.0	978.6
% Change Revenue	23.4	(3.9)	1.9	9.6	14.8
% Change Assets	16.4	(9.5)	(5.3)	(14.1)	24.2

Preferred Div. Coverage	4.7	2.7	1.4
Total Div. Coverage	2.1	1.3	0.8
Interest Coverage	2.9	4.0	3.3
Current Ratio	1.7	1.9	2.2
Operating Margin	3.0	1.6	2.7
Asset Turnover	1.7	1.5	1.5

5 YEAR RATIOS (%)			
Return on Capital	9.8	9.4	7.4
Return on Com. Equity	6.2	1.5	(6.7)
Profit Growth	61.1	98.4	9.5
Revenue Growth	8.7	4.6	2.3
Asset Growth	1.2	(5.1)	(7.0)

BALANCE SHEET (000)			
Cash	72,576	93,010	113,271
Current Assets	554,996	514,257	584,314
Net Fixed Assets	166,827	112,399	135,203
Invest's & Advances	0	0	0
Total Assets	1,016,416	873,541	965,125
Short Term Debt	26,040	52,136	22,444
Current Liabilities	325,753	277,791	267,727
Long Term Debt	219,164	175,376	195,221
Total Liabilities	566,266	480,506	488,849
Total Equity	450,150	393,035	476,276
Total Liab. & Equity	1,016,416	873,541	965,125

CAPITAL (000)			
Total Debt	245,204	227,512	217,665
Preferred Equity	51,784	54,505	152,144
Common Equity	398,366	338,530	324,132

Business:

UNITED DOMINION INDUSTRIES LIMITED provides manufactured products, engineering services, and construction products and services to industrial, energy and construction markets worldwide.

Date		EPS	DPS	Tot Rev	Inc Bex
Mar 93	US	(0.03)	0.05	411,489	129
Dec 92	US	0.28	0.05	461,789	10,746
Sep 92	US	0.17	0.05	443,844	7,529
Jun 92	US	0.27	0.05	441,782	10,054
Mar 92	US	(0.14)	0.05	365,340	(2,645)
Dec 91	US	(0.17)	0.36	333,184	(3,407)
Sep 91	US	0.04	0.05	325,299	5,442
Jun 91	US	0.14	0.05	371,734	8,015

Synopsis:

United Dominion Industries Limited realigned its corporate management structure and vested more autonomy in its business groups. The changes have been designed to decentralize decision making functions, allowing the operating units to become more accountable and entrepreneurial, and to intensify the focus on operating earnings. The operating units will consist of: United Dominion Construction Products and Services; United Dominion Industrial Products; United Dominion Engineering Services; and Dominion Bridge.

Canadian Pacific Limited will reduce its stake in United Dominion from its current 45% to 17%. CP issued debentures last year that could be redeemed for up to 10 million of CP's United Dominion shares on December 15, 1995.

United Dominion is planning to make acquisitions during 1993 in product areas that complement its current operations. The company is in discussions with a pump company that may lead to a deal in 1993. United Dominion had $45-million (U.S.) cash on hand and $354-million (U.S.) of unused credit facilities as at December 31, 1992. The company has tax-loss carry forwards in the United States which it can use to shelter earnings of the businesses from the payment of taxes, which also shields cash flow. United Dominion sold MENCK, a producer of hydraulic steam piling and hammers. The German company, which had break-even results last year, was sold at book value.

Contribution to sales (operating income) for 1992 were: construction products and services, 51% (20%); industrial products, 23% (50%); and engineering services, 26% (30%). Contribution to sales (operating income), excluding the divested businesses, for 1991 were: construction products and services, 51% (9%); industrial products, 28% (48%); and engineering services, 21% (43%). Geographic sales in 1992 (1991) were: the U.S., 74% (61%); Canada, 11% (19%); and Europe, 15% (20%).

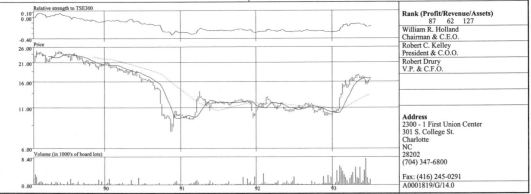

Rank (Profit/Revenue/Assets)
87   62   127

William R. Holland
Chairman & C.E.O.

Robert C. Kelley
President & C.O.O.

Robert Drury
V.P. & C.F.O.

Address
2300 - 1 First Union Center
301 S. College St.
Charlotte
NC
28202
(704) 347-6800

Fax: (416) 245-0291
A0001819/G/14.0

Page	Company	$	Latest year end	Earnings per Share		
				Actual	Estimate this year	Estimate next year
463	BMB Compuscience		9204	(0.37)	n.a.	n.a.
464	Cognos		9302	(0.54)	0.35	0.53
465	Corel Systems		9211	0.97	1.14	1.36
466	Geac Computer		9204	0.50	0.59	0.72
467	I.S.G. Technologies		9206	(0.11)	n.a.	n.a.
468	ISM Information Systems Management		9212	0.12	0.32	0.55
469	SHL Systemhous		9208	(0.23)	0.20	0.57
470	Softkey Software		9301	0.46	0.61	0.69
471	Teleglobe		9112	0.54	0.66	0.98

Estimates from I/B/E/S Inc., 345 Hudson St., New York, NY 10014 (212) 243-3335. In Canada: 6 Lansing Square, Ste. 235, Willowdale, ON M2J 1T5 (416) 496-0977.

Computer Software & Processing

Europe: Information Processing - Industry Report [Apr-21-1993]. MERRILL LYNCH CAPITAL MARKETS reported by Exton, D.

A consensus of recent statistics suggests that the European IT (Information Technology) market will grow by 6.8% in 1994. This compares with a 4.3% forecast for 1993. Software products software services areeach bigger than the PC market and, in aggregate terms, software/services is much bigger than hardware. Germany is the biggest single market within Europe and further economic slowdown will have consequences for the IT market. [RN 1324385]

Multi-Protocol Router Market - Industry Report [Apr-15-1993]. PAINEWEBBER INC. reported by Diwan, A.

The multi-protocol router market is expected to grow rapidly over next three years driven by the fundamental shift from the host-terminal architecture to the networked client-server architecture. Multi-protocol routers provide high gross (greater than 60%) and operating (greater than 20%) margins. This is a result of the high software content, barriers to entry and the ability of vendors to lock in customers. The multi-protocol router market is dominated by two vendors, Cisco Systems and WellfleetCommunications, which control over 70% of the market. [RN 1325348]

Info. Processing - Microcomputers - Industry Report [Apr-7-1993]. MERRILL LYNCH CAPITAL MARKETS reported by Preston, M.S., et al

In the hardware arena, continued strong demand is expected to provide significant revenue gains for leading manufacturers gaining market share, while second-tier vendors will begin to suffer. Gross margins are likely to remain under pressure from continued price reductions and negative foreign currency translation, given the strength in the U.S.dollar. Compaq is expected to record the strongest earnings gains of 127%. In software, new product applications are expected to impact result with most major vendors launching new products. Across the board, strength in operating system and application sales is expected to generate 40% revenue growth for Microsoft. [RN 1319701]

Microcomputer Weekly - Industry Report [Apr-7-1993]. MERRILL LYNCH CAPITAL MARKETS reported by Preston, M.S., et al

According to Storeboard Dealer Survey, PC unit sales have declined sequentially from a peak in seasonally strong December, but remain at the levels of last year's fall surge indicating demand remains healthy. New product cycles continue to dominate the news in both hardware and software arenas. Apple has a plethora of new products to be delivered over the next nine months including PDAs, multimedia devices, services and PowerOpen platforms. Lotus is getting good marks from beta sites for 1-2-3 for Windows 4.0. Sources expect a steady flow of news regarding Windows NT and additional operating system initiatives including a new version of Windows 3 called Chicago should boost Microsoft's stock over the near term. Products and services cited include personal computers, compact disc players, computer hardware, software, databases, spreadsheets, computer operating systems, and video equipment. [RN 1319622]

Mid-Range Computers - Industry Report [Apr-6-1993]. MERRILL LYNCH CAPITAL MARKETS reported by Elling, G.D.

At no time has the computer industry gone through the rapid technological and structural changes that are currently taking place. computer company executives are desperately seeking answers as to where to commit resources and how to refocus energies. While many salesmen are encouraged by the strategic moves that have been undertaken by their companies, operating in a more commoditized world is far different than most are used to and there are varied views as to what it will take to succeed in the future. Pricing pressures remain extremely intense, and while salesmen do not view the overall environment as having become worse, they point to the fact that discounting and special deals have been prevalent for the past 12-to-18 months, and no let up in the competitive pricing environment appears at hand. Most salesmen believe that an improving economy should begin to stimulate overall computer demand, although market disruptions, particularly now that Windows-NT is scheduled for introduction, and the various controversies regarding a standardized UNIX and which chip platform to adopt, are of current concern. [RN 1320589]

Software Industry - Industry Report [May-11-1993]. MERRILL LYNCH CAPITAL MARKETS reported by McClellan, S.T.

The Software Magazine and Sentry Market Research 1993 software market survey indicated that the U.S. software market is forecast to accelerate in growth in 1993 to a 21% rate. This represents the fastest pace since 1986. Total U.S. revenues are expected to be $41 billion (U.S.) in 1993, up from $34 billion (U.S.) a year ago. The typical large data center computer site is expected to increase expenditures on workstation and PC/Local Area Network (LAN) software by 41% in 1993, accounting for some 49% of total software budget, compared to a 42% portion in 1992. This will benefit companies such as Microsoft, Peoplesoft, Oracle, and Sybase. [RN 1330472]

Worldwide Technology Outlook - Industry Report [Apr-20-1993]. SHEARSON LEHMAN BROTHERS, INC. reported by Gumport, M., et al

1993 should be a good year for the semiconductor equipment industry. While parts of the global economy are in recession, there is still moderate worldwide economic growth. [RN1327070]

BMB COMPUSCIENCE CANADA LTD.

Exchanges	Price (Jun24'93)	0.35	Trailing P/E	nm	Stock Symbol
T	Trailing Yield (%)	0.00	Trailing EPS	(0.32)	**BMB**

Period Ending	Apr92	Apr91	Apr90	Apr89	Apr88
Yearly Statistics					
Price-Close	0.50	0.58	0.65	0.90	1.00
Price-High	0.80	1.35	1.20	1.30	1.95
Price-Low	0.40	0.40	0.60	0.75	0.95
P/E-Close	nm	4.14	15.85	5.63	11.91
Dividends per Share	0.00	0.00	0.00	0.00	0.00
Dividend Yield (%)	0.00	0.00	0.00	0.00	0.00
Sales per Share	0.47	0.93	0.99	1.04	0.52
EPS before extra. item	(0.37)	0.14	0.04	0.16	0.08
Cash Flow per Share	(0.21)	0.18	0.08	0.19	0.10
Book Value per Share	1.78	2.16	2.02	1.98	1.83
O/S Common Shares	2,472,314	2,457,564	2,457,564	2,457,564	2,457,564
Total Revenue	1,494,287	2,757,019	2,931,460	2,945,809	2,875,517
Income before extra.	(904,619)	343,475	100,202	394,302	376,710
Cash Flow	(524,427)	449,552	198,637	458,658	442,915
Debt/Equity	0.34	0.26	0.32	0.11	nd
Return on Capital (%)	(13.03)	10.09	3.93	8.13	8.86
Ret. on Com. Equity (%)	(18.60)	6.68	2.04	8.41	5.44
% Change Profit	(363.4)	242.8	(74.6)	4.7	35.1
% Change Revenue	(45.8)	(6.0)	(0.5)	2.4	(19.9)
% Change Assets	(13.6)	0.6	20.5	18.6	(51.5)
Preferred Div. Coverage	np	np	np		
Total Div. Coverage	na	na	na		
Interest Coverage	0.0	3.9	2.6		
Current Ratio	2.7	3.0	2.4		
Operating Margin	(74.4)	4.2	(8.4)		
Asset Turnover	0.2	0.3	0.4		
5 YEAR RATIOS (%)					
Return on Capital	3.6	7.5	0.7		
Return on Com. Equity	0.8	5.1	(1.0)		
Profit Growth	na	21.1	na		
Revenue Growth	(16.1)	(12.1)	(24.5)		
Asset Growth	(9.7)	(6.1)	(12.0)		
BALANCE SHEET					
Cash	3,957,424	3,711,615	3,417,431		
Current Assets	4,225,934	4,859,552	4,646,339		
Net Fixed Assets	1,680,018	1,956,539	1,952,332		
Invest's & Advances	81,025	111,871	291,382		
Total Assets	5,986,977	6,927,962	6,890,053		
Short Term Debt	1,490,910	1,373,133	1,611,024		
Current Liabilities	1,576,455	1,612,821	1,918,387		
Long Term Debt	0	0	0		
Total Liabilities	1,576,455	1,612,821	1,918,387		
Total Equity	4,410,522	5,315,141	4,971,666		
Total Liab. & Equity	5,986,977	6,927,962	6,890,053		
CAPITAL					
Total Debt	1,490,910	1,373,133	1,611,024		
Preferred Equity	0	0	0		
Common Equity	4,410,522	5,315,141	4,971,666		

Business:

BMB COMPUSCIENCE CANADA LTD. designs, sells and installs microcomputer based applications and solutions, including communications hardware and software. The company's products include executive information systems, treasury management systems, office automation systems, and communications gateways. The company has customers in Canada, the United States and worldwide.

Date	EPS	DPS	Tot Rev	Inc Bex
Jan 93	(0.04)	0.00	144	(89)
Oct 92	0.01	0.00	250	24
Jul 92	0.00	0.00	216	9
Apr 92	(0.29)	0.00	208	(723)
Jan 92	(0.05)	0.00	298	(123)
Oct 91	(0.03)	0.00	468	(70)
Jul 91	0.04	0.00	520	11
Apr 91	0.03	0.00	659	60

Synopsis:

Over the first nine months of fiscal 1993, BMB Compuscience Canada Ltd. remained focused on the development of satellite based information systems. BMB is continuing the process of developing its satellite information system NEWSCLIPS. The company during the period added real-time stock quotes in association with North American Quotations (NAQ) of London, Ontario. BMB is also currently examining opportunities with NAQ to offer products to the brokerage community in the U.S. Another product, JobSAT, a satellite communications based job listing system, has so far underperformed for the company. JobSAT is currently being marketed to community colleges, universities and chambers of commerce. BMB continues to develop MANAGER and executive information system (EIS) related products and has recently released a new version of MANAGER III. BMB currently has about $2-million in cash and securities, which will give the company an opportunity to develop the JobSAT and NEWSCLIPS markets.

Fiscal 1992 proved to be a tough year for BMB. Sales of custom software in addition to BMB's proprietary products dropped significantly from previous levels. In fiscal 1993, BMB will concentrate on the further development of THE MANAGER, its principal programming tool and satellite communications software. BMB will continue to support the development of EIS products and laboratory information programs such as QCExpert, a joint development with Perkin-Elmer Corporation. BMB believes there are strong opportunities in the management of satellite broadcast data.

In the fiscal 1992, research and development expenditures were $562,000, down 22% from fiscal 1991.

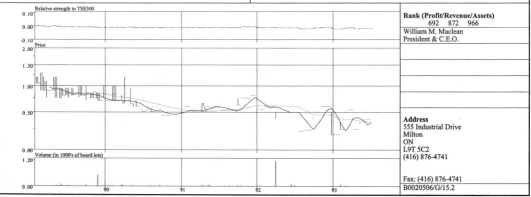

Rank (Profit/Revenue/Assets)
692 872 966

William M. Maclean
President & C.E.O.

Address
555 Industrial Drive
Milton
ON
L9T 5C2
(416) 876-4741

Fax: (416) 876-4741
B0020506/G/15.2

COGNOS INCORPORATED

Exchanges	Price (Jun24'93)		9.00	Trailing P/E		nm	Stock Symbol
TQ	Trailing Yield (%)		0.00	Trailing EPS		(0.61)	**CSN**

Period Ending	Feb93	Feb92	Feb91	Feb90	Feb89
Yearly Statistics					
Price-Close	8.75	12.00	19.00	5.50	8.38
Price-High	12.13	24.00	19.00	9.50	11.00
Price-Low	7.00	8.50	5.13	4.60	6.00
P/E-Close	nm	27.91	52.78	nm	13.51
Dividends per Share	0.00	0.00	0.00	0.00	0.00
Dividend Yield (%)	0.00	0.00	0.00	0.00	0.00
Sales per Share	11.57	11.91	12.93	10.79	10.50
EPS before extra. item	(0.62)	0.43	0.36	(1.64)	0.62
Cash Flow per Share	0.15	1.12	1.16	(0.87)	1.29
Book Value per Share	4.40	4.99	3.05	4.16	5.84
O/S Common Shares	12,851	12,682	10,692	10,459	10,387
Total Revenue	150,666	147,759	137,477	113,558	110,350
Income before extra.	(7,914)	5,244	3,823	(17,109)	6,346
Cash Flow	1,962	13,643	12,285	(9,119)	13,271
Debt/Equity	0.08	0.08	0.17	0.15	0.09
Return on Capital (%)	(8.28)	16.00	18.11	(22.90)	18.01
Ret. on Com. Equity (%)	(13.21)	10.94	10.05	(32.86)	10.89
% Change Profit	(250.9)	37.2	122.3	(369.6)	102.5
% Change Revenue	2.0	7.5	21.1	2.9	29.8
% Change Assets	(5.5)	44.7	15.5	(16.4)	13.3

Business:

COGNOS INCORPORATED develops, markets and supports open tools for developing business applications on a wide range of UNIX and proprietary midrange servers, and supports desktop clients under Microsoft Windows. PowerHouse, the company's flagship product, is used in over 23,000 midrange server installations in 68 countries.

Date	EPS	DPS	Tot Rev	Inc Bex
Feb 93	0.01	0.00	38,666	68
Nov 92	(0.54)	0.00	38,238	(6,921)
Aug 92	(0.10)	0.00	36,834	(1,306)
May 92	0.02	0.00	36,284	245
Feb 92	0.11	0.00	38,345	1,468
Nov 91	0.12	0.00	35,858	1,456
Aug 91	0.14	0.00	37,546	1,674
May 91	0.06	0.00	36,010	646

Preferred Div. Coverage	np	np	np	
Total Div. Coverage	na	na	na	
Interest Coverage	0.0	10.6	8.5	
Current Ratio	1.6	1.8	1.3	
Operating Margin	(3.0)	4.1	5.7	
Asset Turnover	1.3	1.2	1.6	
5 YEAR RATIOS (%)				
Return on Capital	4.2	8.6	11.7	
Return on Com. Equity	(2.8)	1.2	5.1	
Profit Growth	na	(5.2)	33.5	
Revenue Growth	12.0	15.5	24.8	
Asset Growth	8.3	18.9	19.3	
BALANCE SHEET (000)				
Cash	42,332	48,571	10,155	
Current Assets	87,348	93,465	58,185	
Net Fixed Assets	19,630	20,554	19,571	
Invest's & Advances	0	0	0	
Total Assets	114,258	120,920	83,588	
Short Term Debt	551	797	874	
Current Liabilities	53,669	53,223	46,208	
Long Term Debt	4,014	4,438	4,754	
Total Liabilities	57,683	57,661	50,962	
Total Equity	56,575	63,259	32,626	
Total Liab. & Equity	114,258	120,920	83,588	
CAPITAL (000)				
Total Debt	4,565	5,235	5,628	
Preferred Equity	0	0	0	
Common Equity	56,575	63,259	32,626	

Synopsis:

Cognos Inc. is investigating the recruitment of resellers to help deliver its PowerPlay information management system to a wider spectrum of desktop users. Traditionally, the company has relied on its own worldwide sales force but may examine using more traditional sales channels. Cognos wants to expand its network of resellers into the hundreds. For the first three quarters of 1992, about 10% of the company's revenue came from the desktop division.

Cognos initiated a reorganization of its top management earlier in the year after poor financial results for the company. This started with the resignation of company president and C.O.O., Jeff Papows, after three years. The heads of Cognos's underperforming European and U.S. operations are also gone. Previous management was unable to adapt the company's core products and sales force to the increasingly fast paced computer industry. In fiscal 1992, as open systems like Unix gained popularity, Digital Electronics Corporation related revenues at Cognos dropped 17%. Chairman, Michael Potter, realizes the difficulty of transforming Cognos into a fast mover. He added," we're in a dominant position in a low growth market...it's going to be hard to get hyper-growth until we shift more of the business." Growth in the traditional products is expected to remain flat over the next year and then slowly decline. Newer products could make up nearly one-quarter of 1993 sales.

Cognos continues to move from mature established markets with flat returns to newer, high growth markets. The trend has been the movement of revenues from proprietary Hewlett-Packard and Digital markets to newer high growth markets involving UNIX, IBM AS/400 and desktop computing. In the Unix and IBM AS/400 markets, revenues are up over 50%, with software sales in these markets plus desktop computing at 22% of license revenues for the first half of 1992. As newer markets develop, the company will redirect earnings from its older markets to reinvest in the newer markets. Revenues generated from the company's new UNIX and desktop-based products are expected to account for approximately 25% of overall revenues. Spending on research and development is expected to rise 30% in 1993.

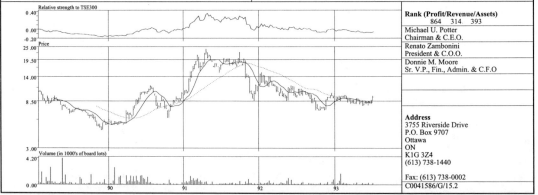

Rank (Profit/Revenue/Assets)
864   314   393

Michael U. Potter
Chairman & C.E.O.
Renato Zambonini
President & C.O.O.
Donnie M. Moore
Sr. V.P., Fin., Admin. & C.F.O

Address
3755 Riverside Drive
P.O. Box 9707
Ottawa
ON
K1G 3Z4
(613) 738-1440

Fax: (613) 738-0002
C0041586/G/15.2

COREL CORPORATION

Exchanges	Price (Jun24'93)		21.50	Trailing P/E		21.29	Stock Symbol
TQ	Trailing Yield (%)		0.00	Trailing EPS		1.01	**COS**

Period Ending	Nov92	Nov91	Nov90	Nov89	Nov88
Yearly Statistics					
Price-Close	21.25	19.00	11.88	6.13	n t
Price-High	24.88	29.50	16.13	7.38	n t
Price-Low	14.75	10.88	3.95	5.38	n t
P/E-Close	20.43	18.63	17.99	16.55	n t
Dividends per Share	0.00	0.00	0.00	0.00	0.00
Dividend Yield (%)	0.00	0.00	0.00	0.00	0.00
Sales per Share	7.64	4.69	2.74	3.14	1.21
EPS before extra. item	1.04	1.02	0.66	0.37	0.02
Cash Flow per Share	1.43	1.24	0.74	0.47	0.06
Book Value per Share	7.22	4.40	3.17	2.51	0.44
O/S Common Shares	13,675	11,318	10,706	10,647	5,932
Total Revenue	94,940	54,851	31,905	21,902	6,605
Income before extra.	11,186	11,357	6,990	2,559	123
Cash Flow	16,871	13,790	7,878	3,246	336
Debt/Equity	nd	nd	nd	0.02	nd
Return on Capital (%)	25.73	46.66	38.53	30.82	7.68
Ret. on Com. Equity (%)	15.06	27.15	23.08	17.45	5.31
% Change Profit	(1.5)	62.5	173.2	1,973.4	109.2
% Change Revenue	73.1	71.9	45.7	231.6	22.8
% Change Assets	77.4	41.8	35.8	741.8	38.0
Preferred Div. Coverage	np	np	np		
Total Div. Coverage	na	na	na		
Interest Coverage	nd	nd	nd		
Current Ratio	13.3	5.4	4.9		
Operating Margin	17.1	34.8	31.5		
Asset Turnover	0.9	0.9	0.7		
5 YEAR RATIOS (%)					
Return on Capital	29.9	na	na		
Return on Com. Equity	17.6	na	na		
Profit Growth	185.4	na	na		
Revenue Growth	77.5	na	na		
Asset Growth	108.7	na	na		
BALANCE SHEET (000)					
Cash	49,720	25,919	21,720		
Current Assets	86,481	51,606	39,202		
Net Fixed Assets	18,832	7,752	2,656		
Invest's & Advances	0	0	0		
Total Assets	105,313	59,358	41,858		
Short Term Debt	0	0	0		
Current Liabilities	6,520	9,589	7,978		
Long Term Debt	0	0	0		
Total Liabilities	6,520	9,589	7,978		
Total Equity	98,793	49,769	33,880		
Total Liab. & Equity	105,313	59,358	41,858		
CAPITAL (000)					
Total Debt	0	0	0		
Preferred Equity	0	0	0		
Common Equity	98,793	49,769	33,880		

Business:

COREL CORPORATION is a software development and marketing company specializing in graphics and SCSI (small computer systems interface) software.

Date	EPS	DPS	Tot Rev	Inc Bex
Feb 93	0.11	0.00	21,557	1,514
Nov 92	0.44	0.00	30,623	4,181
Aug 92	0.32	0.00	29,293	3,762
May 92	0.14	0.00	21,188	1,650
Feb 92	0.14	0.00	14,638	1,593
Nov 91	0.27	0.00	15,454	2,992
Aug 91	0.16	0.00	12,480	1,835
May 91	0.32	0.00	14,107	3,595

Synopsis:

In March 1993, Corel Corporation and Acculogic Inc. formed an partnership to market turnkey SCSI solutions. Also, Corel and NCR Microelectronic Products Division announced a strategic alliance through which both companies will team up to advance SCSI technology. In December 1992, Corel and Future Domain formed an alliance to include Corel's SCSI software with Future's family of host adapters. Also in December, a similar alliance was formed with Buslogic Inc., a supplier of SCSI host adapters. In the first phase of the alliance, Buslogic is responsible for the distribution and supporting of Corel SCSI products. In October 1992, Corel and ALWAYS Technology Corporation announced an agreement to include SCSI software with ALWAYS's host adapters. All these alliances are steps toward securing a standard for connecting all SCSI peripherals.

For fiscal 1992, record sales were aided by increased sales of CorelDraw 3.0, with an installed base for CorelDRAW of over 400,000 users. "CorelDRAW 3.0 represents a major step forward in graphics software. Providing total graphics capability in a single easy-to-use package, CorelDraw 3.0 is ideal for corporate standardization," according to Michael Cowpland, president and C.E.O. of Corel.

In November 1992, Corel and SyDOS, a division of SyQuest Technology formed a joint marketing partnership to supply the lowest cost CorelDraw CD-ROM drive bundle. Under the agreement, SyDOS will ship CorelDRAW together with its Personal CD-ROM product to customers in one package.

Corel has released a network-ready version of CorelDRAW, which should aid systems administrators in corporate settings.

Relative strength to TSE300 / Price / Volume (in 1000's of board lots)

Rank (Profit/Revenue/Assets)
167   390   412

Michael C.J. Cowpland
Chairman, President & C.E.O.

Michael W. Slaunwhite
C.F.O.

Kerry Williams
Director Of Operations

Address
1600 Carling Avenue
Ottawa
ON
K1Z 8R7
(613) 728-8200

Fax: (613) 728-9790
C0002878/G/15.2

GEAC COMPUTER CORPORATION LIMITED

Exchanges	Price (Jun24'93)	11.75	Trailing P/E	55.95	Stock Symbol
T	Trailing Yield (%)	0.00	Trailing EPS	0.21	**GAC**

Period Ending	Apr92	Apr91	Apr90	Apr89	Apr88
Yearly Statistics					
Price-Close	5.13	1.45	1.10	2.42	1.60
Price-High	5.63	2.00	3.20	2.62	3.65
Price-Low	1.45	1.10	1.10	1.35	1.25
P/E-Close	10.25	nm	2.90	11.00	nm
Dividends per Share	0.00	0.00	0.00	0.00	0.00
Dividend Yield (%)	0.00	0.00	0.00	0.00	0.00
Sales per Share	3.74	3.65	3.39	3.74	3.51
EPS before extra. item	0.50	(0.25)	0.38	0.22	(0.55)
Cash Flow per Share	0.62	(0.15)	0.18	0.42	(0.17)
Book Value per Share	2.19	1.68	1.94	1.58	1.47
O/S Common Shares	22,472	22,361	21,530	20,527	19,505
Total Revenue	85,322	82,165	81,186	75,219	68,585
Income before extra.	11,101	(5,507)	8,150	4,520	(9,203)
Cash Flow	13,916	(3,352)	3,891	8,340	(3,278)
Debt/Equity	nd	0.02	0.00	0.06	0.14
Return on Capital (%)	27.09	(10.07)	22.47	14.32	(20.29)
Ret. on Com. Equity (%)	25.59	(13.90)	21.99	14.82	(45.50)
% Change Profit	301.6	(167.6)	80.3	149.1	54.1
% Change Revenue	3.8	1.2	7.9	9.7	7.1
% Change Assets	7.1	1.9	13.6	(2.4)	1.2

Preferred Div. Coverage	na	na	na
Total Div. Coverage	na	na	na
Interest Coverage	143.7	0.0	39.4
Current Ratio	2.8	2.4	3.1
Operating Margin	13.5	3.9	2.3
Asset Turnover	1.2	1.2	1.1
5 YEAR RATIOS (%)			
Return on Capital	6.7	(5.5)	(7.3)
Return on Com. Equity	0.6	(22.8)	(25.6)
Profit Growth	na	na	13.9
Revenue Growth	5.8	4.4	2.2
Asset Growth	4.1	(2.3)	(2.7)
BALANCE SHEET (000)			
Cash	31,462	23,815	12,909
Current Assets	62,139	54,573	51,698
Net Fixed Assets	10,098	11,396	11,727
Invest's & Advances	0	1,482	2,749
Total Assets	72,237	67,451	66,174
Short Term Debt	0	295	32
Current Liabilities	22,554	23,009	16,709
Long Term Debt	0	352	109
Total Liabilities	22,554	23,361	17,618
Total Equity	49,683	44,090	48,556
Total Liab. & Equity	72,237	67,451	66,174
CAPITAL (000)			
Total Debt	0	647	141
Preferred Equity	398	6,627	6,803
Common Equity	49,285	37,463	41,753

Business:

GEAC COMPUTER CORP. LTD. is engaged in the design, manufacture, sale, rental and service of computer systems and software. A Unix applications software provider, the company supplys total automation solutions to selected vertical markets, principally libraries, leasing and asset finance companies, and the property management, hospitality construction, manufacturing and distribution industries.

Date	EPS	DPS	Tot Rev	Inc Bex
Jan 93	(0.26)	0.00	27,815	(7,023)
Oct 92	0.13	0.00	22,998	3,608
Jul 92	0.13	0.00	22,244	3,086
Apr 92	0.21	0.00	23,338	4,699
Jan 92	0.16	0.00	21,055	3,628
Oct 91	0.08	0.00	21,199	1,710
Jul 91	0.05	0.00	19,730	1,064
Apr 91	0.08	0.00	24,212	1,636

Synopsis:

In April 1993, Geac acquired Australia-based Computer Library Services International (Australia) Pty Ltd. (CLSI Australia) for about $1-million. CLSI Australia provides CD-ROM network solutions and database subscriptions to Australian libraries, and distributes the LIBS 100 plus products to the Australian marketplace. CLSI Australia has annual revenues of over $4-million.

For the most recent third quarter, the 32.1% jump in revenues Geac recorded compared to the same period last year, was attributed to the acquisitions of CLSI Inc of the U.S., and the McDonnell Douglas Information Systems hardware service business in Canada. In relation to the CLSI Inc. business, Geac allocated $4-million of the acquisition cost to application software.

Geac's president and C.E.O., Stephen Sadler, has indicated Geac's desire to grow by building revenues through the acquisition of companies with thin margins. By this method, Geac can acquire companies at good prices. An example is the conditional acquisition of NBI Canada Inc., only if the company can arrange a deal with its creditors. NBI had revenues in excess of $2-million last year. As well, Geac recently acquired Florida-based Concord Management Systems Inc., Australia-based Mentat Computer Systems Pty Ltd., U.S.-based CLSI Inc., and the assets of McDonnell Douglas Information Systems Canada. Geac has stated it is not on the lookout for new markets, but will concentrate on computer service. As at January 31, 1993, Geac has a cash balance of $39-million.

The acquired companies Concord and Mentat have combined revenues of about $13-million and were purchased for about $5-million. Concord is a developer and marketer of software for construction companies in North America, and Mentat provides software for the apparel and footwear market. CLSI Inc. provides turnkey solutions and this acquisition is expected to provide an additional $20-million to Geac's library revenue. Geac, once a large scale hardware producer, now derives most of its revenues from the higher margin software and systems support market.

Relative strength to TSE300 / Price / Volume (in 1000's of board lots)

Rank (Profit/Revenue/Assets)		
169	402	473

Donald C. Webster
Chairman

Stephen J. Sadler
President & C.E.O.

David G. B. Scott
V.P., Finance & Administration

Address
11 Allstate Parkway
Suite 300
Markham
ON
L3R 9T8
(416) 475-0525

Fax: (416) 475-3847
G0014748/G/15.2

I.S.G. TECHNOLOGIES INC.

Exchanges	Price (Jun24'93)	14.62	Trailing P/E	nm	Stock Symbol
T	Trailing Yield (%)	0.00	Trailing EPS	(0.09)	ISO

Period Ending	Jun92	Jun91	Jun90	Jun89	Jun88
Yearly Statistics					
Price-Close	10.75	12.56	1.98	1.80	3.75
Price-High	18.50	14.06	3.38	4.14	5.63
Price-Low	10.13	1.88	1.65	1.65	1.58
P/E-Close	nm	4,187.50	nm	nm	nm
Dividends per Share	0.00	0.00	0.00	0.00	0.00
Dividend Yield (%)	0.00	0.00	0.00	0.00	0.00
Sales per Share	1.54	1.90	1.10	0.52	0.47
EPS before extra. item	(0.11)	0.00	(0.43)	(1.01)	(1.82)
Cash Flow per Share	(0.06)	0.05	(0.40)	(0.95)	(1.64)
Book Value per Share	3.64	0.40	0.24	0.67	(0.96)
O/S Common Shares	11,834	6,255	5,736	5,736	1,851
Total Revenue	15,962	12,957	7,304	2,420	1,096
Income before extra.	(917)	16	(2,498)	(3,440)	(3,348)
Cash Flow	(517)	298	(2,274)	(3,250)	(3,039)
Debt/Equity	0.04	1.12	0.47	0.02	na
Return on Capital (%)	(3.06)	5.45	(82.39)	(134.96)	(250.61)
Ret. on Com. Equity (%)	(4.02)	0.82	(95.56)	(329.00)	na
% Change Profit	(5,875.6)	100.6	27.4	(2.7)	(56.6)
% Change Revenue	23.2	77.4	201.8	120.9	290.4
% Change Assets	474.9	108.9	(17.2)	193.3	(6.1)
Preferred Div. Coverage	np	np	np		
Total Div. Coverage	na	na	na		
Interest Coverage	0.0	1.1	0.0		
Current Ratio	9.2	1.3	1.3		
Operating Margin	(13.5)	(3.6)	(47.4)		
Asset Turnover	0.3	1.4	1.6		
5 YEAR RATIOS (%)					
Return on Capital	(93.1)	(113.3)	(99.9)		
Return on Com. Equity	na	na	na		
Profit Growth	na	(52.6)	na		
Revenue Growth	124.3	38.4	13.2		
Asset Growth	93.8	12.2	6.2		
BALANCE SHEET (000)					
Cash	28,666	0	0		
Current Assets	43,197	7,625	3,424		
Net Fixed Assets	672	570	512		
Invest's & Advances	3,935	0	0		
Total Assets	47,854	8,325	3,986		
Short Term Debt	1,779	2,755	597		
Current Liabilities	4,717	5,755	2,571		
Long Term Debt	26	57	49		
Total Liabilities	4,743	5,811	2,620		
Total Equity	43,111	2,513	1,365		
Total Liab. & Equity	47,854	8,325	3,986		
CAPITAL (000)					
Total Debt	1,805	2,812	646		
Preferred Equity	0	0	0		
Common Equity	43,111	2,513	1,365		

Business:

I.S.G. TECHNOLOGIES is a medical company which designs, manufactures and markets full solution medical imaging workstations. Its flagship product is a compact interactive workstation for two and three dimensional analysis of data from computer-based imaging techniques such as CAT or CT scanners and magnetic resonance imagers.

Date	EPS	DPS	Tot Rev	Inc Bex
Mar 93	(0.03)	0.00	4,355	(326)
Dec 92	(0.04)	0.00	4,874	(424)
Sep 92	(0.02)	0.00	4,065	(280)
Jun 92	0.00	0.00	4,405	(22)
Mar 92	(0.02)	0.00	4,067	(246)
Dec 91	(0.05)	0.00	4,119	(350)
Sep 91	(0.05)	0.00	3,215	(299)
Jun 91	0.03	0.00	3,877	186

Synopsis:

In March 1993, ISG Technologies Inc. signed an agreement with the Nuclear Medicine Division of Milwaukee-based GE Medical Systems related to the supply of licenses for the Image Applications Platform (IAP) and other ISG software products. GE Medical intends to incorporate IAP and other ISG software products into future product offerings. This agreement followed an earlier one between the two companies which made IAP available for development use in a broad range of its diagnostic imaging equipment.

ISG and Sweden-based Elekta Instrument AB have entered into an agreement which calls for Elekta to distribute ISG's Viewing Wand product internationally, excluding Japan. This new business formation is said to allow ISG to benefit from Elekta's established worldwide distribution system for its product. Elekta is a market leader in several key segments within the neuroscience field. The wand is currently approved for use in Canada, Italy, the U.K., and Scandinavia, and is awaiting approval from the Food and Drug Administration in the United States. Acceptance into the large U.S. market should directly benefit ISG.

ISG has built upon its relationship with Netherlands-based Philips Medical Systems. ISG had previously been supplying Philips with its Gyroview workstation for the past three years. Under this new five-year agreement, Philips will include ISG's IAP in the Gyroview workstation in addition to extensions to other products. Philips, a division of Philips Electronics, has business activities in 102 countries.

ISG has also signed a licensing agreement with Wisconsin-based NORAN Instruments involving ISG's IAP. The agreement calls for Noran to use IAP as the basis for its confocal microscope platform.

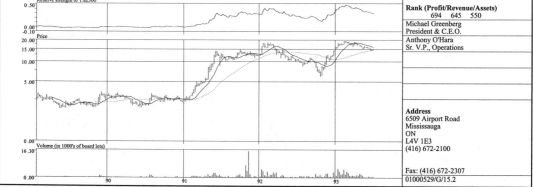

Rank (Profit/Revenue/Assets)
694   645   550

Michael Greenberg
President & C.E.O.

Anthony O'Hara
Sr. V.P., Operations

Address
6509 Airport Road
Mississauga
ON
L4V 1E3
(416) 672-2100

Fax: (416) 672-2307
01000529/G/15.2

ISM INFORMATION SYSTEMS MANAGEMENT CORPORATION

Exchanges	Price (Jun24'93)	13.12	Trailing P/E	437.50	Stock Symbol
T	Trailing Yield (%)	0.00	Trailing EPS	0.03	**ISM.A**

Period Ending	Dec92	Dec91	Mar91	Mar90	Mar89
Yearly Statistics		9M			
Price-Close	8.75	7.13	3.85	6.50	9.00
Price-High	17.25	7.13	6.50	15.00	9.00
Price-Low	6.38	1.75	1.75	6.50	7.50
P/E-Close	291.67	67.22	nm	nm	7.90
Dividends per Share	0.00	0.00	0.00	0.00	0.00
Dividend Yield (%)	0.00	0.00	0.00	0.00	0.00
Sales per Share	19.44	16.19	12.68	11.36	15.83
EPS before extra. item	0.03	0.08	(4.01)	(0.95)	1.14
Cash Flow per Share	1.00	1.81	0.15	0.90	2.62
Book Value per Share	2.49	1.95	1.61	5.62	6.59
O/S Common Shares	20,334	18,085	7,495	7,495	7,495
Total Revenue	378,894	167,545	95,031	85,375	118,674
Income before extra.	507	1,132	(30,056)	(7,137)	5,516
Cash Flow	19,497	18,506	1,139	6,762	19,644
Debt/Equity	1.58	2.38	2.40	0.76	0.64
Return on Capital (%)	7.83	16.50	(49.31)	(7.22)	15.50
Ret. on Com. Equity (%)	1.18	6.38	(110.85)	(15.87)	19.14
% Change Profit	(66.4)	105.0	(321.1)	(229.4)	4,512.0
% Change Revenue	69.6	135.1	11.3	(28.1)	268.2
% Change Assets	3.2	158.6	(33.2)	6.3	73.4

Preferred Div. Coverage	np	np	np
Total Div. Coverage	na	na	na
Interest Coverage	1.2	1.8	0.0
Current Ratio	0.9	0.9	1.0
Operating Margin	5.3	8.6	2.0
Asset Turnover	2.0	1.2	1.3
5 YEAR RATIOS (%)			
Return on Capital	(3.3)	na	na
Return on Com. Equity	(20.0)	na	na
Profit Growth	33.5	na	na
Revenue Growth	63.7	na	na
Asset Growth	26.8	na	na
BALANCE SHEET (000)			
Cash	0	0	0
Current Assets	63,913	65,643	40,002
Net Fixed Assets	33,012	32,947	20,221
Invest's & Advances	16,102	9,933	0
Total Assets	191,262	185,422	71,693
Short Term Debt	21,463	21,368	10,061
Current Liabilities	71,266	76,935	38,336
Long Term Debt	58,152	62,297	18,898
Total Liabilities	140,739	150,211	59,606
Total Equity	50,523	35,211	12,087
Total Liab. & Equity	191,262	185,422	71,693
CAPITAL (000)			
Total Debt	79,615	83,665	28,959
Preferred Equity	0	0	0
Common Equity	50,523	35,211	12,087

Business:

ISM INFORMATION SYSTEMS MANAGEMENT CORPORATION is Canada's largest full service information technology company providing total solutions to meet the changing information systems management needs of private and public sector organizations.

Date	EPS	DPS	Tot Rev	Inc Bex
Mar 93	0.08	0.00	111,993	1,596
Dec 92	(0.10)	0.00	97,643	(1,905)
Sep 92	0.01	0.00	92,898	155
Jun 92	0.04	0.00	94,254	680
Mar 92	0.08	0.00	94,099	1,577
Sep 91	0.01	0.00	67,946	96
Jun 91	0.00	0.00	21,127	37
Mar 91	(3.40)	0.00	28,540	(25,509)

Synopsis:

In May 1993, ISM signed a 10-year, $36-million outsourcing agreement with Toronto-based credit bureau company Equifax Canada. ISM will operate the existing Equifax computing centre facilities in Montreal and manage Equifax's information systems operations. Other recent contracts include: an $8-million contract with Alberta Energy, a $200-million contract with AGT Ltd., a $5.7-million contract with Computing Devices Canada, and a $34-million contract with Consumers Gas.

ISM manages information technology for companies to allow companies to concentrate on their core businesses. Currently, ISM is divesting its poor performing operations and focusing on its own core business. ISM, formed in 1991 from a merger of Westbridge Computer Corp. and STM Systems Corp., now represents the outsourcing arm of IBM Canada, which owns 52% of ISM. ISM will drop businesses like the resale of telephone voice circuits, and focus on outsourcing services for governments and utilities in Canada. ISM has signed deals with the federal Department of Supply and Services and government operations in Manitoba and Saskatchewan. Presently, ISM has no plans to move into international markets.

The key to the company's success will be combining ISM's computing centres with IBM's marketing. ISM plans to establish a computing centre in each province that can handle data management for large organizations and government departments. There are now eight centres in most provinces except Quebec and parts of Atlantic Canada.

In December 1992, ISM acquired Utlas International Canada, a firm that manages computerized cataloguing and reference services for libraries. Utlas has annual revenues of about $13-million. The acquisition represents part of ISM's strategy to tailor computer services to specific industries.

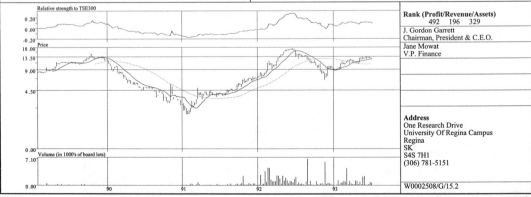

Rank (Profit/Revenue/Assets)
492   196   329

J. Gordon Garrett
Chairman, President & C.E.O.
Jane Mowat
V.P. Finance

Address
One Research Drive
University Of Regina Campus
Regina
SK
S4S 7H1
(306) 781-5151

W0002508/G/15.2

SHL SYSTEMHOUSE INC.

Exchanges	Price (Jun24'93)		13.25	Trailing P/E		nm	Stock Symbol
TMQ	Trailing Yield (%)		0.00	Trailing EPS		(0.15)	**SHK**

Period Ending	Aug92	Aug91	Aug90	Aug89	Aug88
Yearly Statistics					
Price-Close	9.63	5.38	7.13	11.00	7.25
Price-High	16.88	7.50	12.00	12.50	32.00
Price-Low	4.60	3.15	4.70	8.00	7.00
P/E-Close	nm	nm	nm	23.40	32.96
Dividends per Share	0.00	0.00	0.00	0.00	0.00
Dividend Yield (%)	0.00	0.00	0.00	0.00	0.00
Sales per Share	19.01	18.34	18.70	23.85	8.65
EPS before extra. item	(0.25)	(0.53)	(1.10)	0.47	0.22
Cash Flow per Share	0.32	0.55	0.28	1.01	0.61
Book Value per Share	6.42	5.99	6.66	8.92	6.06
O/S Common Shares	43,291	37,846	37,222	32,184	26,262
Total Revenue	743,970	694,063	698,430	640,725	240,743
Income before extra.	(9,521)	(19,892)	(40,585)	12,305	5,813
Cash Flow	12,450	20,585	10,311	26,648	16,202
Debt/Equity	0.69	0.63	0.37	0.44	1.35
Return on Capital (%)	1.38	(1.07)	(5.77)	11.35	5.17
Ret. on Com. Equity (%)	(3.77)	(8.38)	(15.18)	5.51	3.50
% Change Profit	52.1	51.0	(429.8)	111.7	(75.5)
% Change Revenue	7.2	(0.6)	9.0	166.1	36.6
% Change Assets	22.0	14.2	(11.2)	14.9	103.1

Business:

SHL SYSTEMHOUSE is in the business of transformational outsourcing which enables its customers to re-engineer their business processes and sustain competitive advantage through information technology. The company provides a full range of seamless systems management services anywhere in the world, working with customers during planning, building and ongoing management.

Date	EPS	DPS	Tot Rev	Inc Bex
Feb 93	0.03	0.00	240,973	1,261
Nov 92	0.01	0.00	202,402	309
Aug 92	(0.19)	0.00	192,020	(7,389)
May 92	0.00	0.00	185,369	(145)
Feb 92	(0.02)	0.00	181,411	(733)
Nov 91	(0.03)	0.00	185,170	(1,254)
Aug 91	(0.82)	0.00	154,659	(30,922)
May 91	0.11	0.00	179,072	4,039

Preferred Div. Coverage	na	np	np	
Total Div. Coverage	na	na	na	
Interest Coverage	0.4	0.0	0.0	
Current Ratio	1.4	1.3	1.6	
Operating Margin	0.9	2.4	0.6	
Asset Turnover	1.2	1.3	1.5	
5 YEAR RATIOS (%)				
Return on Capital	2.2	7.2	13.5	
Return on Com. Equity	(3.7)	0.7	6.5	
Profit Growth	na	na	na	
Revenue Growth	33.3	45.9	66.1	
Asset Growth	23.5	35.3	83.9	
BALANCE SHEET (000)				
Cash	65,791	28,794	71,544	
Current Assets	366,950	278,307	298,389	
Net Fixed Assets	80,211	63,886	49,929	
Invest's & Advances	29,786	17,795	4,658	
Total Assets	637,542	522,712	457,870	
Short Term Debt	107,317	74,248	79,704	
Current Liabilities	263,720	222,167	192,345	
Long Term Debt	86,549	68,521	11,776	
Total Liabilities	354,676	295,866	210,167	
Total Equity	282,866	226,846	247,703	
Total Liab. & Equity	637,542	522,712	457,870	
CAPITAL (000)				
Total Debt	193,866	142,769	91,480	
Preferred Equity	4,813	0	0	
Common Equity	278,053	226,846	247,703	

Synopsis:

SHL Systemhouse Inc. plans to expand its international business in the rapidly expanding markets of Mexico and South America this year. Last year SHL had a deal valued in excess of $500-million (U.S.) with the Mexican government. The company is negotiating for business in China and is also working towards a partnership arrangement in Japan. As part of its strategy of working with local partners in joint ventures, SHL has acquired the Venezuelan consulting firm Advanced Management Systems CA. SHL's strategy is to find a partner who's willing to provide most of the working capital and employees and then transfer its own technology to the country and begin bidding on local contracts.

SHL and Samsung have formed a joint venture in outsourcing, or managing a client company's main computer operations and data banks. This represents a first step for SHL to export computer services throughout eastern Asia. SHL plans to capitalize on the market-wide shift to client/server computing and the industry trend towards outsourcing.

For the first half of fiscal 1993, improvements in all lines of SHL's business and a substantial $825-million order backlog provided a large jump in revenues. SHL's operations in the U.S. and Latin America posted profits. In April 1993, SHL signed its largest contract to date when Canada Post Corp. agreed to outsource its data processing, telecommunications and computer systems management to them. This contract is believed to be substantially more significant than a $550-million (U.S.) deal last year with Government of Mexico.

SHL will grow through international joint ventures and domestic acquisitions. In North America, SHL recently purchased Rockwood Infomatics of Fredericton, a software development firm specializing in government applications; and Benson, Douglas & Associates of Virginia, a client/server oriented systems integrator. And to improve its UNIX and open systems business, SHL acquired Interactive Systems Corp. of Illinois, a systems integration firm.

Relative strength to TSE300 / Price / Volume (in 1000's of board lots)

Rank (Profit/Revenue/Assets)
884   129   188

John R. Oltman
Chairman & C.E.O.
Paul D. Damp
V.C., Fin. & Admin. & C.F.O.

Address
50 O'Connor Street
5th Floor
Ottawa
ON
K1P 6L2
(613) 236-1428

Fax: (613) 563-9896
S0006061/G/15.2

SOFTKEY SOFTWARE PRODUCTS INC.

Exchanges	Price (Jun24'93)	7 .00	Trailing P/E	22 .58	Stock Symbol
T	Trailing Yield (%)	0 .00	Trailing EPS	0 .31	**SSK**

Period Ending	Jan93	Jan92	Jan91	Nov90	Nov89
Yearly Statistics			14M		
Price-Close	10 .25	7 .75	3 .05	2 .65	2 .40
Price-High	11 .00	8 .00	5 .25	5 .25	2 .55
Price-Low	6 .00	2 .95	2 .00	2 .00	0 .80
P/E-Close	22 .28	20 .95	10 .17	8 .55	17 .14
Dividends per Share	0 .00	0 .00	0 .00	0 .00	0 .03
Dividend Yield (%)	0 .00	0 .00	0 .00	0 .00	1 .38
Sales per Share	2 .71	2 .49	1 .38	1 .29	1 .15
EPS before extra. item	0 .46	0 .37	0 .35	0 .31	0 .14
Cash Flow per Share	0 .58	0 .56	0 .34	0 .34	0 .17
Book Value per Share	3 .43	2 .16	0 .74	0 .69	0 .30
O/S Common Shares	24 ,651	18 ,994	10 ,645	10 ,583	9 ,674
Total Revenue	62 ,612	36 ,891	16 ,092	13 ,097	10 ,396
Income before extra.	10 ,446	6 ,105	3 ,510	3 ,069	1 ,293
Cash Flow	13 ,119	8 ,250	3 ,960	3 ,467	1 ,537
Debt/Equity	0 .17	0 .33	0 .15	0 .22	0 .29
Return on Capital (%)	14 .84	27 .85	41 .25	58 .75	71 .31
Ret. on Com. Equity (%)	16 .56	24 .48	39 .49	60 .09	88 .44
% Change Profit	71 .1	102 .9	(2 .0)	137 .3	161 .8
% Change Revenue	69 .7	167 .5	5 .3	26 .0	901 .7
% Change Assets	77 .4	465 .6	5 .2	96 .1	381 .8

Preferred Div. Coverage	np	56 .0	np
Total Div. Coverage	200 .9	56 .0	na
Interest Coverage	na	14 .9	na
Current Ratio	4 .0	2 .6	3 .5
Operating Margin	16 .7	25 .4	26 .9
Asset Turnover	0 .5	0 .6	1 .2
5 YEAR RATIOS (%)			
Return on Capital	42 .8	(35 .8)	(55 .1)
Return on Com. Equity	45 .8	(33 .1)	(51 .8)
Profit Growth	84 .1	na	na
Revenue Growth	127 .0	126 .6	105 .5
Asset Growth	151 .0	117 .1	43 .5
BALANCE SHEET (000)			
Cash	24 ,639	1 ,580	1 ,404
Current Assets	55 ,037	19 ,598	9 ,949
Net Fixed Assets	7 ,266	4 ,753	694
Invest's & Advances	0	1 ,527	349
Total Assets	113 ,944	64 ,246	11 ,358
Short Term Debt	433	193	538
Current Liabilities	13 ,788	7 ,669	2 ,809
Long Term Debt	14 ,006	13 ,378	627
Total Liabilities	29 ,505	22 ,452	3 ,436
Total Equity	84 ,439	41 ,794	7 ,922
Total Liab. & Equity	113 ,944	64 ,246	11 ,358
CAPITAL (000)			
Total Debt	14 ,439	13 ,571	1 ,165
Preferred Equity	0	723	0
Common Equity	84 ,439	41 ,071	7 ,922

Business:

SOFTKEY SOFTWARE PRODUCTS INC. is in the business of developing and marketing micro computer software solutions for specialized business oriented applications.

Date	EPS	DPS	Tot Rev	Inc Bex
Apr 93	(0 .02)	0 .00	17 ,407	(573)
Jan 93	0 .15	0 .00	21 ,787	3 ,624
Oct 92	0 .10	0 .00	13 ,151	2 ,507
Jul 92	0 .08	0 .00	11 ,967	1 ,870
Apr 92	0 .13	0 .00	14 ,718	2 ,445
Jan 92	0 .13	0 .00	11 ,621	2 ,401
Oct 91	0 .07	0 .00	8 ,249	1 ,092
Jul 91	0 .07	0 .00	6 ,501	1 ,204

Synopsis:

In the first quarter of fiscal 1993, the results for Softkey Software Products were affected by costs associated from its merger with Wordstar International of California, and the sale of its consulting division. These resulted in charges of $3.9-million in the quarter. Softkey plans to sell its Insight Business Consultants, which sells computer systems. The sale of Insight will allow the company to concentrate on marketing software. Insight generated about 16% of Softkey's revenues last year, or $10- million. As a result of the merger, Softkey will close its Mississauga head office and its sales office in Florida, and will move to California subsequent to the merger being finalized. The deal is subject to approval by regulatory authorities and by shareholders of both companies.

The merger will result in company with over $90-million (U.S.) in sales and market capitalization of over $250-million (U.S.). This deal is a reverse takeover of a U.S. firm by a Canadian firm, with the new company essentially run by Softkey's current president and chairman. Softkey shareholders will own or have the right to acquire 75% of Wordstar common shares. Wordstar last year had a 17% jump in revenue but a 33 cents (U.S.) per share loss. Wordstar has had losses in each of its last five years. However, Wordstar's was recently affected by one-time costs after a merger with another small software company, and product acquisition and reorganization charges. Wordstar has slashed its staff by 25% recently and has consolidated facilities.

Wordstar should provide a base for the international distribution of Softkey products. Softkey will gain three new distribution channels including: Wordstar's direct mail program; Wordstar's arrangements with computer makers; and Wordstar's international distribution channels. Both companies have a strategy of acquiring many products and mass-marketing them. The combined company will have about $35-million in cash and no debt. Company officials said funds will be earmarked for acquisitions to broaden the new company's offerings.

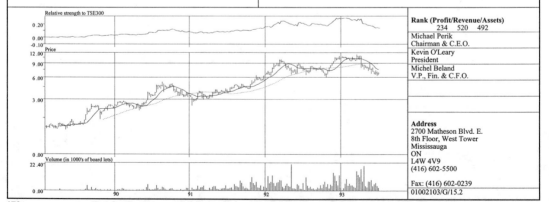

Rank (Profit/Revenue/Assets)
234　520　492

Michael Perik
Chairman & C.E.O.
Kevin O'Leary
President
Michel Beland
V.P., Fin. & C.F.O.

Address
2700 Matheson Blvd. E.
8th Floor, West Tower
Mississauga
ON
L4W 4V9
(416) 602-5500

Fax: (416) 602-0239
01002103/G/15.2

TELEGLOBE INC.

Exchanges	Price (Jun24'93)	17.25	Trailing P/E	nm	Stock Symbol
TM	Trailing Yield (%)	1.62	Trailing EPS	(1.26)	**TGO**

Period Ending	Dec92	Dec91	Dec90	Dec89	Dec88
Yearly Statistics					
Price-Close	13.75	10.88	7.88	10.63	10.25
Price-High	13.94	11.00	10.75	11.82	15.38
Price-Low	11.00	7.38	7.50	9.50	9.75
P/E-Close	nm	20.14	39.38	20.43	10.25
Dividends per Share	0.28	0.28	0.28	0.24	0.10
Dividend Yield (%)	2.04	2.58	3.56	2.26	0.98
Sales per Share	8.03	7.15	9.93	9.66	10.96
EPS before extra. item	(1.19)	0.54	0.20	0.52	1.00
Cash Flow per Share	2.88	3.18	2.13	2.52	3.51
Book Value per Share	9.23	10.26	9.16	9.99	9.65
O/S Common Shares	52,099	39,578	40,694	37,735	35,173
Total Revenue	521,900	459,400	408,700	371,900	380,177
Income before extra.	(50,600)	25,700	8,000	20,100	33,514
Cash Flow	123,000	129,700	86,600	97,200	117,967
Debt/Equity	0.92	1.00	1.01	0.86	0.79
Return on Capital (%)	1.58	9.74	5.17	7.31	13.59
Ret. on Com. Equity (%)	(12.77)	5.68	1.91	5.61	10.85
% Change Profit	(296.9)	221.3	(60.2)	(40.0)	(48.1)
% Change Revenue	13.6	12.4	9.9	(2.2)	8.3
% Change Assets	8.1	20.5	7.7	18.2	5.2
Preferred Div. Coverage	0.0	7.1	9.3		
Total Div. Coverage	0.0	1.7	0.7		
Interest Coverage	0.5	2.0	1.6		
Current Ratio	0.7	0.6	0.5		
Operating Margin	15.6	15.7	14.1		
Asset Turnover	0.2	0.2	0.4		
5 YEAR RATIOS (%)					
Return on Capital	7.5	14.9	16.7		
Return on Com. Equity	2.3	13.1	14.1		
Profit Growth	na	49.7	33.9		
Revenue Growth	8.2	51.1	87.0		
Asset Growth	11.7	76.4	112.4		
BALANCE SHEET (000)					
Cash	6,000	23,600	5,700		
Current Assets	255,200	257,900	180,900		
Net Fixed Assets	1,030,200	820,700	658,100		
Invest's & Advances	1,600	46,100	41,600		
Total Assets	1,500,300	1,388,300	1,151,700		
Short Term Debt	21,000	88,900	59,800		
Current Liabilities	355,900	427,300	336,800		
Long Term Debt	506,500	408,700	358,900		
Total Liabilities	926,700	889,400	736,600		
Total Equity	573,600	498,900	415,100		
Total Liab. & Equity	1,500,300	1,388,300	1,151,700		
CAPITAL (000)					
Total Debt	527,500	497,600	418,700		
Preferred Equity	93,000	93,000	42,500		
Common Equity	480,600	405,900	372,600		

Business:

TELEGLOBE INC. designs, makes and markets data communcations products and services worldwide for customers in the banking, insurance, health care and transportation industries. The company also provides computer systems integration services. The company's subsidiary, Teleglobe Canada of Montreal, is Canada's sole overseas telecommunications carrier.

Date	EPS	DPS	Tot Rev	Inc Bex
Dec 92	0.37	0.07	142,720	17,966
Sep 92	0.27	0.07	126,346	15,032
Jun 92	(1.73)	0.07	109,124	(77,949)
Mar 92	(0.17)	0.07	110,400	(5,700)
Dec 91	0.26	0.07	128,613	12,029
Sep 91	0.13	0.07	105,373	7,081
Jun 91	0.12	0.07	103,954	5,499
Mar 91	0.03	0.07	99,900	1,100

Synopsis:

In May 1993, Teleglobe Inc. completed a $400-million five-year credit facility with a syndicate of financial institutions led by the Royal Bank, Bank of Montreal, and the National Bank. This new facility will replace four existing banking facilities totaling about $300-million and provide additional credits to fund the company's investments, specifically in the telecommunications group. In addition, a $95-million (U.S.) financing agreement guaranteed by BCE Inc., for the Cantat-3 transatlantic cable project, has been arranged with the Toronto-Dominion Bank. BCE will receive certain guarantee fees and a 25% interest in the Teleglobe subsidiary holding Teleglobe's investment in Cantat-3. Cantat-3 will generate more capacity than all existing cables in the Atlantic and will allow Teleglobe to enter the growing markets of Eastern Europe and the Commonwealth of Independent Stares.

With Teleglobe's long-term strategy of concentrating on its international and submarine communications services, the company may eventually sell off its communication products and insurance systems divisions. The two units provided $2.8-million in profits in the first quarter 1993 after $19-million in losses in fiscal 1992. Teleglobe has said its intends to expand its international telecommunications activities by the expansion of its own carrier network and developing strategic alliances with other carriers.

In April 1993, Teleglobe completed a public offering of $125-million unsecured debentures in Canada. The net proceeds are earmarked for the repayment of indebtedness under a term loan incurred to finance the privatization of the corporation.

Teleglobe plans to invest $278-million in 1993, with a large portion going towards the Cantat-3 project. Teleglobe plans to invest about $1-billion in the next five years. As Canada's monopoly overseas long distance carrier and a regulated company, Teleglobe must outline its spending plans with the CRTC.

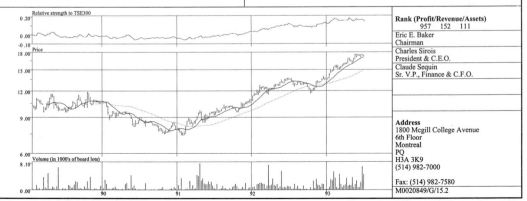

Rank (Profit/Revenue/Assets)
957   152   111

Eric E. Baker
Chairman

Charles Sirois
President & C.E.O.

Claude Sequin
Sr. V.P., Finance & C.F.O.

Address
1800 Mcgill College Avenue
6th Floor
Montreal
PQ
H3A 3K9
(514) 982-7000

Fax: (514) 982-7580
M0020849/G/15.2

Page	Company	$	Latest year end	Earnings per Share		
				Actual	Estimate this year	Estimate next year
475	Agra Industries		9207	(0.15)	0.17	0.84
476	DMR Group		9205	0.35	0.32	0.45
477	FCA International		9206	(0.18)	(0.28)	0.13
478	Intera Information Technologies	$US	9209	(0.37)	0.63	0.78

Estimates from I/B/E/S Inc., 345 Hudson St., New York, NY 10014 (212) 243-3335. In Canada: 6 Lansing Square, Ste. 235, Willowdale, ON M2J 1T5 (416) 496-0977.

AGRA INDUSTRIES LIMITED

Exchanges	Price (Jun24'93)	8.50	Trailing P/E	nm	Stock Symbol
TM	Trailing Yield (%)	1.82	Trailing EPS	(0.58)	**AGR.B**

Period Ending	Ju l92	Ju l91	Ju l90	Ju l89	Ju l88
Yearly Statistics					
Price-Close	7.13	8.00	8.00	9.50	7.50
Price-High	9.00	9.30	9.75	12.00	8.75
Price-Low	7.13	5.70	7.00	6.50	5.50
P/E-Close	nm	nm	114.29	nm	16.30
Dividends per Share	0.16	0.15	0.12	0.12	0.12
Dividend Yield (%)	2.25	1.88	1.50	1.26	1.60
Sales per Share	24.77	21.18	16.79	16.97	17.30
EPS before extra. item	(0.49)	(0.07)	0.07	(0.43)	0.46
Cash Flow per Share	0.86	1.66	1.03	0.13	1.10
Book Value per Share	9.16	9.64	9.88	10.82	7.15
O/S Common Shares	17,854	17,742	17,721	14,691	14,485
Total Revenue	441,095	375,596	274,181	247,089	231,116
Income before extra.	(8,689)	(1,240)	1,188	(6,318)	6,124
Cash Flow	15,337	29,501	16,888	1,956	14,696
Debt/Equity	1.02	0.55	0.37	0.46	0.58
Return on Capital (%)	0.77	5.54	6.61	1.49	10.87
Ret. on Com. Equity (%)	(5.19)	(0.72)	0.71	(4.81)	6.23
% Change Profit	(600.6)	(204.4)	118.8	(203.2)	(11.5)
% Change Revenue	17.4	37.0	11.0	6.9	11.2
% Change Assets	32.2	2.5	6.9	51.2	25.2
Preferred Div. Coverage	np	np	np		
Total Div. Coverage	0.0	0.0	0.6		
Interest Coverage	0.2	2.0	3.0		
Current Ratio	1.4	1.3	1.3		
Operating Margin	2.7	8.3	9.2		
Asset Turnover	1.0	1.1	0.8		
5 YEAR RATIOS (%)					
Return on Capital	5.1	7.8	8.7		
Return on Com. Equity	(0.8)	1.8	2.8		
Profit Growth	na	na	(24.0)		
Revenue Growth	16.2	16.9	15.1		
Asset Growth	22.3	18.0	21.7		
BALANCE SHEET (000)					
Cash	38,063	11,628	40,189		
Current Assets	200,702	126,505	139,954		
Net Fixed Assets	130,838	127,572	111,979		
Invest's & Advances	65,112	63,757	65,054		
Total Assets	438,763	331,833	323,899		
Short Term Debt	47,967	35,280	29,653		
Current Liabilities	139,114	97,665	107,825		
Long Term Debt	118,642	58,634	35,008		
Total Liabilities	275,203	160,807	148,784		
Total Equity	163,559	171,026	175,115		
Total Liab. & Equity	438,763	331,833	323,899		
CAPITAL (000)					
Total Debt	166,609	93,914	64,661		
Preferred Equity	0	0	0		
Common Equity	163,559	171,026	175,115		

Business:

AGRA INDUSTRIES LTD. is a diversifed company with operations across North America. The company is active in three areas: engineering, construction and technology; resource recovery and recycling; and asset development and investments. Agra has engineering projects in Europe, Asia, the United States and the Caribbean.

Date	EPS	DPS	Tot Rev	Inc Bex
Jan 93	(0.09)	0.04	139,184	(1,610)
Oct 92	0.08	0.04	150,674	1,452
Jul 92	(0.54)	0.04	127,852	(9,604)
Apr 92	(0.03)	0.04	98,439	(442)
Jan 92	(0.04)	0.04	100,890	(794)
Oct 91	0.12	0.04	107,093	2,152
Jul 91	0.06	0.04	96,241	1,140
Apr 91	0.07	0.04	97,786	1,141

Synopsis:

Agra Industries Limited's revenue increase for the first half of fiscal 1993 was due primarily to the inclusion of subsidiary Monenco Agra Inc., which was not included in the corresponding period last year. Extra costs in the six months included a $2-million financing charge and $500,000 for restructuring charges related to the acquisition of Monenco.

In February 1993, Agra and Bracknell Corp. won a $124-million contract to design and build a cogeneration plant in Quebec. The actual design and construction of the facility will be done by a 50/50 joint venture between Agra subsidiary Northern Engineering Inc. and The State Group, a division of Bracknell. In December 1992, subsidiary Monenco Agra was awarded a $8-million contract to supply the Telecommunication Authority of Singapore with an integrated frequency management computer system.

In fiscal 1992, Agra's results included after-tax restructuring costs of $1.6-million and $4.5-million of costs associated with discontinued operations. During the year, the restructuring costs were primarily due to the integration of several engineering operations resulting from the purchase of Monenco Group Ltd., and Agra's efforts to improve operating efficiencies. The integration of several Agra engineering companies into Monenco will result in a large engineering company to be renamed Monenco Agra Inc. The discontinued operations were related to the closure of Camrec Facilities Consultants which could not generate sufficient business, and the sale of the Research Foods operation. This is in line with Agra's strategy to focus on its core businesses of engineering, construction and technology, and resource recovery and recycling.

Revenues in the Engineering Construction and Technology segment climbed 19.5% to $294-million, but operating earnings were lower as a result of reduced margins due to heavy competition in a weak service market. Revenues in the Resource Recovery and Recycling segement rose 12% to $37-million. Revenues in the Asset Development and Investment segment increased 13% to $110-million, but operating revenue dipped due to lower margins in the airport retail business.

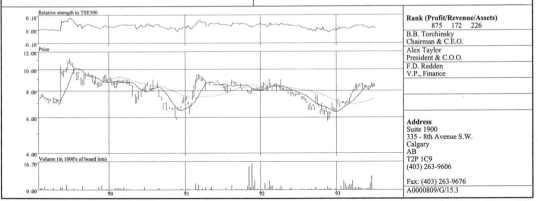

Rank (Profit/Revenue/Assets)
875   172   226

B.B. Torchinsky
Chairman & C.E.O.

Alex Taylor
President & C.O.O.

F.D. Redden
V.P., Finance

Address
Suite 1900
335 - 8th Avenue S.W.
Calgary
AB
T2P 1C9
(403) 263-9606

Fax: (403) 263-9676
A0000809/G/15.3

DMR GROUP INC.

Exchanges	Price (Jun24'93)		5.75	Trailing P/E		19.56	Stock Symbol
TM	Trailing Yield (%)		0.00	Trailing EPS		0.29	**DR.A**

Period Ending	May92	May91	May90	May89	May88
Yearly Statistics					
Price-Close	5.63	4.65	2.95	3.10	3.65
Price-High	6.00	4.75	4.50	4.00	9.38
Price-Low	4.45	2.60	2.55	2.15	3.20
P/E-Close	16.07	10.81	nm	14.76	33.18
Dividends per Share	0.00	0.00	0.00	0.00	0.00
Dividend Yield (%)	0.00	0.00	0.00	0.00	0.00
Sales per Share	16.04	15.50	13.31	10.09	8.07
EPS before extra. item	0.35	0.43	(0.03)	0.21	0.11
Cash Flow per Share	0.64	0.73	0.26	0.40	0.28
Book Value per Share	3.14	2.75	2.35	2.40	2.26
O/S Common Shares	13,401	12,898	12,879	12,719	12,497
Total Revenue	211,800	202,291	171,072	127,609	101,639
Income before extra.	4,632	5,557	(442)	2,604	1,369
Cash Flow	8,487	9,438	3,304	5,014	3,436
Debt/Equity	0.42	0.31	0.35	0.11	0.05
Return on Capital (%)	19.11	28.91	9.77	17.74	8.43
Ret. on Com. Equity (%)	11.95	16.92	(1.45)	8.87	5.09
% Change Profit	(16.6)	1,357.2	(117.0)	90.2	(66.0)
% Change Revenue	4.7	18.2	34.1	25.6	27.1
% Change Assets	27.4	20.2	20.9	28.3	13.6

Preferred Div. Coverage	np	np	np
Total Div. Coverage	na	na	na
Interest Coverage	6.8	7.9	2.5
Current Ratio	1.6	1.6	1.5
Operating Margin	5.8	5.8	2.9
Asset Turnover	2.1	2.5	2.6
5 YEAR RATIOS (%)			
Return on Capital	16.8	21.6	33.6
Return on Com. Equity	8.3	10.8	16.0
Profit Growth	2.9	8.3	na
Revenue Growth	21.4	27.5	27.1
Asset Growth	21.9	35.4	33.9
BALANCE SHEET (000)			
Cash	1,892	5,880	5,179
Current Assets	62,782	50,445	38,586
Net Fixed Assets	10,797	10,819	11,903
Invest's & Advances	3,494	1,054	1,235
Total Assets	100,149	78,630	65,437
Short Term Debt	867	405	455
Current Liabilities	39,615	32,492	24,965
Long Term Debt	16,880	10,517	10,108
Total Liabilities	58,073	43,189	35,173
Total Equity	42,076	35,441	30,264
Total Liab. & Equity	100,149	78,630	65,437
CAPITAL (000)			
Total Debt	17,747	10,922	10,563
Preferred Equity	0	0	0
Common Equity	42,076	35,441	30,264

Business:

DMR GROUP INC. provides information management services. Its fields of activity include: management consulting, systems development and implementation, techical support, education and training, technology development, integrated management, and systems integration.

Date	EPS	DPS	Tot Rev	Inc Bex
Feb 93	0.05	0.00	59,480	713
Nov 92	0.08	0.00	58,090	1,097
Aug 92	0.06	0.00	50,851	759
May 92	0.10	0.00	60,934	1,402
Feb 92	0.08	0.00	51,948	1,063
Nov 91	0.06	0.00	51,498	766
Aug 91	0.11	0.00	47,378	1,401
May 91	0.08	0.00	51,805	1,081

Synopsis:

For the third quarter of 1993, DMR Group Inc. experienced a 33% drop in net earnings compared to the same period last year. This poor performance was attributed to lower results in Canada and the U.S. which offset improved performances in Australia and Europe. All divisions were affected by margin pressures resulting from higher marketing costs and the severity of the recession. In DMR's European operations, results have been hampered by delays in project approval and similar weak market conditions.

DMR continues to build business by attracting new contracts and renewals. In the third quarter, contracts valued at over $30-million were acquired or renewed. Key contracts include a $9.3-million systems integration contract with Revenue Canada for the provision of an automated Goods and Services Tax processing system; and a $27.2-million, five-year systems integration contract with the Quebec Ministry of Energy and Resources.

DMR supplies information technology to corporate and government clients in Australia, Canada, Europe, and the U.S. Approximately half of its revenues is derived from outside Canada.

In late 1992, DMR and Videoway Communications formed a joint venture to develop Vedioway multimedia transactional services. This project is expected to be implemented on Videotron networks when it becomes operational.

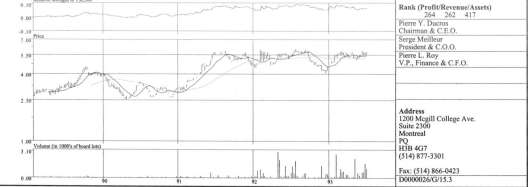

Rank (Profit/Revenue/Assets)
264   262   417

Pierre Y. Ducros
Chairman & C.E.O.

Serge Meilleur
President & C.O.O.

Pierre L. Roy
V.P., Finance & C.F.O.

Address
1200 Mcgill College Ave.
Suite 2300
Montreal
PQ
H3B 4G7
(514) 877-3301

Fax: (514) 866-0423
D0000026/G/15.3

FCA INTERNATIONAL LTD.

Exchanges	Price (Jun24'93)		3.10	Trailing P/E		nm	Stock Symbol
TM	Trailing Yield (%)		1.61	Trailing EPS		(0.29)	**FC**

Period Ending	Jun92	Jun91	Jun90	Jun89	Jun88
Yearly Statistics					
Price-Close	7.13	6.25	10.38	9.38	9.00
Price-High	8.50	11.00	11.75	10.00	17.00
Price-Low	3.85	6.00	8.88	8.00	7.00
P/E-Close	nm	nm	nm	nm	60.00
Dividends per Share	0.05	0.04	0.08	0.08	0.08
Dividend Yield (%)	0.70	0.64	0.77	0.85	0.89
Sales per Share	7.23	6.34	6.77	6.93	7.48
EPS before extra. item	(0.18)	(1.10)	(0.29)	(0.27)	0.15
Cash Flow per Share	0.29	(0.58)	0.21	0.16	0.69
Book Value per Share	3.88	3.85	5.11	5.52	5.95
O/S Common Shares	10,497	10,371	10,363	10,345	10,345
Total Revenue	75,557	66,659	72,008	72,432	79,734
Income before extra.	(1,853)	(11,416)	(3,056)	(2,805)	1,512
Cash Flow	2,984	(6,010)	2,157	1,662	7,155
Debt/Equity	nd	nd	nd	nd	nd
Return on Capital (%)	(4.86)	(22.92)	(10.13)	(8.77)	2.44
Ret. on Com. Equity (%)	(4.60)	(24.60)	(5.55)	(4.73)	2.42
% Change Profit	83.8	(273.5)	(9.0)	(285.5)	(78.4)
% Change Revenue	13.3	(7.4)	(0.6)	(9.2)	(7.5)
% Change Assets	5.5	(19.0)	(7.0)	(9.1)	(2.0)
Preferred Div. Coverage	np	np	np		
Total Div. Coverage	0.0	0.0	0.0		
Interest Coverage	nd	nd	nd		
Current Ratio	1.6	3.0	6.5		
Operating Margin	(3.9)	(13.1)	(10.4)		
Asset Turnover	1.4	1.3	1.1		
5 YEAR RATIOS (%)					
Return on Capital	(8.8)	(4.3)	5.6		
Return on Com. Equity	(7.4)	(4.2)	3.9		
Profit Growth	na	na	na		
Revenue Growth	(2.6)	(4.8)	(0.3)		
Asset Growth	(6.6)	(6.0)	0.3		
BALANCE SHEET (000)					
Cash	12,475	8,197	12,286		
Current Assets	22,306	18,343	28,081		
Net Fixed Assets	19,867	22,815	24,081		
Invest's & Advances	0	1,355	1,327		
Total Assets	54,497	51,638	63,748		
Short Term Debt	0	0	0		
Current Liabilities	13,759	6,087	4,304		
Long Term Debt	0	0	0		
Total Liabilities	13,759	11,764	10,795		
Total Equity	40,738	39,874	52,954		
Total Liab. & Equity	54,497	51,638	63,748		
CAPITAL (000)					
Total Debt	0	0	0		
Preferred Equity	0	0	0		
Common Equity	40,738	39,874	52,954		

Business:

FCA INTERNATIONAL LTD. through its subsidiaries, acts as a full service collection agency. It provides services for commercial, retail, institutional, medical and government clients. The company has operations across Canada and the United States and in the United Kingdom.

Date	EPS	DPS	Tot Rev	Inc Bex
Mar 93	0.01	0.00	17,690	112
Dec 92	(0.18)	0.00	17,814	(1,950)
Sep 92	(0.08)	0.00	18,335	(789)
Jun 92	(0.04)	0.05	20,690	(363)
Mar 92	0.00	0.00	19,823	6
Dec 91	(0.06)	0.06	17,863	(700)
Sep 91	(0.08)	0.00	17,180	(796)
Jun 91	(0.24)	0.00	16,771	(2,491)

Synopsis:

The loss of a major U.S. client will yield FCA International another year of losses. The client represented 10.8% of FCA's 1992 revenue. The client, faced with eliminating a collection agency to reduce its costs, decided to drop FCA.

For the first nine months of fiscal 1993, FCA had collectible accounts of $1.65-billion in its portfolio, up 33% from the previous year. Fees charged depend on the total amount collected, and range from 18% to 50%. About 55% of its business is derived in the U.S., 35% in Canada, and the remaining 10% in Britain. Its subsidiaries, operating under different names, provide a wide range of collection services, including overdue accounts for retail and wholesale businesses, banks, airlines, oil companies, car rental agencies, governments, and telephone and utility companies. FCA has recently been involved in collecting delinquent student loans and health care billings. FCA works with the in-house credit operations of its clients, and acts as an intermediary between its clients and their customers.

In fiscal 1992, FCA's top 10 clients accounted for 36.8% of consolidated gross revenue from operations. The five largest clients in the U.S., Canada, and Britain represented 33%, 50%, and 49%, respectively, of each country's gross revenue from operations. In the U.S., gross revenues from operations jumped 17% due to greater placement volumes and project revenues. In Canada, gross revenues jumped 12% resulting from new clients acquired at the end of fiscal 1991 and increased placements from existing clients.

Relative strength to TSE300
Price
Volume (in 1000's of board lots)

Rank (Profit/Revenue/Assets)
744   415   522

Mark S. Lubotta
Chairman

W. Edwin Jarmain
President & C.E.O.

Robert Di Sante
Exec V.P., Fin. & Corp. Serv.

Address
376 Victoria Ave.
Westmount
PQ
H3Z 1C3
(514) 485-4525

Fax: (514) 485-5178
F0000304/G/15.3

INTERA INFORMATION TECHNOLOGIES CORPORATION

Exchanges	Price (Jun24'93)		Trailing P/E		Stock Symbol
TZQ	11.62		35.23		**IIT.A**
	Trailing Yield (%)	0.00	Trailing EPS	0.33	

Period Ending	Sep92	Sep91	Sep90	Sep89	Sep88
Yearly Statistics	US	US	US	US	US
Price-Close	7.25	12.00	13.88	nt	nt
Price-High	13.60	19.75	24.00	nt	nt
Price-Low	4.50	10.25	10.25	nt	nt
P/E-Close	nm	nm	12.72	nt	nt
Dividends per Share	0.00	0.00	0.00	0.00	0.00
Dividend Yield (%)	0.00	0.00	0.00	0.00	0.00
Sales per Share	12.91	13.60	12.53	14.93	14.99
EPS before extra. item	(0.65)	(0.21)	0.80	0.75	0.61
Cash Flow per Share	0.68	1.13	1.98	1.44	1.63
Book Value per Share	5.95	7.08	7.35	3.20	2.99
O/S Common Shares	5,453	5,453	5,372	2,201	2,201
Total Revenue	71,154	73,794	52,283	42,653	39,016
Income before extra.	(3,573)	(1,145)	3,493	2,411	1,874
Cash Flow	3,755	6,142	8,281	4,002	4,217
Debt/Equity	0.40	0.44	0.36	2.10	1.58
Return on Capital (%)	(3.05)	3.24	12.52	9.38	na
Ret. on Com. Equity (%)	(10.06)	(2.93)	15.01	35.38	na
% Change Profit	(212.1)	(132.8)	44.9	28.7	na
% Change Revenue	(3.6)	41.1	22.6	9.3	na
% Change Assets	(16.9)	3.7	45.5	11.0	na

Preferred Div. Coverage	np	np	np
Total Div. Coverage	na	na	na
Interest Coverage	0.0	1.0	na
Current Ratio	1.2	1.3	1.6
Operating Margin	0.7	5.7	14.1
Asset Turnover	1.2	1.0	0.8
5 YEAR RATIOS (%)			
Return on Capital	na	na	na
Return on Com. Equity	na	na	na
Profit Growth	na	na	na
Revenue Growth	na	na	na
Asset Growth	na	na	na
BALANCE SHEET (000)			
Cash	583	2,242	0
Current Assets	26,112	29,535	29,937
Net Fixed Assets	28,517	35,552	33,958
Invest's & Advances	0	0	0
Total Assets	58,953	70,927	68,404
Short Term Debt	8,008	9,321	6,005
Current Liabilities	21,046	23,436	18,744
Long Term Debt	5,050	7,755	8,287
Total Liabilities	26,508	32,342	28,914
Total Equity	32,445	38,585	39,490
Total Liab. & Equity	58,953	70,927	68,404
CAPITAL (000)			
Total Debt	13,058	17,076	14,292
Preferred Equity	0	0	0
Common Equity	32,445	38,585	39,490

Business:

INTERA INFORMATION TECHNOLOGIES CORPORATION collects, processes and interprets spatial information collected using proprietary airborne radar systems, satellite images and surface and sub-surface survey technologies. It operates in two principal business segments: petroleum and resource management; and mapping and reconnaissance. Main clients include resource companies and government agencies.

Date		EPS	DPS	Tot Rev	Inc Bex
Mar 93	US	0.15	0.00	19,108	828
Dec 92	US	0.12	0.00	18,378	641
Sep 92	US	0.09	0.00	18,513	475
Jun 92	US	(0.03)	0.00	17,698	(159)
Mar 92	US	(0.73)	0.00	16,918	(4,002)
Dec 91	US	0.02	0.00	17,873	113
Sep 91	US	(0.55)	0.00	16,285	(2,967)
Jun 91	US	0.05	0.00	20,810	265

Synopsis:

In May 1993, Intera Information Technologies (Canada) Ltd. won a $950,000 contract to continue research and testing on the synthetic aperture radar system for Energy, Mines and Resources Canada.

For the first two quarters of 1993, Intera continues to return profits as a result of increased revenues and reduced operating costs. The company's restructuring program in mid-1992 aimed to reduce operating costs and to focus and build on Intera's core activities appears to be returning dividends. The petroleum and resource management division experienced a 9% increase in revenues resulting from strong demand for the company's software products and consulting services. The mapping and reconnaissance division experienced a 5% gain in revenues resulting from STAR radar services and mapping products.

In fiscal 1992, the weak economy had the greatest impact on the company's mapping and reconnaissance segment, in addition to reduced sales in the exploration portion of the petroleum and resource production and environmental units. Despite the economy, Intera's R&D budget climbed 31% in the year allocated to the development of ECLIPSE and its related software products. Intera's ECLIPSE software business has been growing and the company has introduced a new three dimensional visualization product called InteraView. InteraView is a product designed to be used in conjunction with graphic software packages. Further, Intera brought Digital Orthoimaging to the production stage which will be used in geographical information system applications. STARMAP, which applies the same principles as Digital, was also brought to the production stage.

In fiscal 1992, revenues derived from the petroleum and resource sector represented 66% of total sales, with the remaining 34% derived from the mapping and reconnaissance sector. Revenues by geographic segment were: the United States 17%, Canada 37%, and the United Kingdom, 46%.

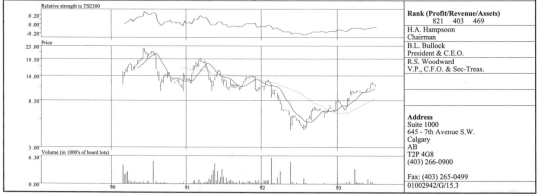

Rank (Profit/Revenue/Assets)
821   403   469

H.A. Hampsoon
Chairman

B.L. Bullock
President & C.E.O.

R.S. Woodward
V.P., C.F.O. & Sec-Treas.

Address
Suite 1000
645 - 7th Avenue S.W.
Calgary
AB
T2P 4G8
(403) 266-0900

Fax: (403) 265-0499
01002942/G/15.3

For further company information, call Globe Information Services 1-800-268-9128 or (416)585-5345

| Page | Company | $ | Latest year end | Earnings per Share | | |
				Actual	Estimate this year	Estimate next year
483	Arbor Capital		9210	0.81	0.86	0.94
484	Astral Communications		9302	0.46	0.74	0.88
485	Banister Inc.		9212	1.21	1.27	n.a.
486	Bovar Inc.		9212	0.03	0.03	0.04
487	Bracknell Corp.		9210	0.48	0.48	0.64
488	CGC Inc.		9212	0.11	0.43	0.64
489	Chai-Na-Ta Ginseng		9205	0.18	n.a.	n.a.
490	Cineplex-Odeon	$US	9212	(0.48)	(0.16)	0.01
491	Cinram Ltd.		9212	0.93	1.09	1.33
492	Derlan Industries		9212	(0.68)	0.00	0.37
493	Four Seasons Hotels		9212	0.32	0.76	1.00
494	Inter City Products		9212	(0.40)	0.25	0.70
495	International Murex Technologies	$US	9212	(0.62)	0.17	n.a.
496	Kaufel Group		9208	0.35	0.57	0.78
497	Lafarge Corp.	$US	9212	(0.30)	0.56	1.41
498	Loewen Group		9212	0.77	0.96	1.15
499	MDS Health Group		9210	0.87	1.01	1.07
500	Moore Corporation		9212	0.60	1.03	1.36
501	Philip Environmental		9212	0.60	0.64	0.76
502	Premdor Inc.		9212	0.28	0.57	0.87
503	Scott Paper		9212	(0.38)	(0.14)	0.28
504	Shaw Industries		9212	0.48	0.81	1.14
505	SNC Group		9212	0.64	0.92	1.43
506	St Lawrence Cement		9212	(0.73)	(0.21)	0.49

Estimates from I/B/E/S Inc., 345 Hudson St., New York, NY 10014 (212) 243-3335. In Canada: 6 Lansing Square, Ste. 235, Willowdale, ON M2J 1T5 (416) 496-0977.

Industrial, nec (Not Elsewhere Classified)

Engineering & Construction Monitor - Industry Report [Apr-21-1993]. SHEARSON LEHMAN BROTHERS, INC. reported by Callaghan, C., et al
The only consistently strong area in the U.S. construction industry during early 1993 has been residential building, which continues to grow at double digit rates over year earlier levels. Public works and highway spending has slowed versus 1992's strong levels. Commercial construction is expected to bottom in 1993. Industrial construction shoud improve during the year, as higher capacity utilization levels lead to capacity additions. [RN 1325072]

Building Materials Industry - Industry Report [Apr-13-1993]. MERRILL LYNCH CAPITAL MARKETS reported by Goldfarb, J.
Notwithstanding the disinflationary trend of the overall economy, prices for many building products are beginning to advance. Those increases primarily reflect tightening balances between supply and demand. Spurred by strength in housing and related markets, consumption is rising; production capacities for most building materials have declined measurably over the past decade. The expansion in construction activity is still in its early stages. As further growth in demand pushes operating rates higher, selling prices should continue upward. Realizations may not rise quite as sharply as in some past cycles, but positive price leverage will still be significant. [RN 1322056]

Building Industry - Industry Report [Apr-2-1993]. MERRILL LYNCH CAPITAL MARKETS reported by Goldfarb, J.
A slow and gradual economic upturn of the type that seems most probable for the next several years, without the interest-rate and inflationary pressures of a faster rebound, could extend the fundamental upcycle in the building industry. Residential alterations and repairs, a large market (90% the size in dollars of new single-family housing construction) that usually demands top-of-the-line products will be at record levels in 1993 and will continue expanding thereafter. This entire industry has downsized and cut costs and break-even points dramatically over the past decade. As the cycle expands, companies in this sector should enjoy significantly positive operating leverage, with large proportions of incremental sales dollars flowing down to their bottom lines. [RN 1320586]

Health Care Strategies And Positioning - Industry Report [Apr-19-1993]. SHEARSON LEHMAN BROTHERS, INC. reported by Brimeyer, J.R., et al
There is a sales slowdown that is occurring in addition to the effects of the political side of health care reform. This has already developed throughout the health care system, affecting pharmaceuticals, medical supplies, and devices. This trend toward sluggish demand and weaker pricing probably began in mid-year 1992. What caused health care reform to be such

a hot political issue, that health care spending has reached intolerable levels in this economy, is the same force behind the slowdown in health care utilization that has already begun. [RN 1325715]

Entertainment Industry - Industry Report [Apr-29-1993] MERRILL LYNCH CAPITAL MARKETS reported by Vogel, H.L.
The entertainment and media businesses are now in the midst of a major transition that is being driven by advances in distribution technology and regulation. In distribution technology, the evolution of data compression algorithms, fiber optic network switching, cheaper storage chips, and faster microprocessors means that entertainment programs can be sliced, and diced and manipulated and distributed in an infinite number of ways. Changes on the regulatory front further appear to support the convergence of telephones, computers, and cable television networks. The American television viewer today already has a set turned on for seven hours a day. [RN 1326641]

Environmental Services - Industry Report [Apr-2-1993]. THE CHICAGO CORPORATION reported by McDonald, J.D., et al
A recent study by Environmental Information Ltd. (EI) indicates that the cost of cleaning up USTs in the United States could exceed $41 billion, significantly more than the EPA's current estimate of $30 billion (U.S.). The majority ($33.7 billion (U.S.)) of EI's projection represents cleanup that has not yet started; only $8 billion (U.S.) accounts for efforts already in progress. Law mandates that pre-1988 unprotected steel tanks must either be replaced with corrosion-resistant models by 1998 or be closed or removed. [RN 1320210]

Canadian Cement Industry - Industry Report [Mar-8-1993]. SCOTIA MCLEOD INC. reported by Proulx, C.
Capacity utilization is increasing rapidly in all regions of the U.S. Overall, the Portland Cement Association (PCA) estimates that the industry reached 87% capacity for the 12-month period ended in November 1992 compared with 79.8% the previous year. As capacity utilization goes up, so will prices and profit. The next construction cycle will not see a repeat of the boom experienced in the 1980s, which led to an oversupply of real estate in many markets. U.S. cement makers are likely to experience higher profitability this cycle, because they have been able to eliminate most of the imports that prevented the industry from reaching profitability in many markets, particularly on the coast. Dumping fees have been imposed on some foreign producers (Venezuela, Japan and Mexico) and this action has made other exporters careful. [RN 1313071]

ARBOR CAPITAL INC.

Exchanges	Price (Jun24'93)	14.00	Trailing P/E	18.42	Stock Symbol
T	Trailing Yield (%)	0.00	Trailing EPS	0.76	**ABO.B**

Period Ending	Oct92	Oct91	Oct90	Oct89	Oct88
Yearly Statistics					
Price-Close	13.00	9.00	7.00	8.50	5.25
Price-High	13.00	10.13	9.00	9.75	12.00
Price-Low	9.00	6.50	6.50	4.90	5.00
P/E-Close	16.05	15.52	9.09	5.78	22.83
Dividends per Share	0.00	0.00	0.00	0.00	0.00
Dividend Yield (%)	0.00	0.00	0.00	0.00	0.00
Sales per Share	10.89	9.27	10.28	9.89	9.30
EPS before extra. item	0.81	0.58	0.77	1.47	0.23
Cash Flow per Share	2.60	1.60	1.90	1.82	2.19
Book Value per Share	9.68	8.87	8.28	7.51	6.04
O/S Common Shares	7,773	7,773	7,773	7,773	7,773
Total Revenue	94,289	83,803	93,098	101,004	83,894
Income before extra.	6,326	4,545	5,980	11,464	1,818
Cash Flow	20,208	12,403	14,749	14,157	17,024
Debt/Equity	0.37	0.47	0.62	0.83	1.46
Return on Capital (%)	14.97	11.42	15.72	24.72	11.23
Ret. on Com. Equity (%)	8.78	6.82	9.74	21.77	3.89
% Change Profit	39.2	(24.0)	(47.8)	530.6	(40.5)
% Change Revenue	12.5	(10.0)	(7.8)	20.4	10.0
% Change Assets	5.0	3.1	0.3	0.8	10.5

Date	EPS	DPS	Tot Rev	Inc Bex
Apr 93	0.27	0.00	25,489	2,064
Jan 93	0.18	0.00	22,893	1,429
Oct 92	0.13	0.00	24,556	1,028
Jul 92	0.18	0.00	23,684	1,430
Apr 92	0.31	0.00	24,757	2,386
Jan 92	0.19	0.00	21,655	1,482
Oct 91	0.22	0.00	22,230	1,780
Jul 91	0.09	0.00	21,046	703

	Oct92	Oct91	Oct90
Preferred Div. Coverage	np	np	np
Total Div. Coverage	na	na	na
Interest Coverage	5.3	3.2	3.3
Current Ratio	3.1	2.5	3.0
Operating Margin	17.1	11.9	15.8
Asset Turnover	0.3	0.3	0.3
5 YEAR RATIOS (%)			
Return on Capital	15.6	15.2	15.7
Return on Com. Equity	10.2	0.0	9.7
Profit Growth	15.7	10.5	13.1
Revenue Growth	4.3	5.6	8.8
Asset Growth	3.8	8.4	12.7
BALANCE SHEET (000)			
Cash	10,583	2,546	15,936
Current Assets	53,036	42,910	56,042
Net Fixed Assets	70,890	71,645	67,307
Invest's & Advances	22,802	25,186	22,488
Total Assets	288,189	274,369	266,119
Short Term Debt	1,982	5,257	5,192
Current Liabilities	16,862	16,900	18,772
Long Term Debt	26,183	27,245	34,859
Total Liabilities	212,955	205,461	201,756
Total Equity	75,234	68,908	64,363
Total Liab. & Equity	288,189	274,369	266,119
CAPITAL (000)			
Total Debt	28,165	32,502	40,051
Preferred Equity	0	0	0
Common Equity	75,234	68,908	64,363

Business:

ARBOR CAPITAL INC. through its related companies owns and operates cemeteries, crematoria and funeral service establishments in Canada and the United States.

Synopsis:

Quarterly results for Arbor Capital released on January 31, 1993, showed a revenue increase of $1.3-million, or 5.8% more than the corresponding period last year on revenue of $22.9-million. Earnings per share dropped by one cent from 19 cents reported a year ago at this time.

As of October 31, 1992, revenues were $94-million and the carrying value of Arbor's assets, together with the care funds held on behalf of its cemeteries, was more than $340-million. At the end of 1992, Arbor had unused available bank lines of credit of $19.4-million (U.S.) sufficient to fulfill its investment strategy.

In Canada, through its principal subsidiary Memorial Gardens Canada Ltd., Arbor owns 44 cemeteries and 21 crematoria and has interests in 47 funeral homes in all provinces of Canada except Newfoundland. Four cemeteries and four funeral homes are also owned in the United States.

In 1992, the company sold Palms Memorial Park in Florida for $2-million (U.S.). That transaction awaits regulatory approval which is expected in April 1993. Arbor has been negotiating for the sale of the remaining assets and operations in the U.S. During 1992, U.S. operations experienced a modest operating loss. It is expected that initiatives to dispose of other under-performing assets will continue, and capital improvements will be required at other locations. As well Arbor is expecting to acquire or construct funeral homes in other markets where growth is expected.

Although the economy seems to be recovering from the most profound effects of the recession, Arbor management does not expect that the recovery will have a significant effect on operating results in 1993. Management focus will be on developing new marketing techniques and expanding products and services to increase sales.

Rank (Profit/Revenue/Assets)
229 391 278

Daniel J. Scanlan
Chairman
John W. Sabine
President
Robert J. Sumsion
Exec. V.P., Fin. & Treasurer

Address
2 Jane Street
Toronto
ON
M6S 4W8
(416) 763-4531

Fax: (416) 763-0381
A0002718/G/16.3

ASTRAL COMMUNICATIONS INC.

Exchanges	Price (Jun24'93)	15.37	Trailing P/E	30.75	Stock Symbol
TM	Trailing Yield (%)	1.79	Trailing EPS	0.50	**ACM.A**

Period Ending	Feb92	Feb91	Feb90	Feb89	Feb88
Yearly Statistics					
Price–Close	11.00	9.38	11.00	10.00	5.25
Price–High	12.50	11.88	14.75	11.00	13.38
Price–Low	9.75	8.25	9.75	5.50	5.00
P/E–Close	16.67	11.57	11.58	15.87	13.13
Dividends per Share	0.25	0.25	0.23	0.18	0.15
Dividend Yield (%)	2.27	2.67	2.05	1.75	2.86
Sales per Share	33.94	33.33	36.36	39.15	28.74
EPS before extra. item	0.66	0.81	0.95	0.63	0.40
Cash Flow per Share	1.41	1.48	2.31	1.80	0.75
Book Value per Share	10.70	10.29	9.74	8.22	7.51
O/S Common Shares	8,503	8,499	8,455	6,780	6,710
Total Revenue	289,214	283,380	287,642	265,325	195,757
Income before extra.	5,599	6,902	7,467	4,240	2,703
Cash Flow	11,951	12,543	18,225	12,174	5,040
Debt/Equity	0.58	0.74	0.40	0.94	0.56
Return on Capital (%)	7.95	10.95	13.26	15.77	7.49
Ret. on Com. Equity (%)	6.28	8.13	10.82	7.96	5.55
% Change Profit	(18.9)	(7.6)	76.1	56.9	31.3
% Change Revenue	2.1	(1.5)	8.4	35.5	8.7
% Change Assets	(5.5)	12.3	13.5	42.6	10.7

Date	EPS	DPS	Tot Rev	Inc Bex
Nov 92	0.09	0.00	81,776	867
Aug 92	0.15	0.15	73,194	1,241
May 92	0.11	0.00	70,901	951
Feb 92	0.15	0.13	66,638	1,302
Nov 91	0.12	0.00	74,585	1,017
Aug 91	0.21	0.13	68,559	1,779
May 91	0.18	0.00	66,113	1,501
Feb 91	0.18	0.13	61,061	1,564

	Feb92	Feb91	Feb90
Preferred Div. Coverage	np	np	na
Total Div. Coverage	2.6	3.2	4.1
Interest Coverage	1.9	1.7	2.7
Current Ratio	1.1	1.1	1.2
Operating Margin	4.0	5.4	6.8
Asset Turnover	1.3	1.2	1.4
5 YEAR RATIOS (%)			
Return on Capital	11.1	10.8	10.5
Return on Com. Equity	7.7	7.5	6.6
Profit Growth	22.1	45.4	30.0
Revenue Growth	9.9	16.4	23.4
Asset Growth	13.7	23.0	27.0
BALANCE SHEET (000)			
Cash	5,412	8,561	16,820
Current Assets	78,868	86,818	104,505
Net Fixed Assets	24,216	25,465	22,951
Invest's & Advances	7,468	7,112	6,353
Total Assets	219,532	232,359	206,880
Short Term Debt	1,479	4,421	7,754
Current Liabilities	69,779	78,157	88,426
Long Term Debt	51,385	60,341	24,867
Total Liabilities	128,581	144,873	124,227
Total Equity	90,951	87,486	82,653
Total Liab. & Equity	219,532	232,359	206,880
CAPITAL (000)			
Total Debt	52,864	64,762	32,621
Preferred Equity	0	0	325
Common Equity	90,951	87,486	82,328

Business:

ASTRAL COMMUNICATIONS offers pay and basic television services in English and French. It owns The Movie Network First Choice, controls Super Ecran and Canal Famille, is the majority partner and operator of the Viewer's Choice Canada pay-per-view service and has a 50% interest in Family Channel.

Synopsis:

Astral Communications took a technological leap in May 1993 when its Movie Network signed a five-year agreement with Telesat, Canada's satellite operator, to use digital video compression technology to multiply the number of channels on which movies could be shown. This follows a year-long test of the technology by the Movie Network, which is owned by Astral's First Choice Communication Corp. of Toronto.

The success of this venture is tied to the development of an industry standard for video compression technology which is to be set this summer. The Canadian operation will then be able to deal with the proposed direct broadcast satellite which is to be launched by Hughes Communication Inc.

This service will compete with the $1-billion-a-year video cassette rental market and will be available in most major cable systems served by the Movie Network by September, even though 75% of small cable systems would not be able to handle four channels.

In the 12 month period ended February 28, 1993, revenues increased 5.7% from $228-million to $304.5-million. Operating earnings after the amortization of broadcast licences almost doubled to $11.3-million from $5.8-million last year. Cash flow amounted to $16.3-million for 12 months, compared with $12-million for same period last year.

In March 1993, CBC-TV and Astral completed a historic three-year deal to distribute CBC programs (covering 40 years of programming) on VHS video cassettes, at the rate of two per month with the initial launch limited to 10 titles.

In March 1993, Hees International Bancorp. Inc. sold its 20% block in Astral to the Greenberg family for an undisclosed price. As a result the Greenberg family got 53% of Astral, which they founded 20 years ago with the merger of Astral Communications Ltd. and Bellevue Pathe Ltd.

Relative strength to TSE300 / Price / Volume (in 1000's of board lots) chart

Rank (Profit/Revenue/Assets)
245   227   308

Harold Greenberg
Chairman
Murray Marchant
V.P. Finance

Address
Maison Astral
2100, Rue Ste-Catherine Ouest
Bureau 900
Montreal
PQ
H3H 2T3
(514) 939-5000
Fax: (514) 939-1515
A0003324/G/16.1

BANISTER INC.

Exchanges	Price (Jun24'93)	15.75	Trailing P/E	12.40	Stock Symbol
TMZA	Trailing Yield (%)	0.00	Trailing EPS	1.27	**BAC**

Period Ending	Dec92	Dec91	Dec90	Dec89	Dec88
Yearly Statistics					
Price-Close	8.88	7.00	8.63	12.13	7.50
Price-High	9.25	9.50	12.50	16.75	10.13
Price-Low	7.00	5.68	7.75	7.38	6.75
P/E-Close	7.34	6.25	nm	nm	125.00
Dividends per Share	0.00	0.00	0.00	0.00	0.00
Dividend Yield (%)	0.00	0.00	0.00	0.00	0.00
Sales per Share	58.19	70.28	117.49	108.28	61.21
EPS before extra. item	1.21	1.12	(1.43)	(0.89)	0.06
Cash Flow per Share	2.59	2.32	(0.52)	(0.94)	0.96
Book Value per Share	11.66	10.45	9.31	10.74	11.60
O/S Common Shares	5,953	5,953	5,953	5,948	5,932
Total Revenue	348,014	421,725	700,697	647,896	366,141
Income before extra.	7,174	6,648	(8,517)	(5,267)	375
Cash Flow	15,395	13,786	(3,082)	(5,596)	5,676
Debt/Equity	0.32	0.38	0.68	0.62	0.28
Return on Capital (%)	14.19	11.09	(4.21)	(4.37)	4.62
Ret. on Com. Equity (%)	10.90	11.30	(14.28)	(7.94)	0.55
% Change Profit	7.9	178.1	(61.7)	(1,504.5)	(67.1)
% Change Revenue	(17.5)	(39.8)	8.2	77.0	79.1
% Change Assets	(2.7)	(32.5)	(5.5)	43.9	17.5

Date	EPS	DPS	Tot Rev	Inc Bex
Mar 93	0.09	0.00	71,710	511
Dec 92	0.55	0.00	88,278	3,230
Sep 92	0.49	0.00	125,336	2,889
Jun 92	0.14	0.00	79,739	816
Mar 92	0.04	0.00	54,520	239
Dec 91	1.10	0.00	102,635	6,510
Sep 91	0.78	0.00	133,053	4,662
Jun 91	(0.46)	0.00	99,110	(2,766)

	Dec92	Dec91	Dec90
Preferred Div. Coverage	np	np	np
Total Div. Coverage	na	na	na
Interest Coverage	6.6	2.7	0.0
Current Ratio	1.3	1.2	1.1
Operating Margin	3.2	1.6	(0.7)
Asset Turnover	2.2	2.5	2.9
5 YEAR RATIOS (%)			
Return on Capital	4.3	2.5	6.1
Return on Com. Equity	0.1	(1.7)	(1.0)
Profit Growth	44.5	(2.7)	na
Revenue Growth	11.2	25.9	43.6
Asset Growth	0.9	12.3	21.7
BALANCE SHEET (000)			
Cash	12,822	11,108	13,322
Current Assets	86,880	95,448	168,921
Net Fixed Assets	59,181	58,835	64,002
Invest's & Advances	3,294	0	0
Total Assets	160,770	165,191	244,632
Short Term Debt	2,624	5,592	15,791
Current Liabilities	64,876	79,955	160,310
Long Term Debt	19,438	17,831	22,011
Total Liabilities	91,365	102,960	189,201
Total Equity	69,405	62,231	55,431
Total Liab. & Equity	160,770	165,191	244,632
CAPITAL (000)			
Total Debt	22,062	23,423	37,802
Preferred Equity	0	0	0
Common Equity	69,405	62,231	55,431

Business:

BANISTER INC. is a Canadian construction company specializing in civil, pipeline, utility, industrial and building construction. The company's ten divisions are active across Canada and in the United States, the Caribbean, China, Kenya and Romania.

Synopsis:

In December 1992, Banister made a public offer for the outstanding shares of Majestic Contractors Limited; 98% of those shares were tendered and the remaining shares have since been acquired. Pipeline construction accounted for about 22% of Banister's 1991 revenue. Assuming those proportions are maintained in 1993, the acquisition of Majestic will boost the pipeline component of Banister's total business to over 40%. Coupled with Banister's pipelines division, this addition to the group has put Banister Inc. into the front rank of large international pipeline contractors, with the largest combined fleet of heavy pipeline construction equipment in Canada.

1992 was one of the most depressed periods for civil construction in Canada. Faced with practically no domestic prospects, the Nuclear Division of Foundation Company of Canada, a subsidiary of Banister, turned its attention to the highly competitive international marketplace. Much effort and resources were directed to tendering projects financed by the Canadian International Development Agency and multi-lateral agencies such as the World Bank.

Significant projects completed in 1992 by The Jackson-Lewis Company, the building construction division of the company, include an office tower for CP Pension Plan in Vancouver, B.C., an office tower for Canada Trust in Kitchener, Ontario, and a computer centre for Confederation Life in Markham, Ontario. In spite of the slump market in the building construction sector, the building group maintained its target volume and work in place was about 10% higher than 1991. The year ahead for this group does not look optimistic, according to the company. Most projects are smaller in value and volumes available may be diminished, even from 1992. It is not anticipated that a significant recovery in the industrial, commercial and institutional sectors will occur until 1994 and such recovery, at that stage, may be modest. Financial attrition will probably lessen competition sometime in 1993, so increased margins may be possible.

Relative strength to TSE300 / Price / Volume (in 1000's of board lots)

Rank (Profit/Revenue/Assets)
213   207   349

J.R. McCaig
Chairman

E.R. Austin
President & C.E.O.

C.N. D'Croix
V.P., Finance & C.F.O.

Address
3660 Midland Avenue
Scarborough
ON
M1V 4V3
(416) 754-8735

Fax: (416) 754-8736
B0000364/G/7.3

BOVAR INC.

Exchanges	Price (Jun24'93)	1.06	Trailing P/E	nm	Stock Symbol
T	Trailing Yield (%)	0.00	Trailing EPS	0.00	**BVR**

Period Ending	Dec92	Dec91	Dec90	Dec89	Dec88
Yearly Statistics					
Price-Close	0.90	1.10	0.60	0.44	3.10
Price-High	1.55	1.70	0.65	4.50	6.20
Price-Low	0.80	0.50	0.20	0.36	2.20
P/E-Close	90.00	13.75	nm	nm	nm
Dividends per Share	0.00	0.00	0.00	0.00	0.00
Dividend Yield (%)	0.00	0.00	0.00	0.00	0.00
Sales per Share	0.92	1.51	1.39	1.01	46.04
EPS before extra. item	0.01	0.08	(0.20)	0.00	(48.07)
Cash Flow per Share	0.12	0.20	0.18	0.09	2.88
Book Value per Share	0.06	(0.99)	(1.12)	(1.00)	(106.97)
O/S Common Shares	55,293	34,950	34,915	34,015	1,923
Total Revenue	48,786	55,576	48,917	35,699	161,634
Income before extra.	773	4,367	(4,951)	(103)	(84,838)
Cash Flow	6,417	6,950	6,141	3,155	5,336
Debt/Equity	18.02	na	na	na	na
Return on Capital (%)	9.12	21.56	4.42	14.05	(55.39)
Ret. on Com. Equity (%)	na	na	na	na	na
% Change Profit	(82.3)	188.2	(4,706.8)	99.9	(1,541.0)
% Change Revenue	(12.2)	13.6	37.0	(77.9)	(13.4)
% Change Assets	18.1	0.1	(7.0)	(33.4)	(60.5)

Business:
BOVAR INC. is an environmental and waste management company providing consulting and technical services. BOVAR manufactures multi-gas monitoring instrumentation and control equipment, and is an owner/operator of waste management facilities. BOVAR offers cost effective engineering solutions for challenging environmental problems.

Date	EPS	DPS	Tot Rev	Inc Bex
Mar 93	0.00	0.00	12,188	323
Dec 92	(0.01)	0.00	12,417	(60)
Sep 92	0.00	0.00	11,384	77
Jun 92	0.01	0.00	11,949	249
Mar 92	0.01	0.00	12,956	507
Dec 91	(0.01)	0.00	14,006	202
Sep 91	0.01	0.00	13,639	650
Jun 91	(0.01)	0.00	12,824	30

Preferred Div. Coverage	np	na	na	
Total Div. Coverage	na	na	na	
Interest Coverage	0.9	1.6	0.3	
Current Ratio	0.7	0.8	0.8	
Operating Margin	10.0	13.8	17.3	
Asset Turnover	0.6	0.8	0.7	
5 YEAR RATIOS (%)				
Return on Capital	(1.2)	(0.5)	(2.8)	
Return on Com. Equity	na	na	na	
Profit Growth	na	na	na	
Revenue Growth	(23.6)	(23.7)	(29.8)	
Asset Growth	(22.0)	(26.9)	(35.1)	
BALANCE SHEET (000)				
Cash	668	984	1,208	
Current Assets	23,968	24,323	26,775	
Net Fixed Assets	52,527	39,796	37,200	
Invest's & Advances	0	0	0	
Total Assets	80,844	68,468	68,432	
Short Term Debt	13,043	12,526	10,617	
Current Liabilities	34,711	29,508	32,893	
Long Term Debt	43,022	51,013	47,765	
Total Liabilities	77,733	80,521	84,871	
Total Equity	3,111	(12,053)	(16,439)	
Total Liab. & Equity	80,844	68,468	68,432	
CAPITAL (000)				
Total Debt	56,065	63,539	58,382	
Preferred Equity	0	22,500	22,500	
Common Equity	3,111	(34,553)	(38,939)	

Synopsis:

BOVAR Inc. continues to position itself as an international player in the environmental services and waste management industries, by expanding its marketing network into the U.S. and internationally. In Canada, BOVAR was successful in increasing capacity by adding to its waste management operations, and during the year it received regulatory approval to expand the Alberta Special Waste Treatment Centre at Swan Hills, Alberta, of which it is a 60% owner. BOVAR also had a new transformer furnace commissioned at a treatment centre which handles PCB contaminated transformers and contaminated metal structures, and it constructed a new state-of-the-art Biomedical Waste Facility at Beiseker, Alberta.

Revenues in 1992 of $48.8-million were down from $53.1-million in 1991. Total revenues in the first quarter of 1993 were $12.2-million compared to $13-million in 1992. First quarter net income was $323,000 (0 cents per share) compared to $507,000 (1 cent per share) in 1992. Income from continuing operations was $474,000 (1 cent per share) compared to $507,000 (1 cent per share) in 1992. Discontinued operations incurred carrying costs of $151,000 related to 22 acres of vacated industrial land and buildings in Richmond, B.C., currently up for sale.

The expansion of the Swan Hills Treatment Centre accounted for $10.4-million of the 1993 capital expenditures of $11.2-million. The centre remains on schedule with the commissioning of the incineration system program targeted for mid-1994.

BOVAR is optimistic about the sales of its continuous emission monitoring systems to Poland and the U.S., and anticipates further international penetration. Its environmental services had low activity levels during the first quarter of 1993, but were successful in booking contracts which will benefit the balance of 1993. In April 1993, BOVAR received a five-year license from Alberta Environment to operate its 20 tonne per day biomedical waste incineration facility at Beiseker, Alberta. This is the first such plant in Canada to meet the new air emission guidelines.

Relative strength to TSE300 / Price / Volume (in 1000's of board lots)

Rank (Profit/Revenue/Assets)
448 477 454
John R. McCaig — Chairman
Paul Fee — President & C.E.O.
Kenneth E. Myers — V.P., Fin., C.F.O. & Secretary

Address
4 Manning Close N.E.
Calgary
AB
T2E 7N5
(403) 235-8300

Fax: (403) 248-3306
B0005970/G/8.1

BRACKNELL CORPORATION

Exchanges	Price (Jun24'93)	6.75	Trailing P/E	14.06	Stock Symbol
T	Trailing Yield (%)	0.00	Trailing EPS	0.48	**BRK**

Period Ending	Oct 92	Oct 91	Oct 90	Oct 89	Oct 88
Yearly Statistics					
Price-Close	5.00	3.20	1.37	1.35	1.15
Price-High	6.00	3.30	2.00	1.68	1.35
Price-Low	2.95	1.10	1.25	0.75	0.55
P/E-Close	10.42	5.16	2.64	4.04	115.00
Dividends per Share	0.00	0.60	0.00	0.00	0.00
Dividend Yield (%)	0.00	18.75	0.00	0.00	0.00
Sales per Share	10.50	11.90	11.44	10.22	na
EPS before extra. item	0.48	0.62	0.52	0.33	0.01
Cash Flow per Share	0.77	0.81	0.59	0.40	0.01
Book Value per Share	1.95	1.05	1.05	0.53	0.12
O/S Common Shares	23,281	17,160	15,219	15,219	12,633
Total Revenue	225,413	203,958	174,665	153,565	232
Income before extra.	10,138	10,535	7,930	5,019	157
Cash Flow	16,386	13,735	8,924	6,032	166
Debt/Equity	nd	0.31	0.37	0.73	nd
Return on Capital (%)	54.52	57.30	44.07	64.36	10.53
Ret. on Com. Equity (%)	31.98	62.06	65.79	103.95	10.53
% Change Profit	(3.8)	32.9	58.0	3,096.8	173.7
% Change Revenue	10.5	16.8	13.7	nm	(90.3)
% Change Assets	40.0	4.6	31.6	2,615.2	(4.4)

Date	EPS	DPS	Tot Rev	Inc Bex
Jan 93	0.11	0.00	53,881	2,457
Oct 92	0.13	0.00	60,801	2,851
Jul 92	0.12	0.00	52,109	2,632
Apr 92	0.12	0.00	66,054	2,682
Jan 92	0.11	0.00	46,449	1,973
Oct 91	0.20	0.00	48,241	3,352
Jul 91	0.13	0.00	57,186	2,256
Apr 91	0.17	0.00	52,570	2,842

Preferred Div. Coverage	np	np	np
Total Div. Coverage	na	1.0	na
Interest Coverage	nd	na	na
Current Ratio	1.9	1.4	1.3
Operating Margin	7.7	5.6	4.2
Asset Turnover	2.1	2.6	2.4
5 YEAR RATIOS (%)			
Return on Capital	46.2	35.6	15.0
Return on Com. Equity	54.9	na	na
Profit Growth	181.5	224.4	243.1
Revenue Growth	148.3	95.5	83.8
Asset Growth	118.6	32.6	22.0
BALANCE SHEET (000)			
Cash	29,733	11,131	14,027
Current Assets	98,297	72,127	68,956
Net Fixed Assets	2,947	2,001	1,659
Invest's & Advances	3,862	0	0
Total Assets	107,861	77,063	73,655
Short Term Debt	0	0	0
Current Liabilities	53,083	51,020	51,697
Long Term Debt	0	5,609	5,940
Total Liabilities	62,383	59,129	57,637
Total Equity	45,478	17,934	16,018
Total Liab. & Equity	107,861	77,063	73,655
CAPITAL (000)			
Total Debt	0	5,609	5,940
Preferred Equity	0	0	0
Common Equity	45,478	17,934	16,018

Business:

BRACKNELL CORPORATION is an industrial specialty services company. Bracknell's main business is conducted through The State Group which provides construction technical services (or multi-trade contracting services) and management services to commercial industrial and institutional clients. Bracknell recently acquired Village Communication and its wholly owned affiliate Cablecom International.

Synopsis:

During February 1993, Bracknell Corp. and Agra Industries Ltd. won a $124-million contract to design and build what will be one of the largest cogeneration plants in Quebec. The 145-megawatt facility, which is to be constructed in Hull, will generate electricity for sale to Hydro-Quebec and steam for processing use in the nearby plants of E.B. Eddy Forestry Products Ltd. and Scott Paper Ltd. The plant, which will be fired by natural gas, is expected to be in service by September, 1994. Actual design and construction of the facility will be undertaken by a 50/50 joint venture of Agra's subsidiary, Northern Engineering Inc., and The State Group, a division of Bracknell, in conjunction with Natural State Construction Group of Longueuil, Quebec.

In February 1993, the company agreed to issue three million special warrants through Midland Walwyn Capital Inc. for distribution by private placement at $7.125 per warrant. Each special warrant would entitle the holder to acquire one common share for no additional payment. The net proceeds of the issue of approximately $20-million will be used to increase bonding capacity and pursue diversification and expansion plans. Pending such use, the net proceeds will be added to Bracknell's working capital.

On December 22, 1992, Bracknell said its joint venture with SNC-Lavalin, a unit of Montreal-based SNC Group Inc., won a $127-million contract for Canada Post Corp.'s community mailbox program. The five-year contract covers engineering, installation, maintenance and snow clearance at the community mailbox sites across Canada. During April 1993, when the work started, 38,000 community mailbox sites were installed across Canada, and 33,300 more are planned in the contract.

In 1992, Bracknell formed Clientech Support Services Inc. The subsidiary provides facilities management as well as operations and maintenance services to public and private sector companies seeking to contract out services that are not a core part of their operations. At year-end, Clientech had a backlog of $69-million.

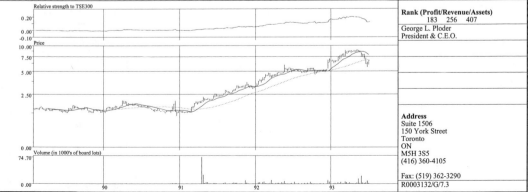

Rank (Profit/Revenue/Assets)
183   256   407

George L. Ploder
President & C.E.O.

Address
Suite 1506
150 York Street
Toronto
ON
M5H 3S5
(416) 360-4105

Fax: (519) 362-3290
R0003132/G/7.3

CGC INC.

Exchanges	Price (Jun24'93)	8.87	Trailing P/E	59.17	Stock Symbol
TM	Trailing Yield (%)	4.96	Trailing EPS	0.15	**GYP**

Period Ending	Dec92	Dec91	Dec90	Dec89	Dec88
Yearly Statistics					
Price-Close	7.60	7.75	8.50	14.00	10.50
Price-High	10.50	11.13	14.13	14.88	14.75
Price-Low	6.25	7.38	7.13	10.25	9.50
P/E-Close	69.09	17.22	11.81	9.27	5.65
Dividends per Share	0.44	0.74	0.84	2.81	0.66
Dividend Yield (%)	5.79	9.55	9.88	20.07	6.29
Sales per Share	5.97	6.64	8.00	9.71	10.72
EPS before extra. item	0.11	0.45	0.72	1.51	1.86
Cash Flow per Share	0.29	0.63	0.89	1.69	2.01
Book Value per Share	1.80	2.14	2.43	2.66	3.95
O/S Common Shares	25,342	25,342	25,342	25,341	25,320
Total Revenue	151,803	168,338	203,336	252,169	273,869
Income before extra.	2,727	11,343	18,283	38,299	47,064
Cash Flow	7,410	15,938	22,679	42,732	50,945
Debt/Equity	0.49	0.39	0.16	nd	nd
Return on Capital (%)	6.16	26.64	43.93	75.64	95.21
Ret. on Com. Equity (%)	5.46	19.61	28.35	45.74	55.45
% Change Profit	(76.0)	(38.0)	(52.3)	(18.6)	(10.6)
% Change Revenue	(9.8)	(17.2)	(19.4)	(7.9)	(3.9)
% Change Assets	(8.4)	(2.4)	(34.8)	10.1	14.7

Date	EPS	DPS	Tot Rev	Inc Bex
Mar 93	0.07	0.11	39,892	1,754
Dec 92	0.04	0.11	34,334	932
Sep 92	0.05	0.11	42,045	1,351
Jun 92	(0.01)	0.11	38,171	(314)
Mar 92	0.03	0.11	38,416	758
Dec 91	0.10	0.11	40,266	2,503
Sep 91	0.14	0.21	44,061	3,522
Jun 91	0.10	0.21	43,091	2,447

	Dec92	Dec91	Dec90
Preferred Div. Coverage	np	np	np
Total Div. Coverage	0.2	0.6	0.9
Interest Coverage	na	32.8	na
Current Ratio	0.9	1.1	1.2
Operating Margin	2.5	11.6	14.8
Asset Turnover	1.6	1.6	1.9
5 YEAR RATIOS (%)			
Return on Capital	49.5	83.1	96.0
Return on Com. Equity	30.9	49.0	55.3
Profit Growth	(45.1)	(23.2)	(7.5)
Revenue Growth	(11.9)	(6.2)	2.8
Asset Growth	(6.0)	(12.7)	(8.2)
BALANCE SHEET (000)			
Cash	0	0	2,627
Current Assets	27,598	36,766	37,641
Net Fixed Assets	45,740	46,819	49,544
Invest's & Advances	0	0	0
Total Assets	96,497	105,316	107,914
Short Term Debt	19,262	17,865	10,061
Current Liabilities	31,612	32,993	31,545
Long Term Debt	2,942	2,971	0
Total Liabilities	50,775	51,170	46,358
Total Equity	45,722	54,146	61,556
Total Liab. & Equity	96,497	105,316	107,914
CAPITAL (000)			
Total Debt	22,204	20,836	10,061
Preferred Equity	0	0	0
Common Equity	45,722	54,146	61,556

Business:

CGC INC. is a building materials company and operates three divisions. CGC Gyspsum makes and markets gypsum wallboard and construction steel. CGC Interiors makes suspended ceilings, ceiling tiles and shower enclosures. CGC Industries makes industrial and consumer products including safety grating and mineral wool insulation.

Synopsis:

CGC Inc.'s first quarter results for 1993 reflect positive signs in the Canadian economy. This, in combination with improved volumes and pricing for gypsum wallboard, has had a favourable impact on earnings. It is anticipated that prices will continue to improve and there will be a gradual increase in demand for CGS's products as the economy strengthens.

Declines in net sales and earnings in 1992 from 1991 were primarily due to a drop of about 12% in the domestic selling price of gypsum wallboard, CGC's major product line, to a 14-year low during the second quarter of 1992. Wallboard volume dipped marginally as a result of the construction recession in Eastern Canada. Residential construction in Eastern Canada continued its four-year decline to 4% below 1991 levels. Non-residential construction also continued its decline to 16% below 1991 levels on a national basis. The weak demand for gypsum wallboard in the United States continued to reduce the company's ability to export to that market. CGC attributed its profit in 1992 to disciplined cost control since revenues declined dramatically due to lower selling prices.

CGC Gypsum is the largest supplier of gypsum wallboard and related products in Eastern Canada. It generated 60% of company sales in 1992 and 1991. The company maintained its number one position in suspended ceilings nationally, as well as increasing market share in other product lines.

The most significant factor in 1992 performance was the erosion in gypsum board pricing due to the dumping of U.S. imports. On January 20, 1993, the Canadian International Trade Tribunal ruled the dumping had caused material injury to Canadian producers. Revenue Canada will impose anti-dumping duties on most gypsum board imported from the United States into Canada for a five-year period.

1992 sales by end-use markets were: new residential, 31%; new non-residential, 24%; repair and renovation, 37%; and industrial processes, 8%.

Rank (Profit/Revenue/Assets)
325 312 422

William R.C. Macdonald
President & C.E.O.

W. Blair Douglas
Sr. V.P., C.F.O. & Sec-Treas.

Address
777 Bay Street
Suite 1800
Toronto
ON
M5W 1K8
(416) 595-8835

Fax: (416) 595-8852
C0000935/G/6.10

CHAI-NA-TA GINSENG PRODUCTS LTD.

Exchanges	Price (Jun24'93)	6.87	Trailing P/E	42.97	Stock Symbol
T	Trailing Yield (%)	0.00	Trailing EPS	0.16	CJG

Period Ending	May92	May91	May90	May89	May88
Yearly Statistics					
Price-Close	5.25	1.90	1.57	2.23	1.73
Price-High	6.13	2.47	2.87	3.33	1.88
Price-Low	2.20	1.33	1.50	1.67	0.67
P/E-Close	29.17	31.67	14.69	55.75	35.71
Dividends per Share	0.00	0.00	0.07	0.03	0.00
Dividend Yield (%)	0.00	0.00	4.26	1.34	0.00
Sales per Share	0.70	0.31	0.36	0.16	0.16
EPS before extra. item	0.18	0.09	0.11	0.04	0.05
Cash Flow per Share	0.54	0.25	0.30	0.10	0.14
Book Value per Share	1.10	0.76	0.68	0.64	0.40
O/S Common Shares	12,427	10,937	10,252	10,252	9,036
Total Revenue	7,971	3,484	3,774	1,578	1,373
Income before extra.	2,006	1,040	1,160	390	389
Cash Flow	6,145	2,800	3,040	971	1,191
Debt/Equity	0.19	0.36	0.16	0.01	0.03
Return on Capital (%)	29.31	19.47	28.11	13.50	25.59
Ret. on Com. Equity (%)	18.33	13.60	17.15	7.67	14.44
% Change Profit	93.0	(10.4)	197.4	0.2	4,212.4
% Change Revenue	128.8	(7.7)	139.2	14.9	127.0
% Change Assets	51.8	42.8	31.7	82.8	45.4

Business:

CHAI-NA-TA GINSENG PRODUCTS LTD. is an agricultural company involved in the cultivation and harvesting of ginseng root and is currently the largest grower of ginseng in North America. The company also has a processing and grading operation in mainland China, operated through a joint venture with the China National Foreign Trade Corporation and a marketing company in Hong Kong.

Date	EPS	DPS	Tot Rev	Inc Bex
Feb 93	0.15	0.00	6,032	1,831
Nov 92	(0.02)	0.00	20	(284)
Aug 92	(0.03)	0.00	10	(319)
May 92	0.06	0.00	3,005	662
Feb 92	0.15	0.00	4,929	1,715
Nov 91	(0.01)	0.00	30	(192)
Aug 91	(0.02)	0.00	7	(179)
May 91	(0.01)	0.00	5	(88)

	May92	May91	May90	
Preferred Div. Coverage	np	np	np	
Total Div. Coverage	na	na	1.7	
Interest Coverage	9.0	26.4	27.9	
Current Ratio	4.7	5.4	1.3	
Operating Margin	50.4	55.7	54.2	
Asset Turnover	0.4	0.3	0.4	
5 YEAR RATIOS (%)				
Return on Capital	23.2	na	na	
Return on Com. Equity	14.2	na	na	
Profit Growth	194.7	na	na	
Revenue Growth	67.5	na	na	
Asset Growth	49.9	na	na	
BALANCE SHEET (000)				
Cash	1,311	942	10	
Current Assets	3,139	1,232	1,662	
Net Fixed Assets	16,304	12,004	7,775	
Invest's & Advances	865	145	0	
Total Assets	20,460	13,478	9,437	
Short Term Debt	0	0	1,135	
Current Liabilities	664	226	1,244	
Long Term Debt	2,635	3,000	0	
Total Liabilities	6,849	5,196	2,435	
Total Equity	13,611	8,282	7,002	
Total Liab. & Equity	20,460	13,478	9,437	
CAPITAL (000)				
Total Debt	2,635	3,000	1,135	
Preferred Equity	0	0	0	
Common Equity	13,611	8,282	7,002	

Synopsis:

In fiscal 1993, Chai-Na-Ta Ginseng Products Ltd. harvested 63 acres or 177,704 pounds of ginseng roots. As of February 28, 1993, the nine months results reflect only half of the harvest being sold. Total sales for the year ending May 31, 1993 are expected to be in excess of $10-million.

Currently the company has 779 acres of ginseng under cultivation. If the ginseng market remains as strong as the last few years, the company projects that in 1994 it will harvest 124 acres of roots and will generate $20.5-million in revenues. In 1995, it will harvest 155 acres and generate $25.5-million, in 1996, 200 acres and $35-million, and in 1997, 300 acres and $50-million.

For 1992, about three million pounds of North American ginseng were produced; Chai-Na-Ta produced about 6% of the total. Of the three million pounds, Hong Kong, Taiwan, Malaysia, Thailand, Singapore and Indonesia consumed approximately 1.5 million pounds leaving only one and one-half million pounds for the world's largest market, China. The company projected that by 1996 there will be approximately five million pounds of North American ginseng produced with Chai-Na-Ta's production comprising 15%.

On May 22, 1991, Chai-Na-Ta announced the formation of a marketing company, North American Ginseng Enterprises Ltd. (NAGEL), in Hong Kong. In April 1992, Chai-Na-Ta took on Tung Fong Hung Medicine Company Limited as a Partner in NAGEL. Tung Fong Hung, a Hong Kong public company, is the largest retailer of Ginseng in South East Asia. NAGEL negotiated and obtained a renewable 20-year joint venture agreement with the China National Pharmaceutical Foreign Trade Corporation and the Wuxi Processed Chinese Herbal Medicine Factory to process, grade and market North American ginseng in China. The joint venture's factory in Wuxi received the first shipment of roots and began processing in November 1992. This will be the Wuxi joint venture's first year of full production, with virtually all of the roots harvest to be processed by the joint venture plant.

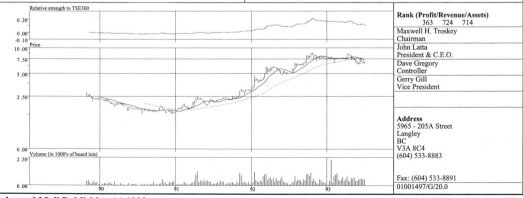

Rank (Profit/Revenue/Assets)
363   724   714

Maxwell H. Troskey
Chairman

John Latta
President & C.E.O.

Dave Gregory
Controller

Gerry Gill
Vice President

Address
5965 - 205A Street
Langley
BC
V3A 8C4
(604) 533-8883

Fax: (604) 533-8891
01001497/G/20.0

CINEPLEX ODEON CORPORATION

Exchanges	Price (Jun24'93)		3.45	Trailing P/E		nm	Stock Symbol
T	Trailing Yield (%)		0.00	Trailing EPS		(0.43)	**CPX**

Period Ending	Dec92	Dec91	Dec90	Dec89	Dec88
Yearly Statistics	US	US	US	US	US
Price-Close	2.42	3.60	2.60	7.75	14.00
Price-High	4.20	7.13	8.50	19.38	16.00
Price-Low	1.97	2.03	2.15	7.50	9.63
P/E-Close	nm	nm	nm	nm	13.44
Dividends per Share	0.00	0.00	0.00	0.00	0.00
Dividend Yield (%)	0.00	0.00	0.00	0.00	0.00
Sales per Share	6.04	9.59	12.89	12.21	12.20
EPS before extra. item	(0.48)	(1.38)	(2.85)	(1.65)	0.85
Cash Flow per Share	0.01	(0.21)	(0.96)	(1.33)	0.38
Book Value per Share	1.96	2.56	3.53	6.31	7.89
O/S Common Shares	101,380	83,362	47,691	47,691	47,539
Total Revenue	518,463	535,398	582,160	631,682	637,621
Income before extra.	(41,349)	(77,212)	(135,934)	(78,637)	40,396
Cash Flow	982	(11,595)	(45,782)	(63,346)	18,227
Debt/Equity	2.27	2.26	3.37	2.06	1.90
Return on Capital (%)	(0.75)	(3.56)	(8.86)	(2.03)	9.09
Ret. on Com. Equity (%)	(20.04)	(40.43)	(57.98)	(23.28)	11.33
% Change Profit	46.4	43.2	(72.9)	(294.7)	16.9
% Change Revenue	(3.2)	(8.0)	(7.8)	(0.9)	27.9
% Change Assets	(7.9)	(6.1)	(22.5)	(12.4)	36.5

Date		EPS	DPS	Tot Rev	Inc Bex
Mar 93	US	(0.11)	0.00	116,649	(10,841)
Dec 92	US	(0.14)	0.00	125,918	(12,714)
Sep 92	US	(0.09)	0.00	133,534	(7,169)
Jun 92	US	(0.09)	0.00	131,090	(7,596)
Mar 92	US	(0.17)	0.00	129,124	(13,870)
Dec 91	US	(0.25)	0.00	121,060	(23,364)
Sep 91	US	(0.31)	0.00	136,580	(15,010)
Jun 91	US	(0.61)	0.00	125,647	(28,935)

	Dec92	Dec91	Dec90
Preferred Div. Coverage	np	np	np
Total Div. Coverage	na	na	na
Interest Coverage	0.0	0.0	0.0
Current Ratio	0.3	0.2	0.4
Operating Margin	(0.9)	(1.3)	(2.6)
Asset Turnover	0.7	0.7	0.7
5 YEAR RATIOS (%)			
Return on Capital	(1.2)	0.8	4.3
Return on Com. Equity	(26.1)	(19.6)	(7.9)
Profit Growth	na	na	na
Revenue Growth	0.8	8.4	36.4
Asset Growth	(4.4)	4.9	52.6
BALANCE SHEET (000)			
Cash	1,350	1,088	1,469
Current Assets	30,653	40,071	65,148
Net Fixed Assets	658,598	710,657	743,869
Invest's & Advances	5,613	6,650	4,673
Total Assets	741,652	805,073	857,782
Short Term Debt	30,991	62,382	31,578
Current Liabilities	120,106	168,895	149,534
Long Term Debt	420,303	419,828	536,029
Total Liabilities	542,686	591,325	689,545
Total Equity	198,966	213,748	168,237
Total Liab. & Equity	741,652	805,073	857,782
CAPITAL (000)			
Total Debt	451,294	482,210	567,607
Preferred Equity	0	0	0
Common Equity	198,966	213,748	168,237

Business:

CINEPLEX ODEON CORP. is engaged in exhibiting and distributing motion pictures. The company operates theatre complexes across North America. MCA Inc. of Universal City, California, and investors related to the Claridge Group of companies are the company's major shareholders.

Synopsis:

Although a former director of Cineplex Odeon Corp., David Fingold, and two companies that his family controls, have been charged with insider trading, the Ontario Securities Commission is not investigating Cineplex.

Cineplex, which operated 1,621 screens in 365 locations in North America, reported a 1992 loss of $41.3 million (U.S.), on revenue of $518.7-million (U.S.), compared with a loss of $77.2-million (U.S.) on revenue of $538.3-million (U.S.) a year earlier. The company hopes the summer line-up of movies will strengthen its financial recovery. Revenue in 1992 fell to $518.7-million (U.S.) from $538.3-million (U.S.) a year earlier, largely because of the sale of theatres in Texas and Washington state, some box office price reductions and a weaker Canadian dollar.

First quarter results of 1993 noted a reduced net loss of $1.8-million (U.S.) on revenues of $116.6-million (U.S.), compared to a net loss of $13.9 million (U.S.) on revenues of $129.1-million (U.S.) in the first quarter of 1992.

In April 1993, Cineplex agreed with its 18-bank syndicate to extend the maturity date of its long-term debt to December 31, 1996. Under the previous terms, the debt would have had to be repaid by December 31, 1994. Factoring in interest and principal payments for 1993, however, the amount outstanding at the end of 1994 would have been $269.4-million.

The new banking arrangement reduced the 1993 principal payment to $39.5-million from $70-million. Cineplex will pay $21-million of that amount by using a $31-million partial prepayment from a supplier. Analysts saw this conversion of debt to equity as diluting the ownership of all other shareholders. Over the past 2-1/2 years, the number of Cineplex shares has more than doubled to 101 million from about 48 million.

Relative strength to TSE300 / Price / Volume (in 1000's of board lots) charts, years 90–93.

Rank (Profit/Revenue/Assets)
956   136   157

E. Leo Kolber
Chairman

Allen Karp
President & C.E.O.

Ellis Jacob
Exec. V.P. & C.F.O.

Address
1303 Yonge Street
Toronto
ON
M4T 2Y9
(416) 323-6600

Fax: (416) 323-6677
C0029495/G/16.1

CINRAM LTD.

Exchanges	Price (Jun24'93)		12.37	Trailing P/E		13.31	Stock Symbol
TM	Trailing Yield (%)		1.62	Trailing EPS		0.46	**CRW**

Period Ending	Dec92	Dec91	Dec90	Dec89	Dec88
Yearly Statistics					
Price-Close	9.06	7.19	3.50	3.44	3.44
Price-High	9.25	7.84	3.56	4.00	3.75
Price-Low	7.13	3.38	2.69	3.00	2.50
P/E-Close	19.28	16.15	10.00	24.55	15.28
Dividends per Share	0.09	0.10	0.06	0.06	0.06
Dividend Yield (%)	1.05	1.39	1.71	1.75	1.75
Sales per Share	3.96	3.54	2.39	2.26	2.62
EPS before extra. item	0.47	0.44	0.35	0.14	0.22
Cash Flow per Share	0.72	0.69	0.57	0.45	0.57
Book Value per Share	3.13	3.19	1.95	1.66	1.49
O/S Common Shares	22,152	19,152	19,152	19,152	15,286
Total Revenue	88,754	69,198	47,978	43,131	40,230
Income before extra.	10,233	8,535	6,743	2,621	3,406
Cash Flow	15,747	13,268	11,004	8,345	8,692
Debt/Equity	nd	0.01	0.02	0.01	0.06
Return on Capital (%)	23.54	21.24	27.64	16.76	22.41
Ret. on Com. Equity (%)	15.70	17.32	19.48	9.60	15.74
% Change Profit	19.9	26.6	157.3	(23.0)	0.5
% Change Revenue	28.3	44.2	11.2	7.2	35.1
% Change Assets	22.7	49.8	19.9	13.5	15.7

Period Ending	Dec92	Dec91	Dec90
Preferred Div. Coverage	np	np	np
Total Div. Coverage	4.6	4.3	5.9
Interest Coverage	nd	na	na
Current Ratio	2.5	4.4	3.3
Operating Margin	14.8	13.5	11.6
Asset Turnover	0.9	0.9	0.9
5 YEAR RATIOS (%)			
Return on Capital	22.3	23.0	27.4
Return on Com. Equity	15.6	16.0	17.9
Profit Growth	24.7	24.4	34.8
Revenue Growth	24.3	21.1	16.6
Asset Growth	23.6	20.7	38.8
BALANCE SHEET (000)			
Cash	36,752	31,875	17,892
Current Assets	55,651	47,896	27,793
Net Fixed Assets	40,579	30,527	24,574
Invest's & Advances	0	0	0
Total Assets	96,230	78,423	52,367
Short Term Debt	0	188	217
Current Liabilities	21,968	10,851	8,385
Long Term Debt	0	231	406
Total Liabilities	27,040	17,251	14,960
Total Equity	69,190	61,172	37,407
Total Liab. & Equity	96,230	78,423	52,367
CAPITAL (000)			
Total Debt	0	419	623
Preferred Equity	0	0	0
Common Equity	69,190	61,172	37,407

Business:

CINRAM LTD. is the largest custom-manufacturer of compact discs and pre-recorded audio and video casette tapes in Canada and is a principal supplier of these products to most of the major record companies in the country.

Date	EPS	DPS	Tot Rev	Inc Bex
Mar 93	0.09	0.02	22,784	1,990
Dec 92	0.18	0.03	27,669	3,963
Sep 92	0.11	0.02	23,651	2,486
Jun 92	0.08	0.03	18,196	1,926
Mar 92	0.09	0.02	19,238	1,858
Dec 91	0.15	0.02	21,421	2,885
Sep 91	0.12	0.03	20,191	2,433
Jun 91	0.08	0.04	14,435	1,557

Synopsis:

Sales for Cinram in 1992 increased by 27% to more than $86-million, and net earnings increased by 20% to over $10-million. The greatest portion of the increase in sales came from higher compact disc (CD) shipments, and to a lesser extent, pre-recorded audio and VHS cassettes. Cinram performance compares favorably to the industry as a whole, which saw an 11.4% increase in sales of all pre-recorded carriers and a 22% increase in CD sales in North America in 1992.

Increases in earnings per share have lagged earnings before taxes, because the number of shares outstanding has increased to 11,076,000 in March 1993. Also, the tax-loss carry-forwards Cinram inherited from the acquisition of Praxis Technologies in 1988 were exhausted in 1991. As a result, 1992 after tax earnings increased 20% over 1991 while pre-tax earnings increased 45%.

Cinram's state-of-the-art manufacturing facilities and economies of scale gives it several competitive advantages that have been beneficial to its ongoing expansion into the United States. Sales in the U.S. accounted for more than one-third of sales in 1992.

Cinram continues to strengthen its management and marketing teams to generate more business for existing and new product lines, and to invest internally to improve efficiencies and reduce future overhead costs further. For instance, it is eliminating expensive processes by using new equipment pioneered by its Nobler Technologies. In 1992, Cinram invested over $17-million in new equipment and over $3-million in research and development.

The compact disc is becoming the most popular pre-recorded music carrier format. Market penetration of CD players in Canadian homes is estimated at 30%, up from 21% in 1991 and 15% in 1990. In the U.S., where trends typically precede Canada, penetration is estimated at 42% of households.

On June 21, 1993, the company sought shareholder approval at its annual meeting for a two-for-one stock split.

Relative strength to TSE300 / Price / Volume (in 1000's of board lots)

Rank (Profit/Revenue/Assets)
180   397   424

Samuel Sokoloff
Chairman Of The Board

Isidore Philosophe
President, C.E.O. & C.O.O.

Lewis Ritchie
Secretary, V.P., Fin. & C.F.O.

Address
2255 Markham Road
Scarborough
ON
M1B 2W3
(416) 298-8190

Fax: (416) 298-0612
01000468/G/6.10

DERLAN INDUSTRIES LIMITED

Exchanges	Price (Jun24'93)	3.90	Trailing P/E	nm	Stock Symbol
T	Trailing Yield (%)	7.18	Trailing EPS	(0.70)	**DRL**

Period Ending	Dec92	Dec91	Dec90	Dec89	Dec88
Yearly Statistics					
Price-Close	4.65	5.75	6.13	9.50	11.75
Price-High	7.00	8.25	9.50	14.38	14.00
Price-Low	4.60	5.25	6.00	9.00	9.50
P/E-Close	nm	nm	8.06	25.00	12.50
Dividends per Share	0.28	0.28	0.28	0.27	0.23
Dividend Yield (%)	6.02	4.87	4.57	2.84	1.96
Sales per Share	18.50	17.85	16.33	24.58	20.68
EPS before extra. item	(0.63)	(0.39)	0.76	0.38	0.94
Cash Flow per Share	0.86	0.60	1.90	1.40	1.70
Book Value per Share	7.02	7.55	8.21	7.69	7.69
O/S Common Shares	15,127	15,396	15,771	16,322	16,986
Total Revenue	283,329	276,640	275,476	416,343	349,821
Income before extra.	(5,701)	(3,925)	12,247	6,440	15,716
Cash Flow	13,226	9,301	30,750	23,689	28,570
Debt/Equity	1.08	0.99	1.07	1.20	0.80
Return on Capital (%)	1.34	1.97	10.57	8.93	14.52
Ret. on Com. Equity (%)	(8.09)	(4.96)	9.61	5.03	12.52
% Change Profit	(45.2)	(132.0)	90.2	(59.0)	22.7
% Change Revenue	2.4	0.4	(33.8)	19.0	27.6
% Change Assets	(8.0)	11.1	(2.0)	14.0	9.8
Preferred Div. Coverage	0.0	0.0	np		
Total Div. Coverage	0.0	0.0	2.7		
Interest Coverage	0.4	0.5	2.2		
Current Ratio	1.4	1.4	1.5		
Operating Margin	2.0	2.7	6.7		
Asset Turnover	0.9	0.8	0.8		
5 YEAR RATIOS (%)					
Return on Capital	7.5	11.2	15.4		
Return on Com. Equity	2.8	7.4	11.7		
Profit Growth	na	na	33.6		
Revenue Growth	0.6	9.5	28.6		
Asset Growth	4.6	20.1	37.8		
BALANCE SHEET (000)					
Cash	3,200	1,170	4,892		
Current Assets	124,866	154,005	158,479		
Net Fixed Assets	118,883	116,672	99,472		
Invest's & Advances	8,472	9,959	9,341		
Total Assets	332,062	360,833	324,845		
Short Term Debt	55,862	64,745	66,362		
Current Liabilities	86,616	109,946	104,781		
Long Term Debt	97,576	84,800	72,545		
Total Liabilities	190,292	209,030	195,445		
Total Equity	141,770	151,803	129,400		
Total Liab. & Equity	332,062	360,833	324,845		
CAPITAL (000)					
Total Debt	153,438	149,545	138,907		
Preferred Equity	35,553	35,553	0		
Common Equity	106,217	116,250	129,400		

Business:

DERLAN INDUSTRIES LTD. is an industrial corporation that acquires and enhances manufacturing companies. The company assumes majority equity positions in each of its subsidiaries, while leaving operating management responsible for day-to-day operations. The company has interests principally in the aerospace and specialty manufacturing industries in the United States and Canada.

Date	EPS	DPS	Tot Rev	Inc Bex
Mar 93	(0.16)	0.07	73,045	(1,438)
Dec 92	(0.47)	0.07	74,656	(5,659)
Sep 92	(0.14)	0.07	64,161	(1,365)
Jun 92	0.07	0.07	73,558	1,957
Mar 92	(0.09)	0.07	71,073	(634)
Dec 91	(0.45)	0.07	68,130	(4,303)
Sep 91	(0.15)	0.07	66,605	(1,642)
Jun 91	0.01	0.07	72,939	802

Synopsis:

While the timing of the North American recovery remains uncertain, there is evidence of an upturn in the U.S. specialty manufacturing market. Derlan's specialty operations are poised to take advantage of an upturn, since they have reduced manufacturing cycle times and developed several new products and export markets. In aerospace, Derlan expects a recovery to lag behind overall economic improvement. However, the strategy of diversifying the aerospace sector into industrial markets and implementing aggressive marketing and cost reduction programs will enable this sector to stabilize operations. Sales to industrial markets in 1992 jumped to 20% of sales in the aerospace sector, up from 5% three years ago.

Throughout 1992 and the first quarter of 1993, the specialty manufacturing sector and the new Mexican joint venture, purchased in early 1993, improved operating performance, which was offset by the continuing impact of depressed commercial and defense aerospace markets. This resulted in pre-tax losses similar to the previous year. There were significantly higher taxes and minority interest charges compared to a year ago, resulting in lower net earnings.

In first quarter 1993, Derlan sold Gormon, and, in the process, completed the sale of its construction operations. To strengthen its two core business sectors, Derlan completed two purchases, one in the United States in 1992 and one in Mexico in early 1993. It sold two small, unprofitable non-core businesses in 1992.

Specialty manufacturing markets began to improve at the end of 1992 and the outlook for this sector is improving. Bookings in the fourth quarter of 1992 were the highest received for 18 months. The divestment of Continental's collision repair division will eliminate losses incurred in 1992. As well, the sector has lower costs, new products and improved production efficiencies.

In 1992, 75% of Derlan's sales were in the United States. The aerospace sector generated 47% of sales and 53% of operating profit.

Rank (Profit/Revenue/Assets)
844   231   260

Dermot G. Coughlan
Chairman & C.E.O.

Allan R. Sutherland
Pres. & C.O.O., Special Mfg.

Terence P. Clark
V.P., Finance

Address
Suite 500
145 King Street East
Toronto
ON
M5C 1G4
(416) 364-5852

Fax: (416) 362-5334
D0000375/G/6.10

FOUR SEASONS HOTELS INC.

Exchanges	Price (Jun24'93)	17.00	Trailing P/E	31.48	Stock Symbol
TM	Trailing Yield (%)	0.65	Trailing EPS	0.54	**FSH**

Period Ending	Dec92	Dec91	Dec90	Dec89	Dec88
Yearly Statistics					
Price-Close	19.38	17.50	16.00	21.13	12.50
Price-High	21.88	20.50	21.00	21.75	13.00
Price-Low	16.13	14.50	13.00	10.38	6.63
P/E-Close	60.55	134.62	18.61	27.80	18.66
Dividends per Share	0.11	0.11	0.11	0.11	0.10
Dividend Yield (%)	0.57	0.63	0.69	0.52	0.80
Sales per Share	3.86	6.29	7.81	9.28	10.53
EPS before extra. item	0.32	0.13	0.86	0.76	0.67
Cash Flow per Share	0.15	0.51	1.30	1.34	1.29
Book Value per Share	8.89	6.23	5.50	4.70	4.26
O/S Common Shares	27,739	22,198	20,088	19,975	19,970
Total Revenue	158,168	180,771	200,768	218,997	240,986
Income before extra.	7,721	2,837	17,322	15,036	13,126
Cash Flow	3,676	11,167	26,175	26,669	25,403
Debt/Equity	1.24	1.07	0.61	0.81	0.58
Return on Capital (%)	1.74	2.85	15.32	17.90	23.15
Ret. on Com. Equity (%)	4.01	2.28	16.95	16.81	20.15
% Change Profit	172.2	(83.6)	15.2	14.6	16.4
% Change Revenue	(12.5)	(10.0)	(8.3)	(9.1)	5.0
% Change Assets	80.9	39.6	4.9	17.2	3.9

Preferred Div. Coverage	na	na	na
Total Div. Coverage	2.8	1.2	7.8
Interest Coverage	0.6	1.0	5.3
Current Ratio	0.8	0.9	0.7
Operating Margin	(11.3)	(1.1)	10.8
Asset Turnover	0.2	0.4	0.7
5 YEAR RATIOS (%)			
Return on Capital	12.2	16.8	21.3
Return on Com. Equity	12.0	16.3	20.3
Profit Growth	(7.4)	(21.6)	38.0
Revenue Growth	(7.2)	(2.6)	2.5
Asset Growth	26.4	18.8	5.8
BALANCE SHEET (000)			
Cash	15,704	27,689	8,087
Current Assets	55,231	67,022	48,249
Net Fixed Assets	72,176	107,188	96,021
Invest's & Advances	283,113	85,736	49,529
Total Assets	610,678	337,578	241,865
Short Term Debt	13,897	36,463	29,615
Current Liabilities	70,923	70,795	70,520
Long Term Debt	291,995	112,532	39,215
Total Liabilities	362,918	198,031	129,507
Total Equity	247,760	139,547	112,358
Total Liab. & Equity	610,678	337,578	241,865
CAPITAL (000)			
Total Debt	305,892	148,995	68,830
Preferred Equity	1,241	1,304	1,812
Common Equity	246,519	138,243	110,546

Business:

FOUR SEASONS HOTELS INC. owns and/or manages 23 medium-sized luxury hotels and resorts worldwide. The company's hotels serve major markets in North America. International Hotels are located in Tokyo, Japan and London, England. The company operates resorts in Dallas, Maui, Nevis, Minaki and Santa Barbara. Other hotels and resorts are under development.

Date	EPS	DPS	Tot Rev	Inc Bex
Mar 93	0.08	0.00	23,854	2,250
Dec 92	0.40	0.06	116,523	9,661
Sep 92	(0.01)	0.00	23,249	(354)
Jun 92	0.07	0.06	16,133	1,604
Mar 92	0.04	0.00	40,794	849
Dec 91	0.11	0.06	134,870	2,395
Sep 91	0.11	0.00	20,072	2,386
Jun 91	0.10	0.06	18,039	2,123

Synopsis:

Four Seasons Hotels Inc. might have to sell undefined non-strategic hotel operations in 1993 to reduce its debt. It raised about $100-million in two equity issues in 1992, but its debt still rose about $100-million as a result of the $200-million purchase of contracts from Hong Kong-based Regent International Hotels Limited in August 1992. To get its desired 1:1 debt-equity ratio, Four Seasons would have to raise about $40-million this year.

Increased occupancy and room rates in the U.S. market and an improved economy boosted the company's net earning for the first quarter of 1993 to $2.3-million, an increase of $1.4-million over the first quarter of 1992. Earnings from management operations increased to $6.2-million, with the profit margin climbing to 44% as compared to 36% for the same period in 1992. Total fee revenues were $14-million, up 76% over last year's quarter. Of this increase, $4.3-million relates to the acquired management contracts.

Four Seasons has opened five new hotels in London, Bali, Milan and New York since November 1992. Together with Regent, Four Seasons operates a total of 45 five-star properties around the world with several others under development. Two hotels are planned to open in Berlin and Prague in 1996. The Regent deal gave Four Seasons 15 additional management agreements, the Regent trademarks and trade names, and a 25% ownership interest in the Regent Hong Kong.

Four Seasons' income is derived partly from equity investments in properties under its management, but primarily through the provision of management services under long-term contracts. Revenue and profits are forecast to rise this year compared to 1992.

Relative strength to TSE300

Price

Volume (in 1000's of board lots)

Rank (Profit/Revenue/Assets)
203   305   192

Isadore Sharp
Chairman & President

H. Roger Garland
Executive Vice President

John L. Sharpe
Executive Vice President

Address
1165 Leslie Street
Toronto
ON
M3C 2K8
(416) 449-1750

Fax: (416) 441-4374
F0000479/G/12.7

INTER-CITY PRODUCTS CORPORATION

Exchanges	Price (Jun24'93)	4.85	Trailing P/E	nm	Stock Symbol
TWA	Trailing Yield (%)	0.00	Trailing EPS	(0.78)	**IPR**

Period Ending	Dec92	Dec91	Dec90	Dec89	Dec88
Yearly Statistics					
Price-Close	7.13	5.88	3.20	93.00	88.50
Price-High	10.13	6.38	8.75	102.00	94.50
Price-Low	5.50	2.70	2.45	84.00	61.00
P/E-Close	nm	nm	0.11	13.68	18.14
Dividends per Share	0.00	0.00	0.00	2.88	2.88
Dividend Yield (%)	0.00	0.00	0.00	3.10	3.25
Sales per Share	36.60	53.88	98.02	127.12	125.64
EPS before extra. item	(0.40)	(1.13)	28.90	6.80	4.88
Cash Flow per Share	2.98	1.38	5.43	3.45	(3.17)
Book Value per Share	5.07	4.20	6.81	63.94	60.46
O/S Common Shares	24,619	17,227	7,227	5,942	5,756
Total Revenue	827,500	670,100	674,300	750,100	719,100
Income before extra.	(4,100)	(9,100)	203,000	50,800	39,800
Cash Flow	67,100	17,100	37,200	20,100	(18,000)
Debt/Equity	1.00	2.03	1.89	0.71	1.07
Return on Capital (%)	2.58	2.08	40.17	10.58	6.17
Ret. on Com. Equity (%)	(9.14)	(23.05)	92.33	10.91	8.15
% Change Profit	54.9	(104.5)	299.6	27.6	(14.0)
% Change Revenue	23.5	(0.6)	(10.1)	4.3	(57.5)
% Change Assets	(4.5)	27.1	(57.3)	(11.1)	(43.0)
Preferred Div. Coverage	0.0	0.0	41.4		
Total Div. Coverage	0.0	0.0	41.4		
Interest Coverage	0.7	0.3	7.7		
Current Ratio	1.8	1.4	1.3		
Operating Margin	3.2	2.4	5.8		
Asset Turnover	1.6	1.2	1.6		
5 YEAR RATIOS (%)					
Return on Capital	12.3	14.2	16.1		
Return on Com. Equity	15.8	20.0	25.9		
Profit Growth	na	na	36.3		
Revenue Growth	(13.3)	(14.4)	(15.5)		
Asset Growth	(23.5)	(22.4)	(24.7)		
BALANCE SHEET (000)					
Cash	12,400	23,800	16,000		
Current Assets	302,600	342,800	270,200		
Net Fixed Assets	187,800	179,200	155,600		
Invest's & Advances	0	0	0		
Total Assets	521,000	545,700	429,300		
Short Term Debt	50,700	138,000	120,200		
Current Liabilities	169,800	250,100	210,300		
Long Term Debt	134,100	132,900	88,200		
Total Liabilities	335,300	412,400	319,100		
Total Equity	185,700	133,300	110,200		
Total Liab. & Equity	521,000	545,700	429,300		
CAPITAL (000)					
Total Debt	184,800	270,900	208,400		
Preferred Equity	61,000	61,000	61,000		
Common Equity	124,700	72,300	49,200		

Business:

INTER-CITY PRODUCTS CORPORATION is a producer of energy related products for residential and light commercial markets. It manufactures heating and cooling equipment through its Heil, KeepRite, Tempstar, Arcoaire Comfortmaker and ZoneAire brands. It also makes spiral welded steel pipe for water transmission projects under the name Thompson Pipe & Steel and refrigeration products under the KeepRite name.

Date	EPS	DPS	Tot Rev	Inc Bex
Mar 93	(0.45)	0.00	164,800	(9,800)
Dec 92	(0.34)	0.00	207,500	(2,300)
Sep 92	(0.15)	0.00	193,800	(1,800)
Jun 92	0.16	0.00	239,900	4,500
Mar 92	(0.07)	0.00	182,900	(300)
Dec 91	0.07	0.00	185,800	100
Sep 91	(0.44)	0.00	200,400	(6,300)
Jun 91	0.41	0.00	175,000	4,200

Synopsis:

For the first quarter 1993, the large increase in Inter-City Products Corp.'s losses compared to the same period last year, was attributed to the weak economy which caused air conditioner and furnace distributors to delay new orders. The company also blamed reduced housing starts in North America. The financial results included restructuring costs of $568,000 related to workers compensation claims resulting from the closing of a plant in Illinois, and refinancing charges of $1.6-million because of the early retirement of the debt of a U.S. subsidiary.

In March 1993, the company announced that its U.S. subsidiary went ahead with a previously announced financing plan to improve operating and financial flexibility. The terms of the deal calls for the U.S. subsidiary to issue $140-million (U.S.) of its Senior Secured notes in a public offering in the U.S. and Canada, and the establishment of a new $135-million (U.S.) Revolving Credit Facility. Proceeds of the public offering and a part of the Revolving Credit is earmarked to repay all of the subsidiary's existing borrowings, and to refinance an existing accounts receivable purchase facility. The company said the new financing arrangement is intended to improve the subsidiary's operating and financial flexibility.

For fiscal 1992, the company's losses declined on a 24% jump in operating revenue versus fiscal 1991. The loss included non-recurring costs of $4.6-million relating to the relocation and integration of the company's heating and cooling product lines in Canada and the U.S. In the year, air conditioner volumes jumped 10% while furnace volumes jumped 22%. The recession and the cool temperatures led to a difficult year for the industry as a whole. The company's Thompson Pipe & Steel operation reported a 46% increase in steel pipe volume to 38,000 tonnes. The company will continue to refocus its manufacturing operations to reduce overall costs. Operating revenues were as follows: heating and cooling, 92%; engineering products, 7%; and corporate and other, 1%.

Relative strength to TSE300 / Price / Volume (in 1000's of board lots)

Rank (Profit/Revenue/Assets)
819   121   206

Robert G. Graham
Chairman & C.E.O.

Henry J. Forrest
President & C.O.O.

Arindra Singh
Sr. V.P., C.F.O. & Secretary

Address
Box 32
20 Queen Street West
Toronto
ON
M5H 3R3
(416) 598-0101

Fax: (416) 598-5288
I0001182/G/5.8

INTERNATIONAL MUREX TECHNOLOGIES CORPORATION

Exchanges	Price (Jun24'93)		6.50	Trailing P/E		nm	Stock Symbol
TA	Trailing Yield (%)		0.00	Trailing EPS		(1.22)	**MXX**

Period Ending	Dec92	Dec91	Dec90	Dec89
Yearly Statistics	US	US	US	US
Price-Close	9.75	15.38	5.38	6.93
Price-High	20.75	16.00	7.70	15.75
Price-Low	5.88	4.00	3.99	2.80
P/E-Close	nm	nm	nm	nm
Dividends per Share	0.00	0.00	0.00	0.00
Dividend Yield (%)	0.00	0.00	0.00	0.00
Sales per Share	4.80	0.23	0.37	0.02
EPS before extra. item	(1.17)	(0.62)	(1.31)	(1.57)
Cash Flow per Share	(0.73)	(0.56)	(1.17)	(1.42)
Book Value per Share	2.17	3.02	0.89	0.03
O/S Common Shares	16,040	13,934	9,395	4,939
Total Revenue	73,359	3,137	1,891	201
Income before extra.	(17,597)	(6,201)	(6,646)	(5,715)
Cash Flow	(10,934)	(5,633)	(5,921)	(5,186)
Debt/Equity	0.06	0.05	0.22	28.81
Return on Capital (%)	(41.14)	(21.62)	(77.09)	na
Ret. on Com. Equity (%)	(45.75)	(24.59)	(155.95)	na
% Change Profit	(183.8)	6.7	(16.3)	na
% Change Revenue	2,238.5	65.9	839.5	na
% Change Assets	26.9	280.1	92.9	na

	Dec92	Dec91	Dec90
Preferred Div. Coverage	np	np	np
Total Div. Coverage	na	na	na
Interest Coverage	0.0	0.0	0.0
Current Ratio	2.2	8.2	4.3
Operating Margin	(12.6)	(259.9)	(290.8)
Asset Turnover	1.2	0.0	0.2
5 YEAR RATIOS (%)			
Return on Capital	na	na	na
Return on Com. Equity	na	na	na
Profit Growth	na	na	na
Revenue Growth	na	na	na
Asset Growth	na	na	na
BALANCE SHEET (000)			
Cash	8,449	37,430	6,461
Current Assets	49,764	40,312	8,242
Net Fixed Assets	9,576	2,070	1,904
Invest's & Advances	0	0	0
Total Assets	59,844	47,146	12,403
Short Term Debt	1,333	2,069	825
Current Liabilities	23,012	4,923	1,932
Long Term Debt	599	115	1,017
Total Liabilities	24,982	5,073	4,043
Total Equity	34,862	42,073	8,360
Total Liab. & Equity	59,844	47,146	12,403
CAPITAL (000)			
Total Debt	1,932	2,184	1,842
Preferred Equity	0	0	0
Common Equity	34,862	42,073	8,360

Business:

INTERNATIONAL MUREX TECHNOLOGIES CORPORATION develops, manufactures and markets medical diagnostic products and services for the diagnosis and monitoring of infectious diseases and other medical conditions.

Date		EPS	DPS	Tot Rev	Inc Bex
Mar 93	US	(0.03)	0.00	20,269	(411)
Dec 92	US	(0.68)	0.00	19,374	(10,282)
Sep 92	US	(0.53)	0.00	19,879	(8,129)
Jun 92	US	0.02	0.00	20,698	300
Mar 92	US	0.04	0.00	14,003	674
Dec 91	US	(0.20)	0.00	1,124	(2,173)
Sep 91	US	(0.13)	0.00	741	(1,375)
Jun 91	US	(0.15)	0.00	652	(1,420)

Synopsis:

International Murex Technologies (IMTC) is still recovering from the February 1992 purchase of the Murex Diagnostic division from the Wellcome Foundation. While an ultimately positive move, the acquisition is still generating losses. IMTC expects to see its plan of integrated internal controls and cost structuring to pay off by 1996, with continued strong sales and licencing revenues rising. IMTC is beginning to realize the beneficial effects of the cost reduction efforts it began to implement in the second half of 1992. The first quarter of 1993 shows a major improvement from the losses incurred in the third and fourth quarters of 1992, which showed a loss from operations of 39 cents (U.S.) per share before restructuring costs of $5.1-million (U.S.) and a goodwill write-off of $3.4-million (U.S.).

Sales of the Single Use Diagnostic System (SUDS/R) HIV-1 Antibody Test have improved during the first half of 1993. In the first quarter of 1993, sales of SUDS/R were $438,000 (U.S.) versus $550,000 (U.S.) for all of 1992. In June 1993, IMTC entered into an exclusive sales and marketing agreement with Medis HF to sell IMTC's rapid SUDS(R) HIV 1+2 test in Scandinavia. The contract stipulates an initial order of 30,000 tests with a 120,000 test minimum for the first year. The Scandinavian market represents 7% of the European population. The contract is expected to be the first of many such arrangements. Distributors will be appointed in certain regions to supplement and complement IMTC's existing international internal sales and marketing organization.

As a result of the broad consolidation and restructuring implemented in September 1992, the company operates one research, manufacturing and distribution facility in each of the U.S., Canada and the U.K.. The two North American facilities are both FDA approved manufacturing sites and the U.K. plant is an ISO 9000 certified design, manufacturing and distribution facility.

Annualized geographical sales distribution in 1992 was: the U.S., 22%; Europe, 55%; and other, 23%.

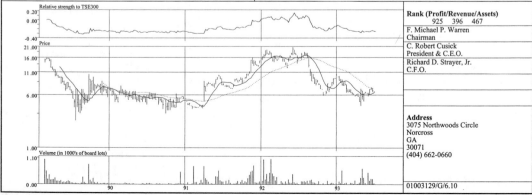

Rank (Profit/Revenue/Assets)
925   396   467
F. Michael P. Warren
Chairman
C. Robert Cusick
President & C.E.O.
Richard D. Strayer, Jr.
C.F.O.

Address
3075 Northwoods Circle
Norcross
GA
30071
(404) 662-0660

01003129/G/6.10

KAUFEL GROUP LTD.

Exchanges	Price (Jun24'93)	8.00	Trailing P/E	20.00	Stock Symbol
TM	Trailing Yield (%)	0.00	Trailing EPS	0.40	**KGL.A**

Period Ending	Aug92	Aug91	Aug90	Aug89	Aug88
Yearly Statistics					
Price-Close	6.00	6.00	7.25	12.00	8.75
Price-High	9.00	8.25	12.63	12.38	12.00
Price-Low	4.90	5.63	7.00	9.00	5.00
P/E-Close	16.67	19.36	14.22	12.50	9.83
Dividends per Share	0.00	0.00	0.00	0.00	0.00
Dividend Yield (%)	0.00	0.00	0.00	0.00	0.00
Sales per Share	8.35	7.82	8.16	8.54	7.34
EPS before extra. item	0.36	0.31	0.51	0.96	0.89
Cash Flow per Share	0.65	0.56	0.65	1.16	1.15
Book Value per Share	6.11	5.70	5.57	5.08	3.32
O/S Common Shares	14,698	14,698	14,698	14,673	12,068
Total Revenue	122,690	114,924	120,129	109,373	88,427
Income before extra.	5,226	4,492	7,430	12,236	10,676
Cash Flow	9,623	8,290	9,493	14,717	13,803
Debt/Equity	0.84	0.71	0.75	0.71	1.34
Return on Capital (%)	7.15	6.59	9.67	18.10	23.88
Ret. on Com. Equity (%)	6.02	5.42	9.50	21.36	30.87
% Change Profit	16.3	(39.5)	(39.3)	14.6	54.1
% Change Revenue	6.8	(4.3)	9.8	23.7	56.9
% Change Assets	19.1	(1.0)	11.5	32.8	75.8

	Aug92	Aug91	Aug90
Preferred Div. Coverage	np	np	np
Total Div. Coverage	na	na	na
Interest Coverage	2.1	2.1	3.4
Current Ratio	1.9	2.5	2.4
Operating Margin	9.0	8.2	10.7
Asset Turnover	0.7	0.7	0.8
5 YEAR RATIOS (%)			
Return on Capital	13.1	18.5	25.8
Return on Com. Equity	14.6	19.9	27.6
Profit Growth	(5.5)	4.0	35.7
Revenue Growth	16.8	33.0	54.8
Asset Growth	25.1	37.1	80.0
BALANCE SHEET (000)			
Cash	23,240	25,135	27,548
Current Assets	105,318	92,993	93,057
Net Fixed Assets	39,831	33,756	34,541
Invest's & Advances	0	0	0
Total Assets	187,403	157,303	158,939
Short Term Debt	32,959	22,297	23,691
Current Liabilities	54,434	36,588	39,311
Long Term Debt	42,265	36,815	37,684
Total Liabilities	97,581	73,472	77,085
Total Equity	89,822	83,831	81,854
Total Liab. & Equity	187,403	157,303	158,939
CAPITAL (000)			
Total Debt	75,224	59,112	61,375
Preferred Equity	0	0	0
Common Equity	89,822	83,831	81,854

Business:

KAUFEL GROUP LTD. is a Quebec-based company specializing in the design, manufacturing and distribution of lighting products and systems for a wide range of industrial, residential, institutional, recreational, mass transit and municipal applications. It is the largest manufacturer and supplier of emergency lighting systems and backup power equipment in North America.

Date	EPS	DPS	Tot Rev	Inc Bex
Feb 93	0.11	0.00	31,912	1,588
Nov 92	0.11	0.00	32,828	1,587
Aug 92	0.12	0.00	34,367	1,743
May 92	0.06	0.00	29,833	867
Feb 92	0.09	0.00	29,741	1,346
Nov 91	0.09	0.00	28,749	1,270
Aug 91	0.09	0.00	29,004	1,323
May 91	0.05	0.00	28,988	734

Synopsis:

Sales for Kaufel Group in the first six months of fiscal 1993 rose by 11% to $64.7-million and net earnings jumped by 23% to $3.2-million, compared to the same period last year. These results are attributable to a slight upturn in the North American economy, as well as a stronger U.S. dollar. In addition, Kaufel's continued efforts to control its material and operating costs have resulted in slightly better margins. Kaufel was profitable throughout the recession.

Over the past two years Kaufel has expanded its operations into Europe by acquiring eight emergency lighting companies in three European countries, adding approximately $50-million of additional revenues on an annualized basis. Kaufel intends to spend until April 1994 integrating these operations before considering further European expansion. Kaufel feels it will be able to expand at a faster pace in Europe than in North America. The European operations appear to have significantly higher margins than those in Canada and the U.S. These acquisitions have added to Kaufel's 10 manufacturing plants in North America.

About 80% of Kaufel's sales in 1992 were generated from emergency lighting products. The rest were from general lighting and plastics and metal products. The company's market share in Canada is 50% and in the United States, about 20%. The rest of the North American market of $250- to $300-million is shared by a number of small companies. Sales in 1992 by country were: Canada, 41%; United States, 50%; and Europe, 9%.

Kaufel's market is a fairly secure one, in that emergency lighting is a legal requirement across North America in all buildings above two floors with more than eight units. A downturn in new construction, which is expected to continue, means demand for replacement emergency lighting should rise as building inspectors visit older units. Replacement sales generate higher margins than new construction sales since they are sold through normal distribution channels and not through tendered bids.

Rank (Profit/Revenue/Assets)
251 337 330

Bruce J. Kaufman
President & C.E.O.

Aslam Khatri
V.P., Finance

Address
1811 Hymus Blvd.
Dorval
PQ
H9P 1J5
(514) 685-2270

Fax: (514) 685-0378
K0000322/G/6.10

LAFARGE CANADA INC.

Exchanges	Price (Jun24'93)	21.62	Trailing P/E	nc	Stock Symbol
TM	Trailing Yield (%)	nc	Trailing EPS	2.07	**LCI.PR.E**

Period Ending	Dec92	Dec91	Dec90	Dec89	Dec88
Yearly Statistics					
Price-Close	18.50	16.13	15.88	21.25	20.00
Price-High	21.63	19.25	23.00	23.63	24.75
Price-Low	14.13	14.25	13.25	18.50	15.50
P/E-Close	nc	nc	nc	nc	nc
Dividends per Share	nc	nc	nc	nc	nc
Dividend Yield (%)	nc	nc	nc	nc	nc
Sales per Share	70.78	74.35	91.08	95.25	85.18
EPS before extra. item	1.88	0.76	7.07	10.48	9.00
Cash Flow per Share	6.22	5.83	11.29	14.37	13.12
Book Value per Share	56.00	54.10	53.34	46.77	36.78
O/S Common Shares	12,008	12,000	12,000	12,000	12,000
Total Revenue	863,631	896,124	1,103,592	1,153,686	1,037,920
Income before extra.	27,226	14,202	84,816	125,747	113,036
Cash Flow	74,640	70,015	135,511	172,425	157,391
Debt/Equity	0.03	0.05	0.06	0.08	0.10
Return on Capital (%)	5.66	4.43	19.95	32.73	35.81
Ret. on Com. Equity (%)	3.43	1.41	13.14	23.90	27.91
% Change Profit	91.7	(83.3)	(32.6)	11.2	30.4
% Change Revenue	(3.6)	(18.8)	(4.3)	11.2	5.0
% Change Assets	0.7	(0.6)	5.1	16.0	9.6

Preferred Div. Coverage	5.9	2.8	14.4		
Total Div. Coverage	5.9	2.8	14.4		
Interest Coverage	11.8	11.3	29.0		
Current Ratio	3.3	3.1	3.1		
Operating Margin	3.3	3.2	12.2		
Asset Turnover	0.8	0.9	1.1		
5 YEAR RATIOS (%)					
Return on Capital	19.7	25.4	29.8		
Return on Com. Equity	14.0	19.0	23.4		
Profit Growth	(20.7)	(25.4)	15.3		
Revenue Growth	(2.7)	1.8	7.7		
Asset Growth	5.9	7.7	9.1		
BALANCE SHEET (000)					
Cash	105,100	78,237	49,197		
Current Assets	440,922	405,196	392,749		
Net Fixed Assets	515,545	547,993	561,724		
Invest's & Advances	46,014	41,292	43,243		
Total Assets	1,022,555	1,015,704	1,022,313		
Short Term Debt	6,460	15,612	4,947		
Current Liabilities	131,989	132,417	128,242		
Long Term Debt	19,096	24,846	39,503		
Total Liabilities	248,324	265,927	282,839		
Total Equity	774,231	749,777	739,474		
Total Liab. & Equity	1,022,555	1,015,704	1,022,313		
CAPITAL (000)					
Total Debt	25,556	40,458	44,450		
Preferred Equity	101,853	100,534	99,348		
Common Equity	672,378	649,243	640,126		

Business:

LAFARGE CANADA INC. produces cement and concrete-related products. The company operates seven cement plants in Canada and serves principal markets from coast to coast. The company also makes ready mix concrete, aggregates and construction materials such as concrete pipe, block and paving stone. Lafarge Corp. of Reston, Va., owns all of the company's common shares.

Date	EPS	DPS	Tot Rev	Inc Bex
Mar 93	(2.19)	nc	98,372	(25,495)
Dec 92	1.03	nc	235,381	15,130
Sep 92	2.42	nc	298,693	28,976
Jun 92	0.81	nc	227,226	9,680
Mar 92	(2.28)	nc	98,947	(26,560)
Dec 91	0.14	nc	220,962	3,659
Sep 91	2.21	nc	321,087	27,350
Jun 91	0.55	nc	239,945	7,678

Synopsis:

Lafarge Canada expects a moderate recovery in business conditions in 1993. It will pursue profitability while de-emphasizing growth through acquisition. Costs will be contained by strict controls on selling and administration expenses and manufacturing costs.

In 1992, sales declined 5% to $849.6-million. Net income improved to $27.2-million from $14.2-million in 1991. The improvement came from divestment gains, cost-reduction programs, a nonrecurring adjustment in cost allocations to Lafarge Corporation and a lower effective income tax rate. The improvement in cement operations was more than offset by a decline in the construction materials group. Although the economy in Western Canada improved in 1992, the recession continued to severely hamper construction activity in Central and Eastern Canada. Results from operations improved strongly during the fourth quarter.

Operating income for the cement group increased 27% from 1991. Results in western Canada improved due to the end of a strike at the Richmond, B.C., plant plus higher shipments and prices. These improvements were partially offset by lower shipments and prices in Central and Eastern Canada due to sluggish construction activity. Cement shipments increased 1% from 1991, while selling prices rose 2% in 1992.

The company's cost of producing a tonne of cement, which is heavily influenced by plant capacity utilization, increased 3% in 1992, mostly as a result of lower production. Cement production fell 3% from 1991, due to a drop in cement demand.

The exchangeable preference shares are entitled to a cumulative dividend equal to the Canadian dollar equivalent of the dividends declared on the Lafarge Corporation common shares. They are exchangeable at any time on a one-for-one basis for Lafarge Corporation common shares and carry voting and liquidation rights which parallel the rights of the common shares of Lafarge Corporation.

Relative strength to TSE300
Price
Volume (in 1000's of board lots)

Rank (Profit/Revenue/Assets)
106 118 153

John D. Redfern
Chairman Of The Board
Michel Rose
President & C.E.O.
Jean-Pierre Cloiseau
Sr. V.P. & C.F.O.

Address
Suite 800
606 Cathcart Street
Montreal
PQ
H3B 1L7
(514) 861-1411

Fax: (514) 861-1123
C0001384/G/6.6

LOEWEN GROUP INC. (THE)

Exchanges	Price (Jun24'93)	26.12	Trailing P/E	30.74	Stock Symbol
TMQ	Trailing Yield (%)	0.15	Trailing EPS	0.85	**LWN**

Period Ending	Dec92	Dec91	Dec90	Dec89	Dec88	Business:
Yearly Statistics						LOEWEN GROUP INC., through its
Price-Close	19.63	15.63	25.00	9.31	5.31	subsidiaries, operates funeral home locations,
Price-High	20.00	17.63	27.63	9.75	5.50	cemeteries, crematoria, and ambulance services
Price-Low	14.63	10.50	16.75	5.06	2.75	in Canada and the United States. It also
P/E-Close	25.49	25.62	49.02	22.99	17.42	operates insurance companies.
Dividends per Share	0.04	0.02	0.00	0.00	0.00	
Dividend Yield (%)	0.20	0.13	0.00	0.00	0.00	
Sales per Share	8.49	6.85	5.26	4.26	3.74	
EPS before extra. item	0.77	0.61	0.51	0.41	0.31	
Cash Flow per Share	1.40	1.10	0.83	0.65	0.58	
Book Value per Share	8.79	6.96	5.49	3.47	1.66	
O/S Common Shares	35,534	32,754	28,391	19,977	14,120	
Total Revenue	295,074	219,497	136,500	75,712	49,634	
Income before extra.	26,125	19,066	12,864	7,201	4,520	
Cash Flow	48,606	35,129	21,636	11,534	7,560	
Debt/Equity	1.07	1.14	1.38	1.24	2.21	
Return on Capital (%)	11.79	12.03	13.10	15.63	18.20	
Ret. on Com. Equity (%)	9.67	9.94	11.09	13.85	20.24	
% Change Profit	37.0	48.2	78.6	59.3	138.1	
% Change Revenue	34.4	60.8	80.3	52.5	77.8	
% Change Assets	34.9	30.2	109.3	61.2	25.2	

Date	EPS	DPS	Tot Rev	Inc Bex
Mar 93	0.28	0.00	95,311	9,985
Dec 92	0.24	0.02	82,382	8,540
Sep 92	0.16	0.00	72,954	5,517
Jun 92	0.17	0.02	70,567	5,614
Mar 92	0.20	0.00	69,171	6,454
Dec 91	0.21	0.01	62,132	6,807
Sep 91	0.11	0.00	52,234	3,570
Jun 91	0.14	0.01	52,578	4,306

Preferred Div. Coverage	np	np	np	
Total Div. Coverage	19.1	29.2	33.8	
Interest Coverage	2.7	2.6	2.5	
Current Ratio	1.7	2.3	1.6	
Operating Margin	22.4	23.6	26.3	
Asset Turnover	0.4	0.4	0.3	
5 YEAR RATIOS (%)				
Return on Capital	14.2	15.2	16.4	
Return on Com. Equity	13.0	15.0	19.6	
Profit Growth	68.9	82.3	103.3	
Revenue Growth	60.2	66.1	66.9	
Asset Growth	49.2	54.9	69.4	
BALANCE SHEET (000)				
Cash	16,093	21,194	12,830	
Current Assets	88,027	71,239	56,082	
Net Fixed Assets	408,126	307,679	230,859	
Invest's & Advances	13,308	7,071	0	
Total Assets	695,507	515,611	396,123	
Short Term Debt	14,685	8,027	15,528	
Current Liabilities	52,937	30,653	36,169	
Long Term Debt	319,738	250,848	199,937	
Total Liabilities	383,167	287,758	240,383	
Total Equity	312,340	227,853	155,740	
Total Liab. & Equity	695,507	515,611	396,123	
CAPITAL (000)				
Total Debt	334,423	258,875	215,465	
Preferred Equity	0	0	0	
Common Equity	312,340	227,853	155,740	

Synopsis:

The largest funeral service company in Canada and the second largest in North America, The Loewen Group Inc., continued to expand in the first quarter, spending $26.2-million on the purchase of 27 funeral homes in 10 states. Since the end of the first quarter, Loewen has spent or is committed to spending $100.3-million on the purchase of 49 funeral homes, nine cemeteries and three crematoria in 12 states and one province. Loewen plans to maintain the acquisition level at $100-million per year.

Loewen owns and operates 478 funeral homes, 41 cemeteries and 19 crematoria and is negotiating the sale of its two insurance operations. During 1992, the company sold off two ambulance services and two small funeral homes for a net gain of $800,000 or 0.3% of revenue.

Growth also showed up in 1993 first quarter revenues which rose by 37.8% to $95.3-million from $69.2-million, and earnings jumped 54.7% to $10-million from $6.5-million. Earnings per share and fully diluted earnings per share both rose 40% to 28 cents per share from 20 cents per share.

Private placements included the delayed funding of up to $60-million (U.S.) of senior guaranteed 10 year notes. The proceeds will be used to repay existing bank indebtedness. In addition to the growing amounts of internally generated cash flow, Loewen intends to continue to access both U.S. and Canadian markets to provide capital for growth.

Loewen's asset base grew to $696-million during 1992, from $516-million the previous year. In addition, the company administers trust assets totaling $193-million.

In 1992 Loewen provided 63,516 funeral services, an increase of 21.7% over 1991, and demographic trends project that even greater volumes of funeral services will be needed over the next 20 years.

Relative strength to TSE300

Rank (Profit/Revenue/Assets)
110 225 184

Raymond L. Loewen
Chairman, President & C.E.O.

Robert B. Lundgren
Sr. V.P., Finance & Corp. Dev.

John T. Turner
Sr. V.P., Operations

Address
4126 Norland Avenue
Burnaby
BC
V5G 3S8
(604) 299-9321

Fax: (604) 299-2369

L0001127/G/16.3

MDS HEALTH GROUP LIMITED

Exchanges	Price (Jun24'93)	12.50	Trailing P/E	18.66	Stock Symbol
T	Trailing Yield (%)	1.17	Trailing EPS	0.67	MHG.B

Period Ending	Oct 92	Oct 91	Oct 90	Oct 89	Oct 88
Yearly Statistics					
Price-Close	14.63	17.25	13.00	13.56	11.06
Price-High	21.00	22.50	14.75	14.38	13.00
Price-Low	14.00	13.00	11.75	10.19	9.56
P/E-Close	10.91	20.29	18.57	21.87	14.27
Dividends per Share	0.15	0.14	0.13	0.10	0.10
Dividend Yield (%)	0.99	0.78	0.96	0.75	0.90
Sales per Share	17.44	14.15	16.20	13.06	12.14
EPS before extra. item	1.34	0.85	0.70	0.62	0.78
Cash Flow per Share	2.04	1.66	1.43	1.06	1.25
Book Value per Share	11.28	9.89	8.00	6.00	5.47
O/S Common Shares	25,822	25,676	21,508	17,198	17,010
Total Revenue	477,335	343,496	304,569	231,144	210,997
Income before extra.	34,615	19,951	13,100	10,890	13,371
Cash Flow	51,955	38,962	26,027	18,289	21,254
Debt/Equity	0.73	0.45	0.68	1.14	0.49
Return on Capital (%)	17.87	13.12	16.07	14.81	22.36
Ret. on Com. Equity (%)	12.70	9.36	9.52	na	15.39
% Change Profit	73.5	52.3	20.3	(18.6)	31.9
% Change Revenue	39.0	12.8	31.8	9.5	22.4
% Change Assets	49.7	25.3	30.9	43.5	17.7

Preferred Div. Coverage	np	np	np
Total Div. Coverage	9.8	6.6	5.9
Interest Coverage	4.8	3.7	2.1
Current Ratio	2.0	3.1	2.0
Operating Margin	12.2	12.1	11.2
Asset Turnover	0.7	0.8	0.9

5 YEAR RATIOS (%)			
Return on Capital	16.8	17.5	18.5
Return on Com. Equity	na	na	na
Profit Growth	27.8	27.6	15.9
Revenue Growth	22.5	19.8	21.0
Asset Growth	32.9	28.8	26.9

BALANCE SHEET (000)			
Cash	88,977	113,225	43,504
Current Assets	247,995	182,175	113,215
Net Fixed Assets	165,268	62,018	60,354
Invest's & Advances	78,464	69,795	54,280
Total Assets	622,877	416,043	332,143
Short Term Debt	32,907	31,760	31,510
Current Liabilities	126,950	59,678	57,789
Long Term Debt	178,303	83,516	84,646
Total Liabilities	331,684	161,994	160,027
Total Equity	291,193	254,049	172,116
Total Liab. & Equity	622,877	416,043	332,143

CAPITAL (000)			
Total Debt	211,210	115,276	116,156
Preferred Equity	0	0	0
Common Equity	291,193	254,049	172,116

Business:

MDS HEALTH GROUP LIMITED is a technology-based health care company providing professionally directed testing and measurement services and systems to physicians, hospitals, nursing homes, industry and government. It operates a network of clinical laboratories in Canada, produces and supplies radioisotope products, and makes and distributes mass spectrometry instruments and medical supplies.

Date	EPS	DPS	Tot Rev	Inc Bex
Jan 93	0.21	0.00	155,183	5,321
Oct 92	0.01	0.07	110,439	512
Jul 92	0.20	0.00	118,444	4,996
Apr 92	0.25	0.07	113,053	6,490
Jan 92	0.88	0.00	135,399	22,617
Oct 91	0.24	0.07	88,397	6,321
Jul 91	0.20	0.00	88,710	4,623
Apr 91	0.25	0.06	88,652	5,493

Synopsis:

In April 1993, MDS Health Group Limited and MDS Health Ventures announced they had received an order from the Mayo Clinic for the Automated Specimen Handling System. This system represents a important economic development opportunity for the company, in so far as the international market is estimated in excess of $500-million.

MDS has exercised its option to acquire the remaining 51% of the shares of Toronto-based Ingram & Bell Inc. Ingram is the largest Canadian-owned manufacturer and distributor of medical supplies and products for use by physicians, hospitals, and the homecare market in Canada.

For the first quarter of 1993, the 50% jump in revenues was attributed primarily to the consolidation of the results of Ingram & Bell, and the consolidation of Medgenix Diagnostics of Belgium, which was acquired by subsidiary Nordion International during the second quarter of 1992. The 12.5% jump in operating income reflected the full impact of the 5% Ontario laboratory fee reduction. Operating income was also affected by the consolidation of Ingram & Bell's results and by the impact on that business of health care funding restraints in the public sector, which resulted in delays to major capital expenditure programs by hospitals and other health care institutions. MDS, specifically its laboratory operations, continues to adjust and adapt to the increased focus on controlling provincial health care costs. MDS will continue to examine the possibility of new cooperative activities with governments, hospitals and other strategic alliances.

Nordion performed well in the quarter and sought to integrate the Medgenix operations. Medgenix strengthened Nordion's position in the European marketplace, but incurred an operating loss in fiscal 1992. The Sciex division achieved record revenues and profitability in fiscal 1992. Investment in technology based health care opportunities continued.

Relative strength to TSE300

Price

Volume (in 1000's of board lots)

Rank (Profit/Revenue/Assets)
84 161 191

Wilfred G. Lewitt
Chairman & C.E.O.
John A. Rogers
President & C.O.O.
Douglas M. Phillips
Sr. V.P., Finance & C.F.O.

Address
100 International Blvd.
Etobicoke
ON
M9W 6J6
(416) 675-7661

Fax: (416) 672-4220
M0003011/G/16.2

MOORE CORPORATION LIMITED

Exchanges	Price (Jun24'93)	21.00	Trailing P/E	nm	Stock Symbol
TMN	Trailing Yield (%)	4.48	Trailing EPS	(0.05)	**MCL**

Period Ending	Dec92	Dec91	Dec90	Dec89	Dec88
Yearly Statistics	US	US	US	US	US
Price-Close	21.88	23.25	25.75	33.25	30.25
Price-High	26.13	32.63	35.63	37.38	39.63
Price-Low	17.63	21.75	25.00	32.00	35.50
P/E-Close	nm	19.48	14.88	11.05	10.01
Dividends per Share	0.94	0.94	0.94	0.88	0.78
Dividend Yield (%)	5.22	4.63	4.26	3.13	3.16
Sales per Share	24.56	25.69	29.08	28.86	27.47
EPS before extra. item	(0.02)	0.91	1.27	2.15	2.01
Cash Flow per Share	1.76	2.10	2.78	3.31	2.84
Book Value per Share	14.83	16.21	16.05	15.27	13.89
O/S Common Shares	99,469	97,744	95,814	94,349	93,050
Total Revenue	2,454,764	2,544,275	2,854,072	2,772,575	2,584,387
Income before extra.	(2,327)	88,074	120,629	201,721	185,996
Cash Flow	174,099	203,642	265,062	310,486	263,146
Debt/Equity	0.06	0.06	0.06	0.06	0.09
Return on Capital (%)	2.28	9.02	13.45	21.33	20.02
Ret. on Com. Equity (%)	(0.15)	5.64	8.10	14.76	15.12
% Change Profit	(102.6)	(27.0)	(40.2)	8.5	27.1
% Change Revenue	(3.5)	(10.9)	2.9	7.3	11.7
% Change Assets	(5.2)	(2.2)	7.8	8.7	(4.7)

Preferred Div. Coverage	np	np	np
Total Div. Coverage	0.0	1.0	1.3
Interest Coverage	2.7	11.3	12.3
Current Ratio	2.9	3.3	2.9
Operating Margin	1.0	4.4	8.5
Asset Turnover	1.2	1.2	1.3
5 YEAR RATIOS (%)			
Return on Capital	13.2	16.9	0.0
Return on Com. Equity	8.7	11.4	12.6
Profit Growth	na	(4.3)	(2.5)
Revenue Growth	1.1	3.5	7.2
Asset Growth	0.7	7.3	10.1
BALANCE SHEET (000)			
Cash	311,993	267,494	279,166
Current Assets	1,063,144	1,095,031	1,180,213
Net Fixed Assets	655,665	696,390	679,275
Invest's & Advances	216,633	227,767	206,172
Total Assets	2,006,959	2,116,973	2,165,690
Short Term Debt	56,411	33,192	37,733
Current Liabilities	366,019	331,948	410,246
Long Term Debt	32,434	58,613	56,244
Total Liabilities	531,451	532,193	628,019
Total Equity	1,475,508	1,584,780	1,537,671
Total Liab. & Equity	2,006,959	2,116,973	2,165,690
CAPITAL (000)			
Total Debt	88,845	91,805	93,977
Preferred Equity	0	0	0
Common Equity	1,475,508	1,584,780	1,537,671

Business:

MOORE CORP. LTD. makes and distributes business forms and related services. The company operates in 57 countries with major markets in the United States, Canada, Europe, Australasia and South America. Its products include business forms, labels, equipment and computer supplies. The company also provides information management services in direct marketing, database management and business communication.

Date		EPS	DPS	Tot Rev	Inc Bex
Mar 93	US	0.23	0.24	597,021	23,161
Dec 92	US	(0.50)	0.24	614,989	(49,424)
Sep 92	US	0.11	0.24	606,338	10,951
Jun 92	US	0.11	0.24	603,211	10,967
Mar 92	US	0.26	0.24	630,226	25,179
Dec 91	US	0.22	0.24	639,970	21,368
Sep 91	US	0.17	0.24	602,964	16,669
Jun 91	US	0.22	0.24	627,683	20,882

Synopsis:

The reduction in income from operations for the first quarter of 1993, compared to the same period last year, for Moore Corporation Limited is mainly due to the very competitive business forms market. Sales of business forms were down $14-million ($5-million due to unfavorable exchange rates) in Europe, and $17-million in the North American operations. The increases in information management services' revenue and operating income were attributed to the large gains in the direct marketing and data base services segments. Interest expense was higher in the first quarter of 1993 compared to last year because of the increased borrowing by Moore's Brazilian subsidiary. The funds were used for working capital requirements and capital investments.

During 1992 a new management group, with headquarters in Paris, was put in place for the European business forms operations. A separate information management services operation was established for the European market to address its unique opportunities and challenges. In 1992, Moore sold its Canadian packaging division and acquired the largest insurance printing centre in the United States.

The restructuring programs for business forms will reduce personnel, eliminate redundant assets and remove excess capacity to lower costs. Operations will be streamlined through the integration of manufacturing facilities. Expected cost for the work force reduction and plant closures is $40-million. The program will make the direct marketing services more efficient and improve the business communications services operations in North America.

Contributions to total sales for 1992 (1991) by geographic segment were: Canada, 9% (11%); United States, 63% (61%); Europe, 16% (16%); and other, 12% (12%). In 1992, the United States and other segments generated operating profits after restructuring costs, while in 1991, Canada and the United States segments generated operating profits after restructuring costs.

Relative strength to TSE300

Price

Volume (in 1000's of board lots)

Rank (Profit/Revenue/Assets)
791 43 76

M. Keith Goodrich
Chairman, President & C.E.O.

Joseph B. Mcarthur
Vice Chairman & C.F.O.

Address
P.O. Box 78
1 First Canadian Place
Toronto
ON
M5X 1G5
(416) 364-2600

Fax: (416) 364-1667
M0005091/G/6.9.2

PHILIP ENVIRONMENTAL INC.

Exchanges	Price (Jun24'93)	9 .37	Trailing P/E	19 .13	Stock Symbol
TM	Trailing Yield (%)	0 .00	Trailing EPS	0 .49	**PEN**

Period Ending	Dec92	Dec91	Dec90	Jun90
Yearly Statistics				6M
Price-Close	10 .00	8 .88	n t	n t
Price-High	10 .50	12 .13	n t	n t
Price-Low	7 .75	7 .75	n t	n t
P/E-Close	16 .67	17 .40	n t	n t
Dividends per Share	0 .00	0 .05	0 .00	0 .00
Dividend Yield (%)	0 .00	0 .56	0 .00	0 .00
Sales per Share	5 .18	3 .93	2 .08	0 .00
EPS before extra. item	0 .60	0 .51	0 .55	na
Cash Flow per Share	1 .10	0 .80	0 .55	0 .00
Book Value per Share	5 .38	4 .44	1 .86	na
O/S Common Shares	31 ,812	28 ,927	19 ,315	0
Total Revenue	157 ,665	102 ,439	36 ,816	15 ,799
Income before extra.	18 ,273	12 ,987	9 ,540	4 ,569
Cash Flow	33 ,314	20 ,481	9 ,540	4 ,569
Debt/Equity	0 .66	0 .59	0 .84	0 .40
Return on Capital (%)	14 .36	18 .86	39 .97	na
Ret. on Com. Equity (%)	12 .21	15 .82	36 .40	na
% Change Profit	40 .7	36 .1	4 .4	na
% Change Revenue	53 .9	178 .2	16 .5	na
% Change Assets	33 .7	231 .5	166 .5	na

Preferred Div. Coverage	np	np	np
Total Div. Coverage	na	10 .8	na
Interest Coverage	4 .8	6 .3	16 .1
Current Ratio	1 .3	0 .7	0 .9
Operating Margin	23 .6	24 .8	48 .4
Asset Turnover	0 .5	0 .4	0 .5
5 YEAR RATIOS (%)			
Return on Capital	na	na	na
Return on Com. Equity	na	na	na
Profit Growth	na	na	na
Revenue Growth	na	na	na
Asset Growth	na	na	na
BALANCE SHEET (000)			
Cash	230	0	4 ,207
Current Assets	45 ,397	28 ,827	17 ,436
Net Fixed Assets	186 ,212	158 ,588	23 ,981
Invest's & Advances	0	0	0
Total Assets	348 ,101	260 ,456	78 ,578
Short Term Debt	5 ,574	21 ,014	9 ,356
Current Liabilities	35 ,428	41 ,214	20 ,205
Long Term Debt	107 ,421	55 ,256	20 ,848
Total Liabilities	177 ,093	132 ,097	42 ,736
Total Equity	171 ,008	128 ,359	35 ,842
Total Liab. & Equity	348 ,101	260 ,456	78 ,578
CAPITAL (000)			
Total Debt	112 ,995	76 ,270	30 ,204
Preferred Equity	0	0	0
Common Equity	171 ,008	128 ,359	35 ,842

Business:

PHILIP ENVIRONMENTAL INC. is a fully integrated waste management company specializing in recycling and is one of Canada'a largest recyclers. The company has operations throughout Ontario, Quebec, British Columbia, Alberta, and in the state of Michigan.

Date	EPS	DPS	Tot Rev	Inc Bex
Mar 93	0 .00	0 .00	36 ,592	4
Dec 92	0 .16	0 .00	42 ,629	5 ,023
Sep 92	0 .20	0 .00	47 ,837	6 ,238
Jun 92	0 .13	0 .00	37 ,469	3 ,951
Mar 92	0 .11	0 .00	29 ,730	3 ,061
Dec 91	0 .16	0 .00	30 ,846	4 ,366
Sep 91	0 .15	0 .00	31 ,928	4 ,007
Jun 91	0 .10	0 .05	23 ,857	2 ,622

Synopsis:

Expansions and acquisitions continue to play an important role in the growth of Philip Environmental. In 1992, the company added five new transfer and processing stations and applied for licenses that will provide it with significantly larger disposal capacities and increase daily receipt limits at its disposal sites. Purchases included Barringer Laboratories of Mississauga, Ontario, which expanded the company's in-house capabilities to test materials and complete R&D projects and lower its costs for outside analytical services. Acquiring Montreal-based Sanivan Inc. broadened Philip's waste operations in Quebec.

Sales in 1992 rose to $157.1-million, an increase of 56.3% over 1991. Net earnings climbed 40.7% to $18.3-million from $12.9-million in 1991. Basic earnings per share were 60 cents, compared to 51 cents last year.

However, the first quarter of 1993 reflected a difficult operating environment as severe winter conditions, reduced pricing and the temporary cancellation of the delivery of waste materials from a large customer combined to reduced profit by $4.5-million. Net earnings for the three months were $4,000, compared to $3-million last year. Sales increased 22.3% from $29.7-million in 1992 to $36.3-million in 1993.

In February 1993, Philip bought the solvent and paint recycling assets and facilities of Varnicolor Chemical Ltd. of Elmira, Ontario. A portion of this property had been contaminated and it is Philip's task to clean up the site. In addition it will be installing and constructing various capital assets at the site to maximize operating efficiencies. The work is expected to take up to one year to complete and will cost an estimated $4-million. Governments will pay for all of the cleanup costs

Indebtedness, under the operating line of credit increased to $11.1-million at March 31, 1993. To boost cash flow, the company negotiated an increase in the operating line of credit.

Relative strength to TSE300

Price

Volume (in 1000's of board lots)

Rank (Profit/Revenue/Assets)
127   306   255
Kenneth Fowler
Chairman
Allen Fracassi
President And C.E.O.
Marvin Boughton
Vice President, Finance
Philip Fracassi
Exec. V.P. And C.O.O.

Address
651 Burlington Street East
P.O. Box 423, Depot 1
Hamilton
ON
L8L 7W2
(416) 544-6687

Fax: (416) 548-8475
P0003131/G/8.1

PREMDOR INC.

Exchanges	Price (Jun24'93)	10.87	Trailing P/E	31.99	Stock Symbol
TM	Trailing Yield (%)	0.00	Trailing EPS	0.34	**PDI**

Period Ending	Dec92	Dec91	Dec90	Dec89	Dec88
Yearly Statistics					
Price-Close	8.88	5.75	1.70	4.40	3.70
Price-High	9.25	5.75	4.30	7.25	6.88
Price-Low	5.00	1.50	1.50	3.10	3.40
P/E-Close	31.70	nm	nm	nm	10.00
Dividends per Share	0.00	0.00	0.04	1.12	0.22
Dividend Yield (%)	0.00	0.00	2.35	25.46	5.95
Sales per Share	13.53	14.36	17.58	17.47	14.98
EPS before extra. item	0.28	(0.09)	(0.14)	(0.35)	0.37
Cash Flow per Share	0.44	0.04	0.02	0.22	0.55
Book Value per Share	3.75	2.65	2.11	2.26	3.25
O/S Common Shares	32,346	26,182	13,622	13,189	9,195
Total Revenue	417,212	285,322	239,437	184,443	135,972
Income before extra.	8,516	(1,734)	(1,889)	(3,696)	3,358
Cash Flow	13,535	874	303	2,294	5,008
Debt/Equity	0.47	1.12	2.48	2.78	0.64
Return on Capital (%)	11.28	2.92	7.75	1.30	17.23
Ret. on Com. Equity (%)	8.93	(3.53)	(6.45)	(12.38)	11.48
% Change Profit	591.1	8.2	48.9	(210.1)	(42.1)
% Change Revenue	46.2	19.2	29.8	35.6	(2.6)
% Change Assets	23.5	53.9	(17.3)	119.0	9.3

Date	EPS	DPS	Tot Rev	Inc Bex
Mar 93	0.10	0.00	126,005	3,172
Dec 92	0.09	0.00	109,675	2,876
Sep 92	0.09	0.00	105,874	2,775
Jun 92	0.06	0.00	107,929	1,908
Mar 92	0.04	0.00	93,734	957
Dec 91	0.02	0.00	85,712	132
Sep 91	0.03	0.00	93,126	728
Jun 91	(0.04)	0.00	55,992	(879)

Preferred Div. Coverage	np	np	np
Total Div. Coverage	na	na	0.0
Interest Coverage	4.2	0.6	0.8
Current Ratio	2.1	1.3	1.2
Operating Margin	4.4	1.3	3.1
Asset Turnover	1.9	1.6	2.0
5 YEAR RATIOS (%)			
Return on Capital	8.1	11.6	18.0
Return on Com. Equity	(0.4)	2.1	8.4
Profit Growth	8.0	na	na
Revenue Growth	24.5	20.9	22.9
Asset Growth	30.3	27.8	23.8
BALANCE SHEET (000)			
Cash	15,321	0	0
Current Assets	138,933	107,300	70,034
Net Fixed Assets	66,301	57,771	32,645
Invest's & Advances	2,357	2,282	2,078
Total Assets	218,765	177,107	115,101
Short Term Debt	26,947	52,480	41,401
Current Liabilities	67,269	82,656	56,156
Long Term Debt	29,677	25,032	29,931
Total Liabilities	97,440	107,688	86,382
Total Equity	121,325	69,419	28,719
Total Liab. & Equity	218,765	177,107	115,101
CAPITAL (000)			
Total Debt	56,624	77,512	71,332
Preferred Equity	0	0	0
Common Equity	121,325	69,419	28,719

Business:

PREMDOR INC. manufactures and distributes new wood doors for residential construction, home repair, renovation, remodelling and commercial use. The company also distributes a complete line of wood mouldings and steel doors.

Synopsis:

For fiscal 1992, the 46% increase in sales for Premdor Inc. was primarily due to acquisitions made in the United States effective July 1, 1991. Sales for the fourth quarter of 1992 were the highest quarterly amount ever reported by the company, a 28% jump over the same quarter last year. This increase was attributed to the steady improvement in housing indicators in the second half of 1992. None of the fourth quarter sales or earnings is attributed to two acquisitions that Premdor completed at the end of the year.

Premdor completed two acquisitions in the U.S. in December 1992. One of the companies, California-based Delta Door increased Premdor's ability to effectively service its customer base on the U.S. West Coast. The other purchase was the assets of Walled Lake Door of Texas. The combined sales of the two companies were approximately $35-million (U.S.) in 1992. Premdor also completed a strategic acquisition in France in January 1993. The purchase of EKEM s.a. is expected to increase Premdor's European sales.

Due to declining housing starts, Premdor has focused primarily on the home improvement market, feeling it represents the growth area of the housing industry. Its marketing strategy include point-of-sale displays, videos and clinics in stores. Premdor will rely on its specialty, the production of wood doors which accounted for 79% of company revenues in 1992. Premdor remains committed to its attempt to expand the market for doors, but does not seek to expand the kinds of products sold.

In April 1992, Premdor shares began to trade in the New York Stock Exchange. This should provide greater liquidity and a broader market for its shares. Premdor's strategy is to continue to expand its markets internationally. It currently has over 70% of its sales, plants, and employees in the U.S. Sales in 1992 were divided geographically as follows: Canada, 29%; and the U.S. 71%. 17% of operating income was derived from Canada, with 83% from the U.S. Export sales from Canada were 2% of total sales, and were principally to Europe.

Rank (Profit/Revenue/Assets)
193   181   309

Saul M. Spears
Chairman

Philip S. Orsino
President & C.E.O.

Robert V. Tubbesing
V.P. & C.F.O.

Address
4120 Yonge Street
Suite 402
Willowdale
ON
M2P 2B8
(416) 250-8933

Fax: (416) 250-9269
P0000487/G/5.8

SCOTT PAPER LIMITED

Exchanges	Price (Jun24'93)	11 .62	Trailing P/E	nm	Stock Symbol
TMV	Trailing Yield (%)	2 .80	Trailing EPS	(0 .60)	**SPL**

Period Ending	Dec92	Dec91	Dec90	Dec89	Dec88
Yearly Statistics					
Price-Close	9 .50	19 .00	16 .75	17 .63	17 .50
Price-High	20 .00	23 .13	19 .50	19 .50	19 .00
Price-Low	8 .75	16 .63	15 .75	16 .63	15 .50
P/E-Close	nm	23 .46	18 .41	14 .94	16 .51
Dividends per Share	0 .40	0 .38	0 .34	0 .32	0 .30
Dividend Yield (%)	4 .21	2 .00	2 .03	1 .82	1 .71
Sales per Share	26 .15	28 .45	31 .28	28 .53	20 .49
EPS before extra. item	(0 .38)	0 .81	0 .91	1 .18	1 .06
Cash Flow per Share	1 .25	2 .59	2 .82	2 .72	2 .02
Book Value per Share	8 .36	9 .14	8 .71	8 .15	7 .29
O/S Common Shares	15 ,281	15 ,281	15 ,281	15 ,281	15 ,281
Total Revenue	399 ,590	434 ,791	477 ,993	445 ,608	313 ,173
Income before extra.	(5 ,792)	12 ,321	13 ,847	17 ,969	16 ,245
Cash Flow	19 ,175	39 ,535	43 ,135	41 ,517	30 ,820
Debt/Equity	1 .36	1 .14	1 .32	1 .36	0 .27
Return on Capital (%)	2 .18	12 .32	13 .64	19 .86	22 .40
Ret. on Com. Equity (%)	(4 .33)	9 .04	10 .75	15 .24	15 .39
% Change Profit	(147 .0)	(11 .0)	(22 .9)	10 .6	11 .9
% Change Revenue	(8 .1)	(9 .0)	7 .3	42 .3	8 .6
% Change Assets	0 .3	(2 .1)	3 .0	80 .1	12 .2

Preferred Div. Coverage	np	np	np
Total Div. Coverage	0 .0	2 .1	2 .7
Interest Coverage	0 .4	2 .0	2 .0
Current Ratio	1 .2	1 .3	1 .3
Operating Margin	1 .6	8 .6	8 .6
Asset Turnover	1 .0	1 .0	1 .1
5 YEAR RATIOS (%)			
Return on Capital	14 .1	18 .5	20 .7
Return on Com. Equity	9 .2	13 .2	14 .4
Profit Growth	na	(1 .0)	4 .3
Revenue Growth	6 .7	10 .6	14 .0
Asset Growth	15 .3	15 .5	18 .0
BALANCE SHEET (000)			
Cash	48	49	49
Current Assets	107 ,678	111 ,610	119 ,538
Net Fixed Assets	303 ,802	299 ,956	303 ,166
Invest's & Advances	0	0	0
Total Assets	416 ,736	415 ,348	424 ,378
Short Term Debt	34 ,118	23 ,901	28 ,845
Current Liabilities	91 ,754	85 ,049	92 ,688
Long Term Debt	139 ,850	134 ,563	146 ,568
Total Liabilities	289 ,007	275 ,715	291 ,259
Total Equity	127 ,729	139 ,633	133 ,119
Total Liab. & Equity	416 ,736	415 ,348	424 ,378
CAPITAL (000)			
Total Debt	173 ,968	158 ,464	175 ,413
Preferred Equity	0	0	0
Common Equity	127 ,729	139 ,633	133 ,119

Business:

SCOTT PAPER LTD. makes and markets household and commercial paper products including bathroom tissue, paper towels and facial tissue. Plant facilities are located in New Westminster, British Columbia, and in Lennoxville, Crabtree, and Hull, Quebec. The company has sales offices across Canada.

Date	EPS	DPS	Tot Rev	Inc Bex
Apr 93	(0 .13)	0 .03	101 ,246	(2 ,014)
Dec 92	(0 .34)	0 .10	102 ,008	(5 ,126)
Sep 92	(0 .15)	0 .10	101 ,429	(2 ,315)
Jun 92	0 .02	0 .10	97 ,941	274
Mar 92	0 .09	0 .10	98 ,212	1 ,375
Dec 91	0 .06	0 .10	100 ,785	880
Sep 91	0 .23	0 .10	110 ,826	3 ,532
Jun 91	0 .21	0 .09	105 ,060	3 ,213

Synopsis:

Scott Paper Ltd. continues to see its industry plagued with too much capacity. Between 1989 and 1991 new paper machines brought into production boosted capacity by 30%. Adding to the increase in supply within the Canadian tissue industry was the elimination of duties on U.S. tissue products coming into Canada. The duties were eliminated over a five-year period ending January 1, 1993. Prices remained lower than a year ago in the first quarter of 1993. This resulted in a loss for the first quarter even though Scott experienced an increase in physical sales volume in the first quarter compared to a year ago.

Scott continues to focus on cutting costs and looking for efficiencies to regain its profitability. One result of this plan has been the reduction in Scott's workforce. In 1992,the number of salaried jobs was reduced by 10%,and in 1993 approximately 10% of fixed hourly rate jobs will be cut. The cost reductions in 1992 were not able to offset the decline in sales and operating revenue.

Total net investment expenditures for 1992 amounted to $29-million. Part of the expenditures were used in the ongoing modernization and efficiency upgrading programs at three operating facilities in Quebec and one in British Columbia. The completion of the upgrade of the original Crabtree recycled fibre facility cost $8.5-million. The upgrade, combined with a new plant that opened in 1991, gives Scott the ability to produce 300 tonnes of recycled fibre per day. Scott purchased a site in Western Canada for a potential recycled fibre facility for $6.3-million. The facility would be to support the Western Canadian manufacturing operations.

Rank (Profit/Revenue/Assets)
845   187   233

Robert T. Stewart
Chairman, President & C.E.O.
John M. Reid
Corp. V.P., Finance

Address
P.O. Box 3600
1111 Melville Street
12th Floor
Vancouver
BC
V6E 3V6
(604) 688-8131
Fax: (604) 643-5543
S0000990/G/6.9.1

SHAW INDUSTRIES LTD.

Exchanges	Price (Jun24'93)	12.87	Trailing P/E	32.19	Stock Symbol
T	Trailing Yield (%)	0.47	Trailing EPS	0.40	**SHL.A**

Period Ending	Dec92	Dec91	Dec90	Dec89	Dec88
Yearly Statistics					
Price-Close	10.00	14.83	9.00	5.83	3.42
Price-High	16.75	15.00	9.17	5.83	3.67
Price-Low	8.50	8.33	5.54	3.50	2.50
P/E-Close	20.83	9.43	10.34	9.31	10.79
Dividends per Share	0.12	0.11	0.09	0.07	0.03
Dividend Yield (%)	1.21	0.74	1.00	1.23	0.98
Sales per Share	9.93	14.09	10.27	8.62	6.15
EPS before extra. item	0.48	1.57	0.87	0.63	0.32
Cash Flow per Share	1.10	2.17	1.31	0.95	0.69
Book Value per Share	5.93	5.45	4.04	3.28	2.84
O/S Common Shares	20,538	20,452	20,088	19,767	19,493
Total Revenue	203,588	285,540	204,788	169,910	119,838
Income before extra.	9,862	31,883	17,411	12,353	6,165
Cash Flow	22,620	44,053	26,136	18,661	13,541
Debt/Equity	0.08	0.11	0.29	0.29	0.12
Return on Capital (%)	15.28	46.96	33.58	32.55	17.81
Ret. on Com. Equity (%)	8.45	33.11	23.85	20.53	11.59
% Change Profit	(69.1)	83.1	40.9	100.4	116.2
% Change Revenue	(28.7)	39.4	20.5	41.8	36.5
% Change Assets	(4.4)	20.1	14.9	37.8	(3.7)

Date	EPS	DPS	Tot Rev	Inc Bex
Mar 93	0.26	0.00	59,944	5,307
Dec 92	0.04	0.06	49,464	926
Sep 92	0.00	0.00	42,661	50
Jun 92	0.10	0.00	50,120	1,978
Mar 92	0.34	0.06	61,343	6,908
Dec 91	0.29	0.00	62,345	5,865
Sep 91	0.47	0.00	82,940	9,618
Jun 91	0.43	0.00	75,571	8,816

Preferred Div. Coverage	np	np	np
Total Div. Coverage	4.1	14.7	10.0
Interest Coverage	45.1	26.4	10.6
Current Ratio	2.4	1.8	1.4
Operating Margin	9.6	18.7	15.4
Asset Turnover	1.3	1.7	1.5
5 YEAR RATIOS (%)			
Return on Capital	29.2	28.0	20.6
Return on Com. Equity	19.5	19.0	13.2
Profit Growth	28.1	71.6	45.3
Revenue Growth	18.2	25.9	17.8
Asset Growth	11.8	17.5	9.9
BALANCE SHEET (000)			
Cash	18,654	16,272	3,128
Current Assets	90,099	94,078	71,463
Net Fixed Assets	70,523	73,466	69,262
Invest's & Advances	0	0	0
Total Assets	161,644	169,001	140,725
Short Term Debt	8,827	10,270	21,546
Current Liabilities	36,966	52,217	50,202
Long Term Debt	1,073	1,843	1,527
Total Liabilities	39,830	57,505	59,629
Total Equity	121,814	111,496	81,096
Total Liab. & Equity	161,644	169,001	140,725
CAPITAL (000)			
Total Debt	9,900	12,113	23,073
Preferred Equity	0	0	0
Common Equity	121,814	111,496	81,096

Business:

SHAW INDUSTRIES LTD. supplies goods and services to the energy industry. The company has operations in Canada, the United States, the United Kingdom, and Australia. Products include drill string components, geophones, wire, cable, tubing, and heat-shrinkable polymeric products. Services include pipeline corrosion protection, thermal insulation systems, and pipeline inspection and repair.

Synopsis:

The growth pattern, established during the past few years at Shaw Industries, was interrupted in 1992 due to the persistent effects of the recession which engendered lower gas and oil prices and reduced capital and operating expenditures in all sectors of the energy industry. Recently, the first signs of a revival together with stronger natural gas prices are prompting increases in all North American pipeline sectors. This escalation of domestic activity levels, combined with the expanded emphasis on international energy markets in all business units, should benefit Shaw in 1993. Shaw will continue its cost reduction, process efficiency, product quality, and product diversification programs to enhance its ability to serve worldwide energy markets.

An increase in drilling activity in Western Canada together with renewed demand for large diameter pipe have combined to strengthen sales and earnings for Shaw, as shown by first quarter results.

The combination of higher natural gas prices plus royalty and tax changes in Alberta have sparked a strong rebound in the Canadian oil patch. In the U.S., however, stronger natural gas prices have yet to create any real impact on exploration and production spending. Drilling in the Gulf of Mexico rose slightly, but land based drilling remained weak leaving overall U.S. activity at a lower level than during the comparable period in 1992. As a result, contributions from the resource products sector were weaker than expected, after a very weak 1992.

The results in the pipeline & tubular products sector improved significantly with gains in the Canadian oil country tubular goods markets plus steady revenue from the pipeline inspection segment.

In 1992, Canadian sales represented 60% of consolidated sales. Net income was particularly depressed due to losses in the U.S. pipe coating and resource products operations.

Relative strength to TSE300

Price

Volume (in 1000's of board lots)

Rank (Profit/Revenue/Assets)		
186	271	347

Leslie E. Shaw
Chairman & C.E.O.

Geoffrey F. Hyland
President & C.O.O.

B.J. Conroy
V.P., Finance

Address
25 Bethridge Rd
Rexdale
ON
M9W 1M7
(416) 743-7111

Fax: (416) 743-8194
S0001899/G/6.10

SNC-LAVALIN GROUP INC.

Exchanges	Price (Jun24'93)		17.50	Trailing P/E		21.88	Stock Symbol
TM	Trailing Yield (%)		0.69	Trailing EPS		0.80	**SNC.A**

Period Ending	Dec92	Dec91	Dec90	Dec89	Dec88	Business:
Yearly Statistics						SNC-LAVALIN GROUP INC. provides
Price-Close	10.50	16.25	13.63	11.75	4.00	engineering, procurement, construction and
Price-High	19.00	20.00	14.63	12.00	8.13	project management services in Canada and
Price-Low	7.88	11.63	9.38	3.85	3.75	abroad. SNC Industrial Technologies Inc.
P/E-Close	16.41	47.79	6.52	5.02	nm	makes products for the military, para-military,
Dividends per Share	0.18	0.36	0.34	0.07	0.14	and industrial markets worldwide. Securiplex
Dividend Yield (%)	1.71	2.22	2.50	0.60	3.50	Technologies produces electronic fire and
Sales per Share	51.08	46.39	41.40	32.53	29.85	control systems for naval and industrial markets
EPS before extra. item	0.64	0.34	2.09	2.34	(3.14)	worldwide.
Cash Flow per Share	2.30	2.13	3.91	3.53	(0.49)	
Book Value per Share	11.66	11.22	9.33	7.46	5.19	
O/S Common Shares	14,670	14,514	11,087	10,747	10,742	
Total Revenue	758,418	581,411	447,628	364,861	320,690	
Income before extra.	9,309	4,197	22,893	26,206	(32,927)	
Cash Flow	33,677	26,723	42,256	37,960	(5,279)	

Date	EPS	DPS	Tot Rev	Inc Bex
Mar 93	0.17	0.03	173,007	2,443
Dec 92	0.45	0.02	256,107	6,477
Sep 92	0.14	0.02	178,526	2,132
Jun 92	0.04	0.05	164,948	609
Mar 92	0.01	0.09	154,437	91
Dec 91	(0.17)	0.09	211,333	(1,932)
Sep 91	0.19	0.09	150,740	2,419
Jun 91	0.07	0.09	114,478	918

	Dec92	Dec91	Dec90
Debt/Equity	0.67	1.00	0.99	1.00	1.83
Return on Capital (%)	9.87	7.62	24.42	22.30	(15.16)
Ret. on Com. Equity (%)	5.58	3.15	24.64	37.07	(46.03)
% Change Profit	121.8	(81.7)	(12.6)	179.6	(673.3)
% Change Revenue	30.4	29.9	22.7	13.8	(22.0)
% Change Assets	(3.2)	90.0	14.7	1.0	(13.9)

Preferred Div. Coverage	np	np	np
Total Div. Coverage	3.5	0.9	5.8
Interest Coverage	2.3	1.9	4.5
Current Ratio	1.1	1.1	1.2
Operating Margin	3.2	3.8	10.6
Asset Turnover	1.2	0.9	1.4
5 YEAR RATIOS (%)			
Return on Capital	9.8	8.7	10.1
Return on Com. Equity	4.9	2.7	4.4
Profit Growth	na	(13.6)	13.5
Revenue Growth	13.0	10.3	14.7
Asset Growth	12.9	13.0	18.3
BALANCE SHEET (000)			
Cash	32,160	23,662	0
Current Assets	378,844	382,984	192,530
Net Fixed Assets	140,336	150,759	103,323
Invest's & Advances	13,585	9,185	8,095
Total Assets	607,846	627,896	330,485
Short Term Debt	34,809	66,541	54,782
Current Liabilities	338,625	353,475	164,717
Long Term Debt	79,604	96,923	47,499
Total Liabilities	436,818	465,121	227,014
Total Equity	171,028	162,775	103,471
Total Liab. & Equity	607,846	627,896	330,485
CAPITAL (000)			
Total Debt	114,413	163,464	102,281
Preferred Equity	0	0	0
Common Equity	171,028	162,775	103,471

Synopsis:

In May 1993, SNC Group Inc. shareholders endorsed a new name for the company that puts the emphasis squarely on its engineering business and away from manufacturing. The consulting engineer and munitions maker was renamed SNC-Lavalin Group Inc. at the company's annual meeting, formally embracing the name of the engineering rival it took over in 1991, Lavalin Inc.

In May's annual meeting, the company also raised the possibility of selling its two manufacturing subsidiaries, munitions maker SNC Technologies Inc. and Securiplex Technologies Inc., which makes fire detection equipment. SNC Technologies and Securiplex accounted for nearly a quarter of the company's $747-million in revenue in 1992, but are a lot less profitable than engineering. At the end of March, the company's backlog of engineering work was $1.2-billion, up from $400-million last year. The company said it is confident it can keep new orders at the same level for most of the year.

In 1992, total revenue rose, reaching $747.1-million compared with $480.8-million in 1991, an increase of 28.6% largely attributable to the acquisition of Lavalin's engineering assets in August 1991. Of this total, engineering-construction accounts for $547.9-million, or 73% of corporate revenues, with $448.8-million from services and $99.1-million from packages. About 40% of revenues came from international markets, an increase of 80% over 1991. Manufacturing operations represent $199.2-million.

During 1992 in engineering, despite the sluggish domestic market, the company succeeded in winning a large contract for the Maritime Coastal Defense Vessel Program. In international markets, the company obtained 74 new projects in 37 countries, among them the Ankara Metro, in Turkey, and an aluminum smelter in South Africa.

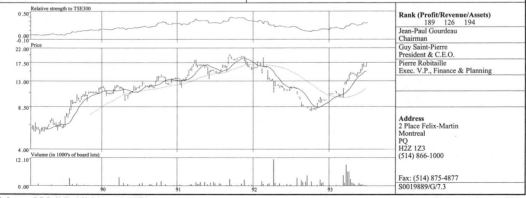

Rank (Profit/Revenue/Assets)
189   126   194

Jean-Paul Gourdeau
Chairman

Guy Saint-Pierre
President & C.E.O.

Pierre Robitaille
Exec. V.P., Finance & Planning

Address
2 Place Felix-Martin
Montreal
PQ
H2Z 1Z3
(514) 866-1000

Fax: (514) 875-4877
S0019889/G/7.3

ST. LAWRENCE CEMENT INC.

Exchanges	Price (Jun24'93)		8.25	Trailing P/E		nm	Stock Symbol
TM	Trailing Yield (%)		5.70	Trailing EPS		(0.91)	**ST.A**

Period Ending	Dec92	Dec91	Dec90	Dec89	Dec88
Yearly Statistics					
Price-Close	6.63	12.25	12.75	17.38	13.50
Price-High	13.00	17.00	19.63	22.25	14.37
Price-Low	6.50	11.88	11.00	13.63	10.25
P/E-Close	nm	nm	21.25	9.76	6.28
Dividends per Share	0.38	0.76	0.76	0.76	0.65
Dividend Yield (%)	5.73	6.20	5.96	4.37	4.82
Sales per Share	10.89	12.33	15.47	17.96	18.18
EPS before extra. item	(0.94)	(0.14)	0.60	1.78	2.15
Cash Flow per Share	(0.20)	0.71	1.51	2.74	3.14
Book Value per Share	7.19	8.42	9.14	9.29	8.22
O/S Common Shares	43,551	42,252	40,810	40,622	40,335
Total Revenue	467,085	504,479	629,970	727,225	732,734
Income before extra.	(39,869)	(5,728)	24,194	72,057	86,602
Cash Flow	(8,415)	29,106	61,470	111,042	126,583
Debt/Equity	0.81	0.62	0.47	0.44	0.50
Return on Capital (%)	(6.96)	2.02	11.55	27.10	36.33
Ret. on Com. Equity (%)	na	(1.57)	6.45	20.33	28.77
% Change Profit	(596.0)	(123.7)	(66.4)	(16.8)	21.9
% Change Revenue	(7.4)	(19.9)	(13.4)	(0.8)	5.1
% Change Assets	2.4	2.4	0.5	6.6	13.7

Preferred Div. Coverage	na	np	np
Total Div. Coverage	0.0	0.0	0.8
Interest Coverage	0.0	0.6	2.9
Current Ratio	2.9	3.5	3.2
Operating Margin	(5.8)	2.3	10.0
Asset Turnover	0.6	0.7	0.9
5 YEAR RATIOS (%)			
Return on Capital	14.0	22.4	27.2
Return on Com. Equity	na	16.6	21.4
Profit Growth	na	na	(6.4)
Revenue Growth	(7.7)	(3.5)	5.0
Asset Growth	5.0	4.5	4.9
BALANCE SHEET (000)			
Cash	0	0	0
Current Assets	231,975	224,313	239,032
Net Fixed Assets	412,916	427,738	430,823
Invest's & Advances	64,332	52,114	17,440
Total Assets	729,955	712,989	695,970
Short Term Debt	0	0	0
Current Liabilities	81,273	63,690	75,067
Long Term Debt	260,177	221,856	175,440
Total Liabilities	406,825	357,327	322,840
Total Equity	323,130	355,662	373,130
Total Liab. & Equity	729,955	712,989	695,970
CAPITAL (000)			
Total Debt	260,177	221,856	175,440
Preferred Equity	10,003	0	0
Common Equity	313,127	355,662	373,130

Business:

ST. LAWRENCE CEMENT INC. manufactures and distributes cement, concrete and aggregates to markets in Quebec, Ontario, the Maritimes and the eastern United States. Operations include cement and ready-mix concrete plants, distribution terminals and quarries and sand pits. Holderbank Financiere Glaris Ltd. of Switzerland, through a subsidiary, controls 60% of the company's shares.

Date	EPS	DPS	Tot Rev	Inc Bex
Mar 93	(0.33)	0.00	57,800	(14,300)
Dec 92	(0.43)	0.28	136,385	(18,169)
Sep 92	(0.05)	0.00	151,000	(2,000)
Jun 92	(0.10)	0.19	126,500	(4,400)
Mar 92	(0.36)	0.19	53,200	(15,300)
Dec 91	(0.02)	0.19	137,366	(925)
Sep 91	0.15	0.19	168,700	6,200
Jun 91	0.05	0.19	139,800	2,200

Synopsis:

There are some indications that St. Lawrence Cement's markets will gradually recover in 1993. This slow recovery, combined with the many cost reductions achieved and planned for 1993, could lead to improved results in 1993.

In the first quarter of 1993, cement sales in Quebec were at last year's levels for this period. Ontario sales were down slightly from last year, after an extremely harsh winter. Sales in the United States were notably higher as the U.S. cement market has definitely gained strength. Given the low-demand outlook and competition from external suppliers, the company must reduce costs. In the first quarter, employees suggested ideas that will help the company save approximately $5.3-million per year.

The 4.4% decline in Canada's cement volume during 1992 was centred in the company's markets. As a result, total sales dropped by 7.4% from 1991, to $467-million. While sales volumes for all product lines except construction declined in 1992, lower cement volumes accounted for 70% of the drop. The $39.9-million loss for 1992 was due mainly to low volumes, and higher bad debts. Low volumes also caused unit costs to be higher, especially in cement, where capacity utilization was only 61%. The industry has high break-even points.

Sales by product line in 1992 were: cement, 38%; concrete, 24%; aggregates, 9%; construction, 22%; and others, 7%. Sales by division in 1992 were: Ontario, 60%; Quebec and the Maritimes, 25%; and the United States, 15%.

In late May 1993 Dominion Bond Rating Service (DBRS) cut its rating on the company's debentures to triple-B (high) from single-A (low) and commercial paper to R-2 (high) from R-1 (low). DBRS expects St. Lawrence's profitability to show slow improvement after two years of losses. However, DBRS said debt was up to 47% of capitalization at March 31, and that the company's balance sheet has weakened during the past two years.

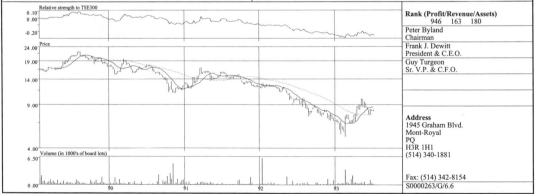

Rank (Profit/Revenue/Assets)
946   163   180

Peter Byland
Chairman

Frank J. Dewitt
President & C.E.O.

Guy Turgeon
Sr. V.P. & C.F.O.

Address
1945 Graham Blvd.
Mont-Royal
PQ
H3R 1H1
(514) 340-1881

Fax: (514) 342-8154
S0000263/G/6.6

For further company information, call Globe Information Services 1-800-268-9128 or (416)585-5345

COMPANY INDEX

Spread the Wealth.

The Report on Business Canada Company Handbook can potentially reward you and your friends through wise investments and business dealings. For copies of this year's book to give as gifts to friends, colleagues or clients, or to order a copy for yourself fill out and return the form below. Call us at (416) 585-5250, or fax the coupon to (416) 585-5249. Special bulk order prices are available for purchases of 50 books or more.

Mail to:
Globe Information Services
444 Front Street W., Toronto, Ontario.
M5V 2S9

Yes! Please send me _____ copy/copies of the Fall 1993 Edition of the REPORT ON BUSINESS CANADA COMPANY HANDBOOK at $49.95 per copy plus $5.00 postage and handling plus $3.85 GST and $4.00 PST (Ontario only) – per copy – for a total of $_____. All sales are final.

Name	Title
Company	
Address	City
Province Postal Code	Telephone
❏ Cheque or money order enclosed ❏ VISA	❏ MasterCard ❏ AmEx
Charge Card #	Expiry Date

Signature   (required to validate order)

A

Abiti-Price Inc. 133
Acklands Limited 343
Agnico-Eagle Mines Limited 27
Agra Industries Limited 475
Air Canada 271
Alberta Energy Company Ltd. 67
Alberta Natural Gas Company Ltd. 435
Alcan Aluminium Limited 3
Algoma Central Corporation 272
American Barrick Resources Corporation 28
Anderson Exploration Ltd. 68
Andres Wines Ltd. 155
Anglo-Canadian Telephone Company 289
Arbor Capital Inc. 483
Archer Communications Inc. 213
Arimetco International Inc. 4
Astral Communications Inc. 484
Atco Ltd. 436
Aur Resources Inc. 29

B

B.C. Bancorp 377
B.C. Pacific Capital Corporation 437
Bachelor Lake Gold Mines Inc. 30
Banister Inc. 485
Bank of Montreal 378
The Bank of Nova Scotia 379
Baton Broadcasting Incorporated 315
BC Gas Inc. 290
BC Sugar Refinery, Limited 156
BC Telecom Inc.
    See British Columbia Telephone Company
BCE Inc. 291
BCE Mobile Communications 316
Belmoral Mines Ltd. 31
Bema Gold Corporation 32
BF Realty Holdings Limited 253
BGR Precious Metals Inc. 395
Biochem Pharma Inc. 191
Biomira Inc. 192
BMB Compuscience Canada Ltd. 463
Bombardier Inc. 214
Bonar Inc. 245
Bovar Inc. 486
Bow Valley Energy Inc. 69
Bracknell Corporation 487
Bramalea Limited 254
Brascade Resources Inc. 438
Brascan Limited 439
Breakwater Resources Ltd. 33
Brenda Mines Ltd. 5
Bright, T.G. & Co., Limited.
    See T.G. Bright & Co. Ltd.
British Columbia Telephone Company 292
BRL Enterprises Inc. 440

Bruncor Inc. 293
Brunswick Mining and Smelting Corporation Limited . . 6
Budd Canada Inc. 183

C

Cabre Exploration Ltd. 70
CAE Industries Ltd. 215
Cambior Inc. 34
Cambridge Shopping Centres Limited 255
Camco Inc. 173
Camdev Corporation 256
Cameco Corporation 7
Campbell Resources Inc. 35
Canada Malting Co. Limited 157
Canada Southern Petroleum Ltd. 71
Canada Trust Income Investments 396
Canada Trustco Mortgage Company 380
Canada Tungsten Inc. 8
Canadian General Investments Limited 397
Canadian Imperial Bank of Commerce 381
Canadian Manoir Industries Limited 174
Canadian Marconi Company 216
Canadian Natural Resources Limited 72
Canadian Occidental Petroleum Ltd. 73
Canadian Pacific Forest Products Limited 134
Canadian Pacific Limited 441
Canadian Roxy Petroleum Ltd. 74
Canadian Satellite Communications Inc. 317
Canadian Tire Corporation, Limited 353
Canadian Utilities Limited 294
Canadian Western Natural Gas Company Limited . . . 295
The Canam Manac Group Inc. 199
CanCapital Corporation 442
Canfor Corporation 135
Canstar Sports Inc. 175
CanWest Global Communications Corp. 318
Cara Operations Limited 354
Carena Developments 257
Cascades Inc. 136
CCL Industries Inc. 246
Celanese Canada Inc. 237
Centra Gas Ontario Inc. 296
Central Capital Corporation 398
Central Fund of Canada Limited 399
Central Guaranty Trustco Limited 382
CFCF Inc. 319
CGC Inc. 488
Chai-Na-Ta Ginseng Products Ltd. 489
Chateau Stores of Canada Ltd. 355
Chauvco Resources Ltd. 75
Chieftain International, Inc. 76
CHUM Limited 320
Cimarron Petroleum Ltd. 77
Cineplex Odeon Corporation 490
Cinram Ltd. 491
Circo Craft Co. Inc. 217

Co-Enerco Resources Ltd. 78
Co-Steel Inc. 200
Coca-Cola Beverages Ltd. 158
Cognos Incorporated 464
Coho Resources Limited 79
Cominco Ltd. 9
Cominco Resources International Limited 36
Computalog Ltd. 80
Consolidated Canadian Express Limited 400
Consolidated Carma Corporation 258
Consolidated Enfield Corp. Ltd. 443
Consolidated HCI Holdings Corporation 259
Consumers Packaging Inc. 247
The Consumers' Company Ltd. 297
Conwest Exploration Company Limited 81
Corby Distilleries Limited 159
Corel Corporation 465
Cornucopia Resources Ltd. 37
Corporate Foods Limited 160
Coscan Development Corporation 260
Cott Corporation 161
Counsel Corporation 444
Coutu, Jean Group (PJC) Inc.
  See Jean Coutu Group (PJC) Inc.
Crestbrook Forest Industries Ltd. 137
Crown Life Insurance Company 421
Crownx Inc. 445
Czar Resources Ltd. 82

D

Dalmys (Canada) Limited 356
Denison Mines Limited 10
Deprenyl Research Limited 193
Derlan Industries Limited 492
Develcon Electronics Ltd. 218
Dia Met Mineral Ltd. 11
Dickenson Mines Limited 38
Discovery West Corp. 83
DMR Group Inc. 476
Dofasco Inc. 201
Doman Industries Limited 138
Dominion Textile Inc. 176
Domtar Inc. 139
Donohue Inc. 140
Dorset Exploration Ltd. 84
Dover Industries Limited 162
Dreco Energy Services Ltd. 85
Du Pont Canada Inc. 238
Dundee Bancorp Inc. 401
Dylex Limited 357

E

E-L Financial Corporation Limited 422
Echo Bay Mines Ltd. 39
Elan Energy Inc. 86
Emco Limited 202
Empire Company Limited 358

Equity Silver Mines Limited 40
Euro-Nevada Mining Corporation Limited 41
Excel Energy Inc. 87

F

Fahnestock Viner Holdings Inc. 402
Fairfax Financial Holdings Limited 423
FCA International Ltd. 477
Federal Industries Ltd. 446
Finning Ltd. 344
First Marathon Inc. 403
Fleet Aerospace Corporation 219
Fletcher Challenge Canada Limited 141
Ford Motor Company of Canada, Limited 184
Fortis Inc. 298
Four Seasons Hotels Inc. 493
FPI Limited 163
Franco-Nevada Mining Corporation Limited 42
FT Capital Ltd. 424

G

G.T.C. Transcontinental Group Ltd. 321
Gandalf Technologies Inc. 220
Geac Computer Corporation Limited 466
Gendis Inc. 359
General Trustco of Canada Inc. 383
Gennum Corporation 221
Gentra Inc. 384
George Weston Limited 360
Gibraltar Mines Limited 12
Glamis Gold Ltd. 43
Glenayre Electronics Ltd. 222
Goldcorp Inc. 44
Golden Knight Resources Inc. 45
Golden Star Resources Ltd. 46
Granges Inc. 13
Great Lakes Power Inc. 447
The Great-West life Assurance Company 425
Great-West Lifeco Inc. 426
Greyhound Lines of Canada Ltd. 273
Greyvest Financial Services Inc. 404
Le Groupe Videotron Ltee 322
Gulf Canada Resources Limited 88

H

Haley Industries Limited 223
Harris Steel Group Inc. 203
Harrowston Inc. 405
Hawker Siddeley Canada Inc. 224
Hayes-Dana Inc. 185
Hees International Bancorp Inc. 406
Helix Circuits Inc. 225
Hemlo Gold Mines Inc. 47
Hillcrest Resources Ltd. 89
Hollinger Inc. 323
Home Oil Company Limited 90
The Horsham Corporation 91

Hudson Bay Mining and Smelting Co., Limited 14
Hudson's Bay Company 361

I

I.S.G. Technologies Inc. 467
Imasco Limited 448
The Imperial Life Assurance Company of Canada . . 427
Imperial Oil Limited 92
Inco Limited 15
Inter-City Products Corporation 494
Intera Information Technologies Corporation 478
International Colin Energy Corporation 93
International Forest Products Limited 142
International Innopac Inc. 248
International Murex Technologies Corporation 495
International Petroleum Corporation 94
International Semi-Tech Microelectronics Inc. 177
International Verifact Inc. 226
Interprovincial Pipe Lines System Inc. 281
Intrawest Corporation 261
Inverness Petroleum Ltd. 95
Investors Group Inc. 407
IPSCO Inc. 204
Irwin Toy Limited 178
The Island Telephone Company Limited 299
ISM Information Systems Management Corporation . 468
Ivaco Inc. 205

J

Jannock Limited 449
The Jean Coutu Group (PJC) Inc. 362
John Labatt Limited 450

K

Kaufel Group Ltd. 496
Kerr Addison Mines Limited 16

L

Labatt, John Limited.
  See John Labatt Limited
Lac Minerals Ltd. 48
Lafarge Canada Inc. 497
Laidlaw Inc. 451
Laurentian Bank of Canada 385
The Laurentian Group Corporation 408
Lawson Mardon Group Limited 249
Linamar Corporation 227
Loblaw Companies Limited 363
The Loewen Group Inc. 498
London Insurance Group Inc. 428

M

Mackenzie Financial Corporation 409
Maclean Hunter Limited 324
MacMillan Bloedel Limited 143
Magna International Inc. 186
Maple Leaf Foods Inc. 164
Maritime Electric Company, Limited 300
Maritime Telegraph and Telephone Company, Limited 301

Mark Resources Inc. 96
Markbourough Properties Inc. 262
Marshall Steel Limited 345
MDS Health Group Limited 499
Melcor Developments Ltd. 263
Metall Mining Corporation 17
Methanex Corporation 239
MICC Investments Limited 429
Midland Walwyn Inc. 410
MinVen Gold Corporation 49
Mitel Corporation 325
Moffat Communications Limited 326
The Molson Companies Limited 165
Montreal Trustco Inc. 386
Moore Corporation Limited 500
Morgan Hydrocarbons Inc. 97
Morrison Petroleums Ltd. 98
Municipal Financial Corporation 411
Muscocho Explorations Ltd. 50

N

National Bank of Canada 387
National Sea Products Limited 166
National Trustco Inc. 388
Newbridge Networks Corporation Limited 228
Newfoundland Capital Corporation Limited 274
Newfoundland Light & Power Co. Limited 302
Newtel Enterprises Limited 303
Noma Industries Limited 229
Noranda Forest Inc. 144
Noranda Inc. 452
Norcen Energy Resources Limited 99
North Canadian Oils Limited 100
The North West Company Inc. 364
Northern Telecom Limited 327
Northgate Exploration Limited 51
Northstar Energy Corporation 101
Northwestern Utilities Limited 304
Nova Corporation of Alberta 282
Nova Scotia Power Inc. 305
Nowsco Well Service Ltd. 102
Numac Oil & Gas Ltd. 103

O

Ocelot Energy Inc. 104
Omega Hydrocarbons Ltd. 105
Onex Corporation 453
The Oshawa Group Limited 365

P

Pacific Northern Gas Ltd. 306
The Pagurian Corporation Limited 412
PanCanadian Petroleum Limited 106
Paramount Resources Ltd. 107
Pe Ben Oilfield Services Ltd. 108
Pegasus Gold Inc. 52
Pennington's Stores Limited 366

Peoples Jewellers Limited 367
Petro-Canada 109
Philip Environmental Inc. 501
Pinnacle Resources Ltd. 110
Pioneer Metals Corporation 53
Placer Dome Inc. 54
Poco Petroleums Ltd. 111
Potash Corporation of Saskatchewan Inc. 18
Power Corporation of Canada 413
Power Financial Corporation 414
Precambrian Shield Resources Limited 112
Premdor Inc. 502
Princeton Mining Corporation 19
PWA Corporation 275

Q

QSound Labs, Inc.
   See Archer Communications Inc.
Quadra Logic Technologies Inc. 194
Quebec Sturgeon River Mines Limited 55
Quebec-Telephone 307
Quebecor Inc. 328
Quebecor Printing Inc. 329

R

Ranchmen's Resources Ltd. 113
Ranger Oil Limited 114
Rayrock Yellowknife Resources Inc. 56
Reitmans (Canada) Limited 368
Renaissance Energy Ltd. 115
Repap Enterprises Inc. 145
Revenue Properties Company Limited 264
Rigel Energy Corporation 116
Rio Algom Limited 20
Rio Alto Exploration Ltd. 117
Rogers Cantel Mobile Communications Inc. 330
Rogers Communications Inc. 331
Rolland Inc. 146
Roman Corporation Limited 454
Rothmans Inc. 167
Royal Bank of Canada 389
Royal LePage Limited 265
Royal Oak Mines Inc. 57
Royal Trustco Limited.
   See Gentra Inc.

S

Samuel Manu-Tech Inc. 206
Saskatchewan Oil and Gas Corporation 118
SBN Systems Inc. 230
Sceptre Resources Limited 119
Schneider Corporation 168
Scott Paper Limted 503
Scott's Hospitality Inc. 455
Scurry-Rainbow Oil Limited 120
The Seagram Company Ltd. 456
Sears Canada Inc. 369

Shaw Communications Inc. 332
Shaw Industries Ltd. 504
Shell Canada Limited 121
Sherritt Gordon Limited 457
SHL Systemhouse Inc. 469
Sico Inc. 240
Silcorp Limited 370
Simcoe Erie Investors Limited 430
Slater Industries Inc. 207
Slocan Forest Products Ltd. 147
SNC-Lavalin Group Inc. 505
Softkey Software Products Inc. 470
Sonora Gold Corp. 58
Southam Inc. 333
Spar Aerospace Limited 231
St. Lawrence Cement Inc. 506
Stelco Inc. 208
Suncor Inc. 122

T

T.G. Bright & Co., Limited 169
Talisman Energy Inc. 123
Tarragon Oil and Gas Limited 124
TCG International Inc. 187
Teck Corporation 21
Tele-Metropole Inc. 334
Teleglobe Inc. 471
Telus Corporation 308
Tembec Inc. 148
The Thomson Corporation 335
TIE/Telecommunications Canada Limited 232
Toronto Sun Publishing Corporation 336
The Toronto-Dominion Bank 390
Torstar Corporation 337
Total Petroleum (North America) Ltd. 125
Traders Group Limited 415
Trans Mountain Pipe Line Company Ltd. 283
Transalta Utilities Corporation 309
TransCanada PipeLines Limited 284
Tri Link Resources Ltd. 126
Trilon Financial Corporation 416
Trimac Limited 276
Triton Canada Resources Ltd. 127
Trizec Corporation Ltd. 266
TVX Gold Inc. 59

U

UAP Inc. 346
Ulster Petroleums Ltd. 128
Unicorp Energy Corporation 310
Unigesco Inc. 458
United Corporations Limited 447
Unitied Dominion Industries Limited 459
United Keno Mines Limited 60
United Westburne Inc. 347
Univa Inc. 371

V

Varity Corporation 209
Versa Services Ltd. 372
Viceroy Resource Corporation 61

W

Wajax Limited 348
Weldwood of Canada Limited 149
West Fraser Timber Co. Ltd. 150
Westar Group Ltd. 277
Westcoast Energy Inc. 285
Westmin Resources Limited 22
Weston, George Limited.
  See George Weston Limited
Wharf Resources Limited 62
WIC Western International Communications Ltd. . . . 338

X

Xerox Canada Inc. 233

3M CANADA INC.
(Private)   MISC. CONSUMER PRODUCTS
1840 Oxford Street East, P.O. Box 5757, London, ON,
N6A 4T1   (519) 451-2500
3M CANADA INC. is a diversified manufacturing company.
Dr. W.E. Coyne, President & General Manager
TOTAL REVENUE ($000)   588,889

20/20 FINANCIAL CORPORATION
(Public)   INVESTMENT COMPANIES AND FUNDS
Suite 500, 2010 Winston Park Drive, Oakville, ON,
L6H 5R7   (416) 829-2020
20/20 FINANCIAL CORPORATION is a holding company which
conducts its business through 20/20 Group Financial Inc., a mutual fund
management company. 20/20 Group Financial Inc. is in the business of
sponsoring, managing and distributing mutual funds in Canada.
Larry R. Lunn, Chairman
TOTAL REVENUE ($000)   24,912

A & A FOODS LTD.
(Public)   WHOLESALE DISTRIBUTORS
1560 Broadway Street, Port Coquitlam, BC,
V3C 2M8   (604) 942-6613
A & A FOODS LTD. is involved in the importing, manufacturing and
distribution of specialty cheese and food products.
Giovanni Camporese, Chairman President & C.E.O.
TOTAL REVENUE ($000)   16,143

A & W FOOD SERVICES OF CANADA LTD.
(Private)   FOOD SERVICES
171 West Esplanade, Suite 300, North Vancouver, BC,
V7M 3K9   (604) 988-2141
A & W FOOD SERVICES OF CANADA LTD. is franchiser and
operator of fast food hamburger restaurants and franchiser and marketer
of soft drinks. The company is wholly owned by U L Canada Inc.
J.J. Mooney, President
TOTAL REVENUE ($000)   271,767

A. G. SIMPSON CO. LIMITED
(Private)   AUTOMOTIVE
675 Progress Avenue, Scarborough, ON, M1H 2W9 (416) 438-6650
A.G. SIMPSON CO. LIMITED is engaged in heavy metal stamping and
auto parts. The company is family owned.
Ben Virgilio, President & C.E.O.
TOTAL REVENUE ($000)   375,000

A.G.F. MANAGEMENT LIMITED
(Public)   INVESTMENT COMPANIES AND FUNDS
31st Floor, TD Bank Tower, Toronto-Dominion Centre, Toronto,
ON, M5K 1E9   (416) 367-1900
A.G.F. MANAGEMENT LIMITED is engaged in the field of investment management. The company has a diversified group of funds
designed to meet a variety of investment objectives, including aggressive
growth, stable growth, and high income. The funds provide professional
management of investments in Canada, the U.S., Europe, Japan and other
countries in Southeast Asia.
C. Warren Goldring, Chairman & C.E.O.
TOTAL REVENUE ($000)   42,912

A.L. VAN HOUTTE LTEE
(Public)   FOOD PROCESSING
8300 19ieme Avenue, Montreal, PQ, H1Z 4J8   (514) 593-7711
A.L. VAN HOUTTE LTEE operates a roasting and distribution of coffee
business. The company also operates, either directly or via franchises 84
cafe-bars and cafe-bistros.
Pierre Van Houtte, Chairman Of The Board
TOTAL REVENUE ($000)   27,921

ABBEY WOODS DEVELOPMENTS LTD.
(Public)   DEVELOPERS
Suite 301, 747 Bute Street, Vancouver, BC,
V6E 1Y2   (604) 685-2868
ABBEY WOODS DEVELOPMENT LTD. is involved with the acqui-
sition, sale and development of real estate property for investment
purposes through its two real estate companies and for clients.
Kuok, Khoon Ho, Chairman
TOTAL REVENUE ($000)   7,508

ABITIBI-PRICE INC.
See page 133 for a full company profile.

ABN AMRO BANK CANADA
(Private)   BANKS
P.O. Box 114, Toronto Dominion Centre, Suite 3402 IBM Tower,
Toronto, ON, M5K 1G8   (416) 367-0850
ABN BANK CANADA is a wholly owned subsidiary of Algemene
Bank Nederland N.V. It offers a comprehensive package of banking
services including corporate and commercial lending, trade finance,
deposit taking, foreign exchange, leasing and risk management products.
It has offices in Toronto, Vancouver and Montreal.
Basil A Beneteau, Chairman
TOTAL REVENUE ($000)   75,443

ACCORD FINANCIAL CORP.
(Public)   CONSULTING
18th Floor, 77 Bloor Street West, Toronto, ON,
M5S 1M2   (416) 961-0007
ACCORD FINANCIAL CORP. through its subsidiaries provides factoring services to companies primarily in textiles, apparel, temporary staff
placement, transportation, footwear, floor coverings, toys and sporting
goods. These services include credit investigation and guarantees, receivables collection, record-keeping and financing.
Ken Hitzig, President
TOTAL REVENUE ($000)   11,091

ACCUGRAPH CORPORATION
(Public)   COMPUTER SOFTWARE & PROCESSING
5822 Cromo Drive, El Paso, TX, 79912   (915) 581-1171
ACCUGRAPH CORP. is engaged in design and development of computer-based software products, specifically addressing the computer-
aided design, computer-aided manufacturing, and computer-aided
engineering markets. The company sells its software in combination with
computer hardware purchased from third party manufacturers.
Hector Holguin, Chairman & C.E.O.
TOTAL REVENUE ($000)   10,085 (US)

ACIER LEROUX INC.
(Public)   WHOLESALE DISTRIBUTORS
1331 Graham Bell Street, Boucherville, PQ, J4B 6A1 (514) 641-4360
ACIER LEROUX INC. operates one of the principal steel service centres in Quebec. In this capacity the company acts as a distributor of steel products and also processes certain products in order to meet the needs of its clientele.
Raymond Leroux, President & C.E.O.
TOTAL REVENUE ($000)   62,870

ACKLANDS LIMITED
See page 343 for a full company profile.

ACTIDEV INC.
(Public)   MANAGEMENT AND DIVERSIFIED
1600 St. Martin Blvd. East, Tower B, Suite 280, Laval, PQ,
H7G 4S7   (514) 662-3272
ACTIDEV INC. is a holding company with a 59.3% interest in Alimentation Couche-Tard Inc. which operates a network of 160 convenience stores. A wholly owned subsidiary, Actigaz Inc., is involved in the retail sale of gasoline.
Alain Bouchard, Chairman
TOTAL REVENUE ($000)   111,161

ADS ASSOCIES LTEE
(Public)   CONSULTING
1220 Boul. Lebourgneuf, Bureau 200, Quebec, PQ,
G2K 2G4   (418) 626-1688
ADS ASSOCIES LTEE is a multidisciplinary group operating mainly in the engineering and construction, technology, and manufacturing sectors.
Paul Drouin, Chairman & C.E.O.
TOTAL REVENUE ($000)   38,143

AETNA LIFE INSURANCE COMPANY OF CANADA
(Public)   INSURANCE - LIFE
P.O. Box 120, 79 Wellington St. W., Aetna Tower, TD Centre, Toronto, ON, M5H 1N9   (416) 864-8000
AETNA LIFE INSURANCE COMPANY OF CANADA is a major Canadian life insurance company offering a comprehensive range of life, annuity and health products to individuals and groups across Canada.
Fraser M. Fell, Chairman
TOTAL REVENUE ($000)   602,000

AG ARMENO MINES & MINERALS INC.
(Public)   METAL MINES
P.O. Box 10332, Pacific Centre, Suite 930, 609 Granville Street, Vancouver, BC, V7Y 1H3   (604) 681-1519
AG ARMENO MINES & MINERALS INC. is involved in the acquisition, exploration and development of natural resource properties.
Bedo H. Kalpakian, President
TOTAL REVENUE ($000)   484

AGNICO-EAGLE MINES LIMITED
See page 27 for a full company profile.

AGRA INDUSTRIES LIMITED
See page 475 for a full company profile.

AGRINOVE, COOPERATIVE AGRO-ALIMENTAIRE
(Non-fin Co-op)   AGRICULTURE
180 Boul. Begin, C.P. 4600, Sainte-Claire, PQ,
G0R 2V0   (418) 883-3301
AGRINOVE, COOPERATIVE AGRO-ALIMENTAIRE is a dairy co-operative suppling capital management services, transportation and sales support to its members. Agrinove has an interest in Groupe Lactel.
Herman Bolduc, Chairman
TOTAL REVENUE ($000)   153,747

AGRO COMPANY OF CANADA LIMITED
(Private)   WHOLESALE DISTRIBUTORS
450 Rue Bridge, Montreal, PQ, H3K 2C6   (514) 937-4241
AGRO COMPANY OF CANADA LIMITED is a grain broker.
Mr. Murray Cormack, President & C.E.O.
TOTAL REVENUE ($000)   305,106

AGROMEX INC.
(Public)   AGRICULTURE
2950 Rue Ontario Est, Montreal, PQ, H2K 1X3   (418) 527-9661
AGROMEX INC. is engaged exclusively in the business of reproducing and fattening hogs.
Robert Desilets, Chairman & President
TOTAL REVENUE ($000)   35,061

AGROPUR, COOPERATIVE AGRO-ALIMENTAIRE
(Non-fin Co-op)   AGRICULTURE
510 Principale Street, Granby, PQ, J2G 7G2   (514) 375-1991
AGROPUR, COOPERATIVE AGRO-ALIMENTAIRE is a dairy based cooperative centred in Quebec, which operates in three divisions: industrial; yogurt and fresh desserts; and fine cheese. The cooperative serves 4,100 members. A subsidiary, Naturel inc., produces and distributes consumer milk products.
Jacques Cartier, Chairman
TOTAL REVENUE ($000)   1,007,122

AIR CANADA
See page 271 for a full company profile.

AKIKO-LORI GOLD RESOURCES LTD.
(Public)   PRECIOUS METALS
Suite 1000, 789 West Pender Street, Vancouver, BC,
V6C 1H2   (604) 687-2038
AKIKO-LORI GOLD RESOURCES LTD. is engaged in the exploration and development of mineral properties in the Ross River-Faro area, Yukon, the Skeena Mining Division, British Columbia and various properties in Ontario.
Michael Levinson, Chairman
TOTAL REVENUE ($000)   (484)

ALBERTA AND SOUTHERN GAS CO LTD
(Private)   GAS PIPELINES
240 - 4th Avenue S.W., Suite 2900, Calgary, AB,
T2P 4L7   (403) 691-7500

ALBERTA AND SOUTHERN GAS CO LTD. purchases natural gas and arranges its transportation and sale, principally to markets in the United States.
Mr. Chuck Schultz, President & C.E.O.
TOTAL REVENUE ($000) 918,738

ALBERTA ENERGY COMPANY LTD.
See page 67 for a full company profile.

ALBERTA HERITAGE SAVINGS TRUST FUND
(Crown)   INVESTMENT COMPANIES AND FUNDS
426 Terrace Building, Edmonton, AB, T5K 2C3   (403) 427-9957
ALBERTA HERITAGE SAVINGS TRUST FUND is a regulated fund established by provincial statute and administered by the Provincial Treasurer. The fund has three basic objectives: to save for the future; to strengthen and diversify the Alberta economy; and to improve the quality of life in Alberta.
Dennis Anderson, Chairman
TOTAL REVENUE ($000) 1,483,236

ALBERTA MORTGAGE AND HOUSING CORPORATION
(Public)   DEVELOPERS
9405 - 50 Street, Edmonton, AB, T6B 2T4   (403) 468-3535
The crown corporation manages extensive social housing, land and real estate, and loan portfolios developed for the benefit of Albertans.
Hon. Raymond A. Speaker, Chairman
TOTAL REVENUE ($000) 501,707

ALBERTA NATURAL GAS COMPANY LTD
See page 435 for a full company profile.

ALBERTA OIL AND GAS LIMITED
(Public)   OIL AND GAS PRODUCERS
Suite 1200, 700 - 4th Avenue S.W., Calgary, AB,
T2P 3J4   (403) 269-3779
ALBERTA OIL AND GAS LIMITED is involved in the acquisiton and development of oil and gas properties.
Paul Stauffer, Chairman
TOTAL REVENUE ($000) 3,804

ALBERTA POWER LIMITED
(Private)   ELECTRICAL UTILITIES
10035 105 Street, Edmonton, AB, T5J 2V6   (403) 420-7310
ALBERTA POWER LIMITED is engaged in the generation, transmission and distribution of electrical energy in Alberta and the Yukon Territory. Alberta Power is 100% owned by Canadian Utilities Limited of Alberta.
J.D. Wood, Chairman & C.E.O.
TOTAL REVENUE ($000) 518,232

ALBERTA WHEAT POOL
(Non-fin Co-op)   AGRICULTURE
Box 2700, 505 - 2nd Street S.W., Calgary, AB,
T2P 2P5   (403) 290-4910
ALBERTA WHEAT POOL is a farmer-owned cooperative that provides fully integreted grain handling, grain marketing and farm supply services to its members through facilities located in Alberta and northeastern

British Columbia. It also owns and operates an export grain terminal in Vancouver, British Columbia.
G.J. Dewar, Chief Executive Officer
TOTAL REVENUE ($000) 995,489

ALCAN ALUMINIUM LIMITED
See page 3 for a full company profile.

ALERT CARE CORPORATION
(Public)   OTHER SERVICES
145 Murray Drive, Aurora, ON, L4G 2C7   (416) 841-2745
ALERT CARE CORPORATION is involved in the construction, development, sale and management of retirement homes.
W. Wayne Barton, President
TOTAL REVENUE ($000) 3,450

ALGO GROUP INC.
(Public)   CLOTHING AND TEXTILES
225 Rue Chabanel Ouest, Montreal, PQ, H2N 2C9   (514) 382-1240
ALGO GROUP INC. operates in the fashion apparel field and its activities include the designing, manufacturing, marketing and importing of ladies, mens and childrens apparel. The company is a converter of fashion fabrics and operates two chains of ladies retail stores. Its operations are conducted in both Canada and the United States.
Joseph Schaffer, Co-Chairman & President
TOTAL REVENUE ($000) 308,161

ALGOMA CENTRAL CORPORATION
See page 272 for a full company profile.

ALGOMA STEEL INC.
(Private)   STEEL
105 West Street, Sault Ste Marie, ON, P6A 5P2   (705) 945-2788
ALGOMA STEEL INC. is an integrated steel producer. It produces sheet and strip, plate, seamless tubular steel, structural shapes and steel rails at its steelworks in Sault Ste. Marie. The company satisfies all of its iron ore requirements from mines which it owns. Dofasco Inc. of Hamilton owns all of the company's common shares.
H. Earl Joudrie, Chairman
TOTAL REVENUE ($000) 429,481

ALGONQUIN MERCANTILE CORPORATION
(Public)   MANAGEMENT AND DIVERSIFIED
Unit 11, 668 Millway Avenue, Concord, ON,
L4K 3V2   (416) 660-7688
ALGONQUIN MERCANTILE CORP. is a diversified company engaged directly or through subsidiaries in the retailing of drugs and related products; providing home health care services; and the wholesaling, packaging and distributing of fresh produce.
Michael Blair, Chief Executive Officer
TOTAL REVENUE ($000) 96,227

ALIMENTATION COUCHE-TARD INC.
(Public)   FOOD STORES
1600 St. Martin Blvd. East, Tower B, Suite 280, Laval, PQ,
H7G 4S7   (514) 662-3272
ALIMENTATION COUCHE-TARD INC. is involved in the convenience store industry. It offers customers four main services: packaged

foods and goods, gasoline service, automated teller machines, and fast food. The company operated 160 convenience stores.
Alain Bouchard, Chairman, President & C.E.O.
TOTAL REVENUE ($000)   111,161

ALL-NORTH RESOURCES LTD.
(Public)   METAL MINES
935 Marine Building, 355 Burrard Street, Vancouver, BC,
V6C 2G8   (604) 687-7169
ALL-NORTH RESOURCES LTD. is involved in the acquisition, exploration and development of natural resource properties.
J.A. Currie, President & C.E.O.
TOTAL REVENUE ($000)   9

ALLELIX BIOPHARMACEUTICALS INC.
(Public)   BIOTECHNOLOGY & PHARMACEUTICALS
6850 Goreway Drive, Mississauga, ON, L4V 1P1   (416) 677-0831
ALLELIX BIOPHARMACEUTICALS INC. focuses on the discovery and development of biopharmaceutical products for tissue repair, immunology and inflammation. Allelix applies advances in the scientific understanding of molecular and cellular biology to develop new approaches for the development of therapeutic products for these conditions.
John R. Evans, Chairman
TOTAL REVENUE ($000)   10,074

ALLIANCE RO-NA HOME INC.
(Private)   WHOLESALE DISTRIBUTORS
34 Henry St., St-Jacobs, ON, N0B 2N0
ALLIANCE RO-NA HOME INC. is a buyer of merchandise for its two 50% shareholders, Le Groupe Ro-Na Dismat Inc. and Home Hardware Stores Limited. Volume purchase rebates earned are allocated to the shareholders.
TOTAL REVENUE ($000)   1,147,768

ALLIEDSIGNAL CANADA INC.
(Private)   TRANSPORTATION EQUIP & COMPNTS
240 Attwell Drive, Etobicoke, ON, M9W 6L7   (416) 675-1411
ALLIEDSIGNAL CANADA INC. is engaged in three industries: areospace, automotive and chemicals. AlliedSignal Canada is wholly owned by Allied Signal Inc.
Ken Kivenko, Chairman& President
TOTAL REVENUE ($000)   356,527

ALLSTATE INSURANCE COMPANY OF CANADA
(Private)   INSURANCE - PROPERTY & CASUALTY
10 Allstate Parkwy, Markham, ON, L3R 5P8   (416) 677-6900
ALLSTATE INSURANCE COMPANY OF CANADA is an insurance carrier. The company is a wholly owned subsidiary of Allstate Life Insurance Company of Northbrook, Illinois.
Raymond H. Kiefer, Chairman
TOTAL REVENUE ($000)   436,618

AMERADA HESS CANADA LTD.
(Private)   OIL AND GAS PRODUCERS
700 - 9th Avenue S.W., Suite 1900, Calgary, AB,
T2P 4B3   (403) 267-6910

AMERADA HESS CANADA LTD. is involved in oil and gas exploration and production.
L. Hess, Chairman
TOTAL REVENUE ($000)   205,668

AMERICA WEST CAPITAL CORP.
(Public)   MANAGEMENT AND DIVERSIFIED
Suite 200, 455 Granville Street, Vancouver, BC,
V6C 1T1   (604) 683-0455
AMERICA WEST CAPITAL CORP. operates in three main industry segments: real estate investments; oil and gas; and sign sales and leases. It also has a new venture in the hospitality industry.
David M. Mercier, Chairman & President
TOTAL REVENUE ($000)   2,084

AMERICAN BARRICK RESOURCES CORPORATION
See page 28 for a full company profile.

AMERICAN EAGLE PETROLEUMS LTD.
(Public)   OIL AND GAS FIELD SERVICES
Suite 1900, Monenco Place, 801 - 6th Avenue S.W., Calgary, AB,
T2P 3W2   (403) 262-8727
AMERICAN EAGLE PETROLEUMS LTD. operates in the petroleum industry.
H. Earl Joudrie, Chairman
TOTAL REVENUE ($000)   19,213

AMERICAN NORTEL COMMUNICATIONS INC.
(Public)   TELECOMMUNICATIONS
Suite 2150, 136 East South Temple St., Salt Lake City, UT,
84111   (801) 578-8000
AMERICAN NORTEL COMMUNICATIONS INC. through its wholly owned subsidiary NorTel Communications USA provides telecommunications services.
Dr. Kenneth D. Rogers, President
TOTAL REVENUE ($000)   1,776

AMERICAN RESERVE MINING CORPORATION
(Public)   PRECIOUS METALS
Suite 420, 625 Howe Street, Vancouver, BC,
V6C 2T6   (604) 683-2130
AMERICAN RESERVE MINING CORPORATION is involved in the acquisition, exploration and development of natural resource properties.
Carl F. Zuber, Chairman, President & C.E.O.
TOTAL REVENUE ($000)   1

AMEX BANK OF CANADA
(Private)   BANKS
101 McNabb Street, Markham, ON, L3R 4H8   (416) 474-8000
AMEX BANK OF CANADA is a federally chartered bank which issues charge cards (Personal Card, Gold Card, Platinum Card, Corporate Card, Optima Card and Lifetime Membership), as well as a variety of lending products and offers an interest bearing account for businesses. It is a unit of New York-based American Express Co..
Alan W. Stark, President
TOTAL REVENUE ($000)   323,641

AMISCO INDUSTRIES LTD.
(Public)   HOME FURNISHINGS
33 5e Rue., Ville de L'Islet, PQ, G0R 2C0   (418) 247-5025
AMISCO INDUSTRIES LTD. is a manufacturer of home furnishings which are sold under the trademark Amisco. The self-assembled furniture is made of steel tubing. Its products are sold in 10 Canadian provinces and 45 American states.
Martin Poitras, Chairman & C.E.O.
TOTAL REVENUE ($000)   22,813

AMOCO CANADA PETROLEUM COMPANY LTD.
(Private)   OIL AND GAS PRODUCERS
240 - 4th Avenue S.W., P.O. Box 200, Calgary, AB,
T2P 4H4   (403) 233-1313
AMOCO CANADA PETROLEUM COMPANY LTD. is engaged in the exploration for and production of crude oil and natural gas, the production and purchase of natural gas liquids, the marketing of liquified petroleum gases, the production and sale of sulphur and the development of mineral properties.
T. Don Stacy, Chairman & President
TOTAL REVENUE ($000)   3,783,000

ANCHOR LAMINA INC.
(Public)   MISC. INDUSTRIAL PRODUCTS
2590 Ouellette Avenue, Windsor, ON,
N8X 1L7   (519) 966-4431
ANCHOR LAMINA INC. is engaged in the production and sale of die sets and related products and services to the metal working and plastic mould industries throughout North America.
Clare Winterbottom, Chairman, President & C.E.O.
TOTAL REVENUE ($000)   44,706

ANDERSON EXPLORATION LTD.
See page 68 for a full company profile.

ANDRES WINES LTD.
See page 155 for a full company profile.

ANGLO-CANADIAN TELEPHONE COMPANY
See page 289 for a full company profile.

ANZ BANK CANADA
(Private)   BANKS
18th Floor, North Tower, P.O. Box 145, Royal Bank Plaza, Toronto, ON, M5J 2J3   (416) 865-0299
ANZ BANK CANADA is a wholly owned subsidiary of Australia and New Zealand Banking Group Limited. The bank provides a comprehensive range of commercial and international trade related banking services to clients, Canadian enterprises and companies with their origins in Australia and New Zealand.
H. Bourke, Gen. Mgr. & C.E.O.
TOTAL REVENUE ($000)   16,640

ARAKIS ENERGY CORPORATION
(Public)   OIL AND GAS PRODUCERS
Suite 630, 800 West Pender Street, Vancouver, BC,
V6C 2V6   (604) 685-7933

ARAKIS ENERGY CORP. is engaged in the acquisition, exploration and development of natural resource properties.
J. Terry Alexander, Chairman, C.E.O. & President
TOTAL REVENUE ($000)   601

ARBOR CAPITAL INC.
See page 483 for a full company profile.

ARBOR RESOURCES INC.
(Public)   OIL AND GAS PRODUCERS
Suite 1000, 675 West Hastings Street, Vancouver, BC,
V6B 1N6   (604) 685-2222
ARBOR RESOURCES INC. is engaged in the exploration, development and production of mineral properties primarily in the Yukon and Ontario.
Richard W. Hughes, President
TOTAL REVENUE ($000)   (404)

ARCHER COMMUNICATIONS INC.
See page 213 for a full company profile.

ARDEN HOLDINGS INC.
(Public)   SPECIALTY STORES
99 Chabanel W., Suite 104, Montreal, PQ,
H2N 1C2   (514) 383-4442
ARDEN HOLDINGS INC. owns and operates 41 retail stores under the names Ardene, Flash, Fantazia, and Audrey Morris. The company sells inexpensive to medium priced fashion jewellery and fashion accessories.
Arden Dervishian, President
TOTAL REVENUE ($000)   21,698

ARGUS CORPORATION LIMITED
(Public)   MANAGEMENT AND DIVERSIFIED
10 Toronto St, Toronto, ON, M5C 2B7   (416) 363-8721
ARGUS CORPORATION LIMITED is involved in a single business activity which is the investment of funds in companies, dividend and interest earning deposits.
Conrad M. Black, Chairman & C.E.O.
TOTAL REVENUE ($000)   17,952

ARIEL RESOURCES LTD.
(Public)   PRECIOUS METALS
Suite 1135, 1188 West Georgia Street, Vancouver, BC,
V6E 4A2   (604) 682-2201
ARIEL RESOURCES LTD. operates the Tres Hermanos gold mine and milling complex 95 kilometres northwest of San Jose in Costa Rica.
William C. Bennett, President
TOTAL REVENUE ($000)   4,014 (US)

ARIMATHAEA RESOURCES INC.
(Public)   PRECIOUS METALS
18th Floor, 100 Front Street West, Toronto, ON,
M5J 1E3   (416) 366-8352
ARIMATHAEA RESOURCES INC. is involved in the business of gold exploration.
Graham Ferguson Lacey, Chairman
TOTAL REVENUE ($000)   130

ARIMETCO INTERNATIONAL INC.
See page 4 for a full company profile.

ARMBRO ENTERPRISES INC.
(Public)   CONTRACTORS
25 Van Kirk Drive, Unit #8, Brampton, ON, L7A 1A6 (416) 454-3737
ARMBRO ENTERPRISES INC. operates in a variety of areas including:
real estate development; road building; construction and aggregates.
George F. Michals, Chairman & C.E.O.
TOTAL REVENUE ($000)   55,994

ARMISTICE RESOURCES LTD.
(Public)   PRECIOUS METALS
6 Tippett Road, Suite B, Downsview, ON, M3H 2V2 (416) 635-1811
ARMISTICE RESOURCES LTD. is a gold exploration company with
properties in Ontario and Manitoba.
Harvey Atkin, Chairman
TOTAL REVENUE ($000)   (27)

ASEA BROWN BOVERI INC.
(Private)   ELECTRICAL & ELECTRONIC
3000 Halpern, St. Laurent, PQ, H4S 1R2   (514) 856-6222
ASEA BROWN BOVERI INC. is an electrical engineering company
which develops, provides, sells and services a wide range of systems and
products generally related to the production, distribution and application
of electricity. ABB is a wholly owned subsidiary of ABB Asea Brown
Boveri Ltd. of Switzerland.
Peter S. Janson, President & C.E.O.
TOTAL REVENUE ($000)   839,046

ASSINIBOINE CREDIT UNION LIMITED
(Fin. Co-op)   CREDIT UNIONS
200 Main Street, 6th Floor, P.O. Box 2, Winnipeg, MB,
R3C 2G1   (204) 958-8550
ASSINIBOINE CREDIT UNION LIMITED offers deposit, loan, and
retail financial services to its members.
Richard Feist, General Manager
TOTAL REVENUE ($000)   31,448

ASTRAL COMMUNICATIONS INC.
See page 484 for a full company profile.

ATCO LTD.
See page 436 for a full company profile.

ATCOR RESOURCES LTD.
(Public)   OIL AND GAS PRODUCERS
Suite 600, 800 - 6th Avenue S.W., Calgary, AB,
T2P 3G3   (403) 292-8000
ATCOR RESOURCES LTD. is engaged in the business of crude oil and
gas exploration and production and in the processing and marketing of
natural gas.
Ronald D. Southern, Chairman
TOTAL REVENUE ($000)   138,687

ATLANTA GOLD CORPORATION
(Public)   PRECIOUS METALS
Suite 1440, 625 Howe Street, Vancouver, BC,
V6C 2T6   (604) 669-0016
ATLANTA GOLD CORPORATION is involved in the acquisition,
exploration and development of precious metal properties. The com-
pany's principal project is in Idaho.
Olaf Tolpinrud, President
TOTAL REVENUE ($000)   3

ATLANTIC COAST COPPER CORPORATION LIMITED
(Public)   METAL MINES
P.O. Box 937, Saint John, NB, E2L 4E3   (506) 632-7171
ATLANTIC COAST COPPER CORPORATION LIMITED is a hold-
ing company with investments in Consolidated Rambler Mines Limited
and Northern Canada Mines, Limited.
D.A. Macfarlane, President & Treasurer
TOTAL REVENUE ($000)   159

ATLANTIC SHOPPING CENTRES LIMITED
(Public)   PROPERTY MGMNT & INVESTMENT
115 King St., Stellarton, NS, B0K 1S0   (902) 755-4440
ATLANTIC SHOPPING CENTRES LIMITED, directly and through
subsidiaries, is engaged primarily in the acquisition, development and
management of commercial real estate comprised mainly of shopping
centres and office buildings located in the Atlantic Provinces.
P.D. Sobey, Chairman & C.E.O.
TOTAL REVENUE ($000)   68,585

ATLANTIS RESOURCES LTD.
(Public)   OIL AND GAS PRODUCERS
Suite 900, 202 - 6th Avenue S.W., Calgary, AB,
T2P 2R9   (403) 233-0921
ATLANTIS RESOURCES LTD. is a Canadian oil and gas exploration
company with reserves and production in both Canada and the United
States.
Lawrence H. Payne, Chairman President & C.E.O.
TOTAL REVENUE ($000)   9,557

ATLAS-GEST INC.
(Private)   CONTRACTORS
2000 Peel Street, Suite 830, Montreal, PQ,
H3A 2W5   (514) 849-5350
ATLAS-GEST INC. is engaged in civil engineering, utilities and build-
ing construction. Atlas-Gest is a wholly owned subsidiary of Dumez
North America of Montreal, Quebec.
Jean-Pierre Noyer, President & C.E.O.
TOTAL REVENUE ($000)   181,969

ATOMIC ENERGY OF CANADA LIMITED
(Crown)   MACHINERY
344 Slater Street, Ottawa, ON, K1A 0S4   (613) 237-3270
ATOMIC ENERGY OF CANADA's commercial operations consist of
nuclear power engineering and design, project management, operating
plant support services, manufacturing and selling of medical and industrial radiation equipment and radio-isotopes, and investment. Research
and development operations consist of basic and applied nuclear research
and development and contract research and development services.

Robert A. Ferchat, Chairman
TOTAL REVENUE ($000) 395,832

AUBERGES DES GOUVERNEURS INC.
(Public) LODGING
777 University, Suite 800, Montreal, PQ, H3C 3Z7 (514) 875-8822
AUBERGES DES GOUVERNEURS INC. and its franchisees operate hotels in the province of Quebec under the trademarks Hotel Des Gouverneurs and Radisson Gouverneurs.
Paul G. Vien, Chairman of the Board
TOTAL REVENUE ($000) 40,030

AUDREY RESOURCES INC.
(Public) METAL MINES
800 Rene-Levesque Blvd. W., Suite 850, Montreal, PQ, H3B 1X9 (514) 878-3166
AUDREY RESOURCES INC. is a producer of zinc, copper, gold and silver. The company is also involved in the acquisition, exploration and development of mineral properties.
Guy Hebert, President & C.E.O.
TOTAL REVENUE ($000) 483

AUR RESOURCES INC.
See page 29 for a full company profile.

AURIZON MINES LTD.
(Public) METAL MINES
Suite 1000, 1177 West Hastings Street, Vancouver, BC, V6E 2K3 (604) 687-6600
AURIZON MINES LTD. is a gold and silver mining company. It owns a 50% interest in The Sleeping Gaint Mine and a 50% interest in the Beaufor property, both in Quebec. The company is also involved in the Beacon property, Connell Corner property, Bruneau property and the Benoist Township porperty, all in Quebec, and the La Reyna project in Mexico. Aurizon owns 56% of Aurex Resources and 22% of Cazador Explorations.
Frank A. Lang, Chairman
TOTAL REVENUE ($000) 2,168

AUTO WORKERS' (OSHAWA) CREDIT UNION LIMITED
(Fin. Co-op) CREDIT UNIONS
322 King St. W., P.O. Box 158, Oshawa, ON, L1H 7L1 (416) 728-5187
AUTO WORKERS' (OSHAWA) CREDIT UNION LIMITED offers full financial services including savings, loans, mortgages and RRSPs/RRIFs to its members.
Steve Nimigom, President
TOTAL REVENUE ($000) 19,474

AUTOSTOCK INC.
(Public) SPECIALTY STORES
8288 Pie IX Boulevard, Montreal, PQ, H1Z 3T6 (514) 593-8300
AUTOSTOCK INC. comprises 9 divisions and subsidiaries engaged in the sale and installation of auto parts: Autopoint Inc., Autostock Distribution, Du-Ro Vitres et accessoires d'autos, Glenayre Communications, Lebeau Vitres d'autos, Lebeau Technicentre, Monsieur Muffler, Octo Freins et Silencieux and Prodiesel.

Gerard Lebeau, Chairman Of The Board
TOTAL REVENUE ($000) 154,637

AUTREX INC.
(Public) MISC. INDUSTRIAL PRODUCTS
50 Bartor Road, Weston, ON, M9M 2G5 (416) 745-3335
AUTREX INC. is engaged in the design, manufacture and sale of electronic equipment instrumentation, and specialized lighting and electrical products through its operating divisions, Adjusta-Post Manufacturing Company of Norton, Ohio, Pylon Electronics Inc. of Ottawa, Toronto, Dartmouth and Montreal, and Bison Instruments of Minneapolis.
Barrie D. Rose, Chairman & C.E.O.
TOTAL REVENUE ($000) 12,069

AVCO FINANCIAL SERVICES CANADA LIMITED
(Private) FINANCE AND LEASING
201 Queens Avenue, London, ON, N6A 1J1 (519) 672-4220
AVCO FINANCIAL SERVICES CANADA LIMITED is engaged in the provision of financial and insurance services. Financial services include consumer loans, sales financing and mortgages. Insurance operations are carried out through a subsidiary, London and Midland General Insurance Company. Avco Financial Services is a wholly owned subsidiary of Textron Inc.
Engene R. Schutt, Exec. V.P., Int'l Operations
TOTAL REVENUE ($000) 258,833

AVCORP INDUSTRIES INC.
(Public) TRANSPORTATION EQUIP & COMPNTS
Suite 200, 1001 Autoroute 440 West, Chomedey, PQ, H7L 3W3 (514) 629-5506
AVCORP industries is engaged in the design, manufacture and sale of an extensive range of aerospace products comprised of four product groups: composite and plastic components, metal structures, aircraft engine overhaul and remanufacture and aerospace design engineering.
Kenneth R. Patrick, Chairman, President & C.E.O.
TOTAL REVENUE ($000) 24,584

AVESTEL CREDIT UNION LIMITED
(Fin. Co-op) CREDIT UNIONS
688 Queensdale Avenue East, Hamilton, ON, L8V 1M1 (416) 387-0770
AVESTEL CREDIT UNION LIMITED provides financial products, services and programs.
Jessie C. Knox, President & Chairperson
TOTAL REVENUE ($000) 29,674

B.C. TREE FRUITS LIMITED
(Non-fin Co-op) FOOD PROCESSING
1473 Water Street, Kelowna, BC, V1Y 1J6 (604) 762-2604
B.C. TREE FRUITS is involved in the marketing and sale of fresh fruit received from British Columbia Fruit Growers' Association member growers through packing houses with which the company has contracts.
Allan Earl, C.E.O.
TOTAL REVENUE ($000) 6,530

B.C. BANCORP
See page 377 for a full company profile.

B.C. CENTRAL CREDIT UNION
(Fin. Co-op)   CREDIT UNIONS
1441 Creekside Drive, Vancouver, BC, V6J 4S7   (604) 734-2511
B.C. CENTRAL CREDIT UNION is a financial services and trade
association for credit unions operating in British Columbia.
Tod Manrell, Chairperson
TOTAL REVENUE ($000)   167,268

B.C. PACIFIC CAPITAL CORPORATION
See page 437 for a full company profile.

B.I.D. BUILDING MATERIALS OF CANADA LTD.
(Private)   WHOLESALE DISTRIBUTORS
312 Dolomite Drive, Suite 208, Downsview, ON,
M3J 3H2   (416) 661-5950
B.I.D. BUILDING MATERIALS OF CANADA LTD. operates as a
buyer for its shareholder companies. It has 200 equal shareholders.
H. Gower, President
TOTAL REVENUE ($000)   340,015

B.Y.G. NATURAL RESOURCES INC.
(Public)   METAL MINES
Suite 801, 602 West Hastings Street, Vancouver, BC,
V6B 1P2   (604) 681-9696
B.Y.G. NATURAL RESOURCES INC. is involved in the acquisition,
exploration and development of mineral properties.
Alan G. Thompson, Chairman
TOTAL REVENUE ($000)   11

BACA RESOURCES LTD.
(Public)   OIL AND GAS PRODUCERS
Suite 1900, 717 - 7th Avenue S.W., Calgary, AB,
T2P 0Z3   (403) 269-5505
BACA RESOURCES LTD. is involved in the acquisition, exploration
and development of oil and gas properties.
William I.M. Turner, Jr., Chairman
TOTAL REVENUE ($000)   4,019

BACHELOR LAKE GOLD MINES INC.
See page 30 for a full company profile.

BANCA COMMERCIALE ITALIANA OF CANADA
(Private)   BANKS
P.O. Box 100, Suite 1800, 130 Adelaide Street West, Toronto,
M5H 3P5   (416) 366-8101
BANCA COMMERCIALE ITALIANA OF CANADA is a wholly
owned subsidiary of Banca Commerciale Italiana and is licenced to
operate as a bank in Canada with full banking powers as a foreign bank
subsidiary.
Donald E. Smith, Chairman Of The Board
TOTAL REVENUE ($000)   121,008

BANCA NAZIONALE DEL LAVORO OF CANADA
(Private)   BANKS
95 Wellington Street West, Suite 2100, P.O. Box 23, Toronto, ON,
M5J 2N7   (416) 365-7777

BANCA NAZIONALE DEL LAVORO OF CANADA is involved in
corporate and commercial banking. The bank is licenced as a foreign
bank subsidiary.
Derek G. Keaveney, Chairman Of The Board
TOTAL REVENUE ($000)   27,725

BANCO CENTRAL OF CANADA
(Private)   BANKS
330 Bay Street, Toronto, ON, M5H 2S8   (416) 365-7070
BANCO CENTRAL OF CANADA is a wholly owned subsidiary of
Banco Central, S.A. of Spain. The bank is licensed to operate in Canada
as a foreign bank with full banking powers.
F. Bustamante, Chief Executive Officer
TOTAL REVENUE ($000)   12,334

BANISTER INC.
See page 485 for a full company profile.

BANK HAPOALIM (CANADA)
(Private)   BANKS
10th Floor, 1 First Canadian Place, P.O. Box 35, Toronto, ON,
M5X 1A9   (416) 367-1710
BANK HAPOALIM (CANADA) is a wholly owned subsidiary of Bank
Hapoalim B.M., Israel, and is licenced to operate in Canada with full
banking powers as a foreign bank subsidiary.
Philip Granovsky, Chairman
TOTAL REVENUE ($000)   10,853

BANK LEUMI LE-ISRAEL (CANADA)
(Private)   BANKS
Bank Leumi Building, 2nd Floor, 3055 Bathurst Street, Toronto,
ON, M6B 3B7   (416) 789-3392
BANK LEUMI LE-ISRAEL (CANADA) is licenced to operate in
Canada with banking powers as a foreign bank subsidiary.
David Friedmann, Chairman
TOTAL REVENUE ($000)   19,325

BANK OF AMERICA CANADA
(Private)   BANKS
4 King Street West, 18th Floor, Toronto, ON,
M5H 1B6   (416) 863-5400
BANK OF AMERICA CANADA is a Canadian chartered bank operating across the country. The bank provides a broad range of financial
services to Canadian corporations and individuals, both domestically and
internationally, including capital markets, project finance, foreign exchange, cash management and commercial lending. The bank is a wholly
owned subsidiary of BankAmerica Corporation.
M. Peter McPherson, Chairman
TOTAL REVENUE ($000)   134,445

BANK OF BOSTON CANADA
(Private)   BANKS
Suite 1400, 500 Rene-Levesque Blvd. W., Montreal, PQ,
H2Z 1W7   (514) 397-9600
BANK OF BOSTON CANADA is licenced to operate in Canada with
full banking powers as a foreign bank subsidiary.
Slater Smith, Chairman
TOTAL REVENUE ($000)   21,035

BANK OF MONTREAL
See page 378 for a full company profile.

BANK OF MONTREAL SECURITIES CANADA LIMITED
(Private)   INVESTMENT HOUSES
First Canadian Place, 16th Floor, Toronto, ON,
M5X 1A1   (416) 867-5000
BANK OF MONTREAL SECURITIES CANADA LIMITED was
incorporated as the holding company for its subsidiary, The Nesbitt
Thomson Corporation Limited, which is a fully-integrated Canadian
investment dealer with investment advisors in Canada and operations in
the United States and the United Kingdom. Bank of Montreal Securities
is a wholly owned subsidiary of Bank of Montreal.
Mathew Barrett, Chairman & C.E.O.
TOTAL REVENUE ($000)   289,695

BANK OF NEW YORK CANADA (THE)
(Private)   BANKS
Suite 1707, 150 King Street West, P.O. Box 54, Toronto,
ON, M5H 1J9   (416) 974-9575
BANK OF NEW YORK CANADA is a wholly owned subsidiary of the
Bank of New York of the United States and is licenced as a bank in
Canada with full banking powers under the Bank Act 1980 as a foreign
bank subsidiary.
Laurence G. Kuhl, President & C.E.O.
TOTAL REVENUE ($000)   11,340

BANK OF NOVA SCOTIA (THE)
See page 379 for a full company profile.

BANK OF TOKYO CANADA (THE)
(Private)   BANKS
P.O. Box 42, Suite 2100, Royal Bank Plaza, South Tower, Toronto,
ON, M5J 2J1   (416) 865-0220
THE BANK OF TOKYO CANADA is a wholly owned subsidiary of
the Bank of Tokyo, Ltd. It offers commercial banking services to
Canadian business and industry on a country-wide basis, with particular
reference to the financing of international trade, commercial lending,
financing for natural resource projects and other traditional and special-
ized banking services.
Toshihiko Hisayama, President & C.E.O.
TOTAL REVENUE ($000)   94,091

BANQUE NATIONALE DE PARIS (CANADA)
(Private)   BANKS
BNP Tower, 1981 McGill College Avenue, Montreal, PQ,
H3A 2W8   (514) 285-6000
BANQUE NATIONALE DE PARIS (CANADA) provides a range of
corporate financial services including private banking, leasing, securities
and trade financing.
Jean Campeau, Chairman
TOTAL REVENUE ($000)   212,542

BARCLAYS BANK OF CANADA
(Private)   BANKS
304 Bay Street, Box No. 1, 5th Floor, Toronto, ON,
M5H 2P2   (416) 359-8000

BARCLAYS BANK OF CANADA is a wholly owned subsidiary of
Barclays Bank plc. The Barclays Group is one of the world's premier
international banking groups, with a network of over 3,500 offices in
more than 76 countries and assets exceeding $300 billion.
William B. Harris, Chairman Of The Board
TOTAL REVENUE ($000)   197,785

BARRINGTON PETROLEUM LTD.
(Public)   OIL AND GAS PRODUCERS
P.O. Box 1958, Station M, Calgary, AB, T2P 2M2   (403) 263-9464
BARRINGTON PETROLEUM LTD. is involved in oil and gas explo-
ration and production.
Brian W. Lawrence, Chairman & C.E.O.
TOTAL REVENUE ($000)   7,484

BASF CANADA INC.
(Private)   CHEMICALS
5850 Cote De Liesse Road, Mont-Royal, PQ,
H4T 1C1   (514) 341-5411
BASF CANADA INC. is a chemical company involved in the production
of computer diskettes, video and audio tapes, and fibres used by both the
textile and carpet industries, among other businesses. It is a wholly owned
subsidiary of BASF Corp. of the United States.
C. von Krafft, President
TOTAL REVENUE ($000)   481,522

BATON BROADCASTING INCORPORATED
See page 315 for a full company profile.

BATTLE CREEK DEVELOPMENTS LTD.
(Public)   OIL AND GAS PRODUCERS
Suite 1400, 300 - 5th Avenue S.W., Calgary, AB,
T2P 3C4   (403) 233-6400
BATTLE CREEK DEVELOPMENTS LTD. is involved in the acquisi-
tion, exploration and development of oil and gas properties.
Leslie C. Cole, President
TOTAL REVENUE ($000)   6,641

BC GAS INC.
See page 290 for a full company profile.

BC RAIL LTD.
(Public)   TRANSPORTATION
P.O. Box 8770, Vancouver, BC,
V6B 4X6   (604) 986-2012
BC RAIL LTD. is the operating arm of the British Columbia Railway
group of companies. BC Rail's principal sources of revenue are the
transport of forest industry related products and of coal from British
Columbia's northeastern coalfields.
David A. Jiles, Chairman
TOTAL REVENUE ($000)   327,897

BC SUGAR REFINERY, LIMITED
See page 156 for a full company profile.

BCE INC.
See page 291 for a full company profile.

BCE MOBILE COMMUNICATIONS INC.
See page 316 for a full company profile.

BEARCAT EXPLORATIONS LTD.
(Public)   OIL AND GAS PRODUCERS
Suite 1200, 520 - 5th Avenue S.W., Calgary, AB,
T2P 3R7   (403) 265-6161
BEARCAT EXPLORATIONS LTD. operates in the oil and gas industry in Canada and the United Kingdom. It also operates in the mining industry in Canada and the United States.
John W. McLeod, President
TOTAL REVENUE ($000)   446

BEATRICE FOODS INC.
(Private)   FOOD PROCESSING
295 The West Mall, Suite 600, Etobicoke, ON,
M9C 4Z4   (416) 626-5500
BEATRICE FOODS INC. is a dairy and food processing company with operations in Ontario, Quebec, Manitoba, Alberta and Saskatchewan. The company is 98.1% owned by Merrill Lynch Capital Partners of New York. The remaing 2% is owned by management.
Don McCarthy, Chairman, President & C.E.O.
TOTAL REVENUE ($000)   817,700

BEAU CANADA EXPLORATION LTD.
(Public)   OIL AND GAS PRODUCERS
Suite 700, 520 - 5th Avenue S.W., Calgary, AB,
T2P 3R7   (403) 266-2400
BEAU CANADA EXPLORATION LTD. is engaged in oil and gas production and drilling.
Thomas Bugg, President & C.E.O.
TOTAL REVENUE ($000)   10,541

BECHTEL CANADA INC.
(Private)   CONTRACTORS
10 Gateway Blvd., Suite 200, Don Mills, ON,
M3C 3N8   (416) 467-3100
BECHTEL CANADA INC. is involved in engineering, procurement, construction management and maintenance.
Rudy Ionides, President & C.E.O.
TOTAL REVENUE ($000)   891,652

BECKER MILK COMPANY LIMITED (THE)
(Public)   FOOD STORES
671 Warden Ave., Scarborough, ON, M1L 3Z7   (416) 698-2591
THE BECKER MILK COMPANY LIMITED operates convenience stores in Ontario, a portion of which are under franchise. The company processes milk and dairy products and has a fully automated blow-molding plant to manufacture plastic one, two and four litre milk jugs.
Frank A. Bazos, Chairman Of The Board
TOTAL REVENUE ($000)   431,195

BELL CANADA
(Public)   TELEPHONE UTILITIES
19th Floor, 1050 Beaver Hall Hill, Montreal, PQ,
H2Z 1S4   (514) 870-1511
BELL CANADA is engaged in the business of providing telecommunications services and equipment.

Raymond Cyr, Chairman
TOTAL REVENUE ($000)   7,904,500

BELMORAL MINES LTD.
See page 31 for a full company profile.

BEMA GOLD CORPORATION
See page 32 for a full company profile.

BENSON PETROLEUM LTD.
(Public)   OIL AND GAS PRODUCERS
Suite 1070, 521 - 3rd Avenue S.W., Calgary, AB,
T2P 3T3   (403) 269-5158
BENSON PETROLEUM LTD. is involved in oil and gas exploration and development. The company owns interests in producing oil and gas properties in Alberta, British Columbia and Columbia, South America.
Stephan V. Benediktson, President
TOTAL REVENUE ($000)   5,083

BENVEST CAPITAL INC.
(Public)   INVESTMENT COMPANIES AND FUNDS
1 Place Ville Marie, Suite 3230, Montreal, PQ,
H3B 3Y2   (514) 877-4299
BENVEST CAPITAL INC. is a merchant bank.
W. John Bennett, Chairman, President & C.E.O.
TOTAL REVENUE ($000)   647

BESTAR INC.
(Public)   HOME FURNISHINGS
4220 Rue Villeneuve, Lac-Megantic, PQ, G6B 2C3   (819) 583-1017
BESTAR manufactures ready-to-assemble furniture. It designs, manufactures and sells over 120 models of ready-to-assemble furniture used mainly as shelving for consumer electronics equipment. The company also designs, manufactures and sells juvenile furniture and home-office furniture.
Paulin Tardif, Chairman, President & C.E.O.
TOTAL REVENUE ($000)   20,340

BETHLEHEM RESOURCES CORPORATION
(Public)   PRECIOUS METALS
Suite 700, 815 West Hastings Street, Vancouver, BC,
V6C 1B4   (604) 687-7444
BETHLEHEM RESOURCES CORPORATION is engaged in the production of base metals and the mining, acquisition, exploration and development of base and precious metal properties in Canada and the western United States. The company is an operator of the copper-zinc Goldstream Mine located near Revelstoke, B.C.
Henry G. Ewanchuk, Chairman
TOTAL REVENUE ($000)   13,052

BF REALTY HOLDINGS LIMITED
See page 253 for a full company profile.

BGR PRECIOUS METALS INC.
See page 395 for a full company profile.

BICC CANADA INC.
(Private)   METAL FABRICATORS
300 Consilium Place, Suite 200, Scarborough, ON, M1H 3G2
BICC CANADA INC. includes the business of its main subsidiaries. These include: BICC Canada Holdings Inc., Balfour Beatty Canada Limited, and Phillips Cables Limited (81.2% interest).
TOTAL REVENUE ($000)   253,793

BIG V PHARMACIES CO. LIMITED
(Private)   SPECIALTY STORES
3 Buchanan Court, Box 5802, London, ON,
N6A 5G1   (519) 686-5081
BIG V PHARMACIES CO. LIMITED is an employee-owned retail pharmacy.
Norman Puhl, Chairman, President & C.E.O.
TOTAL REVENUE ($000)   430,700

BII ENTERPRISES INC.
(Public)   MISC. INDUSTRIAL PRODUCTS
5145 Steeles Avenue West, Weston, ON, M9L 1R5 (416) 749-7800
BII ENTERPRISES INC. manufactures and supplies a broad range of store fixtures and merchandising display products and provides fixturing services to the retail industry.
Milton Shier, Chairman & C.E.O.
TOTAL REVENUE ($000)   118,906

BIOCHEM PHARMA INC.
See page 191 for a full company profile.

BIOMIRA INC.
See page 192 for a full company profile.

BIONAIRE INC.
(Public)   MISC. CONSUMER PRODUCTS
2000 - 32nd Avenue, Lachine, PQ, H8T 3H7   (514) 636-0790
BIONAIRE INC. is involved in the design, manufacture and marketing of air and water treatment and purification products. Its products have been sold principally for home and office use, but it has also developed and is distributing products which have computer and industrial applications. Products are sold through the company's subsidiaries and independent distributors on a worldwide basis.
F. Ross Johnson, Chairman
TOTAL REVENUE ($000)   54,369

BIRD CONSTRUCTION COMPANY LIMITED
(Public)   CONTRACTORS
Suite 206, 5405 Eglinton Avenue West, Etobicoke, ON,
M9C 5K6   (416) 620-7122
BIRD CONSTRUCTION COMPANY LIMITED is engaged in construction on a contract basis in British Columbia, Alberta, Saskatchewan, Manitoba and Ontario, and is also involved in the selling of building supplies in Manitoba.
R.A. Bird, Chairman
TOTAL REVENUE ($000)   124,319

BITECH CORPORATION
(Public)   PRECIOUS METALS
Suite 200, 7030 Woodbine Avenue, Markham, ON,
L3R 6G2   (416) 415-1825
BITECH CORPORATION is primarily engaged in the development of natural gas and petroleum properties in Irkutsk Oblast, Russia. It has mineral properties in Newfoundland and Quebec. Bitech is also engaged in research & development work on the Angelov-Shibley solvent deasphalting process for heavy oil through its wholly owned subsidiary, Bitumen Development Corporation Ltd.
James Wade, President
TOTAL REVENUE ($000)   1

BLACK HAWK MINING INC.
(Public)   METAL MINES
Suite 600, 6 Adelaide Street East, Toronto, ON,
M5C 1H6   (416) 365-5656
BLACK HAWK MINING INC. is engaged in the exploration and development of mineral resource properties. The Knox nickel-cobalt-copper project located in the State of Maine is the company's most advanced project and is in the permitting and feasibility study stage. The Minago nickel project which is located in northern Manitoba is in the advanced exploration stage.
Gordon F. Bub, Chairman & C.E.O.
TOTAL REVENUE ($000)   48

BLUE RANGE RESOURCE CORPORATION
(Public)   OIL AND GAS PRODUCERS
Suite 905, 706 Seventh Avenue S.W., Calgary, AB,
T2P 0Z1   (403) 264-7422
BLUE RANGE RESOURCE CORPORATION is involved in the exploration, development, production, processing and marketing of natural gas and petroleum reserves in Canada.
Gary B. Unrau, President
TOTAL REVENUE ($000)   5,439

BMB COMPUSCIENCE CANADA LTD.
See page 463 for a full company profile.

BMTC GROUP INC.
(Public)   WHOLESALE DISTRIBUTORS
8500 Place Marien, Montreal-Est, PQ, H1B 5W8   (514) 648-5757
BMTC GROUP INC. is a holding company. Its subsidiary, Brault & Martineau Inc., retails furniture and appliances.
Yves Des Groseillers, Chairman, President & C.E.O.
TOTAL REVENUE ($000)   274,780

BNT LTD.
(Public)   INVESTMENT COMPANIES AND FUNDS
Suite 5000, P.O. Box 150, 1 First Canadian Place, Toronto, ON,
M5X 1H3   (416) 359-4630
BNT's only undertaking will be to invest its funds in BCE Inc. common shares. The purpose of the company is to provide a vehicle through which different investment objectives may be satisfied by holding BCE Inc. common shares.
Frederick J. Troop, President & C.E.O.
TOTAL REVENUE ($000)   10,331

BOMBARDIER INC.
See page 214 for a full company profile.

BONAR INC.
See page 245 for a full company profile.

BOUTIQUES SAN FRANCISCO INCORPOREES (LES)
(Public)   CLOTHING STORES
50 De Lauzon, Boucherville, PQ, J4B 1E6   (514) 449-1313
LES BOUTIQUES SAN FRANCISCO INCORPOREES is primarily involved in the retail sale of men's, women's, and children's clothing. Its target customers are fashion-conscious men, women, and children who wish to purchase reasonably priced good quality clothes.
Paul D. Roberge, President & C.E.O.
TOTAL REVENUE ($000)   72,920

BOVAR INC.
See page 486 for a full company profile.

BOW VALLEY ENERGY INC.
See page 69 for a full company profile.

BOWTEX ENERGY (CANADA) CORPORATION
(Public)   OIL AND GAS PRODUCERS
1100 Trimac House, 800 - 5th Avenue S.W., Calgary, AB,
T2P 3T6   (403) 531-1700
BOWTEX ENERGY is an independent Canadian controlled company engaged in the exploration and production of petroleum and natural gas reserves. Most of the company's Canadian activities are in Alberta. The company is represented in the U.S. by its wholly owned subsidiaries Strand Oil & Gas Inc. and Bowtex Energy, Inc.
Harold P. Milavsky, Chairman
TOTAL REVENUE ($000)   12,195

BPCO INC.
(Private)   MISC. INDUSTRIAL PRODUCTS
460 Hanlan Road, Suite 200, Woodbridge, ON,
L4L 3P6   (416) 856-6689
BPCO INC. is involved in the manufacturing and distribution of high quality building materials: roofing, vinyl siding, woodfibre ceiling tiles and structural products, windows and doors, insulation and flooring.
Douglas E. Speeks, President
TOTAL REVENUE ($000)   234,701

BRACKNELL CORPORATION
See page 487 for a full company profile.

BRAMALEA LIMITED
See page 254 for a full company profile.

BRAMPTON BRICK LIMITED
(Public)   MISC. INDUSTRIAL PRODUCTS
225 Wanless Drive, Brampton, ON, L7A 1E9   (416) 840-1011
BRAMPTON BRICK manufactures clay bricks and concrete blocks. The main operations are in Brampton. In addition, the company owns and operates a brick plant in the Quebec City area. The bricks are marketed mainly in Ontario, Quebec and the Atlantic provinces. Concrete blocks are marketed in Southern Ontario. The company's products are used in residential, institutional, commercial and industrial projects.
Jeffrey G. Kerbel, President & C.E.O.
TOTAL REVENUE ($000)   25,020

BRASCADE RESOURCES INC.
See page 438 for a full company profile.

BRASCAN LIMITED
See page 439 for a full company profile.

BREAKWATER RESOURCES LTD.
See page 33 for a full company profile.

BRENDA MINES LTD.
See page 5 for a full company profile.

BRIO INDUSTRIES INC.
(Public)   FOOD PROCESSING
Suite 110, 3728 North Fraser Way, Burnaby, BC,
V5J 5G1   (604) 436-5876
BRIO INDUSTRIES INC. holds the U.S. and Western European distribution rights to Clearly Canadian sparkling mineral water.
Terry Neild, Chairman & President
TOTAL REVENUE ($000)   7,524

BRISTOL-MYERS SQUIBB CANADA INC.
(Private)   MISC. CONSUMER PRODUCTS
111 Gordon Baker Road, Suite 700, Toronto, ON,
M2H 3R1   (416) 490-2800
BRISTOL-MYERS SQUIB CANADA INC. is a manufacturer and distributor of household products.
Gary Findlay, President
TOTAL REVENUE ($000)   469,496

BRITISH COLUMBIA FERRY CORPORATION
(Crown)   TRANSPORTATION
1112 Fort Street, Victoria, BC, V8V 4V2   (604) 381-1401
BRITISH COLUMBIA FERRY CORPORATION is a government of British Columbia crown corporation which operates coastal ferry services.
M. Headley, Chair of the Board
TOTAL REVENUE ($000)   284,791

BRITISH COLUMBIA HYDRO AND POWER AUTHORITY
(Crown)   ELECTRICAL UTILITIES
333 Dunsmuir Street, Vancouver, BC, V6B 5R3   (604) 623-4152
BRITISH COLUMBIA HYDRO AND POWER AUTHORITY is a provincial crown corporation which generates, transmits and distributes electricity to a service area which contains more than 90% of B.C.'s population.
J. Norman Olsen, Chairman
TOTAL REVENUE ($000)   2,371,000

BRITISH COLUMBIA PETROLEUM CORPORATION

(Crown) OIL AND GAS PRODUCERS
Suite 1650, Commerce Place, 400 Burrard Street, Vancouver, BC,
V6C 3A6 (604) 681-5395
BRITISH COLUMBIA PETROLEUM CORPORATION is responsible for monitoring the operations of the deregulated natural gas marketplace to ensure that the public interest is protected and that all participants in the marketplace are treated fairly. Administrative functions include: the issuing of acquisition orders, the issuing of findings of producer support, collection of data and collection of the levy.
William R. Strachan, Chairman
TOTAL REVENUE ($000) 49,142

BRITISH COLUMBIA RAILWAY COMPANY

(Crown) TRANSPORTATION
P.O. Box 8770, Vancouver, BC, V6B 4X6 (604) 986-2012
BRITISH COLUMBIA RAILWAY COMPANY is a provincial crown corporation which provides a fully-integrated rail freight service within B.C. One subsidiary, BCR Properties Ltd., owns and manages the group's non-operating real estate assets. The operating railway subsidiary, B.C. Rail Ltd., derives its revenue mainly from the transportation of forest products, coal, ore, petrochemicals and general freight.
David A. Jiles, Chairman
TOTAL REVENUE ($000) 330,235

BRITISH COLUMBIA SYSTEMS CORPORATION

(Crown) COMPUTER SOFTWARE & PROCESSING
4000 Seymour Place, Victoria, BC, V8X 4S8 (604) 389-3101
BRITISH COLUMBIA SYSTEMS CORPORATION, is a provincial crown corporation providing information technology services for the public sector. Created in 1977 with the enactment of the System Act, BC Systems offers data processing, professional staff services, data and voice communications and information access services.
T. Bulmer, Chairman
TOTAL REVENUE ($000) 171,636

BRITISH COLUMBIA TELEPHONE COMPANY

See page 292 for a full company profile.

BRITISH COLUMBIA TRANSIT

(Crown) TRANSPORTATION
Airport Square, 1200 West 73rd Avenue, Vancouver, BC,
V6P 6M2 (604) 264-5000
BRITISH COLUMBIA TRANSIT is a crown corporation that serves more than 2.8 million people throughout British Columbia. The corporation's 29 conventional transit systems, in greater Vancouver, greater Victoria and 27 communities across the province, carry 151 million passengers annually. The largest contributor to this total is the Vancouver Regional Transit System with 128 passengers.
Eric A. Denhoff, Chairman, Acting President & C.E.O.
TOTAL REVENUE ($000) 507,499

BRITISH GROUP HOLDINGS INC.

(Public) DEVELOPERS
15595 - 24th Avenue, Surrey, BC, V4A 2J4 (604) 536-4443
BRITISH GROUP HOLDINGS INC. is involved in land and real estate development.

Henry John Block, Chairman of the Board
TOTAL REVENUE ($000) 1,801

BRL ENTERPRISES INC.

See page 440 for a full company profile.

BRUNCOR INC.

See page 293 for a full company profile.

BRUNEAU MINERALS INC.

(Public) METAL MINES
1010 Sherbrooke Street West, Suite 1608, Montreal, PQ,
H3A 2R7 (514) 842-6684
BRUNEAU MINERALS is involved in the acquisition, exploration and development of mineral properties.
Jean-Guy Masse, President
TOTAL REVENUE ($000) (6)

BRUNSWICK MINING AND SMELTING CORPORATION LIMITED

See page 6 for a full company profile.

BT BANK OF CANADA

(Private) BANKS
P.O. Box 100, 17th Floor, North Tower, Royal Bank Plaza, Toronto,
ON, M5J 2J2 (416) 865-0770
BT BANK OF CANADA is a commercial bank which provides specialized financial services in selected markets. The company carries on its banking operations through three major working groups: a capital markets group; a fixed income group and; a treasury group.
Richard Marin, Chairman, C.E.O. & President
TOTAL REVENUE ($000) 40,823

BUDD CANADA INC.

See page 183 for a full company profile.

BURNS FOODS (1985) LIMITED

(Private) FOOD PROCESSING
Box 2520, Station M, Calgary, AB, T2P 3X4 (403) 265-8140
BURNS FOODS (1985) LIMITED is engaged in food processing and distributing.
R.J.E. Child, Chairman
TOTAL REVENUE ($000) 670,000

BURNS FRY HOLDINGS CORPORATION

(Private) INVESTMENT HOUSES
Suite 5000, P.O. Box 150, 1 First Canadian Place, Toronto, ON,
M5X 1H3 (416) 359-4000
BURNS FRY HOLDINGS CORPORATION owns 100% of Burns Fry Limited, a full service investment banking and securities dealing firm.
Richard J. Lawrence, Chairman
TOTAL REVENUE ($000) 386,207

C CORP. INC.

(Private) FOOD STORES
3100 Cote-Vertu, Ville Saint-Laurent, PQ, H4R 2J8 (514) 333-5110

C CORP. INC. is a franchisor of five convenience store chains in Quebec, Ontario and Alberta, under the names Provi-Soir, Pinto, Red Rooster, Winks and Winks Express. The company is also involved in the wholesale and retail sale of petroleum products.
Jean Bernier, President
TOTAL REVENUE ($000)   401,374

C.A.M.S. TERRES NOIRES LTEE
(Public)   WHOLESALE DISTRIBUTORS
219 Rang St-Louis, Sherrington, PQ, J0L 2N0   (514) 454-4621
C.A.M.S. TERRES NOIRES LTEE is engaged in agricultural production and the production of distribution of fruits and vegetables.
Benoit Subtil, Pres. & Chef De La Direction
TOTAL REVENUE ($000)   14,718

C-MAC INDUSTRIES INC.
(Public)   ELECTRICAL & ELECTRONIC
3000 Industrial Boulevard, Sherbrooke, PQ, J1L 1V8 (819) 821-4524
C-MAC INDUSTRIES INC. is a microelectronics manufacturer. The company operates in Canada, the United States and England. It manufactures electronic components and backpanels - mounting electronic components on printed circuits and inspecting sophisticated electronic components on printed circuit boards.
Dennis Wood, President & C.E.O.
TOTAL REVENUE ($000)   118,338

CABANO TRANSPORTATION GROUP INC.
(Public)   TRANSPORTATION
6600 Chemin St-Francois, St-Laurent, PQ, H4S 1B7 (514) 332-4341
CABANO TRANSPORTATION GROUP INC., through its subsidiaries, carries on its operations in the areas of general transport and specialized transport of both short and long distances in Ontario, Quebec, the Atlantic provinces and the United States.
J. Norman Morrisson, Chairman & C.E.O.
TOTAL REVENUE ($000)   129,130

CABRE EXPLORATION LTD.
See page 70 for a full company profile.

CAE INDUSTRIES LTD.
See page 215 for a full company profile.

CAISSE CENTRALE DESJARDINS DU QUEBEC (LA)
(Fin. Co-op)   CREDIT UNIONS
1 Complexe Desjardins, Suite 2822, Montreal, PQ,
H5B 1B3   (514) 281-7070
The CAISSE CENTRALE has a threefold mandate. Its primary mandate is to act as financial agent within the Desjardins Group. Increasing and diversifying sources of funds and income needed to fulfill its role in the Desjardins Group and to insure its own group is the second mandate of the Caisse. Its third mandate is to participate in the development of services offered by the Group to large companies.
Claude Beland, Chairman, President & C.E.O.
TOTAL REVENUE ($000)   429,671

CAISSE DE DEPOT ET PLACEMENT DU QUEBEC
(Crown)   INVESTMENT COMPANIES AND FUNDS
1981 Avenue McGill College, Montreal, PQ,
H3A 3C7   (514) 842-3261
The CAISSE is a public pension and insurance fund manager. Its dual mandate consists in achieving an optimal financial return and in contributing through its actions to the dynamism of the Quebec economy, while ensuring the security of capital under its management.
Jean-Claude Delorme, Chairman of the Board
TOTAL REVENUE ($000)   3,290,000

CALDWELL PARTNERS INTERNATIONAL INC. (THE)
(Public)   CONSULTING
64 Prince Arthur Avenue, Toronto, ON, M5R 1B4   (416) 920-7702
CALDWELL PARTNERS INTERNATIONAL INC. is an executive search consulting firm specializing in the recruitment of executives on behalf of its clients. The firm's clients include a broad range of business enterprises, public and private institutions, governments and governmental agencies.
C. Douglas Caldwell, Chairman & Managing Director
TOTAL REVENUE ($000)   9,011

CALEDONIA MINING CORPORATION
(Public)   PRECIOUS METALS
Suite 1, 1775 Meyerside Drive, Mississauga, ON,
L5T 1E2   (416) 564-5213
CALEDONIA MINING CORPORATION is a mining and investment company.
D.S. MacLeod, Chairman & President
TOTAL REVENUE ($000)   1,543

CALGARY CO-OPERATIVE ASSOCIATION LIMITED
(Non-fin Co-op)   DEPARTMENT STORES
8818 Macleod Trail S.E., Calgary, AB, T2H 0M5   (403) 253-0345
CALGARY CO-OPERATIVE ASSOCIATION LIMITED is a consumer cooperative. It operates 14 one-stop shopping centres, which retail food, drugs, petroleum, hardware, dry goods and services. In addition, the co-op has four home improvement centres, a farm service centre, a prefab plant and travel services with four offices.
Bruno A. Friesen, Chairman Of The Board
TOTAL REVENUE ($000)   525,322

CAM-NET COMMUNICATIONS NETWORK INC.
(Public)   TELECOMMUNICATIONS
Suite 700, 885 Dunsmuir Street, Vancouver, BC,
V6C 1N5   (604) 684-9016
CAM-NET COMMUNICATIONS NETWORK INC., through its subsidiaries, provides alternative long distance voice and data telecommunication services to business and residential customers in the provinces of B.C., Ontario and Quebec. The company also provides private long distance telecommunication services to business customers in Calgary, Alberta.
Robert E. Moore, Chairman & C.E.O.
TOTAL REVENUE ($000)   4,687

CAMBIOR INC.
See page 34 for a full company profile.

CAMBRIDGE SHOPPING CENTRES LIMITED
See page 255 for a full company profile.

CAMCO INC.
See page 173 for a full company profile.

CAMDEV CORPORATION
See page 256 for a full company profile.

CAMECO CORPORATION
See page 7 for a full company profile.

CAMPBELL RESOURCES INC.
See page 35 for a full company profile.

CAMPBELL SOUP COMPANY LTD
(Private)   FOOD PROCESSING
60 Birmingham Street, Toronto, ON, M8V 2B8   (416) 251-1131
CAMPBELL SOUP CO. LTD. is engaged in the manufacture of convenience foods such as soups, frozen meals and desserts, juices, sauces and condiments. Its brand names include Campbell's, Le Menu, Swanson, Pepperidge Farm, Prego, A1, Franco American, V-8, and Habitant. The company is wholly owned by Campbell Soup Co. of the United States.
H.M. Baumnstock, Chairman
TOTAL REVENUE ($000)   432,294

CANADA DEPOSIT INSURANCE CORPORATION
(Crown)   INSURANCE - PROPERTY & CASUALTY
1707 - 50 O'Connor St., P.O. Box 2340, Station D, Ottawa, ON,
K1P 5W5   (613) 996-2081
CANADA DEPOSIT INSURANCE CORPORATION is a crown corporation. The objects of the corporation are to provide insurance against the loss of part or all of deposits, to be instrumental in the promotion of standards of sound business and financial practices for member institutions, and to promote and otherwise contribute to the stabilityand competitiveness of the financial system in Canada.
G.L. Reuber, Chairman
TOTAL REVENUE ($000)   308,837

CANADA DEVELOPMENT INVESTMENT CORPORATION
(Crown)   MANAGEMENT AND DIVERSIFIED
Scotia Plaza, Suite 2703, P.O. Box 320, 40 King Street West,
Toronto, ON, M5H 3Y2   (416) 864-0333
CANADA DEVELOPMENT INVESTMENT CORPORATION is a federal crown corporation which is responsible for the divestiture of corporate interests of the crown. It also manages federal shares in mixed ownership enterprises for which divestiture is the ultimate objective, but which may require commercial strengthening before the federal shares can be sold.
Patrick J. Keenan, Chairman
TOTAL REVENUE ($000)   30,897

CANADA LIFE ASSURANCE COMPANY (THE)
(Private)   INSURANCE - LIFE
330 University Avenue, Toronto, ON, M5G 1R8   (416) 597-1456

THE CANADA LIFE ASSURANCE COMPANY is involved in financial protection in the event of certain risks icluding life, medical, dental, disability and general insurance. It accumulates assets in the form of annuity, pension and investment products. It is also involved in financial and investment management.
E.H. Crawford, Chairman
TOTAL REVENUE ($000)   3,911,719

CANADA MALTING CO. LIMITED
See page 157 for a full company profile.

CANADA MORTGAGE AND HOUSING CORPORATION
(Crown)   FINANCE AND LEASING
National Office, 682 Montreal Road, Ottawa, ON,
K1A 0P7   (613) 748-2000
CANADA MORTGAGE AND HOUSING is a crown corporation with the authority to act for the Government of Canada in all matters prescribed by housing legislation, principally the National Housing Act. CMHC's purpose, as embodied in the National Housing Act is, to promote the construction of new houses, the repair and modernization of existing housing, and the improvement of housing and living conditions.
Claude F. Bennett, Chairman Of The Board
TOTAL REVENUE ($000)   1,115,352

CANADA PORTS CORPORATION
(Crown)   TRANSPORTATION
99 Metcalfe Street, 8th Floor, Ottawa, ON, K1A 0N6 (613) 957-6787
CANADA PORTS CORPORATION describes a federal system of ports administered pursuant to the Canada Ports Corporation Act. The corporation handles nearly half of the overall Canadian port traffic and more than 95% of container traffic.
William Marsh, Acting Chairman Of The Board
TOTAL REVENUE ($000)   56,298

CANADA POST CORPORATION
(Crown)   OTHER SERVICES
Confederation Heights, 720 Heron Road, Ottawa, ON,
K1A 0B1   (613) 734-8440
CANADA POST CORPORATION is a Canadian company meeting the advertising, communications and physical distribution needs of Canadian and international customers.
Donald H. Lander, Chairman & C.E.O.
TOTAL REVENUE ($000)   3,872,759

CANADA SAFEWAY LIMITED
(Private)   FOOD STORES
47th Floor, 150-6th Ave S.W., Calgary, AB, T2P 2J6 (403) 260-8600
CANADA SAFEWAY LIMITED operates in the food industry. The company's retail stores are located in Western Canada and Ontario.
R.H. Kinnie, Chairman & C.E.O.
TOTAL REVENUE ($000)   4,360,400

CANADA SOUTHERN PETROLEUM LTD.
See page 71 for a full company profile.

CANADA STARCH COMPANY (1990) INC.
(Private)   FOOD PROCESSING
401 The West Mall, Etobicoke, ON, M9C 5H9   (416) 620-2300

CANADA STARCH COMPANY (1990) INC., manufactures industrial starches and sweetners and consumer food products. Its parent company is CPC International Inc., of Englewood Cliffs, New Jersey .
D.B. Macnaughton, Chairman
TOTAL REVENUE ($000)   396,433

CANADA TRUST INCOME INVESTMENTS
See page 396 for a full company profile.

CANADA TRUSTCO MORTGAGE COMPANY
See page 380 for a full company profile.

CANADA TUNGSTEN INC.
See page 8 for a full company profile.

CANADEX RESOURCES LIMITED
(Public)   TRANSPORTATION
10 Sun Pac Boulevard, Brampton, ON, L6S 4R5   (800) 265-6942
CANADEX RESOURCES is involved in the acquisition, exploration and development of oil and gas and natural resource properties. As well the company is involved in car and truck leasing and school bus operations.
J.A. Riddell, President
TOTAL REVENUE ($000)   10,148

CANADIAN 88 ENERGY CORP.
(Public)   OIL AND GAS PRODUCERS
Canterra Tower, Suite 700, 400 - 3rd Avenue S.W., Calgary, AB,
T2P 4H2   (403) 974-8800
CANADIAN 88 ENERGY CORP. is involved in the pursuit of diversified developments and business opportunities in the areas of oil and gas exploration, gas plants, refining and petrochemical development throughout Western Canada through its wholly owned subsidiaries.
Greg S. Noval, President
TOTAL REVENUE ($000)   2,889

CANADIAN BROADCASTING CORPORATION
(Crown)   BROADCASTING
P.O. Box 8478, 1500 Bronson Avenue, Ottawa, ON,
K1G 3J5   (613) 724-1200
CBC's objective is to develop and provide a national broadcasting service for all Canadians in both official languages, in television and radio, and to provide an international service. Both services should be primarily Canadian in content and character.
Patrick Watson, Chairman
TOTAL REVENUE ($000)   392,440

CANADIAN CO-OPERATIVE WOOL GROWERS LIMITED
(Non-fin Co-op)   WHOLESALE DISTRIBUTORS
Box 130, Carleton Place, ON, K7C 3P3   (613) 257-2714
CANADIAN CO-OPERATIVE WOOL GROWERS are involved in wool marketing, retail clothing, and animal health products and equipment.
Lloyd Ayre, President
TOTAL REVENUE ($000)   2,506

CANADIAN COMMERCIAL CORPORATION
(Crown)   OTHER SERVICES
Metropolitan Centre, 11th Floor, 50 O'Connor Street, Ottawa, ON,
K1A 0S6   (613) 996-0034
CANADIAN COMMERCIAL's objectives are: to provide a government-to-government export contracting service to the private and public sectors in Canada; and to provide a contract management service to foreign governmental customers in order to ensure their satisfaction as to the quality, cost and delivery of Canadian goods and services.
Ruth Hubbard, President
TOTAL REVENUE ($000)   761,629

CANADIAN CONQUEST EXPLORATION INC.
(Public)   OIL AND GAS PRODUCERS
Suite 1100, 736 - 8th Avenue S.W., Calgary, AB,
T2P 1H4   (403) 261-4871
CANADIAN CONQUEST EXPLORATION INC. is an oil and gas company headquartered in Calgary, Alberta. It focuses its operations and those of its wholly owned subsidiary, Universal Explorations Ltd., on the exploration and development of petroleum and natural gas reserves in Alberta and Saskatchewan.
Peter C. Forbes, Chairman
TOTAL REVENUE ($000)   8,891

CANADIAN DAIRY COMMISSION (THE)
(Crown)   AGRICULTURE
2197 Riverside Drive, Ottawa, ON, K1A 0Z2   (613) 998-9490
THE CANADIAN DAIRY COMMISSION has the authority to purchase, store, process, or dispose of dairy products; make payments to milk and cream producers for the purpose of stabilizing the price of industrial milk and cream; investigate matters relating to the production, processing or marketing of any dairy product; help promote the use of dairy products; and receive funds for the disposal of dairy products.
Roch Morin, Chairman & C.E.O.
TOTAL REVENUE ($000)   465,284

CANADIAN FILM DEVELOPMENT CORPORATION
(Crown)   FINANCE AND LEASING
Tour de La Banque Nationale, 600, De La Gauchetiere Ouest, 14e
Etage, Montreal, PQ, H3B 4L8   (514) 283-6363
CANADIAN FILM DEVELOPMENT CORP. was established with the objective of fostering and promoting the development of a feature film industry in Canada
Harvey A. Corn, Chairman
TOTAL REVENUE ($000)   879

CANADIAN FOREMOST LTD.
(Public)   TRANSPORTATION EQUIP & COMPNTS
1616 Meridian Road N.E., Calgary, AB, T2A 2P1   (403) 272-3322
CANADIAN FOREMOST LTD. specializes in the design, manufacture and sales of high-mobility all-terrain vehicles, mineral exploration drilling equipment and associated parts and service, and most recentlythe energy services business. It serves a broad range of global market segments, including oil and gas, utilities, mineral exploration, defense, environmental protection and frontier development.
J.H. Nodwell, Chairman & C.E.O.
TOTAL REVENUE ($000)   18,970

CANADIAN FROBISHER RESOURCES LTD.
(Public)   OIL AND GAS PRODUCERS
Suite 2100, 144 - 4th Avenue S.W., Calgary, AB,
T2P 3N4   (403) 265-0270
CANADIAN FROBISHER RESOURCES LTD. is involved in the
acquisition, exploration and development of oil and natural gas proper-
ties.
Robert W. Lamond, President
TOTAL REVENUE ($000)   3,695

CANADIAN GENERAL INVESTMENTS LIMITED
See page 397 for a full company profile.

CANADIAN HOME SHOPPING NETWORK (CHSN) LTD.
(Public)   SPECIALTY STORES
1400 Castlefield Avenue, Toronto, ON, M6B 4H8   (416) 785-3500
CANADIAN HOME SHOPPING NETWORK (CHSN) LTD. is a retail
merchandiser that markets a variety of consumer products in Canada by
means of a live, televised, shop-at-home service delivered via satellite to
cable television subscribers.
Edward S. Rogers, Chairman Of The Board
TOTAL REVENUE ($000)   48,057

CANADIAN HYDRO DEVELOPERS, INC.
(Public)   OIL AND GAS PRODUCERS
Suite 1204, 333 - 7th Avenue. S.W., Calgary, AB,
T2P 2Z1   (403) 269-9379
CANADIAN HYDRO DEVELOPERS, INC. is a developer of private
hydroelectric power projects.
Jack D. McCleary, President
TOTAL REVENUE ($000)   1,160

CANADIAN IMPERIAL BANK OF COMMERCE
See page 381 for a full company profile.

CANADIAN JOREX LIMITED
(Public)   OIL AND GAS PRODUCERS
2870 Bow Valley Square IV, 250 - 6th Avenue S.W., Calgary, AB,
T2P 3H7   (403) 266-0930
CANADIAN JOREX LIMITED is involved in oil and gas exploration
and production. The company's areas of major interest are Sylvan Lake,
Alberta, Thorsby, Alberta and Farrow, Alberta.
Louis J. Schneider, President & C.E.O.
TOTAL REVENUE ($000)   8,099

CANADIAN LIQUID AIR LTD.
(Private)   MISC. INDUSTRIAL PRODUCTS
1155 Sherbrooke St. W., Montreal, PQ, H3A 2N3   (514) 842-5431
CANADIAN LIQUID AIR LTD. is a producer and marketer of industrial, medical and specialty gases and welding equipment. It is a member
of the Air Liquide group of companies which operates in 58 countries on
five continents and is headed by L'Air Liquide S.A. of France.
Mr. John W. McGill, President & C.E.O.
TOTAL REVENUE ($000)   300,100

CANADIAN MANOIR INDUSTRIES LIMITED
See page 174 for a full company profile.

CANADIAN MAPLE LEAF FINANCIAL CORPORATION INC.
(Public)   INVESTMENT COMPANIES AND FUNDS
Suite 850, 999 West Hastings Street, Vancouver, BC,
V6C 2W2   (604) 684-7411
CANADIAN MAPLE LEAF FINANCIAL CORPORATION is a spe-
cialist corporate finance company. Its operational focus is high growth
mid-market investment and investment management. The company has
extensive experience in Western Canada and the Pacific Rim.
Steven Funk, Chariman & C.E.O.
TOTAL REVENUE ($000)   3,268

CANADIAN MARCONI COMPANY
See page 216 for a full company profile.

CANADIAN NATIONAL RAILWAY SYSTEM
(Crown)   TRANSPORTATION
935 De La Gauchetiere W., Montreal, PQ, H3B 2M9 (514) 399-5430
CANADIAN NATIONAL RAILWAY is a federal crown corporation
engaged primarily in railway transportation and distribution. The major
activity of the company, rail transportation, is conducted across Canada
and the United States. Other operating divisions encompass real estate
and international consulting.
Brian R.D. Smith, Chairman
TOTAL REVENUE ($000)   4,069,550

CANADIAN NATURAL RESOURCES LIMITED
See page 72 for a full company profile.

CANADIAN NEWSCOPE RESOURCES LTD.
(Public)   OIL AND GAS PRODUCERS
Suite 2999, 300 - 5th Avenue S.W., Calgary, AB,
T2P 3C4   (403) 266-1101
CANADIAN NEWSCOPE RESOURCES LTD. is a junior publicly
traded natural resource company with interests primarily in Alberta,
southeastern Saskatchewan, Texas, Louisiana and Mississippi.
Wieland F. Wettstein, Chairman
TOTAL REVENUE ($000)   2,995

CANADIAN NORTHSTAR CORPORATION
(Public)   OIL AND GAS PRODUCERS
Suite 300, 535 - 7th Avenue S.W., Calgary, AB,
T2P 0Y4   (403) 298-0500
CANADIAN NORTHSTAR CORP. is a diversified investment com-
pany headquartered in Calgary, Alberta. The company is active in
merchant banking and investment activities in Canada, with a significant
emphasis in the western Canadian energy sector.
John A. Hagg, Chairman
TOTAL REVENUE ($000)   12,650

CANADIAN OCCIDENTAL PETROLEUM LTD.
See page 73 for a full company profile.

CANADIAN PACIFIC EXPRESS & TRANSPORT LTD.
(Private)   TRANSPORTATION
2255 Sheppard Ave. E., Willowdale, ON, M2J 4Y1   (416) 497-7900

CANADIAN PACIFIC EXPRESS & TRANSPORT LTD. carries on the trucking services of Canadian Pacific Limited, operating as CP Trucks. It provides truckload and less-than-truckload freight service, primarily in Canada. CP Trucks operates in 143 locations in Canada. Its fleet consists of 1,200 trucks, 3,300 highway trailers and 1,000 tractors. About 43% of 1992 revenues were generated in Ontario.
Mr. Ralph Teoli, President & C.E.O.
TOTAL REVENUE ($000)   419,500

CANADIAN PACIFIC FOREST PRODUCTS LIMITED
See page 134 for a full company profile.

CANADIAN PACIFIC HOTELS & RESORTS INC.
(Private)   LODGING
One University Avenue, Suite 1400, Toronto, ON,
M5J 2P1   (416) 367-7111
CANADIAN PACIFIC HOTELS operates over 80 hotels, which it owns, leases, or manages. Hotels are located in city centre and resort locations across Canada and the United States.
Robert S. Demone, Chairman, President & C.E.O.
TOTAL REVENUE ($000)   463,140

CANADIAN PACIFIC LIMITED
See page 441 for a full company profile.

CANADIAN PIONEER ENERGY INC.
(Public)   OIL AND GAS PRODUCERS
Suite 3750, 205 - 5th Avenue S.W., Calgary, AB,
T2P 2V7   (403) 265-9471
CANADIAN PIONEER ENERGY INC. is involved in the acquisition, exploration, development and production of hydrocardon reserves in Canada.
James W. Beckerleg, Chairman
TOTAL REVENUE ($000)   4,288

CANADIAN REYNOLDS METALS COMPANY LIMITED
(Private)   METAL FABRICATORS
Room 802, 1420 Sherbrooke St. W., Montreal, PQ,
H3G 1K9   (514) 842-6487
CANADIAN REYNOLDS METALS COMPANY is a producer of primary aluminium and fabricated finished and semi-finished aluminium products. The company is a wholly owned subsidiary of Reynolds Metals Company of Richmond, Virginia.
William O. Bourke, Chairman & C.E.O.
TOTAL REVENUE ($000)   779,065

CANADIAN ROXY PETROLEUM LTD.
See page 74 for a full company profile.

CANADIAN SALT COMPANY LIMITED (THE)
(Private)   OTHER MINES
755 St. Johns Road, Pointe Claire, PQ, H9R 5M9   (514) 630-0900
CANADIAN SALT COMPANY LIMITED is engaged in the mining of rock salt, which it markets under the Windsor brand name.
William E. Johnston, President
TOTAL REVENUE ($000)   168,312

CANADIAN SATELLITE COMMUNICATIONS INC.
See page 317 for a full company profile.

CANADIAN STRATEGIC HOLDINGS LTD.
(Public)   ELECTRICAL & ELECTRONIC
Suite 1408, 925 West Georgia Street, Vancouver, BC,
V6C 3L2   (604) 685-0448
CANADIAN STRATEGIC HOLDINGS LTD. is involved in the semi-conductor industry.
A.M. Garcia, Chairman
TOTAL REVENUE ($000)   13,563

CANADIAN TIRE CORPORATION, LIMITED
See page 353 for a full company profile.

CANADIAN TURBO INC.
(Private)   INTEGRATED OILS
815 - 8th Avenue S.W., Calgary, AB, T2P 3P2   (403) 294-6400
CANADIAN TURBO INC. owns and operates a crude oil refinery near Calgary. The company markets petroleum products under the brand name Turbo through marketing outlets in Western Canada.
Eric S. Sprott, Chairman, President & C.E.O.
TOTAL REVENUE ($000)   376,148

CANADIAN ULTRAMAR LIMITED
(Private)   INTEGRATED OILS
1356 Pleasant Street, Eastern Passage, NS,
B2Y 3Y9   (902) 465-6340
CANADIAN ULTRAMAR LTD. through its wholly owned subsidiary is engaged in petroleum refining and marketing.
Garry Garcin, Senior Vice President
TOTAL REVENUE ($000)   1,472,154 (US)

CANADIAN UTILITIES LIMITED
See page 294 for a full company profile.

CANADIAN WESTERN BANK
(Public)   BANKS
Suite 2300, 10303 - Jasper Avenue, Edmonton, AB,
T5J 3X6   (403) 423-8888
CANADIAN WESTERN BANK provides loan and deposit services for individuals and business customers. The bank was formed by the amalgamation of Bank of Alberta and Western Pacific Bank on April 29, 1988.
Jack C. Donald, Chairman
TOTAL REVENUE ($000)   50,267

CANADIAN WESTERN NATURAL GAS COMPANY LIMITED
See page 295 for a full company profile.

CANAM MANAC GROUP INC. (THE)
See page 199 for a full company profile.

CANBRA FOODS LTD.

(Public) FOOD PROCESSING
2415 - 2nd Avenue A. North, Lethbridge, AB,
T1H 0G7 (403) 329-5500
CANBRA FOODS LTD. is a fully-integrated company engaged in the edible oil industry. Canola seed is separated into vegetable oil and protein meal for sale in domestic and export markets. Canbra also processes other oils and animal fats into salad oils, margarine or shortening basestocks. These products are sold to end-user manufacturers or packaged for sale to food retailers or to the foodservice industry.
Robert A. Wisener, Chairman
TOTAL REVENUE ($000) 106,730

CANCAPITAL CORPORATION

See page 442 for a full company profile.

CANFOR CORPORATION

See page 135 for a full company profile.

CANGENE CORPORATION

(Public) BIOTECHNOLOGY & PHARMACEUTICALS
3403 American Drive, Mississauga, ON,
L4V 1T4 (416) 673-0200
CANGENE CORPORATION is a biotechnology company involved in the commercialization of innovative technology, discovered and developed at Cangene, in the field of diagnostics and therapeutics.
Eric James, Chairman, C.E.O.
TOTAL REVENUE ($000) 2,712

CANLAN INVESTMENT CORPORATION

(Public) DEVELOPERS
Suite 1180, 1333 West Broadway, Vancouver, BC,
V6H 4C1 (604) 736-9152
CANLAN INVESTMENT CORPORATION is an investment company which generates its revenue primarily from land development. The company's investments consist primarily of a revenue property portfolio.
John B. Ross, President & C.E.O.
TOTAL REVENUE ($000) 33,862

CANON CANADA INC.

(Private) WHOLESALE DISTRIBUTORS
6390 Dixie Road, Mississauga, ON, L5T 1P7 (416) 795-1111
CANON CANADA INC. is engaged in sales and distribution of photographic products, business products, broadcast TV lenses, medical and X-ray equipment. Canon Canada is wholly owned by Canon U.S.A. Inc.
H. Murase, Chairman
TOTAL REVENUE ($000) 452,995

CANPOTEX LIMITED

(Private) WHOLESALE DISTRIBUTORS
Suite 400, 111 Second Ave. South, P.O. Box 1600, Saskatoon, SK,
S7K 3R7 (306) 931-2200
CANPOTEX LTD. is engaged in the export marketing of potash.
Glen Shields, Treasurer
TOTAL REVENUE ($000) 412,350 (US)

CANSTAR SPORTS INC.

See page 175 for a full company profile.

CANTOL LIMITEE - CANTOL LIMITED

(Public) CHEMICALS
199 Steelcase Rd. W., Markham, ON, L3R 2M4 (416) 475-6141
CANTOL LIMITEE - CANTOL LIMITED is engaged in the industrial chemicals industry in Canada and the United States. Sales to the United States market constitute over half of the total revenue generated by the Company.
Simms Shuber, President
TOTAL REVENUE ($000) 7,675

CANUTILITIES HOLDINGS LTD.

(Public) ELECTRICAL UTILITIES
1600 Canadian Western Centre, 909 - 11th Avenue S.W., Calgary,
AB, T2R 1N6 (403) 292-7550
CANUTILITIES HOLDINGS LTD. is a single purpose holding company which owns controlling shares in Canadian Utilities Limited and ATCOR Resources Ltd.
Ronald D. Southern, Chairman, President & C.E.O.
TOTAL REVENUE ($000) 1,375,378

CANWEST GAS SUPPLY INC.

(Private) WHOLESALE DISTRIBUTORS
1285 West Pender Street, Seventh Floor, Vancouver, BC,
V6E 4B1 (604) 661-3321
CANWEST GAS SUPPLY INC., is a marketing company that purchases natural gas primarily in British Columbia, and markets gas throughout B.C., Central Canada and the U.S. CanWest is owned by a group of natural gas producers who hold long term natural gas sales contracts with the company and who have subscribed for shares in the company.
John Anthony, President & C.E.O.
TOTAL REVENUE ($000) 378,377

CANWEST GLOBAL COMMUNICATIONS CORP.

See page 318 for a full company profile.

CANWEST TRUSTCO LIMITED

(Public) INVESTMENT COMPANIES AND FUNDS
One Lombard Place, Suite 600, Winnipeg, MB,
R3B 0X3 (204) 956-2025
CANWEST TRUSTCO LIMITED owns CanWest Trust Company, which operates as a federally chartered trust company in Manitoba, Alberta, Saskatchewan and British Columbia.
Israel Asper, Chairman Of The Board
TOTAL REVENUE ($000) 1,718

CAPE BRETON DEVELOPMENT CORPORATION

(Crown) NON-BASE METAL MINING
P.O. Box 2500, Sydney, NS, B1P 6K9 (902) 842-2848
CAPE BRETON DEVELOPMENT CORPORATION is a federal crown corporation. It operates two coal mines, Prince Colliery and Phalen Colliery and is the largest coal producer in eastern Canada.
M.H. Cochrane, Chairman Of The Board
TOTAL REVENUE ($000) 254,625

Canada Company Handbook

CAPILANO INTERNATIONAL INC.
(Public)   OIL AND GAS FIELD SERVICES
Suite 2615, 22nd Street N.E., Calgary, AB, T2E 7L9 (403) 250-9520
CAPILANO INTERNATIONAL INC. is a Canadian-owned geophysical service company.
M.V. Little, President & C.E.O.
TOTAL REVENUE ($000)   16,944

CAPITAL CITY SAVINGS & CREDIT UNION LTD.
(Fin. Co-op)   CREDIT UNIONS
8723 - 82nd Avenue, Suite 300, Edmonton, AB,
T6C 0Y9   (403) 496-2000
CAPITAL CITY SAVINGS & CREDIT UNION LTD. is a full service credit union.
Ernie Jacobson, Chairman
TOTAL REVENUE ($000)   69,380

CARA OPERATIONS LIMITED
See page 354 for a full company profile.

CARENA DEVELOPMENTS
See page 257 for a full company profile.

CARGILL LIMITED
(Private)   WHOLESALE DISTRIBUTORS
300-240, Graham Avenue, P.O. Box 5900, Winnipeg, MB,
R3C 4C5   (204) 947-0141
CARGILL LIMITED, is an agricultural based company which owns country grain elevators, feed, seed, fertilizer, beef processing and grain terminal facilities in seven provinces. Cargill is a wholly owned subsidiary of Cargill Incorporated of Minneapolis, Minnesota.
K.L. Hawkins, President
TOTAL REVENUE ($000)   1,719,012

CARLSON MARKETING GROUP LTD.
(Private)   OTHER SERVICES
3300 Bloor Street West, Centre Tower, Suite 1400, Toronto, ON,
M8X 2Y2   (416) 236-1991
CARLSON MARKETING GROUP LTD. is a leading full service incentive marketing and promotions company. It develops marketing incentive campaigns, group travel, event marketing, direct marketing such as credit card protection, consumer promotions, retail vacation and corporate travel through P. Lawson Travel.
Curtis L. Carlson, Chairman
TOTAL REVENUE ($000)   491,000

CASCADES INC.
See page 136 for a full company profile.

CASCADES PAPERBOARD INTERNATIONAL INC.
(Public)   PACKAGING AND CONTAINERS
Suite 3625, 1 Place Ville Marie, Montreal, PQ,
H3B 4M7   (514) 393-4160
CASCADES PAPERBOARD INTERNATIONAL INC. is involved in the manufacturing of paperboard, principally from recyclable paper, and in the production of folding cartons and corrugated containers.

Laurent Lemaire, Chairman & C.E.O.
TOTAL REVENUE ($000)   435,573

CASSIDY'S LTD.
(Public)   WHOLESALE DISTRIBUTORS
95 Eastside Drive, Toronto, ON, M8Z 5N7   (416) 231-1222
CASSIDY'S LTD. is engaged in the distribution of hospital, hotel and restaurant equipment, giftware and floor coverings. Operations of the company are conducted in Canada with a small percentage of distribution in the United States. The company is represented in every province except Saskatchewan, Manitoba and Prince Edward Island.
A.T. Brodeur, Chairman of the Board
TOTAL REVENUE ($000)   103,197

CATERPILLAR OF CANADA LTD.
(Private)   MACHINERY
1550 Caterpillar Road, Mississauga, ON, L4X 1E7 (416) 273-3495
CATERPILLAR OF CANADA LTD. is a manufacturer of heavy equipment. Its products include wheel loaders, log skidders, diesel electric generator sets and integrated tool carriers. The company also operates a lift truck distribution centre and replacement parts depot. Caterpillar of Canada is a wholly owned subsidiary of Caterpillar Inc.
Robert Ruel, Toronto Regional District Manager
TOTAL REVENUE ($000)   233,984

CBR MATERIALS CORPORATION OF CANADA
(Private)   CEMENT AND CONCRETE
1015 Fourth St. S.W., Suite 1200, Calgary, AB,
T2R 1J4   (403) 262-2928
CBR MATERIALS CORPORATION OF CANADA, through its main operating subsidiary CBR Cement Canada Limited and other operating divisions and subsidiaries, is involved in manufactured products and construction contracts. It is an indirect wholly owned subsidiary of Cimenteries CBR, S.A..
Donald M. Fallon, Chairman of the Board
TOTAL REVENUE ($000)   400,950

CCL INDUSTRIES INC.
See page 246 for a full company profile.

CELANESE CANADA INC.
See page 237 for a full company profile.

CENTRA GAS MANITOBA CO.
(Private)   GAS UTILITIES
444 St. Mary Avenue, 5th Floor, Winnipeg, MB,
R3C 3T7   (204) 944-9920
CENTRA GAS MANITOBA INC. is a natural gas distribution company.
M.E.J. Phelps, Chairman
TOTAL REVENUE ($000)   256,725

CENTRA GAS ONTARIO INC.
See page 296 for a full company profile.

CENTRAL CAPITAL CORPORATION
See page 398 for a full company profile.

CENTRAL CRUDE LTD.
(Public)   OIL AND GAS PRODUCERS
Suite 301, 55 Yonge St., Toronto, ON, M5E 1J4   (416) 864-1456
CENTRAL CRUDE LTD. is involved in the acquisition, exploration and development of mineral resource properties. The company's most signifcant property is a 40% interest in the Eagle River property which is located in the Mishibishu Lake area of Northwestern Ontario. Hemlo Gold Mines Inc. owns the other 60% interest in the property and acts as the operator.
Richard E. Nemis, President
TOTAL REVENUE ($000)   21

CENTRAL FUND OF CANADA LIMITED
See page 399 for a full company profile.

CENTRAL GUARANTY TRUSTCO LIMITED
See page 382 for a full company profile.

CFCF INC.
See page 319 for a full company profile.

CFS GROUP INC.
(Public)   MISC. INDUSTRIAL PRODUCTS
550 Marshall Avenue, Dorval, PQ, H9P 1C9   (514) 631-7731
CFS GROUP INC. is principally involved in manufacturing and selling coatings, adhesives and refractories. Its main markets are steel mills, iron foundries, aluminum and other nonferrous smelters, furniture manufacturers, the construction and woodworking industries, the packaging industry and the home improvement and sporting goods industries.
Michael Kawaja, President
TOTAL REVENUE ($000)   46,834

CGC INC.
See page 488 for a full company profile.

CGI GROUP INC. (THE)
(Public)   CONSULTING
1130 Sherbrooke West, Suite 700, Montreal, PQ,
H3A 2M8   (514) 841-3200
CGI GROUP provides consulting services in information systems, telecommunications and management, and a range of services in systems management and outsourcing.
Serge Godin, Chairman President & C.E.O.
TOTAL REVENUE ($000)   70,135

CHAI-NA-TA GINSENG PRODUCTS LTD.
See page 489 for a full company profile.

CHANCELLOR ENERGY RESOURCES INC.
(Public)   OIL AND GAS PRODUCERS
Suite 950, 333 - 5th Avenue S.W., Calgary, AB,
T2P 3B6   (403) 233-8426
CHANCELLOR ENERGY RESOURCES INC. is a Calgary based resource company primarily engaged in the acquisition, exploration and development of oil and gas leases in North America. Exploration efforts are concentrated in Western Canada, Texas and Oklahoma.

Robert G. Peters, Chairman
TOTAL REVENUE ($000)   4,265

CHARTER INDUSTRIES LTD.
(Public)   INVESTMENT COMPANIES AND FUNDS
Suite 300, 1290 Van Horne, Outremont, PQ,
H2V 4S2   (514) 277-5353
CHARTER INDUSTRIES LTD. is a public company whose principal activity is investment.
Gordon Fox, Chairman
TOTAL REVENUE ($000)   202

CHARTERWAYS TRANSPORTATION LTD.
(Private)   TRANSPORTATION
P.O. Box 847, Station B, London, ON, N6A 4Z3   (519) 679-9150
CHARTERWAYS TRANSPORTATION LTD. is a school bus operator. Charterways' Canadian fleet comprises approximately 2,500 vehicles operating out of 41 facilities in Ontario. It also operates a freight services business and a storage and distribution business.
Geoff Davies, President & C.E.O.
TOTAL REVENUE ($000)   223,597

CHASE MANHATTAN BANK OF CANADA (THE)
(Private)   BANKS
150 King St. W., 16th Floor, P.O. Box 68, Toronto, ON,
M5H 1J9   (416) 585-3300
CHASE MANHATTAN BANK OF CANADA is a wholly owned subsidiary of Chase Manhattan Overseas Banking Corp., with the ultimate parent The Chase Manhattan Corporation. The company is licensed to operate as a Schedule II bank. The bank specializes in corporate finance and advisory services.
Thomas C. Gardner, President & C.E.O.
TOTAL REVENUE ($000)   33,434

CHATEAU STORES OF CANADA LTD.
See page 355 for a full company profile.

CHAUVCO RESOURCES LTD.
See page 75 for a full company profile.

CHC HELICOPTER CORPORATION
(Public)   TRANSPORTATION
Hangar #1, St. John's Airport, P.O. Box 5188, St. John's, NF,
A1C 5V5   (709) 570-0700
CHC HELICOPTER CORPORATION, through its operating subsidiaries, owns, operates or leases approximately 250 aircraft in nine countries around the world. It offers repair and overhaul facilities in Richmond and Langley, British Columbia, and in Summerside, Prince Edward Island. CHC also operates two flight training schools in Canada: one in Ontario and one in British Columbia.
Craig L. Dobbin, Chairman & C.E.O.
TOTAL REVENUE ($000)   147,662

CHEMICAL BANK OF CANADA
(Private)   BANKS
Suite 900, 100 Yonge Street, Toronto, ON,
M5C 2W1   (416) 594-9800

CHEMICAL BANK OF CANADA is a wholly owned subsidiary of Chemical Banking Corporation, one of the largest commercial banks in the U.S. Through its office in Toronto, it offers a wide range of corporate finance products and banking services to clients and institutions. Through its affiliation with Chemical Bank of New York, the company offers its clients access to a full range of international services.
Maurice H. Hartigan II, Chairman
TOTAL REVENUE ($000)   55,720

CHENI GOLD MINES INC.
(Public)   PRECIOUS METALS
Sun Alliance Building, Suite 200, 580 Hornby Street, Vancouver, BC,
V6C 3B6   (604) 688-2321
CHENI GOLD MINES INC. is engaged in mineral exploration and development activities. Operations at the company's gold and silver mine were terminated on December 16, 1992, and the mine was placed on a care and maintenance basis at that time.
Edwin C. Phillips, Chairman
TOTAL REVENUE ($000)   16,517

CHEVRON CANADA LIMITED
(Private)   INTEGRATED OILS
1500 - 1050 West Pender Street, Vancouver, BC,
V6E 3T4   (604) 668-5300
CHEVRON CANADA LIMITED, is a refiner and marketer of petroleum products and is wholly owned by Chevron Corporation of San Francisco, California.
Ron Kiskis, President & C.E.O.
TOTAL REVENUE ($000)   998,051

CHEVRON CANADA RESOURCES LIMITED
(Private)   OIL AND GAS PRODUCERS
500 - 5th Avenue S.W., Calgary, AB, T2P 0L7   (403) 234-5000
CHEVRON CANADA RESOURCES LTD. is engaged in oil and gas exploration and production. Chevron Canada Resources is a wholly owned subsidiary of Chevron Corporation of San Francisco, California.
J.R. Baroffio, President
TOTAL REVENUE ($000)   998,051

CHIEFTAIN INTERNATIONAL, INC.
See page 76 for a full company profile.

CHO HUNG BANK OF CANADA
(Private)   BANKS
2 Sheppard Avenue East, Suite 1100, North York, ON,
M2N 5Y7   (416) 590-9500
CHO HUNG BANK OF CANADA is licensed to operate in Canada as a foreign bank subsidiary with full banking powers.
C.K. Yun, President
TOTAL REVENUE ($000)   4,122

CHRYSLER CANADA LTD.
(Private)   AUTOMOTIVE
P.O. Box 1621, Chrysler Centre, Windsor, ON,
N9A 4H6   (519) 973-2000
CHRYSLER CANADA LTD. manufactures, distributes and sells automobiles and related parts. The company is 100% owned by Chrysler Corporation of Highland Park, Michigan.

G. Yves Landry, President & C.E.O.
TOTAL REVENUE ($000)   9,478,900

CHUBB INSURANCE COMPANY OF CANADA
(Private)   INSURANCE - PROPERTY & CASUALTY
One Financial Place, 1 Adelaide Stree East, Toronto, ON,
M5C 2V9   (416) 863-0550
CHUBB INSURANCE COMPANY OF CANADA is a property and casualty insurer operating in all provinces and territories. The company is a wholly- owned subsidiary of The Chubb Corporation.
Percy Chubb III, Chairman
TOTAL REVENUE ($000)   217,013

CHUM LIMITED
See page 320 for a full company profile.

CHURCHILL CORPORATION (THE)
(Public)   CONTRACTORS
Suite 2280, Manulife Place, 10180 - 101 Street, Edmonton, AB,
T5J 3S4   (403) 424-8230
THE CHURCHILL CORPORATION is a diversified investment and holding company whose principal business activities are corporate investment, commercial construction, real estate development and financial and advisory services.
Stanton K. Hooper, Chairman
TOTAL REVENUE ($000)   237,158

CIBA-GEIGY CANADA LTD.
(Private)   CHEMICALS
6860 Century Avenue, Mississauga, ON, L5N 2W5   (416) 821-4420
CIBA-GEIGY CANADA LTD. is a chemical company engaged in the pharmaceuticals, agriculturals and plastics and additives industries. The company is wholly owned by CIBA-GEIGY Limited of Switzerland.
Leon Jacobs, President & C.E.O.
TOTAL REVENUE ($000)   433,340

CIMARRON PETROLEUM LTD.
See page 77 for a full company profile.

CINEPLEX ODEON CORPORATION
See page 490 for a full company profile.

CINRAM LTD.
See page 491 for a full company profile.

CIRCO CRAFT CO. INC.
See page 217 for a full company profile.

CITADEL GOLD MINES INC
(Public)   PRECIOUS METALS
150 Signet Drive, Weston, ON, M9L 1T1   (416) 749-9300
CITADEL GOLD MINES INC is involved in the acquisition, exploration and development of precious metals and industrial minerals properties.
Craig Baxter, Chairman & Sec.-Treasurer
TOTAL REVENUE ($000)   767

CITIBANK CANADA
(Private)   BANKS
Citibank Place, Suite 1900, 123 Front Street West, Toronto, ON,
M5J 2M3   (416) 947-5500
CITIBANK CANADA, a wholly owned subsidiary of Citibank, N.A.,
is licensed to operate in Canada as a Schedule B bank with full banking
powers. The company, through its leasing and securities subsidiaries,
offers leasing and investment dealing services through offices across
Canada.
Richard E. Lint, Chairman & C.E.O.
TOTAL REVENUE ($000)   584,311

**CIVIL SERVICE CO-OPERATIVE CREDIT SOCIETY,
LIMITED**
(Fin. Co-op)   CREDIT UNIONS
400 Albert Street, Ottawa, ON, K1R 5B2   (613) 560-6600
CIVIL SERVICE CO-OPERATIVE CREDIT SOCIETY LIMITED
provides full financial services for members, who are employees of the
federal government. Through ATM and branch locations, it offers savings, RRSP, loan services, mortgages and a variety of other financial
services.
Ronald G.E. Fitzgerald, General Manager & C.E.O.
TOTAL REVENUE ($000)   74,064

CLAIRVEST GROUP INC.
(Public)   FINANCE AND LEASING
22 St. Clair Avenue East, Suite 1700, Toronto, ON,
M4T 2S3   (416) 925-9270
CLAIRVEST GROUP INC. is organized to provide merchant banking
services to emerging businesses. These merchant banking services in-
clude advisory services and the facilitation of financings. The company
makes direct investments for its own account in these businesses.
Joseph L. Rotman, Chairman & C.E.O.
TOTAL REVENUE ($000)   6,519

CLEARLY CANADIAN BEVERAGE CORP.
(Public)   FOOD PROCESSING
Suite 1900, 999 West Hastings Street, Vancouver, BC,
V6C 2W2   (604) 683-0312
CLEARLY CANADIAN BEVERAGE CORPORATION is involved
in manufacturing and distributing bottled mineral water and a line of
natural fruit-flavored sparkling waters.
Douglas L. Mason, President & C.E.O.
TOTAL REVENUE ($000)   71,505

CM NT EQUITY CORP.
(Public)   INVESTMENT COMPANIES AND FUNDS
Suite 5000, P.O. Box 150, 1 First Canadian Place, Toronto, ON,
M5X 1H3   (416) 365-4602
CM NT EQUITY will invest its funds in common shares of the Canadian
Imperial Bank of Commerce and pay dividends on the company's
outstanding Class A preferred and common shares. The Class A shares
are owned by CM PREF. CORP. The capital shares will provide their
holder with an investment whose value is linked to changes in the market
value of the CIBC common shares held by CM NT.
Frederick J. Troop, President & C.E.O.
TOTAL REVENUE ($000)   8,354

CM PREF. CORP.
(Public)   INVESTMENT COMPANIES AND FUNDS
Suite 5000, P.O. Box 150, 1 First Canadian Place, Toronto,
M5X 1H3   (416) 365-4602
CM PREF. CORP.'s only undertaking will be to invest its funds in Class
A preferred shares of CM NT EQUITY CORP. and to pay dividends on
the company's outstanding preferred and common shares. This provides
an alternate investment vehicle through which to invest in Canadian
Imperial Bank of Commerce common shares.
Frederick J. Troop, President & C.E.O.
TOTAL REVENUE ($000)   7,953

CML INDUSTRIES LTD.
(Public)   MANAGEMENT AND DIVERSIFIED
550 Cochrane Dr., Unionville, ON, L3R 8E2   (416) 513-8511
CML INDUSTRIES's principal business consists of investing in and
managing secondary manufacturing businesses. The company, through
its wholly owned subsidiaries, is involved in the manufacturing of
envelopes and specialty papers.
Claude Theberge, Chairman & C.E.O.
TOTAL REVENUE ($000)   22,899

CO-ENERCO RESOURCES LTD.
See page 78 for a full company profile.

CO-MAXX ENERGY GROUP INC.
(Public)   OIL AND GAS PRODUCERS
Suite 1110, 605 - 5th Avenue S.W., Calgary, AB,
T2P 3H5   (403) 233-7100
CO-MAXX ENERGY GROUP INC., is a Canadian independent natural
resource company engaged in the exploration for and production of oil
and gas in Alberta and Saskatchewan. Co-Maxx is also engaged in
exploring for gold in northwestern Ontario.
Gerald J. Hipple, President & C.E.O.
TOTAL REVENUE ($000)   2,541

CO-OP ATLANTIC
(Non-fin Co-op)   DEPARTMENT STORES
P.O. Box 750, Moncton, NB, E1C 8N5   (506) 858-6000
CO-OP ATLANTIC is a wholesale central cooperative involved in meat,
grocery, produce, hardware, family fashions, petroleum, and agricultural
products in Atlantic Canada.
Sid Pobihushchy, Chairman & President
TOTAL REVENUE ($000)   441,225

CO-OPERATIVE CREDIT SOCIETY OF MANITOBA
(Fin. Co-op)   CREDIT UNIONS
P.O. Box 9900, 215 Garry Street, Winnipeg, MB,
R3C 3E2   (204) 985-4700
CO-OPERATIVE CREDIT SOCIETY OF MANITOBA serves its
member credit unions' needs primarily in the areas of: depository for
liquidity reserves; centralized services such as cheque clearing, training,
dataprocessing, and advertising; and, representation with related organi-
zation and all levels of government.
Herb Boyce, President Of The Board
TOTAL REVENUE ($000)   75,706

CO-OPERATIVE HAIL INSURANCE COMPANY LIMITED

(Fin. Co-op) INSURANCE - PROPERTY & CASUALTY
P.O. Box 777, 2709 - 13th Avenue, Regina, SK,
S4P 3A8 (306) 522-8891
CO-OPERATIVE HAIL INSURANCE's principal business is the sale of hail insurance to farmers in Manitoba and Saskatchewan.
Arthur E. Missal, Chairman & President
TOTAL REVENUE ($000) 17,691

CO-OPERATIVE TRUST COMPANY OF CANADA

(Fin. Co-op) TRUST, SAVINGS AND LOAN
333 - 3rd Avenue North, Saskatoon, SK, S7K 2M2 (306) 956-1800
CO-OPERATIVE TRUST COMPANY OF CANADA is a national financial institution owned by the Canadian Credit Union system. The company delivers deposit, retirement, mortgage and trust services through the credit union system. Co-operative Trust has 10 branch offices across Canada.
R.W. McVeigh, Chairman
TOTAL REVENUE ($000) 104,924

CO-OPERATORS DATA SERVICES LIMITED

(Non-fin Co-op) COMPUTER SOFTWARE & PROCESSING
1920 College Ave., Regina, SK, S4P 1C4 (306) 347-6200
CO-OPERATORS DATA SERVICES LIMITED provides information system operation, and management, development and support of software products, and professional services related to use of information systems and management of telecommunication facilities. It specializes in delivering solutions to Canadian and international financial services and health care markets.
Jack Morneau, Chairman Of The Board
TOTAL REVENUE ($000) 86,631

CO-OPERATORS GENERAL INSURANCE COMPANY

(Fin. Co-op) INSURANCE - PROPERTY & CASUALTY
Priory Square, Guelph, ON, N1H 6P8 (519) 824-4400
CO-OPERATORS GENERAL INSURANCE COMPANY is licenced to transact general insurance in all provinces and territories except Quebec.
Gordon Sinclair, Chairman
TOTAL REVENUE ($000) 974,592

CO-OPERATORS GROUP LIMITED (THE)

(Fin. Co-op) INSURANCE - PROPERTY & CASUALTY
Priory Square, Guelph, ON, N1H 6P8 (519) 824-4400
CO-OPERATORS GROUP LIMITED (THE) provides a wide range of services including life, property & casualty insurance, annuities & structured settlements, and investment counselling. The company is also engaged in real estate development and property management, data services and communications.
Wayne McLeod, Chairman
TOTAL REVENUE ($000) 1,425,823

CO-OPERATORS LIFE INSURANCE COMPANY

(Fin. Co-op) INSURANCE - LIFE
1920 College Avenue, Regina, SK, S4P 1C4 (306) 347-6200
CO-OPERATORS LIFE INSURANCE COMPANY provides life insurance protection. It is part of The Co-operators Group Limited.

Warren Hanstead, Chairman Of The Board
TOTAL REVENUE ($000) 296,287

CO-STEEL INC.
See page 200 for a full company profile.

COBI FOODS INC.

(Public) FOOD PROCESSING
P.O. Box 1000, Collins Road, Port Williams, NS,
B0P 1T0 (902) 542-5722
COBI FOODS INC. is a food processor engaged in the canning, freezing and freeze-drying of vegetables, other food products and beverages.
George E. Bishop, Chairman Of The Board
TOTAL REVENUE ($000) 80,615

COCA-COLA BEVERAGES LTD.
See page 158 for a full company profile.

COCA-COLA LTD.

(Private) WHOLESALE DISTRIBUTORS
42 Overlea Blvd, Toronto, ON, M4H 1B8 (416) 424-6000
COCA-COLA LTD. is engaged in the production and sale of soft drink and juice products.
Ira C. Herbert, Chairman
TOTAL REVENUE ($000) 295,461

COGAS ENERGY LIMITED

(Public) OIL AND GAS PRODUCERS
Suite 500, 407 - 8th Avenue S.W., Calgary, AB,
T2P 1E5 (403) 233-7350
GOGAS ENERGY LIMITED is engaged in the exploration and development of oil and gas properties in Canada and the United States. The majority of the company's operations are in Canada.
Michael S.P. Cooke, President & C.E.O.
TOTAL REVENUE 7,511

COGECO INC.

(Public) CABLE
1 Place Ville Marie, Suite 3636, Montreal, PQ,
H3B 3P2 (514) 874-2600
COGECO INC. operates television and radio stations, cable television operations, a 37% investment in a television and film production company, and a chain of newspapers in Canada.
Henri Audet, Chairman & C.E.O.
TOTAL REVENUE ($000) 177,779

COGNOS INCORPORATED
See page 464 for a full company profile.

COHO RESOURCES LIMITED
See page 79 for a full company profile.

COLES BOOK STORES LIMITED

(Private) SPECIALTY STORES
90 Ronson Drive, Rexdale, ON,
M9W 1C1 (416) 243-3132

COLES BOOK STORES LIMITED is a retail bookstore chain. It is a subsidiary of Southam Inc. of Toronto.
William Ardell, Chairman
TOTAL REVENUE ($000)   196,852

COLGATE PALMOLIVE CANADA INC.
(Private)   MISC. CONSUMER PRODUCTS
99 Vanderhoof Avenue, Toronto, ON, M4G 2H6   (416) 421-6000
COLGATE PALMOLIVE CANADA INC. manufactures and distributes consumer products. The company is a wholly owned subsidiary of the Colgate-Palmolive Company.
P. Gordon McArthur, President & General Manager
TOTAL REVENUE ($000)   244,000

COLONY PACIFIC EXPLORATIONS LTD.
(Public)   OIL AND GAS PRODUCERS
Suite 800, 601 West Hastings Street, Vancouver, BC,
V6B 5A6   (604) 689-5797
COLONY PACIFIC EXPLORATIONS LTD. is engaged in the exploration and development of mineral properties located in British Columbia and California, and of petroleum and natural gas leases located in Alberta. Operations are primarily conducted in the United States through the company's subsidiaries.
Hugh C. Morris, Chairman Of The Board
TOTAL REVENUE ($000)   458

COLORTECH CORPORATION
(Public)   MISC. INDUSTRIAL PRODUCTS
8027 Dixie Road, Brampton, ON, L6T 3V1   (416) 792-0333
COLORTECH CORPORATION is involved in the manufacture of colour and additive concentrates for the plastic industry.
Howard W. Taylor, Chairman
TOTAL REVENUE ($000)   29,623

COMINCO LTD.
See page 9 for a full company profile.

COMINCO RESOURCES INTERNATIONAL LIMITED
See page 36 for a full company profile.

COMMASSUR INC.
(Private)   INSURANCE - PROPERTY & CASUALTY
2450 Rue Girouard, St-Hyacinthe, PQ, J2S 7C4
COMMASSUR INC., through subsidiaries, operates in the property and casualty insurance industry.
TOTAL REVENUE ($000)   329,573

COMMCORP FINANCIAL SERVICES INC.
(Private)   FINANCE AND LEASING
P.O. Box 5060, 5050 South Service Road, Burlington, ON,
L7R 4C8   (416) 335-7555
COMMCORP FINANCIAL SERVICES is engaged in equipment financing. It was formed by CIBC Leasing buying Norex Leasing.
A.L. Flood, Chairman
TOTAL REVENUE ($000)   172,078

COMMERCIAL UNION LIFE ASSURANCE COMPANY OF CANADA
(Private)   INSURANCE - LIFE
P.O. Box 370, Station A, Scarborough, ON,
M1K 5C3   (416) 296-0700
COMMERCIAL UNION LIFE ASSURANCE COMPANY OF CANADA offers life, accident and sickness insurance.
Gerry S. Stafford, Chairman
TOTAL REVENUE ($000)   180,801

COMMERCIAL UNION OF CANADA HOLDINGS LTD.
(Private)   INSURANCE - PROPERTY & CASUALTY
Commercial Union Tower, TD Centre, P.O. Box 441, Toronto, ON,
M5K 1L9   (416) 361-2500
COMMERCIAL UNION OF CANADA HOLDINGS LTD. is the parent of operating insurance company subsidiaries which provide a wide range of insurance products, both life and property and casualty.
Alastair H. Ross, Chairman Of The Board
TOTAL REVENUE ($000)   388,637

COMPUTALOG LTD.
See page 80 for a full company profile.

COMPUTER BROKERS OF CANADA INC.
(Public)   WHOLESALE DISTRIBUTORS
57 Adesso Drive, Concord, ON, L4K 3C7   (416) 660-1616
COMPUTER BROKERS OF CANADA INC. is a distributor of microcomputers and related hardware products.
Nir Shafrir, Chairman, President & C.E.O.
TOTAL REVENUE ($000)   140,053

COMPUTERTIME NETWORK CORPORATION
(Public)   COMPUTER SOFTWARE & PROCESSING
10340 Cote de Liesse, Lachine, PQ, H8T 1A3   (514) 633-9900
COMPUTERTIME NETWORK CORPORATION is engaged in two major lines of activity:the development, sale and distribution of fourth generation software products; and the execution of computer systems integration contracts and turnkey projects which require the furnishing of both products and services.
Daniel L.J. Benn, President
TOTAL REVENUE ($000)   3,636

CONFEDERATION LIFE INSURANCE COMPANY
(Private)   INSURANCE - LIFE
321 Bloor Street East, Toronto, ON, M4W 1H1   (416) 323-8111
THE CONFEDERATION LIFE GROUP OF COMPANIES operates mainly in Canada, the U.K, and the U.S. Member companies offer individual and group insurance products and services, pension fund management, mutual funds, corporate finance, and trust, treasury and banking services. Confederation Life is a substantial investor in the countries in which it carries on business.
Adam H. Zimmerman, Chairman
TOTAL REVENUE ($000)   3,909,238

CONNAUGHT LABORATORIES LIMITED
(Private)   BIOTECHNOLOGY & PHARMACEUTICALS
1755 Steeles Ave. W., Willowdale, ON, M2R 3T4   (416) 667-2706

CONNAUGHT LABORATORIES LIMITED is engaged in the development, manufacturing and commercialization of human vaccines.
Georges Hibon, Chairman & C.E.O.
TOTAL REVENUE ($000)   263,791

CONPAK SEAFOODS INC.
(Public)   FOOD PROCESSING
33 Pippy Place, P.O. Box 13008, St. John's, NF,
A1B 3V8   (709) 726-3020
CONPAK SEAFOODS INC., a purchaser, processor and marketer of seafood products, is one of the largest inshore seafood companies in Newfoundland, based on sales and assets.
C.M. Blackwood, Chairman
TOTAL REVENUE ($000)   25,288

CONSOLIDATED CANADIAN EXPRESS LIMITED
See page 400 for a full company profile.

CONSOLIDATED CARMA CORPORATION
See page 258 for a full company profile.

CONSOLIDATED ENFIELD CORP. LTD.
See page 443 for a full company profile.

CONSOLIDATED EUROCAN VENTURES LTD.
(Public)   OIL AND GAS PRODUCERS
Suite 1320, 885 West Georgia Street, Vancouver, BC,
V6C 3E8   (604) 689-7842
EUROCAN VENTURES LTD. is engaged in the exploration for, and development of oil and gas in Latin America with exploration properties in Columbia, Chile, Argentina and Peru. The company also has oil and gas production from its 30% interest in the Las Monas area in Columbia, where it is operator-elect.
Lukas H. Lundin, Chairman
TOTAL REVENUE ($000)   4,984 (US)

CONSOLIDATED FIVE STAR RESOURCES LTD.
(Public)   OIL AND GAS PRODUCERS
20 Bertrand Ave, Scarborough, ON, M1L 2P4   (416) 752-5324
CONSOLIDATED FIVE STAR RESOURCES LTD. is engaged in the exploration of mineral claims in the Northwest Territories, Prince Rupert and Slave Lake areas. It also has oil and gas interests in Queensland, Australia.
Edward H.K. Tan, Chairman & President
TOTAL REVENUE ($000)   2,581

CONSOLIDATED HCI HOLDINGS CORPORATION
See page 259 for a full company profile.

CONSOLIDATED HCO ENERGY LTD.
(Public)   OIL AND GAS PRODUCERS
Suite 1830 Sunlife Plaza I, 144 - 4th Avenue S.W., Calgary, AB,
T2P 3N4   (403) 269-8980
CONSOLIDATED HCO ENERGY has moved away from gas exploration and is currently focusing towards oil property acquisition and development.

Daryl H. Connolly, President & C.E.O.
TOTAL REVENUE ($000)   4,142

CONSOLIDATED NEVADA GOLDFIELDS CORPORATION
(Public)   PRECIOUS METALS
Suite 1620, 1801 Broadway, Denver, CO, 80202   (303) 296-3200
CONSOLIDATED NEVADA GOLDFIELDS CORPORATION is involved in the operation, exploration and development of precious metal properties. Its major area of activity is Nevada and South Carolina.
Peter Bojtos, President & C.E.O.
TOTAL REVENUE ($000)   12,573 (US)

CONSOLIDATED NORTH COAST INDUSTRIES LTD.
(Public)   OTHER MINES
Suite 920, 1188 West Georgia Street, Vancouver, BC,
V6E 4A2   (604) 681-0799
CONSOLIDATED NORTH COAST INDUSTRIES LTD. processes oysters.
R.W. Thiessen, President & C.E.O.
TOTAL REVENUE ($000)   198

CONSOLIDATED OASIS RESOURCES INC.
(Public)   METAL MINES
110 567 Avenue Victoria, St. Laurent, PQ, J4P 3R2   (514) 465-4656
CONSOLIDATED OASIS RESOURCES INC. is engaged in the acquisition, exploration and development of mineral properties.
R. Gosselin, President
TOTAL REVENUE ($000)   24

CONSOLIDATED RAMBLER MINES LIMITED
(Public)   EAST COAST FORESTRY
P.O. Box 937, 300 Union Street, Saint John, NB,
E2L 4E3   (506) 632-7171
CONSOLIDATED RAMBLER MINES LIMITED is engaged in the development and harvesting of timberland in Maine, U.S.A. and the exploration of minerals primarily in Newfoundland.
D.A. Macfarlane, President & Treasurer
TOTAL REVENUE ($000)   3,049

CONSOLIDATED RAMROD GOLD CORPORATION
(Public)   METAL MINES
Suite 1440, 625 Howe Street, Vancouver, BC,
V6C 2T6   (604) 682-6477
CONSOLIDATED RAMROD GOLD CORPORATION is engaged in the acquisition and exploration of mineral resource properties in the United States, Canada, Central America and Europe.
Olaf Tolpinrud, President
TOTAL REVENUE ($000)   104

CONSUMERS CO-OPERATIVE REFINERIES LIMITED
(Private)   OIL AND GAS PRODUCERS
P.O. Box 1050, Saskatoon, SK, S7K 3M9   (306) 244-3311
CONSUMERS' CO-OPERATIVE REFINERIES LIMITED manages the Co-op Refinery/ Upgrader Complex in Regina, Saskatchewan. It and the Government of Saskatchewan jointly own the upgrader through NewGrade Energy Inc. Consumers' Co-operative Refineries Limited is a wholly owned subsidiary of Federated Co-operatives Limited.

Vern Leland, President
TOTAL REVENUE ($000)   309,842

CONSUMERS PACKAGING INC.
See page 247 for a full company profile.

CONSUMERS' GAS COMPANY LTD. (THE)
See page 297 for a full company profile.

CONTINENTAL BANK OF CANADA
(Public)   BANKS
c/o Tory Tory DesLauriers &, Binnington, Suite 3000, P.O. Box 270,
TD Centre, Toronto, ON, M5K 1N5   (416) 864-101
CONTINENTAL BANK OF CANADA is in voluntary liquidation. The
bank sold substantially all of its business to Lloyds Bank Canada effective
November 1, 1986.
Harold Corrigan, Chairman & C.E.O.
TOTAL REVENUE ($000)   972

CONTINENTAL CANADA GROUP (THE)
(Private)   INSURANCE - PROPERTY & CASUALTY
1 Adelaide Street East, Toronto, ON, M5C 2V9   (416) 350-4400
THE CONTINENTAL CANADA GROUP provides a full range of
property and casualty insurance coverages and services for both commercial and personal lines. The group is wholly owned by The Continental Corporation (U.S.).
William W. Ward, Chairman & C.E.O.
TOTAL REVENUE ($000)   347,000 (US)

CONTINENTAL GRAIN COMPANY (CANADA) LIMITED
(Private)   WHOLESALE DISTRIBUTORS
900-360 Main Street, Winnipeg, MB, R3C 3Z3   (204) 942-5181
CONTINENTAL GRAIN COMPANY (CANADA) LIMITED,
through its investment in Canagrain International Partnership, is in the
business of buying, trading, selling and transporting of export grain and
grain byproductsin Canada and such other commodities that the Partners
may agree upon. It owns and operates an elevator facility on leased land.
Its parent is Continental Grain Company.
Gerald L. McClintock, President & C.E.O.
TOTAL REVENUE ($000)   186,935

CONTINENTAL PHARMA CRYOSAN INC.
(Public)   BIOTECHNOLOGY & PHARMACEUTICALS
5485 Pare Street, Mont-Royal, PQ, H4P 1P7   (514) 344-4004
CONTINENTAL PHARMA CRYOSAN is a biotechnology business,
through its subsidiary Ibex Technologies Inc. Through another subsidiary, Conpharma Home Healthcare Inc., the company operates a home
health care business in the United States.
Thomas O. Hecht, Chairman, President & C.E.O.
TOTAL REVENUE ($000)   51,277

CONTRANS CORP.
(Public)   TRANSPORTATION
1179 Ridgeway Road, P.O. Box 1210, Woodstock, ON,
L4S 8P6   (519) 421-4600
CONTRANS CORP. is engaged in the truckload movement of a wide
range of general freight as well as specialized commodities in bulk or by

flatbed throughout Ontario and Quebec, Eastern Canada and the United
States.
Stan G. Dunford, Chairman & President
TOTAL REVENUE ($000)   61,736

CONWEST EXPLORATION COMPANY LIMITED
See page 81 for a full company profile.

COOPERATIVE FEDEREE DE QUEBEC
(Public)   AGRICULTURE
9001 Boul. de l'Acadie, Bureau 200, Montreal, PQ,
H4N 3H7   (514) 384-6450
COOPERATIVE FEDEREE DE QUEBEC is an agricultural coopera-
tive with operations in meat packing, poultry products, dairy products,
fruits and vegetables, petroleum products, feeds and fertilizers, agricul-
tural supplies and farm implements.
Jean-Marc Bergeron, Chief Executive Officer
TOTAL REVENUE ($000)   1,564,466

CORAL GOLD CORP.
(Public)   PRECIOUS METALS
Suite 400, 455 Granville Street, Vancouver, BC,
V6C 1T1   (604) 682-3701
CORAL GOLD CORP. holds gold and silver properties in Canada, the
United States and Mexico. Primary emphasis is on the Robertson Project,
open pit gold property in the Northern Nevada gold belt underjoint
venture with Amax Gold Inc.
Louis Wolfin, President
TOTAL REVENUE ($000)   0

CORBY DISTILLERIES LIMITED
See page 159 for a full company profile.

COREL CORPORATION
See page 465 for a full company profile.

CORNUCOPIA RESOURCES LTD.
See page 37 for a full company profile.

CORONET CARPETS INC.
(Private)   HOME FURNISHINGS
7605 Bath Road, Mississauga, ON, L4T 3T1   (416) 678-9595
CORONET CARPETS INC. is a manufacturer of tufted broadloom
carpet in Canada. Its manufacturing operation is vertically integrated
from yarn processing through carpet finishing in one facility in Farnham,
Quebec.
William T. Bodenhamer, Chairman Of The Board
TOTAL REVENUE ($000)   266,383

CORPORATE FOODS LIMITED
See page 160 for a full company profile.

COSCAN DEVELOPMENT CORPORATION
See page 260 for a full company profile.

COSCIENT GROUP INC.
(Public)   ENTERTAINMENT SERVICES
300 Rue Leo-Pariseau, Bureau 2400, C.P. 1145, Montreal, PQ,
H2W 2P4   (514) 284-2525
COSCIENT GROUP INC. is an independent producer in Quebec of
television series, documentaries of all sorts intended for the television
market as well as commercial and promotional audiovisual materials for
corporate clients and institutions.
Richard Laferriere, President & C.E.O.
TOTAL REVENUE ($000)   15,421

COSMAIR CANADA INC.
(Private)   MISC. CONSUMER PRODUCTS
2115 Crescent, Montreal, PQ, H3G 2C1   (514) 335-8000
COSMAIR CANADA INC. is a manufacturer and supplier of cosmetics,
toilet preparations and fragrances. Cosmair Canada is 56% owned by
Nestle S.A. of Switzerland.
G. Peyrelongue, Chairman
TOTAL REVENUE ($000)   175,031

COTT CORPORATION
See page 161 for a full company profile.

COUNSEL CORPORATION
See page 444 for a full company profile.

CRANE CANADA INC.
(Private)   METAL FABRICATORS
5850 Cote de Liesse, 5th Floor, Montreal, PQ,
H4T 1B2   (514) 735-3592
CRANE CANADA INC., is a manufacturer and wholesaler of plumbing
and valve products. Crane is a wholly owned subsidiary of Crane Co.
(U.S.).
R.S. Evans, Chairman
TOTAL REVENUE ($000)   220,272

CREDIT LYONNAIS CANADA
(Private)   BANKS
2000 Mansfield Street, 18th Floor, Montreal, PQ,
H3A 3A6   (514) 288-4848
CREDIT LYONNAIS CANADA is a wholly owned subsidiary of Credit
Lyonnais and has been licenced in Canada as a Schedule B foreign bank
subsidiary since January 1, 1982.
Robert Ganne, Chairman
TOTAL REVENUE ($000)   131,986

CREDIT SUISSE OF CANADA
(Private)   BANKS
Credit Suisse Centre, Suite 1300, 525 University Avenue, Toronto,
ON, M5G 2K6   (416) 351-3500
CREDIT SUISSE OF CANADA is a wholly owned subsidiary of Credit
Suisse of Zurich, Switzerland. It is licenced to operate in Canada under
the Bank Act.
Rudolf W. Hug, Chairman Of The Board
TOTAL REVENUE ($000)   249,048

CREDIT UNION CENTRAL ALBERTA LIMITED
(Fin. Co-op)   CREDIT UNIONS
8500 Macleod Trail S.E., Calgary, AB, T2H 2N1   (403) 258-5900
CREDIT UNION CENTRAL ALBERTA LIMITED provides leader-
ship and services to member credit unions in Alberta.
Don Buehler, Chairman
TOTAL REVENUE ($000)   60,285

CREDIT UNION CENTRAL OF NOVA SCOTIA
(Fin. Co-op)   CREDIT UNIONS
P.O. Box 9200, Station A, 6074 Lady Hammond Road, Halifax, NS,
B3K 5N3   (902) 453-0680
CREDIT UNION CENTRAL OF NOVA SCOTIA provides corporate
financial services to Credit Unions, development support, education and
training services, marketing, printing and data processing services.
Gerald W. Wrigley, Chairman & President
TOTAL REVENUE ($000)   43,589

CREDIT UNION CENTRAL OF ONTARIO LIMITED
(Fin. Co-op)   CREDIT UNIONS
2810 Matheson Blvd. East, Mississauga, ON,
L4W 4X7   (416) 238-9400
CREDIT UNION CENTRAL OF ONTARIO LIMITED is a financial
service and trade association for about 500 credit unions in Ontario.
Allan Lanctot, Chairman
TOTAL REVENUE ($000)   113,187

CREDIT UNION CENTRAL OF PRINCE EDWARD ISLAND
(Fin. Co-op)   CREDIT UNIONS
P.O. Box 968, 281 University Avenue, Charlottetown, PE,
C1A 7M4   (902) 566-3350
CREDIT UNION CENTRAL OF PRINCE EDWARD ISLAND is a
financial cooperative responsible for providing financial and other serv-
ices, as well as leadership, to its members in a manner responsive to the
social needs of people.
Gerard T. Dougan, C.E.O. & Managing Director
TOTAL REVENUE ($000)   3,757

CREDIT UNION CENTRAL OF SASKATCHEWAN
(Fin. Co-op)   CREDIT UNIONS
P.O. Box 3030, Regina, SK, S4P 3G8   (306) 566-1301
CREDIT UNION CENTRAL OF SASKATCHEWAN is the trade and
financial services association for credit unions in Saskatchewan.
Norm Bromberger, Chief Executive Officer
TOTAL REVENUE ($000)   150,684

CRESTBROOK FOREST INDUSTRIES LTD.
See page 137 for a full company profile.

CROWN LIFE INSURANCE COMPANY
See page 421 for a full company profile.

CROWNX INC.
See page 445 for a full company profile.

CS RESOURCES LIMITED
(Public)   OIL AND GAS PRODUCERS
29th Floor, 645 - 7th Avenue S.W., Calgary, AB,
T2P 4G8   (403) 234-8410
CS RESOURCES LIMITED is involved in resources exploitation using
horizontal production technologies.
Richard J. Renaud, Chairman
TOTAL REVENUE ($000)   30,834

CSA MANAGEMENT LIMITED
(Public)   MANAGEMENT AND DIVERSIFIED
Suite 2700, 145 King St. West, Toronto, ON,
M5H 1J8   (416) 865-0326
CSA MANAGEMENT LIMITED provides investment management
services to an investment company and to mutual funds publicly distrib-
uted in Canada which invest substantially all their assets in gold bullion
and gold mining securities. The company also acts as exploration man-
ager to first exploration fund 1986 and 1987, Limited partnership vehicles
for flow-through financing in Canada.
Robert R. McEwen, Chairman, President & C.E.O.
TOTAL REVENUE ($000)   3,129

CSL GROUP INC. (THE)
(Private)   TRANSPORTATION
759 Victoria Square, Montreal, PQ, H2Y 2K3   (514) 288-0231
THE CSL GROUP INC. is a holding company. It is wholly owned by
Passage Holdings Inc.
A.J. Chesterman, Chairman
TOTAL REVENUE ($000)   172,377

CT FINANCIAL SERVICES INC.
(Public)   TRUST, SAVINGS AND LOAN
P.O. Box 5703, London, ON, N6A 4S4   (519) 663-1938
CT FINANCIAL SERVICES INC. is the parent holding company of
Canada Trustco Mortgage Co. Operations consist of the following
segments; intermediary, fiduciary, real estate sales, and real estate invest-
ments.
Peter C. Maurice, President & C.E.O.
TOTAL REVENUE ($000)   4,094,468

CUBE ENERGY CORP.
(Public)   OIL AND GAS PRODUCERS
Suite 800, 926 - 5th Avenue S.W., Calgary, AB,
T2P 0N7   (403) 264-4405
CUBE ENERGY CORP. is a Calgary based Canadian controlled com-
pany whose business is the exploration for, and the development and
production of petroleum and natural gas. The company operates primar-
ily in Western Canada.
Steven P. Dobrowolski, President
TOTAL REVENUE ($000)   5,466

CULINAR INC.
(Private)   FOOD PROCESSING
2 Complexe Desjardins, Suite 2700, P.O. Box 32, Montreal, PQ,
H5B 1B2   (514) 288-3101
CULINAR INC. manufactures, processes, imports, and markets a broad
range of food products. Its main sectors of activity include bakery,
confectionery, cookies, jams and dry bread products. Through the acqisi-

tion of new components, it has expanded its manufacturing and distribu-
tion networks across Canada and the notheastern United States.
Raymond Gagne, Chairman Of The Board
TOTAL REVENUE ($000)   587,208

CUMIS GROUP LIMITED (THE)
(Fin. Co-op)   INSURANCE - LIFE
P.O. Box 5065, Burlington, ON, L7R 4C2   (416) 632-1221
CUMIS GROUP LIMITED is a holding company with interests in:
Cumis Life Insurance; Cumis General Insurance; and Canadian Northern
Shield Insurance.
R.A. Effa, Chairman Of The Board
TOTAL REVENUE ($000)   130,661

CURRAGH INC.
(Public)   METAL MINES
Suite 1900, Box 12, 95 Wellington Street West, Toronto, ON,
M5J 2N7   (416) 363-7111
CURRAGH INC. is a major producer of zinc and lead concentrates. The
company's concentrates are produced from its Faro and Sa Dena Hes
mines in the Yukon.
Clifford H. Frame, Chairman & C.E.O.
TOTAL REVENUE ($000)   355,536

CUSAC INDUSTRIES LTD.
(Public)   PRECIOUS METALS
Suite 510, 700 West Pender Street, Vancouver, BC,
V6C 1G8   (604) 682-2421
CUSAC INDUSTRIES LTD. is engaged in the development of resource
properties primarily in British Columbia.
Guildford H. Brett, President
TOTAL REVENUE ($000)   10

CYANAMID CANADA INC.
(Private)   CHEMICALS
88 McNabb Street, Markham, ON, L3R 6E6   (416) 470-3600
CYANAMID CANADA INC. manufactures and markets pharmaceuti-
cals, surgical products, and agricultural and industrial chemicals. The
company is a wholly owned subsidiary of Ameican Cyanamid Company.
Garry Carlson, President
TOTAL REVENUE ($000)   205,122

CZAR RESOURCES LTD.
See page 82 for a full company profile.

D.A. STUART LTD.
(Public)   CHEMICALS
P.O. Box 430, 43 Upton Road, Scarborough, ON,
M1L 2C1   (416) 757-3226
D.A. STUART LTD. is an international specialty chemical company
which produces and sells specialty lubricants and chemical programs
covering a variety of industrial uses in the metalworking industry. The
primarycustomers are flat roll steel and aluminum companies and auto-
motive manufacturers. About 75% of sales occur in or are exported from
North America, with the balance in Europe.
Dr. Michael Werhahn, Chairman
TOTAL REVENUE ($000)   89,757 (US)

DAI-ICHI KANGYO BANK (CANADA)
(Private)   BANKS
Commerce Court West, Suite 5025, P.O. Box 295, Toronto, ON,
M5L 1H9   (416) 365-9666
DAI-ICHI KANGYO BANK (CANADA) is a wholly owned subsidiary
of the Dai-Ichi Kangyo Bank, Ltd, Japan, and is licensed to operate as a
Schedule II bank in Canada.
Toshiro Motohashi, Chairman, President & C.E.O.
TOTAL REVENUE ($000)   40,603

DAISHOWA FOREST PRODUCTS LTD.
(Private)   EAST COAST FORESTRY
207 Queens Quay West, Suite 800, Toronto, ON,
M5J 1A7   (416) 862-5000
DAISHOWA FOREST PRODUCTS LTD. is a manufacturer of news-
print, paperboard and lumber. It is a wholly owned subsidiary of
Daishowa Paper Mfg. Co. Ltd. of Japan.
Mr. Koichi Kitagawa, President & C.E.O.
TOTAL REVENUE ($000)   329,005

DAIWA BANK CANADA
(Private)   BANKS
P.O. Box 95, Suite 2509, Sun Life Centre, 150 King Street West,
Toronto, ON, M5H 1J9   (416) 979-7177
DAIWA BANK CANADA is a wholly owned subsidiary of The Daiwa
Bank, Ltd, Japan, and is licensed to operate as a bank in Canada with full
banking powers as a foreign bank subsidiary.
Hiroyuki Yamaji, Chairman
TOTAL REVENUE ($000)   20,674

DALMYS (CANADA) LIMITED
See page 356 for a full company profile.

DARIUS TECHNOLOGY LTD.
(Public)   ELECTRICAL & ELECTRONIC
2808 Ingleton Ave., Burnaby, BC, V5C 6G7   (604) 654-1830
DARIUS TECHNOLOGY LTD. is involved in the manufacture and
distribution of personal computers and peripherals.
Benjamin K. Tam, Chairman, President & C.E.O.
TOTAL REVENUE ($000)   30,825

DATA BUSINESS FORMS LIMITED
(Private)   BUSINESS FORMS
2 Shaftsbury Lane, Brampton, ON, L6T 3X7   (416) 791-3151
DATA BUSINESS FORMS LIMITED is engaged in the manufacture
and distribution of business forms.
John H. Greenhough, Chairman
TOTAL REVENUE ($000)   176,418

DATAMARK INC.
(Public)   BUSINESS FORMS
909 Upton, LaSalle, PQ, H8R 2V1   (514) 366-0652
DATAMARK INC. is engaged in the design, manufacture and distribution of high quality business forms and pressure sensitive labels.
Datamark also provides complementary services including warehousing,
forms distribution and form management computerized control systems.
Other activities include commercial printing, direct marketing promotional printing and senstrip products.

Frank Heller, C.E.O. & Chairman
TOTAL REVENUE ($000)   79,994

DATATECH SYSTEMS LTD.
(Public)   COMPUTER SOFTWARE & PROCESSING
1095 McKenzie Avenue, Victoria, BC, V8P 5L4   (604) 479-7117
DATATECH SYSTEMS LTD. is an independent third party computer
maintenance organization, providing service and maintenance for se-
lected types of computers and computer peripheral equipment to the
Canadian private and public sectors.
Earl W. Large, Chairman
TOTAL REVENUE ($000)   16,547

DAVIDSON TISDALE LTD.
(Public)   PRECIOUS METALS
32 Shasfesbury Ave., Toronto, ON, M4T 1A1   (416) 929-0517
DAVIDSON TISDALE MINES LIMITED has business interests in
base and precious metal exploration, as well as real estate development
in the Toronto area. The company is the controlling shareholder of Vital
Pacific Resources Ltd., which has active copper and gold exploration
programs in Ontario, B.C. and Montana. It is also the sole owner of
Aurora Steel Services Inc., a steel fabricating and machine shop.
William G. Dingwall, Chairman
TOTAL REVENUE ($000)   16

DAVIS DISTRIBUTING LIMITED
(Public)   WHOLESALE DISTRIBUTORS
7171 Jane Street, Concord, ON, L4K 1A7   (416) 738-6226
DAVIS DISTRIBUTING LIMITED is a wholesale distributor of to-
bacco products, groceries, confectionery, health and beauty aids, and
sundries to some 3,000 retailers, most of which are located in Southern
Ontario.
Bernard J. Davis, President
TOTAL REVENUE ($000)   235,336

DAYTON MINING CORPORATION
(Public)   METAL MINES
Suite 1610, 200 Burrard Street, Vancouver, BC,
V6C 3L6   (604) 662-8383
DAYTON MINING CORPORATION is developing a large open pit
gold mine in Chile capable of producing in excess of 100,000 ounces of
gold per year
Wayne D. McClay, Chairman, President & C.E.O.
TOTAL REVENUE ($000)   75

DEAK RESOURCES CORPORATION
(Public)   METAL MINES
Suite 501, 155 University Avenue, Toronto, ON,
M5H 3B7   (416) 360-7707
DEAK RESOURCES CORPORATION is the result of the amalgama-
tion of Wilco Mining, Seadrift International Exploration, and Deak
Ariadne Limited.
J. Malcolm Slack, Chairman & C.E.O.
TOTAL REVENUE ($000)   17,125

DELRINA CORPORATION
(Public)   COMPUTER SOFTWARE & PROCESSING
895 Don Mills Road, 500 - 2 Park Centre, Toronto, ON,
M3C 1W3   (416) 441-3676
DELRINA CORPORATION is a software publisher that designs, develops, markets and supports software products for use on personal computers. Delrina's products include software in several categories: forms processing; fax communications; electronic daily planners and content publishing. Delrina is recognized as the technical and market leader for PC forms and fax software sold worldwide.
Dennis Bennie, Chairman President & C.E.O.
TOTAL REVENUE ($000)   19,208

DELTA CATALYTIC CORPORATION
(Private)   CONTRACTORS
400 - 8500 Macleod Trail South, P.O. Box 5244, Station A, Calgary,
T2H 2N7   (403) 258-6411
DELTA CATALYTIC CORPORATION provides engineering, procurement, construction, industrial contract maintenance, and tool and equipment supply services to domestic and international clients.
A.B. Coady, Chairman & C.E.O.
TOTAL REVENUE ($000)   703,583

DELTA HOTELS & RESORTS
(Private)   LODGING
557 Church St., Toronto, ON, M4Y 2E2   (416) 926-7800
DELTA HOTELS & RESORTS is a Canadian privately owned hospitality company with hotels and resorts in Canada, two in the United States and two in Asia.
Jonas J. Prince, Chairman & C.E.O.
TOTAL REVENUE ($000)   260,000

DENBRIDGE CAPITAL CORPORATION
(Public)   INVESTMENT COMPANIES AND FUNDS
Suite 910, 26 Wellington St. E., Toronto, ON,
M4E 1S2   (416) 862-7444
DENBRIDGE CAPITAL CORPORATION is a merchant bank.
TOTAL REVENUE ($000)   7,299

DENISON MINES LIMITED
See page 10 for a full company profile.

DEPRENYL RESEARCH LIMITED
See page 193 for a full company profile.

DERLAN INDUSTRIES LIMITED
See page 492 for a full company profile.

DESJARDINS LIFE ASSURANCE COMPANY INC.
(Fin. Co-op)   INSURANCE - LIFE
200 Avenue des Commandeurs, Levis, PQ,
G6V 6R2   (418) 838-7870
DESJARDINS LIFE ASSURANCE CO. INC. offers the full range of life and health insurance services, on an individual and group basis, through various intermediaries, life underwriters, brokers, specialized consultants or direct distribution network. In addition, the company offers

coverage services designed for members, employees and directors of Desjardins Caisses. It does business mainly in Quebec.
Yves Malo, Chairman
TOTAL REVENUE ($000)   834,109

DESJARDINS TRUSTCO INC.
(Public)   TRUST, SAVINGS AND LOAN
1 Complexe Desjardins, C.P. 34, Succursale Desjardins, Montreal,
PQ, H5B 1E4   (514) 286-3434
DESJARDINS TRUSTCO INC. is the result of arrangements by Mouvement Desjardins to make Desjardins Trustco Inc. the parent corporation of Desjardins Trust (Fiducie Desjardins) and of Desjardins Commercial and Industrial Credit Inc. (Credit Industriel Desjardins Inc.). The company adopted its current corporate name on November 4, 1988.
Paul-Yvon Lesage, Chairman of the Board
TOTAL REVENUE ($000)   347,469

DEUTSCHE BANK (CANADA)
(Private)   BANKS
Suite 1200, 222 Bay Street, P.O. Box 196, Toronto, ON,
M5K 1H6   (416) 369-8800
DEUTSCHE BANK (CANADA) is a wholly owned subsidiary of Deutsche Bank AG, Frankfurt/Main, Germany.
Dr. Ronaldo H. Schmitz, Chairman
TOTAL REVENUE ($000)   105,081

DEVELCON ELECTRONICS LTD.
See page 218 for a full company profile.

DEVJO INDUSTRIES INC.
(Public)   MISC. INDUSTRIAL PRODUCTS
375 Steelcase Road East, Markham, ON, L3R 1G3 (416) 477-7689
DEVJO INDUSTRIES INC. has three wholly owned divisions involved in the manufacture and distribution of proprietary specialty chemical products, and the custom manufactuing of fittings in various alloy metals.
Joseph A. Devine, President
TOTAL REVENUE ($000)   9,602

DEVNIC ENERGY INC.
(Public)   OIL AND GAS PRODUCERS
Suite 1000, 833 - 4th Avenue S.W., Calgary, AB,
T2P 3T5   (403) 297-0230
DEVNIC ENERGY INC. is an independent crude oil and natural gas exploration, development and production company engaged in acquiring petroleum and natural gas rights in Alberta, and exploiting the resulting crude oil and natural gas reserves through production and sale.
Gordon F. Dixon, Chairman
TOTAL REVENUE ($000)   457

DEVRAN PETROLEUM LTD.
(Public)   OIL AND GAS PRODUCERS
300 Princess Avenue, London, ON, N6B 2A6   (519) 672-5520
DEVRAN PETROLEUM LTD. is involved in both conventional oil and gas exploration in Ontario and in horizontal drilling projects in Alberta. One of the company's projects is a joint venture carried on with Telesis Oil and Gas and Pembina Exploration Ltd. in Essex and Kent Counties in Ontario. Devran participates (23%) with CS Resources in horizontal drilling development at Pelican Lake, Alberta.

John F. Cowan, President
TOTAL REVENUE ($000) 6,727

DEVTEK CORPORATION
(Public) ELECTRICAL & ELECTRONIC
100 Allstate Parkway, Suite 500, Markham, ON,
L3R 6H3 (416) 477-6861
DEVTEK CORPORATION is a diversified developer and manufacturer of systems sub-systems and components for the aerospace, defence and electronics markets. The company has a wide range of customers including the Canadian, U.S. and other free-world governments and major North American aerospace, defence and electronics prime contractors.
Helmut Hofmann, Chairman & C.E.O.
TOTAL REVENUE ($000) 224,334

DEXLEIGH CORPORATION
(Public) MANAGEMENT AND DIVERSIFIED
P.O. Box 129, Suite 1500, Commerce Court West, Toronto, ON,
M5L 1K5 (416) 359-8630
DEXLEIGH CORPORATION invests for the long term in real estate and other assets where their value can be enhanced through an orderly restructuring.
R. Bryan McJannet, President & C.E.O.
TOTAL REVENUE ($000) 22,809

DIA MET MINERALS LTD
See page 11 for a full company profile.

DICKENSON MINES LIMITED
See page 38 for a full company profile.

DIGITAL EQUIPMENT OF CANADA LIMITED
(Private) ELECTRICAL & ELECTRONIC
100 Herzberg Road, Kanata, ON, K2K 2A6 (416) 597-3100
DIGITAL EQUIPMENT OF CANADA LIMITED's business consists of design, manufacture, sale and service of networked computer systems, associated peripheral equipment, and related network, communications and software products. Digital Canada is a wholly owned subsidiary of Digital Equipment Corporation of Maynard, Massachusetts.
Winston R. Hindle Jr., Chairman Of The Board
TOTAL REVENUE ($000) 1,076,886

DISCOVERY WEST CORP.
See page 83 for a full company profile.

DISYS CORPORATION
(Public) MISC. CONSUMER PRODUCTS
719 Clayson Road, Toronto, ON, M9M 2H4 (416) 745-6044
DISYS CORPORATION designs, manufactures and markets consumer health, safety and security products and Radio Frequency Identification tags throughout the world.
Steven W. Chepa, Chairman
TOTAL REVENUE ($000) 18,703

DMR GROUP INC.
See page 476 for a full company profile.

DOFASCO INC.
See page 201 for a full company profile.

DOMAN INDUSTRIES LIMITED
See page 138 for a full company profile.

DOMCO INDUSTRIES LIMITED
(Public) HOME FURNISHINGS
1001 Yamaska Street East, Farnham, PQ,
J2N 1J7 (514) 293-3173
DOMCO INDUSTRIES LIMITED is a manufacturer of resilient floor coverings and vinyl tiles in North America. The company produces vinyl floorings which are sold to retail specialty stores, mass merchandisers and home improvement centres as well as builders and the re-modelling trades.
Alberto Cefis, Chairman
TOTAL REVENUE ($000) 163,902

DOMINION OF CANADA GENERAL INSURANCE COMPANY (THE)
(Private) INSURANCE - PROPERTY & CASUALTY
165 University Avenue, 5th Floor, Toronto, ON,
M5H 3B9 (416) 362-7231
DOMINION OF CANADA GENERAL INSURANCE COMPANY writes personal accident, public liability, employer's liability, sickness, automobile, burglary fire, guarantee, personal property, plate glass, steam boiler, forgery and real property insurance. The company is wholly owned by E-L Financial Corporation Limited of Toronto.
Peter S. Gooderham, Chairman
TOTAL REVENUE ($000) 595,842

DOMINION TEXTILE INC.
See page 176 for a full company profile.

DOMTAR INC.
See page 139 for a full company profile.

DONOHUE INC.
See page 140 for a full company profile.

DOREL INDUSTRIES INC.
(Public) MISC. CONSUMER PRODUCTS
4750 Boul des Grandes Prairies, St-Leonard, PQ,
H1R 1A3 (514) 323-5701
DOREL INDUSTRIES INC. is a full line manufacturer and distributor of children's furniture and accessories. The company is also a leading manufacturer of ready-to-assemble furniture.
Leo Schwartz, Chairman
TOTAL REVENUE ($000) 211,555

DORSET EXPLORATION LTD.
See page 84 for a full company profile.

DOVER INDUSTRIES LIMITED
See page 162 for a full company profile.

DOW CHEMICAL CANADA INC.
(Private)　　　　　　　　　　　　CHEMICALS
1086 Modeland Road, Box 1012, Sarnia, ON,
N7T 7K7　　　　　　　　　　　　(519) 339-3131
DOW CHEMICAL CANADA INC. manufacturers chemicals, plastics
and consumer products. Dow Canada is a wholly owned subsidiary of
The Dow Chemical Company (U.S.).
Denis Wilcock, Chairman, President & C.E.O.
TOTAL REVENUE ($000)　　　　　　　1,696,383

DRAMEX CORPORATION
(Public)　　　　　　　　　　METAL FABRICATORS
3555 Pitfield Boulevard, Saint-Laurent, PQ,
H4S 1H3　　　　　　　　　　　　(514) 745-7360
DRAMEX CORPORATION specializes in the manufacturing of stand-
ard and flattened expanded metal, structural grating and decorative metal
patterns, sold under the trademark dramex. Wholly owned subsidiaries,
Braidwood Gear Limited and Cambridge Gear Limited, specialize in the
manufacture of gears and in the distribution of other power transmission
products.
Alan B. Pearson, Chairman & President
TOTAL REVENUE ($000)　　　　　　　18,346

DRECO ENERGY SERVICES LTD.
See page 85 for a full company profile.

DRESDNER BANK CANADA
(Private)　　　　　　　　　　　　BANKS
Suite 1700, 2 First Canadian Place, P.O. Box 430, Toronto, ON,
M5X 1E3　　　　　　　　　　　　(416) 369-8300
DRESDNER BANK CANADA is a subsidiary of Dresdner Bank of
Germany. As a foreign bank subsidiary, the scale of the bank's operations
is limited by the Bank Act, 1980.
Kurt Morgen, Chairman
TOTAL REVENUE ($000)　　　　　　　56,396

DRUG TRADING COMPANY LIMITED
(Private)　　　　　　　WHOLESALE DISTRIBUTORS
1960 Eglinton Ave E, Scarborough, ON, M1L 2M5　(416) 288-1100
DRUG TRADING COMPANY LIMITED is a wholesaler of pharma-
ceuticals and drug store sundry products.
J. Sinclair, Chairman
TOTAL REVENUE ($000)　　　　　　　594,326

DU PONT CANADA INC.
See page 238 for a full company profile.

DUKE SEABRIDGE LIMITED
(Private)　　　　　MANAGEMENT AND DIVERSIFIED
#505, Kapilano 100, 100 Park Royal, West Vancouver, BC,
V7T 1A2　　　　　　　　　　　　(604) 926-0167
DUKE SEABRIDGE LIMITED is a wholesaler of construction materi-
als and industrial equipment and a real estate developer. The company is
wholly owned by the Guinness Family.
Antoine Laoun, President
TOTAL REVENUE ($000)　　　　　　　240,619

DUNDEE BANCORP INC.
See page 401 for a full company profile.

DUNDEE-PALLISER RESOURCES INC.
(Public)　　　　　　　　OIL AND GAS PRODUCERS
Suite 200, 20 Adelaide Street East, Toronto, ON,
M5C 2T6　　　　　　　　　　　　(416) 867-1100
DUNDEE-PALLISER RESOURCES INC. is involved in oil and gas
production and mineral exploration.
Richard W. Brissenden, President
TOTAL REVENUE ($000)　　　　　　　328

DURKIN HAYES PUBLISHING LTD.
(Public)　　　　　　MISC. CONSUMER PRODUCTS
3375 North Service Road, Unit B7, Burlington, ON,
L7N 3G2　　　　　　　　　　　　(416) 335-0393
DURKIN HAYES PUBLISHING LTD. produces full-colour information, activity and story books for children as well as best-selling books
on cassette for sale to distributors, retailers and consumers. The company
also produces books and cassettes for use in combatting illiteracy and
teaching english as a second language. Books and books-on-tape are sold
to distributors, libraries and schools worldwide.
Douglas A.C. Davis, Chairman
TOTAL REVENUE ($000)　　　　　　　3,807

DY 4 SYSTEMS INC.
(Public)　　　　　　ELECTRICAL & ELECTRONIC
21 Fitzgerald Road, Nepean, ON, K2H 9J4
DY 4 SYSTEMS INC. is involved in the design and manufacture of high
end VME open architecture computer systems. These systems are used
in applications that require high reliability when operating in rugged or
harsh environments. Primary applications for the company's systems
include defence, surveillance, space and aerospace.
Danny B. Osadca, Chairman, President & C.E.O.
TOTAL REVENUE ($000)　　　　　　　26,873

DYLEX LIMITED
See page 357 for a full company profile.

DYNACARE INC.
(Public)　　　BIOTECHNOLOGY & PHARMACEUTICALS
Suite 1600, 20 Eglinton Avenue West, Toronto, ON,
M4R 2H1　　　　　　　　　　　　(416) 487-1100
DYNACARE INC. is active in threee aspects of the health care industry.
It operates licensed diagnostic medical laboratories in Ontario and Al-
berta, develops and operates quality retirement residences and seniors'
apartments, and provides nursing and health care services.
Herbert Shapiro, C.E.O.
TOTAL REVENUE ($000)　　　　　　　161,943

E.D.S. OF CANADA LTD.
(Private)　　　COMPUTER SOFTWARE & PROCESSING
300 Consilium Place, Suite 800, Scarborough, ON,
M1H 3G2　　　　　　　　　　　　(416) 290-2700
EDS CANADA provides its customers with a wide range of business
information technology services including Systems Management, Systems Integration, Systems Development and Consulting. EDS Canada is

100% owned by Electronic Data Systems Corporation of the United States.
John D. Bowie, President & C.E.O.
TOTAL REVENUE ($000) 229,000

E-L FINANCIAL CORPORATION LIMITED
See page 422 for a full company profile.

EAGLE PRECISION TECHNOLOGIES INC.
(Public) AUTOMOTIVE
565 West Street, P.O. Box 786, Brantford, ON,
N3T 5R7 (519) 756-5223
EAGLE PRECISION TECHNOLOGIES designs and manufactures metal tube end forming machines, computer numerically controlled metal tube bending machines and machines used in the manufacture of automotive exhaust systems, catalytic converters, shock absorbers and suspension struts. The company's products are presently sold almost exclusively to the automotive industry.
A. Alex Kepecs, Chairman & President
TOTAL REVENUE ($000) 33,794

EASTERN CONSTRUCTION COMPANY LIMITED
(Private) CONTRACTORS
4120 Yonge St., Suite 410, North York, ON,
M2P 2C8 (416) 250-7400
EASTERN CONSTRUCTION COMPANY LIMITED is a general contractor involved in commercial, industrial and institutional construction.
L.L. Odette, Chairman
TOTAL REVENUE ($000) 200,203

ECHO BAY MINES LTD.
See page 39 for a full company profile.

ECLIPSE CAPITAL CORPORATION
(Public) MANAGEMENT AND DIVERSIFIED
148-A James Street, Bracebridge, ON, P1L 1R7 (705) 645-4044
ECLIPSE CAPITAL's principal business is its investment in Alert Care Corporation, a 56% owned subsidiary which manages retirement homes.
W. Wayne Barton, President
TOTAL REVENUE ($000) 3,482

ECONOMIC INVESTMENT TRUST LIMITED
(Public) INVESTMENT COMPANIES AND FUNDS
10th Floor, 165 University Avenue, Toronto, ON,
M5H 3B8 (416) 947-2578
ECONOMIC INVESTMENT TRUST LIMITED is an investment Corporation whose portfolio includes investments in banks and trust companies and the financial, insurance & funds, food, manufacturing, metals & mining, oil, gas & pipelines, communications and transportation industries.
J. Christopher Barron, Chairman Of The Board
TOTAL REVENUE ($000) 5,055

ECONOMICAL MUTUAL INSURANCE COMPANY
(Private) INSURANCE - PROPERTY & CASUALTY
111 Westmount Road South, P.O. Box 2000, Waterloo, ON,
N2J 4S4 (519) 570-8200

ECONOMICAL MUTUAL INSURANCE COMPANY is a property and casualty insurance comapny.
P.H. Sims, Chairman Of The Board
TOTAL REVENUE ($000) 656,393

EDINOV CORPORATION
(Public) MISC. INDUSTRIAL PRODUCTS
115 Labrosse Avenue, Pointe Claire, PQ, H9R 1A3 (514) 694-6611
EDINOV CORPORATION manufactures and distributes specialized industrial fasteners for the industrial and manufacturing sectors.
M.L. Marengere, President & C.E.O.
TOTAL REVENUE ($000) 5,845

EDMONTON POWER
(Crown) ELECTRICAL UTILITIES
10065 Jasper Avenue, Suite 1700, Edmonton, AB,
T5J 3B1 (403) 448-3193
EDMONTON POWER is a fully integrated electric utility, from generation to transmission.
Jack Cresseyerack, Chairman
TOTAL REVENUE ($000) 395,282

EDMONTON TELEPHONES CORPORATION
(Crown) TELEPHONE UTILITIES
P.O. Box 20500, Edmonton, AB, T5J 2R4 (403) 441-2000
EDMONTON TELEPHONES CORPORATION is the largest municipally owned and independent telephone system in Canada. It is a fully integrated operation, providing a complete range of telecommunications products and services to residential and business clients within the Edmonton corporate boundaries. It sells consulting services and terminal products around the world.
J.L. Schlosser, Chairman
TOTAL REVENUE ($000) 276,529

EDPER ENTERPRISES LTD.
(Public) MANAGEMENT AND DIVERSIFIED
Suite 4400, Commerce Court West, Toronto, ON,
M5L 1K5 (416) 865-0430
EDPER ENTERPRISES LTD. is a diversified Canadian company with interests in the natural resources, real estate, financial services and consumer products sectors. Its principal corporate investments include direct and indirect equity interests in Hees International Bancorp Inc., Brascan Limited and Carena Developments Limited.
Peter F. Bronfman, Chairman
TOTAL REVENUE ($000) (117,926)

EL CONDOR RESOURCES LTD.
(Public) PRECIOUS METALS
Suite 1020, 800 West Pender Street, Vancouver, BC,
V6C 2V6 (604) 684-6365
EL CONDOR RESOURCES LTD. is focused on the development of a large scale copper-gold project in Western Canada. Engineering and permitting programs are now underway. Rio Algom Limited owns 7.6% of the company's shares.
Robert G. Hunter, Chairman & C.E.O.
TOTAL REVENUE ($000) 218

ELAN ENERGY INC.
See page 86 for a full company profile.

ELECTROHOME LIMITED
(Public)   ELECTRICAL & ELECTRONIC
809 Wellington St North, Kitchener, ON, N2G 4J6   (519) 744-7111
ELECTROHOME LIMITED operates in two business segments in Canada. The electronics division designs, manufactures and markets internationally a wide range of video display and projection oriented products. The communications segment operates a number of radio and television stations in Alberta and Ontario.
J.A. Pollock, Chairman
TOTAL REVENUE ($000)   127,464

ELI LILLY CANADA INC.
(Private)   CHEMICALS
3650 Danforth Ave, Scarborough, ON, M1N 2E8   (416) 694-3221
ELI LILLY CANADA INC. develops, manufactures and markets life science products of which 77% is pharmaceutical. The company is wholly owned by Eli Lilly and Co. of the United States.
Roy A. Cage, Chairman
TOTAL REVENUE ($000)   215,000

ELLIS-DON INC.
(Private)   CONTRACTORS
2045 Oxford Street East, London, ON, N5V 2Z7   (519) 455-6770
ELLIS-DON INC. operates as a general contractor in the construction business. The company is 100% employee owned.
Donald J. Smith, Chairman & C.E.O.
TOTAL REVENUE ($000)   748,000

EMCO LIMITED
See page 202 for a full company profile.

EMERSON ELECTRIC CANADA LIMITED
(Private)   ELECTRICAL & ELECTRONIC
9999 Highway 48, Markham, ON, L3P 3J6   (416) 294-9340
EMERSON ELECTRIC CANADA LIMITED is engaged in two industry segments commercial and industrial components and consumer products. The company is a wholly owned subsidiary of Emerson Electric Co. of the United States.
Lawrence C. Barrett, President
TOTAL REVENUE ($000)   271,007

EMPIRE COMPANY LIMITED
See page 358 for a full company profile.

EMPIRE LIFE INSURANCE COMPANY (THE)
(Private)   INSURANCE - LIFE
259 King Street East, Kingston, ON, K7L 3A8   (613) 548-1881
THE EMPIRE LIFE INSURANCE COMPANY markets a full range of financial products and services designed to meet the needs of individuals and businesses in Canada.
James W. McCutcheon, Q.C., Chairman Of The Board
TOTAL REVENUE ($000)   332,821

ENCAL ENERGY LTD.
(Public)   OIL AND GAS PRODUCERS
Suite 700, 350 - 7th Avenue S.W., Calgary, AB,
T2P 3N9   (403) 294-1766
ENCAL ENERGY LTD. is involved in the acquisition, exploration and development of oil and natural gas properties.
Michael A. Columbos, President & C.E.O.
TOTAL REVENUE ($000)   5,058

ENERPLUS RESOURCES CORPORATION
(Public)   OIL AND GAS PRODUCERS
Suite 3200, 150 - 6th Avenue S.W., Calgary, AB,
T2P 3Y7   (403) 269-7070
ENERPLUS RESOURCES CORPORATION's operations are to consist of the aquisition, holding, managing and disposing of interests in oil and gas properties and sale of royalty units as interests in the royalty to be paid from the acquired properties.
Marcel J. Tremblay, Chairman, President & C.E.O.
TOTAL REVENUE ($000)   34,455

ENNISTEEL CORP.
(Public)   METAL FABRICATORS
South Street N., P.O. Box 10, Port Robinson, ON,
L0S 1K0   (416) 384-9794
ENNISTEEL CORP. operates steel service centres, which purchase hot rolled steel products from steel mills, warehouse the products, in certain cases cut the steel according to customer's specifications anddeliver such products to steel fabricators and manufacturers. It also operates steel fabricators, which purchase structural steel from whichthey manufacture structural steel products.
Bernard Ennis, President
TOTAL REVENUE ($000)   87,234

ENRON OIL TRADING & TRANSPORTATION CANADA LTD.
(Private)   OIL AND GAS PRODUCERS
400 - 3rd Avenue. S.W., Suite 3550, Calgary, AB, T2P 4H2
ENRON OIL TRADING & TRANSPORTATION CANADA LTD. is engaged in the gathering, transporting and marketing of petroleum and petroleum products in Canada and the United States. The company is a wholly owned subsidiary of Enron Oil Trading & Transportation Company (U.S.).
TOTAL REVENUE ($000)   1,045,548

ENSCOR INC.
(Public)   DEVELOPERS
156 Duncan Mill Road, Unit 12, Don Mills, ON,
M3B 3N2   (416) 449-3535
ENSCOR INC.'s core business has, since 1986, consisted primarily of residential home building and land development in the Greater Toronto area. During the past eighteen months, Enscor has gradually reduced its real estate activities. At this time, Enscor is committed to a complete and orderly withdrawl from the industry, and to the pusuit of acquisition opportunites in the United States.
Sam Reisman, Chairman & C.E.O.
TOTAL REVENUE ($000)   37,919

ENSERV CORPORATION
(Public)   OIL AND GAS FIELD SERVICES
Suite 1505, 505 - 3rd Street S.W., Calgary, AB,
T2P 3E6   (403) 237-7660
ENSERV CORPORATION, is a diversified oil field services company.
Activities include contract drilling of shallow and medium depth oil and
gas wells, well servicing and snubbing operations, rental of production
equipment, natural gas compressor packaging, design, sales, rentals and
service, and the provision of environmental services and equipment.
John B. Zaozirny, Chairman
TOTAL REVENUE ($000)   51,328

ENSIGN RESOURCE SERVICE GROUP INC.
(Public)   OIL AND GAS FIELD SERVICES
Suite 900, 400 - 5th Avenue S.W., Calgary, AB,
T2P 0L6   (403) 262-1361
ENSIGN RESOURCE SERVICE GROUP INC. is involved in contract
drilling and well servicing services to the oil and gas industry.
Donald Jewitt, Chairman
TOTAL REVENUE ($000)   41,741

ENVIRONMENTAL TECHNOLOGIES INC.
(Public)   MISC. INDUSTRIAL PRODUCTS
190 Attwell Drive, Suite 202, Etobicoke, ON,
M9W 6H8   (416) 674-0573
ENVIRONMENTAL TECHNOLOGIES INTERNATIONAL INC.
operates through a number of secondary technology, equipment and
process-oriented businesses in the environmental industry. ETI provides
initial and ongoing financial, marketing, operational, planning, technical
and general management resources to its subsidiaries and associates.
Ron Williams, Chairman, President & C.E.O.
TOTAL REVENUE ($000)   7,567

ENVIRONMENTAL TECHNOLOGIES INTERNATIONAL INC.
(Public)   ENVIRONMENTAL SERVICES
Suite 202, 190 Attwell Drive, Etobicoke, ON,
M9W 6H8   (416) 674-0573
ENVIRONMENTAL TECHNOLOGIES INTERNATIONAL INC.
operates through a number of secondary technology, equipment and
process-oriented businesses in the environmental industry. ETI provides
initial and ongoing financial, marketing, operational, planning, technical
and general management resources to its subsidiaries and associates.
Ron Williams, Chairman
TOTAL REVENUE ($000)   13,005

EPIC DATA INTERNATIONAL INC.
(Public)   ELECTRICAL & ELECTRONIC
7280 River Road, Richmond, BC, V6X 1X5   (604) 273-9146
EPIC DATA INC. designs, manufactures, markets and services elec-
tronic data collection systems and products, primarily for the factory data
collection market.
Helmut M. Eppich, Chairman
TOTAL REVENUE ($000)   25,903

EQUINOX RESOURCES LTD.
(Public)   PRECIOUS METALS
Suite 1500, 625 Howe Street, Vancouver, BC,
V6C 2T6   (604) 684-1175
EQUINOX RESOURCES LTD. is involved in major gold, lead, zinc
and platinum exploration and mining projects in Canada, and the United
States.
Ross J. Beaty, President
TOTAL REVENUE ($000)   1,561

EQUITABLE LIFE INSURANCE COMPANY OF CANADA
(Private)   INSURANCE - LIFE
One Westmount Road North, Waterloo, ON,
N2J 4C7   (519) 886-5110
EQUITABLE LIFE INSURANCE COMPANY OF CANADA is an
independent mutual life insurance company offering a full range of life
insurance, annuities and group plans for individuals and businesses.
Robert J. Collins-Wright, Chairman Of The Board
TOTAL REVENUE ($000)   229,876

EQUITY SILVER MINES LIMITED
See page 40 for a full company profile.

ESPALAU INC.
(Public)   MANAGEMENT AND DIVERSIFIED
1400 4th Avenue, Val d'Or, PQ, J9P 5Z9   (819) 825-1111
ESPALAU INC. specializes in services and products for the mining and
construction industries. It is also active in the hotel sector.
Normand Cliche, President, C.E.O. & Secretary
TOTAL REVENUE ($000)   51,912

ESSTRA INDUSTRIES CORP.
(Public)   MISC. CONSUMER PRODUCTS
Suite 218, 10458 Mayfield Road, Edmonton, AB,
T5P 4P4   (403) 484-3794
ESSTRA INDUSTRIES CORP. is involved in a 122 unit luxury rental
townhouse project in Minneapolos, construction of townhomes in Van-
couver for sale, merchant banking, bridge loans, equity placements,etc.
Frederic S. Martin, Chairman
TOTAL REVENUE ($000)   881

ESTEE LAUDER COSMETICS LTD.
(Private)   MISC. CONSUMER PRODUCTS
161 Commander Blvd., Agincourt, ON, M1S 3K9   (416) 961-1919
ESTEE LAUDER COSMETICS LTD. is a distributor of cosmetic
products. It is a wholly owned subsidiary of Estee Lauder International
Inc..
Anton McBurnie, Exec. V.P. & Managing Director
TOTAL REVENUE ($000)   733,818

ETAC SALES LTD.
(Public)   WHOLESALE DISTRIBUTORS
20 Bertrand Avenue, Scarborough, ON, M1L 2P4   (416) 752-5324
ETAC SALES LTD. is an international trading company whose principal
activity is the importation into Canada of various consumer products. The
company's supplier network is located mostly in the Far East, primarily
in the Peoples' Republic of China, Hong Kong, South Korea, Taiwan,

Indonesia, and Thailand. The customer base includes many of Canada's major department stores, specialty stores and chain stores.
Edward Tan, Chairman
TOTAL REVENUE ($000)   198,065

EURO-NEVADA MINING CORPORATION LIMITED
See page 41 for a full company profile.

EXCEL ENERGY INC.
See page 87 for a full company profile.

EXCO TECHNOLOGIES LIMITED
(Public)   MISC. INDUSTRIAL PRODUCTS
60 Spy Court, Markham, ON, L3R 5H6   (416) 477-3065
EXCO TECHNOLOGIES LIMITED is a design, engineering and high precision machining house operating in the tooling segment of the metalworking industry. The company's technologies have been applied in four separate but related sectors: mould making, mould making services, extrusion tooling and precision machining.
Arthur A. Kennedy, Chairman of the Board
TOTAL REVENUE ($000)   39,500

EXPLORATION OREX INC.
(Public)   METAL MINES
67 Perreault East, Rouyn-Noranda, PQ, J9X 3C1   (819) 797-1400
EXPLORATION OREX INC. is involved in the acquisition, exploration and development of mineral properties.
Michel Roy, President
TOTAL REVENUE ($000)   6

EXPORT DEVELOPMENT CORPORATION
(Crown)   FINANCE AND LEASING
151 O'Connor Street, Ottawa, ON, K1A 1K3   (613) 598-2500
EXPORT DEVELOPMENT CORPORATION is a Canadian crown corporation whose purpose or goal is to facilitate and develop Canada's export trade within the framework of the Export Development Act. The company pursues its purpose by providing insurance guarantee and financing facilities, allowing Canadian firms to compete effectively abroad.
Maureen Sabia, Chairman
TOTAL REVENUE ($000)   660,314

EXPORT PACKERS COMPANY LIMITED
(Private)   WHOLESALE DISTRIBUTORS
250 Summerlea Road, Brampton, ON, L6T 3V6   (416) 792-9700
EXPORT PACKERS COMPANY LIMITED is engaged in food wholesaling and egg processing. The company is wholly owned by the Rubenstein family of Toronto, Ontario.
Max Rubenstein, Chairman
TOTAL REVENUE ($000)   230,861

EXTENDICARE HEALTH SERVICES INC.
(Private)   BIOTECHNOLOGY & PHARMACEUTICALS
3000 Steeles Avenue East, Suite 700, Markham, ON,
L3R 9W2   (416) 470-1400
EXTENDICARE HEALTH SERVICES INC. is a provider in North America of long-term care to the elderly through its nursing and retirement centres. It also offers other health care services including home care,

the provision of institutional pharmacy and medical supplies, and hospital management and development.
Fredende Ladly, President & C.E.O.
TOTAL REVENUE ($000)   807,274

F.W. WOOLWORTH CO. LIMITED
(Private)   DEPARTMENT STORES
33 Adelaide Street West, Toronto, ON, M5H 1P5   (416) 361-2111
F.W. WOOLWORTH CO. LIMITED, is engaged in merchandise retailing. Its parent company is Woolworth World Trade Corp. of New York, New York.
William K. Lavin, Chairman
TOTAL REVENUE ($000)   2,143,355

FAHNESTOCK VINER HOLDINGS INC.
See page 402 for a full company profile.

FAIRFAX FINANCIAL HOLDINGS LIMITED
See page 423 for a full company profile.

FALCONBRIDGE GOLD CORPORATION
(Public)   PRECIOUS METALS
95 Wellington Street West, Suite 1200, Toronto, ON,
M5J 2V4   (416) 946-5700
FALCONBRIDGE GOLD CORPORATION operates the Hoyle Pond mine and the Bell Creek mine and mill which are located in the Timmins area of Ontario and the Blanket and Golden Kopje mines in the Republic of Zimbabwe.
Brian A. Ferguson, Chairman, President & C.E.O.
TOTAL REVENUE ($000)   30,747

FALCONBRIDGE INC.
(Private)   INTEGRATED MINES
Suite 1200, 95 Wellington Street West, Toronto, ON,
M5J 2V4   (416) 956-5700
FALCONBRIDGE INC. is an international resource company engaged in the exploration, mining, processing and marketing of metals and minerals. Products include nickel, ferronickel, copper, zinc, cobalt and precious metals. The company has operations in Canada, Norway, the Dominican Republic and Zimbabwe.
Kjell Nilsson, Chairman
TOTAL REVENUE ($000)   1,670,780

FALVO CORPORATION
(Public)   METAL FABRICATORS
42 Taber Road, Rexdale, ON, M9W 3A8   (416) 748-7000
FALVO CORPORATION is engaged in steel fabrication and the manufacture of other steel products as well as real estate development in Toronto and surrounding areas.
N. Falvo, Chairman
TOTAL REVENUE ($000)   12,308

FAMOUS PLAYERS INC.
(Private)   ENTERTAINMENT SERVICES
130 Bloor Street West, Toronto, ON, M5S 1P5
FAMOUS PLAYERS INC. is engaged in the exhibition of motion pictures. The company is a subsidiary of Paramount Pictures (Canada) Inc.

TOTAL REVENUE ($000)   198,067

FARADAY RESOURCES INC.
(Public)   OIL AND GAS PRODUCERS
Suite 2000, 95 Wellington Street West, Toronto, ON,
M5J 2N7   (416) 362-6721
FARADAY RESOURCES INC. is engaged in the exploration for, and
the development of oil and gas in Alberta. The company is also involved
in mining through investments in Prairie Potash Mines Limited and
Madawaska Mines Limited.
Martin P. Connell, Chairman of the Board
TOTAL REVENUE ($000)   4,703

FARM CREDIT CORPORATION
(Crown)   TRUST, SAVINGS AND LOAN
P.O. Box 4320, 1800 Hamilton Street, Regina, SK,
S4P 4L3   (306) 780-8100
FARM CREDIT's role is to provide mortgage, credit and complimentary
financial services on a breakeven basis to enable Canadian farmers to
establish, develop and maintain viable farm enterprises.
James J. Hewitt, Chairman & C.E.O.
TOTAL REVENUE ($000)   423,358

FARMERS CO-OPERATIVE DAIRY LTD.
(Non-fin Co-op)   FOOD PROCESSING
P.O. Box 8114, Station A, Halifax, NS, B3K 5L8   (902) 835-3373
FARMERS CO-OPERATIVE DAIRY LTD. processes and distributes
a full range of dairy products including milk, cream, yogurt, cheese and
margarine.
Ralph T. Ballam, Chairman
TOTAL REVENUE ($000)   129,130

FCA INTERNATIONAL LTD.
See page 477 for a full company profile.

FCMI FINANCIAL CORPORATION
(Public)   INVESTMENT COMPANIES AND FUNDS
347 Bay Street, 2nd Floor, Toronto, ON, M5H 2R7   (416) 364-1171
FCMI FINANCIAL CORPORATION is engaged in providing manage-
ment and/or advisory services to specialized funds, from which it derives
fee income.
Albert D. Friedberg, Chairman & President
TOTAL REVENUE ($000)   7,853

FEDERAL BUSINESS DEVELOPMENT BANK
(Crown)   TRUST, SAVINGS AND LOAN
P.O. Box 335, Tour de la Place Victoria, Montreal, PQ,
H4Z 1L4   (514) 283-5904
FEDERAL BUSINESS DEVELOPMENT BANK is a crown corpora-
tion that promotes the creation and development of businesses in Canada,
especially small and medium sized businesses. The bank provides term
loans and loan guarantees, venture capital, and a broad range of manage-
ment training, counselling, and planning services.
Bertrand J. Lavoie, Chairman
TOTAL REVENUE ($000)   368,068

FEDERAL INDUSTRIES LTD.
See page 446 for a full company profile.

FEDERAL PIONEER LIMITED
(Private)   ELECTRICAL & ELECTRONIC
19 Waterman Avenue, Toronto, ON, M4B 1Y2   (416) 752-8020
FEDERAL PIONEER LTD. makes and markets electrical equipment.
Products include transformers, circuit breakers, switchgear, low voltage
distribution equipment and high voltage direct current systems. The
company is a wholly owned subsidiary of Sadasi, S.A..
Russell M. Baranowski, President & C.E.O.
TOTAL REVENUE ($000)   226,874

FEDERATED CO-OPERATIVES LIMITED
(Non-fin Co-op)   WHOLESALE DISTRIBUTORS
Box 1050, 401 - 22nd Street East, Saskatoon, SK,
S7K 3M9   (306) 244-3311
FEDERATED CO-OPERATIVES LIMITED operates from its base in
Saskatchewan to co-ordinate the procurement, processing, manufactur-
ing and distribution of goods, and the provision of services to its
member-owners. The cooperative operates in several business segments
including food, petroleum, hardware building materials, crop supplies,
feed supplies and family fashions.
V.J. Leland, President Of The Board
TOTAL REVENUE ($000)   1,717,507

FEDNAV LIMITED
(Private)   TRANSPORTATION
600 De La Gauchetiere West, Suite 2600, Montreal, PQ,
H3B 4M3   (514) 878-6500
FEDNAV LIMITED is a ocean transportation company.
Laurence G. Pathy, President & C.E.O.
TOTAL REVENUE ($000)   337,000 (US)

FIBERGLAS CANADA INC.
(Private)   MISC. INDUSTRIAL PRODUCTS
4100 Yonge Street, Willowdale, ON, M2P 2B6   (416) 733-1600
FIBERGLAS CANADA INC.'s operations consist of two segments: the
insulation group manufactures thermal insulation for residential, commercial and industrial buildings, as well as roof insulation, accoustic
products and other insulation products; the textiles, reinforcements and
chemicals group provides a variety of materials primarily to the glass
fibre reinforced plastics industry.
R. Jones, President & C.E.O.
TOTAL REVENUE ($000)   318,826

FIDUCIE DESJARDINS INC.
(Public)   TRUST, SAVINGS AND LOAN
1 Complexe Desjardins, P.O. Box 34, Desjardins Station, Montreal,
PQ, H5B 1E4   (514) 286-9441
FIDUCIE DESJARDINS INC. offers a range of services specific to a
trust company, such as guaranteed investment certificates, mortgage
loans, portfolio management services for the account of individuals and
businesses, mutual fund units, trustee services to individuals, companies
and pension funds and other related services.
Paul-Yvon Lesage, Chairman of the Board
TOTAL REVENUE ($000)   252,265

FINNING LTD.
See page 344 for a full company profile.

FIRAN CORPORATION
(Public)   AUTOMOTIVE
353 Iroquois Shore Road, Oakville, ON,
L6H 1M3   (416) 844-2870
FIRAN CORPORATION is engaged in: the manufacture of a full line
of recreational vehicles, marketed through an independent franchised
dealer network throughout North America; the design and manufacture
of communications systems for the international air traffic control market; and the manufacture of printed circuit boards for the North American
electronics industry.
D. Morgan Firestone, Chairman, President & C.E.O.
TOTAL REVENUE ($000)   99,534

FIRST B SHARES INC.
(Public)   INVESTMENT COMPANIES AND FUNDS
2 First Canadian Place, Suite 3100, P.O. Box 21, Toronto, ON,
M5X 1J9   (416) 869-3707
FIRST B SHARES INC. is a mutual fund company.
Stuart W. Henry, President
TOTAL REVENUE ($000)   16,817

**FIRST CALGARY FINANCIAL SAVINGS & CREDIT
UNION**
(Fin. Co-op)   FINANCE AND LEASING
Suite 200, 510 16th Ave N.W., Calgary, AB,
T2E 1K4   (403) 230-2783
FIRST CALGARY FINANCIAL SAVINGS & CREDIT UNION is a
full service open bond credit union.
Ron Gillmore, Chairman
TOTAL REVENUE ($000)   55,024

FIRST INTERSTATE BANK OF CANADA
(Private)   BANKS
Suite 4117, Royal Trust Tower, 77 King Street West, Toronto, ON,
M5K 1H1   (416) 865-0250
FIRST INTERSTATE BANK OF CANADA is a wholly owned sub-
sidiary of First Interstate Bank of California. It is licensed to operate as
a bank under the Bank Act with full banking powers as a foreign bank
subsidiary.
Harold J. Meyerman, Chairman
TOTAL REVENUE ($000)   10,868

FIRST MARATHON INC.
See page 403 for a full company profile.

FIRST MARITIME MINING CORPORATION LIMITED
(Public)   METAL MINES
P.O. Box 937, 300 Union Street, Saint John, NB,
E2L 4E3   (506) 632-7171
FIRST MARITIME MINING CORPORATION LIMITED is a holding
company with investments in Brunswick Mining and Smelting Corpo-
ration Limited, Alantic Coast Copper Corporation Limited and Consoli-
dated Rambler Mines Limited.
D.A. Macfarlane, President & Treasurer
TOTAL REVENUE ($000)   1,292

FIRST MERCANTILE CURRENCY FUND, INC. (THE)
(Public)   INVESTMENT COMPANIES AND FUNDS
347 Bay Street, Suite 404, Toronto, ON, M5H 2R7   (416) 364-2724
FIRST MERCANTILE CURRENCY FUND is a closed-end trust devoted to investment in foreign currencies. These investments are made
primarily through the interbank market in the form of forward contracts.
A key objective of the Fund is to correctly anticipate relative movements-
both upward and downward-in the exchange rates of various currencies,
earning profits on the changing spreads between them.
Herbert Alpert, Chairman of the Board
TOTAL REVENUE ($000)   2,209

FLEET AEROSPACE CORPORATION
See page 219 for a full company profile.

FLETCHER CHALLENGE CANADA LIMITED
See page 141 for a full company profile.

FLETCHER CHALLENGE FINANCE CANADA INC.
(Public)   INVESTMENT COMPANIES AND FUNDS
P.O. Box 10058, 9th Floor, Pacific Centre, 700 West Georgia Street,
Vancouver, BC, V7Y 1J7   (604) 668-4242
FLETCHER CHALLENGE FINANCE CANADA INC. does not carry
on, nor does it intend to carry on, any activity. The net proceeds of the
issue will be advanced to businesses of the group (Fletcher Challenge
Limited and all its subsidiaries) and will be used to repay U.S. Dollar and
N.Z. Dollar indebtedness. Proceeds from the indebtedness being repaid
were used by businesses of the group for working capital purposes.
B.D. Cooper, President
TOTAL REVENUE ($000)   34,238

FLETCHER CHALLENGE INVESTMENTS II INC.
(Public)   INVESTMENT COMPANIES AND FUNDS
9th Floor, 700 West Georgia Street, P.O. Box 10058, Pacific Centre,
Vancouver, BC, V7Y 1J7   (604) 654-4372
FLETCHER CHALLENGE INVESTMENTS II INC.'s principal assets
include a long term investment in, and various receivables with, compa-
nies in the Fletcher Challenge group. The majority of the company's
revenues are received by way of dividends on long-term investments.
I. Donald, President & C.E.O.
TOTAL REVENUE ($000)   11,239

FLETCHER CHALLENGE INVESTMENTS INC.
(Public)   INVESTMENT COMPANIES AND FUNDS
9th Floor, 700 West Georgia Street, P.O. Box 10058, Pacific Centre,
Vancouver, BC, V7Y 1J7   (604) 654-4372
FLETCHER CHALLENGE INVESTMENTS INC.'s principal assets
include a long- term investments in, and note receivables from, compa-
nies in the Fletcher Challenge group. The majority of its revenues are
received by way of dividends from the long term investments in Fletcher
Challenge group companies.
I. Donald, President & C.E.O.
TOTAL REVENUE ($000)   30,929

FLETCHER'S FINE FOODS LTD.
(Private)   FOOD PROCESSING
8385 Fraser Street, Suite 3000, Vancouver, BC,
V5X 3X8   (604) 321-6681

FLETCHER'S FINE FOODS LTD. is a pork producer with operations in Red Deer, Edmonton, Vancouver and the United States. It is wholly owned by Alberta Pork Producers Development Corporation.
Brian Perkins, Chairman
TOTAL REVENUE ($000)   208,500

FLUOR DANIEL CANADA INC.
(Private)   CONTRACTORS
Box 8799, Station F, Calgary, AB, T2J 4B4   (403) 259-1110
FLUOR DANIEL CANADA INC. is engaged in engineering, procurement, construction management and maintenance. Fluor Daniel Canada's ultimate parent is Fluor Corporation (U.S.).
John Gallagher, Gen Mgr Operations
TOTAL REVENUE ($000)   463,192

FOOTHILLS PIPE LINES LTD.
(Private)   GAS PIPELINES
P.O. Box 2535, Postal Station M, Calgary, AB,
T2P 2N6   (403) 290-6000
FOOTHILLS PIPE LINES LTD. was established to construct the Canadian portion of the Alaska Natural Gas Transportation System. It transports Canadian natural gas for export to U.S. markets. It is owned in equal shares by Nova Corporation of Alberta and Westcoast Energy Inc..
R.L. PIERCE, C.E.O. & Chairman
TOTAL REVENUE ($000)   169,804

FORD CREDIT CANADA LIMITED
(Private)   FINANCE AND LEASING
The Canadian Road, Oakville, ON, L6J 5C7   (416) 845-2511
FORD CREDIT CANADA LIMITED provides wholesale and retail financing support to Ford automotive dealers and their customers. It is an affiliate of Ford Motor Company of Canada, Limited.
William E. Odom, Chairman Of The Board
TOTAL REVENUE ($000)   724,721

FORD ELECTRONICS MANUFACTURING CORPORATION
(Private)   ELECTRICAL & ELECTRONIC
7455 Birchmount Road, Markham, ON, L3R 5C2   (416) 474-4203
FORD ELECTRONICS MANUFACTURING CORPORATION is the manufacturer of electronic automotive products for Ford Motor Company worldwide. The company is a wholly owned subsidiary of Ford Motor Company of Michigan.
C. Szuluk, President
TOTAL REVENUE ($000)   277,100

FORD MOTOR COMPANY OF CANADA, LIMITED
See page 184 for a full company profile.

FORDING COAL LIMITED
(Private)   NON-BASE METAL MINING
10th Floor, 205 - 9th Avenue S.E., Calgary, AB,
T2G 0R4   (403) 264-1063
FORDING COAL LIMITED mines and processes metallurgical and thermal coal for markets including blast furnace steel producers, utilities and other coal consumers worldwide. Mine sites are located in Alberta and southeastern British Columbia. The company is a wholly owned subsidiary of Canadian Pacific Limited of Montreal, Quebec.

J.H. Morrish, Chairman & C.E.O.
TOTAL REVENUE ($000)   252,055

FORESBEC INC.
(Public)   EAST COAST FORESTRY
1750 Rue Haggerty, Drummondville, PQ, J2C 5P8   (819) 477-8787
FORESBEC INC. is a major producer of hardwoods for export markets.
Guy Boisse, President & C.E.O.
TOTAL REVENUE ($000)   35,413

FORTIS INC.
See page 298 for a full company profile.

FOSTER'S BREWING GROUP CANADA INC.
(Public)   BREWERIES
Suite 1114, North Tower, 175 Bloor Street East, Toronto,
M4W 3R8   (416) 921-0055
FOSTER'S BREWING GROUP CANADA INC. is an indirect, wholly owned subsidiary of Foster's Brewing Group Limited. Foster's Brewing Group Limited is an international brewing company with major subsidiaries in Australia, the United Kingdom and Canada.
Edward T. Kunkel, President
TOTAL REVENUE ($000)   31,009

FOUR SEASONS HOTELS INC.
See page 493 for a full company profile.

FPI LIMITED
See page 163 for a full company profile.

FRANCO-NEVADA MINING CORPORATION LIMITED
See page 42 for a full company profile.

FRASER INC.
(Private)   EAST COAST FORESTRY
27 Rice St, Edmundston, NB, E3V 1S9   (506) 735-5551
FRASER INC. is an integrated producer of forest products based in New Brunswick. From its woodlands, the company produces boxboard, fine papers, market pulp, coated and uncoated ground wood papers and wood products. The company operates a forest tree nursery which produces seedlings for reforestation projects carried out on company lands.
Niall O'briain, President
TOTAL REVENUE ($000)   472,563

FREEWEST RESOURCES INC.
(Public)   METAL MINES
Suite 1525, 800 Rene-Levesque Blvd. W., Montreal, PQ,
H3B 1X9   (514) 878-3551
FREEWEST RESOURCES INC. is a mining exploration company, exploring for precious and base metals in Ontario, Quebec and New Brunswick. Its main asset is its interest in the Holloway project, a joint venture with Hemlo Gold Mines Inc. and Teddy Bear Valley Mines Limited, which is expected to be in production by 1994.
Mackenzie I. Watson, President & C.E.O.
TOTAL REVENUE ($000)   103

FT CAPITAL LTD.
See page 424 for a full company profile.

FUJI BANK CANADA
(Private) BANKS
BCE Place, Canada Trust Tower, P.O. Box 609, Suite 2800, 161
Bay Street, Toronto, ON, M5J 2S1 (416) 865-1020
FUJI BANK CANADA is a Schedule II bank, offering full banking
services.
Tomohiro Kayio, Chairman
TOTAL REVENUE ($000) 65,927

G.T.C. TRANSCONTINENTAL GROUP LTD.
See page 321 for a full company profile.

GAINERS INC.
(Private) FOOD PROCESSING
12525-66 Street, Edmonton, AB, T5J 2H8 (403) 471-0611
GAINERS INC. is engaged in meat packing.
Ian Strang, Chairman & C.E.O.
TOTAL REVENUE ($000) 432,881

GALTACO INC.
(Public) AUTOMOTIVE
Suite 300, 174 Stanley Street, Brantford, ON,
N3S 7S3 (519) 751-1691
GALTACO INC., through its controlled subsidiary Redlaw Industries,
is involved in metal stampings and assemblies for the automotive indus-
try, thermoplastics injection molded parts and thermoset plastic parts for
the shoe industry and recreational vehicle industry, and also the manu-
facture of industrial apparel textiles through its investment in Johnston
Industries Inc.
David L. Chandler, Chairman, President & C.E.O.
TOTAL REVENUE ($000) 47,374

GANDALF TECHNOLOGIES INC.
See page 220 for a full company profile.

GARBELL HOLDINGS LIMITED
(Public) INVESTMENT COMPANIES AND FUNDS
Suite 2402, P.O. Box 53, Royal Trust Tower, Toronto-Dominion
Centre, Toronto, ON, M5K 1E7 (416) 947-1100
GARBELL HOLDINGS LIMITED is an investment holding company.
George R. Gardiner, Chairman
TOTAL REVENUE ($000) 4,207

GAZ METROPOLITAIN, INC.
(Private) GAS UTILITIES
1717 Du Havre Street, Montreal, PQ, H2K 2X3 (514) 598-3737
GAZ METROPOLITAIN INC. is a natural gas distribution company.
Its network covers 95% of the province of Quebec. Gaz is also involved
in the sale and repair of natural gas appliances and the use of natural gas
as a motor vehicle fuel. The company is a wholly owned subsidiary of
Noverco (1991) Inc. of Montreal.
Yves Rheault, Chairman
TOTAL REVENUE ($000) 1,091,396

GEAC COMPUTER CORPORATION LIMITED
See page 466 for a full company profile.

GEDDES RESOURCES LIMITED
(Public) METAL MINES
Suite 1400, Pender Place, 700 West Pender Street, Vancouver, BC,
V6C 1G8 (604) 682-2392
GEDDES RESOURCES LIMITED is engaged in mining exploration
and development.
Howard E. Cadinha, Chairman
TOTAL REVENUE ($000) 42

GENDIS INC.
See page 359 for a full company profile.

**GENERAL ACCIDENT ASSURANCE COMPANY OF
CANADA**
(Private) INSURANCE - PROPERTY & CASUALTY
2 First Canadian Place, Suite 2600, P.O. Box 410, Toronto, ON,
M5X 1J1 (416) 368-4733
GENERAL ACCIDENT ASSURANCE COMPANY OF CANADA is
a property and casualty insurer. The company is 99.9% owned by Scottish
Insurance Corp. Limited of Perth, Scotland.
F. Mercier, Chairperson of the Board
TOTAL REVENUE ($000) 603,397

GENERAL ELECTRIC CANADA INC.
(Private) ELECTRICAL & ELECTRONIC
2300 Meadowvale Blvd., Mississauga, ON,
L5N 5P9 (416) 858-5100
GENERAL ELECTRIC CANADA INC. is engaged in the manufacture
and distribution of appliances, motors, lighting products and other elec-
trical products. The company is a wholly owned subsidiary of General
Electric Company of the United States.
Steven C. Riedel, Chairman & C.E.O.
TOTAL REVENUE ($000) 1,448,660

**GENERAL ELECTRIC CANADIAN HOLDINGS
LIMITED**
(Private) ELECTRICAL & ELECTRONIC
2300 Meadowvale Blvd., Mississauga, ON,
L5N 5P9 (416) 858-5100
GENERAL ELECTRIC CANADIAN HOLDINGS LIMITED amalga-
mated with GE Plastics Limited in July 1992. GE Plastics is the holding
company of GE Canada Limited, which manufactures and distributes
industrial and consumer products.
TOTAL REVENUE ($000) 1,505,300

GENERAL ELECTRIC CAPITAL CANADA INC.
(Private) FINANCE AND LEASING
2300 Meadowvale Blvd., Mississauga, ON, L5N 5P9
GENERAL ELECTRIC CAPITAL CANADA INC. and its subsidiaries
provide time sales, loans, equipment lease financing and real estate
financing. It is a wholly owned subsidiary of General Electric Capital
Corp. of the United States.
TOTAL REVENUE ($000) 394,144

GENERAL LEASEHOLDS LIMITED

(Public)   DEVELOPERS
Suite 600, 2 St. Clair Avenue West, Toronto, ON,
M4V 1L5   (416) 929-1003
GENERAL LEASEHOLDS LIMITED is a public real estate develop-ment company with holdings in Northern and Southern Ontario including major shopping centres and office buildings.
Morey I. Speigel, Chairman & C.F.O.
TOTAL REVENUE ($000)   22,805

GENERAL MILLS CANADA, INC.

(Private)   FOOD PROCESSING
1330 Martin Grove Road, P.O. Box 505, Rexdale, ON,
M9W 4X4   (416) 743-8110
GENERAL MILLS CANADA, INC. conducts operations through six divisions. They are: Lancia-Bravo Foods division (pasta and spaghetti sauce); Blue Water Seafoods division (cooked fish products); Grocery Products (cereals, dessert mixes, granola products); Parker Brothers division (games, toys); Eddie Bauer division (sports clothes); Izod division (men's, ladies' and children's clothing and accessories).
Stephen Demeritt, President & C.E.O.
TOTAL REVENUE ($000)   445,027

GENERAL MOTORS ACCEPTANCE CORPORATION OF CANADA LIMITED

(Private)   FINANCE AND LEASING
3300 Bloor Street West, Suite 2800, Toronto, ON,
M8X 2X5   (416) 234-6600
GENERAL MOTORS ACCEPTANCE CORPORATION OF CAN-ADA LIMITED is engaged in automotive financial services to and through General Motors Dealers in Canada and other automobile deal-erships. GMAC of Canada is wholly owned by GMAC of Detroit, Michigan.
W. James Watson, President
TOTAL REVENUE ($000)   1,016,450

GENERAL MOTORS OF CANADA LIMITED

(Private)   AUTOMOTIVE
1908 Colonel Sam Drive, Oshawa, ON, L1H 8P7   (416) 644-5000
GENERAL MOTORS OF CANADA LIMITED designs, manufac-tures, assembles and sells cars and trucks. It is a wholly owned subsidiary of General Motors Corp..
George A. Peapples, President & General Manager
TOTAL REVENUE ($000)   18,366,900

GENERAL TRUSTCO OF CANADA INC.
See page 383 for a full company profile.

GENNUM CORPORATION
See page 221 for a full company profile.

GENTRA INC.
See page 384 for a full company profile.

GEORGE WESTON LIMITED
See page 360 for a full company profile.

GEORGE WIMPEY CANADA LIMITED

(Private)   CONTRACTORS
80 North Queen Street, Toronto, ON, M8Z 5Z6   (416) 233-5811
GEORGE WIMPEY CANADA LIMITED is engaged in construction and housing and real estate development. The company is wholly owned by George Wimpey plc of London, England.
D.H. Heppell, Chairman
TOTAL REVENUE ($000)   167,237

GESCA LTEE

(Private)   PUBLISHING & PRINTING
7 Rue St Jacques Ouest, Montreal, PQ, H2Y 1K9   (514) 285-6981
GESCA LTEE is engaged in the publication of newspapers, daily and weekly. The company is a wholly owned subsidiary of Power Corpora-tion of Canada.
Roger de Landryne, President
TOTAL REVENUE ($000)   189,677

GESCO INDUSTRIES INC.

(Public)   WHOLESALE DISTRIBUTORS
1965 Lawrence Ave. West, Weston, ON, M9N 1H5   (416) 243-0040
GESCO INDUSTRIES INC. has substantially all of its operations in the floor-covering industry. The company is a distributor of a product line that includes carpeting produced at both their own facilities and outside sources, resilient flooring, cushioned flooring, undercushion and sup-plies.
Norman Shnier, Chairman
TOTAL REVENUE ($000)   114,359

GIBRALTAR MINES LIMITED
See page 12 for a full company profile.

GILLETTE CANADA INC.

(Private)   MISC. CONSUMER PRODUCTS
5450 Cote De Liesse Rd, Montreal, PQ, H4P 1E7   (514) 340-2800
GILLETTE CANADA INC. is a consumer products firm engaged in the manufacture and sale of a wide range of products for personal care or use. Gillette Canada is a wholly owned subsidiary of The Gillette Company.
Mr. D. MacDuff, President
TOTAL REVENUE ($000)   445,853

GLAMIS GOLD LTD.
See page 43 for a full company profile.

GLAXO CANADA INC.

(Private)   CHEMICALS
7333 Mississauga Road North, Mississauga, ON,
L5N 6L4   (416) 819-3000
GLAXO CANADA INC. is a manufacturer of pharmaceuticals. It is a wholly owned subsidiary of Glaxo Holdings, plc.
Mr. Art Pappas, Chairman
TOTAL REVENUE ($000)   286,841

GLENAYRE ELECTRONICS LTD.
See page 222 for a full company profile.

GLENEX INDUSTRIES INC.

(Public)   MANAGEMENT AND DIVERSIFIED
185 Davenport Road, Toronto, ON, M5R 1J1   (416) 962-9292
GLENEX INDUSTRIES operates in two industry segments: entertainment; and oil and gas exploration and development. Entertainment options include the provision of production and post production facilities to the television, advertising and communication industries.
Norman Glick, President & C.E.O.
TOTAL REVENUE ($000)   5,005

GOLDBELT RESOURCES LTD.

(Public)   PRECIOUS METALS
Suite 1200, 885 West Georgia Street, Vancouver, BC,
V6C 3E2   (604) 669-2290
GOLDBELT RESOURCES LTD. is developing a 2.8 million ounce gold tailings recovery project in Kazakhstan. A feasibility study has been completed and gold production, at an initial annual rate of 100,000 ounces per year, is expected to begin in 1994 or 1995.
Mike Muzylowski, Co-Chairman
TOTAL REVENUE ($000)   869

GOLDCORP INC.

See page 44 for a full company profile.

GOLDEN KNIGHT RESOURCES INC.

See page 45 for a full company profile.

GOLDEN QUEEN MINING CO. LTD.

(Public)   PRECIOUS METALS
Suite 1000, 900 West Hastings, Vancouver, BC,
V6C 1E5   (604) 684-4468
GOLDEN QUEEN MINING CO. LTD. is involved in the acquisition, exploration and development of precious metal properties.
Paul Bailly, Chairman & C.E.O.
TOTAL REVENUE ($000)   8

GOLDEN RULE RESOURCES LTD.

(Public)   PRECIOUS METALS
Suite 1450, 125 - 9th Avenue S.E., Calgary, AB,
T2G 0P6   (403) 233-7898
GOLDEN RULE RESOURCES LTD. is engaged in the acquisition and exploration of precious metals properties. The company has land holdings in the LaRonge Greenstone Belt of northern Saskatchewan, and in the Toodoggone Gold Camp in British Columbia.
Glen Harper, President
TOTAL REVENUE ($000)   876

GOLDEN STAR RESOURCES LTD.

See page 46 for a full company profile.

GOLDFARB CORPORATION (THE)

(Public)   CONSULTING
Suite 1700, 4950 Yonge Street, North York, ON,
M2N 6K1   (416) 221-9200
GOLDFARB CORPORATION (THE) primarily performs market research through a partnership, Goldfarb Consultants.

Martin Goldfarb, Chairman & C.E.O.
TOTAL REVENUE ($000)   35,067

GOLDSTAKE EXPLORATIONS INC.

(Public)   PRECIOUS METALS
Suite 202, 1231 Yonge Street, Toronto, ON,
M4T 2T8   (416) 966-3939
GOLDSTAKE EXPLORATION and its wholly owned subsidiary, Goldstake Explorations (S.D.) Inc. a corporation incorporated under the laws of South Dakota, is in resource exploration and development.
Robert B. Cleaver, President
TOTAL REVENUE ($000)   (523)

GOODFELLOW INC.

(Public)   MISC. INDUSTRIAL PRODUCTS
225 Rue Goodfellow, Delson, PQ, J0L 1G0   (514) 635-6511
GOODFELLOW INC. is a diversified distributor and remanufacturer of sawn timber, dressed and rough lumber, prefinished and unfinished flooring and composite and veneer based wood panel products. It also re-manufactures wood products provided by kiln drying, wood preservation and milling. The company serves customers throughout Canada, the United States and abroad.
George D. Goodfellow, Chairman
TOTAL REVENUE ($000)   156,928

GOODYEAR CANADA INC.

(Private)   AUTOMOTIVE
10 Four Seasons Place, Etobicoke, ON, M9B 6G2   (416) 626-4611
GOODYEAR CANADA INC. is a tire and rubber company. Products include new tires and tubes, retreads, automotive belts and hoses, automotive molded parts, auto repair services, industrial rubber, and plastic products and films. The company has operations in Ontario, Quebec and Alberta and store locations across Canada. Goodyear Tire and Rubber Co. of Ohio is the company's major shareholder.
Eugene R. Culler, President & C.E.O.
TOTAL REVENUE ($000)   902,783

GORAN CAPITAL INC.

(Public)   INSURANCE - PROPERTY & CASUALTY
Suite 1101, 181 University Ave., Box 11, Toronto, ON,
M5H 3M7   (416) 594-1155
GORAN CAPITAL INC. is the holding company of Pafco Insurance Company Ltd. and Symons General Ins. Co. of Toronto and Fafco General Ins. Co. of Indiana. The insurance companies provide specialty package programs of property and casualty insurance and high premium automobile insurance coverages. The companies operate in all provinces of Canada and six states in the U.S.
G. Gordon Symons, Chairman, President & C.E.O.
TOTAL REVENUE ($000)   75,939

GRANDUC MINES LIMITED

(Public)   METAL MINES
2500 Three Bentall Centre, P.O. Box 49200, 595 Burrard Street,
Vancouver, BC, V7X 1L1   (604) 689-9111
GRANDUC MINES LIMITED is engaged in the exploration for and development of minerals, primarily copper, gold and silver.
W. Glen Zinn, President
TOTAL REVENUE ($000)   348

GRANGES INC.
See page 13 for a full company profile.

GRAYMONT LIMITED
(Private)   MANAGEMENT AND DIVERSIFIED
999 West Hastings St, Suite 1160, Vancouver, BC,
V6C 2W2   (604) 687-0131
GRAYMONT LIMITED is an investment holding company with diverse interests in Canada and the United States.
Stuart F. Wolfe, President & C.E.O.
TOTAL REVENUE ($000)   184,215

GRE FINANCIAL LTD.
(Private)   INSURANCE - PROPERTY & CASUALTY
R.F. Nicol, 181 University Ave., Suite 700, Toronto, ON,
M5H 3M7   (416) 941-5050
GRE FINANCIAL LTD. is a property and casualty insurance company.
It is wholly owned by GRE Financial of the United Kingdom.
TOTAL REVENUE ($000)   440

GREAT ATLANTIC AND PACIFIC TEA COMPANY, LIMITED (THE)
(Private)   FOOD STORES
5559 Dundas Street West, Islington, ON, M9B 1B9   (416) 239-7171
THE GREAT ATLANTIC AND PACIFIC TEA COMPANY, LIMITED operates a chain of retail food stores and is a wholly owned subsidiary of Great Atlantic & Pacific Tea Company, Inc. of Montvale, New Jersey.
Mr. Nigel Byars, Ex. V.P. & Chief Financial Officer
TOTAL REVENUE ($000)   2,981,191

GREAT EASTERN CORPORATION LIMITED (THE)
(Public)   INVESTMENT COMPANIES AND FUNDS
Suite 2104, Box 60, 1969 Upper Water Street, Halifax, NS,
B3J 3R7   (902) 423-8414
THE GREAT EASTERN CORP. LTD. is an investment company.
Fred S. Fountain, President
TOTAL REVENUE ($000)   6,470

GREAT LAKES POWER INC.
See page 447 for a full company profile.

GREAT LAKES REINSURANCE HOLDINGS LTD.
(Private)   INSURANCE - LIFE
390 Bay Street, Suite 2100, Toronto, ON, M5H 2Y2   (416) 364-2851
GREAT LAKES REINSURANCE HOLDINGS LTD. is an investment and holding company. Its principal investments are in companies engaged in the property and casualty and reinsurance business. Its main consolidated investments are The Great Lakes Reinsurance Company and Great Lakes Reinsurance (U.K.) plc.
TOTAL REVENUE ($000)   174,484

GREAT-WEST LIFE ASSURANCE COMPANY (THE)
See page 425 for a full company profile.

GREAT-WEST LIFECO INC.
See page 426 for a full company profile.

GREEN FOREST LUMBER CORPORATION
(Public)   WHOLESALE DISTRIBUTORS
194 Merton Street, Toronto, ON, M4S 3B5   (416) 489-3336
GREEN FOREST LUMBER CORPORATION is a leading independent North American wholesale distributor of lumber and waferboard. The company also operates two sawmills in Chapleau, Ontario.
John T. Sereny, Chairman President & C.E.O.
TOTAL REVENUE ($000)   215,489

GREENSTONE RESOURCES LTD.
(Public)   METAL MINES
Suite 910, 26 Wellington Street East, Toronto, ON,
M5E 1S2   (416) 862-7300
GREENSTONE RESOURCES LTD. is an international mining company with a large diversified portfolio of advanced projects in precious and base metals.
James S. Anthony, Chairman Of The Board
TOTAL REVENUE ($000)   3,919

GREYHOUND LINES OF CANADA LTD.
See page 273 for a full company profile.

GREYVEST FINANCIAL SERVICES INC.
See page 404 for a full company profile.

GRILLI PROPERTY GROUP INC.
(Public)   DEVELOPERS
3535 Boul. Saint Charles, Bureau 200, Kirkland, PQ,
H9H 5B9   (514) 694-0463
GRILLI PROPERTY GROUP is a Quebec-based company involved in the building and marketing of residential, commercial and industrial properties as well as promoting and selling land for development. It also has operations in the manufacturing industry through its kitchen cabinet and concrete divisions.
Mario Grilli, Chairman & C.E.O.
TOTAL REVENUE ($000)   59,622

GROCERY PEOPLE LTD. (THE)
(Private)   FOOD STORES
14505 Yellowhead Trail, Edmonton, AB, T5L 3C4   (403) 447-5700
THE GROCERY PEOPLE LTD. is in the voluntary wholesale business.
The company is a subsidiary of Federated Co-operatives Limited.
James A. Crawford, President
TOTAL REVENUE ($000)   250,000

GROUPE BOCENOR INC.
(Public)   MISC. CONSUMER PRODUCTS
274 Rue Duchesnay, Sainte-Marie, Beauce, PQ,
G6E 3C2   (418) 387-7723
GROUPE BOCENOR is a manufacturer and distributor of a complete line of windows and doors. The company is also engaged in the distribution of construction materials and renovation in Sainte-Isidore de Beauce . The company sells its products in Quebec, the Maritimes and in Eastern Ontario, under the Bonneville brand name.
Jean-Louis Bonneville, Chairman President & C.E.O.
TOTAL REVENUE ($000)   42,233

GROUPE FOREX INC. (LE)
(Public)   EAST COAST FORESTRY
689 3rd Avenue, P.O. Box 296, Val d'Or, PQ,
J9P 4P3   (819) 825-4841
GROUPE FOREX is a lumber manufacturer which operates three
sawmills in Northern Quebec. The company is a supplier of chips to pulp
and paper companies. The company has sales in Canada and the United
States, as well as overseas.
Jean-Jacques Cossette, Chairman, President & C.E.O.
TOTAL REVENUE ($000)   30,204

GROUPE GOYETTE INC.
(Public)   TRANSPORTATION
2825 Boul. Casavant Ouest, Saint-Hyacinthe, PQ,
J2S 7Y4   (514) 773-9615
GROUPE GOYETTE INC. does business directly or through its wholly
owned subsidiaries, Goyette Transport Ltee, Transport Richelieu Inc. and
Goyterm Inc, in general transport on long and short distances in Quebec,
as well as storage business and intermodal in the Saint-Hyacinthe area
through its entreposage maska division.
Jean-Louis Goyette, President & Chef De La Direction
TOTAL REVENUE ($000)   17,413

GROUPE LAPERRIERE & VERREAULT INC.
(Public)   MISC. INDUSTRIAL PRODUCTS
3100 Rue Westinghouse, Parc Industriel No 2, Trois-Rivieres, PQ,
G9A 5E1   (819) 371-8265
GROUPE LAPERRIERE & VERREAULT INC. is involved in the
design, manufacture and installation of equipment for the pulp and paper
industry, mines, and aluminum plants. The company is also involved in
processing waste water and other environmental projects.
Laurent Verreault, Chairman, President & C.E.O.
TOTAL REVENUE ($000)   208,626

GROUPE POMERLEAU
(Private)   CONTRACTORS
521 Sixieme Avenue, St-Georges de Beauce, PQ,
G5Y 5C4   (418) 228-6688
GROUP POMERLEAU is a general contractor.
Herve Pomerleau, Preident & Director General
TOTAL REVENUE ($000)   231,843

GROUPE PROMUTUEL
(Fin. Co-op)   INSURANCE - PROPERTY & CASUALTY
1091 Chemin Saint-Louis, Bureau 300, Sillery, PQ,
G1S 1E2   (418) 683-1212
GROUPE PROMUTUEL FEDERATION DE SOCIETES MU-
TUELLES D'ASSURANCE GENERALE as a federation of insurance
companies, is a provider of property and casualty insurance in the
province of Quebec. Since 1986 it has offered information processing
services and since 1989 life insurance.
Normand Fontaine, President
TOTAL REVENUE ($000)   9,603

GROUPE RO-NA DISMAT INC. (LE)
(Public)   SPECIALTY STORES
1250 Rue Nobel, Boucherville, PQ, J4B 5K1   (514) 599-5100

LE GROUPE RO-NA DISNAT INC. operates several stores under the
names Le Quincaillier Ro-Na, Le Renovateur Ro-Na, Botanix, Le Quin-
cailleur, Le Chantier, Ambiance and Dismat.
Henri Drouin, Chairman
TOTAL REVENUE ($000)   449,718

GROUPE SANI MOBILE INC.
(Public)   ENVIRONMENTAL SERVICES
Bureau 350, 6500, Boul. de la Rive-Sud, Levis, PQ,
G6V 7M5   (418) 835-3750
GROUPE SANI MOBILE INC. engages in activities related to the
environmental protection, pumping and industrial cleaning sectors.
Louis Lariviere, Chairman & President
TOTAL REVENUE ($000)   36,255

GROUPE SSQ INC.
(Private)   INSURANCE - LIFE
2525 Boul Laurier, P.O. Box 10500, Ste-Foy, PQ,
G1V 4H6   (418) 651-7000
GROUPE SSQ INC. provides life, mutual life, health, property and
casualty insurance through its subsidiaries. It is a wholly owned subsidi-
ary of SSQ Mutuelle de Gestion.
Yves Demers, Chairman & C.E.O.
TOTAL REVENUE ($000)   381,768

GROUPE TRANSAT A.T. INC.
(Public)   TRANSPORTATION
300 Leo Parizeau, Suite 400, C.P. 1114, Succursale Place Du Parc,
Montreal, PQ, H2W 2P4   (514) 987-1616
GROUPE TRANSAT A.T. INC., through its subsidiaries, Vacances Air
Transat A.T. Inc., Air Transat Holidays, Tourbec, Trafic Tours France,
and Air Transat Inc., is involved primarily in travel sales activities and
in commercial air services for passenger transportation.
Jean-Marc Eustache, President & C.E.O.
TOTAL REVENUE ($000)   292,328

GROUPE VAL ROYAL INC.
(Public)   SPECIALTY STORES
159 Jean-Talon West, Montreal, PQ, H2R 2X2   (514) 270-8111
GROUPE VAL ROYAL is a Montreal-area retailer of products related
to construction, renovation and decoration. The company operates two
Val Royal stores, seven Brinco Centre stores and one Reno-Depot
warehouse store. The stores sell a broad range of brand name and private
label goods. A second warehouse store will open in August 1993.
Pierre Michaud, Chairman & C.E.O.
TOTAL REVENUE ($000)   25,688

GROUPE VIDEOTRON LTEE (LE)
See page 322 for a full company profile.

GSW INC.
(Public)   APPLIANCES
P.O. Box 2047, 20 Eglinton West, Suite 1903, Toronto, ON,
M4R 1K8   (416) 489-0640
GSW operates in two industries: water products include pumps and water
heaters; building products include metal and vinyl eaves troughs, factory
built chimnies, fireplaces, stovepipes and barbecue accessories.

R.M. Barford, Chairman
TOTAL REVENUE ($000)   167,037

GUARDIAN CAPITAL GROUP LIMITED
(Public)   INVESTMENT COMPANIES AND FUNDS
18th Floor, 110 Yonge Street, Toronto, ON,
M5C 1T4   (416) 364-8341
GUARDIAN CAPITAL GROUP LIMITED is a financial services and investment company. Through Canadian and international affiliates, subsidiaries and advisors, the company manages portfolios for pension funds, private clients and publicly registered investment funds, and provides administrative and other financial services.
Anthony G.S. Griffin, Chairman
TOTAL REVENUE ($000)   9,877

GUARDIAN INSURANCE COMPANY OF CANADA
(Private)   INSURANCE - PROPERTY & CASUALTY
Suite 700, 181 University Avenue, Toronto, ON,
M5H 3M7   (416) 941-5050
GUARDIAN INSURANCE COMPANY OF CANADA is a property and casualty insurance company.
N. Curtis, Chairman
TOTAL REVENUE ($000)   390,959

GUILLEVIN INTERNATIONAL INC.
(Public)   WHOLESALE DISTRIBUTORS
400 Boul. Montpelier, St-Laurent, PQ, H4N 2G7   (514) 747-9851
GUILLEVIN INTERNATIONAL is a wholesale distributor of electrical material, health-safety and security products and equipment, industrial supplies and equipment, and automation products.
Jeannine Guillevin Wood, Chairman & C.E.O.
TOTAL REVENUE ($000)   407,443

GULF CANADA RESOURCES LIMITED
See page 88 for a full company profile.

GULF INTERNATIONAL MINERALS LTD.
(Public)   OIL AND GAS PRODUCERS
Suite 200, 675 West Hastings Street, Vancouver, BC,
V6B 1N2   (604) 683-9630
GULF INTERNATIONAL MINERALS LTD. is involved in the acquisition, exploration and development of oil and gas properties.
TOTAL REVENUE ($000)   2

GWIL INDUSTRIES INC.
(Public)   METAL FABRICATORS
Suite 650 - West Tower, 555 West 12th Avenue, Vancouver, BC,
V5Z 3X7   (604) 874-4945
GWIL INDUSTRIES INC. is involved in crane services and rentals; the manufacture of polyester resins and related raw materials; wholesale industrial products; analysis of coal samples for the mining industry and management services to the structural steel fabricating industry.
Hugh A. Magee, Chairman & C.E.O.
TOTAL REVENUE ($000)   35,742

H. PAULIN & CO. LIMITED
(Public)   MISC. INDUSTRIAL PRODUCTS
55 Milne Ave., Scarborough, ON, M1L 4N3   (416) 694-3351

H. PAULIN & CO., LIMITED manufactures and distributes industrial fasteners and automotive parts, bolts, nuts, screws and fluid system components to customers in the automotive industry, both original equipment and the aftermarket, agricultural, electrical and appliance industries.
Arthur Paulin, Chairman
TOTAL REVENUE ($000)   38,298

H.E.R.O. INDUSTRIES LTD.
(Public)   MISC. CONSUMER PRODUCTS
2719 Lake City Way, Burnaby, BC, V5A 2Z6   (604) 420-6543
H.E.R.O. INDUSTRIES LTD. is engaged in the design, assembly, and marketing of airless paint sprayers, accessories and colorant tinting dispensers to the paint industry and equipment rental stores.
Bryan H. Ray, President & C.E.O.
TOTAL REVENUE ($000)   6,051

HABSBURG RESOURCES INC.
(Public)   PRECIOUS METALS
1075 North Service Road West, Unit 16, Oakville, ON,
L6M 2G2   (416) 825-9970
HABSBURG RESOURCES INC. is involved in the acquisition, exploration and development of precious metal properties.
Stafford Kelley, President
TOTAL REVENUE ($000)   0

HALEY INDUSTRIES LIMITED
See page 223 for a full company profile.

HALIFAX DEVELOPMENTS LIMITED
(Public)   DEVELOPERS
Suite 400, Duke Tower, Scotia Square, Halifax, NS,
B3J 2V9   (902) 429-3660
HALIFAX DEVELOPMENTS LIMITED is a Nova Scotia based company engaged in development, ownership and management of real estate. The company's major investment is its Scotia Square complex located in Halifax, which houses office and retail space, parking facilities, five residential towers and a hotel.
J.W. Gogan, Chairman Of The Board
TOTAL REVENUE ($000)   32,447

HALIFAX PORT CORPORATION
(Crown)   TRANSPORTATION
P.O. Box 336, Halifax, NS, B3J 2P6   (902) 426-3643
HALIFAX PORT CORPORATION provides port facilities and services in Halifax, Nova Scotia.
Donald Parker, Chairman
TOTAL REVENUE ($000)   11,231

HAMILTON GROUP LIMITED (THE)
(Public)   SPECIALTY STORES
5985 McLauglin Road, Mississauga, ON,
L5R 1B8   (416) 568-4111
THE HAMILTON GROUP LIMITED, through its divison Hamilton Computer Sales and Rentals, is engaged in selling, renting, leasing and servicing computer equipment across Canada.
William J. Young, President
TOTAL REVENUE ($000)   172,826

HAMMOND MANUFACTURING COMPANY LIMITED
(Public) ELECTRICAL & ELECTRONIC
394 Edinburgh Road North, Guelph, ON,
N1H 1E5 (519) 822-2960
HAMMOND MANUFACTURING COMPANY LIMITED manufactures transformers and cabinetry for manufacturers of electrical and electronic equipment, utilities and electrical contractors.
Frederick O. Hammond, Chairman
TOTAL REVENUE ($000) 109,646

HANIL BANK CANADA
(Private) BANKS
36 Lombard Street, Toronto, ON, M5C 2X3 (416) 214-1111
HANIL BANK CANADA is a Schedule II bank. It is a wholly owned subsidary of Hanil Bank, of Seoul, South Korea.
J.H. Park, President & C.E.O.
TOTAL REVENUE ($000) 10,288

HARBOUR PETROLEUM COMPANY LIMITED
(Public) OIL AND GAS PRODUCERS
Suite 1600, 520 - 5th Avenue S.W., Calgary, AB,
T2P 3R7 (403) 265-5522
HARBOUR PETROLEUM COMPANY LIMITED is an oil and gas exploration and development company which has all of its properties located in Alberta, Saskatchewan and British Columbia.
Ronald A. Howard, Chairman
TOTAL REVENUE ($000) 2,459

HARRIS STEEL GROUP INC.
See page 203 for a full company profile.

HARROWSTON INC.
See page 405 for a full company profile.

HARTCO ENTERPRISES INC.
(Public) SPECIALTY STORES
9001 Louis H. Lafontaine Blvd., Anjou, PQ,
H1J 2C5 (514) 354-2299
HARTCO ENTERPRISES INC. operates in the retailing industry. Through its wholly owned division, Hart Department Stores, the company operates a chain of junior department stores. The company is also the franchisor of Compucentre, a network of computer stores catering to the home and small business user, and MicroAge computer stores, which specialize in offering business solutions to the corporate user.
Harry Hart, President & C.E.O.
TOTAL REVENUE ($000) 194,325

HAWKER SIDDELEY CANADA INC.
See page 224 for a full company profile.

HAYES-DANA INC.
See page 185 for a full company profile.

HEES INTERNATIONAL BANCORP INC.
See page 406 for a full company profile.

HELIX CIRCUITS INC.
See page 225 for a full company profile.

HEMLO GOLD MINES INC.
See page 47 for a full company profile.

HENRY BIRKS & SONS LIMITED
(Private) SPECIALTY STORES
1240 Philps Square, Montreal, PQ, H3B 3H4 (514) 397-2511
HENRY BIRKS & SONS LIMITED is a retailer of fine jewellery, giftware and silverware. The company is wholly owned by H. Jonathan Birks.
G. Drummond Birks, Chairman
TOTAL REVENUE ($000) 266,828

HEPCOE CREDIT UNION LIMITED
(Fin. Co-op) CREDIT UNIONS
700 University Avenue, Hydro Place, Toronto, ON,
M5G 1X6 (416) 597-1050
HEPCOE CREDIT UNION LIMITED is one of Canada's largest credit unions. It is a member-owned self-sustained financial cooperative whose purpose is to provide a full range of financial services to its members.
William A.T. Young, C.E.O. & General Manager
TOTAL REVENUE ($000) 57,719

HEROUX INC.
(Public) TRANSPORTATION EQUIP & COMPNTS
755 Thurber Street, Longueuil, PQ, J4H 3N2 (514) 679-5450
HEROUX INC. is engaged in two main businesses. It manufactures aircraft landing gear, servomechanisms, jet engine parts and high-precision machined parts. The company also repairs and overhauls landing gears and servomechanisms.
Sarto Richer, Chairman
TOTAL REVENUE ($000) 84,165

HEWITT EQUIPMENT LIMITED
(Private) WHOLESALE DISTRIBUTORS
5001 Trans Canada, Pointe-Claire-Dorval, PQ,
H9R 1B8 (514) 630-3100
HEWITT EQUIPMENT LIMITED is a heavy equipment and material handling dealer.
James Hewitt, Chairman
TOTAL REVENUE ($000) 202,352

HEWLETT-PACKARD (CANADA) LTD.
(Private) ELECTRICAL & ELECTRONIC
6877 Goreway Drive, Mississauga, ON, L4V 1M8 (416) 678-9430
HEWLETT-PACKARD (CANADA) is engaged in the design and manufacture of precision electronic equipment for measurement, analysis and computation. The company is a wholly owned subsidiary of Hewlett- Packard Company of the United States.
George B. Cobbe, Chairman fo the Board
TOTAL REVENUE ($000) 638,818

HIGH RIVER GOLD MINES LTD.
(Public) PRECIOUS METALS
Suite 1107, 330 Bay Street, Toronto, ON, M5H 2S8 (416) 947-1440

HIGH RIVER GOLD MINES LTD. owns an advanced gold project in Snow Lake, Manitoba. In 1989, its ore reserves were estimated at 4.2 million tons at 0.19 ounces of gold per ton.
Donald A. Whalen, Chairman
TOTAL REVENUE ($000)   0

HIGHLAND VALLEY COPPER
(Private)   METAL MINES
P.O. Box 1500, Logan Lake, BC, V0K 1W0   (604) 575-2443
HIGHLAND VALLEY COPPER is a partnership between Cominco Ltd. (50%), Rio Algom Limited (33.6%) and Teck Corporation (13.9%) (including 2.5% from Highmont) and 2.5% for Highmont Mining Company (excluding Teck's 2.5%).
J.E. Fletcher, Chairman
TOTAL REVENUE ($000)   374

HIGHRIDGE EXPLORATION LTD.
(Public)   OIL AND GAS PRODUCERS
Suite 1500, 630 - 6th Avenue S.W., Calgary, AB,
T2P 0S8   (403) 269-2229
HIGHRIDGE EXPLORATION LTD. is involved in oil and gas exploration and production.
Robert T.M. Vanderham, President
TOTAL REVENUE ($000)   4,968

HIGHWOOD RESOURCES LTD.
(Public)   OIL AND GAS PRODUCERS
12th Floor, 20 Toronto Street, Toronto, ON,
M5C 2B8   (416) 869-0772
HIGHWOOD RESOURCES is engaged in the acquisition, exploration and development of mining properties.
G. Farquharson, President
TOTAL REVENUE ($000)   26

HILLCREST RESOURCES LTD.
See page 89 for a full company profile.

HILLSBOROUGH RESOURCES LIMITED
(Public)   CONSULTING
120 Railroad Street, Brampton, ON, L6X 1G8   (416) 456-0734
HILLSBOROUGH RESOURCES LIMITED carries on its activities through a mining contracting division and a resource property division. The company's contracting division provides contracting and engineering services to the mining industry; its resource property division is involved in acquisition of equity interests in mineral deposits and the related exploration and development of the properties.
C. Alan Smith, Chairman
TOTAL REVENUE ($000)   38,105

HOECHST CANADA INC.
(Private)   CHEMICALS
800 Rene-Levesque Blvd. West, 23rd Floor, Montreal, PQ,
H3R 1z1 514 871-5511
HOECHST CANADA INC., is a manufacturer and wholesaler of chemicals and pharmaceuticals. Its major products are Agro-chemicals, specialty chemicals, pharmaceuticals, fibres, films, pigment, dyestuff and plastic resins. Hoechst Canada is a wholly owned subsidiary of Hoechst AG of Frankfurt, Germany.

A.W. Schuele, President
TOTAL REVENUE ($000)   267,629

HOFFMANN-LA ROCHE LIMITED
(Private)   WHOLESALE DISTRIBUTORS
2455 Meadowpine Blvd., Mississauga, ON, L5N 6L7 (416) 542-5555
HOFFMANN-LA ROCHE LIMITED is a supplier of pharmaceuticals, vitamins, fine chemicals, diagnostics, flavors and fragrances. The company's ultimate parent is Roche Holding Ltd. of Switzerland.
Donald B. Brown, President & Secretary
TOTAL REVENUE ($000)   181,842

HOLLINGER INC.
See page 323 for a full company profile.

HOME CAPITAL GROUP INC.
(Public)   FINANCE AND LEASING
Suite 1910, 145 King Street West, Toronto, ON,
M5H 1J8   (416) 360-4663
HOME CAPITAL operates through one subsidiary, Home Savings & Loan Corp., to provide mortgage lending for both rural and urban properties. Its branch system provides a strong deposit base.
Gerald M. Soloway, Chairman President & C.E.O.
TOTAL REVENUE ($000)   44,483

HOME OIL COMPANY LIMITED
See page 90 for a full company profile.

HOME PRODUCTS INC.
(Public)   SPECIALTY STORES
Suite 120, 10651 Shellbridge Way, Richmond, BC,
V6X 2W8   (604) 273-5445
HOME PRODUCTS INC. is a manufacturer, distrutor and retailer of consumer products, primarily for in-home use.
James Trainor, Chairman
TOTAL REVENUE ($000)   22,500

HONCO INC.
(Public)   METAL FABRICATORS
1191 Chemin Industriel, Bernieres, PQ, G7A 1A6   (418) 831-2245
HONCO INC. manufactures corrugated metal buildings made from pre-shaped structural panels.
Paul Lacasse, President
TOTAL REVENUE ($000)   8,488

HONDA CANADA INC.
(Private)   AUTOMOTIVE
715 Milner Avenue, Scarborough, ON, M1B 2K8   (416) 284-8110
HONDA CANADA INC. is involved in the assembly and distribution of vehicles and the distribution of small engines and parts to dealers throughout Canada. It is 50.16% owned by Honda Motor Co., Ltd. of Japan, and 49.84% owned by American Honda Motor Co., Inc.
Isao Suzuki, Chairman & C.E.O.
TOTAL REVENUE ($000)   2,722,203

HONEYWELL LIMITED
(Private)   ELECTRICAL & ELECTRONIC
The Honeywell Centre, 155 Gordon Baker Road, Willowdale, ON,
M2H 3N7   (416) 499-6111
HONEYWELL LTD. is a manufacturer and distributor of automation
and control products and systems. The company is a wholly owned
subsidiary of Honeywell Inc. (U.S.).
Dave Larkin, President & C.E.O.
TOTAL REVENUE ($000)   418,720

HONGKONG BANK OF CANADA
(Private)   BANKS
Suite 300, 885 West Georgia Street, Hongkong Bank of Canada
Bldg., Vancouver, BC, V6C 3E9   (604) 685-1000
HONGKONG BANK OF CANADA is a wholly owned subsidiary of
HSBC Holdings plc of London, England, and is licensed to operate as a
bank in Canada with full banking powers under the Bank Act 1980 as a
foreign bank subsidiary.
John R.H. Bond, Chairman
TOTAL REVENUE ($000)   950,012

HORNE & PITFIELD FOODS LIMITED
(Private)   FOOD STORES
12831 163rd Street, P.O. Box 10, Edmonton, AB,
T5J 2G9   (403) 447-1470
HORNE & PITFIELD FOODS LIMITED supplies 94 IGA and six
Garden Market supermarkets, 83 M/M stores, 18 Mayfair superettes, 20
Triple S and 56 Reddi Mart convenience through eight distribution
centres and seven cash and carry outlets. It operates in Alberta, Saskatch-
ewan, the Northwest Territories, as well as northern and central British
Columbia.
Wayne Wagner, President & C.O.O.
TOTAL REVENUE ($000)   613,769

HORSHAM CORPORATION (THE)
See page 91 for a full company profile.

HUBBARD HOLDING INC.
(Public)   CLOTHING AND TEXTILES
425 Avenue Marien, Montreal-Est, PQ, H1B 4V7   (514) 645-8833
HUBBARD HOLDING INC. is engaged in the business of applying
dyes and finishes to woven and knitted fabrics.
Robert Lemire, Chairman
TOTAL REVENUE ($000)   10,352

HUDSON BAY MINING AND SMELTING CO., LIMITED
See page 14 for a full company profile.

HUDSON'S BAY COMPANY
See page 361 for a full company profile.

HUDSON'S BAY COMPANY ACCEPTANCE LIMITED
(Private)   FINANCE AND LEASING
501-10310 Jasper Avenue, Edmonton, AB,
T5J 3P7   (403) 423-1311
HUDSON'S BAY COMPANY ACCEPTANCE LIMITED is engaged
in the business of purchasing without recourse accounts receivable
arising out of retail credit sales of Hudson's Bay Company and an
affiliate, Zeller's Inc. It is a wholly owned subsidiary within the Hudson's
Bay Company group.
TOTAL REVENUE ($000)   195,570

HUGHES LANG CORP.
(Public)   PRECIOUS METALS
Suite 1000, 1177 West Hastings Street, Vancouver, BC,
V6E 2K3   (604) 687-6600
HUGHES LANG CORP. is involved in mineral exploration and devel-
opment.
Frank A. Lang, Chairman
TOTAL REVENUE ($000)   308

HUSKY INJECTION MOLDING SYSTEMS LTD.
(Private)   MISC. INDUSTRIAL PRODUCTS
530 Queen St. South, Bolton, ON, L7E 5S5   (416) 951-5000
HUSKY INJECTION MOLDING SYSTEMS LTD. is engaged in
supplying high technology plastic injection molding systems (including
machines, molds, robots and product handling equipment) and hot
runners. Husky Injection exports 90% of its Canadian production. Husky
Injection is 74% owned by an employee group and 26% by Komatsu
Ltd.
Robert Schad, President & C.E.O.
TOTAL REVENUE ($000)   287,445

HUSKY OIL LTD.
(Private)   INTEGRATED OILS
707-8th Avenue S.W., P.O. Box 6525, Postal Station O, Calgary,
AB, T2P 3G7   (403) 298-6111
HUSKY OIL LTD., is a privately-held Canadian-based oil and gas
enterprise engaged in the exploration for, and development, production
purchase, transportation, processing and marketing of, crude oil, natural
gas, natural gas liquids and sulphur, refining of crude oil and marketing
and transportation of refined petroleum products.
S. Murray, Co-Chairman
TOTAL REVENUE ($000)   720,793

HY & ZEL'S INC.
(Public)   SPECIALTY STORES
7171 Yonge St., Thornhill, ON, L3T 2A9   (416) 886-7171
HY & ZEL'S, through its subsidiary, The Warehouse Drug Store Ltd.,
operates 15 retail stores in the Southern Ontario region under the name
Hy & Zel's The Supermarket Drug Store.
Zelick Goldstein, C.E.O.
TOTAL REVENUE ($000)   160,509

HYAL PHARMACEUTICAL CORPORATION
(Public)   BIOTECHNOLOGY & PHARMACEUTICALS
3909 Nashua Drive, Unit 5, Mississauga, ON,
L4V 1R3   (416) 678-6800
HYAL PHARMACEUTICAL CORPORATION is engaged in the development of hyaluronic acid formulations, which enhance, improve and
control the delivery and ultization of active drug compounds in the human
body, while reducing the toxicity of the drug. Hyal is concentrating on
three areas: the treatment of pain, both topically and intravenously; the
treatment of skin cancer; and the treatment of infections.
Donald C. Webster, Chairman
TOTAL REVENUE ($000)   3,343

HYCROFT RESOURCES AND DEVELOPMENT CORPORATION

(Public)   PRECIOUS METALS
Suite 2300, 885 West Georgia Street, Vancouver, BC,
V6C 3E8   (604) 687-2831
HYCROFT RESOURCES AND DEVELOPMENT CORPORATION
is a gold mining company.
Colin F. Kaiser, Chairman, President & C.E.O.
TOTAL REVENUE ($000)   44,960

HYDRO-QUEBEC

(Crown)   ELECTRICAL UTILITIES
75 Boul. Rene-Levesque Ouest, Montreal, PQ,
H2Z 1A4   (514) 289-2211
HYDRO-QUEBEC is a Quebec government owned electrical utility that
ensures the generation, transmission and distribution of almost all the
electricity sold in Quebec. The company has power stations which serve
the needs of the province and allow the company to export power to the
United States.
Richard Drouin, Chairman & C.E.O.
TOTAL REVENUE ($000)   7,002,000

I.G. INVESTMENT MANAGEMENT LTD.

(Private)   INVESTMENT COMPANIES AND FUNDS
One Canada Centre, 447 Portage Avenue, Winnipeg, MB,
R3C 3B6   (204) 943-0361
I.G. INVESTMENT MANAGEMENT LTD. provides investment man-
agement functions for the Investors Group of mutual funds and for
segregated and pooled pension funds. The company is a wholly owned
subsidiary of Investors Group Inc.
Hugh Sanford Riley, President & C.E.O.
TOTAL REVENUE ($000)   174,710

I.M.P. GROUP LIMITED

(Private)   TRANSPORTATION EQUIP & COMPNTS
Suite 400, 2651 Dutch Village Road, Halifax, NS,
B3L 4T1   (902) 453-2400
I.M.P. GROUP LIMITED is involved in aircraft repair & overhaul,
general aviation, sales of commercial fishing supplies and manufactur-
ing. It is a wholly owned subsidiary of Industrial Marine Products
Limited.
K.C. Rowe, Chairman President & C.E.O.
TOTAL REVENUE ($000)   300,000

I.S.G. TECHNOLOGIES INC.

See page 467 for a full company profile.

IATCO INDUSTRIES INC.

(Public)   TRANSPORTATION EQUIP & COMPNTS
1655 Finfar Court, Mississauga, ON, L5J 4K1   (416) 855-8400
IATCO INDUSTRIES INC. is involved in the manufacture of tires for
commercial and industrial offroad vehicles and equipment.
E. Alexander Goldstein, President
TOTAL REVENUE ($000)   2,767

IBM CANADA LIMITED - IBM CANADA LIMITEE

(Private)   ELECTRICAL & ELECTRONIC
3500 Steeles Avenue East, Markham, ON,
L3R 2Z1   (416) 946-9000
IBM CANADA LTD. is a leader in the information technology industry.
IBM Canada is wholly owned by IBM World Trade Corp., of the United
States.
John M. Thompson, Chairman
TOTAL REVENUE ($000)   6,805,000

ICI CANADA INC.

(Private)   CHEMICALS
C-I-L House, 90 Sheppard Ave. E., P.O. Box 200, Station A, North
York, ON, M2N 6H2   (416) 229-7000
ICI CANADA INC. is engaged in the manufacturing of explosives,
paints, agrochemicals, fertilizers and chloralkali products. The company
is a wholly owned subsidiary of Imperial Chemical Industries plc (U.K.).
C.H. Hantho, Chairman & C.E.O.
TOTAL REVENUE ($000)   663,000

IDEAL METAL INC.

(Public)   WHOLESALE DISTRIBUTORS
3399 Francis-Hughes Avenue, Ville De Laval, PQ,
H7L 5A5   (514) 385-0111
IDEAL METAL INC. is a major non-ferrous metal distribution and
processing service centre supplying the metal requirements of manufac-
turing and other key industries in Canada.
Jacques E. Daccord, Chairman
TOTAL REVENUE ($000)   101,379

IFL INVESTMENT FOUNDATION (CANADA) LIMITED

(Public)   INVESTMENT COMPANIES AND FUNDS
Suite 3060, 1501 McGill College Avenue, Montreal, PQ,
H3A 3M8   (514) 286-7241
IFL INVESTMENT FOUNDATION (CANADA) LIMITED is an
investment company whose portfolio includes investments in banking
and finance, building products, consumer merchandising, forest prod-
ucts, manufacturing, petroleum and services, and utilities and pipelines
industries.
A. Scott Fraser, Chairman, President & Treasurer
TOTAL REVENUE ($000)   462

IGLOO VIKSKI INC.

(Public)   WHOLESALE DISTRIBUTORS
195 Brissette Street, P.O. Box 180, Ste-Agathe-des-Monts, PQ,
J8C 3A3   (819) 326-1664
IGLOO VIKSKI INC. is a leading importer and wholesale distributor of
an extensive line of quality sports equipment and apparel.
William P. Glass, Chairman
TOTAL REVENUE ($000)   9,465

IMASCO ENTERPRISES INC.

(Private)   INVESTMENT COMPANIES AND FUNDS
600 De Maisonneuve Blvd. W., 19th Floor, Montreal, PQ,
H3A 3K7   (514) 982-9111
IMASCO ENTERPRISES INC. was incorporated to acquire Genstar
Corporation, and holds approximately 98% of the outstanding common
shares of CT Financial Services Inc. It also consolidates the assets,

liabilities and results of certain other financial services and real estate activities and investments. It is an indirect wholly owned subsidiary of Imasco Limited.
Brian M. Levitt, President
TOTAL REVENUE ($000)   4,437,700

IMASCO FINANCIAL CORPORATION
(Private)   TRUST, SAVINGS AND LOAN
20th Floor, 600 De Maisonneuve Blvd. West, Montreal, PQ,
H3A 3K7   (514) 982-9111
IMASCO FINANCIAL is engaged, through its subsidiaries and investments, in the financial services industry, providing services for both individual and commercial clients in personal banking (deposits and consumer loans) commercial and mortgage lending, real estate brokerage and development, trust & fiduciary services, venture capital investments (U.S.) and mutual fund & mortgage portfolio servicing.
Brian M. Levitt, President
TOTAL REVENUE ($000)   4,371,500

IMASCO LIMITED
See page 448 for a full company profile.

IMPERIAL LIFE ASSURANCE COMPANY OF CANADA (THE)
See page 427 for a full company profile.

IMPERIAL METALS CORPORATION
(Public)   OIL AND GAS PRODUCERS
8th Floor, 601 West Hastings Street, Vancouver, BC,
V6B 5A6   (604) 669-8959
IMPERIAL METALS CORPORATION is active across the entire spectrum of crustal resources on a global basis. While Imperial produces oil and gas from fields in Alberta and B.C., it is primarily a mineral exploration and development company, with deposits of base and precious metals, uranium and coal. The company also derives considerable revenue from management fees.
Peter Geib, Chairman & C.E.O.
TOTAL REVENUE ($000)   3,775

IMPERIAL OIL LIMITED
See page 92 for a full company profile.

IMPERIAL OIL RESOURCES PRODUCTION LIMITED
(Private)   OIL AND GAS PRODUCERS
37-4th Avenue S.W., Suite 1135, Calgary, AB,
T2P 0H6   (403) 237-3737
IMPERIAL OIL RESOURCES PRODUCTION LIMITED is the oil and gas production division of Imperial Oil Limited.
TOTAL REVENUE ($000)   173,708

INCO LIMITED
See page 15 for a full company profile.

INCOME TRUSTCO CORPORATION
(Public)   TRUST, SAVINGS AND LOAN
181 Main Street West, P.O. Box 870, Hamilton, ON,
L8N 3N9   (416) 528-9811

INCOME TRUSTCO CORPORATION is a holding company which, through its subsidiaries, offers financial intermediary, lease financing, trust and real estate services in southern and central Ontario. Operations include deposit services, mortgage lending, mortgage brokerage and administration, consumer lending, lease financing and trust services.
Bernard S. Walman, Chairman & C.E.O.
TOTAL REVENUE ($000)   34,027

INDAL LIMITED
(Private)   METAL FABRICATORS
4000 Weston Rd, Weston, ON, M9L 2W8   (416) 743-1400
INDAL LIMITED is a diversified industrial company with subsidiaries in Canada and U.S. which extrude aluminum, cold rollform and stamp aluminum and steel, diecast zinc, temper and laminate glass and fabricate a broad range of metal, wood and glass products sold principally to residential construction including home improvements; non-residential construction and industrial sector.
Gordon H. Sage, Chairman
TOTAL REVENUE ($000)   902,100

INDUSTRA SERVICE CORPORATION
(Public)   OTHER SERVICES
401 Salter Street, New Westminster, BC, V3M 5Y1   (604) 521-3322
INDUSTRA SERVICE CORPORATION's principal activity is the repair and maintenance of generaing plants used in the pulp and paper and petrochemical industries. These services encompass all aspects of the design, engineering, fabrication, installation, maintenance, repair and modification of boilers, pressure vessels, tubing, piping, dust collection, ancillary equipment and instrumentation.
Wayne E. Shaw, Chairman, President & C.E.O.
TOTAL REVENUE ($000)   54,846

INDUSTRIAL BANK OF JAPAN (CANADA)
(Private)   BANKS
Suite 1102, 100 Yonge Street, P.O. Box 29, Toronto, ON,
M5C 2W1   (416) 365-9550
INDUSTRIAL BANK OF JAPAN (CANADA) is a schedule II bank, which offers a full range of banking services throughout Canada.
Yoh Kurosawa, Chairman
TOTAL REVENUE ($000)   51,677

INDUSTRIAL-ALLIANCE LIFE INSURANCE COMPANY
(Private)   INSURANCE - LIFE
1080 St-Louis Road, Sillery, PQ, G1K 7M3   (418) 684-5000
INDUSTRIAL-ALLIANCE LIFE INSURANCE COMPANY is a major Canadian mutual life insurance company and through its wholly owned subsidiaries, owns or has majority interest in the following companies: General Trustco, Canadian Union Insurance Co.; IST; Equitable General Insurance; Industrial Alliance General Insurance; National Life of Canada; North West Life of Canada; and North West Life of America.
Robert Begin, Chairman
TOTAL REVENUE ($000)   1,762,888

INDUSTRIAL-ALLIANCE LIFE MANAGEMENT CORPORATION
(Private)   INSURANCE - LIFE
1080 St-Louis Road, Sillery, PQ, G1K 7M3   (418) 684-5000

INDUSTRIAL-ALLIANCE LIFE MANAGEMENT CORPORATION is a group of three companies that provide life insurance. The three companies are The National Life Assurance Company of Canada, The North West Life Assurance Company of Canada and North West Life Assurance Company of America. These three companies operate in Ontario and Western Canada as well as in the northwestern United States.
Robert Begin, Chairman
TOTAL REVENUE ($000)   582,768

INGERSOLL-RAND CANADA INC.
(Private)   MACHINERY
3501 St. Charles Blvd., Suite 202, Kirkland, PQ,
H9H 4S3   (514) 695-9040
INGERSOLL-RAND CANADA INC. is engaged in the manufacture, distribution and marketing of machinery and equipment. Ingersoll-Rand Canada is wholly owned by Ingersoll-Rand Company of Woodcliff Lake, New Jersey.
S.J. Zalzal, President & C.E.O.
TOTAL REVENUE ($000)   256,934

INLAND TRUST AND SAVINGS CORPORATION LIMITED
(Public)   TRUST, SAVINGS AND LOAN
Suite 201, 1 Forks Market Road, Winnipeg, MB,
R3C 4L9   (204) 949-4800
INLAND TRUST AND SAVINGS CORPORATION LIMITED is incorporated under the laws of Manitoba and its principal business activity is providing first mortgage loans on residential properties.
Ken Cooper, President
TOTAL REVENUE ($000)   14,570

INSURANCE CORPORATION OF BRITISH COLUMBIA
(Crown)   INSURANCE - PROPERTY & CASUALTY
151 West Esplanade, North Vancouver, BC,
V7M 3H9   (604) 661-2800
INSURANCE CORPORATION OF BRITISH COLUMBIA is a crown corporation which has the power and capacity to act as an insurer and reinsurer in all classes of insurance.
Leonard J. DeVito, Chairman Of The Board
TOTAL REVENUE ($000)   2,104,326

INTENSITY RESOURCES LTD.
(Public)   OIL AND GAS PRODUCERS
Suite 1000, 400 - 5th Avenue S.W., Calgary, AB,
T2P 0L6   (403) 263-3440
INTENSITY RESOURCES LTD. is an oil and gas exploration and development company with properties in Alberta.
Daniel U. Pekarsky, Chairman
TOTAL REVENUE ($000)   14,573

INTER-CITY PRODUCTS CORPORATION
See page 494 for a full company profile.

INTERA INFORMATION TECHNOLOGIES CORPORATION
See page 478 for a full company profile.

INTERMETCO LIMITED
(Public)   MANAGEMENT AND DIVERSIFIED
519 Parkdale Ave. N., P.O. Box 70, Hamilton, ON,
L8N 3B4   (416) 548-9700
INTERMETCO LIMITED is the largest recycler of metal products in Canada; manufactures spiral-weld pipe in Georgia and Pennsylvania and distributes tubular piping, prime pipe piling, sheet piling, beams and hollow structural tubing.
Marvin E. Goldblatt, Chairman
TOTAL REVENUE ($000)   102,672

INTERNATIONAL COLIN ENERGY CORPORATION
See page 93 for a full company profile.

INTERNATIONAL COMMERCIAL BANK OF CATHAY (CANADA)
(Private)   BANKS
Suite 910, 150 York Street, Toronto, ON, M5H 3S5   (416) 947-2800
INTERNATIONAL COMMERCIAL BANK OF CATHAY (CANADA) is a schedule II bank operating in Canada.
Theodore S.S. Cheng, Chairman Of The Board
TOTAL REVENUE ($000)   8,670

INTERNATIONAL CORONA CORPORATION
(Private)   PRECIOUS METALS
Suite 2500, 666 Burrard Street, Park Place, Vancouver, BC,
V6C 2X8   (604) 669-1011
INTERNATIONAL CORONA CORP. is a precious metal mining company with mines in Ontario, Saskatchewan, British Columbia, Nevada and Mexico. The company is also involved in mineral production in Quebec, oil and gas production in Western Canada, and mineral exploration throughout North America. The company has interests in other companies including a 17% interest in Poco Petroleums Ltd. of Calgary.
Norman Anderson, Chairman
TOTAL REVENUE ($000)   313,477

INTERNATIONAL DUNRAINE LIMITED
(Public)   METAL MINES
3rd Floor, 172 King Street East, Toronto, ON,
M5A 1J3   (416) 947-9216
INTERNATIONAL DUNRAINE holds all of capital stock of South Riding Point Holding Ltd. South Riding Point is a Bermuda corporation whose primary operations occur at an oil transshipment facility in the Bahamas. The transshipment facility consists of an offshore jetty and eight crude oil storage tanks.
P. Anthony Novelly, Chairman
TOTAL REVENUE ($000)   11,577 (US)

INTERNATIONAL EPITEK INC.
(Public)   ELECTRICAL & ELECTRONIC
100 Schneider Road, Kanata, ON, K2K 1Y2   (613) 592-2240
INTERNATIONAL EPITEK is a Canadian manufacturer of hybrid micro circuits for the computer, communication, test instrumentation, medical electronics, and various other industries.
Robert W. Corson, President & C.E.O.
TOTAL REVENUE ($000)   8,422

INTERNATIONAL FOREST PRODUCTS LIMITED
See page 142 for a full company profile.

INTERNATIONAL INNOPAC INC.
See page 248 for a full company profile.

INTERNATIONAL INTERLAKE INDUSTRIES INC.
(Public)   OIL AND GAS PRODUCERS
1600 Bow Valley Square II, 205 - 5th Avenue S.W., Calgary, AB,
T2P 2V7   (403) 264-7382
INTERNATIONAL INTERLAKE INDUSTRIES INC. is engaged in
the exploration for, and development of oil, gas and minerals in Alberta
and British Columbia.
Rudolf Seigert, President & C.E.O.
TOTAL REVENUE ($000)   4,616

INTERNATIONAL MAHOGANY CORP.
(Public)   PRECIOUS METALS
Suite 1305, 1090 West Georgia Street, Vancouver, BC,
V6E 3V7   (604) 685-9316
INTERNATIONAL MAHOGANY CORP. and its subsidiaries are
engaged in the exploration and development of mineral resource prop-
erties in Canada, United States and Chile. The company also has sub-
stantial investments in several resource companies listed on the
Vancouver and Toronto Stock Exchanges.
Anton Hendriksz, Chairman
TOTAL REVENUE ($000)   3,560

INTERNATIONAL MINERALS & CHEMICAL CORP.
(CANADA) LTD.
(Private)   OTHER MINES
Box 310, Esterhazy, SK, S0A 0X0   (306) 745-3931
INTERNATIONAL MINERALS & CHEMICAL CORPORATION
(CANADA) LIMITED's business consists primarily of potash mining
operations located in Canada. It is a wholly owned subsidiary of IMC
Fertilizer Group, Inc.
TOTAL REVENUE ($000)   172,462

INTERNATIONAL MUREX TECHNOLOGIES
CORPORATION
See page 495 for a full company profile.

INTERNATIONAL OILTEX LTD.
(Public)   OIL AND GAS PRODUCERS
910 Roslyn Building, 400 - 5th Ave. S.W., Calgary, AB,
T2P 0L6   (403) 266-1094
INTERNATIONAL OILTEX LTD. is involved in the exploration for
and the development and production of oil and gas in Western Canada.
Christopher K.G. Rowe,
TOTAL REVENUE ($000)   1,381

INTERNATIONAL PANORAMA RESOURCE CORP.
(Public)   OIL AND GAS PRODUCERS
P.O. Box 1586, Blaine, WA, 98230   (206) 332-4600
INTERNATIONAL PANORAMA RESOURCE CORP. is involved in
mining exploration in the United States. Mining projects are in southern
Colorado, and Grass Valley, California.

Ray Saadien, President
TOTAL REVENUE ($000)   21 (US)

INTERNATIONAL PETROLEUM CORPORATION
See page 94 for a full company profile.

INTERNATIONAL POTTER DISTILLING
CORPORATION
(Public)   DISTILLERIES
Suite 214, 1285 West Broadway, Vancouver, BC,
V6H 3X8   (604) 738-9463
INTERNATIONAL POTTER DISTILLING CORPORATION manu-
factures and supplies beer, wine and spirits to Canadian markets.
Ian C. Tostenson, President
TOTAL REVENUE ($000)   28,075

INTERNATIONAL PURSUIT CORPORATION
(Public)   OIL AND GAS PRODUCERS
172 King Street East, 3rd Floor, Toronto, ON,
M5A 1J3   (416) 947-9216
INTERNATIONAL PURSUIT recently completed a sale of its wholly
owned subsidiary, Pursuit Athletic Footwear, Inc., giving the company
enough capital to consider future acquisitions in the oil and gas sector.
P.A. Novelly, Chairman
TOTAL REVENUE ($000)   74

INTERNATIONAL SEMI-TECH MICROELECTRONICS
INC.
See page 177 for a full company profile.

INTERNATIONAL UNP HOLDINGS LTD.
(Public)   INVESTMENT COMPANIES AND FUNDS
Suite 409, 120 Adelaide Street West, Toronto, ON,
M5H 1T1   (416) 364-4184
INTERNATIONAL UNP HOLDINGS LTD. is in the business of
investing in existing profitable companies in Poland.
L. George Bonar, Chairman, President & C.E.O.
TOTAL REVENUE ($000)   6,138

INTERNATIONAL VERIFACT INC.
See page 226 for a full company profile.

INTERPROVINCIAL COOPERATIVE LIMITED
(Non-fin Co-op)   WHOLESALE DISTRIBUTORS
Box 1050, Saskatoon, SK, S7K 3M9   (306) 244-3311
INTERPROVINCIAL COOPERATIVE LIMITED is owned and controlled by a number of cooperative wholesalers and the prairie wheat
pools. IPCO coordinates many of the purchases of its member organizations, manufactures agricultural chemicals and owns and controls a
number of trademarks used by its members, the most important of which
is the Co-op trademark.
John Spiering, President Of The Board
TOTAL REVENUE ($000)   189,602

INTERPROVINCIAL PIPE LINE SYSTEM INC.
See page 281 for a full company profile.

INTERTAPE POLYMER GROUP INC.
(Public)   PACKAGING AND CONTAINERS
110 E Montee de Liesse, Ville St. Laurent, PQ,
H4T 1N4   (514) 731-0731
INTERTAPE POLYMER GROUP INC. develops, manufactures and sells a variety of specialized polyolefin plastic packaging products for industrial use.
Eric E. Baker, Chairman
TOTAL REVENUE ($000)   112,360

INTERTEL COMMUNICATIONS INC.
(Public)   TELECOMMUNICATIONS
200 Burrard Street, Suite 800, Vancouver, BC,
V6C 2J3   (604) 669-9777
INTRAWEST CORPORATION operates resorts and real estate.
TOTAL REVENUE ($000)   705

INTRAWEST CORPORATION
See page 261 for a full company profile.

INVENTRONICS LIMITED
(Public)   MISC. INDUSTRIAL PRODUCTS
3900 - 101 Street, Edmonton, AB, T6E 0A5   (403) 461-5010
INVENTRONICS LIMITED is a diversified manufacturing company with plants in Brandon and Edmonton. The company is a supplier of customized sheet metal products and parts to the telecommunication, power, defence and electronics markets.
Don F. Baille, Chairman
TOTAL REVENUE ($000)   11,639

INVERNESS PETROLEUM LTD.
See page 95 for a full company profile.

INVESTORS GROUP INC.
See page 407 for a full company profile.

IONA APPLIANCES INC.
(Public)   APPLIANCES
1110 Hansler Road, P.O. Box 1004, Welland, ON,
L3B 5S1   (416) 734-7476
IONA APPLIANCES INC. manufactures and markets floor care products, including stick vacuums, hand-held vacuums, upright carpet cleaners and vacuum cleaners, and small kitchen appliances including portable and stand mixers, and can openers.
Kenneth Kelman, Chairman
TOTAL REVENUE ($000)   17,278

IPL INC.
(Public)   PACKAGING AND CONTAINERS
140 Rue Commerciale, Saint-Damien, PQ, G0R 2Y0(418) 789-2880
IPL is a major manufacturer of injection and extrusion moulded plastic products. The company manufactures and commercializes a wide range of rigid packaging containers and pails, as well as beverage cases and handling boxes designed for various uses within the food, fishing, chemical, forestry, petrochemical, construction and recycling industries. The company also supplies the automotive industry.

Remi Metivier, Chairman of the Board
TOTAL REVENUE ($000)   65,080

IPSCO INC.
See page 204 for a full company profile.

IRWIN TOY LIMITED
See page 178 for a full company profile.

ISLAND TELEPHONE COMPANY LIMITED (THE)
See page 299 for a full company profile.

ISM INFORMATION SYSTEMS MANAGEMENT CORPORATION
See page 468 for a full company profile.

ISRAEL DISCOUNT BANK OF CANADA
(Private)   BANKS
Suite M100, 150 Bloor Street West, Toronto, ON,
M5S 2Y5   (416) 926-7200
ISRAEL DISCOUNT BANK OF CANADA is a schedule II bank.
Aron Kahana, Chairman
TOTAL REVENUE ($000)   9,466

ITOCHU CANADA LTD.
(Private)   WHOLESALE DISTRIBUTORS
770 - 999 Canada Place, Vancouver, BC, V6C 3E1 (604) 683-5764
ITOCHU CANADA LTD. is involved in the import and export business. It is a wholly owned subsidiary of Itochu Corporation of Tokyo, Japan.
Hiroshi Ooka, President & C.E.O.
TOTAL REVENUE ($000)   1,352,575

ITT CANADA LIMITED
(Private)   AUTOMOTIVE
P.O. Box 138, Toronto-Dominion Centre, Toronto, ON,
M5K 1H1   (416) 863-9666
ITT CANADA is a diversified manufacturing, distribution and service company engaged principally in the manufacture and distribution of automotive parts, pumps, valves, controls and electronic components and in the provision of insurance, financial and hotel services.
Thomas H. Savage C.B.E., Chairman
TOTAL REVENUE ($000)   404,461

IVACO INC.
See page 205 for a full company profile.

J.D.S. INVESTMENTS LIMITED
(Public)   PROPERTY MGMNT & INVESTMENT
Suite 800, 1000 Finch Avenue West, North York, ON,
M3J 2E7   (416) 661-8400
J.D.S. INVESTMENTS LIMITED is a Canadian real estate company engaged in the acquisition, development and management of regional and community shopping centres, office and mixed-use buildings and real estate investments. It has interests in six shopping centres and four office and mixed use buildings, the majority of which are in the Toronto region.

Jack Israeli, Chairman, President & C.E.O.
TOTAL REVENUE ($000)   34,480

JAMES RICHARDSON & SONS, LIMITED
(Private)   WHOLESALE DISTRIBUTORS
Richardson Building, One Lombard Place, Winnipeg, MB,
R3B 0Y1   (204) 934-5811
JAMES RICHARDSON & SONS, LIMITED is a grain, financial and
management holding company. The company's subsidiaries engage in
grain operations, the investment securities industry, real estate, construc-
tion, oil and gas and shipping. The company is wholly owned by the
Richardson family.
George T. Richardson, President & C.E.O.
TOTAL REVENUE ($000)   1,831,850

JANNOCK LIMITED
See page 449 for a full company profile.

JASCAN RESOURCES INC.
(Public)   METAL MINES
Suite 2000, 95 Wellington St. W., Toronto, ON,
M5J 2N7   (416) 362-6721
JASCAN RESOURCES INC. is engaged in the acquisition, exploration
and development of mineral properties with the primary focus being gold,
silver and copper.
Martin P. Connell, Chairman
TOTAL REVENUE ($000)   1,539

JEAN COUTU GROUP (PJC) INC. (THE)
See page 362 for a full company profile.

JEWETT-CAMERON TRADING COMPANY LTD.
(Public)   WHOLESALE DISTRIBUTORS
12670 S.W. Hall Boulevard, Tigard, OR, 97223   (503) 620-1788
JEWETT-CAMERON TRADING COMPANY LTD. distributes and
markets lumber and other building materials in the northwestern United
States and the South Pacific. It also distributes and imports pneumatic air
tools and industrial clamps.
Donald M. Boone, President
TOTAL REVENUE ($000)   25,862 (US)

JIM PATTISON GROUP (THE)
(Private)   MANAGEMENT AND DIVERSIFIED
1055 West Hastings Street, Suite 1600, Vancouver, BC,
V6E 2H2   (604) 688-6764
THE JIM PATTISON GROUP is a diversified organization with con-
sumer oriented lines of businesses that include food, broadcasting,
packaging, transportation and financial services.
Jim Pattison, C.E.O. & Managing Director
TOTAL REVENUE ($000)   2,914,000

JOHN DEERE LIMITED
(Private)   WHOLESALE DISTRIBUTORS
South Service Road, Grimsby, ON, L3M 4H5   (416) 945-9281
JOHN DEERE LIMITED is a manufacturer and wholesaler of agricul-
tural equipment, and a wholesaler of industrial equipment and consumer
products.

G.J. Clark, President & C.E.O.
TOTAL REVENUE ($000)   597,008

JOHN FORSYTH COMPANY INC. (THE)
(Public)   CLOTHING AND TEXTILES
36 Horner Avenue, Toronto, ON, M8Z 5Y1   (416) 252-6231
THE JOHN FORSYTH COMPANY INC. designs and manufactures,
or contracts for the manufacture of a broad range of clothing and
accessories for men and women, and a comparatively smaller range of
similar items for boys and girls. The company also holds the exclusive
licence to market products in Canada under the name of a number of well
known designers.
Oskar Rajsky, President & C.E.O.
TOTAL REVENUE ($000)   97,475

JOHN LABATT LIMITED
See page 450 for a full company profile.

JOHNSON & JOHNSON INC.
(Private)   CHEMICALS
2155 Pie IX Boulevard, Montreal, PQ, H1V 2E4   (514) 251-5151
JOHNSON & JOHNSON INC. is a consumer health care products
company.
G. Ostrou, Chairman & C.E.O.
TOTAL REVENUE ($000)   349,030

JONPOL EXPLORATIONS LIMITED
(Public)   PRECIOUS METALS
Suite 420, 111 Richmond Street West, Toronto, ON,
M5H 2G4   (416) 947-1087
JONPOL EXPLORATIONS LIMITED is involved in the acquisition,
exploration and development of natural resource properties.
John A. Pollock, President & C.E.O.
TOTAL REVENUE ($000)   18

JORDAN PETROLEUM LTD.
(Public)   OIL AND GAS PRODUCERS
Suite 850, Bow Valley Square III, 255 - 5th Avenue S.W., Calgary,
AB, T2P 3G6   (403) 266-1024
JORDAN PETROLEUM LTD. is an oil and gas exploration and devel-
opment company which conducts operations in Canada and the United
States.
Harold V. Pedersen, President
TOTAL REVENUE ($000)   18,982

JORDEX RESOURCES INC.
(Public)   METAL MINES
Suite 2660, 1221 Brickell Ave., Miami, FL, 33131   (305) 530-1875
JORDEX RESOURCES INC. is involved in the acquisition, exploration
and development of mineral properties.
Brian Hinchcliffe, President & C.E.O.
TOTAL REVENUE ($000)   6,893

JOSS ENERGY LTD
(Public)   OIL AND GAS PRODUCERS
Suite 2350, 444 - 5th Ave. S.W., Calgary, AB,
T2P 2T8   (403) 233-7377

JOSS ENERGY LTD is a natural resource enterprise, primarily active in the acquisition, exploration, and development of oil and gas reserves in the Western Canadian sedimentary basin.
Denis J. Cote, Chairman
TOTAL REVENUE ($000)   9,735

JOURNEY'S END CORPORATION
(Public)   LODGING
199 Front Street, Suite 100, P.O. Box 6000, Belleville, ON,
K8N 5E2   (613) 966-8020
JOURNEY'S END is engaged in the development, syndication, management and ownership of limited service motel, hotel and all-suite properties located in Canada from Newfoundland to Saskatchewan and in New York State and Connecticut. The company operates through two divisions - real estate acquisition, development and sales; and management operations.
Maurice H. Rollins, Chairman & C.E.O.
TOTAL REVENUE ($000)   26,103

JOUTEL RESOURCES LIMITED
(Public)   METAL MINES
Suite 1116, 111 Richmond St. West, Toronto, ON,
M5H 2G4   (416) 364-0001
JOUTEL RESOURCES LIMITED is engaged in the exploration and development of mineral properties in British Columbia, Ontario and Quebec. It owns the controlling block of shares in Queenston Mining Inc.
Hugh D. Harbinson, Chairman
TOTAL REVENUE ($000)   (115)

K MART CANADA LIMITED
(Private)   DEPARTMENT STORES
8925 Torbram Road, Brampton, ON, L6T 4G1   (416) 792-4400
K MART CANADA LIMITED is a general merchandise retailer. K Mart Canada is a wholly owned subsidiary of K Mart Corporation of Troy, Michigan.
J. Antonini, Chairman
TOTAL REVENUE ($000)   1,244,354

KAUFEL GROUP LTD.
See page 496 for a full company profile.

KELLOGG CANADA INC.
(Private)   FOOD PROCESSING
6700 Finch Ave W., Etobicoke, ON, M9W 5P2   (416) 675-5200
KELLOGG CANADA INC. is involved in the manufacturing and marketing of ready-to-eat cereals and other quality convenience food products.
Jean-Louis Gourbin, President & C.E.O.
TOTAL REVENUE ($000)   353,831

KELTIC INCORPORATED
(Public)   TRUST, SAVINGS AND LOAN
1809 Barrington Street, Suite 900, Halifax, NS,
B3J 3K8   (902) 429-9911
KELTIC is a financial holding and management company offering financial services and products to individuals, businesses, and organizations in Atlantic Canada.

J. William Ritchie, Chairman & C.E.O.
TOTAL REVENUE ($000)   1,886

KERR ADDISON MINES LIMITED
See page 16 for a full company profile.

KINGSFIELD CAPITAL CORPORATION
(Public)   MANAGEMENT AND DIVERSIFIED
P.O. Box 1268, Lethbridge, AB, T1J 4K1   (403) 752-3213
KINGSFIELD CAPITAL CORPORATION is a management and investment company.
TOTAL REVENUE ($000)   3,110

KINNEY CANADA INC.
(Private)   SPECIALTY STORES
100 Mainshep Road, Weston, ON, M9M 1L5   (416) 742-3590
KINNEY CANADA INC., is a clothing and shoe retailer. Kinney Canada is a wholly owned subsidiary of F.W. WOOLWORTH of New York, New York.
William K. Lavin, Chairman
TOTAL REVENUE ($000)   660,216

KINROSS GOLD CORPORATION
(Public)   PRECIOUS METALS
Suite 400, 185 South State Street, Salt Lake City, UT,
84111   (801) 363-9152
KINROSS GOLD CORPORATION and its wholly owned U.S. subsidiary are involved in the acquisition and development of interests in precious and base metals properties. All of the company's operations are conducted in the United States.
James H. Coleman, Chairman
TOTAL REVENUE ($000)   10,870 (US)

KOREA EXCHANGE BANK OF CANADA
(Private)   BANKS
Suite 600, Edison Centre, 2345 Yonge Street, Toronto, ON,
M4P 2E5   (416) 932-1234
KOREA EXCHANGE BANK OF CANADA is a wholly owned subsidiary of the Korea Exchange Bank, and is licenced to operate as a bank in Canada with full banking powers as a foreign bank subsidiary.
Myung Sun Chang, President & C.E.O.
TOTAL REVENUE ($000)   33,729

KRAFT GENERAL FOODS CANADA INC.
(Private)   FOOD PROCESSING
95 Moatfield Drive, Don Mills, ON, M3B 3L6   (416) 441-5000
KRAFT GENERAL FOODS CANADA INC. is a packaged food products manufacturer. The company is part of the North American group of companies of Kraft General Foods Inc. of the United States. The company's ultimate parent is Philip Morris Companies of New York.
Douglas Smith, President
TOTAL REVENUE ($000)   1,650,774

KRG MANAGEMENT INC.
(Public)   INSURANCE - PROPERTY & CASUALTY
555 Wilson Avenue, North York, ON, M3H 3Y6   (416) 636-4544
KRG MANAGEMENT INC., through wholly owned KRG Insurance Brokers Inc. and 50% owned KRG Life Insurance Agency Inc., provides

to clients professional advices and the related services necessary to implement that advice in the areas of general insurance, life insurance and employee benefits to clients throughout Canada.
Steven H. Wise, President & C.E.O.
TOTAL REVENUE ($000)   4,533

KRONOS CANADA, INC.
(Private)   CHEMICALS
4 Place Ville-Marie, Suite 500, Montreal, PQ,
H3B 4M5   (514) 397-3501
KRONOS CANADA INC. is a manufacturer and wholesaler of pigments and chemicals.
R.P. Beaulne, Chairman
TOTAL REVENUE ($000)   170,643

KRUGER INC.
(Private)   EAST COAST FORESTRY
3285 Rue Bedford, Montreal, PQ, H3C 2V2   (514) 737-1131
KRUGER INC. is a producer of newsprint, coated paper, lightweight coated specialties, 100% recycled board and corrugated containers. It is 98% owned by Joseph Kruger of Quebec.
Joseph Kruger, C.E.O. & President
TOTAL REVENUE ($000)   789,909

KWG RESOURCES INC.
(Public)   PRECIOUS METALS
Suite 3200, 630 Rene-Levesque Blvd. West, Montreal, PQ,
H3B 1S6   (514) 866-6001
KWG RESOURCES INC. is involved in the acquisition, exploration and development of precious metal properties.
Pierre R. Gauthier, Chairman
TOTAL REVENUE ($000)   0

LA TEKO RESOURCES LTD
(Public)   PRECIOUS METALS
180 East 2100 South, Suite 204, Salt Lake, UT,
84115   (801) 466-1437
LA TEKO RESOURCES LTD. is involved in the acquisition, exploration and development of precious metal properties.
Jack Layne, President
TOTAL REVENUE ($000)   75 (US)

LAC MINERALS LTD.
See page 48 for a full company profile.

LAFARGE CANADA INC.
See page 497 for a full company profile.

LAIDLAW INC.
See page 451 for a full company profile.

LAIRD GROUP INC. (THE)
(Public)   PUBLISHING & PRINTING
Suite 100, 73 Laird Drive, Toronto, ON, M4G 3T4   (416) 422-5151
LAIRD GROUP INC. has one continuing business, graphic arts, which contributes over 90% of its operations.

Robert M. Leith, Chairman & C.E.O.
TOTAL REVENUE ($000)   22,214

LAKEWOOD ENERGY INC.
(Public)   OIL AND GAS PRODUCERS
Suite 2020, 1200 McGill College Avenue, Montreal, PQ,
H3B 4G7   (514) 866-1866
LAKEWOOD ENERGY INC. is an energy income fund created for the purpose of aqcuiring and managing a pool of resource assets, primarily comprised of proven producing and proven non-producing properties, purchased primarily from Lakewood limited partnerships. The business of Lakewood Energy is the ownership and exploitation of oil and gas properties secured by a royalty indenture.
Martin Hislop, President & Director
TOTAL REVENUE ($000)   6,676

LAMBERT SOMEC INC.
(Public)   CONTRACTORS
725 Rue Lachance, Quebec, PQ, G1P 2H3   (418) 687-1640
LAMBERT SOMEC is a construction contractor specializing in the electrical, piping, ventilation and air conditioning, and industrial mechanical fields. It carries on business primarily in the commercial construction and industrial construction sectors.
Denis Linteau, President
TOTAL REVENUE ($000)   24,690

LANTIC SUGAR LIMITED
(Private)   FOOD PROCESSING
1 Westmount Square, Westmount, PQ, H3Z 2P9   (514) 939-3939
LANTIC SUGAR LIMITED is engaged in refining and sales of sugar.
W.C. Brown, Chairman and C.E.O.
TOTAL REVENUE ($000)   384,696

LARAMIDE RESOURCES LTD.
(Public)   PRECIOUS METALS
Suite 904, 675 West Hastings Street, Vancouver, BC,
V6B 1N2   (604) 688-3584
LARAMIDE RESOURCES LTD., both directly and through its subsidiary, Vanco Exploration Limited, is engaged in the acquisition, exploration and development of mineral properties. The most advanced project is the Lara property, a 100% owned gold-base metals deposit on southern Vancouver Island.
Albert F. Reeve, President
TOTAL REVENUE ($000)   (39)

LASSONDE INDUSTRIES INC.
(Public)   FOOD PROCESSING
170 5th Avenue, Rougemont, PQ, J0L 1M0   (514) 878-1057
LASSONDE INDUSTRIES INC., through its subsidiaries, is engaged in the business of transforming, conditioning, packaging and marketing food products. It is the largest apple juice manufacturer and distributor in Quebec and the Atlantic provinces.
Pierre-Paul Lassonde, Chairman & President of the Executive Ctte.
TOTAL REVENUE ($000)   115,976

LAURENTIAN BANK OF CANADA
See page 385 for a full company profile.

LAURENTIAN FINANCIAL INC.
(Private)   INSURANCE - LIFE
1100 Rene-Levesque Blvd. West, 20th Floor, Montreal, PQ,
H3B 4N4   (514) 392-6440
LAURENTIAN FINANCIAL INC. and its subsidiaries operate principally in the life insurance and mutual funds industries. Effective January 1, 1991, the company underwent a reorganization such that it is now the holding company for all of The Laurentian Group's life insurance and investment management activities.
Jacques A. Drouin, Chairman
TOTAL REVENUE ($000)   1,574,928

LAURENTIAN GROUP CORPORATION (THE)
See page 408 for a full company profile.

LAWSON MARDON GROUP LIMITED
See page 249 for a full company profile.

LEADER INDUSTRIES INC.
(Public)   MISC. CONSUMER PRODUCTS
1280 Nobel St, Boucherville, PQ, J4B 5H1   (514) 641-4480
LEADER INDUSTRIES INC. manufactures and distributes equipment for the eye and face protection for competitive and recreational sports and also for military usage.
Pierre Habib, Chairman & C.E.O.
TOTAL REVENUE ($000)   6,985

LEDCOR INDUSTRIES LIMITED
(Private)   CONTRACTORS
1066 West Hastings Street, Suite 1000, Vancouver, BC,
V6C 3X1   (604) 681-7500
LEDCOR INDUSTRIES LIMITED is a construction company.
David Lede, Chairman & C.E.O.
TOTAL REVENUE ($000)   198,370

LEHNDORFF CANADIAN PROPERTIES
(Public)   PROPERTY MGMNT & INVESTMENT
360 Bay Street, Toronto, ON, M5H 2V6   (416) 869-7800
LEHNDORFF CANADIAN PROPERTIES is a real estate limited partnership established in 1979 for individual and institutional investors participating on a limited liability basis in the ownership of a large and diversified portfolio of income-producing properties in Canada.
Dr. Hans G. Abromeit, Chairman
TOTAL REVENUE ($000)   3,912

LEON'S FURNITURE LIMITED
(Public)   SPECIALTY STORES
P.O. Box 460, 88 Gordon Mackay Road, Weston, ON,
M9N 3N2   (416) 243-7880
LEON'S FURNITURE LIMITED sells home furnishings, appliances and carpets through a chain of retail facilities and franchises located in Alberta, Manitoba, Ontario, Quebec, the Maritime provinces and in the United States.
Anthony T. Leon, Chairman & C.E.O.
TOTAL REVENUE ($000)   266,320

LEP INTERNATIONAL INC.
(Private)   TRANSPORTATION
401 The West Mall, Etobicoke, ON, M9C 5J5   (416) 620-6570
LEP INTERNATIONAL INC. is an international freight forwarder and customs broker.
Peter Brown, C.E.O. & President
TOTAL REVENUE ($000)   189,974

LESSARD, BEAUCAGE, LEMIEUX INC.
(Public)   CONTRACTORS
225 Montee De Liesse, St-Laurent, PQ,
H4T 1P5   (514) 737-4533
LESSARD, BEAUCAGE, LEMIEUX INC. is a building contractor specializing in the manufacture and installation of windows, greenhouses, atria, curtain-walls and entrances for commercial and industrial buildings. It designs, assembles, manufactures and installs the glass-covered portions of buildings.
Camille Lessard, Chairman, President & C.E.O.
TOTAL REVENUE ($000)   32,036

LEVON RESOURCES LTD.
(Public)   PRECIOUS METALS
Suite 400, 455 Granville Street, Vancouver, BC,
V6C 1T1   (604) 682-3701
LEVON RESOURCES LTD. is an exploration company that develops gold properties in British Columbia.
Louis Wolfin, President
TOTAL REVENUE ($000)   38

LGS GROUP INC.
(Public)   COMPUTER SOFTWARE & PROCESSING
1253 McGill College Avenue, Suite 1070, Montreal, PQ,
H3B 2Y5   (514) 392-9193
LGS GROUP INC. provides information management consulting services. Its fields of activity include systems integration, data processing, office automation and related products.
Raymond Lafontaine, President
TOTAL REVENUE ($000)   50,015

LILYDALE CO-OPERATIVE LIMITED
(Non-fin Co-op)   AGRICULTURE
7727 - 127 Avenue, Edmonton, AB, T5C 1R9   (403) 476-6261
LILYDALE CO-OPERATIVE is an Alberta based cooperative designed to build and maintain a financially viable system of processing and marketing poultry products for Alberta and BC farmers. The company operates a processing division, a hatchery division, a farm division, a further-processing division and a table egg division.
T. Donkersgoed, Chairman
TOTAL REVENUE ($000)   271,351

LINAMAR CORPORATION
See page 227 for a full company profile.

LINCOLN CAPITAL CORPORATION
(Public)   SPECIALTY STORES
51 International Boulevard, Etobicoke, ON,
M9W 6H3   (416) 798-3581

LINCOLN CAPITAL CORPORATION's investment strategy is to acquire significant equity positions in businesses with growth potential. The company is liquidating its merchant banking investments and loans over time, on an orderly basis.
Kenneth Fowler, Chairman & C.E.O.
TOTAL REVENUE ($000)   61,546

LIQUIDATION WORLD INC.
(Public)   SPECIALTY STORES
3900 - 29th Street N.E., Calgary, AB, T1Y 6B6   (403) 250-1222
LIQUIDATION WORLD INC. is a liquidator of distress merchandise from any source through 12 retail outlets, and through auctions.
Dale Gillespie, Chairman, Presidnet & C.E.O.
TOTAL REVENUE ($000)   18,980

LITTON SYSTEMS CANADA LIMITED
(Private)   ELECTRICAL & ELECTRONIC
25 Cityview Drive, Rexdale, ON, M9W 5A7   (416) 249-1231
LITTON SYSTEMS CANADA LIMITED is a defence contractor providing electronic products and repair services as well as other goods and services.
Thomas J. McGuigan, President
TOTAL REVENUE ($000)   381,131

LIVINGSTON GROUP INC.
(Private)   MANAGEMENT AND DIVERSIFIED
405 The West Mall, Etobicoke, ON, M9C 5K7   (416) 626-2828
LIVINGSTON GROUP INC. provides warehousing, distribution and customs brokerage services. Livingston Group is 91.1% owned by Ivest Corporation of London, Ontario.
R.M. Ivey, Chairman
TOTAL REVENUE ($000)   168,941

LLOYD'S NON-MARINE UNDERWRITERS
(Private)   INSURANCE - PROPERTY & CASUALTY
1155 University, Suite 1400, Montreal, PQ,
H3B 1S3   (514) 861-8361
LLOYD'S NON-MARINE UNDERWRITERS is a property and casualty insurer.
John David Rowland, Chairman of Lloyd's
TOTAL REVENUE ($000)   665,448

LOBLAW COMPANIES LIMITED
See page 363 for a full company profile.

LOEB INC.
(Private)   FOOD STORES
400 Industrial Avenue, Ottawa, ON, K1G 3K8   (613) 737-1485
LOEB INC. operates a franchise network of 116 LOEB IGA, LOEB and IGA stores which are supplied through eight distribution centres. It also operates 22 cash and carry outlets that cater to corner stores and institutional customers. LOEB operates in Ontario and western and northwestern Quebec. The company is a wholly owned subsidiary of Provigo Inc.
W. Kipp, President
TOTAL REVENUE ($000)   1,697,800

LOEWEN GROUP INC. (THE)
See page 498 for a full company profile.

LOGIBEC GROUPE INFORMATIQUE LTEE
(Public)   COMPUTER SOFTWARE & PROCESSING
8 Place du Commerce, 3ieme etage, Ile des Soeurs, PQ,
H3E 1N3   (514) 766-0134
LOGIBEC GROUPE INFORMATIQUE LTEE's services and products can be grouped in four main categories: management information services; specialized application software; distribution of equipmentand software; and batch data processing.
Claude Roy, Chairman, President & C.E.O.
TOTAL REVENUE ($000)   6,784

LOGISTEC CORPORATION
(Public)   TRANSPORTATION
360 Rue St-Jacques, Bureau 1500, Montreal, PQ,
H2Y 1P5   (514) 844-9381
LOGISTEC CORPORATION and its subsidiaries form an integrated group of companies servicing the marine industry. The company operates three marines services divisions: stevedoring and terminal; navigation; and shipping agency. Logistec also operates an enviromental services division. Most operations are conducted in Canada, while some offices are located in the United States.
Jacques Paquin, Chairman
TOTAL REVENUE ($000)   74,415

LOKI GOLD CORP.
(Public)   PRECIOUS METALS
Suite 800, 900 West Hastings Street, Vancouver, BC,
V6C 1E5   (604) 684-8123
LOKI GOLD CORPORATION is involved in the acquisition, exploration and development of precious metal properties.
TOTAL REVENUE ($000)   25

LONDON INSURANCE GROUP INC.
See page 428 for a full company profile.

LONDON LIFE INSURANCE COMPANY
(Private)   INSURANCE - LIFE
255 Dufferin Avenue, London, ON, N6A 4K1   (519) 432-5281
LONDON LIFE INSURANCE COMPANY offers life and annuity products to individuals, and life, health and pension products to groups in Canada.
Earl H. Orser, Chairman
TOTAL REVENUE ($000)   2,781,000

LOUVEM MINES INC.
(Public)   PRECIOUS METALS
Suite 2700, 1 Adelaide Street East, Toronto, ON,
M5C 2Z6   (416) 982-7111
LOUVEM MINES INC. holds various participation in exploration properties in the Val d'Or area.
Pierre R. Gauthier, Chairman
TOTAL REVENUE ($000)   3,525

LSI LOGIC CORPORATION OF CANADA, INC.
(Public)   ELECTRICAL & ELECTRONIC
Suite 3410, 150 - 6th Avenue S.W., Calgary, AB,
T2P 3Y7   (403) 262-9292

LSI LOGIC CORPORATION OF CANADA, INC. designs and markets application specific integrated circuits for electronic applications and provides related design and technology services, all based principally on gate array & cell-based semiconductor technology. The company also offers chip sets used in PCs and MIPS and Sparc RISC microprocessors.
Travis Wells, Chairman
TOTAL REVENUE ($000)   53,667

M-CORP INC.
(Public)   FOOD SERVICES
Suite 310, 8250 Decarie Boulevard, Montreal, PQ,
H4P 2P5   (514) 341-5544
M-CORP operates in Quebec through licensees, a total of 131 Limited-menu, family-style specialty restaurants, featuring italian-style submarine sandwiches, pizzas and pastas. Most of the units offer tableservice, while a majority are fully licensed to sell alcoholic beverages. The company is also actively involved in the development and acquisition of commercial real estate.
William M. Reim, Chairman President & C.E.O.
TOTAL REVENUE ($000)   14,647

MAAX INC.
(Public)   MISC. CONSUMER PRODUCTS
600 Route Cameron, C.P. 1030, Ste-Marie, PQ,
G6E 3C2   (418) 387-3646
MAAX INC. is the sole shareholder of Xatec Inc. This company specializes in the manufacture of products made of compound materials. It designs, manufactures and markest fiberglass bathtubs, showers and bathroom accessories, acrylic whirlpools, bathtubs and fiberglass vehicle components.
Placide Poulin, Chairman, President & C.E.O.
TOTAL REVENUE ($000)   25,874

MABAIE INC.
(Public)   DEVELOPERS
Suite 100, 1870 Boul. Des Sources, Pointe-Claire, PQ,
H9R 5N4   (514) 694-0140
MABAIE INC. is a Montreal based real estate developer operating in residential, commercial and industrial real estate.
Bernard Gervais, Chairman, President & C.E.O.
TOTAL REVENUE ($000)   5,426

MACKENZIE FINANCIAL CORPORATION
See page 409 for a full company profile.

MACLEAN HUNTER LIMITED
See page 324 for a full company profile.

MACMILLAN BLOEDEL LIMITED
See page 143 for a full company profile.

MACYRO GROUP INC. (THE)
(Public)   CONTRACTORS
6140 St-Anne Boulevard, L'Ange-Gardien, PQ,
G0A 2K0   (418) 822-0283
MACYRO GROUP INC. specializes in the construction of industrial and commercial type buildings through its subsidiary Rocois Construction Inc. Through other subsidiaries it also manufactures and installs windows and curtain walls used in industrial and commercial construction as well as manufactures doors and windows for the residential sector.
Marc LeFrancois, Chairman, President & C.E.O.
TOTAL REVENUE ($000)   47,515

MADELEINE MINES LTD.
(Public)   METAL MINES
111 Richmond Street West, Suite 916, Toronto, ON,
M5H 2G4   (416) 867-3072
MADELEINE MINES LTD. is involved in mining exploration and development.
Dale McDoulette, President
TOTAL REVENUE ($000)   150

MAGIC FOODS INC.
(Public)   FOOD SERVICES
4800 Dufferin Street, Downsview, ON, M3H 5S9   (416) 979-3436
MAGIC FOODS INC. is in the restaurant and food and beverage business.
Austin P. Page, C.E.O.
TOTAL REVENUE ($000)   2,202

MAGNA INTERNATIONAL INC.
See page 186 for a full company profile.

MALETTE INC.
(Public)   EAST COAST FORESTRY
Highway 101 West, P.O. Box 1100, Timmins, ON,
P4N 7H9   (705) 268-1462
MALETTE INC. is an integrated forest products company. The company is involved in the management and development of forest resources and the production of lumber, wood chips, oriented stand board and bleached kraft pulp and paper.
Gaston Malette, Chairman President & C.E.O.
TOTAL REVENUE ($000)   114,964

MANITOBA HYDRO-ELECTRIC BOARD (THE)
(Crown)   ELECTRICAL UTILITIES
P.O. Box 815, 820 Taylor Avenue, Winnipeg, MB,
R3C 2P4   (204) 474-3233
THE MANITOBA HYDRO-ELECTRIC BOARD is a Manitoba crown corporation responsible for the generation, transmission and distribution of electricity to consumers throughout the province, except for the central portion of the City of Winnipeg.
J.S. (John) McCallum, Chairman
TOTAL REVENUE ($000)   833,200

MANITOBA POOL ELEVATORS
(Non-fin Co-op)   AGRICULTURE
Royal Bank Building, 220 Portage Avenue, Winnipeg, MB,
R3C 3K7   (204) 947-1171
MANITOBA POOL ELEVATORS is a producer-owned cooperative. Departments include country operations, terminals, agri-sales and service. The Pool has 130 active locals and associations operating on behalf of some 18,000 members.
C.H. Swanson, Chairman & President
TOTAL REVENUE ($000)   146,731

MANITOBA PUBLIC INSURANCE CORPORATION (THE)
(Crown)   INSURANCE - PROPERTY & CASUALTY
Box 6300, 9th Floor, 330 Graham Avenue, Winnipeg,
R3C 4A4   (204) 985-7000
MANITOBA PUBLIC INSURANCE CORPORATION conducts a
comprehensive automobile program.
Ruth M. Konzelman, Chairperson
TOTAL REVENUE ($000)   425,905

MANITOBA TELEPHONE SYSTEM (THE)
(Crown)   TELEPHONE UTILITIES
489 Empress Street, P.O. Box 6666, Winnipeg, MB,
R3C 3V6   (204) 941-7314
THE MANITOBA TELEPHONE SYSTEM is a provincially-owned
crown corporation that provides telecommunications services to resi-
dences and businesses in Manitoba.
Tom Stefanson, Chairman
TOTAL REVENUE ($000)   544,026

MANNVILLE OIL & GAS LTD.
(Public)   OIL AND GAS PRODUCERS
Suite 600, 505 - 8th Avenue S.W., Calgary, AB,
T2P 1G2   (403) 266-4024
MANNVILLE OIL & GAS LTD. is an independent, active oil and gas
exploration company, with producing properties in both Alberta and
Saskatchewan. The company also owns petroleum and natural gas leases
and production facilities in both Alberta and Saskatchewan.
S. Douglas Martin, Chairman Of The Board
TOTAL REVENUE ($000)   11,058

MANUFACTURERS LIFE INSURANCE COMPANY (THE)
(Private)   INSURANCE - LIFE
200 Bloor Street East, Toronto, ON, M4W 1E5   (416) 926-0100
THE MANUFACTURERS LIFE INSURANCE COMPANY, or
MANULIFE FINANCIAL, provides an extensive range of products and
services meeting the life insurance, health insurance, pension income and
banking needs of individuals and businesses. Sales and service offices
are located in major cities in Canada, the U.S., the U.K., and Pacific Asia.
The company operates Manulife Bank of Canada and Western Trust
(U.K.).
Thomas A. Di Giacomo, Chairman President & C.E.O.
TOTAL REVENUE ($000)   6,983,417

MAPLE LEAF FOODS INC.
See page 164 for a full company profile.

MAPLE LEAF GARDENS, LIMITED
(Public)   ENTERTAINMENT SERVICES
60 Carlton Street, Toronto, ON, M5B 1L1   (416) 977-1641
MAPLE LEAF GARDENS, LIMITED operates in the entertainment
industry. Besides being the home of the Toronto Maple Leafs Hockey
Club, the Gardens hosts many other entertainment events.
Steve Stavro, Chairman & C.E.O.
TOTAL REVENUE ($000)   47,097

MAPLE LODGE FARMS LTD.
(Private)   FOOD PROCESSING
R.R. 2, Norval, ON, L0P 1K0   (416) 455-8340
MAPLE LODGE FARMS is a poultry processor and manufacturer of
wiener and deli products.
Robert May, C.E.O.
TOTAL REVENUE ($000)   214,000

MARATHON REALTY HOLDINGS INC.
(Private)   DEVELOPERS
Suite 400, 200 Wellington Street West, Toronto, ON,
M5V 3C7   (416) 348-1500
MARATHON REALTY COMPANY LIMITED is a Canadian com-
pany which develops, owns and manages income-producing properties
across Canada and the United States. Marathon's portfolio includes
shopping centres; office, industrial, aviation-related, and residential
buildings; industrial parks; and commercial and agricultural lands. Mara-
thon is a wholly owned subsidiary of Canadian Pacific Limited.
R.K. Gamey, Chairman
TOTAL REVENUE ($000)   516,469

MARINE ATLANTIC INC.
(Crown)   TRANSPORTATION
100 Cameron Street, Moncton, NB, E1C 5Y6   (506) 851-3600
MARINE ATLANTIC INC. is involved in the management and opera-
tion of marine transportation services, a marina maintenance, repair, and
refit service, a marine construction business, and other related services.
A.K. Scales, Chairman of the Board
TOTAL REVENUE ($000)   230,967

MARITIME ELECTRIC COMPANY, LIMITED
See page 300 for a full company profile.

MARITIME LIFE ASSURANCE COMPANY
(Public)   INSURANCE - LIFE
2701 Dutch Village Road, P.O. Box 1030, Halifax, NS,
B3J 2X5   (902) 453-4300
MARITIME LIFE ASSURANCE COMPANY is involved in the life
insurance industry, providing a wide range of life insurance and annuities
on an individual basis, as well as life insurance, health and annuity
products on a group basis across Canada.
John Lindsay, Chairman
TOTAL REVENUE ($000)   616,551

MARITIME TELEGRAPH AND TELEPHONE COMPANY, LIMITED
See page 301 for a full company profile.

MARK RESOURCES INC.
See page 96 for a full company profile.

MARK'S WORK WEARHOUSE LTD.
(Public)   CLOTHING STORES
Suite 30, 1035 - 64th Avenue S.E., Calgary, AB,
T2H 2J7   (403) 255-9220
MARK'S WORK WEARHOUSE LTD. operates a chain of retail stores
in Canada which cater to the workwear sector and to the casual wear

sector of the market. The Company's sales are comprised of three broad commodity groupings; work wear, jeans and casual wear.
Marcus W. Blumes, Chairman, President & C.E.O.
TOTAL REVENUE ($000)   132,742

MARKBOROUGH PROPERTIES INC.
See page 262 for a full company profile.

MARLIN TRAVEL GROUP LTD. (THE)
(Private)   MANAGEMENT AND DIVERSIFIED
1030 Scotia Place, 10060 Jasper Ave, Edmonton, AB,
T5J 3R8   (403) 424-0587
MARLIN TRAVEL GROUP LTD. is engaged in the sale of travel services to retail customers.
Rod Marlin, Chairman
TOTAL REVENUE ($000)   680,831

MARSHALL MINERALS CORP
(Public)   METAL MINES
4776 Bridge Street, Toronto, ON, L2E 2R8
MARSHALL MINERALS CORP. is engaged in the exploration and development of mineral resource properties.
TOTAL REVENUE ($000)   638

MARSHALL STEEL LIMITED
See page 345 for a full company profile.

MARUBENI CANADA LTD.
(Private)   WHOLESALE DISTRIBUTORS
Canada Trust Tower, BCE Place, 161 Bay Street, Suite 2300,
Toronto, ON, M5J 2S1   (416) 368-1171
MARUBENI CANADA is a trading and wholesaling company.
Ryuhei Nakamura, Chairman
TOTAL REVENUE ($000)   1,094,340

MATCO RAVARY INC.
(Public)   SPECIALTY STORES
355 Sir Wilfrid Laurier Blvd., St-Basile-Le-Grand, PQ,
J3N 1M9   (514) 653-7861
MATCO RAVARY INC. sells home construction and renovation supplies through its seven distribution outlets on Montreal's south shore. shore. It carries some 30,000 products aimed at three customer groups: building contractors; handymen and institutions. The company is part of Le Groupe RO-NA Inc., a purchasing and services group formed by independant retailers.
Carmel Chaput, President
TOTAL REVENUE ($000)   55,035

MATSUSHITA ELECTRIC OF CANADA LIMITED
(Private)   WHOLESALE DISTRIBUTORS
5770 Ambler Drive, Mississauga, ON, L4W 2T2   (416) 624-5010
MATSUSHITA ELECTRIC OF CANADA LIMITED is a distributor of electrical goods.
Tom Shikata, President
TOTAL REVENUE ($000)   489,935

MAXX PETROLEUM LTD.
(Public)   OIL AND GAS PRODUCERS
Suite 1960, 700 - 4th Avenue S.W., Calgary, AB,
T2P 3J4   (403) 261-6666
MAXX PETROLEUM LTD. is engaged in oil and gas exploration and development with prospects primarily in Alberta.
Burl N. Aycock, President& C.E.O.
TOTAL REVENUE ($000)   6,812

MAYNE NICKLESS CANADA INC.
(Private)   TRANSPORTATION
1290 Hornby Street, Suite 300, Vancouver, BC,
V6Z 2G4   (604) 665-4700
MAYNE NICKLESS CANADA INC. supplies armoured car/ABM services, courier small parcel air & road transport services, messenger services and guard and patrol services. The company's parent is Mayne Nickless Limited, Melbourne, Australia.
W.T. Bytheway, Chairman
TOTAL REVENUE ($000)   326,375

MAZDA CANADA INC.
(Private)   WHOLESALE DISTRIBUTORS
2075 Kennedy Road, Suite 400, Scarborough, ON,
M1T 3V3   (416) 609-9909
MAZDA CANADA INC. is a wholesaler of Mazda motor vehicles and parts. Mazda Canada is 60% owned by Mazda Motor Corporation of Japan and and 40% owned by Itohchu Corp. Ltd. of Japan.
Toshinori Mori, President & C.E.O.
TOTAL REVENUE ($000)   873,630

MCCAIN FOODS LIMITED
(Private)   FOOD PROCESSING
Main Street, Florenceville, NB, E0J 1K0   (506) 392-5541
MCCAIN FOODS LIMITED, is a privately owned Canadian multinational food processor.
H.Harrision McCain, Chairman
TOTAL REVENUE ($000)   2,741,671

MCDONALD'S RESTAURANTS OF CANADA LTD
(Private)   FOOD SERVICES
McDonald's Place, Toronto, ON, M3C 3L4   (416) 443-1000
MCDONALD'S RESTAURANTS OF CANADA LIMITED and its affiliates operate or license and service a system of quick service restaurants. Mcdonald's restaurants are located in all provinces of Canada and in the Yukon Territory.
George A. Cohon, Senior Chairman
TOTAL REVENUE ($000)   744,078

MCDONNELL DOUGLAS CANADA LTD.
(Private)   TRANSPORTATION EQUIP & COMPNTS
P.O. Box 6013, Toronto A.M.F., Toronto, ON,
L5P 1B7   (416) 677-4341
MCDONNELL DOUGLAS CANADA LTD. manufacturers major components for both commercial and military jet aircraft. The company is wholly owned by McDonnell Douglas Corporation.
Leslie, Gordon, Acting President
TOTAL REVENUE ($000)   461,587

MCGRAW-HILL RYERSON LIMITED
(Public)   PUBLISHING & PRINTING
300 Water Street, Whitby, ON, L1N 9B6   (416) 428-2222
MCGRAW-HILL RYERSON LIMITED operates exclusively as a publisher and distributor of general books, educational, professional, and technical reference materials and educational films.
Hon. E. Jacques Courtois, Chairman Of The Board
TOTAL REVENUE ($000)   40,691

MCMAHON-ESSAIM INC.
(Private)   WHOLESALE DISTRIBUTORS
11011 Blvd. Maurice Duplessis, Montreal, PQ,
H1C 1V6   (514) 643-1000
MCMAHON-ESSAIM INC. is a drug wholesaler with operations in Quebec. It is a subsidiary of Metro-Richelieu Inc.
TOTAL REVENUE ($000)   169,597

MCNELLEN RESOURCES INC.
(Public)   PRECIOUS METALS
Suite 1210, 111 Richmond Street, Toronto, ON,
M5H 2G4   (416) 363-1124
MCNELLEN RESOURCE INC. is engaged in the exploration and development of Canadian mineral properties. The company also owns 50% of the Magino Gold Mine in Wawa, Ontario.
C.H. McNellen, Chairman
TOTAL REVENUE ($000)   5,685

MCR CAPITAL INC.
(Public)   MANAGEMENT AND DIVERSIFIED
106 Avenue Road, Toronto, ON, M5R 2H3   (416) 920-0500
MCR CAPITAL INC. carries on business as an investment management holding company with investments in effectively controlled operating companies and subsidiaries.
Henry Schnurbach, President
TOTAL REVENUE ($000)   13,320

MDC CORPORATION
(Public)   CONSULTING
Suite 102, 939 Eglinton Avenue East, Toronto, ON,
M4G 4E8   (416) 696-2000
MDC CORPORATION is a communications and marketing organization that specializes in below-the-line or non-advertising communications. Through its operating subsidiaries and divisions, the company is involved in the consulting, production and manufacturing sectors of the communications and marketing industry.
Miles S. Nadal, Chairman, C.E.O. & President
TOTAL REVENUE ($000)   25,258

MDS HEALTH GROUP LIMITED
See page 499 for a full company profile.

MEDIS HEALTH AND PHARMACEUTICAL SERVICES INC.
(Private)   WHOLESALE DISTRIBUTORS
3501 St. Charles Blvd, Suite 101, Kirkland, PQ,
H9H 4S3   (514) 694-2100
MEDIS HEALTH AND PHARMACEUTICAL SERVICES INC. is engaged in the distribution of pharmaceuticals products, health and beauty aids, sundries and other drugstore type of merchandise to over 4,800 pharmacy customers across Canada. Medis serves all Canadian provinces from 15 distribution centres and organized into 4 operating regions: Atlantic, Quebec, Ontario and Western.
David R. Friesen, President & C.O.O.
TOTAL REVENUE ($000)   1,625,000

MELCOR DEVELOPMENTS LTD.
See page 263 for a full company profile.

MELLON BANK CANADA
(Private)   BANKS
Suite 2310, South Tower, Royal Bank Plaza, P.O. Box 153, Toronto, ON, M5J 2J4   (416) 362-6051
MELLON BANK CANADA is a wholly owned subsidiary of Mellon Bank, N.A. which has its head office in Pittsburgh. The bank provides financial services to Canadian corporations, Canadian subsidiaries of U.S. corporations, and multinationls.
William B. Amis, Jr., Chairman, President & C.E.O.
TOTAL REVENUE ($000)   24,001

MENTOR EXPLORATION AND DEVELOPMENT CO., LIMITED
(Public)   PRECIOUS METALS
401 Bay Street, Suite 2302, P.O. Box 102, Toronto, ON,
M5H 2Y4   (416) 947-1212
MENTOR EXPLORATION AND DEVELOPMENT CO., LIMITED conducts precious metal exploration and holds investments in precious metals companies.
Paul Penna, Chairman & President
TOTAL REVENUE ($000)   88

MERCEDES-BENZ CANADA INC.
(Private)   WHOLESALE DISTRIBUTORS
849 Eglinton Ave. E., Toronto, ON, M4G 2L5   (416) 425-3550
MERCEDES-BENZ CANADA is a wholesaler of Mercedes-Benz automobiles. The company is wholly owned by Daimler-Benz North America Holding Corp.
S. Paul Halata, President
TOTAL REVENUE ($000)   278,422

MERCHANT PRIVATE LIMITED
(Public)   FINANCE AND LEASING
Suite 5114, Scotia Plaza, 40 King Street West, Toronto, ON,
M5H 3Y2   (416) 360-4115
MERCHANT PRIVATE LIMITED is a financial services company whose principal activity is the management of financial assets for its own account and for the accounts of others. Financial assets consist of investment and mortgage loan portfolios.
John C. Clark, Chairman & C.E.O.
TOTAL REVENUE ($000)   18,174

MERFIN HYGIENIC PRODUCTS LTD.
(Public)   MISC. INDUSTRIAL PRODUCTS
7979 Vantage Way, Delta, BC, V4G 1A6   (604) 946-0677
MERFIN HYGIENIC PRODUCTS is one of the leading specialty manufacturers in North America of air-laid paper products both in converted form and parent rolls. These products are used on a global basis

for industrial wipes, premoistened wipes such as hot towels, baby wipes and household wiping products, absorbent cores in adult incontinence & feminine hygiene products and specialty packaging for food shipments.
Ivan B. Pivko, President & C.E.O.
TOTAL REVENUE ($000)   31,021

MERIDIAN TECHNOLOGIES INC.
(Public)   AUTOMOTIVE
Suite 1700, 2 St. Clair Avenue West, Toronto, ON,
M4V 1L5   (416) 922-2050
MERIDIAN TECHNOLOGIES INC. is a Canadian company whose principal business is the manufacture of aluminum and magnesium high pressure die cast original equipment components for the North American automotive industry.
Anthony F. Griffiths, Chairman
TOTAL REVENUE ($000)   105,153

METALL MINING CORPORATION
See page 17 for a full company profile.

METALORE RESOURCES LIMITED
(Public)   OIL AND GAS PRODUCERS
Rural Route #1, Vittoria, ON, N0E 1W0   (519) 428-2464
METALORE RESOURCES LIMITED is involved in the exploration for and development and production of natural gas and in the exploration for and development of mining properties in Ontario.
George W. Chilian, President
TOTAL REVENUE ($000)   977

METHANEX CORPORATION
See page 239 for a full company profile.

METRO-RICHELIEU INC.
(Public)   FOOD STORES
11011 Boul. Maurice Duplessis, Montreal, PQ,
H1C 1V6   (514) 643-1000
METRO-RICHELIEU INC. is engaged primarily in the purchase and wholesale distribution of food products and general merchandise. Its operating territory extends throughout Quebec and Northern Ontario.
Bernard Belair, Chairman
TOTAL REVENUE ($000)   2,308,619

MICC INVESTMENTS LIMITED
See page 429 for a full company profile.

MIDLAND WALWYN INC.
See page 410 for a full company profile.

MILES CANADA INC.
(Private)   CHEMICALS
77 Belfield Rd, Rexdale, ON, M9W 1G6   (416) 248-0771
MILES CANADA INC. is a manufacturer and distributor of health care products. It is a wholly owned subsidiary of Miles Inc. of the United States.
W.C. Garriock, President
TOTAL REVENUE ($000)   242,070

MINERA RAYROCK INC.
(Public)   METAL MINES
30 Soudan Avenue, Suite 500, Toronto, ON,
M4S 1V6   (416) 489-0022
MINERA RAYROCK INC. is an exploration and mining development company active in Costa Rica, Ecuador and Chile.
David R. Crombie, President & C.E.O.
TOTAL REVENUE ($000)   13

MINNOVA INC.
(Private)   METAL MINES
Suite 3400, Aetna Tower, P.O. Box 19, Toronto-Dominion Centre,
Toronto, ON, M5K 1A1   (416) 364-6400
MINNOVA INC. is a natural resource company exploring, developing and mining a range of minerals, primarily copper, zinc, gold, lead and silver. The company operates gold and copper mines in Quebec, a zinc and copper mine in Ontario. It has other properties in Ontario, Quebec, British Columbia and Nevada. Metall Mining Corporation of Toronto owns 50.4% of Minnova.
Klaus M. Zeitler, Chairman
TOTAL REVENUE ($000)   181,461

MINORCO CANADA LIMITED
(Public)   INTEGRATED MINES
Suite 720, 70 York Street, Toronto, ON, M5J 1S9   (416) 601-9546
MINORCO CANADA LIMITED, also known as Mincan, jointly owns Mingold Resources Inc. with Inspiration Resources Corporation
G.E. Munera, Chairman & President
TOTAL REVENUE ($000)   648

MINVEN GOLD CORPORATION
See page 49 for a full company profile.

MIRAMAR MINING CORPORATION
(Public)   METAL MINES
213 West First Street, North Vancouver, BC,
V7M 1B3   (604) 985-2572
MIRAMAR MINING CORPORATION is involved in the acquisition, exploration and development of mineral properties.
Walter H. Berukoff, President & C.E.O.
TOTAL REVENUE ($000)   1,154

MIRTRONICS INC.
(Public)   MISC. CONSUMER PRODUCTS
106 Avenue Road, Toronto, ON, M5R 2H3   (416) 920-0500
MIRTRONICS INC. operates in one industry being the design, manufacture and sale of fire alarms and life safety equipment products and related systems.
Mark I. Litwin, President
TOTAL REVENUE ($000)   13,322

MITEL CORPORATION
See page 325 for a full company profile.

MITSUBISHI BANK OF CANADA
(Private)   BANKS
P.O. Box 518, Suite 3800, Canada Trust Tower, BCE Place, 161
Bay St., Toronto, ON, M5J 2S1   (416) 365-1940
MITSUBISHI BANK OF CANADA is a schedule II bank, wholly
owned by the Mitsubishi Bank Limited of Tokyo, Japan.
Takeshi Yano, Chairman
TOTAL REVENUE ($000)   63,988

MITSUBISHI CANADA LIMITED
(Private)   ELECTRICAL & ELECTRONIC
P.O. Box 17, Commerce Court Postal Station, Suite 2181
Commerce Court West, Toronto, ON, M5L 1A5   (416) 362-6731
MITSUBISHI CANADA LIMITED produces machinery and engines
and is a buyer and seller of steel. It is a wholly owned subsidiary of
Mitsubishi Corp. of Japan.
S. Eto, President & C.E.O.
TOTAL REVENUE ($000)   1,265,952

MITSUBISHI ELECTRIC SALES CANADA INC.
(Private)   ELECTRICAL & ELECTRONIC
4299 - 14th Avenue, Markham, ON, L3R 0J2   (416) 475-7728
MITSUBISHI ELECTRIC SALES CANADA INC. is a distributor of
electronic components, equipment and consumer electronics and a manufacturer of colour television sets. The company is a wholly owned
subsidiary of Mitsubishi Electric Corporation of Japan.
E. Nishibori, President & C.E.O.
TOTAL REVENUE ($000)   185,000

MITSUI & CO. (CANADA) LTD.
(Private)   WHOLESALE DISTRIBUTORS
20 Adelaide Street East, Suite 1500, Toronto, ON,
M5C 2T6   (416) 947-3899
MITSUI & CO. (CANADA) LTD. is an importer and exporter of steel,
non-ferous metals, machinery, chemical, foodstuff, wood products and
sundry items. The company is wholly owned by Mitsui & Co., Ltd. of
Japan.
Shinji Teshima, President & C.E.O.
TOTAL REVENUE ($000)   2,037,689

MIU INDUSTRIES LTD.
(Public)   COMPUTER SOFTWARE & PROCESSING
17 Skyridge Court, Gormley, ON, L0H 1G0   (416) 888-1580
MIU INDUSTRIES LTD. is the parent company of MIU Automation
Inc., a Toronto-based company engaged in the development and market-
ing of software and hardware products in the computer industry.
Sylvia Gray, Secretary
TOTAL REVENUE ($000)   12

MOBIL MARINE TRANSPORTATION LIMITED
(Private)   TRANSPORTATION
3225 Gallows Road, Fairfax, VA, 22037   (703) 846-3000
MOBIL MARINE TRANSPORTATION LIMITED provides marine
transportation services for its parent and affiliates. It is a wholly owned
subsidiary of Mobil Corp. of the United States.
Allan E. Murray, President & C.E.O.
TOTAL REVENUE ($000)   632,265 (US)

MOBIL OIL CANADA, LTD.
(Private)   OIL AND GAS PRODUCERS
P.O. Box 800, Calgary, AB, T2P 2J7   (403) 260-7910
MOBIL OIL CANADA, LTD. is engaged in exploration for and pro-
duction of oil and gas. The company is wholly owned by Mobil Invest-
ments Canada Inc. (U.S.).
Ron Billings, President
TOTAL REVENUE ($000)   1,755,417

MOFFAT COMMUNICATIONS LIMITED
See page 326 for a full company profile.

MOHAWK OIL CANADA LIMITED
(Private)   OIL AND GAS PRODUCERS
The Mohawk Building, 6400 Roberts Street, Burnaby, BC,
V5G 4G2   (604) 293-4138
MOHAWK OIL CANADA LIMITED is involved in retail motor fuel
sales.
D. Skagan, Chairman
TOTAL REVENUE ($000)   369,307

MOLSON COMPANIES LIMITED (THE)
See page 165 for a full company profile.

MONARCH DEVELOPMENT CORPORATION
(Public)   DEVELOPERS
Heron's Hill, 2025 Sheppard Ave East, Suite 1201, Willowdale, ON,
M2J 1V7   (416) 491-7440
MONARCH DEVELOPMENT CORP. is engaged in land develop-
ment, residential construction and investment in rental properties. The
operations are currently being conducted in two main geographical areas,
Canada and the United States.
E.J. Latimer, President
TOTAL REVENUE ($000)   118,713

MONETA PORCUPINE MINES INC.
(Public)   METAL MINES
Box 1756, 273 - 2nd Avenue, Timmins, ON,
P4N 7W9   (705) 264-2296
MONETA PORCUPINE MINES INC. is in the process of exploring and
developing its mineral properties and has not yet determined whether
these properties contain ore reserves that are economically recoverable.
John Larche, Chairman
TOTAL REVENUE ($000)   0

MONSANTO CANADA INC.
(Private)   CHEMICALS
P.O Box 787, Streetsville P.O., 2330 Argentia Road, Mississauga,
ON, L5M 2G4   (416) 826-9222
MONSANTO CANADA INC. is a manufacturer of industrial and
agricultural chemicals, pharmaceuticals and process control equipment.
Monsanto is wholly owned by Monsanto Company of St. Louis, Mis-
souri.
W.A. Dimma, Chairman
TOTAL REVENUE ($000)   458,498

MONT SAINT-SAUVEUR INTERNATIONAL INC.
(Public)   ENTERTAINMENT SERVICES
350 St-Denis Street, St-Sauveur-Des-Monts, PQ,
J0R 1R3   (514) 227-4671
MONT SAINT-SAUVEUR INTERNAIONAL INC. operates four ski centres, three in Quebec and one in Vermont, a summer water recreation complex, and is involved in construction, sale and rental of housing units in the form of condominiums and single family units.
Jacques G. Hebert, Chairman, President & C.E.O.
TOTAL REVENUE ($000)   24,715

MONTREAL PORT CORPORATION
(Crown)   TRANSPORTATION
Port of Montreal Building, Wing No. 1, Cite du Havre, Montreal, PQ,
H3C 3R5   (514) 283-7050
MONTREAL PORT CORPORATION is involved in the administration of the Port of Montreal.
Andre Gingras, Chairman Of The Board
TOTAL REVENUE ($000)   57,422

MONTREAL TRUSTCO INC.
See page 386 for a full company profile.

MOORE CORPORATION LIMITED
See page 500 for a full company profile.

MORDEN & HELWIG GROUP INC.
(Public)   OTHER SERVICES
155 University Avenue, Suite 600, Toronto, ON,
M5H 3N5   (416) 362-6762
MORDEN & HELWIG GROUP INC. is an independent insurance holding company, which through its subsidiaries provides claim adjusting, appraisal and loss management services to insurance companies and self-insured organizations across Canada, the United States and the United Kingdom.
V. Prem Watsa, Chairman Of The Board
TOTAL REVENUE ($000)   139,315

MORGAN BANK OF CANADA
(Private)   BANKS
P.O. Box 80, Suite 2200, Royal Bank Plaza, South Tower, Toronto,
OM, M5J 2J2   (416) 981-9200
MORGAN BANK OF CANADA is an indirect wholly owned subsidiary of Morgan Guaranty Trust Company of New York, providing corporate finance advice and executing financing transactions as well as underwriting, trading and investing in securities.
Arthur M. Rogers Jr., Chairman
TOTAL REVENUE ($000)   137,562

MORGAN FINANCIAL CORPORATION
(Public)   FINANCE AND LEASING
Suite 910, 340 - 12th Avenue S.W., Calgary, AB,
T2R 1L5   (403) 531-1760
MORGAN FINANCIAL is a life insurance holding company. It owns 99.8% of Westbury Canadian Life Insurance Company of Hamilton, Ontario.
J. Rob Collins, Chairman & C.E.O.
TOTAL REVENUE ($000)   86,696

MORGAN HYDROCARBONS INC.
See page 97 for a full company profile.

MORRISON PETROLEUMS LTD.
See page 98 for a full company profile.

MOTOR COACH INDUSTRIES LIMITED
(Public)   TRANSPORTATION EQUIP & COMPNTS
1149 St. Matthews Avenue, Winnipeg, MB,
R3G 0J8   (204) 786-3301
MOTOR COACH INDUSTRIES LIMITED manufactures inter-city coaches with MCI (USA), a wholly owned subsidiary of The Dial Corp. The company also sells replacement parts for the Canadian after-market and sells finished coaches to the Canadian inter-city coach market which it purchases from MCI (USA).
John R. Nasi, President & C.E.O.
TOTAL REVENUE ($000)   123,967

MOTOROLA CANADA LIMITED
(Private)   ELECTRICAL & ELECTRONIC
4000 Victoria Park Avenue, North York, ON,
M2H 3P4   (416) 499-1441
MOTOROLA CANADA LIMITED is engaged in manufacturing and distributing electronic equipment, systems and components.
Eric Taylor, Chairman
TOTAL REVENUE ($000)   476,085

MPG INVESTMENT CORPORATION LIMITED
(Public)   INVESTMENT COMPANIES AND FUNDS
215 Sydney Street, Cornwall, ON, K6H 3H3   (613) 932-0183
MPG INVESTMENT CORPORATION LIMITED, as a closed-end investment corporation, invests mainly in common shares of Canadian companies listed on recognized stock exchanges. It also has minor investments inforeign companies, bonds and certificates of deposit and cash.
J.K. McBride, President & C.F.O.
TOTAL REVENUE ($000)   1,987

MR. JAX FASHIONS INC.
(Public)   CLOTHING AND TEXTILES
611 Alexander Street, Vancouver, BC, V6A 1E1   (604) 251-8600
MR. JAX FASHIONS INC. designs, manufactures and markets an extensive range of women's traditional and contemporary fashion apparel including pants, skirts, jackets, coats, and blouses under the names Jax, Jaxsport and Studio J.
Joseph Segal, Chairman Of The Board
TOTAL REVENUE ($000)   52,378

MRRM INC.
(Public)   FOOD PROCESSING
1600 Trans Canada Hwy, Suite 100, Dorval, PQ,
H9P 1H7   (514) 683-5583
MRRM is involved in the food processing industry and the ship agency business. The company's main operating subsidiaries are Les Aliments Dainty Foods, which operates as an importer and processor of rice products in Canada; and Robert Reford, which represents ship owners and operators from various offices in Montreal and Toronto. The company also owns two food brokers, one in Ontario and one in Quebec.

L.A.M. Reford, President
TOTAL REVENUE ($000)   36,296

MSV RESOURCES INC.
(Public)   METAL MINES
630 Rene-Levesque Blvd. W., Suite 3240, Montreal, PQ,
H3B 1S6   (514) 875-9033
MSV RESOURCES INC. is involved in the acquisition, exploration and development of mineral properties. Its predecessor is Massval Resources Inc. MSV produces gold and copper.
Mario Caron, President
TOTAL REVENUE ($000)   559

MTC ELECTRONIC TECHNOLOGIES CO. LTD.
(Public)   WHOLESALE DISTRIBUTORS
2580 Viscount Way, Vancouver, BC, V6V 2G8   (604) 278-8788
MTC ELECTRONOC TECHNOLOGIES CO. LTD. is an importer and exporter of electronics to the Peoples' Republic of China.
Miko Leung, Chairman & President
TOTAL REVENUE ($000)   49,547

MTC MORTGAGE INVESTMENT CORPORATION
(Public)   INVESTMENT COMPANIES AND FUNDS
Suite 400, 70 University Avenue, Toronto, ON,
M5J 2M4   (416) 598-2665
MTC MORTGAGE INVESTMENT CORPORATION's objective is to generate a secure stream of income by investing in a portfolio of residential, industrial and commercial mortgages and other qualified investments.
Ian Sutherland, Chairman, C.E.O. & President
TOTAL REVENUE ($000)   2,984

MULTI-CORP INC.
(Public)   MANAGEMENT AND DIVERSIFIED
1424 Canada Trust Tower, 10104 - 103 Avenue, Edmonton, AB,
T5J 0H8   (403) 429-1726
MULTI-CORP INC. is an industrial holding company. United Industrial Equipment Rentals Ltd. is its sole subsidiary.
David F. Edgar, President
TOTAL REVENUE ($000)   4,844

MULTI-MARQUES INC.
(Private)   FOOD PROCESSING
1600 Henri-Bourassa Ouest, Suite 510, Montreal, PQ,
H3M 3E2   (514) 333-7246
MULTI-MARQUES INC. is a manufacturer and distributor of fresh bakery products in Quebec under the trade marks: Gailuron, Durivage, Diana, Bon Matin, and Petite Douceur. It markets under the Aunt May's brand in Ontario, and the Mother's Own brand in New Brunswick.
Hubert Barbeau, Chairman & C.E.O.
TOTAL REVENUE ($000)   267,000

MULTIBANC FINANCIAL CORP.
(Public)   INVESTMENT COMPANIES AND FUNDS
3rd Floor, 161 Bay Street, Toronto, ON, M5J 2T2   (416) 361-8670
MULTIBANC FINANCIAL CORP. was established as a closed end investment fund to acquire a portfolio consisting of common shares of five major Canadian chartered banks. Dividends received are paid to

preferred shareholders of an affiliated company, Multibanc Fiancial Corp. On disposition of the portfolio, capital gains, after redemption of the preferreds, accrue to the holders of Multibanc NT's capital shares.
John B. Newman, Chairman & C.E.O.
TOTAL REVENUE ($000)   5,838

MULTIBANC NT FINANCIAL CORP.
(Public)   INVESTMENT COMPANIES AND FUNDS
3rd Floor, 161 Bay Street, Toronto, ON,
M5J 2T2   (416) 361-8670
MULTIBANC NT FINANCIAL CORP. invested the proceeds of the public issue of its capital shares and the private sale of Class A shares to Multibank Financial Corp. in a portfolio consisting of common shares of Bank of Montreal, Canadian Imperial Bank of Commerce, Bank of Nova Scotia, Royal Bank of Canada and Toronto-Dominion Bank.
John B. Newman, Chairman & C.E.O.
TOTAL REVENUE ($000)   6,068

MUNICIPAL FINANCIAL CORPORATION
See page 411 for a full company profile.

MUNICIPAL SAVINGS AND LOAN CORPORATION
(Public)   TRUST, SAVINGS AND LOAN
The Municipal Tower, P.O. Box 147, 70 Collier Street, Barrie, ON,
L4M 4S9   (705) 734-7500
MUNICIPAL SAVINGS AND LOAN CORPORATION is a financial intermediary involved in investing funds from depositors and shareholders in income-producing assets such as securities, mortgages and other loans.
Maxwell L. Rotstein, Chairman & C.E.O.
TOTAL REVENUE ($000)   128,870

MUSCOCHO EXPLORATIONS LTD.
See page 50 for a full company profile.

MUTUAL LIFE ASSURANCE COMPANY OF CANADA (THE)
(Private)   INSURANCE - LIFE
227 King Street South, Waterloo, ON, N2J 4C5   (519) 888-2290
THE MUTUAL LIFE ASSURANCE COMPANY OF CANADA is a mutual life insurance company which provides life insurance and health insurance products, annuities and a financial planning service for policy holders.
Jack V. Masterman, Chairman
TOTAL REVENUE ($000)   3,600,000

MVP CAPITAL CORP.
(Public)   PRECIOUS METALS
Suite 200, 20 Adelaide Street East, Box 28, Toronto, ON,
M5C 2T6   (416) 867-1100
MVP CAPITAL CORP. operates as a mining finance house by providing capital to public mining exploration and development companies and emerging producers. The company is evolving from a fund of portfolio holdings into a mining house with the majority of its assets committed to direct gold production. The company owns a 91% interest in CamindexMines Limited of Toronto.
Ian M.T. McAvity, President & C.E.O.
TOTAL REVENUE ($000)   7,984

MYTEC TECHNOLOGIES INC.
(Public)   OTHER SERVICES
Suite 430, 10 Gateway Blvd., Don Mills, ON,
M3C 3A1   (416) 467-9738
MYTEC TECHNOLOGIES INC., through its wholly owned subsidiary
Counterforce Inc., provides an electronic monitoring service for burglar
and fire alarms in homes and businesses. As well, the company holds
U.S. and Canadian patents for an invention which incorporates finger-
print identification and holpgraphic optical processing to verify if the user
of a card is actually the owner of the card.
G.J. Tomko, Chairman, President & C.E.O.
TOTAL REVENUE ($000)   3,419

NABISCO BRANDS LTD
(Private)   FOOD PROCESSING
Suite 2700, South Tower, Royal Bank Plaza, Toronto, ON,
M5J 2J4   (416) 867-3800
NABISCO BRANDS is one of Canada's foremost consumer food
manufacturers with two main lines of business being biscuits and grocery
products. Biscuits include such well-known brands as Oreos, Peek
Freens, Dad's cookies and triscuits, Ritz and Premium Plus crackers;
grocery products include Nabisco Shredded Wheat cereals and Milk
Bone pet snacks as well as Aylmer and Del Monte canned vegetables
and fruits.
Raymond J. Verdon, President & C.E.O.
TOTAL REVENUE ($000)   773,399

NATIONAL BANK OF CANADA
See page 387 for a full company profile.

NATIONAL BANK OF GREECE (CANADA)
(Private)   BANKS
1170 Place Du Frere Andre, Montreal, PQ,
H3B 3C6   (514) 954-1522
NATIONAL BANK OF GREECE (CANADA) is a wholly owned
subsidiary of the National Bank of Greece S.A. Athens, Greece, and is
licenced to operate with the full banking powers of a foreign bank
subsidiary.
Demetrios Germidis, Chairman & President
TOTAL REVENUE ($000)   27,092

NATIONAL LIFE ASSURANCE COMPANY OF CANADA (THE)
(Private)   INSURANCE - LIFE
522 University Avenue, Toronto, ON, M5G 1Y7   (416) 598-2122
NATIONAL LIFE ASSURANCE COMPANY OF CANADA, is a
99.8% owned subsidiary of Industrial-Alliance Life Management Corporation of Quebec City. National is engaged in life and health insurance
plus the administration of various segregated funds.
Raymond Garneau, Chairman & C.E.O.
TOTAL REVENUE ($000)   500,005

NATIONAL SEA PRODUCTS LIMITED
See page 166 for a full company profile.

NATIONAL TRUSTCO INC.
See page 388 for a full company profile.

NATIONAL WESTMINSTER BANK OF CANADA
(Private)   BANKS
Suite 2060, South Tower, P.O. Box 10, Royal Bank Plaza, Toronto,
ON, M5J 2J1   (416) 865-0170
NATIONAL WESTMINSTER BANK OF CANADA is a wholly
owned subsidiary of National Westminster Bank plc. It operates as a
Chartered Schedule II bank serving major corporations, governments
fFederal, provincial and municipal) and banking correspondents.
Alastair W. Gillespie, Chairman
TOTAL REVENUE ($000)   73,734

NBD BANK, CANADA
(Private)   BANKS
Suite 1601, North Tower, P.O. Box 112, Royal Bank Plaza, Toronto,
ON, M5J 2J3   (416) 865-0466
NBD BANK, CANADA is a schedule II bank offering services in foreign
exchange, cash management, corporate lending and support of retail
banking operations for small Canadian companies.
William R. Flynn, Chairman Of The Board
TOTAL REVENUE ($000)   31,509

NCR CANADA LTD - NCR CANADA LTEE
(Private)   ELECTRICAL & ELECTRONIC
320 Front Street West, Toronto, ON, M5V 3C4   (416) 599-4627
NCR CANADA LTD., the Networked Computing Resource of AT&T,
develops, manufactures, markets, supports and services enterprise-wide
information systems for worldwide markets. The company is wholly-
owned by NCR Corporation of Dayton, Ohio.
Marcel R. Carrier, President
TOTAL REVENUE ($000)   343,832

NEEDLER GROUP LIMITED
(Public)   CEMENT AND CONCRETE
380 Hardy Road, P.O. Box 1390, Brantford, ON,
N3T 5T6   (519) 753-3408
NEEDLER GROUP LIMITED is involved in the production of aggre-
gates, asphalt, concrete block and paving stone and provide construction
services, operating principally in the Province of Ontario and the State
of New York.
G.H. Christopher Needler, Chairman & C.E.O.
TOTAL REVENUE ($000)   43,933

NESBITT THOMSON CORP. LIMITED (THE)
(Private)   INVESTMENT HOUSES
Sun Life Tower, 150 King St. W., 20th Floor, Toronto, ON,
M5H 3W2   (416) 586-3600
THE NESBITT THOMSON CORP. LIMITED is an investment hold-
ing company which, through its subsidiaries is a fully integrated invest-
ment dealer. Nesbitt Thomson is 75% owned by the Bank of Montreal.
Brian J. Steck, Chairman & C.E.O.
TOTAL REVENUE ($000)   289,285

NESMONT INDUSTRIAL CORPORATION
(Public)   MISC. INDUSTRIAL PRODUCTS
7333 River Road, Tilbury Industrial Park, Ladner, BC,
V4G 1B1   (604) 946-2266
NESMONT INDUSTRIAL CORPORATION through its wholly
owned subsidiary, Nesmont Precious Metals Corporation is a precious

metals refiner of gold, silver, platinum and palladium. Nesmont is capable of bulk processing, concentrating by gravity or floatation, complete assay services using government certified assayers, smelting, refining and fabricating of precious metals.
William K. Nestor, Chairman, President & C.E.O.
TOTAL REVENUE ($000)   28,776

NESTLE CANADA INC.
(Private)   FOOD PROCESSING
1185 Eglinton Avenue East, Don Mills, ON,
M3C 3C7   (416) 467-2020
NESTLE CANADA INC., is engaged in the manufacturing and distribution of food products. Nestle is a wholly owned subsidiary of Nestle S.A. of Vevey, Switzerland.
F. Cella, Chairman, C.E.O. & Market Head
TOTAL REVENUE ($000)   923,000

NEW BRUNSWICK POWER COMMISSION
(Crown)   ELECTRICAL UTILITIES
P.O. Box 2000, Fredericton, NB, E3B 4X1   (506) 458-4444
THE NEW BRUNSWICK ELECTRIC POWER COMMISSION is a provincial crown corporation which provides electric power directly to customers and indirectly through sales to municipal utilities. NB Power is electrically interconnected with neighbouring utilities in Quebec, Nova Scotia, Prince Edward Island and New England.
Raymond J. Frenette, Chairman
TOTAL REVENUE ($000)   991,077

NEW BRUNSWICK RESEARCH AND PRODUCTIVITY COUNCIL (RPC)
(Crown)   CONSULTING
921 College Hill Road, Fredericton, NB, E3B 6Z9   (506) 452-8994
RPC is an independent contract research and development organization that assists clients on a fee-for-service basis. Typical projects involve the design or formulation of innovative products, productivity improvements in resource and manufacturing operations, and prototype development. RPC also offers a wide range of analytical and testing capabilities.
Dr. Knut Grotterod, Chairman
TOTAL REVENUE ($000)   9,604

NEW BRUNSWICK TELEPHONE COMPANY, LIMITED (THE)
(Private)   TELEPHONE UTILITIES
P.O. Box 1430, One Brunswick Square, Saint John, NB,
E2L 4K2   (506) 694-2340
NEW BRUNSWICK TELEPHONE CO. LTD. provides a broad range of modern telecommunications services to its residential and business customers in New Brunswick. Bruncor Inc. of Saint John owns all of the company's common shares.
Terence C. Bird, Chairman
TOTAL REVENUE ($000)   357,175

NEW CACHE PETROLEUMS LTD.
(Public)   OIL AND GAS PRODUCERS
Suite 200, 1301 - 8th Street S.W., Calgary, AB,
T2R 1B7   (403) 245-4333
NEW CACHE PETROLEUMS LTD. is a Canadian owned exploration and development company.

Keith E. Macdonald, President
TOTAL REVENUE ($000)   2,616

NEW DOLLY VARDEN MINERALS INC.
(Public)   OIL AND GAS PRODUCERS
45 Charles Street East, 6th Floor, Toronto, ON,
M4Y 1S2   (416) 968-7384
NEW DOLLY VARDEN MINERALS is engaged in the exploration and development of mineral and natural gas properties.
W.F. Christensen, President
TOTAL REVENUE ($000)   72

NEWALTA CORPORATION
(Public)   OIL AND GAS PRODUCERS
Suite 400, 333 - 11th Street S.W., Calgary, AB,
T2R 1L9   (403) 266-6556
NEWALTA CORPORATION provides a wide range of resource management and environmental services to the oil and gas industry through a network of eight facilities located in Alberta. Newalta provides clean oil terminalling and emulsion treatment. It handles drilling muds, tank bottoms, workover fluids, produced sands and spills, and provides site remediation services.
Felix Pardo, Chairman of the Board
TOTAL REVENUE ($000)   7,837

NEWBRIDGE NETWORKS CORPORATION
See page 228 for a full company profile.

NEWFOUNDLAND AND LABRADOR HYDRO
(Crown)   ELECTRICAL UTILITIES
P.O. Box 12400, St. John's, NF, A1B 4K7   (709) 737-1400
NEWFOUNDLAND AND LABRADOR HYDRO is incorporated under a special act of the province of Newfoundland as a crown corporation. Its principal activity is the development, generation and sale of electric power.
James R. Chalker, Chairman
TOTAL REVENUE ($000)   407,023

NEWFOUNDLAND CAPITAL CORPORATION LIMITED
See page 274 for a full company profile.

NEWFOUNDLAND LIGHT & POWER CO. LIMITED
See page 302 for a full company profile.

NEWFOUNDLAND TELEPHONE COMPANY LIMITED
(Private)   TELEPHONE UTILITIES
Fort William Building, P.O. Box 2110, St John's, NF,
A1C 5H6   (709) 739-2100
NEWFOUNDLAND TELEPHONE CO. LTD. provides telecommunications and information handling services throughout Newfoundland and Labrador. The company is a wholly owned subsidiary of NewTel Enterprises Ltd. of St. John's.
Vincent G. Withers, Chairman, President & C.E.O.
TOTAL REVENUE ($000)   269,676

NEWHAWK GOLD MINES LTD.
(Public)   PRECIOUS METALS
Suite 860, 625 Howe Street, Vancouver, BC,
V6C 2T6   (604) 687-7545
NEWHAWK GOLD MINES LTD. is involved in the acquisition, exploration and development of precious metals mineral properties. It holds a 60% working interest in the Bruceside Sulphurets property and a 100% interest in the Snowfields Sulphurets property, in northwestern British Columbia.
Donald A. McLeod, President & C.E.O.
TOTAL REVENUE ($000)   0

NEWTEL ENTERPRISES LIMITED
See page 303 for a full company profile.

NIAGARA CREDIT UNION LIMITED
(Fin. Co-op)   CREDIT UNIONS
344 Lake Street, P.O. Box 2157 B, St. Catharines, ON,
L2N 4H4   (416) 935-1000
NIAGARA CREDIT UNION LIMITED is a member owned and locally controlled financial institution. It operates in the Niagara region of Ontario.
William Goertz, Cheif Executive Officer
TOTAL REVENUE ($000)   60,582

NII NORSAT INTERNATIONAL INC.
(Public)   ELECTRICAL & ELECTRONIC
Suite 302, 12886 - 78th Avenue, Surrey, BC,
V3W 8E7   (604) 597-6200
NII NORSAT INTERNATIONAL INC. designs, manufactures, distributes and markets electronic products used to receive broadcast communications from satellite terrestrial broadcasting systems.
John Anderson, President & C.E.O.
TOTAL REVENUE ($000)   17,562

NISSAN CANADA INC.
(Private)   WHOLESALE DISTRIBUTORS
5290 Orbitor Dr., Mississauga, ON, L4W 4Z5   (416) 629-2888
NISSAN CANADA INC. is a wholesale distributor of vehicles, forklifts, outboard motors and associated parts. The company is a wholly owned subsidiary of Nissan Motor Co. of Tokyo.
Eisuke (Ace) Toyama, President
TOTAL REVENUE ($000)   808,955

NISSHO IWAI CANADA LTD
(Private)   MANAGEMENT AND DIVERSIFIED
P.O. Box 49293, 1055 Dunsmuir St, Suite 2624, Vancouver, BC,
V7X 1L3   (604) 684-8351
NISSHO IWAI CANADA LTD. is involved in the purchase and sale of merchandise. A substantial portion of transactions entered into by Nissho is for merchandise bought and sold to its parent and affiliated companies. The company acts as an agent in some transactions and as principal in others. It is a wholly owned subsidiary of Nissho Iwai Corporation, a Japanese corporation.
Mr. Masao Yamashita, President & C.E.O.
TOTAL REVENUE ($000)   580,664

NOBLE PEAK RESOURCES LTD
(Public)   PRECIOUS METALS
50 Burnhamthorpe Rd. W., Suite 906, Mississauga, ON,
L5B 3C2   (416) 897-9406
NOBLE PEAK RESOURCES LTD. is engaged in investigation, acquisition, exploration and development of gold and base metal mining operations.
Maureen C. Jensen, President
TOTAL REVENUE ($000)   3

NOMA INDUSTRIES LIMITED
See page 229 for a full company profile.

NORAMCO MINING CORPORATION
(Public)   MANAGEMENT AND DIVERSIFIED
Suite 900, 999 West Hastings Street, Vancouver, BC,
V6C 2W2   (604) 689-1428
NORAMCO MINING CORPORATION is a mining finance house whose principal business has consisted of financing natural resource companies and their respective properties through direct investments to such companies.
R.A. Bruce McDonald, Chairman
TOTAL REVENUE ($000)   952

NORANDA FOREST INC.
See page 144 for a full company profile.

NORANDA INC.
See page 452 for a full company profile.

NORANDA MINERALS INC.
(Private)   INTEGRATED MINES
1 Adelaide Street East, Suite 2700, Toronto, ON,
M5C 2Z6   (416) 982-7111
NORANDA MINERALS INC. is an integrated mining, smelting and refining group. The group operates 23 mines and 10 metallurgical plants in Canada, the United States, Mexico, Norway, the Dominican Republic and Zimbabwe. The company is a wholly owned subsidiary of Noranda Inc.
Alex G. Balogh, President & C.E.O.
TOTAL REVENUE ($000)   2,248,000

NORBORD INDUSTRIES INC.
(Private)   WHOLESALE DISTRIBUTORS
1 Toronto Street, Suite 500, Toronto, ON,
M5C 2W4   (416) 365-0710
NORBORD INDUSTRIES INC. manufactures, markets and distributes wood and wood/fibre composite products for construction and industrial purposes. The company operates mills in Canada, the U.S., the U.K., the Benelux countries, Germany, France and Japan.
Arkadi G. Bykhovsky, President
TOTAL REVENUE ($000)   315,811

NORCEN ENERGY RESOURCES LIMITED
See page 99 for a full company profile.

NORONT RESOURCES LTD.
(Public)   PRECIOUS METALS
111 Richmond St. W., Suite 1210, Toronto, ON,
M5H 2G4   (416) 864-1456
NORONT RESOURCES LTD. is engaged in the acquisition, explora-
tion and development of natural resource properties.
Richard E. Nemis, Chairman, President & C.E.O.
TOTAL REVENUE ($000)   54

NORTH AMERICAN LIFE ASSURANCE COMPANY
(Private)   INSURANCE - LIFE
5650 Yonge Street, North York, ON, M2M 4G4   (416) 229-4515
NORTH AMERICAN LIFE ASSURANCE COMPANY is a mutual
life insurance company with $145 billion of assets under management
and life insurance in force of $74 billion. The company operates through-
out Canada and the U.S., offering a range of financial products and
services, including trust, real estate asset management, investment counselling, annuities and mutual funds.
G.P. Osler, Chairman
TOTAL REVENUE ($000)   1,506,875

NORTH AMERICAN TRUST CO.
(Private)   TRUST, SAVINGS AND LOAN
151 Yonge Street, Toronto, ON, M5C 2W7   (416) 362-7211
North American Trust is a financial services company that provides a
wide range of loan, deposit, investment and trust services through a
network of 30 branches from Montreal to Victoria. It also provides a wide
variety of mortgage, loan, advisory and deposit services to commercial
companies and real estate investors across the country.
Thomas H. Savage, Chariman
TOTAL REVENUE ($000)   274,268

NORTH CANADIAN OILS LIMITED
See page 100 for a full company profile.

NORTH WEST COMPANY INC. (THE)
See page 364 for a full company profile.

NORTH WEST TRUST COMPANY
(Public)   TRUST, SAVINGS AND LOAN
Suite 1800, T-D Tower, Edmonton Centre, 10205 - 101 Street,
Edmonton, AB, T5J 4G1   (403) 429-9300
NORTH WEST TRUST COMPANY is registered as a trust company
under the provisions of the Loan and Trust Corporations Act of Alberta.
It is also licensed to carry on the business of a trust company in the
provinces of British Columbia, Saskatchewan, Manitoba, the Yukon, and
the Northwest Territories.
Gary G. Campbell, Chairman & C.E.O.
TOTAL REVENUE ($000)   90,239

NORTHERN TELECOM LIMITED
See page 327 for a full company profile.

NORTHGATE EXPLORATION LIMITED
See page 51 for a full company profile.

NORTHROCK RESOURCES LTD.
(Public)   OIL AND GAS PRODUCERS
Suite 3500, 700 Second Street S.W., Calgary, AB,
T2P 2W2   (403) 269-3100
NORTHROCK RESOURCES LTD. is involved in the acquisition,
exploration and development of petroleum and natural gas.
V.W. Sutherland, Chairman & C.E.O.
TOTAL REVENUE ($000)   5,153

NORTHSTAR ENERGY CORPORATION
See page 101 for a full company profile.

NORTHWEST DRUG COMPANY LIMITED
(Public)   WHOLESALE DISTRIBUTORS
10931 - 177 Street, P.O. Box 2318, Edmonton, AB,
T5J 2P9   (403) 484-0404
NORTHWEST DRUG COMPANY LIMITED is a full-line, front-store
and pharmaceutical wholesaler in Western Canada, with warehouses in
Edmonton, Vancouver and Winnipeg.
Gowan T. Guest, Q.C., Chairman Of The Board
TOTAL REVENUE ($000)   120,007

NORTHWEST SPORTS ENTERPRISES LTD.
(Public)   ENTERTAINMENT SERVICES
Suite 410, 355 Burrard Street, Vancouver, BC,
V6C 2G8   (604) 681-2226
NORTHWEST SPORTS ENTREPRISES LTD., through its subsidiar-
ies, owns the Vancouver Canucks hockey team. Other operations include
a restaurant at the Coliseum and 14 gallery suites.
Frank Armathwaite Griffiths, Chairman
TOTAL REVENUE ($000)   37,628

NORTHWEST TERRITORIES POWER COMMISSION
(Crown)   ELECTRICAL UTILITIES
Bag 6000, #3 Capital Road, Hay River, NT,
X0E 0R0   (403) 874-5200
NORTHWEST TERRITORIES POWER CORPORATION is a crown
corporation, which operates under the authority of the Northwest Terri-
tories Power Corporation Act. It provides for the construction and
operation of public utility plants in the Northwest Territories.
J.H. Robertson, Chairman & C.E.O.
TOTAL REVENUE ($000)   95,800

NORTHWESTERN UTILITIES LIMITED
See page 304 for a full company profile.

NORTHWOOD PULP AND TIMBER LIMITED
(Private)   WEST COAST FORESTRY
5162 Northwood Pulp Mill Road, Box 9000, Prince George, BC,
V2L 4W2
NORTHWOOD PULB AND TIMBER LIMITED is an integrated forest
products company with operations in central British Columbia. It pro-
duces lumber, plywood and pulp for international markets. The company
is owned 50% by Noranda Forest and 50% by Mead Corporation.
E.M. Karter, Chairman & Sr. V.P.
TOTAL REVENUE ($000)   530,147

NOVA CORPORATION OF ALBERTA
See page 282 for a full company profile.

NOVA SCOTIA POWER INC.
See page 305 for a full company profile.

NOVA SCOTIA RESEARCH FOUNDATION CORPORATION
(Crown)   CONSULTING
101 Research Drive, Woodside Industrial Park, P.O. Box 790,
Dartmouth, NS, B2Y 3Z7   (902) 424-8670
NOVA SCOTIA RESEARCH FOUNDATION CORPORATION was established in 1975 by the Act to Establish the Nova Scotia Research Foundation Corporation. Its purpose is to assist in the economic development of Nova Scotia bypromoting, simulating and encouraging the effective utilization of science and technology by industry and government.
T.B. Nickerson, Chairman President & C.E.O.
TOTAL REVENUE ($000)   6,874

NOVA-COGESCO RESOURCES INC.
(Public)   PRECIOUS METALS
630 Rene-Levesque Blvd. W., Suite 3240, Montreal, PQ,
H3B 1S6   (604) 687-6600
NOVA-COGESCO's principal business consists of acquiring undivided interests in certain mining properties and participating in the exploration and development of such properties.
Mario Caron, President
TOTAL REVENUE ($000)   415

NOVACOR CHEMICALS (CANADA) LTD.
(Private)   CHEMICALS
201 Front Street N, Sarnia, ON, N7T 7V1   (519) 332-1212
NOVACOR CHEMICALS is a Canadian international company engaged in the production of synthetic rubber, rubber latex and other petrochemical products which are sold in more than 90 countries. With plants throughout the world, Novacor is involved in manufacturing, sales, technical support and research and development. The company's output is used mostly by manufacturers who process the products further.
John Feick, President
TOTAL REVENUE ($000)   1,510,000

NOVAGOLD RESOURCES INC.
(Public)   PRECIOUS METALS
1583 Hollis St, Second Floor, Bank Of Canada Building, Halifax, NS,
B3J 1V4   (902) 420-0230
NOVAGOLD RESOURCES INC. is in the business of acquiring, exploring and developing gold properties in the provinces of Nova Scotia and New Brunswick and in the states of New Mexico and Nevada.
Gerald J. McConnell, President
TOTAL REVENUE ($000)   2,708

NOWSCO WELL SERVICE LTD.
See page 102 for a full company profile.

NU-GRO CORPORATION
(Public)   MISC. CONSUMER PRODUCTS
P.O. Box 1148, Woodstock, ON, N4S 8P6   (519) 456-2021
NU-GRO CORPORATION is engaged in blending, packaging, and distributing in Canada and the United States bulk packaged goods such as cat litter, lawn and garden fertilizers, potting soils, and pesticides. Nu-Gro's products are sold under the Hillview, Cirle H Farms, and C-I-L brands, as well as many private labels.
Roger Pascoe, President , C.E.O. & Secretary
TOTAL REVENUE ($000)   31,892

NUGAS LIMITED
(Public)   OIL AND GAS PRODUCERS
Suite 2100, 421 - 7th Ave. S.W., Calgary, AB,
T2P 4K9   (403) 262-7034
NUGAS LIMITED is involved in the exploration, development and production of natural gas in southeastern Alberta and western Saskatchewan.
Gus A. Van Wielingen, Chairman, C.E.O. & C.F.O.
TOTAL REVENUE ($000)   5,010

NUMAC OIL & GAS LTD.
See page 103 for a full company profile.

OCELOT ENERGY INC.
See page 104 for a full company profile.

OCS TECHNOLOGIES CORP.
(Public)   COMPUTER SOFTWARE & PROCESSING
Suite 106, 7011 Elmbridge Way, Richmond, BC,
V7C 4V5   (604) 273-8045
OCS TECHNOLOGIES CORP. is a leading developer and marketer of software products designed to meet the particular needs of a number of large growing markets. These include: law enforcement agencies; correctionalinstitutions; court and prosecutor management; computer aided dispatch for public safety agencies; and natural resource and environmental managers.
Raymond W.G. Foucault, Chairman, C.E.O. & President
TOTAL REVENUE ($000)   5,750

OERLIKON AEROSPACE INC.
(Private)   ELECTRICAL & ELECTRONIC
Byers Casgrain, 1 Place Ville Marie, Suite 3900, Montreal, PQ,
H3B 4M7 404
OERLIKON AEROSPACE INC. is a systems engineering company. Oerlikon is engaged in the design, integration, test and support of advanced defence, communications and electronics systems. Oerlikon also provides full life-cycle support and project management services.
Dr. Anton Menth, Chairman
TOTAL REVENUE ($000)   191,907

OGY PETROLEUMS LTD.
(Public)   OIL AND GAS PRODUCERS
Suite 2270, 140 - 4th Ave. S.W., Calgary, AB,
T2P 3N3   (403) 233-0066
OGY PETROLEUMS LTD. is involved in the acquisition, exploration and development of oil and gas properties and mineral exploration.

William Wolodarsky, President & C.E.O.
TOTAL REVENUE ($000)   1,138

OKANAGAN SKEENA GROUP LIMITED
(Public)   CABLE
4625 Lazelle Avenue, Terrace, BC, V8G 1S4   (604) 635-6316
OKANAGAN SKEENA GROUP LIMITED's business segments comprise: cablevision, the operation of a cable systems for the transmission of radio and television signals; broadcasting, the origination and rebroadcasting of television and radio programs and commercials; and real estate, the investment in and rental of commercial real estate properties.
John Weatherall, Chairman
TOTAL REVENUE ($000)   16,971

OLCO PETROLEUM GROUP INC.
(Public)   WHOLESALE DISTRIBUTORS
2561 Avenue Georges V, Montreal-East, PQ,
H1L 6J7   (514) 645-6526
OLCO is involved, directly and through its subsidiaries, in the downstream activity of the petroleum industry, namely the supply, trading, marketing, storage and distribution of petroleum products.
Wilfred Kaneb, Chairman & C.E.O.
TOTAL REVENUE ($000)   445,273

OLD CANADA INVESTMENT CORPORATION LIMITED
(Public)   INVESTMENT COMPANIES AND FUNDS
Suite 2700, 145 King Street West, Toronto, ON,
M5H 1J8   (416) 865-0470
OLD CANADA INVESTMENT CORPORATION LIMITED is an investment company largely investing in securities of companies listed on stock exchanges.
D.S. Beatty, Chairman Of The Board
TOTAL REVENUE ($000)   564

OLYMEL SOCIETE EN COMMANDITE
(Private)   FOOD PROCESSING
2200 Leon-Pratte, Suite 400, St-Hyacinthe, PQ,
J2S 4B6   (514) 771-0400
OLYMEL, SOCIETE EN COMMANDITE is engaged in slaughtering, cutting and further processing pork and beef.
Jean Bienvenue, Chairman, President & C.E.O.
TOTAL REVENUE ($000)   645,000

OMEGA HYDROCARBONS LTD.
See page 105 for a full company profile.

ONDAATJE CORPORATION (THE)
(Public)   INVESTMENT HOUSES
30A Hazelton Avenue, Toronto, ON, M5R 2E2   (416) 925-3555
ONDAATJE CORPORATION is a merchant banking company which, through its subsidiaries and associated companies, will establish an international operation that will pursue opportunities in North America, South East Asia, Western U.S.A., Central America and Europe.
Christopher Ondaatje, Chairman, President & C.E.O.
TOTAL REVENUE ($000)   65,189

ONEX CORPORATION
See page 453 for a full company profile.

ONTARIO DEVELOPMENT CORPORATIONS
(Crown)   TRUST, SAVINGS AND LOAN
56 Wellesley Street West, 6th Floor, Queen's Park, Toronto, ON,
M7A 2E7   (416) 326-1070
ONTARIO DEVELOPMENT CORPORATIONS is involved in the promotion of economic development and diversification of Ontario's manufacturing, tourism and high technology industries.
G.H. Cowperthwaite, Chairman
TOTAL REVENUE ($000)   30,049

ONTARIO HYDRO
(Crown)   ELECTRICAL UTILITIES
700 University Avenue, Toronto, ON, M5G 1X6   (416) 592-5111
ONTARIO HYDRO is a provincial crown corporation without share capital. Its mission is to help Ontario become a world leader in developing an engery efficient and competitive economy and a leading example of sustainable development. It supplies electric power, provides energy management services, and develops future energy technologies.
Maurice F. Strong, Chairman & C.E.O.
TOTAL REVENUE ($000)   7,900,000

ONTARIO NORTHLAND TRANSPORTATION COMMISSION
(Crown)   TRANSPORTATION
555 Oak Street E., North Bay, ON, P1B 8L3   (705) 472-4500
ONTARIO NORTHLAND TRANSPORTATION COMM. is a crown corporation of the province of Ontario. Its major activities include rail freight and passenger marine, bus, telecommunications, truck transport, air passenger and freight, and real estate development.
M.D. Sinclair, Chairman
TOTAL REVENUE ($000)   144,653

OPTIMA PETROLEUM CORPORATION
(Public)   OIL AND GAS PRODUCERS
P.O. Box 48328, The Bentall Centre, Vancouver, BC,
V7X 1A1   (604) 684-6886
OPTIMA PETROLEUM CORPORATION is involved in the acquisition, exploration and development of oil and gas properties.
William C. Leuschner, Chairman
TOTAL REVENUE ($000)   1,013

ORBIT OIL & GAS LTD.
(Public)   OIL AND GAS PRODUCERS
Suite 2100, 144 - 4th Avenue S.W., Calgary, AB,
T2P 3N4   (403) 264-8900
ORBIT OIL & GAS LTD. is involved in the exploration for, and development and production of petroleum and natural gas in Western Canada and the United States. Substantially all of the Company's activities are conducted jointly with others.
Robert W. Lamond, Chairman
TOTAL REVENUE ($000)   12,157

ORDINATEURS HYPOCRAT INC. (LES)
(Public)   COMPUTER SOFTWARE & PROCESSING
7900 Boulevard Taschereau, Edifice E, Brossard, PQ,
J4X 2T3   (514) 877-5555
ORDINATEURS HYPOCRAT INC. develops software packages for medical clinics and pharmacies.

Yves Marmet, President & C.E.O.
TOTAL REVENUE ($000)   17,120

ORENDA FOREST PRODUCTS LTD.
(Public)   WEST COAST FORESTRY
Suite 409, 545 Clyde Avenue, West Vancouver, BC,
V7T 1C5   (604) 926-4445
ORENDA FOREST PRODUCTS LIMITED is British Columbia logging and forest management company. Its primary products are pulp logs and saw logs.
Hugh W. Cooper, Chairman & President
TOTAL REVENUE ($000)   12,769

OSHAWA GROUP LIMITED (THE)
See page 365 for a full company profile.

OSPREY ENERGY LTD.
(Public)   OIL AND GAS PRODUCERS
Suite 410, 800 - 6th Avenue S.W., Calgary, AB,
T2P 3G3   (403) 264-2624
OSPREY ENERGY LTD. is involved in the acquisition, exploration and development of oil and gas properties.
Norman T. Jeal, President & C.E.O.
TOTAL REVENUE ($000)   2,665

OVERSEAS UNION BANK OF SINGAPORE (CANADA)
(Private)   BANKS
P.O. Box 9, Suite 1000, Standard Life Centre, 121 King Street West,
Toronto, ON, M5H 3T9   (416) 363-8227
OVERSEAS UNION BANK OF SINGAPORE (CANADA) is a schedule II bank, whose business activities include deposits, bills and remittances, trade finance, and loans.
Hee Seng Lee, Chairman
TOTAL REVENUE ($000)   3,130

OXFORD PROPERTIES CANADA LIMITED
(Public)   PROPERTY MGMNT & INVESTMENT
Suite 1700, 120 Adelaide Street West, Richmond-Adelaide Centre,
Toronto, ON, M5H 1T1   (416) 865-8300
OXFORD PROPERTIES CANADA LIMITED is the owner of interests in a portfolio of commercial real estate in Toronto, Edmonton and Calgary.
G. Donald Love, Chairman
TOTAL REVENUE ($000)   86,398

P. LAWSON TRAVEL
(Private)   OTHER SERVICES
3300 Bloor St W, Centre Tower, Suite 1200, Toronto, ON,
M8X 2Y2   (416) 236-1921
P. LAWSON TRAVEL is a travel agency serving both corporate and vacation clients.
John Powell, President
TOTAL REVENUE ($000)   494,538

PACCAR OF CANADA LTD.
(Private)   AUTOMOTIVE
6711 Mississauga Road North, Third Floor, Mississauga, ON,
L5N 4J8   (416) 858-7000

PACCAR OF CANADA LTD. is engaged in heavy duty truck manufacturing, distribution, parts sales and truck leasing. Paccar Canada is wholly owned by Paccar Inc. of the United States.
C.M. Pigott, Chairman & President
TOTAL REVENUE ($000)   365,454

PACIFIC & WESTERN TRUSTCO LTD.
(Public)   TRUST, SAVINGS AND LOAN
P.O.Box 7380, Saskatoon, SK, S7K 4E4   (306) 664-2202
PACIFIC & WESTERN TRUSTCO LTD.'s principal activity is its subsidiary trust company, P & W Trust.
Brian Larrivee, President
TOTAL REVENUE ($000)   3,723

PACIFIC AQUA FOODS LTD.
(Public)   FISHING
Suite 650, 220 Cambie Street, Vancouver, BC,
V6B 2M9   (604) 662-8999
PACIFIC AQUA FOODS is in the business of salmon hatcheries and pen-raised salmon and cultured oysters.
W.O. Morrow, Chairman
TOTAL REVENUE ($000)   8,020

PACIFIC CASSIAR LIMITED
(Public)   OIL AND GAS PRODUCERS
2420 Encor Place, 645-7th Avenue S.W., Calgary, AB,
T2P 4G8   (403) 265-6292
PACIFIC CASSIAR LIMITED is involved in the exploration for, and development of oil, gas and minerals.
Steve Vavra, President
TOTAL REVENUE ($000)   2,341

PACIFIC COAST SAVINGS CREDIT UNION
(Fin. Co-op)   CREDIT UNIONS
722 Cormorant Street, Victoria, BC, V8W 1P8   (604) 380-3100
PACIFIC COAST SAVINGS CREDIT UNION is a credit union in British Columbia.
Gordon Munn, Chairman Of The Board
TOTAL REVENUE ($000)   99,690

PACIFIC NORTHERN GAS LTD.
See page 306 for a full company profile.

PACIFIC SENTINEL GOLD CORP.
(Public)   METAL MINES
800 West Pender Street, Suite 1020, Vancouver, BC,
V8W 1P8   (604) 684-6365
PACIFIC SENTINEL GOLD CORP. is focused on the development of a giant open-pit copper-gold-molybdenum-silver project in Yukon Territory. Ongoing development is expected to lead to substantial metal production.
TOTAL REVENUE ($000)   157

PAGURIAN CORPORATION LIMITED (THE)
See page 412 for a full company profile.

PALLISER FURNITURE LTD.
(Private)   HOME FURNISHINGS
55 Vulcan Avenue, Winnipeg, MB, R2G 1B9   (204) 668-5600
PALLISER FURNITURE LTD. is engaged in furniture manufacturing.
Palliser Furniture is wholly owned by the DeFehr family of Manitoba.
Abram A. Defehr, Chairman
TOTAL REVENUE ($000)   192,900

PALOMA PETROLEUM LTD.
(Public)   OIL AND GAS PRODUCERS
1150 Guinness House, 727-7th Ave S.W., Calgary, AB,
T2P 0Z7   (403) 265-9265
PALOMA PETROLEUM LTD. is involved in the exploration for,
development and production of petroleum and natural gas in Canada.
Substantially all of the company's activities are conducted jointly with
others.
Walter J. Adams, Chairman Of The Board
TOTAL REVENUE ($000)   15,300

PAN PACIFIC PETROLEUM INC.
(Public)   OIL AND GAS PRODUCERS
One Maritime Plaza, Suite 1630, San Francisco, CA,
94111   (415) 986-7545
PAN PACIFIC PETROLEUM INC. is involved in the acquisition,
exploration and development of oil and gas properties.
Lawrence Barker, Jr., Chairman
TOTAL REVENUE ($000)   5,519 (US)

PANCANADIAN PETROLEUM LIMITED
See page 106 for a full company profile.

PANTORAMA INDUSTRIES INC.
(Public)   CLOTHING STORES
2 Lake Road, Dollard-des-Ormeaux, PQ, H9B 3H9   (514) 421-1850
PANTORAMA INDUSTRIES INC. is engaged in the retail sale of
casual clothing at medium prices for men and women.
Robert Wexler, Chairman Of The Board
TOTAL REVENUE ($000)   113,221

PAPERBOARD INDUSTRIES CORPORATION
(Private)   PACKAGING AND CONTAINERS
Suite 403, 2121 Argentia Road, Mississauga, ON,
L5N 2X4   (416) 821-1666
PAPERBOARD INDUSTRIES CORPORATION is an integrated re-
cycled paperboard manufacturer and paperboard packaging supplier.
John Evans, Chairman
TOTAL REVENUE ($000)   600,000

PARAGON PETROLEUM CORPORATION
(Public)   OIL AND GAS PRODUCERS
Suite 500, 407 - 8th Ave S.W., Calgary, AB,
T2P 1E5   (403) 266-5075
PARAGON PETROLEUM CORPORATION is a resource company
engaged in the exploration for and development and production of
petroleum and natural gas in Western Canada.
Michael S.P. Cooke, Chairman & C.E.O.
TOTAL REVENUE ($000)   10,292

PARAMOUNT RESOURCES LTD.
See page 107 for a full company profile.

PARIBAS BANK OF CANADA
(Private)   BANKS
Toronto-Dominion Centre, Royal Trust Tower, P.O. Box 31, Suite
4100, Toronto, ON, M5K 1N8   (416) 365-9600
PARIBAS BANK OF CANADA is a schedule II foreign bank subsidiary
of Banque Paribas providing a broad range of services in the commercial
banking, energy and commodity finance, as well as treasury areas.
Gilles Roman, Chairman
TOTAL REVENUE ($000)   39,777

PARKLAND INDUSTRIES LTD.
(Public)   INTEGRATED OILS
Suite 236, Riverside Office Plaza, 4919 - 59 Street, Red Deer, AB,
T4N 6C9   (403) 343-1515
PARKLAND is an integrated Western Canadian energy company with
activities in refining, retailing and transportation.
Jack C. Donald, Chairman President & C.E.O.
TOTAL REVENUE ($000)   106,064

PARRISH & HEIMBECKER LIMITED
(Private)   WHOLESALE DISTRIBUTORS
360 Main Street, Suite 700, Winnipeg, MB,
R3C 3Z3   (204) 956-2030
PARRISH & HEIMBECKER LIMITED is a wholesaler of grain and
poultry. It also operates flour mills, feed mills, poultry processing plants
and lake ships.
H. Heimbecker, Chairman
TOTAL REVENUE ($000)   688,037

PATHEON INC.
(Public)   INVESTMENT COMPANIES AND FUNDS
Canterra Tower, Suite 4615, 400 - 3rd Ave. S.W., Calgary, AB,
T2P 4H2   (403) 269-6795
PATHEON INC. is currently reviewing a variety of investment oppor-
tunities. In 1989 the company sold all of its construction industry assets.
Richard A.N. Bonnycastle, Chairman, President & C.E.O.
TOTAL REVENUE ($000)   787

PCL CONSTRUCTION GROUP INC.
(Private)   CONTRACTORS
5410 - 99 Street, Edmonton, AB,
T6E 3P4   (403) 435-9711
PCL CONSTRUCTION GROUP INC. is a general contractor. PCL
Construction Group is a wholly owned subsidiary of PCL Construction
Holdings Ltd. of Edmonton, Alberta.
R. Stollery, Chairman
TOTAL REVENUE ($000)   1,456,972

PE BEN OILFIELD SERVICES LTD.
See page 108 for a full company profile.

PEERLESS CARPET CORPORATION
(Public) HOME FURNISHINGS
1 Dawson St, Place Bonaventure, P.O. Box 944, Montreal, PQ,
H5A 1E8 (514) 878-6800
PEERLESS CARPET CORPORATION directly and with its subsidiaries, manufactures broadloom carpet and bathroom broadloom sets. Peerless also distributes other related products. The company is represented in the United States, United Kingdom and Australia through subsidiaries.
Bram Garber, Chairman & C.E.O.
TOTAL REVENUE ($000) 438,402

PEGA CAPITAL CORPORATION
(Public) WHOLESALE DISTRIBUTORS
4275 Village Centre Court, Mississauga, ON,
L4Z 1V3 (416) 897-0915
PEGA CAPITAL CORPORATION is an investment management company with operation in specialty manufacturing and consumer products distribution.
T. Edward R. Butcher, Chairman
TOTAL REVENUE ($000) 10,005

PEGASUS GOLD INC.
See page 52 for a full company profile.

PENGROWTH GAS INCOME FUND
(Public) INVESTMENT COMPANIES AND FUNDS
Suite 3080, 255 - 5th Avenue S.W., Calgary, AB,
T2P 3G6 (403) 233-0224
PENGROWTH GAS INCOME FUND is a closed-end trust established to earn oil and gas royalty income through the purchase of Pengrowth Gas Corporation royalty units. All amounts received by the Fund are distributed to unitholders on a monthly basis. The corporation is managed by Pengrowth Management Ltd.
James S. Kinnear, President & C.E.O.
TOTAL REVENUE ($000) 2,723

PENN WEST PETROLEUM LTD.
(Public) OIL AND GAS PRODUCERS
Suite 900, 665 - 8th Street S.W., Calgary, AB,
T2P 3K7 (403) 237-0120
PENN WEST PETROLEUM LTD. is a Canadian energy company engaged in the acquisition, exploration, development and production of oil and natural gas in Canada and the United States. Operations in the United States are carried out through a wholly owned subsidiary, Penn West Petroleum, Inc., and those in Australia through Penn West Petroleum, Ltd., and Springwest-Page Petroleum N.L.
Denis Russell, President & C.E.O.
TOTAL REVENUE ($000) 7,135

PENNINGTON'S STORES LIMITED
See page 366 for a full company profile.

PEOPLES JEWELLERS LIMITED
See page 367 for a full company profile.

PERKINS PAPERS LTD.
(Public) PAPER PRODUCTS
2345 Autoroute des Laurentides, Laval, PQ,
H7S 1Z7 (514) 688-1152
PERKINS PAPERS LTD. is engaged in the manufacture and sale of sanitary tissue products to the Canadian consumer and industrial markets. Paper towels, bathroom tissue, serviettes, placemats, tablecovers and food wrap are sold in the consumer market under the Budget, Decor, Plush and Rite brand names. A similiar range of products is offered to food chains and merchandisers under private label or generic packaging.
R. Bramwell, President & C.E.O.
TOTAL REVENUE ($000) 73,625

PETERSBURG LONG DISTANCE INC.
(Public) MANAGEMENT AND DIVERSIFIED
166 Pearl Street, Ground Floor, Toronto, ON,
M5H 1L3 (416) 593-4989
PETERSBURG LONG DISTANCE INC., through its investment in Peterstar Company Limited, is a provider of modern international and domestic telecommunications services to the city of St. Petersburg, Russia.
Rupert Galliers-Pratt, Chairman, President & C.E.O.
TOTAL REVENUE ($000) 58,143

PETRO-CANADA
See page 109 for a full company profile.

PETROMET RESOURCES LIMITED
(Public) OIL AND GAS PRODUCERS
Suite 350, 839 - 5th Avenue S.W., Calgary, AB,
T2P 3C8 (403) 269-2627
PETROMET RESOURCES LIMITED is a natural gas exploration, development and production company concentrating its activities in west central Alberta. Its strategy is to own and operate its production facilities,generate prospects internally and to maintain high working interests.
P. Gren Schoch, Chairman
TOTAL REVENUE ($000) 3,067

PETROMONT & CO. LTD. PARTNERSHIP
(Private) CHEMICALS
2931 Marie-Victorin Boulevard, Varennes, PQ,
J3X 1S7 (514) 642-2971
PETROMONT & CO. LTD. PARTNERSHIP operates three petrochemical plants. Petromont is 50% owned by Ethylec Inc. and 50% by Union Carbide Chemicals and Plastics Canada Inc.
Louis M. Riopel, Chairman of the Board
TOTAL REVENUE ($000) 237,677

PETROREP RESOURCES LTD.
(Public) OIL AND GAS PRODUCERS
Suite 1000, 630 - 6th Avenue S.W., Calgary, AB,
T2P 0S8 (403) 264-5565
PETROREP RESOURCES is involved in the exploration for, and the development and production of, crude oil, natural gas and related liquids in Canada. The company is administered and controlled by Petrorep (Canada) Ltd. at its Calgary office. Petrorep (Canada) has 66.8% interest in Petrorep Resources.

Peter S. Ffoulkes-Jones, President
TOTAL REVENUE ($000)   24,272

PETROSTAR PETROLEUMS INC.
(Public)   OIL AND GAS PRODUCERS
Suite 3750, 700 - 2nd Street S.W., Calgary, AB,
T2P 2W2   (403) 265-1142
PETROSTAR PETROLEUMS INC. is an Alberta based resource development company engaged in the exploration for, and development of crude oil and natural gas reserves.
Richard G. Anderson, President
TOTAL REVENUE ($000)   6,231

PHILIP ENVIRONMENTAL INC.
See page 501 for a full company profile.

PHILIPS CANADA LTD.
(Private)   ELECTRICAL & ELECTRONIC
601 Milner Avenue, Scarborough, ON, M1B 1M8   (416) 2925161
PHILIPS CANADA LTD. is a manufacturer & wholesaler of a wide range of consumer and professional electric and electronic products. Philips Canada is a wholly owned subsidiary of N.V. Philips Gloelampen-Fabrieken of Holland.
Eric Versteeg, President
TOTAL REVENUE ($000)   450,527

PHILLIPS CABLES LIMITED
(Public)   METAL FABRICATORS
Suite 300, 100 Consilium Place, Scarborough, ON,
M1H 3E3   (416) 296-0250
PHILLIPS CABLES LIMITED, with its eight factories across Canada, designs, engineers, manufactures and markets wire and cable for the transmission and distribution of electrical energy and telecommunications signals. It has customers in Canada, the United States and worldwide.
D.L. Torrey, Chairman
TOTAL REVENUE ($000)   240,467

PHOENIX CANADA OIL COMPANY LIMITED
(Public)   OIL AND GAS PRODUCERS
Suite 1240, 70 York Street, Toronto, ON, M5J 1S9   (416) 368-4440
PHOENIX CANADA OIL COMPANY LIMITED is engaged in investment in oil and gas properties. The company has oil and gas interests in western Canada, Ecuador and Sri Lanka, as well as investments in base metal and gold mining companies in Saskatchewan, Europe and Africa.
S. Donald Moore, President
TOTAL REVENUE ($000)   4,239

PHOTO ENGRAVERS & ELECTROTYPERS LIMITED
(Public)   PUBLISHING & PRINTING
2250 Islington Ave., Rexdale, ON, M9W 3W4   (416) 743-8920
PHOTO ENGRAVERS & ELECTROTYPERS LIMITED is engaged in the graphic arts business through operations as artists photographers, rotogravure engravers, rotogravure printers and bookbinders.
J.R. Shaw, President
TOTAL REVENUE ($000)   30,244

PINNACLE RESOURCES LTD.
See page 110 for a full company profile.

PIONEER METALS CORPORATION
See page 53 for a full company profile.

PIRELLI CANADA INC.
(Private)   METAL FABRICATORS
425 St-Louis Ru, 1801 McGill College, St-Jean-Sur-Richelie, PQ,
J3B 1Y6   (514) 359-6721
PIRELLI CANADA INC. is a holding company which, through its wholly owned subsidiary, Pirelli Cables Inc., is engaged in the manufacture and sale of electrical wire and cable, including fibre optic communication cables.
Mr. L. Raimondo, President & C.E.O.
TOTAL REVENUE ($000)   173,760

PITNEY BOWES OF CANADA LTD.
(Private)   OTHER SERVICES
150 Ferrand Drive, 12th Floor, Don Mills, ON,
M3C 3B5   (416) 424-2211
PITNEY BOWES is comprised of the Business Systems Group and a Leasing Division. The Business Systems Group is Canada's leading supplier of postage meters and mailing systems. It also supplies shipping and inserting systems, copiers, facsimile machines and related supplies. Pitney Bowes Leasing provides leasing programs for the full line of business systems products and its subsidiaries.
George B. Harvey, Chairman
TOTAL REVENUE ($000)   273,628

PLACE RESOURCES CORPORATION
(Public)   OIL AND GAS PRODUCERS
Suite 1350, 140 - 4th Avenue S.W., Calgary, AB,
T2P 3N3   (403) 262-7114
PLACE RESOURCES CORPORATION is engaged in the exploration, development and production of oil and gas. It has interests in Canada and the United States.
Keith W. Hern, President & C.E.O.
TOTAL REVENUE ($000)   3,437

PLACER DOME INC.
See page 54 for a full company profile.

PLASTI-FAB LTD.
(Public)   MISC. INDUSTRIAL PRODUCTS
Suite 270, 3015 - 5th Avenue N.E., Calgary, AB,
T2A 6T8   (403) 248-9306
PLASTI-FAB LTD. is a national plastics manufacturer whose principal products are insulation and protective packaging, each produced from expanded polystyrene. The company services markets throughout Canada with production facilities in British Columbia, Alberta, Saskatchewan, Manitoba and Ontario.
C. Alan Smith, Chairman
TOTAL REVENUE ($000)   20,740

PLASTIBEC LTEE
(Public)   MISC. INDUSTRIAL PRODUCTS
5 Rue Saint-Alphonse, Sainte-Therese, PQ,
J7E 1G3   (514) 430-9818
PLASTIBEC LTEE manufactures plastic profiles and components by
molding and extrusion processes.
Vic De Zen, President & C.E.O.
TOTAL REVENUE ($000)   58,896

PMC CORPORATION
(Public)   SPECIALTY STORES
285 Midwest Rd., Scarborough, ON, M1P 3A6   (416) 752-4550
PMC CORPORATION carries on two businesses directly and through
wholly owned subsidiaries. Plumbing Mart markets plumbing supplies
and services through franchised dealers. Floorco Limited manufactures,
sells on a wholesale basis, and installs hardwood floors.
Noel R. Rebick, Chairman & C.E.O.
TOTAL REVENUE ($000)   7,681

PMG FINANCIAL INC.
(Public)   FINANCE AND LEASING
20 Adelaide St. E., Suite 1300, Toronto, ON,
M5C 2T6   (416) 366-1513
PMG FINANCIAL INC. is an investment management company.
Lou Elmaleh, Chairman, President & C.E.O.
TOTAL REVENUE ($000)   3,782

POCO PETROLEUMS LTD.
See page 111 for a full company profile.

POLYSAR RUBBER CORPORATION
(Private)   CHEMICALS
1265 Vidal St. S., Sarnia, ON, N7T 7M2   (519) 337-8251
POLYSAR RUBBER CORPORATION manufactures synthetic rubber.
The company is a subsidiary of Bayer AG of Germany.
TOTAL REVENUE ($000)   341,206

PORT OF QUEBEC CORPORATION
(Crown)   TRANSPORTATION
150 Dalhousie, Quebec, PQ, G1K 7P7   (418) 648-3640
Port of Quebec is involved in the administration of ports in Quebec.
Raymond McBain, Chairman
TOTAL REVENUE ($000)   14,376

POTASH CORPORATION OF SASKATCHEWAN INC.
See page 18 for a full company profile.

POWER CORPORATION OF CANADA
See page 413 for a full company profile.

POWER FINANCIAL CORPORATION
See page 414 for a full company profile.

PPG CANADA INC.
(Private)   CHEMICALS
30 St. Clair Avenue West, Toronto, ON, M4V 3A1   (416) 923-5441

PPG CANADA INC. is a manufacturer of flat glass, automotive glass,
coatings and resins, and chemicals. The company is a wholly owned
subsidiary of PPG Industries, Inc. of the United States.
Jim W. Craig, President & C.O.O.
TOTAL REVENUE ($000)   546,045

PRAIRIE OIL ROYALTIES COMPANY, LTD.
(Public)   OIL AND GAS PRODUCERS
715 - 5th Avenue S.W., Calgary, AB, T2P 2X7   (403) 231-0111
PRAIRIE OIL ROYALTIES COMPANY, LTD. produces and sells
crude oil, gas liquids and natural gas in Canada, and is engaged in oil and
gas exploration and development in Western Canada. Minor interests are
also held in exploratory lands in the Arctic Islands.
Barry D. Cochrane, Chairman
TOTAL REVENUE ($000)   32,697

PRATT & WHITNEY CANADA INC.
(Private)   TRANSPORTATION EQUIP & COMPNTS
1000 Boul Marie Victorin, Longueuil, PQ, J4G 1A1   (514) 677-9411
PRATT & WHITNEY CANADA INC. is engaged in the manufacture
of gas turbine engines for air, sea and land applications. The company is
wholly owned by United Technologies Corporation (U.S.).
Elvie E. Smith, Chairman Of The Board
TOTAL REVENUE ($000)   1,426,583

PRAXAIR CANADA INC.
(Private)   CHEMICALS
123 Eglinton Ave East, Toronto, ON, M4P 1J3   (416) 488-1444
LINDE CANADA INC. manufactures chemicals, plastics, and indus-
trial, medical and specialty gases. The company has operations across
Canada. Union Carbide Corp. of Danbury, Connecticutt., holds a 75%
interest in the company.
Gilbert E. Playford, President & C.E.O.
TOTAL REVENUE ($000)   304,959

PRECAMBRIAN SHIELD RESOURCES LIMITED
See page 112 for a full company profile.

PRECISION DRILLING (1987) LTD.
(Public)   OIL AND GAS FIELD SERVICES
Suite 1600, 144 - 4th Avenue S.W., Calgary, AB,
T2P 3N4   (403) 264-4882
PRECISION DRILLING CORPORATION is engaged in the business
of providing contract well drilling and other services in the oil and gas
industry in Alberta.
Hank Swartout, Chairman, President & C.E.O.
TOTAL REVENUE ($000)   31,519

PREMDOR INC.
See page 502 for a full company profile.

PREMETALCO INC.
(Private)   WHOLESALE DISTRIBUTORS
110 Belfield Road, Rexdale, ON, M9W 1G1   (416) 245-7386
PREMETALCO INC. is engaged in industrial distribution.
V.H. Sher, Chairman
TOTAL REVENUE ($000)   183,423

PREMIER CDN ENTERPRISES LTD.
(Public)   OTHER MINES
1785 55th Avenue, Dorval, PQ, H9P 2W3   (514) 631-6700
PREMIER CDN ENTERPRISES LTD. operates primarily in the areas of the extraction, production and marketing of sphagnum peat moss and the production and marketing of peat moss based culture mediums, organic soils, organic fertilizer, conception and manufacturing and material handling equipment, research and development in the biotechnology sector.
Bernard Belanger, President & C.E.O.
TOTAL REVENUE ($000)   66,115

PREMIER CHOIX: TVEC INC.
(Public)   BROADCASTING
2100 Rue Sainte-Catherine Oue, 8th Floor, Montreal, PQ,
H3H 2T3   (514) 939-3150
PREMIER CHOIX: TVEC INC. operates a French language pay TV service, Super Ecran, beemed 24 hours a day to Quebec, Ontario, Eastern Manitoba and the Atlantic provinces. The company also provides a french language specialty channel, Canal Famille, to the same regions.
Harold Greenberg, Chairman
TOTAL REVENUE ($000)   28,936

PRENOR FINANCIAL LTD.
(Public)   TRUST, SAVINGS AND LOAN
Suite 1200, 1100 University Street, Montreal, PQ,
H3B 3A4   (514) 871-7120
PRENOR FINANCIAL LTD. is a financial services holding company which operates through subsidiaries engaged in the following businesses: deposit taking and mortgage lending, mutual fund management and distribution, investment counselling, mortgage brokerage, interim financing and real estate lending and investing.
Serge Rocheleau, President & C.E.O.
TOTAL REVENUE ($000)   131,166

PRENOR GROUP LTD.
(Public)   FINANCE AND LEASING
1100 University Street, Suite 1200, Montreal, PQ,
H3B 3A4   (514) 871-7120
PRENOR GROUP LTD. is a holding company with subsidiaries active in investment management and mutual funds, trust company operations and real estate investments.
Lorne C. Webster, Chairman & C.E.O.
TOTAL REVENUE ($000)   139,091

PRICE CLUB CANADA INC.
(Private)   DEPARTMENT STORES
1010 Rue Sherbrooke Ouest, Suite 1100, Montreal, PQ,
H3A 2R7   (514) 744-8173
PRICE CLUB CANADA INC. operates a chain of retail warehouse stores which offer a diverse line of products to consumers through membership.
TOTAL REVENUE ($000)   1,171,982

PRIME EQUITIES INTERNATIONAL CORPORATION
(Public)   MANAGEMENT AND DIVERSIFIED
11th Floor, 808 West Hastings Street, Box 10, Vancouver, BC,
V6C 2X4   (604) 687-7463

PRIME EQUITIES INTERNATIONAL CORPORATION is a management investment company.
Murray Pezim, Chairman & President
TOTAL REVENUE ($000)   2,137

PRIME RESOURCES GROUP INC.
(Public)   PRECIOUS METALS
Suite 1000, 700 West Pender Street, Vancouver, BC,
V6C 1G8   (604) 684-2345
PRIME RESOURCES GROUP INC. is a gold mining company. It operates the Snip Mine. Production at Eskay Creek, one of North America's richest gold deposits, is expected to begin in 1995. Prime largest shareholder, International Corona owns 54.3% of the shares of Prime.
J.E. Thompson, President & C.E.O.
TOTAL REVENUE ($000)   20,034

PRIMEX FOREST PRODUCTS LTD.
(Public)   WEST COAST FORESTRY
9924 River Road, Delta, BC, V4G 1B5   (604) 583-3665
PRIMEX FOREST PRODUCTS LTD. manufactures and markets lumber products through three operations: Acorn Forest Products Division; Specialty Products Division; and Field Sawmills Limited Partnership. All operation are located in British Columbia.
George L. Malpass, President & C.E.O.
TOTAL REVENUE ($000)   120,328

PRINCE RUPERT FISHERMEN'S CO-OPERATIVE ASSOCIATION
(Non-fin Co-op)   FOOD PROCESSING
P.O. Box 520, Prince Rupert, BC, V8G 3R7   (604) 624-2146
PRINCE RUPERT FISHERMEN'S CO-OPERATIVE ASSOCIATION is a fish processing and procurement cooperative. It also owns a feed production mill.
John Haugan, Chairman
TOTAL REVENUE ($000)   53,503

PRINCE RUPERT PORT CORPORATION
(Crown)   TRANSPORTATION
99 Metcalfe Street, Ottawa, ON, K1A 0N6   (613) 957-6787
PRINCE RUPER PORT CORPORATION was established pursuant to the Canada Ports Corporation Act in 1984. The company controls the area and harbor around Prince Rupert through the regulation of cargo and ship traffic through the port.
Donald H. Seidel, Chaiman
TOTAL REVENUE ($000)   14,304

PRINCETON MINING CORPORATION
See page 19 for a full company profile.

PRISM SULPHUR CORPORATION
(Private)   WHOLESALE DISTRIBUTORS
Suite 3200, 700 - 2nd Street S.W., Calgary, AB,
T2P 2W2   (403) 262-8766
PRISM SULPHUR CORPORATION is an international marketer of Canadian elemental sulphur. The company is owned by 33 Western Canadian oil and gas producers. Shell Canada, Husky Oil, Amoco Canada and Mobil Oil Canada each own 10% of the company.

D.M.G. Stewart, President & C.E.O.
TOTAL REVENUE ($000)   176,272

PROCTER & GAMBLE INC.
(Private)   MISC. CONSUMER PRODUCTS
4711 Young St., North York, ON, M2N 6K8   (416) 730-4711
PROCTER & GAMBLE INC. is a manufacturer and/or distributor of
laundry products, household cleaning products, food and beverage products, health, beauty aids and drug products, industrial chemical products
and lumber, pulp and paper products. The company is a wholly owned
subsidiary of Procter & Gamble Company of Cincinnati, Ohio.
T.A. Moore, President & C.E.O.
TOTAL REVENUE ($000)   1,789,768

PROGAS LIMITED
(Private)   GAS UTILITIES
Suite 4100, 400 - 3rd Avenue S.W., Calgary, AB,
T2P 4H2   (403) 266-0300
PROGAS LIMITED is a natural gas marketer. Progas is owned by 12
corporations each holding 8 1/3%.
Vern Horte, Chairman
TOTAL REVENUE ($000)   452,979

PROMATEK INDUSTRIES LTD.
(Public)   MISC. INDUSTRIAL PRODUCTS
8390 Mayrand, Montreal, PQ, H4P 2C9   (514) 737-7747
PROMATEK INDUSTRIES LTD. designs and manufactures two lines.
The Electrostim line consists of electronic muscle stimulators used for
the treatment of injured muscles and tendons. The Copitrak and Faxtrak
lines consist of office equipment machines which record copier use and
disbursement charges.
Harvey Kofsky, Chairman, President & C.E.O.
TOTAL REVENUE ($000)   4,977

PROMIS SYSTEMS CORPORATION LTD.
(Public)   COMPUTER SOFTWARE & PROCESSING
Suite 500, 175 Bloor Street East, Toronto, ON,
M4W 3R8   (416) 960-0960
PROMIS SYSTEMS CORPORATION LTD. develops and markets
software for use by large scale manufacturers in the management of plant
floor operations designed to enhance manufacturing competitiveness
through higher product quality, faster output and lower production costs.
Elliot Wassarman, President & C.E.O.
TOTAL REVENUE ($000)   14,167 (US)

PRUDENTIAL ASSURANCE GROUP OF COMPANIES
(LIFE)
(Private)   INSURANCE - LIFE
101 Frederick St, P.O. Box 9032, Kitchener, ON,
N2G 4R8   (519) 888-5700
PRUDENTIAL ASSURANCE GROUP OF COMPANIES (LIFE) are
providers of life insurance, health insurance, annuity, pension, and
personal investment products and services. Along with the Property and
Casualty Operations of The Prudential Assurance Company Limited and
subsidiaries owned by Prudential Corporation Canada, are collectively
referred to as the Prudential Assurance Group of Companies.
M.A.P. Beck, President - Life, Health & Pension
TOTAL REVENUE ($000)   971,171

PRUDENTIAL ASSURANCE GROUP OF COMPANIES
(P&C)
(Private)   INSURANCE - PROPERTY & CASUALTY
101 Frederick Street, Box 9031, Kitchener, ON,
N2G 4R7   (519) 888-5700
PRUDENTIAL ASSURANCE GROUP OF COMPANIES (P&C) pro-
vides property and casualty insurance. Along with the life, health and
pension operations of The Prudential Assurance Company Limited and
subsidiaries owned by Prudential Corporation Canada, are collectively
referred to as the Prudential Assurance Group of Companies.
Michael Beck, President
TOTAL REVENUE ($000)   350,565

PUBLIC STORAGE CANADIAN PROPERTIES
(Public)   OTHER SERVICES
Suite 202, 5401 Eglinton Avenue West, Etobicoke, ON,
M9C 5K6   (416) 620-1577
PUBLIC STORAGE CANADIAN PROPERTIES is involved in the
operation of storage facilities.
Kenneth Q. Volk, Jr., Chairman
TOTAL REVENUE ($000)   7,549

PUBLIC STORAGE CANADIAN PROPERTIES IV
LIMITED
(Public)   OTHER SERVICES
Suite 202, 5401 Eglinton Avenue West, Etobicoke, ON,
M9C 5K6   (416) 620-1577
PUBLIC STORAGE CANADIAN PROPERTIES IV LIMITED is a
limited partnership which manages three self-service storage facilities,
also known as mini-warehouses, in Ontario with a view to generating
cash flow from operations to create distributable cash.
Kenneth Q. Volk Jr., Chairman
TOTAL REVENUE ($000)   1,923

PURDEL COOPERATIVE AGRO-ALIMENTAIRE
(Non-fin Co-op)   AGRICULTURE
155 Rue Saint-Jean-Baptiste, C.P. 68, Bic, PQ,
G0L 1B0   (418) 736-4363
PURDEL COOPERATIVE AGRO-ALIMENTAIRE is involved in the
distribution of feed and fertilizers, seafood products and agricultural
machinery.
Napoleon Theberge, Chairman
TOTAL REVENUE ($000)   134,626

PUROLATOR COURIER LTD.
(Private)   OTHER SERVICES
5310 Explorer Dr., Mississauga, ON, L4W 4H6   (416) 624-5454
PCL COURIER HOLDINGS is a courier company that delivers manu-
factured goods and documents. It is a wholly owned subsidiary of Onex
Corporation.
Matthew O. Diggs, Jr., Chairman
TOTAL REVENUE ($000)   552,804

PWA CORPORATION
See page 275 for a full company profile.

QIT-FER ET TITANE INC.
(Private)   METAL MINES
770 Sherbrooke St. W., Suite 1800, Montreal, PQ,
H3A 1G1   (514) 288-8400
QIT-FER ET TITANE is engaged in the mining of Ilmenite and the
manufacture of titanium dioxide, high purity iron and steel billets.
Manufacture of metal powders through its wholly owned subsidiary,
Quebec Metal Powders Limited. The company is a wholly owned
subsidiary of The RTZ Corporation plc.
Gilles Charette, President & C.O.O.
TOTAL REVENUE ($000)   431,000

QUADRA LOGIC TECHNOLOGIES INC.
See page 194 for a full company profile.

**QUAKER OATS COMPANY OF CANADA LIMITED
(THE)**
(Private)   FOOD PROCESSING
Quaker Park, Peterborough, ON, K9J 7B2   (705) 743-6330
QUAKER OATS COMPANY OF CANADA LIMITED manufactures
a wide range of quality food and pet food products. Business divisions
include foods, food service, Gatorade sports beverage and pet foods. The
company is a wholly owned subsidiary of Quaker Oats Company of
Chicago, Illinois.
Jon K. Grant, Chairman & C.E.O.
TOTAL REVENUE ($000)   285,539

QUARTEX CORPORATION (THE)
(Public)   COMPUTER SOFTWARE & PROCESSING
85 Scarsdale Road, Suite 200, Toronto, ON,
M3B 2R2   (416) 445-4823
QUARTEX CORPORATION sells computer systems and software for
business. The systems combine off-the-shelf hardware with custom and
package soft- ware developed by the company. The company also
providesongoing support services to its customers.
Rubin I. Osten, President
TOTAL REVENUE ($000)   17,276

QUARTZ MOUNTAIN GOLD CORP.
(Public)   PRECIOUS METALS
Suite 950, 789 West Pender Street, Vancouver, BC,
V6C 1H2   (604) 662-7557
QUARTZ MOUNTAIN GOLD CORP. is engaged in the acquisition,
exploration and development of mineral properties, primarily in the
United States.
David S. Jennings, President & C.E.O.
TOTAL REVENUE ($000)   16 (US)

QUEBEC GROWTH FUND INC.
(Public)   INVESTMENT COMPANIES AND FUNDS
1000 Rue Sherbrooke Ouest, Bureau 2300, Montreal, PQ,
H3A 3G4   (514) 842-6464
QUEBEC GROWTH FUND INC. is a closed-end investment company
which will invest principally in Quebec companies that it believes offer
significant growth potential.
Andre Marsan, Chairman, President & C.E.O.
TOTAL REVENUE ($000)   345

QUEBEC STURGEON RIVER MINES LIMITED
See page 55 for a full company profile.

QUEBEC-TELEPHONE
See page 307 for a full company profile.

QUEBECOR INC.
See page 328 for a full company profile.

QUEBECOR PRINTING INC.
See page 329 for a full company profile.

QUEENSTON MINING INC.
(Public)   PRECIOUS METALS
Suite 1116, 111 Richmond Street West, Toronto, ON,
M5H 2G4   (416) 364-0001
QUEENSTON MINING INC. is a Canadian public company with a
number of major Ontario and Quebec gold property interests. The
company derives its income from gold production, custom milling and
investments. It also owns 31% of the Thermal Exploration Company.
Hugh D. Harbinson, Chairman, President & C.E.O.
TOTAL REVENUE ($000)   164

QUNO CORPORATION
(Public)   EAST COAST FORESTRY
8 King Street, St. Catharines, ON, L2R 7G2   (416) 688-5030
QUNO CORPORATION is an integrated forest products company. The
company operates pulp and paper mills in Thorold, Ontario and Baie-
Comeau, Quebec. It is active in the development and application of
recycling technology.
John E. Houghton, Chairman
TOTAL REVENUE ($000)   436,120

QUORUM GROWTH INC.
(Public)   INVESTMENT COMPANIES AND FUNDS
Suite 1500, 150 King Street West, Toronto, ON,
M5H 1J9   (416) 971-6998
QUORUM GROWTH INC. has been established to acquire investments
previously made by funds indirectly managed by Quorum Funding Corp.
in emerging growth companies and to make new investments in such
companies or supplementary investments in existing investments.
John R. Yarnell, Chairman
TOTAL REVENUE ($000)   3,355

R.P.M. TECH INC.
(Public)   MACHINERY
184 Route 138, Cap-Sante, PQ, G0A 1L0   (418) 285-1811
R.P.M. TECH INC. is involved in the manufacturing, distribution and
maintenance of heavy machinery. The company's activities are concen-
trated in North America but it also operates in Europe and NorthAfrica.
Marcel Papillon, President & General Manager
TOTAL REVENUE ($000)   16,798

RADIOMUTUEL INC.
(Public)   BROADCASTING
1717 Rene-Levesque Blvd. East, Montreal, PQ,
H2L 4E8   (514) 529-3210

RADIOMUTUEL INC.'s activities mainly consist in the operation of French language radio stations in the province of Quebec. It also operates Musique Plus, a French language music video channel on basic cable, and Omni Outdoor Limited Partnership, an advertising company.
Normand Beauchamp, Chairman, President & C.E.O.
TOTAL REVENUE ($000)   44,556

RALSTON PURINA CANADA INC
(Private)   FOOD PROCESSING
2500 Royal Windsor Drive, Mississauga, ON,
L5J 1K8   (416) 822-1611
RALSTON PURINA CANADA INC. is engaged in the production of animal and poultry feeds and battery products. The company has three divisions: Grocery Products, AGRI and Eveready. Ralston Purina Canada is a 90% owned subsidiary of Ralston Purnia International Holding Company Inc. of Delaware. Ralston Purina Overseas Battery Corp. owns the remaining 10%.
W.L. Lewis, President
TOTAL REVENUE ($000)   300,745

RAM PETROLEUMS LIMITED
(Public)   OIL AND GAS PRODUCERS
435 Exeter Rd., London, ON, N6E 2Z3   (519) 681-2244
RAM PETROLEUMS LIMITED and its consolidated subsidiaries are engaged in oil and gas exploration, development and production in Canada and the United States. A portion of the Company's activities are conducted jointly with others.
Robert Opekar, Chairman, President & C.E.O.
TOTAL REVENUE ($000)   5,486

RAMPART MERCANTILE INC.
(Public)   CONTRACTORS
Unit 2, 10 West Pearce Street, Richmond Hill, ON,
L4B 1B6   (416) 881-3324
RAMPART MERCANTILE INC. is involved in the completion of the interiors of shops and restaurants, principally fast food outlets in malls, which the company carries out through its wholly owned subsidiary North American Store Fixtures Limited. The company also owns a number of shares in T.G. Quickly's and owns a major part of Dunsdon Food Products Ltd.
Dominique Monardo, President
TOTAL REVENUE ($000)   4,044

RANCHMEN'S RESOURCES LTD.
See page 113 for a full company profile.

RANGER OIL LIMITED
See page 114 for a full company profile.

RAYROCK YELLOWKNIFE RESOURCES INC.
See page 56 for a full company profile.

RBC DOMINION SECURITIES LIMITED
(Private)   INVESTMENT HOUSES
P.O. Box 21, Commerce Court South, Toronto, ON,
M5L 1A7   (416) 864-4000

RBC DOMINION SECURITIES LIMITED is an investment holding company which, through subsidiaries, carries on business as a fully integrated Canadian-based investment dealer.
Anthony S. Fell, Chairman & C.E.O.
TOTAL REVENUE ($000)   690,610

REA GOLD CORPORATION
(Public)   PRECIOUS METALS
Suite 2050 - Guinness Tower, 1055 West Hastings Street,
Vancouver, BC, V6E 3V3   (604) 684-7527
REA GOLD CORPORATION is a mining exploration engaged in the acquistion, exploration, development and operation of both precious and base metal properties in Canada, the United States and Latin America.
W. James Hogan, President & C.E.O.
TOTAL REVENUE ($000)   4,983

REALCAP HOLDINGS LIMITED
(Public)   INVESTMENT COMPANIES AND FUNDS
2161 Yonge Street, Suite 604, Toronto, ON,
M4S 3A6   (416) 486-7729
REALCAP HOLDINGS LIMITED is an investment holding company which invests in the resources and the financial services industries.
David S. Ades, Chairman, President & C.E.O.
TOTAL REVENUE ($000)   421

REDFERN RESOURCES LTD
(Public)   PRECIOUS METALS
Suite 205, 10711 Cambie Road, Richmond, BC,
V6X 3G5   (604) 278-3028
REDFERN RESOURCES LTD. is engaged in the exploration and development of mineral properties primarily located in British Columbia.
John A. Greig, Chairman & President
TOTAL REVENUE ($000)   312

REDLAW INDUSTRIES INC.
(Public)   AUTOMOTIVE
174 Stanley Street, Suite 300, Brantford, ON,
N3S 7S3   (519) 751-1691
REDLAW INDUSTRIES INC., through subsidiaries and affiliates, is involved in metal stampings and assemblies for the automotive industry, thermoplastics injection molded parts and thermoset plastic parts for the shoe industry and recreational vehicle industry, and also the manufacture of industrial and apparel textiles through its investment in Johnston Industries Inc.
David Chandler, Chairman, President & C.E.O.
TOTAL REVENUE ($000)   47,374

REDPATH INDUSTRIES LIMITED
(Private)   FOOD PROCESSING
95 Queens Quay East, Toronto, ON, M5E 1A3   (416) 366-3561
REDPATH INDUSTRIES LIMITED is engaged in sugar refining, molasses, animal feeds, corn products, and high intensity sweetners. Redpath is wholly owned by Tate & Lyle plc.
M.D. McEwen, Chairman
TOTAL REVENUE ($000)   216,363

REDSTONE RESOURCES INC.
(Public)   METAL MINES
Suite 1900, Box 2005, 20 Eglinton Avenue West, Toronto, ON,
M4R 1K8   (416) 480-6497
REDSTONE RESOURCES INC. is involved in the acquisition of
non-gold mineral royalties.
Pierre Lassonde, Chairman
TOTAL REVENUE ($000)   1,419

REGIONAL CABLESYSTEMS INC.
(Public)   CABLE
Suite 202, 710 Dorval Drive, Oakville, ON,
L6K 3V7   (416) 338-3133
REGIONAL CABLESYSTEMS INC. carries on cable television opera-
tions in Canada and the United States.
Gary D. Kain, Chairman
TOTAL REVENUE ($000)   50,888

REGIONAL RESOURCES LTD.
(Public)   PRECIOUS METALS
12th Floor, 20 Toronto Street, Toronto, ON,
M5C 2B8   (416) 869-0772
REGIONAL RESOURCES LTD. is involved in the exploration and
development of mineral properties in northern British Columbia and the
Yukon. Its assets include a 82% interest in the Midway silver-lead-zinc
property in northern British Columbia and a 36% interest in Fairfield
Minerals Ltd., which is active in exploration in British Columbia.
G. Farquharson, President
TOTAL REVENUE ($000)   115

REITMANS (CANADA) LIMITED
See page 368 for a full company profile.

RENAISSANCE ENERGY LTD.
See page 115 for a full company profile.

REPAP ENTERPRISES INC.
See page 145 for a full company profile.

REPUBLIC GOLDFIELDS INC.
(Public)   PRECIOUS METALS
1 Dundas Street West, Suite 2402, Box 13, Toronto, ON,
M5G 1Z3   (416) 977-4653
REPUBLIC GOLDFIELDS INC. is a gold producer with properties in
Arizona and in Quebec.
Marc C. Henderson, President
TOTAL REVENUE ($000)   15,175

**REPUBLIC NATIONAL BANK OF NEW YORK
(CANADA)**
(Private)   BANKS
1981 McGill College Avenue, Montreal, PQ,
H3A 3A9   (514) 288-5551
REPUBLIC NATIONAL BANK OF NEW YORK (CANADA) is a full
service bank.
Ezekiel Schouela, Chairman
TOTAL REVENUE ($000)   64,325

RESOQUEST RESOURCES LTD.
(Public)   OIL AND GAS PRODUCERS
Suite 2992, Alberta Stock Exchange Tower, 300 - 5th Avenue S.W.,
Calgary, AB, T2P 3C4   (403) 294-1428
RESOQUEST RESOURCES LTD. is involved in the business of oil and
natural gas exploration, development and production, with its activities
concentrated in Saskatchewan and, to a lesser extent, in Alberta.
William Siebens, Chairman
TOTAL REVENUE ($000)   2,348

RESOURCECAN LIMITED
(Public)   MANAGEMENT AND DIVERSIFIED
P.O Box 5367, Baine-Johnston Centre, 10 Fort William Place,
St. John's, NF, A1C 5W2   (709) 576-1287
RESOURCECAN LIMITED was founded for the purpose of assembling
a pool of capital to invest in Newfoundland based companies, or Cana-
dian companies with operations in Newfoundland or anticipating expan-
sion into Newfoundland.
Hubert G. Harnett, President
TOTAL REVENUE ($000)   35,950

REVENUE PROPERTIES COMPANY LIMITED
See page 264 for a full company profile.

REXFOR
(Crown)   EAST COAST FORESTRY
1195 Rue de Lavigerie, Sainte-Foy, PQ,
G1V 4N3   (418) 659-4530
REXFOR's stock is held by the Quebec government. Its objectives are:
to salvage and exploit the forested areas of the public domain and to carry
out and direct the research required for these purposes; to revalorize by
any appropriate sylvicultural measure, preserve and protect forest and
land intended for forest use; to encourage the establishment and development of the forest industry.
Maurice Bolduc, Chairman Of The Board
TOTAL REVENUE ($000)   27,897

RFC RESOURCE FINANCE CORPORATION
(Public)   METAL MINES
Suite 3400, Aetna Tower, P.O. Box 19, Toronto-Dominion Centre,
Toronto, ON, M5K 1A1   (416) 361-6400
RFC RESOURCE FINANCE CORPORATION owns the Pend Oreille
lead-zinc mine in Washington State, and is continuing to evaluate the
economic potential of the area.
David H. Watkins, President
TOTAL REVENUE ($000)   152

RHONE-POULENC CANADA INC.
(Private)   CHEMICALS
2000 Argentia Rd., Plaza #3, Suite 400, Mississauga, ON,
L5N 1V9   (416) 821-4450
RHONE-POULENC CANADA INC. is a formulator and distributor of
chemicals including specialty chemicals, food ingredients, animal nutri-
tion and crop protection products. Rhone-Poulenc Canada is a wholly
owned subsidiary of Rhone-Poulenc S.A. of Paris, France.
Bernard West, President
TOTAL REVENUE ($000)   201,129

RICHARDSON GREENSHIELDS LIMITED
(Private)   INVESTMENT HOUSES
Richardson Building, One Lombard Place, Winnipeg, MB,
R3B 0Y2   (204) 934-5858
RICHARDSON GREENSHIELDS LIMITED is the sole owner of
Richardson Greenshields of CAnada Limited, a full service investment
dealer. Richardson Greenshields Limted is approximately 74% owned
by the Richardson family of Winnipeg.
G.. Richardson, Chairman
TOTAL REVENUE ($000)   308,615

RICHEY PACIFIC CABLEVISION, LTD.
(Public)   CABLE
Suite 7, 1605 Grand Avenue, San Marcos, CA,
92069   (619) 471-6225
INTERNATIONAL RICHEY PACIFIC CABLEVISION, through its
wholly owned subsidiary, Richey Pacific Cable Vision, owns and oper-
ates private cable television systems.
Steve K. Richey, President & C.E.O.
TOTAL REVENUE ($000)   1,944 (US)

RICHLAND PETROLEUM CORPORATION
(Public)   OIL AND GAS PRODUCERS
Suite 1220, 407 - 2nd Street S.W., Calgary, AB,
T2P 2Y3   (403) 261-4080
RICHLAND PETROLEUM CORPORATION is involved in the acqui-
sition, exploration and development of oil and gas properties. The
company's principal properties are located in Alberta and Saskatchewan.
Richard A.M. Todd, President
TOTAL REVENUE ($000)   2,055

RICHMOND SAVINGS CREDIT UNION
(Fin. Co-op)   CREDIT UNIONS
Professional Centre, 5611 Cooney Road, Richmond, BC,
V6X 3J5   (604) 273-8138
RICHMOND SAVINGS CREDIT UNION offers a complete range of
financial services to individuals and businesses in British Columbia. The
company is active in the insurance business through a wholly owned
subsidiary, Richmond Savings Insurance Services.
Robert W. Garnett, Chairman
TOTAL REVENUE ($000)   95,771

RICHMONT MINES INC.
(Public)   PRECIOUS METALS
68 Avenue Principale, Rouyn-Noranda, PQ,
J9X 4P2   (819) 797-2465
RICHMONT MINES INC. is a gold producer operating the Francouer
Mine. The company is also engaged in the exploration and development
of other gold properties. All five of the properties are within a five mile
radius area, 12 miles west of Rouyn-Noranda, Quebec.
Jean-Guy Rivard, President & C.E.O.
TOTAL REVENUE ($000)   8,974

RIGEL ENERGY CORPORATION
See page 116 for a full company profile.

RIMOIL CORPORATION (THE)
(Public)   OIL AND GAS PRODUCERS
Suite 200, 665 - 8th Street S.W., Calgary, AB,
T2P 3K7   (403) 266-4584
THE RIMOIL CORPORATION is engaged in the exploration and
development of oil and gas properties.
Frank G. Vetsch, Chairman
TOTAL REVENUE ($000)   3,474

RIO ALGOM LIMITED
See page 20 for a full company profile.

RIO ALTO EXPLORATION LTD.
See page 117 for a full company profile.

RIVERSIDE FOREST PRODUCTS LIMITED
(Public)   WEST COAST FORESTRY
820 Guy Street, Kelowna, BC, V1Y 7R5   (604) 762-3411
RIVERSIDE FOREST PRODUCTS LIMITED is in the business of
harvesting timber and producing lumber, plywood, veneer and wood
chips.
Gordon W. Steele, President & C.E.O.
TOTAL REVENUE ($000)   39,749

ROBERT MITCHELL INC.
(Public)   METAL FABRICATORS
350 Decarie Boulevard, Saint-Laurent, PQ,
H4L 3K5   (514) 747-2471
ROBERT MITCHELL INC. is involved in the manufacture of fabricated
metal products and wholesale distribution of pipe, valves and fittings.
George H. Holland, Chairman, President & C.E.O.
TOTAL REVENUE ($000)   68,658

ROBIN HOOD MULTIFOODS INC.
(Private)   FOOD PROCESSING
60 Columbia Way, Markham, ON, L3R 0C9   (416) 940-9600
ROBIN HOOD MULTIFOODS INC. is a diversified food processing
and marketing company. It serves the consumer, industrial, and away-
from- home eating markets with products including flour, bakery ingredients,frozen baked goods, pickles, relishes and other condiments. The
company is indirectly a wholly owned subsidiary of Interational Multifoods Inc. of Minnesota.
Adrian H. Vis, President
TOTAL REVENUE ($000)   397,462

ROCKWELL INTERNATIONAL OF CANADA LTD.
(Private)   TRANSPORTATION EQUIP & COMPNTS
Corporate Office, 135 Dundas Street, P.O. Box 843, Cambridge,
ON, N1R 5X9   (519) 740-8656
ROCKWELL's businesses manufacture various automotive compo-
nents for heavy duty trucks, special-purpose vehicles, light trucks and
passenger cars. Its electronics businesses manufacture and market radio
communication, naval combat, avionics and industrial automation sys-
tems and equipment. They are also involved in the marketing of graphic
equipment.
William E. Hetherington, Chairman
TOTAL REVENUE ($000)   405,446

ROCTEST LTD.
(Public)   MISC. INDUSTRIAL PRODUCTS
665 Rue Pine, Saint-Lambert, PQ, J4P 2P4   (514) 465-1113
ROCTEST LTD. designs, produces and commercializes measurement instruments of high technology used primarily in the fields of geotechnic and of high works structures. These instruments are also used to measure the pressure, the compression and the movements of the grounds and the rocks, the supporting capacity and the deformation.
Jean-Paul Gignac, Chairman Of The Board
TOTAL REVENUE ($000)   9,879

ROGERS CANTEL INC.
(Private)   TELECOMMUNICATIONS
6315 Cote De Liesse, Saint-Laurent, PQ, H4T 1E5   (514) 340-1319
ROGERS CANTEL INC. is a telecommunications company. It is a wholly- owned subsidiary of Rogers Communications Inc..
George A. Fierheller, President & C.E.O.
TOTAL REVENUE ($000)   351,764

ROGERS CANTEL MOBILE COMMUNICATIONS INC.
See page 330 for a full company profile.

ROGERS COMMUNICATIONS INC.
See page 331 for a full company profile.

ROINS HOLDING LIMITED
(Private)   INSURANCE - PROPERTY & CASUALTY
10 Wellington Street East, Toronto, ON, M5E 1L5   (416) 366-7511
ROINS HOLDING LIMITED operating subsidiary is Royal Insurance Canada. The company's ultimate owner is Royal Insurance Holdings plc.
Jock K. Finlayson, Chairman
TOTAL REVENUE ($000)   868,932

ROLLAND INC.
See page 146 for a full company profile.

ROLLS-ROYCE HOLDINGS CANADA INC.
(Private)   TRANSPORTATION EQUIP & COMPNTS
9500 Cote De Liesse, Lachine, PQ, H8T 1A2   (514) 631-3541
ROLLS-ROYCE HOLDINGS CANADA INC. and its subsidiary Rolls-Royce Industries Canada Inc., sells and overhauls engines and designs, manufactures and sells electrical and electronic equipment. It is a subsidiary of Rolls-Royce plc.
Roy Clapinson, President
TOTAL REVENUE ($000)   524,084

ROMAN CORPORATION LIMITED
See page 454 for a full company profile.

ROTHMANS INC.
See page 167 for a full company profile.

ROYAL BANK OF CANADA
See page 389 for a full company profile.

ROYAL CANADIAN MINT
(Crown)   METAL FABRICATORS
320 Sussex Drive, Ottawa, ON, K1A 0G8   (613) 993-3500
ROYAL CANADIAN MINT is Canada's national mint and has the primary responsibility for striking Canadian general circulation and numismatic coinage. It also produces bullion investment coins, in addition to coins for foreign countries. The Mint is a major refiner of gold.
James C. Corkery, Chairman Of The Board
TOTAL REVENUE ($000)   377,971

ROYAL INSURANCE COMPANY OF CANADA
(Private)   INSURANCE - PROPERTY & CASUALTY
10 Wellington Street East, Toronto, ON, M5E 1L5   (416) 366-7511
ROYAL INSURANCE COMPANY OF CANADA is a property and casualty insurer. The company is ultimately owned by Royal Insurance Holdings plc.
Jock K. Finlayson, Chairman
TOTAL REVENUE ($000)   886,400

ROYAL LEPAGE LIMITED
See page 265 for a full company profile.

ROYAL OAK MINES INC.
See page 57 for a full company profile.

ROYAL TRUST COMPANY MORTGAGE CORPORATION (THE)
(Public)   TRUST, SAVINGS AND LOAN
Royal Trust Tower, P.O. Box 7500, Station A, Toronto, ON,
M5W 1P9   (416) 981-7000
THE ROYAL TRUST COMPANY MORTGAGE CORPORATION is in the business of making mortgage loans. Funds for this purpose are obtained through the issue of debentures and promissory notes.
Mr. Michel Petit, President & C.E.O.
TOTAL REVENUE ($000)   8,185

ROYAL TRUST ENERGY INCOME FUND I
(Public)   INVESTMENT COMPANIES AND FUNDS
Suite 3300, Scotia Centre, 700 - 2nd Street S.W., Calgary, AB,
T2P 2W2   (403) 269-0500
ROYAL TRUST ENERGY INCOME FUND I is a closed-end investment trust, created by Royal Trust Energy Corporation, a subsidiary of Royal Trustco. The fund is fully invested in producing oil & gas properties. All net income is paid to unitholders quarterly.
B. Lee Bentley, Chairman Of The Board
TOTAL REVENUE ($000)   3,630

ROYAL TRUST ENERGY INCOME FUND II
(Public)   INVESTMENT COMPANIES AND FUNDS
Suite 3300 Scotia Centre, 700 - 2nd Street S.W., Calgary, AB,
T2P 2W2   (403) 269-0500
ROYAL TRUST ENERGY INCOME FUND II is a closed-end investment trust created by Royal Trust Energy Corporation, a subsidiary of Royal Trustco. The fund is completely invested in producing oil & gas properties. All net income is paid to unitholders quarterly.
B. Lee Bentley, Chairman
TOTAL REVENUE ($000)   4,019

SABRE MARKETING CORPORATION
(Public)   MISC. CONSUMER PRODUCTS
Suite 830, 355 Burrard Street, Vancouver, BC,
V6C 2G8   (604) 682-4007
SABRE MARKETING CORP. distributes and markets a full range of
hair care products under the Joico and Sunglitz brand names. As well,
the group produces and markets its own accessory line and its own hair
care range.
Anton Starling, Chairman
TOTAL REVENUE ($000)   18,545

SAINT JOHN PORT CORPORATION
(Crown)   TRANSPORTATION
133 Prince William Street, P.O. Box 6429, Station A, Saint John, NF,
E2L 4R8   (506) 636-4869
Harbour and Port Administration.
Harry P. Gaunce, Chairman
TOTAL REVENUE ($000)   11,862

SAKURA BANK (CANADA)
(Private)   BANKS
Suite 3601, Commerce Court West, P.O. Box 59, Toronto, ON,
M5L 1B9   (416) 369-8531
SAKURA BANK (CANADA) is a wholly owned subsidiary of the
Sakura Bank Ltd., Japan and is licensed to operate as a bank in Canada
with full banking powers.
A. Takahasi, Chairman Of The Board
TOTAL REVENUE ($000)   48,988

SAMOTH CAPITAL CORPORATION
(Public)   PROPERTY MGMNT & INVESTMENT
Suite 2910 TD Tower, P.O. Box 10064 Pacific Centre, 700 West
Georgia Street, Vancouver, BC,
V7Y 1B6 604 688-08
SAMOTH CAPITAL CORPORATION is engaged in real estate, mer-
chant banking and franchising.
Peter H. Thomas, Chairman & C.E.O.
TOTAL REVENUE ($000)   2,659

SAMUEL MANU-TECH INC.
See page 206 for a full company profile.

SANI-GESTION INC.
(Public)   ENVIRONMENTAL SERVICES
3383 Boulevard De La Chaudiere, Sainte-Foy, PQ,
G1X 4B8   (418) 872-8061
SANI-GESTION INC., through its subsidiaries, operates a domestic,
commercial and industrial garbage collection and transportation busi-
ness. It also sells garbage containers and compactors and operatesthree
dump sites for solid and dry material garbage.
Carol Coulombe, President & Gen. Mgr.
TOTAL REVENUE ($000)   11,388

SANWA BANK CANADA
(Private)   BANKS
Suite 4400, Canada Trust Tower, P.O. Box 525, Toronto, ON,
M5J 2S1   (416) 366-2583

SANWA BANK CANADA is a wholly owned subsidiary of the Sanwa
Bank Limited, Japan, and is licensed to operate as a bank in Canada with
full banking powers under the Bank Act 1980 as a foreign bank subsidi-
ary.
M. Eda, Chairman
TOTAL REVENUE ($000)   97,833

SARATOGA PROCESSING COMPANY LIMITED
(Public)   GAS PIPELINES
1333 West Georgia Street, 12th Floor, Vancouver, BC,
V6E 3K9   (604) 691-5500
SARATOGA PROCESSING COMPANY LIMITED operates a natural
gas processing plant in Coleman, Alberta.
William B. Caswell, President
TOTAL REVENUE ($000)   6,145

SASKATCHEWAN AUTO FUND
(Crown)   INSURANCE - PROPERTY & CASUALTY
2260 11th Avenue, Regina, SK, S4P 0J9   (306) 565-1200
SASKATCHEWAN AUTO FUND offers compulsory automobile insurance under the Automobile Accident Insurance Act. The fund is
administered by Saskatchewan Government Insurance and also operates
a salvage division.
Hon. Dwain Lingenfelter, Chairman
TOTAL REVENUE ($000)   307,881

SASKATCHEWAN GOVERNMENT INSURANCE
(Crown)   INSURANCE - PROPERTY & CASUALTY
2260 - 11th Avenue, Regina, SK, S4P 0J9   (306) 565-1200
SASKATCHEWAN GOVERNMENT INSURANCE offers property
and casualty insurance to Saskatchewan residents. It administers for the
Government of Saskatchewan a program of compulsory automobile
insurance regulated by the Automobile Accident Insurance Act.
Hon. Dwain Lingenfelter, Chairman Of The Board
TOTAL REVENUE ($000)   131,757

SASKATCHEWAN OIL AND GAS CORPORATION
See page 118 for a full company profile.

SASKATCHEWAN POWER CORPORATION
(Crown)   ELECTRICAL UTILITIES
2025 Victoria Avenue, Regina, SK, S4P 0S1   (306) 566-2121
SASKATCHEWAN POWER CORPORATION was established as a
provincial crown corporation to provide electrical services throughout
the province. The Corporation's main functions are the generation,
transmission, distribution, sale and supply of electrical energy.
Hon. Dwain Lingenfelter, Chairman
TOTAL REVENUE ($000)   762,000

SASKATCHEWAN TELECOMMUNICATIONS
(Crown)   TELEPHONE UTILITIES
2121 Saskatchewan Drive, Regina, SK, S4P 3Y2 (306) 777-2008
SASKTEL is a Provincial crown coporation that provides local and long
distance voice, data, image and text services throughout Saskatchewan.
As a member of Stentor, an alliance of Canada's major telecommunications companies, SaskTel provides a full range of national and worldwide
long distance communications services.

Marcel M. Bernard, President & C.E.O.
TOTAL REVENUE ($000)   678,443

SASKATCHEWAN WATER CORPORATION
(Crown)   OTHER SERVICES
111 Fairford Street East, Moose Jaw, SK, S6H 7X9 (306) 694-3900
SASKATCHEWAN WATER CORPORATION is responsible for all
water management functions for the Province of Saskatchewan and also
operates as a water supply utility.
Eldon Lautermilch, Chairman
TOTAL REVENUE ($000)   21,195

SASKATCHEWAN WHEAT POOL
(Non-fin Co-op)   AGRICULTURE
2625 Victoria Avenue, Regina, SK, S4T 7T9   (306) 569-4411
SASKATCHEWAN WHEAT POOL is Canada's largest agricultural
cooperative, and one of the country's major businesses. It provides
services to about 70,000 farmer-owners annually and is actively engaged
in promotion and development of agricultural policy on their behalf.
Leroy Larsen, President
TOTAL REVENUE ($000)   1,877,433

SASKATOON CREDIT UNION, LIMITED
(Fin. Co-op)   CREDIT UNIONS
Second Floor, 309 - 22nd Street East, Saskatoon, ON,
S7K 0G7   (306) 934-9000
SASKATOON CREDIT UNION, LIMITED is a member owned full
service credit union.
W. Trevor Shepstone, President
TOTAL REVENUE ($000)   45,297

SAVANNA RESOURCES LTD.
(Public)   OIL AND GAS PRODUCERS
540 - 5th Avenue S.W., Suite 810, Calgary, AB,
T2P 0M2   (403) 269-5369
SAVANNA RESOURCES LTD. is involved in the acquisition, explo-
ration and development of mining claims and rights.
John M. Alston, President
TOTAL REVENUE ($000)   666

SBN SYSTEMS INC.
See page 230 for a full company profile.

SCEPTRE INVESTMENT COUNSEL LIMITED
(Public)   INVESTMENT COMPANIES AND FUNDS
12th Floor, 26 Wellington Street East, Toronto, ON,
M5E 1W4   (416) 367-9898
SCEPTRE INVESTMENT COUNSEL LIMITED is involved in the
business of providing investment management services to institutional
and private clients.
J. Douglas Grant, Chairman
TOTAL REVENUE ($000)   19,642

SCEPTRE RESOURCES LIMITED
See page 119 for a full company profile.

SCHNEIDER CORPORATION
See page 168 for a full company profile.

SCINTILORE EXPLORATIONS LIMITED
(Public)   METAL MINES
Suite 1506, 141 Adelaide Street West, Toronto, ON,
M5H 3LS   (416) 363-1240
SCINTILORE EXPLORATIONS LIMITED holds interests in mining
claims (exploration stage) in Washington County, Maine and Panet and
Talon Townships, Quebec.
Thedore H. Polisiuk, President
TOTAL REVENUE ($000)   0

SCINTREX LIMITED
(Public)   ELECTRICAL & ELECTRONIC
222 Snidercroft Road, Concord, ON, L4K 1B5   (416) 669-2280
SCINTREX LIMITED is a high-tech company engaged in the research,
design and manufacture of geophysical and geochemical instrumentation, nuclear reactor and military monitoring devices, security instrumentation for explosive detection, analytical instruments for medical and
environmental applications and the provision of ground and airborne
exploration and consulting services worldwide.
Harold O. Seigel, Chairman
TOTAL REVENUE ($000)   13,020

SCOTSBURN CO-OPERATIVE SERVICES LTD.
(Non-fin Co-op)   FOOD PROCESSING
P.O. Box 340, Scotsburn, NS, B0K 1R0   (902) 485-8023
SCOTSBURN CO-OPERATIVE SERVICES LTD. operates in two
business segments: the processing and distribution of dairy products; and
the distribution of frozen foods.
Donald Porter, Chairman
TOTAL REVENUE ($000)   153,645

SCOTT PAPER LIMITED
See page 503 for a full company profile.

SCOTT'S HOSPITALITY INC.
See page 455 for a full company profile.

SCURRY-RAINBOW OIL LIMITED
See page 120 for a full company profile.

SEABOARD LIFE INSURANCE COMPANY
(Private)   INSURANCE - LIFE
2165 West Broadway, P.O. Box 5900, Vancouver, BC,
V6K 4N5   (604) 734-1667
SEABOARD LIFE INSURANCE COMPANY is a member of the
Worldwide Friends' Provident Insurance Group which has assets of
about $15 billion. The company markets its products Canada-wide and
is currently expanding into the Western United States.
Michael C.D. Hobbs, Chairman of the Board
TOTAL REVENUE ($000)   328,587

SEABOARD LUMBER SALES COMPANY LIMITED
(Private)   OTHER SERVICES
1190 Melville Street, Suite 600, Vancouver, BC,
V6E 3W1   (604) 661-9100
SEABOARD LUMBER SALES COMPANY LIMITED is engaged in
the marketing of forest products to overseas markets. Seaboard Lumber
Sales is jointly owned by International Forest Products, Canada Forest
Products and Weldwood of Canada.
Mr. Roberts, President & C.E.O.
TOTAL REVENUE ($000)   389,880

SEAGRAM COMPANY LTD. (THE)
See page 456 for a full company profile.

SEARS ACCEPTANCE COMPANY INC.
(Private)   FINANCE AND LEASING
222 Jarvis Street, Toronto, ON, M5B 2B8   (416) 362-1711
SEARS ACCEPTANCE COMPANY INC. purchases and handles all
customer credit accounts generated by merchandise and service sales
from Sears. Sears Acceptance is owned 100% by Sears Canada Inc. of
Toronto, Ontario.
C. Richard Sharpe, Chairman of the Board
TOTAL REVENUE ($000)   292,700

SEARS CANADA INC.
See page 369 for a full company profile.

SECHURA INC.
(Public)   MANAGEMENT AND DIVERSIFIED
P.O. Box 455, The Stock Exchange Tower, Place Victoria, Montreal,
PQ, H4Z 1J7   (514) 397-7640
SECHURA INC. holds as its only asset $6.7-million in cash following
the disposal of its 49% interest of Quoteplan plc in March 1992. In
January 1991, the company completed a major reorganization which
included the disposal of its home improvement and leisure divisions.
divisions.
David B. Hammond, President
TOTAL REVENUE ($000)   1,425

SECOND CUP LTD. (THE)
(Public)   SPECIALTY STORES
Suite 2900, 3300 Bloor Street West, Toronto, ON,
M8X 2X3   (416) 236-0055
SECOND CUP LTD. is involved in the operation of stores dedicated to
the sale of specialty coffee and related products in Canada by virtue of
its network of franchised and company owned stores.
Michael D. Bregman, Chairman & C.E.O.
TOTAL REVENUE ($000)   7,063

SECURITY HOME MORTGAGE INVESTMENT CORPORATION
(Public)   TRUST, SAVINGS AND LOAN
Suite 2180, Sun Life Plaza II, 140 - 4th Avenue S.W., Calgary, AB,
T2P 3N3   (403) 237-7840
SECURITY HOME MORTGAGE INVESTMENT CORPORA-
TION's business is to generate income by investing in a portfolio of high
quality residential and other mortgages. These investments are funded
through a combination of debt and equity issued by the company.

David M. Cockfield, Chairman
TOTAL REVENUE ($000)   20,327

SECURITY PACIFIC BANK CANADA
(Private)   BANKS
Suite 574, Four Bentall Centre, 1055 Dunsmuir Street, P.O. Box
49295, Vancouver, BC,
V7X 1L3   (604) 669-7325
SECURITY PACIFIC BANK CANADA is a commercial schedule II
bank.
Lorne K. Lodge, Chairman
TOTAL REVENUE ($000)   49,015

SEG EXPLORATION INC.
(Public)   METAL MINES
630 Rene-Levesque Blvd. West, Bureau 3200, Montreal, PQ,
H3B 1S6   (514) 866-6001
SEG EXPLORATION INC is a mining exploration company.
Pierre R. Gauthier, President du conseil
TOTAL REVENUE ($000)   0

SEINE RIVER RESOURCES INC.
(Public)   PRECIOUS METALS
Suite 600, 890 West Pender Street, Vancouver, BC,
V6C 1J9   (604) 669-6952
SEINE RIVER RESOURCES INC. is involved in the acquisition,
exploration and development of precious metal properties and oil and gas
properties.
Bernard Orlande Brynelsen, President, C.E.O & C.F.O.
TOTAL REVENUE ($000)   10 (US)

SENVEST CAPITAL INC.
(Public)   ELECTRICAL & ELECTRONIC
1140 Boul. De Maisonneuve Ouest, Suite 1180, Montreal, PQ,
H3A 1M8   (514) 281-8082
SENVEST CAPITAL INC. is engaged in the business of assembling,
marketing, and servicing electronic article surveillance systems and
microprocessor controlled closed circuit television systems. The com-
pany owns the exclusive Canadian rights to the Sensormatic System
Ekectribuc Detectors used primarily by department and retail stores.
Victor Mashaal, Chairman & President
TOTAL REVENUE ($000)   6,257

SERENPET INC.
(Public)   OIL AND GAS PRODUCERS
Suite 1500, 633 - 6th Avenue S.W., CALGARY, AB,
T2P 2Y5   (403) 262-7633
SERENPET INC. is involved in the exploration, development and
production of petroleum and natural gas in Western Canada.
Gerald D Sutton, Chairman
TOTAL REVENUE ($000)   10,413

SERVICE CORPORATION INTERNATIONAL (CANADA) LIMITED
(Public)   OTHER SERVICES
306 East 11th Avenue, Vancouver, BC, V5T 2C6   (604) 874-7247
SERVICE CORPORATION INTERNATIONAL (CANADA) LIM-
ITED operates 39 funeral homes and two cemeteries in Canada. The

cemeteries and all 39 of the funeral homes are 100% owned. The company and an affiliate of the company are engaged in the marketing of prearranged funeral services, and the company will benefit in the event its funeral homes ultimately provide such funeral services.
W. Blair Waltrip, Chairman, President & C.E.O.
TOTAL REVENUE ($000)   40,805

SFP INTERNATIONAL LTD.
(Public)   INVESTMENT COMPANIES AND FUNDS
Suite 1401, 22 Front St. W., Toronto, ON, M5J 1C4   (416) 601-1997
SFP INTERNATIONAL LTD. is a small business development corporation which invests in early state high technology companies in Onatario. The company is managed by agreement with benbaron venture corporation.
Riccardo Tattoni, Chairman
TOTAL REVENUE ($000)   493

SHANNON ENVIRONMENTAL LTD.
(Public)   ENVIRONMENTAL SERVICES
309 Cherry Street, Toronto, ON, M5A 3L3   (416) 365-2354
SHANNON ENVIRONMENTAL is engaged in the refining of used lubrication oil at a plant in the port industrial district of Toronto.
Richard J. Parton, President
TOTAL REVENUE ($000)   0

SHAW COMMUNICATIONS INC.
See page 332 for a full company profile.

SHAW INDUSTRIES LTD.
See page 504 for a full company profile.

SHELL CANADA LIMITED
See page 121 for a full company profile.

SHELTER OIL & GAS LTD.
(Public)   OIL AND GAS FIELD SERVICES
Suite 3600, 350 - 7th Ave S.W., Calgary, AB,
T2P 3N9   (403) 264-8160
SHELTER OIL & GAS LTD. is involved in resource services through the Blue Bird drilling division and in the exploration and development of oil and gas, and mineral properties.
John A. Tessari, President & C.E.O.
TOTAL REVENUE ($000)   5,674

SHERMAG INC.
(Public)   HOME FURNISHINGS
2171 Rue King Ouest, Sherbrooke, PQ, J1J 2G1   (819) 566-1515
SHERMAG INC. is one of the largest furniture manufacturers in Canada. Its products include solid oak, solid maple and veneer funiture. New divisions manufacture modern design, ready-to-assemble and upholstered furniture.
Serge Racine, Chairman, President & C.E.O.
TOTAL REVENUE ($000)   28,124

SHERRITT INC.
See page 457 for a full company profile.

SHERWOOD CREDIT UNION
(Fin. Co-op)   CREDIT UNIONS
1960 Albert Street, Regina, SK, S4P 2T4   (306) 780-1700
SHERWOOD CREDIT UNION LIMITED is a credit union operating in Saskatchewan providing a wide range of financial services.
Dale Hillmer, Chief Executive Offficer
TOTAL REVENUE ($000)   58,032

SHIRMAX FASHIONS LTD.
(Public)   CLOTHING STORES
3901 Jarry Street East, Montreal, PQ, H1Z 2G1   (514) 729-3333
SHIRMAX owns and operates Shirley K. Maternity, Addition-elle, Thyme en Compagnie and Gigi. Shirley K. Maternity and Thyme en Compagnie are engaged in the retail sale of maternity apparel and Addition-elle in the retail sale of women's large-size apparel.
Max Konigsberg, Chairman, President & C.E.O.
TOTAL REVENUE ($000)   96,771

SHL SYSTEMHOUSE INC.
See page 469 for a full company profile.

SICO INC.
See page 240 for a full company profile.

SIDBEC-DOSCO INC.
(Crown)   STEEL
300 Rue Leo-Pariseau, P.O. Box 2000, Succ. Place Du Parc,
Montreal, PQ, H2W 2S7   (514) 286-8600
SIDBEC-DOSCO INC. manufactures a wide range of steel products. It has three plants in Quebec at Contrecoeur, Montreal and Longueuil and has a fourth plant at Etobicoke, Ontario. Sidbec-Dosco sells its products to service centres, to the construction and household appliance sectors and to the automobile industry.
Pierre Laurin, President du Conseil
TOTAL REVENUE ($000)   466,591

SIEMENS GROUP
(Private)   ELECTRICAL & ELECTRONIC
1180 Courtneypark Drive East, Mississauga, ON,
L5T 1P2   (416) 673-1995
SIEMENS GROUP designs, manufactures, markets and services electrical and electronic products and systems for residential and commercial buildings, utilities, science, governments, industry, automotive OEM and healthcare.
Hon. D.S. Macdonald, Chairman
TOTAL REVENUE ($000)   306,021

SIKAMAN GOLD RESOURCES LTD.
(Public)   PRECIOUS METALS
Suite 1401, 22 Front Street West, Toronto, ON,
M5J 1C4   (416) 867-9087
SIKAMAN GOLD RESOURCES is a Canadian based natural resource company engaged in the exploration and development of gold resource projects. Sikaman has a 25.54% interest in a producing gold mine in Ghana, West Africa, and it is anticipating additional production from its two most advanced gold projects in California, and Manitoba, Canada commencing early 1993.

A. Thomas D. Griffis, President & C.E.O.
TOTAL REVENUE ($000)   299

SILCORP LIMITED
See page 370 for a full company profile.

SIMARD-BEAUDRY INC.
(Public)   MISC. INDUSTRIAL PRODUCTS
4230 Saint-Elzear Blvd East, Laval, PQ,
H7E 4P2   (514) 329-4747
SIMARD-BEAUDRY INC.'s operations are organized into three divisions: the production division, which includes a stone crushing plant, a quarry, a concrete block plant and an asphalt plant; the major projects division, specializing in major civil engineering projects; and the municipal works division, which executes various construction and paving projects.
Mario Beaulieu, Chairman
TOTAL REVENUE ($000)   106,343

SIMCOE ERIE INVESTORS LIMITED
See page 430 for a full company profile.

SIMMONDS COMMUNICATIONS LTD.
(Public)   WHOLESALE DISTRIBUTORS
975 Dillingham Road, Pickering, ON,
L1W 3B2   (416) 287-2789
SIMMONDS COMMUNICATIONS LTD. is a national distributor of audio and communications equipment.
John G. Simmonds, Chairman, President & C.E.O.
TOTAL REVENUE ($000)   15,547

SINO PAC INTERNATIONAL INVESTMENTS INC.
(Public)   MANAGEMENT AND DIVERSIFIED
Suite 515, 800 West Pender Street, Vancouver, BC,
V6C 2V6   (604) 682-3290
SINO PAC INTERNATIONAL INVESTMENTS INC. has investments in mineral exploration, property development and development projects.
S.L. Liang, Chairman
TOTAL REVENUE ($000)   2,115

SINTRA LTD.
(Public)   CONTRACTORS
4984 Place De La Savane, Montreal, PQ, H4P 2M9 (514) 341-5331
SINTRA LTD. is a construction firm whose revenues are derived from the construction of roads and related works, sewer and water lines and civil works, quarries and crushing operations, pipe-line and mechanical works, ready-mix concrete operations and production of bituminous concrete.
Michel Roullet, Chairman
TOTAL REVENUE ($000)   140,737

SKYLINE GOLD CORPORATION
(Public)   PRECIOUS METALS
Suite 301, 675 West Hastings Street, Vancouver, BC,
V6B 1N2   (604) 683-6865
SKYLINE GOLD CORPORATION operates a gold mine in Northwestern British Columbia. Production of precious metals, principally gold.

Ronald C. Shon, President & C.E.O.
TOTAL REVENUE ($000)   4,403

SLATER INDUSTRIES INC.
See page 207 for a full company profile.

SLOCAN FOREST PRODUCTS LTD.
See page 147 for a full company profile.

SM PRAIRIE MANAGEMENT LTD.
(Non-fin Co-op)   FOOD PROCESSING
P.O. Box 190, Saskatoon, SK, S7K 3K7   (306) 244-1335
SM PRAIRIE MANAGEMENT LTD. is a processor of canola and sunflowers in Western Canada and marketer of canola oil and meal products in the North American marketplace. It is jointly owned by the Saskatchewan Wheat Pool and Manitoba Pool Elevators.
TOTAL REVENUE ($000)   187,249

SNC-LAVALIN GROUP INC.
See page 505 for a full company profile.

SNT LTD.
(Public)   INVESTMENT COMPANIES AND FUNDS
Suite 5000, P.O. Box 150, 1 First Canadian Place, Toronto, ON,
M5X 1H3   (416) 359-4630
SNT LTD. invests its funds in The Bank of Nova Scotia common shares. The purpose of the company is to provide a vehicle through which different investment ofjectives with respect to participation in BNS common shares may be satisfied.
Frederick J. Troop, President & C.E.O.
TOTAL REVENUE ($000)   7,434

SOBEYS INC.
(Private)   FOOD STORES
115 King Street, Stellarton, NS, B0K 1S0   (902) 752-8371
SOBEYS INC. primarily distributes food products throughout the four Atlantic provinces, the Gaspe region of Quebec and Southern Ontario.
David F. Sobey, Chairman
TOTAL REVENUE ($000)   2,035,327

SOCANAV INC.
(Public)   TRANSPORTATION
1801 McGill College, Suite 1470, Montreal, PQ,
H3A 2N4   (514) 284-9535
SOCANAV is involved in the marine transportation of bulk liquids and the sale of public transportation vehicles.
Michel Gaucher, Chairman & President
TOTAL REVENUE ($000)   80,281

SOCIETE D'EXPLORATION MINIERE MAZARIN INC.
(LA)
(Public)   METAL MINES
Bureau 301, 81, Rue Saint-Pierre, Quebec, PQ,
G1K 4A3   (418) 694-1123
SOCIETE D'EXPLORATION MINIERE MAZARIN INC. (LA) is involved in the acquisition, exploration and development of mineral properties.

Michel Cyr, Chairman
TOTAL REVENUE ($000)   78

SOCIETE D'EXPLORATION MINIERE VIOR INC.
(Public)   PRECIOUS METALS
81 St-Pierre, Bureau 301, Quebec, PQ, G1K 4A3   (418) 692-2678
SOCIETE D'EXPLORATION MINIERE VIOR INC. is involved in
mining exploration.
Claude St-Jacques,
TOTAL REVENUE ($000)   1,473

**SOCIETE DE PORTEFEUILLE DU GROUPE
DESJARDINS ASSURANCES**
(Fin. Co-op)   INSURANCE - PROPERTY & CASUALTY
6300 Boul. de la Rive-Sud, Levis, PQ, G6V 6P9   (418) 835-4840
SOCIETE DE PORTEFEUILLE DU GROUPE DESJARDINS AS-
SURANCES GENERALES is in the business of selling general insur-
ance.
Serge Simard, President Du Conseil
TOTAL REVENUE ($000)   335,137

SOCIETE GENERALE (CANADA)
(Private)   BANKS
1155 University Street, Suite 1100, Montreal, PQ,
H3B 3A7   (514) 875-0330
SOCIETE GENERALE (CANADA) is licensed to operate as a bank in
Canada with full banking powers. The Company is a wholly owned
subsidiary of Societe Generale, France.
Bernard Lorain, Chairman
TOTAL REVENUE ($000)   88,107

SOCIETE GENERALE DE FINANCEMENT DU QUEBEC
(Crown)   MANAGEMENT AND DIVERSIFIED
600 De La Gauchetiere Ouest, Bureau 1700, Montreal, PQ,
H3B 4L8   (514) 876-9290
SOCIETE GENERALE DE FINANCEMENT DU QUEBEC is a management company wholly owned by the Quebec government. The
group's assets are concentrated in 4 key industries: forest products,
energy equipment, petrochemicals and aluminum production. SGF has
direct and indirect investments in some 15 subsidiaries and affiliated
companies.
Marc G. Fortier, Chairman, President & C.E.O.
TOTAL REVENUE ($000)   625,963

**SOCIETE QUEBECOISE D'EXPLORATION
MINIERE-SOQUEM**
(Crown)   METAL MINES
Place Belle Cour, 2590, Boul. Laurier, Bureau 600, Sainte-Foy, PQ,
G1V 4M6   (418) 658-5400
SOCIETE QUEBECOISE D'EXPLORATION MINIERE-SOQUEM
is involved in the acquisition, exploration and development of mineral
properties.
Albert Jessop, Chairman Of The Board
TOTAL REVENUE ($000)   3,839

**SOCIETE QUEBECOISE D'INITIATIVES
AGRO-ALIMENTAIRES**
(Crown)   AGRICULTURE
Parc Samuel Holland, 1275, Chemin Sainte-Foy, Bureau 284,
Quebec, PQ, G1S 4S5   (418) 643-2238
SOCIETE QUEBECOISE D'INITIATIVES AGRO-ALIMEN-
TAIRES was founded in 1975 with a mission of contributing to the
development of the commercial fisheries and agricultural industries.
Andre Martel, President Du Conseil
TOTAL REVENUE ($000)   (850)

SOCIETE QUEBECOISE D'INITIATIVES PETROLIERES
(Crown)   OIL AND GAS PRODUCERS
1175 Rue de Lavigerie, Suite 180, Sainte-Foy, PQ,
G1V 4P1   (418) 651-9543
SOCIETE QUEBECOISE D'INITIATIVES PETROLIERES's objec-
tive is to explore for, develop, produce, store, transport, purchase, import
and sell hydrocarbons in liquid or gaseous form, directly or in partnership
with other firms.
Louise Sicard, Chairman of the Board
TOTAL REVENUE ($000)   32,309

SODARCAN, INC.
(Public)   FINANCE AND LEASING
1140 De Maisonneuve Blvd. West, Suite 701, Montreal, PQ,
H3A 1M8   (514) 288-0100
SODARCAN, INC. operates in three main sectors, insurance brokerage,
reinsurance brokerage, and actuarial consulting.
Robert Parizeau, Chairman President & C.E.O.
TOTAL REVENUE ($000)   86,376

SODISCO INC.
(Private)   WHOLESALE DISTRIBUTORS
303 Industrial Blvd. East, P.O. Box 70, Victoriaville, PQ,
G6P 6S6   (819) 758-0562
SODISCO INC. is involved in the distribution of hardware and renova-
tion products. Sodisco is wholly owned by Unigesco Inc. of Montreal.
Douglass McDougall, President & C.E.O.
TOTAL REVENUE ($000)   370,700

SOFTKEY SOFTWARE PRODUCTS INC.
See page 470 for a full company profile.

SONOR INVESTMENTS LIMITED
(Public)   INVESTMENT COMPANIES AND FUNDS
Suite 2300, Box 82, 1 Dundas Street West, Toronto, ON,
M5G 1Z3   (416) 971-5101
SONOR INVESTMENTS LIMITED is an investment holding com-
pany.
R. Alan Broadbent, Chairman
TOTAL REVENUE ($000)   321

SONORA GOLD CORP.
See page 58 for a full company profile.

SONY OF CANADA LTD.
(Private)   WHOLESALE DISTRIBUTORS
1370 Sony Place, P.O. Box 9400, Winnipeg, MB,
R3C 3C3   (204) 474-5200
SONY OF CANADA LTD. is engaged in the distribution of sony products in Canada.
Albert D. Cohen, Chairman & C.E.O.
TOTAL REVENUE ($000)   515,563

SOTTOMAYOR BANK CANADA
(Private)   BANKS
1102 Dundas St. W., Toronto, ON, M6J 1X2   (416) 588-8597
SOTTOMAYOR BANK CANADA is a Canadian Schedule II chartered bank.
Fernando T. De Almeida, Chairman
TOTAL REVENUE ($000)   5,999

SOUTHAM INC.
See page 333 for a full company profile.

SOUTHERN COPPER CORP.
(Public)   PRECIOUS METALS
1320-885 West Georgia St., Vancouver, BC,
V6C 3E8   (604) 689-7842
SOUTHERN COPPER CORP. is engaged in the exploration and development of mineral resources properties.
H. Lutz Klingmann, President
TOTAL REVENUE ($000)   4,214

SOUTHLAND CANADA, INC.
(Private)   FOOD STORES
3185 Willingdon Green, Burnaby, BC, V5G 4P3   (604) 299-0711
SOUTHLAND CANADA, INC. operates convenience stores. Southland Canada is a wholly owned subsidiary of Southland Corporation of Dallas, Texas.
Frank Farr, V.P. General Manager
TOTAL REVENUE ($000)   690,932

SPAR AEROSPACE LIMITED
See page 231 for a full company profile.

SPECTRUM SIGNAL PROCESSING INC.
(Public)   ELECTRICAL & ELECTRONIC
8525 Baxter Place, 100 Production Court, Burnaby, BC,
V5A 4V7   (604) 421-5422
SPECTRUM SIGNAL PROCESSING INC. designs and manufactures Digital Signal Processing (DSP) computer hardware and software for a variety of computers based on the IBM PC/XT/AT, VMEBus, SBus and FutureBus+ platforms. Applications of Spectrum's products include multimedia, digital cellular, digital audio, medical diagnostics, radar, sonar, defence communications and surveillance and many more industrial uses.
Michael Mertens, Chairman & C.E.O.
TOTAL REVENUE ($000)   8,586

SPORTS EXPERTS INC.
(Private)   WHOLESALE DISTRIBUTORS
4141 Autoroute Laval Ouest, Laval, PQ, H7P 4W6   (514) 687-5200
SPORTS EXPERTS INC. is a national distributor of leisure wear and sporting goods in Canada.
Jean-Claude Merizzi, President Du Conseil
TOTAL REVENUE ($000)   178,568

SPORTSCENE RESTAURANTS INC.
(Public)   FOOD SERVICES
426 Rue Sainte-Helene, Bureau 300, Montreal, PQ,
H2Y 2K7   (514) 849-9376
SPORTSCENE RESTAURANTS INC. owns and operates 31 La Cage aux Sports chicken and rib restaurants, including 20 franchises. It also owns and operates Biddle's Jazz & Ribs.
Donald W. Seal, Chairman, C.E.O. & C.F.O.
TOTAL REVENUE ($000)   23,504

SR TELECOM INC.
(Public)   ELECTRICAL & ELECTRONIC
8150 Trans Canada Highway, Saint-Laurent, PQ,
H4S 1M5   (514) 335-1210
SR TELECOM INC. designs, manufactures and sells point-to-multipoint microwave radio systems for use by public and private telephone networks worldwide. The company sells primarily to telephone companieswhich use its systems as part of their telephone networks. A second group of customers consists of private users, including power utilities and resource companies.
Donald M. Beaupre, Chairman & C.E.O.
TOTAL REVENUE ($000)   63,285

ST ANDREW GOLDFIELDS LTD.
(Public)   PRECIOUS METALS
166 Pearl Street, Toronto, ON, M5H 1L3   (416) 597-0969
ST ANDREW GOLDFIELDS LTD. is engaged in the development and underground exploration of mining properties. The Company's mining properties are located in Stock Township, District of Cochrane, Ontario.
Herbert S. Gasser, President
TOTAL REVENUE ($000)   9,492

ST. CLAIR PAINT & WALLPAPER CORPORATION
(Public)   MISC. CONSUMER PRODUCTS
2600 Steeles Avenue West, Concord, ON,
L4K 3C8   (416) 738-0080
ST. CLAIR PAINT & WALLPAPER CORPORATION, through its subsidiaries, is a retailer of paints, wallpaper, decorative supplies and related products through its 48 company-owned and 142 franchised locations. The company is also a manufacturer of wall and window coverings.
Louis Litwin, Chairman & C.E.O.
TOTAL REVENUE ($000)   59,192

ST. GENEVIEVE RESOURCES LTD.
(Public)   METAL MINES
Suite 3200, 630 Rene Levesque Blvd. W., Montreal, PQ,
H3B 1S6   (514) 866-6001
ST. GENEVIEVE RESOURCES LTD. is involved in the acquisition, exploration and development of mineral properties.

Pierre R. Gauthier, Chairman
TOTAL REVENUE ($000)   12,858

ST. JOHN'S PORT CORPORATION
(Crown)   TRANSPORTATION
P.O. Box 6178, St. John's, NF, A1C 5X8   (709) 772-4664
ST. JOHN'S PORT CORPORATION manages the port of St. John's, Newfoundland.
Fred Milley, Chairman
TOTAL REVENUE ($000)   3,722

ST. LAWRENCE CEMENT INC.
See page 506 for a full company profile.

ST. LAWRENCE SEAWAY AUTHORITY (THE)
(Crown)   TRANSPORTATION
360 Albert Street, Ottawa, ON, K1R 7X7   (613) 598-4600
ST. LAWRENCE SEAWAY AUTHORITY was established to construct and operate a deep waterway between the Port of Montreal and Lake Erie together with such works and other property, including bridges incidental to the deep waterway, as deemed necessary by the Governor in Council.
Glendon R. Stewart, President
TOTAL REVENUE ($000)   79,453

ST-HUBERT GROUP (THE)
(Private)   FOOD SERVICES
2 Place Laval, Suite 500, Laval, PQ, H7N 5N6   (514) 668-4500
THE ST-HUBERT GROUP is involved in the restaurant business.
Rene Leger, Chairman
TOTAL REVENUE ($000)   190,044

STANDARD BROADCASTING CORPORATION LIMITED
(Private)   BROADCASTING
2 St Clair Ave. West, Toronto, ON, M4V 1L6   (416) 960-9911
STANDARD BROADCASTING CORPORATION LIMITED has operations in broadcasting, comprising the operations of seven radio stations and one television station, production, which consists primarily of video tape duplication and the production of television programs, and cable television. Operations are carried out in Canada and the United States.
Allan Slaight, President & C.E.O.
TOTAL REVENUE ($000)   243,978

STANDARD CHARTERED BANK OF CANADA
(Private)   BANKS
14th Floor, 55 University Avenue, P.O. Box 14, Toronto, ON, M5J 2H7   (416) 363-8521
STANDARD CHARTERED BANK OF CANADA is a wholly owned subsidiary of The Standard Chartered Bank of London, England. The bank operates as a Schedule II bank offering international trade commercial retail banking services with special emphasis on import/export, i.o.c., and trade bill financing for small businesses.
Roderick L. Henry, Chairman
TOTAL REVENUE ($000)   35,298

STANDARD LIFE ASSURANCE COMPANY (THE)
(Private)   INSURANCE - LIFE
1245 Sherbrooke Street West, Montreal, PQ, H3G 1G3   (514) 284-6711
THE STANDARD LIFE ASSURANCE COMPANY is a mutual company headquartered in Montreal and with branch offices in 24 Canadian cities, the Company serves the life insurance and pension needs of the Canadian public, and offers a complete range of financial services to its many clients and policy holders. The company is a branch of Standard Life Assurance Co. of Scotland.
N. Lessels, Chairman
TOTAL REVENUE ($000)   2,098,278

STARMIN MINING INC.
(Public)   PRECIOUS METALS
Suite 1101, 10 King Street East, Toronto, ON, M5C 1C3   (416) 366-8058
STARMIN MINING INC. is engaged in mining exploration, in Canada and throughout the world. Recently Starmin acquired a copper-gold porphyry deposit in the Philippines. This deposit contains in excess of 155 million tons in reserves.
B. Gajaria, President & C.E.O.
TOTAL REVENUE ($000)   35

STATE BANK OF INDIA (CANADA)
(Private)   BANKS
P.O. Box 81, Royal Bank Plaza, N. Tower, Suite 800, Toronto, M5J 2J2   (416) 865-0414
STATE BANK OF INDIA (CANADA) is a wholly owned subsidiary of State Bank of India and is licenced to act as a foreign bank with full banking powers.
N. Krishnan, President & C.E.O.
TOTAL REVENUE ($000)   7,267

STATE FARM GROUP
(Private)   INSURANCE - PROPERTY & CASUALTY
100 Consilium Place, Scarborough, ON,   (416) 290-4100
STATE FARM GROUP is a property and casualty insurance company.
Earl Sheeler, Regional Vice President
TOTAL REVENUE ($000)   606,557

STELCO INC.
See page 208 for a full company profile.

STONE-CONSOLIDATED INC.
(Private)   EAST COAST FORESTRY
800 Rene-Levesque Blvd. West, Montreal, PQ, H3B 1Y9   (514) 875-2160
STONE-CONSOLIDATED INC. is an Eastern Canadian forest products and packaging company. Production and sales operations function under three business groups: pulp and paper; North American packaging; and Europa Carton AG. Pulp and paper operations are centered in Quebec and New Brunswick, North American Packaging has plants across Canada and Europa Carton is headquartered in Germany.
T. Oscar Strangeland, Chairman & C.E.O.
TOTAL REVENUE ($000)   1,939,464

STRATMIN INC.
(Public)   OTHER MINES
Suite 3200, 630 Rene-Levesque Blvd. W., Montreal, PQ,
H3B 1S6   (514) 866-6001
STRATMIN INC. is involved in graphite mining operations and operates
a processing plant located near Mont-Laurier, Quebec.
Pierre Gauthier, Chairman
TOTAL REVENUE ($000)   11,483

STRIKE ENERGY INC.
(Public)   OIL AND GAS PRODUCERS
P.O. Box 12139, Suite 1780, 555 West Hastings Street, Vancouver,
BC, V6B 4N6   (604) 688-7002
STRIKE ENERGY INC. is involved in oil and gas production primarily
in southern Saskatchewan.
Edward S. Sampson, President & C.E.O.
TOTAL REVENUE ($000)   2,259

SUMITOMO BANK OF CANADA
(Private)   BANKS
Suite 1400, P.O. Box 172, Ernst & Young Tower, Toronto Dominion
Centre, Toronto, M5K 1H6   (416) 368-4766
SUMITOMO BANK OF CANADA is a Schedule II bank.
H. Yoshida, President & C.E.O.
TOTAL REVENUE ($000)   33,432

SUMITOMO CANADA LIMITED
(Private)   WHOLESALE DISTRIBUTORS
Suite 7010, 1 First Canadian Place, Toronto, ON,
M5X 1C8   (416) 860-3800
SUMITOMO CANADA LIMITED is an international trading company.
It is a wholly owned subsidiary of Sumitomo Corporation of Japan.
T. Hirano, President & C.E.O.
TOTAL REVENUE ($000)   862,386

SUMMIT RESOURCES LIMITED
(Public)   OIL AND GAS PRODUCERS
Suite 2300, 144 - 4th Avenue S.W., Calgary, AB,
T2P 3N4   (403) 269-4400
SUMMIT RESOURCES LIMITED explores for, develops, produces
and markets crude oil and natural gas in Western Canada.
Ernest S. Rady, Chairman
TOTAL REVENUE ($000)   28,873

SUMNER SPORTS INC.
(Public)   WHOLESALE DISTRIBUTORS
405 Galilee Avenue, Frontenac Industrial Park, Quebec, PQ,
G1P 4M6   (418) 527-5031
SUMNER SPORTS INC. is a wholesale distributor of camping, hunting
and fishing gear and outdoor clothing. It operates in Quebec, Ontario, the
Maritimes and the Western provinces.
Serge Dompierre, President & C.E.O.
TOTAL REVENUE ($000)   20,180

SUN ICE LIMITED
(Public)   CLOTHING AND TEXTILES
1001 - 1st Street S.E., Calgary, AB, T2G 5G3   (403) 261-4780

SUN ICE LIMITED designs, manufactures, markets and distributes an
extensive line of skiwear, golf outerwear and active sports and leisure
wear. These products are distributed to retail stores throughout Canada,
the United States and Europe.
Sylvia Rempel, President & C.E.O.
TOTAL REVENUE ($000)   15,811

SUN LIFE ASSURANCE COMPANY OF CANADA
(Private)   INSURANCE - LIFE
Sun Life Centre, 150 King Street West, Toronto, ON,
M5H 1J9   (416) 979-9966
SUN LIFE ASSURANCE COMPANY OF CANADA is a mutual life
insurance company offering a range of financial services and products
for groups and individuals including life, health and disability insurance,
annuities and pensions. Through subsidiaries, Sun Life offers mutual
funds, investment management services, trust services and savings plans.
Sun Life operates in Canada, the U.S., the U.K., and Asia.
John D. McNeil, Chairman & C.E.O.
TOTAL REVENUE ($000)   8,221,630

SUNCOR INC.
See page 122 for a full company profile.

SURREY METRO SAVINGS CREDIT UNION
(Public)   CREDIT UNIONS
15117 - 101 Avenue, Fourth Floor, Surrey, BC,
V3R 8P7   (604) 581-2661
SURREY METRO SAVINGS CREDIT UNION operates primarily in
the Fraser Valley region of British Columbia. It also operates two
insurance agencies and a property development company. The principal
business of the company is to attract retail deposits to fund conventional
residential first mortgage loans.
William M. Vogel, Chairman
TOTAL REVENUE ($000)   115,753

**SURVIVANCE, COMPAGNIE MUTUELLE
D'ASSURANCE-VIE (LA)**
(Fin. Co-op)   INSURANCE - LIFE
C.P. 10000, 1555, Rue Girouard Ouest, Saint-Hyacinthe, PQ,
J2S 7C8   (514) 773-6051
SURVIVANCE, COMPAGNIE MUTUELLE D'ASSURANCE-VIE
has offices in Quebec and New Brunswick.
Lucien Brosseau, President & Chef De La Direction
TOTAL REVENUE ($000)   44,247

SUZUKI CANADA INC.
(Private)   WHOLESALE DISTRIBUTORS
100 East Beaver Creek Road, Richmond Hill, ON,
L4B 1J6   (416) 889-2600
SUZUKI CANADA INC. is a wholesale distributor of automobiles,
motorcycles and outboard motors. Suzuki Canada is a wholly owned
subsidiary of Suzuki Motor Corporation of Japan.
Masataka Oh, President & C.E.O.
TOTAL REVENUE ($000)   204,891

SWISS BANK CORPORATION (CANADA)
(Private)   BANKS
P.O. Box 103, Suite 780, 207 Queens Quay West, Toronto, ON,
M5J 1A7   (416) 203-2180
SWISS BANK CORPORATION (CANADA) is wholly owned subsidi-
ary of Swiss Bank Corporation of Basle, one of Switzerland's leading
banks.
Alberto Togni, Chairman
TOTAL REVENUE ($000)   187,799

SYNERGISTICS INDUSTRIES LIMITED
(Public)   MISC. INDUSTRIAL PRODUCTS
5915 Airport Road, Suite 425, Mississauga, ON,
L4V 1T1   (416) 673-1213
SYNERGISTICS INDUSTRIES LIMITED engaged in the manufacture
and in Canada and the United States of high quality plastic compounds,
including polyvinyl chloride compounds. These are sold directly to
industrial customers who apply them in the manufacture of numerous
products.
R.A Noble, Chairman & C.E.O.
TOTAL REVENUE ($000)   163,215

SYNEX INTERNATIONAL INC.
(Public)   MANAGEMENT AND DIVERSIFIED
Suite 800, 1188 West Georgia Street, Vancouver, BC,
V6E 4A2   (604) 688-8271
SYNEX INTERNATIONAL INC. is diversified, having three distinct
operating divisions involving energy project funding and development,
engineering consulting services and computer software development and
marketing.
Alan W. Stephens, President & C.E.O.
TOTAL REVENUE ($000)   3,203

T & H RESOURCES LTD.
(Public)   OIL AND GAS PRODUCERS
Suite 420, 111 Richmond Street West, Toronto, ON,
M5H 2G4   (416) 947-1087
T & H RESOURCES LTD. holds interests in several mineral properties.
The company is currently exploring for minerals in Canada and Mexico
and hopes to acquire a permit in the Central African Republic to explore
for diamonds.
John A. Pollock, President & C.E.O.
TOTAL REVENUE ($000)   (56)

T.G. BRIGHT & CO., LIMITED
See page 169 for a full company profile.

TAIGA FOREST PRODUCTS LTD.
(Public)   WHOLESALE DISTRIBUTORS
P.O. Box 80329, Burnaby, BC, V5H 3X6   (604) 438-1471
TAIGA FOREST PRODUCTS LTD. is a distributer of building products
including lumber, panelboards, insulation, wood mouldings, and doors.
Mr. P. Hamill, President & C.E.O.
TOTAL REVENUE ($000)   212,531

TALBORNE CAPITAL CORPORATION
(Public)   TRUST, SAVINGS AND LOAN
777 Hornby Street, Vancouver, BC, V6Z 1S4   (604) 685-2489

TALBORNE CAPITAL has been organized to acquire and hold common shares of First City Trust Company and to act as a financial
intermediary services company. Upon conclusion of the offering, First
City Financial Corporation Ltd. will control 80.3% of the outstanding
common shares of the company which, in turn will control 98.4% of the
outstanding common shares of First City Trust Company.
Brent S. Belzberg, President & C.E.O.
TOTAL REVENUE ($000)   4,205

TALISMAN ENERGY INC.
See page 123 for a full company profile.

TANDEM RESOURCES LTD
(Public)   OIL AND GAS PRODUCERS
P.O. Box 6, Suite 860, 1 First Canadian Place, Toronto,
M5X 1B1   (416) 862-7885
TANDEM RESOURCES LTD. is involved in the acquisition, explora-
tion and development of mineral properties.
Stanley G. Hawkins, President
TOTAL REVENUE ($000)   917

TARO INDUSTRIES LIMITED
(Public)   OIL AND GAS FIELD SERVICES
616 - 58 Avenue S.E., Calgary, AB,
T2H 0P8   (403) 253-8511
TARO INDUSTRIES LIMITED is involved in two business segments:
the oilfield services segment consists of oil and gas well drilling and the
installation and repair of oilfield pumping units; the manufacturing
segment consists of the manufacture of oilwell gear reducers and oilwell
pumping units, design and manufacture of oil and gas production,
processing equipment and general fabrication.
Richard G. Burge, Chairman Of The Board
TOTAL REVENUE ($000)   11,036

TARRAGON OIL AND GAS LIMITED
See page 124 for a full company profile.

TASEKO MINES LIMITED
(Public)   OIL AND GAS PRODUCERS
Suite 1020, 800 West Pender Street, Vancouver, BC,
V6C 2V6   (604) 684-6365
TASEKO MINES LIMITED is focused on the development of Canada's
largest copper-gold project, the Fish Lake deposit. Engineering and
permitting programs are now underway for production feasiblilty.
Robert G. Hunter, Chairman
TOTAL REVENUE ($000)   178

TCG INTERNATIONAL INC.
See page 187 for a full company profile.

TECK CORPORATION
See page 21 for a full company profile.

TECSYN INTERNATIONAL INC.
(Public)   MISC. INDUSTRIAL PRODUCTS
113 - 115 Cushman Road, Unit 62, Box 845, St. Catharines, ON,
L2R 6Z4   (416) 687-8811

TECSYN INTERNATIONAL INC. is a North American manufacturer of synthetic baler twine, tying twines, cable fillers, rope, automotive restraint and convenience nets, and powdered metal products.
Juri Koor, Chairman
TOTAL REVENUE ($000)   31,536

TEE-COMM ELECTRONICS INC.
(Public)   ELECTRICAL & ELECTRONIC
775 Main Street East, Milton, ON, L9T 3Z3   (416) 878-8181
TEE-COMM ELECTRONICS INC. is primarily a manufacturer and distributor of satellite television receiving systems for private homeowners use. The company also sells cable-like television programming from coast tocoast in Canada through its extensive branch network. Tee-Comm also distributes ceiling fans, lighting and other consumer products. also distributes ceiling fans, lighting and other consumer products.
Alvin G. Bahnman, Chairman, President & C.E.O.
TOTAL REVENUE ($000)   37,423

TELE-METROPOLE INC.
See page 334 for a full company profile.

TELEBEC LTEE
(Public)   TELEPHONE UTILITIES
1126 Chemin St-Louis, Sillery, PQ, G1S 1E5   (418) 684-3006
TELEBEC LTEE operates a provincially regulated telephone utility in Quebec.
Louis A. Tanguay, Chairman & C.E.O.
TOTAL REVENUE ($000)   176,912

TELEDYNE CANADA, LIMITED
(Public)   METAL FABRICATORS
15 Brydon Dr, Rexdale, ON, M9W 4M8   (416) 746-2100
TELEDYNE CANADA, LIMITED is engaged in industrial services and metals fabrication. The industrial services segment includes tank trailer transportation, production of mining equipment & vehicles, welding wire and accessories. The metals fabrication segment produces cabs and parts for off-road equipment, warehouses steels and produces carbide inserts, sod harvesters and specialty fork lift trucks.
G.L. Riley, Chairman & President
TOTAL REVENUE ($000)   66,458

TELEGLOBE INC.
See page 471 for a full company profile.

TELEMEDIA INC.
(Public)   PUBLISHING & PRINTING
Suite 500, 1411 Peel Street, Montreal, PQ,
H3A 1S5   (514) 845-6291
TELEMEDIA is engaged in broadcasting, which consists primarily of the operation of radio stations in the provinces of Quebec and Ontario, and publishing, which involves primarily the publishing and distribution of consumer magazines, weekly newspapers, book and consumer coupon distribution.
Philippe De Gaspe Beaubien, Chairman
TOTAL REVENUE ($000)   230,916

TELESAT CANADA
(Private)   TELECOMMUNICATIONS
1601 Telesat Court, Gloucester, ON, K1B 5P4   (613) 748-0123
TELESAT CANADA is a national communications common carrier providing telecommunications and broadcast distribution services. Telesat is 96% owned by an alliance of Canadian telephone companies and Spar Aerospace Limited.
Raymond Cyr, Chairman Of The Board
TOTAL REVENUE ($000)   196,652

TELUS CORPORATION
See page 308 for a full company profile.

TEMBEC INC.
See page 148 for a full company profile.

TESMA INTERNATIONAL INC.
(Private)   AUTOMOTIVE
300 Edgeley Blvd., Concord, ON, L4K 3Y3   (416) 669-5444
TESMA INTERNATIONAL INC. is one of the four principal subsidiaries of Magna International Inc. The company manufactures engine and transmission components, automotive systems and other products.
TOTAL REVENUE ($000)   192,000

TEXACO CANADA PETROLEUM INC.
(Public)   OIL AND GAS PRODUCERS
Suite 3100, 150 -6th Avenue S.W., Calgary, AB,
T2P 4M5   (403) 234-2900
TEXACO CANADA PETROLEUM INC. is a Calgary based company active in the exploration, development, production and marketing of crude oil and natural gas, primarily in Western Canada. The company was incorporated in Canada in September 1988, and began operating in January 1989.
Alan C. Cocks, President & C.E.O.
TOTAL REVENUE ($000)   27,856

TEXTRON CANADA LIMITED
(Private)   ELECTRICAL & ELECTRONIC
40 Westminster St, Providence, RI, 02903   (401) 421-2800
TEXTRON CANADA LIMITED is comprised of various manufactured product businesses, which include the Canadian operations of Bell Helicopter Textron, Homelite, Townsend, Davidson Instrument Panel and Colonial Tool. Textron Canada is owned 65% by Ex-Cello Corporation and 35% by Textron Inc.
B.F. Dolan, Chairman
TOTAL REVENUE ($000)   539,855

THIRD CANADIAN GENERAL INVESTMENT TRUST LIMITED
(Public)   INVESTMENT COMPANIES AND FUNDS
Suite 1601, 110 Yonge Street, Toronto, ON,
M5C 1T4   (416) 366-2931
THIRD CANADIAN GENERAL INVESTMENT TRUST LIMITED is a closed-end investment company which invests in a variety of industries.
E. Louise Morgan, Chairman
TOTAL REVENUE ($000)   3,575

THOMSON CONSUMER ELECTRONICS CANADA, INC.
(Private)   APPLIANCES
6540 Tomken Road, Mississauga, ON, L5T 2E9   (416) 670-6165
THOMSON CONSUMER ELECTRONICS CANADA, INC. is a
manufacturer and distriutor of RCA and GE brand consumer electronic
products and GE brand audio and communication products.
C. David Geise, President
TOTAL REVENUE ($000)   268,400

THOMSON CORPORATION (THE)
See page 335 for a full company profile.

THUNDERWOOD RESOURCES INC.
(Public)   PRECIOUS METALS
Suite 2501, 1 Adelaide Street East, Toronto, ON,
M5C 2V9   (416) 362-8730
THUNDERWOOD RESOURCES INC. is a Canadian mineral explora-
tion company specializing in the exploration for, and development of,
gold and base metal deposits.
James W. Gill, Chairman
TOTAL REVENUE ($000)   81

TIE/TELECOMMUNICATIONS CANADA LIMITED
See page 232 for a full company profile.

TIMMINCO LIMITED
(Public)   MISC. INDUSTRIAL PRODUCTS
10 Bay Street, 9th Floor, Toronto, ON, M5J 2R8   (416) 364-5171
TIMMINCO LIMITED operates two businesses - specialty metals and
industrial adhesives - through two divisions. Timminco Metals is a world
class producer of ferrous and non-ferrous metals for the aluminum,
automotive, aerospace, atomic energy, and iron & steel industries. Timminco Adhesives manufactures and distributes more than 500 adhesives
and coatings.
J. Thomas Timmins, President & C.E.O.
TOTAL REVENUE ($000)   65,301

TINTINA MINES LIMITED
(Public)   PRECIOUS METALS
Suite 804, 920 Yonge St, Toronto, ON, M4W 3C7   (416) 929-2944
TINTINA MINES LIMITED is engaged in the exploration and devel-
opment of mineral resource properties.
C.H. Franklin, President
TOTAL REVENUE ($000)   61

TNT FINANCIAL LTD.
(Public)   INVESTMENT COMPANIES AND FUNDS
Suite 5000, P.O. Box 150, 1 First Canadian Place, Toronto, ON,
M5X 1H3   (416) 359-4630
TNT FINANCIAL LTD. invests its fund in TransAlta common shares.
The net proceeds from the issue of the Capital Shares and the Equity
Dividend Shares offered hereby will be used by the company to satisfy
obligations related to the purchase of TransAlta common shares, such
that there will be one Capital Share and one Equity Dividend Share
foreach TransAlta common share purchased.
Frederick J. Troop, President & C.E.O.
TOTAL REVENUE ($000)   6,546

TOKAI BANK CANADA
(Private)   BANKS
Box 84, Suite 2401, Sun Life Centre, 150 King Street West, Toronto,
ON, M5H 1J9   (416) 597-2210
TOKAI BANK CANADA is a wholly owned subsidiary of the Tokai
Bank, Limited, Japan, and is licenced to operate as a bank in Canada with
full banking powers, as a foreign bank.
Tetsuo Iwasaka, President & C.E.O.
TOTAL REVENUE ($000)   34,143

TOLGECO GROUP INC.
(Public)   METAL FABRICATORS
200 Industriel Blvd, Boucherville, PQ, J4B 2X4   (514) 526-2544
GROUPE TOLGECO is a holding company operating through subsidiaries primarily in the manufacturing of steel cladding, industrial profiles,
joists and studs which are primarily used in industrial, commercial,
agricultural and residential construction. The company is also engaged
in the manufacturing and distribution of materials and specialized products for the construction industry.
J. Serge Vezina, Chairman & V.P. Development
TOTAL REVENUE ($000)   46,140

TOMBILL MINES LIMITED
(Public)   OIL AND GAS PRODUCERS
P.O. Box 28, Toronto-Dominion Centre, Toronto, ON,
M5K 1B8   (416) 362-2192
TOMBILL MINES LIMITED is involved in the exploration for, and
production of oil and gas. The company also holds mineral properties
and investments.
S.R. Horne, President
TOTAL REVENUE ($000)   943

TOROMONT INDUSTRIES LTD.
(Public)   MACHINERY
65 Villiers St, Toronto, ON, M5A 3S1   (416) 465-3518
TOROMONT INDUSTRIES LTD. is a Canadian company with operations in Canada and the United States. Its major operations are in
industrial, commercial and process refrigeration, and gas compression.
Activities include the design, engineering, fabrication, installation and
servicing of refrigeration and gas compression equipment as well as
related parts distribution.
Robert M. Ogilvie, Chairman, President & C.E.O.
TOTAL REVENUE ($000)   184,285

TORONTO HYDRO-ELECTRIC SYSTEM
(Crown)   ELECTRICAL UTILITIES
Toronto Hydro, 14 Carlton Street, Toronto, ON,
M5B 1K5   (416) 599-0400
TORONTO HYDRO-ELECTRIC SYSTEM is Canada's largest mu-
nicipal electric utility, distributing electricity to 210,000 customers in the
city of Toronto.
Robert Coyle, Chairman
TOTAL REVENUE ($000)   729,414

TORONTO SUN PUBLISHING CORPORATION
See page 336 for a full company profile.

TORONTO-DOMINION BANK (THE)
See page 390 for a full company profile.

TORSTAR CORPORATION
See page 337 for a full company profile.

TOSHIBA OF CANADA LIMITED
(Private)   WHOLESALE DISTRIBUTORS
3680 Victoria Park Ave, Willowdale, ON, M2H 3K1   (416) 499-5555
TOSHIBA OF CANADA LIMITED is involved in the wholesale distri-
bution of electronic products. It is a wholly owned subsidiary of Toshiba
Corp. of Japan.
Mr. S. Yoshitake, President & C.E.O.
TOTAL REVENUE ($000)   231,240

TOTAL PETROLEUM (NORTH AMERICA) LTD.
See page 125 for a full company profile.

TOURAM INC.
(Private)   OTHER SERVICES
1440 St Catherine St. W, Suite 800, Montreal, PQ,
H3G 1R8   (514) 876-0700
TOURAM INC. is a engaged in the wholesale travel service business.
Touram is wholly owned subsidiary of Air Canada of Montreal, Quebec.
Gaston G. Gauvreau, Chairman
TOTAL REVENUE ($000)   220,987

TOYOTA CANADA INC.
(Private)   WHOLESALE DISTRIBUTORS
One Toyota Place, Scarborough, ON,
M1H 1H9   (416) 438-6320
TOYOTA CANADA INC. is the Canadian distributor of Toyota vehi-
cles, parts and forklift trucks.
T. Kunii, President
TOTAL REVENUE ($000)   1,618,309

TRACER PETROLEUM CORPORATION
(Public)   OIL AND GAS PRODUCERS
Suite 820, 625 Howe Street, Vancouver, BC,
V6C 2T6   (604) 682-7507
TRACER PETROLEUM CORPORATION is involved in the acquisi-
tion, exploration and development of international oil and gas properties.
Roland C. Siouffi, President & C.E.O.
TOTAL REVENUE ($000)   450

TRADER RESOURCE CORP.
(Public)   PRECIOUS METALS
2nd Floor, 1425 West Pender Street, Vancouver, BC,
V6G 2S3   (604) 682-8320
TRADER RESOURCE CORP. is involved in the acquisition, explora-
tion and development of resource properties. The principal properties of
Trader are: the Mikwam joint venture (with Helmo Gold Mines Inc.) in
Ontario and Quebec; the Papoose Creek project in Ontario; and the
Yellow Giant property located on Banks Island, British Columbia.
Margaret K. Witte, Chairman
TOTAL REVENUE ($000)   1

TRADERS GROUP LIMITED
See page 415 for a full company profile.

TRANS MOUNTAIN PIPE LINE COMPANY LTD.
See page 283 for a full company profile.

TRANS-DOMINION ENERGY CORPORATION
(Public)   HOME FURNISHINGS
1200 McFarlane Tower, 700 - 4th Avenue S.W., Calgary, AB,
T2P 3J4   (403) 261-0601
TRANS-DOMINION ENERGY CORPORATION operates primarily
in two industries - oil and gas and the manufacture and installation of
patented design unitized interior wall systems. In addition, the company
holds investments in companies which operate primarily in the resource
sector.
John P.C. Klemp, Non-Executive Chairman
TOTAL REVENUE ($000)   884

TRANSALTA CORPORATION
(Public)   ELECTRICAL UTILITIES
Box 1900, 110 - 12th Avenue S.W., Calgary, AB,
T2P 2M1   (403) 267-7110
TRANSALTA CORPORATION is a management holding company
with principal operations in the electrical utility industry. The company's
two principal subsidiaries are: TransAlta Utilities Corporation which
conducts regulated electrical utility operations in Alberta; and TransAlta
Energy Corporation which conducts non-regulated operations, including
the operation of independent power facilities.
H.G. Schaefer, Chairman & C.F.O.
TOTAL REVENUE ($000)   1,318,200

TRANSALTA UTILITIES CORPORATION
See page 309 for a full company profile.

TRANSCANADA PIPELINES LIMITED
See page 284 for a full company profile.

TREASURY BRANCHES DEPOSITS FUND
(Crown)   BANKS
9925 - 109 Street, 1200 ATB Plaza, Edmonton, AB,
T5K 2J8   (403) 493-7300
ALBERTA TREASURY BRANCHES is an Alberta crown agency
providing banking services to over 225 locations in the province. It
operates under the authority of the Treasury Branches Act, revised
statutes of Alberta 1980.
A.O. Bray, Superintendent & C.O.O.
TOTAL REVENUE ($000)   791,043

TREMINCO RESOURCES LTD.
(Public)   PRECIOUS METALS
Suite 1110, 625 Howe Street, Vancouver, BC,
V6C 2T6   (604) 687-4450
TREMINCO RESOURCES LTD. is involved in the acquisition, explo-
ration and development of precious and base metals properties. It owns
and operates the Ptarmigan and Tom gold mines near Yellowknife,
Northwest Territories, as well as the Silvana silver-lead-zinc mine near
New Denver, British Columbia.

Roland T. Trenaman, President
TOTAL REVENUE ($000) 9,423

TREND VISION TECHNOLOGIES INC.
(Public) MACHINERY
Suite 500, 455 Granville Street, Vancouver, BC,
V6C 1V2 (604) 669-3332
TREND VISION TECHNOLOGIES INC. is licenced to manufacture and market the 'Kwik Hole' drill pipe stabilizer and downhole tools used in the oil and gas industry. The company also holds the patent for the Turbo-injection system.
M.F. Fuchs, President & C.E.O.
TOTAL REVENUE ($000) 27

TRENTON INDUSTRIES INC.
(Public) MACHINERY
175 Watline Avenue, Mississauga, ON, L4Z 1P2 (416) 890-0207
TRENTON INDUSTRIES INC. is engaged in the precision machining of component parts for a broad range of industries, including manufacturers of office equipment, power generation, forestry, pipeline and areospace products.
V. Edward Daughney, Chairman Of The Board
TOTAL REVENUE ($000) 15,388

TRI LINK RESOURCES LTD.
See page 126 for a full company profile.

TRIAN EQUITIES LTD.
(Public) INVESTMENT COMPANIES AND FUNDS
Suite 1200, 900 West Hastings Street, Vancouver, BC,
V6C 1E7 (604) 688-0601
TRIAN EQUITIES LTD. is a venture capital investment company whose objective is to achieve capital appreciation through investments in businesses believed to have substantial growth and earnings potential.
Raymond A. McLean, President & C.E.O.
TOTAL REVENUE ($000) 863

TRIDEL ENTERPRISES INC.
(Public) DEVELOPERS
4800 Dufferin Street, Downsview, ON, M3H 5S9 (416) 661-9290
TRIDEL ENTERPRISES is a diversified residential builder and construction technology distribution company engaged in two businesses. The residential real estate division develops high-rise condominium lifestyle projects primarily in the greater Metropolitan Toronto area. The construction technology division is a supplier of products to the concrete construction industry.
Angelo Delzotto, Chairman & C.E.O.
TOTAL REVENUE ($000) 391,398

TRILOGY RESOURCE CORPORATION
(Public) OIL AND GAS PRODUCERS
Suite 3800, 150 - 6th Avenue S.W., Calgary, AB,
T2P 3Y7 (403) 261-8750
TRILOGY RESOURCE CORPORATION is petroleum and natural gas corporation.
Gerald L. Roe, Chairman, President & C.E.O.
TOTAL REVENUE ($000) 29,950

TRILON FINANCIAL CORPORATION
See page 416 for a full company profile.

TRIMAC LIMITED
See page 276 for a full company profile.

TRIMARK FINANCIAL CORPORATION
(Public) INVESTMENT COMPANIES AND FUNDS
Suite 5200, P.O. Box 205, Scotia Plaza, Toronto, ON,
M5H 3Z3 (416) 362-7181
TRIMARK FINANCIAL CORPORATION, through its wholly owned subsidiary Trimark Investment Management Inc., is a mutual fund company. It is a sponsor, manager and distributor of mutual funds, with an emphasis on equity portfolios.
Robert C. Krembil, Chairman
TOTAL REVENUE ($000) 43,741

TRIMEL CORPORATION
(Public) BIOTECHNOLOGY & PHARMACEUTICALS
10 Carlson Crt, 8th Floor, Etobicoke, ON, M9W 6L2 (416) 798-3000
TRIMEL CORPORATION is engaged in pharmaceutical product development services and communications. Its operations include: developing novel drug delivery systems, including controlled research release products; pharmaceuticial contract research operations including, labratory testing, clinical research and regulatory services; pharmaceuticial manufacturing services; and electronic info systems.
Eugene N. Melnyk, Chairman
TOTAL REVENUE ($000) 6,729

TRIMIN ENTERPRISES INC.
(Public) METAL FABRICATORS
Suite 1740, 555 West Hastings Street, Vancouver, BC,
V6B 4N5 (604) 688-4693
TRIMIN ENTERPRISES INC. is engaged in the manufacture of iron, steel, aluminum and magnesium castings, the production of plastic films, and the provision of data management services.
James D. Meekison, Chairman
TOTAL REVENUE ($000) 76,983

TRITON CANADA RESOURCES LTD.
See page 127 for a full company profile.

TRIZEC CORPORATION LTD.
See page 266 for a full company profile.

TRU-WALL GROUP LIMITED
(Public) CEMENT AND CONCRETE
150 Ashbridge Circle, Woodbridge, ON, L4L 3R5 (416) 798-7066
TRU-WALL GROUP LIMITED is engaged in forming and pouring concrete. Through joint ventures and subsidiaries, the company constructs houses. The company also has equipment rental income.
L.A. Ursini, President
TOTAL REVENUE ($000) 7,707

TRUSCAN REALTY LIMITED
(Public)   PROPERTY MGMNT & INVESTMENT
Suite 1200, 380 Wellington Street, London, ON,
N6A 4S4   (519) 663-1911
TRUSCAN REALTY LIMITED is a wholly owned subsidiary of
Canada Trustco Mortgage Company and a member of the Canada Trust
group of companies. Its principal business is the acquisition, development
and management of real estate, both for investment purposes and for
occupancy by CT Financial Services Inc. and its subsidiaries.
H. Purdy Crawford, Chairman
TOTAL REVENUE ($000)   117,444

TSC SHANNOCK CORP.
(Public)   WHOLESALE DISTRIBUTORS
4222 Manor Street, Burnaby, BC, V5G 1B2   (604) 433-3331
TSC SHANNOCK's principal business is as a wholesale distributor of
video movies, accessories, cassettes, compact discs and laser videos.
William G. McCartney, President & C.E.O.
TOTAL REVENUE ($000)   51,357

TUDOR CORPORATION LTD.
(Public)   MISC. CONSUMER PRODUCTS
2929 - 15th Street N.E., Calgary, AB, T2E 7L8   (403) 250-7225
TUDOR CORPORATION LTD. is engaged in three major activities:
the exploration and development of oil and gas properties in the United
States and Canada; the manufacture and distribution of the universal skate
sharpener; and its newest endeavour, the manufacture and distribution of
fish leather under the Mermaid Leather Company Ltd.
Lionel Conn, President
TOTAL REVENUE ($000)   2,461

TVX GOLD INC.
See page 59 for a full company profile.

TWINPAK INC.
(Private)   PACKAGING AND CONTAINERS
1840 Route Trans-Canada, Dorval, PQ, H9P 1H7   (514) 684-7070
TWINPAK INC. is a Canadian leader in plastic, paper and composite
material packaging. The company is a wholly owned subsidiary of
Amcor Limited of Australia.
Chris D.V. Nixon, Chairman/CEO, Australia
TOTAL REVENUE ($000)

UAP INC.
See page 346 for a full company profile.

ULSTER PETROLEUMS LTD.
See page 128 for a full company profile.

UNI-SELECT INC.
(Public)   WHOLESALE DISTRIBUTORS
170 Boulevard Industriel, Boucherville, PQ, J4B 2X3 (514) 641-2440
UNI-SELECT INC. is involved in the wholesale distribution and mar-
keting of spare parts for motor vehicles, equipment, tools and accessories.
It carries on business in the provinces of Quebec, Ontario, Nova Scotia,
New Brunswick and Prince Edward Island. Distribution of these parts is

carried out mainly through its members, which are all shareholders of
Uni-Select.
Jean-Louis Dulac, Chairman
TOTAL REVENUE ($000)   218,219

UNICAN SECURITY SYSTEMS LTD.
(Public)   MISC. INDUSTRIAL PRODUCTS
7301 Decarie Blvd., Montreal, PQ, H4P 2G7   (514) 735-5411
UNICAN SECURITY SYSTEMS LTD. is the parent of a group of
international companies engaged in the manufacture of security products
and zinc die cast hardware.
Aaron M. Fish, Chairman & President
TOTAL REVENUE ($000)   126,780

UNICORP ENERGY CORPORATION
See page 310 for a full company profile.

UNIGESCO INC.
See page 458 for a full company profile.

UNILENS VISION INC.
(Public)   MISC. CONSUMER PRODUCTS
Suite 1490, P.O. Box 1011, 885 West Georgia St., Vancouver,
V6C 3E8   (604) 682-7551
UNILENS VISION INC. is a manufacture and marketer of soft and
specialty contact lenses and conducts clinical markets. Unilens Vision
Inc. is a holding company for Unilens U.S.A. Corp. which manufactures
contact lenses.
Ian S. Brodie, President & Director
TOTAL REVENUE ($000)   4,991 (US)

UNILEVER CANADA LTD.
(Private)   MANAGEMENT AND DIVERSIFIED
160 Bloor St. East, Suite 1500, Toronto, ON,
M4W 3R2   (416) 964-1857
UNILEVER CANADA LTD. is engaged in the manufacture and distri-
bution of food products, detergents, personal products and specialty
chemicals. Unilever Canada also operates a national chain of restaurants.
R.A. Goldstein, Chairman & C.E.O.
TOTAL REVENUE ($000)   1,197,398

UNION BANK OF SWITZERLAND (CANADA)
(Private)   BANKS
154 University Avenue, Toronto, ON, M5H 3Z4   (416) 343-1800
UNION BANK OF SWITZERLAND (CANADA) is a schedule II bank.
The bank is a wholly owned subsidiary of Union Bank of Switzerland.
Mathis Cabiallavetta, Chairman
TOTAL REVENUE ($000)   255,160

UNION ENERGY INC.
(Private)   GAS UTILITIES
Penthouse, 21 St. Clair Avenue East, Toronto, ON,
M4T 2T7   (416) 964-6300
UNION ENERGY INC.'s principal investment is Union Gas Limited,
which transports, distributes and stores natural gas in Southwestern
Ontario. Unigas Corp. markets natural gas to custom ers in Alberta,
Central Canada and the Great Lakes region of the United States. It also

owns the St. Clair pipeline. Union Energy was purchased by Westcoast Energy Inc. in November 1992.
Michael J. Phelps, Chairman, President & C.E.O.
TOTAL REVENUE ($000)   1,775,460

UNION GAS LIMITED
(Public)   GAS UTILITIES
50 Keil Dr. N., Chatham, ON, N7M 5M1   (519) 352-3100
UNION GAS LIMITED owns and operates a fully integrated system of natural gas transmission, distribution and storage. It serves over 650,000 residential, commercial and industrial customers throughout southwestern Ontario. The storage and transmission facilities are an important component in the delivery of Western Canada gas to Eastern Canada. The company is regulated by Ontario Energy Board.
Michael J. Phelps, Chairman
TOTAL REVENUE ($000)   1,289,225

UNIROYAL GOODRICH CANADA INC.
(Private)   AUTOMOTIVE
P.O. Box 9000, Kitchener, ON, N2G 4S5   (519) 749-4900
Uniroyal Ltd. is a manufacturer of tires, tire cord, and custom process equipment.
Herbert Heuchert, Vice President, Operations
TOTAL REVENUE ($000)   408,911

UNISYS CANADA INC.
(Private)   ELECTRICAL & ELECTRONIC
2001 Sheppard Ave., North York, ON,
M2J 4Z7   (416) 495-0515
UNISYS CANADA INC. is engaged in the manufacture, sale and service of computer equipment and related products. Unisys Canada is a wholly owned subsidiary of Unisys Corporation (U.S.).
Brian Clark, President & C.E.O.
TOTAL REVENUE ($000)   302,661

UNITED CANADIAN SHARES LIMITED
(Public)   CLOTHING AND TEXTILES
1601 Church Avenue, Winnipeg, MB, R2X 1G9   (204) 633-7042
UNITED CANADIAN SHARES LIMITED is engaged in leather tanning with approximately 52% of its sales from exports.
Robert H. Jones, Chairman Of The Board
TOTAL REVENUE ($000)   62,361

UNITED CO-OPERATIVES OF ONTARIO
(Non-fin Co-op)   WHOLESALE DISTRIBUTORS
P.O. Box 527, Station A, 5600 Cancross Court, Mississauga, ON,
L5A 3A4   (416) 890-8500
UNITED CO-OPERATIVES OF ONTARIO is the largest farm supply and marketing cooperative in the province. The role of the cooperative is as a wholesaler, manufacturer, distributor and retailer in farm products, supplier and services.
Gordon Cummings, C.E.O.
TOTAL REVENUE ($000)   285,614

UNITED CORPORATIONS LIMITED
See page 417 for a full company profile.

UNITED DOMINION INDUSTRIES LIMITED
See page 459 for a full company profile.

UNITED FARMERS OF ALBERTA CO-OPERATIVE LTD.
(Non-fin Co-op)   WHOLESALE DISTRIBUTORS
1016 - 68th Avenue S.W., Calgary, AB, T2V 4J2   (403) 258-4500
UNITED FARMERS OF ALBERTA CO-OPERATIVE LTD. is a member owned farm cooperative. An extensive and diversified range of farm production inputs are distributed by the cooperative which is recognized as the largest farm supply cooperative in Alberta. Farm supplies are available from the 33 farm supply centres and petroleum products are marketed through 131 petroleum outlets and member associations.
J.F. Shindler, Chief Executive Officer
TOTAL REVENUE ($000)   330,423

UNITED GRAIN GROWERS LIMITED
(Public)   AGRICULTURE
P.O. Box 6600, 2800 - 201 Portage Avenue, Winnipeg, MB,
R3C 3A7   (204) 944-5411
UNITED GRAIN GROWERS LIMITED (UGG) is a member owned cooperative agricultural products company. UGG collects wheat through a network of grain elevators throughout Manitoba, Saskatchewan and Alberta as an agent of the Canadian Wheat Board. UGG also operates feed mills, seed plants, anhydrous ammonia and bulk fertilizer plants.
T.M. Allen, Chairman & President of the Board
TOTAL REVENUE ($000)   1,034,268

UNITED KENO HILL MINES LIMITED
See page 60 for a full company profile.

UNITED OVERSEAS BANK (CANADA)
(Private)   BANKS
Suite 310 Vancouver Centre, P.O. Box 11616, 650 West Georgia Street, Vancouver, BC, V6C 4N9   (604) 662-7055
UNITED OVERSEAS BANK (CANADA) is licenced to act as a foreign subsidiary bank. The bank is wholly owned by the United Overseas Bank Limited of Singapore.
Cho Yaw Wee, Chairman
TOTAL REVENUE ($000)   4,401

UNITED RAYORE GAS LTD.
(Public)   OIL AND GAS PRODUCERS
Suite 1120, 520 - 5th Avenue S.W., Calgary, AB,
T2P 3R7   (403) 262-7677
UNITED RAYORE GAS LTD. is involved in the exploration for and development of oil, gas and minerals.
Robert L. Bell, President & C.E.O.
TOTAL REVENUE ($000)   5,662

UNITED TIRE & RUBBER CO. LIMITED
(Public)   AUTOMOTIVE
275 Belfield Rd, Rexdale, ON, M9W 5C6   (416) 675-3077
UNITED TIRE & RUBBER CO. LIMITED operates in one business segment: the design, manufacture, retreading and distribution of tires. The Company is a supplier of tires and other rubber products to the mining, construction and forestry industries with branches across Canada and the United States.

Robert Scolnick, Chairman
TOTAL REVENUE ($000)   30,200

UNITED TRI-STAR RESOURCES LTD.
(Public)   OIL AND GAS PRODUCERS
1600 Bow Valley Square II, 205 - 5th Avenue S.W., Calgary, AB,
T2P 2V7   (403) 269-6977
UNITED TRI-STAR RESOURCES LTD. is a diversified North American energy resource company headquartered in Calgary, Alberta. The company's primary business is the exploration for and development and production of oil and gas in Western Canada.
Rudolf Siegert, President & C.E.O.
TOTAL REVENUE ($000)   1,694

UNITED WESTBURNE INC.
See page 347 for a full company profile.

UNITEL COMMUNICATIONS HOLDINGS INC.
(Private)   TELECOMMUNICATIONS
200 Wellington Street West, Suite 1601, Toronto, ON,
M5V 3C7   (416) 345-2256
UNITEL COMMUNICATIONS HOLDINGS INC. is a telecommunications company.
E.S. Rogers,
TOTAL REVENUE ($000)   440,483

UNIVA INC.
See page 371 for a full company profile.

UNOCAL CANADA LIMITED
(Private)   OIL AND GAS PRODUCERS
150-6th Avenue S.W., Box 999, Calgary, AB,
T2P 2K6   (403) 268-0176
UNOCAL CANADA LIMITED is involved in the exploration, development and production of oil and gas and exploration and mining of coal and minerals. It is a wholly owned subsidiary of Unocal Corp. of the United States.
Fritz Perschon, President
TOTAL REVENUE ($000)   241,506

UPTON RESOURCES INC.
(Public)   OIL AND GAS PRODUCERS
322 - 4th Street, Estevan, SK,
S4A 0T8   (306) 634-6484
UPTON RESOURCES INC. produces crude oil and associated natural gas, and also acts as contract operator and administrator for other oil companies in southeast Saskatchewan.
William R. Dutton, Chairman & President
TOTAL REVENUE ($000)   8,785

URBCO INC.
(Public)   DEVELOPERS
Suite 212, 6131- 6th Street S.E., Calgary, AB,
T2H 1L9   (403) 531-0720
URBCO INC. is a real estate development and management company. It has properties under management in Yellowknife, Northwest Territories, and Calgary, Alberta. The company has a subdivision under development in Okotoks, Alberta.

TOTAL REVENUE ($000)   1,136

UTDC INC.
(Private)   TRANSPORTATION EQUIP & COMPNTS
C/O Bombardier Inc., UTDC Systems Division, P.O. Box 220,
Station A, Kingston, ON, K7M 6R2   (613) 384-3100
UTDC INC. is a manufacturer of rapid transit vehicles. UTDC is 85% owned by Lavalin Industries of Quebec and 15% by the government of Ontario. On February 7, 1992, the mass transit assets of UTDC were sold to Bombardier Inc.
David Pattenden, Chairman & C.E.O.
TOTAL REVENUE ($000)   175,677

VALDEZ GOLD INC.
(Public)   PRECIOUS METALS
20 Adelaide St. E., Suite 200, Toronto, ON, M5C 2T6(416) 867-1100
VALDEZ GOLD INC. owns a 25% interest in the Valdez Creek Project, a producer in Alaska. Cambior operates the project and owns the maining 25% interest.
Ian McAvity, Chairman
TOTAL REVENUE ($000)   4,038

VAN WATERS & ROGERS LTD.
(Private)   WHOLESALE DISTRIBUTORS
9800 Van Horne Way, Richmond, BC, V6X 1W5   (604) 273-1441
VAN WATERS & ROGERS LTD. is a wholesale chemical distributor. The company is wholly owned by Univar Corp. (U.S.).
A.C. McHeight, Chairman
TOTAL REVENUE ($000)   339,625

VANCOUVER CITY SAVINGS CREDIT UNION
(Fin. Co-op)   CREDIT UNIONS
515 West 10th Avenue, Vancouver, BC, V5Z 4A8   (604) 877-7000
VANCOUVER CITY SAVINGS CREDIT UNION is Canada's largest credit union offering a full range of financial services to members.
Robert D. Quart, C.E.O.
TOTAL REVENUE ($000)   323,025

VANCOUVER PORT CORPORATION
(Crown)   TRANSPORTATION
1900 Granville Square, 200 Granville Street, Vancouver, BC,
V6C 2P9   (604) 000-0000
VANCOUVER PORT CORPORATION is a crown corporation responsible for administering the lands and waterways of the Port of Vancouver. The VPC also owns five cargo and cruise terminals, and actively markets port services worldwide. The VPC maintains harbour safety and security through the offices of the Harbour Master and Ports Canada police.
Patrick Reid, O.C., Chairman
TOTAL REVENUE ($000)   64,522

VARITECH INVESTORS CORPORATION
(Public)   INVESTMENT COMPANIES AND FUNDS
P.O. Box 770, Suite 4500, BCE Place, 181 Bay Street, Toronto, ON,
M5J 2T3   (416) 865-0430
VARITECH INVESTORS CORPORATION invests in premium high yielding securities of Canadian corporations according to investment guidelines established by the board of directors. Such securities primarily include preferred shares and convertible preferred shares.

Marlene J. Davidge, Chairman
TOTAL REVENUE ($000)   20,099

VARITY CORPORATION
See page 209 for a full company profile.

VENCAP EQUITIES ALBERTA LTD.
(Public)   INVESTMENT COMPANIES AND FUNDS
Suite 1980, 10180 - 101 Street, Edmonton, AB,
T5J 3S4   (403) 420-1171
VENCAP EQUITIES ALBERTA LTD. is a venture capital company.
Vencap's aim is to seek out, invest in, add value to, and profit from
business opportunities of outstanding potential and benefit to Alberta.
Donald A. Carlson, Chairman
TOTAL REVENUE ($000)   21,488

VENTRA GROUP INC.
(Public)   AUTOMOTIVE
1 Mitten Court, P.O. Box 126, Cambridge, ON,
N1R 5S9   (519) 658-6777
VENTRA GROUP INC. is engaged in molding and finishing of plastic
components for the automotive and other industries. The company
manufactures air, power steering, and brake reservoirs for the truck
industry and has two major metal stamping facilities, both servicing the
automotive and truck industries. The company also has stamping, assembly and E-coat painting facilities for the automotive industry.
Kenneth R. Nichols, President & C.E.O.
TOTAL REVENUE ($000)   42,221

VERONEX RESOURCES LTD.
(Public)   OIL AND GAS PRODUCERS
Suite 701, 475 Howe Street, Vancouver, BC,
V6C 2B3   (604) 669-5650
VERONEX RESOURCES LTD. is a diversified natural resource com-
pany whose principal business is the exploration for and development
and production of oil, natural gas, and precious metals world-wide. The
Company's principal properties are in North America, Indonesia, and
Papua New Guinea.
David A. Hite, Chairman, President & C.E.O.
TOTAL REVENUE ($000)   59 (US)

VERSA SERVICES LTD.
See page 372 for a full company profile.

VIA RAIL CANADA INC.
(Crown)   TRANSPORTATION
P.O. Box 8116, Station A, Montreal, PQ, H3C 3N3   (514) 871-6000
VIA RAIL CANADA INC. provides national rail passenger service.
Marc LeFrancois, Chairman
TOTAL REVENUE ($000)   546,056

VICEROY HOMES LIMITED
(Public)   MISC. CONSUMER PRODUCTS
30 Melford Drive, Scarborough, ON, M1B 1Z4   (416) 298-2200
VICEROY HOMES LIMITED is engaged in the design, manufacture
and distribution of precut packaged and 'factory built' custom homes as
well as the manufacture and distribution of PVC windows, sliding glass
doors, skylights and sunroom windows.

Galylord G. Lindal, President
TOTAL REVENUE ($000)   26,985

VICEROY RESOURCE CORPORATION
See page 61 for a full company profile.

VITRAN CORPORATION INC.
(Public)   TRANSPORTATION
24 Mobile Drive, Toronto, ON, M4A 1H9   (416) 752-1411
VITRAN CORPORATION INC. is a North American multi-divisional
operating company providing services to the freight and environmental
industries. The Freight Transportation Services Group provides a complete range of services for the movement of freight across Canada and
the continental United States. The Environmental Group supplies waste
management services to municipalities and other clients in B.C.
Anthony F. Griffiths, Chairman of the Board
TOTAL REVENUE ($000)   99,361

VOLKSWAGEN CANADA INC.
(Private)   WHOLESALE DISTRIBUTORS
1940 Eglinton Ave East, Scarborough, ON,
M1L 2M2   (416) 288-3000
VOLKSWAGEN CANADA INC. is engaged in importing and distrib-
uting automobiles and their related parts and manufacturing automotive
components. Volkswagen Canada is 100% owned by Volkswagen AG
of Germany.
John E. Kerr, Chairman
TOTAL REVENUE ($000)   768,943

VOLVO CANADA LTD.
(Private)   AUTOMOTIVE
175 Gordon Baker Road, North York, ON, M2H 2N7 (416) 493-3700
VOLVO CANADA LTD. is a manufacturer of automobiles. The com-
pany is a wholly owned subsidiary of Volvo Canadian Holdings Ltd.
Mats Ola Palm, Chairman
TOTAL REVENUE ($000)   236,476

W. G. THOMPSON & SONS LTD.
(Private)   WHOLESALE DISTRIBUTORS
122 George Street, Blenheim, ON, N0P 1A0   (519) 676-5411
W.G. THOMPSON & SONS LTD. operates country grain elevators and
is involved in grains, seeds, fertilizers, pulses and agricultural chemicals.
W.D. Thompson, Chairman & President
TOTAL REVENUE ($000)   200,000

WAJAX LIMITED
See page 348 for a full company profile.

WALL FINANCIAL CORPORATION
(Public)   PROPERTY MGMNT & INVESTMENT
Suite 520, 601 West Broadway, Vancouver, BC,
V5Z 4C2   (604) 872-3555
WALL FINANCIAL CORPORATION is involved in real estate devel-
opment, investment in revenue producing properties and real estate sales.
Peter Wall, Chairman & President
TOTAL REVENUE ($000)   29,782

Canada Company Handbook

WAWANESA MUTUAL INSURANCE COMPANY (THE)
(Private)   INSURANCE - PROPERTY & CASUALTY
191 Broadway Ave, Winnipeg, MB, R3C 3P1   (204) 985-3811
THE WAWANESA MUTUAL INSURANCE COMPANY offers mutual property and casualty insurance.
V.M. Binkley, Chairman
TOTAL REVENUE ($000)   594,691

WELCOME NORTH RESOURCES INC.
(Public)   METAL MINES
15th Floor, 675 West Hastings Street, Vancouver, BC,
V6B 1N2   (604) 687-1658
WELCOME NORTH RESOURCES INC. is involved in the acquisition, exploration and development of mineral properties.
John S. Brock, President
TOTAL REVENUE ($000)   99

WELDWOOD OF CANADA LIMITED
See page 149 for a full company profile.

WEST FRASER TIMBER CO. LTD.
See page 150 for a full company profile.

WEST KOOTENAY POWER LTD.
(Public)   ELECTRICAL UTILITIES
8100 Rock Island Highway, Waneta Plaza, Box 130, Trail, BC,
V1R 4L4   (604) 368-3321
WEST KOOTENAY POWER LTD. is a public utility engaged in the business of generating, transmitting, distributing, and selling electricity in the Southern interior of British Columbia. The company supplies 90% of the electricity purchased by industrial, commercial and residential customers in its service area and is regulated by the British Columbia utilities commission.
J.A. Drennan, President & C.E.O.
TOTAL REVENUE ($000)   98,339

WESTAR GROUP LTD.
See page 277 for a full company profile.

WESTCOAST ENERGY INC.
See page 285 for a full company profile.

WESTERN CO-OPERATIVE FERTILIZERS LIMITED
(Non-fin Co-op)   WHOLESALE DISTRIBUTORS
P.O. Box 2500, Calgary, AB, T2P 2N1   (403) 279-1100
WESTERN CO-OPERATIVE FERTILIZERS LIMITED is involved in the wholesale and distribution of fertilizer.
K. Komitsch, President & C.E.O.
TOTAL REVENUE ($000)   136,819

WESTERN CORPORATE ENTERPRISES INC.
(Public)   MANAGEMENT AND DIVERSIFIED
Suite 200, 1199 West Hastings Street, Vancouver, BC,
V6E 3T5   (604) 682-1317
WESTERN CORPORATE ENTERPRISES INC.'s two principal subsidiaries are Facs Records Centre Inc. which manages and stores paper and magnetic records, and International Aviation Terminals Inc. (IAT),

which operates multi-tenant air cargo tenants at North American airports. IAT is also a 50% partner in the B.C. Government's Air Careprogram to acquire & develop 12 exhaust emission testing stations.
William H. Levine, Chairman
TOTAL REVENUE ($000)   16,348

WESTERN GARNET COMPANY LTD.
(Public)   OTHER MINES
Suite 303, 675 West Hastings Street, Vancouver, BC,
V3B 1N2   (604) 687-6009
WESTERN GARNET COMPANY is involved in the acquisition, exploration and development of mineral resource properties, in particular, but not limited to, industrial grade garnet properties. Its subsidiaries are involved in the mining, milling and marketing of industrial grade garnet.
Joseph H. Whipple, President And C.E.O.
TOTAL REVENUE ($000)   7,106

WESTERN QUEBEC MINES INC.
(Public)   PRECIOUS METALS
137 Church Street, Toronto, ON, M5B 1Y5   (416) 000-0000
WESTERN QUEBEC MINES INC. is involved in the acquisition, exploration and development of mineral properties.
Murray H. Pollitt, Chairman
TOTAL REVENUE ($000)   3,716

WESTFAIR FOODS LTD.
(Public)   FOOD STORES
3225 - 12th Street N.E., Calgary, AB, T2E 7S9 (403) 291-7700
WESTFAIR FOODS is a major wholesaler and retailer of food products in Western Canada. It is a wholly owned subsidiary of Kelly, Douglas & Company, Ltd.
Serge K. Darkanzanli, Chairman & President
TOTAL REVENUE ($000)   2,414,701

WESTFIELD MINERALS LIMITED
(Public)   METAL MINES
Suite 2701, P.O. Box 143, 1 First Canadian Place, Toronto, ON,
M5X 1C7   (416) 362-6683
WESTFIELD MINERALS LIMITED is a mineral resource company that is involved in exploration and mine development. The company holds a substantial portfolio of resource investments. The company owns mineral properties in Ontario, Quebec, Newfoundland and the western United States. Through its investments, the company also has resource interests in Canada, Ireland, Australia and the United States.
John F. Kearney, Chairman
TOTAL REVENUE ($000)   1,208

WESTGROUP CORPORATIONS INC.
(Public)   MANAGEMENT AND DIVERSIFIED
Suite 4600, 400 - Third Avenue S.W., Calgary, AB,
T2P 4H2   (403) 269-1868
WESTGROUP CORPORATIONS INC. is a diversified management corporation.
Thomas F. Stibbard, President & C.O.O.
TOTAL REVENUE ($000)   36,093

WESTINGHOUSE CANADA INC.
(Private)   ELECTRICAL & ELECTRONIC
P.O. Box 2510, Hamilton, ON, L8N 3K2   (416) 528-8811
WESTINGHOUSE CANADA INC. competes globally in the manufacture and sale of electrical, electronic and mechanical products and services. The company is a wholly owned subsidiary of Westinghouse Electric Corp.
Mr. Garry Graham, President
TOTAL REVENUE ($000)   834,680

WESTMIN RESOURCES LIMITED
See page 22 for a full company profile.

WESTMINSTER CREDIT UNION
(Fin. Co-op)   CREDIT UNIONS
422 Sixth Street, New Westminster, BC, V3L 3B2   (604) 525-7384
WESTMINSTER CREDIT UNION is a full service credit union operating in the suburban Vancouver area.
Barry W. Forbes, President & C.E.O.
TOTAL REVENUE ($000)   35,664

WFI INDUSTRIES LTD.
(Public)   BIOTECHNOLOGY & PHARMACEUTICALS
234 Talbot Street West, Leamington, ON, N8H 1P1   (519) 326-5728
WFI INDUSTRIES LTD. is a manufacturer and distributor of residential geothermal heating and cooling systems.
Michael Scholz, Chairman
TOTAL REVENUE ($000)   10,840

WHARF RESOURCES LTD.
See page 62 for a full company profile.

WHITE ROSE CRAFTS AND NURSERY SALES LIMITED
(Public)   SPECIALTY STORES
4938 Highway No. 7, Unionville, ON, L3R 2L5   (416) 477-3330
WHITE ROSE CRAFTS AND NURSERY SALES LIMITED is a specialty retailer of nursery and crafts products in Ontario.
Ron MacLean, President & C.E.O.
TOTAL REVENUE ($000)   124,293

WIC WESTERN INTERNATIONAL COMMUNICATIONS LTD.
See page 338 for a full company profile.

WINDARRA MINERALS LTD.
(Public)   OIL AND GAS PRODUCERS
Suite 700, 555 West Hastings Street, Vancouver, BC,
V6B 4N5   (604) 893-7088
WINDARRA MINERALS LTD. is involved in the exploration for, and production of oil, gas and minerals. The company holds interests in oil and gas properties in Ohio, Oklahoma and Texas in the U.S. and in Alberta, Canada. Also, the company has interests in mineral claims in Ontario and British Columbia.
Ronald H.D. Philp, President
TOTAL REVENUE ($000)   (35)

WINPAK LTD.
(Public)   PACKAGING AND CONTAINERS
100 Saulteaux Crescent, Winnipeg, MB, R3J 3T3   (204) 889-1015
WINPAK LTD. designs and manufactures a comprehensive and varied range of plastic flexible packaging materials for use in vacuum and modified atmosphere packaging, as well as for pharmaceutical and industrial packaging applications. The Portion Packaging division is a leading supplier of individual thermoformed containers and packaging systems used by the dairy and foodservice industries.
A. Aarnio-Wihuri, Chairman
TOTAL REVENUE ($000)   115,829

WINZEN INTERNATIONAL INC.
(Public)   DEVELOPERS
Suite 700, 67 Yonge Street, Toronto, ON, M5E 1J8 (416) 863-0071
WINZEN INTERNATIONAL INC. is involved in real estate brokerage and property management and development.
Victor Zenkovich, President
TOTAL REVENUE ($000)   1,036

WISE STORES INC.
(Public)   DEPARTMENT STORES
845 Deslauriers Street, Ville St-Laurent, PQ,
H4N 1X5   (514) 333-7810
WISE STORES INC. operates 49 junior department stores which offer a wide range of consumer products including wearing apparel, accessories and footwear for men, women and children, houseware and giftware items, linen and bedding, bathroom accessories, window treatments, toys and confectionery items.
Alex Wise, Chairman & President
TOTAL REVENUE ($000)   97,441

XCAN GRAIN POOL LTD.
(Non-fin Co-op)   WHOLESALE DISTRIBUTORS
201 Portage Avenue, Suite 1200, Winnipeg, MB,
R3B 3K6   (204) 949-1388
XCAN GRAIN POOL LTD. is a marketer of grains and foodstuffs. Xcan is jointly owned by Alberat Wheat Pool, Manitoba Pool Elevators and Saskatchewan Wheat Pool.
G.W. Stevenson, Chairman & President
TOTAL REVENUE ($000)   728,538

XEROX CANADA INC.
See page 233 for a full company profile.

XILLIX TECHNOLOGIES CORP.
(Public)   MISC. INDUSTRIAL PRODUCTS
2339 Columbia Street, 2339 Columbia Street, Vancouver, BC,
V5Y 3Y3   (604) 875-6161
XILLIX TECHNOLOGIES CORP. is involved in the development, anufacture and marketing of medical imaging devices for the earlier dectection of cancer. The company's markets are in in the biological and medical sectors, including both research and clinical applications.
Barclay Isherwood, Chairman
TOTAL REVENUE ($000)   837

XL FOODS LTD.
(Public)   AGRICULTURE
Suite 250, 1209 - 59th Avenue S.E., Calgary, AB,
T2H 2P6   (403) 258-3233
XL FOODS operates primarily in agribusiness beef production, which consists of raising, feeding, slaughtering and processing cattle, as well as feed and grain production.
John K. Church, Chairman
TOTAL REVENUE ($000)   231,886

YORBEAU RESOURCES INC
(Public)   PRECIOUS METALS
Suite 2215, 1155 Rene-Levesque Blvd. W., Montreal, PQ,
H3B 4T3   (514) 842-6684
YORBEAU RESOURCES INC. is a gold exploration company with varying interests in 20 mining properties located primarily along the Rouyn-Noranda-Val d'Or axis in northwestern Quebec.
David Crevier, Chairman & Secretary
TOTAL REVENUE ($000)   3

YORK CENTRE CORPORATION
(Public)   PROPERTY MGMNT & INVESTMENT
Suite 15, Empire Centre, 350 Harry Walker Pkwy. N., Newmarket,
ON, L3Y 8L3   (416) 853-1973
YORK CENTRE CORPORATION is a property investment company which concentrates its investments in energy properties, primarily through its subsidiary, Canalands Resources Corporation. The company is also involved in the constuction and sale or leasing of commercial and industrial buildings.
Sinclair M. Stevens, Chairman
TOTAL REVENUE ($000)   571 (US)

ZELLERS INC.
(Private)   DEPARTMENT STORES
5100 De Maisonneuve Blvd. West, Montreal, PQ,
H4A 1Y6   (514) 483-7600
ZELLERS INC. is a national chain of discount department stores. It targets the budget minded customer with 272 stores across Canada mainly in shopping malls. The typical store is 65,000 sq. ft. in size.The company is a wholly owned subsidiary of Hudson's Bay Company of Toronto.

Paul S. Walters, President
TOTAL REVENUE ($000)   3,021,171

ZENON ENVIRONMENTAL INC.
(Public)   ENVIRONMENTAL SERVICES
845 Harrington Court, Burlington, ON, L7N 3P3   (416) 639-6320
ZENON ENVIRONMENTAL INC. develops, manufactures and markets environmental control technologies and operates an environmental testing laboratory. The company specializes in water and waste water treatment processes.
Andrew Benedek, Chairman & C.E.O.
TOTAL REVENUE ($000)   33,156

ZODIAC HURRICANE TECHNOLOGIES INC.
(Public)   MISC. CONSUMER PRODUCTS
10751 River Drive, Richmond, BC, V6X 1Z2   (604) 273-0451
ZODIAC HURRICANE TECHNOLOGIES INC. designs, manufactures and distributes worldwide, rigid inflatable boats which are primarily used by military, coast guard, enforcement agencies and custom authorities.
M. Pinault, Chairman
TOTAL REVENUE ($000)   14,875

ZURICH CANADA
(Private)   INSURANCE - PROPERTY & CASUALTY
400 University Avenue, Toronto, ON, M5G 1S7   (416) 586-2731
ZURICH CANADA is a property and casualty insurer. The company is a wholly owned subsidiary of Zurich Group of Switzerland.
Daniel Damov, Chairman
TOTAL REVENUE ($000)   1,027,920

ZURICH LIFE INSURANCE COMPANY OF CANADA
(Private)   INSURANCE - LIFE
2225 Sheppard Avenue East, Willowdale, ON,
M2J 5C4   (416) 502-3600
ZURICH LIFE INSURANCE COMPANY OF CANADA is a life and health insurance company.
Daniel Damov, Chair of the Board
TOTAL REVENUE ($000)   201,214

Stock Market Information

Price: Closing price of the stock on the date indicated.

Trailing P/E: Price divided by the sum of earnings per share before extraordinary items from the last four quarters listed.

Trailing Yield: The sum of dividends per common share from the last four quarters listed divided by Price, multiplied by 100.

Trailing EPS: The sum of earnings per share before extraordinary items from the last four quarters listed divided by Price.

Yearly Statistics (5 years)

All Companies

Price-Close: Market price as of balance sheet date.

Price-High and Price-Low: High and low market prices during the indicated fiscal year.

P/E Close: Closing market price as of balance sheet date divided by earnings per share before extraordinary items during the indicated fiscal year.

Dividends per Share (Dividends per common share): Presented for annual results for the indicated fiscal year.

Dividend Yield: Dividends per common share divided by closing market price as of balance sheet date, multiplied by 100.

Sales per Share: Main source(s) of revenue, net of excise taxes, trade discounts, returns, and allowances, divided by common shares outstanding at end of indicated fiscal year.

EPS before extra. item (Earnings per share): Earnings before extraordinary items, less preferred-share dividends, divided by average common shares outstanding during indicated fiscal year.

Cash Flow per Share: Cash flow from operations divided by common shares outstanding at end of indicated fiscal year.

Book Value per Share: Common shareholders' equity divided by common shares outstanding at end of indicated fiscal year.

O/S Common Shares (Common shares outstanding at year-end): Total number of common shares outstanding. Includes shares held by subsidiaries and other inter-company holdings. Net of treasury stock.

Total Revenue: Total revenue from operations, less sales and excise taxes, plus income from investments and any other pre-tax income during indicated fiscal year.

Income before extra. (Earnings before extraordinary items): Earnings excluding extraordinary gains and losses during indicated fiscal year.

Cash Flow (Cash flow from operations): Income before extraordinary items plus non-cash items, such as equity income and depreciation, for continuing operations.

Debt/Equity (Debt/equity ratio): Short and long term interest-bearing debt (including capital lease obligations) divided by shareholders' equity. Indicates the extent to which a company is financing its assets with debt, a more risky source of capital than equity.

Return on Capital (Return on average capital): Earnings before extraordinary items, interest expense and income taxes, divided by average capital. Shows how effectively a company is employing its capital to generate profit.

Ret. on Com. Equity (Return on average common equity): Earnings before extraordinary items, less preferred-share dividends, divided by average common shareholders' equity. Shows the rate of return on the investment for the company's common shareholders, the only providers of capital who do not have a fixed return.

% Change Profit: Percentage change in earnings before extraordinary items during the indicated fiscal period.

% Change Revenue: Percentage change in total revenue during the indicated fiscal period.

% Change Assets: Percentage change in total assets during the indicated fiscal period.

Yearly Ratios (3 years)

All Companies

Preferred Div. Coverage (Preferred dividend coverage): Earnings before extraordinary items, divided by preferred-share dividends. Shows how many times over a company can cover its preferred-share dividend obligations from earnings.

Total Div. Coverage (Total dividend coverage): Earnings before extraordinary items, divided by total dividends. Shows how many times over a company can pay its dividends from earnings.

Canada Company Handbook

General Companies

Interest Coverage: Earnings before extraordinary items plus income taxes and interest expense, divided by total interest expense. Shows how many times over a company can cover its interest obligations from earnings.

Current Ratio: Ratio of current assets divided by current liabilities. It is a measure of short term liquidity.

Operating Margin: Operating revenues less operating expenses, divided by operating revenues and multiplied by 100. Shows the percentage of operating revenues a company retains after operating expenses.

Asset Turnover: Total sales divided by total assets. Shows a company's ability to employ its assets productively.

Banks

Capital Ratio: Year-end assets divided by year-end total equity (capital plus reserves). Shows the proportion of a bank's assets that are financed by shareholders' equity and reserves, as opposed to debt or deposits. A higher proportion can make the bank vulnerable to downturns in the business cycle.

Operat. Costs/$100 of Assets (Operating costs per $100 of assets): Operating costs (salaries and benefits, amortization and depreciation, and other expenses) divided by year-end assets. The higher the ratio, the more the bank has spent on operations in relation to its size.

Real Estate Companies

Income prop. (% tot. prop.) and Develop. prop. (% tot. prop.) (Income producing and development properties as a percentage of total property): Shows the proportion of company's total property in income producing and development properties.

5 Year Ratios (3 years)

All Companies

Return on Capital (Five year return on average capital): Simple average of return on capital for the past five years. Shows how well a company has employed its capital over the long term.

Return on Com. Equity (Five year return on average common equity): Simple average of the return on common equity for the past five years. Shows the rate of return on the shareholders' investment over the long term.

Profit Growth (Five year profit growth): Compounded growth rate of earnings before extraordinary items over last five years.

Revenue Growth (Five year revenue growth): Compounded growth rate of total revenue over last five years.

Asset Growth (Five year asset growth): Compounded growth rate of total assets over last five years.

Balance Sheet (3 years)

General Companies

Cash (Cash and short term investments): Includes cash, short term investments, and marketable securities. Does not include cash held in trust.

Current Assets (Total current assets): As presented by the company.

Net Fixed Assets: Gross fixed assets less accumulated depreciation / depletion / amortization plus assets under capital lease, deferred exploration and resource development costs, and mining and oil and gas interests.

Invest's & Advances (Investments and advances): Includes long-term marketable securities, investments at cost, receivables under equipment leases, and all long-term interest-bearing receivables and advances. Includes cash surrender value of life insurance. Also includes non-current investments in unconsolidated subsidiaries, investments at equity, joint venture investments, and advances to and receivables from related entities. Includes dues from employees or other related entities under a share purchase plan. Includes cost investments where the company considers the investment to be in "affiliate."

Total Assets: As presented by the company.

Short Term Debt: Includes bank indebtedness, notes payable, loans and advances payable, cheques issued and outstanding, and other short term interest bearing debt. Includes current portion of long term debt as defined in non-current liabilities. Includes current portion of obligations under capital leases. Includes loans and advances from related entities not in the nature of trade. "Related entities" includes employees, directors, shareholders, and related companies.

Current Liabilities (Total current liabilities): As presented by the company.

Long Term Debt: Includes long term debt, advances, obligations under capital lease, secured debt, mortgages payable, and other interest-bearing long term debt.

Total Liabilities: Total of all liability accounts, excluding preferred shares not presented as equity (rarely used).

Total Equity: As presented by the company.

Total Liab. & Equity (Total liabilities and shareholders' equity): As presented by the company.

Banks

Cash (Cash and deposits): Includes cash and term deposits. May include short term investments.

Total Loans: Includes bank loans and mortgage loans as presented by the bank, and includes all loans and receivables, other than accounts receivable. Includes receivables under equipment leases and secured loans receivable. Does not include accrued interest receivable.

Net Fixed Assets: Gross fixed assets less accumulated depreciation / depletion / amortization.

Total Assets: As presented by the bank.

Total Deposits: Includes demand deposits, short-term deposits, RSP deposits, guaranteed investment certificates and guaranteed accounts.

Subordinated Debt: As presented by the bank.

Total Liabilities: Includes total deposits, liabilities of subsidiaries other than deposits, unspecified deferred credits and subordinated debt.

Total Equity: As presented by the company.

Total Liab. & Equity (Total liabilities and shareholders' equity): As presented by the company.

Finance Companies

Cash (Cash and deposits): Includes cash and term deposits and short term deposits.

Total Loans (Total mortgages and loans): Includes mortgage loans as presented by the company and all other loans and receivables, other than accounts receivable. Includes receivables under equipment leases and secured loans receivable. Does not include accrued loans receivable.

Net Fixed Assets: Includes gross fixed assets less accumulated depreciation / depletion / amortization.

Invest's & Advances: (Investments and advances) Includes bonds, stocks, and other marketable securities, and securities purchased under agreements to resell. Also includes investments in companies accounted for at cost, gold bullion, share exchange memberships, and other investments.

Total Assets: As presented by the company.

Total deposits: Includes demand deposits, short-term deposits, RSP deposits, guaranteed investment certificates and guaranteed accounts.

Insurance Liability: Includes "present value of liabilities under insurance contracts" and "amounts required to provide for unmatured obligations" as presented on the balance sheet of insurance companies. Also includes benefits in course of payment, provision for unreported claims, policyholders' amounts left on deposit, provision for future policy dividends, and experience rating refunds. May include segregated investment fund liabilities.

Long Term Debt: Includes long term debt, advances, obligations under capital lease, secured debt, mortgages payable, and other interest-bearing long term debt.

Total Liabilities: Total of all liability accounts, excluding preferred shares not presented as equity (rarely used).

Total Equity: As presented by the company.

Total Liab. & Equity (Total liabilities and shareholders' equity): As presented by the company.

Real Estate Companies

Cash (Cash and short term investments): Includes cash, short term investments, and marketable securities. Does not include cash held in trust.

Total Real Estate Assets: Includes net income from producing properties after depreciation, properties under development as presented by the company, land and properties held for development as presented by the company, and land and properties held for resale as presented by the company.

Invest's & Advances (Investments and advances): Includes long term marketable securities, investments at cost, receivables under equipment leases, and all long term interest-bearing receivables and advances. Includes cash surrender value of life insurance. Also includes non-current investments in unconsolidated subsidiaries, investments at equity, joint venture investments, and advances to and receivables from related entities. Includes dues from employees or other related entities under a share purchase plan. Includes cost investments where the company considers the investment to be in "affiliate."

Total Assets: As presented by the company.

Bank Indebtedness: Includes bank indebtedness, notes payable, loans and advances payable, cheques issued and outstanding, and other short term interest bearing debt. Includes all items specified as bank debt by the company.

Long Term Debt: Includes long term debt, advances, obligations under capital lease, secured debt, mortgages payable, and other interest-bearing long term debt.

Total Liabilities: Total of all liability accounts, excluding preferred shares not presented as equity (rarely used).

Total Equity: As presented by the company.

Total Liab. & Equity (Total liabilities and shareholders' equity): As presented by the company.

Capital (3 years)

All Companies

Preferred Equity: As presented by the company.

Common Equity: Total equity less preferred equity, as presented by the company.

General Companies

Total Debt: Includes bank indebtedness, notes payable, loans and advances payable, cheques issued and outstanding, and other short term interest bearing debt. Also includes current portion of long term debt, current advances from related entities, and long term debt, advances, obligations under capital lease, secured debt, mortgages payable, and other interest bearing long term debt.

Banks

Total External Debt: Includes subordinated debt as presented by the bank, and liabilities of subsidiaries other than deposits.

Finance Companies

Total Debt: Includes bank indebtedness, notes payable, loans and advances payable, cheques issued and outstanding, and other short term interest bearing debt. Also includes current portion of long term debt, current advances from related entities, and long term debt, advances, obligations under capital lease, secured debt, mortgages payable, and other interest-bearing long-term debt. For investment houses, includes call and other loans due to clients / brokers and dealers.

Real Estate Companies

Total Debt: Includes bank indebtedness, notes payable, loans and advances payable, cheques issued and outstanding, and other short term interest bearing debt. Also includes current portion of long term debt, current advances from related entities, and long-term debt, advances, obligations under capital lease, secured debt, mortgages payable, and other interest-bearing long term debt.

Quarterly Information (8 quarters)

All Companies

EPS (Earnings per share): Earnings (or income) before extraordinary items, less preferred-share dividends, divided by average common shares outstanding.

DPS (Dividends per common share): Presented for fiscal period indicated.

Tot Rev (Total revenue): Total revenue from operations, less sales taxes and excise taxes, plus income from investments and any other pretax income.

Inc Bex (Income before extraordinary items): Earnings excluding extraordinary gains and losses.

Earnings Estimates Information

From I/B/E/S, the Institutional Brokers Estimate System.

Latest year end: Year-end date (year/month) of the actual earnings per share presented.

Earnings per Share Actual: Most recent earnings per share as reported by I/B/E/S. It is the net income of the company divided by the number of shares outstanding.

Earnings per Share Est. this year: Mean or consensus earnings estimates for the next fiscal year end. It is the arithmetic average of all the earnings forecasts for that period. It most closely represents "what Wall Street is saying."

Earnings per Share Est. next year: Mean or consensus earnings estimates for the fiscal year end two years forward. It is the arithmetic average of all the earnings forecasts for that period. It most closely represents "what Wall Street is saying."

Synopsis Information

Banks and Trusts

Capital ratio on risk-adjusted basis: Comprises of Tier 1 and Tier 2 capital as a percentage of risk-adjusted assets.

Under the Bank for International Settlements Guidelines, banks are required to maintain a minimum level of capital based on their risk-adjusted assets. A solid capital base protects depositors and creditors allowing the bank to withstand losses incurred in the normal course of business. This contributes to favorable credit ratings and permits expansion and new initiatives.

Interest rate spread: Net interest income (adjusted to a taxable equivalent basis) divided by average total assets. Net interest income is the difference between interest earned on loans and securities and the interest paid on deposits and/or debentures. There is an inverse relationship between interest rates and the interest rate spread.

Non-performing loans: Those loans and loan substitution securities which have been placed on a non-accrual basis, generally due to non-payment of interest or principal for 90 days or where the collectibility of principal or interest is in significant doubt by management. These loans also include loans which have been re negotiated at a reduced rate.

Mines and Precious Metals

Probable reserves: Probable ore is ore in place for which the tonnage and grade have been computed partly from specific measurements, samples or production data, and partly from projection for a reasonable distance on geological evidence.

Proven or proved reserves: Proven ore is ore in place for which the tonnage and grade have been computed from dimensions revealed in outcrops or trenches or underground workings or drill holes and for which the grade is computed from the results of adequate sampling.

Reserve grade: Estimated metal content of an ore body, based on reserve calculations.

Reserves life index: Reserves remaining at the end of a given year divided by production in that year. Gives the remaining life in years of current reserves at the current production level.

Management and Diversified

Equity investments: Represents between 20% and 50% of the ownership interest in an investee. The choice of equity method reflects the investor's ability to influence the operations of the investee.

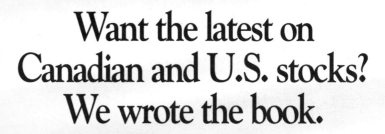

Want the latest on Canadian and U.S. stocks? We wrote the book.

Cross-border tracking is easy, at Green Line.

Receive valuable, unbiased information covering TSE 300 and S&P 100 stocks from Green Line® Investor Services Inc., where you save up to 83%* on the commissions you may be paying your full-cost broker. To receive more information on Green Line and your FREE copy of the Green Line Pocket Stock Guide, complete this card and return it to us. Or FAX it to **1-800-263-2038** (in Toronto, **416-292-6057**).

Yes! I want the latest on stocks and more information on Green Line's services. Please send me information on Green Line Direct Trading and a free copy of the Green Line Pocket Stock Guide.

Name

Address

City   Province   Postal Code

Phone: Home   Business

GREEN LINE
CANADA'S LARGEST DISCOUNT BROKER

TD

Save on commissions with a Green Line® Direct Trading® account.

Imagine how the savings shown here can add up over a period of one year? Why not do your own comparison? You'll find our commission savings can mean the difference between a profit and a loss, and our service is exceptional, too.

Sample Trades Canadian Stocks	Transaction Value	Average full price Commission*	Direct Trading Discount Rate**	Dollar Savings	Savings %
400 shares traded at $4 per share	$1,600	$75	$45	$30	40%
200 shares traded at $25 per share	$5,000	$123	$52	$71	58%
500 shares traded at $20 per share	$10,000	$228	$65	$163	71%
1,000 shares traded at $35 per share	$35,000	$575	$110	$465	81%
1,000 shares traded at $60 per share	$60,000	$648	$110	$538	83%

®   Trade mark of TD Bank. Green Line Investor Services Inc., a wholly-owned subsidiary, is a registered user.
*   These rates are an average of those charged by leading brokerage firms in October, 1992.
** Rates as disclosed subject to change. Minimum commissions will be charged as applicable.

MAIL ➤ POSTE

Canada Post Corporation / Société canadienne des postes

Postage paid
if mailed in Canada

Port payé
si posté au Canada

**Business
Reply**

**Réponse
d'affaires**

0183913699   01

0183913699-M1V4Y5-BR01

```
GREEN LINE  INVESTOR  SERVICES
585  MIDDLEFIELD  RD  UNIT  33
SCARBOROUGH  ON   M1V 9Z9
```